China

Michael Buckley
Alan Samagalski
Rober
Chris
Clem Lin

中国

China – a travel survival kit

4th edition

Published by
  Lonely Planet Publications
  Head Office: PO Box 617, Hawthorn, Vic 3122, Australia
  Branches: PO Box 2001A, Berkeley, CA 94702, USA
                 10 Barley Mow Passage, Chiswick, London W4 4PH, UK
                 71 bis rue du Cardinal Lemoine, 75005 Paris, France

Printed by
  Singapore National Printers Ltd, Singapore

Photographs by

Chris Beall (Retna Pictures) (CB)	Sonia Berto (SB)	Jim Hart (JH)
Richard I'Anson (RI'A)	Clem Lindenmeyer (CL)	Richard Nebesky (RN)
Jo O'Brien (JO)	Alan Samalgalski (AL)	Robert Storey (Storey)
Robert Strauss (Strauss)	Chris Taylor (CT)	

  Front cover: photo by Dallas & John Heaton: Scoopix Photo Library

First Published
  October 1984

This Edition
  March 1994

National Library of Australia Cataloguing in Publication Data

Storey, Robert.
  China – a travel survival kit.

  4th ed.
  Includes index.
  ISBN 0 86442 207 5.

  1. China – Description and travel – Guide-books.
  I. Taylor, Chris, 1961-. II. Lindenmayer, Clem. III. Title (Series : Lonely Planet travel survival kit.)

915.10459

text & maps © Lonely Planet 1994
photos © photographers as indicated 1994
climate charts compiled from information supplied by Patrick J Tyson, © Patrick J Tyson, 1994

Michael Buckley

Michael was raised in Australia and now lives in Canada, where he is a freelance writer and photographer. He is based in Vancouver, but spends part of each year on the road. He has travelled extensively throughout Asia, and has trekked and mountain-biked in the Himalayan and Karakoram ranges. He co-authored the first edition of this book, and is the author of a travelogue *Cycling to Xian*, which is about bicycling across China and Tibet.

Alan Samagalski

Alan left Melbourne University's Genetics Department to work at some legendary Melbourne comedy venues. He then went to India for a lengthy stay before eventually returning home to help research LP's *Australia – a travel survival kit*. After several missions updating travel survival kits for *Hong Kong, Macau & Canton* and *Bali & Lombok*, and co-writing our guides to *China* (first and second editions) and *Indonesia*, he went to South America to write the first edition of *Chile – a travel survival kit*. He now lives in Adelaide.

Robert Storey

A refugee from the Third World (New York City), Robert escaped to Las Vegas where he became a distinguished slot machine repairman. After graduating from the University of Nevada in Las Vegas with a worthless liberal arts degree, he then went on the road and learned to speak Chinese along the way. Today, he is a successful writer, computer hacker, model citizen and a pillar of his community – though no one is quite sure which community that is. His last known address was in Taipei.

Chris Taylor

Chris Taylor spent his formative years in Bristol, England. He emigrated to Australia with his family in the '70s, and has followed a mixed bag of occupations that found him variously in Queensland (Great Keppel Island and Mt Isa), London and Tokyo, in between extended bouts of travel in Asia. After completing a degree in English Literature and Chinese, Chris joined the Lonely Planet team to work on our phrasebook series. More recently he has co-authored *Japan – a travel survival kit*, and written Lonely Planet city guides to *Tokyo* and *Seoul*. He is also author of our *Mandarin Chinese phrasebook*. He currently calls Puli in Taiwan home, and when he's not on the road, occasionally gets to spend some time there.

Clem Lindenmayer

Clem's decidedly scattered 'career' has ranged from dishwasher and telex operator to layabout and habitual traveller. Mountains and languages are his pivotal interests, and for both reasons China eventually caught his attention. Having made the fateful resolution ɔ learn Chinese while on a lengthy solo trek through Lapland, he died the language intermittently for several years in Australia and na before working on the update for this book. Clem is also the r of Lonely Planet's *Trekking in the Patagonian Andes*.

From the Authors

See page 1056 for authors' acknowledgements and for the names of travellers who wrote to Lonely Planet.

This Book

The first edition of this book appeared after Michael Buckley and Alan Samagalski spent many months on the road in China in 1983 followed by many more months at their desks. Alan Samagalski and Robert Strauss researched and wrote the second edition, preparing the way for Joe Cummings and Robert Storey for the third edition. This edition (fourth) was researched by Robert Storey, Chris Taylor and Clem Lindenmayer. All those involved in producing this book greatly appreciate the contributions of those travellers who put so much effort into writing and telling us of their experiences. These people's names appear on page 1056.

From the Publisher

Kay Waters and Sharan Kaur edited this edition. Thanks also to Felicia Zhang for coding and proofing the Chinese script, to Caroline Williamson for checking final script and pinyin, to Dan Levin for sorting out problems with Chinese software, to Vyvyan Cayley for proofing, and to Ann Jeffree for compiling the index.

Glenn Beanland coordinated the mapping and was assisted by Chris Lee-Ack, Valerie Tellini, Ralph Roob, Richard Stewart and Jacqui Schiff. Valerie Tellini, Jacqui Schiff, Louise Keppie and Rachel Black helped with map corrections and the stripping in of Chinese script.

Margaret Jung was responsible for the design, illustrations, cover and layout. Thanks also to Tamsin Wilson and Ann Jeffree for additional illustrations.

Warning & Request

A travel writer's job is never done. Before the ink is dry on a new book, things change, and few places change more quickly than China. At Lonely Planet we get a steady stream of mail from travellers and it all helps – whether it's a few lines scribbled on the back of a used paper plate or a stack of neat typewritten pages spewing forth from our fax machine. Prices go up, new hotels open, old ones degenerate, some burn down, others get renovated and renamed, bus routes change, bridges collapse and recommended travel agents get indicted for fraud.

Remember, this book is meant to be a guide, not the oracle – since things go on changing we can't tell you exactly what to expect all the time. Hopefully this book will point you the right directions and save you some time and money. If you find that China is not identical to the way it's described herein, don't get upset but get out your pen or word processor and write to Lonely Planet. Your input will help make the next edition better.

Your letters will be used to help update future editions and, where possible, important changes will also be included in a Stop Press section in reprints.

We greatly appreciate all information that is sent to us by travellers. Back at Lonely Planet we employ a hard-working readers' letters team to sort through the many letters we receive. The best ones will be rewarded with a free copy of the next edition or another Lonely Planet guide if you prefer. We give away lots of books, but, unfortunately, not every letter/postcard receives one.

Prices – stop press
On 1 April 1994, China increased entrance fees to tourist attractions by up to 400%!

Contents

SOUTHERN & CENTRAL CHINA

CANTON 216

GUANGDONG 252

HAINAN ISLAND 288

HUNAN 301

Map Legend

BOUNDARIES

— · — · — · —	........International Boundary
— · — · — · —	................Internal Boundary
++++++++++++	....National Park or Reserve
- - - - - - - - -	........................The Equator
· · · · · · · · · ·	.........................The Tropics

SYMBOLS

◎ NATIONAL	.....................National Capital
● PROVINCIAL	........Provincial or State Capital
● Major	...............................Major Town
● Minor	...............................Minor Town
■	...........................Places to Stay
▼	...........................Places to Eat
⊠	..................................Post Office
✈	....Airport
i	....................Tourist Information
⊖	.............Bus Station or Terminal
66	............Highway Route Number
☾ ✝ 🕌 ⛪	...... Mosque, Church, Cathedral
∴	...........................Temple or Ruin
✚	.....................................Hospital
※	......................................Lookout
⌂	...................................Lighthouse
⚑	............................Camping Area
⊓	...............................Picnic Area
⌂	................................Hut or Chalet
▲	........................Mountain or Hill
⌒	....Cave
⊢⊣	.... Railway Station
⊒	.........................Road Bridge
+++++	........................Railway Bridge
⇒ ⇐	............................Road Tunnel
→) (←	.........................Railway Tunnel
⌢⌢⌢	....................Escarpment or Cliff
⌣	....Pass

ROUTES

———————	.......Major Road or Highway
- - - - - - - - -	.... Unsealed Major Road
———————	.......................Sealed Road
- - - - - - - - -	.....Unsealed Road or Track
═══════	..............................City Street
++++++++++	...................................Railway
⊶⊸⊶	.... Subway
- - - - - - - - -	......................Walking Track
- - - - - - - - -	..........................Ferry Route
+⊦+⊦+⊦+⊦	.... Cable Car or Chair Lift

HYDROGRAPHIC FEATURES

	.....................River or Creek
	..............Intermittent Stream
	........Lake, Intermittent Lake
	...........................Coast Line
	.....................................Spring
	...................................Waterfall
	.....................................Swamp
	.... Salt Lake or Reef
	...................................Glacier

OTHER FEATURES

	Park, Garden or National Park
	.... Built Up Area
	... Market or Pedestrian Mall
	.........Plaza or Town Square
	.............................Cemetery

Note: not all symbols displayed above appear in this book

Introduction

After being closed for repairs for almost 30 years the Middle Kingdom suddenly swung open its big red doors – but not quite all the way. Comrades, we must increase the production of tourists! China desperately needs the foreign exchange that tourism so conveniently provides, and has done very well out of the deal so far. With several million tourists flocking in every year, the tallest buildings in China are, appropriately, hotels. Money-losing state-run companies have dived into the tourism business and have found it to be extremely profitable – business has been so good that even the People's Liberation Army has opened a few hotels to enhance the military budget.

In the late 1970s the tour groups started rolling in but the prospects for individual travel looked extremely dim. It has always been possible for individuals to travel to the People's Republic of China (PRC), but by invitation only, and until the late 1970s few managed an invite. The first regulars were people from Sweden and France (nations favoured by China) who stepped off the Trans-Siberian Railway in 1979.

In 1981 the Chinese suddenly started issuing visas to solo and uninvited travellers through a couple of their embassies overseas, but mainly through various agencies in Hong Kong. Just about anyone who wanted a visa could get one, but since there was no fanfare, news spread slowly by word of mouth. By 1983 it seemed that just about everyone who landed in Hong Kong was going to China. After all, we'd been waiting over 30 years to travel in the country unfettered by tour guides.

Nowadays the remote travellers' trails of China have been worn down to gullies tramped by curious foreigners who notice that the image of the late '60s and early '70s – hardy peasants and sturdy workers in blue uniforms building a Communist heaven – has changed. Today they see motorcycle gangs (relatively benign) in Canton; daring

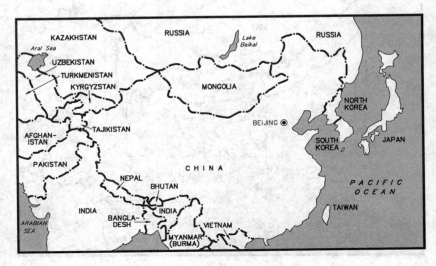

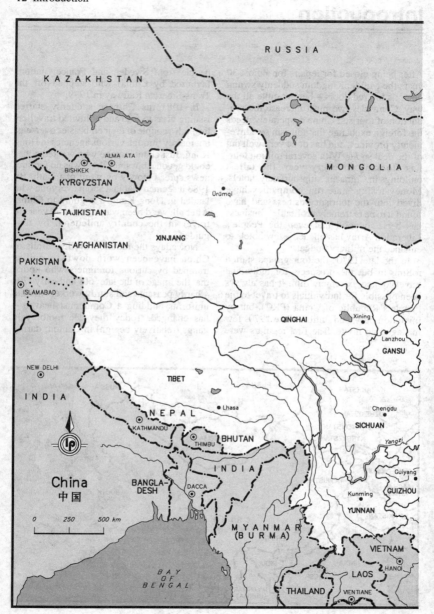

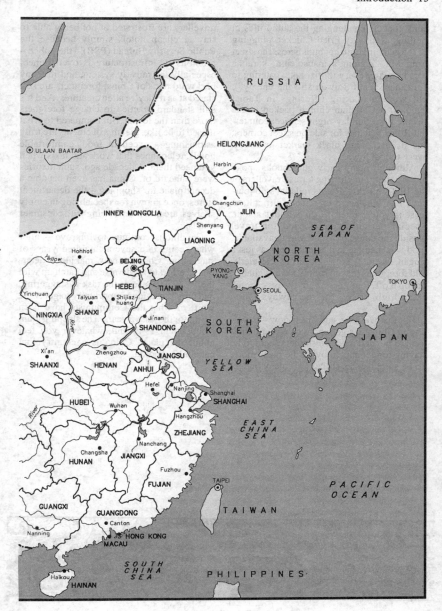

punk rockers challenging the authorities in Beijing; Kentucky Fried Chicken plugging its roasted birds and hot buns across the street from Mao Zedong's mausoleum; karaoke bars in nearly every tourist hotel catering to Taiwanese (isn't Taiwan still the enemy?); old women making offerings in Taoist temples; a Christian church packed to the steeple for a Sunday-night service; counterfeit Rolex watches for sale on street corners; and a burgeoning black market in almost every tourist town.

Although many early guidebooks spoke of the country in glowing terms, travellers of the 1980s quickly discovered that solo journeys in China were extremely difficult, at least if you wanted to go without a tour. Special permits were needed for travel outside the cities, transport was unavailable, food was inedible and 'sanitation' was just a slogan. At empty hotels, sneering desk clerks told foreigners that no rooms were available. To top it off, foreigners were always charged extra high prices for the always-rotten service.

But that was then and this is now – travelling in China has gotten much easier than it used to be, and most Westerners seem to be staying longer and enjoying the place more. To be sure, hassles still exist – many budget travellers are frustrated at not being able to stay at cheap hotels simply because the Public Security Bureau (PSB) – the police – prohibits it. Infrastructure is overstrained, especially the railway system, and in many backward parts of China, foreigners are still stared at as if they're alien creatures. And it's still standard practice to charge foreigners more than the locals. But compared to what it used to be like, the improvements are truly astonishing – excellent food, comfortable hotels, telephones that work and taxis when you need them. A decade ago, such luxuries were unheard of. China has even become a decent place for shopping – the department stores, once known for specialising in empty shelves, are now overflowing with consumer goods.

Conditions continue to improve – after what seems like several hundred years of stagnation, China is now making a determined effort to modernise and catch up with the West. The size of the task is staggering, and now is a unique opportunity to get some whiff of what the Communists have been doing for the last 45 years. The sleeping giant stood up in 1949 and, whatever you feel about the place, China is a country that cannot be ignored.

Facts about the Country

HISTORY

For all peoples, history is an essential link in national identity, but for the Chinese this link somehow seems particularly crucial. In part their history's sheer longevity is responsible: Chinese frequently declaim proudly (and justifiably so) about their 5000 years of continuous history, even if the first couple of thousand years are shrouded in myth. But even more than this it is a profound sense of a shared glorious history that works to hold together the vast mass of 1.1 billion Chinese in nationhood.

Traditionally, new dynasties realigned the past to authorise their grab for power, and even the present regime has done its fair share of scouring the past for precedents that vindicate its changing policies. Mao himself frequently dipped into Chinese history to make his vast Communist experiment more palatable to Chinese sensibilities, and his favourite novel was *The Water Margin*, a prose epic that depicts the lives and struggles of a group of rebels and bandits in the time of the Northern Song.

Similarly, China's rebels, dissidents and social critics frequently veil their attacks in historical allusion. The opening salvo of the Cultural Revolution was an official attack on the Writer Wu Han, whose play about the dismissal of an upright Song Dynasty official, Hai Rui, was an oblique reference to Peng Dehuai, the army marshal who had dared to criticise Mao on the Great Leap Forward, and who was sacked for his troubles.

If in your travels in China you find that

CHINESE DYNASTIES

Xia	2200 – 1700 BC	Eastern Wei	534 – 577
Shang	1700 – 1100 BC	Western Wei	535 – 556
Zhou	1100 – 221 BC	Northern Qi	550 – 577
Western Zhou	1100 – 771 BC	Northern Zhou	557 – 581
Eastern Zhou	770 – 221 BC	**Sui**	589 – 618
Spring & Autumn Period	722 – 481 BC	**Tang**	618 – 907
Warring States Period	453 – 221 BC	**Five Dynasties**	907 – 960
Qin	221 – 207 BC	Later Liang	907 – 923
Han	206 BC – 220 AD	Later Tang	923 – 936
Former Han	206 BC – 24 AD	Later Jin	936 – 946
Later Han	25 – 220 AD	Later Han	947 – 950
Three Kingdoms Period	220 – 280	Later Zhou	951 – 960
Wei	220 – 265	**Liao**	916 – 1125
Shu Han	221 – 263	**Song**	960 – 1279
Wu	222 – 280	Northern Song	960 – 1126
Jin	265 – 420	Southern Song	1127 – 1279
Western Jin	265 – 316	**Western Xia**	1038 – 1227
Eastern Jin	317 – 420	**Jin**	1115 – 1234
Southern & Northern Dynasties		**Yuan (Mongol)**	1271 – 1368
Southern	420 – 589	**Ming**	1368 – 1644
Song	420 – 479	**Qing (Manchu)**	1644 – 1911
Qi	479 – 502		
Liang	502 – 557	**CHINESE REPUBLICS**	
Chen	557 – 589		
Northern		**Republic of China**	1911 – 1949
Northern Wei	386 – 534	**People's Republic of China (PRC)**	1949 –

Chinese tourism is an unfathomable phenomenon, bear in mind that this too has a heavy historical emphasis. Sights are generally appreciated less for what Westerners might feel to be their intrinsic value than for their historical associations. It's not uncommon to find a group of Chinese scrambling up a rock face and ignoring the nearby rolling hills in order to gaze at a misshapen stone inscribed with a poem.

Mythological Beginnings

The Chinese claim a history of 5000 years, but early 'records' are of a mythological and legendary nature. The very existence of the Xia Dynasty, documented in early Chinese histories as the first Chinese dynasty, still awaits archaeological verification.

According to legend, the Xia was preceded by a succession of three sovereigns and five emperors. The first of the three sovereigns, Fuxi, is usually depicted alongside his wife and sister, the goddess Nügua. The two are human from the waist up but have dragons' tails. Nügua is credited with having fashioned human beings from clay and having created the institution of marriage, while Fuxi bestowed the gifts of hunting, fishing and animal husbandry. The ox-headed Shennong, another of the three sovereigns, bestowed agriculture and knowledge of the medicinal properties of plants on the Chinese.

Like the three sovereigns, the five emperors are each credited with having founded certain key elements of the Chinese cultural tradition. For example, the first of them, Huang Di, is said to have brought the agricultural calendar, boats, armour and pottery to the Chinese people. A later emperor, Shun, devised the writing brush. Dynastic rule commenced when the same Shun abdicated in favour of Yu, the first emperor of the Xia.

Xia & Shang Dynasties

Many historians believe that the Xia Dynasty may actually have existed, though not in the terms depicted in Chinese mythology. The dynasty is claimed to have held power for nearly five centuries from 2200 to 1700 BC, before becoming corrupt and being overthrown by the Shang.

There is more evidence of the existence of the Shang than of the Xia. Archaeological finds have shown for certain that a state existed in the Yellow River plain in the present provinces of Shandong, Shanxi and Shaanxi, and that it held power from 1554 to 1045 BC. It was an agricultural society that practised a form of ancestor worship. It was also marked by the presence of what seems to be a caste of high priests who practised divination using so-called oracle bones. Associated with ancestor worship and divination are the Shang bronze vessels, the surfaces of which are covered with extraordinarily detailed linear designs. Like the Xia before it, the Shang fell prey to corruption and degeneracy, and was toppled by the Zhou.

Zhou Dynasty

Like the Shang before it, little is known with any great certainty about the Zhou (1100-221 BC). It is thought that they were a nomadic tribe who came under the influence of the Shang and later displaced it. The Zhou

---

Divination

Divination, as practised by Shang priests, was a unique procedure that involved applying heat to the bones of cattle or to the shells of turtles. Grooves were carved on one side of the bones and into the grooves were inserted heated rods. Cracks that appeared on the other side of the bone could be read for information concerning the outcome of crops or for guidance on almost every aspect of daily life.

For scholars of ancient Chinese, the Shang practice of writing the topic of divination and often the outcome on the bones provide the only surviving record of early Chinese ideographs. Some 50,000 oracle bones and fragments have been unearthed, mainly from storage pits in Xiaotun in Henan. From these, 3000 early Chinese characters have been identified. ■

capital was known as Hao and was near Xi'an, the site that was to become the imperial seat of power for many subsequent Chinese dynasties. The Zhou also established another power centre close to present-day Luoyang in Henan, from where they governed the subjugated Shang. The Zhou social structure seems to have been heavily influenced by the Shang, from whom they inherited the practices of divination and ancestor worship.

Historians generally divide the Zhou period into the Western Zhou (1100-771 BC) and the Eastern Zhou (770-221 BC). The demarcation point is the sacking of the traditional Zhou capital of Hao by barbarian tribes, the transfer of power to Luoyang and a loss of effective control by the Zhou over its feudatory states. Nevertheless, Zhou nobles remained symbolic heads of state over a land of warring kingdoms until 221 BC, when they were displaced by the Qin.

The Eastern Zhou, though riven by strife, is thought of as the crucible of Chinese culture. The traditional Chinese division of the period into the Spring and Autumn period (722-481 BC) and the Warring States period (453-221 BC) doesn't follow any historical logic, but rather refers to the periods covered by two historical books of the same names, written during the period, which were to become cornerstones of the classical education system until the Qing collapsed in 1912. The *Spring & Autumn Annals* is traditionally ascribed to Confucius (551-479 BC), a scholar who wandered from state to state during these troubled times in search of a ruler who would put his ideas for the perfect state into practice.

Confucianism wasn't the only important school of thought to emerge in the Eastern Zhou. The same period saw Laozi pen his *Daode Jing*, or *The Way & its Power* (as it was famously translated by Arthur Waley), the classic text of Taoism. While there were many other competing ideologies in the Eastern Zhou (the Chinese frequently allude to the 'Hundred Schools'), Confucianism and Taoism are two opposing streams that left their mark on all future Chinese thinking,

the former pragmatic and socially oriented, the latter personal and mystical.

Mandate of Heaven

The Zhou period is important for the establishment of some of the most enduring Chinese political concepts. Foremost is the 'mandate of heaven', in which heaven gives wise and virtuous leaders a mandate to rule and removes it from those who are evil and corrupt. It was a concept that was later extended to incorporate the Taoist theory that heaven expresses disapproval of bad rulers through natural disasters such as earthquakes, floods and plagues of locusts.

In keeping with this was the idea that heaven also expressed its displeasure with corrupt rulers through rebellion and withdrawal of support by the ruled. This has been referred to as the 'right to rebellion', a slippery concept, since the right to rebellion could only be confirmed by success.

Nevertheless, rebellious expressions of heaven's will were an essential ingredient in China's dynastic cycle, and mark an essential difference with, say, Japan, where the authority of the imperial family derives from a single lineage that, according to legend, can be traced back to the Sun goddess.

Qin Dynasty

The tenuous authority of the Zhou ended in the 3rd century BC, when the state of Qin united the Chinese, for the first time, into a single empire. However, the First Exalted Emperor Qin Shihuang ruled only from 221 to 207 BC. He is remembered above all for his tyranny and cruelty, and yet historians maintain that the Qin Dynasty bequeathed administrative institutions that were to remain features of the Chinese state for the following 2000 years.

The state of Qin grew in power during the 5th and 4th centuries BC. In 246 BC the state took present-day Sichuan and proceeded to finish off the remaining major kingdoms whose fortunes had variously waxed and waned during the late Eastern Zhou period. By 221 BC the Qin was the only state still standing, and King Zheng took the major step of fashioning his conquests into an empire and giving himself the newly coined title *huángdì*, or emperor.

The principal feature of the Qin Dynasty that was to leave its mark on subsequent Chinese history was the Qin's strong centralised control, dividing its territory into provincial units run by centrally appointed administrators. Both the systems of weights and measures and writing were standardised.

Great emphasis has been placed on the ruthlessness of Qin Shihuang, as King Zheng became known, but while much evidence points to the harshness of Qin rule it is still uncertain whether accounts are not exaggerated.

Labour for the massive project of constructing the Great Wall seems to have been undertaken largely by conscripts, of whom countless numbers perished. Scholars point also to the great 'Burning of the Books', in which according to some accounts all books produced prior to the Qin were destroyed in accordance with imperial edict. It is more commonly thought today that the book burning was limited to books thought to be inimical to laws of the state and that books on many subjects were exempt.

Qin Shihuang's heir to the imperial throne proved ineffectual and, shaken by rebellion, the Qin capital near modern-day Xi'an fell to an army led by the commoner Liu Bang in 207 BC. Liu lost no time in taking the title of emperor and establishing the Han Dynasty.

Han Dynasty

The Han Dynasty ruled China from 206 BC to 220 AD. While it held the reins of power less tightly than the preceding Qin, it nevertheless maintained many of the institutions of the dynasty that it followed. Its history is complicated by the fact that it is often divided into a Western Han and a Eastern Han, with an interregnum of 14 years (9-23 AD), during which the country was governed by the Xin.

The Western Han was a period of consolidation, notable for the true establishment of the Chinese state and military extension of the empire's borders. The Eastern Han, after a brief period of stability, fell prey to a process of weakening and decentralisation of power that in 220 AD saw the abdication of the last of the Han emperors and the beginning of some 400 years of turmoil.

Foreign Contacts

The expansion of the Han brought the Chinese into contact with the 'barbarians' that encircled their world at the centre of all things. This contact was both military and commercial.

To the north, the Xiongnu (a name given to various nomadic tribes of central Asia) posed the greatest threat to China. Military expeditions were sent against these tribes, initially with much success. This in turn provided the Chinese with access to central Asia and was a major factor in opening up the silk routes that carried Chinese silk as far afield as Rome. On the diplomatic front, links were formed with Central Asian tribes, and the great Chinese explorer Zhang Qian provided the authorities with information on the possibilities of trade and alliances in northern India. The same period saw the percolation of Chinese influence into areas that were later to become known as Vietnam and Korea.

Naturally, the Chinese saw their contact with outsiders as a civilising influence on the barbarian inhabitants of the peripheries of the Celestial Empire. Foreigners were expected to offer tribute to the Chinese court and were received as vassals.

Decentralisation of Power

From the collapse of the Han Dynasty in 220 AD to the establishment of the Sui in 581 AD, China was riven by more than four centuries of internal conflict that saw some of the most terrible wars in the nation's history. Curiously, however, the turmoil still allowed for a massive flowering of Buddhism and for cultural consolidation that produced a high-water mark in the arts.

Chinese historians refer to this period as the Wei, Jin and Northern & Southern dynasties. This is slightly deceptive, as in reality the successive competing kingdoms and strongholds of power numbered 19 altogether for the period of 316-439 AD alone. Initially the country divided into three large kingdoms, the Wei governing the area roughly north of the Yangzi River, and the south represented by the Wu to the east and the Shu to the west (Sichuan Province is still often referred to as Shu).

The Wei lasted little more than 40 years. Its successor, the Western Jin, fared not much better. By 306 AD its capital, Luoyang, had fallen to Xiongnu horsemen, issuing in 150 years of bloodshed as competing non-Han tribes jockeyed for absolute power. In the 5th century the Tuoba tribe eliminated all its rivals in the north and its Sinisized rulers set about consolidating their position through such measures as land reform. But they were to fall too, and the north divided into Eastern and Western Wei.

The Western Wei, though numerically weaker than its rival in the north, set up an efficient system of administration and dis-banded Buddhist temples, confiscating much of the faith's accumulated wealth in the process. In 577 AD it defeated the Eastern Wei, and in 581 AD one of its own generals took the reins of power and established the Sui Dynasty. By 589 the Sui had taken control of the much weakened south, and China was once again reunified under a single government.

Sui Dynasty

The Sui Dynasty (589-618 AD) was short-lived but its accomplishments were many. Yang Jian, the Chinese-Tuoba general who established the dynasty, was given the title Wendi, the 'Cultivated Emperor'. He under-took extensive reorganisation of the administration, modelling much of it on the earlier Han institutions; the civil service was strengthened at the expense of aristocratic privilege; and land reform was undertaken. All this, along with revisions of the law code, was to serve as the basis for the institutions of the Tang Dynasty that followed fast on the heels of Sui collapse.

Chinese historians frequently point to Wendi's son, Yangdi, as epitomising imperial mismanagement, but if it had not been for his disastrous military excursions into north-ern Korea the Sui might not have fallen as soon as it did. His massive public works in restoring much of the Great Wall and estab-lishing the Grand Canal (which did much to

achieve the economic cohesion of China), were indeed carried out with much loss of life, but were arguably important elements in the strengthening of the empire. However, his three unsuccessful incursions onto Korean soil put an enormous burden on the national coffers and fanned the flames of revolt.

Tang Dynasty

Faced with disastrous military setbacks in Korea and the country on the brink of anarchy, Yangdi was assassinated by one of his high officials. Meanwhile, another Sui official, posted in the border garrison of Taiyuan, seeing that the writing was on the wall for the Sui, turned his troops back on the capital. His name was Li Yuan (known posthumously as Gaozu) and he was to establish the Tang Dynasty (618-907), for most Chinese the most glorious period in their history.

Gaozu's grab at dynastic succession was not without contest, and it was to take 10 years before the last of his rivals was defeated. Once this was achieved, however, the Tang set about putting the house in order. A pyramidical administration was estab-

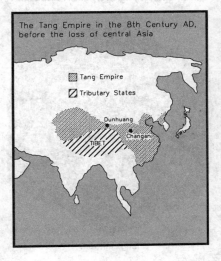

The Tang Empire in the 8th Century AD, before the loss of central Asia

Tang Empire

Tributary States

Dunhuang

Changan

TIBET

lished, with the emperor at its head, two policy-formulating ministries and a Department of State Affairs below this, followed in turn by nine courts and six boards dealing with specific administrative areas. In a move to discourage the development of regional power bases, the empire was divided into 300 prefectures *(zhōu)* and 1500 counties *(xiàn)*, a regional breakdown that persists to this day.

The accession of Gaozu's son Taizong (600-49) to the imperial throne saw a continuation of the early Tang successes. Military conquests re-established Chinese control of the silk routes and contributed to an influx of traders, producing an unprecedented 'internationalisation' of Chinese society. The major cities of Chang'an, Luoyang and Canton, as well as many other trading centres, were home to foreign communities, mainly from central Asia, which brought with them new religions, food, music and artistic traditions. Later in the Tang Dynasty foreign contact was extended to Persia, India, Malaysia, Indonesia and Japan. By the 9th century the city of Canton was said to have a foreign population of 100,000.

The Tang also saw a flourishing of Buddhism. Chinese pilgrims, notably the famous

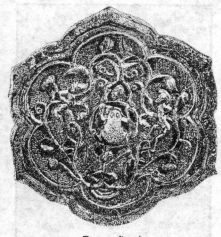

Tang craftwork

wanderer Xuan Zang, made their way to India, bringing back with them Buddhist scriptures that in their turn brought about a Buddhist renewal. Translation, which until this time had extensively Sinicized difficult Buddhist concepts, was undertaken with a new rigour, and Chinese Buddhist texts increased vastly in number. One of the consequences of this, however, was a schism in the Buddhist faith. In reaction to the complexity of many Buddhist texts being translated from Sanskrit, the Chan school, more famously known by its Japanese name Zen, arose. Chan looked to bypass the complexities of scriptural study through discipline and meditation, while another Buddhist phenomenon, the Pure Land School, later to become the most important form of Chinese Buddhism, concerned itself with attaining the 'Western Paradise'.

For Chinese, the apex of Tang dynastic glory was the reign of Xuanzong (685-761), known also by the title Minghuang, or the 'Radiant Emperor'. His capital of Chang'an was one of the greatest cities in the world, with a population of over one million. His court was a magnet to scholars and artists throughout the country, and home for a time to poets such as Du Fu and Li Bai, perhaps China's two most famous rhymers. His reign similarly saw a flourishing of the arts, dance and music as well as a remarkable religious diversity.

Some might say that all this artistic activity was a sign that the empire was beginning to go a bit soft at the core. Xuanzong's increasing preoccupation with the arts, tantric Buddhism, Taoism, one of his consorts Yang Guifei and whatever else captured his fancy largely left the affairs of state to his administrators. An Lushun, a general in the north-east, took this opportunity to build up a huge power base in the region, and before long (755) he made his move on the rest of China. The fighting, which dragged on for nearly 10 years, overran the capital and caused massive dislocations of people and millions of deaths. Although Tang forces regained control of the empire, it was the beginning of the end for the Tang.

More Anarchy & Discord

The 8th and 9th centuries saw a gradual weakening of Tang power. In the north-west Tibetan warriors overran Tang garrisons, while to south the Nanzhao kingdom centred in Dali, Yunnan, posed a serious threat to Sichuan. Meanwhile, in the Chinese heartland of the Yangzi region and Zhejiang, heavy taxes and a series of calamities engendered wide-ranging discontent that culminated in Huang Zhao, the head of a loose grouping of bandit groups, ransacking the capital. From 907 to 959, until the establishment of the Song Dynasty, China was once again wracked by wars between contenders for the mandate of heaven. It is a period often referred to as the Five Dynasties and 10 Kingdoms period.

Song Dynasty

In 959 Zhao Kuangyin, the leader of the palace corps of one of the so-called Five Dynasties (the Later Zhou), usurped power from a seven-year-old head of state. By 976 he had conquered the dozen or so other kingdoms that stood in the way to reunifying China and established yet another dynasty: the Song (960-1279).

The Song is generally divided into the Northern Song (960-1126) and the Southern Song (1127-1279). The reason was the Jurchen Jin Dynasty, which took control of the north from 1126 and drove the Song from its capital Kaifeng to the southern capital of Hangzhou.

Despite the continual threat of powerful forces on its borders (the Tibetan/Tangut Xixia kingdom, the Mongol Liao Dynasty and the Jurchen Jin Dynasty), the Song is memorable for its strong centralised government, a renewal of Confucian learning, a restoration of the examination system that fostered a civilian-dominated bureaucracy, and what has been referred to as a commercial revolution.

The economic progress of the Song period can be attributed in large part to dramatically increased agricultural production. Land reclamation, new rice strains and improved agricultural techniques and tools all had a role to play in this development. At the same time improvements in the transport infrastructure, the rise of a merchant class and the introduction of paper money facilitated the growth of wider markets. This commercial revolution allowed for the growth of more urban centres nourished by the influx of goods from around the country. When Marco Polo arrived in China in the 13th century he found prosperous cities on a grander scale than those he was used to at home in Europe. Historians point to the Song Dynasty as the turning point in China's development of an urban culture.

Mongol Reign (Yuan Dynasty)

Beyond the Great Wall lay the Gobi Desert. Beyond that lay only slightly more hospitable grassland stretching all the way from Manchuria to Hungary and inhabited by nomadic Turkic and Mongol tribes who endured a harsh life as shepherds and horse-breeders. The Mongols, despised for what was considered their ignorance and poverty, occasionally went to war with the Chinese but had always been defeated.

In 1206 after 20 years of internal war, Genghis Khan united the roaming Mongol tribes into a new national entity: the 'Blue Mongols', under the protection of the heavenly sky. In 1211 he turned his attention on China, penetrated the Great Wall two years later and took Beijing in 1215. Stubborn resistance from the Chinese rulers, conflict within the Mongolian camp, and campaigns in Russia delayed the conquest of Song China for many years. Not until 1279 did the grandson of Genghis, Kublai Khan, bring southern China under his sway and establish the Yuan Dynasty (1271-1368). The China ruled by Kublai was the vastest country the world has ever seen.

The Mongols established two capitals: a summer capital of Shangdu in Inner Mongolia and a winter capital of Dadu or, as it's now known, Beijing. They made many administrative changes to the Chinese court, the major difference from the Song being the militarisation of administrative organs. Another major feature of the Yuan Dynasty

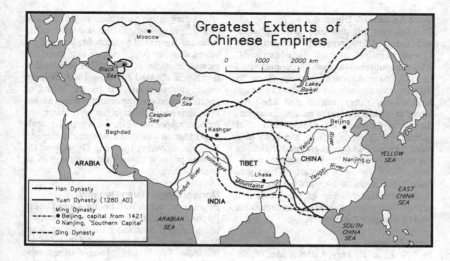

Greatest Extents of Chinese Empires

Moscow

Black Sea

Aral Sea

Caspian Sea

Baghdad

ARABIA

Kashgar

TIBET

Lhasa

Lake Baikal

Beijing

Yellow River

CHINA

Nanjing

Yangzi River

YELLOW SEA

EAST CHINA SEA

Himalaya Mountains

INDIA

ARABIAN SEA

SOUTH CHINA SEA

Han Dynasty
Yuan Dynasty (1280 AD)
Ming Dynasty
● Beijing, capital from 1421
○ Nanjing, 'Southern Capital'
Qing Dynasty

was that Chinese became 3rd and 4th-class citizens in their own country. Society was split into four categories, with the Mongols first, their central Asian allies next, northern Chinese third and southern Chinese last.

The Mongols were harsh in administering their rule, but on the economic front at least they were less interfering than the Chinese dynasties that had preceded them. More work was carried out on China's canal system and roads, offering a further stimulus to trade. The commercial revolution that had gathered pace in the Song continued unabated in the Yuan, with inter-regional and even international trade flourishing. Taxes were heavy, however, except for those of Mongol descent, who were exempt.

The grip of the Yuan Dynasty over its vast empire remained strong almost until the very end, despite internal intrigues and widespread Chinese disaffection with their Mongol rulers. By the middle of the 14th century, however, the country had become convulsed by rebellion. Chief among the rebel groups were the Red Turbans, who were guided in their mission by a belief structure compounded of diverse religious sources, ranging from Buddhism to Mani-

chaeism, Taoism and Confucianism. By 1367 Zhu Yuanzhang, originally an orphan and Buddhist novice, had climbed to the top of the rebel leadership, and in 1368 he established the Ming Dynasty and restored Chinese rule.

Ming Dynasty

Upon establishing the Ming (1368-1644), Zhu Yuanzhang took the name of Hongwu. He established his capital in Nanjing, but in 1402 the second Ming emperor, Yongle, set about building a new seat of imperial power on the site of the old Yuan capital in Beijing. In 1420 Beijing was designated the first capital and Nanjing the second (their names mean 'Northern Capital' and 'Southern Capital' respectively).

Hongwu is remembered for his despotism (he had some 10,000 scholars and their families put to death in two particular paranoid purges of his administration), but he was also a strong leader who did much to set China back on its feet in the aftermath of the Yuan collapse. This consolidation was continued by Yongle, strictly speaking the third but effectively the second Ming emperor. He ruled less autocratically, running the court bureaucracy with a steadier hand than Hongwu had, and he carried out effective campaigns in protection of the Great Wall against the Mongols.

Yongle's reign also saw, for the first time, China developing into a strong maritime nation. Zheng He, a eunuch General of Muslim descent, undertook seven great expeditions that took him and a huge fleet to South-East Asia, Persia, Arabia and even eastern Africa.

In the final years of Ming rule, official corruption, excessive eunuch power, intellectual conservatism and costly wars in defence of Korea (and ultimately China itself) against the Japanese Toyotomi Hideyoshi brought the nation to virtual bankruptcy. A famine in Shaanxi Province coupled with governmental neglect was the spark for a massive peasant rebellion that brought the Ming to a close.

Qing Dynasty

The Manchus to the north had long been growing in power, and looked with keen interest to the convulsions of rebellion in their huge neighbour. Taking advantage of the turmoil in China, they launched an invasion. Initially held back by the Great Wall, they were allowed to pass by a Ming general, who saw an alliance with the Manchus as the only hope for defeating the peasant rebel armies that now threatened Beijing itself. The Manchus lost no time in inflicting a decisive defeat on the peasant forces, and in June 1644 they marched into the Ming capital and made it their own. They proclaimed their new dynasty the Qing (1644-1912), though it was to be four decades before they finally cleared the south of Ming loyalist forces and pacified the whole country. Today's Chinese 'triads' (the modern secret societies generally thought to be involved in criminal activity, especially drug trafficking), are actually the descendants of secret societies originally set up to resist the Manchus.

Although the Manchus concentrated power in their own hands and alienated the Han Chinese, the reign of the early Qing emperors from 1663 to 1796 was a period of great prosperity. The throne was occupied by three of the most able rulers China has known: Kangxi, Yongcheng and Qianlong. The Qing expanded the empire to its greatest limits since the Han Dynasty, bringing Mongolia and Tibet under Qing suzerainty. Reduced taxation and massive flood control and irrigation projects benefited the peasants.

One problem was that the first three emperors' exceptional competence led to a further concentration of power in their hands, a challenge that none of their successors were a match for. Like the Mongols, the Manchu rulers succumbed to the ways of the Chinese and soon became culturally indistinguishable from them, modelling their government on the Ming Dynasty. Thus the isolationism and intellectual conservatism of

---

Eunuchs

An interesting feature of the Ming, and one that was principal in its eventual decline, was the ever-increasing power and numbers of eunuchs in the imperial court. Eunuchs had been employed by Chinese emperors as early as the Han Dynasty, and traditionally their role was to serve the needs of the emperor and his harem in parts of the imperial palace that were off-limits to all adult males barring the emperor himself.

By the early Ming the number of eunuchs in the service of the emperor was already 10,000, and despite imperial edicts forbidding their access to political power they continued to grow in influence and numbers throughout the Ming. Certain eunuchs (perhaps the most infamous of whom is Wei Zhongxian, who practically ruled all China in the 1620s) assumed dictatorlike power and siphoned off massive fortunes while their emperors frollicked with their consorts.

Eunuchs, generally castrated at a young age by their families in the hope that their son would attain the imperial court, probably numbered somewhere between 70,000 and 100,000 in the late years of Ming rule and exercised enormous control over the nation. ■

the Ming was passed on to the Qing. China continued to be an inward-looking nation, oblivious to the technological and scientific revolutions taking place in Europe. The coming of Europeans to China hastened the fall of the Qing and helped mould the China we know today.

Coming of the West

Seafaring Europeans couldn't be held back by a Great Wall; the best the Qing Dynasty could do to keep this latest wave of barbarians as far from the Celestial Court as possible was to limit European access to ports. The first European ships to land in China were those of the Portuguese who arrived in 1516. They were foiled in their attempts to gain a permanent foothold in China until 1557, when permission was granted for them to set up a base at Macau. Over the following century the British, Dutch and Spanish all followed hot on the heels of the Portuguese, and all were equally vociferous in their calls for trading rights and diplomatic relations with China.

These overtures of foreign merchants and their governments were initially ignored or rebuffed by the Qing government. However, in 1760 the port of Canton was opened to foreign trade under the Canton system. The system put all trade under the control of a monopolistic guild known as the Cohong. The Cohong not only controlled trade, but also mediated all foreign dealings with China, effectively keeping the foreigners at a long arm's length from the political centre in Beijing. Initially trade flourished in China's favour, but the red-haired barbarians from the West hadn't sailed around the world in order to build up a record trade deficit, and they soon began to look for a means of balancing the account books. The answer was opium.

In 1773 the British began selling Indian opium to the Chinese. After all, British purchases of tea, silk and porcelain far outweighed meagre Chinese purchases of British wool and spices. But the British ploy to even up the balance of trade naturally went down badly with the Qing authorities.

Opium addiction rose dramatically and, with Chinese silver rapidly disappearing into British pockets, the emperor thundered forth with an edict in 1800 banning the trade. Foreigners, Chinese merchants and corrupt officials duly ignored it.

After much imperial vacillation and hand wringing, in March 1839 Lin Zexiu, an official of great personal integrity, was dispatched to Canton to put a stop to the illegal traffic once and for all. He acted promptly, demanding and eventually getting some 20,000 chests of opium stored by the British in Canton. This, along with several other minor incidents, was just the pretext that hawkish elements in the British government of the day needed to win support for military action against China. In 1840 a British naval force assembled in Macau and moved up the coast to Beihe, not far from Beijing. The Opium War was on.

For the Chinese, the conflicts centred around the Opium trade were a fiasco from start to finish. While the Qing court managed to fob the first British force off with a treaty that neither side ended up recognising, increasing British frustration soon led to an attack on Chinese positions close to Canton.

The resulting treaty ceded Hong Kong to the British and called for indemnities of six million yuan and full resumption of trade. The furious Qing emperor refused to recognise the treaty, and in 1841 British forces once again headed up the coast, taking Fujian and eastern Zhejiang. They settled in for the winter, and in the spring of 1842, their numbers swollen with reinforcements, they moved up the Yangzi duly dispatching all comers. With British guns trained on Nanjing, the Qing spirit for a fight evaporated, and they reluctantly signed the humiliating Treaty of Nanjing.

Taiping Rebellion

The second half of the 19th century saw two uprisings which might have halted the process of Chinese decay: the Taiping and Boxer rebellions. The earliest of them, the Taiping movement, was founded by Hong Xiuquan, a native of Guangdong. Convinced

Unequal Treaties

The first of the many unequal treaties that were foisted on the Chinese by European (later Japanese) greed and Qing incompetence in dealing with the demands of the modern world was the Treaty of Nanjing. It brought the Opium War to a close, but it was also a humiliating slap in the face for the Qing court. According to its terms (there were 12 articles altogether) the ports of Canton, Xiamen, Fuzhou, Ningbo and Shanghai were to be opened to foreign trade; British consuls were to be opened in each of the open ports; an indemnity of 21 million Mexican dollars was to be paid to the British; the Cohong was to be disbanded; and, perhaps most humiliating, Hong Kong was to be ceded to the British 'in perpetuity'.

Unequal treaties followed thick and fast once a precedent had been established in Nanjing. The Treaty of Tianjin, originating in a Chinese refusal to apologise for having torn a British flag and culminating in a combined British-French occupation of Tianjin, provided a further 10 treaty ports and more indemnities. Following complications led to the burning of the Summer Palace by the British and the ceding of the Kowloon Peninsula. Further unequal treaties won the French the Chinese vassal state of Vietnam, gave the Japanese Taiwan, the Pescadores and the Liaodong Peninsula, and eventually opened 50 treaty ports from as far south as Simao in Xishuangbanna to Manzhouli on the Russian frontier. In the space of some 50 years or so, a spate of unequal treaties effectively turned China into a colony of the imperial forces of the day. ∎

that he was on a mission from God and professing to be the younger brother of Jesus Christ, Hong and his followers preached Christianity while smashing Buddhist, Taoist and Confucian idols and razing their temples to the ground. Hong called his movement the 'Heavenly Kingdom of Great Peace', and attempts by the Qing to suppress it only led him to declare open rebellion in 1851.

Marching north from Guangdong, the Taipings captured numerous towns on the Yangzi River; by 1853 they had captured Nanjing and brought southern China under their control. The army consisted of 600,000 men and 500,000 women, and was a highly

Taiping coin

organised and strictly disciplined group that adhered only to the Christian god. Gambling, opium, tobacco and alcohol were forbidden. Women were appointed as administrators and officials, and the practice of foot-binding was abolished along with slavery, prostitution, arranged marriages and polygamy. The peasants were attracted by the Taipings' policy of agrarian reform and fairer taxation. In many ways the Taipings were forerunners of the Communists of the following century.

However, the Taipings failed to gain the support of the Western powers, who initially remained neutral on the issue. In time, the success of the Taipings began to worry the West. It was more expedient dealing with a corrupt and weak Qing government than with the strong, united Taipings. After 1860 the Western powers allied with the Qing and a counter-offensive began. By 1864 the Taipings had retreated to their capital city of Nanjing. A Qing army aided by British army regulars and European and US mercenaries besieged and captured the city, slaughtering the defenders. Hong Xiuquan committed suicide and the rebellion ended.

Decline of the Qing

The years after the Taiping Rebellion were a time of further intrusion into China by the foreign powers. The Qing government grew progressively weaker and the lot of the peasants became increasingly miserable.

In 1861, when China needed a strong government more than ever, six-year-old Emperor Guangxu ascended to the throne. Real power remained in the hands of his aunt the Empress Dowager Wu Cixi, a former concubine. Wu Cixi saw reform and modernisation as a threat to the conservative power base of the Qing Dynasty. Clinging to this belief, she spent the next 48 years presiding over the disintegration of her empire.

The first to go was China's colonial 'possessions'. A war with France from 1883 to 1885 ended Chinese suzerainty in Indo-China and allowed the French to maintain control of Vietnam and eventually gain control of Laos and Cambodia. The British occupied Burma. In 1895 Japan forced the Chinese out of Korea and made them cede Taiwan. Britain, France, Germany and Russia rushed in to map out 'spheres of influence' in a spree of land-grabbing. By 1898 the European powers were on the verge of carving up China and having her for dinner, a meal that was averted only by a US proposal for an 'open-door' policy that would leave China open to trade with any foreign power.

Economically the Chinese government fared disastrously. China, in debt to the Western powers and Japan, began to raise taxes, which added to the general misery of the peasants. Coastal trade by foreign ships developed at the expense of the Chinese junk trade. Foreigners built railways and telegraph lines and opened coal mines and ironworks, using them exploitatively. Missionaries arrived in large numbers, threatening traditional Chinese social structures with their teachings. Chinese students returning from study abroad brought with them anti-Manchu sentiment and European-influenced political ideologies.

An attempt at 'self-strengthening' in 1881 resulted in the building of naval yards, arsenals and railways. One of its products, the modern Chinese army, was resoundingly trounced in a series of defeats during the Sino-Japanese War of the mid-1890s. The Qing court's one hope of salvation lay in the young emperor Guangxu, who had come under the influence of an influential Chinese reformer, Kang Youwei.

In 1898 the court embarked on the so-called 'Hundred Days of Reform'. Rejecting the creed of the self-strengthening movement, which took Chinese learning as the basis for applying Western learning, Kang Youwei and his reformist supporters occupied the court for 100 days, issuing decree after decree in the emperor's name. The experiment was a failure. The Empress Dowager was not amused, and the culprits were rounded up and six of them executed. Kang Youwei fled, the young emperor was placed under palace arrest and the reforming decrees rescinded.

The Qing had long been on a downhill slide and, with this final rejection of internal reform, it basically guaranteed itself a bumpy landing. The Boxer Rebellion was another push in the right direction.

Boxer Rebellion

The Boxers United in Righteousness, as they called themselves, emerged in Shandong in 1898. They originated from secret societies that probably grew in response to growing Christian influence in the area, and their name can be traced back to the martial exercises they practised. Fanatically anti-foreign, they saw 1900 as the dawn of the new age and believed themselves invincible to the bullets of the foreign forces. They might have been a far more effective force had they not lacked an organised leadership. As it was they continued to grow in numbers, and by 1900 groups of them had begun to drift into Beijing and Tianjin, attacking converted Christian Chinese and foreigners.

It was another time of vacillation and hand wringing for the imperial court who, while happy enough to see foreigners being molested on the streets, were fearful of the consequences. Nevertheless, in June 1900 the Empress Dowager issued a declaration of war against the foreign powers in the hope that the Boxers would vanquish the foreigners.

The modernised Qing army held back from the fray, allowing foreign nationals to hold out in the foreign legation compound of Beijing until August, when a combined British, US, French, Japanese and Russian force of 20,000 troops moved in and defeated the Boxers. The empress fled to Xi'an with her court, and the foreign forces levied a massive indemnity on the Qing government.

At the end of the Boxer uprising over 200 foreigners were dead and the Qing was in disarray and on its knees. The foreign forces, nevertheless, preserved the dynasty with Cixi as ruler, seeing a thoroughly defeated Qing as far more compliant entity than anything that might possibly follow it.

Fall of the Qing

With the defeat of the Boxers, even the Empress Dowager realised that China was too weak to survive without reform. But, while the civil service examinations based on the irrelevant thousand-year-old Confucian doctrines were abolished, other court-sponsored reforms proved to be a sham.

Furthermore, by now secret societies aimed at bringing down the Qing Dynasty were legion, even existing overseas, where they were set up by disaffected Chinese who had left their homeland. To make matters worse for the Qing, in 1908 the Empress Dowager died and the two-year-old Emperor Puyi ascended to the throne. The Qing was now rudderless, and quickly collapsed in two events: The Railway Protection Movement and the Wuchang Uprising of 1911.

The railway incident began with the public Chinese sentiment that newly constructed railways should be in Chinese control, not in the hands of the foreigners who had financed and built them. Plans to construct lines to provincial centres using local funds soon collapsed, and the despairing Qing government adopted a policy of nationalisation and foreign loans to do the work. Opposition by vested interests and provincial leaders soon fanned violence that spread and took on an anti-Qing nature. The violence was worst in Sichuan, and troops were taken from the Wuchang garrison in Wuhan to quell the disturbances.

As it happened, revolutionaries in Wuhan, coordinated by Sun Yatsen's Tokyo-based Alliance Society, were already planning an uprising in concert with disaffected Chinese troops. With the garrisons virtually empty, the revolutionaries were quickly able to take control of Wuhan and ride on the back of the large-scale Railway Protection uprisings to victory over all China. Two months later representatives from 17 provinces throughout China gathered in Nanjing to establish the Provisional Republican Government of China. China's long dynastic cycle had come to an end.

Early Days of the Republic

The Provisional Republican Government was set up on 10 October 1911 (a date that is still celebrated in Taiwan as 'Double Tenth') by Sun Yatsen and Li Yuanhong, a military commander in Wuchang. Lacking the power to force a Manchu abdication, they had no choice but to call on the assistance of Yuan Shikai, head of the imperial army and the same man the Manchus had called on to put down the Republican uprisings. The favour cost the Republicans dearly. Yuan Shikai placed himself at the head of the Republican movement and forced Sun Yatsen's resignation.

Yuan lost no time in dissolving the Republican government and amending the constitution to make himself president for life. When this met with regional opposition, he took the natural next step in 1915 of declaring an imperial restoration and pronouncing himself China's latest emperor. Yunnan seceded, taking Guangxi, Guizhou and much of the rest of the south with it, forces were sent to bring the breakaway provinces back into the imperial ambit, and in the confusion Yuan himself passed away. What followed was a virtual warlord era, with no single power strong enough to hold the country together until the Communists established the People's Republic of China (PRC) in 1949.

Intellectual Revolution

Chinese intellectuals had been probing the inadequacies of the old Confucian order and looking for a path to steer China into the 20th century ever since early contact with the West, but a sense of lost possibilities with the collapse of the Republican government and the start of new period of social decay lent an urgency to their worries in the early years of the 1900s. Intellectuals and students were also supported by a sense of nationalism that had been slowly growing in force since the late years of the Qing (many commentators have seen the ideologies of the Taiping and Boxer movements as underpinned by a crude nationalism).

Beijing University became a hotbed of intellectual dissent, attracting scholars from all over China (even Mao was present in his capacity as library assistant), most notably Cai Yuanpei, Hu Shi and Chen Duxiu. In their pursuit of a road to modernisation it seemed as if anything was possible, and intellectuals were merciless in their criticisms of orthodox Chinese society. Some explored ideas of social Darwinism, the Communist Manifesto was translated into Chinese and became the basis for countless discussion groups, others favoured anarchism, and all looked keenly to events unfolding in Russia, where revolutionaries had taken power.

The catalyst for demonstrations that became known as the May Fourth Movement was the decision of the Great Powers in Versailles to pass defeated Germany's rights in Shandong over to the Japanese. A huge public outcry ensued and on 4 May 1919, students took the streets in a protest that combined a sense of nationalist outrage with demands for modernisation. Mass strike action in support of the students took place throughout China. Although the disturbances were quelled and many of the ringleaders temporarily imprisoned, the May Fourth incident became a focus for a vast range of dissatisfactions and inspired a new generation of Chinese leaders.

Perhaps most interesting today is the way in which the student protests at Tiananmen in 1989 echoed the slogans and catchcries of the 1919 protests. Students bearing placards marked with 'Mr Science' and 'Mr Democracy' in 1989 were harking back to 1919, when the same slogans were used – perhaps, in fine Chinese tradition, seeking the authority of historical precedent.

Kuomintang & Communists

After initial setbacks Sun Yatsen and the Kuomintang (the KMT or Nationalist Party), which had emerged as the dominant political force after the fall of the Qing Dynasty, managed to establish a secure base in southern China, and began training a National Revolutionary Army (NRA) with which to challenge the northern warlords.

Since 1920 Russians who had taken part in the Bolshevik Revolution had been coming to China representing the Soviet government and the Communist International (Comintern), the international body dedicated to world revolution. Talks between the Comintern representatives, Li Dazhao and Chen Duxiu, eventually resulted in several Chinese Marxist groups banding together to form a Chinese Communist party (which became the CCP) at a meeting in Shanghai in 1921.

In 1922 CCP members were urged by the Moscow Comintern representatives to join the Kuomintang. There was a great deal of uneasiness within the CCP about doing this since Party members feared the Kuomintang was interested only in a national revolution to unify the country and eliminate foreign interference, rather than in a wider social revolution.

The Russians insisted that a social revolution could not occur without a national revolution first. Soviet military, economic and political advisers were sent to China between 1923 and 1927 to help the Kuomintang, perhaps primarily to help form a buttress against aggressive Japanese ambitions on the Soviet Union's eastern flank. Under threat of the withdrawal of Soviet support, the CCP joined the Kuomintang.

Sun Yatsen's death from cancer in 1925 removed the unifying influence in the faction-ridden Kuomintang. A power struggle emerged between those in the political wing who were sympathetic to the social reform policies of the Communists, and those in the military wing led by Chiang Kaishek. Chiang commanded the NRA and had strengthened his claim as Sun's legitimate heir by marrying Madam Sun Yatsen's sister. He opposed social reform and wished to preserve the capitalist state dominated by a privileged elite of wealthy family members and their associates, and supported by a military dictatorship.

Peasant Movement

Under the direction of CCP member Peng Pai, the Kuomintang set up a Peasant Training Institute in Canton where hundreds of potential peasant leaders from Guangdong, Hunan and other provinces trained for six months before returning to their home provinces to organise the peasants.

The peasant organisations grew much faster than their urban industrial counterparts, and began pressing for radical changes. They demanded that land rent be reduced to only 25% of the crop, that high taxes be removed, that taking land as payment for debts be prohibited, that farm labourers be paid more, and that the landlords' private armies and gangs be abolished.

Impressed by the strength of the peasant movement, Mao Zedong, who taught at the institute during 1925 to 1926, tried to persuade the Kuomintang leadership that the greatest potential for social revolution lay in the countryside. He was ignored as attention was focused on the impending 'Northern Expedition'.

Shanghai Coup

In 1926, in an effort to unify China, the Kuomintang embarked on the Northern Expedition to wrest power from the remaining warlords. Chiang Kaishek was appointed commander in chief by the Kuomintang and the Communists. One force of the NRA moved up through Hunan to take the city of Wuhan, which became the seat of the

Kuomintang government. Meanwhile Chiang Kaishek's force captured Nanchang.

Following this victory Chiang tried to persuade the Soviet advisers and the political and military leaders of the Kuomintang to join him. There was now an obvious struggle for power within the Kuomintang. With the NRA about to move on Shanghai, Chiang took the opportunity to put down both the Communists and his opponents in the Kuomintang.

Shanghai was under the control of a local warlord whose strength was being undermined by a powerful industrial movement organised in the city by the Communists under Liu Shaoqi and Zhou Enlai. Kuomintang strategy called for the Shanghai workers to take over key installations in the city while the NRA advanced on it. In March 1927 a general strike was called and Shanghai industry shut down; police stations and military arsenals were seized and 5000 workers were armed. The NRA entered the city not long afterwards.

Supported by the Shanghai industrialists who were worried about the trade union movement, and by foreigners who feared the loss of trade and privileges, Chiang let loose a reign of terror against the Communists and their sympathisers. With the help of Shanghai's underworld leaders and with

Chiang Kaishek

financial backing from Shanghai bankers and foreigners, Chiang armed hundreds of gangsters, dressed them in Kuomintang uniforms and launched a surprise attack overnight on the workers' militia. About 5000 Shanghai Communists were killed. Massacres of Communists and various anti-Chiang factions followed in other Chinese cities. Zhou Enlai managed to escape by a hair's breadth. Li Dazhao was executed by slow strangulation.

The political leadership of the Kuomintang was thrown into turmoil once again. Since the military supported Chiang Kaishek, the Wuhan government was forced to bow to his wishes. By the middle of 1928 the Northern Expedition had reached Beijing and a national government was established, with Chiang holding both military and political leadership.

Kuomintang Government

Even at the end of the Northern Expedition only about half the country was under direct Kuomintang control; the rest was ruled by local warlords. Despite these and other problems Chiang was obsessed with his campaigns against the Communists, which he continued in the 1930s.

Any prospects of social and rural reform under the Kuomintang were lost. In the cities, labourers were treated little better than beasts of burden. Children were used as slave labour in factories, standing at machines for 12 or 13 hours a day and sleeping under them at night. Women and children were sold as concubines, prostitutes or domestic slaves. The destitute and starving died on the streets and strikes were ruthlessly suppressed by foreign and Chinese factory owners.

In the countryside the Kuomintang 'government' consisted of a Kuomintang-appointed county magistrate who ruled in collusion with the landlords and moneylenders and their private armed guards. Attempts at reform were blocked because it was not in the magistrates' interests to reduce rents or allow the establishment of rural banks with low interest rates for peasants.

The magistrates used money made available by the government at low interest and lent it at higher interest to the poor farmers. If rural reformers persuaded farmers to use fertiliser to increase crop yields, the farmers would have to borrow money at high interest rates to buy fertiliser – then, if a better crop resulted, the local merchants would simply lower the buying price ensuring hardship for the farmers. Peasant protests were often dealt with by the private armies and gangs retained by many landlords, while the peasants' wives and children were taken into the landlords' households as domestic slaves in lieu of paying debts.

Tax collectors had police powers and could imprison peasants for failing to pay taxes and rent. Peasants who did not want to go to jail were forced to borrow money at interest rates of up to 700% a year. In some instances land taxes were collected 60 years in advance. Not only were most peasants destitute, they were terrified of taking any step which would bring them into conflict with armed authority. The Communists quickly realised that the only way to win a social revolution was through the barrel of a gun.

Civil War

After the massacre of 1927 the remaining Communist forces staged insurrections in several towns. Rebel units of the Kuomintang under Zhou Enlai and Zhu De (who held a high-ranking post in the NRA but was sympathetic to the Communists) seized Nanchang and held it for several days until they were driven out by loyal Kuomintang troops. The revolt was a fiasco, but it marked the beginning of the Communist Army.

In Changsha, Mao Zedong organised an uprising of the peasantry, miners and rebel Kuomintang soldiers. Mao's army moved south through Hunan, fighting Kuomintang troops, and climbed into the Jinggangshan mountains on the border between Hunan and Jiangxi. They were reinforced by Zhu De's troops, and a strategy was mapped out to first consolidate control over the Jinggang area and then slowly expand from there.

Mao Zedong

However, the Party hierarchy led by Li Lisan followed the orthodox Marxist theory that revolution must be based in the cities and towns, and ordered the Communist army to attack Nanchang and Changsha. After two costly defeats at Changsha in 1930, Mao and Zhu refused to obey Li's orders to attack Changsha again. There ensued a brief Party war in which a number of anti-Maoists were killed or imprisoned. From then on the power base of the revolution was moved squarely to the countryside and the peasants.

Communist-led uprisings in other parts of the country brought various parts of the country under their control. However, the Communist armies were still small, with limited resources and weapons. The Communists adopted a strategy of guerrilla warfare, emphasising mobility and rapid concentration and deployment of forces for short attacks on the enemy, followed by swift separation once the attack was over. Pitched battles were avoided except where their force was overwhelmingly superior. The strategy was summed up in a four-line slogan:

The enemy advances, we retreat;
The enemy camps, we harass;
The enemy tires, we attack;
The enemy retreats, we pursue.

By 1930 the ragged Communist forces had been turned into an army of perhaps 40,000, and presented such a serious challenge to the Kuomintang that Chiang had to wage a number of extermination campaigns against them. He was defeated each time, and the Communist Army expanded its territory.

The Long March
Chiang's fifth extermination campaign began in October 1933, when the Communists suddenly changed their strategy. Mao and Zhu's authority was being undermined by other members of the Party who advocated meeting Chiang's troops in pitched battles, but this strategy proved disastrous. By October 1934 the Communists had suffered heavy losses and were hemmed into a small area in Jiangxi.

On the brink of defeat, the Communists decided to retreat from Jiangxi and march north to Shaanxi. In China's northern mountains the Communists controlled an area which spread across Shaanxi, Gansu and Ningxia, held by troops commanded by an ex-Kuomintang officer who had sided with the Communists after the 1927 massacre.

There was not one 'Long March' but several, as various Communist armies in the south made their way to Shaanxi. The most famous was the march from Jiangxi Province which began in October 1934, took a year to complete and covered 8000 km over some of the world's most inhospitable terrain. On the way the Communists confiscated the property of officials, landlords and tax-collectors, redistributed the land to the peasants, armed thousands of peasants with weapons captured from the Kuomintang, and left soldiers behind to organise guerrilla groups to harass the enemy. Of the 90,000 people who started out in Jiangxi only 20,000 made it to Shaanxi. Fatigue, sickness, exposure, enemy attacks and desertion all took their toll.

The march proved, however, that the Chinese peasants could fight if they were given a method, an organisation, leadership, hope and weapons. It brought together many people who later held top positions in China after 1949, including Mao Zedong, Zhou Enlai, Zhu De, Lin Biao, Deng Xiaoping and Liu Shaoqi. It also established Mao as the paramount leader of the Chinese Communist movement; during the march a meeting of the CCP hierarchy recognised Mao's overall leadership and he assumed supreme responsibility for strategy.

Japanese Invasion

In September 1931 the Japanese occupied the potentially wealthy but underdeveloped area of Manchuria, setting up a puppet state with the last Chinese emperor, Puyi, as the symbolic head.

Despite the Japanese invasion, Chiang was obsessed with putting down the Communists. 'Pacification first, resistance afterwards' was his slogan. The Communists believed that unless the Japanese were defeated there would be no China left at all, and advocated an anti-Japanese alliance with the Kuomintang. Instead, Chiang launched his extermination campaigns, the last of which forced the Communists to retreat to Shaanxi.

At the end of 1936 Chiang flew to Xi'an to oversee yet another extermination campaign against the Communists. The deadlock was broken in an unexpected manner. In what became known as the Xi'an Incident, Chiang was taken prisoner by his own generals led by Marshal Zhang Xueliang who commanded an army of Manchurian troops. (See the Shaanxi chapter for more details.) Chiang was forced to call off his extermination campaign and to form an anti-Japanese alliance with the Communists. In 1937 the Japanese launched an all-out invasion and, by 1939, had overrun eastern China. The Kuomintang retreated west to Chongqing.

At the end of 1941 America entered the war, after the Japanese bombed Pearl Harbor. The Americans hoped to use the Chinese to tie up as many Japanese troops as possible and to use China as a base for attacking Japanese shipping and troops in South-East Asia. Chiang hoped the Americans would win the war against the Japanese and provide him with the munitions he required to finally destroy the Communists.

From 1938 until the end of the war the Japanese were never seriously harassed by the Kuomintang troops, as Chiang attempted to save his troops for renewed attacks on the Communists once the Americans had defeated the Japanese. The US general Joseph Stilwell, who was sent to China in 1942 by President Roosevelt to improve the combat effectiveness of the Chinese army, concluded that 'the Chinese government was a structure based on fear and favour in the hands of an ignorant, arbitrary and stubborn man...' and that its military effort since 1938 was 'practically zero'.

Defeat of the Kuomintang

Since the defeat of Japan was in the USA's own interest, Chiang saw no need to maintain his alliance with the Communists, reasoning that the Americans would support him regardless.

The Kuomintang-Communist alliance collapsed in 1941 when Kuomintang troops ambushed the rear detachment of one of the Communist armies. This non-combat detachment was annihilated and its commander, Ye Ding, was imprisoned in Chongqing. Chiang then blockaded Communist forces to prevent them from receiving supplies. Although the Communists did not directly retaliate, clashes between the Kuomintang and the Communists were frequent, often developing into all-out civil war.

Nevertheless, the Communist armies and guerrillas expanded into areas occupied by the Japanese. When the war against Japan ended in 1945 the Communist army numbered 900,000 and was backed by militia and several million active supporters. With the surrender of Japan in 1945, a dramatic power struggle began as the Kuomintang and Communist forces gathered in Manchuria for the final showdown.

By 1948 the Communists had captured so much US-supplied Kuomintang equipment and had recruited so many Kuomintang soldiers that they equalled the Kuomintang in both numbers and supplies. Three great battles were fought in 1948 and 1949 which saw the Kuomintang defeated and hundreds of thousands of Kuomintang troops join the

Communists. The Communists moved south and crossed the Yangzi – by October all the major cities in southern China had fallen to them.

In Beijing on 1 October 1949, Mao Zedong proclaimed the foundation of the PRC *(Zhonghua Renmin Gongheguo* in Chinese). Chiang Kaishek fled to the island of Formosa (Taiwan), taking with him the entire gold reserves of the country and what was left of his air force and navy. Some two million refugees and soldiers from the mainland crowded onto the island. President Truman ordered a protective US naval blockade to prevent an attack from the mainland – the USA continued to recognise Chiang's delusion of being the legitimate ruler of all China.

Early Years of the PRC

The PRC started as a bankrupt nation. The economy was in chaos following Chiang's flight to Taiwan with the gold reserves. The country had just 19,200 km of railways and 76,800 km of usable roads, all in bad condition. Irrigation works had broken down and livestock and animal populations were greatly reduced. Industrial production fell to half that of the prewar period and agricultural output plummeted.

With the Communist takeover, China seemed to become a different country. Unified by the elation of victory and the immensity of the task before them, and further bonded by the Korean War and the necessity to defend the new regime from possible US invasion, the Communists made the 1950s a dynamic period. The drive to become a great nation quickly was awesome.

By 1953 inflation had been halted, industrial production had been restored to prewar levels and the land had been confiscated from the landlords and redistributed to the peasants. On the basis of earlier Soviet models, the Chinese embarked on a massive five-year plan that was successful in lifting production on most fronts.

At the same time, the party increased its social control by organising the people according to their work units *(danwei)*, and dividing the country into 21 provinces, five autonomous regions, two municipalities (Beijing and Shanghai), and around 2200 county governments with jurisdiction over approximately one million party sub-branches.

Hundred Flowers

While China was moving from strength to strength on the economic front in the early years of the PRC, immense problems remained in the social sphere, particularly with regard to the question of intellectuals. Many Kuomintang intellectuals had stayed on rather than flee to Taiwan, and still more Overseas Chinese, many of them highly qualified, returned to China soon after Liberation to help in the enormous task of reconstruction. Returning Chinese and those of suspect backgrounds were given extensive re-education courses in special universities put aside for the purpose, and were required to write a self-critical 'autobiography' before graduating. For many it was a traumatic experience.

Meanwhile, writers, artists and film-makers were subject to strict ideological controls guided by Mao's writings on art during the Yan'an period. The issue came to a head around the figure of a writer, Hu Feng, who, in response to an easing of these controls in the early years of the first five-year plan, spoke out about the use of Marxist values in judging creative work. He soon became the object of nationwide criticism and was accused of being in the employ of the Kuomintang. Before long a witch-hunt was on in artistic circles for evidence of further 'Hu Fengism'.

In the upper echelons of the party itself opinions were divided as to how to deal with the problem of the intellectuals. But Mao, along with Zhou Enlai and other influential figures, felt that the party's work had been so successful that it could roll with a little criticism, and in a closed session Mao put forward the idea of 'letting a hundred flowers bloom' in the arts and 'a hundred schools of thought contend' in the sciences.

It was to be a full year before Mao's ideas

were officially sanctioned in April 1957 but, once they were, intellectuals around the country responded with glee. Complaints poured in on everything from party corruption to control of artistic expression, from the unavailability of foreign literature to low standards of living; but most of all, criticisms focused on the CCP monopoly on power and the abuses that went with it. The party quickly had second thoughts about the flowers, and an anti-rightist campaign was launched. Within six months 300,000 intellectuals had been branded rightists, removed from their jobs, and in many cases incarcerated or sent to labour camps.

Great Leap Forward

The first five-year plan had produced satisfactory results on the industrial front, but growth of agricultural yields had been a disappointingly low 3.8%. The state was posed with the difficult problem of how to increase agricultural production to meet the needs of urban populations coalescing around industrialised areas. As with the question of dealing with intellectuals, the party leadership was divided on how to respond. Some, such as Zhou Enlai, favoured an agricultural incentive system. Mao favoured mass mobilisation of the country and inspirational exhortations that he believed would jumpstart the economy into first-world standards overnight.

In the event it was Mao who won the day, and the Chinese embarked on a radical programme of creating massive agricultural communes and drawing large numbers of people both from the country and urban areas into enormous water control and irrigation projects. In Mao's view revolutionary zeal and mass cooperative effort could overcome any obstacle and transform the Chinese landscape into a productive paradise. At the same time Mao criticised the earlier emphasis on heavy industry, and pushed for small local industry to be developed in the communes, with profits going back into agricultural development.

Despite the enthusiastic forecasts, at the end of the day inefficient management, little incentive to work in the common field, and large numbers of rural workers engaged in industrial projects resulted in a massive slump in agricultural output. With industry in confusion and agriculture at an all-time low, China was struck by two disasters: the floods and droughts which ruined the harvests of 1959 and 1960, and the sudden withdrawal in 1960 of all Soviet aid.

Sino-Soviet Split

Droughts and floods were beyond even Mao's ability to control, but in the Great Leap Forward and the Sino-Soviet dispute that led to the withdrawal of Soviet aid he played no small part. Basically Mao's prob-

---

Mao & the Bomb

Mao took extreme exception to Kruschev's policy of peaceful coexistence with the capitalist West. In Mao's view confrontation with the forces of imperialism was an inevitability, while Kruschev drew on Lenin in pointing to the establishment of socialist states and the existence of mass union movements in the West to justify a more conciliatory line.

More interestingly, as the Soviet press dwelt more and more on the horrors of nuclear war, the Chinese remained remarkably sanguine about its aftermath. Drawing on curiously naive statements by Mao himself, the Chinese press maintained that while perhaps half of the human race would be wiped out in a nuclear conflagration, imperialism would be annihilated and the remaining victorious socialist peoples would raise a civilization 'thousands of times higher than the capitalist system' and create 'a truly beautiful future for themselves'.

When the Soviets withdrew their foreign experts in 1960 they took with them scientists working with the Chinese on a Chinese bomb. The soviet scientists shredded all documentation relating to the bomb before leaving, but they had not counted on Chinese ingenuity. Remarkably, piecing the shredded documents together again, they discovered crucial information that allowed them by 1964 to have successfully built and tested their own bomb. ∎

lems with the Soviet Union stemmed from the latter's policy of peaceful coexistence with the USA, Kruschev's de-Stalinisation speech, and what Mao generally felt to be the increasingly revisionist nature of the Soviet leadership. Sino-Soviet relations became ever frostier, with Kruschev reneging on a promise to provide China with a prototype atomic bomb and siding with the Indians in a Sino-Indian border dispute.

In 1960 the Soviets removed all their 1390 foreign experts working in China. With the experts went the blueprints for some 600 projects that the two powers had been working on together including China's nuclear bomb program.

Prelude to the Cultural Revolution

Mao's extreme views, his opposition to the bureaucratisation of the CCP, his roles in the Hundred Flowers movement, the Great Leap Forward and the disintegration of Sino-Soviet relations had all left Mao in an uncomfortable position with the party. There were no doubt feelings that he should be put out to pasture, and Mao himself felt that his vision of the continuing Chinese revolution was becoming increasingly unheeded by his fellows. One man who sought to change all this was Lin Biao, the minister of defence and head of the People's Liberation Army (PLA).

In the early 1960s, Lin had a collection of Mao's sayings compiled into a book that was to become known simply as the Little Red Book, though its real title was *Quotations from Chairman Mao*. Using his position, Lin saw to it that the book became the subject of study sessions for all PLA troops. At the same time PLA propaganda writers produced another significant literary effort: *The Diary of Lei Feng*. Lei Feng was an unknown PLA truck driver who gave everything in his love for Chairman Mao, and who died an unmarked death when a truck backed over him. The book was introduced into the school system as a standard text and Mao exhorted the people to learn from the PLA, which was under his and Lin's control, bypassing the authority of the party.

These general background events show Mao manoeuvring for power in the early '60s, but the precipitating factor for the Cultural Revolution itself was a play by a historian named Wu Han. The revolution was, after all, a *cultural* revolution, and although it quickly deepened its lines of attack into Chinese culture in its broader sense, it was on the literary cultural front that things got underway.

Wu's play *The Dismissal of Hai Rui from Office*, in its depiction of an upright Song official defying the authorities in defence of the people's rights, was felt to be a direct reference to Mao's dismissal of Peng Dehuai, the army marshal who had dared to raise his voice in protest against the Great Leap Forward. The work was attacked on strict Marxist ideological grounds and battle lines were drawn within the party on how to deal with the problem.

The Cultural Revolution (1966-70)

In 1966 the so-called Group of Five led by the current mayor of Beijing, Peng Zhen, met to discuss the Wu Han issue, and although they agreed that it was of great significance they ultimately concluded that it was an academic matter. Jiang Qing, Mao's wife and an erstwhile Shanghai B-grade stage and film actress, felt otherwise, and held a forum in Shanghai to expound her views on the need for a socialist purification of the arts. Lin Biao invited Jiang to coordinate the cultural policy of the PLA as a result. The stage was set for what is properly known as the Great Proletarian Cultural Revolution.

From this point events moved swiftly and unpredictably. There was a multitude of complicated factors for what started as a purge of the arts turning into a mass movement that swept the entire nation into four years of chaos, but basically divisions within the party, political intrigues and broad discontent in the general Chinese populace came together in an explosion of pent-up frustration. For his part, Mao was fed up with the bureaucratisation of the party and the slow pace of change; Lin Biao had ambitions to put his PLA at the vanguard of Chinese cultural policy formulation; throughout China millions of ordinary people had been stifled by the controls of the CCP and angered by official corruption and petty power-mongering.

In Beijing the Group of Five were purged and simultaneously wall posters went up at Beijing University attacking the university administration. Mao officially sanctioned the wall posters and criticisms of party members by university staff and students, and before long students were being issued red armbands and taking to the streets. The Red Guards *(hongweibing)* had been born. By August 1966 Mao was reviewing mass parades of the Red Guards, chanting and waving copies of his little red book.

Nothing was sacred enough to be spared the brutal onslaught of the Red Guards as they went on the rampage through the country. Universities and secondary schools were shut down; intellectuals, writers and artists were dismissed, killed, persecuted or sent to labour in the countryside; publication of scientific, artistic, literary and cultural periodicals ceased; temples were ransacked and monasteries disbanded; and many physical reminders of China's 'feudal', 'exploitative' or 'capitalist' past, including temples, monuments, and works of art were destroyed.

By the end of January 1967 the PLA had been ordered to break up all 'counter-revolutionary organisations', an edict that was interpreted by the PLA as all groups with interests contrary to their own. Thousands of Chinese were killed in the ensuing struggles, notably in Sichuan and in Wuhan, where the PLA took on a coalition of 400,000 Red Guards and workers' groups, killing over 1000 people. The struggles continued through September of 1967, and even Mao and Jiang Qing began to feel that enough was enough. 'Ultra-left tendencies' were condemned and the PLA was championed as the sole agent of 'proletarian dictatorship'.

The Cultural Revolution took a new turn as the Red Guards slipped from power and the PLA began its own reign of terror. The so-called Campaign to Purify Class Ranks was carried out by Workers' Mao-Thought Propaganda Teams on anyone with a remotely suspect background – this could mean anything from having a college education to having a distant cousin who lived overseas. Those who needed re-education were sent to schools in the countryside that combined intensive study and self-criticism with hard labour.

Significance & Repercussions Like most of Mao's well-intentioned experiments, the Cultural Revolution was a disaster of vast proportions. His belief in the possibility of a constantly self-renewing, dynamic society in a state of continual revolution (along the lines laid out by Mao Thought of course), unleashed forces that in the end proved nearly unstoppable. Students and workers needed little encouragement to rise up against the petty officials who had made their lives so miserable, but once the process had started, where did it stop?

At the end of the day new power structures were put into place and many of those for whom the Cultural Revolution really did seem to offer the promise of a new society were locked out of the process. One party that benefited was the PLA, which ended up with a deeper penetration of most government organisations.

Unexpectedly, a major victim of the Cultural Revolution was the man who had done so much to get it started: Lin Biao. In the aftermath of the Cultural Revolution, Mao was troubled by the powers of the PLA, and demanded self-criticisms from senior PLA officers. It is thought that a desperate Lin Biao sought support for an assassination attempt on Mao and, failing to find it, fled with his family to Russia in a Trident jet. The 'renegade and traitor', as the Chinese press labelled him, died when his plane crashed in Mongolia on 13 September 1971.

The sudden reversal in Lin Biao's fortunes, who until a few days earlier had been Mao's chosen successor and second only to Mao in the people's adoring hearts, was for many Chinese the final straw. The neverending policy shifts, the mayhem of the Cultural

Revolution and countless other mistakes left the vast majority of Chinese weary and disillusioned. Though few would speak it aloud, a great many Chinese were disillusioned with the system.

Rise of Zhou Enlai

With Lin dead and Mao's health steadily deteriorating as he approached 80 years of age, Premier Zhou Enlai now exercised the most influence in the day-to-day governing of China. Remarkably, Zhou had survived the Cultural Revolution, though he tended to support the same economic policies as Liu Shaoqi, who had been painted with the same brush as Kruschev and hounded into a premature death in the Cultural Revolution. Zhou's loyalty to Mao, however, appears never to have wavered since Mao assumed supreme leadership of the Party in the 1930s. As premier, Zhou's main preoccupation during the Cultural Revolution was to hold together the administrative machinery of the government.

After the 1969 Congress, Zhou set about reorganising the government structure and restoring and expanding China's diplomatic and trade contacts with the outside world – including the USA. Despite attempts at reconciliation by the Chinese in the 1950s, the USA continued to follow a policy of armed 'containment' of China which aimed to isolate and eventually bring about the collapse of the Communist government.

In 1969 the Nixon administration finally cancelled most of the restrictions against trade, travel, and cultural and journalistic contacts with China; Chinese and US diplomats discussed terms of peaceful coexistence and the ceasing of US armed protection of Taiwan. The Bamboo Curtain finally parted in 1972 when Nixon stepped off the plane at Beijing Airport, to be greeted by Zhou.

Second Coming of Deng Xiaoping

In 1973 Zhou's efforts allowed a return to power of Deng Xiaoping, vilified as China's 'No 2 Capitalist Roader' during the Cultural Revolution. Deng joined Zhou in a faction of 'moderates' or 'pragmatists'. On the other side of the ring were the 'radicals', 'leftists' or 'Maoists', led by Mao's wife Jiang Qing. With their power threatened by the resurgence of Zhou and Deng, the radicals mounted the oddly named 'Criticise Lin Biao and Confucius' campaign – in reality an attack on Zhou and Deng.

While Zhou lived, the inevitable power struggle was kept at bay. However, his health rapidly deteriorated and, in the midst of the radical resurgence, he died in early January 1976. A memorial service was held in the Great Hall of the People in Beijing, from which Mao was inexplicably absent. At the end of the service, Deng Xiaoping too was absent, and the newspapers started to propagate the line that China was once again threatened by high-level party officials who were taking the 'capitalist road'. The post of acting premier went to the fifth-ranking Vice-Premier Hua Guofeng, little known in the West. Deng had been passed over for what appeared to be a compromise candidate for the job.

Tiananmen Incident (1976)

In March 1976, during the Qing Ming Festival, when the Chinese traditionally honour the dead, people began to lay wreaths dedicated to Zhou on the Heroes' Monument in Tiananmen Square; every night, for about a week, huge piles of paper flowers were removed from the square. More and more people came to honour Zhou with wreaths and eulogies until the square was filled with thousands of people. Wreaths were sent by ministries of the central government, departments of the central command of the PLA and other military units as well as factories, schools, stores and communes in the Beijing area.

For the Chinese, Zhou represented both the antithesis of the madness and fanaticism of the Cultural Revolution and its instigators, and the last vestige of goodness and justice in the government – without him everything seemed lost. Though there was some scattered official support for the demonstration in Tiananmen, on the whole it was a rare, spontaneous display of how the Chinese felt about China's general situation. Indirectly it was an attack on Mao and an open defiance of the leftists who had commanded that there be no more mourning for Zhou.

In the early hours of 5 April, the wreaths and poems in Tiananmen were again torn down from the square and carted away. Those who tried to prevent the removal of the tributes were arrested, and guards surrounded the monument. On the same day, tens of thousands of people swarmed into the square, demanding the return of the wreaths and the release of those arrested, only to be attacked and dispersed by thousands of men wearing the armbands of the Workers' Militia and armed with staves.

The subsequent demonstrations and riots became known as the 'Tiananmen Incident'. The demonstrations were declared counter-revolutionary and the blame was laid on Deng. On 7 April a meeting of the Politburo stripped Deng of all office and Hua Guofeng was made vice-chairman of the Party while continuing in his role as premier.

Mao was still in public view but disappeared in the middle of the year. Who had access to him, what he was being told, whether he still had the capacity to grasp and influence any of the events taking place, is unknown. The Chinese were now going through another struggle. Mao had led them against the Kuomintang, the Japan and the USA in Korea, and then into the depths of the Cultural Revolution. Finally at Tiananmen his own people turned against him, just a few blocks from his home behind the walls of the Zhongnanhai government compound.

In late July the massive Tangshan earthquake struck northern China, claiming over a quarter of a million lives. For the Chinese great natural disasters foreshadow the end of dynasties, and once again it seemed as though a cycle of Chinese history had concluded. With the portentous sign from heaven that he had lost the mandate to rule, Mao died in the early hours of 9 September 1976.

The Gang of Four

With Mao gone the two factions had to stand on their own feet. The meat in the sandwich was Hua Guofeng, whose authority rested largely on his status as the chosen successor to Mao Zedong.

Change came swiftly and dramatically. Less than a month after the death of Mao, Hua Guofeng had Jiang Qing and a number of other leftist leaders and their supporters arrested. She and three other principal allies of Mao – Yao Wenyuan, Zhang Chunqiao and Wang Hongwen – were selected as scapegoats for this latest ideological change and became known as the 'Gang of Four'.

They were not to come to trial until 1980, and when it took place it provided a bizarre spectacle, with the blame for the entire Cultural Revolution falling on their shoulders. Jiang Qing remained unrepentant, hurling abuse at her judges and holding famously to the line that she 'was Mao's dog – whoever he told me to bite I bit'. Its meaning was not lost on most Chinese, and privately whispers circulated that the problem had been not a Gang of Four but a 'Gang of Five'. Jiang Qing's death sentence was commuted and she lived on until 1991 under house arrest.

Third Coming of Deng Xiaoping

In the middle of 1977 Deng Xiaoping returned to power for the third time and was appointed to the positions of vice-premier, vice-chairman of the Party and chief of staff of the PLA. His next step was to remove Hua Guofeng. In September 1980 Hua relinquished the post of premier to Zhao Ziyang, a long-standing member of the CCP whose economic reforms in Sichuan in the mid-1970s overcame the province's bankrupt economy and food shortages and won him Deng's favour. In June 1981 Hu Yaobang, a protégé of Deng's for several decades, was named Party chairman in place of Hua.

Final power now passed to the collective leadership of the six-member Standing Committee of the CCP which included Deng, Hu and Zhao. The China they took over was racked with problems, a backward country in desperate need of modernisation. Ways had to be found to rejuvenate and replace an aged leadership (themselves) and to overcome the possibility of leftist backlash. The wasteful and destructive power struggles that had plagued the CCP since its inception had to be eliminated. The need for order had to be reconciled with the popular desire for more freedom; those with responsibility had to be rewarded but watched over in case of misuse of privilege; the crisis in faith in Communist ideology had to be overcome; and a regime now dependent on the power of the police and military for its authority had to be legitimised.

Resolution of a Theological Crisis

Deng was able to ward off immediate threats from the leftists by locking them up, but he still had to deal with a major crisis – what to do with Mao Zedong. One step taken was the resolution on the historical role of Mao Zedong issued in 1981 by the Central Committee of the CCP.

Deng had every intention of pulling Mao off his pedestal and making a man out of the god. However, he couldn't denounce Mao as Khrushchev had denounced Stalin, since Mao had too many supporters in the Party and too much respect among the common people. An all-out attack would have provoked those who would otherwise have begrudgingly fallen in line with Deng and his supporters. Instead a compromise stand was taken.

The resolution cited Mao as a great Marxist and a great proletarian revolutionary, strategist and theorist, saying:

It is true that he made gross mistakes during the Cultural Revolution, but, if we judge his activities as a whole, his contributions to the Chinese Revolution far outweigh his mistakes.

The resolution went on to blame Mao for initiating and leading the Cultural Revolution which 'was responsible for the most severe setback and the heaviest losses suffered by the Party, the state and the people since the founding of the PRC.

1980s & Beyond – Economics in Command

The Deng Xiaoping years have seen a slow but sure freeing up of the Chinese economy, so that by the early '90s China has become the fastest growing economy in the world. This is an achievement which in itself points to major changes not just in economic policy but in the outlooks of the ordinary Chinese that have brought about this success. The early '70s saw the Chinese people dispirited and psychologically scarred by the events of the Cultural Revolution, most of them employed in state enterprises that doled out pay checks whether workers did anything or not. The Chinese system was one in which politics were in command, the philosophy of which is well summed up in the Cultural Revolution saying: 'a socialist train running late is better than a revisionist train running on time'.

In 1978 China embarked on its Four Modernisations (agriculture, industry, national defence, and science and technology) in earnest. The phrase dated back to a 1963 speech of Mao's, but with the fall of the Gang of Four it really began to gather speed. Plans were initiated for the training of some 800,000 technical personnel to administer the modernisations; new universities were established; and a policy of sending students overseas for training was approved. Deng was also at the same time looking for ways to speed up the modernisation process with infusions of foreign technical expertise. In July 1979 four Special Economic Zones were set up in Zhuhai (next to Macau), Shenzhen (next to Hong Kong), and Shantou and Xiamen (both just across the Taiwan Strait from Taiwan).

The same period also saw the 'Responsibility System' being applied to agriculture and industry. Allowing agricultural households and factories to sell their quota surpluses on the open market. All aspects of the economic front have seen a gradual loosening of restraints through the '80s and into '90s.

The overall picture of the Deng years has been of a move away from a centrally planned economy to a market-governed one. Incidents such as the Beijing Massacre of 1989 and the spectre of rampant inflation in 1988 have resulted in periodic tightening of controls, but the late 1991 14th Congress endorsement of Deng Xiaoping's 'reform and opening' policy line 'for 100 years' would seem to indicate that China is set for more of the rapid growth that has marked the last decade.

All this is hardly surprising; there is really nowhere else for the CCP to go. The sudden demise of the Soviet Union was a salutary lesson, and for the Communists plunging ahead with their oxymoronic 'socialist market economy' line provides the promise of affluence with the trade-off of a continued Communist monopoly of power.

Hong Kong & Taiwan

In 1984 a Sino-British agreement allowed for the reversion of Hong Kong to China in 1997. The original 'unequal' Treaty of Nanjing (1840) foisted on China by the UK in the Opium War had ceded Hong Kong to the British 'in perpetuity', but the New Territories adjoining Kowloon were 'leased' to the British for 99 years in 1898. In the event, Britain agreed to hand the entire colony lock, stock and skyscrapers back to China when the New Territories lease expired.

The transition of power looks set to be a bumpy ride. According to the terms of the 1984 agreement, Hong Kong's transfer to Chinese rule is to take place under the concept of 'one country, two systems'. The implementation and administration of this 'system' was laid out in the Basic Law, which promised the former colony a 'high degree of autonomy'. Just how much 'autonomy' though has become a subject of acrimonious debate between the UK and China.

In the aftermath of the Beijing Massacre the people of Hong Kong, who for the most part had been too busy making money to pay much attention to the Sino-British negotiations over their future, suddenly began to sit up and wonder what kind of protections the Basic Law offered them against a regime that put down street protests with machine guns

and tanks. Enter Chris Patten, the UK's latest appointee to the Hong Kong governorship. His attempts to lower the voting age in Hong Kong from 21 to 18 and to extend the democratic make-up of the governing Legislative Council (Legco) have been stonewalled by China.

At present Hong Kong's future remains murky, and the souring of Sino-British relations has affected business confidence and even the progress of projects such as the new airport scheme. It's a situation that the government and people of Taiwan have been watching with great interest.

The Kuomintang government of Chiang Kaishek fled (or 'withdrew', depending on your politics) to Taiwan in 1949 following the Communist takeover and has been there ever since, getting steadily richer and richer and, over recent years, increasingly democratic. At present Taiwan has the world's largest foreign currency reserves, is arguably the most democratic of the 'Four Little Tigers' (or 'Dragons' as the Chinese refer to them), has a lively, uncensored press and has lifted all travel restrictions for its nationals. However, over this remarkable success story lies the shadow of Communist-Kuomintang politics.

The problem is a simple one. The Nationalists (Kuomintang) occupied Taiwan still maintaining their right to govern China itself. The Communists, for their part, maintain that Taiwan is a province of the mainland. Reunification is a prickly issue in Taiwan, particularly since many Taiwanese have now had the opportunity to visit mainland China and see for themselves the kind of system they might have to live under if the two countries came together again.

Most Taiwanese are extremely sceptical of the sincerity of 'one country, two systems' promises and wonder aloud about the possibility of maintaining the freedoms they have won in their own country when the mainland takes such objection to the limited democratic rights being discussed for Hong Kong. At present, everyone seems to be happy to let the situation ride for a while, the Taiwanese continuing to do what they do best (get rich) and the mainland Chinese having a crack at becoming a Big Tiger. Most Chinese, however, feel that once Hong Kong has reverted to China in 1997, Taiwan will be the next major issue on the mainland foreign affairs agenda.

Dissidence & the Beijing Massacre

There has been very little tolerance for outspokenness in the PRC since its inception. Brief moments of free expression have all been smartly followed by crackdowns and tight ideological control. Campaigns against 'spiritual pollution', 'peaceful evolution' and 'bourgeois liberalisation' have all marked a deep-seated fear that the technology transfers and infusions of foreign capital from the West are bringing with them imports of a more threatening nature: democracy and freedom of speech.

The ideological obsessions that marked the early years of the PRC have waned in recent years, though the first year or so following the 1989 Beijing Massacre saw an attempt to dust the cobwebs off old slogans and even Lei Feng, the self-sacrificing PLA officer who sold his soul to Mao, was shunted out of retirement briefly. The truth of it, however, is that the party is ideologically bankrupt, and the central issue nowadays is party power not ideological purity. Deng himself is famously uninterested in the colour of the cat – 'if it catches mice, it's a good cat' – and the tacit deal is that the economy will be allowed to continue on its merry path of liberalisation, the Chinese will be allowed to do what they wanted to do all along (make money), and the party will stay in power – no talk of opposition politics.

For the most part Chinese are fairly happy with this arrangement. But it's a tricky one insofar as the Party has to keep its side of the bargain. When the economy lurches in its stride widespread discontent tends to emerge, bringing the Party under attack on a number of fronts. This can be seen in the events leading up to what has become known as the Beijing Massacre, Tiananmen or, in

Chinese, the 'Student Uprising' *(xuécháo)* or simply 'Fourth of June' *(liùsì)*.

By 1988 the unleashing of free (though limited) market forces, the reduction of state subsidies, and an increase in money supply all combined to bring rapid price inflation to China. Panicking consumers made a run on the banks and used their money to stock up on all manner of goods before prices could be raised. Officially, the inflation rate was reported to be 20%, but many observers thought that 30% was a more realistic figure. Remembering that inflation helped bring down the Kuomintang in 1949, conservative CCP leaders called for a halt to the reforms – at a time when many economists were saying that China needed even more rapid reforms.

Adding fuel to the fires of discontent were increasing reports of corruption at all levels of government. Public discontent with inflation, corruption, nepotism, the lack of individual freedom and the slow pace of reform was a recipe for protest. The catalyst turned out to be the death of Hu Yaobang.

At the age of 73, Hu Yaobang died suddenly from natural causes on 15 April 1989. Although not exactly a hero of the students when he lived, his death served as a rallying point for reformists. On 22 April during the weekend after his death, China's leaders gathered at the Great Hall of the People for an official 'mourning for Hu'. Just outside, in Tiananmen Square, approximately 150,000 students and other activists held their own ceremony which soon turned into a massive pro-democracy protest.

It didn't end there. As the weather warmed up students flocked to Beijing to camp out in the square. By the middle of May, the crowds of protesters in and around the square had swelled to nearly one million. Workers and even policemen joined in. Protests erupted in at least 20 other cities. Approximately 3000 students staged a hunger strike for democracy in the square. Railway workers assisted students wanting to come to Beijing by allowing them free rides on the trains. Students enrolled at Beijing's Art Institute constructed the 'Goddess of Democracy' in

Tiananmen Square – a statue which bore a striking resemblance to America's Statue of Liberty. The students made speeches demanding a free press and an end to corruption and nepotism. Huge pro-democracy demonstrations in Hong Kong, Macau and Taiwan lent support. The arrival of the foreign press corps turned the 'Beijing Spring' into the media event of 1989.

While vehemently denouncing the demonstrations, CCP leaders showed surprising restraint for a while. A major reason for this might have been the fact that Soviet leader Mikhail Gorbachev was scheduled to visit Beijing from 15 May to 18 May for the first Sino-Soviet summit since 1959 – a bloodbath just before his arrival would probably cause him to cancel the trip.

On 20 May, straight after Gorbachev's departure, martial law was declared. Zhao Ziyang was ousted from power because he had openly sympathised with the students. Li Peng assumed control of the party with the backing of Deng Xiaoping and Yang Shangkun. Troops were slow to mobilise, and when they did enter the city they found their way obstructed by huge crowds who'd set up roadblocks. A widely rumoured plan by the military to deploy forces using Beijing's subway system was halted when transit workers shut down the power supply.

By 2 June, 350,000 troops had been deployed around Beijing. In the early hours of the morning on 4 June the 27th Army division attacked. Unlike the troops that had been deployed in Beijing previously, this was a crack division led by a relative of President Yang Shangkun. Other units loyal to Deng were also employed. Heavy tanks and armoured vehicles made short work of the barricades, crushing anyone who got in their way, while troops with automatic weapons strafed the crowds on the streets.

The number of deaths that resulted from the action is widely disputed. Eyewitness accounts have indicated that hundreds died in the square alone, and it's likely that fighting in the streets around the square and in the suburbs of Beijing may have led to several thousand casualties. Hospitals were filled to overflowing, with PLA troops refusing to allow doctors to treat their patients, and rumours of secret mass graves were rife. The truth will probably never be known. What is certain is that the Party lost whatever remaining moral authority it had in the action, and sooner or later will have to deal with widespread recriminations. Nearly a year afterwards, a wall in Beijing was still scrawled with the words: 'all this shall not be forgotten'.

The Future

Every revolution evaporates, leaving behind only the slime of a new bureaucracy.

Franz Kafka

China is at present changing so rapidly that it is anyone's guess where it is all heading. The big question mark is whether the Chinese government will be able to exercise its traditional levels of control over an increasingly affluent, educated and mobile populace. There are already many signs of cracks in the system, but while most Chinese themselves welcome moves towards liberalisation most admit China needs a firm hand to keep things running smoothly and to prevent a breakdown into regional power bases.

The 1992 14th Party Congress saw a major changing of the guard that seems to have been orchestrated from behind the scenes by an aged Deng Xiaoping. A great many reformists with extensive experience managing the booming coastal regions of China were elevated to the politburo. The signs would all indicate that Deng, perhaps prompted by the threat of the Soviet and Eastern European experience, is moving China in a market-oriented, neo-authoritarian direction along the lines of Singapore. State-guided economic growth coupled with strict ideological control are the order of the day.

While these Party changes are important, the question that is occupying more and more China watchers is the gathering inertia of the Chinese economic miracle. It is obvious the central powers are increasingly devolving to a provincial level, while ordinary Chinese themselves are opting out of the system to grasp entrepreneurial opportunities that come their way. Traditional controls like the work unit and housing registration are becoming less relevant as Chinese flock to the coastal regions to take up work in private factories and organisations. As even traditionally conservative organisations such as the PLA experiment with the stock market and private enterprise, Party ideology is becoming less and less relevant. After all, economic success in South Korea and Taiwan brought with it political changes that few would have predicted 10 years ago.

Miron Mushkat, a Hong Kong-based economist, has pointed out that the Chinese economy is 'like a truck with no brakes' and that 'the only way to stop it is to crash it'. Either way, whether the Party lets the truck keep careering onwards or whether it swerves it off the road, it is likely that the Chinese one-party state is also in for a rough ride and some upsets.

GEOGRAPHY

The country is bounded to the north by deserts and to the west by the inhospitable Tibetan Plateau. The Han Chinese, who first built their civilisation around the Yellow River (Huang He), moved south and east towards the sea. The Han did not develop as a maritime people so expansion was halted at the coast; they found themselves in control of a vast plain cut off from the rest of the world by oceans, mountains and deserts.

China is the third-largest country in the world, after Russia and Canada. Only half of China is occupied by Han Chinese; the rest is inhabited by Mongols, Tibetans, Uigurs and a host of other 'national minorities' who occupy the periphery of Han China, in the strategic border areas. The existence of numerous minority languages is why maps of China often have two spellings for the same place – one spelling being the minority language, the other being Chinese. For example, Kashgar is the same place as Kashi.

From the capital, Beijing, the government rules 21 provinces and the five 'autonomous regions' of Inner Mongolia, Ningxia, Xinjiang, Guangxi and Tibet. Beijing, Tianjin and Shanghai are administered directly by the central government. China also controls about 5000 islands and lumps

China & the Spratly Islands

If they were not such a contentious piece of real estate, very few people would have heard of the Spratly Islands. To find them on a map, look out for a parcel of little dots in the South China Sea hemmed in by Malaysia, Brunei, the Philippines, Vietnam and China way to the north. The interesting thing is that all these countries have claims on the islands.

It is tempting to ask what all the fuss is about. After all, this is a collection of 53 specks of land, many of which are reefs and shoals rather than islands. The answer is oil. The absurdity of the answer is that no oil has been discovered in the region, and some experts dispute that any will ever be found. Yet the very possibility that there *might* be oil in the Spratly Islands has set all the countries in the region at loggerheads with each other.

China, the most distant of the claimants, sees its territorial rights to the area as being validated by a historical relationship with the islands that dates back to the Han Dynasty. The ruins of Chinese temples can still be found on some of the islands. Vietnam has for long been a disputant to this claim, and in 1933 the colonial French government of Vietnam annexed the islands. They lost them to Japan in 1939. With Japan's WW II defeat, the question of the Spratly Islands was left unaddressed, and it was not until a Philippine claim in 1956 that the Taiwan Nationalist government reasserted the traditional Chinese claim over the island group by occupying Taiping, the largest of the islands (they are still there). Vietnam followed by hoisting a flag over the westernmost of the islands. The Chinese struck back in 1988 by sinking two Vietnamese ships.

With all the countries of the region embarking on programmes of updating their military capabilities, along with the North Korean nuclear issue, the Spratly Islands remain one of the most potentially destabilising issues in the Asian region. ■

of rock which occasionally appear above water level; the largest of these is Hainan off the southern coast.

Taiwan, Hong Kong and Macau are all firmly regarded by the PRC as Chinese territory, and under the 1984 agreement with the UK, Hong Kong will be handed back to China in 1997. There is conflict with Vietnam concerning sovereignty over the Nansha and Xisha island groups in the South China Sea; Vietnam claims both and has occupied some of the Nansha Islands. In 1989 the Chinese took some of these islands from Vietnam by force. Other disputed islands in the Nansha group are also claimed by the Philippines, Taiwan and Malaysia.

China's topography varies from mountainous regions with towering peaks to flat, featureless plains. The land surface is a bit like a staircase descending from west to east. At the top of the staircase are the plateaus of Tibet and Qinghai in the south-west, averaging 4500 metres above sea level. Tibet is referred to as the 'Roof of the World'. At the southern rim of the plateau is the Himalayan mountain range, with peaks averaging 6000 metres high; 40 peaks rise 7000 metres or more. Mount Everest, known to the Chinese as Qomolangma Feng, lies on the China-Nepal border.

Melting snow from the mountains of western China and the Tibet-Qinghai Plateau provides the headwaters for many of the country's largest rivers: the Yangzi (Chang Jiang), Yellow (Huang He), Mekong (Lancang Jiang) and Salween (Nu Jiang) rivers. The latter runs from eastern Tibet into Yunnan Province and on into Myanmar (Burma).

Across the Kunlunshan and Qilianshan mountains on the northern rim of the Tibet-Qinghai Plateau and the Hengduanshan mountains on the eastern rim, the terrain drops abruptly to between 1000 and 2000 metres above sea level. The second step down on the staircase is formed by the Inner Mongolia, Loess and Yunnan-Guizhou plateaus, and the Tarim, Sichuan and Junggar basins.

The Inner Mongolia Plateau has open terrain and expansive grasslands. Further south, the Loess Plateau is formed of loose earth 50 to 80 metres deep – in the past the soil erosion which accompanied a torrential rainfall often choked the Yellow River. The Yunnan-Guizhou Plateau in the south-west has a lacerated terrain with numerous gorges, rapids and waterfalls, and is noted for its limestone pinnacles with large underground caverns such as those at Guilin and Yangshuo.

The Tarim Basin is the largest inland basin in the world and is the site of the Xinjiang Autonomous Region. Here you'll find the Taklamakan Desert (the largest in China) as well as China's largest shifting salt lake, Lop Nur (Luóbù bó), where nuclear bombs are tested. The Tarim Basin is bordered to the north by the Tianshan mountains. To the east of this range is the low-lying Turpan Depression, known as the 'Oasis of Fire' and the hottest place in China. The Junggar Basin lies in the far north of Xinjiang Province, beyond the Tianshan range.

As you cross the mountains on the eastern edge of this second step of the topographical staircase, the altitude drops to less than 1000 metres above sea level. Here, forming the third step, are the plains of the Yangzi River valley and northern and eastern China. These plains – the homeland of the Han Chinese, their 'Middle Kingdom' – are the most important agricultural areas of the country and the most heavily populated. It should be remembered that two-thirds of China is mountain, desert, or otherwise unfit for cultivation. If you exclude the largely barren regions of Inner Mongolia, Xinjiang and the Tibet-Qinghai Plateau from the remaining third, all that remains for cultivation is a meagre 15 or 20% of land area. Only this to feed a billion people!

In such a vast country, the waterways quickly took on a central role as communication and trading links. Most of China's rivers flow east. At 6300 km long, the Yangzi is the longest in China and the third longest river in the world after the Nile and the Amazon. It originates in the snow-covered Tanggulashan mountains of south-western

Qinghai, and passes through Tibet and several Chinese provinces before emptying into the East China Sea.

The Yellow River, about 5460 km long and the second-longest river in China, is the birthplace of Chinese civilisation. It originates in the Bayan Harshan mountains of Qinghai and winds its way through the north of China into the sea east of Beijing. The third great waterway of China, the Grand Canal, is the longest artificial canal in the world. It originally stretched 1800 km from Hangzhou in south China to Beijing in the north, though most of it is no longer navigable.

CLIMATE

China experiences great diversity in climate. Spread over such a vast area, the country is subject to the worst extremes in weather, from the bitterly cold to the unbearably hot. There isn't really an 'ideal' time to visit the country, so use the following information as a rough guide to avoid temperature extremes. The warmest regions are found in the south and south-west in areas such as Xishuangbanna, the south coast and Hainan Island. In summer, high spots like Emei Shan are a welcome relief from the heat.

North

Winters in the north fall between December and March and are incredibly cold. Beijing's temperature doesn't rise above 0°C (32°F), although it will generally be dry and sunny. North of the Great Wall, into Inner Mongolia or Heilongjiang, it's much colder with temperatures dropping down to -40°C and you'll see the curious sight of sand dunes covered in snow.

Summer in the north is around May to August. Beijing temperatures can rise to 38°C (100°F) or more. July and August are also the rainy months in this city. In both the north and south most of the rain falls during summer.

Spring and autumn are the best times for visiting the north. Daytime temperatures range from 20°C to 30°C (68°F to 86°F) and there is less rain. Although it can be quite hot

during the day, nights can be bitterly cold and bring frost.

Central

In the Yangzi River valley area (including Shanghai) summers are long, hot and humid. Wuhan, Chongqing and Nanjing have been dubbed 'the three furnaces' by the Chinese.

You can expect very high temperatures any time between April and October. Winters are short and cold, with temperatures dipping well below freezing – almost as cold as Beijing. It can also be wet and miserable at any time apart from summer. While it is impossible to pinpoint an ideal time to visit, spring and autumn are probably best.

South

In the far south, around Canton, the hot, humid periods last from around April through September, and temperatures can rise to 38°C (100°F) as in the north. This is also the rainy season. Typhoons are liable to hit the south-east coast between July and September.

There is a short winter from January to March. It's nowhere near as cold as in the north, but temperature statistics don't really indicate just how cold it can get, so bring warm clothes.

Autumn and spring can be good times to visit, with day temperatures in the 20°C to 25°C (68°F to 75°F) range. However, it can be miserably wet and cold, with perpetual rain or drizzle, so be prepared.

North-West

It gets hot in summer, but at least it's dry. The desert regions can be scorching in the daytime. Turpan, which sits in a depression 150 metres below sea level, more than deserves the title of the 'hottest place in China' with maximums of around 47°C (117°F).

In winter this region is as formidably cold as the rest of northern China. In Ürümqi the average temperature in January is around -10°C (14°F), with minimums down to almost -30°C (-22°F). Temperatures in

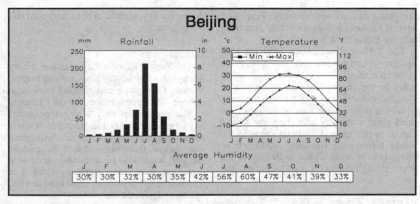

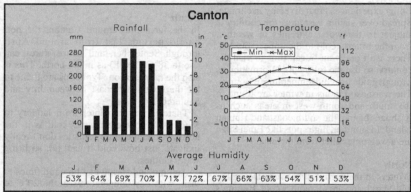

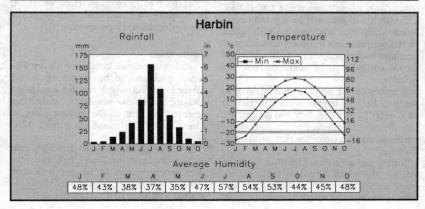

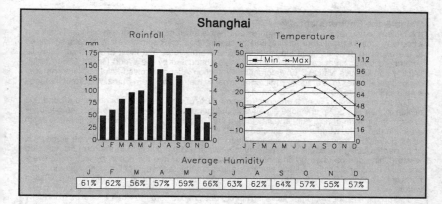

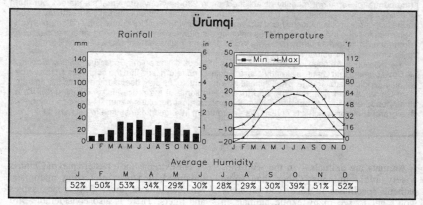

Turpan are only slightly more favourable to human existence.

Tibet

For details of this special region see the Tibet chapter in this book.

FLORA & FAUNA

Given the fact that China is a large country spanning most of the world's climatic zones, it's not surprising that there is a great diversity in plant and animal life. Unfortunately, human beings have had a considerable impact and much of China's rich natural heritage is rare, endangered or extinct. To the

government's credit, more than 300 nature reserves have been established protecting over 1.8% of China's land area. Many animals are officially protected, though illegal hunting and trapping continues. A bigger problem is habitat destruction, caused by agriculture, urbanisation and industrial pollution.

Bird-watching is a possibility, especially in the spring. Some good places for this activity include the Zhalong Nature Reserve in Heilongjiang Province; Qinghai Lake in Qinghai Province; and Poyang Lake in northern Jiangxi Province – China's largest freshwater lake.

China & the Environment

It is difficult to find reliable facts and figures on China's environment, but one thing is certain: it's in a bad way. China's great leaps forward and the current economic boom have largely been sustained at the expense of controls on industrial waste and emissions, and most of the major cities lie smothered under great canopies of smog. Tests conducted by the World Health Organization (WHO) and China's National Environmental Protection Agency showed levels of airborne suspended particulates to average 526 micrograms per sq metre in northern China. WHO recommends a safe limit of 60 to 90 micrograms per sq metre.

The main problem is coal. It provides for some 70% of China's energy needs and around 900 million tonnes of it go up in smoke every year. Sulphur dioxide is another problem. It comes back to earth in the form of acid rain, and has turned the Guangdong-Guangxi-Guizhou-Sichuan basin area into one of the world's worst affected areas.

Air pollution is thought to be exacting a heavy toll on Chinese life expectancy, with some 26% of all deaths being traceable to respiratory disease. Industrial pollution in the form of untreated waste (China dumps three billion tonnes of untreated water into the ocean by way of its rivers annually) threatens China's coastal wetlands and is creating a shortage of drinking water in many parts of the country. Some reports indicate that up to 700 million Chinese are supplied with polluted water.

The problem is not that China lacks legislature designed to curb the worst excesses of industry (the central government recently established some 230 new environmental standards), but that these laws designed to safeguard the environment are rarely implemented. It's not unusual to see huge billboards proclaiming the need to 'Preserve the Environment for Future Generations' plonked right next to huge industrial complexes belching out plumes of viscous-looking smoke and oozing untreated waste into a nearby river. The World Bank maintains that only 32% of China's annual 25 billion tonnes of industrial waste is treated in any way.

He Bochun, a Chinese intellectual, argues in his book *China on the Edge: the Crisis of Ecology & Development* that China is already past the point of no return, and that the country is on the verge of an ecological catastrophe. The Chinese government, for its part, seems to be taking the attitude that China can get rich and dirty, and then spend some of the proceeds on cleaning up. It's a time-honoured tradition, but then China, the world's most populous nation, is perhaps unique in the grand scale on which it is abusing its environment in a race against time to get rich. ∎

Animals are animals – in the wild they wisely avoid humans. Other than some pathetic specimens in zoos, you probably won't get to see many exotic animals in China. However, there is a good deal of wildlife on the luncheon menu – snake, monkey, pangolin, bear, giant salamander and raccoon are among the tastes that can be catered for, not to mention more mundane dog, cat and rat dishes.

Perhaps no animal better represents both the beauty and the struggle of wildlife in China than the panda. These splendid animals are endangered by a combination of hunting, habitat encroachment and natural disasters. Sparsely populated regions of Sichuan, Tibet and Xinjiang provide a habitat for other magnificent creatures including snow leopards, argali sheep and wild yaks.

The extreme north-eastern part of China is inhabited by some interesting mammals: reindeer, moose, musk deer, bears, sables and tigers. There is also considerable bird life – cranes, ducks, bustards, swans and herons are among the winged creatures found in this region.

Plants have fared somewhat better under the crunch of a billion people, but deforestation, grazing and intensive cultivation have taken a toll. One of the rarest trees is the magnificent Cathay silver fir in Guangxi Province. China's last great tracts of forest are in the subarctic north-eastern region near the Russian border. For sheer diversity of vegetation, the area around Xishuangbanna in the tropical south is the richest part of China. This region also provides habitats for herds of wild elephants. Both the creatures and the tropical rainforest are under intense pressure from slash-and-burn agriculture.

Hainan Island also has diverse tropical plant and animal life. There are seven nature reserves on the island, though it's fair to say that more than a few endangered species still end up on the dinner plate.

Perhaps the most beautiful cultivated plant is the bamboo. Bamboo – which is actually a grass rather than a tree – comes in many varieties and is cultivated in south-east China for use as building material and food. Other useful plants include herbs, among them ginseng, golden hairpin, angelica and fritillary.

If you're interested in delving further into China's flora & fauna, two good books on the subject are *Living Treasures* by Tang Xiyang (Bantam Books, 1987) and *The Natural History of China*, by Zhao Ji, et al (Collins, 1990).

GOVERNMENT

Precious little is known about the inner workings of the Chinese government, but Westerners can make educated guesses.

The highest authority rests with the Standing Committee of the CCP Politburo. The Politburo comprises 25 members. Below it is the 210-member Central Committee, made up of younger Party members and provincial Party leaders. At grassroots level the Party forms a parallel system to the administrations in the army, universities, government, and industries. Real authority is exercised by the Party representatives at each level in these organisations. They, in turn, are responsible to the Party officials in the hier-

archy above them, thus ensuring strict central control.

Between 1921 and 1935 the general secretary of the Central Committee and the Politburo held overall leadership of the Party. The significance of this title changed during the Long March when Mao became the Party chairman, assuming power over both Party and government. The post of general secretary was subordinated to him and eventually abolished in 1945. Provision was then made for a chair and four vice-chairs to constitute a Standing Committee of the Politburo.

The Standing Committee of the Politburo still retains supreme power but its members are now accorded a hotchpotch of titles. Foremost on the Standing Committee is general secretary Jiang Zemin. Diminutive Deng Xiaoping no longer holds any official government posts, yet remains the most powerful man in China. Another member of the Standing Committee is the relatively youthful (in his 60s) Premier Li Peng. The post of general secretary was restored in 1956 as a top administrative job and seems to be regaining its original mantle as the foremost leadership position in the Party.

However, in the Chinese political sphere titles and appearances are slippery things and often belie the holder's real power. Hu Yaobang was general secretary until he was suddenly dropped or, to put it officially, 'resigned' the post in a political upheaval in 1987. His successor, Zhao Ziyang, was even more unceremoniously dumped in 1989. The 14th Party Congress of 1992 judged Zhao guilty of 'serious mistakes of judgment and splitting the party' in his handling of the Tiananmen demonstrations of 1989.

The day-to-day running of the country lies with the State Council, which is directly under the control of the CCP. The State Council is headed by the premier. Beneath the premier are four vice-premiers, 10 state councillors, a secretary-general, 45 ministers and various other agencies. The State Council implements the decisions made by the Politburo: it draws up quotas, assesses planning, establishes priorities and organises finances. The ministries include Public Security, Education, Defence, Culture, Forestry, Railways, Tourism, Minority Affairs, Radio & TV, the Bank of China and Family Planning.

Rubber-stamping the decisions of the CCP leadership is the National People's Congress (NPC). In theory the NPC is empowered to amend the constitution and to choose the premier and members of the State Council. The catch is that all these officeholders must first be recommended by the Central Committee, and thus the NPC is only an approving body. Its composition is surprising: there is a sizable number of women, non-Communist Party members, intellectuals, technical people and industrial managers. The army is not well represented and nor are the rural areas which supply only a small fraction of the total of NPC members.

Exactly why so much effort is made to maintain the NPC and give it publicity through TV and newspapers is unknown, but it seems important for the Chinese government to maintain the illusion of democracy. The NPC also chooses the President of the PRC, who at the time of this writing was octogenarian Yang Shangkun. The president, the theoretical head of state, in fact has little political power, although Yang has gained much influence through his connections to the military – his younger half-brother, Yang Baibing, is secretary-general of the Central Military Commission which controls the army.

If the NPC is a white elephant, then the great stumbling block of the Chinese political system is the bureaucracy. There are 24 ranks on the ladder, each accorded its own particular privileges. The term 'cadre' is usually applied to all bureaucrats, but that term includes both the lowliest clerks and the political leaders with real power (from the work-unit leaders to Jiang Zemin) as well as Party and non-Party members.

Despite attacks on the bureaucratic system by the Red Guards it survived intact, if many of its former members did not. Deng's three-year purge (headed by Hu Yaobang) weeded out many officials who might slow down implementation of his new economic policies. Other offenders (according to the *Selected Works of Deng Xiaoping* published in 1983) include the despotic, the lazy, the megalomaniac, the corrupt, the stubborn and the unreliable.

Problems with the Chinese bureaucracy really began with the Communist takeover in 1949. When the Communist armies entered the cities the peasant soldiers were installed in positions of authority as Party representatives in every office, factory, school and hospital.

Once in power these revolutionaries, who had rebelled against the despotism of the Kuomintang, reverted to the inward-looking, conservative values of their rural homes: respectful of authority, suspicious of change, interested in their families' comfort, sceptical of the importance of technology and education, and suspicious of intellectuals. Their only real training had been in the Communist Army, which had taught them how to fight, not how to run a modern state.

During the 1950s Liu Shaoqi and Deng Xiaoping tried to build up a competent bureaucracy, but their training organisations were decimated by Mao's Cultural Revolution. The bureaucratic system survived but new officials had neither the technical competence nor the ideological zeal which was supposed to push China on to greater glories. The slothfulness, self-interest, incompetence and preoccupation with the pursuit of privilege continued.

At grassroots level, the basic unit of social organisation outside the family is the work unit (dānwèi). Every Chinese person is theoretically a member of one, whether he or she works in a hospital, school, office, factory or village, though many Chinese nowadays slip through the net by being self-employed or working in a private operation. For those who are members, tight controls are exercised by the leaders of the unit they belong to.

Nothing can proceed without the work unit. It issues ration coupons for grain, oil, cotton and coal, and it decides if a couple may marry or divorce and when they can have a child. It assigns housing, sets salaries, handles mail, recruits Party members, keeps files on each unit member, arranges transfers to other jobs or other parts of the country, and gives permission to travel abroad. The work unit's control extends into every part of the individual's life.

The Chinese political scene is made up of white elephants, stumbling blocks and work units. There is even a bogeyperson to contend with – the army. The PLA covers the land forces, the navy and the air force; it developed from the Chinese Workers and Peasants Red Army of the 1920s and '30s. The army is currently being trimmed down from about 4.2 million members to around three million. There are also several million workers and peasants in the local militia, which can be mobilised in time of war.

In 1949 the army took control of every institution in China. The Cultural Revolution strengthened its grasp, and there is still a considerable overlap between the Party, army and state. The death of Lin Biao was a major blow to the army's power. Deng dealt another major blow by putting on trial, and subsequently imprisoning, a number of high-ranking military leaders who had supported the Gang of Four. In a delicate transfer of power he has also tried to wean the army away from participation in the political scene and towards target practice and modernisation of equipment and fighting techniques.

Mao held that 'political power grows out of the barrel of a gun'. He also maintained that 'the Party commands the gun and the gun must never be allowed to command the Party'. The gun (or armed forces) has been a burden in Chinese politics because whoever had control of it could do away with their opponents. Mao lost almost all influence in the civilian government during the early 1960s, but his command of the army was the deciding factor in the showdown with Liu Shaoqi.

Likewise, Deng Xiaoping couldn't have made a comeback after Mao's death if the military had completely supported Jiang Qing. Whichever faction can control the military is likely to control the government. As to the other manipulations involved, if you can work out how Deng could come back three times from the political grave then you have probably unlocked the secrets of political power in China today.

Political Dissidence & Repression

If you close the people's mouths and let them say only nice things, it keeps the bile inside.
(From one of the last posters to appear on Democracy Wall)

The events in 1989 showed that not everyone in China is content with the political system, which clearly lacks channels allowing constructive criticism to reach the higher levels of government. In the last decade a handful of extraordinarily courageous political dissidents spoke their minds and paid the price. Many such dissidents though labelled 'counter-revolutionaries' were, ironically, devoted Communists. Once a dissident is convicted as a counter-revolutionary, there is next to no legal recourse since they are stripped at the same time of both political and civil rights.

There are several categories of dissident: members of 'democracy and human rights' movements; individuals protesting unjust treatment by officials, arbitrary arrest, or miscarriage of justice; members of religious organisations; and members of ethnic minorities protesting for political or religious reasons.

Wei Jingsheng, a leading figure in the Democracy Wall Movement, was arrested during the first 'Beijing Spring' of 1979. After a seven-hour trial Wei was sentenced to 15 years imprisonment. Despite rumours of his developing schizophrenia and having died, in the September 1993 lead-up to 2000 Olympics vote, he was released from prison six months short of his full sentence, weakened but sane and alive.

Catholics in China have repeatedly been arrested and imprisoned for refusing to break with the Vatican and join the independent Roman Catholic Church in China. The Roman Catholic Bishop of Shanghai, Ignatius Gong Pinmei, consistently supported independence of the church from the government. Reportedly still detained in Shanghai's main prison, Bishop Gong was arrested in 1955. Sentenced to life imprisonment in 1960, he has spent well over 30 years in prison. Many other Roman Catholic priests and lay Catholics have been arrested and imprisoned. Father Francis Xavier Zhu Shude was first detained in a labour camp in 1953, and was repeatedly sentenced to further imprisonment for carrying out religious duties in the camp. He died there in 1983 at the age of 70, after more than 30 years in detention.

Tibetan dissidents such as Kalsang Tsering, Lobsang Chodag and Thubten Kelsang Thalutsogentsang have been arrested in Lhasa for expressing support for the Dalai Lama and Tibetan independence.

Prisoners are held in a variety of institutions, including prisons, detention centres, labour camps and corrective labour camps. Remote areas such as Tibet, Qinghai, Xinjiang and some provinces in the northeast contain large numbers of such camps, which serve as the equivalent of political exile for dissidents sent there.

The Chinese government rigorously ignores requests for information on dissidents on the grounds that this topic is beyond 'foreign interference': it is strictly an 'internal affair'. Quite possibly South Africa, which has received much criticism from China, could argue that apartheid qualifies as an internal matter. The truth is that any country which denies access to such topics invites conjecture as to the validity of its claims of justice.

More details on this topic can be found in publications such as Amnesty International's China report or *Seeds of Fire – Chinese Voices of Conscience*, edited by Geremie Barmé and John Minford.

ECONOMY

It is obvious to all visitors to China that the country is presently on an economic roll. Wages and living standards are rising significantly in the urban centres, all of which are littered with massive construction projects; the shops are brimming with consumer goodies, stock markets have opened in Shanghai and Shenzhen, the special economic zones are experiencing double-digit annual growth, and Chinese everywhere are rushing in droves to grasp the opportunities presented in the shift from politics-in-command system to an economics-in-command system.

It has not always been like this of course. Apprehensive that foreign trade would bring about economic dependency, Mao had largely isolated China from the world economy. At the same time, private enterprise was anathema to the great cooperative enterprise of the Communist experiment, and self-interest was equated with a feudal and exploitative past. All aspects of the economy, from barber shops and restaurants to steel mills and paddy fields, came under state ownership and rigid state control.

Probably the chief catalyst in the move away from the Mao experiment has been Deng Xiaoping, a tenacious and shrewd politician armed with a bevy of catch cries that underline a pragmatic approach to maintaining Party rule in China. That most of the slogans sanctioning the Chinese entrepreneurial boom are contradictory is irrelevant. The important thing is that the economic freedoms implicit in China's 'socialism with Chinese characteristics', its 'socialist market economy', are clearly trade-offs, allowing individual Chinese to pursue economic interests in return for continued one-party rule. In Deng's most famous disavowal of ideologically structured economics: 'it doesn't matter if the cat is white or black – if it catches mice, it's a good cat'.

What changes have the Deng years seen exactly? The basic changes have been a move away from central planning towards market forces, a decollectivisation of agriculture, and a move away from the concept of high-speed 'great leaps' forward towards balanced agricultural and industrial growth fuelled by foreign trade, science and technology imports and foreign investment. At the heart of this major shift has been an unwavering concentration on the 'Four Modernisations'; namely, industry, agriculture, defence and science & technology. The aim is to transform China into a modern state by the year 2000.

Today the PRC's centrally planned economy has moved to a complex three-tiered system. On the first rung is the state, which continues to control consumer staples (such as grains and edible oils) and industrial and raw materials. On the second rung come private purchases or sales of services and commodities within a price range set by the state. On the third rung is the rural and urban 'free market' in which prices are established between buyer and seller, except that the state can step in if there are unfair practices.

On an ideological level, such economic changes have proved stressful for the Party, which is forced into all manner of contortions to try and avoid the obvious conclusion that China is on its way to becoming a fully fledged capitalist state. But official statements fool no-one. The average Chinese will agree that the vast socialist experiment was a failure and that they hope to see the economic reforms continue in the direction they are currently taking. If Party ideology is strained to near breaking point, the opportunities to get gloriously rich leave few with much time to worry unduly about it.

While the economy is indeed booming, all is not roses on the Chinese economic front. The big problem is spectre of overheating and hyper-inflation. In 1992 GNP grew by 13% and industrial output by a remarkable 21%. At the same time, central, provincial and foreign capital investment grew at record rates, putting price pressures on basic commodities and fuelling inflation. The yuan went on a downhill slide in early '93 (black-market rates for yuan against the US dollar are a good indication of the current value of the yuan in the so-called 'swap shops' that have emerged in China – in August '93 the yuan was running at 10 to 1 against the dollar as opposed to an official exchange rate of 5.65 to 1).

Investment sprees by the central and provincial governments in the meantime created a shortage of funds with which to pay farmers for state crop purchases. Farmers were fobbed off with IOUs and the state printing presses gunned into action to produce more money to pay off the debts.

Many economists feel that the above factors all indicate that the Chinese economy is in for a downturn. The chances are that this will be a temporary phenomenon in the order of the 1988-89 recession. But it's worth bearing in mind that the 1988-89 attempt to stabilise the economy led to the widespread social unrest and the Tiananmen Incident. The last thing the government wants is more trouble of this kind, and hence recent attempts to maintain business-as-usual outlook despite obvious signs that the economy is once again overheating.

Industrial Reform

Prior to 1979 a factory would be allotted a certain quantity of raw materials and told to produce a certain number of units by the appropriate ministry in Beijing. Any profit had to be remitted to the central government. It was then up to the ministry to determine how much of that profit should be returned to the factory in the form of subsidies for repairs, retooling or expansion. Factory managers were essentially cogs in a machine controlled from above.

The reforms of the early Deng years saw the initiation of a long process of devolution of central powers to the sources of production. This process is still ongoing, and the government remains saddled with huge state enterprises that soak up vast amounts of state funds in the way of subsidies and incentives.

The most important of the early reforms was allowing state enterprises to develop so-called 'within' 'without' production plans. According to this, enterprises were allowed to carry out plans of their own after meeting centrally set plan targets with funds economised from allocated funds. Enterprises were given increased freedoms in setting up bonus and incentive schemes for workers, and from 1984 a contract system was set up, providing enterprises with autonomy from the central system in hiring and firing labour.

Critics point out that the reforms have

produced a dual economy of state-run and private enterprises that do not necessarily complement each other. State enterprises are also a drain on the economy insofar as they often have to borrow in order to pay the taxes and profits required by the central government for the maintenance of preferential credit and transport access.

Obviously with this in mind, early '93 saw continued moves by the Chinese government towards widescale privatisation, with the promise that small state enterprises could be sold or leased by public bidding. In late '92 Hong Kong newspapers reported plans by the Guangdong provincial government to privatise *all* its state industries within five years. Such reports should be taken with a pinch of salt, but all the same point to a growing dissatisfaction with the relatively poor performance of the public sector.

Rural Reform

In 1978 the government introduced an agricultural 'responsibility' system which replaced the rigidly collectivised agriculture system instituted under Mao. The system is applied differently from province to province, retaining state-owned farms in the north-east where mechanised agriculture prevails, while in the south-west 'market gardening' controlled by individual villages or families is more appropriate, given the difficult terrain.

Under the system a work team or family was contracted to work a plot of state land. They decided what to grow and when, provided the government with its quota, and were then allowed to sell any surplus at rural free markets and keep the profit. In 1984 a new system was initiated whereby peasants would be granted long land leases with the right to transfer and renew their leaseholds, although it is not possible for peasants or anyone else to actually own land.

Around the end of 1984 it was decided to do away with the quota system which required peasants to sell a certain percentage of their produce to the state. The idea now is that if peasants can get more for their produce in free markets it will encourage

them to increase production. The two exceptions are grain and cotton, over which the state maintains control. The state contracts for grain and cotton then purchases its requirements for more than the market price and permits the rest of the crop to be regulated by the market price. In theory, when the market price is high the state sells its reserves to bring the price down.

Since early 1985, following more than 35 years of rigid price controls, the government has been moving to decontrolling prices for agricultural produce. The existence of the free market along with state-subsidised gives rise to a two-tiered pricing system, and where free-market prices exceed state prices it inevitably gives rise to corruption – those with the right connections can re-sell goods at rates that undercut market prices. In March 1993, Li Peng called for the abolition of controls on prices for grains, one of the few areas where such controls were still applied. It remains to be seen whether such calls are implemented.

Foreign Investment

In sharp contrast to the extreme self-reliance of the Maoist period is China's present open-door policy on foreign investment and joint-venture enterprises with foreign companies.

In an attempt to attract foreign investment to China, the government has set up 'Special Economic Zones' (SEZs) such as Shenzhen County which borders Hong Kong. Low wages, reduced taxation and abundant labour have been used to encourage foreign companies to set up industries in the SEZs. Low production costs mean that Chinese goods can be competitive on the world market. Since 1984, when 14 coastal cities were opened to foreign investment along similar lines, just about every major city and town has been seeking foreign investment. There are hundreds of joint-venture enterprises, from oil and gas exploration in the South China Sea to the construction of several commercial nuclear power plants.

Not all goes smoothly – foreign business people are sometimes driven mad by the

Kafkaesque paperwork for contracts, by the overcharging, or by just plain inefficiency in the use of equipment and even unwillingness on the part of the Chinese to accept advice on increasing production. Interference by government officials is a serious problem. Foreign companies are usually not free to hire and fire employees, and companies are often forced to give the best managerial jobs to those with political connections, rather than to those who are most qualified. Nor are foreign companies free to use incentives like higher pay for deserving employees. Government officials set the salaries, often at exorbitant rates, but the money is not paid to the employee – it first goes to the government, which then deducts anywhere from 50% to 90% for the state.

Another problem is that the Chinese show little respect for intellectual property. Foreign companies who set up high-technology factories in China have often found that once the Chinese learn their manufacturing techniques, the state will set up a new factory in competition with the foreign venture. Because the foreign companies are being charged exorbitant rates for land, labour and materials, they may find themselves unable to compete against the state operation – thus, they are forced to withdraw from China. The foreign companies may own patents and copyrights, but these hold little weight in the Chinese legal system.

The money to finance China's modernisation comes from a number of sources: foreign investment, loans from foreign banks and financial organisations, the tourist industry and – more recently – a fledgling stock market. To raise foreign capital, the Chinese even seem willing, for a price, to allow the Gobi Desert to be used as a dumping ground for nuclear waste from foreign reactors.

China also has vast untapped oil and mineral deposits, particularly in the outlying regions of Qinghai, Tibet and Xinjiang. Another source of foreign money is the Overseas Chinese, who are courted with appeals to patriotism and encouraged to invest in the motherland. Most of the foreign money invested in the Pearl River Delta in Guangdong Province and in the Shenzhen SEZ comes from Hong Kong and Macau and from Overseas Chinese.

Private Enterprise

Besides the peasants who bring their produce to sell in the free markets, there's a new breed of entrepreneur in China – the private urban businessperson and its subspecies the pedlar. Faced with the return of rusticated youth sent away to work during the Cultural Revolution, and growing unemployment amongst young people, the government has even tended to encourage the peddling trades.

The total workforce numbers over 580 million. Around 22% of these are urban employees in state-run and collective enterprises. There are approximately 60% involved in rural work, while 13% are involved in commerce and the service industry. The private businesses and street pedlars may not seem so extraordinary, but barely more than 10 years ago, during the Maoist era, they hardly existed. Free enterprise was a dirty word from the mid-60s until the death of Mao, and during that time there were no kerbside restaurants, hardly any pedlars and no throngs of shoppers browsing and haggling with merchants on the pavements.

Another recent development has been the acceptance of foreign-owned companies in China. Most visitors are likely to come across these in the form of top-end hotels and the occasional department store.

Consumerism

Official figures for urban Chinese incomes are misleading. For a long time they have hovered around Y120 to Y150 (about US$25) per month. The truth of the matter is that urban incomes generally range between Y200 and Y500 if outside sources of income are taken into account. In many cases (private entrepreneurs for example), incomes are much higher than this. You only have to look at the popularity of, say, foreign cigarettes and expensive karaoke parlours to realise that a sizable section of the population is earning more than Y120 a month.

Rising incomes have led to a consumer boom in China. In major cities, foreign companies have opened up retail outlets: Giordano, the Hong Kong clothing chain is a major example, and Nike recently opened a store in Shanghai. Chinese and foreign retailers are even starting to turn their attention to the power of advertising, and billboards that were once given over to government propaganda are now more and more frequently extolling the virtues of a soap powder or a headache cure.

The Back Door

Production of consumer goods still cannot meet demand. The country's industries have been unable to keep pace with the new demand for household appliances, colour TVs, fashionable clothes and other luxury goods by the nouveau riche class of farmers, urban traders and skilled workers which has arisen in the last few years. Nor are they satisfied with Chinese merchandise; they want high status foreign cigarettes, liquor, cameras, cassette players and watches.

Because of the shortages many Chinese still rely on their connections (*guānxi*) to supply them with luxury items. Hong Kong relatives troop over the border laden down with all sorts of presents for their relatives in mainland China. Connections also open the 'back door' – the unauthorised means whereby goods made in state-owned factories and intended for sale in state-owned shops pass into private hands in return for favours or bribes.

The system of privilege is another means by which a few Chinese are able to accumulate a disproportionate share of available luxuries. While few individuals could afford to buy a car, high-ranking cadres will have cars placed at their disposal by the state – which amounts to much the same thing as owning one for as long as they retain their position. Likewise, better quality housing, even hot running water, is still very much the domain of the Chinese elite.

The black market in foreign currency is another product of China's new economic policies. At lower levels, currency is bought from foreigners and resold to other Chinese who use it to buy imported consumer goods. At higher levels, the buyers are usually Chinese enterprises and individuals who use foreign currency to import consumer goods or finance their children's education overseas; the sellers are usually Hong Kong and Macau residents who, having sold their foreign currency at a much higher rate than the official exchange rate, will then buy large quantities of Chinese products which they export for profit.

Results

One of China's most abundant products is statistics. Optimistic figures are constantly produced to prove that these new policies are working. The Chinese press is full of remarkable success stories of prosperous peasants and hard-working entrepreneurs who got rich because of the new economic policies.

With the increase in quantity there has been a dramatic rise in defective goods, or 'dirty radishes', to use the Chinese expression. In 1986, the *China Daily* reported that at least a third of the goods produced in China were defective or did not conform to national standards. 'Red Flag' limousines continued to do nearly four km to the litre, faulty electric blankets electrocuted sleeping elderly people, and hair conditioners left some women bald. Members of the 1984 Chinese expedition to the Antarctic revealed that they suffered extreme discomfort when their parkas, made in Shanghai, proved neither cold-resistant nor waterproof.

The Chinese press recently also blasted counterfeiting and copyright piracy, which have become rampant. Fake Chinese and foreign cigarettes are common, as are counterfeit medicines, wines and watches.

Without a doubt, the economic reforms of the last 10 years have brought an affluence to many Chinese that was unthinkable in the Mao era. Yet the risks still remain immense. Plans to trim state-owned enterprises and China's huge bureaucracy bring with them the threat of massive unemployment that will only slowly be soaked up by China's growth. Moreover, huge discrepancies in incomes are emerging, and the social tensions that result are exacerbated by the inflationary curbing of spending power for those at the bottom end of the income scale. Added to all this is the great uncertainty of what the future holds. Most Chinese worry privately about what will happen when Deng dies.

Despite this, the current mood in China is one of optimism. Most Chinese seem to feel that they are being given opportunities to prove themselves that simply weren't present in the past, and most seem confident that, providing the economic reforms remain on course, China will develop into a major economic power.

POPULATION

The official figures for 1992 show mainland China (excluding Taiwan, Hong Kong and Macau) with a population of 1,158,000,000 (1.1 billion) people. Around a quarter of the total population lives in the cities and towns; the rest live in the villages, many of which are getting so large that they may soon have to be reclassified as cities.

The huge population has to be fed with the produce of around 15-20% of the land they live on, the sum total of China's arable land. The rest is barren wasteland or can only be lightly grazed. Much of the productive land is also vulnerable to flood and drought caused by the vagaries of China's summer monsoons or unruly rivers.

Since the Cultural Revolution, irrigation and flood-control schemes have improved the situation. The Communists have managed to double food production since 1952, but the population has increased by almost the same amount, leaving the quantity of food available per person pretty much to what it was 30 years ago.

More than a quarter of the population is rated by the census as illiterate (people 12 years of age and over who cannot read or who can only read a few words). Those who have been to school number a respectable 600 million, but more than half of them have been to primary school only. There are 4.4 million university graduates and two million undergraduates. Given the formidable nature

of the task, the Communists have certainly made considerable improvements in education. However, the statistics indicate that the staggering population still has very little technical and scientific expertise to draw upon. Even if the Chinese can be adequately fed, the prospect of substantially improving their lot and modernising the country without foreign help is a poor one – as the Chinese government has realised.

Birth Control

Birth-control programmes instituted by the Communist government in the 1950s met with some success, but were abandoned during the Cultural Revolution. The responsibility lies with Mao Zedong, whose decision was probably his greatest mistake. He believed that birth control was a capitalist plot to make China weak and that the country would find strength in a large population. His ideas very much reflected his background – that of the peasant farmer for whom many hands make light work in the fields.

It was not until 1973 that population growth targets were again included in China's economic planning, and campaigns like 'Longer, Later, Fewer' were launched. Planning for the future is a nightmare. Chinese estimates of how many people the country can support range up to 1.4 billion. The current plan is to limit growth to 1.25 billion people by the year 2000, hold that figure steady somehow, and allow birth control and natural mortality to reduce the population to 700 million, which China's leaders estimate would be ideal. Current projections, however, indicate that China's population will be close on 1.5 billion by the year 2010, and that the present population might well double within 50 years.

Huge billboards in cities spell out the goals for the year 2000 – modernisation and population control. The posters look like ads for a Buck Rogers sci-fi movie or Fritz Lang's *Metropolis*: planes, UFOs and helicopters fill the skies, strange vehicles glide down LA-style freeways, and skyscrapers poke out of futuristic cities. Often the only people visible are a smiling couple with their one child, often a girl. The figure on the poster is 1.25 billion, the quota set for the year 2000.

China must be given some credit – it's the only major Third World country to really tackle the population problem seriously. However, it's a daunting task – although Chinese couples are legally only permitted to have one child, it has not been easy to get a billion people to procreate in accordance with government-set quotas.

In recent years the main thrust of the campaign in the cities is to encourage couples to sign a one-child pledge by offering them an extra month's salary per year until the child is 14, plus housing normally reserved for a family of four (a promise often not kept because of the acute housing shortage). If the couple have a second child then the privileges are rescinded, and penalties such as demotion at work or even loss of job are imposed. If a woman has an abortion it entitles her to a vacation with pay.

The legal minimum age for marriage is 22 years for men and 20 for women, but if the woman delays marrying until after 25 then she is entitled to longer maternity leave. Material incentives are also applied in rural areas, sometimes meaning that farming couples get a double-sized plot if they only have one child. All methods of birth control are free; the most common ones are the IUD, female sterilisation and abortion. Forcing women to have abortions and falsifying figures are two methods taken by some local officials in their enthusiasm to meet the 'quotas' in their area.

The birth-control measures appear to be working in the cities, but it's difficult to say what's happening in the villages or if the target of zero growth can ever be reached. The catch is that Chinese agriculture still relies on human muscle and farmers find it desirable to have many children.

The Chinese press has often talked about 'birth guerrillas' – pregnant women who hide out in the countryside until the child is born. Such births may not even be officially recorded, but if the 'guerrilla' is discovered after she has already given birth, she can

expect to face a steep fine, loss of employment and other penalties. As late as 1971 the yearly rate of population increase stood at 2.3%, which would have doubled the population again in another 30 years. Currently the rate is down to 1.4%, though this will still double the population in 48 years.

If the Chinese can be convinced or pressured into accepting birth control, the one thing they cannot agree to accept is the sex of their only child. The desire for male children is deeply ingrained and the ancient custom of female infanticide continues to this day – as the Chinese government and press will freely admit. The *People's Daily* has even called the imbalance of the sexes a 'grave problem', and reported that in one rural area of Hebei Province the ratio of male to female children (under the age of five) was five to one. The paper also reported a case in Zhengzhou (Henan Province) in which two applications for divorce were rejected, having been made by husbands on the grounds that their wives had given birth only to female children. In one attempt to counter this age-old prejudice against female offspring the family planning billboards depict, almost without fail, a rosy-cheeked little girl in the ideal family.

PEOPLE

Han Chinese make up about 93% of the total population; the rest is composed of China's 55 or so minority nationalities, including Mongols and Tibetans. Although minorities account for a bit less than 7% of the population, they are distributed over some 50% of Chinese-controlled territory, mostly in the sensitive border regions.

Some groups, like the Zhuang and the Manchu, have become so assimilated over the centuries that to the Western eye they look indistinguishable from their Han counterparts; only language and religion separate them. Other minority groups no longer wear their traditional clothing except on market or festival days. Some have little or nothing in common with the Han Chinese, like the Turkic-descended Uigurs of Xinjiang who are instantly recognisable by their swarthy

Wives for Sale

As China continues to shed the austerities of the hardline Communist years, many of the old ways are returning. Chinese are going back to their temples, burning paper money for their ancestors and playing mahjong. But the old ways are not necessarily good news. In time-honoured tradition, the sale of wives in rural China is once again coming back into fashion.

Actual figures are difficult to obtain, but the Chinese Xinhua news agency admitted that in 1990 courts prosecuted 10,475 cases of women abducted for sale into the rural marriage market. Chinese sources admit that this number is probably a small percentage of the actual cases.

The central problem seems to be gangs of Chinese men who abduct young women and take them thousands of km from their home towns and then sell them to rural families as brides. The going price: US$450 to US$550. The women are often drugged and raped by the gangs. It is suspected that the shame prevents many of the women from reporting what has happened to them.

Strong efforts are presently being made in China to stamp out the practice. Men who buy brides are liable to prison sentences of five to 10 years, while the 'traffickers' face a life sentence or execution. More than 30 gang members were publicly shot in July 1992 in Shandong Province for abducting women. ■

Caucasian appearance, Turkish-related language, use of Arabic script and adherence to Islam.

Han migrations and invasions over the centuries have pushed many of the minorities into the more isolated, rugged areas of China. Traditionally the Han Chinese have regarded the minority groups as barbarians. Indeed, it was only with the formation of the PRC that the symbol for 'dog' – which was included in the characters for minority

names – was replaced with the symbol for 'man'.

Minority separatism has always been a threat to the stability of China, particularly amongst the Uigurs and the Tibetans who have poor and often volatile relations with the Han Chinese and whose homelands form the border regions of China. The minority regions provide China with the greater part of its livestock and hold vast untapped deposits of minerals.

Keeping the minorities under control has been a continuous problem for the Han Chinese. Tibet and Xinjiang are heavily garrisoned by Chinese troops, partly to protect China's borders and partly to prevent rebellion among the local population. Chinese migration to minority areas has been encouraged as a means of controlling them by sheer weight of numbers. For example, 50 years ago Inner Mongolia had a population of about four million and Xinjiang had 2.5 million. Today those figures are 20 and 13 million respectively. The Chinese government has also set up special training centres, like the National Minorities Institute in Beijing, to train loyal minority cadres for these regions. Since 1976 the government has tried to diffuse discontent by relaxing some of its grasp on the day-to-day life of the minority peoples, in particular allowing temples and mosques closed during the Cultural Revolution to reopen.

Until very recently, the minorities were exempt from China's one-child family planning guidelines. In the coming decade, government officials hope to extend the one-child family policy to minorities too, but this is sure to provoke further hostility against the Han majority.

ARTS

Many people go to China expecting a profound cultural experience. This has led to a lot of disappointment. While major attractions like the Forbidden City and the Dunhuang Buddhist caves still stand intact, many of China's other ancient treasures were ransacked or razed to the ground during the Cultural Revolution. Much of China's precious art including pottery, calligraphy and embroidery was defaced or destroyed.

In the early 1970s, with the new turn in China's foreign policy towards rapprochement with the West, the Chinese government began a superficial revival of their ancient culture to present a more acceptable 'human face' towards the outside world. A few of the ransacked temples and monasteries were restored as showpieces. Exhibitions were set up to display 'archaeological objects found during the Cultural Revolution' in some attempt to cover up the vandalism of that period. These early exhibits were open only to foreigners and Overseas Chinese, as were some antique and art-reproduction shops. A few hundred copies of Chinese classics were reprinted, but these were mainly for export.

While the Chinese government is still trying to eradicate 'feudal' ideas, it's generally accepted that beating and smashing is no way to go about it. In the past few years there's been a determined effort to restore the sites destroyed during the Cultural Revolution, but many of the temples remain derelict or are used as factories or warehouses.

Calligraphy

Calligraphy has traditionally been regarded in China as the highest form of visual art. A fine piece of calligraphy was often valued more highly by a collector of art than a good

painting. Children were trained at a very early age to write beautifully, and good calligraphy was a social asset. A scholar, for example, could not pass his examination to become an official if he was a poor calligrapher. A person's character was judged by their handwriting; if it was elegant it revealed great refinement.

The basic tools of calligraphy are paper, ink, ink-stone (on which the ink is mixed) and brush. These are commonly referred to as the 'four treasures of the scholar's study'. A brush stroke must be infused with the creative or vital energy which, according to the Taoists, permeates and animates all phenomena of the universe: mountains, rivers, rocks, trees, insects and animals. Expressive images are drawn from nature to describe the different types of brush strokes – for example, 'rolling waves', 'leaping dragon', 'startled snake slithering off into the grass', 'dewdrop about to fall' or 'playful butterfly'.

A beautiful piece of calligraphy therefore conjures up the majestic movements of a landscape. The qualities of the brush strokes are described in organic terms of 'bone', 'flesh', 'muscle' and 'blood'. Blood, for example, refers to the quality of the ink and the varied ink tones created by the degree of moisture of the brush.

Calligraphy is regarded as a form of self-cultivation as well as self-expression. It is believed that calligraphy should be able to express and communicate the most ineffable thoughts and feelings, which cannot be conveyed by words. It is often said that looking at calligraphy 'one understands the writer fully, as if meeting them face to face'. All over China, decorative calligraphy can be found in temples, adorning the walls of caves, and on the sides of mountains and monuments.

Painting

Chinese art is like Chinese religion – it has developed over a period of more than 2000 years and absorbed many influences. Looking at Chinese paintings for the first time, the Italian Jesuit priest Matteo Ricci (who reached China in 1582) criticised Chinese painters for their lack of knowledge of the illusionistic techniques of shading, with the result that their paintings 'look dead and have no life at all'. The Chinese were in turn astonished by the oil paintings brought by the Jesuits, which to them resembled mirror images. The Chinese rejected them as paintings because they were devoid of expressive brushwork.

Chinese painting is the art of brush and ink. The basic tools are those of calligraphy, which influenced painting in both technique and theory. The brush line, which varies in thickness and tone, is the important feature of a Chinese painting. Shading is regarded as a foreign technique (introduced to China via Buddhist art from central Asia between the 3rd and 6th centuries), and colour plays only a minor symbolic and decorative role. As early as the 9th century, ink was recognised as being able to provide all the qualities of colour.

Although you will see artists in China painting or sketching in front of their subject, traditionally the painter works from memory and is not so interested in imitating the outward appearance of the subject as in capturing its lifelike qualities and imbuing the painting with the energy permeating all nature.

From the Han Dynasty until the end of the Tang Dynasty, the human figure occupied the dominant position in Chinese painting, as it did in pre-modern European art. Figure painting flourished against a Confucian background, illustrating moralistic themes. Landscape painting for its own sake started in the 4th and 5th centuries. The practice of seeking out places of natural beauty and communing with nature first became popular among Taoist poets and painters. By the 9th century the interest of artists began to shift away from figures and, from the 11th century onwards, landscape has been the most important aspect of Chinese painting.

The function of the landscape painting was to substitute for nature, allowing the viewer to wander imaginatively. The painting is meant to surround the viewer, and there is no 'viewing point' as there is in Western painting.

In the 11th century a new attitude towards painting was formulated by a group of scholar-painters led by Su Dongpo (1036-1101). They recognised that painting could go beyond mere representation; it could also serve as a means of expression and communication in much the same way as calligraphy.

Painting became accepted as one of the activities of a cultured person, along with poetry, music and calligraphy. The scholarly amateur painters were either officials or retired people who did not depend on painting for their income. They painted for pleasure and became their own patrons and critics. They were also collectors and connoisseurs of art, and the arbiters of taste. Their ideas on art were voiced in voluminous writings and in inscriptions on paintings.

Moralistic qualities appreciated in a virtuous person (in the Confucian frame of things) became the very qualities appreciated in paintings. One of the most important was the 'concealment of brilliance' under an unassuming exterior, since any deliberate display of technical skill was considered vulgar. Creativity and individuality were highly valued, but only within the framework of tradition. Artists created their own style by transforming the styles of the ancient masters, seeing themselves as part of the great continuity of the painting tradition. This art-historical approach became a conscious pursuit in the late Ming and early Qing dynasties.

When the Communists came to power, much of the country's artistic talent was turned to glorifying the revolution and bombarding the masses with political slogans. Colourful billboards of Mao waving to cheering crowds holding up the 'little red book' were once popular, as were giant Mao statues standing above smaller statues of enthusiastic workers and soldiers. Music and opera were also co-opted for political purposes.

These days artistic expression is freer, but the government still keeps painters on a tight leash. The colourful political posters glorifying socialism are still much in evidence, though Mao is not.

Funerary Objects

As early as Neolithic times (9000-6000 BC), offerings of pottery vessels and stone tools or weapons were placed in graves to accompany the departed.

During the Shang Dynasty, precious objects such as bronze ritual vessels, weapons and jade were buried with the dead. Dogs, horses and even human beings were sacrificed for burial in the tombs of great rulers. When this practice was abandoned, replicas (usually in pottery) were made of human beings, animals and precious objects. A whole repertoire of objects was produced especially for burial, making symbolic provision for the dead without wasting wealth or making human sacrifice.

Burial objects made of earthenware were very popular from the 1st to the 8th centuries AD. During the Han Dynasty, pottery figures were cast in moulds and painted in bright colours after firing. Statues of attendants, entertainers, musicians, acrobats and jugglers were made, as well as models of granaries, watchtowers, pigpens, stoves and various other things.

Close trade links with the West were illustrated among these models by the appearance of the two-humped Bactrian camel, which carried merchandise along the Silk Road, amongst funerary objects. Warriors with west Asian faces and heavy beards appeared as funerary objects during the Northern Wei Dynasty, a foreign dynasty founded by the Turkish-speaking Tobas of central Asia.

The cosmopolitan life of Tang China was illustrated by its funerary wares; western and central Asians flocked to the capital at Chang'an and were portrayed in figurines of merchants, attendants, warriors, grooms, musicians and dancers. Tall Western horses with long legs, introduced to China from central Asia at the beginning of the 1st century BC, were also popular subjects for tomb figurines.

Other funerary objects commonly seen in Chinese museums are fearsome military figures dressed in full armour, often trampling oxen underfoot. The figures may have served as tomb guardians and may represent the four heavenly kings. These kings guard the four quarters of the universe and protect the state; they have been assimilated into Buddhism and you see statues of them in Buddhist temples.

Guardian spirits are some of the strangest funerary objects. A common one has bird wings, elephant ears, a human face, the body of a lion, and the legs and hooves of a deer or horse, all rolled into one. One theory is that these figures represent Tubo, the earth-spirit or lord of the underworld who was endowed with the power to ward off demons and evil spirits. He was entrusted with guarding the tomb of the deceased. Those figures with human faces may have represented the legendary Emperor Yu. He is said to have been the founder of the legendary Xia Dynasty, and was transformed into Tubo after his death.

Ceramics

Earthenware production has a long history in China. As many as 8000 years ago Chinese tribes were making artefacts with clay. The

primitive 'Yangshao' culture (so named because the first excavation of an ancient agricultural village was made in the region of Yangshao near the confluence of the Yellow, Fen and Wei rivers) is noted for its distinctive pottery painted with flowers, fish, animals, human faces and geometric designs. Around 3500 BC the 'Lungshanoid' culture (so named because evidence of this ancient culture was first found near the village of Lungshan in Shandong Province) was making white pottery and eggshell-thin black pottery.

Pottery-making was well advanced by the Shang period; the most important development occurred around the middle of the dynasty with the manufacture of a greenish glaze applied to stoneware artefacts. During the Han Dynasty the custom of glazing pottery became fairly common. However, the production of terracotta items – made from a mixture of sand and clay, fired to produce a reddish-brown colour, and left unglazed – continued.

During the Southern and Northern dynasties, a type of pottery halfway between Han glazed pottery and true porcelain was produced. The proto-porcelain was made by mixing clay with quartz and the mineral feldspar to make a hard, smooth-surfaced vessel. Feldspar was mixed with traces of iron to produce an olive-green glaze. The technique was perfected under the Tang but few examples survive. Three-coloured glazed vessels were also produced during the Tang Dynasty.

By the 8th century, Tang proto-porcelain and other types of pottery had found an international market, and were exported as far afield as Japan and the east coast of Africa. Chinese porcelain did not reach Europe until the Ming period, and the techniques of making it were not developed there until the 17th century.

Chinese pottery reached its artistic peak under the Song rulers. During this time true porcelain was developed. It was made of fine kaolin clay and was white, thin and transparent or translucent. Porcelain was produced under the Yuan but gradually lost the delicacy and near-perfection of the Song

products. However, it was probably during the Yuan Dynasty that 'blue-and-white' porcelain made its first appearance. This porcelain had blue decorations on a white background; it was made of kaolin clay quarried near Jingdezhen, and mixed with a type of cobalt imported from Persia.

During this period three-colour and five-colour porcelain, with floral decorations on a white background, was produced. Another noted invention was mono-coloured porcelain in ferrous red, black or dark blue. A new range of mono-coloured vessels was developed under the Qing.

During the Qing period the production of coloured porcelain continued with the addition of new colours and glazes and more complex decorations. This was the age of true painted porcelain, decorated with delicate landscapes, birds and flowers. Elaborate designs and brilliant colouring became the fashion. Porcelain imitations of other materials such as gold and silver, mother of pearl, jade, bronze, wood and bamboo, also became popular.

Bronze Vessels

Bronze is an alloy whose chief elements are copper, tin and lead. Tradition ascribes the first casting of bronze to the legendary Xia

Bronze tripod

Dynasty of 5000 years ago. Emperor Yu, the founder of the dynasty, is said to have divided his empire into nine provinces and then cast nine bronze tripods to symbolise the dynasty. However, the discovery in 1928 of the last Shang Dynasty capital at Anyang in Henan Province provided the first solid evidence that the ancient Chinese used bronze.

The Shang ruler and the aristocracy are believed to have used a large number of bronze vessels for sacrificial offerings of food and wine. Through ritual sacrifices the spirits of ancestors were prevailed upon to look after their descendants. The vessels were often buried with the deceased, along with other earthly provisions. Most of the late Shang funeral vessels have short, pictographic inscriptions recording the names of the clan, the ancestor and the vessel's maker, along with important events. Zhou Dynasty bronze vessels tend to have longer messages in ideographic characters; they describe wars, rewards, ceremonial events and the appointment of officials.

The early bronzes were cast in sectional clay moulds, an offshoot of the advanced pottery technology's high-temperature kilns and clay-mould casting. Each section of the mould was impressed, incised or carved with the required designs. By the 5th century BC during the Eastern Zhou period (770-256 BC), bronzes with geometric designs and scenes of hunting and feasting were inlaid with precious metals and stones.

Bronze mirrors were used as early as the Shang Dynasty and had already developed into an artistic form by the Warring States Period (476-221 BC). Ceramics gradually replaced bronze utensils by Han times, but bronze mirrors were not displaced by glass mirrors until the Qing Dynasty.

In China, the mirror is a metaphor for self-inspection in philosophical discussion. The wise person has three mirrors: a mirror of bronze in which to see their physical appearance, a mirror of the people by which to examine inner character and conduct, and a mirror of the past by which to learn to emulate successes and avoid the mistakes of earlier times. The backs of bronze mirrors were inscribed with wishes for good fortune and protection from evil influence. Post-Han writings are full of fantastic stories of the supernatural powers of mirrors. One of them relates the tale of Yin Zhongwen, who held a mirror to look at himself but found that his face was not reflected – soon after, he was executed.

Jade

The jade stone has been revered in China since Neolithic times. While the pure white form is the most highly valued, the stone varies in translucency and colour, including many shades of green, brown and black. To the Chinese, jade symbolises nobility, beauty and purity. Its physical properties have become metaphors for the Confucian ideal of the *jūnzi*, the noble or superior man.

Jade is also empowered with magical and life-giving properties. Taoist alchemists, hoping to become immortal, ate an elixir of powdered jade. The stone was thought to be a guardian against disease and evil spirits. Plugs of jade were placed over the orifices of corpses to prevent the life force from escaping. Opulent jade suits, meant to prevent decomposition, have been found in Han tombs; examples can be seen in the Nanjing Museum and in the Anhui Provincial Museum in Hefei.

Literature

China is home to one of the world's richest literary traditions. Unfortunately, barring many, many years of intensive study, much of it is inaccessible to Western readers. Many of the most important Chinese classics are available in translation, but much of the Chinese literary heritage (in particular its rich corpus of poetry) is untranslatable, though this doesn't stop scholars from trying.

The essential point to bear in mind when discussing Chinese literature is that prior to the 20th century there were two literary traditions: the classical and the vernacular. The classical tradition was the Chinese equivalent of a literary canon, though the principles that informed its structure were vastly different from the principles that are brought to bear in deciding what gets onto an English Literature course in a Western university. The classical canon, largely Confucian in nature, was the backbone of the Chinese education system, a core of texts written in ancient Chinese that had to be mastered thoroughly by all aspirants to the Chinese civil service. The vernacular tradition arose in Ming Dynasty and consisted largely of prose epics written for entertainment and consequently derided as a lower art form beneath the attention of scholars (though they were widely read all the same).

For Western readers it is the vernacular texts, precursors of the contemporary Chinese novel and short story, that are probably of most interest. Most of them are available in translation and provide a fascinating insight into life in China centuries past. Perhaps the three most famous early 'novels' are *The Water Margin (shuǐhú zhuàn)* (also translated as *Rebels of the Marsh)*, *The Dream of the Red Chamber (hónglóu mèng)* (also translated as *The Dream of Red Mansions* and *The Story of the Stone)* and *Journey to the West (xīyóu jì)*.

The Water Margin is the story of a group of rebels in the end of the Northern Song. Early versions of the story are thought to have been around in the 13th and 14th centuries, but it was the version by Jin Shentang dating from 1644 that made the story famous. *Journey to the West* dates back to the 16th century, and the story derives from the true exploits of the Chinese wanderer Xuan Zang, who travelled to India between 629 and 645 AD to collect Buddhist texts. The book is largely comic, and Xuan Zang is accompanied by a pig, a monkey and a feminine spirit. It has been made better known in the West by the Japanese TV series *Monkey*.

For the Chinese, the great classic of vernacular literature is *The Dream of the Red Chamber*. It is the story of domestic life in a scholar family insulated from the greater world, and its documentation of human foibles and family life make the writer, Cao Xueqin, a kind of Chinese Tolstoy. Both *Journey to the West* and *The Dream of the Red Chamber* are published by Penguin classics, the latter coming under the title *Story of the Stone*.

By the early 19th century, Western novels had begun to appear in Chinese translations in increasing numbers. Chinese intellectuals began to look at their own literary tradition more critically, in particular the classical one, which was markedly different in form from the Chinese that was spoken by modern Chinese. Calls for a national literature based on vernacular Chinese rather than the stultifying classical language grew in intensity.

The first of the major Chinese writers to write in vernacular Chinese was Lu Xun, regarded by many as still the greatest of China's 20th-century writers. Most of his works were short stories that looked critically at the Chinese inability to drag their nation into the 20th century. His most famous work, *The Story of Ah Q*, examines the life of a man who is chronically unable to recognise the setbacks in his life as such, much as China itself seemed unable to accept the desperate urgency of the need to modernise. Lao She, another important early novelist, also produced an allegorical work in *Cat City*, but is famous most of all for *The Rickshaw Boy*, a book that has been translated many times into English. It is a social critique of the living conditions of rickshaw drivers in Beijing.

Literary creativity in post-1949 China was greatly hampered by ideological controls. Mao's 'Yan'an Talks on Art & Literature', basically reduced literature to the status of a revolutionary tool, and writers were extolled to seek out ideal forms and to find the 'typical in the individual'. Works that did not show peasants triumphing over huge odds were considered not inspirational enough and condemned as bourgeois.

The years following the Cultural Revolution have seen increased creative freedom in the Chinese literary scene, but it remains an area in which the government maintains careful vigilance. Most writers belong to state-sponsored literary guilds and many write on salary. Naturally they are careful not to bite the hand that feeds them.

One of the most interesting writers in contemporary China is Zhang Xianliang, whose book *Half of Man is Woman* was extremely controversial for its sexual content. Most Western readers find Zhang's sexual politics highly suspect, but his book, now published by Penguin, is worth reading all the same. Wang Shuo is a writer whose work still awaits translation into English, but this must only be a matter of time. Much of his work has been adapted for film and he is popular with the younger generation. For the authorities, however, his stories about disaffected urban youth, gambling, prostitution and confidence tricksters are considered a bad influence. Despite this, his works were recently collected in a four-volume set and are widely available in China.

Blood Red Dusk by Lao Gui (literally 'old devil') is available in English in Panda (the Chinese publisher). It's a fascinatingly cynical account of the Cultural Revolution years. Feng Jicai is a writer who has enjoyed great success in China with stories like 'The Magic Ponytail' and 'A Short Man & His Tall Wife', which have a satirical magic realist touch to them. His often horrific account of the Cultural Revolution *Voices From the Whirlwind* is a collection of anonymous personal accounts of those turbulent years and has recently been published in English by Pantheon Books.

READ HAN SUYIN !

Theatre

Chinese theatre draws on very different traditions to Western theatre. The crucial difference is in the importance of music to Chinese theatre, and thus it is usually referred to as opera. Contemporary Chinese theatre, of which the most famous is Peking Opera, has a continuous history of some 900 years, having evolved from a convergence of comic and balladic traditions in the Northern Song period. From this beginning, Chinese opera has been the meeting ground for a disparate range of forms: acrobatics, martial arts, poetic arias and stylised dance. By the 13th century, opera was referred to as *zaju*,

or literally a 'dramatic miscellany'. Performances were rarely of single dramatic piece, but rather composed of a number of sequences around set themes.

Operas were usually performed by travelling troupes whose social status was very low in traditional Chinese society. In fact their status was on a par with prostitutes and slaves, their children barred from social advancement by a government decree that made them ineligible to participate in public-service examinations. Chinese law also forbade mixed-sex performances, forcing actors to act out roles of the opposite sex. Opera troupes were frequently associated with homosexuality in the public imagination, contributing further to their 'untouchable' social status.

Despite this, opera remained a popular form of entertainment, though it was considered unworthy of the attention of the scholar class. Performances were considered an obligatory adjunct to New Year celebrations, marriages, sometimes funerals and ancestral ceremonies, a practice that continues to a certain extent in Taiwan.

Usually opera performances take place on a bare stage, with the actors taking on stylised roles that are instantly recognisable to the audience. The four major roles are the female role, the male role, the 'painted-face' role (for gods and warriors) and the clown.

Cinema

While most travellers in China manage to get to at least one opera or acrobatics performance, less get around to seeing any Chinese films. Part of the problem of course is purely linguistic. Films are not much fun if you cannot follow the dialogue. Still, a number of recent Chinese releases have enjoyed limited success at Western film festivals and in art-house cinemas, are subtitled into English and are well worth the effort of tracking down. Hong Kong often has screenings of China's more offbeat releases.

Much of the early post-1949 film work was ideologically motivated, rich in sentimentality and heroics, and suffered from poor production values. As can be expected, the years of the Cultural Revolution did nothing to improve this state of affairs. The major turning point took place with the graduation of the first intake of students following the end of the Cultural Revolution from the Beijing Film Academy in 1982. This group of adventurous directors, the most well known of whom are Zhang Yimou, Chen Kaige, Wu Ziniu and Tian Zhuangzhuang, became known collectively as the 'Fifth Generation'.

The first film by any of these directors to come to the attention of film buffs in the West was *Yellow Earth (huáng tǔdì)*, a film that depicts the arrival of a PLA officer in a small Shaanxi village to collect peasant folk songs. The story is simple, but the film powerfully employs the visual element to reveal the tenacity of age-old customs in this barren part of China.

A number of other equally powerful and successful films followed hot on the heels of *Yellow Earth*. Zhang Yimou, a director whose films have continued to reap in awards at European film festivals, made *Red Sorghum (hóng gāoliang)*, a film that was adventurous by Chinese standards in portraying an illicit love affair against the backdrop of the Sino-Japanese War.

Huang Jianxin, a director who has recently reappeared after a long absence with *Stand Up, Don't Bend Over*, released *The Black Cannon Incident (hēipào shìjiàn)*, without a doubt the sharpest satire released by any of the Fifth Generation directors. The story revolves around a Chinese interpreter for a German engineer who returns by post a Chinese chess piece (a black cannon) to a friend who left it behind in his house. The telegram he sends to the friend to tell him he has found the piece and sent it on lands him in a quagmire of Kafkaesque bureaucratic suspicions and accusations.

Other films from the mid-80s in a similar vein were *Old Well*, a film rich with sexual tension; *Swan Song*, the tragic story of a Cantonese opera composer who dies neglected after his best work is stolen and made famous by a music student; *The Big Parade*, *The One & the Eight*, a unique

Chinese depiction of the horrors of China's war with Vietnam; and *The Horse Thief*, a haunting story set in Tibet that sensitively treats Tibetan lifestyles, and customs completely alien to Chinese sensibilities such as the sky burial.

After a hiatus following the Tiananmen Incident, Chinese directors have again resurfaced with some of the best international films of recent years. The joint winners for the 1993 Berlin Golden Bear award were both Chinese films: one mainland Chinese and one Taiwanese. The mainland Chinese winner, *The Women from the Lake of Scented Souls* portrays the unhappiness of a woman who runs a sesame-oil mill. Chen Kaige, the director of *Yellow Earth*, has recently released *Farewell to My Concubine*, which took joint honours at Cannes. Zhang Yimou's recent release, *The Story of Qiuju*, has garnered numerous awards, and is a strikingly frank look at the legal processes of modern China, as a woman seeks for legal redress after her husband is beaten by the local village head.

The good news for Chinese film-goers is that, after many years of such films being deemed unsuitable for local screenings, films such as those of Zhang Yimou are being shown in China.

Music

Traditional Chinese musical instruments include the two-stringed fiddle (*èrhú*), three-stringed flute (*sānxuán*), four-stringed banjo (*yuèqín*), two-stringed viola (*húqín*), vertical flute (*dòngxiāo*), horizontal flute (*dízi*), piccolo (*bāngdí*), four-stringed lute (*pípá*), zither (*gǔzhēng*), ceremonial trumpet (*suǒnà*), and ceremonial gongs (*dàluó*).

Popular Music China is beginning to develop a healthy music industry. Much of it is heavily influenced by the already well established music industries in Taiwan and Hong Kong, but these are in turn influenced by Western musical trends, as the recent popularity of Cantonese rap and Taiwanese-language rock experiments have shown.

China has generally been slow in developing a market for Western music (much of what is available in the shops is of the Carpenter's ilk), but the advent of satellite TV (now widely available) and the popularity of MTV, broadcast via Hong Kong's Star TV network, is set to change all this.

China's first concert featuring a foreign rock group was in April 1985, when the British group Wham was allowed to perform. The audience remained sedate – music fans who dared to get up and dance in the aisles were hauled off by the PSB. Since then, things have become more liberal and China has produced some notable local bands. Perhaps the most famous of China's recent musicians is Cui Jian, who also has a sizable following overseas (mainly in Chinese communities). His songs deal with themes of urban angst previously thought unacceptable by the authorities. Recent years have even spawned a number of heavy metal bands that look almost indistinguishable from their Western counterparts. Tang Dynasty is probably the most successful of these.

The hip young urban Chinese like disco music. On the popular music front, Taiwanese love songs have been enormously successful in China, and Mandarin versions of Hong Kong popular hits produced for the Taiwan and China markets are frequently chart hits. Interestingly, Beijing has a nascent heavy metal and punk scene. There are dance halls in all the major cities, generally alternating between disco, live music and a karaoke session.

Attempts to tailor Chinese classical music, song and dance to Western tastes have resulted in a Frankenstein's monster of Broadway-style spectacular and epic-theatre film score. Chinese rock star Cui Jian released a big hit 'Rock for the New Long March'. In an attempt to show that the geriatric leadership is also hip, government officials authorised a disco version of 'The East is Red'. There are orchestras organised on Western lines which substitute Chinese for Western instruments. A few young Chinese have even caught on to Brazil's erotic dance, the 'lambada' – a clear case of spiritual pollution if there ever was one.

Anyone looking for more interesting examples of Chinese popular music, might want to check out the tapes of Cui Jian. His biggest hit is the album that shows him dressed in a PLA uniform complete with a red blindfold – a symbolic statement if ever there was one. Another recent release is a collection of avant guarde musicians and bands irreverently covering Cultural Revolutionary songs. It's called *Red Rock & Roll* (*hóngsè léigǔn*).

Taijiquan & Gongfu

Known in the West as 'taichi', *taijiquan* (slow motion shadow boxing) has in recent years become quite trendy in many countries. It has been popular in China for centuries. It is basically a form of exercise, but it's also an art and is one form of Chinese martial arts. *Gongfu* (or 'kungfu') differs from taijiquan in that the former is performed at much higher speed and with the intention of doing bodily harm. Gongfu also often employs weapons. Taijiquan is not a form of self-defence but the movements are similar to gongfu's. There are different styles of taijiquan, such as Chen and Yang.

Taijiquan is very popular among old people and also with young women who believe it will help keep their bodies beautiful. The movements are supposed to develop the breathing muscles, promote digestion and improve muscle tone.

A modern innovation is to perform taijiquan movements to the thump of disco music. Westerners find it a remarkable sight to see a large group performing their slow motion movements in the park at the crack of dawn.

Taijiquan, dancing in the park and all manner of exercises, are customarily done just as the sun rises, which means if you want to see it or participate you have to wake up the same time as the chickens, but it's well worth it.

Qigong

As much an art form as a traditional Chinese

medicine, *qigong* cannot easily be described in Western terms but it's rather like faith healing. *Qi* represents life's vital energy, and *gong* is from gongfu. Qigong can be thought of as energy management and healing. Practitioners try to project their qi to perform various miracles, including driving nails through boards as well as healing others.

It's interesting to watch them do it. Typically, they place their hands above or next to the patient's body without actually making physical contact. To many foreigners this looks like a circus act, and indeed even many Chinese suspect that it's nothing but quackery. However, there are many who claim that they have been cured of serious illness without any other treatment but qigong, even after more conventional doctors have told them that their condition is hopeless.

Qigong is not particularly popular in China. Denounced as another superstitious link to the bourgeois past, rampaging Red Guards nearly obliterated qigong and its practitioners during the Cultural Revolution. It's only recently that qigong has made a comeback, but many of the highly skilled practitioners are no longer alive. In China, you are most likely to see qigong in the ever-popular gongfu movies (many imported from Hong Kong and Taiwan), where mortally wounded heroes are miraculously revived with a few waves of the hands.

Does qigong work? It's not easy to say, but there is a theory in medicine that all doctors can cure a third of their patients regardless of what method is used. So perhaps qigong gets this cure rate too.

CULTURE
Who's in Charge?

Although many Chinese workers don't seem to have much work to do, everyone fills a specialised niche. In a hotel, one person (and one person only) is in charge of changing foreign currency for FEC. When that person is off duty, foreign currency transactions cease. Similarly, one person is in charge of bicycle rentals; one person is in charge of long-distance phone calls; one person controls postcard sales at the hotel giftshop; one person has responsibilities for map sales, etc.

The Chinese are loath to do someone else's job because they may be held responsible, especially if things don't go right. You may find it difficult or impossible to conduct some essential business like getting your deposit back when trying to return a rented bicycle if the individual in charge of such important matters is on holiday. This shouldn't be much of a problem in a private business, but in a government-run organisation you never know what you'll be up against. Screaming and yelling isn't advised – unless as a last resort – and then it's unlikely to be effective.

Making Contact

Making contact with Chinese people is not usually as simple as most visitors expect. A Chinese travel guide had this to say about encountering foreign guests:

In trains, boats, planes or tourist areas one frequently comes across foreign guests. Do not follow, encircle and stare at them when you meet. Refrain from pointing at their clothing in front of their faces or making frivolous remarks; do not vie with foreign guests, competing for a seat, and do not make requests at will. If foreign guests take the initiative to make contact, be courteous and poised. Do not be flustered into ignoring them by walking off immediately, neither should you be reserved or arrogant. Do your best to answer relying on translation. When chatting with foreign guests be practical and realistic – remember there are differences between foreign and home life.

Don't provide random answers if you yourself don't know or understand the subject matter. Refrain from asking foreign guests questions about age, salary, income, clothing costs and similar private matters. Do not do things discreditable to your country. Do not accept gifts at will from foreign guests. When parting you should peel off your gloves and then proffer your hand. If you are parting from a female foreign guest and she does not proffer her hand first, it is also adequate to nod your head as a farewell greeting.

Educating a billion Chinese to be courteous to foreigners is a formidable task. For many years few foreigners set foot in the country, let alone met the common people. Whether or not most Chinese people actually like foreigners is open to debate – but they are curious about us and sometimes genuinely friendly, and on the whole it is safe to walk the streets at any time.

Making contact with Chinese people can be frustrating. Inevitably it begins with someone striking up a conversation with you on the street, in your hotel or on a train. Unfortunately many of these conversations have a habit of deteriorating into English lessons. There is also the tendency for every conversation to be a monotonous question and answer session, with the questions always being the same.

Conversations with Chinese people usually begin with 'Can I practise my English with you?' followed by 'What country are you from?' and then 'Are you married?' 'How old are you?' 'Do you have children?' Then come the questions about money – 'How much do you make?' 'Do you have a car?' 'How much does a house cost in your country?' By this time, a crowd will have gathered and everyone will be discussing (in Chinese) your income, material standard of living, and, if the numbers sound good, immigration possibilities.

If you're learning to speak Chinese, you can use these conversations to practise your Chinese. This often works out very well, but a lot depends on your linguistic ability.

You should also remember that the Chinese are highly sensitive about political issues. Almost everyone you meet will criticise the Cultural Revolution – but that's official policy nowadays. You simply can't expect people to express their real views on the present government, though many will in private. At the same time, don't expect these 'real views' to be negative just because you think they should be. Many Chinese people won't broach any political subject at all and may say that they have no interest in politics. Don't expect anyone to be too liberal with their views if they're within earshot of others, especially since a conversation with a foreigner in public places automatically attracts a crowd of onlookers.

The official policy on Chinese talking to foreigners tends to vary. Currently it's encouraged (with reservations) – modernisation of the country requires foreign technology, and if a foreign technical journal is going to be of any use you have to be able to read the thing. Fluency in English is a path to a better job, even a chance to travel overseas to work or study, and that helps explain the enthusiasm with which the Chinese are learning the language and seeking help from stray foreigners.

Not all Chinese approach foreigners out of pure curiosity, desire to practise their language skills, or a desire to make friends. Some will approach you ostensibly to practise English but what they really want is to change your Foreign Exchange Certificates (FEC) for Renminbi (RMB). Others have the strange idea that foreigners can sponsor them for emigration to the USA or Australia (the two most popular destinations). American and Australian teachers in China often find themselves targeted for marriage for this reason. A foreign husband or wife is often referred to as a 'rice ticket' *(fàn piào)* by the Chinese.

Interesting people to talk to are elderly Chinese who learned English back in the 1920s and 1930s when there were large foreign communities in China. Then there are the middle-aged who were learning English just before the Cultural Revolution but were forced to stop and started to pick it up again after a gap of several years. Next comes the younger generation of Chinese who went to school or university after the Cultural Revolution and have been able to take foreign-language courses. Even the level of proficiency attained by self-taught Chinese through English-language programmes on radio or TV is quite remarkable. English is now being taught in high schools, and many young kids have a rudimentary knowledge of the language. Japanese is popular at high school and university levels. You sometimes come across French, German, Russian and Spanish speakers.

If you want to meet English-speaking Chinese then go to the 'English corners' which have developed in many large Chinese cities. Usually held on a Sunday morning in a convenient park, Chinese who speak or are learning English gather to practise the language. Also seek out the 'English Salons' – evening get-togethers at which the Chinese practise English, listen to lectures or hold debates in English. Don't expect to remain a member of the audience for very long; you may soon find yourself giving the evening lecture and struggling to answer hard questions about the outside world.

If you make a Chinese friend and want to stay in contact through letters, then it's suggested that before leaving China you buy several stamps sufficient for letters from China to your home country. The first time you write to your Chinese friend enclose the stamps – say that you had them left over when you departed from China, and that you're sending the stamps because you have no use for them. One of these stamps could be half a day's wage to some Chinese – so for them to write to you really does involve a sacrifice!

While you're in China you can arrange meetings by having your Chinese friend phone your hotel or post a letter. Remember to get your friend to write down his/her address on several envelopes so you can post them. In the towns and cities a letter posted before 9 am should be delivered that same afternoon. It *is* possible to visit people's homes – many Chinese feel greatly honoured by your visit, though others may feel embarrassed by their humble living conditions.

Cultural Differences

The cultural gap can be a bigger obstacle to understanding than the language barrier. On the other hand, cultural differences can be fascinating – try to keep a positive attitude. Some cultural differences you may encounter in China follow.

Face Face can be loosely considered as status and many Chinese people will go to great lengths to avoid 'losing face'. For example, a foreigner may front up at a hotel desk and have a furious row with the receptionist over dorm beds which the foreigner knows exist/are vacant while the receptionist

firmly denies all knowledge of the fact. Regardless of who is right or wrong, the receptionist is even less likely to back down (and 'lose face') if the foreigner throws a fit or becomes violent. Persistent waiting may lead to a 'compromise' whereby the receptionist suddenly goes off duty to be replaced by a colleague who coincidentally finds a spare dorm bed or, after the foreigner tactfully refers to a possible 'misunderstanding', discovers a cheaper alternative. There are many such social mores which can severely maul the nerves of even the most patient of foreigners. It is pointless to steer a collision course toward these barriers, but it is often possible to manipulate your way around them.

Gūanxi In their daily life, Chinese often have to compete for goods or services in short supply and many have been assigned jobs for which they have zero interest and often no training. Those who have *gūanxi* (connections) usually get what they want because the 'connections' network is, of course, reciprocal. Obtaining goods or services through connections is informally referred to as 'going through the back door' (*zǒu hòu mén*). Cadres are well placed for this activity; foreigners are not.

Speaking Frankly People often don't say what they think, but rather what they think you want to hear or what will save face for them. Thus, the staff at the CAAC office may tell you that your flight will be here 'very soon' even if they know it will be delayed for two days.

Smiling A smile doesn't always mean happiness. Some Chinese people smile when they are embarrassed or worried. This explains the situation where the foreign tourist is ranting and raving at the staff in the hotel lobby, while the person behind the desk stands there grinning from ear to ear.

RELIGION

Chinese religion has been influenced by three great streams of human thought:

Taoism, Confucianism and Buddhism. Although each has separate origins, all three have been inextricably entwined in popular Chinese religion along with ancient animist beliefs. The founders of Taoism, Confucianism and Buddhism have been deified. The Chinese worship them and their disciples as fervently as they worship their own ancestors and a pantheon of gods and spirits.

Taoism (dào jiào)

It is said that Taoism is the only true 'homegrown' Chinese religion – Buddhism was imported from India and Confucianism is mainly a philosophy. According to tradition, the founder of Taoism is a man known as Laozi. He is said to have been born around the year 604 BC, but some doubt that he ever lived at all. Almost nothing is known about him, not even his name. *Laozi* translates as 'the old one' or the 'Grand Old Master'.

Legends depict Laozi as having been conceived by a shooting star, carried in his unfortunate mother's womb for 82 years, and born as a wise old man with white hair. The most popular story is that Laozi was the keeper of the government archives in a western state of China, and that Confucius consulted him.

At the end of his life, Laozi is said to have climbed on a water buffalo and ridden west towards what is now Tibet, in search of solitude for his last few years. On the way, he was asked to leave behind a record of his beliefs. The product was a slim volume of only 5000 characters, the *Dao De Jing* or *The Way and its Power*. He then rode off on his buffalo.

At the centre of Taoism is the concept of *Dao*. Dao cannot be perceived because it exceeds senses, thoughts and imagination; it can be known only through mystical insight which cannot be expressed with words. Dao is the way of the universe, the driving power in nature, the order behind all life, the spirit which cannot be exhausted. Dao is the way people should order their lives to keep in harmony with the natural order of the universe.

Just as there have been different interpretations of the 'way', there have also been different interpretations of *De* – the power of the universe. This has led to the development of three distinct forms of Taoism in China.

One form held that 'the power' is philosophical. The philosophical Taoist, by reflection and intuition, orders his or her life in harmony with the way of the universe and achieves the understanding or experience of Tao. Philosophical Taoism has many followers in the West.

The second form held that the power of the universe was basically psychic in nature, and by practising yogic exercises and meditation a number of individuals could become receptacles for Tao. They could then radiate a healing, psychic influence over those around them.

The third form is the 'popular Taoism' which took hold in China. The power of the universe is the power of gods, magic and sorcery. Because popular Taoism has been associated with alchemy and the search for immortality, it often attracted the patronage of Chinese rulers before Confucianism gained the upper hand. It's argued that only philosophical Taoism actually takes its inspiration from the *Dao De Jing*, and that the other labels under which 'Taoism' has been practised used Laozi's name to give themselves respectability. As it is commonly practised in China, Hong Kong and Taiwan, popular Taoist worship is still closely bound up with ghosts, exorcisms, faith healing, fortune telling and magic.

Confucianism (rújiā sīxiǎng)

More a philosophy than a religion, Confucianism has nevertheless become intertwined with Chinese religious beliefs. With the exception of Mao, the one name which has become synonymous with China is Confucius *(Kǒngzi)*. He was born of a poor family around the year 551 BC – in what is now Shandong Province. His ambition was to hold a high government office and to reorder society through the administrative apparatus. At most he seems to have had several insignificant government posts, a few followers and a permanently blocked career. At the age of 50 he perceived his 'divine mission' and for the next 13 years tramped from state to state offering unsolicited advice to rulers on how to improve their governing, while looking for an opportunity to put his own ideas into practice. That opportunity never came, and he returned to his own state to spend the last five years of his life teaching and editing classical literature. He died in 479 BC, aged about 72.

The glorification of Confucius began after his death, and eventually his ideas permeated every level of Chinese society. To hold government office presupposed a knowledge of the Confucian classics, and spoken proverbs trickled down to the illiterate masses. During the Han Dynasty, Confucianism effectively became the state religion – the teachings were made the basic discipline for training government officials and remained so until almost the end of the Qing Dynasty in 1911. In the 7th and 8th centuries temples and shrines were built to Confucius and his original disciples. During the Song Dynasty, the Confucian bible *The Analects* became the basis of all education.

Confucius

It is not hard to see why Confucianism took hold in China. The perpetual conflict of the Spring and Autumn Period had inspired Confucius to seek a way which would allow people to live together peacefully. His solution was tradition. Like others of his time, he believed that there had once been a period of great peace and prosperity in China. This had been brought about because people lived by certain traditions which maintained peace and social order.

Confucius advocated a return to these traditions and also devised values which he thought were necessary for collective wellbeing. He aimed to instil a feeling of humanity towards others and respect for oneself, as well as a sense of the dignity of human life. Courtesy, selflessness, magnanimity, diligence and empathy would naturally follow. His ideal person was competent, poised, fearless, even-tempered and free of violence and vulgarity. The study of 'correct attitudes' became the primary task. Moral ideas had to be driven home to the people by every possible means – at temples, theatres, schools, at home and during festivals, in proverbs and folk stories.

All people rendered homage to the emperor, who was regarded as the embodiment of Confucian wisdom and virtue – the head of the great family-nation. For centuries administration under the emperor lay in the hands of a small Confucian scholar class. In theory anyone who passed the examinations qualified, but in practice the monopoly of power was held by the educated upper classes. There has never been a rigid code of law, because Confucianism rejected the idea that conduct could be enforced by some organisation; taking legal action implied an incapacity to work things out by negotiation. The result, however, was arbitrary justice and oppression by those who held power. Dynasties rose and fell but the Confucian pattern never changed.

There are several bulwarks of Confucianism, but the one which has probably had the most influence on the day-to-day life of the Chinese is *li*, which has two meanings. The first meaning of li is 'propriety' – a set of manners or a knowledge of how to behave in a given situation – and presumes that the various roles and relationships of life have been clearly defined. The second meaning of li is 'ritual' – when life is detailed to Confucian lengths it becomes completely ordered.

Confucian codes of conduct and clearly defined patterns of obedience became inextricably bound up in Chinese society. Women obey and defer to men, younger brothers to elder brothers, sons to fathers. Respect flows upwards, from young to old, from subject to ruler. Age is venerated since it gives everything (including people, objects and institutions) their dignity and worth; the elderly may be at their weakest physically, but they are at the peak of their wisdom.

The family retains its central place as the basic unit of society; Confucianism reinforced this idea, but did not invent it. The key to family order is filial piety – children's respect for and duty towards their parents. Teaming up with traditional superstition, Confucianism reinforced the practice of ancestor-worship. Confucius himself is worshipped and temples are built for him. The strict codes of obedience were held together by these concepts of filial piety and ancestor worship, as well as by the concept of 'face' – to let down the family or group is a great shame for a Chinese.

Buddhism (fó jiào)

Buddhism was founded in India in the 6th century BC by Siddhartha Gautama of the Sakyas. Siddhartha was his given name, Gautama his surname and Sakya the name of the clan to which his family belonged.

The story goes that though he was a prince brought up in luxury, Siddhartha became discontented with the world when he was confronted with the sights of old age, sickness and death. He despaired of finding fulfilment on the physical level, since the body was inescapably subject to these weaknesses.

Around the age of 30 years Siddhartha broke from the material world and sought 'enlightenment' by following various yogic disciplines. After several failed attempts he devoted the final phase of his search to intensive contemplation. One evening as he sat beneath a bo (banyan) tree, so the story goes, he slipped into a deep meditation and emerged having achieved enlightenment. His title 'Buddha' means 'the awakened' or 'the enlightened one'.

Buddha founded an order of monks and preached his ideas for the next four decades until his death around 480 BC. To his followers he was known as Sakyamuni, the 'silent sage of the Sakya clan', because of the unfathomable mystery that surrounded him. It is said that Gautama Buddha was not the only Buddha, but the fourth, and is not expected to be the last.

The cornerstone of Buddhist philosophy is the view that all life is suffering. Everyone is subject to the traumas of birth, sickness, decrepitude and death; to what they most dread (an incurable disease or an ineradicable personal weakness), as well as separation from what they love.

The cause of suffering is desire – specifically the desires of the body and the desire for personal fulfilment. Happiness can only be achieved if these desires are overcome, and this requires following the 'eightfold path'. By following this path the Buddhist aims to attain nirvana. Volumes have been written in attempts to define nirvana; the suttas (discourses of the Buddha) simply say that it's a state of complete freedom from greed, anger, ignorance and the various other 'fetters' of existence.

The first branch of the eightfold path is 'right understanding': the recognition that life is suffering, that suffering is caused by desire for personal gratification and that suffering can be overcome. The second branch is 'right-mindedness' – cultivating a mind free from sensuous desire, ill will and cruelty. The remaining branches of the path require that one refrain from abuse and deceit; that one show kindness and avoid self-seeking in all actions; that one develop virtues and curb passions; and that one practise meditation.

The many varieties of Buddhist meditation use mental exercises to penetrate deep into the psyche, where it is believed the real problems and answers lie, and to achieve a personal experience of the verities of existence.

Buddhism developed in China from the 3rd to 6th centuries AD and was probably introduced by Indian merchants who took Buddhist priests with them on their land and sea journeys to China. Later, an active effort was made to import Buddhism into China. In the middle of the 1st century AD the religion had gained the interest of the Han Emperor Ming, who sent a mission to the West; the mission returned in 67 AD with Buddhist scriptures, two Indian monks and images of the Buddha. Centuries later, other Chinese monks like Xuan Zang journeyed to India and returned with Buddhist scriptures which were then translated from the original Sanskrit to Chinese – a massive job involving Chinese and foreign scholars from central Asia, India and Sri Lanka.

Buddhism spread rapidly in the north of China where it was patronised by various ruling invaders, who in some cases had been acquainted with the religion before they came to China. Others patronised the Buddhist monks because they wanted educated officials who were not Confucians. In the south Buddhism spread more slowly, spreading with Chinese migrations from the north. There were several periods in which Buddhists were persecuted. Their temples and monasteries were sacked and destroyed, but the religion survived. To a people constantly faced with starvation, war and poverty the appeal of this philosophy probably lay in the doctrines of reincarnation and nirvana borrowed from Indian Hinduism.

Buddhist monasteries and temples sprang up everywhere in China, and played a similar role to the churches and monasteries of medieval Europe. Monasteries were guesthouses, hospitals and orphanages for travellers and refugees. With gifts obtained from the faithful, they were able to amass considerable wealth, which enabled them to set up moneylending enterprises and pawnshops. These pawnshops were the poor man's bank right up to the mid-20th century.

The Buddha wrote nothing; the Buddhist writings that have come down to us date from about 150 years after his death. By the time these texts came out, divisions had already appeared within Buddhism. Some writers tried to emphasise the Buddha's break with Hinduism, while others tried to minimise it. At some stage Buddhism split into two major schools: Theravada and Mahayana.

The Theravada or 'doctrine of the elders' school (also called Hinayana or 'little vehicle' by non-Theravadins) holds that the path to nirvana is an individual pursuit. It centres on monks and nuns who make the search for nirvana a full-time profession. This school maintains that people are alone in the world and must tread the path to nirvana on their own; Buddhas can only show the way. The Theravada school is the Buddhism of Sri Lanka, Myanmar (Burma), Thailand, Laos and Cambodia.

The Mahayana or 'big vehicle' school holds that since all existence is one, the fate of the individual is linked to the fate of others. The Buddha did not just point the way and float off into his own nirvana, but continues to offer spiritual help to others seeking nirvana. The Mahayana school is the Buddhism of Vietnam, Japan, Tibet, Korea, Mongolia and China.

The outward difference between the two schools is the cosmology of the Mahayana school. Mahayana Buddhism is replete with innumerable heavens, hells and descriptions of nirvana. Prayers are addressed to the Buddha and combined with elaborate ritual. There are deities and bodhisattvas, a rank of supernatural beings in their last incarnation before nirvana. Temples are filled with images such as the future Buddha, Maitreya, often portrayed as fat and happy over his coming promotion, and Amitabha, a saviour who rewards the faithful with admission to a sort of Christian paradise. The ritual, tradition and superstition that Buddha rejected came tumbling back in with a vengeance.

In Tibet and in areas of Gansu, Sichuan and Yunnan a unique form of the Mahayana school is practised: Tantric or Lamaist Buddhism (*lǎmā jiào* in Mandarin). Tantric Buddhism, often called *Vajrayana* or 'thunderbolt vehicle' by its followers, has been practised since the early 7th century AD and is heavily influenced by Tibet's pre-Buddhist Bon religion, which relied on priests or shamans to placate spirits, gods and demons. Generally speaking, it is much more mystical than other forms of Buddhism, relying heavily on mudras (ritual postures), mantras (sacred speech), *yantras* (sacred art) and secret initiation rites. Priests called *lamas* are believed to be reincarnations of highly evolved beings; the Dalai Lama (see Political Dissidence & Repression) is the supreme patriarch of Tibetan Buddhism.

Chinese Religion

Taoism combines with old animistic beliefs to teach people how to maintain harmony with the universe. Confucianism takes care of the political and moral aspects of life. Buddhism takes care of the afterlife. But to say that the Chinese have three religions – Taoism, Buddhism and Confucianism – is too simple a view of their traditional religious life. At the first level, Chinese religion is animistic with a belief in the innate vital energy in rocks, trees, rivers and springs. At the second level, people from the distant past, both real and mythological, are worshipped as gods. Overlaid on these beliefs are popular Taoism, Mahayana Buddhism and Confucianism.

On a day-to-day level, the Chinese are much less concerned with the high-minded philosophies and asceticism of Buddha, Confucius or Laozi than they are with the pursuit of worldly success, the appeasement of the dead and the spirits, and the seeking of hidden knowledge about the future. Chinese religion incorporates what the West regards as superstition; if you want your fortune told, for instance, you go to a temple. The other important thing to remember is that Chinese religion is polytheistic. Apart from Buddha, Laozi and Confucius there are many other divinities such as hearth gods and gods and goddesses for particular professions.

The most important concept in the Chinese popular religious vocabulary is luck, and the Chinese are too astute not to utilise it. Gods have to be appeased, bad spirits blown away and sleeping dragons soothed to keep luck on one's side. Geomancy (*fēngshuǐ*) is the Chinese technique of manipulating or judging the environment. The location of a window, doorway or (most importantly) an ancestor's grave can have a major impact on your fortune. In Hong Kong, many of the largest skyscrapers were only constructed after careful consultation with a geomancer.

Integral parts of Chinese religion are death, the afterlife and ancestor-worship. At least as far back as the Shang Dynasty there were lavish funeral ceremonies involving the internment of horses, carriages, wives and slaves. The more important the person, the more possessions and people had to be buried with them to meet the requirements of the next world. The deceased had to be kept happy because their powers to inflict punishments or to grant favours greatly increased after death. Even today a traditional Chinese funeral can still be a lavish event.

Chinese Temples

Architecturally, the roof is the dominant feature of a Chinese temple. It is usually green or yellow and is decorated with figures of divinities and lucky symbols such as dragons and carp. Stone lions often guard the temple entrance.

Inside is a small courtyard with a large bowl where incense and paper offerings are burnt. Beyond is the main hall with an altar table, often with an intricately carved front. Here you'll find offerings of fruit and drinks. Behind is the altar with its images framed by red brocade embroidered with gold characters. Depending on the size and wealth of the temple there are gongs, drums, side altars and adjoining rooms with shrines to different gods, chapels for prayers to the dead and displays of funerary plaques. There are also living quarters for the temple keepers. There is no set time for prayer and no communal service except for funerals. Worshippers enter the temple whenever they want to make offerings, pray for help or give thanks.

The dominant colours in a Chinese temple are red, gold or yellow, and green. The orange-to-red colour range represents joy and festivity. White stands for purity and is also the colour of death. Green signifies harmony, of fundamental importance to the Chinese. Yellow and gold herald heavenly glory. Grey and black are the colours of disaster and grief.

The most striking feature of the Buddhist temple is the pagoda. It was probably introduced from India along with Buddhism in the 1st century AD. Because the early pagodas were constructed of wood, they were easily destroyed by fire and subject to corrosion, so materials such as brick, stone, brass and iron were substituted. They were often built to house religious artefacts and documents, to commemorate important events, or as monuments. The Big Goose Pagoda in Xi'an is a monolithic example of pagoda construction.

During the Northern Wei period the construction of cave temples began and was continued during later dynasties. The caves at Longmen near Luoyang, at Mogao near Dunhuang, and at Yungang near Datong are some of the finest examples.

In Buddhist art the Buddha is frequently displayed in a basic triad, with a Bodhisattva (a Buddhist saint who has arrived at the gateway to nirvana but has chosen to return to earth to guide lesser mortals along righteous paths) on either side. Their faces tend to express the emotions of joy, serenity or compassion. Sometimes the bodhisattvas are replaced by the figures of Buddha's first two disciples, the youthful Ananda and the older Kasyapa.

Islam *(yīsīlán jiào)*

The founder of Islam was the Arab prophet Mohammed. Strictly speaking, Muslims believe it was not Mohammed who shaped the religion but God, and Mohammed merely transmitted it from God to his people. To call the religion 'Mohammedanism' is also incorrect, since it implies that the religion centres around Mohammed and not around God. The proper name of the religion is Islam, derived from the word *salam* which primarily means 'peace', and in a secondary sense 'surrender'. The full connotation is something like 'the peace which comes by surrendering to God'. The corresponding adjective is 'Muslim'.

The prophet was born around 570 AD and came to be called Mohammed, which means 'highly praised'. His ancestry is traditionally traced back to Abraham, who had two wives, Hagar and Sarah. Hagar gave birth to Ishmael, and Sarah had a son named Isaac. Sarah demanded that Hagar and Ishmael be banished from the tribe. According to Islam's holy book, the Koran, Ishmael went to Mecca, where his line of descendants can be traced down to Mohammed. There have been other true prophets before Mohammed, but he is regarded as the culmination of them and the last.

Mohammed said that there is only one God, Allah. The name derives from joining *al* which means 'the' with *Illah* which means 'God'. His uncompromising monotheism conflicted with the pantheism and idolatry of the Arabs. Also, his moral teachings and vision of a universal brotherhood conflicted with what he believed was a corrupt and decadent social order based on class divisions.

The initial reaction to his teachings was hostile. He and his followers were forced to flee from Mecca to Medina in 622, where Mohammed built up a political base and an army which eventually defeated Mecca and brought all of Arabia under his control. He died in 632, two years after taking Mecca. By the time a century had passed the Arab Muslims had built a huge empire which stretched all the way from Persia to Spain. Though the Arabs were eventually supplanted by the Turks, the strength of Islam has continued to the present day.

Unlike in many other countries, Islam was brought to China peacefully. Arab traders who landed on the southern coast of China established their mosques in great maritime cities like Canton and Quanzhou, and Muslim merchants travelling the Silk Road through central Asia to China won converts among the Han Chinese in the north of the country. There are also large populations of Muslim Uigur people (of Turkic descent) whose ancestors first moved into China's Xinjiang region during the Tang Dynasty.

Christianity (jīdū jiào)

The earliest record of Christianity in China dates back to the Nestorians, a Syrian Christian sect. They first appeared in China in the 7th century when a Syrian named Raban presented Christian scriptures to the imperial court at Chang'an (Xi'an). This event and the construction of a Nestorian monastery in Chang'an are recorded on a large stone stele made in 781 AD, now displayed in the Shaanxi Provincial Museum in Xi'an.

The next major Christian group to arrive in China were the Jesuits. The priests Matteo Ricci and Michael Ruggieri were permitted to set up base at Zhaoqing in Guangdong Province in the 1580s, and eventually made it to the imperial court in Beijing. Large numbers of Catholic and Protestant missionaries established themselves in China following the invasion of China by the Western powers in the 19th century.

Judaism (yóutài jiào)

Kaifeng in Henan Province has been the home of the largest community of Chinese Jews. Their religious beliefs and almost all the customs associated with them have died out, yet the descendants of the original Jews still consider themselves Jewish. Just how the Jews got to China is unknown. They may have come as traders and merchants along the Silk Road when Kaifeng was the capital of China, or they may have emigrated from India. For more details, see the Kaifeng section in Henan Province.

Religion & Communism

Today the Chinese Communist government professes atheism. It considers religion to be base superstition, a remnant of old China used by the ruling classes to keep power. This is in line with the Marxist belief that religion is the 'opiate of the people'. Nevertheless, in an effort to improve relations with the Muslim, Buddhist and Lamaist minorities, the Chinese government is once again permitting open religious activity. However, only atheists are permitted to be members of the CCP. Since almost all of China's 55 minority groups adhere to one religion or another, this rule precludes most of them from becoming Party members.

Traditional Chinese religious beliefs took a battering during the Cultural Revolution when monasteries were disbanded, temples were destroyed, and the monks were sometimes killed or sent to the fields to labour. Many temples and monasteries are now derelict or have other functions. Although traditional Chinese religion is strong in places like Macau, Hong Kong and Taiwan, the temples and monasteries have a very minor religious role in mainland China.

Since the death of Mao, the Chinese government has allowed many temples (sometimes with their own contingent of monks and novices) to reopen as active places of worship. All religious activity is firmly under state control and many of the monks are caretakers within renovated shells of monasteries. Pilgrimages to burn incense, throw *shèng bēi* (fortune-telling wooden blocks) and make offerings to the gods by burning fake paper money appear to be common practice in temples once more. There are also stories of peasants rebuilding shrines to local gods, consulting geomancy experts before constructing buildings and graves, and burying deceased relatives with traditional religious ceremonies.

Confucius has often been used as a political symbol, his role 'redefined' to suit the needs of the time. At the end of the 19th century he was upheld as a symbol of reform because he had worked for reform in his own day. After the fall of the Qing Dynasty, Chinese intellectuals vehemently opposed him as a symbol of a conservative and backward China. In the 1930s he was used by Chiang Kaishek and the Kuomintang as a guide to proper, traditional values. During the Cultural Revolution Confucius was attacked again. Just what line to take with Confucian teachings remains a problem for the Chinese government, but they are now enjoying some kind of comeback as the government emphasises stability and respect for order and authority.

Christianity is a reminder of foreign intrusion and imperialism. The Western powers in the 19th century used the missionaries as an excuse to expand the areas on Chinese soil under their control, claiming the need to protect the missions. Besides winning religious converts, the missions posed a threat to traditional Chinese society since they introduced an alien religion, science, education and morals.

A common criticism is that many early Chinese Christians were 'rice Christians' – attracted to the power and wealth of the church rather than to the faith itself. True or not, the Chinese Christian churches survived the Communist takeover in 1949. Like the Buddhist temples, they were closed down during the Cultural Revolution; many have since been restored and are once again active places of worship.

In China today, there are believed to be 14 million Muslims, making them the largest identifiable religious group still active in the PRC. The government has not published official figures of the number of Buddhists, but they must be substantial since most Tibetans, Mongolians and Dai people follow Buddhism. There are around three million Catholics and four million Protestants. It's impossible to determine the number of Taoists, but the number of Taoist priests is very small.

Freedom of religion is guaranteed under the Chinese constitution, but it carries a crucial rider that 'religious bodies and religious affairs are not subject to any foreign domination'. In the late 1950s the Chinese government moved to cut off the churches from foreign influence and to place them under the control of the government. The 'Three-Self Patriotic Movement' was set up as an umbrella organisation for the Protestant churches, and the 'Catholic Patriotic Association' was set up to replace Rome as the leader of the Catholic churches.

There is much friction between the government and the Chinese Catholic church because the church refuses to disown the Pope as its leader, and because the Vatican maintains diplomatic relations with Taiwan. In March 1983, four elderly priests who had already spent long terms in prison were again given long prison sentences on charges which included subversion and collusion with foreign countries. It's thought their main offence was maintaining illicit contacts with the Vatican.

The Cultural Revolution resulted in the closure of Muslim mosques though many of these have since been reopened. Of all people in China, the Tibetan Buddhists most felt the brunt of Mao's mayhem. The Dalai Lama and his entourage fled to India in 1959 when the Tibetan rebellion was put down by Chinese troops. During the Cultural Revolution the monasteries were disbanded (some were levelled to the ground) and the theocracy which had governed Tibet for centuries was wiped out overnight. Some Tibetan temples and monasteries have been reopened and the Tibetan religion is still a very powerful force among the people.

LANGUAGE

The official language of the PRC is the Beijing dialect, usually referred to in the West as 'Mandarin'. It's spoken mainly in the north-east and south-west. The official name of Mandarin in China is *pŭtōnghuà*, or 'common speech', but students of the language will come across a bewildering number of other appellations for common speech. The most popular alternatives to using the word *pŭtōnghuà* are *hànyŭ* (Han language), *zhōngwén* and *zhōngguóhuà*, both of which mean simply 'Chinese'.

The word 'Mandarin' derives from the use of the Beijing dialect as a standard language by the scholar class in centuries past, when it was referred to as *guānhuà*. This word has fallen into disuse. The widespread promulgation of a national language based on the Beijing dialect has its origins in the Nation-

Chinglish

Initially you might be puzzled by a sign in the bathroom that reads 'Please don't take the odds and ends put into the nightstool'. In fact this is a warning to resist sudden impulses to empty the contents of your pockets or backpack into the toilet. An apparently ambiguous sign with anarchic implications like the one in the Lhasa Bank of China that reads 'Question Authority' is really just an economical way of saying 'Please address your questions to one of the clerks'. On the other hand, just to confuse things, a company name like the 'Risky Investment Co' means just what it says.

If this all sounds confusing, don't worry. It won't be long before you have a small armoury of Chinglish phrases of your own. Before you know it, you'll know without even thinking that 'Be careful not to be stolen' is a warning against thieves; that 'Shoplifters will be fined 10 times' means that shoplifting is not a good idea in China; that 'Do not stroke the works' (generally found in museums) means 'No touching'; and that 'No gang fighting after drinking the liqueurs' is a warning against the cocktail party brawls that have become an increasingly prevalent social problem in the PRC.

The best advice for travellers in China grappling with the complexities of a new language is not to set your sights too high. Bear in mind that it takes a minimum of 15 years of schooling in the Chinese language and a crash course in English to be able to write Chinglish with any fluency. ■

alist period, when it was called *guóyǔ* ('National language'), a term that is still used in Taiwan. Putonghua, as promulgated by the Communists, differs from the Nationalist guoyu in certain respects (vocabulary and tonal values), but not enough to hamper mutual intelligibility.

Spoken

Dialects Discounting Mandarin, China has six major dialect groups, which themselves subdivide into many dialects. It is thought that around 70% of the population speaks Mandarin. This doesn't mean, though, that Mandarin is their first language. In the countryside, people are more likely to speak only a local dialect, though most younger people will at least understand Mandarin.

The dialect other than Mandarin that most Westerners will have come across is Cantonese, which belongs to the *Yue* group of dialects. It is the language most likely to be spoken in your local Chinese take-away. It has six tones (or nine if you include tonal variations within the six), making it an even more difficult language to master than Mandarin for foreigners. It is spoken in Guangdong, southern Guangxi and Hong Kong. Other dialects abound and few of them are mutually intelligible.

Still, a Cantonese or Hokkienese speaker learning Mandarin has a huge head-start on any non-Chinese student. For a start,

Chinese dialects share the same written system. A Cantonese speaker grows up reading the same text books and newspapers as a Mandarin speaker. They pronounce the words they are reading differently, and the Cantonese speaker might be reading words he or she wouldn't choose to use in daily speech, but speakers of both languages understand the same text. Moreover, with some small exceptions, the grammars of Chinese dialects are almost identical.

Grammar Chinese grammar is far simpler than the grammars of European languages. For a start, there are no articles (a, the), no tenses and no plurals. This immediately does away with biggest hurdles facing students of, say, German or French. Many travellers are intimidated by Chinese but, once they latch onto the basic principle that constructing a Chinese sentence is basically a matter of stringing words together, a great deal of progress can be made quickly.

The basic point to bear in mind is that, like English, Chinese is a subject-verb-object language. In other words, a basic English sentence like 'I (subject) go (verb) to the shop (object)', is constructed in exactly the same way in Chinese. You don't have to conjugate anything and you don't have worry about articles and plurals. Simple.

Obviously we are making it sound a lot easier than it really is, and it's a good idea to

CT, CB,
CT, SB,
CT

Top: The Pearl River, Canton (AS)
Bottom: The blues and greys of a Canton winter (JH)

get hold of a phrasebook like the Lonely Planet *Mandarin Chinese Phrasebook* for a more comprehensive rundown on the Chinese grammar and a comprehensive selection of phrases and vocabulary items. But basically, with the exception of the tones (see the section on Tones below), Chinese is comparable to Bahasa Indonesian as a fairly easy language to pick up on the road.

Written
Chinese is probably the oldest writing system in the world. To look at, it seems like so many little pictures, and hence is often referred to as a language of 'pictographs'. Many of the basic Chinese characters are in fact highly stylised pictures of what they represent, but this element is only part of the story in what is a highly complex system.

Chinese & Computers

The information revolution has finally arrived in China, but its arrival was delayed for many years. Part of the reason had to do with security – until very recently the Chinese government did not even allow individuals to own photocopiers and fax machines. Computers provide an even more powerful tool that enables individuals to exchange information beyond the government's control. Yet the Chinese now recognise that, in order to modernise the country, computers must become readily accessible.

Early personal computers from the 1970s and 1980s couldn't run Chinese software very well – they simply weren't powerful enough. Nowadays, modern desktop computers are easily capable of storing (on disk) and displaying (on screen) the thousands of intricate Chinese characters. However, one part of the machine which still doesn't handle Chinese very well is the keyboard. The keyboards on a typical computer were designed for typing the Roman alphabet, or (with special software) other alphabets like Cyrillic, Arabic, and so on.

The problem is that the Chinese language doesn't have an alphabet. It's hard to imagine anyone designing a keyboard with thousands of keys and it's hard to imagine how anyone could type on such a device. So for now, Chinese is typed on a conventional keyboard. Various input methods are used, each with its strong and weak points. The easiest way is to type romanised Chinese and let the computer translate this into characters. This works up to a point, but many Chinese characters have the same pronunciation, forcing the typist to pick and choose amongst the many possibilities. For example, typing *ji* brings up a display of 122 characters – the user must choose the correct one! Also, the typist must know romanised Chinese – many Chinese people do not. Another input method allows the user to find the correct character by the order of the strokes used in normal Chinese writing – this method works but is very slow. Yet another system requires the operator to memorise a code number for each character – thousands of them! Not surprisingly, few people become proficient at this method.

Programmers in China, Hong Kong, Singapore and Taiwan have been looking for solutions. Experiments have been tried with voice input, bypassing the keyboard entirely. Japanese programmers have worked on the same method. After countless hours of effort and billions of dollars in research grants, the results have been poor – no one has found an adequate substitute for typing.

Input is one side of the equation – the other side is output. Mainland China has adopted a standardised format for the storage of Chinese characters on disk. This system works fine for the official 7000 simplified characters, but Taiwan (which uses traditional characters) has an official list of 13,000 characters to deal with and therefore has adopted its own (incompatible) system. Hong Kong uses the traditional writing system but chips in with an additional 150 characters specifically for Cantonese. Chinese programmers have had to work overtime developing file-format converters and various other tricks to deal with the two (or three?) systems.

In the meantime, the number of computers in China is increasing exponentially. Although many parts are imported, China makes its own personal computers including such brands as Great Wall and Taiji. Most Chinese companies now own PCs, as well as many schools and more well-to-do individuals. And just what are all these machines being used for? Sometimes for accounting, and sometimes for keeping business records – but mostly for playing video games.

And sometimes for making mischief. Software pirating is ubiquitous in China, and so are computer viruses. In 1989 the dreaded 'Li Peng virus' appeared. The virus asked if you liked Premier Li Peng, and those who answered 'yes' had their hard disks wiped out. Partly as a result, the PLA has decided that computer viruses pose a significant military threat and a major effort is now being made to find ways of defeating them. ■

Chinese linguists divide characters into six groups according to their composition. The first group is the pictogram, which is what most Westerners call to mind when they think of Chinese characters. It is a character which is a stylised picture of what it represents; a horse, say, or the moon. The second group, the ideogram, represents its object in abstract terms; thus the word for 'middle' is a vertical line cutting through the centre of a rectangle. The third group, the compound ideogram, is a combination of two or more ideograms to denote an idea or object; thus the combination of three tree ideograms creates the word *sēn*, or 'forest'. The fourth group, the phonogram, is a combination of a meaning element and a phonetic element, and is the most common kind of Chinese character (around 90% of Chinese characters are phonograms). The other two groups, the phonetic loan and derivative character, claim less members and are of more interest to the specialist.

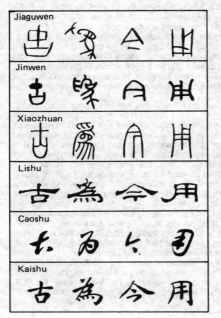

Just how many Chinese characters are there? Well, it is true that with the use of ancient sources it is possible to verify the existence of some 56,000 characters, but the vast majority of these are obsolete and others were variations of the same characters in times before national standards had been imposed. It is commonly felt that a well educated contemporary Chinese might know and use between 6000 and 8000 characters. Students looking at getting through a Chinese newspaper will need to know around 1200 to 1500 characters to get the gist of what's going on, but will probably need between 2000 and 3000 before the going starts to get easy.

The question of how many characters you need to read certain Chinese texts is, however, a little misleading. While the building block of the Chinese language is the monosyllabic Chinese character, Chinese words are usually made up of two or more characters in combination. A student of Chinese, for example, might know the characters for 'look' *(kàn)*, 'home' *(jiā)* and 'dog' *(gǒu)*, but would probably have to look up a dictionary to find out that all three in combination *(kànjiāgǒu)* meant 'watchdog'. A classic example of a less obvious character compound is the combination of *wēi*, meaning 'dangerous' and *jī*, meaning 'opportunity', to create the word 'crisis' *(wēijī)*.

Using a Dictionary One of the big drawbacks of Chinese is that if you don't know the pronunciation of a character (see the following section on Pinyin) it is quite difficult to track it down in a dictionary. It usually takes students of Chinese at least six months of study before they can start using a dictionary effectively.

Basically, the building blocks of Chinese characters are 'radicals'. In Putonghua there are 189 of these radicals (Taiwan guoyu has over 210). A radical is normally on the left-hand side or at the top of the character and it generally gives you a clue as to the character's meaning. The 'water radical', then, can be found in a huge range of characters, from 'mud' to 'soup', and the 'heart radical' can be found in concepts as diverse as 'busy' and 'worry'. For Chinese using a dictionary, the radical is usually obvious, and they can then use this to flip to the section of the dictionary where all the characters with, say, all the water radicals are.

Simplification A final point on Chinese characters is worth making with regard to the simplification process carried out in the PRC. In the interests of promoting universal literacy, in 1954 the Committee for Reforming the Chinese Language was set up by the Beijing Government. Around 2200 Chinese characters have been simplified on systematic grounds.

The reforms were implemented successfully in the PRC, but Chinese communities outside China (notably Taiwan and Hong Kong) continue to use traditional full-form characters. The last few years, probably as a result of large-scale investment by Overseas Chinese and tourism, has seen a return of the full-form characters to China, mainly in advertising (where the traditional characters are considered more attractive) and restaurant, hotel and shop signs. What this means in the long term it is difficult to say. Mainland Chinese insist that simplified characters are here to stay, but the increased usage of traditional characters will probably mean that the two systems will come into competition in China.

Tones

Chinese is a language with a large number of homonyms (words of different meaning but identical pronunciation), and if it were not for its tonal quality it probably would not work very well as a language. Mandarin has four tones (high level, rising, falling-rising and falling), and all Chinese words have one of these as a its tonal value. Examples abound, but the standard one given for beginners is *ma*, which can mean variously, depending on the tone, 'mother', 'hemp',

'horse' or 'scold'. Thus, a nice little exercise for those with an interest in Chinese tones is: *māma qí mǎ, mǎ màn, māma mà mǎ*, which means: 'mother rides a horse; the horse is slow; mother scolds the horse', but then you knew that all along, didn't you?

Actually, as intimidating as this all sounds, English frequent employs all the tones used in Mandarin. The difference is that while we use tonal quality for emphasis or for emotion, for the Chinese the tone is a basic ingredient in the meaning of a word. An angry 'yes!' for example is a falling tone in Mandarin. Still, unless you have a particularly good ear, mastering the Mandarin tones takes a lot of hard work. If you are a beginner, keep trying. In simple sentences the context will generally give the meaning to Chinese after one or two attempts.

high tone	—	*mā* mother
rising tone	╱	*má* hemp or numb
falling-rising tone	⌄	*mǎ* horse
falling tone	╲	*mà* to scold or swear

Pinyin

In 1958 the Chinese officially adopted a system known as *pīnyīn* as a method of writing their language using the Roman alphabet. Since the official language of China is the Beijing dialect, this pronunciation is used. The original idea was to eventually do away with characters completely and just use pinyin. However, tradition dies hard and the idea has gradually been abandoned.

Pinyin is often used on shop fronts, street signs and advertising billboards. Don't expect Chinese people to be able to use pinyin, however. There are also signs in China that adherence to the pinyin system is breaking down. The huge pinyin sign on Guilin railway station, for example, is spelt 'Gveilinz'.

In the countryside and the smaller towns you may not see a single pinyin sign anywhere, so unless you speak Chinese you'll need a phrasebook with Chinese characters if you're travelling in these areas. Though pinyin is helpful, it's not an instant key to communication, since Westerners often don't get the pronunciation and intonation of the romanised word correct.

Since 1979 all translated texts of Chinese diplomatic documents and Chinese magazines published in foreign languages have used the pinyin system of spelling names and places. The system replaces the old Wade-Giles and Lessing systems of romanising Chinese script. Thus under pinyin, 'Mao Tsetung' becomes *Mao Zedong*; 'Chou En-lai' becomes *Zhou Enlai*; and 'Peking' becomes *Beijing*. The name of the country remains as it has been generally written: 'China' in English and German, and 'Chine' in French – in pinyin it's 'Zhongguo'. When Hong Kong (an English version of Cantonese for 'fragrant harbour') goes over to China in 1997 it will become Xianggang.

Maps printed in the PRC still retain a few spellings from minority languages such as Mongolian – thus, Chinese maps still show the city of *Hohhot* (*Huhehaote* in pinyin) and *Ürümqi* (*Wulumuqi*).

Pronunciation The letter **v** is not used in Chinese. The trickiest sounds in pinyin are **c**, **q** and **x**. Most letters are pronounced as in English, except for the following description of the sounds produced in spoken Mandarin.

Vowels

a	as the 'a' in 'father'
ai	as the 'i' in 'I'
ao	as the 'ow' in 'cow'
e	as the 'ur' in 'blur'
ei	as the 'ei' in 'weigh'
i	as the 'ee' in 'meet'; when **i** occurs after **c, ch, r, s, sh, z** or **zh** it sounds more like the 'e' in 'her'
ian	as in 'yen'
ie	as the 'ere' in 'here'
o	as the 'o' in 'or'
ou	as the 'oa' in 'boat'
u	as the 'u' in 'flute'; when preceded by **q, j, x,** or **y,** as **ü** (see following example)
	as the 'oo' in 'woo' in other cases
ü	as in German umlaut 'ü'
ui	as in 'way'
uo	as in 'war'

Consonants

Pinyin consonants are difficult for many English speakers first learning Chinese because their pronunciation differs from that of standard English. A Pinyin *j* is not pronounced as the 'j' in English 'jug' and *z* is not pronounced as in 'zig-zag'. Check the guide below for all the consonants that vary from their English counterparts.

One other point that eludes many beginners is that Pinyin has three pairs of consonants whose pronunciation are the same: *s* and *x*, which are both pronounced like the *s* in 'sock'; *c* and *q*, which are both pronounced like the 'ts' in 'bits'; and *j* and *z*, which are both pronounced like the 'ds' in 'suds'. The reason for this is perfectly logical, but not that easy to explain briefly. Basically, whether, say, a *j* or a *z* is used depends on the value of the vowel following it. Thus *ji* is pronounced 'dzee', while *zi* is pronounced 'dzuh'; *ju* is pronounced 'dzū', while *zu* is pronounced 'dzoo'. Don't worry, once you figure out how it works, it all makes perfect sense.

c	as the 'ts' in 'bits'
ch	as in English, but with the tongue curled back
j	as the 'ds' in 'suds'
h	guttural, as in Scottish 'loch'
q	as the 'ts' in 'bits'
r	as the 's' in 'pleasure'
sh	as in English, but with the tongue curled back
x	as the 's' in 'sock'
z	as the 'ds' in 'suds'
zh	as the 'j' in 'judge' but with the tongue curled back

Consonants (except for **n, ng**, and **r**) never end syllables. In pinyin, apostrophes can separate syllables – writing *ping'an* prevents pronunciation of this word as *pin'gan*.

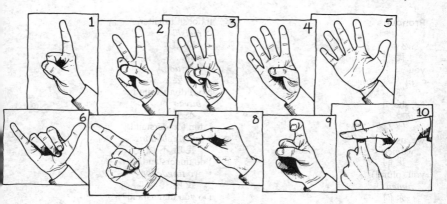

Finger Counting

Gestures

Hand signs are frequently used in China. The 'thumbs-up' sign has a long tradition as an indication of excellence. Another way to indicate excellence is to gently pull your own earlobe between thumb and index finger.

The Chinese have a system for counting on their hands. If you can't speak the language, it would be worth your while to at least learn Chinese finger counting. The symbol for number 10 is to form a cross with the index fingers, but in many locations the Chinese just show a fist.

Behaviour

One way to ask a question in Chinese is to place the verb together with the negative of the verb. One of the commonest examples is *yǒu méiyǒu?* (literally: have not have?). Although grammatically correct, this form of question makes it very easy for the person asked to give the reply that requires the least possible effort, namely, *méiyǒu* (not have).

Nobody leaves China without having learnt this phrase! *Méiyǒu* can mean many things, such as 'not available today', 'not available for you', 'not available because I'm resting' or 'not available because I'm lazy'. To stave off this response for as long as possible, it's worth diving straight in with *wǒ yào* (I want).

Máfán nǐ (literally: cause bother for you) is a useful way to butter up someone to get them to do something for you or to express gratitude for a favour they've just done you. When you've reached an impasse by peaceful means, it often helps to ask *zěnme bàn?* (literally: what to do?). Since some Chinese people only respond to a specific question, this provides them scope to tell you about a room, bus, flight, etc you didn't know about. Sometimes the simplest things seem mighty complicated!

Phrasebooks

Phrasebooks are invaluable – but it's better to copy out the appropriate sentences in Chinese rather than show someone the book; otherwise they'll take it and read every page. Reading place names or street signs is not difficult since the Chinese name is accompanied by the pinyin form; if not you'll soon learn lots of characters just by repeated exposure. A small dictionary with English, pinyin and Chinese characters is also useful for learning a few words.

Lonely Planet publishes a *Mandarin Chinese Phrasebook* as well as the *Tibet Phrasebook*.

Pronouns

I
wǒ
我

you
nǐ
你

he, she, it
tā
他 / 她 / 它

we, us
wǒmen
我们

you (plural)
nǐmen
你们

they, them
tāmen
他们

Useful Phrases

hello
nǐ hǎo
你好！

goodbye
zàijiàn
再见

thank you
xièxie
谢谢

you're welcome
búkèqi
不客气

I'm sorry
duìbùqǐ
对不起

no, don't have
méiyǒu
没有

no, not so
búshì
不是

I am a foreign student.
wǒ shì liúxuéshēng
我是留学生

What's to be done now?
zěnme bàn?
怎么办？

It doesn't matter.
méishì
没事

I want...
wǒ yào...
我要 . . . . .

No, I don't want it.
búyào
不要

I don't understand.
wǒ tīngbudǒng
我听不懂．

I do understand.
wǒ tīngdedǒng
我听得懂．

Do you understand?
dǒng ma?
懂 吗？

Money

How much is it?
duōshǎo qián?
多少钱？

Is there anything cheaper?
yǒu piányì yìdiǎn de ma?
有便宜一点的吗？

That's too expensive.
tài guìle
太贵了．

Bank of China
zhōngguó yínháng
中国 银行

FEC (foreigners' money)
wàihuìjuàn
外汇券

RMB (people's money)
rénmínbì
人民币

change money
huàn qián
换钱

traveller's cheque
lǚxíng zhīpiào
旅行支票

Post & Telecommunications

post office
yóujú
邮局

letter
xìn
信

envelope
xìnfēng
信 封

package
bāoguǒ
包 裹

air mail
hángkōng xìn
航 空 信

surface mail
píngyóu
平 邮

stamps
yóupiào
邮 票

postcard
míngxìnpiàn
明 信 片

aerogramme
hángkōng xìnjiàn
航 空 邮 件

poste restante
cúnjú hòulǐnglàn
存 局 候 领 栏

telephone
diànhuà
电 话

telephone office
diànxùn dàlóu
电 讯 大 楼

telephone card
diànhuà kǎ
电 话 卡

international call
guójì diànhuà
国 际 电 话

collect call
duìfāng fùqián diànhuà
对 方 付 钱 电 话

direct-dial call
zhíbō diànhuà
直 通 电 话

fax
chuánzhēn (or 'fax' as in English)
传 真

Time

What is the time?
jǐ diǎnle?
几 点 了 ？

...hour...minute
...diǎn...fēn
点 ...分...

now
xiànzài
现 在

today
jīntiān
今 天

When?
shénme shíhòu?
什 么 时 候 ？

tomorrow
míngtiān
明 天

the day after tomorrow
hòutiān
后 天

three days ahead
dà hòutiān
大 后 天

in the morning
zǎochén
早 晨

daytime
báitiān
白 天

afternoon
xiàwǔ
下 午

night, evening
wǎnshàng
晚 上

Wait a moment.
děng yīxià
等 一 下

daylight-saving time
xiàlìng shíjiān
夏 令 时 间

Beijing (standard) time
běijīng shíjiān
北 京 时 间

Places

China International Travel Service (CITS)
zhōngguó guójì lǚxíngshè
中 国 国 际 旅 行 社

China Travel Service (CTS)
zhōngguó lǚxíngshè
中 国 旅 行 社

China Youth Travel Service (CYTS)
zhōngguó qīngnián lǚxíngshè
中 国 青 年 旅 行 社

embassy
dàshǐguǎn
大 使 馆

Foreign Languages Bookstore
wàiwén shūdiàn
外 文 书 店

Xinhua Bookstore
xīnhuá shūdiàn
新 华 书 店

Accommodation

hotel
lǚguǎn
旅 馆

small hotel
lǚshè
旅 社

hostel
zhāodàisuǒ
招 待 所

tourist hotel
bīnguǎn, fàndiàn, jiǔdiàn
宾 馆，饭 店，酒 店

dormitory
duōrénfáng
多 人 房

single room
dānrénfáng
单 人 房

double room
shuāngrénfáng
双 人 房

bed
chuángwèi
床 位

economy room
jīngjìfáng
经 济 房

economy room (with bath)
jīngjì tàofáng
经 济 套 房

standard room (with bath)
biāozhǔn tàofáng
标 准 套 房

luxury room (with bath)
háohuá tàofáng
豪 华 套 房

hotel namecard
lǚguǎn de míngpiàn
旅 馆 的 名 片

wash clothes
xǐ yīfú
洗 衣 服

book a whole room
bāofáng
包 房

Transport

I want to go to...
wǒ yào qù...
我 要 去 . . . .

I want to get off
wǒ yào xiàchē
我 要 下 车

luggage
xíngli
行 李

left-luggage room
jìcún chù
寄 存 处

one ticket
yìzhāng piào
一 张 票

I want to depart at...(time)
wǒ yào...diǎn zǒu
我 要 . . . . . 点 开 .

Could you buy a ticket for me?
kěyǐ tì wǒ mǎi yìzhāng piào mā?
可 以 替 我 买 一 张 票 吗 ?

What time does it depart?
jǐdiǎn kāi?
几 点 开 ?

What time does it arrive?
jǐdiǎn dào?
几 点 到 ?

How long does the trip take?
zhècì lǚxíng yào duōcháng shíjiān?
这 次 旅 行 要 多 少 时 间 ?

buy a ticket
mǎi piào
买票

refund a ticket
tuì piào
退票

taxi
chūzū chē
出租车

Air

airport
fēijīchǎng
飞机场

CAAC
zhōngguó mínháng
中国民航

charter flight
bāojī
包机

one-way ticket
dānchéng piào
单程票

round-trip ticket
láihuí piào
来回票

Bus

bus
gōnggòng qìchē
公共汽车

minibus
xiǎo gōnggòng qìchē
小公共汽车

long-distance bus station
chángtú qìchē zhàn
长途汽车站

bus map
jiāotōng dìtú
交通地图

When is the first bus?
tóubān qìchē jǐdiǎn kāi?
头班汽车几点开？

When is the last bus?
mòbān qìchē jǐdiǎn kāi?
末班汽车几点开？

When is the next bus?
xià yìbān qìchē jǐdiǎn kāi?
下一班汽车几点开？

Train

train
huǒchē
火车

ticket office
shòupiào chù
售票处

advance rail ticket office
huǒchē piào yùshòu chù
火车票预售处

railway station
huǒchē zhàn
火车站

main railway station
zhǔyào huǒchē zhàn
主要火车站

hard seat
yìngxí, yìngzuò
硬席，硬坐

soft seat
ruǎnxí, ruǎnzuò
软席，软坐

hard sleeper
yìngwò
硬卧

soft sleeper
ruǎnwò
软卧

middle berth
zhōngpù
中铺

upper berth
shàngpù
上铺

lower berth
xiàpù
下铺

platform ticket
zhàntái piào
站台票

Which platform?
dìjǐhào zhàntái
第几号站台？

upgrade ticket (after boarding)
bǔpiào
补票

first-class waiting room
tóu děng hòuchēshì
头等候车楼

subway (underground)
dìxiàtiělù
地下铁路
subway station
dìtiě zhàn
地铁站

Bicycle
bicycle
zìxíngchē
自行车
I want to hire a bicycle.
wǒ yào zū yíliàng zìxíngchē
我要租一辆自行车
How much is it per day?
yìtiān duōshǎo qián?
一天多少钱？
How much is it per hour?
yíge xiǎoshí duōshǎo qián?
一个小时多少钱？
deposit
yājīn
押金

Boat
boat
chuán
船
hovercraft
qìdiàn chuán
汽垫船
pier
mǎtóu
码头

Toilets
toilet, restroom
cèsuǒ
厕所
toilet paper
wèishēng zhǐ
卫生纸
bathroom (washroom)
xǐshǒu jiān
洗手间

Directions
map
dìtú
地图

Where is the...?
...zài nǎlǐ? ...
. . . . . 在哪里
I'm lost.
wǒ mílùle
我迷路了．
turn right
yòu zhuǎn
右转
turn left
zuǒ zhuǎn
左转
go straight
yìzhí zǒu
一直走
turn around
xiàng huí zǒu
向回走
north
běi
北
south
nán
南
east
dōng
东
west
xī
西

Streets and roads are often split up into sections *(duàn)*. Each section is given a number or (more usually) is labelled according to its relative position to the other sections using compass points. For example, Zhongshan Lu (Zhongshan Rd) might be split into an east section *(dōng duàn)* and a west section *(xī duàn)*. The east section will be designated Zhongshan Donglu and the west will be Zhongshan Xilu.

Geographical Terms
road, trail
lù
路
street
jiē, dàjiē
街，大街

boulevard
dàdào
大道

alley
xiàng, hútong
巷，胡同

cave
dòng
洞

hot spring
wēnquán
温泉

lake
hú
湖

mountain
shān
山

river
hé, jiāng
河，江

valley
gǔ, gōu
谷，沟

waterfall
pùbù
瀑布

Emergency

police
jǐngchá
警察

Fire!
huǒzāi!
火灾

Help!
jiùmìng a!
救命

Thief!
xiǎotōu!
小偷！

Public Security

Public Security Bureau (PSB)
gōng'ān jú
公安局

Foreign Affairs Branch
wài shì kē
外事科

I want to extend my visa...
wǒ yào yáncháng wǒde qiānzhèng...
我要延长我的签证

...by two weeks
...liǎngge xīngqī
两个星期

...by one month
...yíge yuè
一个月

...by two months
... liǎngge yuè
两个月

Alien Travel Permit
wàibīn tōngxíng zhèng
外宾通行政

Medical

I'm sick.
wǒ shēngbìngle
我生病了．

I'm injured.
wǒ shòushāngle
我受伤了

hospital
yīyuàn
医院

pharmacy
yàodiàn
药店

diarrhoea
lādùzi
拉肚子

anti-diarrhoeal drug
huángliánsù
黄连素

laxative
xièyào
泻药

fever
fāshāo
发烧

giardia
āmǐbā fùxiè
阿米巴腹泻
hepatitis
gānyán
肝炎
malaria
nüèjì
疟疾
rabies
kuángquǎn bìng
狂犬病
respiratory infection (influenza)
liúxíngxìng gǎnmào
流行性感冒
tetanus
pòshāngfēng
破伤风

Countries
Australia
àodàlìyà
澳大利亚
Canada
jiā'nádà
加拿大
Denmark
dānmài
丹麦
France
fǎguó
法国
Germany
déguó
德国
Netherlands
hélán
荷兰
New Zealand
xīnxīlán
新西兰
Spain
xībānyá
西班牙
Sweden
ruìdiǎn
瑞典
Switzerland
ruìshì
瑞士

UK
yīngguó
英国
USA
měiguó
美国

Numbers

0	*líng*	零
1	*yī, yāo*	一
2	*èr, liǎng*	二
3	*sān*	三
4	*sì*	四
5	*wǔ*	五
6	*liù*	六
7	*qī*	七
8	*bā*	八
9	*jiǔ*	九
10	*shí*	十
11	*shíyī*	十一
12	*shí'èr*	十二
20	*èrshí*	二十
21	*èrshíyī*	二十一
100	*yìbǎi*	一百
200	*èrbǎi*	二百
1000	*yìqiān*	一千
2000	*liǎngqiān*	两千
10,000	*yíwàn*	一万
20,000	*liǎngwàn*	两万
100,000	*shíwàn*	十万
200,000	*èrshíwàn*	二十万

Studying Chinese

Probably the two best places in the world to learn Chinese are Beijing and Taipei. The advantage of Beijing is that the simplified writing system and pinyin are used. Living expenses are also cheaper than in Taipei, though the schools tend to rip off foreigners at every opportunity. The drawbacks to studying in Beijing are the generally uncomfortable living conditions, and a deliberate xenophobic policy of keeping foreigners separate from Chinese. Foreigners are usually assigned to a separate dormitory and not permitted to live with a Chinese family. The place where most foreigners study in Beijing is the Beijing Language Institute (BLI) (*yǔyán xuéyuán*), east of Qinghua University on the No 331 bus route. There are several other schools that accept foreign students.

In Taipei, or elsewhere in Taiwan, living expenses are high but there are opportunities to work teaching English and it's not difficult to earn enough money to meet all expenses. Foreigners are free to live where they like in Taiwan, and it's not difficult to find some Chinese roommates. A disadvantage to studying in Taiwan is that only the old traditional characters are used, and pinyin is not used at all. Most foreigners also find Taipei to be a crowded, polluted and traffic-clogged city.

There are many places to study in Taiwan.

Probably the best is the National Taiwan Normal University (☎ (02) 3639123), Mandarin Training Centre *(táiwān shīfàn dàxué)*, 129-1 Hoping E Rd, Section 1, Taipei.

Hong Kong is not a particularly good place for studying Mandarin, but it's fine for learning Cantonese. Although about half the population of Hong Kong can speak Mandarin, the local accent is radically different from that heard in Beijing and can be very confusing. The New Asia Yale in China Language School, at the Chinese University in the New Territories, offers courses in both Mandarin and Cantonese.

Facts for the Visitor

VISAS & EMBASSIES

Visas for individual travel in China are easy to get. China will even issue visas to individuals from countries which do not have diplomatic relations with the People's Republic of China (PRC). However, citizens of South Africa can only visit China on an organised tour, and must apply at least one month before their planned arrival in China.

Visas are readily available in Hong Kong and from Chinese embassies in most Western and many other countries. If you can't wait until you get to Hong Kong or if you want to fly direct to China, then inquire first at the nearest Chinese embassy.

In Hong Kong, the cheapest visas (HK$90 for 2½-day service, HK$240 for same day) can be obtained from the Visa Office (☎ 5851794, 5851700) of the Ministry of Foreign Affairs of the PRC, 5th floor, Low Block, China Resources Building, 26 Harbour Rd, Wanchai. You'll have to queue and don't expect so much as a smile, but you'll save a few dollars. It's open Monday to Friday, from 9 am to 12.30 pm and 2 to 5 pm, and on Saturday from 9 am to 12.30 pm. From Tsimshatsui, Kowloon (Hong Kong), the cheapest and easiest way to get there is to take the Star Ferry to Wanchai Pier (not to Central!) – Wanchai Pier is one block away from the China Resources Building. Otherwise, it's a rather long hike from either the Wanchai or Causeway Bay MTR stations.

There are numerous travel agencies in Hong Kong that issue Chinese visas. Besides saving you the hassle of visiting the visa office and queuing, a few travel agents can get you more time than the usual 30 days. For a standard single-entry tourist visa valid for one or two months, issued in two working days, expect to pay around HK$120 to HK$140. For a visa issued in 24 hours, HK$180; issued the same day, HK$280. Dual-entry visas cost double.

Visa applications require two passport-sized photos. Your application must be written in English, and you're advised to have one entire blank page in your passport for the visa.

The visa application form asks you a number of questions – your travel itinerary, means of transport, how long you will stay etc – but you can deviate from this as much as you want. You *don't* have to leave from the place you specify on your visa application form.

If you want more flexibility to enter and leave China several times, multiple-entry visas are available through some travel agencies. This is particularly useful if you intend to follow complicated routes in and out of China via Hong Kong, Macau, Korea, Nepal, Pakistan, Thailand, Mongolia, Russia, etc. Multiple-entry visas cost approximately HK$750 and are valid for six months, allowing an unlimited number of border crossings during this time. But there is a catch – you can only stay in China for 30 days at a time and getting this extended is close to impossible. Another minor catch is that these are in fact business visas, and normally will only be issued if you've been to China at least once before and have a stamp in your passport to prove it.

Certain ports of entry such as Shenzhen issue five-day visas at the border for HK$250. Chinese residents of Hong Kong, Macau and Taiwan can apply for a *huí xiāng zhèng* which entitles them to multiple visa-free entry.

One-month single-entry visas are valid from the date of entry that you specify on the visa application. But all other visas are valid from the date of issue, *not* from the date of entry, so there's no point in getting such a visa far in advance of your planned entry date.

When you check into a hotel, there is usually a question on the registration form asking what type of visa you have. Most travellers aren't sure how to answer. For most, the type of visa is 'L' from the Chinese word for travel *(lüxing)*. This letter is stamped right on the visa. There are seven types of visas, as follows:

L	Travel *(lüxing)*
F	Business *(fangwen)*
D	Resident *(dingju)*
G	Transit *(guojing)*
X	Student *(liu xue)*
Z	Working *(ren zhi)*
C	Stewardess *(chengwu)*

If you ever feel encumbered by the expense and bureaucratic delays of obtaining visas, you might spare a thought for the Chinese, who find it very difficult to leave their own country. While high-ranking cadres and others with the proper connections (or lots of money) can go abroad, the overwhelming majority cannot even obtain a passport. Even those who get a passport must then secure an exit permit – which is even more difficult to get. However, contrary to what many foreigners believe, the Chinese can travel freely *within* their own country – the only limitation being sufficient funds to do so.

Chinese Embassies
Some of the addresses of Chinese embassies and consulates in major cities overseas include:

Australia
15 Coronation Drive, Yarralumla, ACT 2600 (☎ (06) 273 4780, 273 4781)
Consulate: Melbourne (☎ (03) 8220604)

Austria
Metternichgasse 4, 1030 Vienna (☎ (06) 75 31 49, 713 67 06)

Belgium
443-445, Avenue de Tervueren, 1150 Brussels (☎ (02) 771 33 09, 771 26 81)

Canada
515 St Patrick St, Ottawa, Ontario KIN 5H3 (☎ (613) 2342706, 2342682)

Denmark
25 Oregards alle, DK 2900 Hellerup, Copenhagen 2900 (☎ (1) 62 58 06, 61 10 13)

France
11 Ave George V, 75008 Paris (☎ (1) 47.23.36.77, 47.36.77.90)

Germany
Kurfürstenallee 12, 5300 Bonn 2 (Bad Godesberg) (☎ (0228) 36 10 95, 36 23 50)

Italy
56 Via Bruxelles, 56-00198 Rome (☎ (06) 841 34 58, 841 34 67)

Japan
3-4-33, Moto-Azabu, Minato-ku, Tokyo (106) (☎ (03) 34033380, 34033065)

Netherlands
Adriaan Goekooplaan 7, 2517 JX The Hague, (☎ (070) 355 15 15, 355 92 09)

New Zealand
2-6 Glenmore St, Wellington (☎ 4721382, 4721384)

Spain
C/Arturo Soria 113, 28043 Madrid (☎ (01) 519 4242, 519 3651)

Sweden
Lidovagen 8 115 25, Stockholm (☎ (08) 783 67 39, 783 01 79)

Switzerland
Kalecheggweg 10, 3006 Bern (☎ (031) 44 73 33, 43 45 93)

UK
49-51 Portland Place, London WIN 3AH (☎ (071) 636 2580, 636 1835)

USA
2300 Connecticut Ave NW, Washington, DC 20008 (☎ 3282500, 3282517)
Consulates: 3417 Montrose Blvd, Houston, Texas 77006; 104 South Michigan Ave, Suite 1200, Chicago, Illinois 60603; 1450 Laguna St, San Francisco, CA 94115; 520 12th Ave, New York, NY 10036

Visa Extensions
Visa extensions are handled by the Foreign Affairs Section of the local Public Security Bureau (PSB) – the police force. Government travel organisations – like CITS – have nothing to do with extensions so don't bother asking. Extensions can cost nothing for some, Y25 for most nationalities, and Y50 for others. The general rule is that you can get one extension of one month's duration. At an agreeable PSB you may be able to wangle more, especially with cogent reasons like illness (except AIDS) or transport delays, but second extensions are usually only granted for one week with the understanding that you are on your way out of China.

Re-Entry Visas
Most foreign residents of China have multiple-entry visas and don't need a re-entry

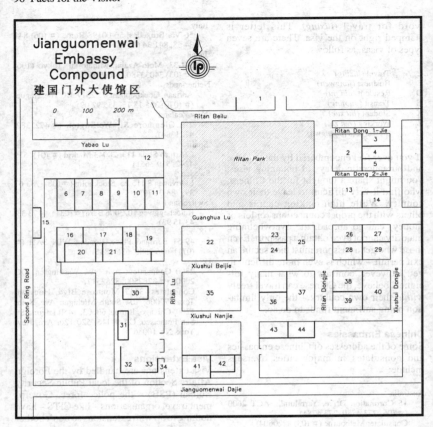

Jianguomenwai
Embassy
Compound
建国门外大使馆区

visa. However, there might be other requirements (tax clearance, vaccinations, etc) – if in doubt, check with the PSB before departing.

Other Visas

See the Train section in the Getting There & Away chapter for info on visas for travelling on the Trans-Siberian Railway.

Foreign Embassies in China

In Beijing there are two main embassy compounds – Jianguomenwai and Sanlitun.

The following embassies are in Jianguomenwai:

Austria
  5 Xiushui Nanjie (☎ 5322061; fax 5321505)
Bangladesh
  42 Guanghua Lu (☎ 5322521)
Bulgaria
  4 Xiushui Beijie (☎ 5322232)
Czech & Slovak
  Ritan Lu (☎ 5321531; fax 5324814)
India
  1 Ritan Donglu (☎ 5321908; fax 5324684)
Ireland
  3 Ritan Donglu (☎ 5322691)

1	North Korea	15	International Post Office	30	Tennis Court
2	Romania	16	Bangladesh	31	Pool
3	Senegal	17	Thailand	32	Tennis Court
4	Guyana	18	Rwanda	33	International Club
5	New Zealand	19	Gabon	34	Taxis
6	Brazil	20	Iraq	35	Czech & Slovak
7	Burundi	21	Philippines	36	Cuba
8	Kuwait	22	Poland	37	Mongolia
9	Chad	23	Colombia	38	USA
10	Greece	24	Sri Lanka	39	Ireland
11	USA (residence)	25	Vietnam	40	Bulgaria
12	Yabao Lu Clothing Market	26	Finland	41	CITIC
13	India	27	Albania	42	Friendship Store
14	UK	28	Egypt	43	Austria
		29	USA	44	Ethiopia

1	北朝鲜	15	国际邮店局	30	网球场
2	罗马尼亚	16	孟加拉国	31	游泳池
3	塞内加尔	17	泰国	32	网球场
4	圭亚那	18	卢旺达	33	国际俱乐部
5	新西兰	19	加蓬	34	出租汽车
6	巴西	20	伊拉克	35	捷克斯洛伐克
7	布隆迪	21	菲律宾	36	古巴
8	科威特	22	波兰	37	蒙古
9	乍得	23	哥伦比亚	38	美国
10	希腊	24	斯里兰卡	39	爱尔兰
11	美国 （房子）	25	越南	40	保加利亚
12	雅宝路	26	芬兰	41	国际大厦
13	印度	27	阿尔巴尼亚	42	友谊商店
14	联合王国	28	埃及	43	奥地利
		29	美国	44	埃塞俄比亚

Israel
Room 405, West Wing, China World Trade Centre, 1 Jianguomenwai Dajie (☎ 5050328)

Japan
7 Ritan Lu (☎ 5322361)

Mongolia
2 Xiushui Beijie (☎ 5321203)

New Zealand
1 Ritan Dong 2-Jie (☎ 5322731; fax 5324317)

North Korea
Ritan Beilu (☎ 5321186)

Philippines
23 Xiushui Beijie (☎ 5322794)

Poland
1 Ritan Lu (☎ 5321235; fax 5325364)

Romania
corner of Ritan Dong 2-Jie and Ritan Donglu (☎ 5323315)

Singapore
1 Xiushui Beijie (☎ 5323926; fax 5322215)

Sri Lanka
3 Jianhua Lu (☎ 5321861; fax 5325426)

Thailand
40 Guanghua Lu (☎ 5321903; fax 5323986)

UK
11 Guanghua Lu (☎ 5321961)

USA
Embassy: 3 Xiushui Beijie (☎ 5323831 ext 274)
Consulate: Bruce Building, 2 Xiushui Dongjie (☎ 5323431 ext 225)

Vietnam
32 Guanghua Lu (☎ 5321125)

The Sanlitun Compound in Beijing is home to the following embassies:

1	Duoweizhai Restaurant	22	Mexico	45	Laos
2	Nepal	23	Switzerland	46	Afghanistan
3	Liberia	24	Denmark	47	South Yemen
4	Beijing International Store	25	Algeria	48	Congo
5	Iran	26	Spain	49	Zambia
6	Lebanon	27	Australia (residence)	50	Chile
7	Tanzania	28	Malaysia	51	Venezuela
8	Oman	29	Togo	52	Holland
9	Singapore	30	Belgium	53	Morocco
10	Niger	31	Ghana	54	Mauritania
11	Burkina Faso	32	Cambodia	55	Mali
12	Jordan	33	Sierra Leone	56	Syria
13	Libya	34	Zaire	57	Yemen
14	Yugoslavia	35	Tunisia	58	France
15	Guinea	36	Madgascar	59	Central African Republic
16	Kenya	37	Uganda	60	PLO
17	Friendship Store	38	Germany	61	Sudan
18	Somalia	39	Nigeria	62	Italy
19	Argentina	40	Pakistan	63	Norway
20	Turkey	41	Sweden	64	Sanlitun Department Store
21	Cameroon	42	Canada		
		43	Hungary		
		44	UNICEF		

1	多味斋	22	墨西哥	43	匈牙利
2	尼泊尔	23	瑞士麦	44	联合国儿童基金会
3	利比里亚	24	丹麦	45	老挝
4	北京国际商店	25	阿尔及利亚	46	阿富汗
5	伊朗	26	西牙	47	南也门
6	黎巴嫩	27	澳大利亚	48	刚国
7	坦桑尼亚	28	马来西亚	49	赞比亚
8	阿曼	29	多哥	50	智利
9	新加坡	30	比利时	51	委内兰拉瑞拉
10	尼日尔	31	加纳	52	荷兰
11	八基那法索	32	柬埔寨	53	摩洛哥
12	约旦	33	塞拉利昂	54	毛里塔尼亚
13	利比亚	34	扎伊尔	55	马里
14	南斯拉夫	35	突尼斯	56	叙利亚
15	几内亚	36	马达加斯加岛	57	也门
16	肯尼亚	37	乌干达	58	法国
17	友谊商店	38	德国	59	中非共和国
18	索马里	39	尼日利亚	60	巴勒斯坦解放党
19	阿根廷	40	巴基斯坦	61	苏丹
20	土耳其	41	瑞典	62	意大利
21	喀麦隆	42	加拿大	63	挪威
				64	三里屯百货商场

Australia
    21 Dongzhimenwai Dajie (☎ 5322331; fax 5324605)
Belgium
    6 Sanlitun Lu (☎ 5321736; fax 5325097)
Cambodia
    9 Dongzhimenwai Dajie (☎ 5321889; fax 5323507)
Canada
    19 Dongzhimenwai Dajie (☎ 5323536; fax 5324072)
Denmark
    1 Sanlitun Dong 5-Jie (☎ 5322431)
Finland
    Tayuan Diplomatic Building, 14 Liangmahe Nanlu (☎ 5321817; fax 5321884)
France
    3 Sanlitun Dong 3-Jie (☎ 5321331)
Germany
    5 Dongzhimenwai Dajie (☎ 5322161; fax 5325336)
Hungary
    10 Dongzhimenwai Dajie (☎ 5321431)
Italy
    2 Sanlitun Dong 2-Jie (☎ 5322131; fax 5324676)
Malaysia
    13 Dongzhimenwai Dajie (☎ 5322531; fax 5325032)
Myanmar (Burma)
    6 Dongzhimenwai Dajie (☎ 5321584; fax 5321344)
Nepal
    1 Sanlitun Xi 6-Jie (☎ 5321795)
Netherlands
    1-15-2 Tayuan Building, 14 Liangmahe Nanlu (☎ 5321131; fax 5324689)
Norway
    1 Sanlitun Dong 1-Jie (☎ 5322261; fax 5322392)
Pakistan
    1 Dongzhimenwai Dajie (☎ 5322504)
Portugal
    Bangonglou 2-72 (☎ 5323497; fax 5324637)
Russia
    4 Dongzhimen Beizhongjie, west of the Sanlitun Compound in a separate compound (☎ 5322051; fax 5324853)
Spain
    9 Sanlitun Lu (☎ 5321986; fax 5323401)
Sweden
    3 Dongzhimenwai Dajie (☎ 5323331; fax 5323803)
Switzerland
    3 Sanlitun Dong 5-Jie (☎ 5322736; fax 5324353)

Consulates There are consulates for Australia, Czech, France, Germany, Hungary, Italy, Japan, Poland, Russia, Singapore, the UK and USA in Shanghai. There are also US,

Japanese, Polish and Thai consulates in Canton, and a US consulate in Shenyang. See the relevant chapters on those cities for details.

DOCUMENTS

Given the Chinese preoccupation with impressive bits of paper, it's worth carrying around a few business cards, student cards and anything else that's printed and laminated in plastic.

These additional IDs are useful for leaving with bicycle-renters, who often want a deposit or other security for their bikes – sometimes they ask you to leave your passport, but you should insist on leaving another piece of ID or a deposit. Some hotels also require you to hand over your passport as security, even if you've paid in advance – an old expired passport is useful for these situations.

If you're travelling with your spouse, a photocopy of your marriage licence just might come in handy should you become involved with the law, hospitals or other bureaucratic authorities. Useful, though not essential, is an International Health Certificate to record your vaccinations.

If you're thinking about working or studying in China or anywhere else along the way, photocopies of university diplomas, transcripts and letters of recommendation could prove helpful.

The International Student Identity Card (ISIC) is of no real use in China, but you can sometimes use it to obtain cheap air fares in other parts of Asia. However, it helps to back up the ISIC with a regular student card and an official-looking letter from your school's registrar. The extra back-up documents are necessary because there's quite a worldwide trade in fake ISIC cards. In addition, there are now maximum age limits (usually 26) for some concessions, and the fake-card dealers have been clamped down on. Nevertheless, fake cards are widely available and usable, although some are of poor quality.

Passport

A passport is essential, and if yours is within

a few months of expiry, get a new one now – many countries will not issue a visa if your passport has less than six months of validity remaining. Be sure that your passport has at least a few blank pages for visas and entry and exit stamps. It could be embarrassing to run out of blank pages when you are too far away from an embassy to get a new passport issued or extra pages added.

Losing your passport is very bad news indeed. Getting a new one takes time and money. However, if you will be staying in China or any foreign country for a long time, it helps tremendously to register your passport with your embassy. This will eliminate the need to send telexes back to your home country to confirm that you really exist.

If you lose your passport, you should certainly have some ID card with your photo – many embassies require this before issuing a new passport. Some embassies will accept a driver's licence but others will not – again, an expired passport will often save the day.

Chinese Documents

Foreigners who live, work or study in China will be issued a number of documents, and some of these can be used to obtain substantial discounts on trains, flights, hotels, museums and tourist sites.

Most common and least useful is the so-called 'white card', a simple student ID card with pasted-on photo and usually kept in a red plastic holder (some call it a 'red card' for this reason). Having one of these supposedly allows you to pay for train tickets in Renminbi (RMB) – it works about 50% of the time. A white card is easily forged – you could reproduce one with a photocopy machine – and the red plastic holders are on sale everywhere. For this reason, you might be approached by touts wanting to sell you a fake one. The fact is that outside major cities like Beijing and Shanghai, railway clerks really have no idea what a white card is supposed to look like – fake ones sometimes work when real ones don't! One French student had a knock-down drag-out battle in Zhengzhou station with a smug booking clerk who threw her absolutely genuine

white card into the rubbish bin and told her it was a fake.

The so-called 'yellow card' (really orange) is not so much a card as a small booklet. The cover is orange and the pages are white. Except for the cover, the book can be easily forged with a photocopier, but there do not seem to be too many fakes around – yet. The value of the yellow card is that it allows foreigners to pay in RMB rather than in Foreign Exchange Certificates (FEC). These seem to work better than white cards.

The 'green card' is a residence permit, issued to English teachers, foreign experts and students who live in the PRC. It's such a valuable document that you'd better not lose it if you have one, or the PSB will be all over you. Foreigners living in China say that if you lose your green card, you might want to leave the country rather than face the music. A green card will permit you to pay Chinese prices in hotels, on flights, trains and elsewhere. In addition, many hotels offer major discounts to green card holders (even five-star hotels!). The green card is not really a card but resembles a small passport – it would be very difficult to forge without modern printing equipment and special paper. Green cards are issued for one year and must be renewed annually.

Travel Permit (tōngxíngzhèng)

In the early 1980s only 130 places in China were officially open to foreign tourists. Then the number swept to 244, and nowadays most of the country is open except for certain remote border areas, especially those inhabited by ethnic minorities. For a long time such permits were required for Tibet, but even there the permit requirement now seems to be suspended (though the rules can change at any time!).

In general, most of the places described in this book are open to foreigners, but one incident (like an ethnic riot in Xinjiang) can cause new permit regulations to be issued overnight. To find out about latest restrictions, it's best to check with the PSB in provincial capitals.

To travel to closed places you officially require an Alien Travel Permit (usually just called Travel Permit). The PSB has wide discretion in issuing you with a permit to a closed place. However, the choice of open places is now so extensive that most travellers won't need to apply. Foreign academics and researchers wanting to poke around remote areas usually need the right credentials or letter of introduction (*jièshào xìn*) before being given a free hand to pursue their lizards, steam trains, yellow-bellied sapsuckers or whatever in remote places.

Travel permits can be demanded from you at hotel registration desks, boat or bus ticket offices, and unusual areas during spot checks by police. If you're off the track but heading towards a destination for which you have a permit, the police will either stop you and cancel the destination, or let you continue on your way.

The permit also lists the modes of transport you're allowed to take: plane, train, ship or car – and if a particular mode is crossed out then you can't use it. If a mode is cancelled it can be reinstated at the next PSB, but that may only be for a single trip from Point A to Point B. You could try and carry on regardless – or you could lose the permit in the next open city and start again.

If you manage to get a permit for an unusual destination, the best strategy is to get to that destination as fast as you can (by plane if possible). Other PSBs do not have to honour the permit and can cancel it and send you back. Take your time getting back – you're less likely to be hassled if you're returning to civilisation. Transit points usually don't require a permit, and you can stay the night.

CUSTOMS

Chinese border crossings have gone from being severely traumatic to exceedingly easy. Although there seem to be lots of uniformed police around, the third degree at Customs seems to be reserved for pornography-smuggling Hong Kongers rather than the stray backpacker.

Note that there are clearly marked 'green channels' and 'red channels', the latter reserved for those with such everyday travel items like refrigerators and colour TV sets.

You're allowed to import 600 cigarettes or the equivalent in tobacco products, two litres of alcoholic drink and one *pint* of perfume. You're allowed to import only 3000 *feet* of movie film, and a maximum of 72 rolls of still film. Importation of fresh fruit is prohibited.

It's illegal to import any printed material, film, tapes, etc 'detrimental to China's politics, economy, culture and ethics'. But don't be too concerned about what you take to read. As you leave China, any tapes, manuscripts, books, etc 'which contain state secrets or are otherwise prohibited for export' can be seized. Cultural relics, handicrafts, gold and silver ornaments, and jewellery purchased in China have to be shown to Customs on leaving. You'll also have to show your receipts; otherwise the stuff may be confiscated. Don't get paranoid – they seldom search foreigners, and in the rare event that they do, they will be mostly concerned that you are not departing with large amounts of Chinese currency (as if anyone would want the stuff).

MONEY
Currency

The basic unit of Chinese currency is the *yuan* – designated in this book by a capital 'Y'. In spoken Chinese, the word *kuai* is often substituted for yuan. Ten *jiao* make up one yuan – in spoken Chinese, it's pronounced *mao*. Ten *fen* make up one jiao, but these days fen are becoming rare because they are worth so little – some people will not accept them.

Absurdly, there are two types of currency in use in China: RMB and FEC.

RMB The Bank of China issuesRenminbi (RMB) or 'People's Money'. Paper notes are issued in denominations of one, five, 10, 50 and 100 yuan; one, two and five jiao; and one, two and five fen. Coins are in denominations of one yuan; five jiao; and one, two and five fen. The one-fen note is small and yellow, the two-fen note is blue, and the five-fen note is small and green – all are next to worthless.

FEC How many countries can you name that have two currencies? The three letters most hated by foreigners and loved by Chinese are Foreign Exchange Certificates (FEC). FEC, or 'tourist money', is issued in China for use by foreigners and compatriots from Hong Kong, Macau and Taiwan.

FEC creates numerous hassles. FEC and RMB are supposed to be worth the same, but in fact they are not. FEC is worth more, but when you pay in FEC you will often receive change in RMB. When you ask for change in FEC, the people you're dealing with will often say that they don't have it. You cannot exchange RMB (legally) when you leave China. If you want to pay for everything in RMB (most foreigners try), you will face constant arguments.

There are no laws governing foreigners using FEC. Because it's convertible, however, everyone wants it. It's very likely that over the next couple of years the RMB will become convertible and the FEC will be abolished.

You're meant to use FEC for all government hotels (private hotels choose for themselves), rail and air transport, as well as international telephone calls or fax. The government does not require you to pay for buses, taxis, postage stamps or food in FEC. In practice, the rules get bent both ways – some hotels and railway stations accept RMB from foreigners, while taxi drivers, restaurants and even some street vendors have gotten into the habit of demanding payment in FEC. There is no legitimate reason why you must pay in FEC for goods which are made in the PRC, but expect continuous vehement arguments if you stand up for your rights. Some people seem to think it's illegal for foreigners to have RMB – it's not.

Some foreign visitors have managed to pay their whole way through China using only RMB, but this requires stamina and an official Chinese student ID card (genuine or

> **Stop Press – FEC abolished**
> Foreign Exchange Certificates were abolished in 1993, shortly after we went to press with this book. Foreigners will no longer have to struggle to pay in local currency. Exchange rates for the yuan have already shifted dramatically, and prices for travellers within China are likely to rise sharply. We look forward to hearing how travellers are managing.

otherwise). You'll probably need a mixture of both RMB and FEC.

Some shops and hotels operate an interesting 'price differential'. You may be asked if you want to pay a given price in FEC or pay about 50% more in RMB. Most hotels simply will *not* accept payment in RMB no matter how hard you plead, cry or rant. Some railway stations have separate booking offices for foreigners which insist on payment in FEC, and air tickets can only be bought in FEC, unless you have the magic green card.

On the other hand, in smaller towns and in the countryside where few foreigners go you'll probably find that the locals have never seen FEC, and you'll have to pay in RMB.

The FEC versus RMB battles can occupy much of your time and energy. In many youth hostels, travellers have a tendency to sit around all day and talk about FEC and changing money. Try not to let this happen to you.

Exchange Rates
At the time of writing, exchange rates were:

Australia	A$1	=	Y3.79
Canada	C$1	=	Y4.33
France	Ffr1	=	Y0.97
Germany	DM1	=	Y3.39
Hong Kong	HK$1	=	Y0.74
Japan	Y100	=	Y5.28
Netherlands	g1	=	Y3.02
New Zealand	NZ$1	=	Y3.17
Switzerland	Sfr1	=	Y3.84
UK	UK£1	=	Y8.52
USA	US$1	=	Y5.72

Changing Money Foreign currency and travellers' cheques can be changed at the main centres of the Bank of China, the tourist hotels, some Friendship Stores, and some of the big department stores. You'll be issued FEC and small change will be made up of RMB one, two and five-fen notes and coins. Hotels usually give the official rate, but some will charge a small commission. A bigger problem is that a few five-star hotels only change money for their own guests – you can always lie and make up a false room number, but this may not work if you're dressed like a slob. The rates charged at various ports of entry (airports, wharves, Hong Kong border, etc) are usually the official rate, so don't be afraid to change as much as you need on arrival.

Always be sure to keep enough money on you to last for at least a few days. Many banks and hotels are unreliable – they run out of FEC, or the one person in charge of FEC takes a holiday and the whole operation shuts down. In some remote areas, travellers have been stuck for several days waiting for the 'FEC person' to show up for work.

Australian, Canadian, US, UK, Hong Kong, Japanese and most West European currencies are acceptable in China. In some of the backwaters, it may be hard to change lesser-known currencies – US dollars are still the easiest to change.

Over the years, the Chinese government has gradually devalued its currency. FEC may be phased out over the next few years, in line with the government's goal of making RMB a convertible currency – this is also a condition of China's entry into the GATT (General Agreement on Tariffs and Trade).

Whenever you change foreign currency into Chinese currency (legally) you'll be given a money-exchange voucher recording the transaction. If you've got any leftover FEC when you leave the country and want to reconvert it to hard currency you *must* have those vouchers – not all of them, but at least equal to *double* the amount of FEC you want to re-exchange. In other words, only 50% of what you originally exchanged can be re-exchanged on departure – the govern-ment is saying that you must spend the rest while in China.

FEC can be taken in and out of the country as you please.

Black Market The words 'Hello, change money' can be heard almost everywhere in China. Thanks to the government's hair-brained FEC idea, the black market has boomed. In addition, there is a bustling black market in Hong Kong and US dollars.

The rate fluctuates wildly, but at the time of writing you could easily gain 70% by purchasing RMB on the black market. Unfortunately, the reports of cheating and outright theft have become so common that it cannot be recommended that you change on the street. Indeed, it would be fair to say that 90% of all street exchanges result in attempted rip-offs (especially in major cities like Canton and Beijing).

You might think you're good at changing money on the street, but we assure you that the rip-off artists are also very good at what they do. There are different techniques. If you're foolish enough to hand over your money first, you're finished – you will be short-changed and nothing short of outright violence will get your money back. But even if you demand that they hand over their cash first, you can still get cheated. In this case, they may claim that *you short-changed them* and demand their money back, and create a very ugly scene (often with the help of accomplices) if you refuse. So you give them back theirs and they give you back yours, but in the process they've removed some large denomination bills and replaced them with small ones (they are skilled magicians!). A crude but effective technique used by some is by simply grabbing the cash out of your hands and running off.

Chinese have the habit of checking all RMB banknotes of large denominations (Y50 and Y100) carefully before accepting them – you'd be wise to copy this practice. Counterfeit currency has become a problem in China, though it's probably not as serious as many Chinese imagine.

It seems to be the experience of most

travellers that female moneychangers are less likely to use threats, intimidation, violence or grab the cash out of your hands. However, female moneychangers have often been known to short-change customers. The very worst thing to do is change with a group of young men on the street – if there's just one of you versus three young men, you might as well just hang a sign around your neck saying 'Rob me'.

Many people have found it fairly easy to change money in small shops, especially in areas where travellers congregate. Indeed, in some of the budget hotels, you can often simply change with the people at the reception desk or the money-exchange counter! The rate in the hotel might not be as good as what the moneychangers offer, but it beats getting robbed. If you need RMB, you can always get it from the banks, but they'll only exchange it on a one-for-one basis (a rotten deal for you, but a great deal for them).

Another possibility is to buy RMB at black-market rates in Hong Kong. Some moneychangers in Tsimshatsui deal in RMB, though the biggest market seems to be concentrated in Sheung Wan near the Macau Ferry Pier. The 'black market' is perfectly legal in Hong Kong – the illegal part is carrying the money across the border. Recent reports indicate that it's now legal to take RMB from Hong Kong to China, though as a foreigner, it would still be wise to be discreet about it. There are big signs at the border crossings warning you about taking RMB into or out of China. We aren't going to advise you to break the law, but we know damn well that most travellers do it. If you do decide to carry RMB across the Chinese border, keep it well hidden, even though you aren't likely to be strip-searched.

There is a black market in more than just foreign currency. One hot item is puppies. In all of China except Tibet, ownership of dogs is prohibited and enforcement is especially strict in the cities. In the past, the Chinese could barely afford to feed themselves, much less dogs. However, rising incomes leads to rising demands for luxuries, and China's nouveaux riches are apparently willing to pay a premium for cutesy, furry little animals to keep around the house. Foreigners occasionally witness some tragicomic scenes of bedraggled dog vendors running down the street, arms clutching three or four yelping puppies, with the police in hot pursuit.

As for bringing things into China to sell, you'll probably find that the Chinese strike too much of a hard bargain to make it worth the trouble.

Travellers' Cheques Besides the advantage of safety, travellers' cheques are useful to carry in China because the exchange rate is actually more favourable than what you get for cash. Cheques from most of the world's leading banks and issuing agencies are now acceptable in China – stick to the major companies such as Thomas Cook, American Express and Bank of America, and you'll be OK.

Credit Cards Plastic is gaining more acceptance in China for use by foreign visitors in major tourist cities. Useful cards include Visa, MasterCard, American Express, JCB and Diners Club. It's even possible to get a cash advance against your card.

It wouldn't be worthwhile to get a credit card especially for your trip to China, but if you already have one you might find it useful. Banks in some of the outlying regions of China can take a long time to debit your account overseas.

Telegraphic Transfers Getting money sent to you while you're in China is a real drag – try to avoid it. On the average, it takes about five weeks for your money to arrive. If you have high-placed connections in the banking system it can take considerably less time, but most travellers are not so fortunate. If you must have money sent to you, try to get it sent to CITIC – the Bank of China appears to be hopeless. At CITIC it is even possible to send money out of China, but only if you have hard currency.

Bank Accounts Foreigners can indeed open bank accounts in China – both RMB and US dollar accounts (the latter only at special foreign-exchange banks). You do not need to have resident status – a tourist visa is sufficient. Virtually every foreigner working in China will tell you that CITIC is far better to do business with than the Bank of China. Automatic-teller machines have been introduced at the Bank of China, but payment is only in RMB.

Costs

How much will it cost to travel in China? That's largely up to the degree of comfort you desire. It also depends on how much travelling you do, and what parts of China you visit. Eastern China is generally more expensive than the west.

If you want to travel on a bottom-of-the-barrel shoestring budget then you have to sleep in dormitories whenever possible, get local price on all train tickets and forgo sleepers. Travelling, however, is *not* an endurance test. If you want to find out how long you can stay away and how little money you can spend doing it, go ahead, but you won't get gold stars each time you sleep on the floor of a train. Your journey can be a miserable experience if you're constantly worried about how far the money is going to stretch and if you force yourself to live in perpetual discomfort. Travelling on too low a budget only allows for a limited experience of a country – you get a one-sided view just like those people who take expensive tours and stay in posh hotels.

China just isn't going to be as cheap and as comfortable as India or South-East Asia; if you want to have a good time in the PRC then spend a bit more money. If you care about your sanity take a sleeper, or get off the train after 12 hours and find a hotel.

In many parts of China it is still possible to travel on US$20 a day, but it requires effort. Generally, the east coast of China is more expensive than the west coast. Accommodation is the biggest expense. The best solution is to find a dorm bed (Y25 or so) but these are not always available. Rooms are invariably expensive – your only hope to cut the tariff is to find another traveller to share a double room with you. Food is dirt cheap

if you avoid classy restaurants. 'Eating Chinese' with a few other people not only gives you a greater variety of food to choose from, it also brings the price down.

Price Gouging Foreigners will inevitably be charged more for most things in China. This situation certainly exists in many other developing countries, but the big difference is that in China, it's official policy. Every business from the airlines and railways to museums and parks are told *by the government* to charge foreigners more. With such official support, many Chinese view ripping off foreigners as their patriotic duty. Sometimes the charge is just a little bit more than a local would pay, but at other times it's 20 times more than the Chinese price. Many foreigners feel that China is the most dishonest country they've ever been to. But just when you reach the end of your tether and you want to hop onto the first flight out of the country, the opposite happens – some total stranger in a restaurant pays for your meal; a passenger you met on the train offers you a free place for the night and lets you borrow the family bicycle; a young student works as your personal tour guide for the entire day and wants nothing in return. Such moments are especially touching in China, because most Chinese are still poor and can hardly afford to be so generous.

Such individual acts of kindness help to restore your faith in humanity – it's a pity that not everyone is like that. Try not to go around China feeling constantly ripped off, but on the other hand, keep your guard up when necessary. To avoid problems, always ask the price first before you get the goods or services rendered. If you can't speak Chinese, write it down.

Tipping

As some compensation for being constantly ripped off, China is at least one of those wonderful countries where tipping is not done and almost no one asks for it. When tips are offered in China, they are offered *before* you get the service, not after – that will ensure (hopefully) that you get better service. All things considered, tipping isn't a good idea because it will make it rough for foreigners who follow you.

Bargaining

Since foreigners are so frequently over-charged in China, bargaining becomes essential. You can bargain in shops, hotels, with taxi drivers, with most people – but not everywhere. In large stores where prices are clearly marked, there is usually no latitude for bargaining. In small shops and street stalls, bargaining is expected, but there is one important rule to follow – be polite. There is nothing wrong with asking for a discount, if you do so with a smile. Some foreigners seem to think that bargaining should be a screaming and threatening contest. This is not only unpleasant for all concerned, it seldom results in you getting a lower price – indeed, in 'face-conscious' China, intimidation is likely to make the vendor more recalcitrant and you'll be overcharged.

You should keep in mind that entrepreneurs are in business to make money – they aren't going to sell anything to you at a loss. Your goal should be to pay the Chinese price, as opposed to the foreigners' price – if you can do that, you've done well.

Consumer Taxes

Although big hotels and fancy restaurants may add a tax or 'service charge' of 10% or more, all other consumer taxes are included in the price tag.

WHEN TO GO

China's peak season for tourism is summer – if you can tolerate the cold of winter, you can avoid the crowds. However, you need to pay careful attention to major public holidays – the Chinese New Year in particular is a horrible time to travel.

WHAT TO BRING

As little as possible. It's much better to buy things as you need them than to throw things away because you've got too much to carry. Lightweight and compact are two words that

should be etched in your mind when you're deciding what to bring. Drill holes in the handle of your toothbrush if you have to – anything to keep the weight down!

That advice having been given, there are some things you will want to bring from home.

Carrying Bags

The first thing to consider is what kind of bag you will use to carry all your goods.

Backpacks are the easiest type of bag to carry and a frameless or internal-frame pack is the easiest to manage on buses and trains. The 'expandable' type are most convenient – a clever arrangement of straps cause these packs to shrink or expand according to how much is inside. Packs that close with a zipper can be secured with a padlock. Any pack can be slit open with a razor blade, but a lock will usually prevent pilfering by hotel staff and baggage handlers at airports.

Chinese-made luggage looks good but is generally of poor quality. Zippers are the biggest problem – we've bought bags where the zippers didn't last a day! The stitching also has a tendency to disintegrate. The only good things we can say about Chinese back-packs is that they're cheap and won't attract much attention like Western models.

Whatever you bring, make it small. A day-pack is useful; you can dump your main luggage in a hotel or the left-luggage room at the railway station and head off. It's good for hiking and for carrying extra food on long train rides. A beltpack is OK for maps, extra film and other miscellanea, but don't use it for valuables such as your travellers' cheques and passport – it's an easy target for pickpockets.

If you don't want to use a backpack, a shoulder bag is much easier to carry than a suitcase. Some cleverly designed shoulder bags can also double as backpacks by rearranging a few straps. Forget suitcases.

Clothes

In theory, you only need two sets of clothes – one to wear and one to wash. Dark coloured clothing is preferred because it doesn't show the dirt – white clothes will force you to do laundry daily. You will, no doubt, be buying clothes along the way – you can find some real bargains in China. However, don't believe sizes – 'large' in Asia is often equivalent to 'medium' in the West.

If you're travelling in the north of China at the height of winter, prepare yourself for incredible cold. You can buy excellent down or quilt jackets in some of the big cities – the khaki-green PLA models make a functional souvenir. Also very cheap and functional are the fur-lined hats with Snoopy ear covers, but they aren't very fashionable. You might want to bring a stocking (ski) cap – they can be bought in China but are somewhat hard to find and often too small or poorly made. By contrast, good sweaters are a bargain in China. You might want to bring fur-lined boots and mittens – mediocre ones can be bought in China but large (Western) sizes are difficult to find. Western long johns are more comfortable and warmer than the Chinese variety.

It's best to bring a Western-made rainsuit with both rainpants and rainjacket. Umbrellas and plastic raincoats can be bought in China, but the quality leaves much to be desired. Chinese nylon rain ponchos are designed for riding bicycles – long in the front but very short in the back, so your bottom gets soaked if there's a tailwind. By contrast, Chinese rainboots are excellent, but again, big-footed Westerners might have difficulty finding the right size.

You shouldn't need a sleeping bag since sheets and blankets are provided even in the hard-sleeper carriages of the trains. If you plan to go camping, a sleeping bag will be a necessity, but opportunities for camping are very limited in China.

In summer, the lightest of clothes will do for daytime wear: T-shirts, sandals and shorts. However, if you go up into the hills it can get very cold, and it can get cold on the trains at night.

The usual standards of Asian decorum apply. While shorts are less acceptable for women, many Chinese women wear them

and you shouldn't get any unpleasant reactions. Skirts and dresses are frequently worn in big cities – in Beijing, miniskirts are in vogue and many young women wear skin-hugging tights. However, bikinis have still not made their debut in China. Make-up and jewellery are becoming increasingly popular in the cities.

The Chinese place little importance on what foreigners wear, as long as they remain within an acceptable level of modesty; casual clothes are always acceptable.

Necessities

Absolutely essential is a good pair of sunglasses, particularly in the Xinjiang desert or the high altitudes of Tibet. Ditto for sunscreen (UV) lotion. A water bottle can be a lifesaver in the western deserts – get one that doesn't leak.

Some pharmaceutical items are hard to find, examples being shaving cream, decent razor blades, mosquito repellent, deodorant, dental floss, tampons and contact lens cleaning solution. Chinese nail clippers are poor quality.

An alarm clock is essential for getting up on time to catch your flight, bus or train – make sure yours is lightweight and bring extra batteries. Size AA rechargeable batteries can be bought in China but the rechargers are bulky – bring a portable one and plug adaptors if you can't live without your Walkman. A gluestick is convenient for sealing envelopes and pasting on stamps.

The following is a checklist of things you might consider packing. You can delete whatever you like from this list.

Passport, visa, documents (vaccination certificate, diplomas, marriage licence photocopy, student ID card), money, money belt or vest, air ticket, address book, reading matter, pen, notepad, gluestick, namecards, visa photos (about 20), Swiss army knife, camera & accessories, extra camera battery, colour slide film, video camera & blank tapes, radio, Walkman & rechargeable batteries, small battery recharger (220 V), padlock, cable lock (to secure luggage on trains), sunglasses, contact lens solution, alarm clock, leakproof water bottle, torch (flashlight) with batteries & bulbs, comb, compass, daypack, long pants, short pants, long shirt, T-shirt, nylon jacket, sweater (only in winter), raincover for backpack, umbrella or rain poncho, razor, razor blades, shaving cream, sewing kit, spoon, sunhat, sunscreen (UV lotion), toilet paper, tampons, toothbrush, toothpaste, dental floss, deodorant, shampoo, laundry detergent, underwear, socks, thongs, nail clipper, tweezers, mosquito repellent, vitamins, laxative, Lomotil, condoms, contraceptives, special medications you use and medical kit (see Health section).

Gifts

Many Chinese people study English and appreciate old English books and magazines. Stamps make good gifts; the Chinese are avid collectors, congregating outside the philatelic sections of the post offices and dealing on the footpath. Odd-looking foreign coins and currency are appreciated. Foreign postcards are sought after, and pictures of you and your family would make very popular gifts.

TOURIST OFFICES

Among the many striking Chinese sayings, a particularly applicable one is 'With one monkey in the way, not even 10,000 men can pass'. The three major monkeys in China today are CITS, the PSB and the mass of little bits of paper collectively referred to as 'red tape'.

Local Tourist Offices

CITS The China International Travel Service (CITS) deals with China's foreign tourist hordes, and mainly concerns itself with organising and making travel arrangements for group tours. CITS existed as far back as 1954 when there were few customers; now they're inundated with a couple of hundred thousand big-noses a year. Unfortunately, after 40 years of being in business, CITS has still not gotten its act together.

CITS can buy train and plane tickets for you (and some boat tickets), reserve hotel rooms, organise city tours, and even get you tickets for the cinema, opera, acrobatics and other entertainment, as well as organise trips to communes and farms, and provide vehicles (taxis, minibuses) for sightseeing or transport.

All train tickets bought through CITS will be tourist-priced (an extra 100% on top of the Chinese price) and there will usually be a small service charge added on to the price of train, boat or plane tickets. CITS has nothing to do with issuing travel permits or visa extensions – for that you must go directly to the PSB. However, if you're on a CITS tour, they are supposed to arrange the permits for you. They can get you permits to places that are normally closed to foreigners but you will have to pay heavily for the privilege.

Generally speaking, solo travellers will rarely have to deal with them. One thing about CITS is fairly consistent – their prices tend to be expensive. Furthermore, CITS has been known to cheat travellers outright – selling 10-day tours but just giving eight, charging for services not rendered, booking tourists onto a bus that breaks down but no refund given, and so on.

The service varies. Some CITS people are friendly and full of useful information about the places they're stationed in – a few may even invite you out to dinner! There are others who are downright rude and only interested in squeezing money out of foreigners – Beijing CITS stands out as a glaring example of the latter. Golmud CITS (in Qinghai Province) is even worse.

They may lie to you – claiming that a certain area is closed to foreigners (except via an expensive CITS tour) when in fact it's open. You may find CITS offices staffed by people who speak sparse or zero English and who got their jobs through the back door. But everything depends on who you're dealing with – some CITS offices deserve eternal praise while others deserve all the abuse you can heap on them.

CITS offices and desks are usually in the major tourist hotels in each town or city open to foreigners; sometimes they are elsewhere but you can get the hotel reception desk to phone them.

Getting information out of CITS is a matter of potluck. In years past, a CITS office was at least an office – you could walk in, sit down at a desk and talk to someone in a casual and friendly manner. That's still possible in the backwaters, but these days the trend is to make all CITS offices into a row of ticket counters – you fill out a form, stand in line, pay your money and leave. Especially in large cities like Beijing and Canton, a 'modern' CITS office looks just like an airport check-in counter.

CTS The China Travel Service (CTS) was originally set up to handle tourists from Hong Kong, Macau and Taiwan, and foreign nationals of Chinese descent (Overseas Chinese). The reason why CITS and CTS were set up as separate organisations supposedly had to do with language. CTS staff were not required to learn English – instead, Mandarin Chinese and Cantonese were the main languages. However, this couldn't explain why Overseas Chinese (many of whom cannot speak Chinese at all) were required to go with CTS tours rather than CITS. Many foreigners couldn't help but get the nagging feeling that race was the real reason – keep the foreign devils away from the Chinese.

These days it makes little difference – CTS has now become a keen competitor with CITS. CITS is trying to cash in on the lucrative Taiwan and Hong Kong markets, while CTS is targeting the Western market which was previously the exclusive domain of CITS. And this competition is for the better, because both CITS and CTS have had a long record for dismal service. It still could stand plenty of improvement, but things have got better. Nevertheless, we periodically get complaints – as one disillusioned traveller wrote:

Although we are seasoned independent travellers, we decided we were better off on a tour in China and contacted CTS via a Hong Kong travel agent. We were *extremely disappointed* with our trip for a number of reasons. The principle one was that the restaurants were extremely dirty and unhygienic. We were paying more than US$350 a day for two and were taken to eat in restaurants that cost Y20 (for foreigners!). The hotel restaurants (where group price was Y38 at the White Swan as an example) were 'too expensive'.

We signed up for a group tour, and when we turned up at the Hong Kong meeting point, we found there were only the two of us. At that point, it was impossible to cancel the trip without forfeiting the entire cost. Being only the two of us increased the costs considerably because we had to support the entire cost of the guide, driver and car, which meant that the value to the two of us was drastically reduced...had we known there would have been only the two of us, we would have gone on our own, stayed at good hotels, skipped some of the uninteresting spots on the itinerary, eaten at *clean* restaurants and probably saved 50% of the overall cost!

Lee S Hubert

Many foreigners use the CTS offices in Hong Kong and Macau to obtain visas and book trains, planes, hovercraft and other transport to China. CTS can sometimes get you a better deal on hotels booked through their office than you could obtain on your own (of course, this doesn't apply to backpackers' dormitories). CTS has 19 branch offices in Hong Kong, and the Kowloon, Mongkok and Wanchai offices are open on Sunday and public holidays. These offices can be crowded – avoid this by arriving at 9 am when the doors open.

CYTS The name China Youth Travel Service (CYTS) implies that this is some sort of student organisation, but these days CYTS performs essentially the same services as CITS and CTS. Being a smaller organisation, CYTS seems to try harder to compete against the big league. This could result in better service, but not necessarily lower prices. CYTS is mostly interested in tour groups, but individual travellers could find it useful for booking air tickets or sleepers on the trains.

Overseas Reps

CITS The main office of CITS in Hong Kong (Tsimshatsui East) can book air tickets to China and has a good collection of English-language pamphlets. The main office and Central branch office are open Monday to Friday from 9 am to 5 pm and Saturday from 9 am to 1 pm; the Mongkok branch office keeps longer hours (Saturday from 9 am to 6.30 pm and half a day on Sunday).

Outside China and Hong Kong, CITS is usually known as the China National Tourist Office. Overseas CITS representatives include:

Australia
China National Tourist Office, 11th floor, 55 Clarence St, Sydney NSW 2000 (☎ (02) 299 4057; fax 290 1958)

France
China National Tourist Office, 51 Rue Saint-Anne, 75002 Paris (☎ (1) 42.96.95.48; fax 42.61.54.68)

Germany
China National Tourist Office, Eschenheimer Anlage 28, D-6000 Frankfurt (☎ (069) 55 52 92; fax 597 34 12)

Hong Kong
Main Office, 6th floor, Tower Two, South Seas Centre, 75 Mody Rd, Tsimshatsui East, Kowloon (☎ 7325888; fax 7217154)
Central Branch, Room 1018, Swire House, 11 Chater Rd, Central (☎ 8104282; fax 8681657)
Mongkok Branch, Room 1102-1104, Bank Centre, 636 Nathan Rd, Mongkok, Kowloon (☎ 3881619; fax 3856157)
Causeway Bay Branch, Room 1104, Causeway Bay Plaza, 489 Hennessy Rd, Causeway Bay (☎ 8363485; fax 5910849)

Japan
China National Tourist Office, 6F Hachidal Hamamatsu-cho Building, 1-27-13 Hamamatsu-cho Minato-ku, Tokyo (☎ (03) 34331461; fax 34338653)

UK
China National Tourist Office, 4 Glentworth St, London NW1 (☎ (071) 935 9427; fax 487 5842)

USA
China National Tourist Office, Los Angeles Branch, 333 West Broadway, Suite 201, Glendale, CA 91204 (☎ (818) 545 7505; fax 545 7506)
New York Branch, Lincoln Building, 60E, 42nd St, Suite 3126, New York, NY 10165 (☎ (212) 867 0271; fax 599 2892)

CTS Overseas representatives include the following:

Australia
Ground floor, 757-759 George St, Sydney, NSW 2000 (☎ (02) 2112633; fax 2813595)

Canada
556 West Broadway, Vancouver, BC V5Z 1E9 (☎ (604) 8728787; fax 8732823)

France
10 Rue de Rome, 75008, Paris (☎ (1) 45.22.92.72; fax 45.22.92.79)

Germany
Düsseldorfer Strasse 14 6000, Frankfurt 1 (☎ (069) 25 05 15; fax 23 23 24)

Hong Kong
Central Branch, 2nd floor, China Travel Building, 77 Queen's Road, Central (☎ 5217163; fax 5255525)
Kowloon Branch, 1st floor, Alpha House, 27-33 Nathan Rd, Tsimshatsui (☎ 7214481; fax 7216251)
Mongkok Branch, 62-72 Sai Yee St, Mongkok (☎ 7895970; fax 3905001)
Wanchai Branch, Ground floor, Southern Centre, 138 Hennessy Rd, Wanchai (☎ 8323888)
China Hong Kong City Branch, 10-12 China Hong Kong City, 33 Canton Rd, Tsimshatsui (☎ 7361863)

Indonesia
PT Cempaka Travelindo, Jalan Hayam Wuruk 97, Jakarta-Barat (☎ (21) 6294256; fax 6294836)

Japan
Nihombashi-Settsu Building, 2-2-4, Nihombashi, Chuo-Ku, Tokyo (☎ (03) 3273-5512; fax 3273-2667)

Macau
Edificio Xinhua, Rua de Nagasaki (☎ 700888, fax 706611)

Malaysia
Yuyi Travel Sdn Bhd, 1st floor, Sun Complex, Jalan Bukit Bintang 55100, Kuala Lumpur (☎ (03) 2427077; fax 2412478)

Philippines
489 San Fernando St, Binondo, Manila (☎ (2) 47-41-87; fax 40-78-34)

Singapore
Ground floor, SIA Building, 77 Robinson Rd, 0106 (☎ 2240550; fax 2245009)

Thailand
559 Yaowaraj Rd, Bangkok 10500 (☎ (2) 2260041; fax 2264712)

UK
24 Cambridge Circus, London WC2H 8HD (☎ (071) 836 9911; fax 836 3121)

USA
2nd floor, 212 Sutter St, San Francisco, CA 94108 (☎ (800) 332 2831, (415) 398 6627; fax 398 6669)
Los Angeles Branch, Suite 138, 223 East Garvey Ave, Monterey Park, CA 91754 (☎ (818) 288 8222; fax 288 3464)

USEFUL ORGANISATIONS
PSB
The Public Security Bureau (PSB) (*gōng'ān jú*) is the name given to China's police, both

uniformed and plain-clothes. Its responsibilities include suppression of political dissidence, crime detection, preventing foreigners and Chinese from having sex with each other (no joke), mediating family quarrels and directing traffic. A related force is the Chinese People's Armed Police Force (CPAPF), which was formed several years ago to absorb cuts in the People's Liberation Army (PLA). The Foreign Affairs Branch *(wài shì kē)* of the PSB deals with foreigners. This branch (also known as the 'entry-exit' branch) is responsible for issuing visa extensions and Alien Travel Permits.

What sets the Chinese police aside from their counterparts in, say, Mexico and South America, is their amiability towards foreigners (what they're like with their own people may be a different story). They'll sometimes sit you down, give you a cup of tea and practise their English – and the number of competent English speakers is surprisingly high.

The PSB is responsible for introducing and enforcing regulations concerning foreigners. So, for example, they bear responsibility for exclusion of foreigners from certain hotels. If this means you get stuck for a place to stay, they can offer advice. Don't pester them with trivia or try to 'use' them to bully a point with a local street vendor. Do turn to them for mediation in serious disputes with hotels, restaurants, taxi drivers, etc. This often works since the PSB wields God-like power – especially in remote areas.

There are a few ways you can inadvertently have an unpleasant run-in with the PSB. The most common way is to overstay your visa. Another risky proposition is to ride your bicycle between cities – in some places, a foreigner riding a bicycle still seems to be a crime. Another possibility is being in a closed area without a permit – fortunately, these days there aren't too many places left in China which require travel permits. Foreign males who are suspected of being 'too friendly' with Chinese women could have trouble with the PSB.

If you do have a run-in with the PSB, you may have to write a confession of your guilt and pay a fine. In more serious cases, you can be expelled from China (at your own expense). But in general, if you aren't doing anything particularly nasty like smuggling suitcases of dope through Customs, the PSB will probably not throw you in prison.

One traveller covered up an expulsion order issued to him by Guiyang PSB. The Wuhan PSB caught up with him, kept him for six days, fined him US$100 and slung him out via Canton. The expulsion was not so much for visiting closed places as for overstaying his visa. (He also used an unusual device to get into Chinese hotels on the way – telling them he was from Xinjiang, where a different language is spoken and a Caucasian face is the norm. Chinese, however, carry all sorts of odd ID, like swimming licences, work-unit cards, bicycle licences and so on.

BUSINESS HOURS & HOLIDAYS

Banks, offices, government departments and the PSB are open Monday to Saturday. As a rough guide only, they open around 8 to 9 am, close for two hours in the middle of the day (often one hour in winter or three during a heat wave in summer), then reopen until 5 or 6 pm. Sunday is a public holiday, but some businesses are open Sunday morning and make up for this by closing on Wednesday afternoon. CITS offices, Friendship Stores and the foreign-exchange counters in the tourist hotels and some of the local branches of the Bank of China have similar opening hours, and are generally open on Sundays as well, at least in the morning.

Many parks, zoos and monuments have similar opening hours, and are also open on Sunday and often at night. Shows at cinemas and theatres end around 9.30 to 10 pm.

Government restaurants are open for early morning breakfast (sometimes as early as 5.30) until about 7.30 am, then open for lunch and again for dinner from around 5 to 8 or 9 pm. The Chinese eat early and go home early – by 9 pm you'll probably find the chairs stacked and the cooks gone home. Privately run restaurants are usually open all

Top: Cobbler on footpath, Canton (RI'A)
Bottom: Rice paddies at Shaoshan (AS)

Left: Blind musician, Kaifeng, Henan (CL)
Right: Yungang caves, Shanxi (AS)
Bottom: Hawkers at Terracotta Army, Xi'an, Shaanxi (AS)

day, and often late into the night, especially around railway stations.

Long-distance bus stations and railway stations open their ticket offices around 5 or 5.30 am before the first trains and buses pull out. Apart from a one or two-hour break in the middle of the day, they often stay open until late at night – say 11 or 11.30 pm.

The PRC has nine national holidays during the year:

New Year's Day
   1 January
Spring Festival
   Usually in February. This is otherwise known as Chinese New Year and starts on the first day of the old lunar calendar. Although officially lasting only three days, many people take a week off from work. Be warned: this is China's only three-day holiday and, unless you have booked a month or two in advance, this is definitely not the time to cross borders (especially the Hong Kong one) or to look for transport or accommodation. Although the demand for accommodation sky-rockets, many hotels close down at this time. Book your room in advance and sit tight until the chaos is over!
International Working Women's Day
   8 March
International Labour Day
   1 May
Youth Day
   4 May – commemorates the student demonstrations in Beijing on 4 May 1919, when the Versailles Conference decided to give Germany's 'rights' in the city of Tianjin to Japan
Children's Day
   1 June
Anniversary of the founding of the Communist Party of China
   1 July
Anniversary of the founding of the Chinese PLA
   1 August
National Day
   1 October – celebrates the founding of the PRC on 1 October 1949

CULTURAL EVENTS

Much of Chinese culture took a beating during the Cultural Revolution and still has not fully revived. Nevertheless, hanging around the appropriate temples at certain times will reward you with special ceremonies and colourful events.

Special prayers are held at Buddhist and Taoist temples on days when the moon is either full or just the thinnest sliver. According to the Chinese lunar calendar, these days fall on the 14th and 15th days of the lunar month and on the last (29th or 30th) day of the month just ending and the 1st day of the new month.

Other notable times when temples are liveliest include the following:

Lantern Festival (yuánxiāo jié)
   It's not a public holiday, but it is very colourful. It falls on the 15th day of the 1st moon (approx. mid-February to mid-March). People take the time to make (or buy) paper lanterns and walk around the streets in the evening holding them.
Guanyin's Birthday (guānshìyīn shēngrì)
   The birthday of Guanyin, the goddess of mercy, is on the 19th day of the 2nd moon (approx. late March to late April) and is a good time to visit Taoist temples.
Mazu's Birthday (māzǔ shēngrì)
   Mazu, goddess of the sea, is the friend of all fishing crews. She's called Mazu in Fujian Province and Taiwan. The name gets changed to Tianhou in Guangdong Province, and in Hong Kong the spelling is 'Tin Hau'. Her birthday is widely celebrated at Taoist temples in coastal regions as far south as Vietnam. Mazu's birthday is on the 23rd day of the 3rd moon (May or June).
Tomb Sweep Day (qīng míng jié)
   A day for worshipping ancestors; people visit the graves of their departed relatives and clean the site. They often place flowers on the tomb and burn ghost money for the departed. Falls on 5 April in the Gregorian calendar in most years, 4 April in leap years.
Water-Splashing Festival (pō shuǐ jié)
   Down in Yunnan Province, this event is held around mid-April (usually 13-15 April). The purpose is to wash away the dirt, sorrow and demons of the old year and bring in the happiness of the new. The event gets staged more often now for tourists.
Ghost Month (guǐ yuè)
   The Ghost Month is the 7th lunar month, or really just the first 15 days (approx. late August to late September). The devout believe that during this time the ghosts from hell walk the earth and it is a dangerous time to travel, go swimming, get married or move to a new house. If someone dies during this month, the body will be preserved and the funeral and burial will be performed the following month. The Chinese government officially denounces Ghost Month as a lot of superstitious nonsense.

Mid-Autumn Festival (zhōngqiū jié)
 Also known as the Moon Festival, this takes place on the 15th day of the 8th moon (approx. October). Gazing at the moon and lighting fireworks are popular activities at this time. This is the time to eat tasty moon cakes.

Birthday of Confucius (kŏngzĭ shēngrì)
 The birthday of the great sage occurs on 28 September of the Gregorian calendar. This is an interesting time to visit Qufu in Shandong Province, the birthplace of Confucius. On the other hand, all hotels in town are likely to be booked out at this time. A ceremony is held at the Confucius Temple starting from around 4 am.

POST & TELECOMMUNICATIONS
Postal Rates

Letters Rates for international surface mail are shown in the table. For air mail add Y0.50 to the figures.

Postcards International postcards cost Y1.10 by surface mail and Y1.60 by air mail to anywhere in the world.

Aerogrammes These are Y1.90 to anywhere in the world.

Printed Matter Rates for international surface mail are shown in the table. Each additional kg above 2000 grams costs Y11. For air mail add Y0.40 to the figures.

Small Packets Rates for international surface mail are shown in the table. For air mail add Y0.40 to the figures.

Parcels Rates vary depending on the country of destination. The charge for a one-kg parcel sent by surface mail from China to the UK is Y52, to the USA Y30.60, and to Germany Y35.60. The charge for a one-kg parcel sent by air mail to the UK is Y82, to the USA Y77, and to Germany Y70.60.

Post offices are very picky about how you pack things; don't finalise your packing until the thing has got its last Customs clearance. Most countries impose a maximum weight limit (10 kg is typical) on packages received – this rate varies from country to country but the Chinese post office should be able to tell you what the limit is. If you have a receipt for the goods, then put it in the box when you're mailing it, since it may be opened again by Customs further down the line.

EMS International express mail (EMS) service charges vary according to country, and whether you are sending documents or parcels. For documents, EMS to Hong Kong and Macau costs Y50; to Japan, Korea and South-East Asia, Y70; to South Asia, Y80; Europe, Canada and the USA, Y95; to the Middle East and Africa, Y105; and to South America, Y115. It's worth noting that EMS is not available to every country.

Registration Fees The registration fee for letters, printed matter and packets is Y1. Acknowledgement of receipt is Y0.80 per article.

Letters

Weight	Rate
0-20 grams	Y1.50
20-50 grams	Y2.90
50-100 grams	Y4.50
100-250 grams	Y8.80
250-500 grams	Y17.90
500-1000 grams	Y34.90
1000-2000 grams	Y49.40

Printed Matter

Weight	Rate
0-20 grams	Y1
20-50 grams	Y1.50
50-100 grams	Y2.80
100-250 grams	Y5.30
250-500 grams	Y9.90
500-1000 grams	Y15.80
1000-2000 grams	Y26.10

Small Packets

Weight	Rate
0-100 grams	Y3.50
100-250 grams	Y7
250-500 grams	Y12.60
500-1000 grams	Y20.90
1000-2000 grams	Y39

staff before mailing). Even at cheap hotels you can usually post letters from the front desk – reliability varies but in general it's OK. In some places, you may only be able to post printed matter from these branch offices. Other parcels may require a Customs form attached at the town's main post office, where their contents will be checked.

Large envelopes are a bit hard to come by; try the department stores. If you expect to be sending quite a few packets, stock up when you come across such envelopes. A roll of strong, sticky tape is a useful item to bring along and serves many purposes. String, glue and sometimes cloth bags are supplied at the post offices, but don't count on it. The Friendship Stores will sometimes package and mail purchases for you, but only goods actually bought at the store.

Private Carriers In a joint venture with China's Sinotrans, fast air freight is offered by two foreign carriers: DHL and UPS. Express document and parcel service is offered by two other foreign carriers: Federal Express and TNT Skypak. Such service is only offered in major cities and doesn't come cheap – costs start at around US$50.

Receiving Mail
There are poste-restante services in just about every city and town, and they seem to work. Unfortunately, since Chinese does not use an alphabet, most post offices don't use alphabetical order. In some cities, the main post office will assign numbers to letters as they are received and post the numbers and names on a notice board. You have to find your name and write down the number(s) of your letters, then tell the clerk at the counter. We've seen some strange names on the notice boards – 'Par Avion, General Delivery', and 'Hold Until Arrival'.

Some major tourist hotels will hold mail for their guests, but this doesn't always work. Many places will hold mail for several months if you write such an instruction on the outside of the letter.

It's worth noting that some foreigners living in China have had their mail opened

Domestic Mail Within the same city, mail delivery for a letter (20 grams and below) costs Y0.10, postcards also Y0.10. Out of town, letters are Y0.20, postcards Y0.15. The fee for registration is Y0.30.

Sending Mail
The international postal service seems efficient, and air-mail letters and postcards will probably take around five to 10 days to reach their destinations. If possible, write the country of destination in Chinese, as this should speed up the delivery. Domestic post is amazingly fast – perhaps one or two days from Canton to Beijing. Within a city it may be delivered the same day that it's sent.

As well as the local post offices there are branch post offices in just about all the major tourist hotels where you can send letters, packets and parcels (the contents of packets and parcels are checked by the post office or parcels pilfered before receipt – and some have had their outgoing mail opened and read. This seems to affect tourists less, although letters with enclosures will almost certainly be opened. Your mail is less likely to be opened if it's sent to cities that handle high volumes of mail, like Canton.

Officially, the PRC forbids certain items from being mailed to it – the regulations specifically prohibit 'reactionary books, magazines and propaganda materials, obscene or immoral articles'. You also cannot mail Chinese currency abroad, or receive it by post. Like elsewhere, mail-order hashish and other recreational chemicals will not amuse the authorities.

Telephone

China's creaky phone system is being overhauled, at least in major cities. Whereas just a few years ago calling from Beijing to Shanghai could be an all-day project, now you can just pick up a phone and dial direct. Making international calls has also become much easier.

Many hotel rooms are equipped with phones from which local calls are free. Local calls can be made from public pay phones (there are some around but not many). China's budding entrepreneurs try to fill the gap – people with private phones run a long cord out the window and stand on street corners, allowing you to use their phone to place local calls for around Y0.50 each – long-distance domestic and international calls are not always possible on these phones, but ask anyway. In the lobbies of many hotels, the reception desks have a similar system – free calls for guests, Y0.50 for non-guests, and long-distance calls are charged by the minute.

You can place both domestic and international long-distance phone calls from main telecommunications offices. The advantage of doing so is that you can pay in RMB rather than FEC, a substantial saving if you're using black-market cash. On the other hand, these offices are a nuisance – you have to fill out forms in Chinese, pay for the call in advance, then wait for perhaps 30 minutes

for someone to gesture to you that you've been connected and can finally pick up the phone and start talking.

Domestic long-distance rates in China vary according to distance, but are cheap. International calls are expensive. Rates for station-to-station calls to most countries in the world are Y18 per minute. Hong Kong is slightly cheaper at Y12 per minute. There is a minimum charge of three minutes. Reverse-charge calls are often cheaper than calls paid for in China. Time the call yourself – the operator will not break in to tell you that your minimum period of three minutes is approaching. After you hang up, the operator will ring back to tell you how much it cost. There is no call cancellation fee.

If you are expecting a call – either international or domestic – try to advise the caller beforehand of your hotel room number. The operators frequently have difficulty understanding Western names, and the hotel receptionist may not be able to locate you. If this can't be done, then try to inform the operator that you are expecting the call and write down your name and room number – this will increase your chances of success.

The phone system in China has improved considerably, but the frustrations of the old days were captured by cartoonist Li Binsheng who once drew a satirical cartoon which depicted an old man standing with a telephone receiver in his hand while his son and grandson waited beside him. The caption for the old man said: ' If I fail to get through, my son will follow; if he fails too, he has his son to follow'.

Direct Dialling Domestic direct dialling (DDD) and international direct dialling (IDD) calls are cheapest if you can find a phone which accepts magnetic cards. These phones are usually available in the lobbies of major hotels, at least in big cities, and the hotel's front desk should also sell the phone cards. These cards come in two denominations, Y20 and Y100 – for an international call, you'll need the latter.

If card phones aren't available, you can usually dial direct from the phones in the

Codes for provincial capitals and major cities

Anhui
    Hefei (0551)
Beijing (01)
Fujian
    Fuzhou (0591)
    Quanzhou (0595)
    Xiamen (0592)
Gansu
    Lanzhou (0931)
Guangdong
    Canton (020)
    Foshan (0757)
    Shantou (0754)
    Shenzhen (0755)
    Zhanjiang (0759)
    Zhuhai (0756)
Guangxi
    Beihai (0779)
    Guilin (0773)
    Nanning (0771)
Guizhou
    Guiyang (0851)
    Zunyi (0852)
Hainan
    Haikou (0750)
    Sanya (0899)
Hebei
    Chengde (0314)
    Shijiazhuang (0311)
    Qinhuangdao (0335)
Heilongjiang
    Harbin (0451)
    Mudanjiang (0453)

Henan
    Kaifeng (0378)
    Luoyang (0379)
    Zhengzhou (0371)
Hubei
    Wuhan (027)
    Yichang (0717)
Hunan
    Changsha (0731)
    Yueyang (0730)
Inner Mongolia
    Baotou (0472)
    Hohhot (0471)
    Xilinhot (0479)
Jiangsu
    Lianyungang (0518)
    Nanjing (025)
    Suzhou (0512)
    Xuzhou (0516)
Jiangxi
    Jiujiang (0792)
    Lushan (07010)
    Nanchang (0791)
Jilin
    Changchun (0431)
    Jilin (0432)
Liaoning
    Dalian (0411)
    Dandong (0415)
    Shenyang (024)
Ningxia
    Guyuan (0954)
    Yinchuan (0951)

Qinghai
    Golmud (0979)
    Xining (0971)
Shaanxi
    Xi'an (029)
    Yan'an (0911)
Shandong
    Ji'nan (0531)
    Qingdao (0532)
    Qufu (05473)
    Weihai (05451)
    Yantai (0535)
Shanghai (021)
Shanxi
    Datong (0352)
    Taiyuan (0351)
Sichuan
    Chengdu (028)
    Chongqing (0811)
    Leshan (0833)
Tianjin (022)
Tibet
    Lhasa (0891)
Xinjiang
    Ürümqi (0991)
Yunnan
    Kunming (0871)
    Simao (0879)
Zhejiang
    Hangzhou (0571)
    Ningbo (0574)
    Wenzhou (0577)

business centres found in most luxury hotels. You do not have to be a guest at these hotels, but equip yourself with a sufficient supply of FEC before dialling – RMB is almost never accepted for international calls.

You can also dial direct from your hotel room. You'll have to ask the staff at your hotel the dial-out code for a direct line (usually a '7' on most switchboards, or sometimes a combination like '78'). Once you have the outside line, dial 00 (the international access code – always the same throughout China) followed by the country code, area code and the number you want to reach. If the area code begins with zero (like '03' for Melbourne, Australia) omit the first zero.

There are a few things to be careful about. The equipment used on most hotel switchboards is not very sophisticated – it's often a simple timer and it begins charging you starting from 30 seconds after you dial '7' (or '78' or whatever) – the timer does not know if your call succeeds or not so you get charged if you stay on the line over 30 seconds, even if you just let the phone ring repeatedly or get a busy signal! On the other hand, if you complete your conversation within 30 seconds and hang up, you don't get charged at all. The hotel switchboard timer keeps running until you hang up, not when the other party hangs up, so replace the receiver immediately when the conversation ends.

The usual procedure is that you make the call and someone comes to your room five or 10 minutes later to collect the cash. If the hotel does not have IDD, you can usually book calls from your room through the switchboard and the operator calls you back, but this procedure is more expensive.

With domestic direct dialling, it's useful to know the area codes of China's cities. These all begin with zero, but if you're dialling into China from abroad, omit the first zero from each code. China's country code is 86. The codes for provincial capitals and major cities are:

Essential Numbers There are several telephone numbers which are the same for all major cities. The problem is that the person answering the phone will likely be Chinese-speaking only – if you're looking to practise your Chinese, this is one way to do it:

local directory assistance	114
long-distance directory assistance	113, 173
HK & Macau directory assistance	115
police hot line	110
fire hot line	119
phone repair	112

Telecommunication for Expats Short-term visitors needn't bother reading this, but those planning to do business, work or study in the PRC have several telecommunication options not available to tourists.

Getting a private telephone installed in your hotel room or apartment is possible in large cities like Beijing or Shanghai, but there are long waiting lists and costs are high. Foreigners are expected to pay their phone bills in FEC (and therefore get priority over locals) but installation can still take months and costs approximately US$2000. To get you own phone line, a residence permit is required.

Though considered a luxury in the West, pagers are far more common in China than telephones – even street vendors have them! This is due to the fact that the number of telephone lines available is inadequate to meet demand, but no such problem exists with pagers. Those with a residence permit can obtain a pager in just a couple of weeks, and the cost is low at around Y25 per month. Those living on a budget, such as foreign students, may well find pagers a more realistic option than having a phone installed.

Cellular telephones are all the rage with status-conscious urban Chinese with money to burn. Despite initial costs of over US$2000 and monthly fees of around US$200, demand easily outstrips the supply of available channels and year-long waiting lists are common in many cities. On the other hand, those who already have a cellular line can sell it to others at a profit, because buying a second-hand line allows one to jump the queue. Indeed, applying for a cellular phone line only to resell it later has become a lucrative business.

Computer buffs may be interested in electronic mail (Email). Chinapac (CNPAC) – China's packet-switching network – has a node in Beijing but nowhere else (yet). To get on line requires a Y300 initial hookup fee, plus Y50 per month service charge. Transferring data is billed by 64-byte segments, plus time calculated at Y0.8 per minute. Compared to most countries, these charges are reasonable. Getting hooked up only takes a couple of days, but finding the person at the phone company who knows anything about it can be a major hassle. The place to go is the Network Management Centre of CNPAC (☎ 6010518), Ministry of Post & Telecommunications, 11 Xi Chang'an Jie, Beijing – good luck trying to explain to the receptionists just what you want. If it helps any, the Chinese name for Email is *diànzǐ yóujiàn*. It's customary for the telecom personnel to give new customers free telecommunication software for their computers – don't accept it unless you want to wind up with a computer virus.

Fax, Telex & Telegraph

Major hotels usually operate a business centre complete with telephone, fax and telex service, not to mention photocopying and perhaps the use of typewriters and word processors. As a rule, you do not have to be a guest at the hotel to use these services, but you certainly must pay. Prices seem to be pretty uniform regardless of how fancy the hotel is, but it's still not a bad idea to ask about the rates first.

Hotels demand payment in FEC – you'll save substantially by faxing from a telecom office and paying with black-market RMB. However, not all telecom offices offer fax service.

International fax and telexes (other than those to Hong Kong or Macau) cost Y23 per minute with a three-minute minimum charge – it's absurdly expensive to send a one-page fax! International telegram rates are usually around Y3.50 per word, and more for the express service. Rates to Hong Kong and Macau are less.

TIME

Time throughout China is set to Beijing time, which is eight hours ahead of Greenwich Mean Time (GMT). When it's noon in Beijing it's also noon in far-off Lhasa, Ürümqi and all other parts of the country. Since the sun doesn't cooperate with Beijing's whims, people in China's far west follow a later work schedule so they don't have to commute two hours' before dawn.

When it's noon in Beijing the time in other cities around the world is:

Frankfurt	5 am
Hong Kong	noon
London	4 am
Los Angeles	8 pm
Melbourne	2 pm
Montreal	11 pm
New York	11 pm
Paris	5 am
Rome	5 am
Wellington	4 pm

The General Office of the State Council started experimenting with daylight-saving time in 1986. It was decreed a 'great success' and made a permanent feature until 1992 – then it was unceremoniously dropped. The Chinese public became mighty confused about what was happening. Chinese people working for foreigners thought the time change only applied to Chinese, not foreigners; trains kept to old schedules, buses used the new time and boats did both; CAAC decided to postpone all flights, including those of foreign airlines, by one hour. For several weeks after daylight-saving time began, and again when it ended, buses were departing at the wrong times, people would show up for work an hour late or leave an hour early. Some cities, especially those near Hong Kong, refused to follow the scheme. Since the Chinese consider regular hours for mealtimes a prerequisite for good health, there was heady debate that this experiment was detrimental to health and could alter the time-balance intervals between meals. Some farmers wondered if it would upset their cows...and so on.

While the experiment is presently moribund, it could be revived again. Just in case it is, the system is: clocks go forward one hour at 2 am on the first Sunday of the second 10 days of April, and are set back one hour at 2 am on the first Sunday of the second 10 days of September.

ELECTRICITY

Electricity is 220 V, 50 cycles AC. Plugs come in at least four designs – three-pronged angled pins (like in Australia), three-pronged round pins (like in Hong Kong), two flat pins (American-style but without the ground wire) or two narrow round pins (European-style). Conversion plugs are easily purchased in Hong Kong but are damn near impossible to find in China. Battery chargers are widely available, but these are generally the bulky style which are not suitable for travelling – buy a small one in Hong Kong. Chinese cities are experiencing power blackouts more frequently in recent years as the demand for power has grown. This is an especially serious problem in summer because of the increasing use of air-conditioning.

Given the situation with power failures, a torch (flashlight) is essential survival gear. Chinese flashlights are awful – 50% of the time they don't work and the bulbs seldom last as long as the batteries. Bring a small but good-quality torch from abroad.

LAUNDRY

Each floor of just about every hotel in China has a service desk, usually near the elevators. The attendant's job is to clean the rooms, make the beds, and collect and deliver laundry. Almost all tourist hotels have a laundry service, and if you hand in clothes one day you should get them back a day or two later. If the hotel doesn't have a laundry, they can usually direct you to one. Hotel laundry service tends to be expensive and you might wind up doing what many travellers do – hand-washing your own clothes. If you plan on doing this, dark clothes are better since the dirt doesn't show up so clearly.

WEIGHTS & MEASURES

The metric system is widely used in China. However, the traditional Chinese measures are often used for domestic transactions and you may come across them. The following equations will help.

Metric	Chinese	Imperial
1 metre	= 3 chi	= 3.28 feet
1 km	= 2 li	= 0.62 miles
1 hectare	= 15 mu	= 2.47 acres
1 litre	= 1 gongsheng	= 0.22 gallons
1 kg	= 2 jin	= 2.2 pounds

BOOKS

There is enough literature on China to keep you reading for the next 5000 years. If you don't have that much time, you might try a few of the following suggested titles.

People & Society

Classics & Fiction The best-known English fiction about China is *The Good Earth* by Pearl S Buck.

Peking by Anthony Grey (Pan Books) is your standard blockbuster by the author of *Saigon*. Not bad.

If you want to read a weighty Chinese classic, you could try *Journey to the West*, available in English in a four-volume set in China and some Hong Kong bookstores. Since much of the action takes place along the Silk Road, it's recommended for travellers following that route.

The Dream of the Red Chamber (also known as *The Story of the Stone*) by Cao Xueqin, is a Chinese classic written in the late 18th century. Published in five volumes by Penguin, it's not an easy read. Fortunately, an abridged edition is available from some of the Friendship Stores and foreign-language bookshops in China, and perhaps from some shops in Hong Kong and abroad.

The third great Chinese classic is *Outlaws of the Marsh*. This is also available in abridged form.

George Orwell's *1984* was ahead of its time in predicting the political trends in the Communist world. *Animal Farm* is perhaps a closer approximation to post-1949 China and its bloated cadres.

Franz Kafka's *The Trial* wasn't written with China in mind, yet his book is a potent reminder of the helplessness of individuals against the all-powerful state bureaucracy.

Recent Accounts Over the last few years, since foreign journalists were permitted to take up residence in China, there has been a spate of books delving into Chinese life, the universe and everything. Most are out of date, but if you read them in succession you can get an overview of the changes which have taken place in China since Mao died.

The Search for Modern China by Jonathan D Spence is the definitive work, often used as a textbook in college courses. If you want to understand the PRC, this is the book to read.

Fox Butterfield's *China – Alive in the Bitter Sea* (Coronet, 1983) is one of the biggest sellers. A harshly critical account, it tells you everything from the location of Chinese labour camps to how women cope with menstruation.

To Get Rich is Glorious (Pantheon Books, 1984) by American scholar and many-times China traveller Orville Schell is a concise and easy-to-read overview of the major changes in China's economic policies and political thinking over the last few years.

A dimmer view of China under Deng Xiaoping is Italian journalist Tiziano Terzani's *Behind the Forbidden Door* (Allen & Unwin, 1986). Terzani, once an avid socialist, became disillusioned after living in China from 1980 to 1984, when he was finally booted out for his critical reporting.

An intriguing and popular book is *The New Emperors* by Harrison E Salisbury. The 'emperors' he refers to are Mao Zedong and Deng Xiaoping.

A moving and now popular book is *Wild Swans* by Jung Chang. The author traces the lives of three Chinese women – the author's grandmother (an escaped concubine with bound feet), her mother and herself.

Chinese Lives by Zhang Xinxin and Sang Ye (Penguin) was written by two Chinese journalists who interviewed Chinese people at all levels of society.

Seeds of Fire: Chinese Voices of Conscience (Far Eastern Economic Review Ltd, 1986) is an anthology of blistering eloquence from authors such as Wei Jingsheng, Liu Qing, Wang Xizhe and Xu Wenli (imprisoned for their roles in the Democracy Movement) and the poet Sun Jingxuan. Wei Jingsheng's description of Q1, China's top prison for political detainees, is utterly horrific.

The issue of human rights is covered in Amnesty International's *China: Violations of Human Rights* – a grim aspect of the country that should not be ignored.

Cultural Revolution The best seller seems to be *Life and Death in Shanghai* by Nien Cheng (Grafton). The author was imprisoned for 6½ years, and this is her gripping story of how she survived.

Other stories from this period include *Born Red* by Gao Yuan (Stanford University Press) and *Son of the Revolution* by Liang Heng and Judith Shapiro (Fontana Paperbacks).

Tiananmen-Inspired If nothing else, the 1989 killings at Tiananmen Square forced foreign journalists to take off the rose-coloured glasses and produce a few hard-hitting critical books.

Tiananmen, the Rape of Peking by Michael Fathers and Andrew Higgins (Doubleday) is probably the best book on the protests.

Beijing Spring by David and Peter Turnley (Asia 2000) is a good pictorial history of the Tiananmen events.

Tiananmen Diary by Harrison Salisbury (Unwin Paperbacks) and *Tiananmen Square* by Scott Simmie and Bob Nixon (Douglas and McIntyre) outline the same story.

Beijing Jeep by Jim Mann (Simon & Schuster) is about the short unhappy romance of American business in China.

History

The classic on the Chinese Revolution is *Red Star Over China* (Pelican, 1972; first published in 1937) by Edgar Snow. Snow managed to get through the Kuomintang blockade of the Communists and spent four months with them in Yan'an in 1936. His book has been criticised as naive in that it glosses over some of the worst aspects of the Communist movement, but it conveys the hope and idealism of the time.

Chinese Shadows by Simon Leys is one of the most critical books on Mao and the Cultural Revolution. It was published in 1974, based on Leys' visits to China in 1972 and 1973. It's interesting to draw comparisons between the China of the post-Mao era and the one that Leys visited.

Roger Garside's *Coming Alive – China After Mao* describes the events which led to the downfall of the 'Gang of Four' and the rise of Deng Xiaoping. Garside served at the US Embassy in Beijing from 1968 to 1970, and was first secretary from 1976 to 1979.

The Dragon Wakes by Christopher Hibbert (Penguin) is a good history from 1793 to 1911.

The Chinese People Stand Up by Elizabeth Wright (BBC) examines China's turbulent history from 1949 up to the brutal suppression of pro-democracy demonstrators in 1989.

The Soong Dynasty by Sterling Seagrave (Sidgwick and Jackson) is one of the most popular books on the corrupt Kuomintang period. Unfortunately, the author severely damaged his credibility when he later published *The Marcos Dynasty* which contains more rumour than fact.

Travel Guides

The classic coffee-table book is *A Day in the Life of China* (Merehurst Press). It's very expensive but you get what you pay for.

Then there's the sort of stuff that fits more into the 'Mad Dogs & Englishmen' genre. You won't fail to be amused by two books by Englishman Peter Fleming, written in the mid-1930s. *One's Company* describes his travels across Siberia and eastern China meeting such notables as Puyi, the puppet-emperor of Japanese-occupied Manchuria. *News from Tartary* describes his epic six-month trek on the backs of camels and donkeys across southern Xinjiang and into the north of Pakistan.

Danziger's Travels by Nick Danziger (Paladin) is a good 'Silk Road' book but the first half of it covers regions outside of China.

In Xanadu by William Dalrymple (Fontana Paperbacks) gives an account of a journey from Jerusalem to Xanadu by two British students.

Behind the Wall by Colin Thubron (Penguin) is an excellent travelogue with lots of insights into Chinese society.

A lively and informative book is *Cycling to Xian* (ITMB, 736A Granville St, Vancouver, BC V6Z 1G3, Canada) by Michael Buckley. The author realistically expresses both the joys and frustrations of travelling through China.

Just in case you didn't know, Lonely Planet (plug No 1) has a few other titles concerning the Chinese world; the *Beijing City Guide* and travel survival kits for *Taiwan* and *Hong Kong, Macau & Canton*.

Dealing with the local language can be a monumental task. To help you on your way, Lonely Planet (plug No 2) publishes the *Mandarin Chinese Phrasebook* and *Tibet Phrasebook*. Berlitz also publishes a phrasebook, *Chinese for Travellers*.

There are, of course, other phrasebooks on the market. Some people use the *Speechless Translator*, which can be bought in Hong Kong; this has columns of Chinese characters and English translations that you string together to form sentences, with no speaking required. Another useful book is *Instant Chinese* (Round Asia Publishing Company, 1985), which you can find in Hong Kong.

Bookshops

If you want good books to read, bring your own. English paperbacks are available from shops in the tourist hotels in the big Chinese cities, but the supply and range are limited. Foreign-language bookshops cater for Chinese who are learning foreign languages, not for Western reading interests – though they often stock classic foreign fiction as well as pirated textbooks. The Beijing Friendship Store has a decent collection of English bestsellers. You can now find English-language Signet classics printed in China and sold in Foreign Languages Bookstores and some hotels for less than Y10 apiece. Mostly they are collections of American and British short stories, and it's not certain how many of these are printed under licence or pirated. Still, for the desperate they're a real bargain.

As a last-ditch measure, the lobbies of many hotels and soft-sleeper waiting rooms at railway stations provide an assortment of free foreign-language booklets explaining China's current version of history (subject to revision on short notice) and recent political pronouncements. Some of these can be amusing and make good collectors' items.

Hong Kong is an excellent place to stock up on books, so take advantage of the opportunity if you're there. Recommended bookstores include:

Joint Publishing Company
  9 Queen Victoria St, opposite the Central Market – good books for Chinese-language study (☎ 5250102)

Peace Book Company
    35 Kimberley Rd, Tsimshatsui – official outlet
    for PRC books & magazines (☎ 8967832)
Swindon Books
    13-15 Lock Rd, Tsimshatsui – large selection
    (☎ 3668033)
Time Books
    Granville & Nathan Rds, Tsimshatsui – lots of
    glossy bestsellers (☎ 7217138)
Wanderlust Books
    30 Hollywood Rd, Central – excellent collection
    of travel books & knowledgeable, English-
    speaking staff (☎ 5232042)

MAPS

One of the big changes to occur in China over
the past decade has been the increase in
availability of good-quality maps. In the
early 1980s, maps were treated as military
secrets. The few that were available were
great works of fiction – doctored to trick the
foreign spies and saboteurs. As China
opened up, it slowly dawned on the Chinese
leadership that the satellite-based maps published in the West were much better quality
than those available in China.

Now the situation has reversed – top
quality maps of almost every Chinese city –
even many small towns – are readily available. Some of these show incredible detail –
bus routes (including names of bus stops),
the locations of hotels, shops and so on. City
maps normally only cost Y1 to Y2 – the cost may
be partly subsidised by the advertisements!

Maps are most easily purchased from
bookstalls or street vendors around railway
and bus stations, from branches of the
Xinhua Bookstore, or from hotel front desks
(even cheap Chinese hotels where foreigners
can't stay). The big problem is this – maps
are almost always in Chinese characters. In
a few major cities like Beijing, you can find
bilingual maps, or sometimes a matched set –
two identical maps, but one in English and one
in Chinese.

The places to look for English-language
editions are the hotel giftshops, Friendship
Stores and sometimes the foreign-language
bookstores. There are also a few atlases –
these only cover major cities and tourist
sites, and most are in Chinese characters
although there are a few English editions

around. English-language editions invariably cost more than the Chinese equivalents.

There seems to be no central place in China
where you can go to purchase maps for the
entire country. The selection at the Xinhua
Bookstore on Wangfujing Dajie in Beijing is
decent, but hardly comprehensive. In Hong
Kong, check out Peace Book Company and
Joint Publishing Company (addresses given in
preceding section under 'Bookstores').

Some of the most detailed maps of China
available in the West are the aerial survey
'Operational Navigation Charts' (Series
ONC). These are prepared and published by
the Defense Mapping Agency Aerospace
Center, St Louis Air Force Station, Missouri
63118, USA. Cyclists and mountaineers
have recommended these highly because of
their extraordinary detail. In the UK you can
obtain these maps from Stanfords Map
Centre, 12-14 Long Acre, London WC2E 9LP
(☎ 071-8361321) or from The Map Shop (☎ 06-
8463146), A T Atkinson & Partner, 15 High St,
Upton-on-Severn, Worcestershire, WR8 OHJ.

MEDIA
News Agencies

China has two news agencies, the Xinhua
News Agency and the China News Service.
The Xinhua (New China) Agency is a
national agency with its headquarters in
Beijing and branches in each province as
well as in the army and many foreign countries. It provides news for the national,
provincial and local papers and radio stations, transmits radio broadcasts abroad in
foreign languages, and is responsible for
making contact with and exchanging news
with foreign news agencies. In Hong Kong,
Xinhua acts as the unofficial embassy.

The main function of the China News
Service is to supply news to Overseas
Chinese newspapers and journals, including
those in Hong Kong and Macau. It also distributes Chinese documentary films abroad.

Chinese-Language Publications

There are nearly 2000 national and provincial newspapers in China. The main one is
Renmin Ribao (the *People's Daily*), with

nationwide circulation. It was founded in 1946 as the official publication of the Central Committee of the Communist Party. Most of these tend to be exceedingly boring though they do provide a brief rundown of world events.

At the other end of the scale there is China's version of the gutter press – several hundred 'unhealthy papers' and magazines hawked on street corners and bus stations in major cities with nude or violent photos and stories about sex, crime, witchcraft, miracle cures and UFOs. These have been severely criticised by the government for their obscene and racy content – they are also extremely popular. There are also about 40 newspapers for the minority nationalities.

Almost 2200 periodicals were published at the last count, of which about half were technical or scientific; the rest were concerned with social sciences, literature, culture and education, or were general periodicals, pictorials or children's publications. One of the better-known periodicals is the monthly *Hongqi* (Red Flag), the main Communist philosophical and theoretical journal.

In China the papers, radio and TV are the last places to carry the news. Westerners tend to be numbed by endless accounts of heroic factory workers and stalwart peasants, and dismiss China's media as a huge propaganda machine. Flipping through journals like *China Today, Women of China* and *China Pictorial* only serves to confirm this view.

Nevertheless, the Chinese press does warrant serious attention since it provides clues to what is happening in China. When Deng Xiaoping returned to public view after being disposed of in the Cultural Revolution, the first mention was simply the inclusion of his name in a guest list at a reception for Prince Sihanouk of Kampuchea, printed in the *People's Daily* without elaboration or comment. Political struggles between factions are described in articles in the Chinese newspapers as a means of warning off any supporters of the opposing side and undermining its position rather than resorting to an all-out, dangerous conflict. The 'Letters to the Editor' section in the *People's Daily* pro-vides something of a measure of public opinion, and complaints are sometimes followed up by reporters.

Newspapers and journals are useful for following the 'official line' of the Chinese government – though in times of political struggle they tend to follow the line of whoever has control over the media.

Foreign-Language Publications

China publishes various newspapers, books and magazines in a number of European and Asian languages. The only English-language newspaper (and one which you are most likely to come across during your travels) is *China Daily*, first published in June 1981; it has two overseas editions (Hong Kong and USA). Overseas subscriptions can be obtained from the following sources:

Hong Kong
    Wen Wei Po, 197 Wanchai Rd (☎ 5722211; fax 5720441)
USA
    China Daily Distribution Corporation, Suite 401, 15 Mercer St, New York, NY 10013 (☎ 212-2190130; fax 2100108)

Although you might stumble across some of the English-language magazines in luxury hotels and Friendship Stores, they are most readily available by subscription. These can be posted to you overseas. The place to subscribe is not in China itself, but in Hong Kong. If interested, contact Peace Book Company (☎ 8967382; fax 8976251), 17th floor, Paramount Building, 12 Ka Yip St, Chai Wan, Hong Kong. You can write, fax or drop by the office for their catalogue. Here's a rundown of what's available in English and other foreign languages:

Beijing Review, a weekly magazine on political and current affairs. Valuable for learning about China's latest half-baked political policies. The magazine is published in English, French, Spanish, German and Japanese.
China Medical Abstracts, a special-interest quarterly magazine in English.
China Philately, a bimonthly magazine in English for stamp collectors.

China Pictorial, a monthly large-format glossy magazine with neat photos, cultural and historical stuff. Available in English, French, Spanish, German and Japanese.

China Screen, a quarterly magazine in English or Chinese with a focus on the Chinese motion-picture industry.

China Sports, an English-language monthly which helps demonstrate the superiority of Chinese atheletes over foreigners.

China Today, a monthly magazine. The magazine was founded in 1952 by Song Qingling (the wife of Sun Yatsen) and used to be called *China Reconstructs*. The name was changed in 1989 because – as one official said – '37 years is a hell of a long time to be reconstructing your country'.

China's Foreign Trade, a monthly publication in English, French, Spanish or Chinese, with a self-explanatory title.

China's Patents & Trademarks, a quarterly magazine in Chinese and English. The title is self-explanatory.

China's Tibet, a quarterly magazine in Chinese or English. Its chief purpose is to convince overseas readers that China's historical claim to Tibet is more than just hot air. Some of the articles about Tibetan culture and religion might prove interesting.

Chinese Literature, a quarterly magazine in English or French. Topics include poetry, fiction, profiles of Chinese writers and so on.

El Popola Cinio, a monthly magazine in Esperanto – good if you want to familiarize yourself with this language.

Kexue Tongbao, a semi-monthly publication in English with a focus on the sciences.

Nexus, a quarterly magazine in English. It is claimed that this is China's first non-government funded magazine in English (who knows?). Articles cover various aspects of Chinese culture and society.

Shanghai Pictorial, a bimonthly magazine available in Chinese or English. Photos of fashionable women dressed in the latest, as well as container ships, cellular telephones and other symbols of Shanghai's developing economy.

Social Sciences in China, a quarterly publication in English. The magazine covers topics like archaeology, economics, philosophy, literature and a whole range of academic pursuits by Chinese scholars.

Women of China, a monthly magazine in English designed to show foreigners that Chinese women are not treated as badly as they really are.

The government also publishes impressive glossy magazines in minority languages such as Tibetan. These appear to be strictly for foreign consumption – they are not available in China.

Imported Publications

In large cities like Beijing, Shanghai and Canton, it's fairly easy to score copies of popular imported English-language magazines like *Time, Newsweek, Far Eastern Economic Review* and *The Economist*. Occasionally you might find European magazines in French or German. Foreign newspapers like the *Asian Wall Street Journal, International Herald-Tribune* and Hong Kong's *South China Morning Post* are also available. Imported periodicals are most readily available from the big tourist hotels, though a few Friendship Stores also stock copies.

To China's credit, foreign-language magazines and newspapers are seldom, if ever, censored, even when they contain stories critical of the PRC. Of course, a different set of rules applies to Chinese-language publications from Hong Kong and Taiwan – essentially, these cannot be brought into China without special permission.

There seems to be no import duty on foreign magazines and newspapers. You do have to pay in FEC, but the prices charged are in line with what you'd pay in Hong Kong or elsewhere.

When the Communist Party committee of Beijing investigated the bustling black market for foreign books, magazines and newspapers they discovered that hotel staff and garbage collectors are well-placed intermediaries for this business. Foreign hotel guests regularly leave behind several tons of foreign publications every month, but resident foreign experts, journalists and diplomats throw out nearly 20 tons.

The Beijing committee analysed printed matter left behind at the Xinqiao Hotel and was pleased to discover that nearly half of the publications had good or relatively good contents. The remaining items contained 'partly erroneous' or 'problematic' material such as 'half-naked advertisements'. When the courageous committee delved into diplomatic dustbins, they discovered that 15% of their haul was 'anti-communist, anti-Chinese, obscene and pornographic' – definitely bottom of the barrel.

Radio & TV

Domestic radio broadcasting is controlled by

the Central People's Broadcasting Station (CPBS). Broadcasts are made in *putonghua*, the standard Chinese speech, as well as in local Chinese dialects and minority languages. There are also broadcasts to Taiwan in putonghua and Fujianese, and Cantonese broadcasts aimed at residents of Guangdong Province, Hong Kong and Macau. Radio Beijing is China's overseas radio service and broadcasts in about 40 foreign languages, as well as in putonghua and several local dialects. It also exchanges programmes with radio stations in a number of countries and has correspondents in some.

If you want to keep up with the world news, a short-wave radio receiver would be worth bringing with you. You can buy these in China, but the ones from Hong Kong are usually more compact and better quality.

Chinese Central Television (CCTV) began broadcasting in 1958, and colour transmission began in 1973. Major cities may have a second local channel, like Beijing Television (BTV). Although they've improved in the past few years, Chinese TV shows are designed to guide the public's moral education. Movies and soap operas urge the people to be good citizens, work and study hard, not to lie, cheat, slash foreigners' backpacks, etc.

Notice Boards

Apart from the mass media, the public notice board retains its place as an important means of educating the people or influencing public opinion. Other people who want to get a message across glue up big wallposters in public places. This is a traditional form of communicating ideas in China and if the content catches the attention of even a few people then word-of-mouth can spread it very quickly. Deng Xiaoping personally stripped from China's constitution the right to put up wallposters.

Public notice boards abound in China. Two of the most common subjects are crime and accidents. In China it's no holds barred – before-and-after photos of executed criminals are plugged up on these boards along with a description of their heinous offences. Other memorable photos include people squashed by trucks, blown-up by fireworks or fried after smoking cigarettes near open petrol tanks. Other popular themes include industrial safety and family-planning. Inspiring slogans such as 'The PLA Protects

The Broadcasting Industry

If the Chinese government thought that TV would provide a useful mechanism for controlling the thoughts of the masses, it was a bad miscalculation. Most Chinese find their public TV boring, and those who have access to video machines consume foreign movies with a passion. Pornography has proven particularly popular, much to the consternation of the authorities. Videotaped Taiwanese programmes have also set the authorities on edge, particularly news broadcasts showing Taiwan's free elections and legal street protests.

Nor is videotape the only threat to the government's stranglehold on the media. Satellite TV has taken the country by storm. Hong Kong's Star TV is particularly popular because it broadcasts in Chinese and does not require a decoder (advertising revenues pay the bill) to receive it. Technically, most of the satellite dishes you see on rooftops in China are illegal. The government could easily tear them down, but to do so would create a problem – loss of revenue. The Chinese now manufacture their own satellite dishes – the military's 'General Staff Department' and the 'Ministry of Radio, Film & TV' make enormous profits by selling them for US$500 apiece.

Satellite dishes and video tape players have given birth to another illegal growth industry – cable TV. Any enterprising individual can simply purchase a satellite dish and video machine, then run cables to neighbouring homes and charge a fee for the service. This not only earns a profit for the entrepreneur, but brings down the cost of receiving foreign programming to a level many Chinese can afford.

Clearly the government is caught in a dilemma – how to control people's access to information and entertainment while attempting to modernise the economy. Stay tuned for the latest episode. ∎

the People' or 'Follow the Socialist Road to Happiness' are also common.

FILM & PHOTOGRAPHY

In China you'll get a fantastic run for your money; for starters there are over a billion portraits to work your way through. Religious reasons for avoiding photographs are absent among the Han Chinese – some guy isn't going to stick a spear through you for taking a picture of his wife and stealing part of her soul – though the taboo may apply to some of the minority groups, and you probably won't be allowed to take photos of statues in Buddhist temples.

Some Chinese shy away from having their photo taken, and even duck for cover. Others are proud to pose and will ham it up for the camera – and they're especially proud if you're taking a shot of their kid. Nobody expects any payment for photos – so don't give any or you'll set a precedent. What the Chinese would go for, though, is a copy of a colour photo, which you could mail to them. People tend also to think that the negative belongs to the subject as well, and they'll ask for both the negative and the print – but through the post there's no argument.

There are three basic approaches to photographing people. One is the polite 'ask for permission and pose it' shot, which is sometimes rejected. Another is the 'no-holds barred and upset everyone' approach. The third is surreptitious, standing half a km away with a metre-long telephoto lens. Many Chinese will disagree with you on what constitutes good subject matter; they don't really see why anyone would want to take a street scene, a picture of a beggar or a shot of an old man driving a donkeycart.

Another objection often brought up is that the subject is not 'dignified' – be it a labourer straining down the street with a massive load on his hand-cart, or a barrel of excrement on wheels. The official line is that peasants and workers are the glorious heroes of China, but you'll have a tough time convincing your photo subject of this.

A lot of Chinese still cannot afford a camera and resort to photographers at tourist places. The photographers supply dress-up clothing for that extra touch. The subjects change from street clothing into spiffy gear and sometimes even bizarre costumes and make-up for the shot. Others use cardboard props such as opera stars or boats. In Beijing one prop is a real car – after all, the average Chinese has about as much hope of owning a car as you've got of hitching on the space shuttle.

The standard shot is one or more Chinese standing in front of something significant. A temple, waterfall, heroic statue or important vintages of calligraphy are considered suitable backgrounds. At amusement parks, Mickey Mouse and Donald Duck get into nearly every photo – Ronald McDonald and the Colonel of Kentucky Fried fame are favourite photo companions in Beijing. If you hang around these places you can sometimes clip off a few portrait photos for yourself, but don't be surprised if your photo subjects suddenly drag you into the picture as an exotic prop!

Buying Film

Imported film is expensive, but major Japanese companies like Fuji and Konica now have factories in China – this has brought prices of colour print film down to what you'd pay in the West, sometimes less. While colour print film is available almost everywhere, it's almost always 100 ASA (21 DIN).

Genuine Chinese brands of film are a big unknown – some are good and some are trash, so you'll just have to experiment if you want to use the stuff. Another big unknown is whether or not these films will work with fully automatic cameras which need to sense the film speed. The letters 'DX' printed on a box of film indicates that it is suitable for automatic cameras, but we have yet to see a Chinese brand carrying this designation.

Black & white film can be found in large cities, but in general it's hard to buy in China – colour photos are now the big thing.

In general, colour slide film is hard to find – check out major hotels and Friendship Stores if you get caught short. When you do find slide film, it's usually expensive and sometimes out-of-date, though last year's slide film is still better than none. Ektachrome and Fujichrome can be found in Beijing and Shanghai – Kodachrome and Agfachrome are close to nonexistent in China.

Polaroid film is rumoured to exist, but if you need the stuff, you'd better bring your own supply.

Finding the special lithium batteries used by many cameras is also hit or miss and you'd be wise to bring a spare. Some cameras have a manual mode which allows you to continue shooting with a dead battery, though the light meter won't work. Fully-automatic cameras totally drop dead when the battery goes.

Video cameras were once subject to shaky regulations but there seems to be no problem now. The biggest problem is recharging your batteries off the strange mutations of plugs in China – bring all the adaptors you can, and remember that it's 220 V.

You're allowed to bring in 8 mm movie cameras; 16 mm or professional equipment may raise eyebrows with Customs. Motion picture film is hard enough to find in the West these days, and next to impossible in China.

Processing

Major cities like Beijing, Shanghai, Canton, Shenzhen and Guilin are equipped with the latest Japanese photoprocessing machines. Quality colour prints can be turned out in one or two hours at reasonable cost.

It's a different situation with colour slides. Ektachrome and Fujichrome can be processed in Beijing and Shanghai but this can be expensive and quality is not assured. If you don't want your slides scratched, covered with fingerprints or over-developed, save the processing until you get home.

Kodachrome film cannot be processed in China or Hong Kong. However, in Hong Kong the photo shops can send it out by express air mail and get it back in four days. The closest countries which process Kodachrome are Japan and Australia.

Undeveloped film can be sent out of China and, going by personal experience only, the dreaded X-ray machines do not appear to be a problem.

Prohibited Subjects

Photography from planes and photographs of airports, military installations, harbour facilities and railroad terminals are prohibited; bridges may also be a touchy subject.

These rules get enforced if the enforcers happen to be around. One traveller, bored at the airport, started photographing the X-ray procedure in clearance. PLA men promptly pounced on her and ripped the film out. In an age where satellites can zoom down on a number plate it all seems a bit absurd, but many countries have similarly ridiculous restrictions on photography.

Taking photos is not permitted in most museums, at archaeological sites and in many temples, mainly to protect the postcard and colour slide industry. It prevents Westerners from publishing their own books about these sites and taking business away from the Chinese-published books. It also prevents valuable works of art from being damaged by countless flash photos – but in most cases you're not allowed to take even harmless natural light photos or time exposures.

Be aware that these rules are generally enforced. If you want to snap a few photos in prohibited spots then start with a new roll of film – if that's ripped out of your camera at least you don't lose 20 other photos as well. Monks can be vigorous enforcers of this rule in temples. They can rip film out of cameras faster than you can cock the shutter – must be some special martial arts training.

HEALTH

Although China presents a few particular health hazards that require your attention, overall it's a healthier place to travel than many other parts of the world. Large cities like Beijing and Shanghai have decent medical facilities – the problem is out in the backwaters like Inner Mongolia, Tibet or Xinjiang.

If you have the time and inclination, you

might want to do some reading to get a better understanding of health hazards, their prevention and treatment. For the technically oriented, the classic medical reference is the *Merck Manual*, a weighty volume which covers virtually every illness known to humanity.

Children, particularly babies and unborn children, present their own peculiar problems when travelling. Lonely Planet's *Travel with Children* by Maureen Wheeler gives a rundown on health precautions to be taken with kids, or if you're pregnant and travelling.

Medical services are generally very cheap in China although hospitals that deal especially with foreigners charge more and ask for payment in FEC. However, they will usually give foreigners better service – Chinese patients usually have to wait for hours in long queues.

In case of accident or illness, it's best just to get a taxi and go to the hospital directly – try to avoid dealing with the authorities (police and military) if possible. One traveller who broke his leg near Dali made the mistake of calling on the police for help. They came with a Land Rover and took him to the military hospital where a cast was put on his leg – he was then charged Y10,000 for this service! A civilian hospital would have charged him less than Y100.

If you're Rh-negative, try not to bleed in China. The Chinese do not have Rh-negative blood and their blood banks don't store it. If you're a type O Rh-negative, then you're in worse luck since you can only accept a transfusion of the same and nothing else – and there aren't very many of us around!

Predeparture Preparations

Health Insurance Although you may have medical insurance in your own country, it is probably not valid in China. But ask your insurance company anyway – you *might* already be covered. A travel insurance policy is a very good idea – the best ones protect you against cancellation penalties on advance-purchase flights, against medical costs through illness or injury, against theft or loss of possessions, and against the cost of additional air tickets if you get really sick and have to fly home. Obviously, the more extensive the coverage, the higher the premiums, but at a minimum you should at least be

---

Massage

Massage (*ànmó*) has a long history in China. It's an effective technique for treating a variety of painful ailments such as chronic back pain and sore muscles. To be most effective, a massage should be administered by someone who has really studied the techniques. An acupuncturist who also practises massage would be ideal.

Traditional Chinese massage is somewhat different from the increasingly popular do-it-yourself techniques practised by people in the West. One traditional Chinese technique employs suction cups made of bamboo placed on the patient's skin. A burning piece of alcohol-soaked cotton is briefly put inside the cup to drive out the air before it is applied. As the cup cools, a partial vacuum is produced, leaving a nasty-looking but harmless red circular mark on the skin. The mark goes away in a few days. Other methods include bloodletting and scraping the skin with coins or porcelain soup spoons.

A related technique is called moxibustion. Various types of herbs, rolled into what looks like a ball of fluffy cotton, are held just near the skin and ignited. A slight variation of this method is to place the herbs on a slice of ginger and then ignite them. The idea is to apply the maximum amount of heat possible without burning the patient. This heat treatment is supposed to be good for such diseases as arthritis.

However, there is no real need to subject yourself to such extensive treatment if you would just like a straight massage to relieve normal aches and pains. Many big tourist hotels in China offer massage facilities, but the rates charged are excessive – around Y100 per hour. You can do much better than that by inquiring locally – the hotel staff might even be able to direct you to such a place if the hotel itself doesn't offer this service. ■

covered for medical costs due to injuries. Read the small print carefully since it's easy to be caught out by exclusions – injuries due to 'dangerous activities' like skiing or bicycling might be excluded, for example.

If you undergo medical treatment, be sure to collect all receipts and copies of your medical report, in English if possible, for your insurance company.

If you purchase an International Student Identity Card (ISIC) or Teacher Card (ISTC), you may be automatically covered depending on which country you purchased the card in. Check with the student travel office to be sure. If you're neither a student nor a teacher, but you're between the ages of 15 and 25, you can purchase an International Youth Identity Card (YIEE) which entitles you to

the same benefits. Some student travel offices also sell insurance to others who don't hold these cards.

Medical Kit You should assemble some sort of basic first-aid kit. You won't want it to be too large and cumbersome for travelling, but some items which could be included are:

Anti-malarial tablets (south-west China only); Band-Aids or gauze bandage with plaster (adhesive tape); a thermometer; tweezers; scissors; UV lotion; insect repellent; multi-vitamins; water sterilisation tablets; chapstick; antibiotic ointment; an antiseptic agent (Dettol or Betadine); any medication you're already taking; diarrhoea medication (Lomotil or Imodium); rehydration mixture for treatment of severe diarrhoea; paracetamol (Panadol), ibuprofen or aspirin for pain

---

Acupuncture

Chinese acupuncture *(zhēnjiŭ)* has received enthusiastic reviews from many satisfied patients who have tried it. Of course, one should be wary of overblown claims. Acupuncture is not likely to cure terminal illness, in spite of any testimonials you might read in Western countries about curing cancer holistically. Nevertheless, acupuncture is of genuine therapeutic value in the treatment of chronic back pain, migraine headaches and arthritis.

For those not already familiar with the term, acupuncture is a technique employing needles which are inserted into various points of the body. In former times, needles were probably made from bamboo, gold, silver, copper or tin. These days, only stainless steel needles of hairlike thinness are used, causing very little pain when inserted. Dirty acupuncture needles can spread disease rather than cure, so good acupuncturists sterilise their needles or use disposable ones. As many as 2000 points for needle insertion have been identified, but only about 150 are commonly used.

One of the most amazing demonstrations of acupuncture's power is that major surgery can be performed using acupuncture alone as the anaesthetic. The acupuncture needle is inserted into the patient and a small electric current is passed through the needle. The current is supplied by an ordinary torch battery.

The exact mechanism by which acupuncture works is not fully understood by modern medical science. The Chinese have their own theories, but it is by no means certain they really know either. Needles are inserted into various points of the body, each point believed by the acupuncturist to correspond to a particular organ, joint, gland or other part of the body. These points are believed to be connected to the particular area being treated by an 'energy channel', also translated as a 'meridian', but more likely it has something to do with the nerves. By means not fully understood, it seems the needle can block pain transmission along the meridian. However it works, many report satisfactory results.

Should you wish to try this technique, there are many hospitals of traditional Chinese medicine in major cities like Guangzhou, Beijing and Shanghai. Many of these hospitals also train Westerners who are eager to learn these methods. In Canton, one popular place with Western students is the Guangzhou Traditional Chinese Medicine Hospital (☎ 886504) *(zhōngyī yīyuàn)* on Zhuji Lu near Shamian Island – they also teach herbal medicine. Some hotels also provide acupuncture services at their clinics, but these are likely to be more expensive.

If you're (justifiably) concerned about catching disease from contaminated acupuncture needles, you might consider buying your own before undergoing treatment. Good quality needles are available in major cities in China and in Hong Kong. Needles come in a bewildering variety of gauges – try to determine from your acupuncturist which type to buy. ■

and fever; antihistamine (such as Benadryl) useful as a decongestant for colds, allergies, to ease reactions to insect bites or stings; a course of antibiotics (probably 30 tablets of 250 mg tetracycline, but check with your doctor); Flagyl (for giardia in Tibet) and contraceptives, if necessary. Most of these medications are available in China at low cost, but finding them when you urgently need them can often prove problematic.

Ideally, antibiotics should be administered only under medical supervision and should never be taken indiscriminately. Overuse of antibiotics can weaken your body's ability to deal with infections naturally and can reduce the drug's efficacy on a future occasion. Take only the recommended dose as prescribed. It's important that once you start a course of antibiotics, you finish it even if the illness seems to be cured earlier. If you stop taking the antibiotics after one or two days, complete relapse is likely. If you think you are experiencing a reaction to any antibiotic, stop taking it immediately and consult a doctor. Antibiotics can be bought cheaply across the counter in many countries in South-East Asia (Taiwan and Thailand are good places to stock up).

Vaccinations Very few people will be required to have vaccinations but there are several that are certainly recommended. If you're arriving within six days after leaving or transiting a yellow fever infected area then a vaccination is required.

Vaccinations which have been recommended by various health authorities include: cholera, meningitis, rabies, hepatitis A, hepatitis B, BCG (tuberculosis), polio,

and TABT (protects against typhoid, paratyphoid A and B, and tetanus) and diphtheria.

You should have your vaccinations recorded in an International Health Certificate. If you are travelling with children, it's especially important to be sure that they've had all necessary vaccinations.

Get your teeth checked and any necessary dental work done before you leave home. Always carry a spare pair of glasses, contact lenses or your prescription in case of loss or breakage.

Basic Rules

Food & Water In many large cities, tap water is not too bad (it's chlorinated) but it's still recommended that you don't drink it without boiling first. In rural areas, the water varies from pretty safe to downright dangerous. Especially after a typhoon and the subsequent flooding, there is a problem with sewers overflowing into reservoirs, thus contaminating the tap water used for drinking and bathing. Outbreaks of cholera and typhoid occur most often after floods so you must be particularly careful at such times – do not even brush your teeth with unboiled water after flooding. Surface water is generally more dangerous than well water, especially if it comes from an area where domestic livestock graze.

Bottled water and soft drinks are widely available in China and should be perfectly safe to drink (how they taste is another matter). There is no problem with contamination of milk products in China, but sometimes yoghurt is stored for prolonged periods without refrigeration – if it smells suspicious, you'd better keep away from it.

Tea and coffee should both be OK since the water should have been boiled. Remember that at high altitude water boils at a lower temperature, so germs are less likely to be killed. You can also boil your own water if you carry an electric immersion coil and a large metal cup (plastic will melt).

Bringing water to a boil is sufficient to kill most bacteria, but 20 minutes of boiling is required to kill amoebic cysts. Fortunately, amoebic cysts are relatively rare and you should not be overly concerned about these, except, again, in Tibet. If you have nothing to boil or purify your water with, you have to consider the risks of drinking possibly contaminated water against the risks of dehydration – the first is possible, the second is definite.

For emergency use, water purification tablets will help, and this is particularly important in Tibet. Water is more effectively sterilised by iodine than by chlorine tablets, because iodine kills amoebic cysts. However, iodine is not safe for prolonged use, and also tastes horrible.

If you can't find tablets, tincture of iodine (2%) or iodine crystals can be used. Two drops of tincture of iodine per litre or quart of clear water is the recommended dosage; the treated water should be left to stand for 30 minutes before drinking. Iodine crystals can also be used to purify water but this is a more complicated process, as you have to first prepare a saturated iodine solution. Iodine loses its effectiveness if exposed to air or damp so keep it in a tightly sealed container. Flavoured powder will disguise the taste of treated water and is a good idea if you are travelling with children.

Out in the western deserts of Xinjiang or high on the Tibetan Plateau, you really need to drink a great deal of water. In such places it's a good idea to carry a water bottle with you (buy one which doesn't leak!). You are dehydrating if you find you are urinating infrequently or if your urine turns a deep yellow or orange; you may also find yourself getting headaches.

When it comes to food, use your best judgement. To be absolutely safe, everything should be clean and thoroughly cooked – you can get diarrhoea from salads and unpeeled fruit. Chinese food is generally well-cooked and raw vegetables are usually pickled. Some of the street markets look pretty grotty, but in general the food is OK.

Shellfish and seafood of any kind pose the greatest risks of all, from spoilage (due to lack of refrigeration) and water pollution. Some of the rivers and bays in China are positively toxic, yet you often see people fishing in them. Better restaurants only buy fish which are raised in commercial ponds, and the fish are kept alive in aquariums until just before cooking – unfortunately, not all restaurants are so scrupulous.

Toilets

Some travellers have given up eating (for a while at least) just to avoid having to use Chinese toilets. Unfortunately, unless your stay in China is extremely brief, you'll have to learn to cope.

Public toilets in China are not the healthiest-looking places – basically they're holes in the ground or ditches over which you squat, and some look like they haven't been cleaned since the Han Dynasty. Many cannot be flushed at all while others are flushed with a conveniently placed bucket of water. Public toilets can often be found in railway stations and the side streets of the cities and towns – many now charge a fee of one or two jiao. Some have very low partitions (without doors) between the individual holes and some have none. Toilet paper is never provided – always keep a stash with you. Dormitory-style hotel rooms are also not equipped with toilet paper.

While it takes some practice to get proficient at balancing yourself over a squat toilet, at least you don't need to worry about whether the toilet seat is clean. Furthermore, experts who study such things (scatologists?) claim that the squatting position is better for your digestive system. Tourist hotels have Western-style 'sit-down' toilets, a luxury you will come to appreciate.

The issue of what to do with used toilet paper has caused some concern. One traveller wrote:

We are still not sure about the toilet paper...in two hotels they have been angry with us for flushing down the paper in the toilet. In other places it seems quite OK though.

In general, if you see a wastebasket next to the toilet, that is where you should throw the toilet paper. The problem is that in many hotels, the sewage system cannot handle toilet paper. This is especially true in old hotels where the antiquated plumbing system was designed in the pre-toilet paper era. Also, in rural areas there is no sewage treatment plant – the waste empties into an underground septic tank and toilet paper will really create a mess in there. For the sake of international relations, be considerate and throw the paper in the wastebasket.

Remember:

men 男

women 女

Other Precautions Sunglasses not only give you that fashionable Hollywood look, but will protect your eyes from the nasty UV rays in the deserts and high-altitude regions of Tibet. Invest in a good-quality pair – in other words, buy them abroad rather than in China. You should also use zinc cream or some other barrier cream for your nose and lips.

If you're sweating profusely, you're going to lose a lot of salt and that can lead to fatigue and muscle cramps for some people. If necessary you can make it up by putting extra salt or soy sauce in your food (a teaspoon a day is plenty), but don't increase your salt intake unless you also increase your water intake.

Everyday Health The normal body temperature is 98.6°F or 37°C; more than 2°C higher is a 'high' fever. A normal adult pulse rate is from 60 to 80 per minute (children from 80 to 100, babies from 100 to 140). You should know how to take a temperature and a pulse rate. As a general rule the pulse increases about 20 beats per minute for each 1°C rise in fever.

Respiration (breathing) rate is also an indicator of illness. Count the number of breaths per minute: between 12 and 20 is normal for adults and older children (up to 30 for younger children, 40 for babies). People with a high fever or serious respira-

tory illness (like pneumonia) breathe more quickly than normal. More than 40 shallow breaths a minute in an adult usually means pneumonia.

Medical Problems & Treatment
Self-diagnosis and treatment can be risky, so wherever possible seek qualified help. Although we give treatment dosages in this section, they are for emergency use only. Medical advice should be sought before administering any drugs.

Sunburn (shài shàng) It's very easy to get sunburnt at high elevations (Tibet), in the deserts (Xinjiang) or the tropics (Hainan Island). Sunburn can be more than just uncomfortable. Among the undesirable effects of frying your hide are premature skin-ageing and possible skin cancer in later years. Sunscreen (UV lotion), sunglasses and a wide-brimmed hat are good means of protection.

Heat Exhaustion (zhòng shǔ) Dehydration or salt deficiency can cause heat exhaustion. Take time to acclimatise to high temperatures and make sure you get sufficient liquids. Salt deficiency is characterised by fatigue, lethargy, headaches, giddiness and muscle cramps, and salt tablets may help. Vomiting or diarrhoea can deplete your liquid and salt levels. Anhydrotic heat exhaustion, caused by an inability to sweat, is quite rare. Unlike the other forms of heat exhaustion it is likely to strike people who have been in a hot climate for some time, rather than newcomers.

Heat Stroke This serious, sometimes fatal, condition can occur if the body's heat-regulating mechanism breaks down and the body temperature rises to dangerous levels. Long, continuous periods of exposure to high temperatures can leave you vulnerable to heat stroke. You should avoid excessive alcohol or strenuous activity when you first arrive in a hot climate.

The symptoms are feeling unwell, not sweating very much or at all and a high body temperature (39°C to 41°C). Where sweating has ceased the skin becomes flushed and red. Severe, throbbing headaches and lack of coordination will also occur, and the sufferer may be confused or aggressive. Eventually the victim will become delirious or convulse. Hospitalisation is essential, but meanwhile get them out of the sun, remove their clothing, cover them with a wet sheet or towel and then fan continually.

Fungal Infections (*pífū bìng*) The most common summertime affliction that visitors to China suffer from is skin disease. This is especially true in the south-east due to the hot, humid climate. The humidity is a bigger problem than the warm weather. The most common varieties of skin problems are 'jock itch' (a fungal infection around the groin), athlete's foot (known to the Chinese as 'Hong Kong feet'), contact dermatitis (caused by a necklace or watchband rubbing the skin) and prickly heat (caused by excessive sweating).

Prevention and treatment of these skin ailments is simply to keep the skin cool, clean, dry and free of abrasions.

For fungal infections, bathe twice daily and thoroughly dry yourself before getting dressed. Standing in front of the electric fan is a good way to get thoroughly dry. Apply an anti-fungal ointment or powder (ointments are better) to affected area – popular brand names are Desenex, Tinactin or Mycota, all available in Hong Kong.

If you're looking for an excuse to wear kinky underwear, this is it. Your underwear needs to be 'breathable' to reduce sweating, so that means light cotton or silk, or very thin 'see-through' nylon – or none at all.

Wear light, loose-fitting cotton clothing when the weather is really hot and humid – not only better for your skin, but also more comfortable. For athlete's foot, wearing open-toed sandals will often solve the problem without further treatment. Cleaning between the toes with warm soapy water and an old toothbrush also helps. Treat contact dermatitis by removing the offending necklace, bracelet or wristwatch. Avoid anything

that chafes the skin, such as tight clothing, especially elastic.

If your skin develops little painful red 'pinpricks', you probably have prickly heat. This is the result of excessive sweating which blocks the sweat ducts, causing inflammation. The treatment is the same – drying and cooling the skin. Bathe often, soak in hot soapy water to get the skin pores open, use a scrub brush to get really clean and dust yourself with talcum powder after drying off. Sleeping in an air-conditioned room will help, but such rooms can be difficult to find if you're on a budget. If all else fails, a trip to the high, cool mountains – or, ironically, to the hot, dry deserts – will do wonders for your itching skin.

Cold Winter in northern China is serious business. Too much cold is probably more dangerous than too much heat, and can lead to the fatal condition known as hypothermia. If you are trekking at high altitudes or simply taking a long bus trip over mountains, particularly at night, be prepared. In regions such as Tibet you should always be prepared for cold even during summer – when the clouds move in, the temperature can drop amazingly fast!

Hypothermia occurs when the body loses heat faster than it can produce it and the core temperature of the body falls. It is surprisingly easy to progress from very cold to dangerously cold due to a combination of wind, wet clothing, fatigue and hunger, even if the air temperature is above freezing. It is best to dress in layers; silk, wool and some high-tech artificial fibres are all good insulating materials. A hat is important, as a lot of heat is lost through the head. A strong, waterproof outer layer is essential, as keeping dry is vital. Carry basic supplies, including food containing simple sugars to generate heat quickly and lots of fluid to drink.

Symptoms of hypothermia are exhaustion, numb skin (particularly toes and fingers), shivering, slurred speech, irrational or violent behaviour, lethargy, stumbling, dizzy spells, muscle cramps and violent bursts of energy. Irrationality may take the form of sufferers claiming they are warm and trying to take off their clothes.

To treat hypothermia, first get the patient out of the wind and/or rain, remove their clothing if it's wet and replace it with dry, warm clothing. Give them hot liquids – not alcohol – and some high-energy, easily digestible food. This should be enough for the early stages of hypothermia, but if it has gone further it may be necessary to place the victim in a warm sleeping bag and get in with them. Do not rub them. Hypothermia dulls sensitivity to pain, and putting someone too near a fire or stove can easily cause burns without anyone realising it. Ditto for putting someone in a too hot bath – you may wind up parboiling them.

Altitude Sickness (*gāo shān fǎnyìng*) Tibet has a few problems all of its own caused by high altitude and thin air. Acute Mountain Sickness (AMS) is the most common problem. Rapid ascent from low altitudes, overexertion, lack of physical fitness, dehydration and fatigue will make it worse. A climber who is elderly, sick or obese is at greater risk. Symptoms include headache, dizziness, lack of appetite, nausea and vomiting. Breathlessness, sleeplessness and a pounding heart are normal at these altitudes and are not part of AMS. If you spend enough time at high elevations, your body will eventually start making more blood cells to carry extra oxygen. If you get altitude sickness, the best cure is to go to a lower altitude. A pain-killer for headache and an anti-emetic for vomiting will also help. The best prevention is to ascend slowly and avoid overexertion in the beginning. Aerobic exercises are good preparation for a trip to high elevations.

AMS is unpleasant, but a far more serious complication is high-altitude pulmonary oedema. This is usually only seen at elevations above 3000 metres about 24 to 72 hours after ascent. Symptoms include coughing up frothy sputum, which usually progresses from white to pink to bloody. A rattling sound in the chest can be heard, often without a stethoscope. The symptoms might be mistaken for pneumonia, but the suddenness of their appearance in a rapidly ascending climber should make you suspect pulmonary oedema. *This is a medical emergency!* Coma and death can follow rapidly – the only effective treatment is to get the victim to a lower elevation as soon as possible. Oxygen helps a little, but only if it's given in the early stages.

Motion Sickness (*yùnchē*) The Chinese are unusually prone to motion sickness – if the person next to you on the bus or ferry starts looking green, move away quickly! Eating lightly before and during a trip will reduce the chances of motion sickness, but the Chinese have the exact opposite idea – the more they throw up, the more they eat.

If you are prone to motion sickness try to find a place that minimises disturbance – near the wing on aircraft, close to midships on boats, near the centre on buses. Fresh air usually helps, reading and cigarette smoke don't. Commercial anti-motion-sickness preparations, which can cause drowsiness, have to be taken before the trip commences; when you're feeling sick it's too late. Ginger is a natural preventative and is available in capsule form.

Diarrhoea (*lā dùzi*) Travellers' diarrhoea has been around a long time – even Marco Polo had it. Diarrhoea is often due simply to a change of diet or bacteria or minerals in the local water which your system is not used to. If you do get diarrhoea, the first thing to do is wait – it rarely lasts more than a few days.

Diarrhoea will cause you to dehydrate, which will make you feel much worse. The solution is not simply to drink water, since it will run right through you. You'll get much better results by mixing your water with oral rehydration salt, a combination of salts (both NaCl and KCl) and glucose. Dissolve the powder in *cool* water (never hot!) and drink, but don't use it if the powder is wet. The quantity of water is specified on the packet. Oralit is also useful for treating heat exhaustion caused by excessive sweating.

If the diarrhoea persists then the usual treatment is Lomotil or Imodium tablets. The maximum dose for Lomotil is two tablets three times a day. Both Lomotil and Imodium are prescription drugs in the West, but are available over the counter in most Asian countries. However, neither is available in China – a good Chinese equivalent is berberine hydrochloride (huáng liǎn sù). Anti-diarrhoeal drugs don't cure anything, but slow down the digestive system so that the cramps go away and you don't have to go to the toilet all the time. Excessive use of these drugs is not advised, as they can cause dependency and other side effects. Furthermore, the diarrhoea serves one useful purpose – it helps the body expel unwanted bacteria.

Activated charcoal – while not actually considered a drug – can provide much relief from diarrhoea and is a time-honoured treatment.

Fruit juice, tea and coffee can aggravate diarrhoea – again, water with oral rehydration salts is the best drink. It will help tremendously if you eat a light, fibre-free diet. Yoghurt or boiled eggs with salt are basic staples for diarrhoea patients. Later you may be able to tolerate rice porridge or plain white rice. Keep away from vegetables, fruits and greasy foods for a while. If you suddenly decide to pig-out on spicy hot Sichuan food, you'll be back to square one. If the diarrhoea persists for a week or more, it's probably not simple travellers' diarrhoea – it could be dysentery and it might be wise to see a doctor.

Giardia (āmǐbā fùxiè) This is another type of amoeba which causes severe diarrhoea, nausea and weakness, but doesn't produce blood in the stool or cause fever. Unlike amoebic dysentery which is most common in the tropics, giardia is found in mountainous and cold regions. Epidemics have been reported in Zermatt, Switzerland; Aspen, Colorado (USA); Leningrad (St Petersburg) in Russia; and Tibet. Mountaineers often suffer from this problem. Just brushing your teeth using contaminated water is sufficient to make you get it. Many kinds of mammals harbour this parasite, so you can get it easily from drinking 'pure mountain water' unless the area is devoid of animals.

Although the symptoms are similar to amoebic dysentery, giardia will not migrate to the liver and other organs – it stays in the intestine and therefore is much less likely to cause long-term health problems.

It can only be cured with an anti-amoebic drug like metronidazole (Flagyl) – again, never drink alcohol while taking Flagyl. Without treatment, the symptoms may subside and you might feel fine for awhile, but the illness will return again and again, making your life miserable.

To treat giardia, the proper dosage of Flagyl is different than for amoebic dysentery. Take one 250 mg tablet three times daily for 10 days. It can sometimes be difficult to rid yourself of giardia, so you might need laboratory tests to be certain you're cured.

Flagyl is not easily obtained in China, though equivalent drugs are available in places like Lhasa where giardia is common. If you're going to be travelling in high mountain areas, it might be prudent to keep your own stock with you.

Dysentery This is not very common in China – many travellers seem to think they have dysentery when all they have is normal diarrhoea.

Bacillary Dysentery Diarrhoea with blood or pus and fever is usually bacillary dysentery. Since it's caused by bacteria infecting the gut, it can be treated with antibiotics like tetracycline, or a sulfa drug, but before you role out the heavy artillery, be sure you've really got this disease. If you do take tetracycline, the usual dose is 250 mg tablets, taken four times daily for about a week. In most cases, bacillary dysentery will eventually clear up without treatment – the exception might be children, who seem to be more vulnerable to this type of infection. Be sure to use water with rehydration salts to prevent dehydration.

Amoebic Dysentery Diarrhoea with blood or pus but without fever is usually amoebic dysentery. This is a disease you should not neglect because it will not go away by itself. In addition, if you don't wipe out the amoeba while they are still in your intestine, they will eventually migrate to the liver and other organs, causing abscesses which could require surgery. Again, it is not common in China, but is easily mistaken for giardia (which *is* common in China – see next section).

The most sure-fire cure for amoebic dysentery is metronidazole (Flagyl), an anti-amoebic drug. It will wipe out amoeba no matter where they reside in the body, even in the liver and other organs. The dosage is three 250 mg tablets (750 mg) three times daily for seven to 10 days. Flagyl is also available in 500 mg tablets, so in that case you take 1½ tablets per dose. If you take Flagyl, *do not* under any circumstances consume alcohol at the same time – not a drop! Flagyl and alcohol together can cause a severe reaction.

Cholera It's not a big problem in China, but cholera tends to travel in epidemics (usually after floods, especially during summer) and outbreaks are widely reported, so you can often avoid problem areas. This is a disease of insanitation, so if you've heard reports of cholera be especially careful about what you eat, drink and brush your teeth with.

Symptoms include a sudden onset of acute diarrhoea with 'rice water' stools, vomiting, muscular cramps, and extreme weakness. You need medical help – but treat for dehydration, which can be extreme, and if there is an appreciable delay in getting to hospital then begin taking tetracycline. See the Dysentery section for dosages and warnings.

Cholera vaccination is not very effective but is still recommended because it will reduce the severity of the disease. The vaccine is only useful for about four to six months, so get the vaccination just before beginning your trip and be revaccinated as often as necessary. The vaccination is cheap and widely available from public health clinics throughout Asia.

Hepatitis *(gān yán)* Hepatitis is a disease which affects the liver. There are several varieties, most commonly hepatitis A and B.

Hepatitis A This occurs in countries with poor sanitation – this would have to include the backward parts of China. It's spread from person to person via infected food or water, or contaminated cooking and eating utensils.

Hepatitis is often spread in China due to the Chinese custom of everybody eating from a single dish rather than using separate plates and a serving spoon. It is a wise decision to use the disposable chopsticks now freely available in most restaurants in China, or else buy your own chopsticks and spoon.

Symptoms appear 15 to 50 days after infection (generally around 25 days) and consist of fever, loss of appetite, nausea, depression, complete lack of energy, and pains around the bottom of your rib cage (the location of the liver). Your skin turns progressively yellow and the whites of your eyes change from white to yellow to orange.

The best way to detect hepatitis is to watch the colour of your urine, which will turn a deep orange no matter how much liquid you drink. If you haven't drunk much liquid and/or you're sweating a lot, don't jump to conclusions since you may just be dehydrated.

The severity of hepatitis A varies; it may last less than two weeks and give you only a few bad days, or it may last for several months and give you a few bad weeks. You could feel depleted of energy for several months afterwards. If you get hepatitis, rest and good food is the only cure; don't use alcohol or tobacco since that only gives your liver more work to do. It's important to keep up your food intake to assist recovery.

A vaccine for hepatitis A came on the market in 1992. At the time of writing it was available in Hong Kong (two shots, two weeks apart). Check with your doctor.

Hepatitis B This is transmitted in the same

three ways as the AIDS (HIV) virus: by sexual intercourse; by contaminated needles; or, in the case of infants, by being inherited from an infected mother. Some Chinese 'health clinics' re-use needles without proper sterilisation – no one knows how many people have been infected this way. Acupuncture can also spread the disease.

There is a vaccine for hepatitis B, but it must be given before you've been exposed. Once you've got the virus, you're a carrier for life and the vaccine is useless. Therefore, you need a blood test before the vaccine is administered to determine if you're a carrier. The vaccine requires three injections each given a month apart, and it's wise to get a booster every few years thereafter. Unfortunately, the vaccine is expensive.

Other Recent research has found other varieties of hepatitis of which little is yet known. Hepatitis C and other strains are considered serious. Fortunately, these are usually spread by blood transfusions and therefore are not diseases that you're going to pick up through casual contact.

Typhoid Typhoid fever is another gut infection transmitted in contaminated water and food. Like cholera, epidemics can occur after floods because of sewage backing up into drinking water supplies. Vaccination against typhoid is useful but not totally effective and it is one of the most dangerous infections, so medical help must be sought.

In the early stages of infection, typhoid victims may feel like they have a bad cold or flu on the way, as early symptoms are a headache, a sore throat, and a fever which rises a little each day until it is around 40°C or more. Without treatment, the illness will either kill you or begin to subside by the third week.

Chloramphenicol is the recommended antibiotic but there are fewer side effects with ampicillin. The adult dosage is two 250 mg capsules, four times a day. Children aged between eight and 12 years should have half the adult dose; younger children should have one-third the adult dose.

Patients who are allergic to penicillin should not be given ampicillin.

Polio Polio is also a disease spread by insanitation and is found more frequently in hot climates. The effects on children can be especially devastating – they can be crippled for life. An excellent vaccination is available, and a booster every five years is recommended.

Diseases Spread by People & Animals

Respiratory Infection The China Syndrome (*liúxíngxìng gǎnmào*), the greatest hazard to your health in China, is a host of respiratory infections which we normally call 'the flu' or just 'the common cold'. You may have heard of the 'Shanghai flu', or various other influenza strains named after Chinese cities. The fact is that China is one vast reservoir of respiratory viruses and practically the entire population is stricken during the winter, but even during the summer it's easy to get ill.

What distinguishes the Chinese flu from the Western variety is the severity and the fact that the condition persists for months rather than days. Like any bad cold, it starts with a fever, chills, weakness, sore throat and a feeling of malaise normally lasting a few days. After that, a prolonged case of coughing and bronchitis sets in, characterised by coughing up large quantities of thick green phlegm, occasionally with little red streaks (blood). It's the bronchitis that really gets you – it makes sleep almost impossible, and this exhausting state of affairs can continue for as long as you stay in the country. Sometimes it even leads to pneumonia.

Why is it such a serious problem in China? Respiratory infections are aggravated by cold weather, air pollution, chain-smoking and overcrowded conditions which increase the opportunity for infection. But the main reason is that Chinese people spit a lot, thereby spreading the disease. It's a vicious circle: they're sick because they spit and they spit because they're sick.

During the initial phase of influenza, bed rest, drinking warm liquids and keeping warm are helpful. The Chinese treat bronchitis with a powder made from the gall bladder of snakes – a treatment of questionable value, but there's probably no harm in trying it. If you continue to cough up green phlegm, run a fever and can't seem to get well, it's time to roll out the heavy artillery – you can nuke it with antibiotics. Tetracycline (250 mg) taken orally four times daily for a minimum of five days is usually highly effective, but note the previously mentioned warnings about using antibiotics.

Finally, if you can't get well in China, leave the country and take a nice holiday on a warm beach in Thailand.

No vaccine offers complete protection, but there are vaccines against influenza and pneumococcal pneumonia which might help. The influenza vaccine is good for no more than a year.

Tetanus (*pò shāng fēng*) There seem to be quite a few motor accidents in rural China. Although there is no vaccination that can protect your bus from getting hit by a logging truck, it would be prudent to get a tetanus vaccination before your arrival in China. If you've already been vaccinated once, you still need a booster every five years to maintain immunity.

Rabies (*kuángquǎn bìng*) China still has a serious problem with this, but the Communists deserve much credit for greatly reducing the threat. Since the Communists came to power in 1949, one of their accomplishments has been to wipe out systematically most of the stray dogs which used to roam the streets of China. This was done to control rabies, improve sanitation and preserve food. While dog lovers may not be impressed by these arguments, it's instructive to visit other poor Third World countries where disease-ridden wild dogs roam the streets, often to end their lives by starving to death.

Although the Chinese have reduced the canine population considerably, packs of wild dogs are still common in Tibetan villages and they are indeed dangerous. Other mammals, such as rats, can also transmit the rabies virus to humans. Also, if you have a scratch, cut or other break in the skin you could catch rabies if an infected animal licked that break in the skin.

If you are bitten by an animal that may be rabid, try to get the wound flushed out immediately with soapy water. It would be prudent to seek professional treatment since rabies carries a nearly 100% fatality rate if it reaches the brain. How long you have from the time of being bitten until it's too late varies – anywhere from 10 days to a year depending on where you were bitten. Those bitten around the face and upper part of the body are in the most immediate danger. Don't wait for symptoms to occur – if you think there's good chance that you've been bitten by a rabid animal, get medical attention promptly, even if it means leaving China.

By all accounts, rabies is a horrible way to go. As the disease works its way through the nervous system towards the brain, the patient experiences terribly painful muscle spasms, especially around the throat. It becomes impossible to drink water – thus, rabies is sometimes called 'hydrophobia'. Death usually occurs from paralysis of the breathing muscles.

A pre-exposure vaccine for rabies exists, though few people bother to get it because the risk of infection is so low. The vaccine will not give you 100% immunity, but will greatly extend the time you have for seeking treatment, and the treatment will not need to be nearly so extensive. If you're planning to travel in the Chinese countryside, and especially in Tibet, this might be worth considering.

Tuberculosis (*jiéhé bìng*) The tuberculosis (TB) bacteria is transmitted by inhalation. Coughing spreads infectious droplets into the air. In closed, crowded spaces with poor ventilation (like a train compartment), the air can remain contaminated for some time. In overcrowded China, it's not hard to see why infection rates are amongst the highest in the world.

In the developed world, TB is usually a relatively mild infection; many people have it at some time in their lives without noticing it, and retain a natural immunity afterwards.

The disease is opportunistic – the patient feels fine, but the disease suddenly becomes active when the body is weakened by other factors such as injury, poor nutrition, surgery or old age. It's now spreading rapidly in the developed world, thanks to AIDS and drug abuse, both of which lower natural immunity – people who are in good health are unlikely to catch the disease. It strikes at the lungs and the fatality rate once it is well established in the body is about 10%.

There are good drugs to treat TB, but prevention is the best cure. If you're only going to be in China for a short time there is no need to be overly worried. TB is usually developed after repeated exposures by people who are not well nourished. Budget travellers – those who often spend a long time staying in cramped dormitories and travelling on crowded buses and trains – are at greater risk than tourists who remain relatively isolated in big hotels and tour buses.

The effective vaccine for TB is called BCG and is most often given to schoolchildren because it must be taken before infection occurs. If you want to be vaccinated, you first must be tested to see if you are already immune from a previous infection – if you are, the vaccination will not be necessary. It is thought to be less effective in adults over 35. The only disadvantage of the vaccine is that, once given, the recipient will always test positive with the TB skin test. Even if you never travel, the TB vaccine could be useful – the disease is increasing worldwide.

Eye Infection Trachoma is a common eye infection which is easily spread by contaminated towels (the kind handed out by restaurants and airlines). The best advice about wiping your face is to use disposable tissue paper. If you think you have trachoma, you need to see a doctor – the disease can damage your vision if untreated. Trachoma is normally treated with antibiotic eye oint-

ments for about four to six weeks. Be careful about diagnosing yourself – simple allergies can produce symptoms similar to eye infections, and in this case antibiotics can do more harm than good.

Sexually Transmitted Disease (STD) The Chinese government for decades pretended that prostitution, premarital and extramarital sex simply didn't exist in the PRC, and that sexually transmitted diseases were a foreign problem.

The Cultural Revolution may be over, but the sexual revolution is blooming in China and STDs are spreading rapidly. Gonorrhoea and syphilis are the most common of these diseases; sores, blisters or rashes around the genitals, discharges or pain when urinating are common symptoms. Symptoms may be less marked or not observed at all in women. Syphilis symptoms eventually disappear completely but the disease continues and can cause severe problems in later years, and if untreated can be fatal. The treatment of gonorrhoea and syphilis is by antibiotics.

There are numerous other sexually transmitted diseases, for most of which effective treatment is available. However, there is neither a cure nor a vaccine for herpes and AIDS. Outside of sexual abstinence, using condoms is the most effective preventative. Condoms are available in China – the word is *băoxiăn tào* which literally translates as 'insurance glove'.

The government announced in early 1993 that foreigners with more than 12 Chinese entry stamps in their passports would have to undergo 'five-minute AIDS tests' right at the border crossing! Exactly how crossing the border 12 times could cause AIDS has not been explained. It seems that Hong Kongers, Taiwanese and others of 'Chinese descent' do not need to undergo the tests – apparently, they are immune to AIDS. There is much suspicion that the real intention was to rake in a little more cash – foreigners must pay for the tests. Whether or not a five-minute AIDS test is accurate has been hotly debated, and at the time of writing it was far from clear whether the rule would actually be enforced or quietly discarded.

The HIV (AIDS) virus can also be spread through infected blood transfusions; most developing countries cannot afford to screen blood for transfusions. It can also be spread by dirty needles – vaccinations, acupuncture, ear piercing and tattooing can potentially be as dangerous as intravenous drug use if the equipment is not clean.

Malaria *(nüèjì)* Malaria is not a big problem in China and you shouldn't worry about it excessively. However, in summer there is a risk in much of southern China, and a year-round risk in tropical regions like Yunnan and Hainan Island.

The parasite that causes this disease is spread by the bite of the *Anopheles* mosquito, though it *rarely* gets passed by blood transfusion. Malaria has a nasty habit of recurring in later years, even if you're cured at the time.

In the 1950s, the World Health Organization (WHO) launched a two-prong attack against malaria, spraying with the pesticide DDT and treating victims with the drug chloroquine. Health authorities confidently predicted that by the year 2000, the malaria parasite would be extinct.

It hasn't worked out that way. The mosquitoes developed resistance against DDT and the malaria parasite developed resistance to chloroquine. Aside from breeding super-mosquitoes, DDT has also proven harmful to the environment and human health. For a while it seemed that the war against malaria was being won; now it is obvious that malaria is staging a comeback and the risk to travellers is increasing.

There are four different types of malaria, but 95% of all cases are one of two varieties: *P vivax* and *P falciparum*. The other two rare types of malaria are similar to *P vivax*.

P vivax malaria is the main type found in China, and although the symptoms are nasty indeed, it is not considered dangerous to life. However, if not adequately treated, the illness will continue to recur, causing chronic ill health.

P falciparum malaria is relatively rare in China but very common in south and southeast Asia. The illness develops 10 to 14 days after being bitten by the mosquito and symptoms consist of high fever with alternate shivering and sweating, intense headaches, and usually nausea or vomiting. Without treatment the condition is fatal within two weeks in up to 25% of cases. It is this variety of malaria which is now showing widespread resistance to the most common antimalarial drug, chloroquine.

The locals have some natural immunity to malaria resulting from generations of exposure; foreigners from non-malarial countries have no such resistance. While it is not yet possible to be inoculated against malaria, limited protection is simple; either a daily or weekly tablet (the latter is more common). The tablets kill the parasites in your bloodstream before they have a chance to multiply and cause illness.

If you're travelling with children or if you're pregnant then the story with antimalarial tablets is more complex (see Lonely Planet's *Travel with Children* for more details). Basically, some antimalarials may stay in your system for up to a year after the last dose is taken and may cause birth defects. So if you get pregnant or are planning to get pregnant within 12 months of taking antimalarials your unborn child could be endangered. It's advisable to check with your physician. With newer drugs there's not much information around on the effects of long-term use. It should be noted that malaria *can* be passed from mother to child at birth. The best precaution is to avoid being bitten in the first place. The *Anopheles* mosquito is only a problem at night. Some Chinese hotels have mosquito nets *(wénzhàang)*. Mosquito repellent is available but you may have trouble finding it, so bring your own. Mosquito coils are readily available *(wénxiāng)*, but a more modern innovation are the 'electric mosquito pads' *(diàn wénxiāng)* on sale at Chinese department stores.

Treating malaria is complicated and something you should not undertake yourself except in an emergency. Blood tests are needed to determine if you in fact have malaria rather than dengue fever (see next section), and the choice of drugs depends on how well you react to them.

For prevention, the most common anti-malarial drugs are chloroquine, maloprim and doxycycline (the latter for very short-term use only), but new drugs are constantly under development. Chloroquine and maloprim are often prescribed by doctors to be taken in combination in order to guard against resistance to either one, but in the long-term this is not a good practice. For China, chloroquine alone should be adequate (not guaranteed though). The Chinese have come up with their own homegrown drug (*qing haosu* – artemesinine) for treating (but not preventing) malaria.

Many travellers are confused about what they should and should not be taking for malaria prevention – you should definitely consult a doctor before taking anything. A brief rundown on common antimalarial drugs follows (note that all dosages are for adults):

Chloroquine The most commonly prescribed drug for malaria prevention, it is extremely effective against *P vivax* malaria but only about 60% effective against *F falciparum*. Chloroquine is safe in pregnancy. Long-term use (over five years) of chloroquine has caused permanent retinal damage to the eyes in some people. Other side effects which have been reported include nausea, dizziness, headache, blurred vision, confusion, and itching, but such problems are rare.

Herbal Medicine

Many foreigners visiting China never try Chinese herbal medicine (*zhōng yào*) because they either know nothing about it or simply don't believe in it. Prominent medical authorities in the West often dismiss herbalists as no better than witch doctors. The ingredients, which may include such marvellous things as snake gall bladder or powdered deer antlers, will further discourage potential non-Chinese customers. Many of the herbs are bitter powders (you may want to load these into empty gelatine capsules if you can't stand the taste). And finally, even true believers are baffled by the wide assortment of herbs available on the shelves of any Chinese pharmacy – it's hard to know where to begin.

Having experimented with Chinese herbs ourselves, we've found several of them to be remarkably effective, but some warnings are in order. Chinese herbalists have all sorts of treatments for stomachaches, headaches, colds, flu and sore throat. They also have herbs to treat long-term problems like asthma. While many of these herbs seem to work, it's much less certain whether Chinese medicine can cure serious illnesses like cancer and heart disease. All sorts of overblown claims have been made for herbal medicines, especially by those who make and sell them. Some gullible Westerners have persuaded themselves that Chinese doctors can cure any disease. A visit to any of China's hospitals will quickly shatter this myth.

Chinese medicine seems to work best for the relief of unpleasant symptoms (pain, sore throat, etc) and for some long-term conditions which resist Western medicines, such as migraine headaches, asthma and chronic backache. But for acute life-threatening conditions, such as a heart attack, it would be foolish to trust your life to herbs.

When reading about the theory behind Chinese medicine, the word 'holistic' appears often. Basically, this means that Chinese medicine seeks to treat the whole body rather than focusing on a particular organ or disease.

Using appendicitis as an example, a Chinese doctor may try to fight the infections using the body's whole defences, whereas a Western doctor would simply cut out the appendix. While the holistic method sounds great in theory, in practice the Western technique of attacking the problem directly often works better. In the case of appendicitis, removing the appendix surgically is 100% effective, though there is always some risk from the surgical procedure itself. On the other hand, in the case of migraine headaches, Chinese herbs may actually prove more effective than Western medical treatments.

Another point to be wary of when taking herbal medicine is the tendency of some manufacturers to falsely claim that their product contains numerous potent and expensive ingredients. For example, some herbal formulas may list rhinoceros horn as an ingredient. Rhinoceros horn, widely acclaimed by herbalists as a cure for fever, is so rare and so expensive that it is practically impossible to buy. Any formula listing rhinoceros horn may, at best, contain water buffalo horn. In

Chloroquine tablets are available in at least two sizes, small (250 mg) or large (500 mg). Make sure you know which you have. The preventative dose is 500 mg weekly (either two small tablets or one large). You have to start taking the tablets two weeks before entering the malarial zone and continue taking them for about four to six weeks after you've left it.

Chloroquine can be used as a treatment for *P vivax*. Treatment dose is 1000 mg initially, then 500 mg at six, 24 and 48 hours.

Maloprim This is an effective malarial preventative especially if combined with chloroquine, but it's expensive. This drug can cause severe (even life-threatening) allergic reactions in sensitive people. Because of the danger of such side effects, maloprim should be taken only once a week even though higher dosages would be more effective. It is not recommended during pregnancy. Long-term use (over three months) can reduce the white blood cell count in some people.

Doxycycline This is a good preventative for the short-term (under one month) traveller. It's definitely not recommended for long-term use.

Doxycycline is a long-acting tetracycline (antibiotic). It is not recommended during pregnancy, breastfeeding or for children under age the age of 10. Side effects include nausea, photosensitivity (severe sunburn) and vaginal yeast infections in women. It should not be taken with milk products.

The preventative dose is 100 mg (one pill) daily. You should start taking doxycycline the day you enter the malarial area, and stop taking it the day you leave. Doxycycline is often taken in combination with chloroquine.

Fansidar This is an effective treatment against *P falciparum* malaria but fansidar is a poor drug against *P vivax*. It is only used as a treatment (not a preventative) because of the risk of severe allergic reactions. Also it is not recommended during pregnancy, espe-

any case, the rhino is a rare and endangered species, and you will not wish to hasten its extinction by demanding rhino-horn products.

Another benefit of Chinese medicine is that there are relatively few side effects. Compared to a drug like penicillin which can produce allergic reactions and other serious side effects, herbal medicines are fairly safe. Nevertheless, herbs are still medicines, not candy, and there is no need to take them if you're feeling fine to begin with. Many Westerners believe that herbs are harmless. In fact, some herbs are mildly toxic, and if taken over a long period of time can actually damage the liver and other organs.

Before shopping for herbs, keep in mind that in Western medicine, doctors talk about broad-spectrum antibiotics, such as penicillin, which are good for treating a wide range of infections. But for many illnesses, a specific antibiotic might be better for a specific type of infection. The same is true in Chinese medicine. A broad-spectrum remedy such as snake gall bladder may be good for treating colds, but there are many different types of colds. The best way to treat a cold with herbal medicine is to see a Chinese doctor and get a specific prescription. Otherwise, the herbs you take may not be the most appropriate for your condition. However, if you can't get to a doctor, you can just try your luck at the pharmacy.

If you visit a Chinese doctor, you might be surprised by what he or she discovers about your body. For example, the doctor will almost certainly take your pulse and then may tell you that you have a slippery pulse or perhaps a thready pulse. Chinese doctors have identified more than 30 different kinds of pulses. A pulse could be empty, prison, leisurely, bowstring, irregular or even regularly irregular. The doctor may then examine your tongue to see if it is slippery, dry, pale, greasy, has a thick coating or maybe no coating at all. The doctor, having discovered that you have wet heat, as evidenced by a slippery pulse and a red greasy tongue, will prescribe the herbs for your condition.

One problem with buying herbs is that there are many fake pharmaceuticals on the market. Counterfeiting is common in China, and the problem extends even to medications. If the herbs you take seem to be totally ineffective, it may be because you've bought sugar pills rather than medicine.

If you spend a good deal of time on buses and boats, you'll get to see how the Chinese deal with motion sickness, nausea and headaches – usually by smearing liniments on their stomach or head. If you want to try these yourself, there are many brands on the market – look for qīng liáng yóu and fēng yóu, or White Flower Oil (bái huā yóu) which comes from Hong Kong. A variation on the theme are salves, the most famous being 'Tiger Balm' which also comes from Hong Kong. And should you strain yourself carrying that heavy backpack around, try applying 'sticky dog skin plaster' (gǒu pí gāo yào) to your sore muscles. You might be relieved to know that these days it's no longer made from real dog skin! ■

cially the last trimester. It should not be taken at all if there is a history of sulfa allergy.

For treatment, three tablets are taken in a single dose. Fansidar is usually taken in combination with quinine.

Quinine This is the drug of choice for treating severe and resistant *P falciparum* malaria and cerebral malaria. It should only be used as a treatment, never as preventative. There is some resistance to quinine and it is a bit less effective against *P vivax* than chloroquine.

Qing Haosu (Artemesinine) This herbal medicine from China has generated much interest in medical circles recently. Qing haosu has been known since at least the 4th century when it was used to treat fevers, but only recently has its antimalarial properties been established. It's important to note that just because this is an 'herbal medicine' does not mean it's harmless. Quinine – made from the bark of the cinchona tree – is also a herbal medicine but it is certainly not harmless. At the time of writing, qing haosu was only available in China because studies have not yet been completed to determine the proper dosage and possible side effects. Preliminary testing in animals suggest it is toxic to the fetus and therefore not recommended in pregnancy.

Dengue Fever This is a mosquito-borne disease which resembles malaria, but is not fatal and doesn't recur once the illness has passed. It is fairly common in parts of southern China during summer, and there have even been outbreaks in Taiwan.

A high fever, severe headache and pains in the joints are the usual symptoms – the aches are so bad that the disease is also called breakbone fever. The fever usually lasts two to three days, then subsides, then comes back again and takes several weeks to pass. People who have had this disease say it feels like imminent death.

Despite the malaria-like symptoms, antimalarial drugs have no effect whatsoever on dengue fever. Only the symptoms can be treated, usually with complete bed rest, aspirin, codeine and an intravenous drip. There is no means of prevention other than to avoid getting bitten by mosquitoes, but once you've had dengue fever, you're immune for about a year. The patient should be kept under a mosquito net until after the fever passes – otherwise there is the risk of infecting others.

Cuts & Bites Take good care of all cuts and scratches. In the subtropical south they take longer to heal and can easily get infected. Treat any cut with care; wash it out with sterilised water, preferably with an antiseptic (Betadine) keep it dry and keep an eye on it. It would be worth bringing an antibiotic cream with you. Cuts on your feet and ankles are particularly troublesome – a new pair of sandals can quickly give you a nasty abrasion which can be difficult to heal. For the same reason, try not to scratch mosquito bites.

Snakes China has a variety of poisonous snakes, the most famous being cobras. *All* sea snakes are poisonous and are readily identified by their flat tails, but opportunities for ocean swimming in China are few and far between. Thanks to American cowboy movies, people often associate snakes with the desert, but they are in fact most common in forested areas, where they have more to eat.

Snakes are not generally aggressive with creatures larger than themselves – they won't chase after you, but they can get nasty if you corner or step on them. To minimise your chances of being bitten while hiking, wear boots, socks and long trousers when walking through undergrowth where snakes may be present. Don't put your hands into holes and crevices.

Snake bites do not cause instantaneous death and antivenins are usually available. Keep the victim calm (sounds easier than it is), wrap the bitten limb tightly, as you would for a sprained ankle, and then attach a splint to immobilise it. Don't wash the wound; any venom remaining on the skin can be used to identify the snake. Then seek medical help, if possible with the dead snake for identification. Don't attempt to catch the snake if there is even a remote possibility of being bitten again. Tourniquets, sucking out the poison and submersion in cold water are now comprehensively discredited.

Bedbugs & Lice Bedbugs live in various places, but particularly in dirty mattresses and bedding. Spots of blood on bedclothes or on the wall around the bed can be read as a suggestion to find another hotel. Bedbugs leave itchy bites in neat rows that swell up, but they generally heal quickly if you don't scratch.

All lice cause itching and discomfort. They make themselves at home in your hair (head lice), your clothing (body lice) or in your pubic hair (crabs). You catch lice through direct contact with infected people or by sharing combs, clothing and the like. Powder or shampoo treatment will kill the lice and infected clothing should then be washed in very hot water.

Women's Health

Gynaecological Problems Poor diet, lowered resistance due to the use of antibiotics for stomach upsets and even contraceptive pills can lead to vaginal infections when travelling in hot climates. Keeping the genital area clean, and wearing skirts or loose-fitting trousers and cotton underwear will help to prevent infections.

Yeast infections, characterised by a rash, itch and discharge, can be treated with a vinegar or even lemon-juice douche or with yoghurt. Nystatin suppositories are the usual medical prescription. Trichomonas is a more serious infection; symptoms are a discharge and a burning sensation when urinating. Male sexual partners must also be treated, and if a vinegar-water douche is not effective medical attention should be sought. Flagyl is the prescribed drug.

The Chinese have various herbal tonics for women only. To help with anaemia and menstrual problems, you could try *sì wù tāng*.

Pregnancy The first four months of pregnancy can be a risky time to travel in remote areas as far as your own health is concerned, as most miscarriages happen during this time and they can occasionally be dangerous. The last three months should be spent within reasonable distance of good medical care. A premature baby will stand a chance of survival as early as 24 weeks if it is born in a well-equipped hospital.

Pregnant women should avoid all unnecessary medication, but vaccinations and malarial prophylactics should still be taken where possible. Check with your physician before embarking on your trip. Additional care should be taken to prevent illness and particular attention should be paid to diet and nutrition. Alcohol, nicotine and other drugs are to be avoided, particularly during the first four months of pregnancy.

WOMEN TRAVELLERS

In general, foreign women are unlikely to suffer serious sexual harassment in China, but there have been reports of problems in Xinjiang (a Muslim area). Wherever you are, it's worth noticing what local women are wearing and how they are behaving, and making a bit of an effort to fit in, as you would in any other foreign country.

We've heard of foreign women being harassed by Chinese men in Beijing's parks or while cycling alone at night, but rape (of foreign women) is not common. This doesn't mean it cannot happen, but most Chinese rapists appear to prefer Chinese victims. The police tend to investigate crimes against foreigners much more closely and more severe penalties (like execution) are imposed if the perpetrator is caught – this provides foreign women with a small but important aura of protection.

Wearing see-through blouses, skimpy shorts or bikinis and going topless at the beach is asking for trouble. While city people in China are hip to the latest fashions (including miniskirts), the countryside is much more conservative. If you want to play safe, wear trousers or a below-the-knee skirt, with a shirt that covers your shoulders. For outdoor wear, sandals are acceptable but thongs (flip flops) are not.

DANGERS & ANNOYANCES
Crime & Punishment

Fictional stories from the official Chinese press paint a picture of exemplary honesty – including the Beijing shop assistant who inadvertently shortchanged a foreign tourist and finally managed to track him down in Lhasa through an advertisement she inserted in the *China Daily*. Another legend involves a foreign businessman who decided to discard a pair of trousers in his hotel room before catching a taxi to the airport. Just as his flight was called, a breathless room-attendant came racing into the airport carrying the trousers. A second attempt to jettison the trousers in another hotel met with the same defeat.

The reality is very different. There is crime in China, as anywhere else in the world, but you can usually avoid trouble by taking simple precautions. It's safer to travel through China than through many other poor countries. Nevertheless, a level of prudence regarding both the safety of yourself and your property is worth maintaining.

Pickpocketing is the most common form of theft and the one you need to carefully guard against. Some thieves may even try to grab your bag and run away, but more common is razoring of bags and pockets in crowded places like buses. Certain cities are worse than others – Canton is notorious. A few travellers have even received serious wounds when poorly skilled pickpockets cut a little too deep in order to get at a money belt.

Since buses in China are usually so packed that passengers are virtually jammed into each other's pockets, there's plenty of scope for theft. If you want to avoid opening wallets or bags on the bus, keep a few coins or small notes ready in an accessible pocket before launching yourself onto the bus. Be careful when sleeping on trains, especially in the hard-seat section – make sure that the pocket with the money is wedged up against the wall, floor or your backpack.

Be careful in public toilets – quite a few foreigners have laid aside their valuables, squatted down to business, and then straightened up again to discover that someone had absconded with the lot!

Hotels are usually safe places to leave your stuff; each floor has an attendant watching who goes in and out. If anything is missing from your room then they're going to be obvious suspects since they've got keys to the rooms. Don't expect them to watch over your room like a hawk – they don't.

Dormitories could be a problem – there have been a few reports of thefts by staff, but the culprits are more likely to be other foreigners! There are at least a few people who subsidise their journey by ripping off their fellow travellers. Most hotels have storage rooms where you check your bags in; some insist that you do. In a few hotels you may have to leave your stuff in the dormitory. This is sometimes locked so that all and sundry don't go wandering in and out. Don't leave your valuables (passport, travellers' cheques, money, air tickets) lying around in dormitories.

A money belt is the safest way to carry valuables, particularly when travelling on buses and trains. During the cooler weather, it's more comfortable to wear a vest (waist-coat) with numerous pockets, but you should wear this under a light jacket or coat since visible pockets invite wandering hands even if sealed with zippers. Keeping all your eggs in one basket is not advised – against possible loss you could leave a small stash of money (say US$50) in your hotel room or buried in your backpack, with a record of the travellers' cheque serial numbers and your passport number. Other things of little or no apparent value to the thief – like film – should be safeguarded, since to lose them would be a real heartbreak to you. Make a copy of your address book before you leave home. And note down ticket numbers – a Swedish couple whose train tickets were stolen in Chengdu were told by the railway booking office that they would have received a refund had they done so.

Small padlocks are useful for backpacks and some dodgy hotel rooms. Bicycle chain locks come in handy not only for hired bikes but for attaching backpacks to railings or luggage racks. The trendy waist-pouches often used by Hong Kong visitors are definitely *not* advisable for valuables. Street tailors are skilled at sewing inside pockets to trousers, jackets and shirts usually for a few yuan, and these can even be sealed with zippers.

The Chinese don't trust each other and there's no reason you should trust them.

They run around with rings full of keys as if they were jailers, everything is scrupulously locked, the walls of buildings have jagged glass concreted to the top and iron bars are fitted on ground-floor windows. Announcements on trains (in Chinese) advise passengers neither to entrust baggage to the care of strangers nor to leave valuables unattended during stops or when going to the dining car.

Perhaps the best way to avoid getting ripped off is to not bring a lot of junk you don't need – Walkmans, video cameras, expensive lenses and jewellery all invite theft.

Loss Reports If something of yours is stolen, you should report it immediately to the nearest Foreign Affairs Branch of the PSB. They will ask you to fill in a loss report before investigating the case and sometimes even recovering the stolen goods.

If you have travel insurance (recommended), it is essential to obtain a loss report so you can claim compensation. For theft of major items, a few countries even permit a tax deduction.

Violence

Street fighting in China is extremely common, yet it seldom leads to serious injury – mostly it's bluff with pushing, shoving, screaming and threats. The Chinese seem to fight with each other for the most petty of reasons – who stepped on whose foot or whose bicycle bumped into another, and so on. The women can be as bad as the men – indeed, it's not uncommon to see a Chinese woman take on a couple of men in a street brawl!

Some foreigners speculate that the Chinese harbour a great deal of rage from all the abuse they endure every day, and that this is their way of letting off steam. Whatever the cause, it's likely that you'll see some amazing street fights in China if you spend any length of time in the country – hundreds of spectators gather to watch (including the police, who sometimes get involved). Fortunately, foreigners are almost never involved in these disputes.

Kill the Rooster to Frighten the Monkey

It's hard to say how China's crime rate compares with those in other countries, though the country has its share of rapists and murderers. 'White collar' crime is also a big problem and the Chinese newspapers regularly report arrests and even the occasional execution of frauds and embezzlers.

The crackdown on corruption has been given extensive coverage in the official press. In Shanghai the sons of three senior cadres were executed for attacks on women. Another Shanghai Party official was jailed for life for accepting over Y30,000 in bribes. Although such sentences were intended to show that all are equal before the law, the centuries-old practice of privilege for high officials and their relatives is unlikely to receive more than a dent.

When the minister and vice minister of astronautics embezzled US$46 million in foreign exchange they were rebuked with 'serious disciplinary warnings within the Party'. Meanwhile, local pickpockets get the death penalty.

Juvenile crime is a growing problem in China's cities. The types of crime committed include murder, rape and theft of large sums of money. The official view is that they are victims of 'spiritual pollution' – influenced by images of foreign criminal cliques portrayed in mass media. Other factors such as unemployment and disillusionment are rarely blamed by the leadership.

Justice in China seems to be dispensed entirely by the police, who also decide the penalty. The ultimate penalty is execution, which serves the purpose of 'killing the rooster to frighten the monkey' or, to phrase this in official terms, 'It is good to have some people executed so as to educate others'. The standard manner of execution is a bullet in the back of the head, often at a mass gathering in some sports stadium. This punishment is usually reserved for rapists and murderers. Afterwards a mugshot and maybe even a photo of the extinguished body gets plugged up on a public notice board. Criminals being paraded on the backs of trucks through the streets of Chinese towns are still a common sight. ■

Most Chinese carry knives (at least the men do), but these are seldom used for anything other than slicing bread. Guns are impossible to buy legally (there is a small black market in military pistols though). That having been said, there have been cases of armed robbery by gangs on trains – knives are the usual weapons. The police have tried to crack down on this – there have been arrests and executions of offenders. The chance of it happening to you is small and you needn't let this deter you from riding the train, but it's a good idea to be aware that it can happen.

Staring Squads

The programme is *Aliens*, you are the star, and cinema-sized audiences will gather to watch. You can get stared at in any Asian country if you have Western racial features, particularly when you go off the beaten track where the locals have seen few or no foreigners. But China is phenomenal for the size and enthusiasm of its staring squads. This is less of a problem in the major tourist centres where the Chinese are used to seeing foreigners, but take one step off the beaten track and you'll very quickly gather a small horde of curious onlookers.

You don't have to do anything to get a crowd. Stop for a minute or two on the street to look at something and several local people will also stop. Before long the number of onlookers swells until you're encircled by a solid wall of people.

If there's anything about you which is deemed 'unusual', the number of spectators increases exponentially. Hairy arms and legs have an enduring fascination for less sophisticated Chinese – curious people may even pluck at the hairs to see if they're real.

Travellers react differently to these crowds. Initially it can be amusing, but gradually the novelty wears off. Then it becomes tedious, and after a while it's outright aggravating to be unable to do the slightest thing without being treated like a circus freak.

Some people get used to being stared at and just laugh at the whole ridiculous situation – others become extremely distraught.

Short of plastic surgery, there are a few things you can do to reduce the size of audiences. You will be less conspicuous if your clothes are similar to those of local people. Keep fancy items like videos cameras tucked away when not in use – Western cargo tends to attract a lot of attention.

An army green backpack attracts less attention than a brightly coloured one. If someone comes up to talk to you on the street, then talk to them as you walk, since a conversation with a foreigner is a magnet for gawkers. If you stand on the street scribbling in a notebook someone is sure to poke their head right over the book to see what you're writing, and sometimes they'll lift it straight out of your hands for a closer inspection.

Travelling with someone else helps; if you've got somebody to talk to it's easier to ignore the crowd. Staring back or an abusive response of any kind is useless (though sometimes it's fun), but often attracts a bigger crowd and occasionally gets you into trouble. Getting out your camera and taking a photo sometimes parts the waves but doesn't send people scurrying for cover. Hiring a bicycle is a good idea – you zoom along so fast the crowds can't accumulate. One way to deal with the staring squads is to ignore them and keep moving.

Laowai!

This is just an extension of the staring-squad problem. *Laowai* literally means 'old outside', but it's just a Chinese idiom for 'foreigner'. It is *not* a term of abuse – in fact it's the politest word for 'foreigner'. Nevertheless, it gets irritating, just as the words 'Hello Mister' in Indonesia begin to sound irritating after you've heard it for the 100th time in the course of 30 minutes. Just why the Chinese are so easily amused by standing next to a foreigner and repeatedly yelling 'Laowai!' is hard to figure out – they must be very bored. You won't get this treatment in relatively sophisticated places like Beijing and Shanghai, but travel through remote backwaters and you'll begin to think everybody has been pre-programmed to say this. Getting visibly angry is of no use.

Noise

After you've been in China a while, you begin to wonder if the entire nation doesn't have a hearing problem – there seems to be a competition for who can speak the loudest, turn the radio or TV up to the highest volume and detonate the most firecrackers.

Even in supposedly relaxing places, it's hard to escape the noise. Silence in nature is not generally appreciated by the Chinese – many parks are 'livened up' with music blasting from speakers hidden amongst the trees. More affluent Chinese carry their own boom boxes. With some effort, you might be able to find a truly quiet place to take a walk – try the deserts of north-west China.

Spitting

The national sport, spitting, is practised by everyone regardless of how well-dressed or sophisticated they try to look. All venues are possible – on board buses and trains, in restaurants, etc. Never walk too closely beside a stationary bus full of passengers, and try not to get caught in the crossfire elsewhere!

There is a reason for all this – most Chinese suffer from chronic bronchitis which clogs the lung passages with mucus. There is much speculation as to why a billion people can't recover from the common cold, but it seems that the spitting itself spreads the very disease which makes people want to spit. If everyone could just agree to stop spitting for a few months, the whole country might be able to get well. Most foreigners who stay in China a few months fall victim to the same condition – don't be surprised if you too become a champion spitter!

It's worth knowing that there are occasional 'crackdown clean-up' campaigns when spitting is banned and the police issue fines to violators. This happens most often in Beijing, especially when some ultra-important foreign dignitary is in town.

Racism

Officially, the PRC condemns racism. The government has been a vehement critic of South Africa's apartheid policies. China's own minorities – at least in theory – hold legal status equal to that of the Han majority.

Despite this outward display of racial harmony, there are some sour notes. In 1997, Hong Kong is to become part of China and Hong Kong citizens will become PRC citizens. But not all – the citizenship offer only applies to those of 'Chinese descent'. There are thousands of people born in Hong Kong who are not Chinese or only partly Chinese. This is especially true of the Indians who were brought in by the British more than a century ago. When 1997 rolls around, they will become stateless because they are the wrong race. Ditto for those of mixed racial heritage – you need 'pure blood' to qualify for a Chinese passport.

Official policy aside, racism exists on the street level as it does in many countries. In China it is not particularly serious – most foreigners are not likely to be refused service in a restaurant or hotel because of racial considerations alone (the language barrier or the laziness of the staff is another matter).

Much depends on just which racial group you belong to. Whites normally only experience minor complications, but Blacks have reported some serious problems. A particularly ugly series of incidents occurred in 1988. The problems started at Hehai University in Jiangsu Province when some African students were found to be dating Chinese women. Riots broke out with students shouting 'kill the black devils'. The riots spread to other campuses and the African students had to be evacuated. The Chinese government mishandled the incidents and several African nations sent official notes of protest to Beijing.

The blatant overcharging of foreigners might seem racist, but the motive is usually sheer greed, not racial discrimination.

Queues

Basically, there are none. People tend to 'huddle' rather than queue – it resembles American-style football but without the protective gear. At larger railway stations the huddles can be a formidable obstacle to getting a ticket. Sometimes it may be worth that extra money to have CITS or your hotel service desk get your tickets, use the separate booking office for foreigners (if one exists) or pay a Chinese person to buy them. Otherwise, take a deep breath, get your adrenalin flowing and jump into the huddle with everyone else. This is China – you have to accept the fact that there's nothing you can do about a billion people!

Beggars

Yes, beggars do exist in China – but there are not as many as there are in countries like India. The beggars tend not to pounce on foreigners – the chief exceptions are the kids who practically have to be removed with a crowbar once they've seized your trouser leg. Some beggars squat on the pavement beside large posters which detail their sad story. Professional beggars are common – sometimes women clutching babies who regurgitate stories about having lost their train tickets and all their money.

Drugs

China takes a particularly dim view of opium and all of its derivatives. The Chinese suffered severely from an opium epidemic which was started by British traders in 1773 and lasted until the Communists came to power – they haven't forgotten! Several heroin smugglers from Hong Kong were caught in Kunming some years ago – within a week they were scheduled for public execution. The local PSB issued a special invitation for the foreign press to attend.

Marijuana is often seen growing by the roadside in China – travellers who have sampled it report that it's very poor quality. Hashish is smoked by some of China's minority groups, especially the Uigurs in Xinjiang Province.

It's difficult to say what attitude the Chinese police will take towards foreigners caught using marijuana – they often don't care what foreigners do if Chinese aren't involved. Then again, you have to remember the old story about 'kill the rooster to frighten the monkey'. If you plan to use drugs and

don't want to become the rooster, discretion is strongly advised!

WORK

There are opportunities to teach English and other foreign languages, or even other technical skills if you're qualified. Teaching in China is not a way to get rich – the pay is roughly US$180 a month, payable in RMB rather than hard currency. While this is about four times what the average urban Chinese worker earns, it won't get you far after you've left China. There are usually some fringe benefits like free or low-cost housing and special ID cards that get you discounts on trains and flights. As a worker in China, you will be assigned to a 'work unit', but unlike the locals you'll be excused from political meetings and the God-like controls over your life that the typical Chinese has to endure.

It's become fairly typical for universities to pressure foreigners into working excessive hours. A maximum teaching load should be 20 hours per week, and even this is a lot – you can insist on no more than 15. Chinese professors teach far fewer hours than this – some hardly show up for class at all since they often have outside business interests.

The main reason to work in China is to experience the country at a level not ordinarily available to travellers. Unfortunately, just how close you will be able to get to the Chinese people depends on what the local PSB allows. In Beijing, where the local PSB is almost hysterical about evil foreign 'spiritual pollution', your students may be prohibited from having any contact with you beyond the classroom, though you may secretly meet them far away from the campus.

Foreign teachers are typically forced to live in separate apartments or dormitories – Chinese students wishing to visit you at your room may be turned away at the reception desk; otherwise they may be required to register their name, ID number and purpose of visit. Since many people are reluctant to draw attention to themselves like this (and they could be questioned by the PSB later), they may be unwilling to visit you at all.

In other words, teaching in China can be a lonely experience, unless you spend all your free time in the company of other expats, but this deprives you of the 'foreign experience' you may be seeking.

Two topics which cannot be discussed in the classroom are politics and religion. Foreigners teaching in Beijing have reported spies being placed in their classrooms. Other teachers have found microphones hidden in their dormitory rooms (one fellow we know took revenge by attaching his Walkman to the microphone wires and blasting the snoops with punk music!).

Rules change – China is opening up slowly, and some provinces are liberalising faster than others. So things might have improved by the time you read this. If interested in working in China, contact a Chinese embassy or the universities directly.

Doing Business

At one time, China was the world's most advanced nation. The Chinese invented gunpowder, rockets, the printing press and paper currency. How did such an advanced nation fall so far behind? Probably because the Chinese also invented bureaucracy.

In bureaucratic China, even simple things can be made difficult – renting property, getting a telephone installed, hiring employees, paying taxes, etc, can generate mind-boggling quantities of red tape. Many foreign business people who have worked in China say that success is usually the result of dogged persistence and finding cooperative officials.

If you have any intention of doing business in China, be it buying, selling or investing, it's worth knowing that most towns and – in large cities – many neighbourhoods, have a Commerce Office (*shāngyè jú*). If you approach one of these offices for assistance, the reaction you get can vary from enthusiastic welcome to bureaucratic inertia. In case of a dispute (the goods you ordered are not what was delivered, etc), the Commerce Office could assist you, provided that they are willing.

Buying is simple, selling is more difficult, but setting up a business in China is a whole different can of worms.

If yours is a high-technology company, you can go into certain economic zones and register as a wholly foreign-owned enterprise. In that case you can hire people yourself without going through the government, enjoy a three-year tax holiday, obtain long-term income tax advantages, import duty-free personal items for corporate and expat use (including a car!). The alternative is listing your company as a representative office, which does not allow you to sign any contracts in China – these must be signed by the mother company. The Foreign Service Company (FESCO) is where you hire employees. FESCO currently demands around US\$325 per month per employee, 75% of which goes to the government.

It's easier to register as a representative office. First find out where you want to set up (a city or special economic zone), then go through local authorities (there are no national authorities for this). Go to the local Commerce Office, Economic Ministry, Foreign Ministry, or any ministry that deals with foreign economic trade promotion. In Beijing, the Haidian High-Technology Zone is recommended if you can qualify, but where you register depends on what type of business you're doing. Contact your embassy first – they can advise you.

The most important thing to remember when you go to register a company is not to turn away when you run into a bureaucratic barrier. Bureaucrats will tell you that everything is 'impossible'. In fact, anything is possible – it all depends on your *guānxì* (connections or relationships). Whatever you have in mind is negotiable – all the rules are not necessarily rules at all.

Tax rates vary from zone to zone, authority to authority – it seems to be negotiable but 15% is fairly standard in economic zones. Every economic zone has a fairly complete investment guide in English and Chinese – your embassy's economic council might have these, and these investment guides are getting to be very clear (but even all these printed 'rules' are negotiable!).

ACTIVITIES
Adventure Sports

Western China in particular offers the type of topography to entice mountaineers, whitewater rafters, hang gliding enthusiasts, and others who want to pursue their adventurous hobbies in the world's highest mountains.

The problem, as always, are those faceless, sombre figures known collectively as 'the authorities'. High-ranking cadres, the PSB, the military, CITS and others in China with the power to extort money know a good business opportunity when they see it. Foreigners have been asked for as much as US$1 million for mountaineering and rafting permits. The amount demanded varies considerably depending on who you're dealing with, and the price is always negotiable.

In many cases, it's doubtful that the law really requires a permit. A Chinese person may climb the same mountain as you without having any authorisation at all, and it may be perfectly legal. But many local governments simply make up the law as they go along. In general, when foreigners do something which is deemed unusual – and hang gliding, bungy jumping, kayaking, etc, are unusual in China – a permit will be required and a fee will be charged. The more unusual the activity, the higher the fee demanded.

Hiking

As opposed to mountaineering (which requires equipment like ropes, ice axes, and so on), normal hiking activities can usually be pursued without permits. The Chinese idea of hiking is often different from the Western concept – most of the peaks climbed are hardly wilderness areas. You can expect and admission gate (charging a small fee, handrails, concrete steps, Chinese characters painted on the rocks, temples, pavilions, trailside souvenir vendors, restaurants and perhaps a hotel or two. Hiking areas of this sort include some of China's famous mountains like Taishan and Emeishan. Still, it can be good fun and exercise, and it's part of the 'China experience'.

Camel & Horseback Riding

The venues are not numerous, but China does offer some opportunities of this sort. Camel rides for tourists have become popular pastimes in places like Inner Mongolia or the deserts around Dunhuang (Gansu Province). There are chances for beautiful trips by horses in the mountains of Xinjiang, or for that matter, in the hills west of Beijing. Costs are negotiable, but in general, the further away from a big city you are, the cheaper it gets.

Exercise & Gymnastics

Swimming pools, gymnasiums, weightlifting rooms, etc, are popular ways to keep fit and enjoy yourself. While swimming pools and gymnasiums exist for the Chinese public, they are generally overcrowded and in poor condition. You'll find better facilities at the tourist hotels, but of course it won't be free (unless you're a guest at the hotel). Most hotels in big cities like Beijing permit non-guests to use the workout rooms, pools, saunas, tennis courts, etc, on a fee basis. This is not a bad idea if you're staying for a month or more – monthly fees typically start at around Y450.

Winter Sports

Beijing's lakes freeze over for a couple of months during winter and ice skating becomes feasible. Further north in Harbin, January temperatures dip to minus 40°C and iceboat racing is a favourite pastime for those who can afford it. North-east China is also the venue for skiing, both the downhill and cross-country variety.

Skiing and ice skating demands specialised gear, and Westerners with big feet often have difficulty finding the right size. If you want to pursue winter sports, you may need to bring your own equipment though some local stuff is available.

Golf

Golf courses have invaded the suburbs of Beijing. As elsewhere, it's a sport of the well-to-do, but that seems to be even more true than usual in China. While green fees are similar to what you'd pay in the West, the cost is astronomical compared to the typical Chinese salary.

Miniature golf also seems ready to make its debut in the PRC. An 18-hole miniature golf course is planned for the roof of the Ürümqi Holiday Inn in Xinjiang.

Taijiquan & Kungfu

For details, see the Arts section in the Facts about the Country chapter.

University Courses

As China continues to experiment with capitalism, universities have found it increasingly necessary to raise their own funds and not depend so much on State largess. For this reason, most universities welcome fee-paying foreign students. Most of the courses offered are Chinese language study, but other possibilities include Chinese medicine, acupuncture, brush painting, music, etc. If you've got the cash, almost anything is possible.

There is considerable variation in the quality of instruction and the prices charged. Tuition alone typically runs from US$1000 to US$3000 per year, sometimes double that, and it may depend on your nationality. The university is supposed to arrange your accommodation (no, it's not free) – living conditions vary from reasonably comfortable to horrific.

It's worth knowing that you'll probably have to pay some additional fees and service charges you weren't told about when you first enrolled. Examples include extra fees for a 'health certificate' or a 'study licence', etc. Sometimes these fees are imposed by the PSB which wants its share of the cash, but often the university itself is pocketing the money – the fees vary from reasonable to ridiculous.

If possible, don't pay anything in advance – show up at the school to assess the situation yourself, and talk to other foreign students to see if they're satisfied. Once you've handed over the cash, don't expect a refund.

HIGHLIGHTS

China has so much of interest to suit such a wide variety of tastes that it's difficult to say which places are best. Nevertheless, we do have some personal favourites. Certainly Yangshuo in Guangxi Province and Dali in Yunnan Province deserve honorable mention – they didn't get to be backpackers' havens for nothing. Tibet has long fascinated travellers, and now that it's open (again), you might as well visit while you still can. Another exotic place on the periphery of China is Xinjiang – Kashgar and the Turpan oasis are both worth checking out.

Cultural buffs will appreciate Xi'an, which also gives you an opportunity to climb one of China's sacred mountains, 2200-metre Huashan. But if you're looking for more impressive scenery, try Emeishan in Sichuan Province – if you prefer your nature more unspoiled and don't mind a rugged trip, check out Sichuan's Jiuzhaigou National Park.

Last but not least, there's Beijing. True, China's capital has traffic jams, crowds and enough politics to make you ill, but it also has the Forbidden City, Summer Palace, the Great Wall, great food and enough of intrinsic interest that many travellers simply run out of time before they've had a chance to see it all.

ACCOMMODATION

One of the main reasons why the Chinese threw the door open to tourism in the 1980s is because they badly needed the foreign exchange. Despite all the government's rhetoric about 'Friendship Hotels' and 'Friendship Stores', the purpose of opening up to tourism has always been to rake in money. Hotel prices are steadily rising towards what you'd pay for a similar standard of accommodation in the West – there aren't too many bargains around. On the other hand, quality has improved – rooms are more luxurious, service has improved and hotel staff are friendlier and more used to dealing with foreigners than a few years ago. In the past, it was common for the staff to simply deny that rooms were available even when the place was empty.

Camping

Camping is possible if you can find a spare blade of grass. If you set up a tent anywhere near civilisation, someone is likely to snitch and the PSB will probably raid your campsite within the hour. Wilderness camping is more appealing, but most such areas in China require special permits and are difficult to reach.

The trick is to select a couple of likely places about half an hour before sunset, but keep moving (by bicycle, foot or whatever) and then backtrack so you can get away from the road at the chosen spot just after darkness falls. Be sure to get up around sunrise and leave before sightseeing locals take an interest.

Hostels

Youth hostels in the Western sense of the word scarcely exist in China. The kinds of cheapie dormitories run by the International Youth Hostel Federation (IYHF) – so common in Europe, Australia, Japan and elsewhere – are not permitted in the PRC. There are a few places which might fit your definition of a hostel, like the very friendly Yangshuo Youth Hostel in Yangshuo (Guangxi Province), or the very unfriendly Guangzhou Youth Hostel in Canton. In most cases, the only 'hostels' in China are dormitory rooms in the old wings of large hotels. Even many of these dormitories are now being renovated and converted into upmarket hotel rooms. Ominously, we found far fewer dormitories during this last trip than in previous journeys.

When dormitories do exist, the staff at the reception desk may be reluctant to tell you. You have to ask about dorms, and sometimes you even have to push the staff a bit ('Are you sure there's no dorm beds; can you check; I don't have much money; I'm just a poor student', etc). Just remember to do your 'pushing' in a friendly manner – a lot of foreigners get hostile with the hotel staff at this point, but that will *not* help your case one iota. If all this produces no result, it's often helpful to try looking lost and using those magic words, *zěnme bàn* (what to do?). The staff might take pity and try to direct you to another hostel, but just remember that they cannot magically produce dormitory beds where none exist.

Universities have their own hostel-dormitories for students, and you can sometimes get a room there because the schools also need the money. There are two problems with this approach – one is that the dorms are typically overcrowded and there simply is no room available; the other problem is that the PSB has the final word and they often frown on this practice. Still, it's a possibility worth looking into – some places like the Central Institute of Fine Arts in Beijing and the Music Conservatory in Shanghai, do accept foreigners when room is available.

Without exception, hostels, dormitories or whatever you'd like to call them, are government-run affairs. Efforts by private individuals to open up budget hostels for foreigners have been sternly rebuked by officials. We personally know one private entrepreneur, an Overseas Chinese, who went to Shanghai recently with the intention of opening up a private youth hostel for foreign travellers. He ran into nothing but solid roadblocks from the PSB. After a month of sheer frustration, he left China totally disillusioned.

Guesthouses

As with hostels, the Western concept of budget guesthouses has been mostly rejected by officials who tightly control such things. By guesthouse, we mean the type of cheapie bed & breakfast hotels typical in Indonesia (where they are called *losmen*), or in Thailand, the Philippines, etc. It's not that these places don't exist in China, it's just that they are forbidden to accept foreigners.

There are a few exceptions – the local PSB has the final say in such matters, and the rules change often enough for you to sometimes get lucky. At railway stations, you'll often see private entrepreneurs carrying placards (in Chinese) trying to solicit passengers as they exit the station. These people work for the guesthouses, usually drawing a commission for every customer they bring in. It could be worth your while to talk to them and see if they'll take you, but don't be surprised if they wave you off.

It's worth noting that the literal Chinese translation of the word 'guesthouse' *(bīnguǎn)* usually denotes an upmarket hotel. Other guesthouses are specifically designated for cadres only, surrounded by high walls, uniformed guards and video cameras.

Hotels

Most of us wind up staying in hotels in China, and unless you're very selective about which cities you visit, hotel accommodation can quickly wipe out your budget. A cheap hotel room in China is anything costing less than Y100; mid-range is about Y100 to Y200, and everything above that is top-end. In many cities, there is nothing available in the cheap range, only one or two mid-range places and everything else is top-end.

That is, of course, if you're a foreigner. There are some excellent, low-priced hotels for Chinese people only. If you front up at a Chinese-only hotel there is little chance that you will get a room. Even if the staff takes pity on you and would like to let you stay, they dare not break the idiotic rules which are under the supervision of the PSB. In some cities (Canton, for example) the rules have little to do with the standard of accommodation, but rather it's a matter of paying taxes – those hotels which are approved to receive foreign guests must pay a steep 'foreigners tax'. Hotels which violate the rules can be fined or shut down.

Some towns apply these rules more strictly than others. In some towns, the PSB doesn't give a hoot where you stay. In other places, exceptions are made for 'persons of Chinese descent'. That means if you look more or less Chinese and claim to be Chinese (even if you're an ethnic Korean or Filipino), you can be admitted with a foreign passport (after being charged double, of course). In remote areas, there may not be any special hotels for foreigners – in this case, you get to stay in a Chinese hotel because nothing else is available.

Discounts If you're a foreign student in the PRC, you can get a discount on room prices. Students usually have to show their government-issued 'green card', though sometimes a fake 'white card' will do the trick. Foreign experts working in China usually qualify for the same discounts as students.

If you are really stuck for a place to stay, it sometimes helps to phone or visit the local PSB and explain your problem. Just as the PSB makes the rules, the PSB can break them – a hotel not approved for foreigners can be granted a temporary reprieve by the PSB and all it takes is a phone call from the right official. Unfortunately, getting such an exemption is not the usual practice.

Hotel Etiquette Most hotels have an attendant on every floor. The attendant keeps an eye on the hotel guests. This is partly to prevent theft and partly to stop you from bringing locals back for the night (this is no joke).

To conserve energy, in many cheaper hotels hot water for bathing in only available in the evening – sometimes only for a few hours a night or once every three days! It's worth asking when/if the hot water will be turned on.

The policy at every hotel in China is to require that you check out by noon to avoid being charged extra. If you check out between noon and 6 pm there is a charge of 50% of the room price – after 6 pm you have to pay for another full night.

Almost every hotel has a left-luggage room (*jìcún chù* or *xínglǐ bǎoguǎn*), and in many hotels there is such a room on every floor. If you are a guest in the hotel, use of the left-luggage room might be free (but not always).

The trend in China over the last few years has been to equip every room – even in the cheap hotels – with TV sets permanently turned to maximum volume. The Hong Kong-style ultra-violent movies are noisy enough, but the introduction of Nintendo-style video games and karaoke microphones (which can be attached to TV sets) has added a new dimension to the cacophony. The combination of screams, screeches, shootings, songs, rings, gongs, beeps and buzzers which reverberate through the vast concrete corridors could force a statue to run away.

Something else to be prepared for is lack

of privacy – what happens is that you're sitting starkers in your hotel room, the key suddenly turns in the door and the room attendant casually wanders in...This is becoming less of a problem as hotel workers learn how to handle foreign visitors, but it's still a frequent occurrence. Don't expect anyone to knock before entering. Your best protection is to prop a chair against the door.

It's also worth noting that privacy is another privilege of rank; the high-ranking cadres live in large houses surrounded by high walls and are driven around in cars with drawn curtains. Those of sufficiently high rank stay in huge government guesthouses, exclusive villas surrounded by walls, guards and 'keep out' signs.

The Chinese method of designating floors is the same as used in the USA, but different from, say, Australia's. What would be the 'ground floor' in Australia is the '1st floor' in China, the 1st is the 2nd, and so on. However, there is some inconsistency – Hong Kong, which uses the British system, has influenced some parts of southern China.

Rental

Most Chinese people live in government-subsidised housing – the price is almost always dirt cheap. For foreigners, the situation is totally different.

If you're going to be working for the Chinese government as a teacher or other type of foreign expert, then you'll almost certainly be provided with cheap or low-cost housing. Conditions probably won't be luxurious, but it should be inexpensive.

The news is not good for those coming to China to do business or work for a foreign company. The cheap apartments available to the Chinese are off limits to foreigners, which leaves you with two choices – living in a hotel, or renting a luxury flat in a compound specifically designated for foreigners.

If you live in a hotel, you might be able to negotiate a discount for a long-term stay, but that's not guaranteed. As for luxury flats and villas, prices start at around US$2000 and reach US$5000 or more. Even at these prices, there is a shortage of flats available

for foreigners in big cities like Beijing and Shanghai.

Considering the sky-high rents, buying a flat or villa might seem like a good idea for companies with the cash. It's actually possible, but the rules vary from city to city. In Xiamen, for example, only Overseas Chinese are permitted to buy luxury villas – real estate speculators from Taiwan do a roaring trade. Shenzhen has long been in the business of selling flats to Hong Kongers, who in turn rent them out to others. Foreigners can buy flats in Beijing (at astronomical prices), and doing this can actually gain you a residence permit.

As for simply moving in with a Chinese family and paying them rent, forget it – the PSB will swoop down on you (and the hapless Chinese family) faster than ants at a picnic.

FOOD

Chinese cooking is justifiably famous, a fine art perfected through the centuries. Quality, availability of ingredients and cooking styles vary by region, but you'll almost always find something to suit your tastes.

You can also put your mind at ease about food shortages – despite China's long history of famines, the country is not short of food. Famines have resulted from natural disasters (droughts, floods, typhoons) and human disasters (wars, the Cultural Revolution, etc), but in China today the transport system is able to quickly move food to those areas that need it. Your biggest problems with food are likely to be figuring out the menus and being overcharged.

While the Chinese make outstanding lunches, dinners and snacks, many foreigners are disappointed by breakfast. The Chinese do not seem to understand the Western notion of eating light in the morning – a typical breakfast could include fried peanuts, pickled vegetables, pork with hot sauce, a horrid greasy breadstick called *yóutiáo*, rice porridge (looks and tastes like wallpaper paste), all washed down with a glass of beer. Just what you had in mind at 7 am.

Places to Eat

Outside of fancy hotel restaurants, prices are generally low. Beware, however, of overcharging – many places think nothing of charging foreigners double or more.

Everyone knows that the price is determined by what you eat as much as by where you eat, but beware – a few exotic dishes are ridiculously expensive and you can't count on the staff to warn you in advance. Certain types of rare fish are worth their weight in gold even if they taste lousy. Bear paws are an exotic delicacy, as outrageously expensive as you'd expect them to be. Snake is expensive but dogmeat is very cheap.

By far one of the most shocking but memorable experiences we had in China occurred in Guilin when we ordered a snake and the cooks killed, skinned and squeezed the red blood out of it in front of our eyes...I paid my equal share of the whopping US$30 bill, but the experience was well worth the price.

In the towns the government-run restaurants are the size of gymnasiums seating several hundred people at any one time. Nor do the Chinese go in for the Western fashion of eating in dimly lit, intimate surroundings. Indeed, Chinese restaurants often resemble aircraft hangers – huge, noisy and brightly lit, and many of the clientele seem to prefer it that way. A few restaurants have small rooms where the elite can eat away from the crowd – cadres and their friends usually hang out in these reclusive surroundings.

As with most things in China, foreigners often end up paying more when the bill arrives at the end of a meal. Sometimes polite insistence will bring the price down, but at other times the locals can be frustratingly stubborn. Check prices and write down the price for every dish when you order. If the menu doesn't have prices, have the waiter write them down. Don't let the price arrive as a neat figure – ask firmly and politely for individual prices, preferably written on a receipt. You can also check the menu again. In case of dispute, you can refer absolutely scandalous overcharging to the PSB. Or you can simply pay what you think it should be

and walk out – the reaction to this tactic may be passive acceptance or physical violence. Good luck.

Many restaurants have a habit of serving enormous helpings – a real problem if you're on your own because they'll often charge you appropriately. Try asking for small helpings – you can always order more if you're still hungry. Small street stalls are good for snacks. If you can't stand the staring any longer then flee to the restaurants in the tourist hotels; most are OK and some are much cheaper than they look.

Large government-owned restaurants have counters where you buy tickets for the food. Then you go to a window facing into the kitchen, hand in your tickets and get your food. Menus and prices are usually chalked up on a blackboard and scrubbed out as the restaurant runs out.

If the language barrier proves impassable, the best way to order a meal in a Chinese restaurant is to point at something that somebody else already has. Some restaurants are cafeteria style and you can just point to what you want. Sometimes somebody takes you in hand, leads you into the kitchen where you can point out what you want, and then buys the tickets for you. Some restaurants with a regular Western clientele have menus in English; most don't. A phrasebook is a big help if you don't speak Chinese.

Tourist hotels almost always have menus in Chinese and English. If not, there's usually someone around who speaks some English. Sometimes they dispense with menus and you pay a flat rate for a set meal.

Snacks

Western-style cakes and sweetbreads are on sale everywhere – with few exceptions, the taste is similar to sawdust. The Chinese are considerably better at making their traditional breads – steamed buns *(mántóu)*, clay-oven bread *(shāobǐng)* and fried bread rolls *(yínsī juǎn)* are notable examples. In general, the Cantonese seem to be better at baking than other Chinese – Cantonese specialties such as coconut cakes and custard tarts get good ratings from Westerners.

Main Dishes

One theory holds that Chinese cooking is famine cooking – almost anything that isn't poisonous gets eaten and almost no part of an animal or plant is wasted. What we now regard as Chinese culinary exotica seems to be an effort to make the most of everything available; they salvage the least appealing ingredients which wealthy nations reject as waste, and make them into appetising food. True or not, the Chinese have some exotic dishes: fish heads, ducks' feet, dog and cat meat, bird saliva, and fish lips and eyeballs, to name a few. Pigs, chickens and ducks have always been a feature of the cuisine because they have unchoosy eating habits and can be raised on very small areas of land.

Traditional Chinese food can be divided into four major categories by geographical region: Beijing (sometimes called Mandarin) and Shandong; Cantonese and Chaozhou; Shanghainese and Jiangzhenese; and Sichuan.

Beijing & Shandong Beijing and Shandong cuisine comes from one of the coldest parts of China. Since this is China's wheat belt, steamed bread and noodles are often eaten instead of rice.

The chief specialty is Beijing duck, served with pancakes and plum sauce. Another specialty is beggar's chicken, supposedly created by a beggar who stole the emperor's chicken and had to bury it in the ground to cook it – the dish is wrapped in lotus leaves and baked all day in hot ashes.

Some good Beijing dishes: chicken or pork with soy sauce; fried dried shredded beef with chilli sauce; stewed mixed vegetables; barbecued chicken; fried shrimp eggs and pork pancakes.

Another specialty is Mongolian hotpot, composed of assorted meats and vegetables cooked in a burner right on the dining table – it's so good in China that it's hard to believe it can be so bad in Mongolia. Hotpot is usually eaten during winter. Mongolian barbecue is a variation featuring a slowly roasted goat or lamb carcass along with a hotpot full of spicy vegetables. If you've eaten the Korean dish *bulgogi*, you've got the idea. A warning though – the price of hotpot depends entirely on the ingredients. It can cost Y20 or Y200 depending on what's thrown into the pot, so ask first to avoid unpleasant surprises.

Bird's nest soup is a specialty of Shandong cooking. Another is sweet-and-sour Yellow River carp – the fish is singed on the outside while still alive and served while still breathing! Not surprisingly, it isn't a big hit with foreigners.

Shanghainese Of all Chinese cuisines, this one gets the poorest reviews by foreigners. Shanghainese cooking is noted for its use of

seafoods, but it's heavy and oily. Many Westerners say it's greasy, tasteless and disgusting, but liberal use of spices can make it almost palatable. Eels are popular, as is drunken chicken, cooked in *Shaoxing* (a potent Chinese firewater a bit like warm sherry). Other things to try are some of the cold-meat-and-sauce dishes, ham-and-melon soup, bean curd (tofu) and brown sauce, braised meat balls, deep-fried chicken, and pork ribs with salt and pepper.

Sichuan This is the hottest of the four major categories – it's great stuff if you like spicy food, but keep the drinking water handy! Specialties include frogs' legs and smoked duck; the duck is cooked in peppercorns, marinated in wine for 24 hours, covered in tea leaves and cooked again over a charcoal fire. Other dishes to try are shrimps with salt and garlic; dried chilli beef; bean curd with chilli; fish in spicy bean sauce and aubergines in garlic.

Cantonese & Chaozhou This is southern Chinese cooking – lots of steaming, boiling and stir-frying. It's the best of the bunch if you're worried about cholesterol and coronaries, as it uses the least amount of oil. It's lightly cooked and not as highly spiced as the other three, with lots of seafood, vegetables, roast pork, chicken, steamed fish and fried rice.

Dim sum is a snack-like variation, served for breakfast and lunch (but never dinner) and consisting of all sorts of little delicacies served from pushcarts wheeled around the restaurant floor. It's justifiably famous and something you should experience at least once, but like many visitors you'll probably get addicted.

The Cantonese are famous for making just about anything palatable: specialties are abalone, dried squid, 1000-year eggs (traditionally made by soaking eggs in horse's urine), shark's fin soup, snake soup and dog stew. Other culinary exotica include anteaters, pangolins *(línglǐ* – a sort of armadillo), cats, rats, owls, monkeys, turtles and frogs. One saying is that the Cantonese eat every-

---

Banquets

The Chinese love them. Cadres try to make a habit of attending banquets as often as possible, which might explain their bulging posteriors. Pigging-out daily at government expense is a privilege rank – hang around big hotel dining rooms and you may get to witness some incredible eating orgies. If you come to China on business or even to teach English, there is a good chance that you'll be invited to a banquet. Visiting delegations, cultural groups, etc, are always given a welcoming banquet by their host organisation.

Dishes are served in sequence, beginning with cold appetisers and continuing through 10 or more courses. Soup is usually served after the main course and is used to wash the food down.

The usual rule is to serve everyone too much. Empty bowls imply that the host hasn't served a sufficient quantity of food, so if you see a bit left in a bowl then leave it there. Similarly, though rice may be the staple, at banquets it is used only as a filler; to consume great quantities of it at a banquet implies you are still hungry and is an insult to your host.

In a formal setting it is impolite to drink alcohol alone; toasts are usually offered to neighbours or to the whole table. It is appropriate for the leader of the guests to offer a toast to everyone at the table, and the Chinese host usually begins the toasts after the first course. Avoid excessive toasting since inebriation is frowned upon.

Toasts are often made with the expression *gān bēi* (dry glass) which literally implies 'empty the cup'. In the course of a banquet there may be several gan bei toasts, but custom dictates that you need only drain your glass on the first one. Subsequent toasts require only a small sip. The Han Chinese don't clink their glasses when toasting.

Don't be late for a formal banquet; it's considered extremely rude. The banquet ends when the food and toasts end – the Chinese don't linger after the meal. You may find yourself being applauded when you enter a large banquet. The Chinese custom is used as a greeting or to indicate approval and it is often OK to applaud back! ∎

thing with four legs but the table. Another Chinese joke is that the Cantonese are industrious people – capable of doing any job except zookeeper.

Despite the unusual ingredients, Cantonese food has long been a favourite of Westerners – Chinese restaurants around the world often include a wide selection of Cantonese dishes on the menu.

Other Exotica If dog and monkey brain seem mundane, one of the stranger Chinese delicacies is pig face. The meat is removed from the head and hot tar is poured over the pig's face. The dried tar is peeled off, removing the hair and leaving the skin intact, which is then used as an ingredient in soup.

Live rat embryos are supposedly a delicacy from Guizhou Province. The dish is nicknamed the 'three squeals' since the embryo squeals when you pick it up with your chopsticks, once again when you dip it in soy sauce, and finally when you put it in your mouth...or so the story goes.

If all this makes you consider becoming a vegetarian, you'll be pleased to know that it is indeed possible to survive in China without eating meat. Although pure vegetarian restaurants are a rarity, it is entirely possible to order tasty vegetable dishes. It could be a problem in places that just have set meals – for example, the dining cars of trains. Learn how to say 'I'm a vegetarian' *(wǒ chī sù)* and specify vegetable dishes when you order. This usually works though sometimes they don't seem to get the message unless you have it written down.

Chopsticks

You'll have to master the art of using chopsticks because there is seldom anything else available besides your hands – disposable wooden chopsticks are now universally available.

Don't worry about making a mess on the table – everyone does. If you want to, raise the bowl right up to your lips and shovel in the rice. This is how the Chinese eat so don't be embarrassed, though it does take practice to master the shovelling process. Spitting

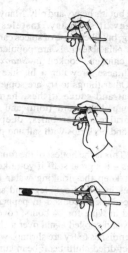

Using chopsticks

bones out on the tablecloth or the floor is standard practice. Nevertheless, there is a proper etiquette to using a toothpick – you should use two hands, one to operate the pick and one to block the view of this process. Just watch how the Chinese do it.

The best way to master chopsticks is to be hungry in a place where there are no knives and forks – the above diagrams might help.

Desserts

The Chinese are not big on dessert. Western influence has added ice cream to the menu in some upmarket establishments, but in general sweet stuff is consumed as snacks and is seldom available in restaurants. Most Chinese finish off a big meal with fruit and tea rather than cake and ice cream.

Fruit

Canned and bottled fruit is readily available everywhere, in department and food stores as well as in dining cars on trains. Good quality fruit – including oranges, mandarins and bananas – is commonly sold in the street markets, though you'll find that the supply and quality drop off severely in winter. Out in the deserts of the north-west, melons are abundant; pineapples and lychees are common along the south-east coast during summer.

Many foreigners who have never eaten sugarcane before make complete fools of themselves the first time they try, much to the amusement of the Chinese. Please be aware that you do not eat or chew the outer (purple coloured) skin of sugarcane – it must be removed with a peeling knife, though experts rip it off with their teeth. Also, you do not actually eat sugarcane, you chew it to extract the sweet juices and then spit out the pulp. If you swallow the pulp, you'll practically choke (but the Chinese audience will have a giggling fit).

Self-Catering

In remote places or on long bus trips it helps to have emergency rations such as instant noodles, dried fruit, soup extract, nuts, chocolate, etc. All this stuff is very cheap in China – railway and bus stations are good places to stock up.

The Chinese can obtain rice and other grains with ration coupons (yōuhuì juàn), which are not issued to foreigners. These days, few things are actually rationed and the coupons are used mainly for getting a discount.

Restaurant Vocabulary

restaurant
  cāntīng 餐厅
I'm vegetarian.
  wǒ chī sù 我吃素
menu
  cài dān 菜单
bill (cheque)
  zhàng dān 帐单
set meal (no menu)
  tàocān 套餐
to eat/let's eat
  chī fàn 吃饭
chopsticks
  kuàizi 筷子

knife and fork
  dāochā 刀叉
spoon
  tiáogēng 调羹

Sample Menu
Rice

plain white rice
  mǐfàn 米饭
watery rice porridge
  xīfàn 稀饭
rice noodles
  mǐfěn 米粉

Bread, Buns & Dumplings

fried roll
  yínsī juǎn 银丝卷
steamed buns
  mántóu 馒头
steamed meat buns
  bāozi 包子
fried bread stick
  yóutiáo 油条
boiled dumplings
  jiǎozi 饺子
prawn cracker
  lóngxiā piàn 龙虾片

Vegetable Dishes

fried rice with vegetables
  shūcài chǎofàn 蔬菜炒饭
fried noodles with vegetables
  shūcài chǎomiàn 蔬菜炒面
spicy peanuts
  wǔxiāng huāshēng mǐ 五香花生米
fried peanuts
  yóuzhà huāshēng mǐ 油炸花生米
spiced cold vegetables
  liángbàn shíjǐn 凉拌什锦
Chinese salad
  jiācháng liángcài 家常凉菜
fried rape in oyster sauce
  háoyóu pácài dǎn 蚝油扒菜胆
fried rape with mushrooms
  dōnggū pácài dǎn 冬菇扒菜胆
fried bean curd in oyster sauce
  háoyóu dòufu 蚝油豆腐
spicy hot bean curd
  mápó dòufu 麻婆豆腐

bean curd casserole
  shāguō dòufu 沙锅豆腐
bean curd & mushrooms
  mógū dòufu 磨菇豆腐
garlic & morning glory
  dàsuàn kōngxīn cài 大蒜空心菜
fried garlic
  sù chǎo dàsuàn 素炒大蒜
fried eggplant
  sùshāo qiézi 素烧茄子
fried beansprouts
  sù chǎo dòuyá 素炒豆芽
fried green vegetables
  sù chǎo qīngcài 素炒青菜
fried green beans
  sù chǎo biǎndòu 素炒扁豆
fried cauliflower & tomato
  fānqié càihuā 炒蕃茄菜花
broiled mushroom
  sù chǎo xiānme 素炒鲜麽
black fungus & mushroom
  mù'ěr huákǒu mó 木耳滑口磨
fried white radish patty
  luóbo gāo 萝卜糕
assorted hors d'oeuvre
  shíjǐn pīnpán 什锦拼盘
assorted vegetarian food
  sù shíjǐn 素什锦

Egg Dishes
preserved egg
  sōnghuā dàn 松花蛋
fried rice with egg
  jīdàn chǎofàn 鸡蛋炒饭
fried tomatoes & eggs
  xīhóngshì chǎo jīdàn 西红柿炒鸡蛋
egg & flour omelette
  jiān bǐng 煎饼

Beef Dishes
fried rice with beef
  niúròusī chǎofàn 牛肉丝炒饭
noodles with beef (soupy)
  niúròu tāng miàn 牛肉汤面
spiced noodles with beef
  niúròu gān miàn 牛肉干面
fried noodles with beef
  niúròu chǎomiàn 牛肉炒面
beef with white rice
  niúròu fàn 牛肉饭

beef platter
  niúròu tiěbǎn 牛肉铁板
beef with oyster sauce
  háoyóu niúròu 蚝油牛肉
beef braised in soy sauce
  hóngshāo niúròu 红烧牛肉
beef with tomatoes
  fānqié niúròu piàn 蕃茄牛肉片
beef with green peppers
  qīngjiāo niúròu piàn 青椒牛肉片
beef curry & rice
  gālí niúròu fàn 咖哩牛肉饭
beef curry & noodles
  gālí jīròu miàn 咖哩牛肉面

Chicken Dishes
fried rice with chicken
  jīsī chǎofàn 鸡丝炒饭
noodles with chicken (soupy)
  jīsī tāng miàn 鸡丝汤面
fried noodles with chicken
  jīsī chǎomiàn 鸡丝炒面
chicken leg with white rice
  jītuǐ fàn 鸡腿饭
spicy hot chicken & peanuts
  gōngbào jīdīng 宫爆鸡丁
fruit kernal with chicken
  guǒwèi jīdīng 果味鸡丁
sweet & sour chicken
  tángcù jīdīng 糖醋鸡丁
sauteed spicy chicken pieces
  làzi jīdīng 辣子鸡丁
sauteed chicken with green peppers
  jiàngbào jīdīng 酱爆鸡丁
chicken slices & tomato sauce
  fānqié jīdīng 蕃茄鸡丁
mushrooms & chicken
  cǎomó jīdīng 草蘑鸡丁
chicken pieces in oyster sauce
  háoyóu jīdīng 蚝油鸡丁
chicken braised in soy sauce
  hóngshāo jīkuài 红烧鸡块
sauteed chicken with water chestnuts
  nánjiè jīpiàn 南芥鸡片
sliced chicken with crispy rice
  jīpiàn guōbā 鸡片锅巴
chicken curry
  gālí jīròu 咖哩鸡肉
chicken curry & rice
  gālí jīròu fàn 咖哩鸡肉饭

chicken curry & noodles
gālí jīròu miàn 咖哩鸡肉面

Duck Dishes

Beijing Duck
běijīng kǎoyā 北京烤鸭
duck with white rice
yāròu fàn 鸭肉饭
duck with noodles
yāròu miàn 鸭肉面
duck with fried noodles
yāròu chǎomiàn 鸭肉炒面

Pork Dishes

pork chop with white rice
páigǔ fàn 排骨饭
fried rice with pork
ròusī chǎofàn 肉丝炒饭
fried noodles with pork
ròusī chǎomiàn 肉丝炒面
pork & mustard greens
zhàcài ròusī 榨菜肉丝
noodles, pork & mustard greens
zhàcài ròusī miàn 榨菜肉丝面
pork with crispy rice
ròupiàn guōbā 肉片锅巴
sweet & sour pork fillet
tángcù zhūròu piàn 糖醋猪肉片
sweet & sour pork fillet
tángcù lǐjī 糖醋里肌
pork fillet with white sauce
huáliū lǐjī 滑溜里肌
shredded pork fillet
chǎo lǐjī sī 炒里肌丝
spicy hot pork pieces
gōngbào ròudīng 宫爆肉丁
fried black pork pieces
yuánbào lǐjī 芫爆里肌
sauteed diced pork & soy sauce
jiàngbào ròudīng 酱爆肉丁
spicy pork cubelets
làzi ròudīng 辣子肉丁
pork cubelets & cucumber
huángguā ròudīng 黄瓜肉丁
golden pork slices
jīnyín ròusī 金银肉丝
sauteed shredded pork
qīngchǎo ròusī 清炒肉丝

shredded pork & hot sauce
yúxiāng ròusī 鱼香肉丝
shredded pork & green peppers
qīngjiāo ròusī 青椒肉丝
shredded pork & bamboo shoots
dōngsǔn ròusī 冬笋肉丝
shredded pork & green beans
biǎndòu ròusī 扁豆肉丝
pork with oyster sauce
háoyóu ròusī 蚝油肉丝
boiled pork slices
shuǐzhǔ ròupiàn 水煮肉片
pork, eggs & black fungus
mùxū ròu 木须肉
pork & fried onions
yángcōng chǎo ròupiàn 洋葱炒肉片
fried rice (assorted)
shíjǐn chǎofàn 什锦炒饭
fried rice Canton-style
guǎngzhōu chǎofàn 广州炒饭

Seafood Dishes

fried rice with shrimp
xiārén chǎofàn 虾仁炒饭
fried noodles with shrimp
xiārén chǎomiàn 虾仁炒面
diced shrimp with peanuts
gōngbào xiārén 宫爆虾仁
sauteed shrimp
qīngchǎo xiārén 清炒虾仁
deep-fried shrimp
zhá xiārén 炸虾仁
fried shrimp with mushroom
xiānmó xiārén 鲜蘑虾仁
squid with crispy rice
yóuyú guōbā 鱿鱼锅巴
sweet & sour squid roll
suānlà yóuyú juàn 酸辣鱿鱼卷
fish braised in soy sauce
hóngshāo yú 红烧鱼
braised sea cucumber
hóngshāo hǎishēn 红烧海参
clams
gé 蛤
crab
pángxiè 螃蟹
lobster
lóngxiā 龙虾

Soup

three kinds seafood soup
  sān xiān tāng 三鲜汤
squid soup
  yóuyú tāng 鱿鱼汤
sweet & sour soup
  suānlà tāng 酸辣汤
tomato & egg soup
  xīhóngshì dàn tāng 西红柿蛋汤
corn & egg thick soup
  fènghuáng lìmǐ gēng 凤凰栗米羹
egg & vegetable soup
  dànhuā tāng 蛋花汤
mushroom & egg soup
  mógu dànhuā tāng 蘑菇蛋花汤
fresh fish soup
  shēng yú tāng 生鱼汤
vegetable soup
  shūcài tāng 蔬菜汤
cream of tomato soup
  nǎiyóu fānqié tāng 奶油蕃茄汤
cream of mushroom soup
  nǎiyóu xiānmó tāng 奶油鲜蘑汤
pickled mustard green soup
  zhàcài tāng 榨菜汤
bean curd & vegetable soup
  dòufū cài tāng 豆腐菜汤
wanton soup
  húndùn tāng 馄饨汤
clear soup
  qīng tāng 清汤

Miscellanea & Exotica

kebab
  ròu chuàn 肉串
goat, mutton
  yáng ròu 羊肉
dogmeat
  gǒu ròu 狗肉
deermeat (venison)
  lùròu 鹿肉
snake
  shé ròu 蛇肉
ratmeat
  lǎoshǔ ròu 老鼠肉
pangolin
  chuān shānjiǎ 穿山甲
frog
  qīngwā 青蛙

eel
  shàn yú 鳝鱼
turtle
  hǎiguī 海龟
Mongolian hotpot
  huǒguō 火锅

Condiments

garlic
  dàsuàn 大蒜
black pepper
  hújiāo 胡椒
hot pepper
  làjiāo 辣椒
hot sauce
  làjiāo jiàng 辣椒酱
ketchup
  fānqié jiàng 蕃茄酱
salt
  yán 盐
MSG
  wèijīng 味精
soy sauce
  jiàng yóu 酱油
vinegar
  cù 醋
sesame seed oil
  zhīmá yóu 芝麻油
butter
  huáng yóu 黄油
sugar
  táng 糖
jam
  guǒ jiàng 果酱
honey
  fēngmì 蜂蜜

DRINKS

Nonalcoholic Drinks

Tea is the most commonly served brew in the PRC; it didn't originate in China but in South-East Asia. Indian tea is not generally available but some of the more modern supermarkets in Canton, Beijing and Shanghai should have it – if you can't live without your Lipton or Twinings, then bring a supply. Coffee addicts will be pleased to find familiar Western brands (Maxwell House, Nescafe) for sale almost everywhere.

Coca-Cola, first introduced into China by

American soldiers in 1927, is now produced in Beijing. Chinese attempts at making similar brews include TianFu Cola, which has a recipe based on the root of herbaceous peony. Fanta and Sprite are widely available, both genuine and copycat versions. Sugary Chinese soft drinks are cheap and sold everywhere – some are so sweet they'll turn your teeth inside out. Jianlibao is a Chinese soft drink made with honey rather than sugar – one of the better brands. Lychee-flavoured carbonated drinks are unique to China and get rave reviews from foreigners. Fresh milk is rare but you can buy imported UHT milk at high prices from Western-style supermarkets in Beijing, Shanghai, Shenzhen and Canton.

A surprising treat is fresh sweet yoghurt, available in many of the more developed parts of China. It's typically sold in what looks like small milk bottles and is consumed by drinking with a straw rather than eating with a spoon. This excellent stuff would make a great breakfast if you could find some decent bread to go with it.

Alcohol

If tea is the most popular drink in the PRC then beer must be number two. By any standards the top brands are great stuff. The best known is Tsingtao (Qingdao), made with a mineral water which gives it its sparkling quality. It's really a German beer since the town of Qingdao (formerly spelled 'Tsingtao') where it's made was once a German concession and the Chinese inherited the brewery. Experts in these matters claim that draft Tsingtao tastes much better than the bottled stuff. Local brews are found in all the major cities of China – notable ones include Zhujiang in Canton and Yanjing in Beijing. San Miguel has a brewery in Canton, so you can enjoy this 'imported' beer at Chinese prices. Real Western imports are sold in Friendship Stores and five-star hotels at five-star prices.

China has probably cultivated vines and produced wine for over 4000 years. Chinese wine-producing techniques differ from those of Westerners. Quality-conscious wine pro-

ducers in Western countries work on the idea that the lower the yield the higher the quality of the wine produced. But Chinese workers cultivate every possible sq cm of earth; they encourage their vines to yield heavily and also plant peanuts between the rows of vines as a cover crop for half the year. The peanuts sap much of the nutrient from the soil, and in cooler years the large grape crop fails to ripen sufficiently to produce a wine comparable to Western ones.

Western producers try to prevent oxidation in the wines, but oxidation produces a flavour which the Chinese find desirable and go to great ends to achieve. The Chinese are also keen on wines with different herbs and other materials soaked in them, which they drink for their health and for restorative or aphrodisiac qualities.

The word 'wine' gets rather loosely translated – many Chinese 'wines' are in fact spirits. Rice wine – a favourite with Chinese alcoholics due to its low price – is intended mainly for cooking rather than drinking. Hejie Jiu (lizard wine) is produced in the southern province of Guangxi; each bottle contains one dead lizard suspended perpendicularly in the clear liquid. Wine with dead bees or pickled snakes is also desirable for its alleged tonic properties – in general, the more poisonous the creature, the more potent the tonic effects.

Tibetans have an interesting brew called *qingke*, a beer or spirit made from barley. Mongolians serve sour-tasting *koumiss*, made of fermented mare's milk with lots of salt added – most Westerners gag on the stuff. *Maotai*, a favourite of the Chinese, is a spirit made from sorghum (a type of millet) and is used for toasts at banquets – it tastes rather like rubbing alcohol and makes a good substitute for petrol or paint thinner.

Chinese women don't drink (except beer) in public – women who hit the booze are regarded as prostitutes. However, Western women can easily violate this social taboo without unpleasant consequences – the Chinese expect weirdness from Westerners anyway. As a rule Chinese men are not big drinkers, but toasts are obligatory at banquets – if you really can't drink, fill your wine glass with tea and say you have a bad stomach. In spite of all the toasting and beer drinking, public drunkenness is strongly frowned upon.

Imported booze – like XO, Johnny Walker, Kahlua, Napoleon Augier Cognac, etc – are highly prized by the Chinese for their prestige value rather than exquisite taste. The snob appeal plus steep import taxes translates into absurdly high prices – don't walk into a hotel bar and order this stuff unless you've brought a wheelbarrow full of cash. If you can't live without Western spirits, be sure to take advantage of your two-litre duty-free allowance on entry to China.

Drinks Vocabulary

beer
píjiǔ 啤酒
whisky
wēishìjì jiǔ 威士忌酒
vodka
fútèjiā jiǔ 伏特加酒
fizzy drink (soda)
qìshuǐ 汽水
Coca-Cola
kěkǒu kělè 可口可乐
tea
chá 茶
coffee
kāfēi 咖啡
water
kāi shuǐ 开水
mineral water
kuàng quán shuǐ 矿泉水
red grape wine
hóng pútáo jiǔ 红葡萄酒
white grape wine
bái pútáo jiǔ 白葡萄酒
rice wine
mǐ jiǔ 米酒
ice cold
bīngde 冰的

TOBACCO

Although the government has made some grumblings about starting an anti-smoking campaign, there is little indication that this is being taken seriously. Nor is it likely to be taken seriously since tax revenues from tobacco sales

is a major source of income for the government. It also seems that few are taking seriously the warnings to be careful with lit cigarettes – in hotel rooms note the burns in the carpets, bedsheets and furniture. Perhaps it's a good thing that Chinese hotels are made from bricks and concrete rather than wood.

If you're the sort of person who gets all upset by people smoking in crowded public places like buses and restaurants, either change your attitude, leave the country or buy a gas mask – the Chinese will be positively offended if you tell them not to smoke. As with drinking hard liquor, smoking in public is largely a male activity – a woman who smokes in public may be regarded as a prostitute.

The Chinese place considerable prestige value on smoking foreign cigarettes. Famous brand names such as Marlboro, Dunhill and 555 are high-priced and widely available – the ultimate status symbol for aspiring Chinese yuppies. Not surprisingly, the counterfeiting of foreign cigarettes has become a profitable cottage industry. As for rolling your own, you occasionally see the older Chinese doing this, but young people sneer at this proletarian activity – much better to spend a full day's pay for a pack of imported pre-rolled cigarettes which will elevate one's social status.

Many foreigners consider Chinese tobacco to have the gentle aroma of old socks, but some good-quality stuff is grown, mostly in Yunnan Province. While American-made Marlboros sell for about Y8 per pack, Chinese-made Red Pagoda Mountain (*hóng tǎ shān*) smokes go for Y12. Zhonghua cigarettes sell for Y10 in the yellow pack or Y20 in a red pack. On the opposite end of the scale, Beijing-made Badaling cigarettes cost a modest Y1.50. Many foreigners are familiar with Double Happiness (*shuāngxǐ*) cigarettes, the only brand so far which has been developed for export.

ENTERTAINMENT

When it comes to nightlife, China is no Bangkok or Hong Kong. Expats congregate in a few well-known pubs in the big hotels.

Beijing Opera participant

Beijing is also known for its Chinese opera, and Shanghai for its acrobatics – see those sections for details. China's English-language newspaper, the *China Daily*, has a reasonably good entertainment section which covers just the major cities favoured by tourists. In every sizable town, big hotels have their discos featuring Chinese music. Video game arcades keep the kids entertained.

Cinemas

Just a few hotels occasionally show English-language movies, but the situation is mostly hopeless. In Chinese cinemas, the dialogue is in Chinese. Many of the films originate in Hong Kong and have English subtitles, but the plot is always the same, which consists of murder, torture and kungfu with liberal quantities of tomato paste splattered in every direction. Just the thing to make you sleep well.

Discos

Beijing has a handful of discos featuring imported rock groups that cater to a purely Western crowd. Outside of these, entertainment is provided by Chinese bands or taped Chinese music. If this suites your tastes, you won't have to look far to find a disco – all big hotels have them, and the music is as loud and the coloured strobe lights just as intense as in the West.

Karaoke

What the Japanese weren't able to accomplish in WW II with bombs and bullets is now being done in a more subtle manner. We don't know whose idea it was, but it originated in Japan and is rapidly spreading. And now karaoke has taken over China – a karaoke bar can be found in just about every hotel, down every side street and there are even floating karaokes on board ships. To find one, look for signs advertising 'KTV' – an abbreviation for 'Karaoke TV' (Japan's answer to MTV).

Warning Besides any mental damage you may suffer from listening to karaoke, these places can be ruinous to your budget. There have been disturbing reports that the 'Tokyo Nightclub Syndrome' has hit China. Basically, foreigners (chiefly male) sitting in a karaoke bar are suddenly joined by an attractive young woman (or maybe several women) who 'just want to talk'. A few drinks are ordered – maybe just Coke or orange juice – and at the end of an hour's conversation a bill of perhaps Y5000 or so is presented to the hapless foreigner. The drinks might only cost Y100, while the other Y4900 is a 'service charge' for talking to the women, who are in fact bar hostesses.

Even more sinister is that these women approach foreigners on the street, ostensibly just to 'practise their English'. Somewhere in the conversation they suggest going to a 'nice place', which happens to be a karaoke bar. What they fail to mention is that they work for the bar and get a percentage of the profits for every sucker they bring in.

It needs to be mentioned that the victims of these schemes are not only foreigners. Overseas Chinese, Hong Kongers, Taiwanese and even mainland Chinese who appear to have money are also targeted. This rip-off system seems to be spreading – we've heard complaints so far from travellers in Canton, Guilin, Hangzhou and Xi'an.

Karaoke

Nowadays karaoke requires little in the way of introduction, even in the benighted West. As most people now know, it is of Japanese origin: a combination of the words *kara*, meaning 'empty', and *oke*, a Japanese contraction of the English word 'orchestra'. The idea is simple enough; the voice track is removed from a particular song, providing the audience with a do-it-yourself pop hit. The results will probably leave you with the impression that 99% of Chinese are completely tone deaf.

From small-time beginnings in Japan, karaoke first took Taiwan and Hong Kong by storm, and then inevitably slipped into China. Today it has become one of the main recreational activities for the Chinese. It's easy to recognise a karaoke parlour; they are usually lit up in neon and have a Chinese sign with the characters for *kālā* (a phonetic rendering of the Japanese) followed by the English letters 'OK'.

It's actually worth checking out a karaoke parlour or two while you are in China, though they are generally not cheap. There are two menus: one for the drinks; one for the songs. Don't expect much in the way of English songs, though you might get a Carpenters track or two (Rod Stewart's *I am Sailing* is a popular English number). It usually costs around Y5 to get up on stage and sing a song, and Chinese clamour for the opportunity. It doesn't matter how badly you sing. You'll get a polite round of applause from the audience when you finish, probably a rapturous round of applause if you have a big nose and blonde hair.

A recent development is the poor-person's karaoke bar, a TV set (a screen that shows a video with a bouncing ball following the lyrics is an essential adjunct to karaoke) set up by the roadside, where you pay a few jiao to sing into a small PA system. The Chinese government, with characteristic market savvy, has responded to the karaoke boom by setting up a department to produce karaoke numbers that give the public an opportunity to musically express their burning ardour for the Party. Perversely, everyone seems to prefer singing Rod Stewart numbers and the latest Taiwanese and Hong Kong pop hits. ■

Game Boy

More paranoid Westerners claim it's part of a sinister plot by the government to brainwash and pacify the public. Whatever the motive, Game Boys have become *de rigueur* in China – even beggars have them. The entire population now spends half their time pushing dots around a handheld video screen – calculating the social consequences will no doubt keep psychologists and sociologists busy for years.

THINGS TO BUY

The Chinese produce some interesting items for export – tea, clothing and Silkworm missiles – the latter not generally for sale to tourists.

Gone are the ration cards and the need for connections to buy TV sets and refrigerators – the consumer boom has arrived. Chinese department stores are like Aladdin's Caves stocked to the rafters with goodies – tourist attractions in themselves.

Unfortunately, quality has not kept pace with quantity. There is an awful lot of junk on sale – zippers which break literally the first time you use them, imitation Walkman's which last a week, electric appliances that go up in smoke the first time they're plugged in, etc. Given this state of affairs, you might wonder how China manages to successfully export so much – the simple fact is that export items are made to a much higher standard while junk is dumped on the local markets. Always test zippers, examine stitching, and in the case of electrical appliances, plug it in and make sure it won't electrocute you before handing over the cash. Chinese sales clerks expect you to do this – they'll consider you a fool if you don't.

Shopping Venues

Hong Kong Emporium Hong Kong department stores overflow with goods from China. Everything – from fake antiques to chopsticks – is available. Prices are sometimes much higher than in China itself, but occasionally lower! However, the main reason for buying in Hong Kong is the quality – the real rubbish that China produces is usually not dumped on the Hong Kong market.

There are two types of stores. The China-products-type stores such as Yue Hwa which sell the domestic, everyday items like clothing, hardware, spectacles and furniture, but also stock luxuries such as silk kimonos and negligees. The China Arts & Crafts stores stock the artsy craftsy, curio/antiquity stuff.

Yue Hwa has several branches, but the best store is at 301-309 Nathan Rd (the northwest corner of Nathan and Jordan roads), Kowloon, right near the Jordan MTR station.

China Arts & Crafts, owned by the PRC, has several branches. Some popular stores in Kowloon are at the New World Centre, Salisbury Rd; the Silvercord Shopping Centre, 30 Canton Rd near Haiphong Rd; Star House, corner of Salisbury and Canton roads; and 233-239 Nathan Rd.

Friendship Stores These stores originally stocked goods either imported from the West or in short supply in the ordinary stores. They were primarily meant for foreigners – locals were unable to shop in these places without permission from the work unit and wads of FEC – of course, exceptions were made for cadres. However, now that Chinese department stores sell imported goods, the whole concept of the Friendship Store is a rather archaic one. Only the large Friendship Stores

Buddha image tourist souvenir

– in Beijing, Shanghai and Canton – are really in a class by themselves for their extraordinary range of goods.

Some Friendship Stores will pack and ship

More Than Meets the Eye...

Once upon a time in China you got what you paid for. A mixed blessing: if the sales clerk said it was top-quality jade then it was top-quality jade and you'd pay through the nose for it. Times have changed – now there are all sorts of cheap forgeries and imitations about, from Tibetan jewellery to Qing coins, phony Marlboro cigarettes, fake Sony Walkmans (complete with fake Maxell cassette tapes), imitation Rolex watches, even fake Garden biscuits (Garden Bakeries is Hong Kong's biggest seller of bread, cakes and biscuits).

While eating counterfeit namebrand biscuits probably won't kill you, phony jewellery is disappointing at best and fake electronic goodies have a life expectancy of a few weeks.

Nor are fakes limited to consumer items – as high technology filters down to the masses, the manufacture of fake railway tickets, fake lottery tickets and fake Y100 RMB notes have become new cottage industries. Cadres now pad their expense accounts with fake receipts, one major reason why State-run companies are losing money. While counterfeiting namebrand goods is supposedly illegal, enforcement has been slack. China's foreign trading partners are none too happy about the fake Rolexes and pirated cassette tapes, and have threatened retaliation if Beijing doesn't crack down. Meanwhile, the government is having a hard enough time stopping the haemorrhage of State funds caused by the fake tickets and receipts.

What to do? It's not easy to say, but if you want to buy things like genuine antiques, try to get an official certificate of verification – just make sure the ink is dry. ∎

your purchases for you. Some imported goods still must be paid for in FEC, but most items can be bought with RMB.

Department Stores The regular Chinese department stores have a rich stock of cheap, everyday consumer items. They're well worth your time.

Hotel Shops These supply foreigners with Western and Japanese film, imported cigarettes and alcohol, Diet Coke, biscuits, Swiss chocolate, souvenirs, toothpaste, postcards, maps, foreign magazines and books. These stores can be expensive, but it's not certain – the five-star hotels tend to charge five-star prices. On the other hand, because of increased competition (there may be several shops in the hotel run leased by different vendors) prices are reasonable in many places.

Street Markets Blankets spread on the pavement and pushcarts in the alleys – this is where you find the lowest prices. All sales are final, forget warranties and no, they don't accept American Express. Nevertheless, the markets are interesting – there is some latitude for bargaining.

Antiques

Many of the Friendship Stores have antique sections, and some cities have antique shops, but prices are high so don't expect to find a bargain. Only antiques which have been cleared for sale to foreigners may be taken out of the country. When you buy an item over 100 years old it will come with an official red wax seal attached. This seal does *not* necessarily indicate that the item is an antique though! A Canadian who bought 'real' jade for Y1500 at a Friendship Store in Guilin later discovered in Hong Kong that it was a plastic fake. After six months of copious correspondence and investigation, the Guilin Tourism Bureau refunded the money and closed down the offending store. You'll also get a receipt of sale which you must show to Customs when you leave the country; otherwise the antique will be confiscated. Imitation antiques are sold everywhere. Some museum shops sell replicas, usually at extravagant prices.

Stamps & Coins

China issues quite an array of beautiful stamps – generally sold at post offices in the hotels. Outside many of the post offices you'll find amateur philatelists with books full of stamps for sale; it can be extraordinarily hard bargaining with these guys! Stamps issued during the Cultural Revolution make interesting souvenirs. Old coins are often sold at major tourist sites; many are forgeries.

Advertising

Advertising for the foreign market is one area the Chinese are still stumbling around in. A TV advertisement in Paris for Chinese furs treated viewers to the bloody business of skinning and cadavers in the refrigerator rooms before the usual parade of fur-clad models down the catwalk. It would be fun to handle the advertising campaigns for their more charming brand names.

There's Pansy underwear (for men) or you can pamper your stud with Horse Head facial tissues. Wake up in the morning with a Golden Cock alarm clock (since renamed Golden Rooster). You can start your breakfast with a glass of 'Billion Strong Pulpy C Orange Drink', or finish your meal with a cup of 'Imperial Concubine Tea'. For your trusty Walkman it may be best to stay away from White Elephant batteries, but you might try the space-age Moon Rabbit variety. Long March car tyres should prove durable, but we aren't too sure about the ginseng product with the fatal name of Gensenocide.

Out of the psychedelic '60s comes White Rabbit candy. Flying Baby toilet paper seems to have been discontinued, but you might still be able to find a pack of Puke cigarettes. The characters for Coca-Cola translate as 'tastes good, tastes happy' but the Chinese must have thought they were really on to something good when the 'Coke Adds Life' slogan got mistranslated and claimed to be able to resurrect the dead. ■

Oddities

If plaster statues are to your liking, the opportunities to stock up in China are abundant. Fat buddhas appear everywhere, and 60-cm-high Venus de Milos and multi-armed gods with flashing lights are not uncommon.

Lots of shops sell medicinal herbs and spices. Export tea is sold in extravagantly decorated tins – you can often get a better deal buying the same thing in the railway stations.

Getting There & Away

AIR

The air ticket alone can gouge a great slice out of anyone's budget, but you can reduce the cost by finding discounted fares. As a general rule, tickets to Hong Kong are cheaper than tickets directly to China. While Hong Kong is a great place to find cheap air fares, China is not – tickets purchased within China are invariably more expensive (usually much more) than those purchased elsewhere. This reflects the fact that there is practically no free-market competition in China, so the government can fix the price at the highest level the market will bear. Thus, a London to Beijing ticket is likely to be half the price of a Beijing to London ticket!

Bargain-Hunting

When you're looking for cheapie fares you have to go to a travel agent rather than directly to the airline, which can only sell fares at full list price. Travel agents often hesitate to sell you the cheapest ticket available, not necessarily because they want to cheat you, but because many budget tickets come with heaps of restrictions which you may find inconvenient. If you want the cheapest ticket, be sure to tell this to the travel agent and then ask what restrictions, if any, apply.

Off-season discounts are available from many airlines. The 'low season' is basically winter, except during the Chinese New Year. The 'shoulder season' is spring and autumn. Summer is the 'peak season' – peak prices are charged and seat availability can be a problem, but there are still ways to get discounts even at this time. If you're flying from the southern hemisphere, seasons are reversed – see the To/From Australia section for details.

There are plenty of discount tickets which are valid for 12 months, allowing multiple stopovers with open dates. These tickets allow for a great deal of flexibility. Just be sure that you check the ticket carefully – some are only valid for six months or even 60 days.

APEX (Advance-Purchase Excursion) tickets are sold at a discount but will lock you into a rigid schedule. Such tickets must be purchased two or three weeks ahead of departure, do not permit stopovers and may have minimum and maximum stays as well as fixed departure and return dates. Unless you definitely must return at a certain time, it's best to purchase APEX tickets on a one-way basis only. There are stiff cancellation fees if you decide not to use your APEX ticket.

Round-the-world (RTW) tickets are usually offered by an airline or combination of airlines, and let you take your time (six months to a year) moving from point to point on their routes for the price of one ticket. The main restriction is that you have to keep moving in the same direction; a drawback is that because you are usually booking individual flights as you go, and can't switch carriers, you can get caught out by flight availabilities, and have to spend more or less time in a place than you wish to.

Some airlines offer student discounts on their tickets – up to 25% to student card holders. Besides having an International Student Identity Card (ISIC), an official-looking letter from the school is also required by some airlines. With most airlines you only qualify for a discount if you are 26 or younger. These discounts are generally only available on ordinary economy-class fares. You wouldn't get one, for instance, on an APEX or a RTW ticket since these are already discounted.

Frequent-flyer deals were pioneered in the USA but have now spread to other countries. The way it works is that you fly frequently with one airline, and eventually you accumulate enough mileage to qualify for a free ticket or some other goodies. First, you must apply to the airline for a frequent flyer account number (some airlines will issue these on the spot or by telephone if you call their head office). A few airlines still require that you have a mailing address in the USA or Canada, but most now don't care where you live.

Every time you buy an air ticket and/or check in for your flight, you must inform the clerk of your frequent flyer account number, or else you won't get credit. Save your tickets and boarding passes, since it's not uncommon for the airlines to fail to give proper credit. You should receive monthly statements by post informing you how much mileage you've accumulated.

Once you've accumulated sufficient mileage to qualify for freebies, you are supposed to receive vouchers by mail. Many airlines have 'black-out periods', or times when you cannot fly for free (Christmas and the Chinese Lunar New Year are good examples). The worst thing about frequent-flyer programmes is that these tend to lock you into one airline, and that airline may not always have the cheapest fares or most convenient flight schedule.

Airlines usually carry babies up to two years of age at 10% of the relevant adult fare, a few may carry them free of charge. Reputable international airlines usually provide nappies (diapers), tissues, talcum and all the other paraphernalia needed to keep babies clean, dry and half-happy. For children between the ages of four and 12 the fare on international flights is usually 50% of the regular fare or 67% of a discounted fare. These days most fares are likely to be discounted.

Airlines

The attitude of the Chinese government has always been to keep lucrative business for itself. Foreigners are just thrown a few scraps, and even this is done grudgingly. This attitude certainly applies to the airline business – very few foreign carriers are permitted to fly into China, and even this was only reluctantly conceded so that China's own airlines could gain access to foreign markets.

The China Aviation Administration of China (zhōngguó mínháng), also known as CAAC, is the official flag carrier of the People's Republic of China (PRC). CAAC is known as Air China on international routes. See the Getting Around chapter for more info on CAAC.

Cathay Pacific (guótài hángkōng), though partly owned by British Airways, is a Hong-Kong-based company well known for good service. Cathay used to be the major foreign player in the China market but has seen its market share reduced in recent years. These days, Cathay doesn't fly into China under its own name, but runs a joint venture with CAAC to operate Hong Kong's other airline, Dragonair.

Dragonair (gǎnglóng hángkōng) started operations in 1985 with a single aircraft. Owned 100% by the PRC, there was much speculation that it would go bankrupt, and it probably would have if Cathay Pacific hadn't bought into it in 1990. Cathay apparently did this to please the Chinese government and to gain air routes to China. Cathay's influence is certainly visible – these days Dragonair's service is top-notch.

Dragonair is closely integrated with Cathay Pacific – you can book a Dragonair flights from Cathay Pacific offices around the world. Also, you can book combined tickets – a seat from Beijing to Vancouver, for example, flying Dragonair from Beijing to Hong Kong and then switching to a Cathay Pacific flight to Canada. Both flights can be included on a single ticket and luggage checked all the way through. If you're a member of Cathay's frequent flyer program (known as the 'Marco Polo Club'), flights on Dragonair can be credited to your mileage total.

To/From Hong Kong

Most travellers heading to the PRC from Hong Kong go by train or ferry, but flying provides a quick and easy way of getting to China's interior.

CAAC runs numerous direct flights between Hong Kong and every major city in China. This includes flights to Beijing, Canton, Chengdu, Guilin, Haikou, Kunming, Shanghai, Tianjin, Xiamen and Xi'an to name a few. Many of these are technically called 'charter flights' and therefore do not appear in the CAAC timetable, even though they operate according to a fixed regular schedule. The charter designation seems to be a ploy to allow the Chinese to avoid making formal agreements on landing rights.

In Hong Kong, travel agents cannot book you onto CAAC flights so you need to go directly to the airline office. There are two such offices in Hong Kong, as follows:

Central, ground floor, 17 Queen's Rd (☎ 8401199)
Kowloon, ground floor, Mirador Mansion, 54-64B Nathan Rd, Tsimshatsui (☎ 7390022)

For other matters besides booking tickets, there is a CAAC business office on the 34th floor, United Centre, 95 Queen's Way, Central.

Both offices tend to be very crowded with long queues, so go early (9 am) when they open. It is possible to buy all of your CAAC tickets from CITS in Hong Kong (both international and domestic), and even from some non-Chinese airlines that have reciprocal arrangements with CAAC. While this should work OK for international flights, this is generally *not* a good idea for Chinese domestic flights.

First of all, it saves you no money whatsoever. Secondly, the tickets issued outside China need to be exchanged for a proper stamped ticket at the appropriate CAAC offices in China – a few of these offices get their wires crossed and refuse to honour 'foreign' tickets. Furthermore, CAAC flights are often cancelled, but you'll have to return the ticket to the original seller in order to get a refund.

Dragonair has flights from Hong Kong to 14 cities in China: Beijing, Changsha, Chengdu, Dalian, Guilin, Haikou, Hangzhou, Kunming, Nanjing, Ningbo, Shanghai, Tianjin, Xi'an and Xiamen. Within China, Dragonair tickets can be bought from CITS or a number of Dragonair representatives listed in this book.

In Hong Kong, any travel agent with a computer can book you onto a Dragonair flight but you can directly contact the ticketing offices of Dragonair (☎ 7360202), Room 1843, Swire House, 9 Connaught Rd, Central; and 12th floor, Tower 6, China Hong Kong City, 33 Canton Rd, Tsimshatsui.

There is virtually no discounting on flights into China and Dragonair's prices are identical to what CAAC charges except in business class.

Hong Kong is a good place to pick up a cheap air ticket to almost anywhere in the world, and you have to go to the travel agents. Remember that prices of cheap tickets change and bargains come and go rapidly, and that some travel agents are more reliable than others. Travel agents advertise in the classified sections of the *South China Morning Post* and the *Hong Kong Standard* newspapers. Some reliable agents we've done business with include:

Traveller Services (☎ 3752222; fax 3752233), Room 1012, Silvercord Tower 1, 30 Canton Rd Tsimshatsui, Kowloon. The efficient staff give fast, reliable and cheap service.

Phoenix Services (☎ 7227378; fax 3698884), Room B, 6th floor, Milton Mansion, 96 Nathan Rd, Tsimshatsui, Kowloon. This is one of Hong Kong's longest running and most reliable operators.

Shoestring Travel (☎ 7232306; fax 7212085), Flat A, 4th floor, Alpha House, 27-33 Nathan Rd, Tsimshatsui – maybe not the friendliest, but cheap and reliable.

Hong Kong Student Travel Bureau or HKSTB (☎ 7213269, 3693804), Room 1021, 10th floor, Star House, Salisbury Rd, Tsimshatsui, Kowloon. Their service is reliable, though they are no longer the cheapest place.

Overcharging The most common way to be ripped off is to simply be overcharged. The technique has become sickenly familiar – you will be quoted an almost ridiculously low air fare and asked to put down a deposit. You'll be given a receipt, the fine print of which says something like 'ticket price not final' and 'deposit not refundable'. When you go back to pick up the ticket, you find that the great bargain-priced tickets are 'all sold out' but much more expensive tickets are now available (sometimes twice the price!). So you buy the more expensive ticket or forfeit the deposit (or some portion of it depending on what the fine print says). This scam is perfectly legal and very common. A word to the wise – if a travel agent asks for a deposit rather than the full amount, you can expect trouble.

The only way to be sure (well, reasonably sure) that there will be no surprises is to pay for the ticket in full. The receipt should clearly say that the ticket has been fully paid for and that no further charges will be necessary. In most cases you still have to come back later in the day or the next day to pick up the ticket because the travel agent has to go to the airline office to get it. If you are buying one of the cheap 'group tickets', you usually have to go to the airport to pick it up.

A word about these group tickets. These are often very cheap, and you don't really have to travel with a group to get one. The usual method of obtaining these tickets is to pay in full at the travel agency, receive a voucher and pick up the ticket *near* the airport check-in counter (not actually right at the counter). We've used this method ourselves and found it usually works OK, but there are often aggravations.

The first is that you've got to find the airline reps with the tickets to exchange your voucher – in one case we (and other passengers) wandered around the Japan Airlines (JAL) ticket counter in Hong Kong for an hour raising hell before the guy with the tickets finally showed up, and nearly missed the flight because of it. In another case, we paid for a one-year round-trip ticket but the ticket presented to us at the airport was only valid for 60 days – after raising more hell, the ticket was exchanged for a proper one. It might have been an innocent mistake, but read your ticket carefully and make sure it's just what you ordered.

To/From Australia

Australia is not a particularly cheap place to fly out of, but from time to time there are some quite good deals going. Shop around, as ticket prices vary.

Some of the cheapest tickets available in

Australia are the Advance Purchase fares. The cost of these tickets depends on whether you fly during the peak season or the low season. The high season for most flights from Australia to Asia is from 22 November to 1 February; if you fly out during peak period expect to pay more for your ticket.

Generally speaking, buying a round-trip or return air ticket works out cheaper than paying for separate or one-way tickets for each stage of your journey, although return tickets are more expensive the longer their validity. Most return tickets to Asia have 45-day, 90-day or 12-month validity.

Cheap flights from Australia to China generally go via one of the South-East Asian capitals such as Kuala Lumpur, Bangkok or Manila. If a long stopover between connections is necessary transit accommodation is sometimes included in the price of the ticket, but if it's at your own expense it may work out cheaper buying a slightly dearer ticket.

Quite a few travel offices specialise in discount air tickets. Some travel agents – smaller ones particularly – advertise cheap air fares in the travel sections of weekend newspapers such as the *Age* and the *Sydney Morning Herald*. Two well-known discounters are STA Travel and Flight Centre. STA Travel has offices in all major cities and at many university campuses, but you don't have to be a student to use STA Travel's services. The Flight Centre has dozens of offices throughout Australia and New Zealand. Both STA Travel and the Flight Centre regularly publish short brochures of their latest deals, including various RTW fares via Asia.

The cheapest way into China is via Hong Kong. The minimum 45-day low-season one-way air fare from Ausralia to Hong Kong is A$750 or A$1100 return, but flights are often heavily booked months in advance. Hong Kong is a convenient transit point for southern China, but too far south if you just want to get to Beijing or the north of the country.

The cheapest return tickets to Beijing are with MAS (Malaysian Air Systems) from Melbourne or Sydney. The fare is A$1305/

A$1410 low season/high season, but you will have to overnight at your own expense in Kuala Lumpur. China Airlines flies direct from Sydney to Beijing (stopping for a Customs control check at Canton Airport) for $A1450 return.

Nippon Airlines has a 90-day ticket to Beijing or Shanghai for A$1499 (A$1699 peak season) which includes one night's accommodation in Tokyo.

For organised tours to China, try Taking Off Tours (☎ 5212458) Suite 3, 618 St Kilda Rd, Melbourne; they have discount air tickets and can also book Trans-Siberian railway tickets from Beijing to Europe.

The departure tax from Australia is A$20 for passengers 12 years and over.

To/From New Zealand

The Flight Centre has a large central office (☎ 3096171) at 3A National Bank Tower, 205-225 Queen St, Auckland. The cheapest return ticket to Hong Kong is an Air New Zealand/Cathay 'companion fare' for NZ$2130 for two people. Qantas flies to Hong Kong via Australia for NZ$1190 (NZ$1690 return). The cheapest tickets to Beijing are with Japan Airlines via Tokyo for NZ$1821/1925 low/high season.

The departure tax from New Zealand is NZ$20. Children under two years of age are exempt.

To/From the UK

British Airways, British Caledonian, Cathay Pacific, Thai, Singapore Airlines, Malaysian Airline System (MAS) and other airlines fly between London (or Manchester) and Hong Kong. All of these forementioned airlines offer discounts; indeed, air-ticket discounting is a long-running business in the UK. The various agents advertise their fares and there's nothing under-the-counter about it at all. There are a number of magazines in the UK which have good information about flights and agents. These include: *Trailfinder*, free from the Trailfinders Travel Centre in Earls Court; and *Time Out* and *City Limits*, the London weekly entertainment guides widely available in the UK.

Discount tickets are almost exclusively available in London. You won't find your friendly travel agent out in the country offering cheap deals. The danger with discounted tickets in the UK is that some of the 'bucket shops' are unsound. Sometimes the backstairs over-the-shop travel agents fold up and disappear after you've handed over the money and before you've got the tickets. Get the tickets before you hand over the cash.

Two reliable London bucket shops are Trailfinders in Earls Court; and the Student Travel Association with several offices.

You can expect a one-way London-Hong Kong ticket to cost from around £330, and a return ticket around £600. London ticket discounters can also offer interesting one-way fares to Australia with a Hong Kong stopover from around £680.

A standard-price one-way ticket with CAAC from London to Beijing will cost £300 (£550 return).

To/From Europe

Fares similar to those from London are available from other European cities.

The Netherlands, Belgium and Switzerland are good places for buying discount air fares. In Antwerp, WATS has been recommended. In Zurich try SOF Travel and Sindbad. In Geneva try Stohl Travel. In the Netherlands, NBBS is a reputable agency.

CAAC has flights between Beijing and Belgrade, Bucharest, Frankfurt, London, Moscow, Paris, Athens and Zurich. Other international airlines operate flights out of Beijing but there are very few, if any, cut-rate fares from the Chinese end. Try the Russian airline Aeroflot and the Rumanian airline Tarom.

To/From the USA

There are some very good open tickets which remain valid for six months or one year (opt for the latter unless you're sure), but don't lock you into any fixed dates of departure. For example, there are cheap tickets between the US west coast and Hong Kong with stopovers in Japan, Korea and Taiwan for very little extra money – the departure dates

Top: Fire buckets, Great Mosque, Xi'an, Shaanxi (CL)
Bottom: The Terracotta Soldiers, Xi'an, Shaanxi (AS)

Top: Ling Yin Temple, Hangzhou, Zhejiang (RI'A)
Bottom: Sunrise over Huangshan, Anhui (AS)

can be changed and you have one year to complete the journey. However, be careful during the peak season (summer and Chinese New Year) because seats will be hard to come by unless reserved months in advance.

Usually, and not surprisingly, the cheapest fares to China are offered by bucket shops owned by ethnic Chinese. San Francisco is the bucket shop capital of America, though some good deals can be found in Los Angeles, New York and other cities. Bucket shops can be found through the Yellow Pages or the major daily newspapers. Those listed in both Roman and Chinese scripts are usually discounters. A more direct way is to wander around San Francisco's Chinatown where most of the shops are – especially in the Clay St and Waverly Place area. Many of these are staffed by recent arrivals from Hong Kong and Taiwan who speak little English. Enquiries are best made in person and be sure to compare prices – cheating is not unknown.

It's not advisable to send money (even cheques) through the post unless the agent is very well established – some travellers have reported being ripped off by fly-by-night mail-order ticket agents.

Council Travel is the largest student travel organisation, and though you don't have to be a student to use them, they do have specially discounted student tickets. Council Travel has an extensive network in all major US cities and is listed in the telephone book.

One of the cheapest and most reliable travel agents on the US west coast is Overseas Tours (☎ (800) 3238777 in California, (800) 2275988 elsewhere), 475 El Camino Real, Room 206, Millbrae, CA 94030. Another good agent is Gateway Travel (☎ (214) 9602000, (800) 4411183), 4201 Spring Valley Rd, Suite 104, Dallas, TX 75244 – they seem to be reliable for mail order tickets.

The cheapest fares through these agents are likely to be on Korean Air (KAL), the Taiwan-based China Airlines (CAL), Philippine Airlines (PAL) and Thai International Airways (THAI). American-based carriers like Delta, North-West and United also offer competitive fares plus frequent flyer credit, the only drawback being that their open return tickets are usually only valid for six months rather than one year (if you're flying one-way or will complete the return journey in six months this hardly matters). At the time of writing, North-West Airlines was offering the most generous frequent flyer credits.

One-way trips usually cost 35% less than a round trip. From Hong Kong, one-way fares to the American west coast start from about US$350 (with APEX restrictions). Return APEX tickets begin at US$640. APEX fares to New York start from US$460 one way, US$630 return on CAL.

For direct flights from the USA to China the general route is from San Francisco (with connections from New York, Los Angeles and Vancouver in Canada) to Tokyo, then Beijing, Shanghai or several other cities in China. It's entirely possible to go through to Beijing and then pick up the return flight in Shanghai. Tickets from the USA directly to China will cost around US$200 to US$300 more than tickets to Hong Kong, even though the flying distance is actually shorter.

In the USA, departure taxes are included in the price of the ticket so there is no additional charge at the airport.

To/From Canada

Travel CUTS is Canada's national student travel agency and has offices in Vancouver, Victoria, Edmonton, Saskatoon, Toronto, Ottawa, Montreal and Halifax. You don't have to be a student to use their services.

Getting discount tickets in Canada is much the same as in the USA. Go to the travel agents and shop around until you find a good deal. In Vancouver try Kowloon Travel, Westcan Treks and Travel CUTS.

Canadian Pacific Airlines are worth trying for cheap deals to Hong Kong although Korean Air may still be able to undercut them.

In general, air fares from Vancouver to Hong Kong or China will cost about 5% to 10% more than tickets from the US west coast.

In Canada, departure taxes are included in the original price of the ticket and there is no additional charge at the airport.

Besides numerous flights to Hong Kong, CAAC has two flights weekly which originate in Toronto, then fly onward to Vancouver, Shanghai and Beijing (in that order).

To/From Bangladesh

Dragonair now has flights from Dhaka to Kunming.

To/From Singapore

There are heaps of direct flights between Singapore and Hong Kong. A good place for buying cheap air tickets in Singapore is Airmaster Travel Centre. Also try STA Travel. Other agents advertise in the *Straits Times* classifieds.

CAAC has flights from Singapore to Canton, Xiamen and Beijing.

To/From Indonesia

Garuda Airlines has direct flights from Jakarta to Hong Kong, and from Denpasar to Hong Kong via Jakarta. CAAC has flights originating in Jakarta which continue onwards to Surabaya and then to Canton, Xiamen or Beijing.

Cheap discount air tickets out of Indonesia can be bought from travel agents at Kuta Beach in Bali and in Jakarta. There are numerous airline ticket discounters around Kuta – several on the main strip, Jalan Legian. In Jakarta, shop around for the best price from travel agents along Jalan Jaksa.

To/From Thailand

Bangkok is one of Asia's hot spots when it comes to finding bargain basement prices on air tickets.

There is a twice-weekly flight from Beijing to Bangkok via Canton (you can pick up the flight in Canton too), but it's not cheap at 9100 baht one way. There is also a very popular flight from Kunming to Bangkok via Chiang Mai on Thai Airways. A typical one-way fare from Bangkok to Kunming is 4000 baht; return 45-day tickets are 5100 baht.

Some of the Bangkok-Canton flights continue on to Shantou in China's Guangdong Province.

To/From Malaysia

Penang is one of the cheapest places in the world to purchase air tickets. CAAC has direct flights from Penang to Canton and Xiamen, though these won't come cheaply. You will be far better off flying to Hong Kong first if you want to save some money.

To/From Pakistan

CAAC has direct flights from Beijing to Karachi three times weekly.

To/From Turkey

There is a once-weekly flight between Beijing and Istanbul, stopping at Ürümqi en route. This ticket is outrageously expensive if bought in China (over US$1000), but travel agents in Istanbul can give generous discounts.

To/From Nepal

There are direct flights between Lhasa and Kathmandu twice a week, but you need to get the Chinese visa somewhere besides Kathmandu.

To/From Myanmar (Burma)

There is a once-weekly flight from Beijing to Rangoon with a stopover in Kunming. You can pick up the flight in Kunming too, but must have a visa for Myanmar – available in Beijing, not Kunming. You can stay in Myanmar for only two weeks and usually have to have an air ticket out of the country before they'll give you a visa. If the present political chaos continues, visits will remain an expensive and uncertain proposition.

To/From Japan

CAAC has several flights a week from Beijing to Tokyo and Osaka, via Shanghai. Japan Airlines (JAL) flies from Beijing and Shanghai to Tokyo, Osaka and Nagasaki. There are flights between Dalian and Fukuoka/Tokyo on All Nippon Airways.

Chinese visas obtained in Japan are outrageously expensive – US$80 to US$120 depending on which agent you use. You'll save money if you can obtain the visa elsewhere, but remember that Chinese tourist visas are normally only valid for one to three months from date of issue so it's useless to obtain it far in advance.

To/From South Korea

Diplomatic relations between the PRC and South Korea were only established in 1992. Since then, flights between Seoul and Tianjin have been opened on Asiana Airlines. The reason why there are no direct Seoul-Beijing flights is because CAAC wants to monopolise the route. The Chinese originally proposed that the Koreans fly Seoul-Shanghai and CAAC fly Seoul-Beijing. The Koreans refused, so Seoul-Tianjin emerged as the eventual face-saving compromise. Weird.

To/From North Korea

If you can get a visa for North Korea (a big *if*), there's a weekly flight between Beijing and Pyongyang for US$110. Getting a seat should be no problem – the planes are mostly empty.

To/From Philippines

CAAC has a twice-weekly flight from Beijing to Manila and a weekly flight from Canton to Manila. The cheapest option is the direct flight from Xiamen to Manila four times a week.

To/From Russia

Any air ticket you buy in Russia is likely to be expensive. You're not paying for fine service, you're paying for the lack of competition. Aeroflot, the only Russian airline, is well known for frequent cancellations, high prices, poor safety and lost or stolen luggage.

A direct Moscow to Beijing flight costs US$1200, and foreigners are required to pay in dollars even for domestic flights within Russia – forget any rumours you've heard about cheap rouble-denominated tickets. Nevertheless, there are a couple of tricks for

reducing the cost significantly. One of the best ways is to take a domestic flight from Moscow to the Siberian city of Irkutsk, then fly internationally from Irkutsk to Shenyang in north-east China. The combined Moscow-Irkutsk-Shenyang ticket costs US$495. From Shenyang, you can take a domestic flight to Beijing on CAAC for Y220. Taking this route may be slower and less convenient, but the saving of over US$700 is a powerful incentive.

To/From Vietnam

China Southern Airlines flies jointly with Vietnam Airlines between Ho Chi Minh City and Canton via Hanoi, using Soviet-built Tupolev 134 aircraft which are due to retire soon. The Guangzhou-Hanoi flight takes 1½ hours; Guangzhou-Ho Chi Minh City (US$270 one way) takes 4½ hours. There are two flights weekly.

The Beijing-Hanoi flight on China Southern Airlines now stops at Nanning (capital of China's Guangxi Province) en route – you can board or exit the plane there. Unfortunately, this flight is a favourite with traders ('smugglers' as far as the authorities are concerned). This not only makes it difficult to get a ticket, but travellers arriving in Hanoi on this flight have reported vigorous baggage searches and numerous Customs hassles. Going the other way, arrival in Nanning *might* be a little bit smoother, but don't count on it – Chinese Customs officers are diligently on the lookout for drugs, and if you look like 'the type', expect a thorough going over.

LAND

For most travellers, 'overland' to China means from Hong Kong or Macau by rail or bus. Another very popular route is the Trans-Siberian railway from Europe. Exotic routes include Tibet to Nepal and Xinjiang to Pakistan or Kazakhstan.

The borders with Vietnam and Laos closed in 1979, but Vietnam has reopened though getting across often requires ingenuity. It is not possible to travel overland to Myanmar (Burma). The borders with

Afghanistan and Bhutan are also out of bounds.

At the time of writing, India was about to open its border with China for trade at Garbyang, Uttar Pradesh, just north of the Nepalese border; it remains to be seen whether travellers will be able to use this route. Another possible border opening getting some press recently was Thailand and Xishuangbanna via a land crossing through either Laos or Myanmar. The logistics of getting this one off the ground look fairly insurmountable, but only time will tell.

Foreigners are not usually allowed to drive cars or motorbikes around China and are therefore not usually allowed to take them in. Bicycles are allowed on some routes but not others – the regulations governing the use of bicycles is in a constant state of confusion.

To/From Hong Kong

Train There are several ways to make the crossing between Hong Kong and Canton, but local train is by far most popular. The local train is least expensive. For more than double the price, you can go by the very popular Hong Kong-Canton express train.

In theory you're allowed to take bicycles on the express train, stowed in the freight car, but this has often been difficult in practice. Some people have had their machines impounded.

In Canton it's very difficult to buy tickets for trains unless you go through CITS – which means you can forget about getting Chinese price.

For the timetable and prices for this train, see the Canton chapter.

Bus The Chinese are building (very slowly) a super-highway from Hong Kong to Canton and Zhuhai. Eventually, we can expect to see some sort of Hong Kong-Canton express bus service. Some of the luxury resort hotels in Shenzhen run weekend bus excursions across the border – these cater to the Hong Kong market and few foreigners are likely to make use of these services.

To/From Macau

On the other side of the border from Macau is the Special Economic Zone (SEZ) of Zhuhai. The Macau-Zhuhai border is open from 7 am to 9 pm and cyclists can ride across. Most people just take a bus to the border and walk across.

For full details, see the Zhuhai section of the Canton chapter.

To/From Pakistan

The Karakoram Highway leading from Kashgar in China's Xinjiang Province into northern Pakistan was closed during and after the civil disturbances in Kashgar in 1990, but since 1992 has reopened for individual travel. Leaving China for Pakistan takes you through the dramatic snow-covered Karakoram mountain ranges. The road closes every winter, between about November and May, depending on the snow. For full details, see the Karakoram Highway section of the Xinjiang chapter.

Some cyclists have succeeded in riding across the Pakistani border, some have had to put their bikes on a bus, and some have been refused permission altogether.

To/From Kazakhstan

At present there is a direct daily bus service between Ürümqi and Alma Ata, and this is probably the easiest way to travel between China and Kazakhstan. At the time of writing, visas for Kazakhstan were being issued on the border. You need to organise a Chinese visa beforehand, however. Trains between the two cities only run once a week, and work out more expensive than the bus. Some travellers have travelled from Alma Ata to Yining, and made their way from there to Kashgar or Ürümqi. If you enter China this way, make sure that your entry stamp does not restrict your place of exit to the same place – some travellers have found that they were expected also to exit by way of the border town of Khorgos.

To/From Nepal

The good news is that the Lhasa-Kathmandu road reopened in 1993 after being closed to foreigners for over three years. The bad news is that there are still a few substantial bureaucratic hurdles to clear, a shortage of public transport on the Chinese side and a major problem with corruption (also on the Chinese side). But keep your ear to the travellers' grapevine, because all of these hurdles could suddenly disappear if Beijing cracks the whip – or new barriers could also be erected just as quickly.

To begin with, if you are entering Tibet from Nepal, you must have a visa for China. That *should* be no problem except that the Chinese embassy in Kathmandu has been issuing visas stamped with the words 'not valid for entry into Tibet'. However, if you've obtained a Chinese visa elsewhere (Hong Kong or Bangkok, for instance), then there's no problem.

Well, no problem with visas, that is. Transport is the next hurdle. At the time of writing there were public buses operating on the Nepalese side right up to the border, but there's not much activity on the Tibetan side. People going from Lhasa to Nepal normally get to the border by rented jeep – since the jeeps return home empty, the drivers are more than happy to find travellers waiting at the border looking for rides to Lhasa. Prices average out at Y700 to Y1000 per person to Lhasa, but there is a fair amount of latitude for bargaining. The problem is you might have to wait a while for an available jeep. There are regular bus services to Shigatse, from where there are daily buses to Lhasa, but buses between Lhasa and the border only run three or four times a month.

Walking from the border to Lhasa is not recommended, but going by bicycle might be feasible. The trouble is the Chinese authorities. At the time of writing, some travellers were being allowed to go by bike and some weren't. The Chinese themselves do not seem to know the rules, and finding out what will be permitted next week or next month requires a knowledge of astrology, crystal ball reading or tarot cards.

Finally, there is this matter of corruption. This doesn't affect you so much when leaving Tibet, but if you want to get to Tibet from the Chinese side, you need to go past officials whose job is to separate you from your cash and put it into their pockets. Going from Lhasa to Golmud by bus seems to be no hassle – the problem is if you want to go the other way. The bus company, CITS and Golmud PSB have a scam going – foreigners must pay at least four times the domestic price. Into whose pocket this vast sum of cash is going is a matter of speculation.

There are other scams involving transport to Tibet from the Chinese side. See the Tibet chapter for more details.

To/From North Korea

There are twice-weekly trains between Beijing and Pyongyang. Visas can be obtained (with difficulty) from the North Korean representative office in Macau. The North Korean Embassy in Beijing is also worth a try, but the staff there seem to be very uncooperative. Should you succeed in getting a North Korean visa, your time in that country will be both tightly controlled and expensive. For full details, see Lonely Planet's *North-East Asia on a shoestring* or *Korea – a travel survival kit*.

To/From Vietnam

This recently opened border still sees very few travellers.

Hanoi-Pingxiang On this route, it is necessary to travel to the Vietnamese border town of Langsön by train or bus. From there you can hitch a ride on a motorcycle up to the border post. The nearest town on the Chinese side is Pingxiang (Guangxi). There are regular buses and two trains a day to Nanning (takes three or four hours).

The obstacles to doing this crossing are not insurmountable, but it will require a little persistence. If you plan to use this route you should specify Langsön as your point of exit when applying for a Vietnamese visa. In Hanoi you will have to organise an exit permit (US$10) to take this crossing.

Travelling the other way from China to Vietnam is a little more difficult in that the Vietnamese border guards are not particularly happy about travellers turning up. You will need to have already organised a Vietnamese visa (they are not available on the border or in Nanning), and the nearest visa issuing offices are in Hong Kong and Beijing. Expect long delays on the border.

Kunming-Hanoi As of 18 May 1993 this land route between Kunming and Hanoi was reopened. With direct access to Kunming, this route is likely to be of even more interest to travellers than the Hanoi-Pingxiang route.

Those coming from China will need to have a Vietnamese visa (there's no way around this one). If your visa does not specify the entry point as Laocai (the Vietnamese border town), you will need to pay US$20 for an 'entry permit'. Access to Vietnam from Kunming is via the town of Hekou. Both buses and trains run there from Kunming. Buses (Y50 RMB) take 14-16 hours on a surprisingly good but mountainous road. Trains to Hanoi from the Kunming north railway station take around 18 hours and cost Y120 hard sleeper. From the Vietnamese border town of Laocai, it is necessary to travel on to Pholu, either by bus or you can hitch a ride on a motorcycle. From Pholu, there are reasonably frequent bus services on to Hanoi.

TRAIN

The Trans-Siberian Railway connects Europe to Asia, and has proved to be a popular route with Western (and more recently, Japanese) travellers.

There is some confusion of terms here – there are, in fact, three railways. The 'true' Trans-Siberian line runs from Moscow to the eastern Siberian port of Nakhodka, from where one can catch a boat to Japan. This route does not go through either China or Mongolia. There is also the Trans-Manchurian line which crosses the Russia-China border at Zabaikalsk-Manzhouli, also completely bypassing Mongolia. The Trans-Mongolian line connects Beijing to Moscow, passing through the Mongolian capital city, Ulaan Baatar.

Most readers of this book are not interested in the first option since it excludes China – your decision is basically between the Trans-Manchurian or the Trans-Mongolian. In fact, it makes little difference. The Trans-Mongolian is marginally faster but requires you to purchase an additional visa and endure another border crossing, but you do at least get to see the Mongolian countryside roll past your window.

There are different classes but all are acceptably comfortable. In deluxe class there are two beds per cabin while economy class has four beds.

Which direction you go makes a difference in cost and travelling time. The trains from Beijing take 1½ days to reach Ulaan Baatar. The journey from Moscow to Ulaan Baatar is four days.

There are major delays (six to ten hours) at both the China-Mongolia and Russia-Mongolia borders during which time you will not have your passport thanks to rigorous Customs inspection of all the freight being carried by 'passengers'. Very little is actually confiscated, but Customs officers try to extract import duty from the traders. On the other hand, those holding passports from Western countries typically sail right through Customs without their bags even being opened, which is one reason why people on the train will approach you and ask if you'll carry some of their luggage across the border. During this time, you can get off the train and wander around the station, which is just as well since the toilets on the train are locked during the whole inspection procedure. You will not have your passport at this time – the authories take it away for stamping. When it is returned, inspect it closely – sometimes they make errors like cancelling your return visa for China.

On the Chinese side of the Russian or Mongolian border, about two hours are spent changing the bogies (undercarriage wheels). This is necessary because Russia, Mongolia and all former East Bloc countries use a wider rail gauge than China and the rest of the world. The reason has to do with security – it seems the Russians feared an invasion by train.

Ticketing Hassles

The international trains are very popular, so popular that it's hard to book this trip anytime except during winter. Travel agents in Europe say that it's even difficult to get an October booking in April! It's best to plan ahead as far as possible.

The reason for the popularity of the train actually has little do with tourism. It has much to do with politics and economics. The 'travellers' on the Trans-Siberian fall into three classes; traders (smugglers), immigrants (mostly illegal) and actual travellers.

The traders are an interesting case. They take advantage of the economic disparities between China, Russia, eastern Europe and Mongolia. The traders buy up ridiculously cheap subsidised goods in Russia and Mongolia for sale in China and elsewhere, and then purchase inexpensive Chinese goods like clothing for sale in Mongolia, Russia and Poland. Due to the scarcity of goods in Russia, there tends to be more freight moving from China to Eastern Europe than the other way around. However, some valuable items move from west to east, such as deer antlers which figure so prominently in Chinese aphrodisiac recipes.

Among the more bizarre (and cruel) cargo items are puppy dogs. The puppies are bought in Russia, drugged, stuffed into bags and smuggled into China – not all survive this rough treatment. It's illegal to own dogs in Beijing, but China's nouveaux riches (especially the wives of cadres) are apparently willing to pay a premium for cutesy, furry little animals to keep around the house, and so the black market exists. Sadly, once the cutesy little puppies grow up and become decidedly less cutesy, they are often abandoned.

In free-market economies, all this trading (except for the puppies) would be perfectly legal and the goods would be transported by freight train or container ship, declared on arrival with perhaps some Customs duty paid. In the 'planned' economies, imports and exported are rigidly controlled by the State and free trade is more or less illegal.

However, the planners have left open one giant loophole; passengers on the international trains are permitted to bring luggage for no extra charge. And so they do; *lots* of 'luggage'. In fact, in a four-bed passenger compartment, it's not so unusual for only one actual person to be travelling using four passenger tickets, with the entire compartment stacked to the ceiling with boxes, bags and shipping crates. Needless to say, this creates considerable chaos at the railway stations when everyone tries to board the train with tons of luggage. Just how much longer this situation will be tolerated before the authorities crack down is unknown. In the meantime, international train tickets are becoming more and more difficult to get, but it is still possible.

Immigrants are another major class of rail passengers, though there are fewer now due to heavy crackdowns. Many of these people are economic (and sometimes political) refugees from Sri Lanka, Bangladesh, Nigeria and other countries with sick economies and civil wars. It's fairly easy for these people to obtain visas for China, so they came to Beijing. From there, they head to Moscow by train and finally to Western Europe.

The refugees face some serious obstacles along the way. Western European nations don't want them, so they won't be issued visas, and without a visa for a Western European country, the Russians also won't issue visas to people from Third World nations. Organised criminal syndicates help the refugees (after receiving a substantial cash payment) with forged visas. Refugees get as far as the border with Germany, or to Paris via an Aeroflot flight from Moscow. The forged visas are discovered on arrival, but then the refugees apply for political asylum. An application for political asylum takes many months to investigate before being rejected or accepted, and during this time the refugees work and pay off the money they borrowed to get to Europe. If their application is finally rejected, they move on to another Western country and try again, or else simply 'disappear'.

Tickets

From Europe Travel Service Asia (☎ (07) 371-4963, fax (07) 371-4769), Kirchberg 15, 7948 Dürmentingen, Germany, is highly recommended for low prices and good service. These people have been on the train themselves and have travelled to Mongolia, and they know what they're talking about.

In the UK, one of the experts in budget rail travel is Regent Holidays (UK) Ltd (☎ (0272) 211711; telex 444606; fax (0272) 254866), 15 John St, Bristol BS1 2HR. Another agency geared towards budget travellers is Progressive Tours (☎ (071) 2621676), 12 Porchester Place, Connaught Square, London W2 2BS.

Several travellers have recommended Scandinavian Student Travel Service (SSTS), 117 Hauchsvej, 1825 Copenhagen V, Denmark. This organisation has branch offices in Europe and the USA, and provides a range of basic tours for student or budget travellers, mostly during summer.

From China In theory, the cheapest place to buy a ticket is at the office of China International Travel Service (CITS) in the Beijing International Hotel. The problem with this theory is that CITS doesn't make advance reservations by phone, fax or through their Hong Kong office. In other words, you first must go to Beijing and fight like everyone else for a ticket, with a good chance that the next seat available will be three months later. There are no queues at the CITS office, just an unruly mob. A Beijing-Moscow ticket (if you can get one) costs US$175. Contrary to what CITS brochures say, Trans-Siberian tickets bought from Beijing CITS are basically nonrefundable – after a vociferous argument, you might get back 20% of the purchase price if you're lucky.

Your other alternative is to buy from a private travel agent. This will always be more expensive than CITS because the agents must purchase their tickets from CITS too. However, it may well work out cheaper to go through a travel agent – hanging around Beijing for three months or making a separate trip to Beijing just to buy a ticket will also cost you money. Almost all of these agents are based in Hong Kong.

The best organised of the Trans-Siberian ticket vendors is Monkey Business, officially known as Moonsky Star (☎ 7231376, fax 7236653), 4th floor, Block E, Flat 6, Chungking Mansions, 30 Nathan Rd, Tsimshatsui, Kowloon. Monkey Business also maintains an information office in Beijing at the Qiaoyuan Hotel (new building), room 716 (☎ 3012244 ext 716), but it's best to book through their Hong Kong office as far in advance as possible. A booking can be done by telephone or fax and a deposit can be wired to them. One advantage of booking through them is that they keep all their passengers in a group (for mutual protection against theft). Monkey Business can also arrange visas and stopover tours to Mongolia and Irkutsk (Siberia).

You can get a very similar deal from Phoenix Services (☎ 7227378) in Room B, 6th floor, Milton Mansion, 96 Nathan Rd, Tsimshatsui, Kowloon.

Another Hong Kong agent selling Trans-Mongolian tickets is Time Travel (☎ 3666222, fax 7395413), 16th floor, Block A, Chungking Mansions, 30 Nathan Rd, Tsimshatsui, Kowloon. Their current cheapest price for a Beijing-Moscow ticket is US$245. Their price is competitive but they offer no services beyond the ticket and cannot organise visas.

You can organise tickets and visas through Wallem Travel (☎ 5286514), 46th floor, Hopewell Centre, 183 Queen's Rd East, Wanchai, Hong Kong. However, this place is more into booking pricey tours than selling tickets – see the Tours section for details.

No matter where you buy your ticket, an extra Y3.50 is added to the price for the mandatory purchase of a CITS booklet entitled *Guide Book For International Railway Passenger*. It looks impressive, with colour glossy photos, timetables and other info – sadly, the information is about 90% wrong.

Black Market Once upon a time, black-market tickets were so common that it seemed like everyone on the train had one.

Indeed, you were almost a fool not to buy one. The way it worked was that people with connections would go to Budapest and buy Beijing-Moscow tickets in bulk for around US$50 a piece, then take the tickets to Beijing and sell them for about US$150. A nice little business, while it lasted.

The good old days are gone. Eastern European countries no longer sell tickets for ridiculously cheap subsidised prices. Not that the black market has disappeared – it's still around. The problem is that the black-market scene has turned ugly. Rather than being cheaper, black-market tickets are now more expensive than tickets you could buy yourself – it's simply the law of supply and demand. In Moscow, Russian gangsters buy up big blocks of tickets and sell them at whatever price the market will bear. In Beijing, the black market is dominated by Uygurs (from China's Xinjiang Province) and local Chinese thugs. In order for anyone to be able to buy up so many tickets, connections on the inside are needed, which requires the payment of considerable bribes. The typical black-market price for a four-bed compartment from Beijing to Moscow is around US$2000, subject to some seasonal variation.

If you attempt to buy a ticket from CITS, it's likely you'll be asked to 'come back tomorrow'. When you come back, you'll probably be told again to 'come back tomorrow'. This may continue for five days or so, at the end of which time you *might* get a ticket, but probably not. If you do, you'll be told that somebody 'cancelled' and that's why the ticket is suddenly available. This is nonsense – nobody cancels because CITS doesn't refund cancelled tickets. What happens is that CITS sells the tickets out the back door to black marketeers – if any remain unsold, the black marketeers return them on the very last day and CITS tries to flog them off to the hopeful 'come back tomorrow' people.

There is also a problem with cheaper Russian tickets partially denominated in roubles which are valid for Russian passport holders only. Black marketeers sell these Russian tickets to gullible foreigners who then find they can't use them. There has also been a problem with forged tickets. Once you try to get on the train and realise that your ticket is worthless, just try filing a complaint with your local black marketeer.

Black marketeers hang out around the CITS booking office in Beijing and will hustle any likely-looking customers. We suggest that you ignore them. At the time of writing, the Chinese police were taking a keen interest in breaking the black market or getting their share of the profits, whichever comes first. Hopefully, the situation will improve.

Needs, Problems & Precautions

Bring plenty of cash US dollars in small denominations for the journey – only in China can you readily use the local currency. In China, food is plentiful and readily available from both the train's dining car and vendors in railway stations. In both Russia and Mongolia, food quality is poorer, but meals are available on the train. Once you get off the train it's a different story – food can be extremely difficult to buy in both Russia and Mongolia, and if you don't want to starve, bring plenty of munchies like biscuits, instant noodles, chocolate and fruit. No alcohol is sold on the Russian and Mongolian trains, but a limited selection of booze can be bought in the Chinese dining car. Except for beer, most Chinese alcohol tastes like low-grade jet fuel and you'd be wise to purchase your own stash before boarding the train.

Showers are only available in the deluxe carriages. In economy class, there is a washroom. You can manage a bath with a sponge but it's best to bring a large metal cup (available in most Chinese railway stations) and use it as a scoop to pour water over yourself from the washbasin. The metal cup is also ideal for making coffee, tea and instant soup. Hot water is available on the trains.

There is much theft on the train, so never leave your luggage unattended, even if the compartment is locked. Make sure at least one person stays in the compartment while the others go to the dining car. A lot of theft is committed by Russian gangs who have master keys to the compartments, so don't assume that a 'foreign face' means honesty.

Mongolians, Russians and Polish passengers boarding the train will usually have mountains of luggage, which they will often try to put into your compartment. If there is even one Mongolian, Russian or Polish person staying in your compartment you're going to have a difficult time preventing this. If you're all foreigners, stand up for your rights aggressively, because if you don't you will truly be buried in bags. Many people riding the train are bringing back goods to sell, and they don't mind using your compartment as their cargo bin. If they get hassled by Customs at the border (very likely) they'll say the bags belong to you. These arguments over where would-be traders put their luggage is one of the worst aspects of making this journey.

The Chinese have now 'cracked down' and a luggage limit of 35 kg per passenger is being enforced – there are scales at the railway station and it's likely your luggage will be weighed. However, the new rules haven't done much to cut down on the cargo – a few dollars in the right pocket can perform well-known miracles. The weight limits might better be thought of as 'guidelines'.

It's important to realise that food in the dining car is priced in local currency. This is true even in Mongolia or Russia. Many foreigners have the mistaken impression that they must pay in US dollars. The railway staff will gladly accept your dollars instead of roubles or togrogs at some ridiculous exchange rate, which means you'll be paying many times the real price. There are black-market moneychangers at border railway stations, but all the usual dangers of black-market exchanges apply.

Books

A popular book about this journey is the *Trans-Siberian Handbook* by Bryn Thomas – Trailblazer Publications, distributed through Roger Lascelles in the UK.

Visas

Russian If you ride the train through Russia, you have a choice between getting a transit visa or a tourist visa. There is a very big difference between the two. Transit visas are valid for a maximum of 10 days and tourist visas are required if the journey is broken. In practice, you can stay in Moscow for three days on a transit visa and apply for an extension when you arrive. This only really works if you're going from Beijing to Moscow rather than the other way – otherwise you'll miss your train to Beijing. Trying to extend a tourist visa is much more expensive – the hotel 'service bureau' will do it for you through Intourist, but only with expensive hotel bookings.

With a tourist visa, you can stay in Russia much longer, but you will pay heavily for the privilege. All hotels must be booked through Intourist in advance of arrival. The attitude of Intourist is to milk travellers for every cent they can get (who said they aren't capitalists?). For a two-star hotel, expect to pay around US$65 outside of Moscow, and US$135 a day in Moscow. The hotel bookings must be confirmed by telex (which you will also have to pay for) and the whole bureaucratic procedure takes about three weeks. On a transit visa, you can sleep in the station or in one of the rapidly proliferating cheap private hostels.

Before you can get a transit visa, you must have a ticket in hand or a ticket voucher. A transit visa can be issued the same day or take two to five days depending on how much you pay. There are two fees you must pay; a visa application fee and a bizarre 'consular fee' for certain nationalities. Visa application fees are US$18 for a visa issued in five days; US$27 if issued in three days; and US$55 if issued the same day. The consular fee varies according to which passport you hold; free for Aussies, Kiwis, Canadians, Brits and Americans, but Swiss citizens pay US$50, it's US$35 for the Dutch and Austrians have the honour of paying US$80. Three photos are required. The embassy does not keep your passport, so you are free to travel while your application is being processed.

Someone can apply for the visa on your behalf and use a photocopy of your passport (all relevant pages must be included). If you want to change an already-issued transit visa, this will cost you US$18. Reasons for changing could be if you want go on a different date or change the final destination (Budapest instead of Berlin, for example). Russian embassies are closed during all Russian public holidays: New Year's Day (1 January), Women's Day (8 March), Labour Day (1 & 2 May), Victory Day (9 May), Constitution Day (7 October), and October Revolution (7 & 8 November).

In Beijing, the Russian Embassy (☎ 5322051, 5321267) is at Beizhongjie 4, just off Dongzhimen and west of the Sanlitun Embassy Compound. Opening hours are Monday to Friday from 9 am to noon. You can avoid the long queues at the Beijing Embassy if you apply at the Russian Consulate (☎ 3242682) in Shanghai, 20 Huangpu Lu, opposite the Pujiang Hotel. However, their opening hours are brief: Tuesday and Thursday from 10 am until 12.30 pm.

The Russian Consulate in Budapest is at Nepkoztarsasag utca 104 (open Monday, Wednesday and Friday from 10 am to 1 pm).

Mongolian The Mongolian Embassy in Beijing is open all day, but the visa section keeps short hours – only on Monday, Tuesday, Thursday and Friday from 8.30 am to 11.30 am. They close for all Mongolian holidays, and they shut down completely for the entire week of National Day (Naadam), which officially falls on 11-13 July. In the UK, the Mongolian Embassy (☎ (01) 9370150, 9375235) is at 7 Kensington Court, London W85 DL.

Visas cost US$22 (US$28 for UK citizens) if picked up the next day, or US$26 (US$36 for UK citizens) for same-day delivery. Some nationalities can get visas for free (India, Finland etc). One photo is required for a tourist visa but none is needed for a transit visa.

It's easy enough to get a transit visa, but obtaining a tourist visa requires the same bureaucratic somersaults as required for getting a Russian tourist visa.

Polish Most travellers between Western Europe and Moscow go via Poland, though there are alternative routes via Finland or Hungary. A Polish visa is not needed by nationals of Austria, Belgium, Denmark, Finland, France, Germany, the Netherlands, Italy, Luxembourg, Malta, Norway, Sweden, Switzerland and the USA. Polish visas are required for Australians, British and New Zealanders, and cost US$32. You get a discount on these fees if you have a student (ISIC) card. These prices are for transit visas; tourist visas cost even more.

In China, there is a Polish Embassy in Beijing and a Polish Consulate in Canton. Poland has embassies in most Western European capitals. Two photos are needed.

Hungarian Americans, Canadians and most West Europeans (including UK citizens) don't need a visa. Australians and New Zealanders do (US$18); two photos are required. Get a tourist rather than transit visa since Hungary is worth visiting.

Unless you travel in a group, the selection of travelling companions for the journey is delightfully or excruciatingly random – a judgment upon which you have five or six days to ponder.

On the trip you can get stuck in the cross-fire of political debates, retreat to a chess game, an epic novel or epic paralytic drinking bouts, or teach English to the train attendant. The scenery is mostly melancholy birch trees, but there are some occasionally fascinating views – snow on the Mongolian Desert and the scenery around Lake Baikal, the deepest lake in the world.

At sub-zero temperatures you can exercise along the platform, start snowball fights or wonder about the destination of teenage recruits milling around a troop train. In these stations, make sure your luggage is secure – during the few minutes that you're out on the platform a sneak thief could pinch your camera and other valuables.

A chess set soon makes friends. The Russians produce not only talented players but also courteous ones – perhaps as a gesture of friendship they'll quickly cede the first game but the rest are won with monotonous regularity. Prodigious amounts of alcohol disappear down Russian throats, so expect a delighted interest in consuming your hoard of Chinese alcohol, for which there is plenty of time. On the other hand, if you want to repulse freeloaders you might try injecting them with a bottle of one of those ghastly Chinese liquers – the recipient is either going to stagger out in absolute revulsion or remain vaccinated and your stock is doomed.

For those interested in barter or fund-raising: tea, watches, jeans and Walkman cassette recorders are all sources of inspiration to passengers.

SEA
To/From Hong Kong
Canton The overnight ferry between Hong Kong and Canton is one of the best and most popular ways of entering or exiting China. The vessels are large, clean and very comfortable – but bring a light jacket because the air-conditioning is fierce!

If you're in a hurry, there are hovercraft and jetcats (jet-powered catamarans) which make the Hong Kong-Canton run in three hours.

There is also a daily ferry which connects Canton to Macau.

For complete information on doing this trip, see the Canton chapter.

Shanghai Several boats ply the south-east coast between Hong Kong and Shanghai, with departures approximately once every five days. Many people take the boat when

they leave China to return to Hong Kong – the trip gets rave reviews. Details of tickets and fares for the trip are given in the Shanghai section.

In Hong Kong, tickets for the boat can be bought from the offices of China Travel Service or from the China Merchants Steam Navigation Company (☎ 5440558, 5430945), 18th floor, 152-155 Connaught Rd, Central District, Hong Kong Island.

Other Ships from Hong Kong A couple of boats travel to Chinese ports on the south-east coast. These are worth investigating since the coast is one of the most attractive parts of China, and some of the most interesting towns are located here.

To/From Shantou The ship runs approximately four times weekly in each direction and the cruise takes 14 hours. There is considerable variation in price according to class. For tickets purchased in Hong Kong, fare is HK$221 (economy) to HK$970 (suite). The same tickets purchased in Shantou are Y139 to Y672.

To/From Xiamen The *Jimei* runs between Hong Kong and Xiamen. It departs from Hong Kong every Tuesday at 1 pm, arriving in Xiamen 22 hours later. Departures from Xiamen are on Monday at 3 pm.

To/From Hainan Island Two boats, the *Donghu* and *Malan*, run approximately five times monthly between Haikou and Hong Kong, taking 18 hours to complete the journey. Another boat, the *Shan Cha*, runs twice a month between Sanya and Hong Kong via Haikou. In Hong Kong, buy tickets from CTS. Tickets bought in Hong Kong cost from HK$296 for 3rd class to HK$425 for deluxe class. In Haikou, tickets cost 20% less and can be bought from CTS – those booked at the hotels cost more.

To/From Wuzhou There is a direct hovercraft from Hong Kong to Wuzhou. It departs Hong Kong on even-numbered dates from the China Ferry Terminal at 7.20 am. The trip takes around 10 hours. Tickets in Hong Kong can be bought at the China Travel Service and from some of the other agencies that issue China visas. Round-trip tickets can also be booked, but the ticket only remains valid for one month.

From Wuzhou you can get a bus to Guilin or Yangshuo, but unless you want to take the night bus to Yangshuo (it arrives around 3 am) you will have to spend the night in Wuzhou. Returning to Hong Kong, the hovercraft departs Wuzhou on odd-numbered dates at 7.30 am. Check the departure time before leaving.

To/From Japan
There is a regular boat service between Shanghai and Osaka/Kobe. The ship departs once weekly, one week to Osaka and the next week to Kobe, and takes two days. Off-season it's kind of empty but can be crowded during summer. The cost is US$130.

Another ship runs from Kobe to Tanggu (near Tianjin). Departures from Kobe are every Thursday at noon, arriving in Tanggu the next day. Economy/first-class tickets cost US$247/333. The food on this boat gets poor reviews so bring a few emergency munchies. Tickets can be bought in Tianjin from the shipping office (☎ 312243) at 89 Munan Dao, Heping District. In Kobe, the office is at the port (☎ 3215791).

To/From Korea
There is a twice-weekly boat between Inchon in South Korea and Weihai in Shandong, leaving Inchon every Wednesday and Saturday at 4 pm and arriving at Weihai the next day at 9 am. The cost is US$90 (economy class), US$110 (2nd class), and US$130 (1st class). Tickets are available in China from CITS in Weihai. The decrepit CTS office in Yantai also sells these tickets, if anyone here bothers to show up for work.

There is also a twice-weekly boat running between Inchon and the Chinese port of Tianjin. This costs US$110 and is probably preferable to the Weihai boat unless you want to visit Qingdao in Shangdong Province.

In Seoul, tickets can be bought from the Universal Travel Service (UTS) behind City Hall, just near the Seoul city tourist information centre, or from the Unification Church's Seil Tour System, 3th, Dowon Building, 292-20 Tohwa-Dong, Mapo-Gu, Seoul (☎ 7016611).

TOURS
Tour groups are still considered the darlings of Chinese who have to deal with foreigners. It is much easier for the Chinese if you arrive in a tour group, if all your accommodation is pre-booked, and if everyone sits down at the same time to eat. If there's a CITS interpreter on hand someone doesn't have to struggle with a phrasebook or pidgin English. Groups don't make a nuisance of themselves by trying to go to closed places, and they usually channel complaints through the tour leader rather than hassle the desk clerk. Most importantly, tour groups spend more money.

Are tours worth it to you? Unless you simply cannot make your own way around, then probably not. Apart from the expense, they tend to screen you even more from some of the basic realities of China travel. Most people who come back with glowing reports of the PRC never had to travel proletariat class on the trains or battle their way on board a local bus in the whole 10 days of their stay. On the other hand, if your time is limited and you just want to see the Forbidden City and the hills of Guilin, then the brief tours from Hong Kong, though expensive, might be worth considering.

One thing you will never be able to complain about on a tour is not being shown enough. Itineraries are jam-packed and the Chinese expect stamina from their guests. The tour may include an early breakfast, a visit to a market, a morning's sightseeing, an afternoon visit to a school and a shopping session, and it may not finish until 10 pm after a visit to the local opera.

Stays in cities are short and in your few weeks in China you're whisked from place to place at a furious rate.

Nor could you complain about the quantity of food – you may complain about the quality or degree of imagination involved in the cooking, but there is no way the Chinese will let you starve.

One advantage of being on a tour is that you may get into places that individuals often can't – such as factories and steam locomotive storage repair depots.

From Hong Kong & Macau

There are innumerable tours you can make from Hong Kong or Macau. The best people to go to if you want to find out what's available are the Hong Kong travel agents, the Hong Kong Student Travel Bureau or China Travel Service (CTS).

We could go on endlessly regurgitating all the tours to China. A lot of people seem to enjoy the one-day tours to the Special Economic Zones (SEZs) – Shenzhen near Hong Kong and Zhuhai near Macau. The tour to Shenzhen costs HK$580, which includes admission to Splendid China (which you can easily see for yourself for a fraction of the cost). The Zhuhai tour seems to be more rewarding but costs HK$800. The day tours include lunch, transport and all admission fees.

There are one-day tours to Canton and tours of several days' length which include Canton, Zhongshan, Shiqi, Zhaoqing and Foshan. Many other combinations are possible.

Essentially the same tours can be booked in Macau. This can be done at the CTS office (ground floor, Metropole Hotel, 63 Rua de Praia Grande) or the travel agents in the large tourist hotels which have English-speaking staff.

Tours further afield are also available in Hong Kong. Prices aren't cheap, but it depends on where you're going – a five-day Canton-Guilin tour costs HK$3500 and a nine-day Canton-Guilin-Beijing tour is HK$8000.

Warning We have had many negative comments from people who have booked extended tours through CTS and CITS. Although the one-day tours seem to be OK, tours further afield frequently go awry. The most significant complaints have been about ridiculous overcharging for substandard accommodation and tours being cut short to make up for transport delays. Some people have booked a tour only to find that they were the sole person on the tour. No refunds are given if you cancel – you forfeit the full amount. Other travellers report additional charges being tacked on which were not mentioned in the original agreement.

CITS drivers have been known to show up with all their relatives who want to tag along for free – they sometimes even expect the foreigner to pay for all their meals and accommodation. One traveller reported booking a week-long tour – the female driver showed up with her boyfriend and asked if he could come along. The traveller foolishly agreed. At the first lunch stop, the driver and her boyfriend took off and left the foreigner behind – the couple then apparently spent the rest of the week enjoying a honeymoon at the traveller's prepaid hotel rooms! When the irate traveller finally made her way back to the CITS office to complain, she was given the runaround but no refund, and in the end she just left China in a fit of frustration.

From Western Countries

These tours are handled by innumerable travel agents and any of them worth their commission will still tell you that you can't go to China except on a tour. They usually offer the standard tours that whip you round Beijing, Shanghai, Guilin, Xi'an, etc.

In an attempt to spice up the offerings the Chinese have come up with some new formulas. These include honeymoon tours (how many in the group?); acupuncture courses; special-interest tours for botanists, railway enthusiasts, lawyers and potters; trekking tours to Tibet and Qinghai; women's tours; bicycle tours, and Chinese-language courses. Check with your local travel agent.

Volunteer Expeditions

Some organisations need paying helpers to assist on projects. This is a contribution to the cost of the project and you have to pay your own air fares and living expenses to and on site. On many of these projects they expect you to work hard – it may be emotionally rewarding but don't necessarily expect it to feel like a holiday.

In the USA you can order the book *Volunteer! The Comprehensive Guide to Voluntary Service in the US and Abroad* published by the Council on International Educational Exchange (CIEE). You can contact their publications office (☎ (212) 6611450), CIEE, Publications Department, 205 East 42nd St, New York, NY 10017, USA.

Wilderness Tours

Mountaineering, trekking, camping, whitewater rafting, kayaking and cross-country skiing tours to China are organised by various agents in the west, but the prices are too high for low-budget travellers. Trekking is administered and arranged by the Chinese Mountaineering Association under the same rules that apply to mountaineering in China. The CMA makes all arrangements for a trek with the assistance of provincial mountaineering associations and local authorities.

The first few trekkers were allowed into China only in 1980 and the first groups were organised in 1981. Because trekking comes under the mountaineering rules, all treks must be near one of the peaks open for mountaineering – these regions span the country and vary from the plains of Tibet to the lush bamboo forests of Sichuan Province and the open plains of Xinjiang.

Various travel agents will book you through to these operators. Scan their literature carefully – sometimes the tours can be done just as easily on your own. What you want are places that individuals have trouble getting into.

If you can afford it, a few mountaineering, horse riding, trekking, cycling, sailing and rafting tour operators are:

USA
  Nonesuch Whitewater (☎ 707-8236603; fax 8231954), 4004 Bones Rd, Sebastopol, CA 95472 (rafting)

Boojum Expeditions (☎ 406-5870125) 14543 Kelly Canyon Rd, Bozeman MT 59715 (horseback trips)
  Mountain Travel (☎ 415-5278100), 6420 Fairmount Ave, El Cerrito, CA (trekking)
  Wilderness Travel (☎ 510-5480420), 801 Allston Way, Berkeley, CA (trekking)
  REI Adventures (☎ 800-6222236, 206-8912633), PO Box 1938, Sumner, WA 98390 (trekking & cycling)
  Backroads (☎ 800-5332573, 510-5271555), 1516 5th St, Berkeley, CA 94710 (cycling)
  Ocean Voyages (☎ 415-3324681), 1709 Bridgeway, Sausalito, CA 94965 (sailing)
  Also check the special outings issues of *Sierra* magazine, published by the Sierra Club (☎ (415) 7762211), 730 Polk St, San Francisco, California 94109.
Australia
  World Expeditions
  Formerly Australian Himalayan Expeditions (☎ 02-496634), 159 Cathedral St, Woolloomooloo, Sydney, 2011.
  Tail Winds Bicycle Touring, PO Box 32, O'Connor, ACT, 2601.
  The Trekking Company, GPO Box 1900, Canberra, ACT 2601.
UK
  Regent Holidays Ltd (☎ (0272) 211711), 15 John Street, Bristol BS1 2HR is a specialist in relatively economical tours.
  Voyages Jules Verne (☎ (071) 7234084), 21 Dorset Square, London NW1 6QG (for more upmarket tours).
Hong Kong
  Several operators organise interesting trips, such as cycling and commune living:
  Hong Kong Student Travel Bureau (HKSTB) (☎ 7213269 or 3693804), Room 1021, 10th floor, Star House, Salisbury Rd, Tsimshatsui, Kowloon;
  China Youth Travel Service (CYTS), Room 904, Nanyang Commercial Bank Building, 151 des Voeux Rd, Hong Kong Island. (CYTS is the younger arm of CITS and it liaises with many foreign student organisations and groups.)
  Mera Travel Services Ltd, Room 1308, Argyle Centre, Phase 1, 688 Nathan Rd, Kowloon does trekking tours to Tibet, Nepal and India.

LEAVING CHINA

In general, there are few hassles on departure. Baggage may be x-rayed even at land and water crossings but the machines are supposedly 'film-safe'. Antiques or things which look antique could cause hassles with Customs, and it's illegal to carry RMB out of the country – at least be discrete if you intend to violate the rules. Lest you need to be reminded, most of China's neighbours (Hong Kong, for example) take a *very* dim view of drugs.

Departure Tax

If leaving China by air, the departure tax is Y60, payable in FEC unless you can produce a magic student card.

Getting Around

AIR

The Civil Aviation Administration of China (CAAC), for many years China's only domestic and international carrier, has officially been broken up and private carriers have been allowed to set up operations in China. This doesn't mean that CAAC is out of business – it now assumes the role of 'umbrella organisation' (whatever that is) for its numerous subsidiaries. The seven major divisions of CAAC are Air China, China Eastern, China Southern, China Northern, China Southwest, China Northwest, and Xinjiang Airlines. For the most part fleets have been substantially upgraded since the old CAAC days, and extensive work has gone into improving traffic control and navigation equipment.

In addition to the divisions of the CAAC network, there is also a bewildering array of private lines taking to the Chinese skies. Many of them serve a small number of destinations, linking one major city with other major cities around China (as is the case with Shanghai Airlines), but others, such as Yunnan Airlines, have extensive routings. The best advice for sorting through this is to shop around for flights; prices vary little, but it's worth checking what kind of plane is being used for a flight you want to take – the old Russian varieties are less likely to reach their destinations than the Boeings. As a general rule of thumb, the smaller private airlines are much more likely to be using Soviet-built CAAC hand-me-downs than modern aircraft. This usually makes prices

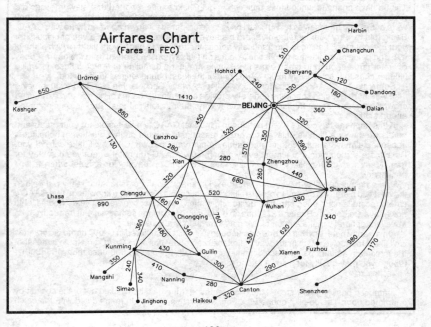

Airfares Chart
(Fares in FEC)

slightly cheaper, but you have to build into this the increased risks.

Timetables

In its role as 'umbrella organisation', CAAC still publishes a combined international and domestic timetable in both English and Chinese in April and November each year. These can be bought at most CAAC offices in China or from the CAAC office in Hong Kong (Ground floor, Gloucester Tower, des Voeux Rd, Central District, Hong Kong Island (☎ 5216416)). The timetable could also serve as a useful phrasebook of Chinese place names, but it's filled with misspellings.

As well as the overall CAAC timetable, former CAAC units and private airlines also publish their own timetables. You can buy these in ticket offices around China.

Fares

Foreigners pay a surcharge of 75% of the fare charged local Chinese people. Unlike the situation with trains, there is no way past this CAAC regulation, unless you are a foreign expert or have a legitimate residence permit. If you do somehow happen to get the Chinese price and it's discovered, your ticket will be confiscated and no refund given. Children over 12 are charged adult fare.

Cancellation fees depend on how long before departure you cancel. On domestic flights, if you cancel 24 hours before departure you lose 10% of the fare; if you cancel between two and 24 hours before the flight you lose 20%; and if you cancel less than two hours before the flight you lose 30%. If you don't show up for a domestic flight, you are entitled to a refund of 50%.

Tales of the Unexpected

Things have changed since times past, when old China hands reported that stewardesses did revolutionary dances in the aisle to take nervous passengers' minds off the extreme danger they were subjecting themselves to. But it still pays to be prepared for anything when flying with CAAC. Being told to carry your luggage on board because it's too big; being thrown a bag of biscuits for your in-flight meal; having to run frantically across the runway to board your flight *(which* plane is it?); and being given life-jacket inflation lessons on flights thousands of km from the nearest body of water large enough to crash a plane in: these are just a sampling of the countless inventive little touches that collectively make CAAC one of the least boring airlines in the world.

Some say that CAAC stands for China Airlines Always Cancels, the standard excuse being 'bad weather'. Evening check-ins generally provide entertaining scenes of hoarse and exhausted crowds who have spent the last eight hours waving their tickets in the air and screaming at the airport staff.

If this happens to you, it's worth bearing in mind that CAAC is responsible for your meals and hotels whenever a flight is delayed beyond a reasonable amount of time. Just what constitutes 'reasonable' may be subject to interpretation; in general, however, CAAC will take care of you. Delays are so common that almost every airport has a CAAC-run hotel where you can stay for free. Many foreign travellers don't realise this and wind up paying for a hotel when it isn't necessary.

While delays can play havoc with your travel itinerary, it's the crashes that really put paid to the best laid plans. It's difficult to obtain reliable statistics, but it's common knowledge that CAAC's safety record is not a good one. The upgrading of the CAAC fleet over recent years (most flights nowadays are done by Boeing 737s) has no doubt improved things somewhat, but frequent China travellers generally make a point of flying as infrequently as possible.

On a happy note, anyone unfortunate enough to be killed or injured in CAAC domestic crashes isn't likely to receive much in the way of financial compensation. The CAAC timetable states that the maximum amount paid for accidental injury or death will be Y20,000 (less than US$4300) – though you may qualify for a ticket refund too.

A classic:

...amused passengers watched the pilot (returning from the toilet) locked out of the cockpit by a jammed door. The co-pilot opened the door from within, then both men fiddled with the catch

Baggage

On domestic and international flights the free-baggage allowance for an adult passenger is 20 kg in economy class and 30 kg in 1st class. You are also allowed five kg of hand luggage, though this is rarely weighed.

When purchasing a ticket, you may be asked to buy luggage insurance. It's certainly not compulsory though some staff give the impression it is – the amount you can actually claim if your bags are lost is pathetically low.

Stand-By

This exists on CAAC-affiliated flights. Some seats are always reserved in case a high-ranking cadre turns up at the last moment. If no one shows up it should be possible to get on board.

Reservations

In theory, you can reserve seats without paying for them. In practice, this doesn't always work. The staff at some booking offices will hold a seat for more than a week – other offices will only hold a seat for a few hours so you can run to the bank and change money. Until you've actually paid for and received your ticket, nothing can be guaranteed. On some routes, competition for seats is keen and people with connections can often jump the queue – if you're only holding a reservation, you might be bounced. If you do decide just to make a reservation rather than purchase a ticket, be sure to get the reservation slip filled out and signed – sometimes they want to hold it, sometimes you can take it with you and bring it back when you want to pick up the ticket.

---

and succeeded in locking themselves out of the cockpit. As passengers stared in disbelief the pilot and co-pilot attacked the door with a fire-axe, pausing for a moment to draw a curtain between themselves and the audience.

Hijackings have added a new dimension to the fire-axe routine. In January 1983 a hijacker fatally shot a pilot after ordering a diversion to Taiwan; the hijacker was then axed by the navigator. Heroics in the air is the Chinese way of dealing with the menace of pirates aloft – the motherland does not like to lose planes, especially to Taiwan.

In July 1982 a Shanghai-bound plane was hijacked by five Chinese youths armed with sticks of dynamite, who ordered the plane to go to Taiwan. The pilot's response was to fly around in circles until the fuel was almost exhausted, whereupon the crew led passengers in an attack on the hijackers with umbrellas and mop handles.

The CAAC version of this near-calamity reads, 'The heroic deeds of the crew...showed the firm standpoint of their love for the Party and our socialist motherland...they feared no sacrifice...' The captain of the flight was awarded a special title created by the State Council – 'anti-hijacking hero'. Similar honours were bestowed on the crew of a plane hijacked to South Korea on 5 May 1983.

One of CAAC's nastiest crashes occurred in October 1990 at Canton's Baiyun Airport – 127 passengers were killed. The cause was an abortive hijacking. As a result, Taiwan's government announced that hijackers would no longer receive political asylum and would immediately be returned to the mainland – where they would most likely receive the customary bullet in the back of the head. However, Taiwan still offers large rewards (paid in gold) to defecting Chinese air-force pilots because the Communists still make verbal military threats against Taiwan.

The year 1992 was a particularly bad one for CAAC, when it managed to score a fifth of the world's total air passenger fatalities for that year. A Soviet-built tri-jet Yak42 did not quite manage to take to the air in Nanjing – of the 116 passengers, 106 died. But new aircraft have also been falling out of the sky with unusual frequency too. The worst crash was a China Southern Airlines Boeing 737-300, which went down in November 1992 near Guilin, killing all 141 passengers on board. The Chinese refused to allow foreigners to inspect the wreckage and examine the 'black box' flight recorder. It's no secret that China wants to replace imported high-technology equipment with domestically produced stuff – there is much speculation that China is now testing out homemade spare parts in new aircraft. ∎

More and more booking offices have been computerised over recent years. These offices allow you to purchase a ticket to or from any other destination on the computer reservation system. If the city you want to fly from is not on the system, you'll have to go there first and buy the ticket in person from the local booking office.

Airport Tax

There is an airport tax of Y15 on domestic flights. On international flights there is an airport departure tax of Y60. Bear in mind, however, that the whole situation with airport tax has become very unstable, with airports around China making things up as they go along.

In Chengdu, for example, the airport tax of Y15 applied only to flights within Sichuan Province, and an airport tax of Y45 was required for domestic flights elsewhere around China. In Jinghong, there is an airport tax of Y30 – Y15 airport tax and Y15 towards the construction of the new airport!

Service

Despite the break-up of CAAC and the existence of private airlines, service is still not that good on domestic flights, though it has definitely improved. On international flights, however, there is a concerted attempt to keep up appearances, and the flight attendants wear spiffy uniforms and make-up and are trained in Japan. On domestic flights you'll probably be given a little bag or two of sweets, or a key ring as a souvenir – it almost justifies the 75% tourist surcharge.

BUS

Long-distance buses are one of the best means of getting around the country. Services are extensive and main roads are usually bumpy but passable at least. Also, since the buses stop every so often in small towns and villages, you get to see bits of the countryside you wouldn't if you only travelled on the trains. Bus travel generally works out to be comparable to hard-seat train travel in terms of expense, and at present there is no foreigner double-pricing rule,

though demands for FEC payment are starting to creep in in one or two places (notably Xinjiang) that see a lot of foreigners and where bus travel is the only onward option.

It's a good idea to book a seat in advance. All seats are numbered. Bus stations are often large affairs with numerous ticket windows and waiting halls. There is a special symbol for a bus station which appears on maps and is meant to resemble the steering wheel of the bus. The symbol is:

Safety is another consideration. Accidents are frequent, especially on winding mountain roads. Foreigners have been injured and killed in bus crashes – there is very little you can do to protect yourself. The government-run buses seem to be somewhat safer than the private ones – if a driver of a government bus causes an accident, they can be imprisoned.

If possible, try to avoid sitting at the rear of the bus since it's painful for the shock-absorbers in your back. Many long-distance buses are equipped with a cassette tape player and stereo speakers in order to allow the drivers to blast out your eardrums with screeching music – select a seat as far away from the speakers as possible.

Alternatively, try buying some music tapes you like and give them to the driver in the hope that he'll play them (find some classical music or Chinese rock). Chinese law requires drivers to announce their presence to cyclists, and for this they use a tweeter for preliminaries, a bugle or bullhorn if they get annoyed and an ear-wrenching air-horn when they're really stirred up.

While things have improved over recent years, the condition of the roads and the buses themselves make bus travel a rather slow means of transport. It's safe to reckon times for bus journeys by calculating the distance against a speed of 25 km/h. Buses will often creak into higher speeds than this (notably on downhill stretches), but by the time you've added all the stops and uphill slogs, the average will rarely be much higher. Unusual driving standards compound the problem. As a rule, Chinese drivers are loathe to change gears and would appear to prefer coming to an almost absolute standstill on a slope rather than changing from third into second. Petrol-saving ploys include getting up to the highest speed possible and then coasting to a near standstill, before starting the process again. Engines are switched off for stops of any kind, even if it's only a matter of seconds.

Astronaut-type backpacks are a nightmare to stow on buses – there's little space under the seats, overhead racks hardly big enough to accommodate a loaf of bread, and sparse space in the aisles. If you intend doing a lot of bus travel then travel light! In China, unlike other Asian countries, people do not ride on the roof – though luggage is sometimes stowed there.

In recent years night buses have become increasingly frequent. These get mixed reviews – they are more dangerous and few but the Chinese can sleep on a crowded jolting bus. On popular routes like Kunming to Dali, sleeper buses *(wòpùchē)* have been introduced – they are usually around double the price of a normal bus service, but many travellers swear by them. Some have comfortable reclining seats, while others even have two-tier bunks. On runs of over 12 hours where sleeper buses have not been introduced there will often be an overnight stop. This is not always the case, however. Increasingly buses are using two drivers and doing 24-hour runs in a single stint – one Dutch traveller we met did 36 hours straight on a bus from Kunming to Nanning!

Privately-owned minibuses are increasingly competing with public buses on medium-length routes. Although they're often a bit cramped, you always get a seat (or at least a knee to sit on), and you can bargain the fare down. Drivers will often try to make you pay extra for bulky luggage.

Finally, the buses provide stops in places you had never counted on visiting: breakdowns are frequent and can occur anywhere. This is a special treat for the locals, who are temporarily entertained by the rare spectacle of a small herd of big noses while the bus is being repaired (or stripped and sold for scrap metal). But breakdowns are not the only reason you might get temporarily dumped in the great unknown:

One German traveller on the bus journey from Wuzhou to Yangshuo was surprised when his bus started competing with the bus ahead for roadside passengers. After getting up perilously close to its rear bumper and blasting furiously on an armoury of horns, his driver managed, in a hair-raising exhibition of reckless abandon and daredevilry, to sweep around the opposition on a blind bend and be first to get to a group of prospective passengers just around the corner. The other driver, determined not to let his fellow get away with such deviously unsporting behaviour, pulled up and started thumping him through the window.

A decisive knock-out proving elusive in such cramped quarters, the two soon leapt out of their buses to continue the punch-up on the roadside. Things were beginning to look grim for the German's driver, when a wailing siren announced the arrival of the boys in green. Without even a glance at the passengers of the two buses, they handcuffed the two drivers, threw them unceremoniously into the back of their van and drove off. It was five hours before new drivers were dispatched to the scene of the crime.

Food It's a very mixed bag out there. In about 50% of the cases, drivers take you to the filthiest and most expensive little hovels they can find with the worst food imaginable. It seems that these places are owned by their friends or relatives and the drivers get a commission. It's depressing because buses usually drive right past many perfectly acceptable restaurants, but the drivers refuse to stop. But sometimes you get lucky – there are at least a few honest drivers out there. Your best defence is to stock up on sufficient munchies before you board the bus.

TRAIN
Trains are the best way to get around in reasonable speed and comfort. The network covers every province except Tibet, and that's not for want of trying (experts have

advised the Chinese that it is impossible to build a line up to Lhasa – it would involve drilling tunnels through ice). There are an estimated 52,000 km of railway lines in China, most of them built since 1949 when the system had either been blown to bits or was nonexistent in certain regions.

The safety record of the railway system is good – other than getting your luggage pinched or your pocket picked, there isn't much danger on trains. However, the Chinese have a habit of throwing rubbish out the windows even as the train moves through a station. Avoid standing too close to a passing train, lest you get hit by flying beer bottles or chicken bones.

Classes

In socialist China there are no classes; instead you have hard seat, hard sleeper, soft seat and soft sleeper.

Hard Seat Except on the trains which serve some of the branch or more obscure lines, hard seat is not in fact hard but is padded. But it's hard on your sanity and you'll get little sleep on the upright seats. Since hard seat is the only thing the locals can afford it's packed to the gills, the lights stay on all night, passengers spit on the floor, and the carriage speakers endlessly drone news, weather, information and music. Hard seat is OK for a day trip; some foreigners can't take more than five hours of it, while others have a threshold of 12 hours or even longer. A few brave, penniless souls have even been known to travel *long-distance* this way – some role out a mat on the floor under the seats and go to sleep on top of the gob.

Hard Sleeper These are comfortable and only a fixed number of people are allowed in the sleeper carriage. The carriage is made up of doorless compartments with half a dozen bunks in three tiers, and sheets, pillows and blankets are provided. It does very nicely as an overnight hotel. The best bunk to get is a middle one since the lower one is invaded by all and sundry who use it as a seat during the day, while the top one has little headroom.

The top bunks are also where the cigarette smoke floats about and it's usually stinking hot up there in summer even with the fans on full blast.

The worst possible bunks are the top ones at either end of the carriage or right in the middle; they've right up against the speakers and you'll get a rude shock in the morning about 6 am. Lights and speakers in hard sleeper go out at around 9.30 to 10 pm. Few ordinary Chinese can afford hard sleeper; those who use it are either the new class of nouveau-riche or privileged cadres on their way to conferences whose travel is being paid for by the State.

Soft Seat On shorter journeys (such as Shenzhen to Canton) some trains have soft-seat carriages. The seats are comfortable and overcrowding is not permitted. Smoking is prohibited, a significant advantage unless you enjoy asphyxiation. If you want to smoke in the soft-seat section, you can do so only by going out into the corridor between cars. Soft seat costs about the same as hard sleeper and is well worth it. Unfortunately, soft-seat cars are a rarity.

Soft Sleeper Luxury. Softies get the works, with four comfortable bunks in a closed compartment – complete with straps to stop the top fatso from falling off in the middle of the night, wood panelling, potted plants, lace curtains, teacup set, clean washrooms, carpets (so no spitting), and often air-con. As for those speakers, not only do you have a volume control, you can turn the bloody things off! Soft sleeper costs twice as much as hard sleeper, and almost the same price as flying (on some routes even *more* than flying!). It's relatively easy to get soft sleeper because few Chinese (except high-ranking cadres who charge it to their State expense accounts) can afford it. Travelling in soft sleeper should be experienced once – it gives you a good chance to meet the ruling class.

Train Types Train composition varies from line to line and also from day to night, and largely depends on the demand for sleepers on that line. A typical high-frequency railway line has about 13 carriages: six hard seat, perhaps one soft seat, three hard sleeper, one soft sleeper, one dining car and one guard/baggage van.

Half or even a whole carriage may be devoted to crew quarters on the longer trips. If the journey time is more than 12 hours then the train qualifies for a dining car. The dining car often separates the hard-seat carriages from the hard-sleeper and soft-sleeper carriages.

The conductor is in a little booth in a hard-seat carriage at the middle of the train – usually carriage No 7, 8 or 9 (all carriages are numbered on the outside). Coal-fired samovars are found in the ends of the hard-class sections, and from these you can draw a supply of hot water. On long trips, however, the water often runs out. The disc-jockey has a little booth at the end of one of the cars with a door marked *Boyinshi*, which apart from the reel-to-reel tape, radio and record player also contains the attendant's bed.

On some of the small branch lines there are various kinds of passenger carriages – some have long bench seats along the walls, others are just cattle cars without seats or windows.

Different types of train are usually recognisable by the train number:

Nos 1-90 These are special express and usually diesel-hauled. They have all classes and there is a surcharge for the speed and superior facilities. The international trains are included in this group.

Nos 100-350 Trains in this approximate number range make more stops than the special expresses. They have soft and hard sleepers, but fewer of them. The speed surcharge is half that of the special expresses but the difference in overall price is minimal.

Nos 400 & 500 These are slow, and stop at everything they can find. They may have hard wooden seats and no sleepers. They should have soft seats, but these will be equivalent to the hard seats on the fast trains. The trains have antique fittings, lamps and wood panelling, and are usually steam-pulled. There is no speed surcharge as there is no speed.

No 700 These trains take suburban routes.

Apart from the speed breakdown, the numbers don't really tell you much else about the train. As a general rule, the outbound and inbound trains have matching numbers; thus train Nos 79/80 divide into No 79 leaving Shanghai and going to Kunming, and No 80 leaving Kunming and going to Shanghai.

However, there are for example at least six different trains listed in the Chinese train timetable under Nos 301/302, and the sequence-number match is not always reliable. Trains also appear to shift numbers from one timetable to the following year's timetable, so train No 175 becomes train No 275. Simple.

Reservations & Tickets

Buying hard-seat tickets at short notice is usually no hassle, though you will not always be successful in getting a reserved seat. Buying a ticket for a sleeper can be problematic – indeed, it can be damn near impossible if you try to do it yourself. If you try to buy a sleeper ticket at the railway station and the clerk just says *meiyou*, you'll have to seek the assistance of a travel agent. This can mean CITS, CTS, CYTS and travel agents affiliated with hotels. However, many CITS and CTS offices no longer do rail bookings. If you run into this problem, the best thing is to ask at the reception desk of your hotel (unless you're staying in a grotty dump). Most hotels have an in-house travel agent who can obtain train tickets. You'll have to pay FEC and a service charge of perhaps Y20 or so, but it's probably worth it to avoid 30 hours in hard-seat hell. You must give your passport to the travel agency when they go to buy your ticket, but an old expired passport will do just fine.

Tickets for sleepers can easily be obtained in major cities, but not in quiet backwaters. Hard sleepers are particularly difficult to get, but your chances improve significantly if you buy the ticket several days in advance. There is a three-day advance-purchase limit, presumably to prevent tickets being hoarded by scalpers.

Another alternative is to try the railway ticket advance booking offices (the big towns all have several of these) but the chance of success here is usually no better than at the railway station. See the Black-Market Tickets section for another alternative.

You can buy tickets the night before departure or on the day of departure from the railway station. This often involves long queues, and in large cities the 'queues' can become near-riots. Some stations are better than others. Hard-seat tickets bought on the same day will usually be unreserved – you get on board and try and find a seat. If there are no seats, you'll either have to stand or find a place for your bum amongst the peanut shells, cigarette butts and spittle.

If you're buying a ticket from the railway station, then you should write down clearly on a piece of paper what you want: train number, time, date, class of travel. The appropriate characters and phrases can be copied from a phrasebook. Learn a few key phrases like 'tomorrow' and 'hard sleeper'. English-speaking Chinese people are always willing to translate and there are usually one or two around in the larger places.

If you have a sleeper ticket the carriage attendant will take it from you and give you a metal or plastic chit – when your destination is close he or she will swap it back and give you the original ticket. Keep your ticket until you get through the barriers at the other end, as you'll need to show it there.

Platform Tickets An alternative to all the above is not to bother with a ticket at all and simply walk on to the train. To do this, you need to buy a platform ticket *(zhàntái piào)*. These are available from the station's information booth for a few jiao. You then buy your ticket on the train. This method is usually more hassle than it's worth, but may be necessary if you arrive at the station without enough time to get your ticket.

Black-Market Tickets These certainly exist and many travellers have made use of them. The way it works is that some local Chinese buy up hard sleepers on the most popular lines (which frequently sell out), then sell these tickets to travellers (both Chinese and

foreigners) at a profit. The black marketeers usually stand outside the station hawking their tickets. This is supposedly illegal, but they often pay off the local police.

Since foreigners have to pay double anyway, black-market tickets can be a bargain even if they cost more than the usual Chinese price. However, be sure you know just what you're looking for as far as a legitimate ticket goes! Otherwise, you could be buying a worthless piece of cardboard, or a hard seat when you expected a hard sleeper. Ticket counterfeiting has become a new growth industry in China.

Getting Aboard
As soon as the train pulls into the station, all hell breaks loose. In the hope of getting a seat, hard-seat passengers charge at the train, often pushing exiting passengers back inside. Some would-be travellers climb through the windows. Railway attendants – often female – try to keep order, sometimes using night-sticks or bamboo poles. If you have a reserved seat or sleeper, you can let the crowd fight it out for awhile, then peacefully find your carriage and claim your rightful place. If you don't have a reserved seat, you're going to have to join the fray. The sensible option is to head for either the very front or the very rear of the train. Most passengers attack the middle of the train – the part closest to the platform entrance gate.

Upgrading
If you get on the train with an unreserved seating ticket, you can seek out the conductor and upgrade *(bǔpiào)* yourself to a hard sleeper, soft seat or soft sleeper if there are any available. It is rare that you will be charged foreigners' prices or even asked to pay FEC for this service, and though there are risks involved (no sleepers left) it is sometimes the cheapest way (or only way) to get a sleeper or even a seat. On some trains it's easy to do but others are notoriously crowded. A lot of intermediary stations along the railway lines can't issue sleepers, making upgrading the only alternative to hard seat.

If the sleeper carriages are full then you

may have to wait until someone gets off. That sleeper may only be available to you until the next major station which is allowed to issue sleepers, but you may be able to get several hours of sleep. The sleeper price will be calculated for the distance that you used it for.

Ticket Validity

Tickets are valid for one to seven days, depending on the distance travelled. On a cardboard ticket the number of days is printed at the bottom left-hand corner. If you go 250 km it's valid for two days; 500 km, three days; 1000 km, three days; 2000 km, six days; about 2500 km, seven days.

Thus if you're travelling along a major line you could (theoretically) buy one ticket and break the journey where you feel like it. This will only work for unreserved hard seats. The advantage of this method is that you can keep away from railway ticket windows for a while; you can get off, find a refreshing hotel, and get back on board the next day on the same ticket.

So much for theory – nothing is consistent in China. In some stations, the railway workers won't let you board unless you hold a ticket for the exact date and time of departure. If you buy a ticket for a morning train (unreserved hard seat) and try to take a later train the same day, they may refuse to let you board even though the ticket is still valid!

Given the fact that the rules are subject to the unpredictable whims of various railway workers, you'll probably wind up just buying tickets for the exact time and date you intend to depart.

Timetables

There are paperback train timetables in both Chinese and English. The English timetables are hard to find in China. In some stations (like Beijing and Shanghai main railway stations) there is a special booking office for foreigners, and these usually have the English timetables. They can also be found in Hong Kong – Swindon's Bookstore and Joint Publishing Company sell them. The English name is simply *China Railway Timetable*.

No matter where you get them, the timetables are so excruciatingly detailed that it's a drag working your way through them. Even the Chinese complain about this.

Thinner versions listing the major trains can sometimes be bought from hawkers outside the railway stations. Hotel reception desks and CITS offices have copies of the timetable for trains out of their city or town.

Thomas Cook publishes an overseas train timetable, which includes China – single copies are expensive but you might get a xerox of the relevant pages from your friendly neighbourhood travel agent.

Railway Stations

Some railway stations require that luggage be X-rayed before entering the waiting area. The reason is that China has to deal with people transporting huge quantities of explosive chemicals, firecrackers and gunpowder for making firecrackers – there have been several disastrous explosions. Occasionally, gory photographs of the results are tacked up in stations.

If the horde of starers in the waiting room is annoying, you can usually head to the soft-class waiting rooms. If you don't have a soft-class ticket, they might still let you in if you've got a foreigner's FEC ticket (the foreigner's ticket looks different). These soft-class waiting rooms can also serve as overnight hotels if you arrive at some disgusting hour of the morning; the staff might let you sleep there until 5 or 6 am (don't count on it though) when you can get a bus to the hotel. You might also be able to put up here if you arrive in or are in transit through a place closed to foreigners. Some soft-class waiting rooms require a Y1 ticket which includes free tea.

Just about all railway stations have left-luggage rooms *(jìcún chù)* where you can safely dump your bags for a few RMB.

Smile – It Helps As far as foreigners are concerned, many railway staff in China are exceedingly polite and can be very helpful –

Distances by rail (km) - Major Cities

	Bei	Shan	Can	Chan	Wuha	Nanj	Qin	Xi'an	Kunm	Chen	Chon
Beijing	Bei										
Shanghai	1462	Shan									
Canton	2313	1811	Can								
Changsha	1587	1187	726	Chan							
Wuhan	1229	1534	1084	358	Wuha						
Nanjing	1157	305	2116	1492	1229	Nanj					
Qingdao	887	1361	2677	1951	1593	1056	Qin				
Xi'an	1165	1511	2129	1403	1045	1206	1570	Xi'an			
Kunming	3179	2677	2216	1592	1950	2982	3512	1942	Kunm		
Chengdu	2048	2353	2544	1920	1887	2048	2412	842	1100	Chen	
Chongqing	2552	2501	2040	1416	1774	2552	2916	1346	1102	504	Chon
Zhengzhou	695	1000	1618	892	534	695	1059	511	2453	1353	1857

Distances by rail (km) - Eastern Provinces

	Han	Shan	Suz	Wux	Nanj	Shao	Nanc	Fuz	Xia	Cant
Hangzhou	Han									
Shanghai	189	Shan								
Suzhou	275	86	Suz							
Wuxi	317	128	42	Wux						
Nanjing	494	305	219	177	Nanj					
Shaoxing	60	249	335	377	554	Shao				
Nanchang	636	825	911	953	1130	59	Nanc			
Fuzhou	972	1161	1247	1289	1466	990	622	Fuz		
Xiamen	1187	1376	1462	1504	1681	1247	838	603	Xia	
Canton	1633	1811	1897	1936	2116	1640	1042	1608	1834	Cant
Beijing	1651	1462	1376	1334	1157	1711	2005	2623	2838	2313

Distances by rail (km) - South-West Provinces

	Bei	Sha	Nan	Wuh	Zhu	Can	Liu	Nann	Che	Cho	Guiy
Beijing	Bei										
Shanghai	1462	Sha									
Nanchang	2005	825	Nan								
Wuhan	1229	1545	776	Wuh							
Zhuzhou	1638	1136	367	409	Zhu						
Canton	2313	1811	1042	1084	675	Can					
Liuzhou	2310	1808	1039	1081	672	1079	Liu				
Nanning	2565	2063	1294	1336	927	1334	255	Nann			
Chengdu	2048	2353	2236	1887	1869	2544	1574	1829	Che		
Chongqing	2552	2501	1732	1774	1365	2040	1070	1325	504	Cho	
Guiyang	2540	2038	1269	1311	902	1577	607	862	967	463	Guiy
Kunming	3179	2677	1908	1950	1541	2216	1246	1501	1100	1102	639
Guilin	2134	–	–	–	–	903	176	–	–	–	–

Distances by rail (km) - North-Eastern Provinces

	Bei	Tia	Jinz	Shen	Chan	Har	Qiq	Jil	Dan	Dal	Jin
Beijing	Bei										
Tianjin	137	Tia									
Jinzhou	599	462	Jinz								
Shenyang	841	704	242	Shen							
Changchun	1146	1009	547	305	Chan						
Harbin	1388	1251	789	547	242	Har					
Qiqihar	1448	1311	849	760	530	288	Qiq				
Jilin	1287	1150	688	446	128	275	563	Jil			
Dandong	1118	981	519	277	582	824	1037	723	Dan		
Dalian	1238	1101	639	397	702	944	1157	84	674	Dal	
Ji'nan	494	357	819	1061	1366	1608	1668	1507	1338	1458	Jin
Jiamusi	1894	–	–	–	–	506	–	–	–	–	–
Mudanjiang	–	–	–	–	–	357	–	–	–	–	–

Distances by rail (km) - North-West Regions

	Bei	Zhen	Xi'an	Lan	Xini	Ürüm	Hoh
Beijing	Bei						
Zhengzhou	695	Zhen					
Xi'an	1165	511	Xi'an				
Lanzhou	1813	1187	676	Lan			
Xining	2098	1403	892	216	Xini		
Ürümqi	3774	3079	2568	1892	2108	Ürüm	
Hohhot	668	1363	1292	1145	1361	3037	Hoh
Yinchuan	1346	1654	1143	467	683	2359	678

how they treat their fellow Chinese is another matter. The staff may bend over backwards to assist you, particularly if you smile, behave friendly and look lost. Sometimes they'll invite you to sit with them or even give you their own train seats. Even when all the sleepers are supposedly full, they sometimes manage to find one for foreigners – it pays to be nice. Unfortunately, many foreigners take out their frustrations on the railway staff – this just makes it tough for all who follow.

Costs

Calculation of train prices is a complex affair based on the length of the journey, speed of the train and relative position of the sun and moon. There are a few variables such as air-con charges, whether a child occupies a berth or not – but nothing worth worrying about. The express surcharge is the same regardless of what class you use on the train.

The most important thing to remember is the double-pricing system on Chinese trains. Most foreigners are required to pay 100% more than People's Republic Chinese for their railway tickets. Other fares apply to Overseas Chinese, Chinese students, foreign students and foreign experts in China. (All train fares mentioned in this book are standard tourist price, unless otherwise stated.)

Trains are naturally cheaper than planes, but if you get a tourist-price soft sleeper then the gap between train and air travel narrows considerably. Often the difference is so small that, given the savings in time and trouble, it's definitely worth considering flying.

Tourist price is the real crunch – it will clean your wallet out. Maybe a higher price can be justified for the sleepers, since they are hard to get and foreigners are given priority. But to sit in hard-seat hell, it doesn't seem fair – you pay double to ride in the same agony!

Calculating Ticket Prices Some typical Chinese prices are given in the table. Use it as a rough guide only because fares vary slightly depending on the class of train and factors such as surcharges for air-con. Prices given are for express trains; in the case of hard sleepers, for the middle berth; and in the case of soft sleepers, for the upper berth. Remember that if you buy a non-black-market ticket you'll be paying double the figures given here. All of the following prices are in RMB.

Distance in km	Hard Seat	Hard Sleeper	Soft Sleeper
100	6		
500	27	42	77
1000	44	69	131
1500	62	96	179
2000	76	118	220
2500	92	144	271
3000	108	169	318
3500	122	191	357

Train fares are related to distance travelled, so it's possible to estimate the fare you would expect to pay for any particular journey if you know the distance. See the distance tables in this chapter.

Getting Cheaper Tickets Tourist-price tickets are slips of paper with various details scribbled all over them. Chinese-price tickets are little stubs of cardboard. Getting a Chinese-priced ticket is possible but becoming more difficult. Officially the only foreigners entitled to local Chinese-priced tickets are foreign students studying in the PRC, and certain foreigners authorised to live and work in China.

In the past travellers have been using all sorts of impressive-looking 'student cards' or made-in-Hong-Kong imitations of the 'white card' and 'red card' (which authorises foreigners to pay local price) to pass themselves off as students. Although more railway stations are catching on to these

tricks, it's surprising how often they still work. It used to be possible to use a Taiwan student card (Taiwan is officially considered part of China), but this trick usually no longer works.

Officially, Overseas Chinese, Hong Kongers and Taiwanese are also required to pay tourist prices and pay in FEC. In actual practice, anyone who looks Chinese (even Japanese) can usually wind up getting local Chinese price. It appears that race is the major consideration. Most Overseas Chinese will gladly buy your ticket for you if you ask them to – they also hate the system and take satisfaction in sabotaging it.

You can also get a local Chinese person to do it and give them a tip, but exercise caution – they could get into trouble, or they could pocket your money and run away. It's best to have them pay first with their own cash and then reimburse them, though many will not have the cash to do this.

Students are your best bet if you want someone to buy tickets for you – they appreciate any tip you give them and they are usually (but not always) honest.

Most railway workers don't care if you get a Chinese-priced ticket, with the sole exception of Canton railway station where the rules seem to be enforced. However, if you do get on the train with a Chinese-priced ticket the conductor can still charge you the full fare, or you could be stopped at the railway station exit gate at your destination, have your tickets checked and be charged the full fare. In practice, this seldom happens.

Some railway stations have separate booking offices for foreigners. As a rule they'll charge you tourist price; you can sometimes wangle local price, though they might make you pay in FEC. On the credit side, you don't have to wait in formidable queues and you can often get a sleeper – so if you do have to pay tourist price, stop bitching and consider your money well spent!

Food The cheapest meals are the 'rice boxes' brought down the carriages on trolleys and distributed to those who previously bought meal tickets. Tickets are sold by one of the train staff who walks through the train shortly before the trolley comes through. The boxes of rice, meat and vegetables cost around Y3 – filling, though some travellers have got the runs from them.

Trains on longer journeys have dining cars. Meals cost a couple of yuan. For breakfast you've got a choice of soup and maybe two plates of meat and/or vegetables, with cheap noodles for breakfast. There is a separate sitting for passengers in the soft-class carriages – as a foreigner you can join in even if you're in hard class, and sometimes you can get a Western breakfast. Some foreigners have been charged excessive prices for food ordered after the main sitting – check the price first.

After about 8 pm when meals are over you can probably wander back into the dining car. The staff may want to get rid of you, but if you just sit down and have a beer it may be OK. One Chinese-speaking traveller recalls getting drunk in the dining car with the train crew, one of whom stood up and loudly cursed the powers that be, saying they were all rotten to the core. He was threatened with ejection from the train at the next stop if he didn't sit down and shut up!

It's worth stocking up with your own supplies for long train trips – particularly if you're an obsessive nibbler. Jam, biscuits and fruit juice can be bought at department stores beforehand. If you like coffee or tea then bring your own – the trains have boilers at the end of the hard-class carriages. Sometimes the dining car will have canned fruit for sale, even whole chickens in plastic bags. At station stops you can buy food from the vendors.

We were allowed to spend one night from Zhanjiang to Guilin in the dining car when it wasn't occupied by people eating there. We ended up there after a futile attempt to upgrade to hard sleeper. Eventually we had to pay Y15 each for the sake of staying there, but it was still less horrible than hard seat.

TAXI
Long-distance taxis are usually booked through CITS or from hotels. They generally ask excessive fees in FEC – the name of the game is negotiate. Private entrepreneurs are becoming more common and they charge considerably less than CITS.

In places frequented by tourists it's possible to book private minibuses – with a group this can be worthwhile for getting to certain isolated sites. For example, it's almost essential to book a minibus to see the sights around the desert oasis of Turpan in Xinjiang Province. Drivers can usually be found hanging around bus stations and hotels. Chances are good that you won't have to look for them – they will be looking for you.

CAR & MOTORBIKE
For those who would like to tour China by car or motorcycle, the news is bleak – basically it's impossible unless you go with a large group (accompanied by PSB the whole way), apply for permits months in advance and pay through the nose for the privilege. It's not like India where you can simply buy a motorcycle and head off on your own.

That having been said, there are a few hopeful signs. Beijing and Shanghai have recently introduced the concept of drive-away car rental. It's experimental and so new we can't tell you too much about it – the Chinese are making up the rules as they go along. But it seems that armed with nothing more than an international driver's licence, a credit card and wads of cash (for a deposit), you can rent a car in Beijing or Shanghai but nowhere else. The catch – besides the expense – is that you can only drive within the city limits. You can't simply rent a car in Beijing and head off to Xi'an or Lhasa, so don't try it. Tourists are not yet permitted to rent motorcycles or purchase motor vehicles.

Foreign residents (as opposed to tourists) are governed by a different set of regulations. A Chinese driver's licence is required. In order to get one, you must first secure a residence permit. Then you must hand in your native country's driver's licence (not an international driver's licence) – the PSB keeps this licence and issues you a Chinese one. When you leave China, you must turn in your Chinese licence and your native country's licence will be returned to you. To complicate things even more, you need to prove you have a car before the licence can be issued! Foreign residents face the same restrictions about driving outside the city – basically it's forbidden without special permits.

BICYCLE

Probably the first time the Chinese saw a pneumatic-tyred bicycle was when a pair of globe-trotting Americans called Allen and Sachtleben bumbled into Beijing around 1891 after a three-year journey from Istanbul. They wrote a book about it called *Across Asia on a Bicycle*. The novelty was well received by the Qing court, and the boy-emperor Puyi was given to tearing around the Forbidden City on a cycle.

Today there are over 250 million bikes in China, more than can be found in any other country. Some are made for export, but most are for domestic use. Production can never keep up with demand because the Chinese will do anything to lay their hands on one rather than be at the mercy of the bus system. Chinese bicycles and tricycles are workhorses, used to carry anything up to a 100-kg slaughtered pig or a whole couch...you name it. Until very recently, Chinese bikes all looked the same – heavy gearless monsters made out of waterpipe and always painted black. Although the black beasts are still the most popular design (because they last a long time and are relatively cheap), sleak new multi-geared models in a variety of colours have made their debut.

But bicycles are not just put to practical uses; some Chinese are great bicycle tourists. An 85-year-old martial arts expert has spent three years pedalling over 16,000 km across China and plans to continue for another three years. A retired Chinese couple did 10,000 km from Gansu to Guangdong in two years. A 69-year-old retired worker set off on a self-made tricycle, the back of which could be converted into a bed and kitchen!

One of the factors in the enormous success of the bicycle in China must be that Chinese cities are so flat. The long, wide avenues, flat as pancakes (one exception is hilly Chongqing where there's hardly a bike in sight) lend themselves to cycling.

Rental

There are now established bicycle hire shops that cater to foreigners in most tourist centres. The majority operate out of hotels popular with foreigners, but there are also many independent hire shops. Even in towns

that don't see much tourist traffic there are often hire shops catering to Chinese who are passing through. They are usually happy to hire bikes to foreigners as well. Surprisingly, medium-size cities often have better bike-rental facilities than large metropolises.

Day hire, 24-hour hire or hire by the hour are the norm. It's possible to hire for a stretch of several days, so touring is possible if the bike is in good condition. Rates for Westerners are typically Y1 per hour or Y7 to Y10 per day – some places are more or less expensive depending on the competition. Some big hotels charge ridiculous rates – the Hyatt in Tianjin was asking Y10 per hour last time we checked!

If you hire over a long period you should be able to reduce the rate. Most hire places will ask you to leave some sort of ID. Sometimes they ask for your passport, which is asking a lot. Give them some other ID instead, like a student card or a driver's licence. Old expired passports are really useful for this purpose. Some hire shops may require a deposit, but that should certainly not be more than the actual value of the bike.

If you're planning on staying in one place for more than about five weeks, it's probably cheaper to buy your own bike and either sell it or give it to a friend when you leave.

Before taking a bike, check the brakes (are there any?), get the tyres pumped up hard – and make sure that none of the moving parts are about to fall off. Get the saddle raised to maximum leg-power. It's also worth tying something on – a handkerchief, for example – to identify your bicycle amidst the zillions at the bicycle parks.

Parking

In most larger towns and cities bicycles should be parked at designated places on the sidewalk. This will generally be a roped off enclosure, and bicycle-park attendants will give you a token when you park there; the charge is usually two or three jiao. If you don't use this service, you may return to find that your bike has been 'towed' away. Confiscated illegally parked bicycles make their way to the police station. There will be a fine in retrieving it – probably a few yuan.

Licences & Repairs

A bike licence is obligatory for Chinese but is not necessary for a foreigner. Some cities have bicycle licence plates, and in Beijing bikes owned by foreigners have special licence plates so they can't be sold to a Chinese. If a person has an accident or is drunk while riding a bike, a fine can be imposed and the bike impounded (there are posters to this effect in Chinese cities). Police also occasionally stop cyclists to do spot checks on the brakes and other equipment. Bike-repair shops are everywhere and repairs are dirt cheap (say Y2 a shot).

Hazards

It's difficult to miss the ubiquitous picture displays around Chinese cities exhibiting the gory remains of cyclists who didn't look where they were going and wound up looking like Y3 worth of fried dumplings. These displays also give tips on how to avoid accidents and show 're-education classes' for offenders who have had several accidents. Take care when you're riding and don't give the authorities the opportunity to feature a foreigner in their next display.

Night riding is particularly hazardous. Most motorised transport in China only uses its headlights to flash them on and off as a warning for cyclists up ahead to get out of the way. It pays to be particularly alert for their presence behind you. On country roads look out for those UFO-style walking tractors, which often have no headlights at all.

Your fellow cyclists are another factor in the hazard equation. Most Chinese cyclists have little more than an abstract grasp of basic road courtesy and traffic rules. Be prepared for cyclists to suddenly swerve in front of you, to come hurtling out of a side road, or even to head straight towards you against the flow of the traffic. This is not to mention situations where you yourself are the traffic hazard: beware of the cyclist who spots you, glides by staring gape-mouthed, crashes into something in front and causes the traffic following to topple like tenpins.

The dog, bane of cyclists the world over, is less of a problem in China than elsewhere. This is because Fido is more likely to be stir-fried than menacing cyclists on street corners. One exception to this rule is Tibet and parts of Qinghai. Be particularly careful if cycling around Lhasa.

Bicycle theft does exist. The bicycle parks with their attendants help prevent this, but keep your bike off the streets at night, or at least within the hotel gates. If the hotel has no grounds then take the bike up to your room. Most hired bicycles have a lock around the rear wheel which nimble fingers can pick in seconds. You can increase security by buying and using a cable lock, widely available from shops in China.

Tours

Organised bicycle tours for groups have operated in China since the beginning of 1981. The range of tours has been extended to include the Silk Road, Inner Mongolia and Tibet.

For bike tours around Guangdong, Guangxi and Hainan try Bike China Tours (☎ 9847208), GPO Box 9484, Hong Kong: these have very small groups, are flexible, and are recommended by some travellers. Another company specialising in biking tours in different regions of China is Tail Winds Bicycle Touring (☎ (06) 249 6634), PO Box 32, O'Connor, ACT 2601, Australia. In the USA, trips of this nature are advertised in cycling magazines.

Freestyle

Prior to 1987, border guards and police officials in remote areas were often puzzled by the sudden appearance of muddy foreign bikers whizzing through from Canton to Kunming, Shanghai to Xi'an, Kathmandu to Lhasa, etc. Unfortunately, now that the novelty has worn off, officials have decided that they need to 'do something' about the influx of foreign bikers. Horror stories abound. Two Americans were intercepted at Kunming Airport after flying in from Hong

Kong with mountain bikes. The ensuing wrangle with Customs took several weeks before the officials, who had been coveting the bikes, graciously agreed to let the foreign couple sell them for a song to a local department store. Foreigners have crossed the border from Hong Kong and Macau without incident, only to be intercepted by local officials in remote areas and fined and even had their bikes confiscated.

The legalities of cycling from town to town are open to conjecture. In China, there is hardly any rule of law; local officials can pretty much do what they want with you. Most of the time, the police won't bother you, but some officials can't stand seeing foreigners bicycling through China – they expect you to be travelling by taxi and tour bus. After all, foreigners are universally regarded as rich and bicycles are meant for poor peasants. No respectable cadre would be caught dead riding a bicycle – they prefer limousines. Most Chinese can't figure out why foreigners would even want to cycle around China.

The other problem is the one of 'open' and 'closed' areas. Many previously closed areas have opened up in recent years, but there are still large tracts of land that the Chinese authorities feel are undeveloped for 'tourism'. Cyclists tend to end up in places where the locals have never heard of FEC, or worse still don't know that foreigners can't stay in any hotel that has a spare bed.

If you get caught in a closed area, it is unlikely to be while you are on the road. The long arm of the law keeps firm tabs on transients via hotels. If you're staying overnight in closed places, try to arrive late and leave between 4 and 5 am. If the authorities do catch up with you they will demand a fine and usually send you back to the nearest open area you came from, although occasionally you will be allowed to proceed with the greatest possible haste to your destination – providing it's open. Fines vary from Y50 to Y100, though any more than Y50 is probably excessive. There is some latitude for bargaining in these situations, and you should request a receipt (shōujù).

Top: Near Upper Cable-Car Station, Huangshan, Anhui (CL)
Bottom: The Bund, Shanghai (AS)

Left: Scaling Tai Shan, Shandong (AS)
Right: Parking zone, Beijing (Storey)
Bottom: Chasing the tourist dollar, Beijing (Storey)

Camping is possible if you can find a spare blade of grass. The trick is to select a couple of likely places about half an hour before sunset, keep pedalling and then backtrack so you can pull off the road at the chosen spot just after darkness falls.

One problem with Western bikes is that they attract a lot of attention. Another problem is the unavailability of spare parts. One Westerner brought a fold-up bicycle with him – but in most places it attracted so much attention that he had to give it to the locals to play with until the novelty wore off. One advantage of the fold-up bike is that you can stick it in a bag and stow it on the luggage racks of the trains, unfold it when you arrive at your destination and zip off, no hassles. They are, however, useless for long-distance travel and can be very expensive in the West.

It's essential to have a kick-stand for parking. A bell, headlight and reflector are good ideas. Make sure everything is bolted down, otherwise you'll invite theft. A cage-less water bottle, even on a Chinese bike, attracts too much attention. Adhesive reflector strips get ripped off.

Off the Road

Most travellers who bring bikes take at least a couple of breaks from the rigours of the road, during which they use some other means of transport. The best option is bus. It is generally no problem stowing bikes on the roofs of buses and there is seldom a charge involved. Air and train transport are more problematic.

Bikes are not cheap to transport on trains; they can cost as much as a hard-seat fare (Chinese price). (Boats are cheaper, at around a third of the 3rd-class passenger fare – usually a pittance.) Trains have quotas for the number of bikes they may transport. As a foreigner you will get preferential treatment in the luggage compartment and the bike will go on the first available train. But your bike won't arrive at the same time as you unless you send it on a couple of days in advance. At the other end it is held in storage for three days free, and then incurs a small charge.

The procedure for putting a bike on a train and getting it at the other end is as follows:

- Railway personnel would like to see a train ticket for yourself (not entirely essential).
- Go to the baggage transport section of the station. Get a white slip and fill it out to get the two or three tags for registration. Then fill out a form (it's only in Chinese, so just fill it out in English) which reads: 'Number/ to station x/send goods person/receive goods person/total number of goods/from station y'.
- Take the white slip to another counter, where you pay and are given a blue slip.
- At the other end (after delays of up to three days for transporting a bike) you present the blue slip, and get a white slip in return. This means your bike has arrived. The procedure could take from 20 minutes to an hour depending on who's around. If you lose that blue slip you'll have real trouble reclaiming your bike.

Chinese cyclists spend ages at the stations mummifying their bicycles in cloth for transport. For the one scratch the bike will get it's hardly worth going through this elaborate procedure. Again, you can avoid all of this by taking a fold-up bicycle.

The best bet for getting your bike on a bus is to get to the station early and put it on the roof. Strictly speaking, there shouldn't be a charge for this, but in practice the driver will generally try to extort a few yuan out of you. Bypass this sort of thing by putting it on the roof and unloading it yourself. The driver won't like it, but you'll normally be allowed to proceed all the same.

Transporting your bike by plane can be expensive, but it's often less complicated than by train. Some cyclists have not been charged by CAAC, others have had to pay 1% of their fare per kg of excess weight.

Buying a Bike

Until very recently, there were only four basic types of bike available in China: small wheel, light roadster (14 kg), black hulk (22 kg) and farmers' models (25 to 30 kg). The average price for an average bike is around Y150, or around a month's wages for a city worker. This situation is changing rapidly (especially in the big cities) as mountain bikes and racing bikes invade the Chinese market. Already, in places like Yangshuo, mountain bikes are available for hire, and in cities like Beijing, Shanghai, Canton and Chengdu very good mountain bikes can be bought at prices that are competitive with the prices you'd have to pay at home.

Some travellers have saved themselves the bother of bringing bikes across the border by buying mountain bikes or racers in Canton. You won't get the range that is available at home or in Hong Kong, but you're likely to save some hassle and quite a bit of money.

In Hong Kong there's a Raleigh agent, British Bicycle Company, and bike shops in the Mongkok area of Kowloon as well as over on Hong Kong Island. Hong Kong bikes are related to the Chinese versions, so Raleighs and Chinese-brand parts should be roughly compatible – or at least your Chinese bicycle repairer should know what they're looking at. You can also buy three-speed bikes in Hong Kong.

HITCHING

Many people have hitchhiked in China, and some have been amazingly successful. It's not officially sanctioned, so don't bother trying to get permission. The best way to get a lift is, like anywhere else, to head out to main roads on the outskirts of town. There are usually lots of trucks on the roads, and even army convoys are worth trying.

Much depends on where you are; in some parts the novelty of hitchhikers has worn off among the locals. Otherwise, hitching is a good way of getting to closed or isolated areas, or to places where there is poor public transport.

Hitching in China is rarely free – passengers are expected to offer at least a tip. Some drivers might even ask for an unreasonable amount of money – try to establish a figure early on in the ride to avoid problems later. Communicating can be a problem if you don't speak Chinese.

As far as we know, there is no Chinese signal for hitching, so just try waving down the trucks. Unless you speak Chinese, you'll need to have where you want to go written down in Chinese – otherwise there's no hope of being understood.

While China is a relatively safe country in which to hitch, bear in mind that hitching invariably carries an element of risk. Exercise caution, and if you're in any doubt as to the intentions of your prospective driver, say no. A lone female would be wise to travel with a male companion.

BOAT

Apart from the ships which ply the coast of China (see the introductory Getting There & Away chapter for details), several inland shipping routes are worth considering. For details of each trip see the appropriate sections in this book. Boat travel is the slowest but often cheapest means of transport in China, though recent price hikes mean that it is no longer the bargain it once was.

The best known trip is the three-day boat ride along the Yangzi River from Chongqing to Wuhan. Some people find this a dull trip but it's a good way to get from Chongqing to Wuhan, and it's a relief from the trains. You can also carry on down the Yangzi River and the Huangpu River to Shanghai. From Shanghai there is the boat to Qingdao.

From Canton to Wuzhou along the West (Xi) River is popular with low-budget travellers as it is the cheapest way to get from Canton to Guilin and Yangshuo, disembarking at Wuzhou and then continuing on by bus to Guilin or Yangshuo. The Li River boat trip from Guilin to Yangshuo is a popular tourist ride which takes six hours.

You can also travel the Grand Canal from Hangzhou to Suzhou, and flit off on various other boats in this district. There are no passenger boats on the Yellow River.

LOCAL TRANSPORT

Long-distance transport in China is not really a problem – the dilemma occurs when you finally make it to your destination. As in US and Australian cities where the car is the key to movement, the bicycle is the key in China, and if you don't have one, life is more difficult. Walking is not usually recommended, since Chinese cities tend to be very spread out.

To/From the Airport

Your plane ticket does not include the cost of transport between the CAAC office and the airport; expect to pay between Y5 and Y15 for airport buses. The departure time of the bus will be noted on your ticket. You can also take a taxi to the airport.

Bus

Apart from bikes, buses are the most common means of getting around in the cities. Services are fairly extensive and the buses go to most places you want to go. The problem is that they are almost always packed. If an empty bus pulls in at a stop then the battle for seats ensues, and a passive crowd of Chinese suddenly turns into a stampeding herd. Even more aggravating is the slow traffic. You just have to be patient, never expect anything to move rapidly, and allow lots of time to get to the railway station to catch your train. One consolation is that buses are cheap, rarely more than two jiao per trip.

Good maps of Chinese cities and bus routes are readily available and are often sold by hawkers outside the railway stations. When you get on a bus, point to where you want to go on the map, and the conductor (who is seated near the door) will sell you the right ticket. They usually tell you where to get off.

You may be offered a seat in a crowded bus, although this is becoming less common in the big cities. It's that peculiarly Chinese politeness which occasionally manifests itself, and if you're offered a seat it's best to accept as refusal may offend.

Taxi

These do not cruise the streets (anything to save petrol) except in major cities, but the situation is improving due to rising affluence. You can always summon a taxi from the tourist hotels which sometimes have separate booking desks. You can hire them for a single trip or on a daily basis – the latter is

worth considering if you've got the money or if there's a group of people who can split the cost. Some of the tourist hotels also have minibuses on hand.

While most taxis have meters, they are a pure formality (except in large cities) and usually only get switched on by accident. Sometimes you're better off without the meter – as elsewhere in the world, Chinese taxi drivers don't mind taking you for a 20-km ride to a place just across the street. Taxi prices should be negotiated before you get into the taxi, and bargaining is usual (but keep it friendly – nastiness on your part will result in a higher price!). Don't be surprised if the driver attempts to change the price when you arrive, claiming that you 'misunderstood' what they said – if you want to get nasty, *this* is the time to do it. If your spoken Chinese isn't perfect, write the price down clearly and make sure the driver agrees, to avoid 'misunderstandings' later. Prices should always be in RMB, not FEC, unless the driver made it clear from the beginning that FEC is expected.

It's important to realise that most Chinese cities impose limitations on the number of passengers that a taxi can carry. The limit is usually four, though minibuses can take more, but drivers are usually unwilling to break the rules and risk trouble with the police. We witnessed a vicious argument in Beijing between eight foreigners and a taxi driver – the driver refused to take all eight people in one trip, saying it was illegal and he could get into trouble. He was willing to make two trips, but the foreigners figured that was just his way of trying to charge double and therefore rip them off. The driver was, in fact, telling the truth.

Scooter Taxi

These are a fairly recent phenomenon, and if you turn a blind eye to the hazards, it's a quick and cheap way of getting around. As in Thailand, the deal is that you get a ride on the back of someone's motorcycle. Most rides cost only a few yuan and drivers provide a helmet. Obviously, there is no meter so fares must be agreed to in advance.

Pedicab *(sānlúnchē)*

A pedicab is a pedal-powered tricycle with a seat to carry passengers. Chinese pedicabs have the driver in front and passenger seats in the back, the opposite of some countries (Vietnam, for example).

Pedicabs congregate outside railway and bus stations and sometimes outside the tourist hotels. Unfortunately, most of the drivers are so aggressive that you have to ask yourself if it's worth bothering with them. Almost without exception a reasonable fare will be quoted, but when you arrive at your destination it'll be multiplied by 10. So if you're quoted a fare of Y3 it becomes Y30, and if you're quoted Y30 it becomes Y300.

The best bet is to write it down, get the driver to agree three or four times, and then when he tries to multiply by 10, hand over the exact change and walk away. At this point the smiling friendly driver will suddenly be transformed into an exceedingly menacing beast – you just have to stand your ground. It's worse if there are two of them, so *never* get into a pedicab if the driver wants his 'brother' to come along for the ride (a common situation). The 'brother' is there to threaten and bully you into paying up when you inevitably balk at being ripped off.

The situation is less likely to turn ugly when the driver is female, but women pedicab drivers are fairly rare. And if she happens to have a 'brother' who wants to come along for the ride, find another driver. In many cases, a taxi works out to be cheaper than a pedicab because the chances of being ripped off are less.

Pedicabs versus rickshaws: A rickshaw is a two-wheeled passenger cart pulled by a man on foot. It was invented in Japan, where the word *jin-rikusha* means 'human-powered vehicle'. It was introduced into China in the late 19th century, where it was called *yángchē* (foreign vehicle). The rickshaw eventually became a symbol of human exploitation – one person pulling another in a cart – and disappeared from China in the 1950s. Its replacement, the pedicab – sometimes mistakenly called a rickshaw – is a tricycle with a seat for one or two passengers.

Motortricycle (Auto-pedicab) *(sānlún mótuōchē)*

The motortricycle – for want of a better name – is an enclosed three-wheeled vehicle with a driver at the front, a small motorbike engine below and seats for two passengers behind. They congregate outside the railway and bus stations in larger towns and cities. Some of these vehicles have trays at the rear with bench seats along the sides so that several people can be carried at once.

Pedicab

TOURS

Some of the one-day tours are reasonably priced and might be worth the cost for all the trouble they can save you. Some remote spots are difficult to reach and a tour might well be your only option.

Basically, tours come in three varieties: for foreigners, for Overseas Chinese and for local Chinese.

Tours aimed at foreigners are usually organised by CITS, CTS or CYTS, though a few private operators are also getting into the act. An English-speaking guide (or French, German, whatever) is supplied. Tours can be organised for very small groups, but costs are high and payment will always be in FEC.

The tours for Overseas Chinese are geared towards large groups and there's a heavy emphasis on shopping, feasting and posing for photos. There's also a tendency towards regimentation – the tour leader (usually female) waves a flag and uses a megaphone to keep the tourist troops in line. The tourists wear some sort of ID badge and a yellow hat (a non-Tibetan version of the Yellow Hat Sect?). Another significant difference is that the guide will speak Chinese. Even if you speak *putonghua* fluently, don't be so certain that you'll understand what's being said – many of the guides speak Cantonese or Taiwanese, depending on what the group demands. The prices that Overseas Chinese pay for these tours is not particularly cheap and payment is in FEC, but you'll eat well and the circus atmosphere is free.

If price is the main consideration, going on tour with the local Chinese is the cheapest option. Payment will always be in RMB unless they're trying to cheat you. Meals might not even be included and the bus could be an old rattletrap, but these tours can be great fun. Don't expect the guides to speak anything but Chinese – possibly just the local dialect. Sometimes the buses will whiz through what Westerners would consider interesting spots and make long stops at dull places for the requisite photo sessions. You might have difficulty getting a ticket if your Chinese isn't good and they think you're too much trouble.

SOUTHERN AND
CENTRAL CHINA

Canton 广州

Known to the Chinese as Guangzhou (*guǎngzhōu*), Canton is one of the oldest cities in China, the capital of Guangdong Province and, for over 1000 years, one of the main gateways to the country. The first town to be established on the site of present-day Canton dates back to the Qin Dynasty. The first foreigners to come here were the Indians and Romans, who appeared as early as the 2nd century AD. By the Tang Dynasty (500 years later) Arab traders were visiting and a sizable trade with the Middle East and South-East Asia had grown.

Initial contact with modern European nations was made in the early 16th century when the Portuguese were allowed to set up base downriver in Macau in 1557. Then the Jesuits came and in 1582 were allowed to establish themselves at Zhaoqing, a town north-west of Canton, and later in Beijing itself. The first trade overtures from the British were rebuffed in 1625, but the imperial government finally opened Canton to foreign trade in 1685.

In 1757 a new imperial edict restricted all foreign trade to Canton, indicating how little importance was placed on trade with the Western barbarians.

The fuse to the Opium wars was lit in 1757 when by imperial edict a Canton merchants' guild, the Co Hong, gained exclusive rights to China's foreign trade. Westerners were permitted to reside in Canton from September to March only, and were restricted to Shamian Island, where they had their factories. They had to leave their wives and families downriver in Macau (though not all found this to be a hardship) and were forbidden to learn Chinese or deal with anyone except the Co Hong. The traders complained about the restrictions and about the trading regulations, which changed from day to day. Nevertheless, trade flourished – mainly in China's favour, because the tea and silk had to be paid for in hard cash, normally silver.

Trade in China's favour was not what the Western merchants had in mind. In 1773 the

British unloaded 1000 chests at Canton, each containing 150 pounds of Bengal opium. The intention was to balance, and eventually more than balance, their purchases of Chinese goods. The Chinese taste for opium, or 'foreign mud' as it was called, amounted to 2000 chests a year by about 1800. Emperor Dao Guang, alarmed at the drain of silver from the country, issued an edict banning the drug trade. But the foreigners had different ideas, and with the help of the Co Hong and corrupt Cantonese officials the trade expanded.

In 1839 opium was still the key to British trade in China. The emperor appointed Lin Zexu commissioner of Canton with orders to stamp out the opium trade once and for all. It took Lin just one week to surround the British in Canton, cut off their food supplies and demand that they surrender all the opium in their possession. In stiff-upper-lip tradition the British stuck it out for six weeks until they were ordered by their own superintendent of trade, Captain Elliot, to surrender 20,000 chests of opium. Elliot tried negotiating with Kishen, Lin's representative, but when this failed he attacked Canton in the first Opium War. The attack was ended by the Convention of Chuen Pi, which ceded Hong Kong Island to the British. A later treaty ceded the island and a piece of Kowloon 'in perpetuity'.

In the 19th century, Canton became a cradle of revolt. The leader of the anti-dynastic Taiping Rebellion, Hong Xiuquan (1814-1864), was born at Huaxian, northwest of Canton, and the early activities of the Taipings centred around this area. Canton was also a stronghold of the republican forces after the fall of the Qing Dynasty in 1911. Sun Yatsen, the first president of the Republic of China, was born at Cuiheng village south-west of Canton. In the early 1920s, Sun headed the Kuomintang (Nationalist Party) in Canton, from where the republicans mounted their campaigns against the northern warlords. Canton was also the centre of activities of the fledgeling Communist Party.

These events were nothing new. Centuries before, the southerners had gained a reputation for thinking for themselves, and rebellions and uprisings had been a feature of Canton from the time of its foundation. The northerners regarded their southern compatriots with disdain, or as one 19th-century northern account put it:

The Cantonese...are a coarse set of people...Before the times of Han and Tang, this country was quite wild and waste, and these people have sprung forth from unconnected, unsettled vagabonds that wandered here from the north.

One of China's boomtowns, Canton and nearby Special Economic Zones (SEZs) like Shenzhen and Zhuhai are hardly representative of the rest of the country. Nor is this part of China particularly beautiful – heavy industrialisation and a booming economy have created undesirable side effects such as pollution, heavy traffic and overcrowding. However, China could be heading the same way economically as Canton, making it a good place to catch a glimpse of some of the successes, pitfalls, fallacies and curious results of the new economic policies.

Orientation

Canton's major streets are usually split into numbered sectors (Zhongshan 5-Lu, etc), or labelled by compass points (Huanshi Donglu).

Information

CITS There is an enormous CITS office (☎ 6666271; fax 6678048) at 179 Huanshi Lu next to the main railway station, but they have little information. It's one big ticket office and the only thing the overworked clerks are likely to say to you is 'Next please' (don't count on the 'please'). You can buy tickets here for trains, planes, hovercraft and ships. The office is open from 8.30 to 11.30 am and from 2 to 5 pm.

PSB The PSB (☎ 3331060) is at 863 Jiefang Beilu, opposite the road which leads up to the Zhenhai Tower.

Money Every large tourist hotel cashes travellers' cheques and changes Hong Kong and US dollars; some even give a FEC advance on credit cards. The black-market moneychangers are professional thieves, especially those on Shamian Island.

Post & Telecommunications Canton's area code is 020. All the major tourist hotels have post offices where you can send letters and packets containing printed matter.

If you're posting parcels overseas you have to go to the post office at 43 Yanjiang Xilu near the riverfront and Shamian Island. Get the parcel contents checked and fill out a Customs form.

Adjacent to the railway station is the main post office, known locally as the Liuhua post office (*liúhuā yóu jú*).

If you require private air freight, there is service available from DHL (☎ 3355034) and UPS (☎ 8889006).

The telecommunications office is across from the railway station on the east side of Renmin Beilu. Most hotels have direct-dial service to Hong Kong which is quite cheap. All the main tourist hotels have 'business centres' offering domestic and international telephone, fax and telex facilities.

Consulates There are several consulates which can issue visas and replace stolen passports.

Depending on what passport you hold, the Polish Consulate can be useful if you want to do the Trans-Siberian. These days most Western nationalities do not require a visa for Poland.

The US Consulate might be better named the 'Emigration Information Centre'. If you go there with some other intention besides emigrating to the USA, the staff will be so happy to see you they might throw a party.

Japan
    Garden Hotel Tower, 368 Huanshi Donglu
    (☎ 3338999)
Poland
    Shamian Island, near the White Swan Hotel
Thailand
    Room 316, White Swan Hotel, Shamian Island
    (☎ 8886968 ext 316)
USA
    1 Shamian Nanjie, Shamian Island (☎ 8888911;
    fax 8862341)

Medical Services If you get sick you can go to one of the hospitals or to the medical clinic for foreigners – Guangzhou No 1 People's Hospital (☎ 3333090) (dìyī rénmín yīyuàn), 602 Renmin Beilu.

If you're staying on Shamian Island or the riverfront, a nearby good hospital is the Sun Yatsen Memorial Hospital (☎ 8882012) (sūn yìxiān jìniàn yīyuàn), 107 Yanjiang Xilu next to the Aiqun Hotel. Not much English is spoken here but the medical facilities are pretty good and the prices low.

Just next to Shamian Island and the Qingping Market is the Guangzhou Hospital of Traditional Chinese Medicine (☎ 8886504) (zhōngyī yīyuàn) at 16 Zhuji Lu. If you want to try acupuncture and herbs, this is the place to go. Many foreigners come here to study Chinese medicine rather than to be patients.

Warning Canton is easily the most dangerous city in China. Because it is widely perceived as the richest place in China, a large number of immigrants from the countryside have poured into the city in search of instant wealth. Needless to say, most become disillusioned when they find that money doesn't grow on trees, and many turn to begging and theft.

There is little physical danger in walking

the streets, but pickpocketing is a problem, especially on crowded buses. You should also be cautious of bag snatchers, especially around the railway station. Some thieves use bicycles as their getaway vehicle – they grab the bag right out of your hand and are gone before you know what's happened.

Peasant Movement Institute
(nóngmín yùndòng jiǎngxí suǒ)
农民运动讲习所
Canton's Peasant Movement Institute was built on the site of a Ming Dynasty Confu-

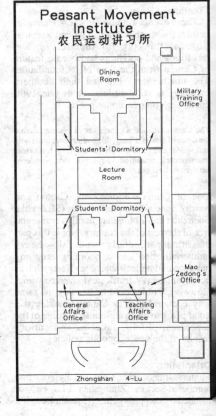

cian temple in 1924. In the early days of the Communist Party, its members (from all over China) were trained at the Institute. It was set up by Peng Pai, a high-ranking Communist leader who believed that if a Communist revolution was to succeed in China then the peasants must be its main force. Mao Zedong – of the same opinion – took over as director of the institute in 1925 or 1926. Zhou Enlai lectured here and one of his students was Mao's brother, Mao Zemin. Peng was executed by the Kuomintang in 1929, and Mao Zemin was executed by a warlord in Xinjiang Province in 1942.

The buildings were restored in 1953 and are now used as a revolutionary museum. There's not a great deal to see: a replica of Mao's room, the soldiers' barracks and rifles, and old photographs. The institute is at 42 Zhongshan 4-Lu.

Memorial Garden to the Martyrs
(lièshì língyuán) 烈士陵园

This memorial is within walking distance of the Peasant Movement Institute, east along Zhongshan 4-Lu to Zhongshan 3-Lu. It was officially opened in 1957 on the 30th anniversary of the December 1927 Canton uprising.

In April 1927, Chiang Kaishek ordered his troops to massacre Communists in Shanghai and Nanjing. On 21 May the Communists led an uprising of peasants on the Hunan-Jiangxi border, and on 1 August they staged another in Nanchang. Both uprisings were defeated by Kuomintang troops.

On 11 December 1927 the Communists staged another uprising in Canton, but this was also bloodily suppressed by the Kuomintang. The Communists claim that over 5700 people were killed during or after the uprising. The memorial garden is laid out

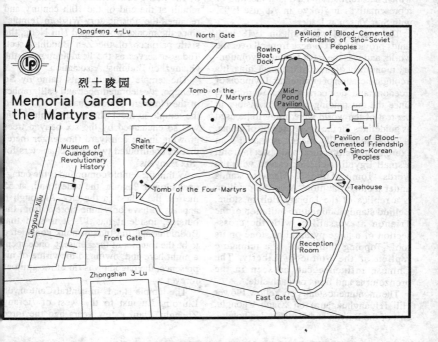

烈士陵园
Memorial Garden to the Martyrs

on Red Flower Hill (Honghuagang), which was one of the execution grounds.

There's nothing of particular interest here, though the gardens themselves are attractive. You'll also see the Pavilion of Blood-Cemented Friendship of the Sino-Soviet Peoples and the Pavilion of Blood-Cemented Friendship of the Sino-Korean Peoples.

Mausoleum of the 72 Martyrs & Memorial of Yellow Flowers
(huánghuā gǎng qīshí'èr lièshì mù)
黄花岗七十二烈士墓

This memorial was built in memory of the victims of the unsuccessful Canton insurrection of 27 April 1911. (It was not until October 1911 that the Qing Dynasty collapsed and a Republic of China was declared in the south of the country.) The uprising had been planned by a group of Chinese organisations which opposed the Qing and which had formally united at a meeting of representatives in Tokyo in August 1905, with Sun Yatsen as leader.

The memorial was built in 1918 with funds provided by Chinese from all over the world, and was the most famous revolutionary monument of pre-Communist China. It's a conglomeration of architectural symbols of freedom and democracy used worldwide, since the outstanding periods of history in the rest of the world were going to be used as guidelines for the new Republic of China.

What that really means is that it's an exercise in architectural bad taste. In front, a small Egyptian obelisk carved with the words 'Tomb of the 72 Martyrs' stands under a stone pavilion. Atop the pavilion is a replica of the Liberty Bell in stone. Behind stands a miniature imitation of the Trianon at Versailles, with the cross-section of a huge pyramid of stone on its roof. Topping things off is a miniature replica of the Statue of Liberty. The Chinese influence can be seen in the bronze urns and lions on each side.

The monument stands on Yellow Flower Hill (Huanghuagang) on Xianli Zhonglu, east of the Baiyun and New Garden hotels.

Sun Yatsen Memorial Hall
(sūn zhōngshān jìniàn táng)
孙中山纪念堂

This hall on Dongfeng Lu was built in honour of Sun Yatsen, with donations from Overseas Chinese and from Canton citizens. Construction began in January 1929 and finished in November 1931. It stands on the site of the residence of the governor of Guangdong and Guangxi during the Qing Dynasty, later used by Sun Yatsen when he became president of the Republic of China. The Memorial Hall is an octagonal Chinese monolith some 47 metres high and 71 metres wide; seating capacity is about 4000.

Temple of the Six Banyan Trees
(liù róng sì huā tǎ) 六榕寺花塔

The temple's history is vague, but it seems that the first structure on this site, called the 'Precious Solemnity Temple', was built during the 6th century AD, and was ruined by fire in the 10th century. The temple was rebuilt at the end of the 10th century and renamed the 'Purificatory Wisdom Temple' since the monks worshipped Hui Neng, the sixth patriarch of the Zen Buddhist sect. Today it serves as the headquarters of the Guangzhou Buddhist Association.

The temple was given its name by Su Dongpo, a celebrated poet and calligrapher of the Northern Song Dynasty who visited the temple in the 11th or 12th century. He was so enchanted by the six banyan trees growing in the courtyard (no longer there) that he contributed two large characters for 'Six Banyans'.

Within the temple compound is the octagonal Flower Pagoda, the oldest and, at 55 metres, the tallest in the city. Although it appears to have only nine storeys from the outside, inside it has 17. It is said that Bodhidharma, the Indian monk considered to be the founder of the Zen sect, once spent a night here and, owing to the virtue of his presence, the pagoda was rid of mosquitoes forever.

The temple stands in central Canton, on Liurong Lu just to the west of Jiefang Zhonglu. Until a few years ago the three large Buddha statues stood in the open courtyard. The main hall was rebuilt in 1984. The buddhas have been painted and several other shrines opened. One shrine houses a statue of Hui Neng.

I would like to suggest that you make a point of reminding readers that many of the temples listed are 'working'; they're not there for tourists. At Liu Rong Si...some Americans and French were happily snapping shots of the kneeling worshippers; some even snuck up in front of the altar to do so. My Chinese friend said her blood was close to boiling...she did indeed seem awfully close to losing her temper.

Bright Filial Piety Temple
(guāngxiào sì) 光孝寺

This temple is one of the oldest in Canton. The earliest Buddhist temple on this site possibly dates as far back as the 4th century AD. The place has particular significance for Buddhists because Hui Neng was a novice monk here in the 7th century. The temple buildings are of much more recent construction, the original buildings having been destroyed by fire in the mid-17th century. The temple is on Hongshu Lu, just northwest of the Temple of the Six Banyan Trees. A section of the complex now houses the Guangdong Antique Store.

Five Genies Temple
(wǔ xiān guān) 五仙观

This Taoist temple is held to be the site of the appearance of the five rams and celestial beings in the myth of Canton's foundation – see the section on Yuexiu Park for the story.

The stone tablets flanking the forecourt commemorate the various restorations that the temple has undergone. The present buildings are comparatively recent, as the earlier Ming Dynasty buildings were destroyed by fire in 1864.

The large hollow in the rock in the temple courtyard is said to be the impression of a celestial being's foot; the Chinese refer to it by the name of 'Rice-Ear Rock of Unique Beauty'. The great bell, which weighs five tonnes, was cast during the Ming Dynasty – it's three metres high, two metres in diameter and about 10 cm thick, probably the largest

in Guangdong Province. It's known as the 'calamity bell', since the sound of the bell, which has no clapper, is a portent of calamity for the city.

At the rear of the main tower stand life-size statues with archaic Greek smiles; these appear to represent four of the five genies. In the temple forecourt are four statues of rams, and embedded in the temple walls are inscribed steles.

The temple is at the end of an alleyway whose entrance is on Huifu Xilu. Huifu Xilu runs westwards off Jiefang Nanlu. Hours are daily from 8.30 to 11.30 am and from 2.30 to 5.30 pm. Next door is 'Tom's Gym' with equipment that dates back to the Stone Age.

Sacred Heart Church
(shí shì jiàotáng) 石室教堂

This impressive edifice is known to the Chinese as the 'house of stone', as it is built entirely of granite. Designed by the French architect Guillemin, the church is an imitation of a European Gothic cathedral. Four bronze bells suspended in the building to the east of the church were cast in France; the original coloured glass was also made in France, but almost all of it is gone.

The site was originally the location of the office of the governor of Guangdong and Guangxi provinces during the Qing Dynasty, but the building was destroyed by British and French troops at the end of the second Opium War in the 19th century. The area was leased to the French after the signing of the Sino-French 'Tianjin Treaty'. Construction of the church began in 1863 and was completed in 1888. It's on Yide Xilu, not far from the riverfront, and is normally closed except on Sunday when mass is held. All are welcome.

Another church you may find interesting is the Zion Christian Church at 392 Renmin Zhonglu. The building is a hybrid, with a traditional European Gothic outline and Chinese eaves. It's an active place of worship.

Huaisheng Mosque
(huáishèng sì guāng tǎ) 怀圣寺光塔

The original mosque on this site is said to have been established in 627 AD by the first

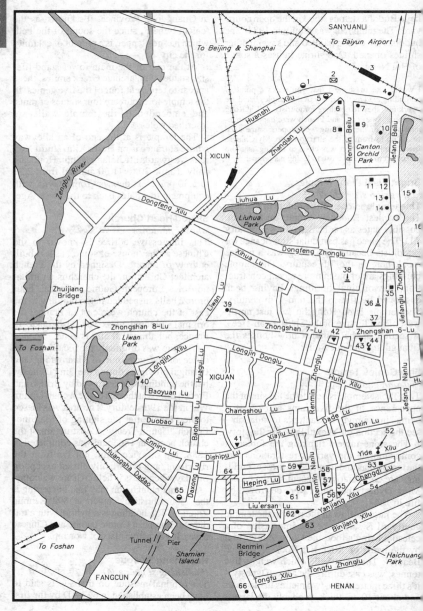

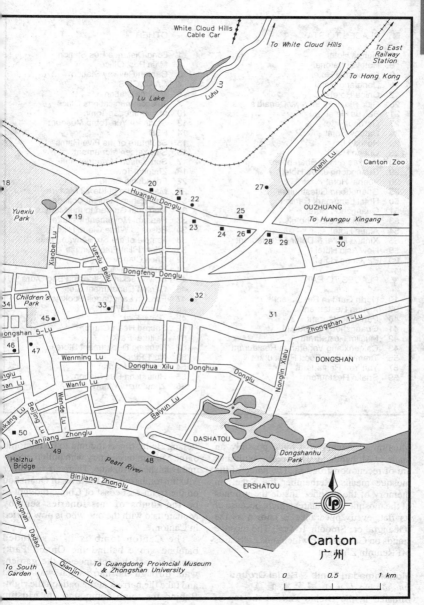

White Cloud Hills
Cable Car

To White Cloud Hills

To East
Railway
Station

Luhu Lu

To Hong Kong

Lu Lake

Xianli Lu

Canton Zoo

18

Yuexiu
Park

20

Huanshi Donglu

21

22

27

OUZHUANG

To Huangpu Xingang

Xiaobei Lu

Yuexiu Beilu

19

25

23

24 26

28 29

30

Dongfeng Donglu

Children's
Park

34

45

33

32

31

Zhongshan 1-Lu

Nonglin Xialu

DONGSHAN

ongshan 5-Lu

46

47

Wenming Lu

Donghua Xilu

Donghua

Donglu

nglu
an Lu

Wanfu Lu

Baiyun Lu

Dongshanhu
Park

Wende Lu

ikang Lu

Beijing Lu

50

Yanjiang Zhonglu

DASHATOU

49

Haizhu
Bridge

Pearl River

48

ERSHATOU

Binjiang Zhonglu

Jiangnan Dadao

Qianjin Lu

Canton
广州

To South
Garden

To Guangdong Provincial Museum
& Zhongshan University

0   0.5   1 km

■ PLACES TO STAY

6	Liuhua Hotel
8	Hotel Equatorial
9	Friendship Hotel
11	Dongfang Hotel
12	China Hotel
20	Gitic Plaza Hotel & McDonald's
21	Baiyun Hotel
23	Garden Hotel
24	Cathay Hotel
25	Holiday Inn
26	Ocean Hotel
28	Hakkas & Hua Shan hotels
29	Guangdong Jinye Hotel
30	Yuehai Hotel
35	Guangdong Guesthouse
50	Hotel Landmark Canton
51	Guangzhou Hotel
53	Furama and GD hotels
54	Aiqun Hotel
56	Xinhua Hotel & Datong Restaurant
58	New Asia Hotel
60	Bai Gong Hotel

▼ PLACES TO EAT

19	North Garden Restaurant
37	Xiyuan Restaurant
40	Panxi Restaurant
41	Guangzhou Restaurant
42	Muslim Restaurant
43	Caigenxiang Vegetarian Restaurant
55	Timmy's Fast Food Restaurant
57	Yan Yan Restaurant
59	Snake Restaurant

OTHER

1	Long-Distance Bus Station
2	Main Post Office
3	Canton Railway Station
4	CAAC/CITS
5	Minibus Station
7	Telecommunications Office
10	Mohammedan Tomb
13	Southern Yue Tomb Museum
14	PSB
15	Sculpture of the Five Rams
16	Sun Yatsen Monument
17	Sun Yatsen Memorial Hall
18	Zhenhai Tower
22	Friendship Store
27	Mausoleum of the 72 Martyrs
31	Zhongshan Medical College
32	Memorial Garden to the Martyrs
33	Peasant Movement Institute
34	Buses to White Cloud Hills
36	Temple of the Six Banyan Trees
38	Bright Filial Piety Temple
39	Chen Clan Academy
44	Huaisheng Mosque
45	Down Jacket & Sleeping Bag Store
46	Canton Department Store
47	Foreign Languages Bookstore
48	Dashatou Wharf
49	Tianzi Pier
52	Sacred Heart Church
61	Cultural Park
62	Nanfang Department Store
63	No 1 Pier
64	Qingping Market
65	Huangsha Bus Station
66	Zhoutouzui Wharf

Muslim missionary to China, possibly an uncle of Mohammed. The present buildings are of recent construction. The name of the mosque means 'Remember the Sage', in memory of the prophet. Inside the grounds of the mosque is a minaret which, because of its flat, even appearance is known as the 'Guangta' or 'Smooth Tower'. The mosque stands on Guangta Lu, which runs eastwards off Renmin Zhonglu.

Mohammedan Tomb & Burial Ground
(mùhǎn mò dé mù) 穆罕默德墓
Situated in the Orchid Park at the top of Jiefang Beilu, this is thought to be the tomb of the Muslim missionary who built the original Huaisheng Mosque. There are two other Muslim tombs outside the town of Quanzhou on the south-east coast of China, thought to be the tombs of missionaries sent by Mohammed with the one who is now buried in Canton.

The Canton tomb is in a secluded bamboo grove behind the Orchid Park; continue past the entrance to the garden, walk through the narrow gateway ahead and take the narrow stone path on the right. Behind the tomb compound are Muslim

■ PLACES TO STAY

6　流花宾馆
8　贵都酒店
9　友谊宾馆
11　东方宾馆
12　中国大酒店
20　广东国际大厦/麦当劳
21　白云宾馆
23　白花园酒店
24　国泰宾馆
25　文化假日酒店
26　远洋宾馆
28　嘉应宾馆/华山宾馆
29　广东金页大厦
30　粤海大厦
35　广东迎宾馆
50　广华宾馆
51　广州宾馆
53　富丽华大酒店/广东大酒店
54　爱群大厦/大同饭店
56　新华酒店
58　新亚酒店
60　白宫酒店

▼ PLACES TO EAT

19　北园酒家
37　西园饭店
40　泮溪酒家
41　广州酒家
42　回民饭店
43　菜根香素菜馆
55　添美食
57　人人菜馆
59　蛇餐馆

OTHER

1　广东省汽车客运站
2　邮政总局（流花邮局）
3　广州火车站
4　中国民航／中国国际旅行社
5　小公共汽车站
7　国际电话大楼
10　穆斯林德汉墓
13　南越王墓汉外事科
14　公安局石像纪
15　五羊中山像纪念碑
16　孙中山纪念堂
17　孙中山楼
18　镇海楼商店
22　友谊商店
27　黄花岗七十二烈士墓
31　中山医科大学第一医院
32　中烈士陵园
33　农民运动讲习所
34　开往榕白云山的汽车站
36　六榕寺花塔
38　光孝寺
39　陈氏书院戒陈家词
44　怀圣寺光塔
45　工农服装百货
46　广州外文书店
47　大头码头
48　沙字码头
49　天字室教堂
52　石化公园大厦
61　文方号头头
62　南平市场
63　一清沙站
64　黄沙车站
65　沙头嘴码头
66　洲头嘴码头

graves and a monumental stone arch. The tomb came to be known as the 'Tomb of the Echo' or the 'Resounding Tomb' because of the noises that reverberate in the inner chamber.

Liu'ersan Lu
(liù'èrsān lù) 六二三路

Just before you reach the south end of Renmin Lu, Liu'ersan Lu heads west. 'Liu er san' means '6 2 3', referring to 23 June 1925, when British and French troops fired on striking Chinese workers during the Hong Kong-Canton Strike.

Qingping Market
(qīngpíng shìchǎng) 清平市场

The market came into existence in 1979. Although such private (capitalist) markets are a feature of all Chinese cities today, it was one of Deng Xiaoping's more radical economic experiments at that time. Deng probably did not realise that he was also creating one of Canton's more radical tourist attractions – if you want to buy, kill or cook it yourself, this is the place to come since the market is like a take-away zoo. Near the entrance you'll find the usual selection of medicinal herbs and spices, dried starfish, snakes, lizards, deer antlers, dried scorpions, leopard and tiger skins, bear paws, semi-toxic mushrooms, tree bark and unidentifiable herbs and plants.

Further up you'll find the live ones waiting to be butchered. Sad-eyed monkeys rattle at the bars of their wooden cages; tortoises crawl over each other in shallow tin trays; owls sit perched on boxes full of pigeons; fish paddle around in tubs aerated with jets of water. You can also get bundles of frogs, giant salamanders, pangolins (ant-eaters), dogs and racoons, alive or contorted by recent violent death – which may just swear you off meat for the next few weeks.

The market is on the north side of Liu'ersan Lu and spills out into Tiyun Lu, which cuts east-west across Qingping Lu.

Shamian Island
(shāmiàn) 沙面
Liu'ersan Lu runs parallel to the north bank of Shamian Island. The island is separated from the rest of Canton by a narrow canal to the north and east, and by the Pearl River to the south and west.

Shamian means 'sand surface', which is all the island was until foreign traders were permitted to set up their warehouses (factories) here in the middle of the 18th century. Land reclamation has increased its area to its present size: 900 metres from east to west, and 300 metres from north to south. The island became a British and French concession after they defeated the Chinese in the Opium wars, and is covered with decaying colonial buildings which housed trading offices and residences.

The French Catholic church has been restored and stands on the main boulevard. The old British church at the western end of the island has been turned into a workshop, but is betrayed by bricked-up Gothic-style windows. Today most of the buildings are used as offices or apartment blocks and the area retains a quiet residential atmosphere detached from the bustle across the canals.

Another 30,000 sq metres of land was added to the south bank of the island for the site of the 35-storey White Swan Hotel, which was built in the early 1980s.

Just near the island, by the riverbank on Yanjiang Lu near the Renmin Bridge overpass, stands the Monument to the Martyrs of the Shaji Massacre (as the 1925 massacre was known).

Cultural Park
(wénhuà gōngyuán) 文化公园
The Cultural Park – just north-east of Shamian Island – was opened in 1956. Inside are merry-go-rounds, a roller-skating rink, an aquarium with exhibits from Guangdong Province, nightly dance classes, acrobatic shows, films and live performances of Cantonese opera (sometimes in full costume).

One of the most breathtaking motorcycle stunt shows you'll ever see is held here in the evenings. Just as interesting is to watch the deadpan audience – no applause, no reaction. A foreigner walks down the street and all of China turns to stare, but a motorcycle stuntman performs a 360-degree mid-air flip and people act like it's nothing.

Haichuang Park
(hǎichuáng gōngyuán) 海幢公园
Renmin Bridge stands just east of Shamian Island and connects the north bank of the Pearl River to the area of Canton known as Henan, the site of Haichuang Park. This would be a nondescript park but for the remains of what was once Canton's largest monastery, the **Ocean Banner Monastery**. It was founded by a Buddhist monk in 1662, and in its heyday the monastery grounds covered 2½ hectares. After 1911 the monastery was used as a school and soldier's barracks. It was opened to the public as a park in the 1930s. Though the three colossal images of the Buddha have gone, the main hall remains and is now used at night as a dance hall (live band). During the day the grounds are full of old men chatting, playing cards and chequers, and airing their pet birds.

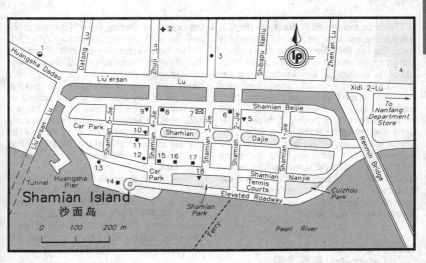

Shamian Island
沙面岛

0   100   200 m

■ PLACES TO STAY	18 Redhouse Cafe
6 Victory Hotel (new annexe)	**OTHER**
8 Victory Hotel	
14 White Swan Hotel	1 Huangsha Bus Station
15 Guangzhou Youth Hostel	2 Hospital of Traditional
16 Shamian Hotel	Chinese Medicine
17 Pearl Inn	3 Qingping Market
	4 Cultural Park
▼ PLACES TO EAT	7 Post Office
	11 Polish Consulate
5 Jing Ji Restaurant	12 Happy Bike Rental Station
9 Bakery	13 US Consulate
10 Li Qin Restaurant	

■ PLACES TO STAY	10 利群饮食店
	18 红房子
6 胜利宾馆（新楼）	
8 胜利宾馆	**OTHER**
14 白天鹅宾馆	
15 广州青年招待所	1 黄沙车站
16 沙面宾馆	2 中医医院
17 夜明珠酒店	3 清平市场
	4 文化公园
▼ PLACES TO EAT	7 邮局
	11 波兰领事馆
5 经济餐厅	12 租自行车店
9 面包店	13 美国领事馆

The large **stone** which decorates the fish pond at the entrance on Tongfu Zhonglu is considered by the Chinese to be a tiger struggling to turn around. The stone came from Lake Tai in Jiangsu Province. During the Qing Dynasty the wealthy used these rare, strangely shaped stones to decorate their gardens. Many are found in the gardens of the Forbidden City in Beijing. This particular stone was brought back by a wealthy Cantonese merchant in the last century. The Japanese took Canton in 1938 and plans were made to ship the stone back to Japan, though this did not happen. After the war the stone was sold to a private collector and disappeared from public view. It was finally returned to the park in 1951.

Yuexiu Park
(yuèxiù gōngyuán) 越秀公园
This is the biggest park in Canton, covering 93 hectares, and includes the Zhenhai Tower, the Sun Yatsen Monument and the large Sculpture of the Five Rams.

The **Sculpture of the Five Rams**, erected in 1959, is the symbol of Canton. It is said that long ago five celestial beings wearing robes of five colours came to Canton riding through the air on rams. Each carried a stem of rice, which they presented to the people as an auspicious sign from heaven that the area would be free from famine forever. Guangzhou means Broad Region, but from this myth it takes its other name, City of Rams or just Goat City.

The **Zhenhai Tower**, also known as the Five Storey Pagoda, is the only part of the old city wall that remains. From the upper storeys it commands a view of the city to the south and the White Cloud Hills to the north. The present tower was built during the Ming Dynasty, on the site of a former structure. Because of its strategic location it was occupied by the British and French troops at the time of the Opium wars. The 12 cannon in front of the tower date from this time (five of them are foreign, the rest were made in nearby Foshan). The tower now houses the City Museum with exhibits which describe the history of Canton from Neolithic times until the early part of this century.

The **Sun Yatsen Monument** is south of the Zhenhai Tower. This tall obelisk was constructed in 1929, four years after Sun's death, on the site of a temple to the goddess Guanyin (Kuanyin). The obelisk is built of granite and marble blocks and there's nothing to see inside, though a staircase leads to the top where there's a good view of the city. On the south side of the obelisk the text of Dr Sun's last testament is engraved in stone tablets on the ground.

West of the Zhenhai Tower is the Sculpture of the Five Rams. South of the tower is the large sports stadium with a seating capacity of 40,000. The park also has its own roller-coaster. There are three artificial lakes: Dongxiu, Nanxiu and Beixiu – the last has rowboats which you can hire.

Orchid Park
(lánpǔ) 兰圃
Originally laid out in 1957, this pleasant little park is devoted to orchids – over 100 varieties. A great place in summer, but a dead loss in winter, when all you will see are rows of flowerpots.

The Y2 admission fee includes tea by the small pond. The park is open daily from 7.30 to 11.30 am and from 1.30 to 5 pm; it's closed on Wednesday. It's at the northern end of Jiefang Beilu, not far from the main railway station.

Southern Yue Tomb Museum
(nán yuè wáng mù) 南越王汉墓
The museum is also known as the 'Museum of the Western Han Dynasty of the Southern Yue King's Tomb'. It stands on the site of the tomb of Emperor Wen, the second ruler of the Southern Yue Kingdom dating back to 100 BC. The Southern Yue Kingdom is what the area around Canton was called during the Han Dynasty (206-220 AD). It's an excellent museum with English explanations. More than 500 rare artefacts are on display.

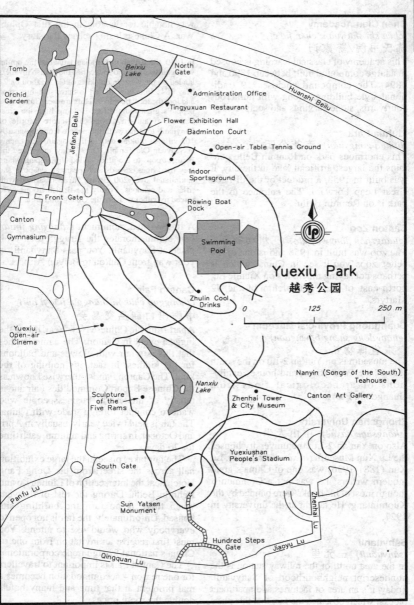

Tomb

Orchid
Garden

Beixiu Lake

North
Gate

Huanshi Beilu

Administration Office

Tingyuxuan Restaurant

Flower Exhibition Hall

Badminton Court

Open-air Table Tennis Ground

Indoor
Sportsground

Rowing Boat
Dock

Jiefang Beilu

Front Gate

Canton
Gymnasium

Swimming
Pool

Yuexiu Park
越秀公园

Zhulin Cool
Drinks

0   125   250 m

Yuexiu
Open-air
Cinema

Nanxiu Lake

Nanyin (Songs of the South)
Teahouse ▼

Sculpture
of the
Five Rams

Zhenhai Tower
& City Museum

Canton Art Gallery

Yuexiushan
People's Stadium

South Gate

Panfu Lu

Sun Yatsen
Monument

Zhenhai Lu

Hundred Steps
Gate

Jiaoyu Lu

Qingquan Lu

Chen Clan Academy
(chén shì shū yuàn; chén jiā cí)
陈氏书院/陈家词

This academy of classical learning is housed in a large compound built between 1890 and 1894. The compound encloses 19 traditional-style buildings along with numerous courtyards, stone carvings and sculptures.

Liuhua Park
(liúhuā gōngyuán) 流花公园

This enormous park on Renmin Beilu contains the largest artificial lake in the city. It was built in 1958, a product of the ill-fated Great Leap Forward. The entrance to the park is on Renmin Beilu.

Canton Zoo
(guǎngzhōu dòngwùyuán) 广州动物园
The zoo was built in 1958 and is one of the better zoos you'll see in China, which is perhaps not saying much. It's on Xianlie Lu, north-east of the Mausoleum of the 72 Martyrs.

Guangdong Provincial Museum
(guǎngdōng shěng bówùguǎn)
广东省博物馆
The museum is on Yan'an 2-Lu on the south side of the Pearl River, and houses exhibitions of archaeological finds from Guangdong Province.

Zhongshan University
(zhōngshān dàxué) 中山大学
Also on Yan'an 2-Lu, the university houses the Lu Xun Museum *(lǔ xùn bówùguǎn)*. Lu Xun (1881-1936) was one of China's great modern writers; he was not a Communist though most of his books were banned by the Kuomintang. He taught at the university in 1927.

Sanyuanli
(sānyuánlǐ) 三元里
In the area north of the railway station is the nondescript neighbourhood of Sanyuanli. Today, it's an area of factories and apartment blocks, which obscures the fact that this place was notable for its role in the first Opium War. A Chinese leaflet relates the story:

In 1840, the British imperialists launched the opium war against China. No sooner had the British invaders landed on the western outskirts of Guangzhou on 24 May 1841 than they started to burn, slaughter, rape and loot the local people. All this aroused Guangzhou people's great indignation. Holding high the great banner of anti-invasion, the heroic people of Sanyuanli together with the people from the nearby 103 villages took an oath to fight against the enemy at Sanyuan Old Temple. On 30 May, they lured the British troops to the place called Niulangang where they used hoes, swords and spears as weapons and annihilated over 200 British invaders armed with rifles and cannons. Finally the British troops were forced to withdraw from the Guangzhou area.

A little-visited monument *(kàngyīng jìniàn bēi)* commemorates the struggle that took place at Sanyuanli. You pass Sanyuanli on your way from Canton to Baiyun Airport.

Canton Fair
(zhōngguó chūkǒu shāngpǐn jiāoyì huì)
中国出口商品交易会
Apart from the Chinese New Year, this is the biggest event in Canton. The name implies that this is a fair with clowns and balloons for the kiddies. In fact, it's nothing of the kind. The Canton Fair is otherwise known as the Chinese Export Commodities Fair and is mostly of interest to businesspeople who want to conduct foreign trade with China. The fair is held twice yearly, usually in April and October, in spring and autumn, each time for 20 days.

The fair takes place in the large exhibition hall across the street from the Dong Fang Hotel, near the intersection of Liuhua Lu and Renmin Beilu. During the rest of the year when there is no fair, the building sits unused. Unfortunately, the fair is not open to everybody who would like to attend. You must first receive an invitation from one of China's national foreign trade corporations.

The Canton Fair is important to travellers for one reason – accommodation becomes a real problem at that time and many hotels double the room prices.

Pearl River Cruises

(zhūjiāng yóulǎnchuán) 珠江游览船
The northern bank of the Pearl River is one of the most interesting areas of Canton, filled with people, markets and dilapidated buildings. A tourist boat ride down the Pearl River runs daily from 3.30 to 5 pm and costs Y10. Boats leave from the pier just east of Renmin Bridge. They take you down the river as far as Ershatou and then turn around and head back to Renmin Bridge.

From April to October there are night cruises for tourists. Departures are from Pier 2 (just south of the Nanfang Department Store). Phone ☎ 8861928, 4412629 or 8885188 for information about the cruise.

The White Swan Hotel on Shamian Island also offers an evening cruise from 6 to 9 pm, including dinner on the boat.

Tourist Train Excursions

The luxurious Tourist Hotel Train is geared towards those with a fair bit of money and some holiday time. Catering mostly for Hong Kongers and foreigners, it's a luxury hotel on wheels. There are side trips to the limestone pinnacles and caves (seen by boat) at Chunwan, the rock formations at Zhaoqing, the Guo En Pagoda in Xinxing county and the Dianbai Longtoushan seaside resort. An evening is spent at the thermal spa of Longshan Holiday Village. The train has its own beauty salon, bar, karaoke lounge and disco.

The train heads westwards from Canton to Foshan, Sanshui, Zhaoqing and Maoming before turning back. You can get off at Maoming and continue on if you like, though that somewhat defeats the purpose (three days of luxurious revelry). To increase the romance, the train uses a steam locomotive.

The cost for a three-day excursion is HK$2800 for two people (the price is the same for one person). All is included – food, accommodation, tour guide, etc.

For further information, contact the Guangdong Sanmao Railway Company (☎ 7765139 ext 0163 or 0169), 374 Huanshi Donglu, just on the east side of the Garden Hotel. The schedule is subject to change but should be about once weekly, probably more often during summer.

Places to Stay – bottom end

On Shamian Island near the massive White Swan Hotel is the *Guangzhou Youth Hostel* (☎ 8884298) *(guǎngzhōu qīngnián zhāodàisuǒ)*, at 2 Shamian 4-Jie. By default, this place wins the title of 'backpackers' headquarters' in Canton since there is little else in this price range that is open to foreigners. The hostel was gutted by a fire in 1992 but has been reopened with new paint, new furniture, new prices (higher) but the same old sassy staff. Fairly comfortable dormitory rooms cost Y45 per person; fairly grotty private singles are Y50 while more comfortable doubles are Y120 to Y138.

The only other place that could qualify as budget accommodation is the *CITS Hostel* (☎ 6664263) *(guólǚ zhāodàisuǒ)* right behind CITS on the east side of the railway station. Singles/doubles cost Y53/63. Dormitories as such don't exist unless there are at least two foreigners staying in this place who are willing to share a room. The hostel really caters to locals and has a depressing appearance, but the rooms are clean.

The *Airport Hotel* (☎ 6661700) *(báiyún jīchǎng bīnguǎn)*, right next to the main terminal of Canton's Bayun Airport (12 km north of city centre), is a fairly cheap place to stay by Canton's standards. All rooms have air-con and are reasonably clean, with prices starting around Y110.

Places to Stay – middle

Pearl River Area The *Shamian Hotel* (☎ 8888124; fax 8861068) *(shāmiàn bīnguǎn)*, at 50 Shamian Nanjie, is only a few steps to the east of the Guangzhou Youth Hostel on Shamian Island. Doubles with twin beds come in three standards costing Y133, Y167 and Y197. This place is popular and at times can be booked up by tour groups.

On the east side of the Shamian Hotel is the *Pearl Inn* (☎ 8889238; fax 8861068) *(yèmíngzhū jiǔdiàn)*, a fancy place known for its good restaurant, bar, sauna, disco and aggressive air-con. Standard/deluxe doubles/twins cost Y130/144 while triples are Y189 and deluxe suites are Y288.

Also on Shamian Island is the *Victory Hotel* (☎ 8862622; fax 8862413) *(shènglì bīnguǎn)*. There's a lack of English signs, but the hotel is easily identified – it looks like a seafood restaurant with big fish tanks outside. It's at the corner of Shamian 4-Jie and Shamian Beijie. Standard doubles cost Y150 to Y182 while cushier rooms are Y256 to Y345. At the time of writing, there was a new annexe under construction two blocks to the east, near the post office; although prices have yet to be determined, it looks like this will be an upmarket place.

The *Aiqun Hotel* (☎ 8866668; fax 8883519) *(àiqún dàjiǔdiàn)* is at 113 Yanjiang Xilu (at the corner of Changdi Lu). Opened in 1937 but fully refurbished, this grand old place overlooks the Pearl River. Given the high standards, prices are reasonable (for Guangzhou anyway) at Y150/219 for singles/doubles, or Y242 for a deluxe twin with riverfront view. The hotel seems to have restaurants tucked away in every corner – if you're not afraid of choking on the prices, check out the rooftop revolving restaurant.

The *Bai Gong Hotel* (☎ 8882313; fax 8889161) *(bái gōng jiǔdiàn)* is a pleasant and friendly place to stay, though the staff speak little English. It's near the river at 17 Renmin Nanlu. Singles (often full with long-term business travellers) are Y98, but you'll probably have to settle for a double (Y148) or a suite (Y198). From the railway station, take bus No 31 and get off at the river.

Across the street from the Bai Gong is the *New Asia Hotel* (☎ 8884722) *(xīnyà jiǔdiàn)*, at 10 Renmin Nanlu, where singles are Y158 and doubles are Y169 to Y189. It's a huge, elegant-looking place that's popular with Hong Kongers but attracts few foreigners. There is no English sign on the hotel and the staff's English-speaking ability consists of 'Hello', but it's not a bad place to stay.

Just to the south of the New Asia is the *Xinhua Hotel* (☎ 8882688) *(xīnhuá dàjiǔdiàn)* at 4 Renmin Nanlu. This is another large, Chinese-speaking place geared towards the Hong Kong crowd. Singles/doubles are reasonably priced at Y126/147.

The *GD Hotel* (☎ 8883601) *(guǎngdōng dàjiǔdiàn)* is at 294 Changdi Lu, one block north of the Aiqun Hotel and next to the palatial Furama Hotel. It's large and attractive, and has rooms for Y140, Y180 and Y300. No-one here speaks English so they prefer foreigners who speak Chinese, though all with FEC are welcome.

Railway Station Area Certainly one of the best deals in this neighbourhood is the *Friendship Hotel* (☎ 6679898; fax 6678653) *(yǒuyì bīnguǎn)* at 698 Renmin Beilu. On 'side B' of the hotel, doubles are Y88 and Y108, while those on 'side A' cost Y180 and Y198. The adjoining Apollo Fast Food Restaurant is a cheap place to eat.

The *Liuhua Hotel* (☎ 6668800; fax 6667828) *(liúhuā bīnguǎn)* is the large building directly opposite the railway station at 194 Huanshi Xilu. At one time this place was the lap of luxury in Canton, but it seems to be going steadily downhill; much of the current clientele are cadres visiting Canton 'on business'. The harried staff at reception speak little English. Standard doubles range in price from Y180 to Y298. The cheaper rooms are on the ground floor and can be noisy – look over the room first before deciding whether you want to stay here.

North-East Area The *Hua Shan Hotel* (☎ 7763868; fax 7760668) *(huá shān bīnguǎn)*, 420 Huanshi Donglu, is certainly one of the better deals in this trendy neighbourhood. Singles, if you can get them, start at Y98 while doubles are Y168 and Y188. The staff at reception seem to be very friendly though not much English is spoken.

Just on the east side of the Hua Shan Hotel is the *Guangdong Jinye Hotel* (☎ 7772888; fax 7787759) *(guǎngdōng jīnyè dàshà)*, 422 Huanshi Donglu. Prices for standard doubles are Y158 and Y168, or you can pay Y338 for a suite.

The *Hakkas Hotel* (☎ 7771688; fax

7770788) (jiāyíng bīnguǎn), 418 Huanshi Donglu, is aimed at the business traveller. Singles/doubles start at Y189/207 and range up to Y345 for a suite.

Places to Stay – top end
Pearl River Area Some top-end hotels in the Pearl River Area are:

White Swan Hotel (☎ 8886968; fax 8861188) (*báitiāné bīnguǎn*), 1 Shamian Nanjie. Standard/deluxe doubles Y575/690, suites Y920 to Y1207.

Furama Hotel (☎ 8863288; fax 8863388) (*fùlìhuá dàjiǔdiàn*), 316 Changdi Lu. Singles/doubles Y345/374, suites Y690.

Guangzhou Hotel (☎ 3338168; fax 3330791) (*guǎngzhōu bīnguǎn*), Haizhu Square. Standard doubles start at Y262.

Hotel Landmark Canton (☎ 3355988; fax 3336197) (*huáshà dàjiǔdiàn*). Standard doubles start at Y456, suites up to Y2166.

Railway Station Area
Around the railway station, you can try the following:

Hotel Equatorial (☎ 6672888; fax 6672582) (*guìdū jiǔdiàn*), 931 Renmin Beilu. Doubles cost Y287.

Guangdong Guesthouse (☎ 3332950; fax 3332911) (*guǎngdōng yíng bīnguǎn*), 603 Jiefang Beilu. Standard/deluxe doubles cost Y250/310.

Dongfang Hotel (☎ 6669900; fax 6681618) (*dōngfāng bīnguǎn*), 120 Liuhua Lu. Singles cost Y350 to Y410, doubles Y460 to Y490.

China Hotel (☎ 6666888; fax 6677014) (*zhōngguó dàjiǔdiàn*). Superior/deluxe doubles cost Y517/575, deluxe suite Y1150.

North-East Area
There are several top-end places in the north-east part of the city:

Baiyun Hotel (☎ 3333998; fax 3336498) (*báiyún bīnguǎn*), 367 Huanshi Donglu. Doubles on lower floor cost Y158 to Y228, 5th floor upwards Y288 to Y328.

Garden Hotel (☎ 3338989; fax 3350467) (*huāyuán jiǔdiàn*), 368 Huanshi Donglu. Doubles cost Y518 to Y573, suites Y1364 to Y8184.

Ocean Hotel (☎ 7765988; fax 7765475) (*yuǎnyáng bīnguǎn*) 412 Huanshi Donglu. Singles/doubles start from Y220/350.

Holiday Inn (☎ 7766999; fax 7753126) (*wénhuà jiàrì jiǔdiàn*), 28 Guangming Lu. Doubles start at Y575.

Yuehai Hotel (☎ 7779688; fax 7788364) (*yuèhǎi dàshà*), 472 Huanshi Donglu. Doubles cost Y238, Y388 and Y418.

Cathay Hotel (☎ 7753888; fax 7766606) (*guótài bīnguǎn*), 376 Huanshi Donglu. Doubles/triples cost Y230/300, suites Y450 and Y600.

Gitic Plaza Hotel (☎ 3311888; fax 3311666) (*guǎngdōng guójì dàshà*). Doubles cost Y793, deluxe suites Y1138; discounts up to 50% offered.

Places to Eat
The Chinese have a saying that to enjoy the best in life, one has to be 'born in Suzhou, live in Hangzhou, eat in Canton and die in Liuzhou'. Suzhou is renowned for beautiful women, Hangzhou for scenery and Liuzhou for the finest wood for coffin-making. Not many travellers have enthusiasm for dying in Liuzhou, but when it comes to eating, Canton is a pretty good place to stuff your face.

Chinese Food On Shamian Island, most budget travellers head for *Li Qin Restaurant (lì qún yǐn shídiàn)* on Shamian Dajie near the Victory Hotel. It's distinguished by a large tree growing right inside the restaurant and out through the roof. Prices are very low and the food is excellent. The owner's daughter is obsessed with playing cards – if you can play too, you should have an instant friend.

The *Pearl Inn (yèmíngzhū jiǔdiàn)* is just to your right as you face the Shamian Hotel on Shamian Nanjie. They have good and cheap dim sum on the ground floor restaurant. There is also a coffee shop serving Western breakfasts.

Also on Shamian Island is the *Victory Restaurant*, attached to the Victory Hotel. Prices are amazingly reasonable for such a high standard of service. The Chinese food is good, but seafood can be expensive. An English menu is available.

Jing Ji Restaurant (jīngjì cāntīng) on Shamian 2-Jie has a name which translates as 'economical restaurant'. Though it's not the cheapest on Shamian Island, it's not unreasonable either. The attached bakery is OK too.

The *Redhouse (hóng fángzi)* is in the park on Shamian Nanjie, Shamian Island. The building is indeed red and it's a pleasant cafe, but prices are not especially cheap.

There are a couple of good places close to the riverfront. Foremost is the *Datong* (☎ 8888988) *(dàtóng jiǔjiā)* at 63 Yanjiang Xilu, just around the corner from Renmin Lu. The restaurant occupies all of an eight-storey building overlooking the river. Specialties of the house are crisp fried chicken and roast suckling pig. The crisp-roasted pig skin is a favourite here. This is a great place for morning dim sum.

Close to the Datong Restaurant is the *Yan Yan Restaurant* (☎ 8885967) *(rénrén càiguǎn)*, 28-32 Xihao 2-Lu, a side street which runs east from Renmin Lu. Look for the pedestrian overpass which goes over Renmin Lu up from the intersection with Yanjiang Lu. The steps of the overpass lead down into a side street and the restaurant is opposite them.

The *Aiqun Hotel* has a great restaurant on the 14th floor. Besides the food, it's worth coming up here just for the views overlooking the Pearl River.

One of the city's best-known restaurants is the *Guangzhou* (☎ 8888388) *(guǎngzhōu jiǔjiā)*, 2 Wenchang Nanlu near the intersection with Dishipu Lu. The four storeys of dining halls and private rooms are built around a central garden courtyard, where potted shrubs, flowers and landscape paintings are intended to give the feeling (at least to the people in the dingy ground-floor rooms) of 'eating in a landscape'. Specialties of the house include shark fin soup with shredded chicken, chopped crabmeat balls and braised dove. It tends to be expensive and reservations are sometimes necessary.

The *Muslim Restaurant* (☎ 8888991) *(huímín fàndiàn)* is at 325 Zhongshan 6-Lu, on the corner with Renmin Lu. Look for the Arabic letters above the front entrance. It's an OK place, but go upstairs since the ground floor is dingy.

North of Zhongshan Lu is Dongfeng Lu, which runs east-west across the city. At 202 Xiaobei Lu, which crosses Dongfeng, is the *North Garden Restaurant* (☎ 3330087) *(běiyuán jiǔjiā)*. This is another of Canton's 'famous houses', a measure of its success being the number of cars and tourist buses parked outside. Specialties of the house include barbecued chicken liver, steamed chicken in huadiao wine, stewed fish head with vegetables, fried boneless chicken (could be a first for China) and stewed duck legs in oyster sauce. Good value.

In the west of Canton, the *Panxi* (☎ 8815718) *(bànxī jiǔjiā)*, 151 Longjin Xilu, is the biggest restaurant in the city. It's noted for its dumplings, stewed turtle, roast pork, chicken in tea leaves and a crabmeat-sharkfin consommé. Its famed dim sum is served from about 5 to 9.30 am, at noon and again at night. Dim sum includes fried dumplings with shrimp, chicken gizzards, pork and mushrooms – even shark fin dumplings! You can try crispy fried egg rolls stuffed with chicken, shrimp, pork, bamboo shoots and mushrooms. Monkey brains are steamed with ginger, scallions and rice wine, and then steamed again with crab roe, eggs and lotus blossoms.

In the same general direction is the *Taotaoju* (☎ 8885769) *(táotáojū),* 20 Dishipu Lu. Originally built as a private academy in the 17th century, it was turned into a restaurant in the late 19th century. Tao Tao was the name of the proprietor's wife. Dim sum is the specialty here; you choose sweet and savoury snacks from the selection on trolleys that are wheeled around the restaurant. Tea is the preferred beverage and is said to be made with Canton's best water – brought in from the Nine Dragon Well in the White Cloud Hills.

Beijing Lu has two of Canton's 'famous' restaurants. The *Wild Animals Restaurant* *(yěwèixiāng fàndiàn)* at No 247 is where you can feast on dogs, cats, deer, bear paws and snake. Once upon a time they even served tiger. Highly recommended is the *Taipingguan* (☎ 3332938) *(tàipíngguǎn cāntīng)* at 344 Beijing Lu, which serves both Western and Chinese food. Zhou Enlai fancied their roast pigeon.

The *South Garden Restaurant* (☎ 4449211) *(nányuán jiǔjiā)* is at 142 Qianjin Lu and the menu features chicken in honey and oyster sauce or pigeon in plum sauce. Qianjin Lu is on the south side of the Pearl River; to get to it you have to cross Haizhu Bridge and go down Jiangnan Dadao. Qianjin Lu branches off to the east.

Just to the west of Renmin Lu at 43 Jianglan Lu is the *Snake Restaurant* (☎ 8883811) *(shé cānguǎn),* with the snakes on display in the window. The restaurant was originally known as the 'Snake King Moon' and has an 80-year history. To get to the restaurant you have to walk down Heping Lu, which runs west from Renmin Lu. After a few minutes turn right into Jianglan Lu and follow it around to the restaurant on the left-hand side. Creative snake recipes include fricasseed assorted snake and cat meats, snake breast meat stuffed with shelled shrimp, stir-fried colourful shredded snakes, and braised snake slices with chicken liver. Way back in the 1320s the Franciscan friar Odoric visited China and commented on the snake-eating habits of the southern Chinese:

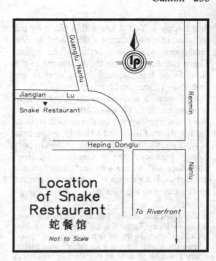

Location of Snake Restaurant
蛇餐馆
Not to Scale

There be monstrous great serpents likewise which are taken by the inhabitants and eaten. A solemn feast among them with serpents is thought nothing of.

Vegetarian Food The *Caigenxiang Vegetarian Restaurant* (☎ 3344363) *(càigēnxiāng sùshíguǎn),* 167 Zhongshan 6-Lu, is one of the few places in Canton where you don't have to worry about accidentally ordering dogs, cats or monkey brains.

Fast Food The China Hotel's *Hasty Tasty Fast Food* shop (which opens on to Jiefang Beilu) should make you feel at home. It looks and tastes exactly like any Hong Kong or US fast-food venue, with banks of neon lights in the ceiling, laminex tables and food served in the finest paper and plastic packaging.

Timmy's (☎ 882012) *(tiān měi shí)* 382 Changdi Lu near the Aiqun Hotel, serves slightly modified Western fast food, including the familiar French fries, hot apple pie and ice cream in a cup. The hamburgers are an acquired taste but the fried chicken can compete with the best.

Fairwood Fast Food (dà kuàihuó) is indeed a branch of the Hong Kong instant-food chain by the same name (which means 'big happy'). You'll know this place by the red plastic clown face by the door. As fast food goes, you could certainly do worse. There is a Fairwood in the basement of the Nam Fong International Plaza next to the Friendship Store on Huanshi Donglu.

McDonald's arrived on the Canton fast-food scene in 1993. Currently, there is only one branch in the city, on the ground floor of the 63-storey Gitic Plaza Hotel. At the time of writing, McDonald's had branches in only four Chinese cities – Canton, Beijing, Shenzhen and Xiamen. Robert Storey recalls the days of deprivation, before the golden arches came to the PRC:

It was a hot and steamy summer afternoon. I was sitting in Hasty Tasty, Canton's premier fast-food restaurant, enjoying the air-conditioning and sipping a large Coke with ice. As I sat there contemplating where I would go next in this sizzling weather, a foreign tourist stepped up to the counter. His name was George.

George's wife was sitting at a table by the door. She wore a purple jump suit, gaudy fake jewellery, horn-rimmed sunglasses and enough perfume to be a fire hazard. Her hair – flaming orange and held rigid by hair spray – looked like two jiao worth of cotton candy. She was carefully explaining to her two children how she would break both their arms if they didn't shut up and stop fighting with each other.

As George approached the counter, the waitress grinned at him. Perhaps she did that to all the customers, or perhaps it had something to do with the way George was dressed – in pink shorts, a flowered shirt and a white sunhat embroidered with a picture of a fish and the words 'Sea World'.

'May I take your order?' the waitress said. George looked relieved, obviously pleased that the waitress could speak English. 'Excuse me, I don't want to order anything right now, but could you tell me where's the nearest McDonald's?'

'Sorry sir,' the waitress replied, 'we don't have McDonald's in Canton. I have never eaten there. But they have in Hong Kong – I saw on television.'

You might as well have hit him with a freight train. Shock, horror, disbelief – you could see it in his face. George turned his back on the waitress without saying another word and trudged fearfully towards the table where his wife and two charming children were sitting.

'Well George,' she bellowed, 'where's the McDonald's?'

'They haven't got one here,' he answered coarsely. Immediately the two kids started yelling, 'We want a Big Mac!'

'Shut up!' George explained. 'We have to go back to Hong Kong!' I could see he was starting to panic. He slung his big camera over his shoulder, grabbed a shopping bag full of tourist junk purchased at the Friendship Store, and headed out the door with his wife and two children behind him. I watched from the window as they flagged down a taxi, and wondered if they were indeed heading for Hong Kong.

Robert Storey

Things to Buy

The intersection of Beijing Lu and Zhongshan Lu is the top shopping area in the city.

At 295 Beijing Lu (corner with Xihu Lu) is the Guangzhou Department Store *(guǎngzhōu bǎihuò dàlóu)*, the other main store in town.

Canton's main department store is the Nanfang *(nánfáng dàshà)* at 49 Yanjiang 1-Lu, just to the east and opposite the main entrance to the Cultural Park. You can also enter the store from the Yanjiang Lu side by the Pearl River.

There are two Friendship Stores in Canton. The main one is next to the Baiyun Hotel on Huanshi Donglu. This store has a particularly good supermarket, so if you have a craving for Cadbury chocolate bars or Swiss cheese, this is the place to come.

The other Friendship Store is next to the China Hotel on the corner of Liuhua Lu and Jiefang Beilu. Both Friendship Stores accept all main credit cards and can arrange shipment of goods back to your country.

Canton's first true shopping mall is Nam Fong International Plaza *(nánfāng guójì guǎngchǎng)* immediately to the east of the Friendship Store on Huanshi Donglu. There is a decent Hong Kong-style supermarket here, but the mall is heavily geared towards luxury items like jewellery, perfume, lipstick and the latest fashions.

If you're heading to north China in winter and don't already have a good down jacket, get one in Canton. Your life depends on it! You can pick up a decent down jacket for less than Y200 at *(gōngnóng fúzhuāng chǎng)* 310 Zhongshan 4-Lu, on the north side of the street and east of Beijing Lu and the Children's Park. This store also sells top-quality down sleeping bags.

The Friendship Stores have antique sections, but another place that plugs these wares is the touristy Guangzhou Antique Shop (☎ 3334229) at 146 and 162 Wende Beilu.

The Foreign Languages Bookstore at 326 Beijing Lu has mostly textbooks and some notable English classics, but it's slim pickings if you'd like some contemporary blockbusters. The nearby Xinhua Bookstore at 336 Beijing Lu is the main Chinese bookstore in the city and has a good collection of maps.

Getting There & Away

Air To give pilots a challenge, Canton's Baiyun Airport is right next to the White Cloud Hills, Canton's only mountains. It's 12 km north of the city centre. The facilities are pretty grotty, but a new airport is under construction with a projected opening date sometime in 1997.

In Canton, the CAAC office is at 181 Huanshi Lu, to your left as you come out of the railway station. It has separate telephone numbers for domestic (☎ 6662969) and international (☎ 6661803). You can also book air tickets in the White Swan Hotel and the China Hotel. The office is open from 8 am to 8 pm daily. There is an inexpensive bus that runs directly from the CAAC office to Baiyun Airport and back again.

International Flights There are at least four daily flights (usually more) from Hong Kong on CAAC for HK$400. The flight takes 35 minutes.

There are direct flights between Canton and a number of other foreign cities including: Bangkok, Hanoi, Jakarta, Kuala Lumpur, Manila, Melbourne, Penang, Singapore, Surabaya and Sydney.

Singapore Airlines (☎ 3358999) has an office on the mezzanine floor of the Garden Hotel, 368 Huanshi Donglu. Malaysian Airline System (☎ 3358828) is also in the Garden Hotel, Shop M04-05.

Domestic Flights For domestic flights, the airport departure tax is Y30. Foreigners must, of course, pay in FEC.

Domestic flights with air fares from Canton are as follows:

Destination	Fare	Destination	Fare
Baotou	Y1040	Beihai	Y310
Beijing	Y980	Changchun	Y1440
Changde	Y390	Changsha	Y290
Changzhou	Y610	Chengdu	Y670
Chongqing	Y590	Dalian	Y1120
Dandong	Y1400	Fuzhou	Y350
Guilin	Y300	Guiyang	Y420
Haikou	Y320	Hangzhou	Y540
Harbin	Y1550	Hefei,	
Hohhot,		Hengyang	Y210
Huangshan	Y460	Huangyan	Y560
Jilin	Y1490	Ji'nan	Y820
Kunming	Y570	Lanzhou	Y1030
Lianyungang	Y780	Liuzhou	Y260
Luoyang	Y690	Meixian	Y300
Mudanjiang	Y1670	Nanchang	Y320
Nanjing	Y610	Nanning	Y280
Ningbo	Y580	Qingdao	Y930
Qiqihar	Y1610	Sanya	Y370
Shanghai	Y620	Shantou	Y350
Shashi	Y450	Shenyang	Y1300
Shijiazhuang	Y910	Taiyuan	Y850
Tianjin	Y980	Ürümqi	Y1910
Wenzhou	Y630	Wuhan	Y430
Xiamen	Y290	Xi'an	Y760
Xiangfan	Y590	Xining	Y1070
Yantai	Y1040	Yichang	Y460
Yiwu	Y550	Zhanjiang	Y350
Zhengzhou	Y670		

Bus Buses ply both international and domestic routes. A small sample of what's on offer includes the following:

To/From Macau If you want to go directly from Macau, Kee Kwan Motors, across the street from the Floating Casino, sells bus tickets to Canton. One bus takes you to the border at Zhuhai while a second bus takes you from there to Canton four hours later. The trip takes about five hours in all. On weekdays, buy your ticket the evening before departure.

This international bus is not necessarily the best way to make this journey. Having to get off the Macau bus, go through immigration and Customs, wait for all your fellow passengers (and their enormous luggage), and then re-board another bus is a time-wasting and confusing exercise. It's usually faster to cross the Macau-Zhuhai border by foot and catch a minibus from Zhuhai to Canton. In Macau, bus No 3 runs between the Jetfoil Pier and the China border, via the Hotel Lisboa, Avenida Almeida Ribeiro and the Floating Casino.

To/From Shenzhen Privately owned aircon minibuses line up opposite the Shenzhen Railway Station near the Hong Kong border. The fare price is posted on a sign where the minibuses line up, and at the time of writing was Y38. The drivers in Shenzhen often ask for Hong Kong dollars but will reluctantly accept RMB. Keep a calculator handy to see which works out cheaper. The trip takes five hours.

From Canton to Shenzhen, minibuses operate from a bus station in front of the Liuhua Hotel, which is across the street from the Canton Railway Station. The east side of the bus station (closest to the Liuhua Hotel) is where the big government-run buses are. These are cheaper but slower and less comfortable. On the west side of this bus station is where you get the minibuses.

To/From Zhuhai From the Zhuhai Bus Station, which is to the west of the Customs building, you can catch buses to Canton and other parts of Guangdong Province.

From Canton, buses to Zhuhai depart from the bus station across the street from the railway station, west of the Liuhua Hotel. There are two kinds of buses – minibuses and government-run buses. The minibuses are preferable and cost Y30.

Train Canton is also blessed with international and domestic train services. Getting sleepers on the domestic routes can be difficult. It's also worth knowing that the staff in Canton's railway station are strict about foreigners using Chinese-priced tickets – if you don't have what appears to be a valid red card, you won't be allowed to board.

.Whatever you do, be careful near the railway station. The whole area is a den of thieves – everything from pickpockets to bag slitters and purse snatchers. There are people selling black-market (Chinese price) tickets outside the station, but the tickets are printed in Chinese so be sure you know what you're buying.

To/From Hong Kong The express train between Hong Kong and Canton is comfortable and convenient. The train covers the 182-km route in 2½ hours. However, it is much cheaper to take a local train to Shenzhen and then another local train to Canton.

In Hong Kong, tickets can be booked up to seven days before departure at China Travel Service (CTS) or the Hunghom Station for HK$197, but the weekend and holiday tariff is HK$229. Children aged between five and nine years are charged HK$91. Return tickets are also sold, but only seven to 30 days before departure.

You're allowed to take bicycles on the express train, and these are stowed in the freight car.

Timetables change, but the following was current at the time of writing:

Train	From	To	Depart	Arrive
96	Kowloon	Canton	7.50 am	10.30 am
98	Kowloon	Canton	8.35 am	11.15 am
92	Kowloon	Canton	12.25 pm	3.05 pm
94	Kowloon	Canton	2.10 pm	4.50 pm
91	Canton	Kowloon	8.15 am	10.55 am
93	Canton	Kowloon	10 am	12.40 pm
95	Canton	Kowloon	4.13 pm	6.53 pm
97	Canton	Kowloon	6 pm	8.40 pm

To/From Shenzhen The local train from Shenzhen to Canton is cheap and reasonably fast, but there are often long queues for tickets, and seats can be difficult to come by at peak times. Hard seats (the Chinese equivalent of 2nd class) are Y25. Soft seats (1st class) cost Y50. There are several trains per day from Shenzhen to Canton, but the schedules change so often that it's not worth quoting them here. The trip takes between 2½ and three hours.

Many of the local trains from Shenzhen now stop at the new East Station. It may be nice and new, but it's also a long way from anywhere. Just follow the crowd to take a bus or minibus to the main train station. The express trains all go to the main Canton Railway Station.

In Canton, you can buy train tickets from CITS several days in advance. Otherwise, you can join the queues at the railway station.

To/From Beijing Trains head north from Canton to Beijing, Shanghai and every province in the country except Hainan Island and Tibet. Sleepers can be booked several days in advance at CITS in Canton. You can also book domestic railway tickets at CTS in Hong Kong for more than double the price! Fares to Beijing are Y182 (hard seat), Y296 (hard sleeper) and Y537 (soft sleeper). The fastest express trains to Beijing take 33 hours (if on time), but most trains require 36 hours or more.

Boat Canton is the major port on China's southern coast, offering high-speed catamaran services or slower overnight ferries to a number of destinations.

To/From Hong Kong There are two types of ships plying the route between Hong Kong and Canton: jetcat (jet-powered catamaran) and a slow, overnight ferry.

The jetcat (named *Liwanhu*) takes three hours from Hong Kong to Canton. It departs from Hong Kong once daily from China Hong Kong City, Tsimshatsui at 8.15 am and costs HK$153 on weekdays or HK$174 on weekends and public holidays. In Canton, departures are from Zhoutouzui Wharf at 1 pm. Tickets can be bought at the wharf and some major hotels if you give them enough advance notice. The ticket costs Y111 on weekdays or Y126 on weekends.

There is also a hovercraft departing from Hong Kong at 9 am, but this only goes as far as the port of Huangpu, 24 km east of Canton. This is not so convenient, so try to

avoid getting on this one by mistake. On the rare chance that you find yourself in Huangpu, the hovercraft returns to Hong Kong at 2.45 pm.

The Pearl River Shipping Company runs two overnight ferries between Hong Kong and Canton – the *Tianhu* and the *Xinghu*. This is an excellent way to get to Canton from Hong Kong and saves you the cost of one night's accommodation. The ships are clean, fully air-con, have comfortable beds and a good Chinese restaurant. One ship leaves Hong Kong daily from China Hong Kong City in Tsimshatsui at 9 pm and arrives in Canton the following morning at 6 am. In Canton the other ship departs at 9 pm and arrives in Hong Kong at 6 am.

Ferry tickets to Canton can be bought most cheaply in China Hong Kong City. You can also buy them at CTS for an extra HK$20 service fee.

Second class has dormitory beds, which

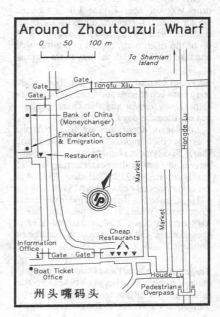

Around Zhoutouzui Wharf

0   50   100 m

To Shamian Island

Gate

Gate
Gate

Tongfu Xilu

Bank of China (Moneychanger)

Embarkation, Customs & Emigration

Restaurant

Hongde Lu

Market

Market

Cheap Restaurants

Information Office

Gate   Gate

Boat Ticket Office

Houde Lu

Pedestrian Overpass

州头嘴码头

are quite comfortable – the biggest problem might be noisy neighbours. A 1st-class ticket gets you a bed in a four-person cabin with private bath. Special class is a two-person cabin with bath. VIP class is like your own little hotel room.

Tickets purchased in Canton are about 10 to 15% cheaper than those bought in Hong Kong. On holidays there is an extra Y15 charge.

Class	Status	From HK	From Canton
VIP	private	HK$638	Y472
Special	2-bed cabin	HK$240	Y165
First	4-bed cabin	HK$205	Y139
Second	dormitory	HK$160	Y105

If you can't get a cabin or a bunk then buy a seat ticket and go to the purser's office as soon as you are on board. The purser distributes leftover bunks and cabins, but get in quick if you want one.

Bus No 31 (not trolley-bus No 31) will drop you off near Houde Lu in Canton, which leads to Zhoutouzui Wharf. To get from the wharf to the railway station, walk up to the main road, cross to the other side and take bus No 31 all the way to the station.

To/From Macau There is a direct overnight ferry between Macau and Canton. Two ships – the *Dongshanhu* and the *Xiangshanhu* – run on alternate days.

In Macau, departures are from the pier near the Floating Casino (*not* the Jetfoil Pier). The boat leaves Macau at 8 pm and arrives in Canton the next morning at 7.15 am. Fares are M$93 in 2nd class, M$124 in 1st class; special class costs M$176.

In Canton, departures are from Zhoutouzui Wharf at 8.30 pm. The fare is Y48 in 2nd class, Y58 in 1st and Y79 in special class. There is an extra Y7 charge on holidays.

To/From Wuzhou/Yangshuo You can purchase a combination boat/bus ticket (Y60) to make an overnight trip from Canton to Yangshuo via Wuzhou. The boat has dormitory accommodation and is reasonably comfortable. The boat departs from Dashatou Wharf in Canton daily at 12.30 pm and terminates at Wuzhou, where you pick up the bus.

To/From Hainan Boats to Haikou (Hainan Island) depart daily at 9 am from Canton's Zhoutouzui Wharf and the trip takes 25 hours. Starting from 5th class and moving upmarket, prices are Y43, Y49, Y65 and Y91.

There are also daily boats to Sanya on Hainan Island, departing from Zhoutouzui Wharf at 3 pm. Prices are nearly the same as those on the Haikou boat.

To/From Xiamen Boats run between Canton and Xiamen (Fujian Province) approximately once a week. In descending order, fares are Y102, Y85, Y53, Y47 and Y36. Departures are from Canton's Zhoutouzui Wharf at 8 am.

To/From Wenzhou Wenzhou (Zhejiang Province) has boats to/from Canton about once weekly. Fares are Y175, Y150, Y125, Y93 and Y69. In Canton, departures are from Zhoutouzui Wharf at 8 am.

Getting Around

Canton proper extends for 60 sq km, with most of the interesting sights scattered throughout, so seeing the place on foot is impractical. Just the walk from the railway station to the hotels on Shamian Island is about six km – good exercise but not recommended for beginning each day's sightseeing.

Bus Canton has an extensive network of motor and electric trolley-buses which will get you just about anywhere you want to go. The problem is that they are almost always packed. Once an empty bus pulls in at a stop, a battle for seats ensues and a passive crowd suddenly turns into a stampeding herd.

Even more aggravating is the tedious speed at which buses move, accentuated by the drivers' peculiar habit of turning off their motors and letting the bus roll to the next stop. You just have to be patient. Never expect anything to move rapidly and allow lots of time to get to the railway station to catch your train. Sometimes you may find you'll give up and walk. One consolation is that buses are cheap – you'll rarely pay more than two jiao per trip.

Good Chinese maps of the city with bus routes are sold by hawkers outside the railway station and at some of the tourist hotel bookshops. Get one! There are too many bus routes to list them all here, but a few of the important routes are:

No 31 Runs along Gongye Dadao Bei, east of Zhoutouzui Wharf, crosses Renmin Bridge and goes straight up Renmin Lu to the main railway station at the north of the city.

No 30 Runs from the main railway station eastwards along Huanshi Lu before turning down Nonglin Xia Lu to terminate in the far east of the city. This is a convenient bus to take if you want to go from the railway station to the Baiyun and Garden hotels.

No 5 Starting from the main railway station, this bus takes a similar route to No 31, but instead of crossing Renmin Bridge it carries on along Liu'ersan Lu, which runs by the northern side of the canal separating the city from Shamian Island. Get off here and walk across the small bridge to the island.

Minibus Minibuses seating 15 to 20 people ply the streets on set routes. If you can find out where they're going, they're a good way to avoid the crowded buses. The front window usually displays a sign with the destination written in Chinese characters.

Taxi Taxis are available from the main hotels 24 hours a day. You can also catch a taxi outside the railway station or hail one in the street – a first for China. Demand for taxis is great, particularly during the peak hours: from 8 to 9 am and during lunch and dinner hours.

Taxis are equipped with meters and drivers use them unless you've negotiated a set fee in advance. If you want to pay in RMB rather than FEC, Hong Kong dollars or US dollars, expect an occasional argument.

Legally, the drivers must accept RMB and it says so right on the meter. Contrary to what some drivers will tell you, there is no such thing as an 'FEC taxi' except maybe a hotel taxi (which you pay in advance directly to the hotel, not to the driver).

The cost of a taxi varies depending on what type of vehicle it is. The cost per km (after flag fall) is displayed on a little sticker on the right rear window. For the cheapest taxis, the sticker displays the number 1.60. Flag fall for these taxis is Y6, which takes you one km, after which you are charged at the rate of Y1.60 for every additional km, though the meter clicks Y0.80 every ½-km interval. The taxis marked Y2.00 cost Y7.20 at flag fall and Y2 per km with the meter clicking Y1 every ½ km. In the 1.60 taxis, a trip from the railway station to Shamian Island would cost around Y12.

Taxis can be hired for a single trip or chartered on an hourly or daily basis. The latter is worth considering if you've got the money or if you're in a group which can split the cost. If you hire for a set period of time, negotiate the fee in advance and make it clear which currency you will pay with.

Bicycle Shamian Island has at least two places to rent bicycles – finding bikes for rent elsewhere in the city takes luck. The Happy Bike Rental Station is opposite the White Swan Hotel and across the road from the Guangzhou Youth Hostel.

The Guangzhou Youth Hostel rents bicycles to their guests. A Y100 deposit is required unless you leave your passport. Bicycle theft is a problem, so you'd be wise to buy a cable lock (widely available) and try to leave the bike only in designated bicycle parks where it will be watched by attendants.

AROUND CANTON
White Cloud Hills
(báiyún shān) 白云山

The White Cloud Hills, in the north-eastern suburbs of Canton, are an offshoot of Dayu Ling, the chief mountain range of Guangdong Province. The hills were once dotted with temples and monasteries, though

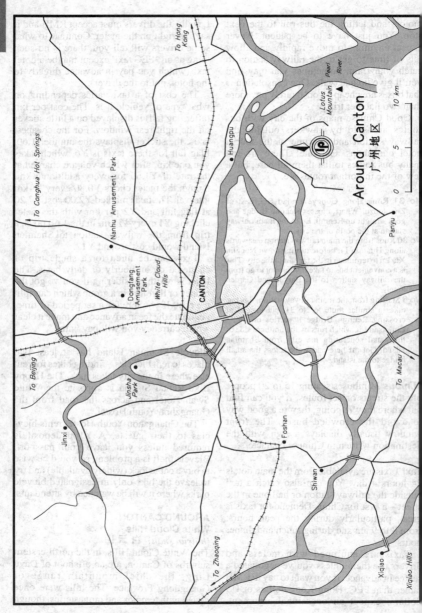

Around Canton
广州地区

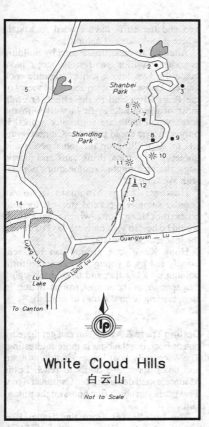

1	Liaoyang Clinic
2	Mingzhu Building
3	White Cloud Billowing Pines
4	Dajinzhong Reservoir
5	Nanfang Amusement Park
6	Star Touching Peak
7	Shanzhuang Inn
8	Twin River Villa
9	Dripping Water Crag
10	Southern Sky First Peak
11	Cheng Precipice
12	Nengren Temple
13	Cable Car
14	Jingtai Hollow

1	疗养院
2	明珠楼
3	白云松涛
4	大金钟水库
5	南方乐园
6	摩星岭
7	山庄旅舍
8	双溪别墅
9	滴水岩
10	天南第一峰
11	白云晚望
12	能仁寺
13	白云索道
14	景泰坑

White Cloud Hills 白云山

Not to Scale

no buildings of any historical significance remain. The hills are popular with the local people who come here to admire the views and slurp cups of tea. The Cloudy Rock Teahouse by a small waterfall on the hillside is recommended if you want to do the same.

At the southern foot of the hills is Lu Lake (lù hú), also called Golden Liquid Lake, which was built for water storage in 1958 and is now used as a park.

The highest peak in the White Cloud Hills is Star Touching Hill (mōxīng líng). At 382 metres it's considerably less tall than Hong Kong's famed Victoria Peak (554 metres),

but anything higher than a kiddy's sandcastle is a mountain in the Pearl River Delta area. On a clear day, you can see a panorama of the city – the Xiqiao Hills to one side, the North River and the Fayuan Hills on the other side, and the sweep of the Pearl River. Unfortunately, clear days are becoming a rarity in Canton.

The Chinese rate the evening view from Cheng Precipice as one of the eight sights of Canton. The precipice takes its name from a Qin Dynasty tale:

It is said that the first Qin Emperor, Qin Shi Huang, heard of a herb which would confer immortality on whoever ate it. Cheng On Kee, a minister of the emperor, was dispatched to find it. Five years of wandering brought Cheng to the White Cloud Hills where the herb grew in profusion. On eating the herb, he found that the rest of it disappeared. In dismay and fearful of returning empty-handed, Cheng threw himself off the precipice, but having been assured immortality from eating the herb, he was caught by a stork and taken to heaven.

The precipice, named in his memory, was formerly the site of the oldest monastery in the area. However, these days the precipice is usually just called the White Cloud Evening View (báiyún wǎnwàng).

Getting There & Away The White Cloud Hills are about 15 km from Canton and make a good half-day excursion. Express buses leave from Guangwei Lu, a little street running off Zhongshan 5-Lu to the west of the Children's Park, about every 15 minutes. The trip takes between 30 and 60 minutes, depending on traffic. There is also a cable car from the bottom of the hill near Lu Lake.

Nanhu Amusement Park
(nánhú lèyuán) 南湖乐园
This is one way to kill half a day. Aside from the roller coaster, water slide, Dodgem cars, skating rink and go-carts, the park has a tree-shaded lake and a good restaurant.

The park is north-east of the city in an area of rolling hills – avoid it on weekends, when it.is packed.

Air-con minibuses depart from near the main entrance of the railway station and go directly to the amusement park.

Another amusement park nearer to Canton is called Dongfang Leyuan, but it's not nearly as pleasant or scenic as Nanhu.

Lotus Mountain
(liánhuā shān) 莲花山
This interesting and exotic place is only 46 km to the south-east of Canton and makes an excellent full-day trip. The name Lotus Mountain might conjure up images of some holy mountain like Emeishan or Huangshan. In fact, it's nothing like that.

Lotus Mountain is an old quarry site. Most people wouldn't think of a quarry as being attractive, but this place is an exception. The stonecutting ceased several hundred years

ago and the cliffs have eroded to a state where it looks almost natural.

Attempts to dress up the area by building pagodas, pavilions and stone steps have made the area into a sort of gigantic rock garden. Dense vegetation and good views of the Pearl River add to the effect. Overall, most of the buildings fit in well with the scenery and there are some nice walks. If only someone could persuade Chinese tourists to stop filling up the lotus ponds and gorges with bottles, drink cans and plastic bags, the area might become more popular with Westerners.

However, Lotus Mountain is now a popular summer weekend stop-off for tour boats from Hong Kong, which means that it would be best to visit on weekdays or during the low season (winter).

Hong Kong tour groups can be seen, usually led by a young woman in uniform holding up a big flag and talking through a megaphone as the tourist troops march in step, leaving behind a trail of rubbish.

Getting There & Away You can get there by bus or boat, but the boat is more interesting. The once-daily boat leaves Canton at 8 am and takes about 2½ hours to reach Lotus Mountain, and departing for Canton at 4 pm. That gives you about five hours on the mountain.

The boat leaves from the Tianzi Pier (tiānzì mǎtóu) on Yanjiang Lu, one block east of Haizhu Square and the Haizhu Bridge. It's not a bad idea to buy a ticket one day in advance. There are mahjong tables on the boat and you won't have any trouble finding partners if you want to participate.

Buses depart from the railway station area in Canton. In theory the bus should be faster than the boat, but with Canton's traffic jams it works out about the same. Soft drinks are available on the boat, but no food.

The major hotels in Canton also run tours to Lotus Mountain, and ditto for CTS in Hong Kong. If you like big crowds, a tour is the way to go but will cost considerably more than doing it yourself.

Jinsha Park

(jīnshātān dùjià cūn) 金沙滩度假村
If you like cruising on riverboats, you might enjoy having a look upstream from Canton.

Jinsha Park is gradually being developed into a standard Chinese carnival. There is also a picnic ground and beach with a changing room, a restaurant and a place selling soft drinks near the beach. The river is muddy but cleaner than in Canton. The full name for this place in Chinese means 'golden sands beach holiday village' – the Chinese have a tendency to exaggerate. If you're determined to swim in the Pearl River, be sure you've had your hepatitis vaccination.

The place where the boat turns around is Jinxi *(jīnxī)*. The village is a small community of no particular interest in itself, but the boat trip is pleasant. Few foreign visitors come here, but it will give you a view of life in the countryside.

Getting There & Away Catch the boat from the No 1 ferry pier, opposite the Nanfang Department Store on Yanjiang 1-Lu. A morning departure is at 9.30 am and there is a second boat at 4 pm (at least during summer). The morning boat from Canton, which will drop you off at Jinshan Park about noon, continues upstream, returning at 3 pm. Jinxi is the last stop. After a lunch break the boat is turned around and returns to Canton.

Conghua Hot Springs

(cōnghuà wēnquán) 从化温泉
The springs are 85 km north-east of Canton in a pleasant forested valley with a river flowing through it. Twelve springs have been found with temperatures varying from 30°C to 40°C, the highest being over 70°C.

Foreigners come here to enjoy the comfort of soaking in hot water during Canton's chilly winter. The Chinese come here because they believe the hot springs can cure everything: arthritis, dermatitis, migraine headaches, high blood pressure, constipation, impotence – the lot. One tourist leaflet even claims relief for 'fatigue of the cerebral cortex' and gynaecological disease.

Unfortunately, there are no longer any outdoor pools. The water is piped into the private bathrooms of nearby hotels, so you'll have to enjoy the water without the benefit of open-air scenery. Nevertheless, Conghua is a pleasant place to visit.

Places to Stay Judging by the amount of hotel construction going on, the Chinese appear to be developing a hot springs Disneyland. Depending on how you feel about the CTS, you can try the *CTS Travel Hotel (lǚyóu bīnguǎn)* which is just next to the Happy Forever Restaurant. The *Wenquan Binguan* charges Y192 to Y236 for a double. Other choices include the *Hot Springs Hotel (wēnquán dàjiǔdiàn)* and *Guangdong Hot Springs Guesthouse (guǎngdōng wēnquán bīnguǎn)*. *Wenquan Shanzhuang* was under construction at the time of writing and looks like it will be a mammoth resort village.

Touts representing smaller private hotels meet arriving buses – it might be worth talking to them. Prices range from around Y60 to Y100 for a double.

Getting There & Away Buses to Conghua depart throughout the day from the long-distance bus station on Huanshi Xilu near Canton East Railway Station. Probably more convenient are the buses departing from the Huangsha Bus Station on Huangsha Dadao near Shamian Island. Some buses go directly to the hot springs, but most of the buses terminate in the town of Conghua, an ugly place 16 km from the hot springs. In that case, you have to catch another bus (20 minutes, Y2.30) to the hot springs *(wēnquán)*. A bus from Canton to Conghua town costs Y10.50, or Y12.50 directly from Canton to the hot springs.

The one-way trip takes three hours, or more depending on traffic. From Huangsha Bus Station, there are two departures directly to the hot springs at 7.35 and 10.35 am; departures to Conghua town are at 8, 9 and 10 am, 1.40, 2.30, 3.30, 4, 4.30, 5 and 5.30 pm.

The place is thick with bodies at the weekend, so try to avoid going then. If you do go on a weekend or holiday, buy a return

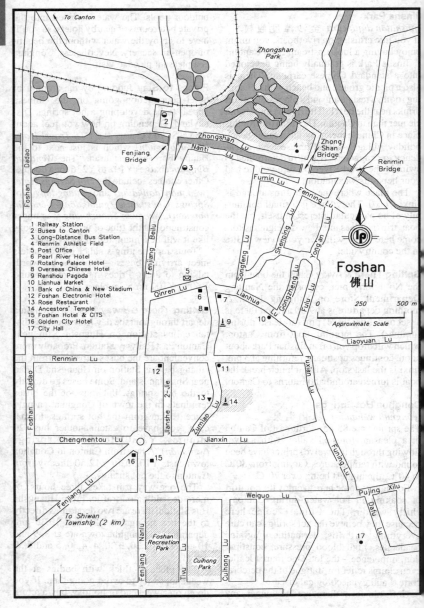

1   Railway Station
2   Buses to Canton
3   Long-Distance Bus Station
4   Renmin Athletic Field
5   Post Office
6   Pearl River Hotel
7   Rotating Palace Hotel
8   Overseas Chinese Hotel
9   Renshou Pagoda
10 Lianhua Market
11 Bank of China & New Stadium
12 Foshan Electronic Hotel
13 Rose Restaurant
14 Ancestors' Temple
15 Foshan Hotel & CITS
16 Golden City Hotel
17 City Hall

Foshan
佛山

0   250   500 m
Approximate Scale

```
1  火车站
2  开往广州的汽车站
3  长途汽车站
4  人民体育场
5  邮电局
6  珠江大酒店
7  旋宫酒店
8  华侨大厦
9  仁寿寺
10 莲花市场
11 中国银行/新广场
12 电子宾馆
13 玫瑰酒家
14 祖庙
15 佛山宾馆/中国国际旅行社
16 金城大酒店
17 市政府
```

ticket to Canton on arrival because the buses fill up fast at those times.

Foshan

(fóshān) 佛山
Just 28 km south-west of Canton is the town of Foshan (Buddha Hill). The story goes that a monk travelling through the area enshrined three statues of Buddha on a hilltop. After the monk left, the shrine collapsed and the statues disappeared. Hundreds of years later, during the Tang Dynasty (618 to 907 AD), the Buddha figurines were suddenly rediscovered, a new temple was built on the hill and the town was renamed.

Whether or not the story is true, from about the 10th century onwards the town became a well-known religious centre.

Since the 10th or 11th century Foshan has been notable as one of the four main handicraft centres of old China. The other three were Zhuxian in Henan Province, Jingdezhen in Jiangxi and Hankou in Hebei. The nearby town of Shiwan (which is now virtually an extension of Foshan) became famous for its pottery, and the village of Nanpu (which is now a suburb of Foshan) developed the art of metal casting. Silk weaving and papercutting also became important industries and now Foshan

papercuts are a commonly sold tourist souvenir in China.

Foshan has developed into a mid-sized city complete with heavy traffic, factories and busy business travellers from Hong Kong – no respite here from Canton. However, it is smaller, a bit easier to get around and a welcome change of scenery.

Information CITS (☎ 353338; fax 352347) is in the Foshan Hotel at 75 Fenjiang Nanlu. CTS (☎ 223828) is in the Overseas Chinese Hotel at 14 Zumiao Lu.

Lianhua Market *(liánhuā shìchǎng)* This market is considerably smaller than the Qingping Market in Canton, but it's still worth a look. You can stock up on dried fish, turtles, frogs, lizards, dogs and snakes.

Ancestors' Temple *(zǔ miào)* Foshan's number one tourist attraction, the Ancestors' Temple, is attracting large tour groups from Hong Kong and elsewhere. Recognising the opportunity, several hotels and restaurants have sprouted in the neighbourhood, but the temple grounds are still quiet and peaceful.

At the southern end of Zumiao Lu, the original temple was built during the Song Dynasty in the latter part of the 11th century, and was used by workers in the metal-smelting trade for worshipping their ancestors. It was destroyed by fire at the end of the Yuan Dynasty in the mid-1300s and was rebuilt at the beginning of the Ming Dynasty during the reign of the first Ming Emperor, Hong Wu. The Ancestors' Temple was converted into a Taoist temple because the emperor worshipped a Taoist god.

The temple has been developed through renovations and additions in the Ming and Qing dynasties. The structure is built entirely of interlocking wooden beams, with no nails or other metal used at all. It is roofed with coloured tiles made in Shiwan.

The main hall contains a 2500-kg bronze statue of a god known as the Northern Emperor (Beidi). He's also known as the Black Emperor (Heidi) and rules over water and all its inhabitants, especially fish, turtles and snakes. Because South China was prone to floods, people often tried to appease Beidi by honouring him with temples and carvings of turtles and snakes. In the courtyard is a pool containing a large statue of a turtle with a serpent crawling over it, into which the Chinese throw one, two and five-fen notes, plus the odd drink can.

The temple also has an interesting collection of ornate weapons used on ceremonial occasions during the imperial days. The Foshan Museum is in the temple grounds, as is the Foshan Antique Store and an arts & crafts store. The temple is open daily from 8.30 am to 4.30 pm.

Places to Stay The cheapest place to stay in Foshan is the *Pearl River Hotel* (☎ 287512) *(zhū jiāng dàjiǔdiàn)* which has doubles for Y120 and Y150, triples for Y180 and quads for Y200. It's on Qinren Lu in the centre of town, across the street from the post office.

Around the corner and just opposite Renshou Pagoda is the *Overseas Chinese Hotel* (☎ 223828; fax 227702) *(huáqiáo dàshà)*, 14 Zumiao Lu. Singles cost Y135 and Y195 while doubles are Y195, Y220 and Y330.

Rotating Palace Hotel (☎ 285622) *(xuángōng jiǔdiàn)*, is in the centre of town at the corner of Zumiao Lu and Lianhua Lu. A double costs Y265. The hotel doesn't rotate but the rooftop restaurant does, and even if you don't eat there, you can pay a visit to the 16th floor for a sweeping view of Foshan's haze and industrial smokestacks.

Foshan Electronic Hotel (☎ 288998; fax 225781) *(diànzi bīnguǎn)*, 101 Renmin Lu, has doubles ranging from Y218 to Y295. This 19-storey building is readily identified by a large red 'FEG' on the roof (Foshan Electronic Group). The hotel features receptionists who giggle uncontrollably at every foreigner who approaches the front desk.

The *Golden City Hotel* (☎ 357228; fax 353924) *(jīnchéng dàjiǔdiàn)*, 48 Fenjiang Nanlu, is pleasant enough, though the location at a noisy intersection is not especially aesthetic. Doubles cost Y280 to Y333, while suites start from Y530 and go to Y2070.

The *Foshan Hotel* (☎ 353338; fax 352347) *(fóshān bīnguǎn)*, 75 Fenjiang Nanlu, is notable as the home of CITS. Singles are Y96 though these seem to be permanently 'all full'. Doubles are Y220 and Y360.

Places to Eat The *Rose Restaurant* on Zumiao Lu just opposite the Ancestors' Temple is one of the better places in town.

Getting There & Away There is a little-used airport seven km north-west of the city. Unless you charter your own flight, you aren't likely to arrive this way.

The easiest way to Foshan from Canton is to catch one of the numerous minibuses at the Huangsha Bus Station on Huangsha Dadao (just west of Shamian Island and Liu'ersan Lu. The slower local minibuses take over an hour and cost Y3, while minibuses using the expressway take about 45 minutes and cost Y5.

You can also catch buses to Foshan from the bus terminal next to the Liuhua Hotel, near the railway station.

The bus from Canton heads into Foshan

To Canton

Foshan Station

FOSHAN

0   0.5   1 km

Canton-Zhanjiang Hwy (Fenjiang Zhonglu)

Ancestors' Temple

Nanhai County

To Xiqiao Hills

SHIWAN

Around Foshan
佛山地区

from the north. First stop is Foshan Railway Station.

Taking the train from Canton to Foshan (30 minutes) might seem like a good way to beat the maddening traffic. However, the time you waste organising the ticket at Canton's chaotic railway station and waiting for the train will more than make up for what you waste sitting on the bus in a traffic jam. Still, it's worth considering the train, especially if you're heading west, because the line from Canton passes through Foshan, then continues westwards to Sanshui, Zhaoqing, Maoming and Zhanjiang (the gateway to Hainan Island).

The schedule will doubtless change, but at the time of writing there were six departures daily from Canton, at 7.25, 8.30 and 11 am, 2.10, 6.10 and 6.45 pm. Going the other way, departures from Foshan station are at 7.14 and 9.40 am, 12.39, 4.55, 5.38 and 7.06 pm. Westbound trains depart from Foshan for Sanshui at 6.50 and 10.30 am, 12.40 and 3.45 pm.

For the busy business traveller, there are now direct express trains to/from Hong Kong. These cost Y190 and take three hours. Currently, there are two trains daily, departing from Kowloon's Hunghom Station at 4.28 and 6.10 pm. Going the other way, departures from Foshan are at 11.50 am and 1.32 pm.

Getting Around You won't have to look too hard for the two-wheeled taxis – they will be looking for you. Motorcycle drivers wearing red safety helmets greet minibuses arriving from Canton and practically kidnap disembarking passengers. The drivers assume that every foreigner wants to head immediately for the Ancestors' Temple. If that's not where you want to go, make that clear straight away.

There aren't too many pedicabs, but you will see them about town. Foshan's pedicabs are really designed for hauling freight – there are no seats, just a cargo area behind the driver. Fares are negotiable.

Shiwan
(shìwān) 石湾
Two km south-west of Foshan, Shiwan

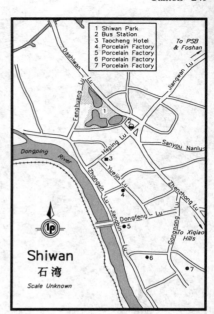

1	石湾公园
2	公共汽车站
3	陶城宾馆
4	陶瓷厂
5	陶瓷厂
6	陶瓷厂
7	陶瓷厂

township is known mostly for its porcelain factories. Although there is nothing of outstanding scenic interest here, you might want to take a look if you have an interest in pottery. Bus Nos 9 and 10 go to Shiwan. You can catch bus No 9 in front of the Ancestors' Temple, or No 10 on Fenjiang Xilu. From the Ancestors' Temple, you could walk to Shiwan in 30 minutes.

The only accommodation place accepting foreigners is the *Taocheng Hotel (táochéng bīnguǎn)* at the corner of Heping Lu and Yuejin Lu.

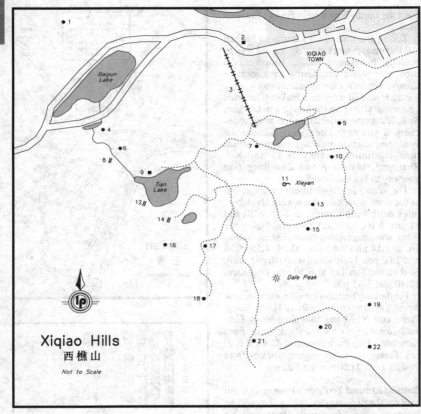

Xiqiao Hills
西樵山
Not to Scale

Xiqiao Hills
(xīqiáo shān) 西樵山
Another scenic spot, these hills are 68 km south-west of Canton. Seventy-two peaks (basically hills) make up the area. There are 36 caves, 32 springs, 28 waterfalls and 21 crags. The summit is very rocky but, rising to a piddling 345 metres, it's certainly not a difficult climb.

At the foot of the hills is the small market town of Xiqiao and around the upper levels of the hills are scattered several centuries-old villages. One of the big sights (at least for the Chinese) is a waterfall called Water Flies

1	Xingtou Village		12	Youchuihong Waterfall	
2	Xiqiao Hotel		13	Wuye Well	
3	Cable Car		14	Zuochuihong Waterfall	
4	Baiyun Cave & Kuiguang Hall		15	Biyun Village	
5	Jade Crag (Yuyan)		16	Yunduan Village	
6	Yuanquan Fairy House		17	Dishui Crag	
7	Shipai Village		18	Yunlu Village	
8	Water Flies 1000 Metres (waterfall)		19	Heaven's Bed (Tianchuangge)	
9	Tianhu Hotel/Restaurant		20	Donggu Rock	
10	Baishan Village		21	Sifang Bamboo Grove	
11	Xieyan Spring		22	Shiyan Crag	

1	杏头村	8	飞流千尺天	15	碧云村
2	西樵饭店	9	天湖饭店	16	云端村岩
3	缆车	10	白山村	17	滴水路村
4	白云洞 / 奎光楼	11	蟹眼泉	18	云窗阁
5	玉珠岩	12	右垂虹瀑	19	天窗阁
6	云泉仙馆	13	无叶井	20	天冬菇石
7	石牌村	14	左垂虹瀑	21	四方竹园
				22	石燕岩

1000 Metres (*fēi liútiān chǐ*). Most of the area is made accessible by stone paths. It's popular with Chinese tourists, but foreigners of any kind are rare.

Getting There & Away Buses to the hills depart from the Foshan Bus Station on Daxin Lu, which runs west off Jiefang Nanlu.

Guangdong 广东

Capital: Canton (Guangzhou)

Over 2000 years ago when the Chinese were carving out a civilisation centred on the Yellow River, southern China remained a semi-independent tributary state peopled by native tribes, the last survivors of which today form minority groups. It was not until the Qin Dynasty (221-207 BC), when the northern states were united for the first time under a single ruler, that the Chinese finally conquered the southern regions. Revolts and uprisings were frequent and the Chinese settlements remained small, dispersed amongst a predominantly aboriginal population.

Chinese emigration to the south began in earnest around the 12th century AD. The original tribes were killed by Chinese armies, isolated in small pockets, or pushed further south. By the 17th century the Chinese had outgrown Guangdong, and population pressure forced them to move into adjoining Guangxi and Sichuan provinces, which had been depopulated after rebellions in the mid-17th century.

Because of these migrations the people of Guangdong are not a homogeneous group. The term 'Cantonese' is sometimes applied to all people living in Guangdong Province but more commonly it refers to those who shared the language and culture.

What the migrants from the north found beyond the mountainous areas of northern and western Guangdong was the Pearl River Delta, a region agriculturally richer than any in China except for the Yangzi and Yellow river areas. The abundant waterways, heavy rainfall and warm climate allowed wet-rice cultivation.

The people of Guangdong Province spearheaded Chinese emigration to the USA, Canada, Australia and South Africa in the mid-19th century, spurred on by the gold rushes in those countries and by the wars and growing poverty in their own country. The image which most Westerners have today of a 'Chinatown' is based on Guangdong's

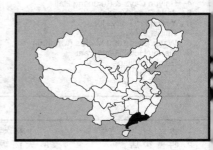

chief city, Canton. It is mostly Cantonese food which is eaten and the Cantonese dialect which is most spoken among the Chinese populations from Melbourne to Toronto to London.

SHENZHEN
(shēnzhèn) 深圳

'The mountains are high and the emperor is far away,' says an ancient Chinese proverb – meaning that life can be relatively free if one keeps far enough away from the central government. Shenzhen is more than 2300 km from Beijing but within sight of Hong Kong, and a living example of the wisdom of this ancient proverb.

Shenzhen is a border town with Hong Kong and officially labelled a Special Economic Zone (SEZ). The Shenzhen SEZ came into existence in 1980. Three other SEZs were established at the same time: Zhuhai (near Macau), Shantou in the eastern part of Guangdong Province and Xiamen in Fujian Province.

As the first and most important of China's SEZ's, Shenzhen has received the closest possible scrutiny from Beijing. During the first few years of operation, it was deemed a failure, especially by hard-line Communist opponents of economic reform. Amongst the problems cited was the tendency for Shenzhen to attract imported goods which

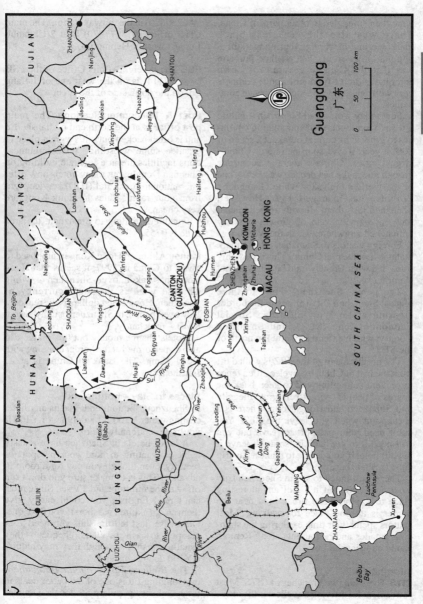

Guangdong 广东

were then smuggled to other parts of China. There was also the ceaseless black marketeering in foreign currency (still a popular profession). Yet another problem was that the Chinese government's own enterprises didn't (and still don't) compete very well against more efficient private companies.

Few today would call Shenzhen a failure – it's a boomtown. If the population continues to grow at its current breakneck speed of 20% a year, it will soon be one of China's largest cities. China's average economic growth rate in the last decade was 10% – one of the world's highest – while Guangdong Province has managed 18%. However, Shenzhen tops them all with a phenomenal 45%, a dizzying rate of growth possibly unmatched anywhere else in the world.

Foreign visitors to Shenzhen often remark that it is 'not the real China'. This is certainly true – it's what China would be if it were not Communist.

The name 'Shenzhen' refers to three places: Shenzhen City (opposite the border crossing at Lo Wu); Shenzhen Special Economic Zone (SEZ); and Shenzhen County, which extends several km north of the SEZ.

The northern part of the SEZ is walled off from the rest of China by an electrified fence to prevent smuggling and to keep back the hoards of people trying to emigrate illegally into Shenzhen and Hong Kong. There is a checkpoint when you leave the SEZ. You don't need your passport to leave but you will need it to get back in, so don't leave it in your hotel if you decide to make a day trip outside Shenzhen.

There isn't much to see in Shenzhen City (*shēnzhèn shì*), but it's still an interesting place to explore. The urban area near the border is a good place for walking. Most visitors spend their time exploring the shopping arcades and restaurants along Renmin Nanlu and Jianshe Lu.

Information
CITS There are two branches of CITS. Most convenient for arriving travellers is the office

(☎ 2239670) in the railway station. The main CITS office (☎ 5577970) is at 2 Chuanbu Jie, just west of Heping Lu.

PSB The Foreign Affairs Office of the PSB (☎ 5572114) is on the west end of Jiefang Lu, on the north side of the street.

Post & Telecommunications The main post office is at the north end of Jianshe Lu and is often packed out – it's a great place to practice sumo wrestling. Telecommunications facilities are in a separate building on Shennan Donglu, but many hotels now offer international direct dial (IDD) service right from your room. Rates to Hong Kong are very cheap.

For direct dialling to Shenzhen, the area code is 0755.

Money Although Hong Kong is supposed to revert to China in 1997, it seems that Hong Kong has taken over Shenzhen – while Chinese yuan is the legal currency of Shenzhen, Hong Kong dollars is the real one. However, people in Shenzhen usually accept RMB – reluctantly.

Hotels change money but this magic can also be performed at the border crossing with Hong Kong. The Bank of China is at 23 Jianshe Lu.

Places to Stay – bottom end
In Shenzhen, 'bottom end' means any hotel costing under Y200 for a double, or Y100 if you're exceptionally lucky.

A lot of hotels in Shenzhen have a nasty habit of wanting to hold your passport as security, even though you pay for a room in advance. This is to make sure you don't run off with the furniture and TV set. Since most can't read English, you could easily give them an old expired passport if you have one. Otherwise, just tell the staff you need your passport to cash travellers' cheques – they usually accept this though they may require a Y100 deposit instead.

The *Binjiang Hotel* (*bīnjiāng dàjiǔdiàn*) on Hongling Lu is one of the better deals in town and very popular with locals. Doubles

Pearl River Delta
珠江三角洲

0   25   50 km

Conghua

CANTON (GUANGZHOU)

FOSHAN

Lotus Mountain

Dongguan

Huiyang

Shunde

Humen

PEOPLE'S REPUBLIC OF CHINA

SHENZHEN SPECIAL ECONOMIC ZONE

JIANGMEN

ZHONGSHAN

Lo Wu

Mirs Bay

Shekou

New Territories

KOWLOON

Xiangzhou

Lantau

Hong Kong Island

HONG KONG

Gongbei

MACAU

ZHUHAI SPECIAL ECONOMIC ZONE

SOUTH CHINA SEA

GUANGDONG

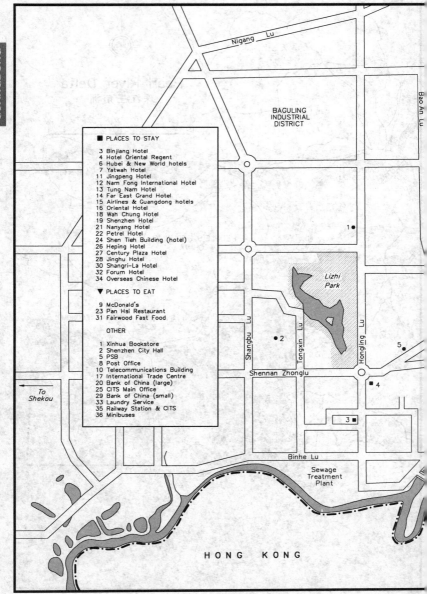

■ PLACES TO STAY

3 Binjiang Hotel
4 Hotel Oriental Regent
6 Hubei & New World hotels
7 Yatwah Hotel
11 Jingpeng Hotel
12 Nam Fong International Hotel
13 Tung Nam Hotel
14 Far East Grand Hotel
15 Airlines & Guangdong hotels
16 Oriental Hotel
18 Wah Chung Hotel
19 Shenzhen Hotel
21 Nanyang Hotel
22 Petrel Hotel
24 Shen Tieh Building (hotel)
26 Heping Hotel
27 Century Plaza Hotel
28 Jinghu Hotel
30 Shangri-La Hotel
32 Forum Hotel
34 Overseas Chinese Hotel

▼ PLACES TO EAT

9 McDonald's
23 Pan Hsi Restaurant
31 Fairwood Fast Food

OTHER

1 Xinhua Bookstore
2 Shenzhen City Hall
5 PSB
8 Post Office
10 Telecommunications Building
17 International Trade Centre
20 Bank of China (large)
25 CITS Main Office
29 Bank of China (small)
33 Laundry Service
35 Railway Station & CITS
36 Minibuses

Nigang Lu

Bao An Lu

BAGULING
INDUSTRIAL
DISTRICT

Lizhi
Park

Shangbu Lu

Tongxin Lu

Hongling Lu

Shennan Zhonglu

To
Shekou

Binhe Lu

Sewage
Treatment
Plant

HONG KONG

GUANGDONG

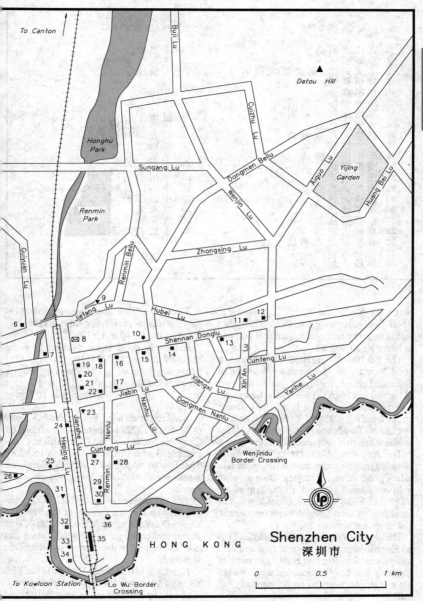

To Canton

Bui Lu

Datou Hill

Honghu Park

Cuizhu Lu

Dongmen Beilu

Arguo Lu

Yijing Garden

Huang Bei Lu

Sungang Lu

Renmin Park

Wenjin Lu

Guiyuan Lu

Renmin Beilu

Zhongxing Lu

Jiefang Lu

9

Hubei Lu

11

12

6

8

10

Shennan Donglu

13

Lu

7

19 18

16

15

14

Cunfeng Lu

20

17

Xin An

Yanhe Lu

21

Jiabin Lu

Xiangxi Lu

22

Nanhu Lu

Nanlu

23

Dongmen Nanlu

24

Heping Lu

Jianshe Lu

Cunfeng Lu

Wenjindu Border Crossing

25

27

28

26

29

Renmin

31

30

32

36

HONG KONG

Shenzhen City

深圳市

33

35

34

0   0.5   1 km

To Kowloon Station

Lo Wu Border Crossing

GUANGDONG

■ PLACES TO STAY

3 宾江大酒店
4 晶都酒店
6 湖北宾馆／新世界大酒店
7 日华宾馆
11 京鹏宾馆
12 南方国际大酒店
13 东南国际大酒店
14 远东大酒店
15 航空和广东酒店
16 东方酒店
18 华中国际酒店
19 深圳酒店
21 南洋酒店
22 海燕大酒店
24 深铁大厦
26 和平酒店
27 新都酒店
28 京湖大酒店
30 香格里拉大酒店
32 富临大酒店
34 华侨大厦

▼ PLACES TO EAT

9 麦当劳
23 洋溪酒家
31 大快活

OTHER

1 新华书店
2 深圳市政府
5 公安局外事科
8 邮局
10 电信大楼
17 国贸大厦
20 中国银行
25 中国国际旅行社
29 中国银行
33 洗衣店
35 火车站
36 小公共汽车站

---

cost Y83, Y123 and Y150. Try paying in RMB first; otherwise use FEC. This place seems to give a bad exchange rate if you pay in Hong Kong dollars.

The *Yat Wah Hotel (rìhuá bīnguǎn)* has a good location on the north-west corner of Shennan Lu and Heping Lu, just to the west of the railway tracks. The outside looks a bit tattered, but the interior is all right. Room prices are Y85, Y95 and Y130, plus 10% on weekends. This is one of the cheapest places in Shenzhen that will accept foreigners.

The *Jing Peng Hotel* (☎ 2227190) *(jīngpéng bīnguǎn)* is a elegant-looking place that offers good value for money. Doubles with twin beds are Y148 and Y188. Triples are Y188 and Y238 while suites are Y388. The hotel has its own billiard room, restaurant, gift shop and karaoke bar.

The *Jinghu Hotel (jīnghú dàjiǔdiàn)* has no English sign but is easy to find and centrally located on Renmin Nanlu just south of Cunfeng Lu. Singles/doubles are Y96/185 but the singles seem to be permanently 'all full'.

The *Shen Tieh Building* (☎ 5584248) *(shēntiě dàshà)* on Heping Lu is good value. Doubles are Y140 and Y190.

Relatively good value is offered by the *Oriental Hotel* (☎ 2234118; fax 2234123) *(dōngfāng jiǔdiàn)*, at 136 Shennan Donglu. Singles/doubles cost Y126/175 and triples are Y217. There is an additional 10% surcharge.

Also recommended is the *Heping Hotel* (☎ 2252111, 2228149) *(hépíng jiǔdiàn)*, 63 Chuanbu Jie, is near the CITS office. Comfortable doubles/triples start at Y160/200. There is an added 10% service charge on weekends though this buys you no extra service.

The *Shenzhen Hotel* (☎ 2238000; fax 2222284) *(shēnzhèn jiǔdiàn)* at 156 Shennan Donglu has doubles for Y180 and Y210. This is a reasonably elegant and friendly place and not bad value for the money by Shenzhen standards.

Nearby at 140 Shennan Donglu is the *Wah Chung Hotel* (☎ 2238060) *(huázhōng guójì jiǔdiàn)*. Spacious doubles cost Y198 and

Y246 and triples Y245. There is a 10% service charge and rooms cost 10% more on weekends.

The *Nanyang Hotel* (☎ 2224968) *(nányáng jiǔdiàn)* has doubles for Y177 (HK$240) and triples for Y222 (HK$300). This reasonably luxurious hotel is well known for its disco. It's on Jianshe Lu, north of Jiabin Lu.

The oddly-named *Petrel Hotel* (☎ 2232828; fax 2221398) *(hǎiyàn dàjiǔdiàn)* on Jiabin Lu is a 29-storey tower offering reasonably priced doubles for Y170 (HK$230), Y244 (HK$330) and Y318 (HK$430) plus 10% service charge. The hotel's brochure clearly explains the name thus: 'Petrel hover at sea of the red sun shine upon'.

The *Hubei Hotel* (☎ 5573272) *(húběi bīnguǎn)* and adjacent New World Hotel *(xīn shìjiè bīnguǎn)* are on the corner of Jiefang Lu and Guiyuan Lu. Both were under renovation at the time of writing but appeared to be decent mid-range hotels. They are near McDonald's, if that's a consideration.

Places to Stay – middle

In Shenzhen, 'mid-range' would have to be defined as a hotel costing between Y200 and Y300.

The *Overseas Chinese Hotel* (☎ 5573811) *(huáqiáo dàshà)* is run-down; doubles cost Y235 or Y361 and it's really not worth it. Its only real advantage is that it's very close to the railway station.

The *Airlines Hotel* (☎ 2237999; fax 2237866) *(hángkōng dàjiǔdiàn)*, 130 Shennan Donglu, has singles/doubles for Y222/259 (HK$300/350). It's modern, clean and ruthlessly air-con.

The *Bamboo Garden Hotel* (☎ 5533138; fax 5534835) *(zhúyuán bīnguǎn)* is somewhat inconveniently located at Dongmen Beilu near the intersection with Aiguo Lu. However, it is a luxurious place and is known for its excellent restaurant. Many tour groups make a lunch stop here, though lately they are being pulled away by new restaurants near Splendid China. You can book rooms from the Hong Kong office (☎ 3674127). Doubles cost Y236 (HK$320) to Y259 (HK$350).

Guangdong Hotel (☎ 5895108; fax 5769381) *(yuèhǎi jiǔdiàn)* is a sparkling glass and concrete edifice on Shennan Donglu. Rooms cost Y288 (HK$390), Y310 (HK$420), Y333 (HK$450) and Y399 (HK$540) plus 10%. In the same neighbourhood is the *Far East Grand Hotel* (☎ 2205369; fax 2200239) *(yuǎndōng dàjiǔdiàn)*, at 104 Shennan Donglu. Singles are Y259 (HK$350) and doubles are Y333 (HK$450) and Y360 (HK$487) plus 10%.

Nearby is the *Tung Nam Hotel (dōngnán guójì dàjiǔdiàn)* on Shennan Donglu. At the time of writing, it was closed for remodelling but should be open by the time you read this.

Places to Stay – top end

Nam Fong International Hotel (☎ 2256728; fax 2256936) *(nánfāng guójì dàjiǔdiàn)*, eastern end of Shennan Donglu. Doubles cost Y318 (HK$430), Y355 (HK$480) and Y392 (HK$530) plus 10% service charge.

Century Plaza Hotel (☎ 2220888; fax 2234060) *(xīndū jiǔdiàn)*, Cunfeng Lu, between Jianshe Lu and Renmin Nanlu; standard/deluxe doubles cost Y444/518 (HK$600/700), plus 10% surcharge.

Forum Hotel (☎ 5586333; fax 5561700) *(fúlín dàjiǔdiàn)*, 67 Heping Lu; doubles cost Y510 (HK$690) and Y584 (HK$790).

Hotel Oriental Regent (☎ 2247000; fax 2247290) *(jīngdū jiǔdiàn)*, south-east corner of Shennan Zhonglu and Hongling Lu; doubles cost Y414 (HK$560), Y466 (HK$630) and Y503 (HK$680).

Shangri-La Hotel (☎ 2230888; fax 2239878) *(xiānggé lǐlā dàjiǔdiàn)*, facing railway station; doubles cost Y606 (HK$820), Y695 (HK$940) and Y888 (HK$1200) plus 10%.

Places to Stay – resorts

These places defy description, but are a bit like Club Med, Disneyland, old European castles and Hong Kong's Ocean Park all rolled into one. They offer discos, saunas, swimming pools, golf courses, horseback riding, roller coasters, supermarkets, palaces, castles, Chinese pavilions, statues and monorails. The huge (and surprisingly cheap) dim sum restaurants become nightclubs in the evening, with Las Vegas-style floor shows.

Weekday prices are about HK$250 to HK$350 for a double, which often includes a free breakfast and transport to and from the Shenzhen border crossing (railway station area). They often throw in free use of their other facilities (sauna, disco, swimming pool) or else offer sizable discounts to hotel guests. Shenzhen's notable resorts include:

Honey Lake Resort (☎ 7745061; fax 7745045) *(xiāngmì hú dùjià cūn)* West of Shenzhen City, it has doubles for HK$288 on weekdays or for up to HK$368 on weekends. Contact the two Hong Kong booking offices (☎ 7989288 or 8656210). Hotel guests receive a 20% discount in the restaurant, amusement park, sauna and other facilities.

Shenzhen Bay Hotel (☎ 6600111; fax 6600139) *(shēnzhèn wān dàjiǔdiàn)*, Overseas Chinese Town. Doubles cost HK$368 on weekdays or HK$498 on weekends. Its Hong Kong booking office (☎ 3693368) is in the New World Office Building, Tsimshatsui. Hotel guests have free use of the swimming pool, nightclub shows and other facilities. Guests also receive a discount at the shopping centre.

Shiyan Lake Hot Springs Resort (☎ 9960143) *(shíyán hú wēnquán dùjià cūn)* Doubles range from HK$248 to HK$398 on weekdays or from HK$278 to HK$430 on weekends. This place is about five km north-west of Shenzhen, outside the SEZ.

Silver Lake Resort Camp (☎ 2222827; fax 2242622) *(yín hú lǚyóu zhōngxīn)* Doubles range from HK$278 to HK$418 on weekdays or from HK$328 to HK$450 on weekends.

Xiaomeisha Beach Resort (☎ 5550000) *(xiǎoméishā dàjiǔdiàn)* Doubles cost HK$228 to HK$328 which includes breakfast and a 20% discount on other meals. Weekend rates are higher.

Xili Lake Resort (☎ 6660022; fax 6660521) *(xīlì hú)* Doubles range from HK$230 to HK$376 on weekdays or from HK$278 to HK$430 on weekends.

Places to Eat

For the backpacker on a budget, Shenzhen is no picnic. You'll find the usual assortment of cheap noodle shops in side alleys. Self-catering is a possibility as grocery stores, supermarkets, bakeries and fruit stalls seem to be on every corner.

Dim sum breakfast and lunch is available in all but the scruffiest hotels. Usually the dim sum restaurants are on the 2nd or 3rd floor rather than by the lobby. Prices are slightly lower than in Hong Kong. You'll have to pay

in Hong Kong dollars in the nicer hotels but you may get away with RMB elsewhere.

The *Oriental Hotel*, on the corner of Renmin Nanlu and Shennan Donglu, has a Western-style restaurant on the ground floor. You have to pay in Hong Kong dollars, but prices are about as cheap as you can find in Shenzhen if you need Western food.

One of Shenzhen's best restaurants is the *Pan Hsi Restaurant* (☎ 2238081) *(bànxī jiǔjiā)* at 33 Jianshe Lu.

Shenzhen is the site of China's first *McDonald's*, a major tourist attraction which draws Chinese from all over the country. A second McDonald's has been built in the west end of town and more are sure to follow, but you might want to visit the original site for historical reasons. It's on the north side of Jiefang Lu.

Fairwood Fast Food (dà kuàihuó) offers Hong Kong-style fast food and charges Hong Kong dollars. It's not bad though. The restaurant is on the west side of Heping Lu just north of the towering Forum Hotel.

Entertainment

All the main hotels and resort areas have discos, nightclubs and karaoke bars.

Getting There & Away

Air Shenzhen's new Huangtian Airport is rapidly becoming one of China's busiest. Flights and their fares are listed in the table.

Destination	Fare	Destination	Fare
Beihai	Y410	Beijing	Y1170
Changchun	Y1630	Changsha	Y360
Chengdu	Y910	Chongqing	Y810
Dalian	Y1500	Fuzhou	Y640
Guilin	Y370	Guiyang	Y590
Haikou	Y420	Hangzhou	Y850
Harbin	Y1650	Kunming	Y870
Lanzhou	Y1300	Meixian	Y360
Nanchang	Y610	Nanjing	Y1050
Nanning	Y460	Ningbo	Y680
Qingdao	Y1290	Sanya	Y590
Shanghai	Y930	Shantou	Y400
Shenyang	Y1500	Taiyuan	Y980
Tianjin	Y1100	Ürümqi	Y1940
Wenzhou	Y540	Wuhan	Y590
Xi'an	Y1030	Xiamen	Y540
Yantai	Y1190	Zhanjiang	Y390

Shenzhen officials harbour ambitions to make Huangtian into an international airport. Plans call for setting up a separate Customs and Immigration terminal for China-bound passengers and Hong Kong-bound passengers.

You can purchase air tickets at the Airlines Hotel (hángkōng dàjiǔdiàn) at 130 Shennan Donglu in central Shenzhen.

Bus From Hong Kong, there are buses Shenzhen run by Citybus, by Motor Transport Company of Guangdong & Hong Kong Ltd at the Canton Rd bus terminal, and by CTS. For most travellers, buses are not a good option unless you are on a tour.

There are long-distance buses to Fuzhou, Xiamen and other coastal cities, departing from the Overseas Chinese Travel Service (huáqiáo lǚyóu bù), next to the Overseas Chinese Hotel on Heping Lu.

There are frequent minibuses between Canton and Shenzhen. In Canton, buses depart from next to the Liuhua Hotel, across the street from the railway station. In Shenzhen, departures are from just east of the railway station next to the Hong Kong border crossing. The fare is Y40 and the ride takes five hours.

Train The Kowloon-Canton Railway (KCR) offers the fastest and most convenient transport to Shenzhen from Hong Kong. Trains to the border crossing at Lo Wu begin from Hunghom Station in Tsimshatsui East. Unless you want to walk to Hunghom, it's easiest to take the MTR to Kowloon Tong Station, then change to the KCR. There are frequent departures throughout the day and the electric trains start at 6.40 am. The fare from Hunghom Station to Lo Wu is HK$25. The last train from Hunghom to Lo Wu is at 8.50 pm. The border closes at 9 pm. From Hunghom to Lo Wu is 34 km and takes 37 minutes. Avoid taking this train on weekends, when it's packed to overflowing and the stampede at the border crossing is incredible.

There are frequent local trains between Canton and Shenzhen and the journey takes about three hours. Tourist prices are Y20 (hard seat) and Y46 (soft seat). The trains are often packed and there are long queues to buy tickets.

Boat Hoverferries run between Hong Kong and Shekou, a port on the west side of Shenzhen. There are three daily departures from the ferry terminal at China Hong Kong City on Canton Rd in Tsimshatsui, Kowloon, at 8 and 10.15 am, and 3.30 pm. There are four additional departures from the Macau ferry terminal on Hong Kong Island at 8.20 and 9.30 am, and at 2 and 4.30 pm. The fare is HK$69 and the trip takes 45 minutes. Departures from Shekou to Kowloon are at 9.15 am, 2.30 and 5 pm. Departures from Shekou to Hong Kong Island are at 8.15 and 10.45 am, and 3.15 and 4.45 pm. The fare is Y35.

There is one jetcat (jet-powered catamaran) daily from Macau to Shekou. It departs from Macau at 8.30 am and arrives at 10 am. The cost is M$79.

There are three daily jetcats running between Shekou and Zhuhai SEZ (north of Macau).

Getting Around

To/From the Airport There are shuttle buses between the airport and the Airlines Hotel (hángkōng dàjiǔdiàn) at 130 Shennan Donglu in downtown Shenzhen. Minibuses and taxis also add to the choices, but remember that in Shenzhen's traffic, getting to the airport can take a long time.

If you want to travel directly between the airport and Hong Kong, there is now a rapid boat service (jetcat) taking 60 minutes to complete the journey, which is at least twice as fast as the bus. The sole ticketing agent in Hong Kong is the branch office of CTS (☎ 7361863) in Kowloon's China Hong Kong City Ferry Terminal on Canton Rd. In Shenzhen, you can purchase tickets right at the airport. The price is steep and based on season (what is the high season for visiting an airport?): high/low season deck class costs HK$213/163; super-deck class is HK$413/313; a VIP cabin costs HK$2478/1878 but at that price why not charter a helicopter? There are eight sailings daily.

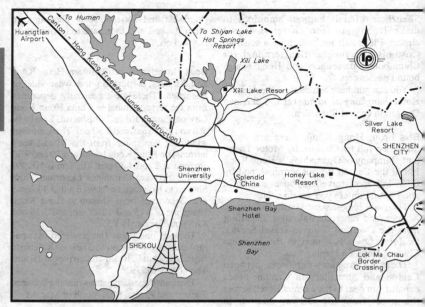

Bus Shenzhen has some of the best public transport in China. The city bus is OK. It's also dirt cheap and not nearly as crowded as elsewhere in China.

The minibuses are faster. These are privately run and cheap, but if you can't read the destination in Chinese characters, you will need help.

Taxi Taxis are abundant but not so cheap, because their drivers have been spoilt by free-spending tourists. There are no meters, so negotiate the fare before you get in. Make sure you understand which currency is being negotiated – drivers will usually ask for payment in Hong Kong dollars.

AROUND SHENZHEN CITY
Splendid China

(jǐnxiù zhōnghuá) 锦绣中华

This is the mainland's answer to Taiwan's *Window on China*. The tourist brochure for Splendid China says 'visit all of China in one day'. You get to see Beijing's Forbid-

den City, the Great Wall, Tibet's Potala Palace, the Shaolin Temple, the gardens of Suzhou, the rock formations of Guilin, the Tianshan Mountains of Xinjiang, the Stone Forest in Yunnan, Huangguoshu Waterfall and even some sights in Taiwan. The catch is that everything is reduced to a fraction of life size.

This place gets mixed reviews from travellers. Some find it intriguing, but others call it a 'bad Disneyland without the rides'. It's more of a carnival than a serious attempt to give you an overview of China, but the Chinese positively flock to this place. If nothing else, Splendid China will give you an idea of the country's best known sights – it could help you decide just what parts of China you'd really like to visit.

Splendid China is at the western end of the SEZ, near Shenzhen Bay. From the railway station there are frequent minibuses. If you're entering Shenzhen by hoverferry, you could take a taxi from Shekou.

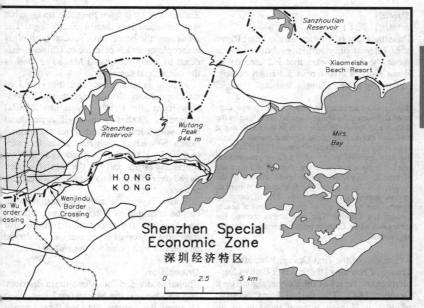

Sanzhoutian
Reservoir

Xiaomeisha
Beach Resort

Shenzhen
Reservoir

Wutong
Peak
944 m

Mirs
Bay

HONG
KONG

o Wu
order
ossing

Wenjindu
Border
Crossing

Shenzhen Special
Economic Zone
深圳经济特区

0   2.5   5 km

China Folk Culture Villages
(zhōngguó mínsú wénhuà cūn)
中国民俗文化村

Adjacent to Splendid China, the China Folk Culture Villages seeks to do the same thing – give you a chance to see all of China in one day. In this case, rather than admiring miniaturised temples and mountains, you get to see full-sized ethnic minorities. To add to the effect, there are over 20 re-creations of minority villages including a cave, Lama temple, drum tower, rattan bridge and a statue of Guanyin (Kuanyin), the Goddess of Mercy. Just to remind you of China's claim to Taiwan, the 'Gaoshan' (high mountain) minority was invented to represent Taiwan's 10 aboriginal tribes. As of yet there are no representatives of Hong Kong's 'foreign devil' minority.

Overseas Chinese Town
(huáqiáo chéng) 华侨城

This is not really meant to be a tourist attrac-tion, but rather a residential area for upper crust Overseas Chinese investors who operate businesses in Shenzhen.

The CTS (Hong Kong branch) has invested heavily in this place, and there is an Overseas Chinese Town CTS branch office (☎ 6601163). If you're interested in coming here to invest or speculate in real estate (a popular Hong Kong activity) this is the office to contact.

The main interest for lower to middle-income travellers is to see how the other half lives and perhaps make use of the newly built shopping centres. The Overseas Chinese Town is just to the north of Splendid China.

Shekou
(shékǒu) 蛇口

A small city at the western end of the Shenzhen SEZ, Shekou is of only minor interest to tourists. A direct hoverferry service links Shekou to Hong Kong Island.

HUMEN
(hǔmén) 虎门

The small city of Humen on the Pearl River is of interest only to history buffs curious about the Opium wars that led directly to Hong Kong's creation as a British colony. According to one Chinese leaflet:

Humen was the place where the Chinese people captured and burned the opium dumped into China by the British and American merchants in the 1830s and it was also the outpost of the Chinese people to fight against the aggressive opium war. In 1839, Lin Zexu, the then imperial envoy of the Qing government, resolutely put a ban on opium smoking and the trade of opium. Supported by the broad masses of the people, Lin Zexu forced the British and American opium mongers to hand over 20,285 cases of opium...and burned all of them at Humen beach, Dongguang County. This just action showed the strong will of the Chinese people to resist imperialist aggression...

At the end of the first Opium War, after the Treaty of Nanking, there was a British Supplementary Treaty of the Bogue, signed on 8 October 1843. The Bogue Forts *(shājiǎo pàotái)* at Humen is now the site of an impressive museum which commemorates the destruction of the surrendered opium which sparked the first Opium War. There are many exhibits, including the large artillery pieces and other relics, and the actual ponds in which Commissioner Lin Zexu had the opium destroyed. When the new museum opened, there was a special exhibition commemorating the 150th anniversary of the war.

The only problem with this place is getting there. No buses go directly to Humen, but buses and minibuses travelling from Shenzhen to Canton go right by. You could ask to be let off at the Humen access road, and then get a taxi, hitch or walk the five km into town.

ZHUHAI
(zhūhǎi) 珠海

From any hilltop in Macau, you can gaze to the north and see a mass of modern buildings just across the border in China. This is the Zhuhai SEZ. Like the Shenzhen SEZ,

Zhuhai was built from the soles up on what was farmland less than a decade ago. The areas near the beach have several high-class resort playgrounds catering to Chinese residents of Hong Kong and Macau as well as the occasional foreigner.

Zhuhai is changing, and the speed of development is almost frightening. Travellers from the 1980s (even *late* 1980s) remember Zhuhai as a small agricultural town with a few rural industries and a quiet beach. Nowadays, high-rise hotels, factories and workers' flats have crowded out the few remaining farms, and half the beach has been paved over to make way for a new waterfront freeway.

Zhuhai is so close to the border that a visit can be arranged as a day trip from Macau, and you can see many of the sights just travelling by foot. Or you can use Zhuhai as an entry or exit point for the rest of China.

Orientation

Zhuhai is divided into three main districts. The area nearest the Macau border is called Gongbei, the main tourist zone. To the northeast is Jida, the eastern part of which has Zhuhai's harbour *(jiǔzhōu gǎng)*. The northernmost section of the city is called Xiangzhou, an area of worker flats and factories.

Information

The CTS office (☎ 885777) is at 4 Shuiwan Lu, opposite the Gongbei Palace Hotel. The PSB (☎ 222459) is in the Xiangzhou District on the south-west corner of Anping Lu and Kangning Lu.

The most useful post office is on Qiaoguang Lu, in Gongbei. You can make IDD calls from your own room in most hotels. The area code for Zhuhai is 0756.

Things to See

Most visitors start their exploration of Zhuhai from the area near the Macau border. It's worth taking a look at the **Gongbei Market** on Yuehua Lu, next to the Overseas Chinese Hotel. It's reasonably clean and not nearly as exotic as the Qingping Market in

GUANGDONG

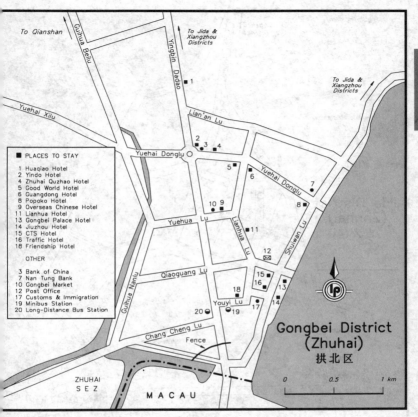

Gongbei District
(Zhuhai)
拱北区

0   0.5   1 km

PLACES TO STAY
1 Huaqiao Hotel
2 Yindo Hotel
4 Zhuhai Quzhao Hotel
5 Good World Hotel
6 Guangdong Hotel
8 Popoko Hotel
9 Overseas Chinese Hotel
11 Lianhua Hotel
13 Gongbei Palace Hotel
14 Jiuzhou Hotel
15 CTS Hotel
16 Traffic Hotel
18 Friendship Hotel

OTHER
3 Bank of China
7 Nan Tung Bank
10 Gongbei Market
12 Post Office
17 Customs & Immigration
19 Minibus Station
20 Long-Distance Bus Station

■ PLACES TO STAY

1 华侨宾馆
2 银都酒店
4 拱北大厦
5 好世界酒店
6 粤海酒店
8 步步高大酒店
9 华侨大酒店
11 莲花大厦
13 拱北宾馆
14 九洲酒店

15 华侨大厦
16 交通大厦
18 友谊酒店

   OTHER

3 中国银行
7 银行
10 拱北市场
12 邮电局
17 海关
19 小公共汽车站
20 长途汽车站

GUANGDONG

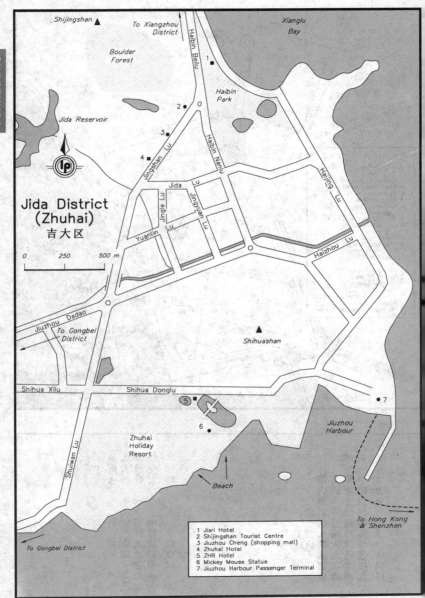

Jida District (Zhuhai)
吉大区

1 Jiari Hotel
2 Shijingshan Tourist Centre
3 Jiuzhou Cheng (shopping mall)
4 Zhuhai Hotel
5 ZHR Hotel
6 Mickey Mouse Statue
7 Jiuzhou Harbour Passenger Terminal

```
1  假日酒店
2  石景山旅游中心
3  九洲城
4  珠海宾馆
5  珠海度假村
6  米老鼠
7  九洲港客运站
```

Canton – they keep the dogmeat hidden when the tour buses come through. It's best in the evening.

The **beach** is the top attraction during the summer months. The nicest stretch of beach is in the Zhuhai Holiday Resort at the south end of the Jida District and west of Jiuzhou harbour. The walk along the coastline from Gongbei to this beach is very pleasant – be sure to wander around the resort itself.

West of Haibin Park in the Jida District is an area called **Shijingshan Tourist Centre** (*shíjǐngshān lǚyóu zhōngxīn*). The tourist centre itself is no big deal, just some gardens, an artificial lake, a supermarket and shops selling tourist junk. However, if you go inside the centre and head towards the back, you'll find some stone steps going uphill. Follow them up and up and you'll quickly find yourself in a forest with big granite boulders all around. Keep climbing to the ridgetop – you'll be rewarded with outstanding views of Zhuhai City, Zhongshan and Macau.

On the south side of Shijingshan Tourist Centre is **Jiuzhou Cheng** (see Jida District map). From the outside, you'll probably think it's some kind of restored Ming Dynasty village. Inside, you'll find that it's a fashionable shopping centre where everything is priced in Hong Kong dollars.

Places to stay – middle
The *Friendship Hotel* (☎ 886683; fax 885212) (*yǒuyí jiǔdiàn*), is at 2 Youyi Lu (Friendship St) Gongbei, near the border gate between Lianhua Lu and Yingbin Dadao. Doubles cost Y120 to Y150, and you must leave a refundable Y100 deposit to ensure that you don't run off with the TV or the toilet.

The *Lianhua Hotel* (☎ 885637) (*liánhuā dàshà*), 13 Lianhua Lu, Gongbei, is in the heart of Zhuhai's liveliest market district. The hotel has no English sign on the door but is easy enough to find. Singles/doubles cost Y70/118.

The *CTS Hotel* (☎ 885777) (*huáqiáo dàshà*), 4 Shuiwan Lu, Gongbei, is operated by guess who? Doubles cost as little as Y72, though these are often full and you might have to settle for fancier facilities costing Y138.

Just next door is the *Traffic Hotel* (☎ 884474) (*jiāotōng dàshà*) at 1 Shuimen Lu, Gongbei, with doubles for Y180.

A little further from the border is the *Overseas Chinese Hotel* (☎ 885183) (*huáqiáo dàjiǔdiàn*), on the north side of Yuehua Lu between Yingbin Dadao and Lianhua Lu, right next to the Gongbei Market. Doubles are Y108 to Y136.

The *Huaqiao Hotel* (☎ 885123) (*huáqiáo bīnguǎn*) on Yingbin Dadao in Gongbei, one block north of Yuehai Donglu, has double rooms for Y160 and Y186. It's a good quiet place to stay with an excellent restaurant.

The *Popoko Hotel* (☎ 886628) (*bùbùgāo dàjiǔdiàn*) is at 2 Yuehai Donglu, on the corner with Shuiwan Lu near the waterfront in Gongbei. Doubles come in four flavours costing Y170, Y180, Y220 and Y240. This is quite an attractive hotel on the inside and the lower-priced rooms seem quite a bargain.

Tucked away in the forested grounds of Haibin Park is the quiet (except on weekends) *Jiari Hotel* (☎ 333277) (*jiàrì jiǔdiàn*). Doubles cost Y180 to Y300. Haibin Park is in the Jida District north-east of Gongbei, within walking distance of the Shijingshan Tourist Centre and luxurious Zhuhai Hotel.

Zhuhai Quzhao Hotel (☎ 886256) (*gǒngběi dàshà*) on Yuehai Donglu in Gongbei looks palatial on the outside, but has doubles for as little as Y138. Nevertheless, it doesn't seem to be popular, possibly because of the exceedingly unfriendly staff.

Places to Stay – top end
The *Good World Hotel* (☎ 880222) (*hǎo*

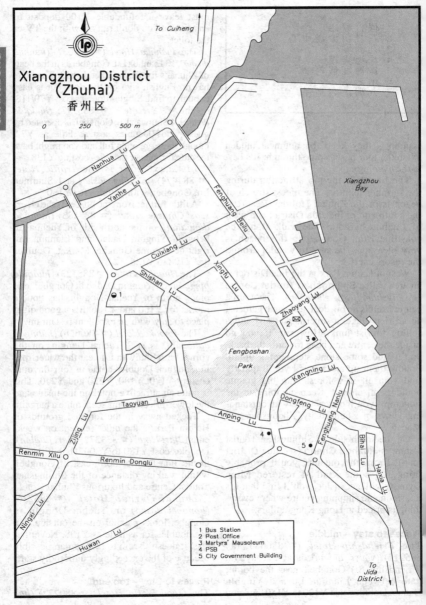

Xiangzhou District (Zhuhai)
香州区

0   250   500 m

To Cuiheng

Xiangzhou Bay

Nanhua Lu

Yanhe Lu

Fenghuang Beilu

Cuixiang Lu

Xingfu Lu

Shishan Lu

Zhaoyang Lu

Fengboshan Park

Kangning Lu

Dongfeng Lu

Taoyuan Lu

Anping Lu

Fenghuang Nanlu

Bihai Lu

Renmin Xilu

Renmin Donglu

Ning xi Lu

Zijing Lu

Huwan Lu

Haixia Lu

1 Bus Station
2 Post Office
3 Martyrs' Mausoleum
4 PSB
5 City Government Building

To Jida District

1	车站
2	邮局
3	烈士陵园
4	公安局外事科
5	市政府

shìjiè jiǔdiàn) at 82 Lianhua Lu, Gongbei is a fine place at the lower end of the top-end accommodation. Deluxe doubles are Y250. There is a 10% surcharge with another 10% on weekends or 20% on major holidays.

The *Gongbei Palace Hotel* (☎ 886833; fax 885686) (*gǒngběi bīnguǎn*) is the most luxurious place close to the border. It's by the waterfront on Shuiwan Lu near Qiaoguang Lu, about a one-minute walk from the border crossing. Among the facilities are a disco, video game arcade, sauna and swimming pool (including water slide). Unfortunately, the beach is too rocky for swimming. The hotel runs bus tours of the surrounding area. Like most top-end places in Zhuhai, they ask for payment in Hong Kong dollars but will reluctantly accept FEC. Deluxe twins cost Y420 (HK$570) or take advantage of the cheaper villas where singles/twins are Y296/355 (HK$400/480). There is an additional 15% service charge. At least these prices keep out the riff-raff.

Adjacent to the Gongbei Palace is the *Jiuzhou Hotel* (☎ 886851) (*jiǔzhōu jiǔdiàn*). Once known as a budget hotel, it has moved upmarket; doubles start at Y207 and skyrocket to Y363 for cushier rooms. It's on the waterfront on Shuiwan Lu near Qiaoguang Lu and south of the Gongbei Palace Hotel, a stone's throw from the border.

Guangdong Hotel (☎ 889115; fax 885063) (*yuèhǎi jiǔdiàn*), 34 Yuehai Donglu, Gongbei, is a flashy place where standard doubles cost Y310 (HK$418) and deluxe singles/doubles are Y316/332 (HK$428/448). There is a 15% surcharge and Hong Kong dollars are definitely favoured.

The ultra-modern *Yindo Hotel* (☎ 883388; fax 883311) (*yíndū jiǔdiàn*) in Gongbei is a gleaming glass and steel high-rise dominat-ing Zhuhai's skyline. Amenities include a bowling alley and miniature golf course. Standard twins start at Y342; somewhat cosier rooms are Y400, Y456 and Y513. Or you can rent the presidential suite for a mere Y6840. There is a 15% surcharge plus 10% more on weekends and 20% more on holidays. The hotel is on the corner of Yuehai Lu and Yingbin Dadao.

The *Zhuhai Holiday Resort* (☎ 332038; fax 332036) (*zhūhǎi dùjià cūn*) or *ZHR* is a five-star resort in Jida with the best beach in Zhuhai and amenities such as a bowling alley, roller rink, tennis courts, club house, go-cart racing, horse riding, camel riding, disco, karaoke, video game parlour and sauna. This is a place to wrap yourself in luxury if you can afford it and don't mind the fact that it doesn't look or feel much like traditional China. The resort is on the shore-line north-east of Gongbei near Jiuzhou Harbour. Single rooms in the main hotel start from Y272 (HK$368), but a villa for two people is a better deal at Y235 (HK$318). There is a 15% surcharge.

The *Zhuhai Hotel* (☎ 333718; fax 332339) (*zhūhǎi bīnguǎn*) in Jida is another playground for the upper crust. However, it doesn't have the benefit of a beach, which makes it much less worth the expense. Nevertheless, it caters to every whim and has a sauna, tennis courts, billiard room, swimming pool, nightclub and even mahjong rooms. Doubles cost Y287 (HK$388), Y435 (HK$588) and Y495 (HK$668), while villas start at Y730 (HK$988). There is also a 15% surcharge. Children under 12 are free if sharing the same accommodation. You can book in Macau (☎ 552275).

Getting There & Away

To/From Macau Simply walk across the border. In Macau, bus Nos 3 and 5 lead to the Barrier Gate, from where you make the crossing on foot. The Macau-Zhuhai border is open from 7 am to 9 pm.

To/From Canton Buses to Zhuhai depart from the bus station across the street from the railway station, just west of the Liuhua

Hotel. The large government buses are cheaper, but less frequent, slower and more crowded. Minibuses from this station are air-con, cost Y30 and leave according to a posted schedule. Unscheduled minibuses cost Y25 and cruise in front of the station in a circular direction (south on Renmin Beilu then back on Zhanqian Lu) looking for passengers. All buses and minibuses accept payment in RMB.

Going the other way, buses from Zhuhai to Canton depart from the main bus terminal on Youyi Lu, directly opposite the Customs building (the border checkpoint). The minibus station is also on Youyi Lu, one block west of the Customs building.

To/From Hong Kong Jetcats (jet-powered catamarans) between Zhuhai and Hong Kong do the trip in about 70 minutes. Departure times are at 7.45 and 11 am and at 2.30 pm. Boats depart from the ferry terminal at China Hong Kong City on Canton Rd in Tsimshatsui, and cost HK$151 on weekdays and HK$161 on weekends.

Going the other way, departures are from Jiuzhou harbour in Zhuhai at 9.30 am, 1 and 4.45 pm. Even when you buy the ticket in Zhuhai, you must pay in Hong Kong dollars! If you argue long enough and loud enough, however, the staff will eventually allow you to pay in FEC after tacking on an extra 50% 'service charge'. In Zhuhai, the official fare is supposed to be HK$118.

To/From Shenzhen A high-speed ferry operates between the port of Shekou in Shenzhen and Jiuzhou harbour (jiǔzhōu gǎng) in Zhuhai (Jida). There are five departures daily in each direction. From Shenzhen, the first boat is at 9 am and the last is at 4.30 pm. From Zhuhai, the first departure is at 8.20 am and the last is at 3 pm. Despite the fact that this is a domestic service, foreigners must pay in Hong Kong dollars! The fare for the fast boats is HK$110, but the staff on the Zhuhai side inexplicably seem to add on an extra HK$20 above the ticket price! If you argue, they tell you to swim.

Getting Around

Bus Zhuhai has a decent public transport system. The routes are clearly shown on the Zhuhai city map and you shouldn't have any trouble figuring it out. Minibuses ply the same routes and cost Y2 for any place in the city. Minibuses will stop in the public bus stops and most other places, but cannot stop right in major intersections.

Taxi You are most likely to use taxis to shuttle between your hotel and the boats at Jiuzhou harbour. Zhuhai taxis have no meters and fares are strictly by negotiation. Drivers typically try to charge foreigners double. A fair price from the Macau border to Jiuzhou harbour is around Y25, but given China's inflation rate, it's best to first ask a neutral bystander (try the desk clerks at your hotel) what the current proper fare is.

AROUND ZHUHAI

In the village of Cuiheng, north of the city limits of Zhuhai, is **Dr Sun Yatsen's Residence** (sūn zhōngshān gùjū). China's most famous revolutionary, Dr Sun Yatsen was born in a house on this site on 12 November 1866. That house was torn down after a new home was built in 1892. This second house is still standing and open to the public. The site also has a museum, but the Chinese have turned the place into something of a circus. Admission is Y1.

Dr Sun dedicated his life to the overthrow of the corrupt and brutal Qing (Manchu) Dynasty. His goal was to do away with dynasties altogether and establish a Chinese republic based on Western democratic principles. He organised several uprisings, all of which failed. As a result, he spent much of his life in exile because of a price on his head. There is no doubt that he would have faced a horrible death by torture if the emperor had succeeded in capturing him.

When the actual revolution came in 1911, Dr Sun wasn't in China. Still, there is no denying his role as a major organiser and instigator of the revolution. Sun Yatsen is widely regarded as the father of his country and has been deified by both the Communist Party and the Nationalists in Taiwan. He briefly served as the first president of the Republic of China. He died in 1925 from liver cancer at the age of 59. His wife was Soong Chingling, the sister of Soong Mayling (Madam Chiang Kaishek).

Just before you reach the Zhuhai City limits, you pass **Pearl Land** *(zhēnzhū lèyuán)*, another Chinese amusement park, which isn't worth stopping for unless you're really into roller coasters.

In Cuiheng there are two hotels – the huge *Cuiheng Hotel (cuìhēng bīnguǎn)* and the

smaller *Cuiheng Jiudian*. You're unlikely to want to spend the night here unless you're a Sun Yatsen-ophile.

There are frequent minibuses to Cuiheng departing from Gongbei near the border checkpoint. The fare was Y8 last time we went and the bus wasn't in good shape – the door fell off.

ZHONGSHAN CITY
(zhōngshān shì) 中山市
The administrative centre of the county by the same name, Zhongshan City is also

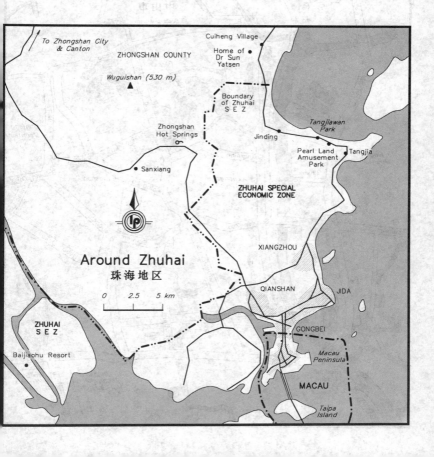

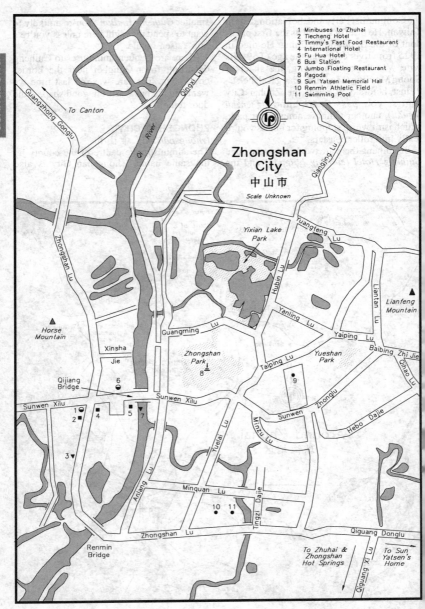

1 Minibuses to Zhuhai
2 Tiecheng Hotel
3 Timmy's Fast Food Restaurant
4 International Hotel
5 Fu Hua Hotel
6 Bus Station
7 Jumbo Floating Restaurant
8 Pagoda
9 Sun Yatsen Memorial Hall
10 Renmin Athletic Field
11 Swimming Pool

Zhongshan
City
中山市

Scale Unknown

To Canton

Qi River

Guangzhong Gonglu

Qingxi Lu

Qianging Lu

Yixian Lake
Park

Yuangfeng Lu

Zhongshan Lu

Hubin Lu

Lianfeng
Mountain

Liantan Lu

Horse
Mountain

Guangming Lu

Yanling Lu

Yaiping Lu

Baibing Zhi Jie

Xinsha
Jie

Zhongshan
Park
8

Taiping Lu

Yueshan
Park
9

Qihao Jie

Qijiang
Bridge

6

Sunwen Xilu

Zhonglu

Sunwen

Hebo Dajie

Sunwen Xilu

1
2 4

5 7

3

Yuelai Lu

Minzu Lu

Anlang Lu

Minquan Lu

10 11

Renmin
Bridge

Zhongshan Lu

Tingzi Dajie

Qiguang Donglu

Qiguang Lu

To Zhuhai &
Zhongshan
Hot Springs

To Sun
Yatsen's
Home

1	开往朱海的小汽车
2	铁城酒店
3	添美食
4	国际酒店
5	富华酒店
6	汽车站
7	珍宝海鲜舫
8	烟墩山宝塔
9	孙中山纪念堂
10	人民体育场
11	游泳池

known as Shiqi. An industrial city, it bears little resemblance to Zhuhai and could hardly be called a main tourist attraction. Still, you must pass through here if doing the circuit from Cuiheng to Zhongshan Hot Springs. The city is worth perhaps 45 minutes of time to walk around.

Things to See

The one and only scenic spot in town is **Zhongshan Park**, which is pleasantly forested and dominated by a large hill *(yāndūn shān)* topped with a pagoda. It's visible from most parts of the city so it's easy to find. It's nice and quiet in the park (except on Sunday) and a climb to the top of the pagoda will reward you with a sweeping view of the city's factories and air pollution. Perhaps this explains why the English translation of the hill's name is 'smoky mound'.

There is a large **Sun Yatsen Memorial Hall** *(sūn zhōngshān jìniàn táng)* on Sunwen Zhonglu to the east of Zhongshan Park. The car park is often jammed with tour buses from Macau, though there is nothing special about this place. The most worthwhile sight is the old, rusting MIG fighter parked on the lawn, a relic of the Korean War.

Apart from the pagoda in Zhongshan Park, the other dominant feature on the skyline of Zhongshan City is the **Fu Hua Hotel**, a huge golden building topped with a revolving restaurant. The hotel has a disco, sauna, bowling alley, billiard room and swimming pool. You might be curious as to why anybody would build this stunning resort hotel in the middle of an industrial wasteland such as Zhongshan City. I asked numerous Hong Kongers this question and the answer was always the same – everyone is here on business.

Places to Stay

Should you be so taken with Zhongshan City that you want to stay, the cheapest place accepting foreigners is the *Tiecheng* ('Iron City') *Hotel* (☎ 823803; fax 821103) *(tiěchéng jiǔdiàn)* at Zhongshan Lu and Sunwen Xilu. Doubles start at Y130 plus a 10% service charge.

Across the street is the *International Hotel* (☎ 824788; fax 824736) *(guójì jiǔdiàn)*, 1 Zhongshan Lu, where doubles cost Y318 to Y410.

Top of the line is the *Fu Hua Hotel* (☎ 822034; fax 828678) *(fùhuá jiǔdiàn)*, which has doubles for Y318. If you want to spend your honeymoon here, there are honeymoon suites for Y488 and the presidential suite goes for a trifling Y3700. There is a 10% service charge.

Most likely, you won't want to stay in Zhongshan City unless you decide to open a factory there.

Places to Eat

In addition to the usual abundance of cheap noodle shops, elegant seafood dining is available at the *Jumbo Floating Restaurant* *(zhēnbǎo hǎixiān fǎng)* on the Qi River.

Fast food has made its debut in Zhongshan City. *Timmy's (tiān měi shí)* on Zhongshan Lu (south of Sunwen Xilu) can satisfy a sudden attack of uncontrollable lust for French fries, hamburgers and milkshakes.

Getting There & Away

The quickest way out of town is to catch a minibus from the car park of the Tiecheng Hotel.

AROUND ZHONGSHAN

The Zhongshan Hot Springs *(zhōngshān wēnquán)* resort has indoor hot springs and a golf course. If you're a real enthusiast of either activity, you might want to

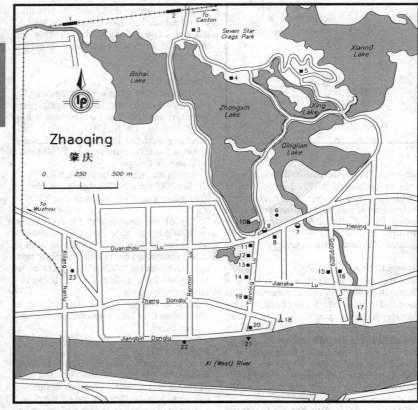

Zhaoqing
肇庆

spend a night here. Otherwise, you'll probably just want to look around briefly and then head back to Gongbei. Considering the palatial surroundings, the *Zhongshan Hot Springs Hotel* (☎ 683888; fax 683333) isn't horribly expensive but they like Hong Kong dollars. Doubles are Y148 (HK$200) to Y259 (HK$350) plus 10% service charge.

A minibus drops you by the entrance to the resort, then it's a ½-km walk to the hotel. For Y1 you can hire someone to carry you on the back of a bicycle. You won't have to look for them as they'll be looking for you. To get back to Gongbei, flag down any minibus you see passing the resort entrance. A minibus from the hot springs to Gongbei costs Y4.

ZHAOQING

(zhàoqìng) 肇庆

For almost 1000 years people have been coming to Zhaoqing to scribble graffiti on its cliffs or inside its caves – often poems or essays describing how much they liked the rock formations they were drawing on.

If you're going to Guilin or Yangshuo, you

■ PLACES TO STAY

3	Bohailou Hotel	波海楼
4	Songtao Hotel	松涛滨馆
5	Xingyan Hotel	星岩宾馆
8	Star Lake Hotel	星湖大厦店
10	Huguang Hotel	湖光大酒店
11	Huaqiao Hotel	华侨大厦
12	Duanzhou Hotel	端州大酒店
14	Xinhua Hotel & Bookstore	新华旅店／新华书店
15	Jinye Hotel	金叶大厦
16	Huata Hotel	花塔酒店
19	Holiday Hotel	假日酒店
20	Yuehai Hotel	粤海大厦

▼ PLACES TO EAT

| 21 | Floating Restaurant | 海鲜舫 |

OTHER

1	Main Railway Station	肇庆火车站
2	Seven Star Crags Railway Station	七星岩火车站
6	Star Lake Amusement Park	星湖游乐园
7	Long Distance Bus Station	市汽车站
9	Local Bus Station	公共汽车站
13	Bicycle Rentals	租自行车店
17	Chongxi Pagoda	崇禧塔
18	Yuejiang Temple	阅江楼
22	Passenger Ferry Terminal	肇庆港客运站
23	Plum Monastery	梅庵

could easily give this place a miss, but it's fair to say that Zhaoqing is the most beautiful place in all of Guangdong Province.

Orientation

Zhaoqing, 110 km west of Canton on the Xi River, is bounded to the south by the river and to the north by the immense Seven Star Crags Park. Zhaoqing is a small place and much of it can be seen on foot.

Seven Star Crags

(qī xīng yán) 七星岩

Zhaoqing's premier attraction, the Seven Star Crags is a group of limestone towers – a peculiar geological formation abundant in the paddy fields of Guilin and Yangshuo. Legend has it that the crags were actually seven stars that fell from the sky to form a pattern resembling the

Big Dipper. In keeping with their celestial origin each has been given an exotic name like 'Hill Slope' and 'Toad'. The artificial lakes were built in 1955, and the park is adorned with concrete pathways, arched bridges and little pavilions.

The crags are in a large park on the north side of town. Hire a bicycle and head off along the paths away from the lake. Old villages, duck ponds, door gods, buffalo swimming in ponds, strange pavilions and caves can all be found.

Chongxi Pagoda

(chóngxī tǎ) 崇禧塔

This nine-storey pagoda on Tajiao Lu in the south-east was in a sad state after the Cultural Revolution, but was restored in the 1980s.

Around
Zhaoqing
肇庆地区

0   1   2 km

Seven Star
Crags

Bohai
Lake

Dong
Lake

Zhongxin
Lake

GAOYAO COUNTY

Qinglian
Lake

Huguang
Lake

ZHAOQING CITY

To Dinghushan

Flowery
Pagoda

Yuejiang
Tower

Xi (West) River

On the opposite bank of the river are two similar pagodas. Tajiao Lu, a quiet riverside street, has interesting old houses.

Yuejiang Temple
(yuèjiāng lóu) 阅江楼
This is a restored temple about 30 minutes' walk from the Chongxi Pagoda, just back from the waterfront at the eastern end of Zheng Donglu.

Plum Monastery
(méi ān) 梅庵
This small monastery by a lake is in the western part of town off Zheng Xilu.

Dinghushan
(dǐnghú shān) 鼎湖山
Twenty km east of Zhaoqing, this is one of the best scenic spots in Guangdong, at least equal to the Seven Star Crags. Apart from its streams, brooks, pools, hills and trees, the mountain is noted for the Qingyuan Temple,

built towards the end of the Ming Dynasty. Dinghushan can be visited as a day trip from Zhaoqing.

Places to Stay
Many budget travellers stay at the *Huata Hotel* (☎ 232423) *(huātǎ jiǔdiàn)*, 5 Gongnong Beilu. Doubles with shared bath are Y50, or Y84 with private bath. Carpeting makes it Y109, or you can bask in luxury for Y165 and Y193.

The *Duanzhou Hotel* (☎ 233215) *(duānzhōu dàjiǔdiàn)*, 77 Tianning Beilu, is certainly one of the better deals in town. Although it looks frightfully expensive on the outside, singles/doubles cost Y58/98. Just how long it will stay so reasonable is uncertain.

The *Xinhua Hotel* (☎ 22574) *(xīnhuá lǚdiàn)* on Tianning Beilu is just behind the Xinhua Bookstore (everybody in Zhaoqing is getting into the hotel business!). Rooms start at Y70.

Another reasonable alternative is the *Holiday Hotel* (☎ 221688; fax 221898) *(jiàrì jiǔdiàn)* at the southern end of Tianning Beilu. Singles/doubles are Y138/180.

The *Xinghuwan Songyuan* (☎ 227521) is a collection of three hotels right in Seven Star Crag Park. On the north side is the *Bohailou Hotel (bōhǎilóu)*, attractive and quiet but not as placid as the other two. More towards the centre of the park is the *Xingyan Hotel (xīngyán bīnguǎn)* and just to the west of that is the very pleasant *Songtao Hotel* (☎ 224412) *(sōngtāo bīnguǎn)*. Doubles cost Y88, Y128, Y168 and Y200, and a room for four is Y250.

On the lake but not quite as nice is the *Huguang Hotel* (☎ 224904, 224905) *(húguāng jiǔdiàn)*. Rooms are Y135, Y150 and Y160. The hotel is just inside the main gate on Duanzhou Lu.

The *Yuehai Hotel (yuèhǎi dàshà)* on Jiangbin Donglu and Tianning Nanlu, is on the banks of the Xi River and was under renovation at the time of writing. It looks like it will be a mid to upmarket place when reopened.

Jinye Hotel (☎ 221338; fax 221368) *(jīnyè*

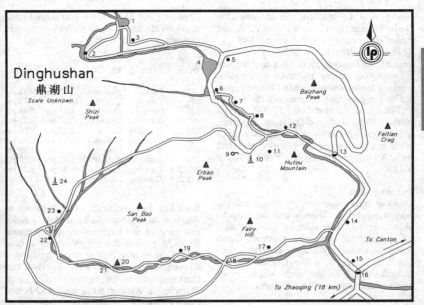

Dinghushan
鼎湖山
Scale Unknown

1	Heaven Lake (Tianhu)
2	Cliff Face Plank Path (Lantianzhandao)
3	No 1 Hydroelectric Station
4	Grass Pond
5	No 2 Hydroelectric Station
6	Twin Rainbow Bridge (Shuanghongfeqian)
7	Tingpu Pavilion
8	Sun Yatsen Swimming Area
9	Gulong Spring
10	Qingyun Temple
11	Tea Flower Pavilion (Huachage)
12	Half Mountain Pavilion
13	Bus Station
14	Archway
15	Kengkou Store
16	Kengkou Bus Station
17	Crane Viewing Pavilion
18	Ping Lake
19	Lion's Roar Rock (Shihoushi)
20	Pearl Mouth Mountain (Hanzhujian)
21	White Goose Pond (Bai'etan)
22	Leaping Dragon Pool (Yuelongtan)
23	Leaping Dragon Nunnery (Yuelong'an)
24	White Cloud Temple

1	天湖	
2	连天栈道	
3	水电一站	
4	草塘	
5	水电二站	
6	双虹飞堑	
7	听瀑亭	
8	孙中山游泳处	
9	古龙泉	
10	庆云寺	
11	花茶阁	
12	半山亭	
13	鼎湖山汽车站	
14	牌楼	
15	坑口商店	
16	坑口汽车站	
17	望鹤亭	
18	平湖	
19	狮吼石	
20	含珠涧	
21	白鹅潭	
22	跃龙潭	
23	跃龙庵	
24	白云寺	

dàshà) is at the southern end of Gongnong Beilu. Doubles cost from Y178 to Y238, and suites are available for Y488 and Y588.

Huaqiao Hotel (☎ 232952) *(huáqiáo dàshà)*, 90 Tianning Beilu, has an excellent location but prices to make you pause. Singles/doubles cost Y298/Y438 and triples Y598; the presidential suite goes for Y3628.

The *Star Lake Hotel* (☎ 221188) *(xīnghú dàshà)*, 37 Duanzhou 4-Lu, is a multistorey, glass high-rise that looks ridiculously out of place in a town noted for its parks, lakes and hills. All this gaudiness costs Y280, Y303 or Y325.

Places to Eat

One can only hope that the Songs and the Jesuits ate better. There's nothing remarkable to be had here. The bus station has a cheap, tolerable restaurant; there are cheap restaurants along Duanzhou Lu and Tianning Lu. There is a *Floating Restaurant* *(hǎixiān fǎng)* on the river which serves seafood and attracts Hong Kongers.

Getting There & Away

Bus There are buses to Zhaoqing from Canton's long-distance bus station. The fare is Y20. There are half a dozen buses a day and the trip takes about 2½ hours. Try to avoid returning to Canton on a weekend afternoon; traffic jams are common on this road.

Privately run minibuses operate between Zhaoqing and Canton. In Zhaoqing the minibus ticket office is inside the main gate of the Seven Star Crags Park.

Train Be careful – there are two railway stations in Zhaoqing. All trains stop at the main railway station *(zhàoqìng huǒchē zhàn)* but only train Nos 351 and 356 stop at the Seven Star Crags railway station *(qīxīngyán huǒchē zhàn)*. If you get into a taxi and say you want to go to the railway station, drivers will automatically assume you mean the main railway station.

Trains from Canton cost Y25 (hard seat) and take two to three hours. All trains also stop at Foshan. Train Nos 69 and 70 connect

Zhaoqing and Shenzhen – you do not need to get off at Canton if you wish to go straight through.

Train No	From	To	Depart	Arrive
351	Canton	Zhaoqing	7.25 am	9.51 am
69	Canton	Zhaoqing	11.07 am	1.20 pm
353	Canton	Zhaoqing	4.45 pm	7.43 pm
355	Canton	Zhaoqing	7 pm	9.25 pm
352	Zhaoqing	Canton	7.15 am	9.56 am
354	Zhaoqing	Canton	10.12 am	12.50 pm
70	Zhaoqing	Canton	2.25 pm	4.30 pm
356	Zhaoqing	Canton	5.45 pm	8.22 pm
282/283	Zhanjiang	Zhaoqing	6.30 pm	3.59 am
281/284	Zhaoqing	Zhanjiang	11.59 pm	10.20 am

Boat The dock and ticket office for boats to Wuzhou and Canton is at 3 Jiangbin Donglu, just west of the intersection with Renmin Nanlu. It appears that only lower-class boat tickets can be bought here since Zhaoqing is an intermediate stop. Boats to Wuzhou and Canton depart in the early evening. From Zhaoqing to Wuzhou takes around 12 hours. From Zhaoqing to Canton is a 10-hour trip. The boat is not popular because it's so slow. In Canton, departures are from Dashatou Wharf.

In the tourist season (summer and holidays), there are direct boats to/from Hong Kong.

Getting Around

The local bus station is on Duanzhou Lu, a few minutes' walk east of the intersection with Tianning Lu. Bus No 1 runs to the ferry dock on the Xi River. Bus Nos 4 and 5 go to the Plum Monastery.

The railway station is well out of town near the north-west corner of the lake. A taxi into town costs Y12 or you can grab a minibus for Y2.

Aside from walking, the best way to get around Zhaoqing is by bicycle. There is a hire place diagonally opposite the main entrance to the Seven Star Crags, and another south of the Duanzhou Hotel in Tianning Lu. They ask exorbitant fees if you have a foreign face, but will accept Y10 per day.

ZHANJIANG

(zhànjiāng) 潮州

Zhanjiang is a major port on the southern coast of China, and the largest Chinese port west of Canton. It was leased to France in 1898 and remained under French control until WW II. Today the French are back, but this time Zhanjiang is a base for their oil-exploration projects in the South China Sea.

You're most likely to come to Zhanjiang if you're on your way from Canton or Nanning to Hainan Island. It's a good place to wander around at night when the crowds are out in the streets, but is rather dusty and boring during the day – too many concrete blocks, drab streets and slums.

Perhaps to liven things up the Chinese have opened some coral reefs to snorkelling and scuba diving. However, Sanya in Hainan Island is a better place to pursue such activities.

Orientation & Information

Zhanjiang is divided into two parts. The north section is called the Chikan District *(chìkǎn qū)* and the south is Xiashan *(xiàshān qū)*. The CTS (☎ 228775) has a small office in the Canton Bay Hotel, 16 Renmin Lu.

Places to Stay

Xiashan District (South) The southern part of town is the most convenient for travellers and has the widest selection of hotels.

The *Canton Bay Hotel* (☎ 281966; fax 281347), 16 Renmin Lu, offers both cheap and luxurious rooms. Budget doubles with electric fan and private bath cost Y48. With air-con and carpeting, the tariff for doubles is Y108 to Y156. This is probably the best of the lot in the low to mid-range category. range.

The *Zhanjiang Traffic Hotel* (☎ 221129) *(zhànjiāng jiāotōng jiǔdiàn)*, 33 Jiefang Lu, is convenient for the railway station. Unfortunately, it's a grotty place although at the time of writing it was under renovation.

The *Friendship Hotel* is a popular place in the centre of town. Singles/doubles/triples are Y53/80/93.

The *Cuiyuan Hotel* (☎ 221688, 225167), 124 Minzhi Lu, is a small but very comfortable hotel. Rooms cost Y80, Y90 and Y100.

The *Haiwan Hotel* on Renmin Lu is also the location of the International Seamen's Club and boasts a karaoke bar. Doubles cost Y105 and Y135. Just around the corner is the *Zhangang Hotel*, which has similar prices.

The *Haifu Grand Hotel (hǎifù dàjiǔdiàn)* by the harbour is indeed grand. A 'sea view' room costs Y138 and a 'city view' room is Y128. Suites are Y238. There is a 10% service charge.

The *Haibin Hotel* (☎ 286888; fax 280747) *(hǎibīn bīnguǎn)* at 32 Haibin 2-Lu is a luxurious Hong Kong joint venture on the outskirts of the southern part of town. Double rooms are Y200. The hotel boasts tree-shaded grounds, an outdoor pool and a sauna.

Chikan District (North) In the northern part of town, only two hotels accept foreigners.

The *Chikan Hotel* (☎ 337611) *(chìkǎn bīnguǎn)*, 2 Yuejin Lu, has rooms starting from Y80.

The *Zhanjiang Guesthouse* (☎ 315388; fax 310603) *(zhànjiāng yíng bīnguǎn)*, 3 Yuejin Lu, is the best appointed in this part of town, with rooms at Y100.

Getting There & Away

Air The CAAC office (☎ 224415) is at 23 Renmin Nan Dadao, but CTS in the Canton Bay Hotel can arrange tickets for you. There are three weekly 'charter flights' between Zhanjiang and Hong Kong.

There are daily flights from Zhanjiang to Canton (Y350) and Shenzhen (Y390), and once-weekly flights to/from Beijing (Y1200) and Changsha (Y480).

Bus There are plenty of buses to Canton from both the north and south bus stations, as well as from the Canton Bay Hotel (CTS office) and elsewhere. The trip takes about 11 hours. But there's one catch – they all run

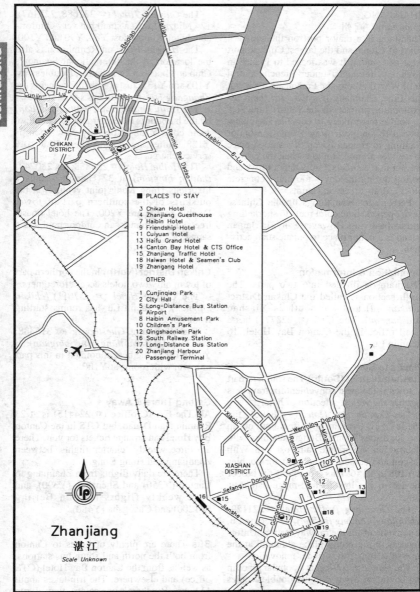

PLACES TO STAY

3 Chikan Hotel
4 Zhanjiang Guesthouse
7 Haibin Hotel
9 Friendship Hotel
11 Cuiyuan Hotel
13 Haifu Grand Hotel
14 Canton Bay Hotel & CTS Office
15 Zhanjiang Traffic Hotel
18 Haiwan Hotel & Seamen's Club
19 Zhangang Hotel

OTHER

1 Cunjinqiao Park
2 City Hall
5 Long-Distance Bus Station
6 Airport
8 Haibin Amusement Park
10 Children's Park
12 Qingshaonian Park
16 South Railway Station
17 Long-Distance Bus Station
20 Zhanjiang Harbour
   Passenger Terminal

Zhanjiang
湛江
Scale Unknown

■ PLACES TO STAY

3 赤坎宾馆
4 湛江迎宾馆
7 海滨宾馆
9 友谊宾馆
11 翠园饭店
13 海富大酒店
14 广州湾华侨宾馆/中国旅行社
15 湛江交通旅店
18 海湾宾馆/海员俱乐部
19 湛港宾馆

OTHER

1 寸金桥公园
2 市政府
5 湛江汽车客运站
6 飞机场
8 海滨游乐中心
10 儿童公园
12 青少年公园
16 湛江火车站
17 霞山汽车客运站
20 湛江港客运站

at night, because the Chinese prefer to sleep during the journey. The fare is Y80 for a bus with air-con and nonstop bloodbath kungfu videos from Hong Kong. There are also numerous buses to Shenzhen. Only one bus a day goes to Zhaoqing, departing from the inconvenient north bus station.

Train Trains to Guilin, Nanning and Canton leave from the south railway station. From Zhanjiang to Guilin takes about 13 hours. From Zhanjiang to Nanning takes about 9½ hours.

Train No	From	To	Depart	Arrive
281/284	Canton	Zhanjiang	9.30 pm	10.20 am
282/283	Zhanjiang	Canton	6.30 pm	6.27 am

Boat You can take a bus-boat combination to Haikou on Hainan Island. A bus takes you from Zhanjiang to Hai'an on the Leizhou Peninsula (five hours), where you take a boat to Haikou (two hours). The bus station at Hai'an is about 100 metres uphill from the harbour. The harbour ticket office is a dingy place, but you can deposit baggage here. Combined bus/boat tickets cost Y45.

Getting Around

There are two railway stations and two long-distance bus stations, one each in the northern and southern parts of town. The southern railway station is the main one.

Bus No 1 runs between the two parts. This bus may be designated by a double-headed arrow (surrounded by calligraphy) rather than by a numeral.

There are many motorcycles with sidecars cruising the streets; Y5 is enough for all locations within a couple of km from where you disembark.

SHANTOU

(shàntóu) 汕头

Considering the length of the southern and south-eastern coasts of China, they are remarkably deficient in seaports. The main problem is the constant accumulation of silt and mud rendering the natural harbours cramped and shallow. Only a few places, like Xiamen and Hong Kong, are fortunate enough to have unlimited deep-water accommodation. On top of that, the mainland ports are handicapped by the mountainous country which surrounds many of them, making communication and transport of goods difficult.

Previously known to the outside world as Swatow, Shantou is the chief port of eastern Guangdong. As early as the 18th century the East India Company had a station on an island outside the harbour, when the town was little more than a fishing village on a mudflat. The port was officially opened up to foreign trade in 1860 with the Treaty of Tianjin, which ended another Opium War. The British were the first to establish themselves here, though their projected settlement

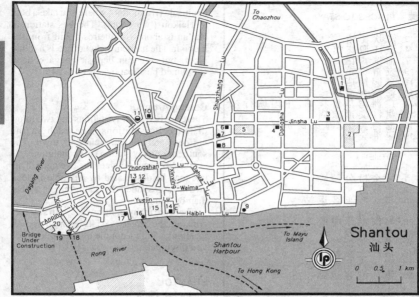

had to relocate to a nearby island due to local hostility. Before 1870 foreigners were living and trading in Shantou town itself.

Today Shantou is the first major stop on the long haul along the coast road from Canton to Fujian. This colourful, lively place is the centre of a unique local culture that extends as far north as Chaozhou. Shantou and the surrounding area has its own language (called *Chao Shan* in Mandarin – a combination of Chaozhou and Shantou – or *tae jiu* by the people themselves) and its own cuisine. Because many of the Overseas Chinese living in Thailand come from the Shantou-Chaozhou area, it's not unusual to see the occasional business sign written in the Thai language as well as Chinese.

Shantou was one of China's original four SEZs, the other three being Shenzhen, Xiamen and Zhuhai. With China's increas-

ingly export-dependent economy, the designation 'SEZ' means much less than it used to, but there is no doubt that Shantou benefited from its special status.

Orientation
Most of Shantou lies on a peninsula, bounded in the south by the ocean and separated from the mainland in the west and the north by a river and canals. The bulk of the tourist amenities are in the western part of the peninsula.

Information
You'll find the PSB on Yuejin Lu, near the corner of Nanmai Lu. The CTS office (☎ 233966) is in the Huaqiao Hotel. They sell bus tickets to Canton, Shenzhen and Xiamen, boat tickets to Hong Kong and air tickets to wherever CAAC flies.

The Bank of China has a branch in the Huaqiao Hotel, and the black-market

■ PLACES TO STAY	▼ PLACES TO EAT
1 Longhu Hotel	2 Longhu Amusement Park
3 Jinlong Hotel	5 Jinsha Park
4 International Hotel	7 CAAC
6 Swatow Peninsula Hotel	9 Stone Fort
8 Huaqiao Hotel, CTS &	11 Long Distance Bus Station
Bank of China	15 Renmin Square
10 Hualian Hotel	16 Shantou Wharf Passenger Terminal
12 Taiwan Hotel	17 International Seamen's Club
13 Xinhua Hotel	18 Buses to Canton
14 Gymnastic Hotel	19 Local Ferry
	20 Xidi Park

■ PLACES TO STAY	▼ PLACES TO EAT
1 龙湖宾馆	2 龙湖乐园
3 金龙宾馆	5 金砂公园
4 国际大酒店	7 民航售票处
6 鸵岛宾馆	9 石炮台
8 华侨大厦 /中国旅行社 /	11 汽车客货运站
中国银行	15 人民广场
10 滑联酒店	16 汕头港客运站
12 台湾宾馆	17 国际海员俱乐部
13 新华酒店	18 往广州汽车站
14 体育宾馆	19 西堤客运公司客运站
	20 西堤公园

'change money' people are present in plague proportions just outside (even inside!) the door. Extreme caution is advised – rip-offs do happen.

There's a post office at 415 Zhongshan Lu, near the intersection with Shanzhang Lu.

Things to See

There's not much in Shantou to 'see' as such, but its intrinsic interest makes it worth a visit. The town is small enough to do a circuit of in a day.

The best area to explore is the southwestern section around Anping Lu, Xidi Lu and Shengping Lu. This is a dilapidated harbourside area, but it is now being built up.

Poking around the neighbourhood, you'll find the ruins of a temple at the corner of Minzu Lu and Zhongshan Lu. Further down Minzu Lu is a shop where you can stock up on cobras and lizards. Carry on to the eastern waterfront where there's a breakwater boat shelter, fishing hovels and lean-tos with little statues of their gods.

Places to Stay – middle

There are no dormitories, but mid-range hotel prices are very reasonable for such a large city. Shantou is a popular tourist destination for Chinese Thais, who generally have less money than their Hong Kong or Taiwanese counterparts, so this keeps hotel prices lower than might be expected.

The *Swatow Peninsula Hotel* (☎ 231261,

316668; fax 25013) (*túodǎo bīnguǎn*) on Jinsha Lu is no relation to the Hong Kong Peninsula, but is the best bargain in town. Very comfortable rooms with private bath and *no* TV (what a blessing!) are Y63. If you want to pay extra to have your eardrums blasted by your neighbours' kungfu movies, TV rooms cost Y110 to Y280.

Another cheapie but goodie is the friendly *Xinhua Hotel* (☎ 273710) (*xīnhuá jiǔdiàn*) at 121 Waima Lu. Doubles are Y98 to Y158.

Just next door is the *Taiwan Hotel* (☎ 276400) (*táiwān bīnguǎn*). Fortunately, it does not charge Taiwanese prices. Singles/doubles are reasonable at Y140/169, with higher-class rooms costing Y182, Y247 and Y312.

The *Hualian Hotel* (☎ 228389) (*huálián jiǔdiàn*), 2 Hushan Lu, is just opposite the main bus station. Built right over a department store, you'll also have no trouble finding a place to shop. Doubles are Y117 and Y130; triples are Y175.

The *Huaqiao Hotel* (☎ 319888) (*huáqiáo dàshà*) on Shanzhang Lu is the home of CTS and half the moneychangers east of Canton. Singles are Y125 to Y154; doubles are Y145 to Y209; triples are Y180.

The *Gymnastic Hotel* (*tǐyù bīnguǎn*) on Haibin Lu has little to recommend it besides its harbour view. If you're stuck for a place to stay, you can consider it – double rooms are Y145 and not worth it.

Places to Stay – top end

The *Longhu Hotel* (☎ 260706; fax 260708) (*lónghú bīnguǎn*) on Beishan Lu in the north-east part of town has doubles from Y280 to Y360.

The *Jinlong Hotel* (☎ 311635) (*jīnlóng bīnguǎn*) on Jinsha Zhonglu has doubles beginning at Y280.

The *International Hotel* (☎ 251212) (*guójì dàjiǔdiàn*) on Jinsha Zhonglu is one of the upper upmarket places, with doubles starting at Y380. The Palace Revolving Restaurant on the top floor has views of the harbour and old sections of town.

Places to Eat

Street markets set up at night and this is where you'll find the cuisine Shantou is famous for. Rice noodles (called *kwetiaw* locally) are also a specialty. All along Minzu Lu are a number of stalls specialising in delicious wonton (*húndùn*).

If you're staying at the *Swatow Peninsula Hotel*, check out the Western Restaurant in the back. There's excellent food at low prices, although as usual, no English menu.

Things to Buy

There are several porcelain factories in the Shantou area, producing some interesting glazes and finishes not made elsewhere in southern China. They also produce the *gong fu cha* (tea) sets which are almost obligatory pieces of household ware in the Shantou area. Embroidered cloth goods are produced in Shantou. Arts & crafts shops near the ferry docks cater to departing Hong Kongers.

Getting There & Away

Air The CAAC office (☎ 251915) is at 46 Shanzhang Lu, a few minutes' walk south of the intersection with Jinsha Lu. It's usually more convenient to buy from CTS next door in the Huaqiao Hotel.

Shantou has flights three times weekly to Bangkok, and twice daily to Hong Kong. Domestic flights and fares are:

Destination	Fare	Destination	Fare
Beijing	Y950	Canton	Y350
Chengdu	Y850	Chongqing	Y890
Dalian	Y1010	Guilin	Y400
Harbin,		Nanjing,	
Kunming	Y760	Shanghai	Y520
Shenyang,			
Shenzhen	Y400	Tianjin	Y960
Wenzhou	Y360		

Bus There are frequent departures to Canton (Y60, nine hours), Shenzhen (Y70, eight hours), Chaozhou (Y5, one hour) and Xiamen (Y50, eight hours).

The situation with bus terminals is a little bit confused. Besides the main bus terminal (*qìchē kèhuò yùn zhàn*), there is another even busier bus terminal on the south-west corner of the peninsula specialising in buses to Canton and Shenzhen. This terminal was built here to take advantage of the vehicular ferry, but this ferry might go out of operation after the new bridge is completed, so just where the bus terminal will move to is still unknown.

Not to worry – all tourist hotels including cheapish ones offer some sort of bus ticketing service. Prices vary (as does the condition of the bus), but you might want to shop around for a departure time that suits your schedule.

Train A railway line from Shantou to Canton is slowly being built, and is years away from completion.

Boat There are boats plying the route between Hong Kong and Shantou. In Hong Kong, departures are from China Hong Kong City Ferry Terminal in Tsimshatsui, Kowloon. In Shantou, departures are from Shantou Wharf Passenger Terminal (☎ 271513) (*shàntóu gǎng kèyùn zhàn*), one block west of the Gymnastic Hotel. The ship runs approximately four times weekly in each direction and the cruise takes 14 hours. There is considerable variation in price according to class. For tickets purchased in Hong Kong, fare is HK$221 (economy) to HK$970 (suite). The same tickets purchased in Shantou are Y139 to Y672.

Getting Around

Pedicabs and motortricycles hover outside the long-distance bus station and tourist hotels and charge about Y3 for most trips in the town centre. Taxis cost about Y10. The local public buses are the usual horror, but there are minibuses for Y2 going any-where in the city. Shantou is small enough for a good deal of the town to be seen on foot.

AROUND SHANTOU

Not far out of the city is **Mayu Island** (*māyǔ dǎo*), which makes a good day trip. A boat leaves from the waterfront at 9 am every day and returns at 2.30 pm. The hour-long ride takes you through the fishing area with close-ups of the fisherfolk and their equipment. On an ordinary weekday the boat is filled with people toting bags of food and sacrificial offerings. Follow the crowd from the landing to the Temple of the Mother of the Heavenly Emperor (*tiānhòu miào*), built in 1985 with funds supplied by Overseas Chinese. The site has apparently always been holy to this deity, and this is where the fisherpeople burn incense before they leave in the morning.

Evidently the island has been developed to keep pace with the worshippers' enthusiasm; there is a new hotel (*māyǔ bīnguǎn*) and restaurant building as well as marked trails for getting around the island. There are no cars, and the beaches and views are refreshing after spending several months in large Chinese cities. According to the villagers, the island was settled mainly during the Japanese occupation, although there were a few people living here before then.

CHAOZHOU

(*cháozhōu*) 潮州

Chaozhou is an ancient commercial and trading city dating back 1700 years. It is situated on the Han River and surrounded by the Golden and Calabash hills.

The chief sight is the **Kaiyuan Temple** (*kāiyuán sì*), which was built during the Tang Dynasty to house a collection of Buddhist scriptures sent here by Emperor Qian Long. The temple was reduced almost to rubble during the Cultural Revolution, but has since been restored with help from Overseas Chinese donors.

On the cliffs at the foot of the Calabash Hills by the shores of the West Lake are the

GUANGDONG

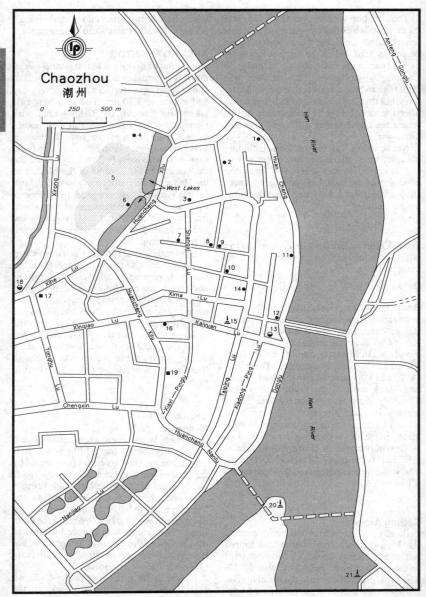

Chaozhou
潮州

0   250   500 m

West Lakes

Han River

Huan Cheng

Xihu

Xirong Lu

Huancheng

Xihe Lu

Huancheng Lu

Xinqiao Lu

Fengbu Lu

Chengxin Lu

Nanjiao Lu

Shangxi Lu

Xima · Lu

Kaiyuan Lu

Xixi — Ping Lu

Xihu

Leping Lu

Xiadong — Ping

Nanlu

Huancheng

Dongju

Anteng — Gongju

Han River

4
1
2
5
West Lakes
6
3
7
8 9
10
11
14
18
17
16
12
15
13
19
20
21

Moya carvings depicting local landscapes and the customs of the people, as well as poems and calligraphy; they date back 1000 years. South-east of Chaozhou is the seven-storey **Phoenix Pagoda** (*fènghuáng tǎ*) built in 1585.

Still further south-east of Chaozhou is the more difficult to reach **Sanyuan Pagoda** (*sānyuán tǎ*).

There are frequent buses from Shantou to Chaozhou. There's also an Overseas Chinese Hotel (*huáqiáo fàndiàn*) in Chaozhou.

Hainan Island 海南岛

Population: five million
Capital: Haikou

Hainan Island *(hǎinán dǎo)* is a large tropical island off the southern coast of China which was administered by the government of Guangdong Province until 1988 when it became Hainan Province.

The island lies close to Vietnam, and its military importance increased sharply in 1978. The conflict with Vietnam was initiated by the flight of as many as 250,000 ethnic Chinese from that country due to persecution. Vietnam's subsequent invasion of Cambodia was the last straw for China (the Khmer Rouge were Chinese allies). In February 1979, China attacked to 'teach the Vietnamese a lesson'. When Foreign Minister Huang Hua announced on 16 March that the Chinese troops were being pulled back, the invasion was proclaimed a great success by the Chinese leadership, though clearly the People's Liberation Army troops had been whipped by the Vietnamese, with probably 20,000 Chinese troops killed or wounded in just two weeks of fighting.

The Chinese were afraid that the Vietnamese alliance with the Soviet Union, their domination of Laos and their occupation of Cambodia were part of a Soviet plan to set up a hostile front on China's southern borders. After Vietnam's retreat from Cambodia in 1989 and the collapse of the Soviet Union in 1991, these fears have subsided.

However, serious territorial disputes with Vietnam remain over the Spratly and Paracel islands to the south of Hainan.

The Spratlys, which consist of hundreds of tiny islets, are closer to Borneo than to either China or Vietnam. They are claimed by virtually every country in the vicinity, including the Philippines, Malaysia, Indonesia, China, Taiwan and Vietnam. In 1988, Vietnam lost two ships and 70 sailors in a clash with China over the Spratlys.

Like Xishuangbanna in Yunnan Province, Hainan is popular as a winter refuge, but it

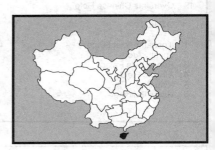

certainly isn't the 'Asian Hawaii' dished up in some tourist brochures. Development of tourist facilities on the island is clearly geared towards those Hong Kong and Overseas Chinese who favour quickie or 'auto-pilot' tours. In actual fact, the island still has a long way to go to develop a tourism infrastructure to handle group tourism.

Haikou is a fairly busy city with little to recommend it beyond a bit of old architecture and karaoke nightlife, if you're into that. With a bit of effort you can escape for a hike around minority areas in the mountains, or without any effort at all you can find a beach to sit on. Winter sees all sorts down on the Sanya beaches: Beijing cadres attending meetings that produce more suntans than dialectics; foreign students giving their nerves and stomachs badly needed R&R; droves of Scandinavians abandoning their climate to polar bears. The island also occasionally attracts foreign cyclists.

CLIMATE

Typhoons are a regular event on Hainan, usually between May and October – during the past 50 years there has been at least one every year. Although they bring the island vital rain, typhoons also have an awesome capacity for destruction. If Hainan is part of your tight travel schedule, remember that typhoons can cripple all transport and com-

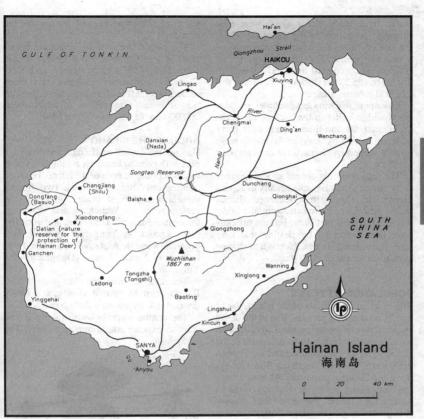

GULF OF TONKIN

Hai'an

Qiongzhou Strait

HAIKOU

Xiuying

Lingao

River

Chengmai

Ding'an

Wenchang

Danxian
(Nada)

Nandu

Songtao Reservoir

Dunchang

Changjiang
(Shilu)

Qionghai

Dongfang
(Basuo)

Baisha

SOUTH
CHINA
SEA

Xiaodongfang

Datian (nature
reserve for the
protection of
Hainan Deer)

Qiongzhong

Ganchen

Wuzhishan
1867 m

Wanning

Tongzha
(Tongshi)

Xinglong

Ledong

Baoting

Yinggehai

Lingshui

Xincun

SANYA

Hainan Island
海南岛

Anyou

0   20   40 km

munication with the mainland for several days at a time.

ECONOMY

Historically, Hainan has always been a backwater of the Chinese empire, a miserable place of exile and one of the poorest regions in the country. When Li Deyu, a prime minister of the Tang Dynasty, was exiled to Hainan he dubbed it 'the gate of hell'.

Times are changing – the entire island of Hainan has been established as a Special Economic Zone (SEZ) and hopes to lure foreign investment. More recently, the State Planning Commission gave Hainan authority at province level over economic management but not over financial affairs – and with good reason.

In 1985, mismanagement of the island's financial affairs caused some extremely red faces among Communist Party officials. Two years previously, Beijing had allocated Hainan massive sums of scarce foreign exchange to modernise the transport infrastructure. Officials on the island indulged, at just about every conceivable level, in a 14-month corruption bonanza. Over US$1.5 billion was used to buy 90,000 cars and trucks from Hong Kong which were then illegally 'funnelled' to the mainland where the rare goods sold like hot cakes to produce a massive profit. For good measure, the officials' shopping list included 2.9 million TV sets, 252,000 video recorders and 122,000 motorcycles.

Elsewhere in China lesser crimes are punished with a bullet in the back of the neck; on Hainan, the top three Communist Party officials in this pyramid of rake-offs were merely sacked and required to criticise their conduct.

The legacy of this absurd shopping spree is the island's unbelievable density of Japanese vehicles. Having imported more vehicles in one year than are imported annually in the whole of the rest of China, Hainan officials have been informed by Beijing that they have squandered Hainan's foreign exchange allocation for the next 10 years.

POPULATION & PEOPLE

The original inhabitants of the island, the Li and Miao minority peoples, live in the dense tropical forests covering the Limulingshan mountains that stretch down the centre of the island. The Li probably settled on Hainan 3000 years ago after migrating from Guangdong and Guangxi provinces. Although there has been a long history of rebellion by the Li against the Chinese, they aided the Communist guerrillas on the island during the war with the Japanese. Perhaps for this reason the island's centre was made an 'autonomous' region after the Communists came to power.

Until recently the Li women had a custom of tattooing their bodies at the age of 12 or 13. Today, almost all Li people except the elderly women wear standard Han dress. However, when a member of the Li dies, traditional Li costume is considered essential; otherwise the ancestors will not be able to recognise or accept the new arrival.

The Miao (Hmong) people spread from southern China across northern Vietnam, Laos and Thailand. In China they moved south into Hainan as a result of the Chinese emigrations from the north, and now occupy some of the most rugged terrain on the island.

The coastal areas of the island are populated by Han Chinese. Since 1949, Chinese from Indonesia and Malaysia and later Chinese-Vietnamese refugees have been settled here. All told, Hainan has a population of around five million, of which about 700,000 are Li and 40,000 are Miao.

AROUND THE ISLAND

Haikou, the capital of Hainan, and Sanya, a port with popular beaches, are the two major towns at opposite ends of the island. For road connections between these two places there's a choice of three highways: the eastern route via Wenchang and Wanning; the central route via Dunchang and Tongzha (also known as Tongshi); and the less popular western route via Danxian (also known as Nada), Basuo (Dongfang) and Yinggehai.

The eastern route is the most popular one. If you want to take it slowly, it's easily divided into stages on a daily basis.

The central route is worth taking if you want to explore ethnic minority areas. The

best mountain scenery is between Sanya and Qiongzhong – after that it's flat and plain.

The western route is scenic but this part of the island is very undeveloped for tourism, which might be one of its attractions. There are few hotels beyond the most basic, which means you'll pay lower prices but conditions can be pretty grotty. Since foreigners are so rare in this region, expect to be the best show in town. One spot in the west perhaps worth looking at is the Institute of Tropical Plants *(rèdài zhìwù yánjiūsuǒ)* near Danxian *(dànxiàn)* and the Nature Reserve for the Protection of the Hainan Deer at Datian. To the east of Datian is the town of Xiaodong-fang, the site of the Li minority's 'Loving Festival' on the third day of the third lunar month (around April). China's largest open-cut iron mine is at Shi Lu (also called Changjiang) *(chāngjiāng)*, which is linked by railway with Basuo, a shabby port. There is reportedly a beautiful stretch of road between Basuo and Sanya which passes the saltworks at Yinggehai.

HAIKOU
(hǎikǒu) 海口

Haikou, Hainan's capital, lies on the northern coastline at the mouth of the Nandu River. It's a port town and handles most of the island's commerce with the mainland.

It's certainly not the most beautiful spot on the island, but it's a friendly city. For most travellers, Haikou is merely a transit point on the way to the beaches at Hainan's southern tip. However, those interested in old southern Chinese architecture may find it worth a day or two. In the town centre, along and off Xinhua Nanlu, are rows of original buildings with the unmistakable Sino-Portuguese influence seen in Chinese colonies throughout South-East Asia: spots like Macau, Malacca (Malaysia) and Penang (Malaysia).

Orientation

Haikou is split into three fairly separate sections. The western section is the port area. The centre of Haikou has all the tourist facilities. On the south side of the airport is another district seldom visited by travellers.

Along Xinhua Nanlu you'll find the town's older buildings, which are reminiscent of Sino-Portuguese architecture once found from Macau to Singapore.

Information

CTS The main CTS office (☎ 773288) is hidden behind the Overseas Chinese Hotel I in a dilapidated building.

Money The Bank of China is in a new, modern building called the International Financial Centre at 33 Datong Lu. There are moneychangers in nearly every tourist hotel and heaps of illegal moneychangers swarming through the streets.

Post The main post office is on Changdi Dadao near the river, but most upmarket hotels offer postal services.

Places to Stay – middle

For foreigners, there are no really cheap places to stay in Haikou, which is the main reason why backpackers don't dawdle here.

The *Overseas Chinese Hotel I* (☎ 773288) *(huáqiáo dàshà)*, 17 Datong Lu, used to be the fanciest place in town but has since been surpassed by a wide margin. It's a bit tattered around the edges but all rooms have private bathroom and it's certainly not bad. Singles are Y109, doubles Y130 to Y143, triples Y139 and suites are Y260. Be careful not to confuse this place with the newer (and much more expensive) Overseas Chinese Hotel II. The designation 'I' and 'II' is something we invented – both places are called the Overseas Chinese Hotel. In Chinese, the cheap one is the *dàshà* and the expensive one is the *bīnguǎn*.

The *Nanhai Hotel* (☎ 773474) *(nánhǎi jiǔdiàn)* is the cheapest place in town if you can get one of the rooms without air-con. Doubles/triples without air-con are Y60/75. With air-con, the tariff runs to Y120 for a double and Y135 for a triple. The hotel is on the west side of Jichang Donglu near Daying Houlu. If you tell the staff you want a dormitory, it's possible they'll put you in a room with other foreigners (if there are any).

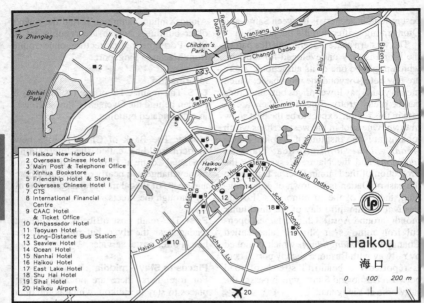

1 Haikou New Harbour
2 Overseas Chinese Hotel II
3 Main Post & Telephone Office
4 Xinhua Bookstore
5 Friendship Hotel & Store
6 Overseas Chinese Hotel I
7 CTS
8 International Financial Centre
9 CAAC Hotel & Ticket Office
10 Ambassador Hotel
11 Taoyuan Hotel
12 Long-Distance Bus Station
13 Seaview Hotel
14 Ocean Hotel
15 Nanhai Hotel
16 Haikou Hotel
17 East Lake Hotel
18 Shu Hai Hotel
19 Sihai Hotel
20 Haikou Airport

Haikou
海口

0   100   200 m

1 海口新港宾馆	11 桃园酒店
2 海华侨宾馆	12 长途汽车站
3 市邮电局	13 望海国际大酒店
4 新华书店	14 海洋宾馆
5 友谊大酒店	15 南海酒店
6 华侨大大厦	16 海口宾馆
7 中国旅行社	17 东湖大酒店
8 国际金融大厦	18 蜀海酒店
9 民航售票处	19 四海大酒店
10 国宾大酒店	20 海口机场

Further south on Jichang Donglu is the *Shu Hai Hotel (shǔhǎi jiǔdiàn)* where doubles are Y120 and Y180. It's not particularly recommended.

A reasonable alternative is the *Taoyuan Hotel* (☎ 772998) *táoyuán jiǔdiàn*, a new place on Daying Houlu opposite the CAAC office. Singles are reasonably priced at Y105 and Y120 while doubles are Y160, Y180 and Y190.

Or you can cross the street and stay at the *CAAC Hotel*, which is also the CAAC booking office *(mínháng shòupiàochù)* where rooms cost Y126 and Y160.

The *Friendship Hotel (yǒuyì dàjiǔdiàn)* (☎ 224712) is behind the Friendship Store at 2 Datong Lu (enter the hotel from the alley to the left as you face the store). Rooms are priced at a not very friendly Y158 and Y238.

The *Seaview Hotel* (☎ 773381) *(wànghǎi*

guójì dàjiǔdiàn) is a very fancy place and seems quite reasonable for what you get. Singles go for Y149 to Y175 and doubles are Y208 to Y250.

At the time of writing, the *Ocean Hotel* (hǎiyáng bīnguǎn) on Jichang Donglu was almost ready to open its doors. Prices are set to be in the mid to upper range.

A sharp-looking hotel close to the airport is the *Sihai Hotel* (☎ 793812) (sìhǎi dàjiǔdiàn), 25 Jichang Donglu Zhongduan, where doubles are Y180 and Y200.

Places to Stay – top end
The *East Lake Hotel* (☎ 772333; fax 774827) (dōnghú dàjiǔdiàn), 8 Haifu Dadao is the flash place in Haikou and charges flash prices; a double with no windows costs Y336. Having windows brings the tariff to Y420, or you can go deluxe for Y503.

Next door, the *Haikou Hotel* (☎ 772266) (hǎikǒu bīnguǎn) has overpriced doubles for Y368.

The *International Financial Centre* (☎ 773088; fax 772113) (guójì jīnróng dàshà), 33 Datong Lu, is in fact a hotel, the Bank of China and a number of business offices all rolled into one skyscraper. It's an impressive place with impressive prices. Doubles start at Y266 and climb all the way up to Y740 for the executive suite.

The *Ambassador Hotel* (☎ 773606; fax 798026) (guóbīn dàjiǔdiàn), 44 Haixiu Dadao, is just as ridiculously overpriced as all the other upmarket places in Haikou. Expect to pay Y310 for a double.

The *Overseas Chinese Hotel II* (☎ 772776) (huáqiáo bīnguǎn) deserves honourable mention for its ridiculously inconvenient location on Binhai Dadao in the north-western part of the city.

Places to Eat
The restaurants at the *Overseas Chinese Hotel* serve acceptable food, but are quite expensive.

There are several cheap places in the vicinity of the main market along Xinhua Nanlu and on Jiefang Xilu. They serve the usual rice, meat and vegetable fare for

around Y8. Along the north end of Datong Lu is a night market with outdoor tables and lots of seafood. You buy your fish, prawns, chickens or whatever by the *jīn* (500 grams) or *bàn jīn* (250 grams); fish prices start at around Y10 per jin; chicken and prawns should be about Y18 per jin.

Hainan is one of the few places in China where you can enjoy fresh tropical fruits such as pineapple, jackfruit and sugar cane.

Getting There & Away
Air There are daily flights between Haikou and Hong Kong (HK$960) on CAAC and Dragonair. Dragonair (☎ 338131, 772117) has a representative in room 103, Heping Mansion, Heping Nanlu. The CAAC flights are technically charters and therefore do not appear in the CAAC timetable.

The CAAC office (☎ 772615) is on Daying Houlu behind the huge Bank of China. CAAC flies daily between Haikou and the following cities:

Destination	Fare	Destination	Fare
Beijing	Y1250	Canton	Y320
Changsha	Y550	Chengdu	Y880
Chongqing	Y630	Dalian	Y1450
Fuzhou,		Harbin	Y1850
Guiyang	Y460	Kunming	Y520
Shanghai	Y880	Shenyang	Y1560
Shenzhen	Y420	Tianjin	Y1170
Wuhan	Y690	Xi'an	Y920
Xiamen	Y540		

Bus The bus station has departures to all major destinations on the island. However, buses to Sanya (and points in between) conveniently stop at the car parks of the Overseas Chinese Hotel I and the East Lake Hotel.

Modern buses and minibuses charge around Y45 for the run to Sanya and take six hours for the journey. The dinosaur buses are cheapest at around Y20, but take a couple of hours longer and you might have to share a seat with sacks of rice and the occasional live chicken.

Tickets are also sold for deluxe buses running direct to Canton, Shenzhen and Hong Kong. However, the combined boat/bus journey can be very tedious when it includes night travel at high speed with nonstop pornographic kungfu videos.

Boat There are two harbours in Haikou, but most departures are from Haikou New Harbour (*hǎikǒu xīngǎng*) at the terminal of bus line No 7 near the Overseas Chinese Hotel II.

Boats leave Haikou about once an hour for the 1½-hour trip to Hai'an on the Leizhou Peninsula, where you get connecting transport to Zhanjiang. The combined bus/boat ticket is available at the harbour for Y46, but it's much better if you can buy a boat ticket only, since it's often very difficult and time-consuming to find your bus in Hai'an. Unfortunately, the ticket office in Haikou usually refuses to sell you a boat ticket only. Like many travellers (both Chinese and foreign) you may wind up buying the boat/bus ticket and still have to pay for a separate bus from Hai'an to Zhanjiang (Y20).

There are infrequent boats directly from Haikou to Zhanjiang. Boats also run between Haikou and Beihai in Guangxi Province.

There are daily boats between Haikou and Canton. Departures are at 9 am from Canton's Zhoutouzui Wharf and the trip takes 25 hours. Starting from 5th class and moving upmarket, prices are Y43, Y49, Y65 and Y91. It's worth paying a little extra to avoid the large dorm below deck, particularly if the boat is pitching and your bunk is next to the toilets. Third class will get you into an eight-bed dorm on deck. Watch out for petty thievery and take your own food – the food on board is poor. In Haikou you can buy tickets from the booking office in the Overseas Chinese Hotel.

Two boats, the *Donghu* and the *Malan*, run approximately five times monthly between Haikou and Hong Kong, taking 18 hours to complete the journey. Another boat, the *Shan Cha*, runs twice a month between Sanya and Hong Kong via Haikou. In Hong Kong, buy tickets from CTS. Tickets bought in Hong Kong cost from HK$296 for 3rd class to HK$425 for deluxe class. In Haikou, tickets cost 20% less and can be bought from CTS – those booked at the hotels cost more.

Getting Around

To/From the Airport Haikou Airport is two km from the centre and a reasonable taxi fare is Y10. Bus No 7 runs between the airport and Haikou New Harbour.

Bus The central area of Haikou is small and easy to walk around, but there is a workable bus system. The fare is two jiao for any destination in the city.

Taxi There are three standards of taxis, indicated by a sticker (on the rear side window) which shows the charge per km. The three levels are Y1, Y1.40 and Y1.60, but this doesn't mean very much since there are no meters – bargain the fare with the driver before heading off. Figure on an average fare of Y10 for any place in the city.

Motortricycle Motortricycles charge Y2 per km. These are becoming a rarity in Haikou but are still popular elsewhere on the island.

WENCHANG
(wénchāng) 文昌

The coconut plantations called Dong Jiao Ye Lin and Jian Hua Shan Ye Lin are a short ride out of town at Qing Lan Gang. Minibuses by the riverside in Wenchang will take you to Qing Lan Gang, where you can take a ferry to the stands of coconut palms and mile after mile of beach. Another way to get to the same plantation is to take the direct bus to Dong Jiao from Haikou's main bus station.

There are a few new resort hotels and villas being built at the beach. Expect prices to be on the high side.

Buses leave for Wenchang from Haikou's main bus station; or you can catch a Sanya-bound bus from outside the Overseas Chinese Hotel I or East Lake Hotel. The 73 km could be done as a day trip.

XINGLONG
(xīnglóng) 兴隆

Since 1952, over 20,000 Chinese-Vietnamese and Overseas Chinese refugees (mostly from Indonesia or Malaysia) have settled at the **Xinglong Overseas Chinese Farm** (xìnglóng huáqiáo cūn) The farm concentrates on tropical agriculture – rubber and coffee are important cash crops here. Many of the members speak English and may be able to organise transport to Miao villages, but many of the guides (including the motorcycle drivers) are not worth the money they ask for.

Places to Stay

Xinglong is worth a stay, but it is no longer cheap. The hotels have hot spring baths, which can be scalding hot – if there's no cold water available, you'll just have to let it cool in the tub before diving in. The hotels are concentrated in an area three km from the town. From the bus stop to the hotels costs Y1 on the back of a motorcycle, or Y2 in a motorcycle with sidecar.

One 'lower end' place is the *Yancao Dujiacun* (☎ 52089) charging Y170 (pay in RMB!) for a comfortable double. Also at the lower end of the price scale is the nearby *Youdian Dujiacun* (☎ 52051, 52052) which charges Y140 (but FEC). Another 'economy' place is the *Yinyan Dujiacun* (☎ 52348) where doubles/triples are Y160/180. Relatively luxurious is the *Xinglong Hot Springs Resort* (☎ 52014, 52383) (*wēnquán dùjià zhōngxīn*) charging Y146 and Y180.

An excellent place to stay is the sparkling new *Taiyanghe Holiday Centre* (☎ 52122) (*tàiyánghé dùjià zhōngxīn*), where rooms are Y200 and Y220. Also in this price bracket is the relatively small *Binlangyuan* where rooms are Y220 (downstairs) and Y240 (upstairs).

Moving upmarket, there's the large and fancy *Xinglong Hot Springs Guesthouse* (☎ 52367) (*xīnglóng wēnquán bīnguǎn*) which has an outdoor pool. The tariff is Y350 for a double.

The top of the market belongs to the *Kangle Garden Resort* (☎ 343133) (*kānglè yuán dàjiùdiàn*). This place features a large outdoor hot-springs pool plus a cool-water swimming pool. However, you cannot go nude here – don't forget, this is China, not Europe. Other facilities include tennis courts and karaoke bar. Prices are from Y260 for a

double to Y760 for a villa. There is an additional 10% 'service charge'.

Things to Buy

Xinglong coffee is exquisite – it's so good you may want to bring a few boxes home with you. You can easily buy this coffee in Haikou (perhaps even more cheaply than in Xinglong!) from any grocery store. It costs less than Y3 for a 100-gram box. Be aware that this isn't instant coffee – the Chinese prepare it like they make tea, by dumping a heaped teaspoon of coffee grounds into a cup of scalding water and letting it steep. Trying to filter out the coffee grounds between your teeth while drinking the brew is a bit of a challenge. Since disposable coffee filters are unknown in China, travellers have to improvise – some have reported mixed success from using toilet paper.

XINCUN
(xīncūn) 新村

Xincun is populated almost solely by Danjia (Tanha) minority people who are employed in fishing and pearl cultivation. In recent years, typhoons have repeatedly blown away the pearl and oyster cultivation farms, but the harbour area, fish market and nearby Monkey Island are worth an afternoon ramble.

Buses travelling the eastern route will drop you off at a fork in the road about three km from Xincun. It should then be easy to get a lift on a passing minibus and hitch or walk into Xincun. Frequent minibuses run directly from Lingshui and Sanya to Xincun.

MONKEY ISLAND
(hóuzi dǎo) 猴子岛

About a thousand Guangxi monkeys *(Macaca mulatta)* live on this narrow peninsula near Xincun. The area is under state protection and a special wildlife research centre has been set up to investigate all the monkey business.

A shack on the beach at Xincun functions as a booking office selling return ferry tickets. They also sell a booklet put together in Chinese by the research centre. It includes exhaustive monkey data and an appendix which lists the monkeys' favourite plants like a menu.

The ferry put-puts from Xincun to Monkey Island in 10 minutes. From the island pier, motorcycles with sidecars will take you to the monkey enclosure (*hóuzi yuán*). You can also get there on foot: walk along the beach road to the left for about one km, then follow the road leading uphill to the right for another 1½ km.

At the entrance a stall sells tickets, and peanuts for the monkeys. Apart from feeding times at 9 am and 4 pm, it's a case of the monkeys seeing you and not vice versa. You can often hear them crashing around and chattering in the shrubs on the hillside; occasionally a wild, woolly head pops out of the top branches to see what's happening or to scream at you.

SANYA

(*sānyà*) 三亚

Sanya is a busy port and tourist resort on the southern tip of Hainan Island. The town lies on a peninsula parallel to the coast and is connected to the mainland on one side by two bridges.

The harbour area is protected to the southeast by the hilly Luhuitou Peninsula. On the western outskirts of Sanya there's a community of around 5000 Hui, the only Muslim inhabitants of Hainan.

The main part of town lacks any special features except perhaps for the local minority women who try to get you to change money.

A Chinese tourist pamphlet points out that 'Nobody goes sightseeing to Sanya without coming to Hainan'. This, we must agree, is indisputable.

Things to See

Most travellers head for Sanya for a few leisurely days at the beach. The popular beaches are at Dadonghai, Luhuitou Peninsula and Tianya Haijiao.

You'll find a fine beach at **Dadonghai** (*dàdōnghǎi*), which has a hotel and plenty of sand, surf and shade. It's about three km east of Sanya and easily reached by bus for Y1. Dadonghai also has the greatest variety of places to stay.

There's only one hotel at the **Luhuitou Peninsula** (*lùhuítóu*). The beaches are too rocky for swimming but pleasant for walks. The usual route to the hotel is not over the hills, but via a road which follows the seashore. It's possible to do this pleasant walk from the town to the hotel in about an hour. You must first cross a narrow channel by ferry and then continue on by motorcycle and sidecar.

The name Luhuitou means 'deer turns its head' and is associated with an old legend.

A young Li hunter who lived near Five Fingers Mountain (*wǔzhǐshān*) pursued a young doe to the southernmost tip of the island. When the creature realised it was trapped it turned its head to gaze at the hunter. Just as the hunter raised his bow to shoot, the doe changed into a beautiful girl and the astonished hunter dropped his bow. The two fell in love and lived happily ever after.

On the tip of Luhuitou Peninsula is the **Hainan Experimental Marine Research Station**, which specialises in pearl cultivation. The use of pearls in China can be traced back 4000 years; cultured pearls were created over 900 years ago during the Song Dynasty.

There's an overrated beach at **Tianya Haijiao** (*tiānyà hǎijiǎo*) (literally 'edge of the sky, rim of the sea') about 24 km west of

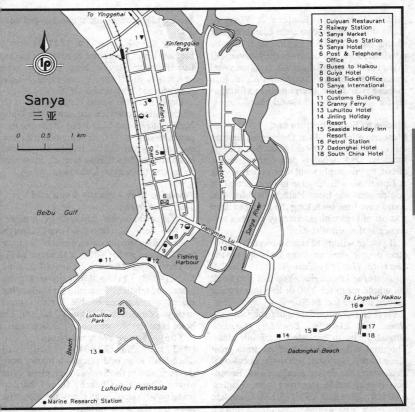

Sanya
三亚

0   0.5   1 km

To Yinggehai

Xinfengqiao
Park

Beibu Gulf

Jiefang Lu

Shengli Lu

Chedong Lu

Sanya River

Cangmen Lu

Fishing
Harbour

Luhuitou
Park

Beach

Luhuitou Peninsula

Marine Research Station

Dadonghai Beach

To Lingshui Haikou

1	Cuiyuan Restaurant
2	Railway Station
3	Sanya Market
4	Sanya Bus Station
5	Sanya Hotel
6	Post & Telephone Office
7	Buses to Haikou
8	Guiya Hotel
9	Boat Ticket Office
10	Sanya International Hotel
11	Customs Building
12	Granny Ferry
13	Luhuitou Hotel
14	Jinling Holiday Resort
15	Seaside Holiday Inn Resort
16	Petrol Station
17	Dadonghai Hotel
18	South China Hotel

HAINAN ISLAND

1	翠园酒家	7	往海口汽车站	
2	火车站	8	贵亚大酒店	
3	三亚商场	9	三亚港客运站	
4	三亚汽车站	10	三亚国际大酒店	
5	三亚宾馆	11	海关楼	
6	邮店局	12	小渡船	
13	鹿回头宾馆			
14	金陵渡假村			
15	滨海渡假村			
16	加油站			
17	大东海大酒店			
18	南中国大酒店			

Sanya, with a few large rocks, no shade and not much else. It's popular with the droves of Chinese tourists who queue to have their pictures taken in front of rocks with carved characters. Catch any bus travelling west

from Sanya bus station. The trip takes about 45 minutes.

To the east of Sanya is Dragon Tooth Bay (*yálóng wān*), another sightseeing spot.

Close to Sanya are **Xidao Dongdao**

(*xīdǎo dōngdǎo*) (Eastern & Western Hawksbill islands), two coral islands clearly visible from Luhuitou Peninsula. It may be possible to find a boat from the harbour out to the islands, where the inhabitants use coral for housing and tacky souvenirs. A site close to these islands has been opened to foreigners for scuba-diving and snorkelling.

Places to Stay – bottom end

Most travellers head for Dadonghai first, as this is where the best sandy beach is. Unfortunately, Dadonghai is fast turning into a circus, so you might want to consider staying at Luhuitou, which is far more peaceful. If you're arriving from Haikou by bus, you could save time by asking the driver to drop you off at Dadonghai. An easy point of reference is the petrol station.

If you're willing to share a room with two other people, there are three-bed dorms in the *Seaside Holiday Inn Resort (bīnhǎi dùjiàcūn)* in Dadonghai. You can also book the whole room for Y90 or live in a regular air-con double for Y120.

Over on Luhuitou Peninsula, the *Luhuitou Hotel (☎ 214659, 274786) (lùhuítóu bīnguǎn)* sits in secluded semi-splendour. The mini-villas in lush gardens are a great place to rest, and well worth the occasional hassle with the frosty receptionists. Reception is just inside the front gate. Singles/doubles/triples cost Y92/115/138. Complete suites are also available at higher prices. Opposite reception is a shop which sells maps (in Chinese) of Sanya, canned drinks, shell necklaces and coconut shell carvings.

There are two routes from town to the Luhuitou Hotel. Cars usually drive up over the hill and deposit you at the gate by reception. Walkers and motorcycles with sidecars generally avoid the climb by taking the beach road from the back gate, a much more scenic and interesting route. From the south end of Sanya, turn left just before hitting the waterfront, then right through some grubby alleys until you find the *mǎtóu* (ferry terminal). For Y0.30 an old woman sells you a ticket for the motorboat which takes you to the other side. From there, the ride by motor-

cycle and sidecar is about two km and costs Y4.

The *Sanya Hotel (☎ 274703) (sānyà bīnguǎn)* is in the centre of town on Jiefang Lu. If you're staying here and you want beach life, you'll have to commute. Singles cost Y66 and Y90, doubles Y90 to Y110.

Down from the Sanya Hotel, almost at the southernmost point of the town, the *Guiya Hotel (guìyà dàjiǔdiàn)* is one of the cheapest places to stay, at Y60 for a double. It's clean, quiet and not bad at all but, like the Sanya Hotel, lacks a nearby beach. However, it's convenient for getting the ferry to Luhuitou.

Places to Stay – middle & top end

The *Dadonghai Hotel (☎ 214008; fax 214006) (dàdōnghǎi dàjiǔdiàn)* is a glittering five-storey building at 6 Yuya Dadao, the 'tourist alley' on the eastern end of Dadonghai. Doubles go for Y158, Y188 and Y192.

The *Jinling Holiday Resort (☎ 214081; fax 214088) (jīnlíng dùjiàcūn)* is a grand place, and relatively peaceful for Dadonghai. Prices are also reasonable for this much luxury – doubles/triples are Y242/306. The hotel is on the western end of Dadonghai.

The *Sanya International Hotel (☎ 273068; fax 275049) (sānyà guójì dàjiǔdiàn)* is an odd place – a luxury hotel on the island in the Sanya River, close to the town. There's no beach, so it's hard to imagine who would stay here – perhaps business travellers attending a convention in Sanya. Rooms cost Y295, Y237 and Y333.

The *South China Hotel (☎ 213888; fax 214005) (nán zhōngguó dàjiǔdiàn)* is at the very end of Yuya Dadao, almost right on the beach. This Hong Kong joint-venture resort has all the trimmings – massage parlour, karaoke bar, tennis courts, water slides and a private beach where non-guests must pay admission (but you can sneak in from the beach side). All this tinsel costs Y328 in the budget rooms, or up to Y2500 for deluxe villas.

Places to Eat

The restaurant at the *Luhuitou Hotel* can be good when there are enough guests to inspire the kitchen staff. The two restaurants just outside the back entrance of the hotel are good but overpriced.

On Yuya Dadao, the tourist street of Dadonghai, there are heaps of seafood restaurants (some types of fish are quite expensive, so check the price). Places to try include the *Pipe Fish King Restaurant* and the *Sichuan Haixian*. Near the petrol station along the Haikou-Sanya highway are some cheap places to eat, including the *Shenyang Restaurant*. These cheaper places may be living on borrowed time as the big push is on to make Dadonghai into an upmarket resort.

In Sanya itself, there are plenty of restaurants and street stalls to try. The restaurant on the 2nd floor of the *Sanya Hotel* has a balcony view, bamboo decor, outstanding food, low prices and is run by friendly people, the only drawback being that there is no English menu.

Some of the locals prefer the Cuiyuan Restaurant *(cuìyuán jiǔjiā)* in the north end of town, but it hardly seems worth it to go that far for a meal.

Things to Buy

Southern Hainan is famous for its cultured pearls, but watch out for fakes. Tourists have been known to pay 100 times the going price for authentic-looking plastic.

Getting There & Away

Air At the time of writing, Sanya Airport was closed for renovation, but when it re-opens there will be international flights to Hong Kong and beyond.

Also anticipated are daily flights to Canton (Y370) and Shenzhen (Y590). Reception at the major hotels may be able to book plane tickets; otherwise try the CAAC office, which is inconveniently located at the western end of town. It is very likely that a new CAAC office will be opened in a better location when the renovated airport is completed.

Bus From Sanya bus station there are frequent buses and minibuses to most parts of Hainan. Deluxe buses for Haikou (Y45; if

they demand FEC, argue) also depart from the Sanya, Luhuitou and Dadonghai hotels. The express buses to Haikou take six hours to cover the 320-km route.

Train The railway line is mostly used for hauling freight, but there is sporadic passenger service between Sanya and Dongfang on the west coast. Travel by this method is very slow.

Boat There is a daily boat from Canton, departing from Zhoutouzui Wharf at 3 pm. The trip takes over 25 hours. Ticket prices are Y39, Y50, Y67 and Y94.

A boat service direct from Hong Kong to Sanya is allegedly in the works, but there's been no final word as to when this might come about.

The boat ticket office is close to the harbour, past the bus station at the southern end of Jiefang Lu.

Getting Around

The airport is a 30-minute drive from the town by taxi.

Motorcycles with sidecars cruise the streets all day. It can be quite a blast, motoring around like a WW II general in a bathtub. The real fare is usually half the asking fare.

A motorcycle and sidecar from the centre of Sanya to Dadonghai costs about Y4. To the Luhuitou Hotel from the harbour should cost about the same.

Bikes can be hired for Y10 per day at the back gate of the Luhuitou Hotel.

TONGZHA

(tōngzhà) 通什

In Mandarin Chinese, the name of this place is really Tongshi *(tōngshí)*, but everyone in Hainan calls it by the local name, Tongzha. Whatever you want to call it, this is the capital of the Li and Miao Autonomous Prefecture.

Minorities make the tourist cash register tinkle here. Busloads of Hong Kongers, Taiwanese and even mainlanders come here for minority watching and leave behind bundles of cash in the process. The town has obviously had some outside investment to transform all the major buildings into modern high-rises; there's even a supermarket.

Just how much of the local culture you see is real and how much is a show for the free-spending tourists is becoming increasingly debatable. The 'Li Village' has folk-song and dance shows with tourists getting dressed up in local garb. You can try to escape to some real villages – there are several Miao villages dotted around the edge of town. From Tongzha you could take local buses to Mao'an, Maodao or Maogan, for example.

Near Tongzha, at 1867 metres, Mount Five Fingers *(wǔzhǐshān)* is Hainan's highest mountain.

Places to Stay

There are several hotels in Tongzha, but there is currently such a shortage of rooms that you'll probably be forced upmarket. The flashiest is the *Tongzha Holiday Resort (dùjià lǚyóu shānzhuāng)* with doubles for Y150. To remind you that this is Minority territory, the roof of the lobby is pyramid-shaped to give the feel of a straw hut, and minority women serve drinks or invite guests to dance and sing. It's a great chance for visitors to play the primitive in luxury.

The *Wuzhishan Guesthouse (wǔzhǐshān bīnguǎn)* charges Y100 for a double.

QIONGZHONG

(qióngzhōng) 琼中

The route between Tongzha and Qiongzhong passes through thick forest. Qiongzhong is a small hill-town with a lively market; the nearby waterfall at Baihuashan falls over 300 metres.

Hunan 湖南

Population: 60 million
Capital: Changsha

Hunan *(húnán)* lies on some of the richest land in China. Its main period of growth occurred between the 8th and the 11th centuries when the population increased fivefold, spurred on by a prosperous agricultural industry and by migrations from the north. Under the Ming and the Qing dynasties it was one of the empire's granaries, and vast quantities of Hunan's rice surplus were shipped to the depleted regions to the north.

By the 19th century Hunan was beginning to suffer from the pressure of population. Land shortage and landlordism led to widespread unrest among the Chinese farmers and the hill-dwelling minority peoples. The increasingly desperate economic situation led to the massive Taiping Rebellion of the mid-19th century and the Communist movement of the 1920s.

The Communists found strong support amongst the poor peasants of Hunan, and a refuge on the mountainous Hunan-Jiangxi border in 1927. Some of the most prominent Communist leaders were born in Hunan: Mao Zedong, Liu Shaoqi (both of whose villages can be visited), Peng Dehuai, Hu Yaobang and others. Hua Guofeng, a native of Shanxi, became an important provincial leader in Hunan.

Most of the inhabitants are Han Chinese. Hill-dwelling minorities can be found in the border regions of the province. They include the Miao, Tujia, Dong (a people related to the Thais and Lao) and Yao. In the far north of the province there is, oddly enough, a pocket of Uigurs.

CHANGSHA
(chángshā) 长沙

The site of Changsha has been inhabited for 3000 years. By the Warring States Period (476-221 BC) a large town had grown up here. The town owes its prosperity to its location on the fertile Hunan plains of central

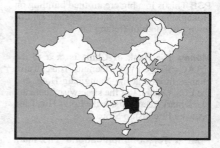

China and on the Xiang River, where it rapidly grew as a major trading centre of agricultural produce.

In 1904 the city was opened to foreign trade as a result of the 1903 Treaty of Shanghai between Japan and China. The 'most-favoured nation' principle allowed foreigners to set themselves up in Changsha, and large numbers of Europeans and Americans came to build factories, churches and schools. The medical centre was originally a college established by Yale University.

Today Changsha has a population of around three million people.

Orientation

Most of Changsha lies on the eastern bank of the Xiang River. The railway station is at the far east of the city. From the station Wuyi Lu leads to the river, neatly separating the city's northern and southern sections. From Wuyi Lu you cross the Xiang River bridge to the western bank, passing over Long Island in the middle of the river. Most of the sights and tourist facilities are on the eastern side of the river.

Information

CITS The local CITS office (☎ 439757) is located on the 4th floor of the building behind the Lotus Hotel. The staff there speak some English. The Xiangjiang Hotel can assist with transport bookings as well.

PSB This is in a big cream-tiled building on Huangxing Lu, over on the western end of town just south of Jiefang Lu.

Money The Bank of China is next to the CAAC office on Wuyi Donglu. You can also change money at the Xiangjiang Hotel and the Lotus Hotel: For the streetwise, there are black marketeers outside the Lotus Hotel and near the Friendship Store.

Post & Telecommunications The main post and telecommunications office is on the corner of Wuyi Lu and Cai'e Lu in the centre of town. There are other useful post offices at the railway station and the Xiangjiang Hotel.

Maps Several colourful variations of the local city transport map are on sale at kiosks around the railway station. The shop at the Lotus Hotel sells one of the better versions.

Hunan Provincial Museum
(húnán bówùguǎn) 湖南博物馆
The Hunan Provincial Museum is on Dongfeng Lu within walking distance of the Xiangjiang Hotel. The exhibits are in three main buildings The first section covers revolutionary history while the two other buildings are devoted to the 2100-year-old Western Han tombs at Mawangdui, some five km east of the city centre, whose excavation was completed in 1974.

Not to be missed are the mummified remains of a Han Dynasty woman. Her preserved body is housed in the basement and is viewed from the floor above through perspex. The organs have been removed and are laid out on display. Another building houses the enormous solid outer timber casks.

The only sign of the tombs above ground were two earthen mounds of similar size and height standing close together. The body was found in the eastern tomb, in a chamber 16 metres underground and approached from the north by a sloping passageway. The walls of the tomb were covered in a thick layer of charcoal surrounded by a layer of pounded earth, which appears to have kept out moisture and prevented the decay of the body and other objects in the tomb.

At the bottom of the tomb was a chamber made of wooden planks, containing an outer, middle and inner coffin. In the coffin was the corpse of a woman of about 50 years of age wrapped in more than 20 layers of silk and linen, with the outer layer bound in nine bands of silk ribbon.

Large quantities of silk garments and fabrics were found in the tomb as well as stockings, shoes, gloves and other pieces of clothing. One of the most interesting objects, now on display in the museum, is a painting on silk depicting the underworld, earth and heaven. The tomb also held lacquerware, pottery containing food, musical instruments (including a 25-stringed wooden instrument called a *se zither*, a set of reed pipes and a set of bamboo pitch-pipes) and a collection of wooden tomb figurines. Other finds included bamboo boxes containing vegetables and grain seeds, straw mats, medicinal herbs, seals and several hundred pieces of money made of unbaked clay with clear inscriptions. Numerous bamboo slips with writing on them listed the names, sizes and number of the objects.

The museum is open daily except Monday from 9 am to noon and from 2.30 to 5.20 pm. Entry to all three sections is Y2 for students and Chinese and Y5 for foreigners. Bus Nos 3 and 103 run north along Dongfeng Lu past the museum.

Maoist Pilgrimage Spots
Scattered about the city are a number of Maoist pilgrimage spots. The **Hunan No 1 Teachers' Training School** (*dìyī shīfàn xuéxiào*) is where Mao attended classes between 1913 and 1918, and where he returned as a teacher in 1920-21. The school was destroyed during the civil war, but has since been restored. Although of historical interest, there's not much to see; the main

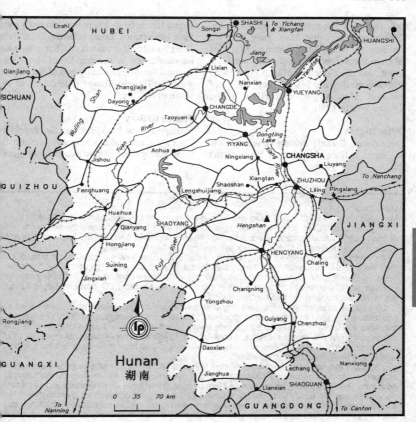

ttraction is a sort of Mao 'shrine' with anners, photos, candles and attendants with lack armbands. To get there take the No 1 us from outside the Xiangjiang Hotel.

The **Former Office of the Hunan (Xiang istrict) Communist Party Committee** *hōngguó gōngchǎndǎng zǎoqī huódòngde fang)* is now a museum that includes Mao's ving quarters and an exhibition of photos nd historical items from the 1920s. On the ame grounds is a large museum containing Mao exhibition and some archaeological lics – mainly pottery, tools, weapons and bins.

About 60 km from Changsha is the **Home & Tomb of Yang Kaihui**. Discounting an unconsummated arranged childhood marriage, Yang was Mao's first wife. Post-reform governments have tended to promote Yang as his favourite as a counter to the vilified Jiang Qing. Yang was the daughter of one of Mao's teachers at the Hunan No 1 Teachers' Training School in Changsha, a member of a wealthy Hunanese landowning family. Mao seems to have influenced Yang Kaihui towards radicalism, and also to marriage in 1920 when she was 25 years old. She was arrested by the Kuomintang in 1930 and executed after she refused to denounce the Communist Party and Mao. Yang had two children by Mao: Mao Anqing, who was taken to the Soviet Union after his mother's arrest, and the elder son Mao Anying, who was arrested with his mother but later released. Mao Anying was killed in the Korean War in 1950.

Other Sights

The **Loving Dusk Pavilion** *(àiwǎntíng)* is on Yuelu Hill on the western bank of the Xiang River, from where you can get a good view of the town. **Long Island** *(júzizhōu)* or Long Sandbank, from which Changsha takes its name, lies in the middle of the Xiang River. The only remaining part of the old city walls is **Tianxin Tower** *(tiānxīngé)* in the south of the city.

Places to Stay

Unhappily for backpackers, the hotels in Changsha that take foreigners are mostly upmarket places. There's plenty of good

Mao Zedong

Mao was Hunan's main export. Mao was born in the Hunanese village of Shaoshan, not far from Changsha, in 1893. His father was a poor peasant who had been forced to join the army because of heavy debts. After several years of service he returned to Shaoshan, and by careful saving through small trading and other enterprises managed to buy back his land.

As 'middle' peasants Mao's family owned enough land to produce a surplus of rice with which they were able to buy more land. This raised them to the status of 'rich' peasants. Mao's father began to deal in grain transport and sales, buying grain from the poor farmers and taking it to the city merchants where he could get a higher price for it. As Mao told US journalist Edgar Snow, 'My family ate frugally, but had enough always'.

Mao began studying in the local primary school when he was eight years old and remained at school until the age of 13, meanwhile working on the farm and keeping accounts for his father's business. His father continued to accumulate wealth (or what was considered a fortune in the little village) by buying mortgages on other people's land. Creditors of other peasants would be paid off in lump sums, and these peasants would then have to pay back their loans to Mao's father, who would profit from the interest rates.

Several incidents influenced Mao around this time. A famine in Hunan and a subsequent uprising of starving people in Changsha ended in the execution of the leaders by the Manchu governor. This left a lasting impression on Mao, who '...felt that there with the rebels were ordinary people like my own family and I deeply resented the injustice in the treatment given to them'. He was also influenced by a band of rebels who had taken to the hills around Shaoshan to defy the landlords and the government, and by a radical teacher at the local primary school who opposed Buddhism and wanted people to convert their temples into schools.

At the age of 16, Mao left Shaoshan to enter middle school in Changsha, his first stop on the footpath to power. At this time he was not yet an anti-monarchist: '...indeed, I considered the emperor as well as most officials to be honest, good and clever men'. He felt however, even at an early age, that the country was in desperate need of reform. He was fascinated by stories of the ancient rulers of China, and learned something of foreign history and geography.

In Changsha, Mao was first exposed to the ideas of revolutionaries and reformers active in China, heard of Sun Yatsen's revolutionary secret society and read about the abortive Canton uprising of 1911. Later that year an army uprising in Wuhan quickly spread and the Qing Dynasty collapsed. Yuan Shikai made his grab for power and the country appeared to be slipping into civil war. Mao joined the regular army but resigned six months later, thinking the revolution was over when Sun handed the presidency to Yuan and the war between the north and south of China did not take place.

Mao became an avid reader of newspapers and from these was introduced to socialism. He decided to become a teacher and enrolled in the Hunan Provincial First Normal (Teachers' Training) School, where he was a student for five years. During his time at the Teachers' Training School, he inserted an advertisement in a Changsha newspaper 'inviting young men interested in patriotic work to make contact with me...'. Among them was Liu Shaoqi, who later became

cheap accommodation for locals, of course, but they're quite determined in excluding non-Chinese from their registers. One Chinese hotel that will probably accept you, however, is the *Binhua Hotel (bīnhuá bīnguǎn)* on Bayi Lu. The Binhua has beds in triple rooms for Y23 (with bathroom) and Y18 (without). Beds in doubles with attached shower cost Y51. There's a noisy karaoke nightclub on the 2nd floor that blasts away most evenings until midnight.

The *Lotus Hotel (fúróng bīnguǎn)* (☎ 401888), is a multistoreyed building favoured by foreign tourists because of its central location. Bottom-range singles cost Y114 and doubles are from Y124 to Y222. The *Xiangjiang Hotel* (☎ 408888) *(xiāngjiāng bīnguǎn)* is at 2 Zhongshan Donglu. This place used to offer dorm accommodation, but renovations have shifted it upmarket. Their cheapest standard doubles now go for US$48. To get there, take bus No 1 from the railway station and get off at the fourth stop, which is right outside the hotel.

president of the PRC, Xiao Chen who became a founding member of the Communist Party, and Li Lisan.

'At this time', says Mao, 'my mind was a curious mixture of ideas of liberalism, democratic reformism and utopian socialism...and I was definitely antimilitarist and anti-imperialist.' Mao graduated from the Teachers' Training School in 1918, and went to Beijing where he worked as an assistant librarian at Beijing University. In Beijing he met future co-founders of the Chinese Communist Party: the student leader Zhang Guodao, Professor Chen Duxiu and university librarian Li Dazhao. Chen and Li are regarded as the founders of Chinese Communism. It was Li who gave Mao a job and first introduced him to the serious study of Marxism.

Mao was very much the perplexed convert, a nationalist who found in Marxist theory a programme for reform and revolution in China. He did not found Chinese Communism but was introduced to it by Beijing intellectuals. On returning to Changsha, Mao became increasingly active in Communist politics. He said at this time:

'I became more and more convinced that only mass political power, secured through mass action, could guarantee the realisation of dynamic reforms.'

He became editor of the *Xiang River Review*, a radical Hunan students' newspaper. He continued working in the New People's Study Society and also took up a post as a teacher. In 1920 he was organising workers for the first time and from that year onwards considered himself a Marxist. In 1921, Mao went to Shanghai to attend the founding meeting of the Chinese Communist Party. Later he helped organise the first provincial branch of the Party in Hunan, and by the middle of 1922 the Party had organised trade unions among the workers and students.

Orthodox Marxist philosophy saw revolution spreading from the cities as it had in the Soviet Union. The peasants, ignored through the ages by poets, scholars and political soothsayers, had likewise been ignored by the Communists. But Mao took a different stand and saw the peasants as the lifeblood of the revolution. The Party had done very little work among them but in 1925 Mao began to organise peasant trade unions. This aroused the wrath of the landlords and Mao had to flee to Canton, where the Kuomintang and Communists held power in alliance with each other. Mao proposed a radical redistribution of the land to help the peasants, and supported (and probably initiated) the demands of the Hunan Peasants Union to confiscate large landholdings. Probably at this stage he foresaw the need to organise and arm them for a struggle against the landlords.

In April 1927, Chiang Kaishek launched his massacre of the Communists. The Party sent Mao to Changsha to organise what became known as the 'Autumn Harvest Uprising'. By September the first units of a peasant-worker army had been formed, with troops drawn from the peasantry, Hengyang miners and rebel Kuomintang soldiers. Mao's army moved south through Hunan and climbed up into the Jinggangshan mountains to embark on a guerrilla war against the Kuomintang. This action eventually culminated in the 1949 Communist takeover. ■

HUNAN

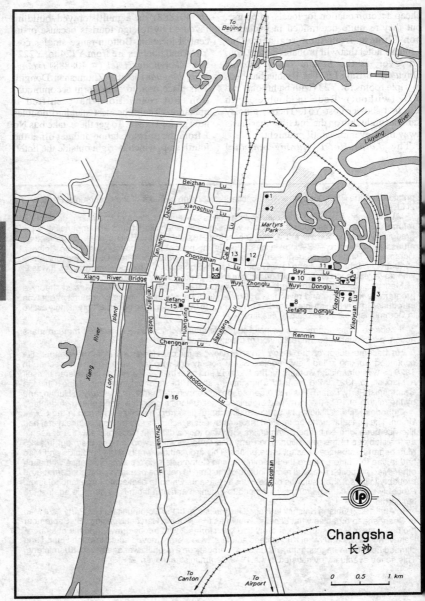

Xiang River

Long Island

Xiang River

To Beijing

Liuyang River

Beizhan Lu

Xiangchun Lu

Dazao

Yanjiang

Martyrs' Park

Zhongshan Lu

Cai Lu

13
12

14

Xiang River Bridge

Wuyi Xilu

Wuyi Zhonglu

11
Bayi Lu

10
9
4
5

Wuyi Donglu

Xiaoyiso

6 Lu

3

8

Jiefang Donglu

Jiefang Lu

15

Huangxing

Jianxiang

Chengnan Lu

Renmin Lu

Xiaoyuan

Laodong Lu

16

Shuyuan Lu

Shaoshan Lu

To Canton

To Airport

Changsha
长沙

0   0.5   1 km

1	Hunan Provincial Museum
2	Monument to the Martyrs
3	Railway Station
4	Long-Distance Bus Station
5	Kaiyun Restaurant
6	Bank of China
7	CAAC Office
8	Hua Tian Hotel
9	Lotus Hotel & CITS
10	Friendship Hotel
11	Binhua Hotel
12	Former Office of the Hunan Communist Party Committee
13	Xiangjiang Hotel
14	Post Office
15	PSB
16	Hunan No 1 Teachers' Training School

1	省博物馆
2	烈士纪念碑
3	火车站
4	长途汽车站
5	开云楼
6	中国银行
7	中国民航售票处
8	华天大酒店
9	芙蓉宾馆和中国国际旅行社
10	友谊商店
11	宾华宾馆
12	中共湘区委员会旧址
13	湘江宾馆
14	邮局
15	公安局
16	第一师范学校

The newest luxury accommodation in town is the *Hua Tian Hotel* (☎ 442888) *(huátiān Dàjiŭdiàn)* at 16 Jiefang Lu, just off Shaoshan Lu. This is a modern joint-venture tower block; rates range from US$58 for a standard double to US$388 for a deluxe suite.

Places to Eat

Hunanese food, like that of neighbouring Sichuan Province, makes use of plenty of chillies and hot spices. The *Kaiyunlou Hotel*

(☎ 443136) *(kāiyúnlóu jiŭjiā)* is on Wuyi Donglu near the corner of Xiaoyuan Lu. Although government-run it's cheap and surprisingly good, but doesn't have an English menu. There's also a good Hunan-style fast-food place on Chezhan Lu just south of the railway station. For 'international cuisine', try *Kiddies Restaurant* on Wuyi Lu. It has Western fast food (chicken and French fries, etc) as well as Chinese takeaways. The bigger hotels, such as the Lotus and Xiangjiang also have good restaurants.

The adventurous might like to sample betel nut *(bīnglang)*, sold at small street stalls all around town. When chewed, the woody flesh, which has an overpowering, spicy-sweet taste, produces a mild, semi-narcotic effect. Once should be enough to satisfy your curiosity.

Getting There & Away

Air The main CAAC office (☎ 23820) is at 5 Wuyi Donglu, around the corner from the railway station. The Lotus Hotel also has a CAAC booking office. Together CAAC and their associated local airline, Southern China Airlines, have 19 flights weekly to Beijing (Y730) and 15 weekly to Canton (Y290). Other useful flights include Shanghai (Y480, six weekly); Chengdu (Y470, four weekly); Kunming (Y560, three weekly); and Xi'an (Y480, Sundays). There are also two weekly flights to Hong Kong (US$170).

Bus The long-distance bus station is conveniently located near the railway station. There are departures for Yueyang (four daily) and several to Nanchang and Shaoshan. There are also daily sleeping-berth coaches to Canton (Y140, 18 hours); Hefei (Y195, 30 hours); Zhuhai (Y140, 21 hours); Nanjing (Y190, 30 hours); and Zhengzhou (Y170, 26 hours). The bus station closes at 6 pm.

Train There are two Canton-Changsha-Beijing expresses daily in either direction. Other important routes via Changsha are Beijing-Kunming-Guilin, Canton-Xian-Lanzhou, and Shanghai-Changsha. Not all trains to Shanghai, Kunming and Guilin stop

HUNAN

in Changsha, so it may be necessary to go to Zhuzhou first and change there. There is also a train daily to Shaoshan (Y5), leaving at 7 am. Counter No 6 at the Changsha railway station is for foreigners.

SHAOSHAN
(shāoshān) 韶山

The village of Shaoshan, about 130 km southwest of Changsha, has a significance to Chinese Communism which far overshadows its minute size, for this is where Mao Zedong was born. In the '60s, during the Cultural Revolution's headier days, some three million pilgrims came here each year, and a railway line and a paved road were built from Changsha to transport them. After Mao's death, the numbers declined and, as memories of the Cultural Revolution's excesses gradually fade, the village is undergoing a tourist revival. In 1993 Shaoshan held celebrations to mark the centenary of Mao's birth.

Shaoshan is hardly typical of Chinese villages, considering the number of tourists who have passed through since it was established as a national shrine. Despite the obvious impact of tourism, however, the surrounding countryside has retained its original rural charm. Traditional adobe houses dot this landscape of mountains and lush rice paddies. Apart from its historical significance, Shaoshan is a great place to get away from those grim, grey cities.

Orientation
There are two parts to Shaoshan: the new town clustered around the railway and bus stations, and the original Shaoshan village about seven km away. From the railway station you can pick up tour minibuses to the main sites. Public buses and motortricycles also meet the train from Changsha. The long-distance bus station is just down to the right from the main street corner.

Mao's Childhood House
(máozédōng tóngzhì gùjū)
毛泽东同志故居

This is the first building you come to as you reach Shaoshan, and is the village's principle shrine. It's a fairly large structure with mud walls and a thatched roof. It's no different from millions of other mud-brick dwellings in China – except for the painstaking restoration. As exhibits there are a few kitchen utensils, original furnishings and bedding, as well as photos of Mao's parents. In front of the house is a pond, and on the other side is a pavilion where Chinese tourists pose for photos with the house in the background.

Museum of Comrade Mao
(máozédōng tóngzhì jìniànguǎn)
毛泽东同志纪念馆

Devoted to the life of Mao, the museum opened in 1967 during the Cultural Revolution. Unfortunately there are no English captions, but the exhibits are graphic enough. There were originally two wings, exact duplicates of each other, so that more visitors could be accommodated at the same time. Today only one set of exhibits exists.

Other Sights
If you came looking for Mao souvenirs, you'll find every kind of Mao kitsch on sale in the **tourist market** *(lǚyóu shìcháng)*. Fancy a set of Mao chopsticks decorated with His picture? Or how about a Mao cigarette lighter that chimes 'The East is Red' when you flick the lid? Of course there're also more conventional Maobilia – like Mao badges, Mao rings and Mao bracelets, as well as those Mao portrait good-luck charms that Chinese drivers attach to their windscreens and car mirrors. The market is a short distance uphill from Mao's Childhood House.

Dripping Water Cave *(dīshuǐdòng)* is 4½ km up from Shaoshan village. Retreating to his native Shaoshan in June 1966, Mao lived in this cave for 11 days, probably thinking up new slogans for the Cultural Revolution that he had just begun. Nearby are the Mao clan's family tombs. You can get a bus up here from the parking lot opposite the post office.

Shaoshan Peak *(shāofēng)* is the prominent, conical-shaped mountain visible from the village. There is a lookout pavilion on the summit, and the 'forest of steles' on the lower

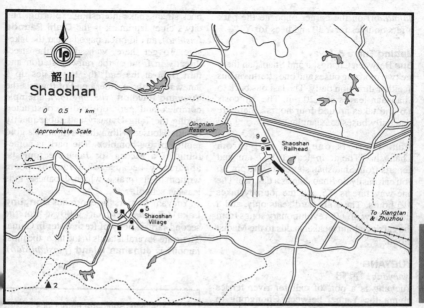

韶山
Shaoshan

0   0.5   1 km
Approximate Scale

Qingnian Reservoir

Shaoshan Railhead

Shaoshan Village

To Xiangtan & Zhuzhou

1	Dripping Water Cave
2	Shaoshan Peak
3	Hongri Hotel
4	Museum of Comrade Mao
5	Mao's Childhood House
6	Shaoshan Guesthouse
7	Railway Station
8	Entertainment City Hotel
9	Long-Distance Bus Station

1	滴水洞
2	韶山峰
3	红日饭店
4	毛泽东同志纪念馆
5	毛泽东同志故居
6	韶山宾馆
7	火车站
8	娱乐城大酒店
9	长途汽车站

slopes has stone tablets engraved with Mao's poems. The area is less frequented than other sites in Shaoshan and has some nice walks along quiet paths through pine forests and stands of bamboo. From Shaoshan village take a minibus south to the end of the road at Feilaichuan (*fēiláichuán*).

Places to Stay

The friendly *Shaoshan Guesthouse* (*shāoshān bīnguǎn*) (☎ 682127) in Shao-

shan village is in a convenient location. The guesthouse has doubles for Y80 or Y40 per bed, and their suite goes for Y500. Up the road is the cheaper *Hongri Hotel (hóngrì fàndiàn)*, a smaller, family-run hotel. They have clean, no-frills accommodation for Y6 per bed in small dorms and there's also a cheap restaurant downstairs.

Back in the new town many good cheap places can be found close to the bus station. The *Entertainment City Hotel (yùlèchéng dàjiǔdiàn*) on the corner opposite the park offers doubles for Y30 and beds for Y12.

Getting There & Away

Bus Between Changsha and Shaoshan there are two morning buses and one afternoon bus in either direction daily. The last bus back to Shaoshan leaves at 2.20 pm. The trip costs Y6 and takes around four hours. There are also daily buses to Xiangtan.

Train There is one train daily from Changsha. The train leaves at 7 am and departs from Shaoshan station at 3.40 pm, so you can easily do Shaoshan as a day trip. The one-way fare is Y5 and the journey takes 3½ hours. There are hard seats only, and a steady flow of '60s revolutionary songs from the carriage loudspeakers adds to the Maoist mood.

YUEYANG

(yuèyáng) 岳阳

Yueyang is a port of call for river ferries plying the Yangzi between Chongqing to Wuhan. The Wuhan-Canton railway passes through this small provincial city, so if you're heading to Canton you can get off here instead of going all the way to Wuhan. The opposite bank of the river is a vast green plain punctuated by villages. A ferry regularly takes trucks and buses across the river.

Information & Orientation

Yueyang is situated just south of the Yangzi River on the north-eastern shore of Dongting Lake, where the lake flows into the river. Yueyang has two quite separate sections. Yueyang proper is really the southern part, where the railway and bus stations as well as most of the hotels and sites are located. Some 17 km away to the north at Chenglingji (*chénglíngjī*) is the city's main port. Most Yangzi ferries dock here, but there are also two smaller local docks in the main (southern) part of Yueyang, where long-distance ferries sometimes call in.

Things to See

Yueyang has a 'port city' atmosphere, and its back streets make interesting exploring. The city's chief landmark is the **Cishi Pagoda** (*císhì tǎ*), an old brick pagoda near the lakeside. To get there, walk down the street directly in front of the railway station and turn right at the end; the tower lies up a laneway. At the northern end of town is the **Yueyang Pavilion** (*yuèyáng lóu*), a temple complex and park originally constructed during the Tang Dynasty and subsequently rebuilt. Housed within the pavilion is a gold replica of the complex. The park is something of a Mecca for Japanese tourists, apparently because of a famous poem written in its praise which Japanese kids learn at school.

Yueyang borders the enormous **Dongting Lake** (*dòngtǐng hú*), at 3900 sq km the second-largest body of fresh water in China. There are several islands in the lake; the most famous is **Junshan Island** (*jūnshān dǎo*),

1	Yueyang (Southern) Ferry Dock
2	Xuelian Hotel
3	Yueyang Pavilion
4	Yueyang Hotel
5	Nanyuepo Dock
6	Cishi Pagoda
7	Yuezhou Hotel
8	Railway Station
9	Yunmeng Hotel
10	Long-Distance Bus Station
11	Xiangwan Hotel

1	岳阳轮船客运站
2	雪莲宾馆
3	岳阳楼
4	岳阳宾馆
5	南岳坡码头
6	慈氏塔
7	岳州饭店
8	火车站
9	云梦宾馆
10	长途汽车站
11	湘宛宾馆

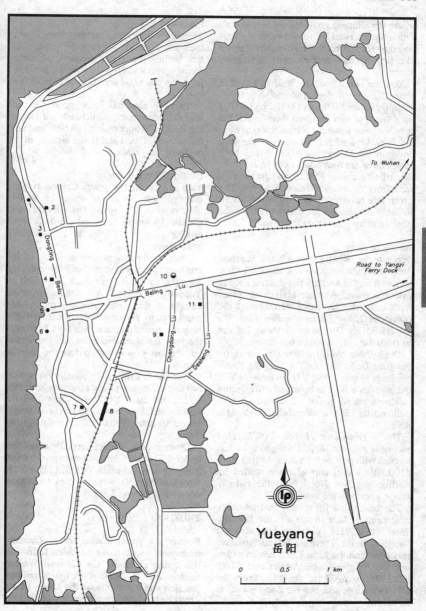

To Wuhan

Road to Yangzi
Ferry Dock

HUNAN

1
2
3
4
6
7
8
9
10
11

Dongting Beilu
Baling Lu
Chengdong Lu
Deshen Lu

Yueyang
岳阳

0   0.5   1 km

where the Chinese grow 'silver needle tea'. When the tea is added to hot water it's supposed to remain on the surface, sticking up like tiny needles and emitting a fragrant odour.

You can board boats to Junshan Island at either Nanyuepo dock (*nányuèpō mǎtou*), centrally located at the end of Baling Lu (bus No 2 more or less gets you there), or at the new Yueyang *southern* ferry dock (*yuèyáng lúnchuán kèyùnzhàn*) just north of Yueyang Pavilion on Dongting Beilu. From both places there are four boats daily to Junshan; the earliest leaves at 7.30 am and the last boat back from the island departs 4.30 pm. The return fare is only Y7, and it's worth a visit not only for the tea plantations but for the other farming activity on the island.

Places to Stay

Opposite the railway station is the Yuezhou Hotel (*yuèzhōu fàndiàn*). For about Y10 you get a spartan but sanitary flat-mattress bed in a double room. Another convenient place that's only slightly more upmarket is the *Xiangwan Hotel* (*xiāngwǎn bīnguǎn*). It's just off Baling Daqiao on Desheng Lu, not far from the long-distance bus station.

The *Xuelian Hotel* (*xuělián bīnguǎn*) is on Dongting Beilu just north of Yueyang Pavilion. Beds in quads cost Y16, in doubles Y20 and in suites Y50. The hotel and surrounding buildings are of quaint traditional Chinese architecture. It's a cheerful, low-budget place.

The *Yunmeng Hotel* (☎ 221115) (*yúnméng bīnguǎn*) at 25 Chengdong Lu has doubles with private bathroom starting from Y100. It's a dull sort of place staffed by indifferents. Bus No 4 from the railway station goes past the hotel.

The best value for money and probably most central place in town is the *Yueyang Hotel* (☎ 23011) (*yuèyáng bīnguǎn*) on Dongting Beilu. There's a Friendship Store next door and the local CITS has an office here too. Singles/doubles/triples cost Y160/200/240; it's Y700 for the suite. From the railway station, take bus No 2 and get off at the second stop.

Places to Eat

Yueyang's better restaurants often display their menu outside – in cages! Their specialties include hedgehog, snakes, pheasant, frogs, egrets and assorted rodents, but don't let it put you off – not all local cuisine is so exotic.

Yueyang also has some good fish and seafood restaurants, particularly on Dongting Beilu. Cheaper places can be found near the railway station and in the vicinity of the northern ferry dock.

Getting There & Away

Yueyang is on the main Canton-Beijing railway line. There are trains to Wuhan (3½ hours), Changsha (two hours) and Canton (13 hours). There are also daily buses to Changsha (Y14) from the long-distance bus station.

Most of the Yangzi ferries dock at the northern part of Yueyang (not to be confused with the southern ferry dock just north of Yueyang Pavilion). All tickets must be bought at the ticket office here. Private minibuses to Yueyang railway station regularly meet arriving boats. Bus No 1 from near the ferry terminal also takes you into town, but the last stop is well before the railway station.

Upriver to Chongqing usually takes four full days. Chinese-priced fares are: 2nd class Y255; 3rd class Y117; 4th class Y92 (in egalitarian China there is no 1st class). Rapid ferries are scheduled to called in at 6 am and 9 pm.

Downriver to Wuhan normally takes just under 10 hours. Chinese ticket prices from Yueyang are: 2nd class Y47; 3rd class Y22; 4th class Y16.50. Rapid ferries to Wuhan depart at 7 am and 8 am.

ZHUZHOU

(*zhūzhōu*) 株州

Formerly a small market town, Zhuzhou underwent rapid industrialisation following the completion of the Canton-Wuhan railway line in 1937. As a major railway junction and a port city on the Xiang River, Zhuzhou has since developed into an important coal and freight reloading point, as well as a manufacturing centre for railway equipment, locomotives and rolling stock. The only reason foreigners usually come here is to change trains, but although there's really nothing much in Zhuzhou to see, it's a pleasant enough place for a short stopover.

Places to Stay & Eat

The joint-venture *Qingyun Hotel* (☎ 224851) *(qìngyún dàshà)* opposite the railway station has singles from Y178 and doubles from Y208. More affordable is the *Zhuzhou Guesthouse* (☎ 222637) *(zhūzhōu bīnguǎn)* on Xinhua Xilu. They've got beds in doubles for Y30. To get there from the railway station head right past the Qingyun Hotel. At the next main intersection turn left and continue past the traffic roundabout. The hotel is just before the bridge up the driveway on the right.

The Qingyun Hotel has a good but a rather expensive restaurant. Near the railway station are cheaper food stalls and small restaurants.

Getting There & Away

Zhuzhou is at the junction of the Beijing-Canton and the Shanghai-Kunming railway lines. From Changsha it's just one hour by express train.

Most buses between Zhuzhou and Xiangtan leave and depart from the long-distance bus station on Xinhua Lu. It's a 10-minute walk to the railway station: turn right and cross the railway bridge then turn left again at the next intersection.

HENGYANG
(héngyáng) 衡阳

Hengyang is another of southern China's small industrial cities. It's on the railway junction where the Guilin-Nanning and Beijing-Canton lines intersect, and people travelling from Canton to Guilin often find themselves here briefly between train connections. Hengyang has important lead and zinc-mining industries, but was badly damaged during WW II. Despite post-1949 reconstruction, Hengyang still lags notice-

ably behind its neighbour down the Xiang River, Zhuzhou.

Places to Stay & Eat

The *Hengyang Hotel (héngyáng fàndiàn)* is across the river on Xiangjiang Lu. Beds in damp doubles with non-functional bathroom cost Y10 a night, but you'll probably have to bargain for that price. Take bus No 1 from the railway station and get off three stops after the bridge. More convenient and comfortable is the *Huiyan Hotel (huíyàn bīnguǎn)* on Guangdong Lu which charges Y120 for a nice double room and Y25 per bed in a triple. From the railway station it's a 10-minute walk straight along the main road.

The Huiyan has a classy restaurant next door specialising in hotpots *(huǒguǒ)*. Some of the small eating places around the railway station are a bit on the sleazy side, so choose carefully.

Getting There & Away

Hengyang is a major railway junction with direct trains to Wuhan, Canton and Guilin among other places. Trains to Changsha take three hours, and tourist-price hard seats cost Y24.

XIANGTAN
(xiāngtán) 湘潭

Once a river port and market centre, Xiangtan stagnated early this century when the railway took away much of its trade. The Kuomintang gave its industry a kick in the late 1930s and the Communists expanded it. Today Xiangtan is a rather flat, hot, drab town of 300,000 people on the Shanghai-Kunming railway line.

There are regular buses from Xiangtan to Zhuzhou (1¼ hours) and buses to Changsha. There are also buses to Shaoshan which take 1½ hours to make the trip and pass several small villages on the way.

HUAIHUA
(huáihuà) 怀华

Huaihua is a small, drab town in western Hunan built around a railway junction. It's not the sort of place you'd choose to come to, but if you're on the way to or from Zhangjiajie, Yaqueling or Liuzhou there are train connections from here. Beijing-Kunming, Chengdu-Canton and Shanghai-Chongqing expresses run via Huaihua. There are also slower trains from Guiyang, Canton and Liuzhou, terminating in Huaihua.

The *Haohua Guesthouse (háohuá kèfáng)* is five minute's walk down down the main street from the railway station. Their cheapest beds are Y30 or Y160 for a double. None of the other hotels will take foreigners.

WULINGYUAN SCENIC AREA
(wǔlíngyuán fēngjǐngqū) 武陵源风景区
Parts of the Wuling mountains *(wǔlíngshān)* in north-western Hunan have been set aside as nature reserves collectively known as the Wulingyuan Scenic Area, encompassing the localities of Zhangjiajie, Sangzhi, Tianzishan and Suoxiyu. The Wulingyuan area is home to three of the province's minority peoples – the Tujia, Miao and Bai nationalities, many of whom continue to speak their languages and maintain their traditional culture.

The mountains have gradually eroded to form a peculiarly spectacular landscape of craggy peaks and huge rock columns rising out of the luxuriant subtropical forest. There are waterfalls, limestone caves (including Asia's largest cave chamber), fresh clearwater streams and rivers suitable for organised rafting trips. There are many possible short and extended hikes, but even if you don't intend doing any walking it's a nice place to spend some time.

Several towns serve as access points to Wulingyuan, but the most popular way in is via **Dayong** and **Zhangjiajie**. Dayong is a small town near the railway line, while the tourist village of Zhangjiajie is situated at nearly 600 metres above sea level in the Wuling foothills. Zhangjiajie is surrounded by sheer cliffs and vertical rock outcrops and is an attractive place.

A fee (locals Y8, foreigners Y15) must be paid at the main entrance gate to the Zhangjiajie forest reserve just below the village. Chinese maps showing walking trails, some with key tourist sites marked in English, are on sale in Zhangjiajie.

Places to Stay & Eat
You'll probably find it more convenient and interesting to stay in Zhangjiajie, but in Dayong a number of hotels also take foreigners.

Diagonally opposite the Dayong bus station is the *Dule Hotel (dūlè bīnguǎn)* where a spartan double room is Y30 a night and dorm beds Y12. The *Wuling Guesthouse (wǔlíng bīnguǎn)* on Jiefang Lu (past the Puguang Temple) charges Y90 for very nice double rooms with bathroom, TV and lots of hot water.

In Zhangjiajie just about all the places seem willing to take foreigners. Just uphill from the bus station is the *Zhangjiajie Hotel (zhāngjiàjiè bīnguǎn)*. Their cheapest beds are Y10 in triples or Y25 in double rooms with bathroom that look out over a fish pond in a garden courtyard. The *Xiangdian Mountain Inn (xiāngdiàn shānzhuāng)* is just uphill from the bridge, 50 metres off the main road. This hotel has modern, clean doubles for Y100.

The best in town seems to be the *Pipaxi Guesthouse (pípāxī bīnguǎn)*, where standard doubles go for Y130 and suites for around Y200. The Pipaxi is situated at the village entrance, so you can save yourself a 10-minute walk back uphill by getting dropped off here. There are simple eating houses scattered around the village, and the better hotels also have their own restaurants. For those hiking overnight in Wulingyuan, basic Chinese hostels exist along most of the popular trail routes. Some people do a return circuit hike from Zhangjiajie via Sangzhi, Tianzishan and Suoxiyu.

Getting There and Away
From Changsha there are train connections to Dayong via the railway junction at Huaihua. If you're coming from the Yangzi port of Yichang you must change trains in Yaqueling. The train from Yichang to

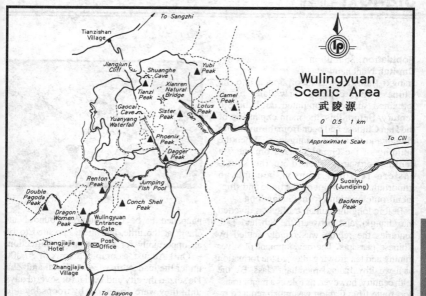

Wulingyuan
Scenic Area
武陵源

0   0.5   1 km
Approximate Scale

Yaqueling takes one hour, from Yaqueling to Dayong around 5½ hours. Confusingly, Dayong railway station is called 'Zhangjiejia', even though Zhangjiajia is actually 42 km north-west of here. In the tourist season (from early April until late October) direct buses also run to and from Changsha and Hengyang.

Minibuses to Zhangjiajie village pick up incoming passengers at Dayong railway station. The trip takes one hour and costs Y6. The main part of Dayong is across the river, 14 km from the railway station. Minibuses run frequently between the railhead and Dayong town centre (bus No 3 passes by the bus station).

Jiangxi 江西

Population: 35 million
Capital: Nanchang

Jiangxi *(jiāngxī)* was incorporated into the Chinese empire at an early date, but it remained sparsely populated until the 8th century. Before this, the main expansion of the Han Chinese had been from the north into Hunan and then into Guangdong. When the building of the Grand Canal from the 7th century onwards opened up the south-eastern regions, Jiangxi became an important transit point on the trade and shipment route overland from Guangdong.

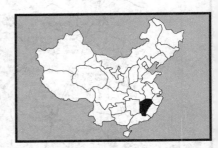

Before long the human traffic was diverted into Jiangxi, and between the 8th and 13th centuries the region was rapidly settled by Chinese peasants. The development of silver mining and tea growing allowed the formation of a wealthy Jiangxi merchant class. By the 19th century, however, its role as a major transport route from Canton was much reduced by the opening of coastal ports to foreign shipping – which forced the Chinese junk trade into a steady decline.

Jiangxi also bears the distinction of having been one of the most famous Communist guerrilla bases. It was only after several years of war that the Kuomintang were able to drive the Communists out onto their 'Long March' to Shaanxi.

NANCHANG
(nánchāng) 南昌

The capital of Jiangxi Province, Nanchang is largely remembered in modern Chinese history for the Communist-led uprising of 1 August 1927.

After Chiang Kaishek staged his massacre of Communists and other opponents in March 1927, what was left of the Communist Party fled underground and a state of confusion reigned. At this time the Party was dominated by a policy of urban revolution, and the belief was that victory could only be won by organising insurrections in the cities. Units of the Kuomintang Army led by Communist officers

happened to be concentrated around Nanchang at the time, and there appeared to be an opportunity for a successful insurrection.

On 1 August, a combined army of 30,000 under the leadership of Zhou Enlai and Zhu De seized the city and held it for several days until they were driven out by troops loyal to the Nanjing regime. The revolt was largely a fiasco, but it is remembered in Chinese history as the beginning of the Communist Army. The Army retreated from Nanchang south to Guangdong, but part of it, led by Zhu De, circled back to Jiangxi to join forces with the ragtag army that Mao Zedong had organised in Hunan and led into the Jinggangshan mountains.

Not all of Nanchang's history has been so tumultuous – in fact, the name means 'southern prosperity'. It was founded back in the Eastern Han Dynasty and became a busy trading city, a major staging post on the trade route from Guangdong to Beijing, and a major distribution point for the kaolin pottery of nearby Jingdezhen. Since 1949 it has grown into another of China's multi-purpose, industrial-urban sprawls, with something like 2½ million inhabitants.

Orientation

Nanchang is bounded in the north by the Gan River and in the west by the Fu River, which branches off the Gan. Bayi Dadao goes north

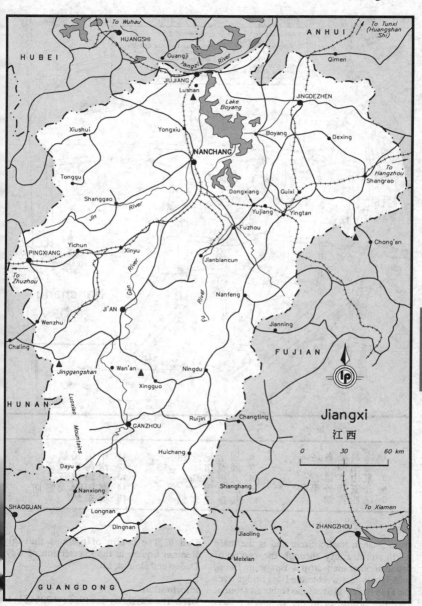

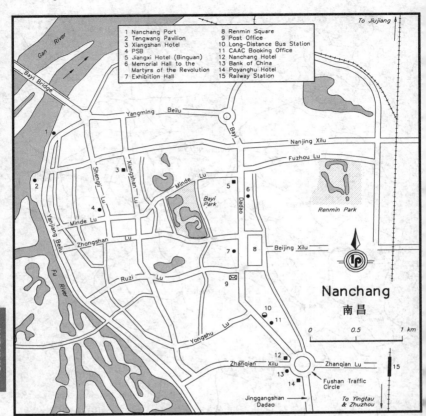

1	Nanchang Port	8	Renmin Square		
2	Tengwang Pavilion	9	Post Office		
3	Xiangshan Hotel	10	Long-Distance Bus Station		
4	PSB	11	CAAC Booking Office		
5	Jiangxi Hotel (Binguan)	12	Nanchang Hotel		
6	Memorial Hall to the Martyrs of the Revolution	13	Bank of China		
7	Exhibition Hall	14	Poyanghu Hotel		
		15	Railway Station		

1	南昌港客运站	6	烈士纪念馆	11	中国民航
2	腾王阁	7	展览馆	12	南昌宾馆
3	象山宾馆	8	人民广场	13	中国银行
4	公安局外事科	9	邮电局	14	鄱阳湖大酒店
5	江西宾馆	10	长途汽车站	15	火车站

from Fushan traffic circle and is the main north-south artery through the centre of town; another main strip is Yangming Beilu, which cuts east-west to the Bayi bridge over the Gan River. Most of the sights and tourist facilities are on or in the vicinity of Bayi

Dadao. The centre of town is the ugly Renmin Square at the intersection of Bayi Dadao and Beijing Lu.

Information
CITS The CITS has its office (☎ 226681) in

the building behind the rear car park at the Jiangxi Hotel (Binguan).

PSB This is in the new cream-tiled high-rise building on Shengli Lu, about 100 metres north of Minde Lu.

Money The main Bank of China is opposite the Nanchang Hotel on Zhanqian Xilu. The Jiangxi Hotel (Binguan) also has a money-changing service.

Post There is a post office on the ground floor of the Jiangxi Hotel, and another on the corner of Bayi Dadao and Ruzi Lu, just south of the Exhibition Hall.

Maps An English-language tourist map of the city has been produced, but in Nanchang it can be hard to get hold of – ask at the shop in the lobby of the Jiangxi Hotel (Binguan). City transport maps in Chinese are sold around the bus and railway stations. Otherwise try the two Xinhua bookstores on Bayi Dadao – one at Renmin Square and the other between the bus station and Fushan traffic circle.

Things to See

A fairly nondescript city, Nanchang has been called 'the poor person's Beijing'. Bayi Dadao is colour deprivation at its worst – a length of grey-on-grey concrete blocks. More interesting are the side streets in the centre of town, where the occasional outdoor market eases the monotony.

On Bayi Dadao in the heart of Nanchang is **Renmin Square**. Here you'll find the **Monument to the Martyrs**, a sculpture of red-tiled flags and a stone column topped with a rifle and fixed bayonet. Opposite the square is the **Exhibition Hall**, an immense building adorned with a giant red star – a nostalgic tribute to Stalinist architecture.

Pride of the city is the massive **Tengwang Pavilion**, erected in 1989, allegedly on the same site as 28 previous reconstructions. Originally built in the Tang period, the modern nine-storey granite pavilion is situated on the banks of the Fu River and houses

exhibit rooms, teahouses and the inevitable souvenir shops. On the top floor is a traditional Chinese music and dance theatre. Entry costs Y10 for Chinese and students, Y20 for foreigners.

Most of the other sights are reminders of the Communist Revolution and include the **Memorial Hall to the Martyrs of the Revolution** on Bayi Dadao north of Renmin Square; the **Residence of Zhou Enlai & Zhu De** on Minde Lu; and the **Former Headquarters of the Nanchang Uprising**, now a museum, near the corner of Shengli and Zhongshan Lu.

Places to Stay

The *Xiangshan Hotel (xiàngshān fàndiàn)* on Xiangshan Beilu is still the only place catering for the thin trickle of low-budget travellers visiting Nanchang. The hotel has beds in triple dorms for Y15, but you'll have to press the staff a bit if you want one. For Y40 their doubles with bathroom are not bad value. (These prices haven't gone up in recent years, but given China's high inflation rate they may have risen by the time you read this.) Take bus No 5 for nine stops from the railway station; the bus stop is almost outside the hotel.

The newly built *Poyanghu Hotel* (☎ 224002) *(póyánghú dàjiǔdiàn)* on the south-west side of Fushan traffic circle has sunny, clean doubles for Y100 and spacious suites for Y380. It's a friendly place, convenient for the bus and railway stations. A few doors north at 2 Bayi Dadao is the *Nanchang Hotel* (☎ 64811) *(nánchang bīnguǎn)*, another of the city's prefab high-rise constructions. Here fairly average doubles cost Y145, while slightly better versions are Y210. They have small dorms as well, but foreigners aren't allowed in.

Two local establishments go by the English name 'Jiangxi Hotel', although their names in Chinese use different words (and characters) for 'hotel'. The *Jiangxi Hotel* (☎ 221131) *(jiāngxī bīnguǎn)* at 78 Bayi Dadao is where most foreign tourists seem to put up. The building is an interesting relic of early 1960s socialist architecture. Room rates are: standard double US$40/45; suite US$80; deluxe suite US$228. To get there take bus No 2 from the railway station. The other *Jiangxi Hotel (jiāngxī fàndiàn)* is a dreary, overpriced place just down the road. The *fandian* is worth mentioning only to avoid confusion with its namesake, the *binguan*.

Places to Eat

The Jiangxi Hotel (Binguan) has restaurants serving Chinese and Western cuisine. Good streets for food are Shengli Lu and Zhongshan Lu. A recommended local place is the *Huadu Restaurant (huádū dàjiǔdiàn)*, specialising in hotpots and fish dishes. It's on Shengli Lu, five minutes' walk north of Minde Lu, and has an English menu upstairs. For fast food try the *Hunky Dory Nice Food Co*, about ½ km south of Renmin Square on Bayi Dadao.

Getting There & Away

Air The most convenient CAAC office (☎ 223656) is on Bayi Dadao next to the bus station. Scheduled flights go to Beijing (Y700, nine a week), Canton (Y320, eight a week), Fuzhou (Y220, two weekly) and Shanghai (Y320, daily). During the tourist season there are also irregular flights to Xi'an. The airport is at Xiangtang, 40 km south of the city centre.

Bus Nanchang's long-distance bus station is on Bayi Dadao between Renmin Square and Fushan traffic circle. From here there are air-con buses to Changsha (Y45, seven daily), Jiujiang (Y15, six daily), and to the porcelain-producing centre of Jingdezhen (Y28, eight daily). There are also direct buses to the mountain resorts of Jinggangshan in Jiangxi's south-western mountains (Y29, five per day) and Lushan hill station to the north (Y15, daily in summer only).

Train Counter No 9 at Nanchang railway station is for foreigners. Nanchang lies just off the main Canton-Shanghai railway line but most trains make the short detour north via the city. There are express trains each day

■	PLACES TO STAY
1	景德镇宾馆
2	景德镇宾馆合资
6	景德镇饭店
8	华光饭店
	OTHER
3	中国国际旅行社
4	中国银行
5	邮电局
7	新华书店
9	火车站
10	长途汽车站
11	陶瓷历史博览区

to the Yangzi port of Jiujiang (Y12, 2½ hours). On board, staff hand out token gifts to passengers and strictly enforce the no-smoking rule.

Boat The small Nanchang ferry terminal is just south of the Bayi bridge. An alternative way of getting to Jingdezhen is to catch a 6.30 am boat (Y18) across Lake Boyang to the town of Boyang, then take a bus connection to Jingdezhen. In summer, tourist cruise boats also leave from here.

Getting Around

From Nanchang railway station, the most useful public transport routes are trolley-buses No 2 and No 201 which go up Bayi Dadao past the long-distance bus station and bus No 5 running north along Xiangshan Beilu. The city has few pedicabs and motortricycles, but there are plenty of taxis at the stations and better hotels.

JINGDEZHEN
(jǐngdézhèn) 景德镇

Jingdezhen is an ancient town once famous for the manufacture of much-coveted porcelain. The city has maintained its position as a major producer of Chinese ceramics, but quality seems to have been compromised by mass production. The skyline of Jingdezhen is dominated by

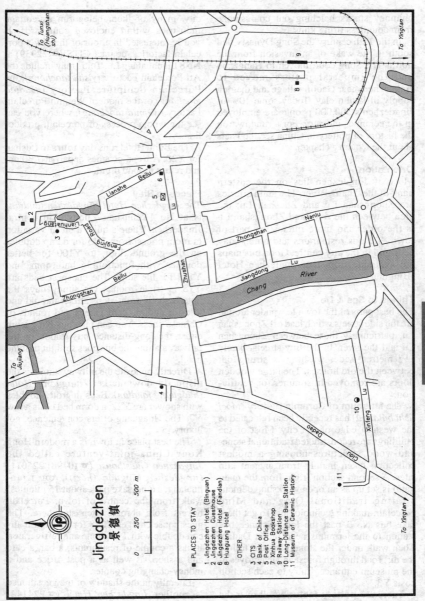

JIANGXI

Jingdezhen 景德镇

0   250   500 m

To Tunxi (Huangshan shi)

To Yingtan

To Jiujiang

To Yingtan

Lianshe

Beilu

Lianhuatang

Road

Fengluo

Zhushan

Zhongshan

Beilu

Zhongshan

Lu

Zhongshan

Nanlu

Jiangdong Lu

Chang River

Cidu

Dadao

Xinfeng

Lu

PLACES TO STAY
- 1 Jingdezhen Hotel (Binguan)
- 2 Jingdezhen Guesthouse
- 6 Jingdezhen Hotel (Fandian)
- 8 Huaguang Hotel

OTHER
- 3 CITS
- 4 Bank of China
- 5 Post Office
- 7 Xinhua Bookshop
- 9 Railway Station
- 10 Long-Distance Bus Station
- 11 Museum of Ceramic History

chimney stacks belching out coal smoke from countless firing kilns.

In the 12th century the Song Dynasty fled south in the wake of an invasion from the north. The Song court moved to Hangzhou and the imperial potters moved to Jingdezhen, near Gaolin village and the rich supply of kaolin clay. Today some 10% of Jingdezhen's 300,000 people are employed in the ceramics industry. For a rundown on the history of pottery in China see the Facts about the Country chapter.

Orientation

Most of Jingdezhen lies on the eastern bank of the Chang River. The main arteries are Zhongshan Lu and Zhushan Lu; the area between the river and Zhongshan Lu is the older and more interesting part of town. Various restaurants and hotels may be found in the city centre. Good bus maps are available from the Jingdezhen Hotel (Binguan).

Things to See & Do

The best parts of the town to wander around are the side streets which lead off Zhongshan Lu, particularly those between Zhongshan Lu and the river. In the tiny streets, barely 1½ metres wide, washing is strung out between the old houses. The large wooden doors are removed in summer for ventilation.

The **Museum of Ceramic History** (*táocí lìshǐ bólǎnqū*) has recently been relocated to the western edge of the city. Most of the buildings are reconstructed traditional stone-and-wood structures housing a modest collection taken mainly from ancient kiln sites. A second section (right from the main gate) is set up as an open workshop demonstrating traditional Qing and Ming porcelain-making technologies. To get there take bus No 3 past the long-distance bus station to the terminus near Taodu Dadao. Then walk under the stone gate and follow the dirt road through forest and tea groves to the museum entrance. Entry to each section costs Y3.

There are **pottery factories** all over the city, many of them being run as cottage industries within enclosed courtyards. If you're interested in a tour of the city's porcelain factories, contact CITS (☎ 22939) at No 8 Lianhuatang Lu. Tours may include the Art Porcelain Factory (*yìshù táochǎng*), the Porcelain Sculpture Factory (*měidiāo táochǎng*) or the modern Weimin Porcelain Factory (*wèimín táochǎng*), where you can see the whole process of porcelain production.

The Bailu Hotel runs **day tours** to Lushan for Y20. Air-con coaches depart at 7.30 am and return around 4 pm.

Places to Stay

The *Jingdezhen Hotel (jǐngdézhèn fàndiàn)* is at No 1 Zhushan Zhonglu in central Jingdezhen. There's quite a bit of variation in room prices, from Y45 for damp doubles on the ground floor, to Y100 for better doubles with functioning bathroom, and Y180 for the suite. The cheapest beds are Y18 in triple rooms. On sunny days the hotel's shady front steps attract the old and idle for endless card games and rounds of Chinese chess. You can take bus No 2 from either the long-distance bus station or the railway station; the bus goes straight past the hotel.

Directly opposite the railway station is the distinctly downmarket *Huaguang Hotel (huáguāng fàndiàn)*. Beds in grotty doubles with shower are Y22; a dorm bed costs a low Y7. The Huaguang offers convenience, not luxury.

The best place in town is a modern Hong Kong-China joint-venture called the *Jingdezhen Guesthouse* (☎ (0798) 225011) *(jǐngdézhèn bīnguǎn (hézī))*, on Lianhuatang, a quiet lake park about 15 minutes' walk from the centre of town. Porcelain buyers from abroad often stay here. The guesthouse charges Y228 for a standard air-con double with TV, phone and refrigerator. It has a couple of restaurants, a bar, a cafe and a shop, as well as a post office and a money-changing counter.

Literally in the shadow of the guesthouse is another *Jingdezhen Hotel* (☎ 224144) *(jǐngdézhèn bīnguǎn)*. This is the older place right behind; clean triples with shared bathroom cost US$21 and standard doubles cost US$24. Compared to its nearby namesake this hotel is a trifle run-down, but it's reasonable value for money.

Things to Buy

Porcelain products are sold in places around the city, particularly on Lianshe Nanlu, opposite the Jingdezhen Hotel (Fandian). The Porcelain Friendship Store *(yǒuyì shāngdiàn)* is at 13 Zhushan Lu.

Getting There & Away

Bus Daily buses run to Yingtan (Y15, four hours), Jiujiang (Y15, 4½ hours) and Nanchang (Y42 air-con bus, Y22 standard). There is also a daily bus to the town of Boyang, south-west of Jingdezhen. From there you can take a boat across Lake Boyang to Nanchang. To get to the mountain resort of Huangshan first catch a bus to Tunxi (Huangshan Shi) then change for Huangshan village.

Train If you're heading north there are trains to Shanghai and Nanjing via Tunxi (Huangshan Shi; 3½ hours, Y48 soft seat, Y32 hard seat) and Wuhu. There is one daily express train to Nanchang via Jingdezhen (six hours, Y30 hard seat, Y46 soft seat), but for better connections first go to the railway junction at Yingtan (3½ hours).

Getting Around

Real taxis are almost nonexistent in Jingdezhen, but there are plenty of pedicabs and motortricycles. The centre of town is small enough to walk around in anyway. Bus No 2 runs from the long-distance bus station, through the centre of town past the Jingdezhen Hotel (Fandian), and out to the railway station.

JIUJIANG

(jiǔjiāng) 九江

Situated near Lake Boyang, which drains into the Yangzi, Jiujiang has been a port since ancient times. Because of its prime location it became one of the leading market towns for tea

and rice in southern China. After it was opened to foreign trade in 1862 the city developed into a port serving nearby Hubei and Anhui provinces as well as Jiangxi itself, but Jiujiang has remained a medium-sized city.

For most travellers, Jiujiang is just a jumping-off point on the way to Lushan, but it's a pleasant enough place to spend a day or so.

Orientation & Information

Jiujiang stretches out along the southern bank of the Yangzi River. Two interconnected lakes divide the older north-eastern part of the city from a newer industrial sprawl off to the south. The long-distance bus station is on the city's eastern side and the railway station over to the west, while the main river port is more conveniently situated close to the heart of town. There is a CITS office (☎ 223390) at 28 Nanhu Lu.

Things to See

The small **Nengren Temple** *(néngrénsì)* on Yuliang Nanlu is worth a short visit. In the temple grounds is a disused Yuan Dynasty pagoda *(dàshèngtǎ)*. The museum is housed in quaint old buildings on **Yanshuiting** *(yānshuǐtíng)*, a tiny island in Gantang Lake. It's a tranquil spot near the centre of town and is connected to the shore by a short bridge. The museum has small exhibits of clothing, ceramics, imperial knights' armour and weaponry, but there are no captions in English.

Places to Stay

The most central place where foreigners can stay is the *Dongfeng Hotel (dōngfēng fàndiàn)* on Xunyang Lu. The prices haven't changed in years: dorm beds are Y10; doubles with shower are Y40. Rooms facing the back are a bit quieter. Bus Nos 1 and 4 run past the hotel from both the long-distance bus station and the railway station.

A few hundred metres further along Xunyang Lu is a new high-rise building, the *Bailu (White Deer) Hotel* (☎ 224404) *(báilù*

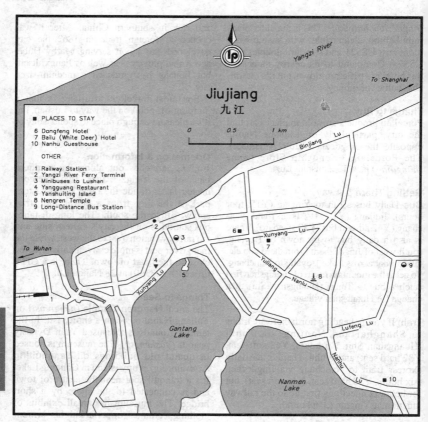

Jiujiang 九江

PLACES TO STAY
6 Dongfeng Hotel
7 Bailu (White Deer) Hotel
10 Nanhu Guesthouse

OTHER
1 Railway Station
2 Yangzi River Ferry Terminal
3 Minibuses to Lushan
4 Yangguang Restaurant
5 Yanshuiting Island
8 Nengren Temple
9 Long-Distance Bus Station

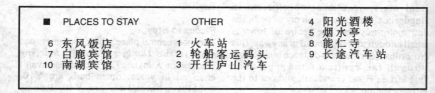

■ PLACES TO STAY	OTHER	
6 东风饭店	1 火车站	4 阳光酒楼
7 白鹿宾馆	2 轮船客运码头	5 烟水亭
10 南湖宾馆	3 开往庐山汽车	8 能仁寺
		9 长途汽车站

bīnguǎn). Their 14th-floor doubles have private bathroom and TV, and cost Y90. These are rooms with a view – on a clear day you might even see Lushan.

The *Nanhu Guesthouse* (☎ 225041)

(nánhú bīnguǎn) at 77 Nanhu Lu is another of China's old run-down tourist hotels, facing either a thorough renovation or eventual demolition. It's set in leafy gardens on a quiet lakeside spot a couple of km out of

town, but unfortunately there's no public transport out there. The cheapest doubles – mind the loose floorboards – cost Y80 and better ones up to Y160.

Places to Eat

You'll find the best street food in the lanes around the docks. There are also plenty of cheap eating houses here, but for something a bit more classy try the *Yangguang Restaurant (yángguāng jiǔlóu)*. It's on Xunyang Lu, a short way past Yanshuiting Island. They've got a shorter version of their menu in English upstairs.

Getting There & Away

Air Jiujiang Airport is 30 km south-west of the city. There is one flight to Beijing (Y630) and one to Shanghai (Y280) each week.

Bus Minibuses for Lushan leave from the corner of Xunyang Lu and the street leading to the ferry terminal whenever they have enough passengers. You can also get minibuses from the railway station, or an 8.00 am minibus from outside the Dongfeng Hotel. Scheduled public buses to Lushan leave from the long-distance bus station (gate 3) between 7.30 and 1.30 pm. The fare for all Lushan buses is about Y5.

There are at least five departures to Jingdezhen each day from the long-distance bus station. Tickets are Y15, and the 4½-hour trip includes a short ferry ride across the mouth of Lake Boyang. Other daily buses go to Nanjing (Y39) and Nanchang (Y18). Minibuses to Nanchang can also be picked up at the dock area.

Train There are several Jiujiang-Nanchang expresses each day; the train takes 2½ hours and one-class-only tickets cost Y12. A railway line is being built across the Yangzi through southern Anhui. When finished it will directly link the provincial capital of Hefei with Jiujiang and Nanchang.

Boat A large, white-tiled ferry terminal has just been completed in Jiujiang. Almost all long-distance boats plying the Yangzi seem to call in here. Local-price ferry tickets upriver to Chongqing cost: Y325 (2nd class), Y151 (3rd class) and Y115 (4th class); downriver fares to Shanghai are: Y144 (2nd class), Y67 (3rd class) and Y51 (4th class). (First class still doesn't exist in nominally socialist China.)

Getting Around

Bus Nos 1, 4 and 14 run from the long-distance bus station to the railway station via the centre of town. You can get motortricycles from around the bus and railway stations, and the dock.

LUSHAN

(lúshān) 庐山

Lushan was established as a mountain resort town by European and American settlers late last century as an escape from lowland China's sweaty summers. They left a fascinating hotch-potch of colonial buildings, from quaint stone cottages reminiscent of southern Germany to small French-style churches and more grandiose hotels built in classical Victorian architecture. The bus ride from the plains of Jiangxi to the top of Lushan is dramatic – and slightly nerve-racking – as the road winds its way around the mountainsides, looking down on sheer cliffs. Over the long drop below you can see vast expanses of patchwork fields.

Lushan's gentleness belies the area's significance in the destiny of over one billion Chinese. Although perhaps a symbol of China's ruthless exploitation by foreign powers, the country's post-1949 revolutionaries favoured these cool uplands as a site for Party conferences. It was here in 1959 that the Central Committee of the Communist Party held its fateful meeting which eventually ended in the dismissal of Peng Dehuai, sent Mao almost into a political wilderness and provided the seeds of the rise and fall of Liu Shaoqi and Deng Xiaoping.

In 1970, after Mao had regained power, another meeting was held in Lushan, this time of the Politburo. Exactly what happened is shrouded in as much mist as the mountains, but it seems that Lin Biao clashed with Mao, opposed his policies of *rapprochement* with the USA and probably proposed the continuation of the xenophobic policies of the Cultural Revolution. Whatever – by the following year, Lin was dead.

Orientation & Information

The point of arrival in Lushan is the charming resort village of Guling (*gǔlǐng*), perched 1167 metres high at the northern end of the range. Two km before Guling is the entrance gate, where you must pay an entry fee (Y12.50 for foreigners). Guling village is where the shops, post office, bank and the long-distance bus station are located. Nestled into the surrounding hills are scores of tourist hotels, sanatoriums and factory work units' holiday hostels. The CITS office, uphill from the Lushan Hotel, is quite well organised and helpful. Detailed maps of Lushan showing roads and walking tracks are available from shops in Guling.

Things to See

Lushan has enough sites of historical and scenic interest to keep you here for a couple of days.

Built by Chiang Kaishek in the 1930s as a summer getaway, **Meilu Villa** (*měilú biéshù*) was named after the general's wife, Song Meilu. It's not a particularly grand house, but well worth a visit. Although the original gardens were probably much more spacious and better maintained than today, the villa has evidently been kept much as it was. It costs Y1 to get in.

The **Peoples' Hall** (*rénmín jùyuàn*), built in 1936 and the venue for the Chinese Communist Party's historic 1959 and 1970 get-togethers, has been turned into a museum. On display are photos of Mao, Zhou and other members of the Party elite taking it easy between meetings. The main auditorium is decked out with the predictable red flags and Mao-era decor.

At Lushan's north-western rim, the land falls away abruptly to give some spectacular views across the densely settled plains of Jiangxi. A long walking track south around these precipitous slopes passes the **Fairy Cave** (*xiānrén dòng*) and continues to the **Dragon Head Cliff** (*lóngshǒuyá*), a natural rock platform tilted above a vertical drop of hundreds of metres.

A place of interest to Chinese visitors is the **Three Ancient Trees** (*sānbǎoshù*) not far by foot from Lulin Lake; 500 years ago Buddhist monks planted a ginkgo and two cedar trees near their temple, now an abandoned ruin. Tourists used to climb onto the branches to have their photos taken, but a high wall now protects the trees from this indignity.

The **Lushan Museum** (*bówùguǎn*) beside Lulin Lake commemorates the historic 1970 meeting with a photo collection and Mao's huge bed. Scrolls and inscribed steles displaying the poetry and calligraphy of Li Bai and other Chinese poet-scholars who frequented Lushan can also be seen, as well as exhibits on local geology and natural history. Unfortunately, none of the labels are in English.

The **Botanical Garden** (*zhíwùyuán*), is mainly devoted to sub-alpine tropical plants that thrive in the cooler highland climate. In the open gardens there are flowering rhododendrons, camellias and conifers, and hothouses with a cactus collection and species of palms and hibiscus. Admission is only Y1.

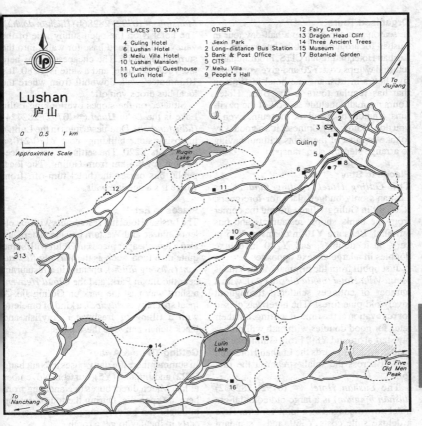

Lushan 庐山

0   0.5   1 km

Approximate Scale

■ PLACES TO STAY	OTHER	12 Fairy Cave
4 Guling Hotel	1 Jiexin Park	13 Dragon Head Cliff
6 Lushan Hotel	2 Long-distance Bus Station	14 Three Ancient Trees
8 Meilu Villa Hotel	3 Bank & Post Office	15 Museum
10 Lushan Mansion	5 CITS	17 Botanical Garden
11 Yunzhong Guesthouse	7 Meilu Villa	
16 Lulin Hotel	9 People's Hall	

To Jiujiang

Ruqin Lake

Guling

Lulin Lake

To Five Old Men Peak

To Nanchang

JIANGXI

■ PLACES TO STAY	OTHER
4 牯岭饭店	1 街心公园
6 庐山宾馆	2 长途汽车站
8 美庐别墅村	3 银行和国际邮局
10 庐山大厦宾馆	5 中国国际旅行社
11 云中美宾馆	7 美庐别墅
16 芦林饭店	9 人民剧院
	12 仙人洞
	13 龙首崖
	14 三宝树
	15 博物馆
	17 植物园

Organised Tours

In season you can pick up a half-day tour in Lushan for around Y12 at the bus station, the Lushan Hotel or through CITS. From Jiujiang, return day trips cost Y20 and give you about five hours in Lushan; one hotel in Jiujiang that has regular tours is the Bailu Hotel. Tours normally include several of the pavilions, a nature hike and the museum. Even if you don't know any Chinese, it's a good way to take in most of the sights without having to arrange step-by-step transport.

Places to Stay

The *Guling Hotel (gǔlǐng fàndiàn)* is Lushan's only budget place for foreigners. It's right in Guling village around the corner from the bank, shops, restaurants and bus terminal. Beds are Y10 in dorms or Y15 in very basic doubles, and Y200 in deluxe doubles in a large annexe opposite.

Just uphill from the original Meilu Villa is *Meilu Villa Hotel (měilú biéshù cūn)*, with a number of cottages scattered throughout lovely old pine forest. The hotel was closed for renovation at the time of writing, but their rates for good doubles with bath will probably start at around Y80. From Gulin take the road downhill towards the Lushan Hotel and go left across the small stream at the first fork.

The *Lushan Hotel* (☎ (0792) 282932) *(lúshān bīnguǎn)* is a large old colonial-era hotel now managed as a joint venture. Here a deluxe suite costs Y380, and a standard double Y200. All rooms are well heated and have phone and (satellite) TV. The hotel also has 'standard basic' doubles in a separate wing for Y62. It's a 20-minute downhill walk from the bus station.

The *Yunzhong Guesthouse* (☎ (0492) 282547) *(yúnzhōng bīnguǎn)* is on the wooded slopes above Gulin. It's a spread-out group of buildings with something of the atmosphere of a large summer vacation camp. Rooms start at Y100 for a double with bath. The Yunzhong is most easily reached via the road past the Lushan Hotel, though this is a tiring walk uphill.

Next door to the People's Hall is *Lushan*

Mansion (☎ (0792) 282860) *(lúshān dàshà)*. The hotel is on the open sunny side of the valley and is a good base for walks into the surrounding hills. The cheapest rooms here are Y150 a double, and a suite is Y380. It's 10 minutes' walk downhill from where the local bus drops you off.

Situated on the slopes overlooking Lulin Lake is the *Lulin Hotel* (☎ (0792) 282424) *(lúlín fàndiàn)*. Doubles/triples in the Lulin's imposing stone buildings cost Y170/210; a quad costs Y220. The setting is very peaceful, but several km from Guling. The local public bus passes the hotel turn-off, from where it's a one-km walk.

Places to Eat

The Lushan Hotel has restaurants with excellent Chinese and Western cuisine. There are also a few cheaper places in Gulin with some quite nice food, such as the *Wusong Restaurant (wùsōng jiǔlóu)*, upstairs in a restaurant near the Jiexin Park, and the *Cloud Heaven*, a short way past the park on Guling Jie. A local specialty is *shíyúpái*, a kind of omelette with a filling of freshwater crayfish and black lichen native to these parts.

Getting There & Away

In summer there are daily buses to Nanchang (Y22) and Jiujiang (Y5), but from November to late March direct buses to Nanchang from here are sporadic. During the tourist season numbers can be very high, so try to arrive early in the day to get a room.

Getting Around

If you like country walking, exploration on foot is the ideal way to go. Paths and small roads crisscross Lushan, so getting around is easy. It's also the best way to avoid the hoards of Chinese tourists who bus up by the truckful from the sticky lowlands in summer.

YINGTAN

(yīngtán) 鷹潭

Nanchang is north of the main Shanghai-Canton line and though most trains make the short detour, you may have to catch some at the railway junction town of Yingtan. If you do stop here, walk down the main street leading from the railway station. The street ends in a T-intersection in front of a park. Turn right for the old part of town by the river. You might try getting a boat to the other side and exploring.

Places to Stay & Eat

There are three cheap Chinese hotels, including an *Overseas Chinese Hotel (huáqiáo fàndiàn)*, on the main street near the railway station. Dormitory beds go for a few yuan, rooms for less than Y50. There are lots of food stalls on the street beside the railway station.

Getting There & Away

The long-distance bus station is on the main street next to the Overseas Chinese Hotel. There are buses to Jingdezhen, and trains to Fuzhou, Xiamen, Shanghai, Canton and Kunming. There is also a branch line to Jingdezhen via Guixi.

JINGGANGSHAN
(jǐnggāng shān) 井岗山

The remote Jinggangshan region in the Luoxiao mountains along the Hunan-Jiangxi border played a crucial role in the early Communist movement. After suffering a string of defeats in an urban-based revolution in the cities, in 1927 Mao led a core of 900 men into the refuge of these misty hills. They were soon joined by other companies of the battered Communist Army led by Zhu De, and from here began the Long March.

Orientation & Information

The main township, Ciping (also called Jinggangshan), up in the mountains at 820 metres, is an attractive place built around a small lake. The local CITS (☎ 222504) is in the grounds of the Jinggangshan Hotel (Binguan). The Xinhua Bookshop near the museum sells a Chinese tourist map of Ciping which also shows hiking trails in the hills.

Things to See

The **Jinggangshan Revolutionary Museum** *(jǐnggāngshān gémìng bówùguǎn)* is devoted to the Kuomintang and Communists' struggle for control of the Hunan-Jiangxi area in the late 1920s. The collection includes Nationalist and Communist Army war paraphernalia and has exhibits showing military strategies and troop movements. The explanations are all in Chinese, but the collection is graphic enough for you to get the gist of things. Entry costs Y2.

The **Former Revolutionary Quarters** *(gémìng jiùzhǐ qún)* in Ciping served as the Communist centre of command between 1927 and 1928. Mao lived temporarily in one of the four crude mud-brick buildings.

Jinggangshan is a major scenic area with large expanses of natural highland forest; the area boasts an interesting species of square-stemmed bamboo and some 26 kinds of alpine azaleas that bloom from late April. There are some great walks into the hills around Ciping, such as to **Five Fingers Peak** *(wǔzhǐfēng)*, a mountain featured on the back of the Y100 banknote, and to the **Five Dragon Pools** *(wǔlóngtán)*.

Places to Stay & Eat

The *Jinggangshan Hotel (jǐnggǎngshān fàndiàn)*, a short walk down from the bus station, has beds in four-person dorms for just Y8 and doubles with shower for Y38.

The other *Jinggangshan Hotel* (☎ (0791) 22272) *(jǐnggǎngshān bīnguǎn)* is where the Party top brass choose to stay – Mao, Lin Biao, Deng and Li Peng have all put up here. The place has just been renovated, and charges around Y140 for doubles and Y200 for a suite. The hotel is 15 minutes' walk from the bus station; go downhill, right at the first road, then right again. There's no sign on the main gate.

There are good cheap restaurants on the main street down from the bus station. For something a bit more romantic, try the place on the island in the middle of the lake.

JIANGXI

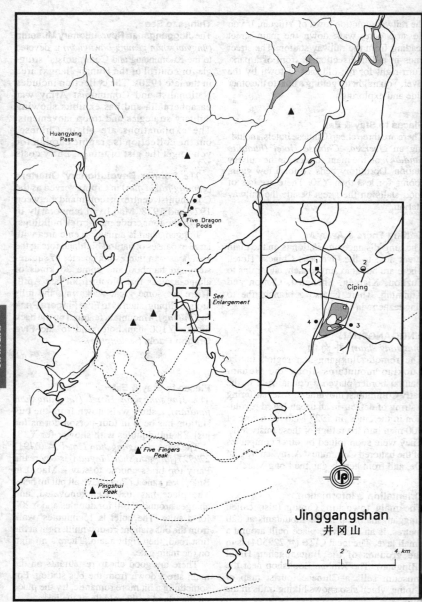

Huangyang Pass

Five Dragon Pools

See Enlargement

Ciping

1

2

4

3

Five Fingers Peak

Pingshui Peak

Jinggangshan
井冈山

0   2   4 km

1	Jinggangshan Hotel (Binguan) & CITS
2	Long-Distance Bus Station
3	Former Revolutionary Quarters
4	Revolutionary Museum

1	井冈山宾馆/中国国际旅行社
2	长途汽车站
3	革命旧址群
4	革命博物馆

Getting There & Away

From Nanchang there are five direct buses to Ciping/Jinggangshan each day (Y29, eight hours). It's a nice ride through lush countryside of high bamboo fences, old stone bridges, water wheels and flocks of ducks waddling about the rice paddies. A daily bus from Ciping goes to Hengyang (Y25.50) in Hunan Province via the beautiful Huangyang Pass, but the road is prone to icing over in cold weather.

JIANGXI

Hubei 湖北

Population: 50 million
Capital: Wuhan

Site of the great industrial city and river port of Wuhan, slashed through by the Yangzi River and its many tributaries, and supporting a population of almost 50 million, Hubei *(húběi)* is still one of China's most important provinces.

The province actually comprises two quite different areas. The eastern two-thirds is a low-lying plain drained by the Yangzi and its main northern tributary, the Han River. The western third is an area of rugged highlands with small cultivated valleys and basins dividing Hubei from Sichuan. The plain was settled by the Han Chinese in 1000 BC. Around the 7th century it was intensively settled and by the 11th it was producing a rice surplus. In the late 19th century it was the first area in the Chinese interior to undergo considerable industrialisation.

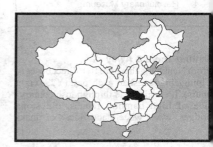

WUHAN
(wǔhàn) 武汉

With a population of over three million, Wuhan is one of China's largest metropolises. It's actually a conglomeration of what were once three independent cities: Hankou, Hanyang and Wuchang.

Wuchang was established during the Han Dynasty, became a regional capital under the Yuan and is now the seat of the provincial government. It used to be a walled city but the walls have long since gone.

Hankou, on the other hand, was barely more than a village until the Treaty of Nanjing opened it to foreign trade. There were five foreign concession areas in Hankou, all grouped around present-day Zhongshan Lu. Arriving in 1861, the British were the first on the scene, followed by the Germans in 1895, the Russians in 1896, the French in 1896 and the Japanese in 1898. With the building of the Beijing-Wuhan railway in the 1920s, Hankou really began to expand and became the first major industrial centre in the interior of China. Many of the European-style buildings from the concession era have remained, particularly along Yanjiang Dadao in the north-east part of town. Government offices now occupy what were once the foreign banks, department stores and private residences.

Hanyang has been outstripped by neighbouring Hankou and today is the smallest municipality. It dates back to 600 AD, when a town first developed on the site. During the second half of the 19th century it was developed for heavy industry. The plant for the manufacture of iron and steel which was built at Hanyang in 1891 was the first modern one in China and it was followed during the early 1900s by a string of riverside factories. The 1930s depression and then the Japanese invasion totally ruined Hanyang's heavy industries and since the revolution light industry has been the main activity.

Not many people go out of their way to get to Wuhan, but a lot of people pass through the place, since this is the terminal of the Yangzi ferries from Chongqing. Livelier, less grimy and more modern than Chongqing, it's a stepping-stone on the way to the comparatively sparkling, cosmopolitan citadels of Nanjing and Shanghai.

Like those cities, Wuhan has been a fortunate place in unfortunate times. In Wuhan in

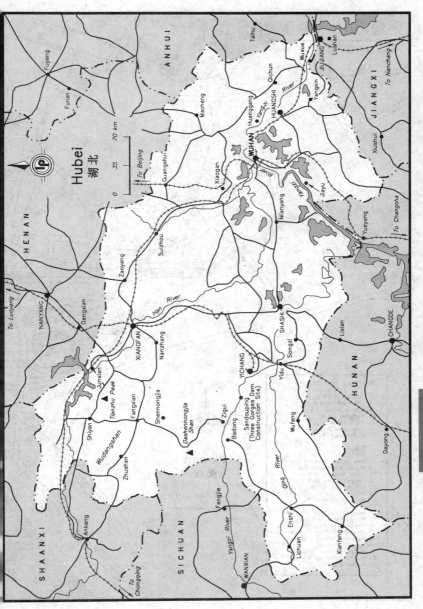

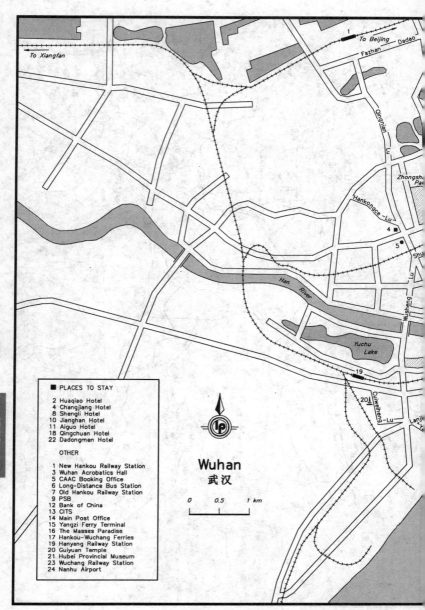

To Xiangfan

To Beijing
Dadao
Fazhan
Qingnian Lu
Zhongsh Par
Hankongce -Lu
4 ■
5 ●
Shu
Han River
Wusheng
Yuchu Lake
19
20
Cuiweheng -Lu
Lanji

■ PLACES TO STAY

2 Huaqiao Hotel
4 Changjiang Hotel
8 Shengli Hotel
10 Jianghan Hotel
11 Aiguo Hotel
18 Qingchuan Hotel
22 Dadongmen Hotel

OTHER

1 New Hankou Railway Station
3 Wuhan Acrobatics Hall
5 CAAC Booking Office
6 Long-Distance Bus Station
7 Old Hankou Railway Station
9 PSB
12 Bank of China
13 CITS
14 Main Post Office
15 Yangzi Ferry Terminal
16 The Masses Paradise
17 Hankou-Wuchang Ferries
19 Hanyang Railway Station
20 Guiyuan Temple
21 Hubei Provincial Museum
23 Wuchang Railway Station
24 Nanhu Airport

Wuhan
武汉

0   0.5   1 km

HUBEI

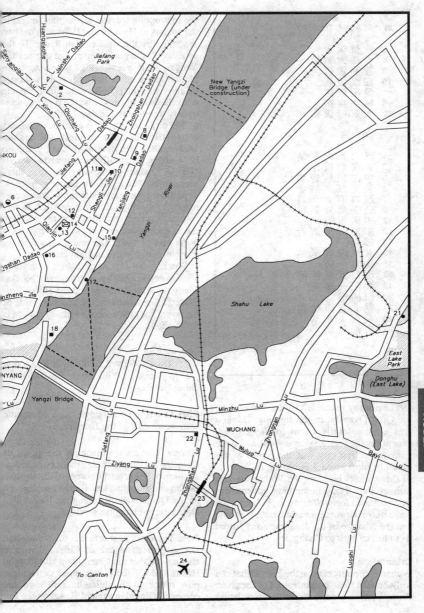

■ PLACES TO STAY

2	花桥饭店
4	长江大酒店
8	胜利饭店
10	江汉饭店
11	爱国饭店
18	晴川宾馆
22	大东门饭店

OTHER

1	汉口新火车站
3	武汉杂技厅
5	中国民航售票处
6	长途汽车站
7	汉口旧火车站
9	公安局外事科
12	中国银行
13	中国国际旅行社
14	邮局
15	武汉港客运站
16	民众乐园
17	汉口武昌渡船
19	汉阳火车站
20	归园寺
21	湖北省博物馆
23	武昌火车站
24	南湖机场

1911 an army revolt led to the downfall of the Qing Dynasty; in the fighting, Hankou was almost totally burnt to the ground, except for the foreign concessions along the river front. The city was the centre of the bloodily suppressed 7 February 1923 strike of the workers building the Wuhan-Beijing railway line. The Kuomintang government first retreated from Nanjing to Wuhan in the wake of the Japanese invasion, until bombing and the advance of the Japanese army forced them further west to Chongqing.

Orientation

Wuhan is the only city on the Yangzi that can truly be said to lie on both sides of the river. From Wuchang on the south-eastern bank, the metropolis spreads across the Yangzi to the sectors of Hankou and Hanyang, the two separated by the smaller Han River. To the south of Wuhan an older bridge crosses the Yangzi, while a new bridge is nearing completion at the city's northern end. A shorter bridge spans the Han River to link Hanyang with Hankou. Ferries cross the rivers continuously throughout the day.

The city's real centre is Hankou *(hànkǒu)*, especially the area around Zhongshan Dadao, although 'central' Wuhan seems to be shifting gradually northwards, across Jiefang Dadao, Hankou's principle thoroughfare. Most of Hankou's hotels, department stores, restaurants and street markets are within this sector, which is surrounded by quieter residential areas. Hankou has an enormous new railway station five km north-east of town; the main Yangzi River ferry terminal is also in Hankou.

Wuchang is a modern district with long, wide avenues lined by drab concrete blocks. Many recreational areas and the Hubei Provincial Museum are on the Wuchang side of the river. The city's second railway station is in Wuchang.

Information

CITS The CITS (☎ 238340) is in Hankou at No 48 Jianghan Yilu (opposite the Xuan Gong Hotel).

PSB This is at 206 Shengli Lu, a 10-minute walk north-east of the Jianghan Hotel.

Money The main branch of the Bank of China is in Hankou in an ornate old concession-era building on the corner of Zhongshan Dadao and Jianghan Lu. Tourist hotels, such as the Qingchuan and Jianghan hotels also have money-changing services.

Post The main post office is on Zhongshan Dadao near the Bank of China. If you're staying at either the Changjiang Hotel or the Hankou Hotel there is a more convenient post office (with philatelic sales) on the corner of Qingnian Lu and Hangkongce Lu.

Maps There must be a dozen city maps of varying usefulness on sale around Wuhan. Xinhua bookshops and some hotels sell a glossy new bilingual version that indicates, in English, places of interest to tourists.

Guiyuan Temple
(guīyuán sì) 归元寺

Doubling as a curiosity shop and active place of worship is this Buddhist temple, with buildings dating from the late Ming and early Qing dynasties.

The main attractions are the statues of Buddha's disciples in an array of comical poses. A few years ago the statues were out in the open, and the smoking incense and sunshine filtering through the skylights gave the temple a rare magic. Alas, no longer.

Other statues in the temple include the Maitreya Buddha and Sakyamuni. Beggars gather outside the temple, and professional photographers inside snap souvenir shots of people posing in front of rocks and puddles. Monks occasionally bang a gong or tap a bell for the amusement of the masses.

To get there take bus No 45 down Zhongshan Dadao and over the Han River bridge; there's a stop within walking distance of the temple. The temple is on Cuiweiheng Lu at the junction with Cuiwei Lu; a trinket market lines Cuiwei Lu.

Yangzi River Bridge
(wǔhàn chángjiāng dàqiáo)
武汉长江大桥

Wuchang and Hanyang are linked by this great bridge – it's over 1100 metres long and 80 metres high. The completion of the bridge in 1957 marked one of Communist China's first great engineering achievements, because until then all road and rail traffic had had to be laboriously ferried across the river. A second trans-Yangzi road bridge is being built in the north of Wuhan.

Hubei Provincial Museum
(húběishěng bówùguǎn)
湖北省博物馆

The museum is a must if you're interested in archaeology. Its large collection of artefacts came from the Zhenghouyi Tomb, which was unearthed in 1978 on the outskirts of Suizhou City. The tomb dates from around 433 BC, in the Warring States Period. The male internee was buried with about 7000 of his favourite artefacts, including bronze ritual vessels, weapons, horse and chariot equipment, bamboo instruments and utensils, and gold and jade objects. Most impressive is the massive set of bronze bell chimes – enough to make Mike Oldfield's eyes water. Other musical instruments found in the tomb included a wooden drum, stringed instruments and a kind of flute similar to pan-pipes.

The museum is beside Donghu (East Lake) in Wuchang. Take bus No 14 from the Wuchang ferry (the dock closest to the bridge) to the terminal.

In summer you can do a scenic day trip that includes the museum, taking a ferry over from Hankou to Wuchang, then boarding bus No 36 to Moshan Hill. Take another ferry across the lake to East Lake Park, walk to the museum, then get bus No 14 to Yellow Crane Tower, and finally a ferry back to Hankou.

Wuhan University
(wǔhàn dàxué) 武汉大学

Wuhan University is beside Luojia Hill in Wuchang. It was founded in 1913, and many of the charming campus buildings originate from that early period. The university was the site of the 1967 'Wuhan Incident' – a protracted battle during the Cultural Revolution with machine gun nests on top of the library and supply tunnels dug through the hill. For a bit of Cultural Revolution nostalgia take bus No 12 to the terminal.

Places to Stay – bottom end

Over to your right as you leave Hankou railway station is the *Jinyan Hotel (jīnyàn fàndiàn)*. Prices quoted for beds are Y27 in a double with bath, Y16 without bath and Y13 in a dorm. Like Hankou station, the hotel is brand new.

The *Aiguo Hotel (àiguó fàndiàn)* on Zhongshan Dadao is still the only budget place in central Hankou that lets in non-

Chinese, but this filthy, damp hole is recommended only to that hard core of travellers prepared – or determined – to rough it. The cheapest dorm beds with communal shower and toilet cost Y20, and singles/doubles are Y30/Y50. Some rooms are not quite so disgusting – check yours beforehand. The place is rumoured to be due for demolition, but – for better or worse – has escaped the sledgehammer for the time being.

A much nicer place in Hankou is the *Huaqiao Hotel (huāqiáo fàndiàn)* on Huiji Lu. It's a simple but well-run Chinese hotel – the sign has no English or pinyin – situated in a narrow market street near Jiefang Park. They have beds in four-person dorms for Y15, simple doubles for Y30 or Y50 with bathroom. It's quite a way north of the centre of town, but bus Nos 68 (from Wuhan ferry dock) and 24 (from Zhongshan Dadao) pass close by.

If you're staying across the river, try the *Dadongmen Hotel (dàdōngmén fàndiàn)* at the intersection of Wuluo Lu and Zhongshan Lu, convenient to Wuchang railway station. It's a large place with plenty of good basic rooms ranging in price from Y18 per bed in a double to Y12 in quads, or Y21 for a single. The Dadongmen's only major drawback is traffic noise, but rooms not fronting the street are quieter.

Places to Stay – middle

The *Shengli Hotel* (☎ 231241) *(shènglì fàndiàn)*, an old British-built guesthouse on the corner of Shengli Jie and Siwei Lu, has moved decidedly upmarket since it had a thorough renovation some years ago. Standard doubles now cost Y180, but out the back they've still got a few cheaper rooms (with 24-hour hot water) around a leafy courtyard. You should be able to bargain them down to around Y70. The place is a bit out of the way, but there are plenty of buses along Shengli Jie.

Places to Stay – top end

The *Jianghan Hotel* (☎ 211600) *(jiānghàn fàndiàn)*, at 245 Shengli Jie just around the corner from the old (now disused) Hankou

railway station, is the place to stay if you can afford it. Built by the French in 1914 as the Demin Hotel, it's one of the best examples of colonial architecture in this part of China. Room rates range from US$55 for a double to a cool US$300 for the suite, plus a 10% surcharge. The hotel has its own post office, shops and an excellent restaurant. The taxi fare from Hankou station is around Y20.

The *Changjiang Hotel* (☎ 562828) *(chángjiāng dàjiŭdiàn)* on the (north-west) corner of Jiefang Dadao and Nianqing Lu has doubles from US$80 a night. Immediately opposite is the *Hankou Hotel* (☎ 557841) *(hànkŏu fàndiàn)* which is similar but somewhat cheaper. Both are quite good hotels, but this intersection now resembles a freeway junction due to the recent construction of a noisy traffic overpass.

Next door to the Qingchuan Pavilion on Qingchuan Jie is the 24-storey *Qingchuan Hotel* (☎ 446688) *(qíngchuān fàndiàn)*, near the Yangzi bridge in Hanyang. The location is not as inconvenient as it might seem, since Hankou is just a short ferry ride away. Rates carry a 10% surcharge and vary according to season; standard rooms are Y88 to Y95 for a single, and Y142 to Y176 a double, but better rooms cost up to US$240 (luxury suite).

Places to Eat

Wuhan has some pretty good eating houses in all price ranges. Popular local snacks include fresh catfish from the nearby East Lake and charcoal-grilled whole pigeons served with a sprinkling of chilli. Good streets for night food are Minsheng Lu and Jianghan Lu, both running off Zhongshan Dadao. Better restaurants can be found along Shengli Lu: the *Prince Saloon* is next door to the Jianghan Hotel, and in a restored concession building on the corner of Tianjin Lu and Shengli Lu is an excellent and reasonably priced restaurant specialising in smorgasbord hotpots. For those who like their food fast and greasy, the *Orient Express (dōngfāng kuàichē)* on Jiefang Dadao opposite Zhongshan Park has hamburgers and fried chicken.

The *Laotongcheng Restaurant (lăotōng-*

HUBEI

chéng dòupí guǎn), at 1 Dazhi Lu on the corner with Zhongshan Dadao, serves a tasty snack called *dòupí* for which the all-important characters are:

豆皮

While it may look like a stuffed omelette, it's actually made with a bean curd base – its name translates as 'bean skin' – and is served rolled around a filling of rice and diced meat. The Laotongcheng was apparently a favourite of Mao's, though presumably he didn't have to push and shove with the proletariat to get his doupi. Doupi is no great delicacy, but at less than Y1 a serving you can't go wrong.

Entertainment

The recently opened Wuhan Acrobatics Hall *(wǔhàn zájìtīng)* on Jianshe Dadao in northern Hankou is a circular building with a striking red-dome roof that resembles a small enclosed stadium. The hall houses a troupe of Chinese acrobats – one of the best and largest in the country. At the time of writing it was still difficult to ascertain the frequency of scheduled performances, so if you're interested either go there yourself or contact CITS.

The Masses' Paradise *(mínzhòng lèyuán)* on Zhongshan Dadao in Hankou is a kind of 'fun palace' in the best of sideshow traditions. The ordinary people of Wuhan often come here at night to enjoy themselves. The large three-storey building is built around a central courtyard and houses karaoke bars and teahouses, shooting galleries, billiard rooms and a dancing hall. What's on seems to depend on the day of the week and the time of year, but attractions have been known to include acrobatic shows, stand-up comic routines, folk song and dance performances, stunt acts and Beijing Opera. The general admission charge of Y3 includes entry to most activities.

Getting There & Away

The best way of getting to eastern destinations such as Nanjing and Shanghai is by air or river ferry rather than the circuitous rail route.

Air CAAC (☎ 357949) has its main ticket office in Hankou at 217 Liji Beilu. It offers air connections to virtually all major cities in China, including daily flights to Beijing (Y570), Canton (Y430) and Shanghai (Y380), and several each week to Nanjing, Fuzhou, Xi'an, Kunming and Hong Kong (Y1000). There are buses from CAAC's Hankou office to the airport at Nanhu south of Wuchang.

Bus The main long-distance bus station is in Hankou on Jiefang Dadao between Xinhua Lu and Jianghan Lu. There are daily departures to Nanchang, Changsha, Xiamen, Xiangfan (north-western Hubei), Hefei and Bozhou (northern Anhui).

Train Wuhan is on the main Beijing-Canton line; express trains to Kunming, Xi'an and Lanzhou run via the city. All trains that go through Wuhan to other destinations stop at both Hankou and Wuchang railway stations; it's usually more convenient to get off at Hankou even though the new station is a fair way out. At Hankou station, hard and soft sleepers must be booked in the small ticket office (windows No 4 or 5) between the waiting halls and the main ticket office. There is also a railway ticket office in central Hankou where Zhongshan Dadao briefly divides (opposite the No 7 bus stop). They've only got hard-seat tickets and might not serve foreigners, but it's worth a try. Note that many southbound trains originating at Wuhan actually depart from Wuchang station rather than Hankou.

Some sample sleeper-ticket prices for foreigners are: Beijing Y365 (soft) or Y192 (hard), Zhengzhou Y172 (soft) or Y91 (hard), Canton Y325 (soft) or Y170 (hard), Changsha Y133 (soft) or Y70 (hard).

Boat You can take ferries from Wuhan along

the Yangzi River either west to Chongqing or east to Shanghai (see the Yangzi River section for details).

Getting Around

Bus routes crisscross the city but getting where you want to go may mean changing at least once. A useful bus is the No 38 which passes the Jianghan Hotel to and from the new Hankou railway station. Motortricycles and pedicabs wait outside the two main railway stations, the Yangzi boat terminal as well as the smaller ferry docks. You'll probably find that the Hankou-Wuchang ferries are a more convenient way of crossing the river than taking a bus over the Yangzi bridge.

YANGZI RIVER: WUHAN TO CHONGQING & SHANGHAI

Wuhan more or less marks the halfway point in the long navigable stretch of the Yangzi from Chongqing down to Shanghai. From Wuhan numerous ferries go up and down the river, some running its entire length.

Boat tickets can be bought at the main Yangzi ferry terminal in Hankou, through CITS, or the service desks at tourist hotels. There is officially no 1st class, so you can only buy tickets for 2nd, 3rd and 4th class. Second class is a two-person cabin, 3rd class is a 10-person dormitory and 4th class is a 20-person dormitory. Food and beer are sold on board; you can also get off at any of the many stops along the way for provisions.

Foreigners' ticket prices (in yuan) and travel times are from Wuhan to the following destinations:

	2nd Class	3rd Class	4th Class	Journey Time
Jiujiang	112	52	40	one night
Wuhu	239	111	85	30 hours
Nanjing	272	126	97	36 hours
Shanghai	401	186	143	48 hours
Yueyang	101	4	3	one night
Yichang	235	10	6	32 hours
Chongqing	511	264	216	five days

Heading downriver on leaving Wuhan, the steamer passes through Huangshi in eastern Hubei Province. This town lies on the south-

ern bank of the river and is being developed as a centre for heavy industry. Nearby is an ancient mining tunnel dating back to the Spring and Autumn Period; it contained numerous mining tools, including bronze axes. Near the border with Jiangxi on the north bank is the town of Wuxue, noted for the production of bamboo goods.

The first major town you come to in Jiangxi is Jiujiang, the jumping-off point for nearby Lushan. The mouth of Lake Boyang is situated on the Yangzi River and at this point on the southern bank of the river is Stone Bell Mountain, noted for its numerous Tang Dynasty stone carvings. This was also the place where Taiping troops were garrisoned for five years, defending Jinling, their capital.

The first major town you approach in Anhui Province is Anqing, on the north bank, in the foothills of the Dabie mountains. Next comes the town of Guichi, from which you can get a bus to the spectacular Huangshan (Yellow mountains). The town of Tongling lies in a mountainous area in central Anhui on the southern bank, west of Tongguanshan. Tongling has been a copper-mining centre for 2000 years, and is a source of copper for the minting of coins. Still in Anhui Province, and at the confluence of the Yangzi and Qingyi rivers, is Wuhu, also a jumping-off point for Huangshan. Just before Anhui Province ends is the city of Manshan, the site of a large iron and steel complex.

In Jiangsu Province the first large city you pass is Nanjing, followed by Zhenjiang, then the port of Nantong at the confluence of the Tongyang and Tonglu canals. The ferry then proceeds along the Yangzi and turns down the Huangpu River to Shanghai. The Yangzi empties into the East China Sea.

WUDANGSHAN
(wǔdāng shān) 武当山

The Wudangshan mountains stretch for 400 km across north-western Hubei Province. The highest summit is the 1600-metre high Tianzhu Peak, situated south-east of Shiyan, whose name translates as 'Pillar Propping up the Sky' or 'Heavenly Pillar Peak'.

The Wudangshan are a sacred range to the Taoists, and a number of Taoist temples were built here during the construction sprees of the Ming emperors Cheng Zu and Zhen Wu. Noted temples include the Golden Hall on Heavenly Pillar Peak, which was built entirely of gilded copper in 1416; the hall contains a bronze statue of Ming Emperor Zhen Wu, who became a Taoist deity. The Purple Cloud Temple stands on Zhanqifeng Peak, and the Nanyan Temple perches on the South Cliff.

SHENNONGJIA
(shénnóngjià) 神农架

The Shennongjia district in remote north-western Hubei has the wildest scenery in the province. With heavily forested mountains reaching over 3000 metres, the area is famous for the sightings of wild, ape-like creatures, a Chinese equivalent of the Himalayan Yeti or the North American Bigfoot. The stories are interesting, but the creatures seem to be able to distinguish between peasants and scientists – molesting the former and evading the latter. The best way into the Shennongjia area is by bus from Yichang.

The Three Gorges (Sanxia) Dam

When completed in about 2008, the Three Gorges (Sanxia) Dam will be the world's largest water storage reservoir. First put forward more that a decade ago, the dam proposal was finally given the go-ahead by the Chinese government only in 1992. This colossal project involves the construction of a two-km wide, 185-metre high dam wall across the Yangzi River at Sandouping, 38 km upstream from the existing Gezhou Dam. The aims of the project are to supply electricity, to improve the river's navigability and to protect against flooding.

The Three Gorges Dam is a cornerstone in government efforts to channel economic growth from the dynamic coastal provinces towards the more backward Chinese hinterland. The dam's hydroelectric production – reckoned to equal almost one-fifth of China's current generating capacity – is intended to power the continuing industrialisation of the upper Yangzi Basin.

Navigation upriver from Yichang has always been hindered by rather unfavourable conditions for shipping. Although passing the dam itself will be an inconvenience for ships – the Three Gorges Dam will have five passage locks compared to just one lock on the Gezhou Dam – the navigability of the upper Yangzi will be drastically improved by the widening of shipping lanes and the creation of a more constant water level within the new lake. Inundation will eliminate strong river currents, and obstacles dangerous to navigation such as sand bars and submerged rocks will disappear completely.

At least as important will be the dam's role in flood control. The Yangzi is prone to repeated flooding, often causing great loss of life. Several catastrophic floods have occurred this century, in 1931, 1935, 1954 and more recently in 1991, when over two thousand people are believed to have perished.

However, the massive scale of the Three Gorges Dam project has caused disquiet amongst environmentalists and economists, arousing some of the most outspoken criticism of government policy in China since 1989.

The social and environmental implications of the dam, which will create a vast 550-km long lake stretching deep into Sichuan Province, are profound indeed. When the backwaters build up behind the dam wall the great inland port of Chongqing will become the world's first metropolis situated on the banks of a major artificial lake. An estimated two million people living in the inundated areas will need to be relocated. Some destruction of the natural and scenic splendour of the Three Gorges will be unavoidable, though how the dam will affect Yangzi River tourism – still in its infancy – is uncertain.

Construction of the dam will be enormously expensive, with a final cost probably somewhere in the vicinity of US$20,000,000,000 (that's twenty billion US dollars). Economists at home and abroad have warned that it may be imprudent for China to concentrate such investment into one single project. The scenario of dam failure would – at the very least – be a financial catastrophe. ■

HUBEI

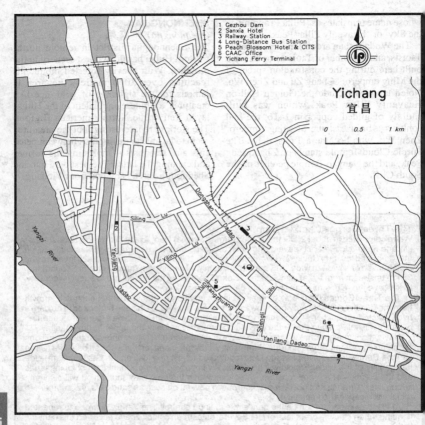

1 Gezhou Dam
2 Sanxia Hotel
3 Railway Station
4 Long-Distance Bus Station
5 Peach Blossom Hotel & CITS
6 CAAC Office
7 Yichang Ferry Terminal

Yichang
宜昌

0   0.5   1 km

HUBEI

YICHANG
(yíchāng) 宜昌

Situated just below the famous Three Gorges, Yichang is the gateway to the Upper Yangzi and was a walled town as long ago as the Sui Dynasty. The city was opened to foreign trade in 1877 by a treaty between Britain and China, and a concession area set up along the river front south-east of the old city.

Today Yichang is best known for the nearby Gezhou Dam, and the city is to be the construction base for the massive Three Gorges hydroelectric project now being built

at Sandouping, 40 km upstream. There's otherwise precious little worth seeing in this grimy, unwelcoming city, but it's a useful jumping-off point for more interesting places.

Places to Stay

With very few of the cheaper hotels willing to take foreigners, cheap accommodation is hellishly hard to find in Yichang. The *Peach Blossom Hotel* (☎ 442244) *(táohuālíng bīnguǎn)* in the middle of town on Kangzhuang Lu has doubles from Y190; the CITS office is next door. The *Three Gorges*

1	葛洲坝
2	三峡宾馆
3	火车站
4	长途汽车站
5	桃花岭饭店/中国国际旅行社
6	中国民航售票处
7	宜昌港

Hotel (☎ 224911) *(sānxiá bīnguǎn)* at 38 Yanjiang Dadao on the waterfront has similar prices. Take bus No 11 from the station or No 2 from the dock.

Getting There & Away

Yichang has a small airport with one flight to Wuhan every evening and three flights a week to Canton.

The long-distance bus station is to the left of the railway station along Dongshan Dadao. There are several daily buses to Yaqueling and one at 6.00 am each day to Songbai in the Shennongjia area.

The town is linked by a 40-km section of track to the rail junction at Yaqueling *(yāquèlǐng)*. Some trains run directly between Yichang and Xiangfan, Beijing and Wuhan (via Xiangfan), but to pick up connections to Dayong or Huaihua first go to Yaqueling.

All passing river ferries call in at Yichang ferry terminal. Travellers often find the two-day boat trip through the Yangzi gorges between Chongqing (Sichuan Province) and Yichang quite long enough, and some disembark or board here rather than spend an extra day on the river between Yichang and Wuhan. If you're going upriver, the Chinese-price fares to Chongqing are: Y178 (2nd class), Y83 (3rd class) and Y63 (4th class). Bus Nos 3 and 4 run from the railway station to near the ferry terminal.

Henan 河南

Population: 80 million
Capital: Zhengzhou

The Yellow River snakes its way across the north of Henan *(hénán)*, where it all began. About 3500 years ago the Chinese were turning their primitive settlements into an urban-centred civilisation governed by the Shang Dynasty.

Excavations of Shang Dynasty towns have shown that these were built on the sites of even more ancient settlements. The Shang civilisation was not founded by people migrating from western Asia, as was once thought, but was part of a continuous line which had been developing here since pre-historic times.

The Shang Dynasty ruled from the 16th to the 11th century BC and controlled an area which included parts of what are today Shandong, Henan and Hebei provinces. To the west of their territory the powerful Zhou people arose and conquered the Shang; the last Shang emperor supposedly hurled himself into the flames of his burning palace.

The first Shang capital, perhaps dating back 3800 years, is believed to be the site of Yanshi, west of modern-day Zhengzhou. Around the middle of the 16th century BC the capital was moved to Zhengzhou, where the walls of the ancient city are still visible. Later the capital moved to Yin, near the modern town of Anyang, in the north of Henan.

The only clues as to what Shang society was like are found in the remnants of their cities, in divining bones inscribed with a primitive form of Chinese writing, and in ancient Chinese literary texts. Apart from the walls at Zhengzhou, all that has survived of their cities are the pounded-earth foundations of the buildings, stone-lined trenches where wooden poles once supported thatched roofs, and pits used for storage or as underground houses.

Today Henan, one of the smaller Chinese provinces, is also one of the most densely

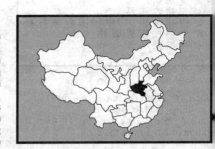

populated – with over 80 million people squashed in; only Sichuan Province has more human mouths to feed. It was the centre of Chinese civilisation during the Song Dynasty, but lost political power when the government fled south from its capital at Kaifeng, in the wake of an invasion from the north in the 12th century. Nevertheless, with such a large population on the fertile (though periodically flood-ravaged) plains of the unruly Yellow River, Henan remained an important agricultural area.

Henan's urban centres rapidly diminished in size and population with the demise of the Song. It was not until the Communist take-over in 1949 that they once again expanded. Zhengzhou was transformed into a sizable industrial city – Luoyang, Kaifeng and Anyang have also been industrialised but not to such a great extent.

For modern travellers, the biggest drawcard in Henan is the Longmen Caves near Luoyang.

ZHENGZHOU
(zhèngzhōu) 郑州

Zhengzhou is a 12-hour train ride from Shanghai and Beijing and a couple of decades behind them in progress. Because of its importance as a railway junction, Zhengzhou was made the capital of Henan Province after 1949. Since 1950 the popula-

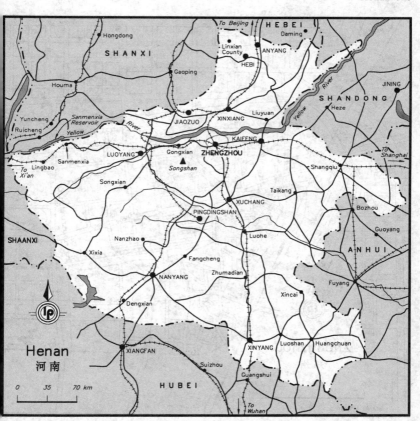

Henan
河南

0   35   70 km

tion has increased tenfold from around 100,000 people to over one million.

Zhengzhou gave the Communists the opportunity to create a whole new city – one that might, perhaps, have reflected their own concept of the ideal regional capital. What the architects and town-planners came up with, however, is a thoroughly uninspiring urban landscape that is itself educational. Even among China's wide field of nondescript major cities, Zhengzhou would have to be one of the ugliest.

Viewed from the heights of its taller buildings, the city reveals itself as a sea of low-rise red brick residential blocks interspersed with haphazardly placed factories and smokestacks like giant Lego blocks plonked down between the narrow, twisting alleys. Zhengzhou's broad, tree-lined boulevards, which serve as thoroughfares for tens of thousands of bicycles, are one of the city's few minor graces.

Orientation

All places of interest to tourists lie within the section of the city east of the railway line.

The liveliest part of town is around the railway and long-distance bus stations, with

Zhengzhou
郑州

0	0.5	1 km

To Beijing
To Yellow River
Jinshui Lu
Minggong Lu
Renmin Park
Taikang Lu
Erqi Lu
Zhangzhai Jie
Renmin Lu
Shangcheng Lu
Jiefang Lu
Fayuan Jie
Zhengxing Jie
Xi Dajie
Zhongyuan Lu
Daxue Lu
Fushun Jie
Dehua Jie
Malu
Chengnan Lu
Xiong'er River
Longhai Donglu
To Shaolin Monastery
To Canton
Huanghe Lu
Jinshui Lu
Chengdong Lu
Wall
Dong Dajie
To Kaifeng
Fenghuang Lu
To Shanghai

street stalls, restaurants and markets. North-east of the railway station, five roads converge at the prominent Erqi Pagoda (or 'February 7th Memorial Tower') to form a large traffic circle marking Zhengzhou's most central point. Erqi Lu runs north from the Erqi Pagoda past the CAAC office to intersect with Jinshui Lu near Renmin Park; the Provincial Museum and the Henan International Hotel are east along Jinshui Lu.

Information

The local entry-exit office is up a short laneway off Jinshui Lu, a few minutes' walk

west of the T-intersection with Chengdong Lu. CITS is in a small office on the ground-floor lobby in the Henan International Hotel.

The Bank of China is at 16 Huayuankou Lu. The tower building beside the square in front of the railway station houses the main post and telecommunications centre. The Henan International Hotel also offers a postal service.

Shang City Ruins

(shāngdài yízhǐ) 商代遗址

On the eastern outskirts of Zhengzhou lie the remains of an ancient city from the Shang

1	Bank of China
2	PSB
3	Henan International Hotel & CITS
4	Guotai Restaurant
5	Provincial Museum
6	Henan Guesthouse
7	Friendship Hotel
8	CAAC
9	Asia Hotel
10	Erqi Pagoda (February 7th Tower)
11	Zhengzhou Hotel
12	Long-Distance Bus Station
13	Zhongyuan Mansions
14	Railway Station
15	Post Office
16	Shang City Ruins

1	中国银行
2	公安局外事科
3	河南国际饭店／中国国际旅行社
4	国泰酒家
5	省博物馆
6	河南宾馆
7	友谊饭店
8	中国民航售票处
9	亚细亚大酒店
10	二七塔
11	郑州饭店
12	长途汽车站
13	中原大厦
14	火车站
15	邮政大楼
16	商代遗址

period. Long, high mounds of earth indicate where the city walls used to be, now cut through by modern roads. This is one of the earliest relics of Chinese urban life. The first archaeological evidence of the Shang period was discovered near the town of Anyang in northern Henan. The city at Zhengzhou is believed to have been the second Shang capital, and many Shang settlements have been found outside the walled area.

Excavations here and at other Shang sites suggest that a 'typical' Shang city consisted of a central walled area containing large buildings (presumably government buildings or the residences of important people, used for ceremonial occasions) surrounded by a ring of villages. Each village specialised in such products as pottery, metalwork, wine or textiles. The village dwellings were mostly semi-underground pit houses, while the buildings in the centre were rectangular and above ground.

Excavations have also uncovered Shang tombs. These are rectangular pits with ramps or steps leading down to a burial chamber in which the coffin was placed and surrounded with funeral objects such as bronze weapons, helmets, musical instruments, oracle bones and shells with inscriptions, silk fabrics, and ornaments of jade, bone and ivory. Among these, depending on the wealth and status of the deceased, have been found the skeletons

of animals and humans – sacrifices meant to accompany their masters to the next world. Study of these human skeletons suggests they were of a different ethnic origin from the Shang – possibly prisoners of war. This and other evidence has suggested that Shang society was not based on the slavery of its own people. Rather, it was a dictatorship of the aristocracy with the emperor/father-figure at the apex.

There are two sites where you can see part of the ruins. The portion that still has some of the wall standing is in the south-eastern section of the city. Bus Nos 2 and 8 stop nearby – get off at the stop called East Gate (*dōng mén kǒu*). Bus No 3 runs through the old Shang City. The other set of ruins is in Zijingshan Park (*zǐjīngshān gōngyuán*) near the Henan International Hotel.

Henan Provincial Museum

(*hénán shěng bówùguǎn*) 河南省博物馆
The museum is at 11 Renmin Lu, at the intersection with Jinshui Lu, readily identifiable by the large Mao statue. It has an interesting collection of artefacts discovered in Henan Province, including some from the Shang period. There's also an exhibition on the February 7th revolt but, unfortunately, there are no English captions. The Erqi

Pagoda, in the centre of Zhengzhou, commemorates the 1923 strike organised by workers building the railway from Wuhan to Beijing. The strike was bloodily suppressed.

Yellow River
(huánghé) 黄河

The Yellow River is just 24 km north of Zhengzhou and the road passes near the village of Huayuankou, where in April 1938 Kuomintang general Chiang Kaishek ordered his troops to blow up the river dikes to halt the Japanese advance. This desperately ruthless tactic was successful for only a few weeks and at the cost of drowning some one million Chinese people and making another 11 million homeless and starving. The dike was repaired with American help in 1947 and today the point where it was breached has an irrigation sluice gate and Mao's instruction, 'Control the Yellow River', etched into the embankment.

The river has always been regarded as 'China's sorrow' because of its propensity to flood. It carries masses of silt from the loess plains and deposits them on the riverbed, causing the water to overflow the banks. Consequently, the peasants along the river bank have had to build the dikes higher and higher each century. As a result, parts of the river flow along an elevated channel which is often as much as 1½ km wide and sometimes more than 15 metres high!

The river has been brought partially under control through the building of upstream dams and irrigation canals which divert the flow. The largest of these is the Longyang Dam in Qinghai Province, which is also a major source of hydroelectric power.

Mangshan is the site of Yellow River Park, on the south bank of the river. You can buy minibus tickets out to the Yellow River Park at a small booth opposite the Zhengzhou Hotel.

Renmin Park
(rénmín gōngyuán) 人民公园

This park is interesting not for its scenic beauty but for the entranceway, which looks like someone's attempt to re-create either the Lunan Stone Forest or the Tiger Balm Gardens – enough said. The park itself has little to offer but family circuses sometimes set up shop here, performing such feats as wrapping their bodies in wire, or lying down with a concrete block on their stomach while dad takes to it with a sledgehammer. You can play that venerated Chinese sport of ping pong on the concrete tables in the park if you've got some bats and a ball. The entrance to the park is on Erqi Lu.

Places to Stay

Cheaper hotels pay local touts to seek out and bring back new guests, but most are still nervous about letting in foreigners.

Opposite the railway station is *Zhongyuan Mansions (zhōngyuán dàshà)*, a cavernous white tower with untold numbers of rooms in various adjoining annexe buildings. It's more than a trifle run-down, but handy if you're just passing through. A simple double is Y30, while Y90 gets you one of their better doubles, complete with functioning bathroom. It costs Y23 a night in a small dormitory, and Y10 in an uncomfortably tight 17-bedder. There's plenty of night activity (and noise) in the streets below. The *Zhengzhou Hotel (zhèngzhōu fàndiàn)*, left as you leave the railway station, has similar prices.

The *Friendship Hotel (yǒuyì fàndiàn)* is on the corner of Erqi Lu and Jinshui Lu. Prices range from just Y10 for their cheapest dorm beds up to Y68 per bed in a double suite. The place is close to Renmin Park, but it's popular with Chinese travellers and often full. Bus Nos 6, 24 and 32 from the railway station will all get you there.

The *Henan Guesthouse* (☎ 345522) *(hénán bīnguǎn)* is opposite Renmin Park on Jinshui Lu. The hotel is in the middle price-range, with standard doubles for Y80, or Y60 without bathroom. It's a laid-back sort of place, set back from the street in pleasant gardens. Take bus No 24 from the railway station.

The newest and best place in downtown Zhengzhou is the *Asia Hotel* (☎ 668866) (*yàxìyà dàjiǔdiàn*), a joint venture facing the Erqi Pagoda from its central location on the sharp corner of Jiefang Lu and Zhengxing Jie. Their price for a single with bathroom is Y210, Y248 for a double, and Y418 for a luxury suite.

Over in the city's eastern suburbs on Jinshui Dadao is the *Henan International Hotel* (☎ 556600, 553888) (*hénán guójì fàndiàn*). Rooms start at Y218 for a double and Y328 for a suite; all have air-con as well as TV, phone and private fridge. Sharing the same compound is the extravagant three-storey *Regent Palace* (☎ 550122) (*lìjīng dàshà*), whose doubles are from Y330 upwards. Between them these hotels have several karaoke/disco bars, cafes and shops as well as four outstanding Chinese and Western restaurants. CITS is in the lobby of the International and there is a CAAC ticket office on the ground floor of the Regent Palace. Bus No 2 from in front of the railway station gets you to these hotels.

The *Zhongzhou Guesthouse* (☎ 524255) (*zhōngzhōu bīnguǎn*), next door at 115 Jinshui Dadao, was being renovated at the time of writing, but will probably offer doubles for something like Y180 after it reopens.

Places to Eat

Food stalls around town sell bowls of opaque noodles called *liáng fěn*, popular in Henan as in many parts of north-western China. It's made by first boiling a kind of bean paste that cools to form a solidified loaf that can be sliced into broad strips and then either wok-fried or served in soup with a tossing of vinegar or hot chilli.

The best place for street food seems to be along Fushou Jie near the railway station. If you're planning to dine out, most of the classier restaurants are on Jinshui Lu between Chengdong Lu and Huayuankou Lu. Here you'll find the pricey but excellent *Guotai Restaurant* (☎ 555285) (*guótài dàjiǔdiàn*) serving mainly Cantonese cuisine; the cheaper *Rose Garden* (*méiguīyuán cāntīng*) has typical Hui (Chinese-Islamic) dishes.

The *Greenland Hotel* (*gélínlán dàjiǔdiàn*), in the new high-rise building overlooking the railway station square, has a revolving restaurant on the top floor with a good range of Western-style food. They've got an English menu too.

Getting There & Away
Air The CAAC office (☎ 222433) is at 38 Bei

Erqi Lu. From Zhengzhou there are scheduled flights to 22 cities in China, including Beijing (Y350, four a week); Canton (Y670, daily), Xi'an (Y240, six a week); Shanghai (Y440, three a week); Kunming (Y780, twice weekly) and Ürümqi (Y1370, once a week). The airport is on the eastern outskirts of the city.

Bus From the Zhengzhou long-distance bus station (diagonally opposite the railway station) there are air-con buses to Luoyang (Y15, three hours) approximately every half-hour, six scheduled departures to Kaifeng (Y6.50, two hours) and several to Anyang (Y20, 4½ hours) every day. You can also take overnight sleeping-berth coaches (wòpùchē) to Beijing (Y112), Xi'an (Y89) and Wuhan (Y87). Minibuses leave irregularly from the square in front of the railway station for Shaolin (Y10), and less frequently to Luoyang (many go via Shaolin) and to Kaifeng.

Train Zhengzhou is one of the most important junctions in the Chinese rail network, and numerous express and rapid trains run via the city; you could well find yourself here 'in transit' for a few hours. The ticket office at Zhengzhou railway station is often crowded out, but foreigners can buy tickets more easily at counters 1 and 2 or at the advance booking office at 193 Erqi Lu. Convenient connections are to Beijing (Y241, soft sleeper; Y136, hard sleeper; 12 hours), Shanghai (Y298, soft sleeper; Y157, hard sleeper; 14 hours), Xi'an (Y190, soft sleeper; Y110, hard sleeper; 10 hours), Wuhan (Y172, soft sleeper; Y91, hard sleeper; nine hours) Canton (23 hours), Luoyang (four hours) as well as Taiyuan and Datong.

Getting Around
Since most of the sights and tourist facilities are well away from the city centre, walking is a laborious means of getting about. Despite Zhengzhou's flat and spread-out topography, the local entrepreneurs don't appear to have discovered the bike rental business yet. Bus No 2 gets you from the

railway station to the Henan International Hotel, while the No 3 runs through the old Shang city. Taxis pick up people outside the railway station but motortricycles are no longer allowed to enter the last street block before the station.

AROUND ZHENGZHOU
Shaolin Monastery
(shǎolín sì) 少林寺
David Carradine never trained here, but China's most famous martial arts tradition was indeed developed by Buddhist monks at Shaolin Monastery, 80 km west of Zhengzhou.

Each year, thousands of Chinese enrol at Shaolin's martial art schools. Large classes of enthusiastic young trainees – many no older than nine or 10 – can often be seen in the monastery grounds ramming a javelin through their imaginary opponent's body or kicking into a sparring dummy with enough force to wind an elephant.

According to legend, Shaolin was founded in the 5th century AD by an Indian monk, Bodhidharma, who preached Chan (Zen) Buddhism. The story goes that for relief between long periods of meditation, Bodhidharma's disciples imitated the natural motions of birds and animals, developing these exercises over the centuries into a form of unarmed combat. The monks have supposedly intervened continually throughout China's many wars and uprisings – always on the side of righteousness, naturally – and perhaps as a result, their monastery has suffered repeated sackings. The most recent round of destructive visits was in 1928 when a local warlord had a go, then again in the early '70s by bands of Red Guards.

In spite of the fires and vandalism many of the monastery buildings are still standing, though most have had any original charm restored out of them. One of the most impressive and photogenic sights is the Forest of Dagobas (shǎolín tǎlín) situated outside the walls past the temple, each dagoba built in remembrance of a monk.

Nowadays Shaolin is something of a tourist trap catering to the hordes of Chinese tourists who are bussed in every day. The way from the main bus parking area to the monastery is thick with food stalls, ice-cream sellers, street photographers and small souvenir shops selling imitation scimitars along with other junk. There's a martial arts museum and a giant buddha for the kids to play on.

The monastery sits on Songshan, a mountain sacred to Taoists. On the same mountain is the Taoist Zhongyue Temple, supposedly founded during the Qin Dynasty, and site of the oldest surviving pagoda in China.

The main gate-ticket (*ménpiào*) is Y6 for students and Y12 for all other foreigners; it costs another Y5/10 to get into the Shaolin temple itself.

Getting There & Away

Shaolin is well off the main road between Zhengzhou and Luoyang. One way of getting there is to take one of the frequent but unscheduled private minibuses from in front of the railway station in either city. Minibuses from Zhengzhou cost Y10, and (depending on what route they take) sometimes stop at either Zhongyue Temple, the

tombs near Dahuting or the Songyue Pagoda.

Public buses to Shaolin leave roughly half hourly from the long-distance bus stations in both Zhengzhou (Y8) and Luoyang (Y5), and are generally cheaper and quicker than minibuses.

Gongxian County

(gǒngxiàn) 巩县

Gongxian County lies on the railway line which runs west from Zhengzhou to Luoyang. During the Northern Wei Dynasty a series of Buddhist caves was cut and a temple built on the bank of the Yiluo River. However, the main attractions of the area are the great tombs built by the Northern Song emperors.

The county is bounded in the south by Songshan and in the north by the Yellow River. The Yiluo River is a branch of the Yellow River and cuts through the centre of the county.

The Buddhist cave temples are at the foot of Dalishan on the northern bank of the Yiluo River. Construction of the caves began in 517 AD and additions were made during the

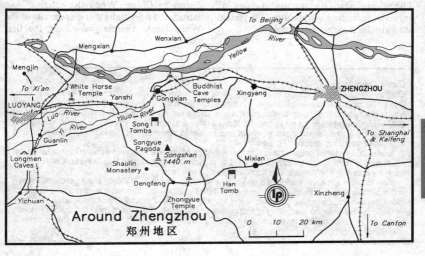

Eastern and Western Wei, Tang and Song dynasties. There are now 256 shrines containing over 7700 Buddhist figures.

The Song Tombs are scattered over an area of 30 sq km. Seven of the nine Northern Song emperors were buried here; the other two were captured and taken away by the Jin armies who overthrew the Northern Song in the 12th century.

After the vicissitudes of more than 800 years of history and repeated wars, all that remain of the tombs are the ruined buildings, the burial mounds and the statues which line the sacred avenues leading up to the ruins. About 700 stone statues still stand, and these have a simple and unsophisticated but imposing manner about them.

Some of the earlier statues, such as those on the Yongan and Yongchang tombs, utilise very plain lines and are characteristic of the late Tang Dynasty style. The statues of the intermediate period on the Yongding and Yongzhao tombs are carved with more exquisite, harmonious proportions. Later statues, such as those on the way to the Yongyu and Yongtai tombs, tend to be more naturalistic and lifelike. The statues of people include civil officials, foreign envoys and military leaders. There are also numerous statues of animals, including a *jiaoduan*, a mythical animal which symbolises luck.

Buses running between Zhengzhou and Luoyang pass by the tombs turn-off, though the tombs themselves are some distance from the highway. You can also charter a taxi or motortricycle out to the tombs and/or the Buddhist cave temples from Gongxian, on the Zhengzhou-Luoyang road and rail route.

LUOYANG
(luòyáng) 洛阳

Luoyang is one of the richest historical sites in China. Founded in 1200 BC, it was the capital of 10 dynasties before losing its rank in the 10th century AD when the Jin moved their capital to Kaifeng. In the 12th century Luoyang was stormed and sacked by Jurchen invaders from the north and never really recovered from the disaster. For centuries it remained a squalid little town vegetating on the edge of a vanished capital. By the 1920s it had only 20,000 inhabitants. It was the Communists who built a new industrial city similar to Zhengzhou at Luoyang, a vast expanse of wide avenues and endless brick and concrete apartment blocks now housing over a million people.

Looking at it today, it's hard to imagine that Luoyang was once the centre of Buddhism in China. When the religion was introduced from India this was the site of the White Horse Temple *(báimǎ sì)*, the first

---

Cave Dwellings

On the road from Zhengzhou to Luoyang you'll see some of China's interesting cave dwellings. Over 100 million Chinese people live in cave houses cut into dry embankments, or in houses where the hillside makes up one or more walls. These are not peculiar to Henan Province: a third of these dwellings are found in the dry loess plateau. Some communities use both caves and houses; the former are warmer in winter and cooler in summer, but also tend to be darker and less ventilated than ordinary houses.

Sometimes a large square pit is dug first and then caves are hollowed into the four sides of the pit. A well is sunk in the middle of the yard to prevent flooding during heavy rains. Other caves, such as those at Yan'an, are dug into the side of a cliff face.

The floors, walls and ceilings of these cave dwellings are made of loess, a fine yellowish-brown soil which is soft and thick and makes good building material. The front wall may be made of loess, mud-brick, concrete, bricks or wood, depending on the availability of materials.

Ceilings are shaped according to the quality of the loess. If it is hard then the ceiling may be arched; if not, the ceiling may rise to a point. Besides the doors and windows in the front wall, additional vents may let in light and air. ■

Buddhist temple built in China. At this temple Indian Sanskrit scriptures were first translated into Chinese. When the city was the imperial capital under the Northern Wei Dynasty there were supposed to be 1300 Buddhist temples operating in the area. At the same time, work was begun on the magnificent Buddhist Longmen Cave temples outside the city.

Orientation

Luoyang is spread across the northern bank of the Luo River. The Luoyang railway station, a large new white-tiled building with a loud chiming clock, is in the north of the city. Luoyang's chief thoroughfare is Zhongzhou Lu, which meets Jinguyuan Lu running down from the railway station at a central T-intersection. The old city is east of the old west gate at Xiguan and sections of the original walls can still be seen. Throughout the maze of narrow streets and winding laneways stand many older houses which are interesting to explore on foot.

Information

The CITS office (☎ 413701) is on the 2nd floor of the ugly white building immediately behind the Friendship Guesthouse. There is also a CITS branch in the Peony Hotel. The PSB is on the corner of Kaixuan Lu and Tiyuchang Lu. It's reportedly a good place to get a visa extension.

The Bank of China is on the corner of Yanan Lu and Zhongzhou Xilu (opposite the Friendship Store). The main post and telephone office is at the T-intersection of Zhongzhou Lu and Jingguyuan Lu.

White Horse Temple

(báimǎ sì) 白马寺

The Ming and Qing buildings of the White Horse Temple, perhaps the most venerable Buddhist temple in China, are built on the site of the original temple. The story of the temple's origin is interesting. In 67 AD the second emperor of the Han Dynasty sent two envoys to India to collect Buddhist scriptures. Their journey preceded that of the Tang Dynasty monk Xuan Zhuang (whose

story is told in the classic novel *Journey to the West*) by 500 years. When the envoys reached Afghanistan they met two Indian monks who gave them Buddhist scriptures and statues. The four then returned to Luoyang and had the temple built. The story goes that, since the scriptures and statues were carried to Luoyang on the back of a white horse, the temple was named the White Horse Temple. In front of the temple are two Song Dynasty stone horses. To the east is a 13-storey pagoda built sometime between the 10th and 12th centuries. The two Indian monks lived in the temple, translating scriptures and lecturing on Buddhist teachings and Indian culture; they are still buried there today.

The temple is 13 km east of Luoyang. To get there take bus No 5 or 9 to Xiguan traffic circle at the edge of the old city walls. Walk east to the stop for bus No 56, which will take you to the temple. On weekdays the temple tends to be a quiet and relaxing place. The entry price for foreigners is Y12.

Wangcheng Park

(wángchéng gōngyuán) 王城公园

At the rear of the park are a tiny zoo and two Han Dynasty tombs. Paintings and bas-reliefs can still be seen on the stone doors but the coffins have long gone. There's also an underground 'theme park' with moving dinosaur models and an assortment of polystyrene ghouls. The Peony Festival centred in Wangcheng Park is held from April 15 to 25, when thousands of Chinese tourists descend on Luoyang to view the peony flowers. If nature fails to provide sufficiently resplendent blooms, fake peonies are attached to the bushes.

Luoyang Museum

(luòyáng bówùguǎn) 洛阳博物馆

The museum is next to the park and houses a collection of early bronzes, Tang figurines and implements from the Stone Age. There are some eye-catching pieces but no English captions. Bus No 2 from the railway station area goes to the museum.

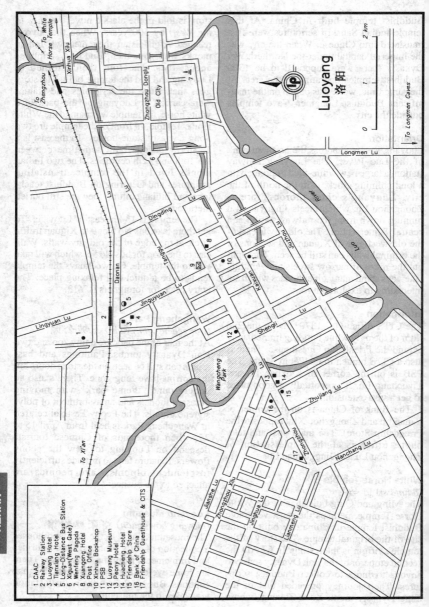

Luoyang 洛阳

0 1 2 km

1 CAAC
2 Railway Station
3 Luoyang Hotel
4 Tianxiang Hotel
5 Xiguan (West Gate)
6 Wenfeng Pagoda
7 Xuangong Hotel
8 Post Office
9 Xinhua Bookshop
10 Luoyang Museum
11 PSB
12 Peony Hotel
13 Huacheng Hotel
14 Friendship Store
15 Bank of China
16 Friendship Guesthouse & CITS

To White Horse Temple
To Zhengzhou
Xinhua Xilu
Zhongzhou Donglu
Old City
To Longmen Caves
Longmen Lu
Lu
Dingding Lu
River
Lu
Daonan
Jiuzhou Lu
Lingyuan Lu
Jinguyuan
Tangyu
Kaixuan Lu
Lu
Shengli Lu
Wangcheng Park
To Xi'an
Zhujiang Lu
Nanchang Lu
Jianshe Lu
Zhongzhou Xilu
Jinghua Lu
Lanmeng Lu
Zhongzhou

HENAN

1	中国民航售票处
2	火车站
3	洛阳旅社
4	天香旅社
5	长途汽车站
6	西关
7	文峰塔
8	旋宫大厦
9	邮电局
10	新华书店
11	公安局
12	洛阳博物馆
13	牡丹大酒店
14	花城饭店
15	友谊商店
16	中国银行
17	友谊宾馆/中国国际旅行社

Longmen Caves

(*lóngmén shíkū*) 龙门石窟

In 494 AD the Northern Wei Dynasty moved its capital from Datong to Luoyang. At Datong the dynasty had built the impressive Yungang Caves where works of typical Buddhist art can be seen. A common motif, for instance, is a triad in which the Buddha is flanked by bodhisattvas, though sometimes these are replaced by Ananda and Kasyapa, Buddha's first disciples. Bodhisattvas generally have expressions of benign tranquillity; they are saints who have opted to return to earth instead of entering nirvana, so that they might help others to follow the path of righteousness. You'll find many flying apsaras (celestial beings similar to angels and often depicted as musicians or bearers of flowers and incense).

At Luoyang the dynasty began work on the Longmen Caves. Over the next 200 years, more than 100,000 images and statues of Buddha and his disciples were carved into the cliff walls on the banks of the Yi River, 16 km south of the city. It was an ideal site. The hard texture of the rock, like that at Datong, made it very suitable for being carved. The caves of Luoyang, Dunhuang and Datong represent the peak of Buddhist cave art.

Apart from natural erosion, at Luoyang there has been much damage done to the sculptures during the 19th and 20th centuries by Western souvenir hunters who beheaded just about every figure they could lay their saws on. These heads now grace the museums and private paperweight collections of Europe and North America. Among these were two murals which were entirely removed and can now be seen at the Metropolitan Museum of Art in New York, and the Atkinson Museum in Kansas City. Oddly enough, the caves appear to have been spared the ravages of the Cultural Revolution. Even during the most anarchic year of 1967 the caves were reported to be open, no-one was watching over them and anybody could go in and have a look.

The art of Buddhist cave sculpture largely came to an end around the middle of the 9th century as the Tang Dynasty declined. Persecution of foreign religions in China began, with Buddhism as the prime target. Although Buddhist art and sculpture continued in China, it never reached the heights it had enjoyed previously.

Binyang Caves (*bīnyáng dòng*) The main caves of the Longmen group are on the west bank of the Yi River. They stretch out along the cliff face on a north-south axis. The three Binyang Caves are at the north end, closest to the entrance. All were begun under the Northern Wei and, though two were finished during the Sui and Tang dynasties, the statues all display the benevolent saccharine expressions which characterised the Northern Wei style.

Ten Thousand Buddha Cave (*wànfó dòng*) Several minutes' walk south of the Binyang Caves is the Tang Dynasty Ten Thousand Buddha Cave, built in 680. In addition to the legions of tiny bas-relief buddhas which give the cave its name, there is a fine big buddha and images of celestial dancers. Other images include musicians playing the flute, *pípá* (a plucked stringed instrument), cymbals and *zheng* (a 13 to 14-stringed harp).

HENAN

Lotus Flower Cave (*liánhuā dòng*) This cave was carved in 527 AD during the Northern Wei Dynasty and has a large standing buddha, now faceless. On the ceiling are wispy apsaras drifting around a central lotus flower. A common symbol in Buddhist art, the lotus flower represents purity and serenity.

Ancestor Worshipping Temple (*fèngxiān sì*) This is the largest structure at Longmen and contains the best works of art. It was built between 672 and 675 AD, during the Tang Dynasty. The roof is gone and the figures lie exposed to the elements. The Tang figures tend to be more three-dimensional than the Northern Wei figures, standing out in high relief and rather freer from their stone backdrop. Their expressions and poses also appear to be more natural but, unlike the other-worldly figures of the Northern Wei, the Tang figures are meant to be awesome.

The seated central Buddha is 17 metres high and is believed to be Vairocana, the supreme, omnipresent divinity. The face is thought to be modelled on that of the all-powerful Empress Wu Zetian of the Tang Dynasty.

As you face the Buddha, to the left are statues of the disciple Ananda and a bodhisattva wearing a crown, a tassel and a string of pearls. To the right are statues (or remains) of another disciple, a bodhisattva, a heavenly guardian trampling on a spirit, and a guardian of the Buddha.

Medical Prescription Cave South of the Ancestor Worshipping Temple is the tiny Medical Prescription Cave whose entrance is filled with 6th-century stone steles inscribed with remedies for common ailments.

Guyang Cave Adjacent to the Medical Prescription Cave is the much larger Guyang Cave, cut between 495 and 575 AD. It's a narrow, high-roofed cave featuring a buddha statue and a profusion of sculpture, particularly of flying apsaras. This was probably the first cave of the Longmen group to be built.

Shiku Cave This cave is a Northern Wei construction. It's the last major cave and has carvings depicting religious processions.

Getting to the Caves From the Luoyang railway station area, bus No 81 goes to the Longmen Caves. From the Friendship Guesthouse, take bus No 60 which leaves from the far side of the small park opposite the hotel. Bus No 53 from Xiguan traffic circle also runs past the caves.

Half-day minibus tours including the Longmen Caves, White Horse Temple and possibly other sights around Luoyang depart sporadically from in front of the railway station. The price is negotiable, but Chinese

The mighty celestial guardian - Ancestor Worshipping Temple

tourists seem to pay about Y20. Some hotels run their own tours out to the caves as well.

Places to Stay

Directly opposite the railway station is the *Luoyang Hotel (luòyáng lǔshè)* where doubles without bathroom cost Y40. With its grotty toilets, scowling staff and rows of 'overflow' beds along the hotel's noisy hallways, this is rather a depressing place.

A far more pleasant budget alternative is the *Huacheng Hotel (huáchéng fàndiàn)* at 49 Zhongzhou Xilu, which has beds in triple rooms for Y15 and doubles from Y40. It's not all that central, but bus Nos 2, 4 and 11 will get you there.

Around the corner on Jinguyuan Lu is the *Tianxiang Hotel* (☎ 337846) *(tiānxiāng lǔshè)*. It's a big place with a good choice of rooms. The cheapest dorm beds are Y12, simple doubles Y40 and doubles with bathroom Y80 or Y100; the suite goes for Y280.

The *Xuangong Hotel (xuángōng dàshà)* is in a good central location on Zhongzhou Lu near its junction with Jinguyuan Lu. This tower block hotel has doubles with bathroom from Y160.

The *Friendship Guesthouse* (☎ (0379) 412780) *(yǒuyí bīnguǎn)* at 6 Xiyuan Lu is where foreign tour groups generally stay and charges Y196/262 for standard singles/doubles. The place is a bit inconveniently situated on the western side of town. To get there, take bus No 4 from the main railway station and get off at the seventh stop; it's a five-minute walk from there to the hotel. For a taxi, expect to pay around Y60 from Luoyang Airport or Y20 from the main railway station.

The *Peony Hotel* (☎ (0379) 413699) *(mǔdan dàjiǔdiàn)* is a new high-rise joint venture at 15 Zhongzhou Xilu. With its cheapest rooms at Y520 it's well and truly in the upmarket bracket. It's got a high-class bar and a couple of upmarket restaurants.

Places to Eat

Luoyang is situated far enough west to give the local street food a slight Islamic touch. Cheap common snacks include *jiǎnpào*, small fried pastries filled with chopped herbs and Chinese garlic, and *dòushāgāo*, a sweet 'cake' made from ground yellow peas and jujubes (Chinese dates), sold by street vendors for about Y0.30 a slice. At night the street stalls around the railway station sell cheap and very good *shāguǒ*, a kind of meat and vegetable casserole cooked with bean noodles in a small earthenware pot.

You'll find better 'sit-down' restaurants along Zhongzhou Lu. The *Tianxiang Hotel* has a good and inexpensive restaurant with an English menu.

Getting There & Away

Air The CAAC office (☎ 335301) is in an unlikely and inconvenient location up a short lane off Dao Beilu. Bus No 83 passes it on the way to the small Luoyang Airport. There are flights to Xi'an (Y180, four a week), Canton (Y690, five a week), Beijing (Y370, three a week) and Shanghai (Y319, twice weekly) as well as Fuzhou (Y700) Chongqing (Y440) and Shenzhen (Y890). There are also charter flights to Hong Kong (Y1500).

Bus The long-distance bus station is diagonally opposite the main railway station. There are daily buses to Zhengzhou (Y15, air-conditioned; three hours) and Shaolin (Y5). You can also get direct buses to Anyang and Ruicheng (in south-western Shanxi Province) from here.

Coach buses fitted with sleeping berths leave in the evening from outside the railway station for Xi'an (Y65, 10 hours), Taiyuan (Y65, 11 hours), Wuhan (Y85, 15 hours) and Yantai in Shandong Province (Y168, 23 hours).

Train From Luoyang there are direct trains to Beijing (soft sleeper Y235, hard sleeper Y118, 13 hours), to Shanghai (soft sleeper Y325, hard sleeper Y170, 18 hours), and to Xi'an (soft sleeper Y85, hard sleeper Y148, eight hours). There are some direct trains north to Taiyuan and south to Xiangfan and Yichang. Yichang is a port on the Yangzi River, where you can pick up the Chongqing to Wuhan ferry.

HENAN

Getting Around

Luoyang is ideal for getting around by bicycle. Bikes can be rented outside the Tianxiang Hotel and around the railway station. They're classic old Chinese brands like 'Flying Pigeon', all in the standard colours of black or black. The going rate is about Y1 per hour or Y5 for a day.

ANYANG

(ānyáng) 安阳

Anyang, north of the Yellow River near the Henan/Hebei border, is now believed to be the site of Yin, the last capital of the ancient Shang Dynasty and one of the first centres of an urban-based Chinese civilisation.

Peasants working near Anyang in the late 19th century unearthed pieces of polished bone inscribed with an ancient form of Chinese writing, which turned out to be divining bones with questions addressed to the spirits and ancestors. Other inscriptions were found on the undershells of tortoises as well as on bronze objects, suggesting that the late Shang capital once stood here in the 14th century BC.

The discoveries attracted the attention of both Chinese and Western archaeologists, though it was not until the late 1920s that work began on excavating the site. These excavations uncovered ancient tombs, the ruins of a royal palace, workshops and houses – proof that the legendary Shang Dynasty had indeed existed.

Museum of the Yin Ruins

(yīnxū bówùyuàn) 殷墟博物馆

A museum has recently been established at the Yin site, but its collection is still disappointingly limited; it includes reassembled pottery and oracle bone fragments as well as jade and bronze artefacts. An excavation site is being prepared for public viewing. Bus No 1 from near the corner of Jiefan Lu and Zhangde Lu goes past the museum turn-off.

Places to Stay & Eat

The *Fenghuang Hotel (fēnghuáng bīnguǎn)* on Jiefang Lu near its intersection with Xihuancheng Lu seems willing to take foreigners and charges Y25 for a double. There's a good restaurant on the ground floor and you can rent bikes right outside.

The *Anyang Guesthouse* (☎ 422219) *(ānyáng bīnguǎn)* at No 1 Youyi Lu is the only tourist hotel in town. It has various doubles with bathroom for Y30, Y80 and Y160 and cheapest dorm beds for Y10.

Getting There & Away

From Anyang long-distance bus station there are connections to Zhengzhou (Y20, 4½ hours), Linxian (Y5, leaving half-hourly), Taiyuan (Y40, a rough 10-hour ride across the Taihangshan) and to Luoyang. Anyang is on the main Beijing-Zhengzhou railway line. Other rail links go to Taiyuan (Y21 hard seat, Chinese price; 13 hours) and Linxian (Y3, one daily; 8.30 am train).

AROUND ANYANG

To the west of Anyang, in the foothills of the Taihangshan close to Henan's border with Shanxi Province, lies **Linxian County** *(línxiàn)*.

Linxian is a rural area which rates with Dazhai and Shaoshan as one of the 'holy' places of Maoism, since this is the location of the famous Red Flag Canal. To irrigate the district, a river was re-routed through a tunnel beneath a mountain and then along a new bed built on the side of steep cliffs. The Communists insist that this colossal job, carried out during the Cultural Revolution, was done entirely by the toiling masses without the help of engineers and machines.

The statistics are impressive: 1500 km of canal was dug, hills were levelled, 134 tunnels were pierced, 150 aqueducts were constructed and enough earth was displaced to build a road one metre high, six metres wide and 4000 km long. All this was supposedly done by hand and was a tribute to Mao's vision of a self-reliant China.

Critics have called it an achievement worthy of Qin Shihuang, who pressed millions into building the Great Wall. They say that this sort of self-reliance only committed the peasants and workers to endless back-breaking toil. It would have made more sense to put the energy to some productive use and, with the profit, buy a pump and lay a pipeline to bring the water straight over the hill.

KAIFENG
(kāifēng) 开封

Kaifeng is a medium-sized city east of Zhengzhou. Its size belies the fact that this was once the prosperous imperial capital of China during Northern Song times.

With the invasion from the north in 1127 the Song fled south, where their poets wrote heart-rending verse as their beautiful capital was pillaged. Kaifeng never recovered from the assault and was never properly restored. All that remains today of the imperial splendour is a scroll painting in Beijing's Forbidden City which depicts the bustling town centre as it once was.

Restored and rebuilt Qing Dynasty structures with carved and painted wooden designs survive in parts of the old city, along with newer but interesting early 20th-century buildings. Alas, even little Kaifeng must move with the times, and whole blocks have recently been demolished to make way for...who knows what? Eroded, pounded-earth city walls surround Kaifeng on all sides, frequently interrupted by roads or new buildings. Kaifeng's population has grown little in the past 60 years, from *only* 280,000 in 1923 to just over 300,000 today, which makes it something of an odd-town-out in China's urban population boom.

The most intriguing members of Kaifeng's population are the Chinese Jews. Just how the Jews came to China is unknown. The story of the scattering of the '10 tribes' is one possibility, but according to another theory, Jews first arrived in China as traders and merchants along the Silk Road when Kaifeng was still a capital. Chinese historians, however, believe their Jewish population are descendants of immigrants from Jewish communities on the south-west coast of India.

In China, Jews have official status as a national minority, and for some time Kaifeng's Jewish population has had plans –

Kaifeng's Israelites

Father Nicola Trigault translated and published the diaries of the Jesuit priest Matteo Ricci in 1615, and based on these diaries he gives an account of a meeting between Ricci and a Jew from Kaifeng. The Jew was on his way to Beijing to take part in the imperial examinations, and Trigault writes:

'When he (Ricci) brought the visitor back to the house and began to question him as to his identity, it gradually dawned upon him that he was talking with a believer in the ancient Jewish law. The man admitted that he was an Israelite, but he knew no such word as 'Jew'.'

Ricci found out from the visitor that there were 10 or 12 families of Israelites in Kaifeng. A 'magnificent' synagogue had been built there and the five books of Moses had been preserved in the synagogue in scroll form for over 500 or 600 years. The visitor was familiar with the stories of the Old Testament, and some of the followers, he said, were expert in the Hebrew language. He also told Ricci that in a province which Trigault refers to as 'Cequian' at the capital of 'Hamcheu' there was a far greater number of Israelite families than at Kaifeng, and that there were others scattered about. Ricci sent one of his Chinese converts to Kaifeng, where he confirmed the visitor's story.

Today several hundred descendants of the original Jews live in Kaifeng and, though they still consider themselves Jewish, the religious beliefs and the customs associated with Judaism have almost completely died out. The original synagogue was destroyed in a Yellow River flood in 1642. It was rebuilt but destroyed by floods again in the 1850s. This time there was no money to rebuild it. Christian missionaries 'rescued' the temple's scrolls and prayer books in the late 19th century, and these are now in libraries in Israel, Canada and the USA.■

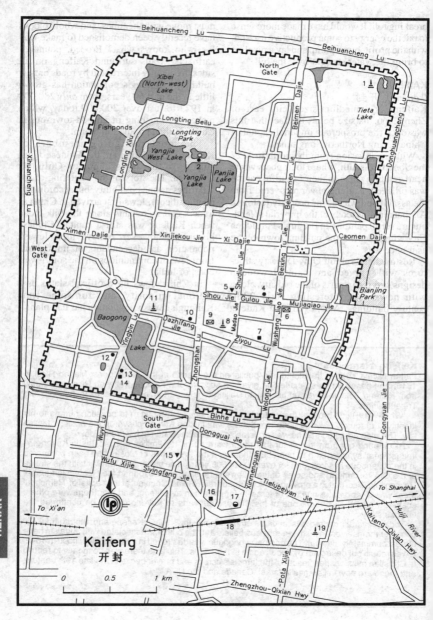

Kaifeng
开封

0   0.5   1 km

To Xi'an

To Shanghai

1	Iron Pagoda
2	Longting (Dragon Pavilion)
3	Ruins of Kaifeng Synagogue
4	Bank of China
5	Jiaozi Guan Restaurant
6	Post Office
7	Kaifeng Guesthouse
8	Xiangguo Temple
9	Post Office
10	PSB
11	Yanqing Taoist Temple
12	Museum
13	CITS
14	Dongjing Hotel
15	Tianjin Restaurant
16	Bianliang Hotel
17	Long-Distance Bus Station
18	Railway Station
19	Fan Pagoda

1	铁塔
2	龙亭
3	开封犹太教堂遗址
4	中国银行
5	饺子馆
6	邮电局
7	开封宾馆
8	相国寺
9	邮电局
10	公安局
11	延庆观
12	博物馆
13	中国国际旅行社
14	东京大饭店
15	天津饭馆
16	汴梁旅社
17	长途汽车站
18	火车站
19	繁塔

still unfulfilled – to rebuild its synagogue and establish a Jewish museum in the city. A small Christian community also lives in Kaifeng alongside a much larger local Muslim minority; you may come across their churches and mosques in Kaifeng's back-streets.

Orientation

The long-distance bus station and the railway station are both outside and about one km to the south of the old city walls; the rest of Kaifeng is mostly within the walled area. The city's pivotal point is the intersection of Sihou Jie and Madao Jie; the street market here is particularly lively at night. The surrounding restaurants, shops and houses are of mainly traditional Chinese wooden architecture. Not far away are the Kaifeng Guesthouse and the Xiangguo Temple.

Information

The PSB is on Dazhifang Jie, 50 metres west of Zhongshan Lu. CITS (☎ 555131) has a new office at 14 Yingbin Lu, next to the Dongjing Hotel. The Bank of China is on Gulou Jie about half a km north of the Kaifeng Guesthouse.

There are post and telephone offices near the corner of Zhongshan Lu and Ziyou Lu, and on the corner of Mujiaqiao Jie and Wusheng Jiao Jie.

Xiangguo Temple

(xiàngguó sì) 相国寺

The temple is next door to a large Chinese-style market. Originally founded in 555 AD but frequently rebuilt over the next 1000 years, Xiangguo Temple was completely destroyed in 1644 when the Yellow River floodgates were opened in a disastrous attempt to halt a Manchu invasion. The current buildings date from 1766 and have had a thorough going-over since then. There's an enormous old cast-iron bell on the right as you go in; entry costs Y4.

Iron Pagoda

(tiě tǎ) 铁塔

Built in the 11th century, the Iron Pagoda is actually made of normal bricks but covered in specially coloured tiles that look like iron. You can climb to the top of this impressive structure. The tiles on the lower levels have damaged buddha images – possibly the result of Red Guard sledgehammers. Take bus No 3 from near the long-distance bus

HENAN

station to the route terminal; it's a 15-minute walk from there.

Other Sights

The large local **museum** *(kāifēng bówùguǎn)* on Yingbin Lu just south of Baogong Lake has a diverse collection that deals mainly with Kaifeng's Song Dynasty period, the local Jewish community and Chinese revolutionary history. **Longting Park** *(lóngtíng gōngyuán)* is covered mostly by lakes; on its drier northern rim near the **Longting** (Dragon Pavilion) there is a small children's fun park with sideshows and bumper-car rides; old men often sit here playing Chinese chess in the shade. The very small **Yanqing Taoist Temple** *(yánqìng guān)* has interesting architecture and a strange, 13-metre-high pagoda. The oldest existing building in Kaifeng is **Fan Pagoda** *(fán tǎ)*, south-east of the railway station.

If you want to see the **Yellow River**, take local bus No 6 or a motortricycle to Liuyuan *(liǔyuán)*, 11 km north of Kaifeng. Ferries cross the river at this point too.

Places to Stay

Virtually no restrictions apply as to where foreigners can stay in Kaifeng. Indeed, the atmosphere is so relaxed that one suspects the local authorities might actually be trying to encourage foreign tourists to come here – evidence that Kaifeng leads the way in China's gradual opening. All this means you have a wide choice of accommodation possibilities. You'll find the two main hotel areas are around the railway station and in the centre of town.

The *Bianliang Hotel (biànliáng lǚshè)* on Zhongshan Lu, about 100 metres up from the railway station, has doubles with crude bathrooms for Y34 and dorm beds from Y4 to Y9. There's hot water for a few hours in the evening. A similarly priced place is the *Dongfeng Hotel (dōngfēng lǚshè)* across the road, with single rooms without bathroom for Y10.

The *Bian Hotel (biàn dàlǚshè)* is the big four-storey building you see to the left as you leave the bus station. Despite its grandish appearance this place is rather basic inside – none of the rooms come with private bathroom – but with singles from Y9 and doubles for Y15 it's OK considering what you pay.

Another good-value place is the *Dajintai Hotel (dàjīntái lǚguǎn)* on Gulou Jie (nearly opposite the Bank of China). It's a central yet quiet location in a small courtyard just behind the street front, and offers double rooms with bathroom (including 24-hour hot water) for Y24.

In the mid-price range is the *Bianjing Hotel* (☎ (0378) 552012) *(biànjīng fàndiàn)* on the corner of Dong Dajie and Beixing Jie at the north-eastern edge of town in the Muslim quarter. It's an older pre-fab concrete building with little character of its own, but there's plenty of activity on the surrounding streets. There's also a popular restaurant in the back of the hotel compound. They charge Y10 per bed in triples and Y96 for nice doubles with attached shower facilities. To get there take bus No 3 from the long-distance bus station and get off at the sixth stop.

The *Kaifeng Guesthouse* (☎ (0378) 555589) *(kāifēng bīnguǎn)* on Ziyou Lu is the most central of the better hotels and where tour groups often put up. The original Russian-built structure has recently undergone (apparently its first) major renovation. The price for a standard double is Y84, while a luxury suite goes for Y280. Take bus No 5 from the railway station and get off at Xiangguo Temple.

South of Baogong Park on Yingbin Lu is the newish *Dongjing Hotel* (☎ (0378) 558938) *(dōngjīng dàfàndiàn)*, probably a joint-venture operation. The staff speak quite good English and are helpful and friendly. Prices for doubles in the hotel's four separate wings vary from Y60 to Y100, and Y300 for a suite. It's inconveniently located, but at least the museum and CITS are nearby. Bus No 9 from the railway station goes past here.

Places to Eat

Despite its small size, Kaifeng offers a fair variety of street food, which is particularly good at the night market near the corner of

Sihou Jie and Madao Jie. Worth sampling there is *ròuhé*, a local snack of fried vegetables and pork (or mutton in its Islamic version) stuffed into a 'pocket' of flat bread.

The eating places around the railway station have a decidedly unhygienic look and are probably best left alone, but the simple *Tianjin Restaurant (tiānjīn fànzhuāng)* five minutes' walk up Zhongshan Lu offers a good alternative.

As its name suggests, the busy government-run *Jiaozi Guan Restaurant (jiǎozi guǎn)* specialises in *jiaozi* – Chinese dumplings with a meat or vegetable filling – but upstairs there's a much wider selection of dishes. It's on the corner of Shudian Lu and Sihou Jie in a three-storey traditional Chinese building with a quaint old wooden balcony.

Getting There & Away

Bus Private minibuses to Zhengzhou collect passengers from in front of the railway station. Scheduled public buses to Zhengzhou (Y6.50, two hours) depart from the long-distance bus station. The Kaifeng-Zhengzhou road passes through numerous villages lined with fragrant paulownia trees and Chinese poplars.

There are quite a few direct buses to Luoyang, but it may still work out quicker changing at Zhengzhou. There are also three regular daily buses to Anyang (Y22) via Zhengzhou and a daily bus to Bozhou (Y13). The fastest and cheapest way to get to Qufu from Kaifeng is an eight-hour bus route via Heze and Yanzhou, passing the Yellow River on the way.

Train Kaifeng lies on the railway line between Xi'an and Shanghai and trains are frequent. Expresses to Zhengzhou take about 1½ hours and about 13 hours to both Shanghai and Xi'an. You can also get direct trains south to Bozhou and Hefei in Anhui Province from here.

Getting Around

Kaifeng is a small place built on a flat river plain, so bicycles are a handy means of transport; you can rent a bike from right outside the CITS building for Y3 per day. Bus routes cover all sights of likely interest to tourists.

Shaanxi 陕西

Population: 30 million
Capital: Xi'an

The northern part of Shaanxi *(shǎnxī)* is one of the oldest settled regions of China, with remains of human habitation dating back to prehistoric times. This was the homeland of the Zhou people, who eventually conquered the Shang and established their rule over much of northern China. It was also the homeland of the Qin, who ruled from their capital of Xianyang near modern-day Xi'an and were the first dynasty to rule over all of eastern China. Shaanxi remained the political heart of China until the 9th century. The great Sui and Tang capital of Xi'an was built there and the province was a crossroads on the trading routes from eastern China to central Asia.

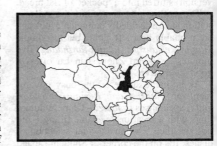

With the migration of the imperial court to pastures further east, Shaanxi became a less attractive piece of real estate. Rebellions afflicted the territory from 1340 to 1368, again from 1620 to 1644, and finally in the mid-19th century, when the great Muslim rebellion left tens of thousands of the province's Muslims dead. Five million people died in the famine from 1876 to 1878 and another three million in the famines of 1915, 1921 and 1928. It was probably the dismal condition of the Shaanxi peasants that gave the Communists such willing support in the province in the late 1920s and during the ensuing civil war. From their base at Yan'an the Communist leaders directed the war against the Kuomintang and later against the Japanese, before being forced to evacuate in the wake of a Kuomintang attack in 1947.

Some 30 million people live in Shaanxi, mostly in the central and southern regions. The north of the province is a plateau covered with a thick layer of wind-blown loess soil which masks the original landforms. Deeply eroded, the landscape has deep ravines and almost vertical cliff faces. The Great Wall in the far north of the province is something of a cultural barrier, beyond which agriculture and human existence were always precarious ventures.

Like so much of China, this region is rich in natural resources, particularly coal and oil. The Wei River, a branch of the Yellow River, cuts across the middle of the province. This fertile belt became a centre of Chinese civilisation. The south of the province is quite different from the north; it's a comparatively lush, mountainous area with a mild climate.

XI'AN
(xī'ān) 西安

Once the focus of China, Xi'an vied with its contemporaries, Rome and later Constantinople, for the title of greatest city in the world. Over a period of 2000 years Xi'an has seen the rise and fall of numerous Chinese dynasties, and the monuments and archaeological sites in the city and the surrounding plain are a reminder that once upon a time Xi'an was a booming metropolis.

The earliest evidence of human habitation dates back 6000 years to Neolithic times, when the plain was lush and green and primitive Chinese tribes established their villages. The legendary Zhou established their capital on the banks of the Fen River near present-day Xi'an.

Xianyang
Between the 5th and 3rd centuries BC, China

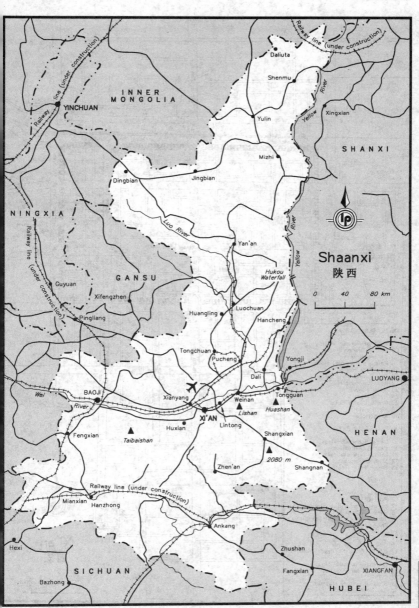

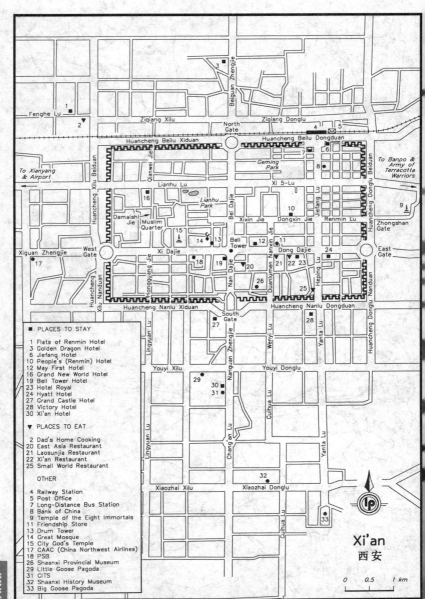

Xi'an
西安

■ PLACES TO STAY
1 Flats of Renmin Hotel
3 Golden Dragon Hotel
6 Jiefang Hotel
10 People's (Renmin) Hotel
12 May First Hotel
16 Grand New World Hotel
19 Bell Tower Hotel
23 Hotel Royal
24 Hyatt Hotel
27 Grand Castle Hotel
28 Victory Hotel
30 Xi'an Hotel

▼ PLACES TO EAT
2 Dad's Home Cooking
20 East Asia Restaurant
21 Laosunjia Restaurant
22 Xi'an Restaurant
25 Small World Restaurant

OTHER
4 Railway Station
5 Post Office
7 Long-Distance Bus Station
8 Bank of China
9 Temple of the Eight Immortals
11 Friendship Store
13 Drum Tower
14 Great Mosque
15 City God's Temple
17 CAAC (China Northwest Airlines)
18 PSB
26 Shaanxi Provincial Museum
29 Little Goose Pagoda
31 CITS
32 Shaanxi History Museum
33 Big Goose Pagoda

0   0.5   1 km

SHAANXI

split into five separate states locked in perpetual war, until the state of Qin conquered everyone and everything. Emperor Qin Shihuang became the first emperor of a unified China and established his capital at Xianyang near modern-day Xi'an. His longing for immortality gave posterity a remarkable legacy of these ancient times – a tomb guarded by an army of thousands of terracotta soldiers.

The Qin Dynasty was unable to withstand the death of Qin Shihuang. In 206 BC it was overthrown by a revolt led by a commoner, Liu Pang. Pang established the Han Dynasty which lasted a phenomenal 400 years, during which time the boundaries of the empire were extended deep into central Asia. Despite its longevity, the dynasty was never really secure or unified. It collapsed in 220 AD, making way for more than three centuries of disunity and war. Nevertheless the Han empire had set the scene for later emperors' dreams of Chinese expansion, power and unity. This dream was taken up by the Sui and the Tang and encapsulated in their magnificent capital of Chang'an.

Chang'an

The new city was established in early 582 AD on the fertile plain where the capital of the Han Dynasty had once stood, and on which modern-day Xi'an now stands. After the collapse of the Han, the north of China was ruled by foreign invaders and the south by a series of weak and short-lived Chinese dynasties. When the Sui Dynasty united the country after a series of wars, the first emperor, Wen Ti, ordered the new capital of Chang'an to be built. It was a deliberate reference back to the glory of the Han period, a symbol of reunification.

The Sui were short-lived and in 618 AD they were replaced by the Tang. Under the Tang, Chang'an became the largest city in Asia, if not the world. At the height of Tang power Chang'an was a cosmopolitan city of courtiers, merchants, foreign traders, soldiers, artists, entertainers, priests and bureaucrats, with a million people within the city walls and perhaps another million outside. The thriving metropolis of commerce, administration, religion and culture was the political hub of the empire and the centre of a brilliant period of creativity.

The city's design was based on traditional Chinese urban planning theories as well as on innovations introduced under the Sui. The outer walls of the new city formed a rectan-

SHAANXI

gle which ran almost 10 km east-west and just over eight km north-south, enclosing a neat grid system of streets and wide avenues. The walls were made of pounded earth faced with sun-dried bricks, and were probably about 5½ metres high and between 5½ and nine metres thick at the base, penetrated by 11 gates. Within these walls the bureaucracy and imperial court were concentrated in a separate administrative city and a palace city which were also bounded by walls, a design probably based on the highly developed Northern Wei capital of Luoyang. Situated on a plain bounded by mountains, hills and the Wei River (which flowed eastward to join the Yellow River), the city was easy to defend against invaders.

The scale of Chang'an was unprecedented, perhaps an expression of the Sui and Tang rulers' vision of an expanded empire, but with power more centralised than anything their predecessors had imagined. With the final conquests in the south in 589 AD, Wen Ti was able to embark on an administrative reorganisation of the empire. A nationwide examination system enabled more people from the eastern plains and the increasingly populous southern regions to serve in the government bureaucracy in Chang'an, thus ensuring that the elite were drawn from all over the country, a system continued and developed by the Tang.

Communications between the capital and the rest of China were developed, mainly by canals which linked Chang'an to the Grand Canal and to other strategic places – another system also developed and improved by the Tang. Roads were built radiating from the capital, with inns for officials, travellers, merchants and pilgrims. These systems enabled Chang'an to draw in taxes and tribute and enforce its power. They extended to the sea ports and caravan routes which connected China to the rest of the world, allowing Chang'an to import the world's ideas and products. The city became a centre of international trade, and a large foreign community established itself there. Numerous foreign religions built temples and mosques, including Muslims, the Zoroastri-

ans of Persia, and the Nestorian Christian sect of Syria. The growth of the government elite and the evolution of a more complex imperial court drew vast numbers of people to serve it. By the 8th century the city had a phenomenal population of two million.

Towards the end of the 8th century the Tang Dynasty and its capital began to decline. From 775 onwards the central government suffered reverses at the hands of provincial warlords and Tibetan and Turkic invaders. The setbacks exposed weaknesses in the empire, and though the Tang still maintained overall supremacy they gradually lost control of the transport networks and the tax collection system on which their power depended. The dynasty fell in 907 AD and China once again broke up into a number of independent states. Chang'an was eventually relegated to the role of a regional centre.

Xi'an

The modern-day city of Xi'an stands on the site of Chang'an. In the 19th century Xi'an was a rather isolated provincial town, a condition which persisted until the completion of a railway line from Zhengzhou in 1930. After 1949 the Communists started to industrialise the city and it now supports a population of some three million people. As the capital of Shaanxi, Xi'an has been a major recipient of investment from the Chinese government, aimed at creating new inland industrial centres as a counterbalance to the increasing dominance of the large industrial centres of the coast. At first glance the city looks little different from other modern Chinese industrial cities, but scattered about are many reminders of its imperial past. Today, Xi'an is one of the biggest open-air museums in China.

Orientation

Xi'an retains the same rectangular shape that characterised Chang'an, with streets and avenues laid out in a neat grid pattern.

The central block of the modern city is bounded by the city walls. The centre of town is the enormous Bell Tower, and from here run Xi'an's four major streets: Bei, Nan,

Top: Kunming Lake, Beijing (Storey)
Left: Summer Palace, Beijing (Storey)
Right: Lama Temple, Beijing (Storey)

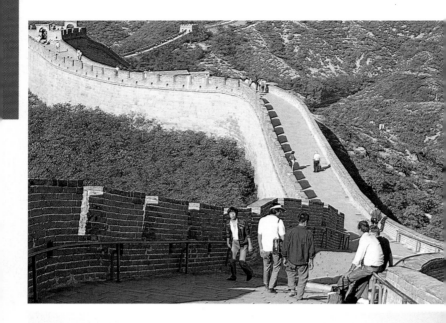

Top: The Great Wall, Beijing (AS)
Bottom: Marble Boat, Kunming Lake, Beijing (Storey)

Dong and Xi Dajie. The railway station stands at the north-east edge of the central city block. Jiefang Lu runs south from the station to intersect with Dong Dajie.

Most of the tourist facilities can be found either along or in the vicinity of Jiefang Lu or Xi and Dong Dajie. However, many of the city's sights like the new Shaanxi History Museum, the Big Goose and Little Goose pagodas and Banpo Neolithic Village are outside the central block. Further afield on the plains surrounding Xi'an are sights such as the Entombed Warriors at Xianyang, Famen Temple, the Tomb of Qin Shihuang and the Army of Terracotta Warriors near Lintong.

Information

CITS The CITS (☎ 735600) has its main office on Chang'an Beilu, a few minutes' walk south of the Xi'an Hotel. There are more central CITS branches at the Jiefang Hotel (☎ 713329 ext 237) and the Bell Tower Hotel (☎ 775046).

PSB This is at 138 Xi Dajie, a 10-minute walk west of the Bell Tower. It's open every day except Sunday from 8 am to noon and from 2.30 to 6 pm.

Money The main Bank of China (☎ 772312) is at 223 Jiefang Lu, just up from Dong 5-Lu. It's open from 9 to 11.45 am, and from 2 until 4.30 pm. Two other useful branches where foreigners can change money are on Xi Dajie and Dong Dajie. Banks in Xi'an demand a hefty 7½% service charge for cashing travellers' cheques into both FEC and US dollars. Many of the hotels also have money-changing services but they often refuse to serve non-guests. Some of the small restaurants popular with Western travellers do foreign currency-RMB swaps.

Post & Telecommunications The most convenient post and telephone offices are next to the railway station and on Bei Dajie at the corner of Xixin Jie.

Maps Hawkers at Xi'an railway station wave cheap bus maps in the face of arriving passengers; some indicate the main features in English. Several rather more expensive bilingual tourist maps are also sold around town, chiefly at hotel shops or outside the main sights.

Bell Tower
(zhōnglóu) 钟楼
The Bell Tower is a huge building in the centre of Xi'an that you enter through an underpass on the north side of the tower. The original tower was built in the late 14th century, but was rebuilt at the present location in 1739 during the Qing Dynasty. A large iron bell in the tower used to mark the time each day, hence the name. Upstairs is an elaborate waxworks display of Qin, Han and Tang emperors of Chang'an. Entry to the Bell Tower and the wax exhibit both cost Y10 or (Y3 for students).

Drum Tower
(gǔlóu) 鼓楼
The Drum Tower, a smaller building to the west of the Bell Tower, marks the Muslim quarter of Xi'an. Foreigners pay an entry price of Y5. Beiyuanmen is an interesting old street of traders and craftspeople running north directly from the Drum Tower, and has recently undergone major restoration.

City Walls
(chéngqiáng) 城墙
Xi'an is one of the few cities in China where old city walls are still visible. The walls were built on the foundations of the walls of the Tang Forbidden City during the reign of Hong Wu, first emperor of the Ming Dynasty. They form a rectangle with a circumference of 14 km. On each side of the wall is a gateway, and over each stand three towers. At each of the four corners is a watchtower, and the top of the wall is punctuated with defensive towers. The wall is 12 metres high, with a width at the top of 12 to 14 metres and at the base of 15 to 18 metres.

Air-raid shelters were hollowed out of the walls when the Japanese bombed the city, and during the Cultural Revolution caves were dug to store grain. Most sections have been restored or even rebuilt but others have disappeared completely (though they're still shown on the maps), so unfortunately it's not possible to walk right around Xi'an along the city walls. There are access ramps up to the wall just east of the railway station, near Heping Lu, at South Gate (*nánmén*) beside the Provincial Museum and some obscure steps at the eastern end of the south wall; tickets cost Y6.

Big Goose Pagoda
(*dà yàn tǎ*) 大雁塔
This pagoda stands in what was formerly the Temple of Great Maternal Grace in the south of Xi'an. The temple was built about 648 AD by Emperor Gao Zong (the third emperor of the Tang Dynasty) when he was still crown prince, in memory of his deceased mother. The buildings that stand today date from the Qing Dynasty and were built in a Ming style.

The original pagoda was built in 652 AD with only five storeys, but it has been renovated, restored and added to many times. It was built to house the Buddhist scriptures brought back from India by the travelling monk Xuan Zang, who then set about translating them into 1335 Chinese volumes. The impressive, fortress-like wood-and-brick building rises 64 metres. You can climb to the top for a view of the countryside and the city.

The Big Goose Pagoda is at the end of Yanta Lu, at the southern edge of Xi'an. Bus No 41 from the railway station goes straight there. The entrance is on the southern side of the temple grounds. Foreigners pay Y10 at the main gate, plus Y15 to climb the pagoda (student concessions are available).

On the east side of the temple is the newly-built Tang Dynasty Arts Museum (*tángdài yìshù bówùguǎn*) with a collection specifically devoted to the Tang period in Xi'an (admission Y5).

Little Goose Pagoda
(*xiǎo yàn tǎ*) 小雁塔
The Little Goose Pagoda is in the grounds of the Jianfu Temple. The top of the pagoda was shaken off by an earthquake in the middle of the 16th century but the rest of the structure, 43 metres high, is intact. The Jianfu Temple was originally built in 684 AD as a site to hold prayers to bless the afterlife of the late Emperor Gao Zong. The pagoda, a rather delicate building of 15 progressively smaller tiers, was built from 707 to 709 AD and housed Buddhist scriptures brought back from India by another pilgrim.

You can get to the pagoda on bus No 3, which runs from the railway station through the south gate of the old city and down Nanguan Zhengjie. The pagoda is on Youyi Xilu just west of the intersection with Nanguan Zhengjie. Entry to the grounds is Y5 for foreigners, plus Y4 more to climb to the top of the pagoda for a panorama of Xi'an's apartment blocks and smokestacks.

Great Mosque
(*dà qīngzhēnsì*) 大清真寺
This is one of the largest mosques in China. The present buildings only date back to the middle of the 18th century, though the mosque might have been established several hundred years earlier. It stands north-west of the Drum Tower and is built in a Chinese architectural style with most of the grounds taken up by gardens. Still an active place of worship, the mosque holds several prayer services each day. The mosque is open from 8 am to noon, and from 2 to 6 pm. The courtyard of the mosque can be visited, but only Muslims may enter the prayer hall.

The Great Mosque is five minutes' walk from the Drum Tower: go under the arch then take the second tiny lane leading left to a small side street. From here the mosque is a few steps along to the right past souvenir shops; it costs Y12 to get in.

Shaanxi Provincial Museum
(*shǎnxī shěng bówùguǎn*) 陕西省博物馆
Once the Temple of Confucius, the museum houses a fine collection devoted largely to the history of the Silk Road. Among the artefacts is a tiger-shaped tally from the Warring States Period, inscribed with ancient Chinese characters and probably

used to convey messages or orders from one military commander to another.

One of the more extraordinary exhibits is the Forest of Steles, the heaviest collection of books in the world. The earliest of these 2300 large engraved stone tablets dates from the Han Dynasty.

Most interesting is the Popular Stele of Daiqin Nestorianism, recognisable by the small cross at the top. The Nestorians were an early Christian sect who differed from orthodox Christianity in their belief that Christ's human and divine natures were quite distinct. Nestorian Christianity spread eastwards to China via the Silk Road, and Marco Polo mentions making contact with members of the sect in Fuzhou in the 13th century.

The Popular Stele was engraved in 781 AD to mark the opening of a Nestorian church. The tablet describes in Syrian and Chinese how a Syrian disciple named Raban came to the imperial court of Xi'an in 635. Raban presented Christian scriptures which were translated and then read by the emperor. The emperor, says the stone, was impressed and ordered that a monastery dedicated to the new religion be established in the city.

Other tablets include the Ming De Shou Ji Stele which records the peasant uprising led by Li Zhicheng against the Ming, and the 114 Stone Classics of Kaichen from the Tang Dynasty inscribed with 13 ancient classics and historical records.

All of the important exhibits have labels in English. The museum entrance is on a side street which runs off Baishulin Lu, close to the South Gate of the old city wall. It's open from 8.30 am to 6 pm. Admission for foreigners is Y20 and students Y3.

Shaanxi History Museum
(shǎnxī lìshǐ bówùguǎn)
陕西历史博物馆
Built in huge classical-Chinese style, the museum was opened in 1992 and is one of Xi'an's major attractions. The collection is chronologically arranged and includes material previously housed in the Provincial Museum, though many objects have never been on permanent display before.

The section on the ground floor deals with Chinese prehistory and the early dynastic period, starting with palaeolithic Langtian Man and the more recent New Stone Age settlements at Lintong and Banpo between 7000 and 5000 years ago. There are many pieces of neolithic pottery, ancient jade carvings and arrowheads. Particularly impressive are several enormous Shang and Western Zhou Dynasty bronze cooking tripods and other vessels from Yantou, Qin burial objects, bronze arrows and crossbows, ancient ceramic water pipes and four original terracotta warrior statues taken from near the Tomb of Qin Shihuang.

Upstairs, the second section is devoted to Han, Western Wei and Northern Zhou Dynasty relics. There are some interesting goose-shaped bronze lamps and a set of forged-iron transmission gears, which are surprisingly advanced for their time.

The final, third section has mainly Sui, Tang, Ming and Qing Dynasty artefacts. The major advances in ceramic-making techniques during this period are most evident, with intricately crafted terracotta horses and camels, fine pale-green glazed *misi* pottery and Buddhist-inspired Tang Dynasty statues. There are also items from the Famen Temple including a gold and silver tea set and some superbly designed Ming and Qing pottery with rose and peony decorations.

To get there from the railway station, take bus No 5 or 14. Foreigners enter and leave the museum via doors to the left of the main entrance. Photography is strictly prohibited and you must deposit (free of charge) any hand luggage in the lockers provided. Admission is Y38, but holders of a valid student card pay only Y10. All exhibits include labels and explanations in English. The museum is open every day from 8.30 am to 5.30 pm.

Old Xi'an
Xi'an's old **Muslim Quarter** centred around the Great Mosque has retained much of its original character. The backstreets to the north and west of the mosque have been

home to the city's Hui community for centuries. Walking through the narrow laneways lined with old mud-brick houses, you pass butcher shops, sesame oil factories, smaller mosques hidden behind enormous wooden doors and proud, stringy-bearded men wearing white skull-caps. Good streets to explore are Nanyuan Men, Huajue Xiang and Damaishi Jie, which runs north off Xi Dajie through an interesting Islamic food market.

The **Temple of the Eight Immortals** (*bā xiān ān*) is Xi'an's largest Taoist establishment and an active place of worship. Scenes from Taoist mythology are painted around the temple courtyard. To get there take a No 10, 11, 28 or 42 bus east along Changle Lu and get off two stops past the city walls, then continue 100 metres on foot and turn right (south) under a green-painted iron gateway into a market lane. Follow this, turning briefly right then left again into another small street leading past the temple. The entrance is on the southern side of the temple grounds. You can also reach the temple by following the street running directly east from Zhongshan Gate. Entry is Y5.

The **City God's Temple** (*chéng huáng miào*) is built in old-style heavy wooden architecture with a blue tiled roof, and possibly dates from the early Qing period. The building is sadly dilapidated and currently being used as a warehouse, but this gives it a definite 'unrestored charm'. The temple is 10 minutes' walk west of the Drum Tower at the end of a long roofed-over market running north off Xi Dajie. There's no English sign, so look for the large red Chinese characters above the entrance immediately west of the Xijing Hotel.

Organised Tours

One-day tours allow you to the see all the sights around Xi'an more quickly and conveniently than if you did it yourself. Itineraries differ somewhat, but there are two basic tours: a 'Western Tour' and an 'Eastern Tour'. There are also tours of the sights within the city area that leave from the square in front of the railway station. CITS-organised tours are more expensive than those run by other operators, but the cheaper tours usually won't leave until they have enough people and tend to give you less time at each place.

Eastern Tour The eastern tour (*dōngxiàn yóulǎn*) is the most popular since it includes the Army of Terracotta Warriors as well as the Tomb of Qin Shihuang, Banpo Museum and Huaqing Pool. The CITS-run Eastern tour costs Y95 with transport only, or Y210 including lunch and all entry tickets. The coach leaves Xi'an around 9 am and returns by 5 pm, and will pick you up from your hotel. An English-speaking guide is provided and you usually get two hours at the warriors and Qin Shihuang's tomb, although many tourists complain that the CITS tour spends too long at the boring Huaqing Pool. Essentially the same tour can be done for far less by taking one of the Chinese minibus tours; you can buy tickets for Y15 at a kiosk in front of the railway station or outside the Bell Tower Hotel. The Jiefang Hotel also does the Eastern Tour (excluding Banpo Museum) for Y20.

Western Tour The longer Western Tour (*xīxiàn yóulǎn*) includes the Xianyang City Museum, some of the Imperial Tombs, the Qian Tomb and sometimes also Famen Temple. The CITS organises a Western tour costing Y120, but it doesn't leave every day. The cheapest minibus tours are Y25 and depart from outside the railway station. The Jiefang Hotel runs buses on the standard Western Tour for Y30, or Y40 including Famen Temple.

Places to Stay – bottom end

The *Flats of Remin Hotel* (☎ 722352) (*rénmín dàshà gōngyù*) is at No 9 Fenghe Lu. Beds in mini-dorms go for Y20, and old-style doubles with bathroom are Y80. There's 24-hour hot water for showering and a relatively cheap laundry service. The place is north-west of the city outside the old walls, but the hotel regularly sends its own scout with a minibus to snap up arriving train passengers – if he misses you, take bus No 9 from the railway station and get off after six stops. You can rent bikes at reception for Y5 a day or Y1 per hour.

Another place where budget travellers often end up is the *Victory Hotel* (☎ 713184) *(shènglì fàndiàn)* just south of Heping Gate. The hotel has recently had a minor facelift, but its rooms are as grotty as ever and the toilets quite disgusting – what the Victory really needs is a complete overhaul and new management. Beds in simple triples start at Y20 and doubles with bathroom are Y80. Buses No 5 and No 41 (among others) go past the hotel from the railway station.

The *Golden Dragon* (☎ 723371) *(jīnlóng dàjiǔdiàn)* is north of the North Gate on Beiguan Zhengjie. Some travellers have managed to get a bed here in a small, clean, air-con dorm for Y20, or (after some bargaining) a nice double with bathroom for Y70. This hotel also employs spies to seek out backpackers at the railway station, but you can otherwise get there by catching a No 28 bus and getting off after three stops.

Places to Stay – middle

The *May First Hotel* (☎ 712212) *(wǔyī fàndiàn)* is at 351 Dong Dajie, a short distance from the Bell Tower. Foreigners favour this place for its friendliness and central location. Its rates have risen disproportionately in recent years, but at Y99 for a double with private bath it's still not bad value.

The *Jiefang Hotel* (☎ 713329) *(jiěfàng fàndiàn)* diagonally across the wide square to your left as you leave the railway station, has a convenient location that for many foreign travellers is decisive. The Jiefang lets out single beds in standard doubles for Y60 (or Y120 for two people) and with a bit of persuasion will give you a bed in a small dorm for Y45. Their nicer doubles cost Y180.

The enormous *People's (Renmin) Hotel* (☎ 715111) *(rénmín dàshà)* is at 319 Dongxin Jie. Built in classic early-1950s Stalinist architecture softened with Chinese features, two recently added multistorey wings have spoilt the building's original

street view. With a bit of bargaining, you can get a double for Y120.

The *Bell Tower Hotel* (☎ 779200) *(zhōnglóu fàndiàn)* diagonally opposite the Bell Tower in the centre of town has been likened to an aircraft hangar. Rates are seasonal, but the bottom price for a double is US$44. There's a good Cantonese restaurant on the 2nd floor. To get there take the No 101 trolley-bus from the railway station and get off at the Bell Tower.

Places to Stay – top end

The *Xi'an Hotel* (☎ 751796) *(xī'ān bīnguǎn)* at 36 Chang'an Lu has doubles from US$55 a night. It's about two km south of the city walls but bus No 3 from the railway station runs straight past it.

A more central alternative is the *Hotel Royal* (☎ 710305) *(xī'ān huángchéng bīnguǎn)* at 334 Dong Dajie near the Friendship Store, where a standard twin costs US$90. It's a new Sino-Japanese joint venture with shops and restaurants – by all accounts the sushi bar is good.

The *Grand Castle Hotel* (☎ 731800) *(cháng'ān chéngbǎo dàjiǔdiàn)* at 12 Huancheng near the South Gate is another of Xi'an's luxury high-rise hotels. Standard doubles are US$110.

The *Grand New World Hotel* (☎ 716868) *(gǔdū dàjiǔdiàn)* at 48 Lianhu Lu on the north-west side of the old city near the Muslim quarter has doubles from US$115.

The *Hyatt Hotel* (☎ 731234) *(kǎiyuè fàndiàn)* is at Dong Dajie and Heping Lu. It has a range of rooms from US$110 for a standard double to US$1000 for the 'presidential suite' – plus a 15% surcharge.

Places to Eat

How you experience Xi'an's street-food scene depends largely on when you visit. In winter the entire population seems to get by on endless bowls of noodles, but at other times of the year you should find more variety. A good night-food street is Dongxin Jie between Jiefang Lu and Zhongshan Gate. Much of the local street food is of Islamic origin, and some common dishes are:

fěnrèròu, made by frying chopped mutton in a wok with fine-ground wheat; dark brown sorghum or buckwheat noodles called *héletiáo*; and *mǐgāo*, deep-fried rice cakes with a sweet rose-water filling.

For Muslim-Chinese 'haute cuisine' try the 3rd-floor section of the *Laosunjia Restaurant (lǎosūnjia fànzhuāng)* on the corner of Duanlumen and Dong Dajie. It's opposite the Friendship Store and is readily identified by its green dome roof with an Islamic moon-crescent on top. They serve a delicious local hotpot called *shuànguōzi*, made by dipping uncooked meat and vegetable slices into a boiling chafing dish.

Two popular meeting places for foreign backpackers are *Dad's Home Cooking* near the Flats of Renmin and the *Small World Restaurant (xiǎo shìjiè cāntīng)* on Heping Lu just inside the city wall, whose menus variously include hash brownies, porridge, french toast and money-changing.

The cheap downstairs restaurant in the *May First Hotel (wǔyī fàndiàn)* is good for staple northern-China food like pork dumplings and hearty bowls of noodles. It's popular with locals and always busy. Upstairs is a more upmarket restaurant with an English menu listing 'barbecued gourd in honey' and other delicacies.

The *East Asia Restaurant* (☎ 718410) *(dōngyà fàndiàn)* was founded in 1916 in Shanghai, but moved to Xi'an in 1956. The restaurant's better sections on the 2nd and 3rd floors have arguably the city's best Chinese cuisine. The East Asia is south-east of the Bell Tower at 46 Luoma Shi, a lane running off Dong Dajie.

The *Xi'an Restaurant* (☎ 716262) *(xī'ān fànzhuāng)* is at 298 Dong Dajie. In the cheap section downstairs, the house specialty is a salty fried dumpling called *guōtiē*. Upstairs is geared mainly to banquets, but they also have a section for general guests with a shorter menu in English. The food ranges from mediocre to outstanding.

If you believe their blurb, the *Qujiangchun Restaurant* (☎ 773572) *(qǔjiāngchūn jiǔjiā)* at 192 Jiefang Lu specialises in 'Tang Dynasty cuisine' and has waiters in costume.

Actually it does have some very fine food, but this restaurant is no place for budget travellers.

Things to Buy

Huajue Xiang *(huàjuè xiàng)* is a narrow alley running beside the Great Mosque with many small souvenir and 'antique' shops – it's great for browsing. This is one of the best places in China to pick up souvenirs like name chops or a pair of chiming steel balls. Bargaining is the order of the day.

The Friendship Store is east of the Bell Tower, on Nanxin Jie just north of the intersection with Dong Dajie. Like the hawkers outside the terracotta soldiers hangar, the Friendship Store sells sets of mini-warriors in sealed one-kg net-bags for the tellingly low sum of Y5 – they're rubbish. Larger, mantelpiece versions are priced between Y60 and Y120. For the really keen, larger-than-life terracotta warrior replicas with a well-crafted 'genuine' look go for Y36,000 apiece, though how much extra it would cost you to get one of these brutes home is anyone's guess.

Around town you'll also find worthy conversation pieces like carved-stone ink trays used in Chinese calligraphy and a wide range of jade products from earrings to cigarette holders. There are plenty of silks too, but you're probably better off buying these closer to their source (Suzhou, Shanghai etc) than in Xi'an. Street hawkers sell delicate miniature wire furniture and ingenious little folded bamboo-leaf insects such as crickets and cicadas, which make cheap and attractive souvenirs. For the environmentally indifferent, there are ivory items and the occasional tiger's paw.

Getting There & Away

Air Xi'an is one of the best-connected cities in China. Here, CAAC is called 'China Northwest Airlines' (☎ 42264, 43815) *(zhōngguó xīběi hángkōng gōngsī)*, and its booking office is on the south-eastern corner of Xiguan Zhengjie and Laodong Lu, 1½ km from West Gate. It's a fair way out, but you can get there on trolley-bus No 101 from the railway station or the Bell Tower. The office is open from 8.30 to 11.30 am, and from 3 to 8 pm, but it may be more convenient to buy air tickets from CITS. There's also another CAAC-affiliated company calling itself 'Shaanxi United Airlines', whose small booking office is conveniently located beside the People's (Renmin) Hotel gate.

Some important CAAC destinations and fares include:

Destination	Fare	Destination	Fare
Baotou	Y370	Beijing	Y520
Canton	Y760	Changchun	Y980
Changsha	Y480	Chengdu	Y320
Chongqing	Y300	Dalian	Y690
Dunhuang	Y760	Fuzhou	Y760
Guilin	Y550	Haikou	Y920
Hangzhou	Y610	Hanzhong	Y150
Harbin	Y1020	Hohhot	Y450
Ji'nan	Y450	Kunming	Y610
Lanzhou	Y280	Luoyang	Y180
Nanchang	Y540	Nanjing	Y550
Qingdao	Y610	Qinhuangdao	Y610
Shanghai	Y680	Shantou	Y950
Shenzhen	Y1030	Taiyuan	Y260
Ürümqi	Y1150	Wuhan	Y370
Xiamen	Y960	Yinchuan	Y280
Yulin	Y240	Zhengzhou	Y240

Check the CAAC timetable for the current listings.

There are also four weekly flights to Hong Kong for Y1550 (one way), but it works out much cheaper to fly to Canton (or even Shenzhen) then take a train or boat to Hong Kong.

Bus The most central long-distance bus station is opposite Xi'an railway station. Some useful connections are to Huashan, Ankang, Yan'an and Ruicheng (south-western Shanxi). Evening buses with sleeping berths go to Zhengzhou (Y95), Yichang (Y135), Yinchuan (Y110) and Luoyang (Y60) from here.

There is also a large bus terminal on Huancheng Nanlu west of the South Gate.

Train There are direct trains from Xi'an to Ürümqi, Beijing, Shanghai, Chengdu, Taiyuan, Hefei, Qingdao and Wuhan. For Chongqing and Kunming change at Chengdu; for Guilin and Canton change at Wuhan.

The foreigners' ticket office is on the 2nd floor of the railway station above the ticket office for Chinese. Same-day tickets can usually be bought immediately at windows 1 and 2, but for other tickets you must first book at the windows near the stairs. Some travellers manage to buy Chinese-price train tickets at another ticket office 100 metres from the south-west side of the Lianhu Lu/Bei Dajie intersection, but they normally only sell hard seats. Fares in yuan for foreigners are:

Destination	Hard Seat	Hard Sleeper	Soft Sleeper
Beijing (22 hours)	140	205	390
Canton (43 hours)	18	285	510
Chengdu (19 hours)	95	155	270
Guilin (35 hours)	170	275	490
Lanzhou (15 hours)	85	140	240
Luoyang (8 hours)	65	95	160
Shanghai (26 hours)	150	225	420
Taiyuan (12 hours)	90	145	220
Tianjin (24 hours)	140	200	390
Tianshui (8 hours)	65	95	160
Ürümqi (56 hours)	220	325	650
Zhengzhou (12 hours)	75	125	190

Getting Around

To/From the Airport The new airport is 40-odd km north-west of Xi'an. CAAC's shuttle buses run only between the airport and their ticket office (Y11, 50 minutes each way), so you'll need other transport to or from your hotel. For a taxi expect to pay about Y120 in either direction.

Bus & Taxi Xi'an's packed public buses are a pickpocket's paradise, so watch your wallet when you ride them. More comfortable minibuses run on the same routes and charge around Y2 for most central destinations. Taxis wait at tourist hotels, the railway station and the airport. You can rent bikes at the Flats of Renmin and Jiefang hotels. Local buses go to all the major sights in and around the city such as Banpo Neolithic Village and the Army of Terracotta Warriors, but taking a tour may be the most practical way of reaching them or distant sights.

AROUND XI'AN
Most of the really interesting sights are outside the city. The two biggest drawcards are the Banpo Neolithic Village and the Army of Terracotta Warriors near the Tomb of Qin Shihuang.

Banpo Neolithic Village
(bànpō bówùguǎn) 半坡博物馆
This rates as Xi'an's No 2 attraction, surpassed only by the Army of Terracotta Warriors. The earliest known agricultural villages in China were uncovered north of the Qinlingshan mountains, near the eastward bend of the Yellow River where it's joined by the Fen and Wei rivers. The term 'Yangshao culture' is used because the first example was found near Yangshao Village. The oldest Yangshao-type village is Banpo, which appears to have been occupied from 4500 BC until around 3750 BC. The village was discovered in 1953 and is on the eastern bank of the Chan River in a suburb of Xi'an. A large hall has been built over what was part of the residential area of the village, and there are adjacent buildings housing pottery and other artefacts. Pottery found south of the Qinlingshan mountains has suggested that even earlier agricultural villages may have existed there, but this is speculation.

The Banpo ruins are divided into three areas: a residential area, a pottery-manufacturing area and a cemetery. These include the remains of 45 houses or other buildings, over 200 storage cellars, six pottery kilns and 250 graves (including 73 for dead children).

The earlier houses are half underground, in contrast to the later houses which stand on ground level and have a wooden framework. Some huts are round, others square, with doors facing south in both cases. There is a hearth or fire-pit in each house. The main building materials were wood for the framework and mud mixed with straw for the walls.

The residential part of the village is surrounded by an artificial moat, 300 metres long, about two metres deep and two metres wide. It protected the village from attacks by wild animals and from the effects of heavy rainfall in what was originally a hot and humid environment. Another trench, about two metres deep, runs through the middle of the village. To the east of the residential area is the pottery kiln centre. To the north of the village lies the cemetery where the adult dead were buried along with funerary objects like earthen pots. The children were buried in earthen pots close to the houses.

The villagers survived by hunting, fishing and gathering, but had begun to farm the surrounding land and keep domestic animals. Their stone tools included axes, knives, shovels, millstones, arrowheads and fishing-net sinkers. Bone objects included needles and fish hooks. Earthenware pots, bowls, basins and jars were used for storage and cooking; there was even a simple earthen vessel for steam cooking. Much of the pottery is coloured and illustrated with geometric patterns or animal figures like fish or galloping deer. The outside edges of some of the vessels are carved with what appears to be a primitive form of writing. Personal ornaments like hairpins, beads and rings were made of bone, shell, stone or animal teeth. A museum at the site sells a book called *Neolithic Site at Banpo Near Xi'an*, which describes the objects on view. Foreigners pay Y10 to get in.

Getting There & Away The eastern tour to the Army of Terracotta Warriors usually includes Banpo Neolithic Village. The best way of getting there by public transport is the No 105 trolley-bus from just north of the Bell Tower or bus No 11 from the railway station, both of which pass the Banpo site. To get to

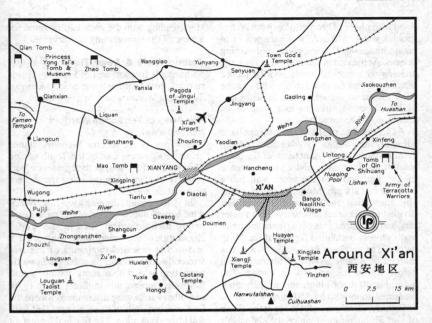

Around Xi'an
西安地区

the warriors from Banpo, catch a bus to Lintong from the stop 50 metres north of the main road (Changdong Donglu) then change at Lintong.

Tomb of Qin Shihuang
(qín shǐhuáng líng) 秦始皇陵

Qin Shihuang was the first emperor of a united Chinese people. His tomb is covered by a huge mound of protective earth that apparently hasn't been disturbed since Qin Shihuang's interment more than 2000 years ago.

In the 3rd century BC China was split into five independent and warring states. In the year 246 BC, at the age of 13, Ying Zheng ascended the throne of the state of Qin and assumed the title 'Shi Huang' or First Emperor. One by one the Qin defeated the other states, until the last fell in 222 BC. The emperor united the country, standardising the currency and the written script. He also burned books and was a cruel tyrant who was

secretive and suspicious in his last days, fearing assassination and searching for an elixir of immortality. His tyrannical rule lasted until his death in 210 BC. His son held out for four years until he was overthrown by the revolt which established the Han Dynasty.

When Qin Shihuang ascended the throne of Qin, construction of his final resting place began immediately. After he conquered the other states, work on the tomb was expanded on an unprecedented scale.

The *Historical Records* of Sima Qian, a famous historian of the 1st century BC, relate that the tomb contains palaces and pavilions filled with rare gems and other treasures, and is equipped with crossbows which automatically shoot intruders. The ceiling was inlaid with pearls to simulate the sun, stars and moon. Gold and silver cast in the form of wild geese and ducks were arranged on the floor, and precious stones were carved into pines. The walls of the tomb are said to be lined with plates of bronze to keep out underground water. Mercury was pumped in to create images of flowing rivers and surging oceans. At the end of the interment rites, the artisans who worked inside and the palace maids who had no children are said to have been forced to remain in the underground palace – buried alive so that none of its secrets could be revealed.

As to the size of the entire necropolis, a Ming Dynasty author in *Notes about Mount Lishan* states that the sanctuary of the mausoleum has four gates and a circumference of 2½ km, and that the outer wall has a perimeter of six km. Modern surveys of the site show that the necropolis is indeed divided into an inner sanctuary and an outer city, and measurements of the inner and outer walls closely match the figures of the Ming author. The southern part of the complex is marked by a large mound of rammed earth below which the emperor is buried. The mound is 40 metres high and at the bottom measures about 480 by 550 metres.

Frankly, there's not a lot to see at the Tomb of Qin Shihuang itself, since the site hasn't been excavated yet. You can climb the stone

Terracotta soldiers

steps leading onto the great earth mound for a view of the surrounding countryside.

Getting There & Away The Tomb of Qin Shihuang is five km east of Lintong. Buses running from Lintong to the nearby Army of Terracotta Warriors pass by the tomb.

The Army of Terracotta Warriors
(bīngmǎyǒng) 兵马俑 料

The Army of Terracotta Warriors stands about 1500 metres east of the Tomb of Qin Shihuang and is thought to represent a perpetually vigilant force guarding the ancient imperial necropolis.

In 1974 peasants digging a well uncovered what turned out to be one of the most fascinating archaeological sites in the world. Excavation of the underground vault of earth and timber revealed thousands of life-size terracotta soldiers and their horses in battle formation – a whole army which would follow its emperor into immortality. In 1976, two other vaults were discovered close to the first one, but each of these was refilled with soil after excavation. The first and largest pit has been covered with a roof to become a huge exhibition hall.

The underground vault measures about 210 metres east to west and 60 metres from north to south. The pit varies in depth from five to seven metres. Walls were built running east to west at intervals of three metres, forming corridors. In these corridors, on floors laid with grey brick, are arranged the terracotta figures. Pillars and beams once supported a roof.

The 6000 terracotta figures of warriors and horses face east in a rectangular battle array. The vanguard appears to be three rows of 210 crossbow and longbow bearers who stand at the easternmost end of the army. Close behind is the main force of armoured soldiers holding spears, dagger-axes and other long-shaft weapons, accompanied by 35 horse-drawn chariots. Every figure differs in facial features and expressions. The horsemen are shown wearing tight-sleeved outer robes, short coats of chain mail and windproof caps. The archers have bodies and limbs positioned in strict accordance with an ancient book on the art of war.

Many of the figures originally held real weapons of the day, and over 10,000 pieces have been sorted out to date. Bronze swords were worn by the figures representing the generals and other senior officers. Surface treatment made the swords resistant to rust and corrosion so that after being buried for more than 2000 years they were still sharp. Arrowheads were made of a lethal metal alloy containing a high percentage of lead.

The second vault, excavated in 1976 but refilled, contained about 1000 figures. The third vault contained only 68 warriors and one war chariot and appeared to be the command post for the soldiers in the other vaults. Archaeologists believe the warriors discovered so far may be part of an even larger terracotta army still buried around Qin Shihuang's tomb. Excavation of the entire complex and the tomb itself could take decades.

Almost as impressive is a pair of bronze chariots and horses unearthed in 1980 just 20 metres west of the Tomb of Qin Shihuang and now housed in a small museum (*qín yŏng bówùguăn*) within the enclosure of the warriors site.

Visitors are not permitted to take photos at the site (ostensibly to protect the figures from light damage caused by camera flashes, but one suspects also to boost postcard and slide sales) and people who infringe this rule can expect to have their film confiscated. If you decide to take a few sly shots and get caught try to remember that the attendants are just doing their job.

The management realise that the same foreign tourists who marvel at the warriors will also pay good money to see them, and as a result ticket prices have been raised progressively in recent years. Admission to the site now costs Y50, plus an additional Y15 for the museum. Student discounts are available.

Getting There & Away You can see the site as part of a tour from Xi'an (see Organised Tours in the Xi'an section). The warriors are seven km from the town of Lintong, which is 30 km east of Xi'an. Buses to Lintong leave from the eastern side of Xi'an railway station. The fare is Y3. Some trains also stop in Lintong. From the bus station in Lintong public buses and private minibuses continually make the trip out to the warriors (Y2 one way), passing the Tomb of Qin Shihuang two km before they get there.

Huaqing Pool
(*huáqīng chí*) 华清池
The Huaqing Pool is 30 km east of Xi'an below Lishan. Water from hot springs is funnelled into public bathhouses that have 60 pools accommodating 400 people. During the Tang Dynasty these natural hot baths were a favoured retreat of emperors, who often came here to relax with their concubines.

The Huaqing Pool leaves most visitors cold, but going for a dip is well worthwhile. If you don't fancy strolling around the gardens with swarms of excited Chinese tourists, try the museum up the road or take a walk on one of the paths leading up through the forest behind the complex. There is a Taoist temple on Lishan dedicated to the 'Old Mother' Nu Wa who created the human race and patched up cracks in the sky after a catastrophe. On the mountain's summit are beacon towers built for defence during the Han Dynasty. Admission to Huaqing Pool is Y15 for foreigners, plus an additional Y10 for entry to the bathhouse.

Getting There & Away Huaqing Pool is just one km south of Lintong, which can be reached by public bus from Xi'an. The Eastern Tour organised from Xi'an visits the Huaqing Pool (see Organised Tours in the Xi'an section), but some tours stop for an excessively long two hours. Buses back to Xi'an can be caught from the parking lot opposite the entrance.

Xianyang
(*xiányáng*) 咸阳
This little town is half an hour's bus ride from Xi'an. The chief attraction is Xianyang

City Museum (*xiányáng shì bówùguǎn*) which houses a remarkable collection of 3000 miniature terracotta soldiers and horses, discovered in 1965. Each figure is about half a metre high. They were excavated from a Han Dynasty tomb. Admission to the Entombed Warriors is Y30, with an extra ticket needed for entry to the special exhibition hall.

Getting There & Away To get to Xianyang Museum from Xi'an, take bus No 3 from the railway station to the terminal and then get bus No 59. Get off at the terminal in Xianyang. Up ahead on the left-hand side of the road you'll see a clock tower. Turn right at this intersection and then left at Xining Jie. The museum is housed in a former Ming Dynasty Confucian temple on Zhongshan Jie, which is a continuation of Xining Jie. The entrance is flanked by two stone lions. It's about a 20-minute walk from the bus terminal.

Imperial Tombs

Apart from the tomb of Qin Shihuang, a large number of other imperial tombs dot the Guanzhong plain surrounding Xi'an. The easiest way to get there is by tour from Xi'an (see the Xi'an Organised Tours section for details).

In these tombs are buried the emperors of numerous dynasties, as well as empresses, concubines, government officials and high-ranking military leaders. Construction of an emperor's tomb often began within a few years of his ascension to the throne and didn't finish until he died.

The Tang tombs can be visited, and there's a touch of intrigue in the stories behind them. The most famous is the Qian Tomb, the joint resting place of Tang Emperor Gao Zong and his wife Empress Wu Zetian. Gao Zong ascended the throne in 650 AD after the death of his father, Emperor Tai Zong. Empress Wu was actually a concubine of Tai Zong who also caught the fancy of his son, who

---

The Xi'an Incident

Nowadays, Lishan is hardly worth the effort of going there, as Chiang Kaishek would probably attest. His visit turned out to be most inauspicious. On 12 December 1936 he was arrested in Lishan by his own generals, supposedly clad only in his pyjamas and dressing gown, on the slopes of the snow-covered mountain up which he had fled. A pavilion marks the spot and there's a simple inscription, 'Chiang was caught here'.

In the early 1930s Kuomintang General Yang Huzheng was the undisputed monarch of those parts of Shaanxi not under Communist control. In 1935 he was forced to share power when General Zhang Xueliang arrived with his own troops from Manchuria in the wake of the Japanese occupation. Zhang assumed the office of 'Vice-Commander of the National Bandit Suppression Commission'.

In October and November 1935 the Kuomintang suffered severe defeats at the hands of the Communists and thousands of soldiers went over to the Red Army. Captured officers were given a period of 'anti-Japanese tutelage' and were then released. Returning to Xi'an, they brought Zhang reports of the Red Army's desire to stop the civil war and unite against the Japanese. Chiang Kaishek, however, stubbornly refused to turn his forces against the Japanese and continued his war against the Communists. On 7 December 1936 he flew to Xi'an to oversee another 'extermination' campaign against the Red Army.

Zhang Xueliang flew to Yan'an, met Zhou Enlai and became convinced of the sincerity of the Red Army's anti-Japanese policies. A secret truce was established. On the night of 11 December Zhang met the divisional commanders of his Manchurian army and the army of General Yang. A decision was made to arrest Chiang Kaishek. The following night the commander of Zhang's bodyguard led the attack on Chiang Kaishek's residence at the foot of Lishan and took him prisoner along with most of his general staff. In the city the 1500 'Blueshirts' (the police force controlled by Chiang's nephew and credited with numerous abductions, killings and imprisonments of Chiang's opponents) were disarmed and arrested.

A few days later, Zhang sent his plane to collect three representatives of the Red Army and

made her his empress. Gao died in 683 AD, and the following year Empress Wu dethroned her husband's successor Emperor Zhong Zong. She reigned as an all-powerful monarch until her death around 705 AD. Nowadays it's fashionable to draw comparisons between Empress Wu and the late Jiang Qing, Mao's disgraced last wife.

Zhao Tomb *(zhāo líng)* The Zhao Tomb set the custom of building imperial tombs on mountain slopes, breaking the tradition of building tombs on the plains with an artificial hill over them. This burial ground on Jiuzongshan, 70 km north-west of Xi'an, belongs to the second Tang emperor, Tai Zong, who died in 649 AD.

Of the 18 imperial mausoleums on the Guanzhong plain, this is probably the most representative. With the mountain at the centre, the tomb fans out to the south-east and south-west. Within its confines are 167 lesser tombs of the emperor's relatives and high-ranking military and government officials.

Burying other people in the same park as the emperor was a custom dating back to the Han Dynasty. Tai Zong won support and loyalty from his ministers and officials by bestowing on them the great favour of being buried in attendance on the Son of Heaven.

Buried in the sacrificial altar of the tomb were six statues known as the 'Six Steeds of Zhaoling', representing the horses which the emperor used during his wars of conquest. Some of the statues have been relocated to museums in Xi'an.

Qian Tomb *(qián líng)* One of the most impressive tombs is the Qian Tomb, 85 km north-west of Xi'an on Liangshan. This is the burial place of Emperor Gao Zong and Empress Wu.

The tomb consists of three peaks; the two on the south side are artificial, but the higher northern peak is natural and is the main part

---

bring them to Xi'an: Zhou Enlai, Ye Jianying and Bo Gu. Chiang Kaishek feared he was going to be put on trial and executed, but instead the Communists and the Manchurian leaders told him their opinions of his policies and described the changes they thought were necessary to save the country. Whatever Chiang did or did not promise to do, the practical result of the Xi'an Incident was the end of the civil war.

Zhang released Chiang Kaishek on Christmas Day and flew back with him to Nanjing to await punishment. It was a face-saving gesture to Chiang. Zhang was sentenced by a tribunal to 10 years' imprisonment and 'deprivation of civil rights for five years'. He was pardoned the next day. The extermination campaign against the Red Army was called off and the Kuomintang announced that their first task now was to recover the territory lost to the Japanese.

Nevertheless, Chiang began organising what he hoped would be a quiet decimation of the Communist forces. By June 1937 Chiang had moved the sympathetic Manchurian army out of Shaanxi and replaced it with loyal Kuomintang troops. He planned to disperse the Communists by moving the Red Army piecemeal to other parts of the country, supposedly in preparation for the war against the Japanese. The Communists were only extricated from their precarious position by Japan's sudden and all-out invasion of China in July 1937. Chiang was forced to leave the Red Army intact and in control of the north-west.

Chiang never forgave Zhang Xueliang and never freed him. Thirty years later he was still held prisoner on Taiwan. General Yang was arrested in Chongqing and towards the end of WW II was secretly executed. Another reminder of this period is the office which the Communist Party set up in Xi'an to liaise with the Kuomintang. The office was disbanded in 1946, and after 1949 it was made into a memorial hall to the Eighth Route Army. It's on Beixin Lu, in the north of the city's central block. ∎

of the tomb. Walls used to surround the tomb but these are gone. South-west of the tomb are 17 smaller tombs of officials.

The grounds of the imperial tomb boast a number of large stone sculptures of animals and officers of the imperial guard. There are 61 (now headless) statues of the leaders of minority peoples of China and of the representatives of friendly nations who attended the Emperor's funeral.

The two steles on the ground each stand over six metres high. The 'Wordless Stele' is a blank tablet; one story goes that it symbolises Empress Wu's absolute power, which she considered inexpressible in words.

Prince Zhang Huai's Tomb (zhāng huái mù) Of the smaller tombs surrounding the Qian Tomb only five have been excavated. Zhang was the second son of Emperor Gao Zong and Empress Wu. For some reason the prince was exiled to Sichuan in 683 and died the following year, aged 31 (a pillow across the face perhaps?). Empress Wu posthumously rehabilitated him. His remains were brought to Xi'an after Emperor Zhong Zong regained power. Tomb paintings show horsemen playing polo, but these and other paintings are in a terrible state.

Princess Yong Tai's Tomb (yǒng tài gōng zhǔ mù) Nearby is the Tomb of Princess Yong Tai with tomb paintings showing palace servants. The line engravings on the stone outer coffin are extraordinarily graceful. Yong Tai was a granddaughter of the Tang emperor Gao Zong, and the seventh daughter of Emperor Zhong Zong. She was put to death by Empress Wu in 701 AD, but was rehabilitated posthumously by Emperor Zhong Zong after he regained power.

Mao Tomb (mào líng) The Mao Tomb, 40 km from Xi'an, is the resting place of Emperor Wu, the most powerful ruler of the Han Dynasty, who died in 87 BC. The cone-shaped mound of rammed earth is almost 47 metres high, and is the largest of the Han imperial tombs. A wall used to enclose the mausoleum but now only the ruins of the

gates on the east, west and north sides remain. It is recorded that the emperor was entombed with a jade cicada in his mouth and was clad in jade clothes sewn with gold thread, and that buried with him were live animals and an abundance of jewels.

Famen Temple
(fǎmén sì) 法门寺
Famen Temple is 115 km north-west of Xi'an and was built during the Eastern Han Dynasty in 300 AD.

In 1981, after torrential rains had weakened the temple's ancient brick structure, the entire western side of the 12-storey pagoda collapsed. The subsequent restoration work produced a sensational discovery. Below the pagoda in a sealed crypt built during the Tang Dynasty to contain four sacred finger bones of the Buddha (known as *sarira*) were over 1000 sacrificial objects and royal offerings including stone-tablet Buddhist scriptures, gold and silver items, and some 27,000 coins. These relics had been completely forgotten for over 1000 years. A museum housing part of the collection has been built on the site. After the excavations had finished the temple was reconstructed in its original form.

The best way to visit Famen Temple is to take an Eastern Tour from Xi'an (see the Xi'an Organised Tours section). Some tours don't include the temple so check before you book. Foreigners' entry prices are: Y10 to the temple, Y15 to the crypt and Y15 to the museum; the pagoda itself is not (yet) open to the public.

HUASHAN
(huàshān) 华山
The 2200-metre-high granite peaks of Huashan, 120 km east of Xi'an, tower above the plains to the north, forming one of China's sacred mountain areas. A tortuous 15-km stepped path leads to the top; in one famous section called Green Dragon Ridge the way has been cut along a narrow rock ridge with sheer cliffs on either side. At the top a circuit trail links Huashan's four main summit peaks. From Huashan village at the

base of the mountain it usually takes between six and nine hours to reach the top, so it's best to stay overnight at one of the mountain hotels. Several narrow and almost vertical 'bottleneck' sections are dangerous when the route is crowded, particularly under wet or icy conditions. The gate ticket price for foreigners is Y25, plus another Y5 'registration fee'.

Places to Stay & Eat

Huashan village has plenty of budget and mid-range accommodation. There is a good CITS-run hotel on the left 20 metres before you come to the entrance gate; doubles with bath cost Y30 per person and singles are Y50. The *Xiyue Hotel (xīyuè fàndiàn)* a short way down the street has dorm beds from Y12. The *Huashan Guesthouse (huàshān bīnguǎn)* on Jianshe Lu near the bus station has nice doubles for Y100; the back rooms have mountain views. There are many cheap tourist restaurants along the street leading up to the entrance gate.

There are a few small hotels along the climb and others are scattered among Huashan's summit peaks; conditions in most are extremely primitive. The best hotel on the mountain is the *East Peak Guesthouse (dōngfēng fàndiàn)*. It's an attractive stone building with some great views and has rooms for Y35. The hotel has electricity, but no washing facilities at all. Simple meals are available at all the mountain hotels; prices reflect the cost of lugging the grub up here.

Getting There & Away

If you're coming from Xi'an, the best access to Huashan is by bus from the long-distance bus station (Y10, 2½ hours). Although Huashan village is on the Xi'an-Luoyang railway line, many trains don't stop at the local station, so you may have to get off at Mengyuan, 15-odd km east of Huashan. From Mengyuan there are regular minibuses to Huashan.

HUANGLING

(huánglíng) 皇陵

Halfway between Xi'an and Yan'an is the town of Huangling. The tomb on nearby Qiaoshan is supposedly that of the Yellow Emperor Huang Di. Huang is said to be the father of the Chinese people, one of the 'Five Sovereigns' who reigned about 5000 years ago and by wars of conquest unified the Chinese clans. He is credited with numerous inventions and discoveries: silkworm cultivation, weaving, writing, the cart, the boat, the compass, building bricks and musical instruments. You can stay overnight in this town if you're taking the bus up from Xi'an to Yan'an.

YAN'AN

(yán'ān) 延安

Yan'an, 270 km from Xi'an in northern Shaanxi Province, is just a small city of 40,000 people, but together with Mao's birthplace at Shaoshan it has special significance as a major Communist pilgrimage spot. Between the years 1936 and 1947 this was the headquarters of the Chinese Communists. The 'Long March' from Jiangxi ended in 1936 when the Communists reached the northern Shaanxi town of Wuqi. The following year they moved their base to Yan'an.

Orientation

Yan'an is spread out along a 'Y' shaped valley formed where the east and west branches of the Yan River meet. The town centre is clustered around this junction, while the old Communist Army headquarters is at Yangjialing on the north-western outskirts of Yan'an. The new railway station is at the far southern end of town about seven km from the centre.

Things to See

At the **Former Revolutionary Headquarters** *(gémìng jiùzhǐ)* you can see the assembly hall where the first Central Committee meetings were held and the nearby simple dugouts built into the loess earth where Mao, Zhu De, Zhou Enlai and other senior Communist leaders lived, worked and wrote. The nearby **Yan'an Revolutionary Museum** *(yán'ān gémìng jìniànguǎn)* has an extensive collection of revolutionary para-

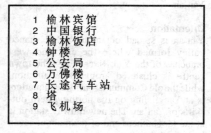

1	榆林宾馆
2	中国银行
3	榆林饭店
4	钟楼
5	公安局
6	万佛楼
7	长途汽车站
8	塔
9	飞机场

phernalia – old uniforms, weaponry and many photographs and illustrations. There's even a horse (stuffed) that was allegedly ridden by Mao himself. Unfortunately there are no English labels. The **Precious Pagoda** *(bǎotǎ)*, built during the Song Dynasty, stands on a prominent hillside south-east of the river junction. The **Ten Thousand Buddha Cave** *(wànfó dòng)* dug into the sandstone cliff beside the river has relatively intact Buddhist statues and wall inscriptions.

The CITS (☎ 216285) at the the Yan'an Hotel organises tours.

Places to Stay

The *Liangmao Hotel* (☎ 212777) *(liángmào dàshà)* at 120 Qilipu Dajie near the railway station is a new and friendly place with nice doubles for Y70. Its dining hall is also good value. The *Yan'an Hotel* (☎ 213122) *(yán'ān bīnguǎn)* is a typical 1950s-style Chinese hotel catering largely to visiting People's Liberation Army officers. Foreigners pay Y140 for a standard double with bathroom. The hotel restaurant is cheap.

Getting There & Away

Regular flights to Yan'an ceased after the railway line opened in 1992, and only the odd charter now flies here. From the long-distance bus station in Xi'an there are some 12 buses daily to Yan'an (Y24). It's a rough ride. A new railway line links Yan'an with Xi'an via an interesting route along the Luo

River, which it crosses on numerous bridges. Chinese-price fares from Xi'an to Yan'an are: Y19 (hard seat), Y33 (soft seat), Y66 (hard sleeper).

YULIN
(yúlín) 榆林
Yulin lies on the fringe of Inner Mongolia's Mu Us Desert in far-north Shaanxi. During the Ming Dynasty Yulin was a fortified garrison town and patrol post serving the Great Wall.

Until now Yulin's remoteness and relative poverty have kept the old town largely untouched by the 'white-tile' trend in Chinese architecture, which is rapidly destroying what remains of the country's older buildings. Along the narrow brick lanes near the unrestored bell tower are traditional family houses with tiny courtyards hidden behind low enclosure walls and old stone gates. The city's old Ming walls are mainly still standing, though in places their original outer brick layer has been removed (probably for housing). A large three-tier fortress and beacon tower *(zhènběitái)* lies 7½ km north of town.

Places to Stay & Eat
In Yulin, two hotels (out of a total of three) accept foreigners. The *Yulin Hotel (Fandian)*

(yúlín fàndiàn) two km north of the bus station on Xinjian Lu quotes Y80 for a double. The *Yulin Hotel (Binguan)* (☎ (0912) 23974) *(yúlín bīnguǎn)* on Xinjian Lu two km just outside the city walls has beds in reasonable doubles with bathroom for Y120. Both have good, cheap dining halls.

Getting There & Away
Air The only regular air link is with Xi'an; there is one flight every day except Sunday (Y260 one way). You can buy tickets at the tiny airport across the river, or book at the Yulin Hotel (Binguan).

Bus There is one direct daily bus each way between Xi'an and Yulin, but it's more convenient and less tiring to stop in Yan'an. There are three normal buses each day between Yan'an and Yulin (Y26) and one sleeping-berth bus (Y44). There is one daily bus at 5.30 am to Yinchuan (Y39, 14 hours) following a route close to the Great Wall. There are also half-hourly buses to the railhead at Daliuta, from where you can catch a train to Baotou in Inner Mongolia.

Train Scheduled services should arrive in Yulin around 1999, when a planned railway line north of Yan'an is due to be completed.

Shanxi 山西

Population: 30 million
Capital: Taiyuan

Shanxi *(shānxī)*, especially the southern half, was one of the earliest centres of Chinese civilisation and formed the territory of the state of Qin. After Qin Shihuang unified the Chinese states, the northern part of Shanxi became the key defensive bulwark between the Chinese and the nomadic tribes to the north. Despite the Great Wall, the nomadic tribes still managed to break through and used Shanxi as a base for their conquest of the Middle Kingdom.

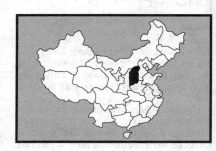

When the Tang Dynasty fell, the political centre of China moved away from the northwest. Shanxi went into a rapid economic decline, though its importance in the northern defence network remained paramount. Strategic importance coupled with isolation and economic backwardness was not an unusual situation for any of China's border regions, then or now.

It was not until the intrusion of the foreign powers into China that any industrialisation got under way. When the Japanese invaded China in the 1930s they carried out further development of industry and coal mining around the capital of Taiyuan. True to form, Shanxi was a bastion of resistance to this invasion from the north, this time through the Communist guerrillas who operated in the mountainous regions.

After 1949 the Communists began a serious exploitation of Shanxi's mineral and ore deposits, and the development of places like Datong and Taiyuan as major industrial centres. Some of the biggest coal mines can be found near these cities, and the province accounts for a third of China's known coal deposits.

Shanxi means 'west of the mountains' and is named after the Taihang range which forms its eastern border. To the west it is bordered by the Yellow River. The province's population of about 30 million people is relatively light by Chinese standards, unless you consider the fact that almost 70% of the province is mountainous. The Taihang range, which also includes the Wutaishan mountains, runs from north to south and separates the province from the great North China Plain to the east. The Central Shanxi Basin crosses the central part of the province from north to south in a series of valleys. This is the main farming and economic area. Most of the farmland is used to grow crops, though the north-west is the centre of the province's animal husbandry industry.

Despite its intended future as an industrial bastion, Shanxi's wealth lies in its history. The province is a virtual gold mine of temples, monasteries and cave-temples – a reminder that this was once the political and cultural centre of China. The main attraction is the Yungang Buddhist Caves at Datong.

TAIYUAN
(tàiyuán) 太原

The first settlements on the site of modern-day Taiyuan date back 2500 years. By the 13th century it had developed into what Marco Polo referred to as 'a prosperous city, a great centre of trade and industry'.

Like Datong, Taiyuan became an important frontier town, but despite its prosperity it has been the site of constant armed conflict. The trouble with Taiyuan was that it was

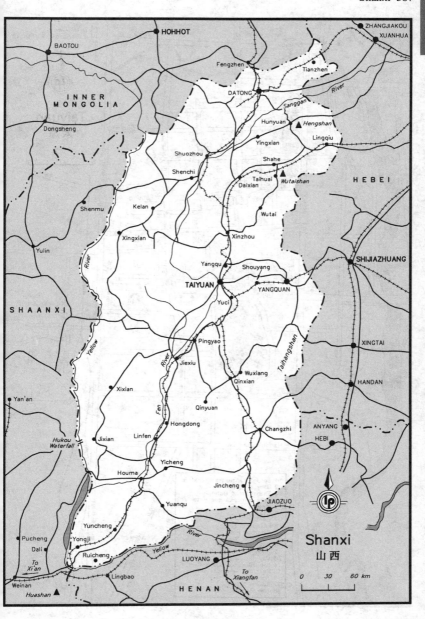

Shanxi
山西

0   30   60 km

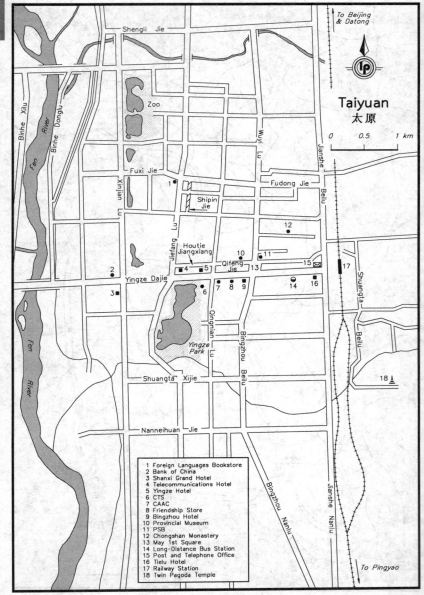

Taiyuan
太原

1 Foreign Languages Bookstore
2 Bank of China
3 Shanxi Grand Hotel
4 Telecommunications Hotel
5 Yingze Hotel
6 CTS
7 CAAC
8 Friendship Store
9 Bingzhou Hotel
10 Provincial Museum
11 PSB
12 Chongshan Monastery
13 May 1st Square
14 Long-Distance Bus Station
15 Post and Telephone Office
16 Tielu Hotel
17 Railway Station
18 Twin Pagoda Temple

1	外文书店
2	中国银行
3	山西大酒店
4	电信大酒店
5	迎泽大宾馆
6	中国旅行社
7	中国民航
8	友谊商店
9	并州饭店
10	山西省博物馆
11	公安局
12	崇善寺
13	五一广场
14	长途汽车站
15	邮电大楼
16	铁路宾馆
17	火车站
18	双塔寺

always in somebody else's way, situated on the path by which successive northern invaders entered China intent on conquest. As some indication of the importance of bloodshed in the city's life, there were once 27 temples here dedicated to the god of war.

The Huns, Tobas, Jin, Mongols and Manchus, among others, all took turns sweeping through Taiyuan. If it wasn't foreign invasion which afflicted the city, then it was the rise and fall of Chinese dynasties during periods of disunity; the town passed from one army to another as different rulers vied for power. Nevertheless, Taiyuan managed to survive.

In the latter part of the 19th century, Taiyuan moved rapidly towards industrialisation, helped by its proximity to some of the world's largest deposits of iron and coal. From 1889 it started to develop as a modern city, with the encouragement of Western powers. In the next 20 years Taiyuan gained a rail link to Hebei, electricity and a telephone system, not to mention a university and military academy. Development was pushed along by the warlord Yan Xishan, who ruled Shanxi virtually as his own private empire after the fall of the Manchu Dynasty. The coal mines were also developed by the Japanese invaders during the 1930s and '40s.

The Communists began the serious industrialisation of Taiyuan, along with other regions of Shanxi, after 1949. Today the city looks very much like its modern counterparts, Zhengzhou and Luoyang, with wide avenues and extensive residential blocks with numerous factories and smokestacks. Amid the industrial monuments are some interesting Chinese Buddhist temples and artwork.

Orientation
Taiyuan lies mainly on the eastern side of the Fen River. The railway station is at the eastern end of Yingze Dajie, Taiyuan's main thoroughfare. The long-distance bus station is roughly half a km west of the railway station on Yingze Dajie, and most tourist sights and facilities are also on or close to this street. The centre of town is May 1st Square.

Information
CTS The CTS (☎ 443377) has an office on the 3rd floor of the circular cream-tiled building behind the small regional bus terminal opposite the Yingze Hotel. The staff are helpful and speak good English (as well as German and Japanese).

PSB This is on a lane near May 1st Square.

Money The Bank of China has its main branch on Yingze Dajie, west of Xinjian Lu. The tourist hotels also change money.

Post & Telecommunications The main post and telephone office is in a white multistorey building diagonally opposite the railway station. There is also a modern telecommunications centre on the corner of Yingze Dajie and Jiefang Lu.

Yingze Park
(yíngzé gōngyuán) 迎泽公园
The Ming Library *(míngdài cángjīng lóu)*, an ornate building in Yingze Park, is worth seeing. The entrance to the park is on the opposite side of the road, to the west of the Yingze Guesthouse.

Chongshan Monastery
(chóngshàn sì) 崇善寺

This Buddhist monastery was built towards the end of the 14th century on the site of an even older monastery, said to date back to the 6th or 7th century. The main hall contains three impressive statues; the central figure represents Guanyin, the goddess of mercy, who has 1000 hands and eyes. Beautifully illustrated book covers show scenes from the life of Buddha. Also on display are Buddhist scriptures of the Song, Yuan, Ming and Qing dynasties. The monastery is on a side street running east off Wuyi Lu.

Twin Pagoda Temple
(shuāngtǎ sì) 双塔寺

The temple has two identical Ming Dynasty pagodas, each a 13-storey octagonal structure almost 55 metres high. The pagodas are built entirely of bricks carved with brackets and cornices to imitate Chinese wooden pagodas of ancient times. You can get halfway there by taking the No 19 bus from in front of the railway station and getting off one stop after the railway bridge. From there walk the few steps back to Shuangta Beilu, turn left (south) and follow this road for 20 minutes to the temple.

Provincial Museum
(shānxī shěng bówùguǎn) 山西省博物馆

This is on Qifeng Jie, north-west of May 1st Square. The museum is in the Chunyang Palace *(chúnyáng gōng)*, which used to be a temple for offering sacrifices to the Taoist priest Lu Dongbin, who lived during the Tang Dynasty. The temple was built during the Ming and Qing dynasties.

Places to Stay
The *Tielu Hotel (tiělù bīnguǎn)* a couple of hundred metres down Yingze Dajie from the railway station is about the only low-budget place in town that accepts foreigners, but it's nearly always full. The cheapest beds are in spartan doubles without bath and cost Y34.

The *Telecommunications Hotel* (☎ 433865) *(diànxìn dàjiǔdiàn)* just east from the corner of Jiefang Lu and Houtie Jiangxiang has nice

doubles with bathroom for Y90. Take the No 1 bus four stops from the railway station.

Just east of May 1st Square at 32 Yingze Dajie is the *Bingzhou Hotel* (☎ 442111) *(bìngzhōu fàndiàn)* whose 'special' prices for foreigners are Y138/156 for singles/doubles.

The *Yingze Hotel* (☎ 443211) *(yíngzé bīnguǎn)* at 51 Yingze Dajie has a newer west block where they put their occasional foreign guests, charging them Y145/200. The old east building is supposedly for Chinese only, but it does have a dormitory. You may be able to coax the rude and uncooperative hotel staff into finding you a dorm bed (for about Y30), but it's best to enlist the help of the CITS across the road – it usually works.

The joint-venture *Shanxi Grand Hotel* (☎ 227569) *(shānxī dàjiǔdiàn)* at 5 Xinjian Nanlu is the most upmarket place in town, with doubles costing Y270 and suites Y1200. It's a fair way from the town centre but you can get there on bus No 1 from the railway station.

Places to Eat
On the Taiyuan street-food menu are local favourites like pigs' hooves *(zhūjiǎo)* stewed in cauldrons and a savoury pancake called *luòbǐng* cooked over coals on a lens-shaped hot-plate. The local variant of Chinese noodles, called *liángpí*, is often dumped into steaming bowls of spiced soup.

Shipin Jie ('food street') a pedestrian zone with a Chinese archway and many old-style buildings has over 30 restaurants serving food in the very cheap to quite upmarket price ranges.

The restaurant on the ground floor of the Telecommunications Hotel is not bad. The *Háohuá Restaurant* on the 7th floor of the Yingze Hotel is pretty good too and has a limited English menu.

Getting There & Away
Air The local CAAC (☎ 442903) is at 38 Yingze Dong Dajie. Useful direct flights go to: Beijing (Y260, six a week); Canton (Y850, 13 a week) Shanghai (Y620, five a

week), and Xi'an (Y260, four a week) as well as Baotou, Changsha, Chengdu, Dalian, Fuzhou, Guilin, Haikou, Hangzhou, Hohhot, Nanjing, Shenyang, Shenzhen, Tianjin, Wenzhou, Wuhan, Xiamen and Zhengzhou.

Bus Minibuses to Datong (Y25) leave irregularly from outside the railway station; there are scheduled services to Datong and Wutaishan (Y21, nine hours) from the long-distance bus station. There are also early-morning sleeper buses *(wòpùchē)* leaving from the square in front of Taiyuan railway station to Datong (Y44), Luoyang (Y65), Zhengzhou (Y76), Beijing (Y80) and Tianjin (Y86).

Train At the railway station, foreigners can buy same-day tickets from window No 17, and there is an advanced booking office upstairs in a separate building immediately left as you leave the ticket office.

From Taiyuan, Shijiazhuang is the closest rail junction on the main Beijing-Canton line, but for southern or eastern destinations like Canton and Shanghai it's best to change trains in Zhengzhou. There are direct trains south to Xi'an via Yuncheng, or north to Beijing via Datong.

Some foreigners' ticket prices are: Datong Y30 (hard seat), Y48 (soft seat), Y80 (hard sleeper), eight hours; Zhengzhou Y187 (soft sleeper), Y99 (hard sleeper), 10 hours; Xi'an Y211 (soft sleeper), Y111 (hard sleeper), 12 hours; Beijing Y172 (soft sleeper), Y91 (hard sleeper), 10½ hours; Hohhot Y211 (soft sleeper), Y111 (hard sleeper); and Shijiazhuang Y41 (soft seat only), four hours.

AROUND TAIYUAN
Jinci Temple
jìncí sì) 晋祠寺

This ancient Buddhist temple is at the source of the Jin River by Xuanwang Hill, 25 km south-west of Taiyuan. It's not known for sure when the original buildings were constructed, but there have been numerous additions and restorations over the centuries, right up to Qing Dynasty times. The temple probably dates back at least 1000 years.

As you enter the temple compound the first major structure is the Mirror Terrace, a Ming building used as an open-air theatre. The name is used in the figurative sense to denote the reflection of life in drama.

Zhibo's Canal cuts through the temple complex and lies west of the Mirror Terrace. Spanning this canal is the Huixian (Meet the Immortals) bridge, which provides access to the Terrace for Iron Statues. At each corner of the terrace stands an iron figure cast in 1097 AD. Immediately behind the statues is Duiyuefang Gate, with two iron statues out the front. Behind the gate is the Offerings Hall built in 1168 to display temple offerings.

A bridge connects the Offerings Hall with the Goddess Mother Hall, the oldest wooden building in the city and one of the most interesting in the temple complex. In front of the temple are large wooden pillars with carvings of fearsome dragons. Inside are 42 Song Dynasty clay figures of maidservants standing around a large seated statue of the Sacred Lady herself. She is said to be the mother of Prince Shuyu of the ancient Zhou Dynasty, and the temple was built in her memory during the Northern Song period. It's suggested that the original building was constructed by the prince as a place to offer prayers and sacrifices to his mother. Today, people still throw money on the altar in front of the statue. Next to the Sacred Lady Hall is the Zhou Cypress, an unusual tree which has supposedly been growing at an angle of about 30° for the last 900 years.

South of the Sacred Lady Hall is the Nanlao (Forever Young or Everlasting) Spring over which stands a pavilion. To the west of the spring is the two-storey Shuimou Lou (Water Goddess House), originally built in 1563. On the ground floor is a statue of the goddess cast in bronze. On the upper storey is a shrine with a seated statue of the goddess surrounded by statues of her female servants.

In the north of the temple grounds is the Zhenguan Baohan Pavilion, which houses four stone steles inscribed with the hand writing of the Tang emperor Tai Zong. The Memorial Halls of Prince Shuyu include a shrine containing a seated figure of the prince surrounded by 12 Ming Dynasty female attendants, some holding bamboo flutes, pipes and stringed instruments. In the south of the temple grounds is the Sacred Relics Pagoda, a seven-storey, octagonal building constructed at the end of the 7th century.

To get to Jinci Temple you can take a No 8 bus from the bus terminal one block east of May 1st Square.

Shuanglin Monastery
(shuānglín sì) 双林寺

Shuanglin Monastery, 110 km south-west of Taiyuan, is worth the effort of getting to. It contains exquisite painted clay figurines and statues dating from the Song, Yuan, Ming and Qing dynasties. Most of the present buildings date from the Ming and Qing dynasties, while the majority of sculptures are from the Song and Yuan dynasties. There are something like 2000 figurines in total.

A visit to Shuanglin is probably best done as a return day trip from Taiyuan by train. Take a train to Pingyao, then hire a pedicab out to the temple. Two good train connections are the No 375 departing from Taiyuan at 11.07 am and arriving in Pingyao at 1 pm and the No 376 back from Pingyao at 3.59 pm. The Chinese-price fare is Y7 (hard seat one way).

WUTAISHAN
(wǔtáishān) 五台山

Wutaishan, centred around the beautiful monastic village of Taihuai *(táihuái)*, is one of China's sacred Buddhist mountain areas. Taihuai lies deep in an alpine valley enclosed by the five peaks of Wutaishan, the highest of which is the 3061-metre northern peak Yedoufeng, known as the roof of northern China. Taihuai itself has 15 or so old temples and monasteries, and many others dot the

1	Bishan Temple
2	Bus Station
3	Tayuan Temple
4	Fenglin Temple
5	Liangcheng Hotel
6	Puhua Temple
7	Friendship Hotel
8	Yunfeng Hotel
9	Nanshan Temple
10	Longquan Temple
11	Zhenhai Temple

1	碧山寺
2	汽车站
3	塔院寺
4	风林寺
5	凉城宾馆
6	普化寺
7	友谊宾馆
8	云峰宾馆
9	南山寺
10	龙泉寺
11	镇海寺

nearby and more distant mountainsides. Part of the charm of Wutaishan is its relative inaccessibility, which spared the area from the worst of the Cultural Revolution and still keeps development to a minimum.

The Tayuan Temple with its large, white, bottle-shaped pagoda built during the Ming Dynasty is the most prominent in Taihuai. The Xiantong Temple has seven rows of halls, totalling over 400 rooms. The small Guangren Monastery, run by Tibetan monks, contains some fine examples of early Qing wood carvings. The Nanshan Temple, built during the Yuan Dynasty on the nearby slopes of Nanshan contains frescoes of the fable 'Pilgrimage to the West'.

Other sights include the marble archway of the Longquan Temple and the 26-metre-high buddha and carvings of 500 arhats in the Shuxiang Temple. The Luohou Temple contains a large wooden lotus flower with eight petals, on each of which sits a carved Buddhist figure; the big flower is attached to a rotating disk so that when it turns, the petals open up and the figures appear.

About 60 km from Nanshan Temple is the Foguang Temple (*fóguāng sì*), which was built during the Northern Wei Dynasty.

Information

Travel to the Wutaishan area requires an Alien Travel Permit, which you can get from the PSB after you arrive. The CITS is at the Yunfeng Hotel. Chinese-language maps are available locally from shops and hotels.

Places to Stay

There are two foreigners' hotels. The *Friendship Hotel* (*yǒuyì bīnguǎn*) about two km below Taihuai charges Y180 for a double with bathroom. Dorms are Y20 per bed, but there are no showers. The *Yunfeng Hotel* (*yúnfēng bīnguǎn*) is three km below the village and has rooms from Y120.

Getting There & Away

There are daily buses to Wutaishan from Taiyuan via Wutai (Y15). The largely unsurfaced and frequently dusty road can make it a rather tortuous nine-hour ride. At Wutai you can get a bus to the Foguang Temple. There is a daily bus to Wutaishan from Datong via Xinzhou (Y21, 9½ hours). A more adventurous way to reach Taihuai from Datong is to get the public bus to Shahe, then a private minibus over the scenic pass road below Yedoufeng.

DATONG

(*dàtóng*) 大同

In 220 AD the Han Empire was separated into three kingdoms. Rivalry between them left China open to invasion from the north, and though the other kingdoms were subjugated by the Wei Kingdom (which took the dynasty name of Jin) it was a shaky unification. A series of kingdoms rose and fell in the north until the Toba, a Turkic-speaking people, came to power at the end of the 4th century and, by the middle of the 5th century, had conquered all of northern China, forming the Northern Wei Dynasty.

The success of the Tobas in ruling the northern Chinese was not due to their numbers, which were relatively small, but to their adoption of a Chinese style of administration and to the intermarriage of Chinese gentry and Toba aristocracy. Northern Wei times appear to have been a very active period of development, particularly in agriculture, irrigation and trade, as well as a cultural high point, despite continuing wars and social instability. Buddhist teachings of personal salvation and nirvana began taking root among the Chinese people, and Buddhism was made a state religion.

The Northern Wei rulers established their capital at Datong, an important centre because of its strategic location just south of the Great Wall and near the border with Inner Mongolia. The town had been fortified under the Han. When the Wei set up their capital here it became the political hub of the dynasty, until the court moved to Luoyang in 494 AD. Outside the modern-day city is the greatest legacy of the period, the Yungang Buddhist Caves.

Apart from the caves, there are few reminders that Datong was once northern China's imperial city. Although this city of

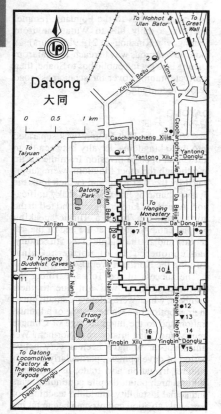

Datong
大同

0   0.5   1 km

To Hohhot &
Ulan Bator

To
Great
Wall

1	Railway Station & CITS
2	Old Long-Distance Bus Station
3	Bank of China
4	New Long-Distance Bus Station
5	PSB
6	Main Post & Telephone Office
7	Huayan Monastery
8	Drum Tower
9	Nine Dragon Screen
10	Shanhua Temple
11	Xinkaili (Buses to Yungang Caves)
12	CAAC
13	Yaxuyuan Restaurant
14	Yungang Hotel & CITS
15	Hongqi Restaurant
16	Datong Hotel

1	火车站/中国国际旅行社
2	长途汽车站旧址
3	中国银行
4	新长途汽车站
5	公安局
6	邮电大楼
7	华严寺
8	鼓楼
9	九龙壁
10	善化寺
11	新开里
12	中国民航
13	雅叙园酒家
14	云冈宾馆/中国国际旅行社
15	红旗大酒店
16	大同宾馆

more than a million people has retained more of its original appearance than most Chinese cities of comparable size, recent earthquakes and/or deliberate demolitions have destroyed whole blocks of streets. Today Datong is one of the country's most depressing cities – ugly, polluted and poor, and all accentuated by its status as one of China's leading producers of coal.

Orientation

The pivotal point of Datong is the intersection just north of the Drum Tower in the large old city. Apart from the Yungang Caves, the historic sights such as Huayan Monastery and the Nine Dragon Screen are all inside the crumbling old city walls, but most of the modern infrastructure is outside them in the surrounding post-1949 sprawl. At Datong's northern end is the railway station, to the west the post office and in the south the city's two tourist hotels. The new long-distance bus station is on Yantong Xilu, near the original north-western corner of the city walls.

Information

CITS Datong has two CITS offices: a branch

at the railway station (☎ 624464 ext 3755) and another at the Yungang Hotel (☎ 522265). The CITS runs regular tours of the city and Yungang Caves.

PSB This is on Xinjian Beilu, north of the large department store.

Money The most convenient branch of the Bank of China is on Caochangcheng Jie. The main office is on Xinjian Nanlu near the end of the No 6 bus route. The Yungang Hotel also offers a money-changing service.

Post & Telecommunications The main post and telephone office is the large central building with the clock tower.

Maps The Xinhua Bookstore diagonally opposite the main post office sells maps of Datong with places of interest to tourists shown in English. You can also pick up maps from hawkers around the railway station.

Datong Locomotive Factory
(dàtóng jīchē chǎng) 大同机车厂
This factory was the last in China making steam engines for the main railway lines. In 1989 it finally switched over to the production of diesel and electric engines. However, the factory still maintains a museum housing about seven old steam locomotives.

A factory inspection is reportedly rather educational. One US tourist said it reminded him of working in the US shipyards in the 1940s. You may be aghast at the safety conditions. After wandering through the factory you enjoy the ultimate experience of rail buffs – a ride in the cabin of one of the locomotives.

The factory is on the city's south-western outskirts. You can only see it as part of a CITS tour. Unfortunately the CITS city tours no longer include the factory, so they might have to arrange a special visit.

Nine Dragon Screen
(jiǔlóng bì) 九龙壁
This is one of Datong's several 'dragon screens' – tiled walls depicting fire-breath-

ing dragons made from separate glazed-ceramic plates. The Nine Dragon Screen was originally part of the gate of the palace of Ming Dynasty emperor Hong Wu's 13th son, and is eight metres high, over 45 metres long and two metres thick. The Nine Dragon Screen is a short way east of the Da Dongjie/Da Beijie intersection; you can get there on bus No 4 from the railway station.

Huayan Monastery
(huáyán sì) 华严寺
The Huayan Monastery is on the western side of the old city. The original monastery dates back to 1140 and the reign of Emperor Tian Juan of the Jin Dynasty.

Mahavira Hall is one of the largest Buddhist halls still standing in China. In the centre of the hall are five gilded Ming Dynasty buddhas seated on lotus thrones. The three statues in the middle are carved out of wood; the other two are made of clay. Around them stand bodhisattvas, soldiers and mandarins. The ceiling is decorated with colourful paintings – originally dating from the Ming and Qing dynasties but recently restored – and supported by massive wooden beams.

Bojiajiaocang Hall (Hall for the Conservation of Buddhist Scriptures of the Bojia Order) is smaller but more interesting than the main hall. It contains 29 coloured clay figures made during the Liao Dynasty (916-1125 AD) representing the Buddha and bodhisattvas. The figures give the monastery a touch of magic lacking in other restored temples.

Huayan Monastery is about half a km east from the post office at the end of a small lane running south off Da Xijie. Bus No 4 passes it. Entry to each hall costs Y12.

Shanhua Temple
(shànhuà sì) 善化寺
The Shanhua Temple is in the south of Datong just within the old city walls. Built during the Tang Dynasty, it was destroyed by fire during a war at the end of the Liao Dynasty. In 1128 more than 80 halls and pavilions were rebuilt, and further restora-

tion was done during the Ming Dynasty. The main hall contains statues of 24 divine generals. There is a small dragon screen within the monastery grounds. Admission is Y10.

Places to Stay

Only two hotels in Datong are officially allowed to take foreigners, but the helpful CITS at the railway station can get you into one of the inexpensive Chinese hotels if no other cheap accommodation is available.

The *Yungang Hotel* (☎ (0352) 521601) (*yúngāng bīnguǎn*) at 21 Yingbin Donglu has doubles from Y180. There is a dormitory on the 3rd floor of the separate CITS building to the right from the compound gate. It has beds in three-person rooms for Y27 and hot showers in the evening.

The *Datong Hotel* (☎ (0352) 232476) (*dàtóng bīnguǎn*) was undergoing a total facelift when we checked, but is expected to have doubles with bath for around Y200 after reopening. It will probably have dorm beds too.

To get to either of the hotels take bus No 15 from the railway station. For the Datong Hotel get off at the 12th stop (just after the bus turns sharply left). For the Yungang Hotel, get off at the stop after that, before crossing the intersection.

Places to Eat

Datong is certainly no gourmet's paradise, but fortunately there are a few good restaurants near the tourist hotels. The *Hongqi Restaurant* (*hóngqí dàjiǔdiàn*) across the road from the main gate of the Yungang Hotel has expensive and cheaper sections. Another nearby place is the *Yaxuyuan Restaurant* (*yǎxùyuǎn jiǔjiā*) on Nanguan Nanjie.

Getting There & Away

Air An airport south of the city is being upgraded to enable jets to land, but at the time of writing there were still no commercial flights to Datong. There is a CAAC booking office (☎ 525357) on Nanguan Nanjie which can book flights for air routes other than to/from Datong.

Bus There are regular buses from the new long-distance bus station to Taiyuan (Y25 or Y44 for a sleeper) and Wutaishan (Y21, 9½ hours). Some readers have mentioned a scenic bus route through the mountains via Hunyuan near Hengshan to Lingqiu (Y10, four hours), from where there are trains to Beijing. However, to go to this area foreigners are supposed to obtain an Alien Travel Permit. (Lingqiu is still not officially open, apparently because it has some kind of military installation.)

Train A railway line north-east to Beijing and a northern line to Inner and Outer Mongolia meet in a 'Y' junction at Datong. (Trans-Siberian trains via Ulaan Baatar come through here.) There are daily expresses to: Lanzhou via Hohhot and Baotou (Y390 soft sleeper, Y205 hard sleeper, 27 hours); Beijing (Y135 soft sleeper, Y76 hard sleeper, seven hours), Taiyuan (seven hours) and Xi'an. The CITS at the railway station can buy train tickets for you at very short notice for a service fee of Y30.

AROUND DATONG
Yungang Buddhist Caves
(*yúngāng shíkū*) 云冈石窟

Unless you admire coal dust and grey buildings, the caves are the only outstanding sight in Datong. The Yungang Buddhist Caves are cut into the southern cliffs of Wuzhoushan, 16 km west of Datong next to the pass leading to Inner Mongolia. The caves contain over 50,000 statues and stretch for about one km east to west. On top of the mountain ridge are the remains of a huge, mud-brick, 17th-century Qing Dynasty fortress. As you approach the caves you'll see the truncated pyramids which were once the watchtowers.

History Most of the caves at Datong were carved during the Northern Wei Dynasty between 460 and 494 AD. Yungang (Cloud Ridge) is the highest part of Wuzhoushan's sandstone range and is on the north bank of the river of the same name. The Wei rulers once came here to pray to the gods for rain.

The Yungang Caves appear to have been modelled on the Dunhuang Caves of Gansu Province, which were dug in the 4th century AD and are some of the oldest in China. Recent studies suggest that the Kongwang grottoes at Lianyungang (a coastal city by the Yellow Sea) were dug 200 years earlier. Buddhism may have been brought to China not only overland along the Silk Road but by sea from Burma, India and Sri Lanka.

It was in India that methods of cutting out cave temples from solid rock first developed. At the Dunhuang Caves the statues are terracotta since the rock was too soft to be carved, but here at Datong are some of the oldest examples of stone sculpture to be seen in China. Various foreign influences can be seen in the Yungang Caves: there are Persian and Byzantine weapons, lions and beards, Greek tridents and the acanthus leaves of the Mediterranean, as well as images of the Indian Hindu gods Vishnu and Shiva. The Chinese style is reflected in the form of bodhisattvas, dragons and flying apsaras (celestial beings rather like angels).

Some think the gigantic buddhas at Bamiyan in Afghanistan may have inspired the Yungang statues. The first caves at Yungang had enormous buddhas in the likenesses of five Northern Wei emperors. In fact, the first Northern Wei emperor, Daiwu, had been declared a 'living Buddha' in 416 AD because of his patronage of Buddhism.

Work on the Yungang Caves fizzled out when the Northern Wei moved their capital to Luoyang in 494. Datong then declined in importance and the caves appear to have been deliberately abandoned. In the 11th and 12th centuries the Liao Dynasty founded by northern invaders saw to some repairs and restoration. Datong itself houses some gems of Liao architecture and sculpture. More repairs to the caves were carried out during the Qing Dynasty. The Datong Caves are probably more impressive than those at Luoyang, and seem to have suffered less vandalism.

From east to west the caves fall into four major groups, though their numbering has nothing to do with the order in which they were constructed. The present appearance of the caves is also misleading – the whole front of the caves was formerly covered with multistorey buildings.

Caves 1-4 These early caves with their characteristic square floor plan are at the far eastern end, separated from the others. Caves 1 and 2 each contain carved pagodas. Cave 3 is the largest in this group, though it contains only a seated buddha flanked by two bodhisattvas. Between this group of four caves and the others is a monastery dating back to 1652, with pavilions hugging the cliff face.

Caves 5 & 6 Yungang art is seen at its best in these two caves. The walls are wonderfully carved with illustrations of Buddhist tales and ornate processions.

Cave 5 contains a colossal seated buddha almost 17 metres high. The faded paint gives you some idea of the original colour schemes: bronze face, red lips and blue hair. Many of the smaller images in this cave have been beheaded. On the whole, however, the sculptures and paintings in Caves 5 and 6 are better preserved than those in other caves since they're protected from the elements by the wooden towers built over the entrances. Cave 5 also contains a five-storey pagoda perched on the back of an elephant, carved on the upper part of the south wall.

Cave 6 contains a richly carved pagoda covered with scenes from religious stories. The entrance is flanked by fierce guardians. In the centre of the rear chamber stands a two-storey pagoda-pillar about 15 metres high. On the lower part of the pagoda are four niches with carved images, including one of the Maitreya Buddha (the future Buddha). The life story of Gautama Buddha from birth to his attainment of nirvana is carved in the east, south and west walls of the cave and on two sides of the pagoda. A relief on the east wall of the rear chamber of Cave 6 shows Prince Gautama's encounter with a sick man; the prince rides a horse while his servant protects him with an umbrella (a symbol of royalty) but cannot prevent him from seeing human suffering. Pilgrims walk around the chamber in a clockwise direction.

Cave 8 Cave 8 contains carvings with Hindu influences that have found their way into Buddhist mythology. Shiva, with eight arms and four heads and seated on a bull, is on one side of the entrance. On the other side is the many-armed, multi-faced Indra, perched on an eagle.

Caves 9 & 10 These have front pillars and interesting smaller figures with humorous faces. Some carry musical instruments.

Caves 11-13 These caves, which you can't enter, were apparently carved in 483 AD. Cave 12 contains apsaras with musical instruments and Cave 13 has a 15-metre high statue of Buddha, its right hand propped up by a figurine.

Caves 16-20 These caves were carved in 460 AD and have oval floors. The roofs are dome-shaped to make room for the huge buddhas – some standing, some sitting, all with saccharine expressions.

The cross-legged giant buddha of Cave 17 represents the Maitreya Buddha. The cave walls are covered with thousands of tiny buddhas; carving them is considered a meritorious act.

The walls of Cave 18 are covered with sculptures of Buddha's disciples, including one near the Buddha's elbow who has a long nose and Caucasian features.

The seated buddha of Cave 20 is almost 14 metres high. The front wall and the wooden structure which stood in front of it are believed to have crumbled away very early on, and the statue now stands exposed. It is thought to represent the son of Northern Wei Emperor Daiwu who is said to have been a great patron of Buddhism but later, through the influence of a minister, came to favour Taoism. Following a revolt which he blamed on the Buddhists, Daiwu ordered the destruction of their statues, monasteries and temples, and the persecution of Buddhists. This lasted from 446 to 452 AD. Daiwu was

murdered in 452 AD, though he had apparently repented of his cruel persecution. His son is said to have died of a broken heart, having been unable to prevent his father's atrocities, and was posthumously awarded the title of emperor. Daiwu's grandson (and successor) restored Buddhism. The statue in Cave 20 has distinctly non-Chinese features. The inlaid spot-like *urna*, a hairy wart between the brows which is a distinguishing mark of the Buddha, is missing. A carved moustache is faintly visible.

Next door is Cave 19, which is the largest cave and contains a 16-metre-high seated statue thought to represent Emperor Daiwu. It is possible that he was deliberately carved with his palm facing forwards – the 'no fear' gesture – in an attempt to abate the painful memories of his persecution of Buddhism.

Cave 21 onwards These caves are small and in poor condition. Cave 51 contains a carved pagoda.

Getting There & Away Buses No 3 and No 10 from the terminal at Xinkaili on the western edge of Datong go past Yungang Caves. You can get to Xinkaili on bus No 2 from the railway station or bus No 17 from outside the Datong Hotel. From Xinkaili it's half an hour's ride to the caves.

Admission to the caves is Y15 (or Y5 for students). You are not supposed to take photos – many visitors seem to get away with it anyway – but excellent sets of 20 slides of the caves cost only Y25.

The Great Wall
(chángchéng) 长城

The Great Wall is about an hour's drive north of Datong and forms much of the border separating Shanxi Province and Inner Mongolia. The wall here is completely unrestored, so you'll need to imagine that this long ruin of old bricks and pounded earth was once China's main defence against invasion from the north. You can take a minibus going to Fengzhen from outside the railway station or a public bus from the long-distance bus station; make sure the driver knows where you want to get off. The trip out to the wall is a good opportunity to see some of the sparsely populated countryside of far northern Shanxi.

Hanging Monastery
(xuánkōng sì) 悬空寺

The Hanging Monastery is just outside the town of Hunyuan, 75 km south-east of Datong. Built precariously onto sheer cliffs above Jinlong Canyon, the monastery dates back more than 1400 years. Having been reconstructed several times through the centuries, it now has some 40 halls and pavilions. They were built along the contours of the cliff face using the natural hollows and outcrops, plus wooden beams for support. The buildings are connected by corridors, bridges and boardwalks and contain bronze, iron, clay and stone statues of gods and buddhas. Some long-overdue repairs have been made to the monastery in recent years and some sections have been closed off. Admission to the Hanging Monastery costs Y15.

The CITS in Datong runs regular tours, with an English-speaking guide, to the Hanging Monastery and the Wooden Pagoda for Y60. They can also arrange tours for around Y250 per car or minibus, so for larger groups it often works out cheaper per person. Chinese tours costing Y20 and taking four to five hours leave from around 7 am, from near the long-distance bus station on Yantong Xilu.

Alternatively, you can take a direct public bus from Datong to Hunyuan, just 3½ km from the Hanging Monastery. The earliest bus leaves at 9 am and the last bus back to Datong leaves Hunyuan at 3.30 pm. Some travellers stay overnight in Hunyuan and return to Datong the next day. In Hunyuan you can stay at the Hengshan Guesthouse *(héngshān bīnguǎn)* or the government hostel *(zhèngfǔ zhāodàisuǒ)*.

Wooden Pagoda
(mùtǎ) 木塔

This 11th-century pagoda at Yingxian *(yìngxiàn)*, 70 km south of Datong, is one of the oldest wooden buildings in the world. It's said that not a single nail was used in the construction of the nine-storey, 97-metre structure.

Tours of the Hanging Monastery often include the Wooden Pagoda, but you can also get to Yingxian by public bus. From Datong the earliest bus to Yingxian leaves at 8.20 am and takes a little under three hours; from Hunyuan (near the Hanging Monastery) the 9 am bus to Yingxian reaches Yingxian around 10 am.

YUNCHENG
(yùnchéng) 运城

Yuncheng is in the south-western corner of Shanxi Province, near where the Yellow River completes its great sweep through far northern China and begins to flow eastwards. The small city is locally famous for the gutsy little orange tractors that are assembled here and often seen chugging along country roads. At Jiezhou *(jiězhōu)* 13 km to the south of Yuncheng is the large **Guandi Temple**, originally constructed during the Sui Dynasty but destroyed by fire in 1702 and subsequently rebuilt. At Ruicheng, 80 km further south, is **Yongle Taoist Temple**, which has valuable frescoes dating from the Tang and Song dynasties. The temple was moved to Ruicheng from its original location beside the Yellow River in the early '60s when the Sanmenxia dam was built.

Places to Stay

The *Huanghe Hotel (huánghé dàshà)*, near the first street corner on the left as you leave the railway station, has good doubles for Y176 and dorm beds for Y20. The *Yuncheng Hotel* (☎ (0359) 224779) *(yùnchéng bīnguǎn)* on Hongqi Lu has rooms from Y25 and a CITS office.

In Ruicheng the *Yongle Hotel (yónglè fàndiàn)* at the town's main intersection has beds in clean basic doubles for Y20. (Yongle Temple is three km directly south along this road.)

Getting There & Away

Yuncheng is on the Taiyuan-Xi'an railway line; all trains including daily expresses stop here. There are also direct bus connections to Yuncheng from Luoyang (Y22, six hours). The trip includes a ferry ride across the Sanmenxia dam and goes through an interesting landscape of eroded gorges and small fields levelled out of the loess earth.

Bus No 11 from Yuncheng railway station drops you off right at Guandi Temple in Jiezhou. From Yuncheng's long-distance bus station there are hourly departures to Ruicheng (Y6, 2½ hours). On the way, the bus passes Jiezhou before climbing the cool sub-alpine slopes of Zhongtiaoshan; it's a nice trip. From Ruicheng you can get an early-morning bus to Xi'an.

Top: Close-up of handle on large pot, Forbidden City, Beijing (RI'A)
Bottom: Interior roof of the Temple of Heaven, Beijing (AS)

Top: View from Moon Hill, Yangshuo, Guangxi (AS)
Bottom: Street scene, Chengdu, Sichuan (CL)

THE EAST

Fujian 福建

Population: 26 million
Capital: Fuzhou

The coastal region of Fujian (*fújiàn*) has well-established trading ports, which for centuries enjoyed substantial contact with the outside world. Early on, its great seaports developed a booming trade which transformed the region from a frontier into one of the centres of the Chinese world.

The Fujians were also the emigrants of China, leaving the Middle Kingdom for South-East Asia in great numbers. Exactly why this happened is unknown. One theory is that the prosperity of the ports caused a population explosion, and as land became scarce the only direction to go was out of China. The other theory is that the money never got beyond the ports, so the interior remained poor but the ports provided a means of escape.

Whatever the reason, ports like Xiamen were stepping stones for droves of Chinese people heading for Taiwan, Singapore, the Philippines, Malaysia and Indonesia. In 1718 the Manchus attempted to halt Chinese emigration with an imperial edict recalling all subjects who were in foreign lands. Finding this ineffectual, in 1728 the court issued another proclamation declaring that anyone who did not return to China would be banished and those captured would be executed. Chinese emigration was only made legal by the Convention of Peking which ended the fourth Opium War in 1860.

Nowadays, many descendants of the original emigrants send money to Fujian, and the Chinese government is trying to build up a sense of patriotism in the Overseas Chinese to get them to invest more money in their 'homeland'.

Just as most Hong Kongers trace their cultural roots to Guangdong Province, most Taiwanese consider Fujian to be their ancestral home. Fujian's local dialect, *minnanhua* (south-of-the-Min-River-language) is essentially the same as Taiwanese, though both

places officially speak Mandarin Chinese. Not surprisingly, the Taiwanese are the biggest investors in Fujian and the most frequent visitors. Some have even built retirement homes in Fujian.

Fujian is a lush, attractive province. The rugged, mountainous interior is beautiful but very poor. By contrast, the port towns on the narrow coastal strip are prosperous and developing fast for tourism and business.

FUZHOU
(*fúzhōu*) 福州

In the 1320s the Franciscan friar Odoric spent three years in China on a missionary venture. He came via India and after landing in Canton travelled eastwards, where he:

...came unto a city named Fuzo, which contains 30 miles in circuit, wherein are exceeding great and fair cocks, and all their hens are as white as the very snow, having wool instead of feathers, like unto sheep. It is a most stately and beautiful city and stands upon the sea.

Odoric's woolly hens are in fact what poultry-breeders call Fleecy Persians, though the Chinese call them Velvet-Hair Fowls. While the Chinese still breed chickens in makeshift pens in their backyards, Fuzhou seems to have lost its fame both as a poultry farm and as a stately and beautiful city.

Although the thriving port of Fuzhou is the capital of Fujian and exports much of the region's agricultural produce, the city itself is a letdown after colourful towns like Xiamen and Quanzhou. Fuzhou looks very much like the dull industrial towns of the north, with long avenues, concrete-block buildings and expansive suburbs, yet the economy is still based heavily on fishing and agriculture.

Fuzhou was founded in the 6th century AD and rapidly became a commercial port specialising in the export of tea. Its name actually means 'wealthy town' and, in terms

of wealth, Fuzhou was second only to Quanzhou. Marco Polo passed through Fuzhou towards the end of the 13th century, several years before Odoric's visit, and described the town as:

...an important centre of commerce in pearls and other precious stones, because it is much frequented by ships from India bringing merchants who traffic in the Indies. Moreover it is not far from the port of Zaiton (Quanzhou) on the ocean, a great resort of ships and merchandise from India; and from Zaiton ships come...as far as the city of Fu-chau (Fuzhou). By this means many precious wares are imported from India. There is no lack here of anything that the human body

FUJIAN

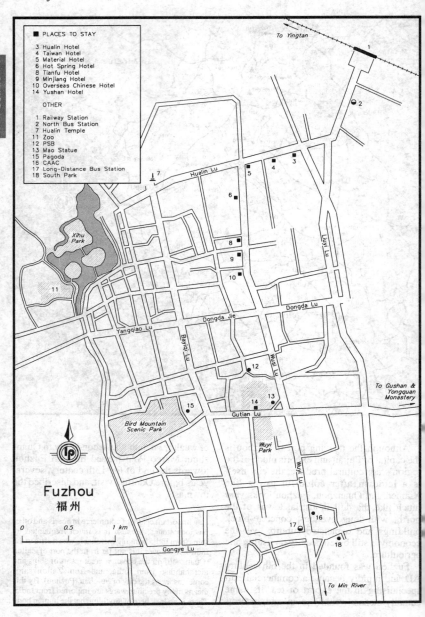

PLACES TO STAY
3 Hualin Hotel
4 Taiwan Hotel
5 Material Hotel
6 Hot Spring Hotel
8 Tianfu Hotel
9 Minjiang Hotel
10 Overseas Chinese Hotel
14 Yushan Hotel

OTHER
1 Railway Station
2 North Bus Station
7 Hualin Temple
11 Zoo
12 PSB
13 Mao Statue
15 Pagoda
16 CAAC
17 Long-Distance Bus Station
18 South Park

To Yingtan

Hualin Lu

Luyi Lu

Xihu Park

Dongda Lu

Dongda Jie

Yangqiao Lu

Bayiqi Lu

Wusi Lu

To Gushan & Yongquan Monastery

Gutian Lu

Bird Mountain Scenic Park

Wuyi Park

Wuyi Lu

Fuzhou
福州

0   0.5   1 km

Gongye Lu

To Min River

■ PLACES TO STAY

3 华林宾馆
4 台湾饭店
5 物质大厦饭店
6 温泉大大饭店
8 天福大酒店
9 闽江饭店
10 华侨大厦
14 于山宾馆

OTHER

1 火车站
2 长途汽车北站
7 华林寺
11 动物园
12 公安局外事科
13 毛主席像
15 八塔
16 民航售票处
17 长途汽车站
18 南公园

---

three apostles of the 70 who went through the world preaching. And they declared that it was these three who had instructed their ancestors in the faith long ago, and that it had been preserved among them for 700 years.

The Christians who Polo met were probably Nestorians, descendants of a Syrian sect whose religion had been carried into China via the Silk Road. What eventually happened to the Nestorian Christians in Fuzhou is unknown, although Polo claims there were 700,000 such households in southern China – probably an exaggeration. A more recent addition to the Christian community was the converts made by the Western missionaries during the 19th and 20th centuries, since Fuzhou was a centre of both Catholic and Protestant missionary activity.

Fuzhou is second only to Xiamen as a centre of Taiwanese investment. The money that the town has recently attracted is reflected in a lot of pricey new hotels and restaurants.

---

requires to sustain life. There are gardens of great beauty and charm, full of excellent fruit. In short it is a good city and so well provided with every amenity that it is a veritable marvel.

Despite its prosperity, Fuzhou had a reputation for revolts. Polo noted that the city had a large garrison of soldiers, as there were frequent rebellions in the district. Nevertheless, Fuzhou's status as an important trading centre and port continued over the centuries and quickly drew the attention of Western traders, who began to arrive in the area in the 16th century. But they couldn't set up shop until 200 years later, when the Treaty of Nanking ended the second Opium War and opened Fuzhou to foreign traders in 1842.

Oddly, Fuzhou had a long history as a centre of Chinese Christianity. Marco Polo describes a Christian sect that worshipped here and writes that his father and uncle:

...enquired from what source they had received their faith and their rule, and their informants replied: 'From our forefathers'. It came out that they had in a certain temple of theirs three pictures representing

Orientation

Most of Fuzhou lies on the northern bank of the Min River. The few tourist attractions are scattered. Most of the activity is in the central part of town, roughly between the bus and railway stations, where you'll also find the hotel and tourist facilities.

Wusi Lu and Dongda Lu are the main streets for expensive hotels, restaurants, shops and nightlife.

Information

CITS The main CITS office (☎ 552052; fax 537447) is just north of the Overseas Chinese Hotel. There is also a representative office inside the hotel itself. CITS offers tours of Fuzhou and can book air, bus and train tickets.

PSB This office is on Xian Ta Lu which runs south off Dongda Lu.

Money There is a money-changing counter on the ground floor of the Taiwan Hotel, the Overseas Chinese Hotel and the Hot Spring

Hotel. The area near the Overseas Chinese Hotel attracts many moneychangers who are notorious for ripping off tourists.

Things to See

Fuzhou is pleasant enough, but there's not a great deal to see. The northern and southern sections of the town are separated by the Min River, and the two old stone bridges which link the halves have lost their former charm.

On a fine day it can be interesting to watch the junks or the squadrons of sampans dredging the riverbed for sand. Across the Min River is **Nantai Island**, where the foreigners established themselves when Fuzhou became an unequal treaty port in the 19th century.

In the centre of town is a windswept square presided over by an enormous **statue of Mao Zedong**. The statue was erected to commemorate the 9th National Congress of the Communist Party where Maoism was enshrined as the new state religion and Lin Biao was officially declared Mao's successor.

In the north-west of Fuzhou is **West Lake Park** (*xīhú gōngyuǎn*) on Hubin Lu, where you'll find the **Fujian Provincial Museum** (*fújiànshěng bówùguǎn*).

Immediately east of the town, on **Drum Hill** (*gǔ shān*), is **Yongquan Monastery** (*yǒngquán sì*). The hill takes its name from a large, drum-shaped rock at the summit. The monastery dates back 1000 years and is said to house a collection of 20,000 Buddhist scriptures – of which almost 700 are written in blood. There is a spa next to the monastery.

Fuzhou has a number of other recent fake temples built to impress Taiwanese tourists so that they'll believe that China has the same kind of religious freedom that exists in Taiwan.

Places to Stay – bottom end

In Fuzhou, there are precious few places that qualify as budget accommodation. The best deal for a single traveller is the *Yushan Hotel* (☎ 551668) (*yúshān bīnguǎn*) pleasantly located in a park on Gutian Lu. Singles/doubles are Y50/88. From the long-distance bus station a pedicab should cost no more than Y5; it's about Y10 from the railway station.

One of the best deals relatively close to the railway station is the *Hualin Hotel* (☎ 570193) (*huálín bīnguǎn*), 36 Hualin Lu. Very comfortable doubles cost Y96.

Nearby, on the south-east corner of Hualin

Lu and Wusi Lu, is the *Material Hotel* (☎ 573168) *(wùzhì dàshà)*. At Y81 for a double, it's about the cheapest place in town that accepts foreigners.

Places to Stay – middle

The *Overseas Chinese Hotel* (☎ 557603; fax 550648) *(huáqiáo dàshà)* on Wusi Lu is very well organised – the rooms are clean, the friendly staff speak good English and the hotel's travel service actually serves you. Doubles cost Y132.

The *Taiwan Hotel* (☎ 570570) *(táiwān fàndiàn)* calls itself the 'Home of Taiwan Compatriots', but all with hard currency are welcome. Fancy doubles cost Y178. Facilities include a sauna, bar and disco.

Just north of the Overseas Chinese Hotel on Wusi Lu is the three-star *Minjiang Hotel* (☎ 557895), where doubles cost Y230 and suites are Y454 and Y862.

Tianfu Hotel (tiānfú dàjiùdiàn) on Wusi Lu offers considerable luxury for Y190. It's just north of the Minjiang Hotel.

Places to Stay – top end

The *Hot Spring Hotel* (☎ 551818, 535150) *(wēnquán dàfàndiàn)*, Wusi Zhonglu, is the fanciest place in town. Doubles cost Y391 to Y431; suites Y747 to Y3956.

Numerous other expensive hotels are sprouting like weeds all along Wusi Lu.

Places to Eat

Just west of the Taiwan Hotel is a large collection of outdoor sidewalk restaurants where you can eat for Y5 or so. Similar offerings are available all around the railway station.

The expensive restaurants line the east side of Wusi Lu, opposite the Hot Springs Hotel and other upmarket establishments.

For fast-food addicts, *California Fried Chicken* is just on the north side of the Overseas Chinese Hotel.

Getting There & Away

Air The CAAC office (☎ 551988) is on Wuyi Zhonglu, tickets can be bought here or at CITS. There are flights from Hong Kong,

and domestic flights and fares from Fujian are:

Destination	Fare	Destination	Fare
Beijing	Y840	Canton	Y350
Changsha	Y370	Chengdu	Y890
Dalian	Y840	Haikou,	
Harbin	Y1240	Hangzhou	Y260
		Ji'nan,	
Lanzhou	Y1070	Kunming	Y970
Nanjing	Y370	Shanghai	Y340
Shenyang	Y1020	Shenzhen	Y640
Taiyuan	Y850	Tianjin	Y810
Wuhan	Y400	Xi'an	Y760
Zhengzhou	Y590		

Bus There is a north long-distance bus station near the railway station, but the main bus station is in the south opposite the CAAC office. Buses head south along the coast from Fuzhou to Quanzhou (Y20) and Xiamen (Y35). Northbound buses go to Wenzhou (Y40, nine hours) and Ningbo (Y80). Much of the route between Fuzhou and Ningbo is spectacular – terraced rice paddies cling to cloud-shrouded mountainsides – but it's slow going.

Just south of the Overseas Chinese Hotel are ticket offices for air-con buses. Many of these are long-distance overnighters going to such places as Hangzhou, Shanghai, Canton and Shenzhen. To pass the time, you get to watch depraved kungfu videos. These buses leave from the major hotels.

Train The railway line from Fuzhou heads north and connects the city with the main Shanghai-Canton line at the Yingtan junction. A branch line splits from the Fuzhou-Yingtan line and goes to Xiamen. There are direct trains from Fuzhou to Beijing, Shanghai, Nanchang and Xiamen. The rail route to Xiamen is circuitous, so you'd be better off taking the bus.

Boat Passenger ships from Fuzhou depart from the nearby port town of Mawei, southeast of Fuzhou, but don't go there expecting to find a bustling harbour full of ships and junks. The port is a boring sprawl of apartment blocks with a Friendship Store and

International Seamen's Club. You can get to Mawei by train from the Fuzhou railway station.

From Mawei you can take a ship to Shanghai. CITS does not handle tickets – you have to buy them either at the booking office on Dong Dajie in Fuzhou, from the port at Mawei. Timetables vary but these boats usually go about every five days.

Getting Around

Fuzhou is a sprawling city, which makes it difficult to get around by foot. Pedicabs will go anywhere in the central part of the city for Y5 to Y7. Taxis are available. The bus network is good and bus maps are available at the railway station or hotels.

XIAMEN

(xiàmén) 厦门

Xiamen was founded around the mid-14th century, in the early years of the Ming Dynasty. There had been a town here since Song times, but the Ming built the city walls and established Xiamen as a major seaport and commercial centre. In the 17th century

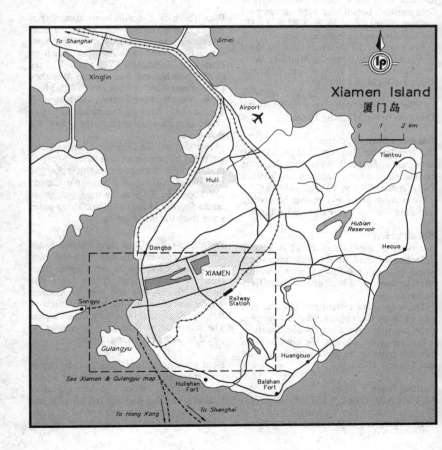

it became a place of refuge for the Ming rulers fleeing the Manchu invaders. From here Ming armies fought their way north again under the command of the pirate-general Koxinga.

From 1516 the Portuguese, based on an island close to Xiamen, traded surreptitiously with the Chinese for 50 years. The Chinese government is supposed to have finally discouraged the Chinese traders by lopping the heads off 90 of them. In 1575 the Spanish arrived and succeeded in building up a substantial trade in raw silk which was shipped to Manila and then to Mexico, but that also came to an end.

The Dutch arrived in 1604 but failed to gain a footing in Xiamen. After seizing Taiwan, however, they maintained a secret trade from the island of Quemoy until Koxinga appeared and put an end to their

commercial aspirations. The opportunity offered by the Dutch expulsion was taken up by the British, who opened up trade with the new regime on Taiwan and even established a base in Xiamen. However, by the early 1700s trade with Westerners only took place intermittently and secretly.

Things changed dramatically with the Opium wars of the 19th century. In August 1841 a British naval force of 38 ships carrying artillery and soldiers sailed into Xiamen harbour, forcing the port to open. Xiamen then came under the control of an assortment of foreigners, mainly the 'round-eye' British and the 'dwarf-barbarian' Japanese. By the early part of the century the Belgians, Danes, French, Germans, Dutch and Americans all had consulates here. The close, offshore island of Gulangyu was established by the European settlers as a foreign enclave.

Koxinga

When the Ming Dynasty collapsed in 1644, under the weight of the Manchu invasion, the court fled to the south of China. One after the other, a varied succession of Ming princes assumed the title of emperor, in the hope of driving out the barbarians and ascending to the Dragon Throne. One of the more successful attempts (which focused on the port of Xiamen) was by an army led by Zheng Chenggong, known in the West as Koxinga.

Koxinga's origins are a mystery. His father is said to have run away to Japan and married a Japanese woman – Koxinga's mother. His father returned to China as a pirate, raiding the Guangdong and Fujian coasts and even taking possession of Xiamen. Exactly how and why Koxinga came to be allied with the defunct Ming princes is unknown. One story claims that a prince took a liking to Koxinga when he was young and made him a noble. Another story says that Koxinga was a pirate-warrior like his father who, for some reason, teamed up with one of the refugee princes.

Koxinga used Xiamen as a base for his attacks on the Manchus in the north. He is said to have had under his command a fleet of 8000 war junks, 240,000 fighting men, and all the pirates who infested the coast of southern China – a combined force of 800,000. He is supposed to have used a stone lion weighing 600 pounds to test the strength of his soldiers; those strong enough to lift and carry it were enlisted in the vanguard of the army. His warriors wore iron masks and armour, and carried long-handled swords to maim the legs of enemy cavalry horses.

Koxinga's army fought its way to the Grand Canal, but was forced to retreat to Xiamen. In 1661 he set sail with his army for Taiwan, then held by the Dutch. He attacked the Dutch settlement at Casteel Zeelandia (not far from Taiwan's west coast city of Tainan) and after a six-month siege the Dutch surrendered. Koxinga hoped to use Taiwan as a stepping stone for invading the mainland and restoring the Ming Dynasty to power but, a year or two later, he died. The Manchus finally conquered the island in the early 1680s.

While Koxinga may have been a pirate and a running-dog of the feudal Ming princes, he is regarded as a national hero because he recovered Taiwan from the Dutch, which is roughly analogous to the mainland's ambition to recover the island from the Kuomintang! Those in China who reinterpret (rewrite?) history seem to have forgotten that Koxinga was forced to retreat to Taiwan after his defeats on the mainland and that the 'liberation' of Taiwan was superfluous to his plans. In reality, his story more closely parallels that of the Kuomintang, a regime which fled to Taiwan but awaits the day when it will invade and seize control of the mainland. ■

When Chiang Kaishek fled to Taiwan in 1949 he left Quemoy (now called Jinmen) and Matsu (Mazu) islands armed to the hilt with Kuomintang troops, hoping to use them as stepping-stones to invade the mainland from Taiwan. In 1958 the People's Liberation Army started bombarding the islands with artillery shells. In the West this crisis is only dimly remembered but, at the time, the USA and Taiwan had a Mutual Security Treaty and it seemed that the USA was about to enter a war for the sake of Chiang's pathetic regime. Kuomintang troops still occupy the islands. Quemoy is within view of Xiamen.

Today, Xiamen is a bustling place. It was opened to tourists in 1980 and in the following year became a Special Economic Zone (SEZ) in the hope of attracting Taiwanese investors, just as Shenzhen was made an SEZ to entice Hong Kongers.

Overseas Chinese are now permitted to buy homes and live in Xiamen on a permanent basis if they so desire. The original idea was to attract Taiwanese pensioners to retire and spend the remainder of their days (and their pensions) in the 'homeland'. Instead, the chief result has been to attract real estate speculators – Overseas Chinese who buy luxury flats and villas in the hope of selling them later for a tidy profit. Speculation has indeed caused a building boom, and real estate prices in Xiamen have been going through the roof. Fortunately, most of this new development is taking place in the suburban districts and the central part of Xiamen near the waterfront retains its very unusual (for China at least) colonial architecture. Gulangyu is especially well preserved. A laid-back town of over 300,000 people, Xiamen has a very different feel from China's inland towns, making this a worthwhile place to visit.

In 1912 the American missionary Reverend Pitcher described the waterfront district of Xiamen (which was once called Amoy) in the following terms:

A city! But not the kind of city you have in mind. There are no wide avenues, beautiful residences, magnificent public and mercantile buildings. All is directly opposite to this condition of things. The streets are narrow and crooked...ever winding and twisting, descending and ascending, and finally ending in the great nowhere. The wayfaring man, tho' wise, is bound to err therein. There is no street either straight, or one even called 'Straight' in Amoy. Then in addition to the crookedness, they must add another aggravation by making some of them very narrow. There are streets in Amoy so narrow that you cannot carry an open umbrella, but there are others ten, twelve, and fifteen feet wide. Of course they are crowded...alive with a teeming throng...Here every aspect of Chinese life passes before you, presenting grotesque pictures. Here goes the motley crowd, from the wretched beggar clothed in filthy rags to the stately mandarin adorned in gorgeous array.

Today, the streets are wider but still teem with people. The beggars Pitcher described as 'spending idle hours picking out the vermin from their dirty and ragged garments' are conspicuous by their absence and the mandarins have been replaced by privileged cadres, or busloads of Taiwanese tourists. Nowadays, Xiamen conveys an air of prosperity – it's a lively, colourful town of over 300,000 people, with many reminders of bygone turmoils.

Orientation

The town of Xiamen is on the island of the same name, which lies just off the mainland.

The island is connected to the mainland by a long causeway which carries a railway, road and footpath. The first section of the causeway connects the town of Xinglin on the mainland to the town of Jimei at the tip of a peninsula due east of Xinglin. The second section connects Jimei to the north of Xiamen Island.

The interesting part of Xiamen is the western (waterfront) district directly opposite the small island of Gulangyu. This is the old area of town, known for its quaint architecture, parks and winding streets.

The central district includes the railway station. Everything about one km east of the railway station is regarded as the eastern district. Both the central and eastern districts are new development areas and very tacky-looking. Like other recently built Chinese cities, it's a world of concrete high-rises and wide boulevards, thoroughly devoid of trees and lacking imagination.

Information

CITS This office (☎ 551825) is on the 15th floor of the Zhenxing Building (*zhènxīng dàshà*), Hubin Beilu. This CITS office has its act together – the staff are knowledgeable and friendly, though they are geared towards group tours. You can book air tickets here.

PSB Opposite the Xinqiao Hotel is a large, red-brick building; the wide footpath on the right-hand side (as you face it) leads to the PSB.

Money The Bank of China is at 10 Zhongshan Lu, near the Lujiang Hotel. There are many black-market moneychangers around the Xinqiao Hotel – rip-offs are not unusual.

Gulangyu Island
(gǔlàngyǔ) 鼓浪屿

Neither Gulangyu nor Xiamen were considered island paradises when Westerners landed in the 1840s. By 1860, however, they had well-established residencies on Gulangyu and, as the years rolled by, churches, hospitals, post and telegraph offices, libraries, hotels and consulates were built. In 1903 the island was officially designated an International Foreign Settlement, and a municipal council with a police force of Sikhs was established to govern it. Today, the only reminders of the settlement are the charming colonial buildings which blanket the island – and the sound of classical piano wafting from the villa-style houses! Many of China's most celebrated musicians have come from Gulangyu.

'In the past few years', says one of the tourist leaflets, 'many foreign visitors... plunged into the sea, indulging themselves in the waves, or lay on the golden sandy beach, being caressed by the sunshine, and made friends with the young people of Gulangyu. When the foreigners go away, they say: I am sure to come back again.' China is hardly a sun-worshipper's paradise but there are two beaches on Gulangyu: the East Beach and the West Beach. The first is overpopulated and has placid and scungy water, and the second belongs to the army and is off limits. On the beaches are a number of old, disused concrete blockhouses which appear to have ringed the entire island at one time.

Sunlight Rock *(rìguāng yán)* is the highest point on Gulangyu. It's an easy climb up the steps to the top where there's an observation platform and a great view across Gulangyu and the harbour. The large colonial building at the foot of Sunlight Rock is the **Koxinga Memorial Hall** *(zhèngchénggōng jìniànguǎn)*. Inside is an exhibition partly dedicated to the Dutch in Taiwan, and the rest to Koxinga's throwing them out. There are no English captions but it is still worth a look and, from the verandahs of the upper storeys, there is a fine view across the island. The hall is open daily from around 8 to 11 am and 2 to 5 pm.

The ferry to Gulangyu leaves from the pier just north of Xiamen's Lujiang Hotel. You don't pay to go from the mainland to the island, but to get back by ferry you must buy a ticket at the pier on Gulangyu. Ferries run from about 5 am to midnight.

Transport around Gulangyu is by foot; there are no buses, cars or pedicabs. It's a small island and the sights are within easy walking distance of each other.

Nanputuo Temple
(nánpǔtuó sì) 南普陀寺

On the southern outskirts of Xiamen town, this Buddhist temple was built during the Tang Dynasty more than a thousand years ago. It was ruined in a battle during the Ming Dynasty but rebuilt during Qing times.

You enter the temple through Tian Wang (Heavenly King) Hall where the welcoming Maitreya Buddha sits cross-legged, exposing his protruding belly. On either side are a pair of guardians who protect him. Standing behind the Maitreya Buddha is Wei Tuo, another Buddhist deity who safeguards the doctrine. He holds a stick which points to the ground – traditionally, this indicates that the temple is rich and can provide visiting

FUJIAN

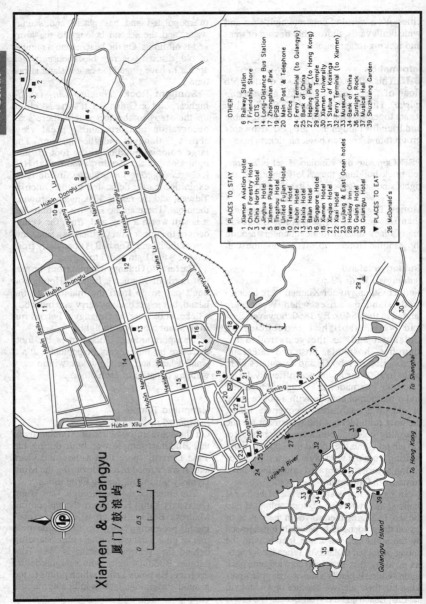

Xiamen & Gulangyu
厦门/鼓浪屿

0   0.5   1 km

PLACES TO STAY

- 1 Xiamen Aviation Hotel
- 2 China Forestry Store
- 3 China North Hotel
- 4 Jinghua Hotel
- 5 Xiamen Plaza Hotel
- 8 Tingzhou Hotel
- 9 United Fujian Hotel
- 10 Taiwan Hotel
- 12 Hubin Hotel
- 15 Baixia Hotel
- 16 Singapore Hotel
- 18 Xiamen Hotel
- 21 Xinqiao Hotel
- 22 Xixi Hotel
- 23 Lujiang & East Ocean hotels
- 28 Holiday Inn
- 35 Gulang Hotel
- 38 Gulangyu Hotel

▼ PLACES TO EAT

- 26 McDonald's

OTHER

- 6 Railway Station
- 7 Friendship Store
- 11 CITS
- 14 Long-Distance Bus Station
- 17 Zhongshan Park
- 19 PSB
- 20 Main Post & Telephone
  Office Terminal (to Gulangyu)
- 24 Ferry Terminal (to Gulangyu)
- 25 Bank of China
- 27 Haning Pier (to Hong Kong)
- 29 Nanputuo Temple
- 30 Xiamen University
- 31 Statue of Koxinga
- 32 Ferry Terminal (to Xiamen)
- 33 Museum
- 34 Bank of China
- 36 Sunlight Rock
- 37 Musical Hall
- 39 Shuzhuang Garden

Lujiang River

To Shanghai

To Hong Kong

Gulangyu Island

■ PLACES TO STAY	▼ PLACES TO EAT
1 厦门航空宾馆	26 麦当劳
2 中林宾馆	
3 北方宾馆	OTHER
4 京华饭店	
5 东南亚大酒店	6 厦门火车站
8 汀州大厦	7 友谊商场
9 福联大饭店	11 中国国际旅行社
10 台湾大酒店	14 长途汽车站
12 湖滨饭店	17 中山公园
13 海峡酒店	19 公安局外事科
15 白兰饭店	20 邮电局
16 新加坡大酒店	24 轮渡码头 （往鼓浪屿）
18 夏门宾馆	25 中国银行
21 新侨酒店	27 和平码头 （往香港）
22 夏西饭店	29 南普陀寺
23 鹭江大厦/东海大厦酒店	30 厦门大学院
28 假日大酒店	31 郑成功塑像
35 鼓浪别墅	32 轮渡码头 （往厦门）
38 鼓浪屿	33 博物馆
	34 中国银行
	36 日光岩
	37 音乐厅
	39 菽庄花园

monks with board and lodging (if the stick is held horizontally it means the temple is poor and is a polite way of saying find somewhere else to stay).

Behind Tian Wang Hall is a courtyard and on either side are the Drum and Bell towers. In front of the courtyard is Daxiongbao (Great Heroic Treasure) Hall, a two-storey building containing three buddhas which represent Sakyamuni in his past, present and future lives. The biography of Sakyamuni and the story of Xuan Zang, the monk who made the pilgrimage to India to bring back the Buddhist scriptures, are carved on the lotus-flower base of the buddha figure.

Inlaid in the buildings to the left and right of Daxiongbao Hall are eight stone tablets, inscribed in the handwriting of Emperor Qianlong of the Qing Dynasty. Four tablets are in Chinese and the others in the peculiar Manchu script. All record the Manchu government's suppression of the 'Tian Di Society' uprisings. The tablets were origi-nally erected in front of the temple in 1789, but were inlaid in the walls when the temple was enlarged around 1920.

The Dabei (Great Compassion) Hall con-tains four bodhisattvas. Worshippers throw divining sticks at the feet of the statues in order to seek heavenly guidance.

At the rear of the temple complex is a pavilion built in 1936 which stores Buddhist scriptures, calligraphy, wood-carvings, ivory sculptures and other works of art – unfortunately it's closed to visitors. Behind the temple is a rocky outcrop gouged with poetic graffiti; the big red character carved on the large boulder simply means 'Buddha'.

To get to the temple, take bus No 1 from outside the Xinqiao Hotel, or bus No 2 from the intersection of Zhongshan Lu and Siming Lu.

Xiamen University
(xiàmén dàxué) 厦门大学
The university is next to the Nanputuo

Temple, and was established with Overseas Chinese funds. The older buildings which face the shoreline are not without a certain charm, though most of the campus is a scattered collection of brick and concrete blocks. The campus entrance is next to the bus No 1 and bus No 2 terminal.

The Museum of Anthropology, on the university grounds, is worth a visit if you're down this way. After entering the campus, turn right at the first crossroads and walk until you come to a roundabout. The museum is the old stone building on the left with the cannon at the front. It has a large collection of prehistoric stone implements and pottery from China, Taiwan and Malaya, as well as human fossil remains. There are collections of porcelain, bronzes, jade and stone implements, coins, and inscribed Shang Dynasty bones and tortoise shells. You'll also see some fine calligraphy, exquisite paintings, glazed clay figurines, sculptures, clothing and ornaments from the Shang and Zhou periods through to Ming and Qing times.

Places to Stay – bottom end

Western District The *Xiaxi Hotel (xiàxī fàndiàn)*, next to Xiaxi Market off Zhongshan Lu and not far from the Xinqiao Hotel, is one of the cheapest places with a good location. Decent rooms cost Y60. To get there from the railway station take a minibus for Y1. From the bus station it's probably better to walk (about 20 minutes) or take a pedicab.

Central District The bottom end of the market belongs to the *Hubin Hotel* (☎ 225202; fax 229964) *(húbīn fàndiàn)* where very basic singles are Y27 and more salubrious rooms cost Y55 and Y65. The hotel is on Huzhong Lu.

The *Taiwan Hotel* (☎ 553808) *(táiwān jiǔdiàn)* on Hubin Donglu has very reasonably priced doubles for Y80.

The *Haixia Hotel (hǎixiá jiǔbīn)* near the long-distance bus station has doubles for Y80 and Y90.

Eastern District The *Jinghua Hotel* (☎ 554471) *(jīnghuá fàndiàn)* looks like an expensive high-rise hotel but in fact has cheap accommodation. Budget singles are Y80 but most rooms are doubles costing Y120 and up. The hotel is one km east of the railway station on Xiahe Lu – a pedicab from the station should cost around Y3.

Places to Stay – middle

Western District A really excellent place to stay is the *Xiamen Hotel* (☎ 222265; fax 221765) *(xiàmén bīnguǎn)*, 16 Huyuan Lu. The location can't be beaten – the hotel is built in a park. There is also a swimming pool and disco. All this luxury costs Y110/160 for singles/doubles.

The *Lujiang Hotel* (☎ 223235; fax 224813) *(lùjiāng dàshà)*, 3 Haihou Lu is opposite the Gulangyu ferry terminal. It once had the run-down charisma of an old colonial building but renovations have transformed it. However, prices are still reasonable; singles cost Y130 and doubles Y160 to Y180. There's a rooftop coffee garden which is very relaxing, with views across the harbour. Bus No 3 from the railway station and minibuses terminate at the Gulangyu ferry terminal just outside the hotel.

The *Bailan Hotel (báilán fàndiàn)* is a small but new and very clean place on Gugong Lu. Rooms start at Y118.

Xinqiao Hotel (☎ 238388; fax 238765) *(xīnqiáo jiǔdiàn)* is an old but classy place at 444 Zhongshan Lu. Singles range from Y161 to Y218 and doubles from Y230.

The *Singapore Hotel* (☎ 226668; fax 225950) *(xīnjiāpō jiǔdiàn)*, 113-121 Xi'an Lu next to a park certainly has a salubrious location but just barely qualifies as mid-range accommodation. Singles/doubles are Y180/222, but some bargaining is possible here in the off season.

Gulangyu Island There are two tourist hotels on Gulangyu Island, neither of which does very good business because of the inconvenience of carrying luggage where there are no motor vehicles or pedicabs. Most convenient (closest to the ferry) is the

Gulangyu Hotel (☎ 231856) (*gǔlàngyǔ bīnguǎn*), 25 Huangyan Lu, which has doubles for Y140. On the western side of the island (furthest from the ferry) is the *Gulang Hotel* (*gǔlàng biéshù*) which is more expensive but often empty. At both hotels, when vacancies are high you should be able to bargain the rates downwards.

Central District The *Tingzhou Hotel* (☎ 566588; fax 566228) (*tīngzhōu dàshà*) is on Hubin Donglu just opposite the railway station. It's a clean and modern-looking place and rooms cost Y160.

Eastern District Lianhua Nanlu is a street in the Eastern District that is packed-out with new hotels. At the lower end is the *China North Hotel* (*běifāng bīnguǎn*) with rooms for Y109 and Y150. Next door is the more salubrious *China Forestry Hotel* (☎ 562828) (*zhōnglín bīnguǎn*), 18 Lianhua Nanlu, where all doubles are Y180 (but they also accept RMB).

Places to Stay – top end
Western District The *East Ocean Hotel* (☎ 221111; fax 233264) (*dōnghǎi dàshà jiǔdiàn*) is near the Gulangyu ferry terminal. The cheapest singles are Y201 but most rooms cost Y316 and suites are Y488.

The *Holiday Inn* (☎ 220313; fax 234441) (*jiàrì dàjiǔdiàn*), 2 Zhongshan Lu, needs no introduction. Room prices range from Y546 for standard doubles to Y3335 for the presidential suite.

Central District The *Xiamen Plaza Hotel* (☎ 558888; fax 558877) (*dōngnán yà dàjiǔdiàn*), 908 Xiahe Lu, is literally just a stone's throw from the railway station. Rooms in this tower of luxury cost Y460 to Y603, with a 30% discount during the off season.

The *United Fujian Hotel* (☎ 555888; fax 557335) on Hubin Nanlu is another luxury resort catering to the Taiwanese crowd. Doubles cost Y265 plus 10% surcharge.

Places to Eat
Xiamen is 'seafood city', with many seafood restaurants along Zhongshan Lu and its side streets. It's hardly worth recommending any one place in particular; just look around until you find something that looks good (but they all do). There are plenty of fresh pineapples, frogs and peppers and a local lobster specialty called dragon shrimp (*lóngxiā*).

Xiamen holds the distinction of being the third city in China to acquire a McDonald's (after Shenzhen and Beijing).

Getting There & Away
Air Xiamen Airlines is what CAAC calls itself in this part of China. CITS books air tickets, as do some major hotels. The CAAC office (☎ 225942) is at 230 Hubin Nanlu.

CAAC offers flights to Hong Kong, Jakarta, Manila, Penang and Singapore. The flight from Manila seems to be very popular with budget travellers. You can also fly between Xiamen and Manila with Philippines Airlines (☎ 225456), 4th floor, Flat J, Seaside Building, Lujiang Dao. On the same floor in Flat F you'll find Dragonair (☎ 225433), which offers flights between Xiamen and Hong Kong for HK$1000.

There has long been speculation about when flights between Xiamen and Taipei will be permitted – since 1949, the only flights on this route have been hijackings.

Domestic flights and fares from Xiamen are:

Destination	Fare	Destination	Fare
Beijing	Y890	Canton	Y290
Changchun,		Changzhou	Y530
Changsha	Y430	Chengdu	Y950
Chongqing	Y760	Dalian	Y960
Guilin	Y440	Guiyang	Y630
Haikou	Y540	Hangzhou	Y360
Harbin	Y1360	Hefei	Y450
Ji'nan	Y700	Kunming	Y840
Lanzhou	Y1120	Nanjing	Y470
Ningbo	Y410	Qingdao	Y790
Shanghai	Y430	Shenyang	Y1120
Shenzhen	Y540	Taiyuan	Y950
Tianjin	Y860	Ürümqi	Y2110
Wenzhou	Y290	Wuhan	Y460
Xi'an	Y960	Yantai	Y870
Yiwu	Y300	Zhengzhou	Y650

Bus Buses to the towns on the south-east coast depart from the long-distance bus station. Destinations include Fuzhou (Y40), Quanzhou (Y12) and Shantou (Y50). You can also get buses straight through to Canton and Shenzhen.

There are many privately run air-con buses with ticket offices around the major hotels. You can pick up a minibus to Quanzhou at the railway station.

Train The 'missing link' in China's railway system is a set of tracks from Canton to Xiamen and up the east coast of Fujian. At present, there is a railway line under construction from Canton to Shantou (close to the Fujian border), but no plans yet for a connection to any cities in Fujian.

The existing railway line from Xiamen heads north and connects with the main Shanghai to Canton line at the Yingtan junction. Another line runs from Yingtan to Fuzhou.

From Xiamen there are direct trains to Yingtan, Shanghai, Fuzhou and possibly Canton. The train to Fuzhou takes a circuitous route, and unless you want to travel by night you're better off taking the bus.

Tourist-price fares from Xiamen to Shanghai are Y69 (hard seat), Y117 (hard sleeper) and Y251 (soft sleeper).

Boat Ships to Hong Kong leave from the Passenger Station of Amoy Port Administration on Tongwen Lu, about 10 minutes' walk from the Lujiang Hotel. There is a ticket office at the passenger station. There is one ship, the *Jimei*, between Xiamen and Hong Kong. It departs from Hong Kong every Tuesday at 1 pm, arriving in Xiamen 22 hours later. Departures from Xiamen are on Monday at 3 pm.

Getting Around

The airport is 15 km east of the waterfront district, or about eight km from the Eastern District. Taxis ask around Y30.

Frequent minibuses run between the railway station and Lujiang Hotel for only Y1. The service is extensive but the buses are always extremely crowded. Taxis are available from the railway station, tourist hotels and sometimes while cruising the streets. Fares for most places in town are Y10.

The interesting Western District can be seen on foot. Pedicabs are ubiquitous but the real fare is usually half of the asking fare, and no matter what is agreed, on the drivers will often demand more on arrival.

There are no buses, cars, pedicabs or bicycles on Gulangyu – it's walking only.

AROUND XIAMEN

Jimei School Village *(jíměi xuéxiào cūn)* is a much-touted tourist attraction on the mainland north of Xiamen Island. The school is a conglomeration and expansion of a number of separate schools and colleges set up by Tan Kahkee (1874-1961). Tan was a native of the area who migrated to Singapore when he was young and became a rich industrialist. He set a fine example to other Overseas Chinese by returning some of that wealth to the mother country – the school now has around 20,000 students. The Chinese-style architecture has a certain appeal which may make a trip worthwhile.

YONGDING

(yǒngdìng) 永定

Yongding is an out-of-the-way place in the south-western part of Fujian. It's in a rural area dominated by small mountains and farmland, and wouldn't be worth a footnote if it weren't for some unusual architecture.

Known as 'earth buildings' *(tǔ lóu)*, these large, circular edifices resemble fortresses and were probably designed for defence. The buildings were constructed by the Hakkas, one of China's ethnic minorities. Coming from Henan Province in northern China, the Hakka people first moved to the Guangdong and Fujian provinces in the south to escape severe persecution in their homelands. The name Hakka means 'guests' – today, Hakka communities are scattered all over South-East Asia.

For some reason, Japanese tourists are drawn like magnets to view the earth buildings – perhaps they know something we don't.

To reach the earth buildings, first take a train or bus to Longyan, and from there a bus to Yongding. New hotels are being built in Yongding to accommodate the Japanese tour groups, but prices might be on the high side.

QUANZHOU
(quánzhōu) 泉州

Long before the large port of Xiamen became a centre for domestic and foreign trade, there was another city nearby – Zaiton, a major port until the end of the 14th century. There is some debate as to its site, but Zaiton is generally accepted to have been where the present-day city of Quanzhou is situated, to the north-east of Xiamen.

The port was probably one of the greatest commercial centres in the world – from here Chinese silks, satins, sugar and spices were exported to India, Arabia and western Asia. When Marco Polo visited he raved about it as:

...a great resort of ships and merchandise...for one spice ship that goes to Alexandria or elsewhere to pick up pepper for export to Christendom, Zaiton is visited by a hundred. For you must know that it is one of the two ports in the world with the biggest flow of merchandise.

Marco Polo also remembered Zaiton as a place where many people came to have figures 'pricked out on their bodies with needles'. He had seen tattooists at work elsewhere on his travels; their 13th-century methods involved the customer being tied hand and foot and held down by two assistants while the artist pricked out images and then applied ink to the incisions. Polo writes that, during this time, the victim 'suffers what might well pass for the pains of Purgatory. Many even die during the operation through loss of blood.'

Kublai Khan's invasion fleets set sail from Zaiton for Japan and Java. With tariffs imposed on all imported goods, this city was an important source of refills for the Khan's treasury.

In the middle of the 14th century, towards the end of the Yuan Dynasty, Zaiton's prosperity began to decline because of fierce fighting. When the first Ming emperor, Hong Wu, came to power, his isolationist policies reduced foreign trade to a trickle. And as if that wasn't enough, the fate of the city was finally sealed by the silting up of its harbour.

Today there are few reminders of Quanzhou's former glory. Nevertheless, it's a lively little town with narrow streets, wooden houses, and numerous shops and restaurants. Of late, a number of Taiwanese citizens have built retirement homes in the area, so the ratio of old architecture to new is fast dwindling.

Orientation
Quanzhou lies on the north bank of the Jin River. The main street is Zhongshan Lu, a colourful street draped in trees and crammed with shops and a steady stream of bicycles. The Kaiyuan Temple, Quanzhou's main attraction, lies in the north-western part of town. There's also a scattering of sights in the hills to the north-east.

Information
CTS This office (☎ 222192) is just on the north side of the Golden Fountain Hotel.

PSB This is at 334-336 Dong Jie, a few minutes' walk east of the intersection with Zhongshan Lu.

Money You can change money at the Bank of China at the corner of Jiuyi Lu and Zhongshan Lu. The black market is just outside the Overseas Chinese and Golden Fountain hotels.

Post The multistorey post office and telecommunications building is opposite the Friendship Hotel on the corner of Jiuyi Lu and Dongda Lu.

Kaiyuan Temple
(kāiyuán sì) 开元寺
The Kaiyuan Temple is distinguished by its pair of tall pagodas. It was founded in the 7th century during the Tang Dynasty but reached

FUJIAN

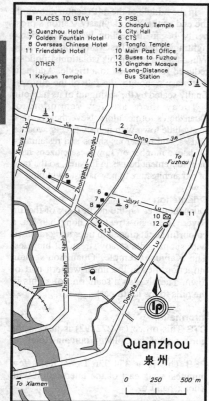

■ PLACES TO STAY	2 PSB
	3 Chongfu Temple
5 Quanzhou Hotel	4 City Hall
7 Golden Fountain Hotel	6 CTS
8 Overseas Chinese Hotel	9 Tongfo Temple
11 Friendship Hotel	10 Main Post Office
	12 Buses to Fuzhou
OTHER	13 Qingzhen Mosque
	14 Long-Distance
1 Kaiyuan Temple	Bus Station

Quanzhou
泉州

0   250   500 m

■ PLACES TO STAY

5 泉州酒店
7 金泉酒店
8 华侨大厦
11 友谊宾馆

OTHER

1 开元寺
2 公安局外事科
3 崇福寺
4 市政府
6 中国旅行社
9 铜佛寺
10 邮电局
12 往福州汽车站
13 清真寺
14 长途汽车站

its peak during Song times when 1000 monks lived here. The present buildings, including the pagodas and the main hall, are more recent. The main hall contains five large, gilded buddhas and on the ceiling above them are peculiar winged apsaras – celestial beings similar to angels. Behind the main hall stands the Guanyin Temple with its saffron-robed buddha.

Within the grounds of the Kaiyuan Temple behind the eastern pagoda is a museum containing the enormous hull of a Song Dynasty seagoing junk which was excavated near Quanzhou.

The temple is on Xi Jie, in the north-west part of town. From the Overseas Chinese Hotel the walk is lengthy but interesting.

Qingzhen Mosque
(*qīngzhēn sì*) 清真寺
On Tonghuai Jie, just south of the Overseas Chinese Hotel, is a mosque originally built in 1009 during the Song Dynasty for Quanzhou's large Muslim population. This is the oldest mosque in eastern China. There's also a small museum which has captions in Arabic, English and Chinese.

Other Temples
Quanzhou has its share of temples, in various stages of repair. One is the Tongfo Temple in the park opposite the Overseas Chinese Hotel; get up early to watch the taiji workouts. Another is the Chongfu Temple in the north-east part of town.

Places to Stay
The *Friendship Hotel* (☎ 223952) (*yǒuyí bīnguǎn*), Wenling Lu Zhong Duan, is the best deal in town. Clean doubles with private bath cost Y50. There is practically no other cheap hotel in Quanzhou open to foreigners.

If you can get one of the economy rooms, the second-cheapest is the *Golden Fountain Hotel* (☎ 225078) (*jīnquán jiǔdiàn*). Doubles range in price from Y103 to Y460 plus 10% surcharge.

Just next door is the *Overseas Chinese Hotel* (☎ 222192) (*huáqiáo dàshà*). Rooms cost Y200 to Y1150.

The *Quanzhou Hotel* (☎ 229958; fax 212128) (*quánzhōu jiǔdiàn*), 22 Zhuangfu Xiang, is approached from a side alley off Zhongshan Lu. It charges Y200 to Y680.

Places to Eat

Quanzhou is a great place for seafood – perhaps better than Xiamen – with a couple of seafood restaurants near the Overseas Chinese Hotel.

Getting There & Away

The long-distance bus station is in the southeastern part of town, but you can also catch both north and south-bound buses along Dongda Lu. Minibuses to Xiamen (three hours) cost Y12 after bargaining. Buses to Fuzhou (four hours) are around Y20 to Y30.

Near the Overseas Chinese Hotel are ticket offices for air-con express buses, but you might still have to go to the bus station to board the bus – be sure you know where the bus actually departs from. Some of the express buses go all the way to Canton and Shenzhen.

Getting Around

There are no city buses in Quanzhou and transport within the city is by Quanzhou-style pedicab – a bicycle with a little wooden sidecart which seats two people (the drivers are predatory!). Buses to nearby places leave from the square at the north end of Zhongshan Lu.

AROUND QUANZHOU

North of Quanzhou is **Qingyuanshan** (*qīngyuánshān*) – the name basically translates as the 'pure water-source mountains'. Regardless of water quality, it's a reasonably scenic mountain area dotted with a few caves, tombs and statues.

The Buddhist caves (*qīngyuán dòng*) on the mountain were destroyed during the Cultural Revolution, though some people still pray in front of the empty spaces where the statues used to be. According to an old woman who lives on the mountain, two Red Guard factions fought each other here during the Cultural Revolution, using mortars! Also found on the mountain is the 'rock that moves' (there's a large painting of it hanging in the dining room of the Overseas Chinese Hotel). It's one of these nicely shaped and balanced rocks which wobbles when you give it a nudge – we're told that to see it move you have to place a stick or a piece of straw lengthways between the rock and the ground and watch it bend as someone pushes on the rock.

The Muslim tomb (*qīngyuánshān shèngmù*) is thought to be the resting place of two Muslim missionaries who came to China during the Tang Dynasty. There are a number of Muslim burial sites on the northeastern and south-eastern outskirts of Quanzhou for the thousands of Muslims who once lived at Quanzhou. The earliest dated tombstone belongs to a man who died in 1171. Many tombstone inscriptions are written in Chinese, Arabic and Persian, giving names, dates of birth and quotations from the Koran.

The largest statue on the mountain is a stubby statue of Laozi (*lǎojūn yán*), the legendary founder of Taoism. Locals claim that Kuomintang soldiers used the statue for target practice but there's no sign of bullet holes.

The highest point in the area reachable by road is now home to a large TV broadcasting tower (*diànshì tái*).

Getting There & Away

Qingyuanshan is certainly too far from Quanzhou to walk, and the hilly terrain makes it impossible to travel by pedicab. The cheapest way for an individual traveller to see the area would be to join a minibus tour with some of the locals or Overseas Chinese. This is best arranged through one of the hotels, though on Sundays and holidays there may be plenty of minibuses looking for passengers around the railway station area. Chartering a taxi or minibus could be worthwhile if you can form a small group.

MEIZHOU
(méizhōu) 湄州

About halfway between Quanzhou and Fuzhou is Putian County. Just offshore is the island of Meizhou, known for its scenic beauty and dotted with temples.

Believers in Taoism credit Meizhou as being the birthplace of Mazu, Goddess of the Sea. Mazu is known by a number of names: Tin Hau in Hong Kong, Thien Hau in Vietnam, and so on. As the protector of sailors and fishing folk, Mazu enjoys high prestige and importance in coastal provinces like Fujian.

Mazu's birthday is celebrated according to the lunar calendar, on the 23rd day of the third moon, and at this time the island comes alive. During the summer months, it's also a popular spot for Taiwanese tourists.

You reach Meizhou by first taking a bus to Putian and then a ferry to the island. The temple is simply called the Mazu Temple *(mázǔ miào)*.

WUYISHAN
(wǔyíshān) 武夷山

Far in the north-west corner of Fujian is Wuyishan, an attractive region of hills, cliffs, rivers and forests. While not really spectacular, it is pretty and has now become the prime scenic spot for Taiwanese tour groups, who descend on the place by the busload. The one advantage this might have is that there are now high-standard (but expensive) hotels in the area. Besides the upmarket prices, another drawback is that it can become crowded during holiday times, but the off season (when it's cold) can be a good time to visit.

From Fuzhou, you can reach Wuyishan by first taking a train to Nanping. From Nanping to Wuyishan takes three hours by bus. An airport is under construction.

Zhejiang 浙江

Population: 40 million
Capital: Hangzhou

Zhejiang is one of China's smallest provinces. Traditionally one of the most prosperous, Zhejiang *(zhèjiāng)* has always been more important than its size would indicate.

The region falls into two distinct sections. The area north of Hangzhou is part of the lush Yangzi River delta, which is similar to the southern region of Jiangsu Province. The south is mountainous, continuing the rugged terrain of Fujian Province. Intensely cultivated for a thousand years, northern Zhejiang has lost most of its natural vegetation cover and is a flat, featureless plain with a dense network of waterways, canals and irrigation channels. The Grand Canal also ends here – Zhejiang was part of the great southern granary from which food was shipped to the depleted areas of the north.

The growth of Zhejiang's towns was based on their proximity to the sea and their location in some of China's most productive farmland. Hangzhou, Ningbo and Shaoxing have all been important trading centres and ports since the 7th and 8th centuries AD. Their growth was accelerated when, in the 12th century, the Song Dynasty moved court to Hangzhou in the wake of an invasion from the north. Silk was one of the popular exports and today Zhejiang is known as the 'land of silk', producing a third of China's raw silk, brocade and satin.

Hangzhou is the province's capital. To the south-east of the city are several places you can visit without backtracking. A road and a railway line run east from Hangzhou to Shaoxing and Ningbo. From Ningbo you could take a bus to Tiantaishan, continue south to Wenzhou and down the coast road into Fujian Province. Jiaxing, on the railway line from Hangzhou to Shanghai, is also open, as is Huzhou in the far north of Zhejiang Province on the shores of Lake Taihu.

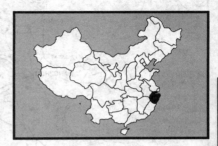

HANGZHOU
(hángzhōu) 杭州

When Marco Polo passed through Hangzhou in the 13th century he described it as one of the finest and most splendid cities in the world. Though Hangzhou had risen to prominence when the southern end of the Grand Canal reached here at the start of the 7th century, it really came into its own after the Song Dynasty was overthrown by the invading Jurchen.

The Jurchen were ancestors of the Manchus, who conquered China five centuries later. The Song capital of Kaifeng, along with the emperor and the leaders of the imperial court, was captured by the Jurchen in 1126. The rest of the Song court fled south, finally settling at Hangzhou and founding the Southern Song Dynasty.

China had gone through an economic revolution in previous years, producing huge and prosperous cities, an advanced economy, and a flourishing inter-regional trade. With the Jurchen invasion, the centre of this revolution was pushed south from the Yellow River Valley to the lower Yangzi Valley and to the coast between the Yangzi River and Canton.

While the north remained in the hands of the invaders (who rapidly became Sinicised), in the south Hangzhou became the hub of the Chinese state. The court, the

ZHEJIANG

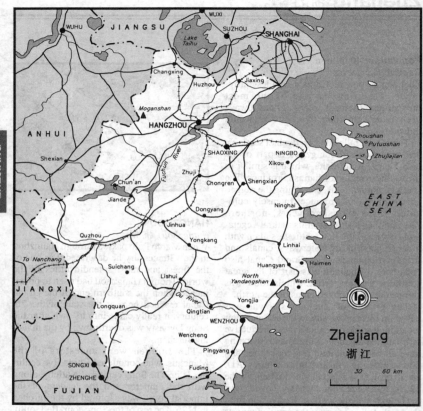

military, the civil officials and merchants all congregated in Hangzhou, whose population rose from half a million to 1¾ million by 1275. The city's large population and its proximity to the ocean promoted the growth of river and sea trade, and of naval and ship-building industries.

When the Mongols swept into China they established their court at Beijing. Hangzhou, however, retained its status as a prosperous commercial city. The Franciscan Friar Odoric visited it in the 1320s and described it as follows:

Never in my life did I see so great a city. It contains in circuit a hundred miles. Neither saw I any plot thereof, which was not thoroughly inhabited. I saw many houses of ten or twelve stories high, one above the other. It has mighty large suburbs containing more people than the city itself. Also it has twelve principal gates; and about the distance of eight miles, in the highway to every one of these gates stands a city as big by estimation as Venice...In this city there are more than eleven thousand bridges...I marvelled much how such an infinite number of persons could inhabit and live together.

Life has not always been so peaceful in Hangzhou. In 1861 the Taipings laid siege to and captured the city; two years later the imperial armies took it back. These campaigns reduced almost the entire city to ashes, annihilated or displaced most of the population, and finally ended Hangzhou's significance as a commercial and trading centre. Few monuments survived the devastation, and most of those that did became victims of the Red Guards a hundred years later.

Hangzhou lies in the area known as Jiangnan or 'South of the River', which covers southern Jiangsu and the northern Zhejiang provinces, one of the most prosperous regions of China. At first glance it seems a century away from the austerity of other Chinese cities – the buildings near the lake are particularly attractive. But behind the fancy exteriors a more humble life usually prevails. Permanent residents number fewer than a million, but on weekends they're flooded out by Chinese day-trippers from Shanghai, Suzhou or Wuxi.

Hangzhou is famous for its West Lake, a large freshwater lake surrounded by hills and gardens, its banks dotted with pavilions and temples. The lake gives rise to what must be one of China's oldest tourist blurbs: 'Above there is heaven, below there is Suzhou and Hangzhou'.

Hangzhou is one of China's big tourist attractions; its popularity is on a par with Guilin's. The downside is that around the hotels, vendors swarm like flies to plug their wares – 'change money' is the universal greeting given to foreigners, followed by 'longjing tea' and 'boat ride'. Fortunately, you can escape to more outlying areas – there is enough pleasant semi-rural territory around Hangzhou to keep you amused for several days.

Orientation
Hangzhou is bounded to the south by the Qiantang River and to the west by hills. Between the hills and the urban area is large West Lake, the region's premier scenic attraction. The eastern shore of the lake is the developed touristy district where you have to climb over 'change money' and 'longjing tea' people, but the western shore is mostly quiet and rural.

Information
CITS This office (☎ 552888; fax 556667) is at 1 Shihan Lu in a charming old building (*wànghú lóu*) near the Wanghu Hotel.

Money There are money-changing counters at most tourist hotels. The main Bank of China branch is at 140 Yan'an Beilu near Qingchun Lu.

Warning Hangzhou is fast gaining a notorious reputation for 'karaoke rip-off' schemes. Friendly young women approach well-heeled visitors and suggest going to a karaoke. After a few drinks, a bill that could bankrupt a Third World country is suddenly presented, while the woman (who gets a commission) suddenly disappears.

Temple of Inspired Seclusion
(*língyǐn sì*) 灵隐寺
Lingyin Si, roughly translated as 'Temple of Inspired Seclusion' or 'Temple of the Soul's Retreat', is really Hangzhou's main attraction. It was built in 326 AD and, due to war and calamity, has been destroyed and restored no fewer than 16 times.

The Cultural Revolution might have seen it razed for good but for the intervention of Zhou Enlai. Accounts vary as to what exactly happened, but it seems there was a confrontation between those who wanted to save the temple and those who wanted to destroy it. The matter eventually went all the way up to Zhou, who gave the order to save both the temple and the sculptures on the rock face opposite. The monks, however, were sent to work in the fields. In the early 1970s a few of the elderly and invalid monks were allowed to come back and live out their last few years in a small outbuilding on the hillside behind the temple.

The present buildings are restorations of Qing Dynasty structures. At the front of the temple is the Hall of the Four Heavenly Guardians and (in the middle of it) a statue of Maitreya, the future Buddha, sits on a platform flanked by two dragons. Behind this hall is the Great Hall, where you'll find

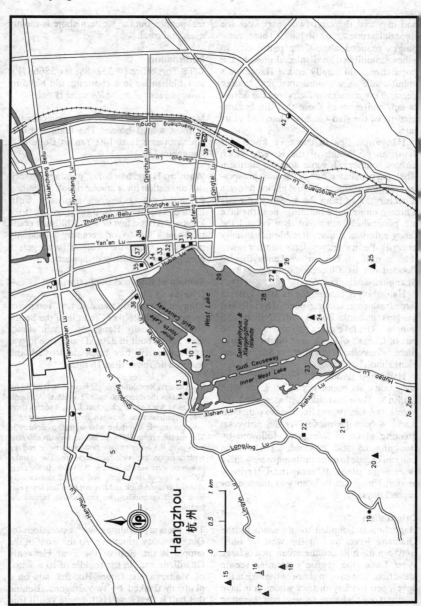

Hangzhou
杭州

ZHEJIANG

■ PLACES TO STAY

6 Yellow Dragon Hotel
9 Xinxin Hotel
13 Hangzhou Shangri La Hotel
21 Liu Tong Hotel
22 Zhejiang Hotel
26 Qingbo Hotel
30 Zhonghua Hotel
31 Huanhu Hotel
32 Xihu Hotel
33 Huaqiao Hotel
35 Wanghu Hotel
39 Xinhua Hotel

▼ PLACES TO EAT

12 Louwailou Restaurant

OTHER

1 Hangzhou Passenger Wharf
2 Long Distance Bus Station
3 Hangzhou University
4 West Bus Station
5 Zhejiang University
7 Yellow Dragon Cave
8 Precious Stone Hill
10 Solitary Hill
11 Zhejiang Provincial Museum
14 Yue Fei Mausoleum
15 Northern Peak
16 Temple of Inspired Seclusion
17 Beauty Peak
18 Peak that Flew from Afar
19 Dragon Well
20 South Peak
23 Huagang Park
24 Xizhao Hill
25 Phoenix Hill
27 Bicycle Rentals
28 Liulangwenying Park
29 Children's Park
34 Friendship Store
36 CITS
37 Zhejiang Medical College
38 Bank of China
40 Main Post Office
41 Railway Station
42 South Bus Station

■ PLACES TO STAY

6 黄龙饭店
9 新新饭店
13 杭州香格里拉饭店
21 六通宾馆
22 浙江宾馆
26 清波饭店
30 中华饭店
31 环湖饭店
32 西湖饭店
33 华侨饭店
35 望湖宾馆
39 新华饭店

▼ PLACES TO EAT

12 楼外楼菜馆

OTHER

1 客运码头
2 长途汽车站
3 杭州大学
4 长途汽车西站
5 浙江大学
7 黄龙洞
8 宝石山
10 孤山
11 浙江省参钢
14 岳飞墓园
15 北高峰
16 灵隐寺
17 美高峰
18 飞来峰
19 龙井
20 南高峰
23 花港公园
24 夕照山
25 风凰山
27 租自行车店
28 柳浪问莺公园
29 儿童公园
34 友谊商店
36 中国国际旅行社
37 浙江医科大学
38 中国银行
40 邮电局
41 火车站
42 长途汽车南站

find the magnificent 20-metre-high statue of Siddhartha Gautama sits. This was sculptured from 24 blocks of camphorwood in 1956 and was based on a Tang Dynasty original. Behind the giant statue is a startling montage of 150 small figures.

Facing the temple is Feilai Feng (*fēilái fēng*), the 'Peak that Flew from Afar'. Some praise must go to the Chinese (or the Indians) for accomplishing the first successful solo flight of a mountain! This name, so the story goes, came from an Indian monk who visited Hangzhou in the 3rd century and said that the hill looked exactly like one in India and asked when it had flown to China. The rocky surface of the hill is chiselled with 330 sculptures and graffiti from the 10th to the 14th centuries. The earliest sculpture dates back to 951 AD and comprises a group of three Buddhist deities at the right-hand entrance to the Qing Lin Cave. Droves of Chinese people clamber over the sculptures and inscriptions to have their photo taken; the most popular backdrop is the laughing Maitreya (the fat buddha at the foot of the ridge). There is a vegetarian restaurant beside the temple.

To get to the temple take bus No 7 to the terminal at the foot of the hills west of Hangzhou. Behind the Lingyin Temple is Northern Peak, which can be climbed via cable car. From the summit there are sweeping views across the lake and city.

Zhejiang Provincial Museum
(*zhèjiāng bówùguǎn*) 浙江省博物馆
This interesting museum is on Solitary Hill Island (*gǔshān*), a short walk from the Hangzhou Shangri-La Hotel. Its buildings were part of the holiday palace of Emperor Qianlong in the 18th century. Most of the museum is concerned with natural history; there's a large whale skeleton (a female *Rhachianectos glaucus cope*) and a dinosaur skeleton. We had one letter from someone who said that visitors should be sure to have the Ming Dynasty eye-wash bowl demonstrated(?!).

Mausoleum of General Yue Fei
(*yuè fēi mù*) 岳飞墓
During the 12th century when China was attacked by Jurchen invaders from the north, General Yue Fei (1103-41) was commander of the Song armies. Despite his successes against the invaders, he was recalled to the Song court where he was executed by a treacherous court official called Qin Gui. Twenty years later, in 1163, Song emperor Xiao Zong rehabilitated him and had his corpse reburied at the present site. Yue was eventually deified.

The mausoleum of this soldier-patriot is in a compound bounded by a red-brick wall on Huanhu Lu, a few minutes' walk west of the Hangzhou Shangri-La Hotel. It was ransacked during the Cultural Revolution but has since been restored.

Inside is a glazed clay statue of the general and, on the wall, paintings of scenes from his life – including one of his back being tattooed with the words 'Loyal to the Last'.

Precious Stone Hill
(*bǎoshí shān*) 宝石山
The original Protect Chu Tower (*bǎochù tǎ*) was erected on Precious Stone Hill in 938 during the Song Dynasty. It was built to ensure the safe return of Hangzhou's Prince Qian Chu from an audience with the emperor. In China there is an old saying that goes something like, 'Keeping company with the emperor is like keeping company with a tiger' – you had to make sure you didn't get eaten. The present tower is a 1933 reconstruction, 45½ metres high and resembling a stone-age rocket ship. It stands just north of Huanhu Lu (follow the steps) on the northern side of the lake. In the early morning you may find elderly Chinese women practising taiji there and old men airing their birds. From the tower there are tracks south along the ridge through bamboo groves; dotted along the tracks are temples and shrines.

Six Harmonies Pagoda
(*liùhé tǎ*) 六和塔
To the south-west of the city stands an enormous rail-and-road bridge which spans the Qiantang River. Close by is the 60-metre-

high octagonal Six Harmonies Pagoda named after the six codes of Buddhism. As a legacy of the feudal past, the pagoda was cited for demolition during the Cultural Revolution, but since this would have required an army of experts the project was called off. The pagoda was originally built as a lighthouse although it was also supposed to have some sort of magical power to halt the tidal bore which thundered up the Qiantang River in mid-September every year.

West Lake
(xī hú) 西湖

There are 30 lakes in China called Xi Hu, but this one is by far the most famous. It is a pretty sight, but if you travel 1000 km just for the water you'll probably be disappointed. The lake was originally a lagoon adjoining the Qiantang River. In the 8th century the governor of Hangzhou had it dredged; later a dike was built which cut it off from the river completely.

The lake is about three km long and a bit under three km wide. Two causeways, the Baidi and the Sudi, split the lake into sections. The causeways each have a number of arched bridges, large enough for small boats and ferries to pass under. The sights are scattered around the lake, though most of them tend to be uninspiring pavilions or bridges with fanciful names. However, the whole being greater than the sum of the parts, it's still a pretty place to wander around and has a romantic feel on a fresh night.

The largest island in the lake is Solitary Hill *(gǔshān)* – the location of the Provincial Museum, the Louwailou Restaurant and Zhongshan Park *(zhōngshān gōngyuǎn)*. During the 18th century Zhongshan Park was once part of an imperial palace, but was renamed after 1911 in honour of Sun Yatsen. The Baidi causeway links the island to the mainland.

Most of the other sights are connected with famous people who once lived there – poets, an emperor, perhaps an alchemist who bubbled up longevity pills. One of these sights is the Pavilion for Releasing Crane on Solitary Hill Island. It was built in memory of the Song poet Lin Hejing who, it is said, refused to serve the emperor and remained a bachelor his whole life. His only pastimes were planting plum trees and fondling his crane.

Hangzhou's botanical gardens even have a sequoia (a coniferous tree) presented by Richard Nixon on his 1972 visit.

Santanyinyue *(sāntán yìnyuè)* is another island in the lake. Most guidebooks and maps refer to it as 'Three Pools Mirroring the Moon' but, in fact, the island is named after three poles which stick out of the water. According to the story, in mid-August, when the moon is at its largest and roundest, it is reflected in the water between the three poles. At this time the locals put lighted candles in the hollow tops of the poles. Hence, the correct translation of the name should be something like 'Three Poles Fixing the Moon'. (Santanyinyue is next to Xiaoyingzhou Island in the southern part of the lake.)

If you want to contemplate the moon in the privacy of your own boat there are a couple of places around the lake where you can hire paddle boats and go for a slow spin. Boats can also be chartered for a lake cruise from the small docks along the eastern side of the lake. On Sundays and holidays, many Chinese families charter covered boats for picnic outings.

Other Sights

Some of the more interesting areas for walking are in the eastern part of town,

around the scungy canals which cut through the urban areas. There are lots of quaint brick and wooden houses, and washing hung out to dry along the narrow lanes.

The **Hangzhou Zoo** has Manchurian tigers, though to our untrained eyes they looked no different from other tigers.

About 60 km north of Hangzhou is Moganshan. Pleasantly cool at the height of summer, Moganshan was developed as a resort for Europeans living in Shanghai and Hangzhou during the colonial era.

Places to Stay – bottom end

Hangzhou's proximity to Shanghai means there is a weekend stampede for hotel rooms, especially cheap ones. Despite the plethora of places to stay, at times accommodation can be very tight. If you arrive on a Saturday night, you'd better bring camping gear or be prepared to pay something like Y300 for a bed. Arriving early in the day is recommended, particularly during the summer school holidays.

At the bottom of the market is the *Xihu Hotel* (☎ 761601) *(xīhú fàndiàn)*, 89 Hubin Lu. Room prices start at Y34 – the low prices are in spite of the hotel being just across the street from the lake.

Also right on the eastern side of the lake is the colonial-style *Huanhu Hotel* (☎ 765491) *(huánhú fàndiàn)*, 54 Hubin Lu. Standard doubles go for Y86.

The *Xinhua Hotel (xīnhuá fàndiàn)* on the eastern end of Jiefang Lu is next to the post office and convenient for the railway station. Rooms cost Y60, Y80 and Y140.

The *Xinxin Hotel* (☎ 777101) *(xīnxīn fàndiàn)*, 58 Beishan Lu, on the northern shore of the lake looks like a good place to stay and is reasonable at Y99. However, it seems to be almost permanently 'all full'.

On the western side of the lake is the Zhejiang Hotel (☎ 777988) *(zhèjiāng bīnguǎn)*, 68 San Tai Shan. It is rather isolated on the outskirts of Hangzhou, in a quiet woodland setting. Building No 1 has a dormitory for foreigners at a modest Y20, though it's none too clean. Doubles are available in building No 5, but at Y160

they're no bargain. Fancier buildings have rooms for Y200. Reminiscent of a convalescent home, this quiet and relaxing hotel was (so the story goes) the personal headquarters of all-purpose arch-villain and traitor, Marshal Lin Biao. Underneath the grounds is a labyrinth of tunnels and rooms which appear to have been used as a military command post. These have been flung open to the general public, and Chinese tour groups are led through them – check out the massive indoor swimming pool.

To get to the hotel take bus No 28 from near the long-distance bus station; get off anywhere north of the lake and switch to a bus No 27 to the hotel. The last No 27 bus is around 6.30 pm. From the railway station take bus No 7 to the west side of the lake and then change to bus No 27. Coming back from the hotel, bus No 27 terminates on Pin Hai Lu, which is a street running off Yan'an Lu close to the eastern shore of the lake.

Places to Stay – middle

Just off the eastern side of the lake is the very pleasant *Zhonghua Hotel* (☎ 727094) *(zhōnghuá fàndiàn)*, 55 Youdian Lu. Singles cost Y130 to Y160, doubles Y160 to Y210. The canned soft drinks placed in your room are free!

South of the Zhejiang Hotel on the remote west side of the lake is the garden-style *Liu Tong Hotel* (☎ 773377; fax 772529) *(liùtōng bīnguǎn)*, 32 Faxiang Xiang, with rooms costing Y150 to Y250.

Places to Stay – top end

The convenient *Huaqiao Hotel* (☎ 774401) *(huáqiáo fàndiàn)*, 15 Hubin Lu, is on the eastern shore of the lake. Doubles cost from Y270.

A short distance to the north on Wangcheng Xilu is the very comfortable *Wanghu Hotel* (☎ 771942) *(wànghú bīnguǎn)*. Doubles cost Y290.

The *Qingbo Hotel (qīngbō fàndiàn)* on Nanshan Lu near the south-eastern shore of the lake offers salubrious accommodation from around Y200.

Top of the market is the *Hangzhou*

Shangri-La Hotel (☎ 777951; fax 773545) *(hángzhōu xiānggé lǐlā fàndiàn)*, also just called the *Hangzhou Hotel (hángzhōu fàndiàn)*. It's on the northern side of the lake surrounding by spacious forested grounds. Doubles with a hillside view cost Y632, or Y862 for a view of the lake.

Places to Eat

There are relatively few restaurants right on the lakeside – real estate is too valuable here. Go east from the lake one block to find Yan'an Lu – this road and all the small side streets spilling off it are a good place to look. There are dozens of choices – just one possibility is the *Nanfang Restaurant* (☎ 763235) *(nánfāng dàjiǔjiā)*. If you've overdosed on Chinese food, you can try the *Haifeng Western Restaurant* (☎ 762640) *(hǎifēng xī cāntīng)* at No 59. Other streets worth exploring for culinary delights include Jiefang Lu, Zhongshan Lu and all the small side alleys.

The *Louwailou* (☎ 729023) *(lóuwài lóu)*, 30 Waixihu on Solitary Hill Island has good, cheap food. Its specialties are West Lake fish in vinegar sauce, and boneless fish in sauce.

Things to Buy

Hangzhou is well known for its tea, especially longjing or Dragon Well green tea, which is grown in the Longjing District west of West Lake. Unlike most Chinese people, Hangzhou residents take great care in selecting the water and utensils with which to brew their tea, and visiting teahouses is a popular local pastime. The taste for tea carries over into Hangzhou cuisine, which features many tea-flavoured dishes. Among the local specialties are freshwater shrimp stir-fried with longjing tea leaves and carp stuffed with tea leaves. You won't have any trouble finding the longjing tea vendors – you'll practically have to beat them off with a stick.

The Foreign Languages Bookstore (☎ 773883) at 34 Hubin Lu is worth a look.

Getting There & Away

Air The CAAC office (☎ 554259) is at 160 Tiyuchang Lu. Dragonair (☎ 554488 ext 2040) has a representative in the Yellow Dragon Hotel *(huánglóng fàndiàn)* on Shuguang Lu, but booking at CITS might be more convenient. Both CAAC and Dragonair offer daily flights to/from Hong Kong for HK$1090. Domestic connections include the following flights and fares:

Destination	Fare	Destination	Fare
Beijing	Y600	Canton	Y540
Changchun	Y1000	Changsha,	
Dalian	Y580	Chengdu	Y900
Fuzhou	Y260	Guilin	Y610
Harbin	Y1040	Huangyan	Y190
Kunming		Shanghai	Y120
Lanzhou	Y890	Shenyang	Y920
Shenzhen	Y850	Taiyuan	Y590
Ürümqi	Y1820	Wenzhou	Y200
Wuhan	Y320	Xiamen	Y360
Xi'an	Y610		

Bus The long-distance bus station is on Hushu Nanlu just north of the intersection with Huancheng Lu. There are several buses a day to Shanghai (Y11), Tunxi (Y13), Hefei and Tiantaishan.

Train There are direct trains from Hangzhou to Fuzhou, Nanchang, Shanghai and Canton, and east to the small towns of Shaoxing and Ningbo. For trains to the north you must first go to Shanghai. Hangzhou railway station has a separate ticket booking office for foreigners – it's through a doorway in the main booking hall.

Tourist-price tickets from Hangzhou to Shanghai are Y14 for a hard seat. The trip takes about three hours, and there are numerous trains daily.

Tourist-price tickets to Canton are Y96 (hard seat), Y146 (hard sleeper) and Y320 (soft sleeper). The trip takes about 28 hours, but depends on the train.

Trains to Canton go via Nanchang, the capital of Jiangxi Province, or via the railway junction of Yingtan.

From Yingtan a branch line extends to Fuzhou and Xiamen (both in Fujian Province on the south-east coast). There are direct trains from Hangzhou to Fuzhou. There is no direct train from Hangzhou to Xiamen; you must first go to Shanghai. However, you can catch a train to Fuzhou and then catch a bus to Xiamen.

Boat You can take a boat up the Grand Canal from Hangzhou to Suzhou. Boats leave twice a day at 5.30 am and 5.50 pm from the dock near the corner of Huancheng Lu and Hushu Nanlu, in the northern part of town. Tickets are available from the booking office at the dock and cost Y9, Y12, and Y20 depending on the class of service. For more details see the Suzhou section in the Jiangsu chapter.

Getting Around

To/From the Airport Hangzhou's airport is 15 km from the city centre; taxi drivers ask around Y40 to Y45 for the trip.

Bus A very useful bus is No 7, which connects the railway station to the major hotel area on the eastern side of the lake. Bus No 1 connects the long-distance bus station to the east shore and bus No 28 connects it to the lake's western side. Bus No 27 is useful for getting between the eastern and western sides of the lake.

Taxi Metered taxis are ubiquitous but the drivers are cut-throats. They will often take you for a complete drive around the lake when the place you want to get to is only a couple of blocks away. Prices for taxis depend on the size of the vehicle. The official price for larger taxis is Y12.60 at flagfall for the first three km and Y1.80 for each additional km. It's only two to three km from the railway station to most hotels on the popular eastern side of the lake.

Bicycle Renting a bike to ride around the lake is a great idea. Surprisingly, bike rentals are not nearly as popular as you'd expect. One place which rents bikes is just across the street from the Qingbo Hotel but the sign is in Chinese.

Boat Boat tours of the lake are popular with the Chinese. You'll hardly have to look for a boat – just stand along the east shore of the lake and the boat-ticket vendors will come to you.

SHAOXING
(shàoxīng) 绍兴

Shaoxing is in the centre of the waterway system on the northern Zhejiang plain. The waterways are part of the city's charm – Shaoxing is an attractive place, notable for its rivers (subject to flooding), canals, boats and arched bridges.

Since early times, it's been a major administrative town and an agricultural market centre. From 770 to 211 BC, Shaoxing was capital of the Yue Kingdom.

Information

There is a CITS office (☎ 533252; fax 535262) at 20 Fushan Xilu. Tourist hotels should be able to change money – if not, the Bank of China is at 225 Renmin Lu.

King Yu's Mausoleum
(yǔ líng) 禹陵

The first Chinese Dynasty – which may have existed only in legends – held power from the 21st to the 16th century BC. The founder was Yu (or King Yu, though it's hard to know the appropriate title). Yu is credited with

1	火车站
2	长途汽车站
3	戒珠寺
4	蔡元培故居
5	市政府
6	华侨饭店
7	市中医院
8	绍兴饭店
9	大善寺
10	周恩来祖居
11	八字桥
12	青藤书屋
13	儿童公园
14	太平天国壁画
15	鲁汛纪念馆
16	三味书屋
17	秋瑾故居

ZHEJIANG

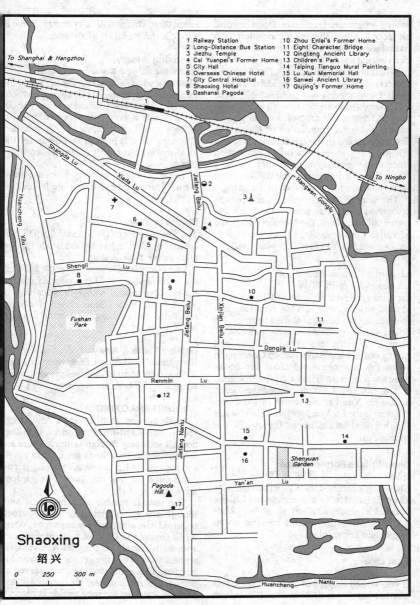

To Shanghai & Hangzhou

1 Railway Station
2 Long-Distance Bus Station
3 Jiezhu Temple
4 Cai Yuanpei's Former Home
5 City Hall
6 Overseas Chinese Hotel
7 City Central Hospital
8 Shaoxing Hotel
9 Dashansi Pagoda
10 Zhou Enlai's Former Home
11 Eight Character Bridge
12 Qingteng Ancient Library
13 Children's Park
14 Taiping Tianguo Mural Painting
15 Lu Xun Memorial Hall
16 Sanwei Ancient Library
17 Qiujing's Former Home

Shangda Lu

Xiada Lu

Jiefang Beilu

Hengwen Gonglu

To Ningbo

Huancheng Xilu

Shengli   Lu

Fushan
Park

Jiefang Beilu

Xinjian Beilu

Dongjie Lu

Renmin   Lu

Jiefang Nanlu

Shenyuan
Garden

Yan'an   Lu

Pagoda
Hill

Shaoxing
绍兴

0   250   500 m

Huancheng   Nanlu

having engineered massive flood control projects – given Shaoxing's position in a river basin laced with canals, that would have been a useful hobby.

Whether or not Yu and his flood-control projects ever existed can be debated endlessly by historians and archaeologists, but CITS needs no convincing – Yu is big business. A temple and mausoleum complex to honour the great-grandfather of China was first constructed in the 6th century. Not surprisingly, it's required a bit of renovation since then – nobody is quite sure just how many times it has been rebuilt. The latest version is four km south-east of Shaoxing.

The temple and mausoleum complex is composed of several parts – the huge 24-metre tall Main Hall, the Memorial Hall, the Meridian Gate *(wǔmén)* and Goulou Pavilion. A statue of Yu graces the Main Hall.

Lu Xun's Former Home
(lǔ xùn zǔjū) 鲁迅祖居
Lu Xun (1881-1936), one of China's best-known writers, was born in Shaoxing and lived here until he went abroad to study. He later returned to China, teaching at Zhongshan University in Canton in 1927 and hiding out in Shanghai's French Concession when the Kuomintang decided his books were too dangerous. His tomb is in Shanghai.

You can visit Lu Xun's former residence at 208 Lu Xun Lu. Nearby at 18 Duchangfangkou is the Lu Xun Memorial Hall *(lǔ xùn jìniàn guǎn)* and adjacent library *(lǔ xùn túshūguǎn)*.

Zhou Enlai's Former Home
(zhōu ēnlái zǔjū) 周恩来祖居
Shaoxing's other famous personage was Zhou Enlai, Mao's old comrade and Chiang Kaishek's nemesis. Zhou spent his childhood in Shaoxing before moving on to bigger and better things.

East Lake
(dōng hú) 东湖
If you've had enough of historical sites, you can do what the locals do and head out to East Lake, three km from the city centre. There is a temple *(dōng hú sì)* by the lake.

Shaoxing Winery
(shàoxīng niàng jiǔ chǎng) 绍兴酿酒厂
Shaoxing wine *(shàoxīng huādiāo jiǔ)* is the local firewater, brewed in Shaoxing and sold all over China. The Chinese are crazy about the stuff and it even gets exported, but foreigners give it mixed reviews. An imitation Shaoxing wine is brewed in Taiwan for the local market but hasn't taken the world by storm.

The winery is in the north-western part of town. Your only hope of getting inside is a CITS tour.

Places to Stay
The *Shaoxing Hotel* (☎ 535881; fax 538795) *(shàoxīng fàndiàn)* at 9 Huanshan Lu has doubles for Y100 and up.

The *Overseas Chinese Hotel* (☎ 532323) *(huáqiáo fàndiàn)* at 91-5 Shangda Lu is the main tourist place, with rooms starting at Y150. Some of the Chinese hotels are being renovated and may start accepting foreigners.

Getting There & Away
Hangzhou-Ningbo trains and buses all stop in Shaoxing. Most of the foreign tourists you see getting off here are Japanese.

AROUND SHAOXING
Considered one of Shaoxing's 'must see' spots, the **Lanting Pavilion** *(lánting)* doesn't see many foreign visitors. There are actually several pavilions here, set in pleasant gardens which are worth visiting if you don't mind the trek out there. The gardens were built in 1548.

The area is notable as a historical site, though the great historical event which occurred here was hardly momentous. Wang Xizhi (renowned Chinese calligrapher) met with some friends here in 353 AD. He later wrote a story about the get-together with his buddies. This earth-shaking event served as the excuse for building the pavilions and gardens – at least the park setting is nice.

Lanting Pavilion is 14 km south-west of the city – the long distance discourages visitors who aren't on a tour.

NINGBO
(níngbō) 宁波

Like Shaoxing, Ningbo rose to prominence in the 7th and 8th centuries as a trading port from which ships carrying Zhejiang's exports sailed to Japan and the Ryukyu Islands and along the Chinese coast.

By the 16th century the Portuguese had established themselves here, working as entrepreneurs in the trade between Japan and China, since the Chinese were forbidden to deal with the Japanese.

Although Ningbo was officially opened to Western traders after the first Opium War, its once-flourishing trade gradually declined as Shanghai boomed. By that time the Ningbo traders had taken their money to Shanghai and formed the basis of its wealthy Chinese business community.

Ningbo today is a bustling city of over 250,000 people, with fishing, textiles and food processing as its primary industries. Travellers come here mainly in transit on the way to nearby Putuoshan, Zhejiang's premier tourist attraction.

Information

There's a CTS (☎ 368690) office in the Ningbo Hotel at 65 Mayuan Lu. The Friendship Store is within spitting distance at 70 Mayuan Lu, adjacent to the Asia Gardens Hotel.

Places to Stay

The best budget place accepting foreigners is the *Yuehu Hotel* (☎ 363370) *(yuèhú fàndiàn)*, at 59 Yanhu Jie. The hotel is in an interesting neighbourhood along the shore of Moon Lake. Doubles cost Y60.

The *Ningbo Erqing Building* (☎ 302234) *(níngbō èrqīng dàshà)*, 2 Changchun Lu, is a good two-star hotel with rooms for around Y100. Minibuses to the passenger ferry terminal go right by the hotel, but it's within walking distance of the railway station.

The *Ningbo Hotel* (☎ 366334) *(níngbō fàndiàn)*, 65 Mayuan Lu, is two blocks north of the railway station and is a middle to top-range hotel, but there are some budget rooms in the old wings where foreigners have found rooms for less than Y100. Just next door is the more expensive *Asia Gardens Hotel* (☎ 366888; fax 362138) *(yàzhōu huáyuán bīnguǎn)*, 72 Mayuan Lu.

The *Huaqiao Hotel* (☎ 363175) *(huáqiáo fàndiàn)*, 130 Liuting Jie, is also within walking distance of the railway station. Expect to pay between Y150 and Y300.

Far to the east is the *Yonggang Hotel* (☎ 334621) *(yǒnggǎng fàndiàn)*, 105 Baizhang Donglu. Because of the inconvenient location, this place might have rooms when the other hotels are full. Expect to pay around Y180 or more.

Just opposite the railway station is Ningbo's fanciest accommodation, the 26-storey *Golden Dragon Hotel* (☎ 318888; fax 312288) *(jīnlóng fàndiàn)*. Singles/doubles cost Y170/195 and suites are Y420.

Getting There & Away

Air The CAAC ticket office (☎ 334202) is at 91 Xingning Lu. There are international flights to Hong Kong four times weekly. Domestic flights and fares from Ningbo are:

Destination	Fare	Destination	Fare
Beijing	Y670	Canton	Y580
Chengdu,		Harbin	Y1010
Guilin	Y660	Lanzhou	Y970
Qingdao	Y430	Shanghai	Y120
Shenyang	Y990	Shenzhen	Y680
Wuhan	Y370	Xiamen	Y410
Xi'an	Y750		

Bus There are two bus stations in town. Most long-distance buses depart from the south bus station *(qìchē nánzhàn)*, just one block from the railway station. From here you get buses to Wenzhou (nine hours), Hangzhou (six hours) and Shanghai. Tickets are fairly easy to obtain, though the buses are often crowded.

The north bus station *(qìchē běizhàn)* is important to travellers mainly because it offers an alternative route (besides direct

ZHEJIANG

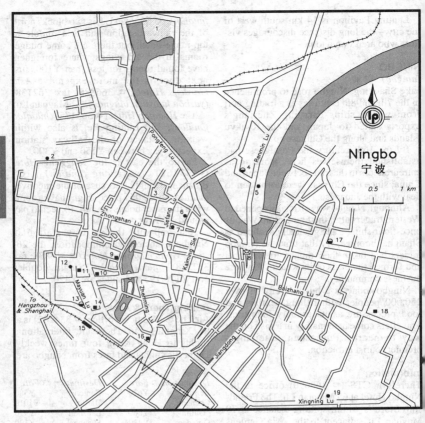

Ningbo 宁波

0   0.5   1 km

ferry) to Putuoshan (see the Putuoshan section for details).

Train The ticket office in the Ningbo railway station is a sight to behold – a sea of human bodies all pulling, pushing, punching, biting, scratching and perhaps killing in the hope of purchasing that magic piece of cardboard that gets one onto a train. Don't even think of diving into that slithering mass of arms and legs without your wallet buried under several layers of pickpocket-proof clothing. It's hard to estimate how long it would actually take to purchase a ticket – perhaps half

ZHEJIANG

■ PLACES TO STAY

9	Yuehu Hotel
10	Huaqiao Hotel
11	Ningbo & Asia Garden Hotels
14	Golden Dragon Hotel
16	Ningbo Erqing Building
18	Yonggang Hotel

OTHER

1	Zoo
2	Radio & TV Tower
3	Zhongshan Park
4	North Bus Station
5	Passenger Ferry Terminal
6	City Hall
7	PSB
8	Main Post Office
12	CTS
13	South Bus Station
15	Railway Station
17	East Bus Station
19	CAAC

■ PLACES TO STAY

9	月湖饭店
10	华侨饭店
11	宁波饭店/亚洲华园
14	金龙饭店
16	宁波二轻大厦
18	甬港饭店

OTHER

1	动物园
2	电台发射塔
3	中山公园
4	汽车北站
5	轮船码头
6	市政府
7	公安局外事科
8	邮电局
12	中国旅行社
13	汽车南站
15	火车站
17	汽车东站
19	民航售票处

a day. Ask the staff at your hotel if they can buy the ticket for you – most will do so with at least one day's notice. It's well worth the small service charge.

Train No	From	To	Depart	Arrive
366	Ningbo	Hangzhou	7.10 am	11.22 am
18	Ningbo	Hangzhou	10.25 am	1.59 pm
370	Ningbo	Hangzhou	5.30 pm	9.30 pm
452	Ningbo	Shanghai	4 am	6.58 pm
354	Ningbo	Shanghai	8.25 am	4.57 pm
352	Ningbo	Shanghai	1.32 pm	9.13 pm
8	Ningbo	Shanghai	10 pm	5 am
365	Hangzhou	Ningbo	noon	8.02 am
551	Hangzhou	Ningbo	9 pm	1.40 pm
369	Hangzhou	Ningbo	9.55 pm	5.35 pm
353	Shanghai	Ningbo	5 am	9.35 am
7	Shanghai	Ningbo	6 am	11.03 pm
351	Shanghai	Ningbo	4.16 pm	7.30 am
17	Shanghai	Ningbo	7.20 pm	3.20 pm

Boat Most useful departures are from the passenger ferry terminal *(lúnchuán mǎtóu)* near the north bus station. A few odd boats depart from Zhenhai wharf *(zhènhǎi mǎtóu)* which is 20 km (40 to 50 minutes by bus) north-east of Ningbo.

Many travellers are interested in the boat to Putuoshan (see the Putuoshan section for details). Also useful is the daily boat service between Ningbo and Shanghai (12 hours). There's a twice-monthly boat to Hong Kong (50 hours).

Getting Around
To/From the Airport Ningbo's Lishe Airport is a 20-minute ride from town. A taxi should cost around Y30 to Y40. The CAAC ticket office (☎ 334202) is at the airport rather than in the city, but hotels and CITS can obtain tickets.

Other The bus service is extensive; good bus maps are for sale at the railway station. Frequent minibuses (Y1) connect the railway station to the passenger ferry terminal and the north bus station. A taxi across town costs about Y10. Pedicabs are ubiquitous, but the drivers are cut-throat artists.

PUTUOSHAN
(pǔtuóshān) 普陀山

Putuoshan is the China we all dream about – temples, pagodas, arched bridges, narrow alleys, fishing boats, artisans and monks – the China we see on postcards and coffee-table books. Distinctly lacking are the noise, pollution, concrete-block housing developments, billboards, political slogans and teeming masses that characterise modern Chinese cities.

The island is small enough for you to reach everywhere on foot, though there are a few minibuses. The easternmost part of the island near Fanyin Cave is certainly worth your time – there are some small but fascinating temples along the route and stunning vistas of the sea. It's also worth investigating the tunnels on the south-western corner of the island near Guanyin Cave – apparently these once served a military purpose.

Because of its remoteness, Putuoshan sees relatively few foreign visitors, but Chinese tour groups come through here in large enough numbers to threaten the island's serenity. The best way to avoid the crowds is to visit during the off season, which basically means don't come during holidays or in the summer. It's also worth keeping in mind that accommodation on the island is limited, and visiting during peak times could mean an impromptu camping trip.

Places to Stay

There are at least a dozen reasonably high-standard hotels that are perfectly adequate, but only two accept foreigners. However, it seems that all the hotels accept Overseas Chinese.

The *Sanshengtang Hotel* (☎ 691277) *(sānshèng táng fàndiàn)* is a great place to stay. The outside of the building looks like an old monastery, but rooms are perfectly modern right down to the colour TV sets. Doubles with private bath cost Y70, or Y35 if you're a student with Chinese ID.

By contrast, the *Xilei Xiaozhuang Hotel* (☎ 61505; fax 227712) *(xīlěi xiǎozhuāng)* is an architectural horror. It's not that the hotel is ugly, but alongside Putuoshan's temples

and pagodas, it's about as inconspicuous as a nudist camp. The hotel 'proudly features' a Western restaurant, banquet hall, tourist souvenir junk shop, bar, business centre, beauty salon, meeting rooms (gives the cadres an excuse to come here at the State's expense) and billiard den. All these comforts cost a minimum of around Y190.

Places to Eat

Forget the expensive hotel food – Putuoshan offers a whole collection of unnamed hole-in-the-wall restaurants where a great meal costs Y10 or so. The biggest concentration

1	龙头墩
2	岗陀鹅耳枥
3	普济禅寺
4	慧佛洞
5	古天佛亭
6	海云亭
7	香财洞
8	善音洞
9	梵海亭
10	望雨禅寺
11	法枝庵
12	杨屏山庄
13	锦泉饭店
14	双乘庵
15	大物馆
16	文阳洞
17	朝人洞
18	仙宝塔
19	多厅/市场
20	餐济禅寺
21	普未小庄
22	息通庵
23	圆龟听法石
24	二天理局
25	西管圣堂饭店
26	三趣亭
27	正肯去观音院
28	不音跳
29	观天门
30	南岸牌坊
31	海船码头
32	
33	轮

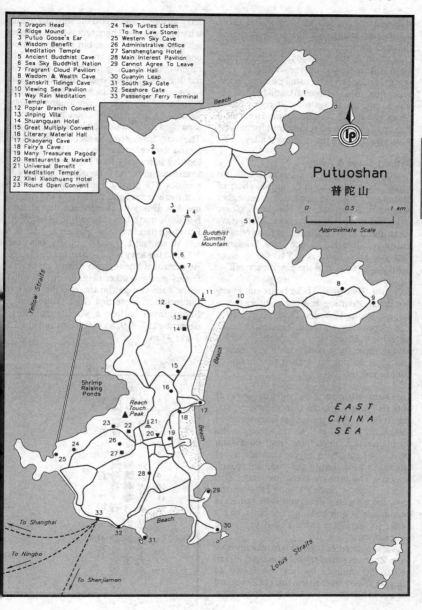

1 Dragon Head
2 Ridge Mound
3 Putuo Goose's Ear
4 Wisdom Benefit
  Meditation Temple
5 Ancient Buddhist Cave
6 Sea Sky Buddhist Nation
7 Fragrant Cloud Pavilion
8 Wisdom & Wealth Cave
9 Sanskrit Tidings Cave
10 Viewing Sea Pavilion
11 Way Rain Meditation
   Temple
12 Poplar Branch Convent
13 Jinping Villa
14 Shuangquan Hotel
15 Great Multiply Convent
16 Literary Material Hall
17 Chaoyang Cave
18 Fairy's Cave
19 Many Treasures Pagoda
20 Restaurants & Market
21 Universal Benefit
   Meditation Temple
22 Xilei Xiaozhuang Hotel
23 Round Open Convent
24 Two Turtles Listen
   To The Law Stone
25 Western Sky Cave
26 Administrative Office
27 Sanshengtang Hotel
28 Main Interest Pavilion
29 Cannot Agree To Leave
   Guanyin Hall
30 Guanyin Leap
31 South Sky Gate
32 Seashore Gate
33 Passenger Ferry Terminal

Putuoshan
普陀山

0   0.5   1 km
Approximate Scale

ZHEJIANG

Beach

Buddhist
Summit
Mountain

Yellow Straits

Shrimp
Raising
Ponds

Reach
Touch
Peak

EAST
CHINA
SEA

Beach

Beach

To Shanghai

To Ningbo

To Shenjiamen

Beach

Lotus Straits

of restaurants is along one narrow alley in the centre (see map), but there are scattered places elsewhere.

Seafood is the specialty, but be careful when you order as some types of fish are very expensive indeed. The usual chicken, pork, duck, rice, tofu (bean curd), stir-fried vegetables, etc, are all on offer at rock-bottom prices. Near the Sanshengtang Hotel is a line-up of old women selling fruit for half the price you'd pay in the restaurant alley.

Getting There & Away

Putuoshan being a small island with no airport, boats are the only option, short of swimming. You can approach from either Ningbo or Shanghai, but Ningbo is closer and offers more frequent service. Many travellers prefer to enter the island from Ningbo and exit to Shanghai, or vice versa. Whatever ship you take, there is a Y10 fee to enter Putuoshan, payable at the pier on arrival.

To/From Shanghai These boats run every two days, departing at 3 pm in either direction and taking 12 hours. Tickets cost Y20 to Y58 depending on class. The lower decks resemble a refugee ship – it's probably worth paying more for a comfortable seat even if you have to put up with a few hours of kungfu videos.

To/From Ningbo You've got several options. Simplest is the direct ferry, departing from Ningbo's passenger ferry terminal (lúnchuán mǎtóu) at 8.30 am. Going in the other direction, departures from Putuoshan are at 7.40 am (there might be an additional afternoon boat during the summer crunch season). The journey takes just under five hours. Tickets cost Y9 to Y21 – in the crowded economy deck you'll be buried in peanut shells, gob and cigarette butts, so it's better to spend the extra Y12 if you value your sanity.

A less convenient option is to take the boat from Zhenhai wharf (zhènhǎi mǎtóu) 20 km (40 to 50 minutes by bus) north-east of Ningbo. If you want to use this option, board the bus in Ningbo at 6.40 am at the passenger ferry terminal, and board the ship at Zhenhai wharf at 7.30 am. There seems to be no great advantage to this route, but it shaves about one hour off the time you spend at sea. You might consider going this way if tickets for the direct boat from Ningbo are all sold out.

Another option is to travel by bus from Ningbo to the port of Shenjiamen (shěnjiāmén) on the island of Zhoushan, which is separated from Putuoshan by a narrow strait. The bus from Ningbo gets to Zhoushan Island by vehicular ferry. The total bus journey is roughly four hours and the ferry from Shenjiamen to Putuoshan takes only 30 minutes. The great advantage of this route is that there are several departures throughout the day. Buses to Shenjiamen depart from Ningbo's north bus station (qìchē běizhàn). Ferries depart from Shenjiamen at 7.10, 8, 9 and 10 am and 1, 3 and 4 pm. The bus costs Y12 and the ferry is Y3 – there are no classes. Be careful at Shenjiamen – there are several ferries going to other neighbouring islands, so be sure you get on the one that goes to Putuoshan. The ferries from Putuoshan to Shenjiamen follow a similar schedule, departing at 7, 8, 9, and 10.30 am and at 1.15, 2 and 4 pm.

1	泗苏
2	轮船码头
3	凉帽礁
4	钓鱼奇石
5	白云奇石
6	月岙
7	鸟龟洞州
8	外樟塘鸟岙
9	满大洞塘鸟石
10	大外洞塘鸟岙
11	外小鸟基石塘
12	小寺岙
13	寺大岙
14	大渔湖映月
15	十里金沙
16	大王岩
17	小澎安
18	

ZHUJIAJIAN
(zhūjiājiān) 朱家尖

Just south of Putuoshan is a larger island called Zhujiajian. It has a collection of small temples and fine rural scenery, but it's certainly not the magic sort of place that Putuoshan is. Nevertheless, it might be worth a visit, particularly if you are travelling during the peak summer season when Putuoshan is packed out. Foreigners of any kind are a rarity in Zhujiajian – expect to be a tourist attraction for the locals.

To reach Zhujiajian, take a bus from Ningbo's north bus station to Shenjiamen (four hours, Y12), then a short ferry ride.

XIKOU
(xīkǒu) 西口

About 60 km south of Ningbo is the small town of Xikou, the home of Chiang Kaishek. It has, surprisingly, become a Chinese tourist destination. Not so surprisingly, many visitors from Taiwan also come here.

Despite local rumours that Chiang's body was secretly returned to China for burial at Xikou, his remains in fact reside in Taiwan

1 Sisu
2 Ferry Terminal
3 Cool Hat Pond
4 Catch Fish Reef
5 White Cloud Strange Stone
6 Moon Isle
7 Bird Turtle Cave
8 Camphor Tree Isle
9 Full Pond Bird Rock
10 Big Cave Isle
11 Outer Pond
12 Bird Stone Pond
13 Temple Foundation
14 Big Isle
15 Fishing Lake To Reflect the Moon
16 Ten Mile Golden Sand
17 King's Crag
18 Little Splash

Zhujiajian
朱家尖

0   1.5   3 km

at Cihu, south of Taipei. Chiang's relatives have persistently maintained that when the Kuomintang 'retakes the mainland', the body will be returned to its proper resting place at Xikou.

TIANTAISHAN
(tiāntái shān) 天台山

Tiantaishan is noted for its many Buddhist monasteries, which date back to the 6th century. While the mountain itself may not be considered sacred, it is very important as the home of the Tiantai Buddhist sect, which is heavily influenced by Taoism.

From Tiantai it's a 3½-km hike to the **Gouqingsi Monastery** at the foot of the mountain (you can stay overnight here). From the monastery a road leads 25 km to **Huadingfeng** (over 1100 metres high) where a small village has been built. On alternate days public buses run up to Huadingfeng. From here you can continue by foot for one or two km to the **Baijingtai Temple** on the summit of the mountain.

On the other days the bus goes to different parts of the mountain, passing **Shiliang Waterfall**. From the waterfall it's a good five to six-km walk along small paths to Huadingfeng.

Tiantaishan is in the east of Zhejiang. Buses link it with Hangzhou, Shaoxing, Ningbo and Wenzhou.

WENZHOU
(wēnzhōu) 温州

Wenzhou is an ancient city founded at the end of the 4th century. As a result of another treaty with Britain, its ocean port was opened to foreign trade in 1877, though no foreign settlement developed. The few foreigners who did come here were missionaries and trade officials – the latter mainly concerned with the once-profitable tea trade.

Wenzhou is once again prosperous, at

■ PLACES TO STAY

3 Dongou Hotel
9 Mochi Hotel
10 Xin'ou Hotel
11 Wenzhou Grand Hotel
13 Lucheng Hotel
14 Huaqiao Hotel
16 Jiushan Hotel
17 Xinghua Hotel
18 Ouchang Hotel
19 Shuixin Hotel
20 Jingshan Hotel

OTHER

1 Ferries to Jiangxin Island
2 Passenger Ferry Terminal
4 East Bus Station
5 Seamen's Club
6 Post & Telephone Office
7 City Hall
8 Renmin Stadium
12 South Bus Station
15 West Bus Station
21 CAAC

■ PLACES TO STAY

3 东瓯大厦
9 墨池饭店
10 新瓯饭店
11 温州大酒店
13 鹿城饭店
14 华侨饭店
16 九山饭店
17 杏花楼饭店
18 瓯昌饭店
19 水心饭店
20 景山宾馆

OTHER

1 麻林码头
2 温州港客运站
4 汽车东站
5 国际海员俱乐部
6 邮电局
7 市政府
8 人民广场
12 汽车南站
15 汽车西站
21 民航售票处

least by China's present standards. Given a boost by a new economic zone in the eastern suburbs, this small city is fast becoming one of Zhejiang's major business centres.

Despite the thriving businesses, Wenzhou has not been wrecked by new development. Noticeably absent (at least for now) are the concrete high-rises that have made many of China's cities resemble military bases. Wenzhou is a colourful town of old houses, narrow busy streets and an almost charming waterfront.

Wenzhou is worth your time if you're doing the coastal route. However, there is one major problem – a serious shortage of accommodation.

Orientation
The city is bounded on the north by the Ou River *(ōu jiāng)* and on the south by the much smaller Wenruitang River. The most interesting areas are along Ou River and major streets like Jiefang Beilu.

Things to See
The major scenic site is **Jiangxin Island** *(jiāngxīn dǎo* or *jiāngxīn gūyǔ)* in the middle of the Ou River. The island is a park dotted

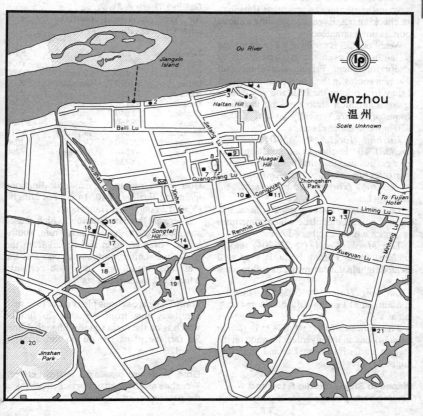

with pagodas, a lake and footbridges. You can easily reach Jiangxin Island by ferry from the pier *(mǎxíng mǎtóu)* just west of the passenger ferry terminal.

Another place worth seeing is **Jinshan Park** *(jǐngshān gōngyuán)* on the south-west perimeter of the city.

Places to Stay – bottom end

A real headache! Things may improve after some new construction, but at the time of writing, finding reasonably priced accommodation in Wenzhou was a major hassle. You can usually find a room if you don't mind paying around Y300 – otherwise, your best bet is to take a night bus so you arrive early in the morning when other travellers are checking out. Even then, finding a cheap room is not guaranteed.

Wenzhou PSB is aware of the problem and has authorised even the grottiest hotels to accept foreigners. Private individuals can also rent rooms in their homes to foreigners if they first inform the PSB and pay a tax – again, a situation almost unique in China. Room prices are typically around Y30 to Y50 at the cheaper places.

Jiushan Hotel (☎ 233901) *(jiǔshān fàndiàn)*, 101 Lucheng Lu, is just opposite the west bus station. Similar accommodation is on offer just next door at the *Xinghua Hotel* (☎ 224904) *(xìnghuā lóu fàndiàn)*, 83 Lucheng Lu.

The *Shuixin Hotel (shuǐxīn fàndiàn)*, Ge'an Lu, is a quiet place which sometimes has space when the others don't.

The *Mochi Hotel* (☎ 225304) *(mòchí fàndiàn)*, at 88 Jiefang Beilu, is very well located right in the centre and therefore often full.

Lucheng Hotel (☎ 333956) *(lùchéng fàndiàn)*, at 31 Liming Xilu, has rooms starting at Y27.

The *Fujian Hotel* (☎ 334953) *(fújiàn fàndiàn)* has an inconvenient location on the eastern end of Liming Lu and therefore might have rooms.

Places to Stay – middle & top end

Finding an expensive room is considerably easier. If you don't mind paying up to Y300, try one of the following:

Wenzhou Grand Hotel (☎ 235991) *(wēnzhōu dàjiǔdiàn)*, 61 Gongyuan Lu.

Huaqiao Hotel (☎ 223911) *(huáqiáo fàndiàn)*, 77 Xinhe Jie.

Dongou Hotel (☎ 227901) *(dōngoū dàshà)*, excellent location on the Ou River, doubles Y105 to Y200.

Ouchang Hotel (☎ 234931) *(oūchāng fàndiàn)*, 71 Xueshan Lu. This is the most expensive place in town, with rooms costing over Y200.

Jinshan Hotel (jīnshān bīnguǎn), very inconveniently located in Jinshan Park south-west of the city.

Xueshan Hotel (☎ 223981) *(xuěshān fàndiàn)*, also very inconveniently located in Jinshan Park and only reachable by taxi.

Getting There & Away

Air Wenzhou is well connected by air to other Chinese cities:

Destination	Fare	Destination	Fare
Beijing	Y790	Canton	Y630
Changsha	Y410	Chengdu	Y900
Dalian	Y1080	Hangzhou	Y200
Harbin	Y1290	Kunming	Y960
Lanzhou	Y1150	Nanjing	Y340
Qingdao	Y540	Shanghai	Y300
Shantou	Y360	Shenyang	Y1130
Shenzhen	Y540	Taiyuan	Y810
Tianjin	Y780	Ürümqi	Y2030
Wuhan	Y640	Xiamen	Y290
Xi'an	Y730		

Bus Buses run to all major destinations including Fuzhou (Y40, 14 hours), Ningbo (Y30, 12 hours) and Hangzhou.

There are three bus stations, which causes some confusion. As a general rule, southbound buses arrive at and depart from the south bus station, northbound buses at the west bus station and some (no certainty which) use the east bus station.

Train There are serious plans afoot to extend a railway line from Wenzhou to Jinhua, which is on the main Canton-Shanghai line. So far, the plans remain on the drawing board.

Boat There are passenger ferries between Wenzhou and Shanghai. For tickets, check at the passenger ferry terminal.

ZHEJIANG

Getting Around

The city has an extensive but crowded bus system that is difficult to cope with. Tiny Fiat taxis are used to manoeuvre Wenzhou's tight streets. The fare is Y7 between the east, west and south bus stations. Pedicab fares are from Y4 to Y10 for any destination in the city. The drivers seem to be a little bit less mercenary than their counterparts in neighbouring Fujian Province.

CHUN'AN COUNTY
(chún'ān xiàn) 淳安县

Chun'an County, in western Zhejiang, is known for its Lake of a Thousand Islands. Worth investigating would be a route from Hangzhou – you'd cross the lake by boat, and perhaps take a bus to Huangshan in Anhui Province.

Anhui 安徽

Population: 55 million
Capital: Hefei

The provincial borders of Anhui *(ānhuī)* were defined by the Qing government and, except for a few changes to the boundary with Jiangsu, have since remained pretty much the same. Northern Anhui forms part of the North China Plain where the Han Chinese settled in large numbers during the Han Dynasty. The Yangzi River cuts through the southern quarter of Anhui and the area south of the river was not actually settled until the 7th and 8th centuries.

Anhui's historical and tourist sights are mainly in the south, and hence more accessible from Hangzhou or Shanghai than from the provincial capital, Hefei. Most famous of the areas open to foreigners are the spectacular Huangshan (Yellow Mountains), in the far south of the province, and the nearby Jiuhuashan. The Yangzi River ports of Guichi and Wuhu are convenient jumping-off points for the Jiuhuashan and Huangshan mountains.

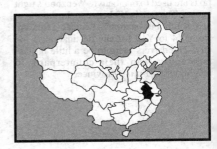

HEFEI
(héféi) 合肥

Hefei is the rather nondescript capital of Anhui Province. It's not an unpleasant place, though from a tourist's viewpoint there's not much going for it either. It was a quiet market town before1949, but expanded to become an industrial centre and now has a population of over 500,000. If you're stuck for something to see, you could go to the Mingjiao Temple, which has a large Yuan Dynasty cast-iron bell, or the Tomb of Bao Zheng, where there are pleasant gardens.

Places to Stay

You'll be hard pressed to find a room in Hefei for under Y120. If you're desperate, try the *Overseas Students' Dormitory at Anhui University* (☎ 254253) *(ānhuī dàxué liúxuéshēng sùshè)*, which can usually give you a bed in a triple with bath for around Y50. Take bus No 10 from the railway station.

Closest to the railway station at 68 Changjiang Lu is the *Overseas Chinese Hotel* (☎ 252221) *(huáqiáo fàndiàn)*, which charges Y140 for a double. Cheaper but further out is the *Meishan Hotel* on Meishan Lu, where doubles start at Y120. The best place in town is the *Anhui Hotel* (☎ 334559) *(ānhuī fàndiàn)* at No 2 Meishan Lu, in a high-rise block overlooking the park; it has doubles from Y260.

Getting There & Away

Useful flights from Hefei include Beijing (Y480, five weekly), Canton (Y540, daily) and Shanghai (Y200, six weekly), plus weekly charter flights to Hong Kong (US$185). You can get buses to Huangshan (Y28), Hangzhou (Y41) and Nanjing; there is also a daily sleeper-bus to Canton (Y197, 36 hours). Hefei is connected by direct trains to Ji'nan, Beijing and Zhengzhou, southwards to the port of Wuhu on the Yangzi, and westwards to Xi'an. CAAC is next door to the Anhui Hotel.

BOZHOU
(bózhōu) 亳州

Bozhou lies in Anhui's far north-west, near the border with Henan. It's not a particularly attractive place, but this small regional city

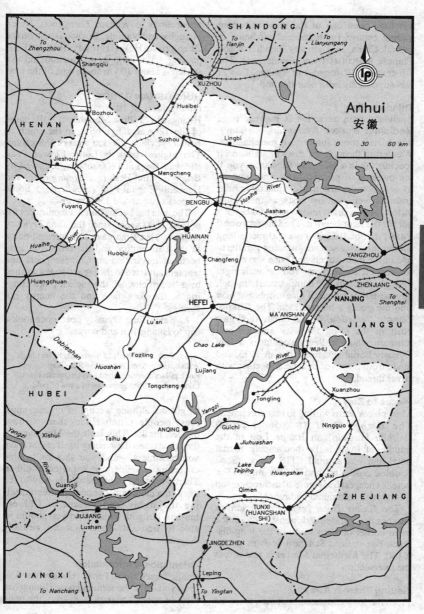

Anhui
安徽

has long been one of the most important trading centres for traditional medicine in central China, and attracts merchants and Chinese herbalists from a wide area. The 5th-century BC founder of Taoism, Lao Zi was supposedly born near Bozhou.

Things to See

Bozhou's main attraction is its very large **Medicinal Market** (*zhōngyào shìchǎng*), which has some interesting merchandise. Wandering through the rows of stalls, each specialising in a particular substance, you'll see mounds of pressed herbs and flowers, roots of obscure origin, rocks and other minerals, as well as wasp nests, animal skins, tortoise shells, dried insects and snakes – it's not for the faint-hearted. The **Underground Pass** (*yǐn bīn dìxiàdào*) is a 600-metre-long subterranean passageway running parallel to one of the main streets and once served as a secret route for soldiers. You can walk right through the narrow, damp tunnel, though anyone tall or prone to claustrophobia may find the going a bit confined. The **Guandi Temple** (*huāxìlóu*) has an ornate tiled gate built in the Qing Dynasty and a small museum whose collection includes a Han Dynasty burial suit unearthed in 1973, and made from pieces of jade held together with silver thread.

Places to Stay

Most places seem willing to take foreigners. The *Bozhou Hotel* (☎ (05681) 22048) (*bózhōu bīnguǎn*) on Banjie Lou in the middle of town is Bozhou's main tourist hotel and has a small CITS office. Good doubles cost Y60 and Y80 a night. The hotel's cheapest beds are Y20 in three-person dorms with communal bathroom.

The *Gujing Hotel* (*gǔjǐng dàjiǔdiàn*) is another new white-tiled monstrosity on the main corner one km south of the long-distance bus station. Standard doubles go for Y160. The Medicinal Market is just across the intersection.

Getting There & Away

From the long-distance bus station there are connections to Wuhan, Zhengzhou, Hefei, Shanghai and Nanjing. Bozhou is also on the Zhengzhou-Hefei railway line and all passing trains stop here. Bozhou railway station is about 10 km south-east of the city.

HUANGSHAN RANGE
(huángshān) 黄山

Huangshan (Yellow Mountains) is the name of the 72-peak range lying in the south of Anhui Province, 280 km west of Hangzhou. The highest peak is Lotus Flower Peak (*liánhuā fēng*) at 1800 metres, followed by Bright Summit Peak (*guāngmíng dǐng*) and Heavenly Capital Peak (*tiāndū fēng*). Some 30 peaks rise above 1500 metres.

The area has been a famous scenic spot for at least 1200 years, since the Tang Dynasty emperor Tian Biao gave it its present name in the 8th century, and the range has long been an inspiration to Chinese poets and painters attracted to the jagged peaks washed by a 'sea of clouds', the ancient pines clinging to the rock face and the nearby hot springs.

Li Bai, a Tang Dynasty poet, once took a trip to Huangshan and wrote:

Huangshan is hundreds of thousands of feet high,
With numerous soaring peaks lotus-like,
Rock pillars shooting up to kiss empyrean roses,
Like so many lilies grown amid a sea of gold.

Li got the altitude wrong, of course, since most people climb Huangshan without oxygen masks. This isn't the Himalayas – though at times the scenery itself might leave you breathless – and you shouldn't come expecting a 'wilderness experience' either. There are stone steps the whole way to the top of the mountain, concrete paths connecting the sights, and masses of Chinese tourists, but with some effort you should be able to find side-paths that are virtually deserted.

Orientation & Information

Public buses from Tunxi (Huangshan Shi) drop you off at the terminal near Huangshan Gate in upper Tangkou (*tāngkǒu*), the main village at the foot of the range. This is the most convenient place to pick up a mountain map, store your excess baggage or buy some snacks. Clustered around the hot springs 2½ km further up the valley is another resort built on both sides of the gushing Taohua (Peach Blossom) Stream, where you'll find tourist hotels, sanatoriums, a bank and a post office. The road ends halfway up the mountain at the lower cable-car station (890 metres above sea level) where the eastern steps begin. Other hotels are scattered on various trails around the summit area.

Getting Up & Down

There are three basic routes to the top: the short, hard way (eastern steps); the longer, harder way (western steps); and the very short, easy way (cable car). Regardless of how you get up Huangshan, you'll first have to pay the entrance fee (foreigners' price Y33, no concessions). This can be done at the start of the eastern steps near the lower cable-car station, or at the entrance gate in the forest where the western steps begin.

Cable Car The eight-minute cable-car ride is the least painful way up. For Y5 minibuses take you from Huangshan Gate to the lower cable-car station. From here the round-trip cable-car fare is Y34 for foreigners. There are *no* student concessions, *no* one-way tickets, nor are tickets sold at the cable car's upper station. The queues can get quite long, with waiting times often exceeding one hour.

On Foot There are two basic walking routes up Huangshan: the *western steps* from above the hot springs, and the *eastern steps* which lead up below the cable-car line.

Eastern Steps The 7½-km eastern-steps route can be climbed comfortably in about three hours. It can be a killer if you push yourself too hard, but it's definitely easier than going up the western steps.

Purists can extend the eastern-steps climb by several hours by setting out from Huangshan Gate, where a stepped path crosses the road at several points before con-

necting with the main eastern-steps trail at the lower cable-car station. If you have enough time, the recommended route is a 10-hour circuit hike taking the eastern steps to the top, then descending back to the hot springs resort via the western steps. While Huangshan's cut-stone stairways undoubtedly make climbing easier, the constant even spacing between steps seems to tire the leg muscles more quickly.

Western Steps The 15-km western-steps route has some of Huangshan's most spectacular scenery, following a precarious route hewn out of the sheer rock cliffs. It is, however, double the length and at least twice as strenuous as the eastern steps, and much easier to enjoy if you're clambering down rather than gasping your way up. The western steps descent begins at the Flying Rock (*fēilái shí*), a rectangular boulder perched on an outcrop half an hour from the Beihai Hotel and goes over Bright Top Peak (*guāngmíng dǐng*), where there is an odd-shaped weather station and hotel.

Not to be missed on the western steps is the exhilaratingly steep and exposed stairway to Heavenly Capital Peak, directly adjacent to the Jade Screen Tower Hotel. Young lovers bring locks engraved with their names up here and fix them to the chain railings, symbolising that they're 'locked' together. The western path continues down past the Mid-Level Temple (*bànshān sì*) back to the hot springs resort.

Guides & Porters

If you think you're having a hard time, spare a thought for the daily army of lean and agile porters lugging someone else's cargo of 50 kg or more up the mountain – crates of drink bottles, baskets of food, even the odd flabby tourist.

Guides are not really necessary since the mountain paths are very easy to follow and you can't get lost for long. CITS can organise an English-speaking guide for around Y200 per day. Private individuals sometimes offer their services as guides too – but it's unlikely you'll find one who speaks enough English.

ANHUI

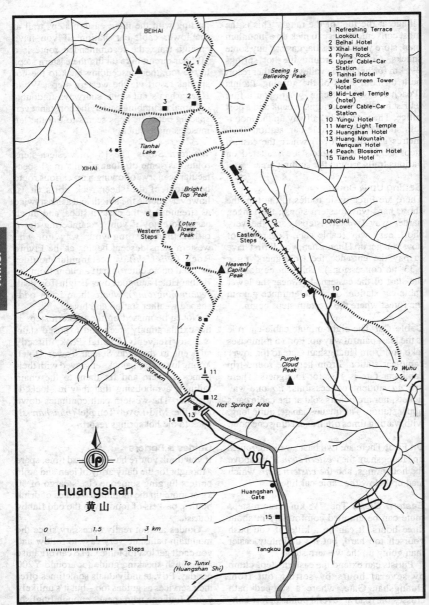

BEIHAI

Seeing is
Believing Peak

1 Refreshing Terrace
  Lookout
2 Beihai Hotel
3 Xihai Hotel
4 Flying Rock
5 Upper Cable-Car
  Station
6 Tianhai Hotel
7 Jade Screen Tower
  Hotel
8 Mid-Level Temple
  (hotel)
9 Lower Cable-Car
  Station
10 Yungu Hotel
11 Mercy Light Temple
12 Huangshan Hotel
13 Huang Mountain
   Wenquan Hotel
14 Peach Blossom Hotel
15 Tiandu Hotel

Tianhai Lake

XIHAI

Bright
Top Peak

DONGHAI

Lotus
Flower
Peak

Western
Steps

Cable Car

Eastern
Steps

Heavenly
Capital
Peak

Taohua Stream

Purple
Cloud
Peak

To Wuhu

Hot Springs Area

ANHUI

Huangshan
黄山

0   1.5   3 km

▪▪▪▪▪▪▪▪▪ = Steps

LP

Huangshan
Gate

Tangkou

To Tunxi
(Huangshan Shi)

1	清凉台
2	北海宾馆
3	西海宾馆
4	飞来石
5	白岭索道站
6	天海宾馆
7	玉屏宾馆
8	半山寺
9	云谷寺索道站
10	云谷山庄
11	慈光阁
12	黄山宾馆
13	黄山温泉大酒店
14	桃源宾馆
15	天都山庄

If you're feeling really decadent, you can make your ascent in a makeshift sedan chair carried on bamboo poles by two porters. Again, CITS can arrange this for a set fee of around Y400 (up and down) – including insurance in case they drop you – or you can bargain with the porters on the mountain for a considerably lower price. The porters usually carry passengers up one day and bring them down the next.

On the Summit

Paved trails lead to lookout points around Huangshan's interesting summit area. Since you're taking the trouble and expense to get up here, you may as well stay a night or two.

One of the highlights of climbing Huangshan is watching sunrise over the Beihai, a 'sea' of low cloud blanketing the valley to the north with 'island' peaks protruding from it. Every morning before daybreak the Chinese throng the Fresh Breeze Terrace (five minutes from the Beihai Hotel) to view the natural spectacle. Hotels supply thick padded jackets for the occasion. It's communal sightseeing at its best and the noise generated by several hundred Chinese tourists is almost as incredible as the sunrise itself! Fortunately, most of them hurry back to eat

breakfast shortly afterwards, leaving you to enjoy the mountains in peace.

Places to Stay & Eat

There are five locations with hotels and restaurants in the Huangshan area. Prices and availability of beds can vary a lot according to seasonal demand.

Tangkou (*tāngkŏu*) You'll find the cheapest and most accessible hotels in Tangkou.

The *Tiandu Hotel* (☎ (0559) 562160) (*tiāndū shānzhuāng*), 700 metres downhill from Huangshan Gate charges Y40 for a bed in a three-person room, and Y160 for an air-con double. It's the closest place to the bus terminal.

The *Tangkou Hotel* (☎ (0559) 562400) (*tāngkŏu bīnguăn*) is at the bottom end of the village, 200 metres off the main road. If you intend staying in Tangkou you can ask to be dropped off here rather than at the bus terminal a few km uphill at Huangshan Gate. The place has improved greatly since it was renovated not so long ago, and now offers the best value in town. Simple doubles go for Y40 and nicer doubles with private bath for Y120. There's hot water in the morning and at night.

Further along the road near the stream is the *Free and Unfettered Hotel* (☎ (0559) 562571) (*xiāoyáo bīnguăn*). Their cheapest doubles are Y35, or Y100 for something rather better. The friendly staff know a bit of English.

There's a row of good cheap restaurants on the main road just below the Tiandu Hotel. In Tangkou proper you'll find several small, private restaurants on the cobblestone street next to the stream, and others scattered through the village. Some local specialties are roast mountain frogs and wild mushrooms, as well as locally grown Ma Fou green tea.

Hot Springs Around the hot springs resort 2½ km further uphill are several more hotels.

Beside the hot springs bathhouse is the *Huangshan Hotel* (☎ (0559) 562320) (*huángshān bīnguǎn*), which has beds in basic quads for Y20 and beds in doubles for Y30. For a wash you'll have to go next door.

Just across the bridge is the brand new *Huang Mountain Wenquan Hotel* (☎ (0559) 562788) (*huángshān wénquán dàjiǔdiàn*). For Y120 all you get here is a rather dreary double on the hotel's lowest level, but their rooms for Y280 are much better.

Higher up the hillside is the newly renovated *Peach Blossom Hotel* (☎ (0559) 562666) (*táoyuán bīnguǎn*), with doubles for US$60 and US$80, and beds in three-person rooms for US$10. It's a big place with a CITS office and a bank; the staff can speak pretty good English.

The Huang Mountain and the Peach Blossom each have two restaurants. Cheaper meals are not as easy to find, but there are a few simple restaurants around the hot springs, and noodle vendors on the street in the mornings and evenings.

Lower Cable-Car Station There is one hotel here – the *Yungu Hotel* (☎ (0559) 562444) (*yúngǔ shānzhuāng*), down the steps from the car park in front of the station. It has doubles for Y180. This location has little to recommend it, unless you've climbed from Tangkou in the afternoon and need a night's sleep before tackling the rest of the steps.

Summit Area There are two tourist hotels within easy walking distance of the upper cable-car station. During the tourist season, especially, it's advisable to reserve a room as these hotels are very popular with foreign and Chinese tourists alike. Most of the other places on the mountain are cheaper and don't have any showering facilities to speak of.

The *Beihai Hotel* (☎ (0559) 562555) (*běihǎi bīnguǎn*) has comfortable and warm doubles with bath for Y200. Rooms in the tacky barracks-style accommodation out the front cost Y40.

The joint-venture *Xihai Hotel* (☎ (0559) 262132/3) (*xīhǎi bīnguǎn*), further west along the trail is a real 'mountain hotel'

designed by Swedish architects. Doubles start at US$100. All rooms have heating and 24-hour hot water.

The Xihai and the Beihai both have a bar and full-service restaurants serving Western and Chinese food but, inconveniently, are open only for a few hours around lunch and dinner time. Cheaper meals are available from stalls and simple restaurants nearby.

Western Steps Highest up is the *Tianhai Hotel (tiānhǎi bīnguǎn)* just down from Bright Top Peak, with dorm beds from Y25 and doubles for Y60.

Further down the mountain at a spectacular 1660-metre-high lookout near Heavenly Capital Peak is the *Jade Screen Tower Hotel* (☎ (0559) 562540) (*yùpínglóu bīnguǎn*). The rates and conditions reflect this hotel's relative inaccessibility: a simple double is Y150, and washing arrangements are basic indeed. The next place you'll come to is the small *Mid-Level Temple (bànshān sì)* at 1340 metres. It only has a small dorm, and is best considered as emergency accommodation.

Considering its location, the Jade Screen Tower Hotel has a very cheap dining hall beside the tiny courtyard, and a better restaurant upstairs. The Mid-Level Temple has a teahouse serving simpler meals and refreshments.

Getting There & Away

Air The airport serving Huangshan is at Tunxi (Huangshan Shi). CAAC has flights to Shanghai (four a week), Canton (six a week), Shenzhen (three a week) Beijing (a four week), Hefei (three a week), Guilin (twice weekly) and Kunming (twice weekly). There are also seasonal charter flights to Tunxi from Hong Kong.

Bus Buses from Tunxi (Huangshan Shi) cost Y8 and take 2½ hours to reach Huangshan Gate. In summer other direct buses come from Hefei (Y28, eight hours), Shanghai (Y34, 10 hours), Hangzhou (Y16), Suzhou and Jingdezhen. There are also buses from the Yangzi River ports of Wuhu and Guichi.

Train Trains from Hefei and Nanjing via Wuhu pass through Tunxi (Huangshan Shi). For connections from southern destinations first go to Yingtan (Jiangxi Province) and change trains there.

TUNXI (HUANGSHAN SHI)
(túnxī (huángshān shì)) 屯溪 （黄山市）
The old trading town of Tunxi (Huangshan Shi) is roughly 80 km south-east by road from Huangshan. As indicated by its rechristened Chinese name (meaning 'Huangshan City') Tunxi is significant to travellers only as a jumping-off point for the Huangshan area.

Regular buses run between Tunxi and Tangkou in the Huangshan mountains. There are other scheduled bus services to Shanghai, Hangzhou, Hefei, Nanjing and Jingdezhen, and direct trains to Hefei, Yingtan (via Jingdezhen) and Wuhu. The local airport receives many weekly flights from Beijing, Canton and Shanghai as well as other regional Chinese cities.

JIUHUASHAN
(jiǔhuá shān) 九华山
It might not be quite as spectacular, but one way to escape the trampling hordes of Huangshan is to head north-west to Jiuhuashan.

The Chinese poet Li Bai, who for a time lived in seclusion on Jiuhuashan, wrote:

Looking far ahead from Jiujiang,
I saw the peaks of Mount Jiuhua
Emerging from the Heavenly River
Like nine beautiful lotus flowers.

Jiuhuashan is regarded as one of China's four sacred Buddhist mountains (together with Pu Tuo in Zhejiang, Emei in Sichuan and Wutai in Shanxi). Third-century Taoist monks had been the first to build thatched temples at Jiuhuashan, but with the rise of Buddhism these were gradually replaced by stone monasteries. Jiuhuashan owes its importance to

a Korean Buddhist disciple, Kim Kiao Kak, who arrived in 720 and founded a worshipping place for Ksitigarbha, the guardian of the earth. Annual festivities are held on the anniversary of Kim's death (the 30th day of the 7th lunar month) when pilgrims flock to Jiuhuashan. In its heyday during the Tang Dynasty as many as 5000 monks and nuns worshipped at Jiuhuashan, living in more than 300 monasteries. Today only some 70 temples and monasteries survive in the hills around Jiuhuashan.

Orientation & Information
Jiuhua village lies at 600 metres, about halfway up the mountain (or, as the locals say, at roughly navel-height in a giant buddha's pot-belly). The bus stops just below the main gate where you must pay an entrance fee to Jiuhuashan (foreigners Y16, or Y8 with student card). From here Jiuhua Jie, the narrow main street, leads up past cheap restaurants, souvenir stalls and hotels. The village square is built around a large pond along a side street off to the right. Several 'pictorial' maps in Chinese showing mountain paths can be bought in the village.

Places to Stay
At the bottom of the village is the beautiful, palace-style *Qiyuan Monastery (qǐyuán sì)* which has beds in large, very basic dormitories for Y7. Directly across the square from the monastery is the *Julong Hotel* (☎ (05630) 811368) *(jùlóng bīnguǎn)*, which looks better from the outside than it really is. A standard double with bathroom costs Y100. Much better value is the *Bell Tower Hotel* (☎ 05630) 811251) *(jiǔhuáshān zhōnglóu fàndiàn)* at the top of the main street, where heated doubles cost Y60 with private bathroom and colour TV. The hotel also has an annexe next door with beds for Y15 in spartan two-person rooms.

Getting There & Away
In summer there are direct buses to Jiuhuashan from Huangshan via Qingyang (Y12, six hours including a ferry across the large Taiping Reservoir), Shanghai and

ANHUI

Nanjing. Outside the tourist season, however, you'll probably have to change in Qingyang, from where there are roughly seven buses daily to Jiuhuashan all year round.

WUHU & GUICHI
(wŭhú, guìchí) 芜湖 , 和贵池
Wuhu is a Yangzi River port and a useful railway junction. Railway lines branch off south to Tunxi, east to Shanghai via Nanjing and, from the northern bank of the river, another line heads north to Hefei. There are also buses to Huangshan and Jiuhuashan from Wuhu. To the west of Wuhu is the Yangzi port of Guichi, which has buses to Huangshan and Jiuhuashan.

Shanghai 上海

Population: 12 million

Shanghai *(shànghǎi)*: Paris of the East, Whore of China, Queen of the Orient; city of bums, adventurers, pimps, swindlers, gamblers, sailors, socialites, dandies, drug runners. Humiliation, indignation, starvation, back-alley corpses, coolies, rickshaw drivers, deformed beggars, child prostitutes, scab-ridden infants, student activists, strikers, intellectuals, Communists, rebels, foreign armies supporting foreign business interests. Trendsetter, snob, leader, industrial muscle, birthplace of the revolution (the label that keeps the Beijing bureaucrats awake at night)...a hybrid of Paris and New York in the 1930s with millions trampling the streets where the millionaires once trod...one way or another Shanghai has permeated the Western consciousness.

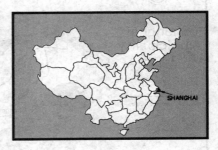

History

To seize the tail of this leviathan you have to go back to the 1840s. At that time Shanghai (the name means 'by the sea') was a prosperous weaving and fishing town – but not an important one – and was walled to keep out the Japanese pirates that roamed the China coast. Shanghai, at the gateway to the Yangzi, was in an ideal position to develop as a trading port. In 1842, after the first Opium War, the British forcibly opened up a concession there, and the French followed in 1847. An International Settlement was established in 1863 and a Japanese enclave in 1895, all completely autonomous and immune from Chinese law.

Spurred on by massive foreign investment, coupled with an inexhaustible supply of cheap Chinese labour, Shanghai quickly became a booming port and industrial city. In the mid-18th century it had a population of a mere 50,000 – by 1900 it had reached its first million, partly caused by the flood of refugees who came here when the Taiping rebels took Nanjing in 1853. The foreign population grew from a few thousand adventurers in the 1860s to some 60,000 by the 1930s.

The International Settlement had the tallest buildings in Asia in the 1930s, the most spacious cinemas, and more motor vehicles than any eastern metropolis or in all other Chinese cities combined. Powerful foreign financial houses had set up here: the Hong Kong & Shanghai Banking Corporation; the Chartered Bank of India, Australia & China; and the National City and Chase Manhattan banks of New York. There were the blue-blood British firms of Jardine & Matheson, Sassoons and others that got their start with the opium trade, and newer but aggressive American firms that had *everything* for sale.

Guarding it all were the American, French and Italian marines, British Tommies and Japanese Bluejackets. Foreign ships and submarines patrolled the Yangzi and Huangpu rivers and the coasts of China. They maintained the biggest single foreign investment anywhere in the world – the British alone had £400 million sunk into the place. After Chiang Kaishek's coup against the Communists in 1927, the Kuomintang cooperated closely with the foreign police and with Chinese and foreign factory owners to suppress labour unrest. The Settlement police, run by the British, arrested Chinese labour leaders and handed them over to the

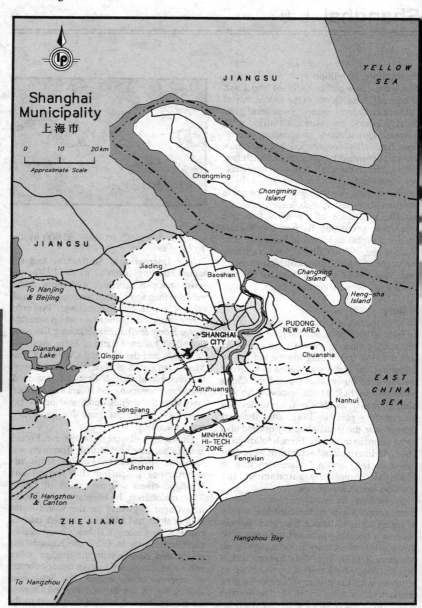

SHANGHAI

Shanghai Municipality
上海市

0   10   20 km
Approximate Scale

YELLOW SEA

JIANGSU

JIANGSU

To Nanjing
& Beijing

Chongming

Chongming
Island

Changxing
Island

Heng-sha
Island

Jiading

Baoshan

SHANGHAI
CITY

PUDONG
NEW AREA

Chuansha

Dianshan
Lake

Qingpu

EAST
CHINA
SEA

Xinzhuang

Songjiang

Nanhui

MINHANG
HI-TECH
ZONE

Jinshan

Fengxian

To Hangzhou
& Canton

ZHEJIANG

Hangzhou Bay

To Hangzhou

Kuomintang for imprisonment or execution, and the Shanghai gangs were repeatedly called in to 'mediate' disputes inside the Settlement.

If you were rich you could get anything in the Shanghai of the 1920s and 1930s: dance halls, opium dens, gambling halls, flashing lights and great restaurants, plus the dimmed lights of the brothels and your choice of 30,000 prostitutes. Supporting it all were the Chinese, who worked as beasts of burden and provided the muscle in Shanghai's port and factories. Shanghai was the largest manufacturing city in Asia, with more than 200,000 workers employed in the factories. American journalist Edgar Snow, who came to Shanghai in the late 1920s, wrote of the hundreds of factories where little boy and girl slave workers laboured 12 or 13 hours a day, and of little girls in silk filature factories – all of them, like most contract labour in Shanghai, literally sold into these jobs as virtual slaves for four or five years – unable to leave the heavily guarded, high-walled premises day or night without special permission.

When the Communists came to power in 1949 one of the first things they wanted to do was turn Shanghai into a showcase of how Communism really worked. And to some extent they were successful – the eradication of the slums, the rehabilitation of the city's hundreds of thousands of opium addicts, and the elimination of child and slave labour were all staggering achievements. Unfortunately, they also eliminated most of the city's businesses, causing the economy to stagnate for some 40 years.

Climate

The best times to visit Shanghai are spring and autumn. In winter, temperatures can drop well below freezing, with a blanket of drizzle. Summers are hot and humid with temperatures as high as 40°C. So, in short, you'll need silk longjohns and down jackets for winter, an ice block for each armpit in summer – and an umbrella won't go astray in either season.

Government

Shanghai is politically one of the most important centres in China – and one of the political flashpoints. The meeting which founded the Chinese Communist Party (CCP) was held here back in 1921. Shanghai was an important centre of early Communist activity when the Party was still concentrating on organising urban workers. Mao also cast the first stone of the Cultural Revolution in Shanghai, by publishing in the city newspapers a piece of political rhetoric he had been unable to get published in Beijing.

Most extraordinary, during the Cultural Revolution a People's Commune was set up in Shanghai, modelled on the Paris Commune of the 19th century. (The Paris Commune was set up in 1871 and controlled Paris for two months. It planned to introduce socialist reforms such as turning over management of factories to the workers' associations.) The Shanghai Commune lasted just three weeks before Mao ordered the Army to put an end to it, and thus China was finished with this form of socialism for a long time.

The so-called 'Gang of Four' had their power base in Shanghai. The campaign to criticise Confucius and Mengzi (Mencius) was started here in 1969, before it became nationwide in 1973 and was linked to Lin Biao. Shanghai's history as the most radical city in China, the supporter of dogmatic Maoism, one of the focuses of the Cultural Revolution, and the power base of Mao's wife, is rather strange when you consider that the city is now, perhaps with the exceptions of Canton and Shenzhen, the most capitalist and the most consumer-oriented in China. If you can work out how a whole city can change its loyalty from orthodox Maoism to *laissez faire* capitalism then you have probably gone a long way to understanding what makes the Chinese world tick.

Economy

Overpopulation and unemployment are severe problems in Shanghai. Some economists claim that China's switch to light industry over the last 10 years or so is due to the fact that it can absorb up to three times the number of workers that heavy industry can, and at the same time increase the general standard of living. People are so numerous in Shanghai that the weekly day off is staggered; shipyard workers don't rub shoulders with textile workers on the streets. Overcrowded as it is, Shanghai still enjoys a high living standard in comparison with the rest of China, at least in terms of wages, consumer goods and educational opportunities.

When the Communists came to power they set about downplaying Shanghai's economic role. Besides closing brothels and opium dens, priority in industrial development (under the first Five-Year Plan launched in 1953) was given to the strategically less vulnerable and poorer cities and towns of the interior – Shanghai's vital economic contacts with the outside world shrank drastically. In 1956 the coastal regions were again reaffirmed as logical places for an industrial base, possibly because of the ease of importing and exporting goods by sea. That resulted in another (but smaller) boom for Shanghai, and in the late 1950s the city's limits were extended to encompass the surrounding counties, giving the city more control over its supply of food and raw materials. In 1963 Zhou Enlai put his personal seal of approval on the city, and output for certain facets of its economy was given priority.

The city drifted along economically until 1990, with the announcement of massive plans to develop Pudong on the east side of the Huangpu River. Foreign companies are taking the plans seriously – the city's hotels are overflowing with foreign financiers working on one project or another. Along with Canton and Shenzhen, Shanghai is one of China's hottest economic prospects. New skyscrapers seem to pop up overnight, bridges and tunnels are being built, factories belch out smoke and finished goods for exports. Shanghai accounts for over 15% of China's total industrial output and is a major source of technical expertise.

Population

Shanghai has a population of at least 12 million people – but that figure is deceptive since it takes into account the whole municipal area of 6100 sq km. Nevertheless, the central core of some 220 sq km has over 6½ million people, which must rate as one of the highest population densities in China, if not the world. In 1955 a plan was announced to reduce the city's population by one million. Some estimates put the number of people moved out of Shanghai at two million since 1949; perhaps three-quarters of these were young people 'sent down' to the countryside during the Cultural Revolution. Whatever the actual figure, Chinese officials will tell you that the professionals and technicians were 'persuaded' to go to the interior to start new schools, colleges and hospitals. Meanwhile, many of the 'exiled' young people who try to creep back into the city are nabbed and shipped back out again.

Orientation

Shanghai municipality covers a huge area, but the city proper is a more modest size. Within the municipality is the island of Chongming, part of the Yangzi River delta – worth a footnote because it's the second-

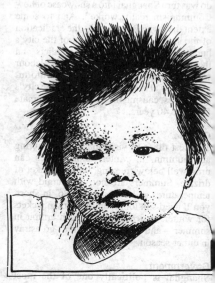

largest island in China (or third if you recognise China's claim to Taiwan).

The city is divided into a number of districts. The central area is known as Huangpu, which spans both sides of the Huangpu River. Other notable neighbourhoods include Hongkou and Yangpu in the north-east, Zhabei and Putuo in the north-west, Jing'an and Changming in the west, Luwan, Nanshi and Xuhui in the south. To the far north is Baoshan, a major port area on the Yangzi River. To the east is the Pudong New Area, the site of Shanghai's major new development scheme.

Street names are given in pinyin, which makes navigating easy, and many of the streets are named after cities and provinces. In the central district (around Nanjing Lu) the provincial names run north-south, and the city names run east-west. Some roads are split by compass points, such as Sichuan Nanlu (Sichuan South Rd) and Sichuan Beilu (Sichuan North Rd). Some of the monstrously long roads are split by sectors, such as Zhongshan Dong Erlu and Zhongshan Dong Yilu, which mean Zhongshan East 2nd Rd and Zhongshan East 1st Rd, respectively – simple!

There are four main areas of interest in the city: the Bund from Suzhou Creek to the Shanghai Harbour Passenger Terminal (Shiliupu wharf); Nanjing Donglu (a very colourful neighbourhood); Frenchtown, which includes Huaihai Zhonglu and Ruijin Lu (an even more colourful neighbourhood); and the Jade Buddha Temple and the side trip along Suzhou Creek.

Information

CITS The headquarters of CITS (☎ 3217200) is at 33 Zhongshan Dong 1-Lu (on the Bund), but more useful is the CITS ticket office (☎ 3234067) at 66 Nanjing Donglu (next to the Peace Hotel). Trains, planes and boats can be booked here with several days' advance notice. For last-minute tickets, go directly to CAAC, the railway station or harbour (whichever is relevant). CITS will book tickets for the Trans-Siberian to Europe, but they often want a month's notice.

CITS has astronomically priced excursions to Suzhou, Wuxi and beyond, but it does more economical city tours. It handles tickets for the Huangpu River trip, but these will be cheaper at the source, which is virtually across the road.

The staff of Shanghai CITS are hopelessly overworked – you'll just have to be patient when getting information from them. Some useful info, such as train timetables to Hangzhou, is laid out on the counter under glass and behind three ranks of customers. The office is open on Saturday and for half a day on Sunday.

PSB The office (☎ 3215380) is at 210 Hankou Lu, one block north of Fuzhou Lu, near the corner with Henan Zhonglu.

Money There are money-changing counters on the premises of almost every hotel, even cheapie ones like the Pujiang and the Haijia. Credit cards are more readily accepted in Shanghai than in other parts of China.

Most tourist hotels will accept the main ones like Visa, American Express, Master Card, Diners, and JCB, as will banks and friendship stores (and related tourist outlets like the Antique & Curio Store). The enormous Bank of China right next to the Peace Hotel is hopelessly crowded, but worth a peak inside for its ornate interior.

Post & Telecommunications The larger tourist hotels have post offices from where you can mail letters and small packages.

The express mail service and poste restante is at 276 Bei Suzhou Lu. Letters to London take just two days – or so they advertise.

The international post and telecommunications office is at the corner of Sichuan Beilu and Bei Suzhou Lu. The section for international parcels is in the same building but around the corner at 395 Tiantong Lu.

Express parcel and document service is available from several foreign carriers. You can contact DHL (☎ 3279596), UPS (☎ 3213862), Federal Express (☎ 4311627) or TNT Skypak (☎ 5371642).

Long-distance calls can be placed from

SHANGHAI

hotel rooms and do not take long to get through. The international telegraph office, from which you can make long-distance phone calls and send international telexes and telegrams, is on Nanjing Donglu next to the Peace Hotel.

Foreign Consulates There are several in Shanghai. If you're doing the Trans-Siberian journey and have booked a definite departure date, it's much better to get your Russian visa here than face the horrible queues at the Russian embassy in Beijing.

Australia
  17 Fuxing Xilu (☎ 4334604; fax 4331732)
Czech & Slovak
  5th floor, New Town Mansion, 55 Loushanguan Lu, Hongqiao (☎ 2757203; fax 2759033)
France
  Room 2008, Ruijin Building, 205 Maoming Nanlu (☎ 4336273; fax 4336286)
Germany
  181 Yongfu Lu (☎ 4336951; fax 4714448)
Hungary
  Room 1810, Union Building, 100 Yan'an Donglu (☎ 3261815; fax 3202855)
Italy
  127 Wuyi Lu (☎ 2524373)
Japan
  1517 Huaihai Zhonglu (☎ 4336639; fax 4331008)
Poland
  618 Jianguo Xilu (☎ 4339288)
Russia
  20 Huangpu Lu (☎ 3242682; fax 3069982)
Singapore
  400 Wulumuqi Zhonglu (☎ 4331362; fax 4334150)
UK
  244 Yongfu Lu (☎ 4330508; fax 4333115)
USA
  1469 Huaihai Zhonglu (☎ 4336880; fax 4314122)

Bookshops Back in 1949 the bookshops removed the porn from the shelves and set up displays of Marx and company overnight. During the Cultural Revolution, it was mostly eulogies to Mao & Co.

The selection has improved in the last few years, but Shanghai is still light years behind Hong Kong. Nevertheless, this is one place where you can replenish your stash – there are numerous foreign-language outlets in Shanghai if you take the tourist hotel bookshops into account. The main Foreign Languages Bookstore is at 390 Fuzhou Lu. Next door is a stationery shop, if you need writing supplies as well. Of special interest is the branch at 201 Shandong Zhonglu, which sells old books in foreign languages. At 424 Fuzhou Lu is the Classics Bookshop. There are other specialist bookshops around Shanghai, if you can read Chinese. Fuzhou Lu is and always has been the bookshop hunting ground.

A small range of foreign newspapers and magazines is available from the larger tourist hotels (eg Park, Jinjiang, Sheraton Huating) and some shops. Publications include the *Wall Street Journal, International Herald Tribune, Asiaweek, The Economist, Time* and *Newsweek.* The latter two make good gifts for Chinese friends.

The Xinhua Bookstore at 345 Nanjing Donglu has mostly Chinese books but it's also the place to pick up the big wall maps of Shanghai, the People's Republic and the world (as the Chinese see it). The biggest selection of Chinese periodicals is found at 16 Sichuan Beilu – and while the lingo might not make these seem worth browsing through, there are oddities, such as the comic book rental section, to dive into.

Get a copy of Pan Ling's *In Search of Old Shanghai* (Joint Publishing Company, Hong Kong, 1982) for a rundown on who was who and what was what back in the bad old days.

Media Shanghai has broken new ground, being the first Chinese city to publish its own English-language newspaper for foreigners – *Shanghai Culture & Recreation.* Actually, this statement needs to be qualified – the newspaper is published by the Jinjiang Group Holding Company. At present, the newspaper comes out only twice monthly (the 2nd & 17th of each month) but this may increase in future. For subscription or advertising information, you can call Jinjiang Holdings (☎ 3264000, 3291327) or drop by the office on the 23rd floor of the Union Building, 100 Yan'an Donglu. Free copies of

he paper are available from the soft-seat
waiting room at Shanghai main railway
station, and from major hotels.

Shanghai's radio stations are a little more hip
than in most other Chinese cities. Radio Shanghai (103.7 MHz) sometimes plays Top-40 hits
from the West, especially on weekends, though
often at odd hours like midnight. The TV stations sometimes broadcast foreign films –
check the *Shanghai Culture & Recreation*
newspaper for the schedule.

Maps An English map of Shanghai is available from the Friendship Store – it's not a
very good map but it's better than nothing. A
much better one is the bilingual *Map of
Shanghai Pudong New Area* – all the
Chinese characters are the traditional ones as
used in Hong Kong and Taiwan.

Currently, the most popular is the traffic
map *shànghǎi shìqū jiāotōng tú*. This one is
totally in Chinese characters (no pinyin!) but
is the best one for the bus routes. It's available from street hawkers, bookshops, hotel
giftshops and everywhere else.

If you want a bilingual map, get the Hong-
Kong-published *Map of Shanghai*, which is
sometimes available in China (you can buy
it in Hong Kong from most large bookshops). This map has streets and destinations
written in Chinese characters (traditional) as
well as English – very useful.

The enormous wall map (*shànghǎi shìqū
tú*) is in Chinese simplified characters exclusively and sold only at Chinese bookshops,
but it makes intriguing wallpaper that will
impress your friends.

Medical Services Shanghai is credited with
the best medical facilities and most advanced
medical knowledge in China. Western medicines are sold at the Shanghai No 8
Drugstore at 951 Huaihai Zhonglu.

Foreigners are referred to Shanghai No 1
People's Hospital (☎ 3240100) (*shànghǎi
shì dìyī rénmín yīyuàn*) at 190 Bei Suzhou
Lu; or to Ruijin Hospital (☎ 4370045) (*ruìjīn
yīyuàn*) at 197 Ruijin 2- Lu.

What Was What
Shanghai gives you the chance to discover
what building was what, when, how, and
why. It's a bit like a giant game of Monopoly:
Jimmy's Kitchen, St Petersburg Restaurant,
Delmonte's Casino, the Lido, Roxy's, Kabul
Rd, Oxford St, Luna Park, Singapore Park.
Most of the taller structures are deadwood from
the 1930s; the buildings rapidly changed func-
tion after the Japanese invasion of 1937.

The old **Chinese city** is now identified by
the Zhonghua-Renmin ring road, which
encloses a shoddy maze of cobbled alleyways, with some newer buildings to the
south. The old walls used to be surrounded
by a moat, but these walls were torn down in
1912.

The **International Settlement** (*shànghǎi
zūjiè*) started off as small tracts of land on the
banks of the Huangpu, north of the old
Chinese city, and eventually grew to several
km in width. The British-dominated Settlement was a brave new world of cooperation
by the British, Europeans and Americans
(the Japanese were also included but were
considered suspect). It's fairly easy to
discern. If you draw a line directly north
from the Jing'an Guesthouse to Suzhou
Creek, then the area is everything from
Yan'an Lu up to Suzhou Creek in the north,
and to the Huangpu River in the east. The
ritziest place to live was west of today's
Xizang Lu (now the Jing'an District) – villas
spread this way as far as the zoo. The foreign
embassies were grouped on either side of the
Waibaidu bridge; the Friendship Store used
to occupy the buildings of the old British
Consulate, and the former Seamen's Club
used to be the Soviet Consulate.

Throwing a pincer around the top of the
Chinese city and lying on the southern flank
of the International Settlement was the
French Concession (*fǎguó zūjiè*). The east-
west dividing line between the French
Concession and the International Settlement
is the present-day Yan'an Lu (previously
known as Avenue Foch in the west, and
Avenue Edward VII in the east). The French
strip of the Bund (south of Yan'an) was
known as the Quai de France. Roughly, the

SHANGHAI

boundaries of Frenchtown can be drawn by heading south from the Dahua Guesthouse on Yan'an Lu to the Xujiahui traffic circle, east along Zhaojiabang Lu and Xujiahui Lu to the Hunan Stadium, then up alongside the western border of the Chinese city as far as Yan'an Donglu – and then tack on the pincer between Yan'an Donglu and the northern rim of the Chinese city. Not all of Frenchtown was densely inhabited back then, and in any case the name is a bit of a misnomer as there weren't too many French there to begin with. Like the other concessions it was 90% Chinese, and in any case the most numerous foreign residents in Frenchtown were White Russians. Vietnamese troops were used by the French as a police force (just as the British used Sikhs in their concessions). For villa and mansion architecture the French concession holds the most surprises – there's a rather exclusive air to the elegant townhouses and apartment blocks. The core of things is around the present Jinjiang Hotel and Huaihai Lu.

The original **central district** (shì zhōngxīn) was bounded by today's Xizang Lu, Yan'an Lu, Suzhou Creek and the Huangpu River. If you bisect that with Nanjing Lu, then the key wining and dining shopping and administrative/hotel area is the slab south of Nanjing Lu as far as Yan'an Lu with Nanjing Donglu being the chief culprit. This is today's Huangpu District.

The area north of the central district and up as far as Suzhou Creek used to be the **American Settlement**. The area on the other side of the creek, east of Zhejiang Beilu and along the banks of the Huangpu, used to be the **Japanese Concession** (rìběn zūjiè). These areas eventually became a Chinese industrial suburb, the **Hongkou District**, and are not of great interest, although the bridges above the polluted sections along Suzhou Creek are good for observing tugs and barges – there's a great deal of industry and warehouses along these banks. The major universities, Tongji and Fudan, are right up north. The main factory zones, shipyards, warehouses and new high-rise housing developments are in the sector north-east of here.

Over on the other side of the railway tracks to the west and the north of the city are rings of new industrial suburbs – **satellite towns**

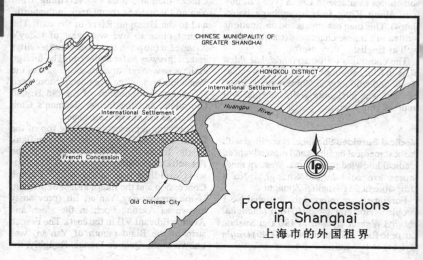

Foreign Concessions
in Shanghai
上海市的外国租界

where the workers live in high-rises adjacent to their factories and plants – the Soviet model. The area due south of the old Chinese city and Frenchtown is similar. The housing projects sprang up, as they did in other Chinese cities, in the 1950s, and were erected outside the original city limits. The initial building programme concentrated upon the construction of about 10,000 dwelling units in north-eastern Shanghai, and another 10,000 in southern, northern and western Shanghai. These satellite towns are about eight km from the centre of Shanghai, and they have their own schools, day-care centres, markets and hospitals.

The Bund
(wàitān) 外滩

The Bund is an Anglo-Indian term for the embankment of a muddy waterfront. The Bund is an apt description – between 1920 (when the problem was first noticed) and 1965 the city of Shanghai sank several metres. Correction of the problem involved pumping water back into the ground, but the Venetian threat is still there. Concrete rafts are used as foundations for high-rises in this spongy mass.

The Bund is a great meeting place for local Chinese and foreigners alike. People stroll up and down in search of vicarious excitement, which is often provided by street performers or free-marketeers. Pedlars sell anything from home-made underwear to naughty pictures. In the morning it's an exhibition place for taiji and martial arts; at night it's a lovers' lane.

Though startling to behold in a Chinese city, the edifices that line the Bund are no special wonder. The exteriors are a solemn mix of neo-classical 1930s Chicago and New York with a bit of monumental Egypt thrown in for good measure. To the Europeans, the Bund was Shanghai's Wall Street, and it saw a fever of trading as the city's fortunes rose and fell with each impending crisis. The buildings changed function several times as the crises got the better of traders, but originally they were banks, trading houses, hotels, residential buildings, commercial buildings and clubs.

One of the most famous traders was Jardine Matheson & Company. They registered in Canton in 1832, and dug into the China trade two years later when the British parliament abolished the East India Company's monopoly of the place. In 1848 Jardine's purchased the first land offered for sale to foreigners in Shanghai and set up shop shortly after, dealing in opium and tea. Today, Jardine Matheson owns just about half of Hong Kong and they're not finished with Shanghai either – they have an office across the way at Shanghai Mansions. James Matheson's nephew Donald, who inherited most of the Matheson side of the fortune, served in China from 1837 to 1849. By the age of 30 he'd had it, went to England, and later became the chairman of the Executive Committee for the Suppression of the Opium Trade.

At the north-western end of the Bund were, or are, the British Public Gardens (now called Huangpu Park), which were off limits to Chinese during the colonial era. A notorious sign at the entrance said 'No Dogs or Chinese Allowed'. A Sikh guard stood at the gateway; the British had brought in an Indian force to protect themselves after the Boxer Rebellion of 1900.

While the Bund may no longer be full of noisy hawkers, tramcars, Oldsmobiles, typists, black marketeers, sailors, taipans and rickshaws, its function is still very much the same – only this time it's the foreigners who come to kowtow to the Chinese trading establishments now set up here. The Customs House (built in 1927) is still a Customs house. An exterior readily identifiable by the dome on top is the Hong Kong & Shanghai Bank, completed in 1921 – one of the most impressive hunks of granite in colonial Asia. The rowdy RAF Club used to be up in the dome. Today the bank houses the Shanghai People's Municipal Government (City Hall, CCP and People's Liberation Army headquarters) so there's little chance of seeing the interior. As for the HK & Shanghai Bank, it has a more modest office further north.

The statues that lined the Bund were stripped away; the whereabouts of the pair of bronze lions that once stood outside the HK

& Shanghai Bank remain a mystery. It was first thought that they had been melted down for cannons by the Japanese, but later the Chinese claimed they had found them. Several Western sources mention seeing the lions in the early 1970s – it's possible that they were brought out for the making of a movie.

One interior that you can visit is the Tung Feng Hotel at the bottom of the Bund near Shiliupu wharf; as you sweep through the double doors and cross the marble paving, you'll come to what looks like a railway concourse. This will give you an idea of how the Dongfeng started life. This was the Shanghai Club, the snootiest little gang this side of Trafalgar Square. Membership was confined to upper-crust Brits, men only. To the left of the entrance is a Suzhou-style restaurant where you'll find the Long Bar, a 33-metre span of thick wood now hacked into three separate pieces. Opposite was the smoking room, now a Cantonese-style restaurant, where the members, replete, would doze with their copies of the *Times*, freshly ironed by the room-boys.

Nanjing Lu & the Central District

Nanjing Donglu (Nanjing Road East), from the Peace to the Park hotels, is the golden mile of China's commerce. Some display windows will stop you in your tracks! Just about everything can be found here, though back in Hong Kong it would be cheaper.

Before 1949 Nanjing Lu was a mixture of restaurants, nightclubs and coffin-makers. The most prestigious department stores were there, and still are, including Wing On's (now the No 10 Department Store), Sun Sun's (now the No 1 Food Store), and The Sun (now the No 1 Department Store).

A stroll down Nanjing Lu at night offers eye-catching window displays and neon signs. Shanghai has the best reputation in China for the art of hairdressing. Both hairdressing and hairdressers were victims of the Cultural Revolution, but this symbol of decadence is now back in fashion (note all the Chinese who now have curly hair).

By day, from 9 am to 6 pm, only buses are allowed on Nanjing Lu, which otherwise turns into a pedestrian thoroughfare. You'll see why there's such a keen one-child-only campaign in Shanghai; the human tide on Nanjing Lu has to be seen to be believed.

At the end of Nanjing Donglu you come to another shopping drag, Nanjing Xilu (once called Bubbling Well Rd, before the well was sealed over). Dividing the sections for a bit of a breather are Renmin Square and Renmin Park, once the Shanghai Racecourse. The old Racecourse Clubhouse is now the Shanghai Municipal Library, and the building is among the oldest in the city.

The nondescript parkland and the desert-like expanses of paving at Renmin Square are where all those large meetings and rallies were held back in the '60s and '70s. In April 1969, 2½ million people poured in here to demonstrate against the Soviet Union after clashes on the border (though even that figure didn't top the peaceful 10 million who'd gathered for the May Day celebrations in Beijing in 1963). The area is also used for paramilitary training; under Renmin Square is a large air-raid shelter. Near Renmin Square is Jiangyin Lu, where you'll find Shanghai's chief goldfish market.

An interesting store at the dividing line of Nanjing Donglu and Nanjing Xilu is the *Shanghai Plants & Bird Shop*, at 364 Nanjing Xilu. It sells bonsai plants, pots, tools, birdcages, goldfish and funeral wreaths. This is possibly one of the few places in the city where you'll find fresh flowers for sale. Most Shanghai locals will queue up to buy plastic flowers – they last longer and are cheaper than the real thing.

The central area bounded by Nanjing Donglu, Xizang Zhonglu, Jinling Donglu and Sichuan Zhonglu is a good place to rummage around. A lot of it is administrative, as it was under the International Settlement. Fuzhou Lu is a good alleyway to explore, with its bookshops and small restaurants, which were once a collection of teahouses covering for brothels.

Shanghai Museum

(shànghǎi bówùguǎn) 上海博物馆

On Henan Nanlu, just off Yan'an Donglu, is the Shanghai Museum. It contains a fair collection of bronzes (graduated bells, knives, axeheads, chariot ornaments), ceramics, paintings and some terracotta figures from Xi'an. There is a shop on the 2nd floor where bronzes, scrolls and ceramics can be bought. It's open from 9 am to 3.30 pm.

Frenchtown

(fǎguó zūjiè) 法国租界

The core of Frenchtown – the former French concession – is the area around Huaihai Lu and the Jinjiang Hotel. The area was inhabited mainly by White Russian émigrés who numbered up to a third of the foreign population in the 1920s and '30s. They ran cafes and tailoring businesses along Huaihai, and took jobs as riding instructors, bodyguards or prostitutes.

The cafes and tailoring outlets in today's Shanghai still centre around Huaihai Lu and the 1930s architecture is still standing. The area offers some good shopping (mainly shoes, household decorations and some second-hand goods) and excellent bakeries. The Parisian touch is about as chic as China gets. The street leading west off the northwestern tip of the Jinjiang Hotel is intriguing for its squat, double-storey architecture, where underwear flaps from the former residences of the rich, or a duck on a pole hangs out to dry.

Site of the 1st National Congress of the Communist Party

(zhōnggòng yīdàhuìzhǐ) 中共一大会址

One activity which the French, and later the Kuomintang, did not take to, was political meetings – these were illegal. The Chinese Communist Party was founded in July 1921 in a French Concession building, at a meeting of delegates from the various Communist and Socialist organisations around China.

This building is usually recorded as being at 76 Xingye Lu – but according to the street signs in the area it stands at the corner of

---

The French Way

Back in the old days the French Concession had a different set of laws from the International Settlement. The French licensed prostitution and opium smoking, while the Internationals just turned a blind eye. With such laws, and because of its proximity to the old Chinese city, a number of China's underworld figures were attracted to the French side of things.

On Xinle Lu, a kind of cul-de-sac which is the first diagonal street to the west of Xiangyang Park, is the Donghu Guesthouse (at No 167). This used to be the headquarters of the Great Circle Gang. Chief mobster was Du Yuesheng, boss of the gang. After a career as a sweet-potato vendor, Du got his start in the police force of the French Concession, where he used his position to squeeze money out of the local opium merchants. In 10 years he had risen to a high position in the Chinese gangs that controlled the opium trade in the Yangzi Valley – they were said to contribute the equivalent of US$20 million annually to the French authorities. In return the French allowed them to use the concession as a base for their operations. By the 1930s Du was on first-name terms with the Nanjing government leaders, and Chiang Kaishek even appointed him 'chief of the bureau of opium suppression'.

In March 1927, as the Kuomintang troops approached Shanghai on their Northern Expedition, the Communist-led workers rose in revolt and took over the Chinese part of Shanghai as planned. But Chiang had different ideas. Financed by Chiang's supporters among the Chinese bankers in Shanghai, escorted by foreign police, and provided with rifles and armoured cars by the International Settlement, Du Yuesheng's gangs launched an attack on the workers, killing between 5000 and 10,000 people, many of them Communists and left-wing Kuomintang. The attack wiped out the Shanghai Communists at a stroke, and was followed by further massacres in Canton, Changsha and Nanchang, forcing the Communists to move the focus of their movement to the countryside. ∎

Huangpi and Ximen Lu, further south of Xingye Lu (see the map for directions). Captions are in English and the building is closed on Monday and Thursday.

Sun Yatsen's Residence
(sūn zhōngshān gùjū) 孙中山故居

At 7 Xianshan Lu, formerly the Rue Molière, is the former residence of Dr Sun Yatsen. He lived for six years in this house not far from Fuxing Park, supported by Overseas Chinese funds. After Sun's death, his wife, Song Qingling (1893-1981), continued to live here until 1937, constantly watched by Kuomintang plain-clothes police and French police. Her sister (Song Meiling) had married Chiang Kaishek in 1927 and her brother (T V Soong) was finance minister to Chiang and a dealer in banking fortunes (and possibly the richest man in China at that time). Song Qingling was close to the Communists, so it must have made for interesting dinner conversation. The two-storey house is set back from the street, furnished the way it used to be (though it was looted by the Japanese).

Fuxing Park is also worth a stroll if you're in the area – locals airing the kids off, playing chess, etc.

There is a second, less popular Sun Yatsen residence at Huaihai Zhonglu, 605 Xiang, Hao (No 3 Lane 605, Huaihai Middle Rd).

Mandarin Gardens (Yuyuan) Bazaar
(yùyuán shāngchǎng) 豫园商场

At the north-eastern end of the old Chinese city, the bazaar area centres on what is known as Mandarin Gardens *(yùyuán)*, and includes the Temple of the Town Gods. Many foreigners consider this to be one of the most interesting places in Shanghai, but it gets some 200,000 visitors daily – avoid it on weekends! While there's nothing of historical interest left, it's one of those great place. where people just come to gawk, mix, buy, sell and eat (see the Places to Eat section) - it's all lively and entertaining enough.

The Pan family, rich Ming Dynasty officials, had Mandarin Gardens built for them. The gardens took 18 years (from 1559 to 1577) to throw together and much less time to destroy. They were bombarded during the Opium War in 1842, which is ironic since the deity in the Temple of the Town Gods is supposed to guarantee the peace of the

---

The First Supper

We don't really know if the 'First Supper' was as cool, calm and collected as the present museum makes out. We don't even know if this really was where the meeting took place, exactly who was there, how many were there, the actual date or what happened. Nevertheless, the museum has been organised here in what is supposed to be the house of one of the delegates, Li Hanjun. Two foreigners are also said to have been in attendance.

Simon Leys, in his book, *Chinese Shadows*, drops 12 names in the attendance list. According to him, what happened to them afterwards doesn't reflect too well on Communist history. Only Mao Zedong and Dong Biwu, elder statesman of the Party and a remarkable political all-rounder, survived in good standing until their natural deaths in the 1970s.

As for the others, four were executed by the Kuomintang or provincial warlords; four defected to the Kuomintang and of these four, two went over to the Japanese. Another delegate, Li Da, remained loyal to the Party and eventually became president of Wuhan University after Liberation; he is supposed to have died of injuries inflicted on him by the Red Guards in 1966. The host, Li Hanjun, appears to have left or to have been excluded from the Party early on, but his execution by the Kuomintang in 1927 rehabilitated him.

The story continues that the delegates' meeting was disrupted by the intrusion of an outsider – presumably a spy – and, fearing a raid by the French police, they left the premises and later continued their meeting on a houseboat in Jiaxing, halfway to Hangzhou. The Shanghai building is supposed to have been damaged during the massacre of 1927, again at the hands of the Japanese. ■

region. In the mid-19th century the gardens became the home base of the Society of Small Swords, who joined with the Taiping rebels and inflicted considerable casualties on the adjacent French Concession. The French responded promptly by destroying them. There's a museum devoted to the uprising and its demise within the gardens. The area was again savaged during the Boxer Rebellion. The gardens close early for lunch.

The **Temple of the Town Gods** *(chénghuángmiào)* first appeared in the Song Dynasty, and disappeared somewhere towards the end. The main hall was rebuilt in 1926 with reinforced concrete and has recently undergone renovation, after being used as a warehouse.

Fanning out from the temple and the gardens is the Mandarin Gardens shopping area – a Disneyland version of what the authorities think tourists might think is the real China. You enter the main area via the **Wuxingting Teahouse** *(wǔxíng cháguǎn)*, a five-sided building set in a pond and looking as old as tea itself. It's pleasant to sit on the upper floor over a 60-fen pot of tea, but stay clear of the coffee and cocoa! The zigzag bridges leading to the teahouse were once full of misshapen beggars at every turn, something to try and visualise as you take in the present scenery. The surrounding bazaar has something like 100 small shops selling the tiny, the curious and the touristy. There are lots of places for Chinese snacks. You can get hankies emblazoned with Chinese landmarks – every time you blow your nose it will remind you of China. You can also get antiques, fans, scissors, bamboo articles, steamed ravioli, vegetarian buns, wine and meat dumplings, chicken and duck-blood soup, radish-shred cakes, shell carvings, paintings, jigsaws, and so on.

Jade Buddha Temple
(yùfó sì) 玉佛寺

From the Mandarin Gardens Bazaar you can hop on bus No 16 and ride all the way out to the Jade Buddha Temple. The ride takes in half of Shanghai en route, and most likely half the population will get off the bus with you.

The temple is an active one, with 70 resident monks at last count. It was built between 1911 and 1918. The exterior is readily identifiable by the bright saffron walls. Inside, the centrepiece is a two-metre-high white jade buddha (some say it's alabaster), which was installed here after it had been brought by a monk from Burma to Zhejiang Province in 1882. This seated buddha, encrusted with jewels, is said to weigh 1000 kg. A smaller, reclining buddha from the same shipment lies on a redwood bed.

In the large . hall are three gold-plated buddhas, and other halls house ferocious-looking deities. Artefacts abound (not all are on display) and some 7000 Buddhist sutras line the walls. Should you arrive at the right time, a ceremony may be in progress. Also in the precincts is a branch of the Antique & Curio Store that sells miniature sandalwood drums and gongs, replicas of the larger ones used in ceremonies.

The temple was largely inactive from 1949 to 1980, as the monks were disbanded and the temple used for other functions. During the Cultural Revolution the place was saved from destruction only by a telegram (so the story goes) direct from the State Council. No doubt the recent picking up of activity is partly due to the tourist trade. The fact is that Shanghai, being so young, has few temples to show off.

The Jade Buddha Temple is popular with Overseas Chinese. No photography is permitted. The temple closes for lunch between noon and 1 pm and is open daily except on some special occasions such as the Lunar New Year in February – that's when Chinese Buddhists, some 20,000 of them, descend on the place.

An interesting route to the Jade Buddha Temple is along Suzhou Creek. It's a long walk there, and you may prefer to take the bus part of the way. The creek (water and banks heavily polluted) is home to sampans, small craft and barges, with crews delivering goods from the Yangzi reaches. There are stacks of bridges along the route and from

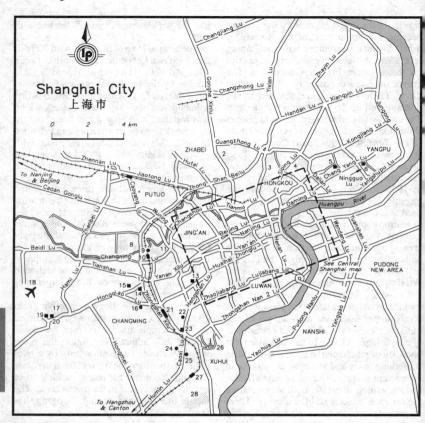

Shanghai City
上海市

these you'll get a decent view of the river life. Warehouses occasionally block the paths along the banks. On the way is a former church which is now a research institute for the electric-light industry.

Tomb of Lu Xun (Hongkou Park)
(hóngkǒu gōngyuǎn) 鲁迅公园
Lu Xun (1881-1936) was a novelist and essayist, and was regarded as the founder of modern Chinese writing. He was also revered as a scholar and a teacher. Though he was not a Communist, most of his books

were banned by the Kuomintang and he had to stay in hiding in the French Concession. His message to Chinese youth read:

Think, and study the economic problems of society...travel through the hundreds of dead villages, visit the generals and then visit the victims, see the realities of your time with opened eyes and a clear mind, and work for an enlightened society, but always think and study.

Lu Xun is best remembered for *The True Story of Ah Q*, the story of an illiterate coolie whose experiences through the first revolution of 1911 show the utter failure of that

■ PLACES TO STAY

5	Haijia Hotel
6	Changyang Hotel
13	Nanying Hotel
14	Galaxy Hotel & Hongqiao State Guesthouse
15	Yangtze New World & Westin Taipingyang hotels
19	Nikko Longbai Hotel
20	Cypress Hotel
23	Sheraton Huating Hotel

OTHER

1	West Railway Station
2	Zhabei Park
3	Tomb of Lu Xun & Hongku Park
4	Peace Park
7	Beixinjing Nursery Garden
8	Changfeng Park
9	Shanghai University
10	Changning Railway Station
11	Zhongshan Park
12	Tianshan Park
16	Wanguo Cemetery & Song Qingling's Tomb
17	Shanghai Zoo
18	Hongqiao Airport
21	Xujiahui Railway Station
22	Guangqi Park
24	Martyrs' Cemetery
25	Caoxi Park
26	Longhua Park & Pagoda
27	Xinlonghua Railway Station
28	Botanical Gardens

■ PLACES TO STAY

5	海佳饭店
6	长阳饭店
13	南鹰饭店
14	银河宾馆/虹桥迎宾馆
15	扬子江大酒店/太平洋大饭店
19	日航龙柏饭店
20	龙柏饭店
23	华亭宾馆

OTHER

1	西火车站
2	闸北公园
3	鲁迅公园
4	和平公园
7	北新泾苗圃
8	长风公园
9	上海大学
10	长宁火车站
11	中山公园
12	天山公园
16	万国公墓/宋庆龄陵园
17	上海动物园
18	虹桥机场
21	徐家汇火车站
22	光启公园
24	烈士陵园
25	漕溪公园
26	龙华公园
27	新龙华火车站
28	植物园

event to reach down to the ordinary people. Constantly baffled, seeing everything through a fog of ignorance and superstition, knowing words but not their meaning, he goes from one humiliation to the next, but each time rationalises his defeats into moral victories. Even when he is executed for a crime he did not commit, he goes cheerily to his death singing from a Chinese opera he does not understand: 'After 20 years I will be reborn again a hero'. Lu Xun's writings are published in English by the Foreign Languages Press and are widely available.

Lu Xun's tomb is some distance up Sichuan Beilu, in Hongkou Park. There's a pompous statue of the writer which would have horrified him. The statue was cast in 1961 and replaces an earlier concrete model, which would also have horrified him. His brother in Beijing wrote to another writer in Hong Kong:

I have just seen a photograph of the statue they put up in front of Lu Xun's tomb in Shanghai; really, this is the supreme mockery! How could this personage sitting as on a throne be the effigy of someone who hated all solemn attitudes?

A museum in Hongkou Park tells the story of Lu Xun from the Communist point of view in Chinese.

Pudong New Area
(pǔdōng xīnqū) 浦东新区

Larger than Shanghai itself, the Pudong New Area is on the eastern bank of the Huangpu River. Before 1990, when development plans for Pudong were first announced, this was an area of boggy farmland supplying vegetables to Shanghai's markets. Now the vegies will have to be grown elsewhere, because this is a Special Economic Zone (SEZ).

The plans for developing Pudong were announced barely six months after the 1989 Tiananmen Massacre, at a time when foreigners were more than a little sceptical of grand pronouncements from Beijing. But Shanghai is not Beijing and the proposals proved to be more than wishful thinking – Pudong is now China's largest development project. Although Pudong's development has barely started, government officials already boast that Pudong will overtake Shenzhen.

Feverish construction is going on, mostly basic infrastructure which will be needed to attract industries. Two new bridges and two tunnels have been built to connect Pudong to central Shanghai, and more are planned. A huge new coal-burning powerplant will be built. The Waigaoqiao harbour area is being upgraded into a major container port. A new telephone exchange is being built to handle the undersea fibre optic telecommunications cable (China's first) which will reach Pudong's shores. A 24-hour international airport will be built to supplement Shanghai's existing Hongqiao Airport.

All this costs money, something not in surplus supply even in relatively prosperous Shanghai. However, it is clear that if China wants to catapult itself into a modern economic power (or superpower?), the investment will have to be made. Unless interference from Beijing (always a possibility) derails the project, Shanghai officials

---

Kids
Children (especially males) have always been highly prized in Chinese society, but even more so now that couples can only have one. At least in big cities like Shanghai, kids are pampered to such an extent that the Chinese newspapers campaign against parents turning their children into 'little emperors'. Pampering plus the housing shortage might explain why children don't move away from home until they get married – or sometimes not until long after they get married. And when they grow up, the kids are expected to take care of the parents in old age.

To the foreign eye, Chinese kids are the most baffling section of the population. Nappyless, hardly ever crying or looking worried – who knows what goes on inside their heads? Around the city are Children's Palaces, where extra-curricular activities take place and special interests are pursued. In theory this supplements regular schooling – but it has overtones of an elitist educational system. The one most visited by group tours (you can get in by yourself if you push) is on Yan'an Zhonglu, just west of Jing'an Park. The building really is a palace that once belonged to the Kadoorie family, and was then known as Marble House. The children here make model aeroplanes, play video games, attend classes in drawing, drama, music – and practise how to love their country and impress tourists.

A stark contrast to the kids' palace is the Peiguang Middle School. Drop down here in the early morning when the kids are doing their exercises in the courtyard just off the street (to the sound of 'Oh Canada'). The school is along Xizang Zhonglu, on the corner of Jiujiang Lu, which is one block south of Nanjing Donglu. The school used to be the notorious Laozhu Police Station in the concession days.

Children's stores are among the places where parents and their (usually one) offspring gather. Try the bookstore at 772 Nanjing Xilu, the Xiangyang at 993 Nanjing Xilu (toys, clothing and furniture), the foodstore at 980 Nanjing Xilu (cakes and cookies), the shoe and hat shop at 600 Nanjing Donglu, and the clothing store at 939 and 765 Huaihai Zhonglu.

In the entertainment line, much-publicised child prodigies pop up at the Conservatory of Music (see the Entertainment section). Shanghai has its own film animation studio – China's equivalent of Disneyworld products. There's also a troupe called the Children's Art Theatre. ∎

anticipate that Pudong will become the Hong Kong of the north. A decade ago, people would have laughed at them – no-one is laughing now.

Other Sights

A further 20 km north of Hongkou Park, towards the banks of the Yangzi and requiring a longer bus ride, is Jiading County, with a ruined Confucian temple and a classical garden.

South-west of central Shanghai and nearing a bend in the Huangpu River (within reach of Frenchtown) is the **Longhua Pagoda** (*lónghuá tǎ*). This fell into disrepair, was used by the Red Guards as an advertising pole, and has since undergone renovation for the tourist trade. The pagoda is 40 metres high, octagonal, with upturned eaves; it is said to date from the 10th century but has probably been rebuilt a couple of times. The surrounding temple is largely restructured concrete, but the statuary of ferocious figures is impressive. The temple's once-famous peach blossoms have now disappeared.

The Xujiahui area bordering the western end of Frenchtown once had a Jesuit settlement, with an observatory (still in use). **St Ignatius Cathedral**, whose spires were lopped off by Red Guards, has been restored and is open once again for Catholic services. It's at 158 Puxi Lu, in the Xujiahui District.

Further south-west of the Longhua Pagoda are the **Shanghai Botanical Gardens** (*shànghǎi zhíwùyuǎn*), with an exquisite collection of 9000 miniatures.

The **Shanghai Exhibition Centre** is west of the city centre. Drop in here for a mammoth view of Soviet palace architecture. There are irregular displays of local industrial wares and handicrafts.

Out near the airport is **Shanghai Zoo**, which has a roller-skating rink, children's playground and other recreational facilities. To the west of that is the former **Sassoon Villas**. At Qingpu County, 25 km west of Shanghai, they've made up for the dearth of real antiquities and temples by creating a new scenic area for tourists to visit.

On the way to the town of Jiaxing, by rail or road, is Sunjiang County, 20 km southwest of Shanghai. The place is older than Shanghai itself. On Tianmashan, in Sonjiang County, is the **Huzhou Pagoda**, built in 1079 AD. It's the leaning tower of China, with an inclination now exceeding the tower at Pisa by 1½ degrees. The 19-metre-high tower started tilting 200 years ago.

Huangpu River Trip

(*huángpǔ jiāng yóulǎn chuán*)
黄浦江游览船

There are three main perspectives on Shanghai – from the gutters, from the heights (aerial views from the battlements of the tourist fortresses) and from the waters. The Huangpu River offers some remarkable views of the Bund and the riverfront activity. The junks that cut in and out of the harbour bring back memories so old you probably last saw them in some pirate movie. Back in the 1920s you would have arrived in Shanghai by boat, and today's touring vessels seem to ham it up, imitating the colonial style of that era. About the only negative aspect of a boat trip is the sulphurous smell of the river itself, which is severely polluted.

Huangpu tour boats depart from the dock on the Bund, slightly north of the Peace Hotel. There are several decks on the boat, but foreigners are forced upmarket into special class A or special class B. Departure times are 8.30 am and 1.30 pm, with possible extra departures in the summer and on

SHANGHAI

Sunday. The schedule may become erratic in winter due to bad weather.

Tickets can be purchased in advance from CITS at the Peace Hotel (there's a small surcharge), or at the boat dock – but there's no real need if you're taking upper deck since it is unlikely to be full. The boat takes you on a 3½-hour, 60-km round trip, northward up the Huangpu to the junction with the Yangzi River, to Wusongkou and back again along the same route. On the return run they show videos on the lower deck – usually bloodthirsty kungfu flicks.

Shanghai is one of the world's largest ports; 2000 ocean-going ships and about 15,000 river steamers load and unload here every year. Coolies used to have the back-breaking task of loading and unloading, but these days the ports are a forest of cranes, derricks, conveyor belts and forklifts. The tour boat passes an enormous variety of craft – freighters, bulk carriers, roll-on roll-off ships, sculling sampans, giant praying-mantis cranes, the occasional junk and Chinese navy vessels (which aren't supposed to be photographed).

Festivals

There are three events of significance. The Mid-autumn Festival (15th day of the 8th moon in the lunar calendar) is when they lay on the mooncakes – the festival recalls an uprising against the Mongols in the 14th century when plans for the revolt were passed around in cakes. Mooncakes are usually filled with a mixture of ground lotus, sesame seeds and dates, and sometimes duck egg. The Shanghai Music Festival is in May. The Shanghai Marathon Cup is in March and is one of the top sporting events in the country. The latter two festivals were suspended during the Cultural Revolution. Hotel space may be harder to come by at these times, and at Lunar New Year in February.

Places to Stay – bottom end

It's 'No Dogs or Foreigners' at the cheap Chinese hotels. Shanghai is an expensive place to stay, even more so than Canton. The salvation for budget travellers is a small collection of somewhat run-down places which still dish out dorm beds for around Y20. Another option is to stay in one of the hotels in the outlying districts, which offer mid-range accommodation. Your best bet is to avoid the peak season (summer) when most bottom-end places fill up.

The *Pujiang Hotel* (☎ 3246388) (*pǔjiāng fàndiàn*), at 15 Huangpu Lu, is the only centrally located place that offers dorms and low-cost (by Shanghai standards) rooms. Dorm beds cost Y30, including a decent breakfast. The dorms are usually booked by mid-afternoon (around 10 am seems to be the best time to show up). There are also grotty four-bed rooms for Y160, grottier five-bed rooms for Y175 and higher-standard doubles for Y180. The Pujiang used to be the Astor House Hotel, one of the most elegant in the early concession days, before it was dwarfed by Shanghai Mansions. Today the Pujiang is a bit run-down but it still has character, something lacking in the modern places. Take bus No 65 from near the main railway station to Beijing Donglu and then walk east and left up the the Bund over Suzhou Creek to the hotel.

If the Pujiang's full, you can almost always get a bed at the *Haijia Hotel* (☎ 5411440) (*hǎijiā fàndiàn*), 1001 Jiangpu Lu, in the north-eastern part of town. Beds are Y15 to Y30 per person depending on room size. Very large doubles with air-con and private bathroom are available for Y140. To get there from the Pujiang Hotel area, take bus No 22 east along Daming Donglu (behind the Pujiang). The bus soon turns onto Changyang Lu; when you see/smell the tobacco factory, get off at the next stop, at Jiangpu Lu. The Haijia is a one-minute walk north of Changyang Lu on the left-hand side of Jiangpu Lu. Coming from the main Shanghai railway station, bus Nos 310 and 70 stop almost in front of the hotel.

In the same neighbourhood is the excellent *Changyang Hotel* (☎ 5434890) (*chángyáng fàndiàn*), at 1800 Changyang Lu. The hotel is very modern but quite a bargain, with singles/doubles for Y100/120.

Bus No 22 from the Bund area runs right past the hotel.

Another place to try is the *Conservatory of Music* (☎ 4372577) *(yīnyuè xuéyuàn)*, 20 Fenyang Lu, off Huaihai Zhonglu. The foreign student dorm will take non-students when there's room, but it's often full (best bet is during the summer). The cost is Y22 per person in a double with shared bathroom. To find it, take the first left after passing through the main gate.

Places to Stay – middle

The *Chun Shen Jiang Hotel* (☎ 3205710) *(chūn zhōng jiāng bīnguǎn)*, 626 Nanjing Donglu, has long been known as a good mid-range hotel with a great location. At the time of writing, it was undergoing renovation. No prices were available, but there is a chance the cost will rise into the top-end category.

The *Yangtze Hotel* (☎ 3207880; fax 3206974) *(yángzi fàndiàn)* is at 740 Hankou Lu, one block east of Renmin (People's) Park. It was built back in 1934 and is an old American-style hotel. Doubles cost Y200 to Y240 – not dirt cheap but quite a bargain for this neighbourhood. Take bus No 109 from the railway station to People's Park on Nanjing Donglu.

The *Nanying Hotel* (☎ 4378188) *(nányīng fàndiàn)*, at 1720 Huaihai Zhonglu, is in the south-western part of the city. Very comfortable doubles cost Y168.

Places to Stay – top end

We're sorry to say that nowadays the vast majority of the hotels in Shanghai fall into the top-end (over Y300) category. But this is Shanghai, and the history and the character of the old palatial hotels is one of the reasons to come here. However, the furnishings and Art-Deco opulence are fading steadily, gradually being replaced by the anonymous Holiday Inn-style aesthetic.

Interior renovations at the Park, Shanghai Mansions, and Jinjiang have taken their toll, but if there's one place left in Shanghai that will give you a sense of the past, it's the *Peace Hotel (the old Cathy)* (☎ 3211244; fax 3290300) *(hépíng fàndiàn)*, at 20 Nanjing Donglu. On the ground floor of the 12-storey edifice are the sumptuous lobby, shops, bookstore, bank, video games parlour, snooker tables, cafe and barber. The scalp

---

The Cathay

The Peace Hotel is a ghostly reminder of the immense wealth of Victor Sassoon. From a Baghdad Jewish family, he made millions out of the opium trade and then ploughed it back into Shanghai real estate and horses. Sassoon's quote of the day was 'There is only one race greater than the Jews, and that's the Derby'. His office-cum-hotel was completed in 1930 and was known as Sassoon House, incorporating the Cathay Hotel. From the top floors Victor commanded his real estate – he is estimated to have owned 1900 buildings in Shanghai.

The Cathay Hotel fell into the same category as the Taj in Bombay, the Stanley Raffles in Singapore and the Peninsula in Hong Kong as *the* place to stay. Sassoon himself resided in what is now the VIP section below the green pyramidal tower, complete with Tudor panelling. He also maintained a Tudor-style villa out near Hongqiao Airport just west of the zoo. Anyone who was anyone could be seen dancing in the Tower Restaurant. The likes of Noel Coward (who wrote *Private Lives* in the Cathay) entertained themselves in this penthouse ballroom.

Back in 1949 the Kuomintang strayed into the place, awaiting the arrival of the Communists. A Western writer of the time records an incident in which 50 Kuomintang arrived, carrying their pots and pans, vegetables and firewood, and one soldier was overheard asking where to billet the mules. After the Communists took over the city, the troops were billeted in places like the Picardie (now the Hengshan Guesthouse on the outskirts of the city), where they spent hours experimenting with the elevators, used bidets as face-showers, and washed rice in the toilets – which was all very well until someone pulled the chain. In 1953 foreigners tried to give the Cathay to the CCP in return for exit visas. The government refused at first, but finally accepted after the payment of 'back taxes'. ■

massage service has a good reputation. To get to the hotel take bus No 64 from the railway station. Drop in and examine the decor – it's staggering! High ceilings, chandeliers, brass doorplates, ornate mirrors, Art-Deco lamps and fixtures, and 1930s calligraphy. Go up to the Dragon & Phoenix Restaurant on the 8th floor for great views across the Bund and the Huangpu River. The south wing used to be the Palace Hotel and was built in 1906; the brass plumbing within is original. The cost of all this history for standard singles/ doubles is Y333/402, and climbs all the way to Y1725 for a 'national deluxe' suite. The national deluxe suites are intentionally laid out in 1930s Art-Deco style to represent the concessions of the time – French, British, American, Japanese, not to mention Chinese. To all of the foregoing prices is added a 10% surcharge.

The *Tung Feng Hotel* (☎ 3218060) (*dōngfēng fàndiàn*), 3 Zhongshan Dong 1-Lu, is a grand but lesser-known establishment right on the Bund at Yan'an Donglu. Modernisation has caught up with the place – the huge Kentucky Fried Chicken on the ground floor does not date from the Kuomintang era. At Y300 for a double, rooms cost considerably more than the chicken wings, but you're paying for the location. There is also another branch (☎ 3235304) at Sichuan Zhonglu.

The *Park Hotel* (☎ 3275225; fax 3276958) (*guójì fàndiàn*), 170 Nanjing Xilu, overlooks Renmin Park. Erected in 1934, the building is one of Shanghai's best examples of Art-Deco architecture from the city's cultural peak. With recent renovations, however, the interior has lost all its old world charm. Singles/doubles start at Y316/402 plus 10% surcharge. The rooms are quite comfortable and the service is efficient. The best views of Shanghai are from the men's toilets on the 14th floor. Take bus No 64 from the railway station. Taxi drivers know the Park Hotel by its Chinese name or as the 'International Hotel'.

Shanghai Mansions (☎ 3246260; fax 3269778) (*shànghǎi dàshà*) is at 20 Suzhou Beilu, near the Pujiang Hotel on the same side of Huangpu River at the junction with Suzhou Creek. It's owned by the Hengshan Group, which also owns the more moderately priced Pujiang and Yangtze hotels. Standard double rooms (no singles) cost Y287 to Y391. For a suite toward the top of the hotel with a waterfront view and balcony and perhaps a grand piano...but if you've got that sort of money then there's no need to ask the price. The Mansions are rather dull compared to other Shanghai hotels but try and make it to the rooftop because the views are stunning!

The 20-storey brick building was constructed in 1934 as a posh British residential hotel. Since it was on the fringes of the International Settlement near the Japanese side of town, it was quickly taken over at the outset of the Sino-Japanese War in 1937. The Japanese stripped the fittings (like radiators) for scrap metal, and the same fate befell other Shanghai hotels during the occupation. As for the billiard tables, these were sawn off at the legs to fit the smaller stature of Japanese enthusiasts. The place used to be known as Broadway Mansions; after the Japanese surrender and before 1949, the US Military Advisory Group to the Kuomintang set up shop on the lower floors, while the upper section was used by the foreign press and one floor was devoted to the Foreign Correspondents' Club.

The *Seagull Hotel* (☎ 3251500; fax 3241263) (*hǎiōu bīnguǎn*), 60 Huangpu Lu, is on the waterfront a minute's walk from the Pujiang Hotel and Shanghai Mansions. Clean doubles cost Y320. A moderately priced restaurant on the 2nd floor serves Chinese and European dishes with generous helpings, and the adjacent Seagull Bar provides the nightlife.

The *Pacific Hotel* (☎ 3276226; fax 3269620) (*jīnmén dàjiǔdiàn*), 104 Nanjing Xilu, was previously called the Overseas Chinese Hotel (*huáqiáo fàndiàn*) and most Shanghai residents still call it that. The hotel is easily recognisable by the distinctive clock tower with the big red star on it, and by the fabulously ornate foyer. Doubles cost Y380 to Y450. This is one of Nanjing Lu's more historic hotels.

The traditional-style *Jinjiang Hotel* (☎ 2582582) *(jǐnjiāng fàndiàn)* is at 59 Maoming Nanlu. This is not to be confused with its annexe, the adjacent, modern, high-rise *Jinjiang Tower* (☎ 4334488; fax 4333265) *(xīn jǐnjiāng dàjiǔdiàn)* at 161 Changle Lu. Both places are so vast you need a map to find your way around – a brochure with map is available in the north building. The colossus stretches north-south along an entire block, with two gates on the western side. Rates for the old annexe start at Y350, or Y632 at the new high-rise annexe (add a 15% surcharge). To get to the Jinjiang take bus No 41 from the railway station; bus No 26 goes there from the Bund area.

If you don't stay at the Jinjiang you should at least drop down and have a look at it; it's located in what used to be the old French Concession, an interesting alternative to the Bund since the surrounding area is now mostly residential. The residents of the hotel, though, need never venture out since this fortress-like building has all you need to survive. Nixon stayed here in 1972, if that's any recommendation. Apart from his fingerprints, check out the North Building, a 14-storey block once called the Cathay Mansions and built as an exclusive French apartment block with amazing wood-panelling and iron chandelier period pieces. Additional attractions of the Jinjiang include the Jin Li Restaurant on the ground floor of the South Building (with 24-hour service); a dance hall and Western-style restaurant on the 11th floor of the North Building; and a Hong Kong-style disco called the *Club d'Elegance* on the ground floor of the West Building. Check out the expensive, though elegant, *Cafe Reve*.

The *Sheraton Huating Hotel* (☎ 4391000; fax 2550830) *(huátíng bīnguǎn)*, 1200 Caoxi Beilu, is a totally modern hotel at the south edge of the city – it has no sense of history, but slick accommodation for the well-to-do. The hotel also boasts a bowling alley. Prices start at Y575.

Other top-end hotels in Shanghai also fall into the modern category. Like the Sheraton Huating, the most luxurious are huge complexes located towards the south-west outskirts of the city (en route to Hongqiao Airport). These hotel complexes attempt to create self-contained international cities (after Beijing models like the Beijing Lido),

complete with multiple restaurants, lounges, discos, hair salons, swimming pools, fitness centres, business centres and shopping centres.

Slightly less expensive are those modern hotels closer to the city centre – Shanghai Hotel, the Jing'an Guesthouse and the Hengshan Guesthouse. All of these places cost over Y300 and you can be sure that all rooms come with a minimum of air-con, colour TV, phone and refrigerator.

Bailemen Hotel (bǎilèmén dàjiǔdiàn) 1728 Nanjing Xilu (☎ 2568686; fax 2566869)

Baolong Hotel (bǎolóng bīnguǎn) 70 Yixian Lu (☎ 5425425; fax 6632710)

Cherry Hill Villa (yīnghuā dùjià cūn) 77 Nonggong Lu (☎ 2758350; fax 2756457)

City Hotel (chéngshì jiǔdiàn) 5-7 Shanxi Nanlu (☎ 2551133; fax 2550211)

Cypress Hotel (lóngbǎi fàndiàn) 2419 Hongqiao Lu (☎ 2558868; fax 2756739)

Dahua Guesthouse (dàhuá bīnguǎn) 914 Yan'an Xilu (☎ 2512512; fax 2512702)

East Asia Hotel (dōngyà fàndiàn) 680 Nanjing Donglu (☎ 3223223)

Equatorial Hotel (guójì guìdū dàfàndiàn) 65 Yan'an Xilu (☎ 2791688; fax 2154033)

Galaxy Hotel (yínhé bīnguǎn) 888 Zhongshan Xilu (☎ 2755888; fax 2750201)

Gaoyang Hotel (gāoyáng bīnguǎn) 879 Dong Daming Lu (☎ 5413920; fax 5458696)

Garden Hotel (huāyuán fàndiàn) 58 Maoming Nanlu (☎ 4331111; fax 4338866)

Hengshan Hotel (héngshān bīnguǎn) 534 Hengshan Lu (☎ 4377050; fax 4335732)

Hilton Hotel (jìng'ān xī ěrdùn jiǔdiàn) 250 Huashan Lu (☎ 2550000; fax 2553848)

Holiday Inn Yinxing (yínxīng jiàrì jiǔdiàn) 388 Panyu Lu (☎ 2528888; fax 2528545)

Hongqiao State Guesthouse (hóngqiáo yíng bīnguǎn) 1591 Hongqiao Lu (☎ 4372170; fax 4334948)

Huaxia Hotel (huáxià bīnguǎn) 38 Caobao Lu (☎ 4360100; fax 4333724)

International Airport Hotel (guójì jīchǎng bīnguǎn) 2550 Hongqiao Lu, Hongqiao Airport (☎ 2558866; fax 2558393)

JC Mandarin Hotel (jǐncāng wénhuà dàjiǔdiàn) 1225 Nanjing Xilu (☎ 2791888; fax 2791822)

Jianguo Hotel (jiànguó bīnguǎn) 439 Caoxi Beilu (☎ 4399299; fax 4399714)

Jing'an Hotel (jìng'ān bīnguǎn) 370 Huashan Lu (☎ 2551888; fax 2552657)

Jinshajiang Hotel (jīnshājiāng dàjiǔdiàn) 801 Jinshajiang Lu (☎ 2578888; fax 2574149)

Jinshan Hotel (jīnshān bīnguǎn) Jingyi Donglu, Jinshanwei (☎ 7941888; fax 7940931)

SHANGHAI

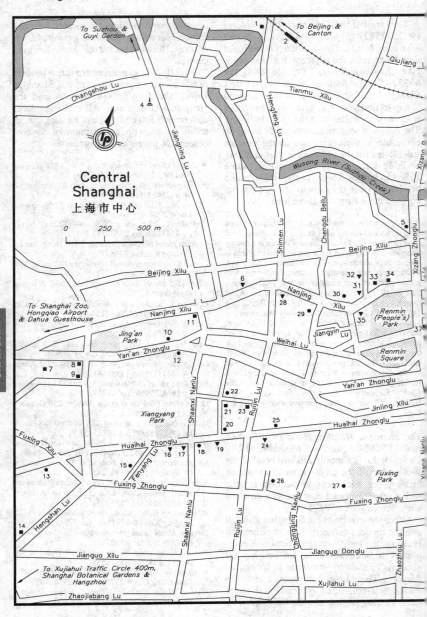

Central Shanghai
上海市中心

0   250   500 m

To Suzhou &
Guyi Garden

To Beijing &
Canton

Qiujiang L

Changshou Lu

Tianmu Xilu

Hengfeng Lu

Jiangning Lu

Wusong River (Suzhou Creek)

Shimen Lu

Chengdu Beilu

Xizang Zhonglu

Beijing Xilu

Beijing Xilu

To Shanghai Zoo,
Hongqiao Airport
& Dahua Guesthouse

Nanjing Xilu

Nanjing
Xilu

Nanjing

Jing'an
Park

Weihai Lu

Jiangyin Lu

Renmin
(People's)
Park

Renmin
Square

Yan'an Zhonglu

Yan'an Zhonglu

Xiangyang
Park

Shaanxi Nanlu

Rujin Lu

Jinling Xilu

Huaihai Zhonglu

Fuxing Xilu

Huaihai Zhonglu

Fenyang Lu

Chongqing Nanlu

Fuxing
Park

Fuxing Zhonglu

Hengshan Lu

Fuxing Zhonglu

Xizang Nanlu

Jianguo Xilu

Shaanxi Nanlu

Rujin Lu

Jianguo Donglu

Zhaozhou

To Xujiahui Traffic Circle 400m,
Shanghai Botanical Gardens &
Hangzhou

Xujiahui Lu

Zhaojiabang Lu

SHANGHAI

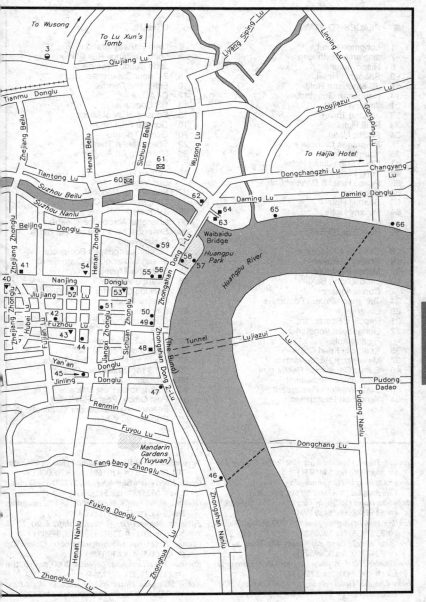

To Wusong

To Lu Xun's Tomb

Qiujiang Lu

3

Tianmu Donglu

Liyang Siping Lu

Linping Lu

Gongping Lu

Zhoujiazui Lu

Zhejiang Beilu

Henan Beilu

Sichuan Beilu

Wusong Lu

Tiantong Lu

60 ⊠

61 ⊠

To Haijia Hotel

Dongchangzhi Lu

Changyang Lu

Suzhou Beilu

Suzhou Nanlu

62

Daming Lu

Daming Donglu

64

Beijing Donglu

63

65

66

Zhejiang Zhonglu

41

54

Henan Zhonglu

59

Dong 1-Lu

Waibaidu Bridge

Huangpu Park

Huangpu River

40

Nanjing Donglu

Zhongshan Dong 1-Lu

58

Jiujiang Lu

52

51

55 56

57

Zhejiang Zhonglu

Hubei Lu

42

Fuzhou Lu

50

49

7

43

Jiangxi Zhonglu

Sichuan Zhonglu

Fujian Lu

44

Yan'an Donglu

48

Tunnel

Lujiazui Lu

Pudong Dadao

45

Jinling Donglu

47

Renmin Lu

Fuyou Lu

Mandarin Gardens (Yuyuan)

Fang bang Zhonglu

46

Pudong Nanlu

Dongchang Lu

Fuxing Donglu

Zhongshan Nanlu

Henan Nanlu

Zhonghua Lu

Zhonghua Lu

SHANGHAI

SHANGHAI

■ PLACES TO STAY

1 Longmen Hotel
7 Jing'an Guesthouse
8 Hilton Hotel
9 Shanghai Hotel
11 JC Mandarin Hotel
14 Hengshan Guesthouse
21 Jinjiang Hotel
23 Jinjiang Tower
33 Park Hotel
34 Pacific Hotel
   (Overseas Chinese Hotel)
38 Yangtze Hotel
41 Chun Shen Jiang Hotel
48 Tung Feng Hotel
56 Peace Hotel & Bank of China
62 Shanghai Mansions
63 Seagull Hotel
64 Pujiang Hotel

▼ PLACES TO EAT

6 Children's Foodstore
16 Shanghai Bakery
17 Meixin Restaurant
19 Laodacheng Bakery/
   Confectionary
24 Tianshan Moslem Foodstore
28 Luyangcun
31 People's Restaurant
32 Gongedelin Vegetarian
   Restaurant
35 Kentucky Fried Chicken
37 Meiweizhai Restaurant
40 Sunya Cantonese Restaurant
43 Xinghualou Restaurant
53 Deda Western Restaurant
54 Yangzhou Restaurant

OTHER

2 Main Railway Station
3 Long Distance Bus Station
4 Jade Buddha Temple
5 24 hour Department Store
10 Exhibition Centre
12 CAAC
13 US Consulate
15 Conservatory of Music
18 Gongtai Fruit Store
20 Guotai Theatre
22 Shanghai Art Theatre
25 Shanghai Art Academy
   Exhibition Hall
26 Former Residence of
   Sun Yatsen
27 Site of First National
   Congress of the CCP
29 TV Tower
30 Shanghai Acrobatics Theatre
36 Shanghai No 1 Department Store
39 Great World
42 Foreign Languages Bookstore
44 Shanghai Antique & Curio Store
45 Shanghai Museum
46 Shiliupu Wharf
47 Booking Office for Yangzi River &
   Coastal Boats
49 City Hall
50 Customs House
51 PSB
52 Xinhua Bookstore
55 CITS (ticket office)
57 Wharf for Huangpu Tour Boats
58 CITS (Administrative Office)
59 Friendship Store
60 International Post Office
61 Post Office (Poste Restante)
65 International Passenger Terminal
66 Gongpinglu Wharf

Lantian Hotel (lántiān bīnguǎn) 2400 Siping Lu (☎ 5485906; fax 5485931)

Longhua Hotel (lónghuá yíng bīnguǎn) 2787 Longhua Lu (☎ 4399399; fax 4392964)

Magnolia Hotel (báiyùlán bīnguǎn) 1251 Siping Lu (☎ 5456888; fax 5459499)

Nanjing Hotel (nánjīng fàndiàn) 200 Shanxi Nanlu (☎ 3221455; fax 3206520)

New Asia Hotel (xīnyà dàjiǔdiàn) 422 Tiantong Lu (☎ 3242210; fax 3269529)

New Garden Hotel (xīnyuàn bīnguǎn) 1900 Hongqiao Lu (☎ 4329900; fax 2758374)

Nikko Longbai Hotel (rìháng lóngbǎi fàndiàn) 2451 Hongqiao Lu (☎ 2559111; fax 2559333)

Novotel Shanghai Yuanlin (nuòfùtè yuánlín bīnguǎn) 201 Baise Lu (☎ 4701688; fax 4700008)

Ocean Hotel (yuǎnyáng bīnguǎn) 1171 Dong Daming Lu (☎ 5458888; fax 5458993)

Olympic Hotel (àolínpīkè jùlèbù) 1800 Zhongshan Nan 2-Lu (☎ 4391391; fax 4396295)

Portman Shangri-La (bōtèmàn dàjiǔdiàn) 1376 Nanjing Xilu (☎ 2798888; fax 2798999)

Qianhe Hotel (qiānhè bīnguǎn) 650 Yishan Lu (☎ 4700000; fax 4700348)

Rainbow Hotel (hóngqiáo bīnguǎn) 2000 Yan'an Xilu (☎ 2753388; fax 2757244)

Regal Shanghai Hotel (fùháo wàimào dàjiǔdiàn) 1000 Quyang Lu (☎ 5428000; fax 5448432)

■ PLACES TO STAY

1 龙门饭店
7 静安宾馆
8 静安希尔顿酒店
9 上海沧文华大酒店
11 锦沧文华大酒店
14 衡山宾馆
21 锦江饭店
23 新锦江大酒店
33 国际饭店
34 金门大酒店 /
  华侨饭店
38 扬子饭店
41 春申江宾馆
48 东风饭店
56 和平饭店 /
  中国银行
62 上海大厦
63 上海鸥饭店
64 浦江饭店

▼ PLACES TO EAT

6 儿童食品店
16 上海食品厂

17 美心酒家
19 大昌回民食品厂
24 老天山村酒家
28 绿扬民饭店
31 功人民蔬菜处
32 肯德基家乡鸡
37 美味雅粤菜馆
40 新花楼
43 杏花楼
53 德大西菜社
54 扬州饭店

OTHER

2 上海火车站
3 长途汽车站
4 玉佛寺
5 二十四百货商店
10 上海展览中心
12 中国民航
13 美国领事馆
15 中音乐学院
18 公泰水果店
20 国泰剧院
22 艺术剧院

25 画院美术馆
26 孙中山故居
27 中共一大会址
29 中电视台场
30 大杂技场
36 第一百货商店
39 世界书店
42 外文书店
44 文物商店
45 上海博物馆
46 十六铺码头
47 轮船售票处 (长江)
49 上海市人民政府
50 海关楼
51 公安外事科
52 新华书店
55 中国国际旅行社
57 浦江游船码头
58 国际旅行社总局
59 友谊商店
60 国际邮局
61 总邮局
65 国际客运站
66 公平路码头

SHANGHAI

Ruijin Hotel (ruìjīn bīnguǎn) 118 Ruijin 2-Lu (☎ 4331076; fax 4374861)

Seventh Heaven Hotel (qī chóngtiān bīnguǎn) 627 Nanjing Donglu (☎ 3220777; fax 3207193)

Shanghai Hotel (shànghǎi bīnguǎn) 505 Wulumqi Beilu (☎ 4712712; fax 4331056)

Silk Road Hotel (sīchóuzhī lù dàjiǔdiàn) 777 Quyang Lu (☎ 5429051; fax 5426659)

Sofitel Hyland Hotel (hǎilún bīnguǎn) 505 Nanjing Donglu (☎ 3205888; fax 3204088)

Sunshine Hotel (yángguāng dàjiǔdiàn) 2266 Hongqiao Lu (☎ 4329220; fax 4329195)

Swan Cindic Hotel (tiāné xìnyí bīnguǎn) 111 Jiangwan Lu, Hongkouqu (☎ 3255255; fax 3248002)

Tianma Hotel (tiānmǎ dàjiǔdiàn) 471 Wuzhong Lu (☎ 2758100; fax 2757139)

West Garden Hotel (xīyuán fàndiàn) 2384 Hongqiao Lu, Changning District (☎ 2557173)

Westin Taipingyang (wēisītīng tàipíngyáng) 5 Zunyi Nanlu (☎ 2758888; fax 2755420)

Xianxia Hotel (xiānxiá bīnguǎn) 555 Shuicheng Lu (☎ 2599400; fax 2517492)

Xijiao Guesthouse (xījiāo bīnguǎn) 1921 Hongqiao Lu (☎ 4336643; fax 4336641)

Xincheng Hotel (xīnchéng fàndiàn) 180 Jiangxi Zhonglu (☎ 3213030; fax 3217365)

Xingguo Guesthouse (xīngguó bīnguǎn) 72 Xingguo Lu (☎ 4374503; fax 2512145)

Yangtze Hotel (yángzi fàndiàn) 740 Hankou Lu (☎ 3225115; fax 3206974)

Yangtze New World (yángzi jiāng dàjiǔdiàn) 2099 Yan'an Xilu (☎ 2750000; fax 2750750)

Yunfeng Guesthouse (yúnfēng bīnguǎn) 1665 Hongqiao Lu (☎ 4328900; fax 4328954)

Places to Eat

Shanghai has a couple of its own specialties and is noted for its seafood (such as the freshwater crab that appears around October to December). Most Chinese food tends towards the oily side, but Shanghai-style cooking is the Persian Gulf of Chinese cuisine. Still, there's plenty of good food around, but at times your meal may be so greasy it will slide off your chopsticks.

Eating in the major restaurants can be an abysmal experience, as there is intense competition from the masses for tables and seats. Restaurants are forever packed in Shanghai and you may need some local help to overcome the language problems even if you speak Chinese – the locals just don't like to admit that Shanghai is not the national language.

> Shanghai is expensive and any government-run restaurant should carry with it a government health warning: they are rude, will undoubtedly overcharge you and follow this up with plenty of physical presence bordering on intimidation. If caught in such a spot, stand your ground and remember not to go there again!
>
> **Neil Richards**

Lunch (around 11.30 am to 2 pm) is sometimes OK but dinner (from 5 to 7 pm) is a rat race. In these busy restaurants the waiters will try and get rid of you either by telling you that there are no tables, or by directing you to the cadre and foreigners' rooms – with their elegant decor and beefed-up prices. If it eases your digestion, back in the inflation-ridden China of 1947 a couple had dinner one evening in a Shanghai hotel and found their bill came to 250 million yuan!

If you want to spend more time eating, and at local prices, then try restaurants a bit off the track, perhaps around the old French Concession area. You could also try the smaller places on Fuzhou Lu, where the greasy-spoon prices drop to a few yuan per head. On the other hand, if it's good food (either Chinese or Western) you want, in surroundings that echo the days of the foreign concessions, then splash out on the restaurants in the old colonial hotels (for details, see the Hotel Food section later in this chapter). It's one aspect of Shanghai not to be missed.

Also not to be missed in Shanghai is the ease and delight of snack-eating. You'll get waylaid for hours trying to make it along the length of Nanjing Lu, stumbling out of a pastry shop and wiping off the smudges of lemon meringue pie, chocolate and cream, only to fall immediately into the sweet store next door. The tourist hotels have a good range of cakes, chocolate eclairs and ice-cream sundaes to get you started. The offerings for breakfast from the Chinese

snack shops are so good you may be converted yet!

Common Chinese breakfast fare is the *yóutiáo*, a somewhat greasy doughnut stick – but deep-fried variations in the doughnut line are smaller and much more palatable. Western snacks are a fad among the young of Shanghai: sandwiches are awful, the coffee is terrible, cream cakes are almost edible and the cocoa is disgusting, but the pastries are better than those you find elsewhere in China (which isn't saying much). These snack hang-outs have lots of character and there are lots of characters to be observed.

One thing worth noting – if you wander into a Nanjing Lu restaurant and see a couple in matching suits with red roses in their lapels, and orange soft drinks on every table – then forget it, it's a wedding party. Around dinnertime all the Nanjing Lu restaurants seem to be occupied by them.

Nanjing Donglu Towards the Bund are two semi-Western-style coffee shops that are immensely popular with young Chinese – one is the *Deda Western Restaurant* (☎ 3218499) (*dédà xī cānshè*) at 359 Sichuan Donglu. The other is *East Sea Restaurant* (☎ 3211940) (*dōnghǎi fàndiàn*) at 143 Nanjing Donglu. Both serve a variety of Chinese and Western dishes but almost everyone orders 'Spanish coffee', coffee with ice cream – also check out the lemon meringue pie and other cakes. Further west on the right is the *Yangzhou Restaurant* (☎ 3225826) (*yángzhōu fàndiàn*) at 308 Nanjing Donglu, which has, as the name implies, Yangzhou-style food, including the famous *yángzhōu chǎofàn*, a delicious fried rice dish.

The *Sichuan* (☎ 3222246) (*sìchuān fàndiàn*) at No 457 has hot and spicy food, including camphor-tea duck and some rather strange-tasting chicken. Don't let them herd you into the private annexes. Stand your ground in the pleb section and fill up for a fraction of the price. It's a lively place at lunchtime; grab the back of someone's chair (everybody else does) and wait for them to go.

The *Sunya Cantonese Restaurant* (☎ 3206277) (*xīnyǎ yuè càiguǎn*) at No 719 has foreigners' cubicles on the 3rd floor with railway-carriage wood panelling and Cantonese food. The lower floors are bare and bright like any self-respecting Chinese restaurant, but foreigners are often charged double anyway (we were). Keep your own record of what you ate and try the moderately priced dishes for lunch and dinner – yum cha is between 6.30 and 9.30 am. On the ground floor is a pastry shop that's often empty. The *Yangunlou Restaurant* in the next block, on the same side of the street, is renowned for its Beijing duck. Across the road is an enormous sweet and cake shop the size of a department store.

Two blocks further, turn left on Yunnan Lu; in the evenings (from 5 to 10 pm) you'll discover a marvellous 'food street' of sorts – it's a great place to sample local fare at local prices. Among the selections are fried wonton, noodle soups and shish kebab. Always settle on the price first before putting in an order.

Nanjing Xilu The *Luzhou Western Restaurant* (☎ 3278254) (*lùzhōu xī càiguǎn*) at 473 Nanjing Xilu is catching on with the city's trendy crowd. If you'd rather eat genuine proletariat dishes, check out the *People's Restaurant* (☎ 2584363) (*rénmín fàndiàn*) at No 226.

For snacks, try the *Wangjiasha Snack Bar* (☎ 2535202) (*wángjiāshā diǎnxīn diàn*) at No 805, off Shimen Lu, for chicken, shrimp in soup, or sweet and salty glutinous dumplings.

Fuzhou Lu Outside the Yunnan Lu night market, this street provides the best chance of getting a feed at low prices in the city centre. Make sure you try places other than those listed here; there are plenty around.

The *Xinghualou Restaurant* (☎ 3282747) (*xìnghuā lóu*) at No 343 has snacks, cakes and refreshments downstairs, including a kind of dim sum. Upstairs you'll get Cantonese food, including 'stewed wild cat' and snake.

The *Meiweizhai Restaurant* (☎ 3222258) (*měiwèzhāi*) at No 600 serves Suzhou and Wuxi styles à la carte or in cheap set meals.

Near the corner of Fuzhou Lu and Xizang Lu, at No 710, is *Da Xi Yang*, a Muslim fastfood restaurant with a clean, tasty buffet. It's open from 10 am to 10 pm. Around the corner on Xizang Lu is a much grubbier and cheaper Muslim place.

Yuyuan Bazaar Area For Chinese-style snacks there's nowhere better than the *Yuyuan Bazaar* (☎ 3111106), also known as the *Mandarin Gardens Bazaar* (*yùyuán lǚyóu shāngchéng*). Officially, it's at 41 Jiujiaochang Lu, the western side of Mandarin Gardens. Among the offerings are Nanxiang dumplings (served in a bamboo steamer), pigeon-egg dumplings (shaped like a pigeon egg in summer), vegetarian buns and spicy cold noodles.

Also in the Yuyuan Bazaar area, the *Old Shanghai Restaurant* (☎ 3289850) (*shànghǎi lǎo fàndiàn*) at 242 Fuyou Lu is a major restaurant specialising in 'Shanghai cuisine' which has been around since day one – it's now housed in a new building. The 2nd floor is air-conditioned and used mainly for banquets, but you could try at lunchtime.

The *Green Wave Gallery* (☎ 3265947) (*lǜbōláng cāntīng*), 125 Yuyuan Lu, serves main courses and more expensive snacks; a seafood dinner may consist of black carp raised in the Lotus Pond under the winding bridge. Snacks include crabmeat buns, lotus root and bamboo shoot shortbread, three-shred eyebrow crispcakes and phoenix-tail dumplings (whatever they are).

Old French Concession Area Try the *Shanghai Western Restaurant* (☎ 4374902) (*shànghǎi xī càiguǎn*) at 845 Huaihai Zhonglu.

The *Meixin* (☎ 4373991) (*měixīn jiǔjiā*) at 314 Shaanxi Nanlu, near Huaihai Zhonglu, serves Cantonese crisp duck and chicken.

The *Red House* (☎ 2565748) (*hóng fángzi xī càiguǎn*) at 37 Shaanxi Nanlu was formerly Chez Louis and things haven't gone so well since Louis left; the food is generally terrible, but the snacks are better so long as they've got the right liqueur (baked Alaska and Grand Marnier soufflé); foreigners are expected to use the more expensive top floor but the ground floor is cheaper.

Along Huaihai Zhonglu is a string of confectioneries. The *Canglangting* (☎ 283876) at 9 Chongqing Nanlu south of Huaihai has glutinous rice cakes and Suzhou-style dumplings and noodles. The *Tianshan Moslem Foodstore (tiānshān huímín shípǐndiàn)* at 671 Huaihai has Muslim delicacies, sweets and cakes. The *Laodachang Bakery & Confectionery (lǎodàchāng shípǐndiàn)* at No 875 has a downstairs bakery with superb ice cream in season; upstairs is a cafe where they spray ice cream over everything; it also offers meringues and macaroons – open until 9.30 pm.

Hotel Food The big tourist hotels have excellent Chinese and Western food. Dining hours are around 7 to 9 am for breakfast, 11.30 am to 2 pm for lunch and 5.30 to 8 pm for dinner. While some of the offerings in the ritzier parts of the hotels are on the expensive side, a Cantonese dim sum or Western breakfast can be surprisingly cheap. The coffee shop in the south wing of the *Peace Hotel* serves a cheap breakfast of toast and three eggs, though coffee costs US$1 per cup (maybe you can sneak in a jar of instant and order hot water?).

If you like Japanese food, be prepared to pay Japanese prices. You can get raw fish with mustard sauce at the Japanese restaurant in the *Westin Taipingyang Hotel* (☎ 2758888) at 5 Zunyi Nanlu. Another venue catering to this market is the *Kawakyu Japanese Restaurant* (☎ 4712712) in the Shanghai Hotel at 505 Wulumuqi Beilu. The *Sakura Japanese Restaurant* (☎ 4331111) is in the Garden Hotel at 58 Maoming Nanlu. The *Benkay Restaurant* (☎ 2559111) in the Hotel Nikko Longbai at 2451 Hongqiao Lu does a mean teriyaki.

If you're not prone to motion sickness, you could give the revolving restaurants a whirl, but hold onto your wallet because these rides aren't cheap. The *Blue Heaven Revolving Restaurant* (☎ 4334488) in the Jinjiang Tower at 161 Changle Lu is one possible moving target.

Also inside the Jinjiang complex at 59 Maoming Nanlu is something called 'Food St' – an arcade (not a street) of restaurants. While the exotic seafood (like seaslug) is expensive, there are quite cheap vegetable and pork dishes – on the other hand, if you've never eaten a seaslug then this might be the time to spend some money and find out what it's like.

The *Park Hotel* has several restaurants. On the 14th floor (it's actually the 12th since two of the floors are below ground) is a restaurant that used to be called the Sky Terrace; a section of the roof could be rolled back to allow patrons to dine under the stars. Apparently the gizmo is still in place though we haven't heard of anyone getting the planetarium effect.

We hate to admit it, but the best hotel food these days is being served at the more modern joint-venture hotels, which can afford to pay for the best chefs in China. *Luigi's* (☎ 4391000) at the Sheraton Huating has excellent Italian food. The *Guan Yue Tai* in the same building does Cantonese cuisine. Italian food is also available at *Giovanni's* (☎ 2758888 ext 3302) in the Westin Taipingyang Hotel.

The Holiday Inn has its *Tian Yuan Cantonese Restaurant*. The *Botania Brasserie* in the Regal Shanghai Hotel is excellent. We could go on, regurgitating lists of outstanding hotel restaurants – unfortunately, you could also find yourself regurgitating when the bill arrives.

Vegetarian Food Vegetarianism became something of a snobbish fad in Shanghai at one time; it was linked to Taoist and Buddhist groups, then to the underworld, and surfaced on the tables of restaurants as creations shaped like flowers or animals. Khi Vehdu, who ran the Jing'an Temple in the 1930s, was one of the most celebrated exponents. The nearly two-metre-tall abbot had a large following – and each of his seven concubines had a house and a car. The Jing'an Temple was eventually divested of its Buddhist statues and turned into a factory.

The *Jade Buddha Temple Vegetarian Restaurant* (☎ 2585596) (*yùfó sì sùzhāi*) at 170 Anyuan Lu certainly has an authentic and congenial atmosphere, not to mention good food.

The *Gongdelin* (☎ 3271532) (*gōngdélín shūshíchù*) at 43 Huanghe Lu is a branch of the Beijing establishment with the same name. It's a government-run place featuring mock seafood, mock duck and roasted brandough. The restaurant is just around the corner from the Park Hotel on Nanjing Xilu.

A couple of shops specialise in vegetarian food; these include the *Hongkouqu Grain Store* (☎ 3240514) at 62 Linping Lu, which is good for fresh peanut butter, tahini, grains, beans and vegetable oils. The *Sanjiaodi Vegetable Market* at 250 Tanggu Lu in the Hongkou District, north of the Bund, is a large indoor market selling fresh vegetables and bean-curd products, and ready-to-cook dinners, fish and meat. The *Yuyuan Bazaar* area has snack bars serving vegetarian food.

Fast Food There's no getting away from it – the Chinese are just as easily addicted to fast food as Westerners. *Kentucky Fried Chicken* (☎ 3275947) (*kěndéjī jiāxiāng jī*) has made its debut at 231 Nanjing Xilu. And if imitation is the sincerest form of flattery, the Colonel should be proud of the fake Chinese Kentucky Fried Chicken just next door. There is another Kentucky Fried in the Tung Feng Hotel (right on the Bund) at 3 Zhongshan Dong 1-Lu. Other venues include 800 Changning Lu and 69 Wuning Lu.

Cafes Shanghai's cafes are open until around 10 pm – just follow the neon. These are meeting and gossip hang-outs where the coffee is dreadful and the cakes are lousy, but if you've wondered what it must have been like in a Parisian cafe in the 1930s, then the ambience is definitely there.

After they get booted out of the shoe stores along Huaihai Zhonglu, young and old folk head for the upstairs section of the *Laodachang Bakery* (☎ 4374809) (*lǎodàchāng shípǐnchǎng*) which is open until around 10 pm – you can choose cakes downstairs first if you want to. In case things get a bit out of hand there are little round coasters under the glass tops of the tables upstairs at the Laodachang, reminding people of the one-child policy – with graphics of a woman feeding rabbits.

Entertainment

Like elsewhere in China, nightlife in Shanghai is now politically acceptable and starting to make a comeback. It's pretty tame by pre-1949 standards and tends to be heavy on awful karaoke bars, but it's rewarding enough if you make the effort. Back in the pre-revolutionary days the acrid smell of opium hung in the streets, bevies of bar girls from the four corners draped themselves over rich men; there were casinos, greyhound and horse-racing tracks, strings of nightclubs, thousands of brothels, lavish dinners and several hundred ballrooms.

The Kuomintang dampened the nightlife by imposing a curfew. When the Communists took over they wiped out in a year what the missionaries had failed to do in a hundred years. Since the average Chinese has to get up at the crack of dawn there's a self-imposed curfew of around 10 pm – nevertheless there are Chinese couples lolling about on the walkways and park benches of the Bund late into the night. Decadent foreign devils who don't need to get up early can rage on (as much as this place will allow) until around 1 am.

Before the Communist takeover, one of the major sources of diversion was the Great World Amusement Centre, offering women, earwax extractors, magicians, mahjong, jugglers, freak shows, dancing, slot machines, story-tellers, barbers, shooting galleries, pickpockets and a bureau for writing love letters. Today the place has been turned into the Shanghai Youth Palace and stands at the corner of Yan'an Lu and Xizang Lu. Since 1983 the place has been hosting 'Youth

SHANGHAI

Evenings' where 30-year-olds come in the hope of finding a husband or wife.

Bars & Clubs Alas, the Jinjiang Club is no more. Housed in a remarkable building opposite the main gates of the Jinjiang Hotel, this place had the most extraordinary nightlife museum in the PRC. The dazzling collection of interiors was thrown up in the 1920s and was then known as the *Cercle Sportif Français* – the French Sporting Club. It closed its doors in 1949, underwent a 30-year silence (when it was rumoured to be either a military training centre or Mao's Shanghai residence) and was reopened in 1979 for foreigners and high-ranking Chinese. It has now been renovated and reopened as the luxury Garden Hotel, retaining some of the original fittings. Instead, try the Jinjiang Hotel across the road, which has a bar and (Y250 cover charge!) disco. Also buried within the Jinjiang complex is the Petit Auditorium, where concerts are staged (mostly sedate chamber music rather than heavy metal).

Each of the elite European/American-style hotels (eg the Sheraton Huating, Shanghai Hilton and Yangtze New World) has at least one international nightclub where businesspeople and technical reps shake it as best they can. One place worth checking out might be the Trader's Pub (☎ 2791888 ext 5307) in the Shanghai JC Mandarin Hotel – it's open from 7 pm to 1 am daily except Monday.

Performing Arts There are some 70 cinemas and theatres and 35 performing troupes in Greater Shanghai – with a little help from the numerous English speakers in this place it should be possible to delve into the local listings, which may include top-notch travelling troupes. This is probably the best place in China to get a look at the local entertainment scene: acrobatics, ballet, music, burlesque, opera, drama, puppets, sporting events...a couple of venues are listed here to give you some idea of what's in stock.

The Shanghai Art Theatre *(shànghǎi yìshù jùyuàn)* is just down the road from the Jinjiang Hotel, and is housed in what used to be the Lyceum Theatre. The theatre was completed in 1931 and was used by the Shanghai Amateur Dramatic Society – a favourite haunt of the Brits. The theatre company of the same name started up in 1929, the first drama troupe of the Communist Party. Nowadays there are all sorts of unexpected performances here – anyone for *Equus* in Mandarin?

The Shanghai Film Studio continues to produce some of the better material in China. Film-making in Shanghai has a long tradition – as old as movie-making can be. One of the starlets of the B-grade set back in the 1930s was Jiang Qing. It's potluck whether you'll find a good movie or not, but it won't cost more than a few jiao to find out. A good gauge of a film's popularity is the bike parking outside – if it spreads for two blocks then it must be a hit!

The Conservatory of Music (☎ 4370137) *(yīnyuè xuéxiào)* at 20 Fenyang Lu off Huaihai Zhonglu in Frenchtown is a treat not to be missed by classical music lovers. The conservatory was established in 1927 and its faculty members were mainly foreign – after WW I, Shanghai was a meeting place for talented European musicians. The most enthralling aspect of the conservatory is the child prodigies. Back in 1979 Yehudi Menuhin was passing through here and picked 11-year-old violinist Jin Li for further instruction in England; the kid enthralled audiences in London in 1982 with his renditions of Beethoven. Other wonders, products of the special training classes set up in the 1950s, have gone to the West on cultural-exchange visits. The conservatory was closed during the Cultural Revolution, but Beethoven et al. have now been rehabilitated along with the conservatory. Performances take place on Sunday evenings at 7 pm. Tickets are usually sold out a few days beforehand, though. Also try the opera at the People's Opera Theatre on Jiu Jiang Lu.

There are several professional orchestras in Shanghai, including the Shanghai Philharmonic and the Shanghai National Orchestra. The latter specialises in native instruments.

Cinemas Cinemas sometimes show imported Western films with Chinese subtitles, or Chinese films with English subtitles. A schedule is published in the English-language *Shanghai Culture & Recreation* newspaper. You can try ringing the cinemas, but don't expect the staff to speak English. Notable cinemas include:

Songshan (☎ 3283482); Changcheng (☎ 3281989); Huaihai (☎ 3271800); Ruijin (☎ 2532833); Xinhua (☎ 2537855); Rihui (☎ 4335155); Cathay (☎ 4732980); Donghu (☎ 4734142); Peace Twin-Hall (☎ 3224954).

Gyms The largest indoor sports venue in Shanghai is the Shanghai Gymnasium at the south-western corner of the city. It's air-con, has computer-controlled scoreboards and seats 18,000.

Acrobatics Acrobats are pure fun and are China's true ambassadors. Donating pandas may sooth relations but it's the acrobats who capture the international imagination. The Shenyang Acrobatic Troupe toured the USA before the two countries established diplomatic relations, and Chinese troupes have gone to 30 countries with not a dud response.

The Shanghai Acrobatics Theatre *(shànghǎi zájì chǎng)* has stunning shows almost every evening. Some people find the animal acts a bit sad, but in general reactions to the shows have been enthusiastic. Sometimes performing tigers and pandas (not together) show up as an added bonus. Tickets for the regular shows are around Y5 but scalpers buy them up ahead of time to resell on the day of the show for Y60 or more. Some suckers pay, but you can bargain with scalpers – if you wait until the very last minute, the price drops dramatically (Y10 is easily possible as they have no use for an unsold ticket). Buying from the ticket office doesn't seem to work – it's permanently 'sold out' even though the show is rarely half full. CITS will also book seats for a fee. Performances start around 7 pm. The theatre is on Nanjing Xilu, a short walk west of the Park Hotel on the same side of the street.

Golf If hitting a ball around a lawn is your type of entertainment, this need can be catered for at the Shanghai Country Club

The Chinese Circus

Circus acts go back 2000 years in the Middle Kingdom; effects are obtained using simple props: sticks, plates, eggs and chairs; and apart from the acrobatics there's magic, vaudeville, drama, clowning, music, conjuring, dance and mime thrown into a complete performance. Happily, it's an art which gained from the Communist takeover and which did not suffer during the Cultural Revolution. Performers used to have the status of gypsies, but now it's 'people's art'.

Most of the provinces have their own performing troupes, sponsored by government agencies, industrial complexes, the army or rural administrations. About 80 troupes are active in China, and they're much in demand – scalpers make huge profits. You'll also see more bare leg, star-spangled costumes and rouge in one acrobat show than you'll see anywhere else in China – it's something of a revelation to see dressed-up and made-up Chinese!

Acts vary from troupe to troupe. Some traditional acts haven't changed over the centuries, while others have incorporated roller skates and motorcycles. A couple of time-proven acts that are hard to follow include the 'balancing in pairs' with one man balanced upside down on the head of another and mimicking every movement of the partner below, mirror image, even drinking a glass of water! Hoop-jumping is another: four hoops are stacked on top of each other and the person going through the very top hoop may attempt a backflip with a simultaneous body-twist.

The 'Peacock Displaying its Feathers' involves an array of people balanced on one bicycle. According to the Guinness Book of Records a Shanghai troupe holds the record at 13, though apparently a Wuhan troupe has done 14. The 'Pagoda of Bowls' is a balancing act where the performer, usually a woman, does everything with her torso except tie it in knots, all the while casually balancing a stack of porcelain bowls on foot, head or both – and perhaps also balancing on a partner. ■

(☎ 9728111; fax 9728520) *(shànghǎi xiāngcūn jùlèbù)* in Zhujiajiao, Qingpu County. This activity is not exactly for those travelling on a limited budget – the fees are near Western levels. Green fees are highest on weekends. If you don't happen to have a set of golf clubs and shoes in your backpack, these can be rented.

Shooting Psychologists say that blowing off some anger every once in a while is good for us. If CITS, FEC and the railway ticket office have been getting to you, good therapy can be provided at the Shanghai Marksmen Shooting Club (☎ 6651641) *(shànghǎi shèshǒu shèjí jùlèbù)*. The club is at 666 Guangzhong Lu in the Hongkou District – take bus No 79.

Things to Buy

Good buys in Shanghai are clothing (silks, down jackets, traditional Chinese clothing, stencilled T-shirts, embroidered clothing), antiques (real or otherwise), tea (chrysanthemum and Dragon Well tea from Hangzhou), stationery...the list goes on and on, so just regard this place as one big department store. All consumer urges are catered for here.

Major shopping areas in Shanghai besides crowded Nanjing Donglu are Huaihai Zhonglu, Ruijin Lu, Sichuan Beilu, Jinling Donglu and Nanjing Xilu.

One good place to look for down jackets is Zhongya Down & Feather Products Store (☎ 2582261) at 990-2 Nanjing Xilu.

Some smaller streets offer specialties. Shimen Yilu has clothing and houseware stores. Over in Frenchtown is the Gujin Brassiere Store (☎ 4736714) at 863 Huaihai Zhonglu. In the same neighbourhood, the Straw Products Shop at 167 Ruijin offers a fine variety of things woven from straw for bargain prices.

You can shop around the clock in Shanghai. For example, the Caitongde Traditional Chinese Medicine Shop (☎ 3207418) at 320 Nanjing Donglu is open 24 hours a day.

The Friendship Store *(yǒuyí shāngdiàn)*, once housed in the former UK consulate on the Bund, has moved around the corner to a multistorey building at 40 Beijing Donglu. This place sells a lot of touristy junk, but useful things too like books in English, maps, silk underwear and other goodies. The Friendship Store also houses a Western-style supermarket.

The Shanghai Antique and Curios Store (☎ 3210019) *(wénwù shāng diàn)* at 192-226 Guangdong Lu is a major tourist outlet.

Shanghai is a good place to stock up on slide film, a rare item in most parts of China. The latest Japanese photoprocessing machines are available to crank out one-hour prints, but save your slide film processing for Hong Kong or elsewhere.

Getting There & Away

Shanghai has rail and air connections to places all over China, ferries up the Yangzi River and many boats along the coast, and buses to destinations in adjoining provinces.

Air CAAC's useful international flights include those to Brussels, Fukuoka, Hong Kong, Los Angeles, Nagasaki, Nagoya, New York, Osaka, Paris, San Francisco, Tokyo, Toronto and Vancouver. CAAC has announced plans to add direct flights from Shanghai to Seoul, Bangkok and Singapore in the near future. Dragonair also flies between Shanghai and Hong Kong for HK$1290. Northwest and United fly to the USA (with a brief change of aircraft in Tokyo) and Canadian International can get you to Canada.

Daily (usually several times daily) domestic flights connect Shanghai to every major city in China. Somewhat less than daily flights serve obscure backwaters. CAAC flies between Shanghai and the following destinations:

Destination	Fare	Destination	Fare
Beijing	Y590	Canton	Y620
Changchun,	Y900	Chengdu	Y890
Changsha	Y480	Chongqing	Y770
Dalian	Y530	Dandong	Y620
Fuzhou	Y340	Guilin	Y700
Guiyang	Y850	Haikou	Y880
Hangzhou	Y120	Harbin	Y920
Hefei	Y200	Huangshan	Y240
Jilin	Y900	Ji'nan	Y420
Kunming	Y1020	Lanzhou	Y950
Lianyungang	Y240	Mudanjiang	Y990
Nanchang	Y320	Nanjing	Y140
Nanning	Y870	Ningbo	Y120
Qingdao	Y350	Qinhuangdao	Y670
Qiqihar	Y1020	Shantou	Y520
Shenyang	Y680	Shenzhen	Y930
Shijiazhuang	Y560	Taiyuan	Y620
Tianjin	Y570	Ürümqi	Y1820
Wenzhou	Y300	Wuhan	Y380
Xiamen	Y430	Xi'an	Y680
Yantai	Y420	Zhengzhou	Y440

CAAC's main office (☎ domestic 2535953, international 2532255) is at 789 Yan'an Zhonglu, with ticket sales counters in the Jinjiang Hotel, Cypress Hotel, Peace Hotel and Shanghai Hotel. China Eastern Airlines (☎ 2472255) is at 200 Yan'an Xilu; China Northwest Airlines (☎ 2558868 ext 5423) is in the Hotel Nikko Longbai at 2451 Hongqiao Lu; Shanghai Airlines (☎ 2558558) is at the airport but travel agents peddle their tickets in the city centre. For all domestic flights, you can buy tickets from CITS, but remember that if CITS tells you a flight is 'all full', try the airline offices because CITS has a fixed number of tickets allocated and is not aware of other seats.

Several other international airlines have Shanghai offices:

Aeroflot
    East Lake Hotel, Donghu Lu
Air France
    Hongqiao Airport (☎ 2558866)

Canadian Airlines International
    Room 109, Jinjiang Hotel, 59 Maoming Nanlu
    (☎ 2582582)
Dragonair
    Room 123, North Wing, Jinjiang Hotel, 59
    Maoming Nanlu (☎ 4336435)
Japan Airlines
    Room 201, Ruijin Building, 205 Maoming Lu,
    1202 Huaihai Zhonglu (☎ 4333000)
Korean Air
    Rooms 104 & 105, Hotel Equatorial, 65 Yan'an
    Xilu (☎ 2588450)
Northwest Airlines
    Room 207, Level 2, East Podium, Jinjiang Hotel,
    59 Maoming Nanlu (☎ 2798100)
Singapore Airlines
    Room 208, East Wing, Shanghai Centre, 1376
    Nanjing Xilu (☎ 2798000)
United Airlines
    Shanghai Hilton Shopping Arcade, 250 Huashan
    Lu (☎ 2553333)

Bus The long-distance bus station is on Qiujiang Lu, west of Henan Beilu. There are several buses a day to Hangzhou, Wuxi and Changzhou.

There is another ticket office at Renmin Square, opposite the junction of Fuzhou Lu and Xizang Zhonglu, which has tickets for buses to Suzhou. The boarding points for the buses are marked on the ticket in Chinese (at the time of writing there were two boarding points for the Suzhou bus – one on Gongxing Lu near Renmin Square, and one on Huangpu Beilu Kou near the main station), so check where to board the bus when you buy a ticket.

Because the Shanghai-Nanjing highway corridor is so busy, rail is a better option for getting to towns along this route.

Train Shanghai is at the junction of the Beijing-Shanghai and Beijing-Hangzhou lines. Since these branch off in various directions, many parts of the country can be reached by direct train from Shanghai.

Your train may arrive or depart from either the main station (see Central Shanghai map) or the west station (see Shanghai city map). For departures, be sure you know which is which.

Travel times from Shanghai are: Beijing 17½ hours; Canton 33 hours; Guilin 29 hours; Fuzhou 22½ hours; Kunming 62 hours; Hangzhou 3½ hours; Nanjing four hours; Qingdao 24 hours; and Xi'an 27 hours.

There are over a dozen trains a day on the Shanghai-Hangzhou line, and numerous trains on the Shanghai-Nanjing line, stopping at major towns like Zhenjiang, Changzhou and Wuxi on the way. Train No 1 is a special express service to Nanjing that stops only in Wuxi.

Getting Chinese-priced tickets is difficult in Shanghai if you don't have a Chinese face. Having a Chinese person buy it for you is one option – otherwise, consider plastic surgery.

There are three locations for foreigners to buy tickets, and though you'll have to pay foreigner prices, you can at least avoid the horrible queues in the station. The soft-seat waiting room in the Shanghai Railway Station is best place to purchase tickets on short notice (even same-day departures). For next-day departures, you can also try the Longmen Hotel (☎ 3170000 ext 5315) next to the railway station at 777 Hengfeng Lu (ticket office open from 2.30 pm to 9 pm). Your third option is CITS, adjacent to the Peace Hotel, but that office asks for six days' notice, though it can sometimes be managed in three days.

Boat Boats are definitely one of the best ways of leaving Shanghai – they're also the cheapest. For destinations on the coast or inland on the Yangzi, they may even sometimes be faster than trains, which have to take rather circuitous routes. Smaller, grottier boats handle numerous inland shipping routes.

Tickets for larger boats (like the Hong Kong to Shanghai ferries) are handled by CITS, which charges a commission. In Hong Kong you buy the tickets from CTS.

Tickets for all domestic passenger shipping out of Shanghai can be bought from the ticket office at 1 Jinling Donglu.

Considering how cheap boats are, you ought to consider taking a class or two above the crowd. It won't cost you that much more to do so.

The Hong Kong route was re-opened in 1980 after a gap of 28 years. Three passenger ships now ply the route: the *Shanghai*, the *Haixin* and the *Jinjiang*. A lot of travellers leave China this way and the 2½-day trip gets rave reviews. There are departures every five days.

Ships depart from the international passenger terminal to the east of Shanghai Mansions. The address is Wai Hong Qiao Harbour, Taipin Lu No 1. Passengers are requested to be at the harbour three hours before departure. Tickets can be bought from CITS or from the ticket office at 1 Jinling Donglu.

When you take into account the luxurious living, the trip is cheap. Ships come complete with dance floor, library, swimming pool...just about the classiest things sailing regularly around Chinese waters.

Boats to Putuoshan run every two days, departing at 3 pm in either direction and taking 12 hours. Tickets cost Y20 to Y58 depending on class.

The main destinations of ferries up the Yangzi River from Shanghai are Nantong, Nanjing, Wuhu, Guichi, Jiujiang and Wuhan. From Wuhan you can change to another ferry which will take you to Chongqing. If you're only going as far west as Nanjing then take the train – much faster than the boat.

Tickets can be bought from the booking hall at the corner of Jinling Donglu and Zhongshan Dong 2-Lu. Foreigners are escorted to window No 1 on the 2nd floor to make sure they pay the tourist price in FEC (there is a 95% surcharge on the Chinese price for foreigners). Daily departures are from Shiliupu wharf.

If money is more important than time, the most sensible way to head west from Shanghai is along the river. Wuhan, for example, is over 1500 km by rail from Shanghai. For about half the hard-sleeper train fare you can get a berth in 4th class on the boat. For a bit more than a tourist-priced hard-sleeper ticket on a train you'd probably be able to get a bed in a two-person cabin on the boat.

The frequency of coastal shipping varies

according to destination. Some of the 5000-tonne liners have staterooms with private bathroom in 1st and special classes – wood panelling, red velvet curtains, the works. The ship should have a restaurant, bar, snack shops, but this depends on the boat. Second and 3rd class are split into A and B fares, with A having just a bit better accommodation and service than B. Popular destinations include Canton, Ningbo, Qingdao and Wenzhou.

Ships to Canton (six times a month), Qingdao (daily), Dalian and Fuzhou leave from Gongpinglu wharf, to the east of Shanghai Mansions. Ships to Ningbo and Wenzhou leave daily from the Shiliupu dock. However, check the departure point when you buy your ticket!

The boat to Qingdao departs daily, with the exception of a few odd days of the month. It takes about 26 hours, while the train takes 24 hours. Second class on the liner is roughly equivalent to the price of a hard seat on a train (if you get the Chinese price) and the boat would be much more comfortable. Boat connections like Shanghai to Dalian, then Dalian to Tianjin, can be made, though you may find the huge number of passengers using the cheaper services a problem when getting tickets.

Getting Around
The sights in Shanghai are spaced a fair distance apart. Not only that, but vehicles swarm everywhere, with a host of noise generators to announce their oncoming right of way: buses and traffic police have megaphones, bells, buzzers, hooters, honkers, screechers, flashing lights; taxis may just as well have a permanent siren attached; pedestrians have no early warning system and rely on fast legs. If you've got the energy, then walking through Shanghai's various neighbourhoods is fascinating.

To/From the Airport Hongqiao Airport is 18 km from the Bund and getting there takes about 30 minutes if you're lucky, or over an hour if you're not. There is a bus from the CAAC office on Yan'an Lu to the airport. Major hotels like the Jinjiang have an airport

shuttle. Taxis from the Bund cost approximately Y45.

Bus Buses are often packed to the hilt and at times impossible to board. The closest thing to revolutionary fervour in Shanghai today is the rush-hour bus ambushes. Once on board, keep your valuables tucked away since pickpocketing is easy under such conditions, and foreigners make juicy targets.

Contrary to popular belief, buses are not colour coded. The bus map is. Routes 1 to 30 are for trolley-buses (now supplemented by regular buses). Buses 1 to 199 operate from 5 am to 11 pm. Buses in the 200 and 400 series are peak-hour buses, and 300 series buses provide all-night service. Suburban and long-distance buses don't carry numbers – the destination is in characters. Some useful buses are listed here:

No 18 runs from the front of the main railway station (it originates further north-east at Hongkou or Lu Xun Park) and proceeds south down Xizang Lu, and then south to the banks of the Huangpu.

No 64 gets you to the railway station from the Pujiang Hotel – catch it near the Pujiang on Beijing Donglu close to the intersection with Sichuan Zhonglu. The ride takes 20 to 30 minutes.

No 65 runs from behind the main railway station, passes Shanghai Mansions, crosses Waibaidu bridge, then heads directly south along the Bund (Zhongshan Lu) as far as the Bund can go.

No 49 from the PSB terminal heads west along Yan'an Lu. Nos 48 and 42 follow similar routes from Huangpu Park, south along the Bund, west around the Dongfeng Hotel, then link westbound along Yan'an Lu. No 26 starts in the city centre a few streets west of the Bund, drops to the Yuyuan Bazaar, then goes west along Huaihai Lu.

No 16 is a good linking bus for all those awkward destinations. It runs from the Jade Buddha Temple to Yuyuan Bazaar, then on to a ferry hop over the Huangpu River.

No 11 travels the ring road around the old Chinese city.

No 71 can get you to the CAAC office, from where you can catch the airport bus. Catch No 71 from Yan'an Donglu close to the Bund.

Underground The Shanghai subway is being built at a feverish pace and portions of it could be in operation by the time you read this. The authorities say that the first section to be opened will run along Huaihai Zhonglu.

Taxi Taxis operate out of the tourist hotels. You can flag them down on the street too, but they are often occupied, at least during peak hours. Different taxis charge different fares – a sticker on the rear window designates the per km charge (Y0.90 to Y1.60). Flag fall for a Y1.20 per km taxi is Y10.80 which in theory should carry you nine km but it seems like only five, after which you pay Y1.20 per km.

Car Anji Car Rental Company in Shanghai is said to be the first company in China to experiment with renting cars to foreigners at the airport on arrival. The service has not proven immensely popular yet, but might catch on. Just why anyone would want to drive a car is Shanghai is the big question.

Hotel Transport The Sheraton Huating has a free hourly shuttle to the Bund and other central areas. Other major hotels may offer the same service for their guests.

Jiangsu 江苏

Population: 65 million
Capital: Nanjing

With China's most productive land, Jiangsu (*jiāngsū*) is symbolic of agricultural abundance and has long been known as the land of 'fish and rice' – these two pictographs are even contained in the original Chinese character for the province. The southern part of Jiangsu lies within the Yangzi Basin, a tapestry landscape of greens, yellows and blues contrasting with whitewashed farm houses. Woven into this countryside is a concentration of towns and cities with one of the highest levels of industrial output in China.

As far back as the 16th century, the towns on the Grand Canal set up industrial bases for silk production and grain storage, and are still ahead of the rest of the nation. While heavy industry is based in Nanjing and Wuxi, the other towns concentrate more on light industry, machinery and textiles. They're major producers of electronics and computer components, and haven't been blotted out by the scourges of coal mining or steelworks. Today southern Jiangsu is increasingly being drawn into the rapidly expanding economy of nearby Shanghai.

The stretch from Nanjing down to Hangzhou in Zhejiang Province is heavily touristed, but north of the Yangzi there's not really much to talk about; it's a complete contrast – decayed, backward and lagging behind the rest of the province. In the north the major port is at Lianyungang and there's a big coal works in Xuzhou.

Jiangsu is hot and humid in summer, yet has overcoat temperatures in winter (when visibility can drop to zero). Rain or drizzle can be prevalent – but it's gentle rain, adding a misty soft touch to the land. The natural colourings can be spectacular in spring. Heavy rains fall in spring and summer, but autumn is fairly dry.

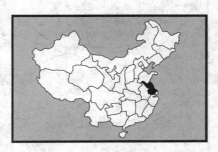

NANJING
(nánjīng) 南京

> Over Chungshan swept a storm, headlong
> Our mighty army, a million strong, has crossed the Great River.
> The city, a tiger crouching, a dragon curling, outshines its ancient glories;
> In heroic triumph heaven and earth have been overturned.
> **Mao, from his poem, 'The People's Liberation Army Captures Nanjing'**

The assault on Nanjing by the Communist Army in April 1949 was not the first time that the heaven and earth of the city had been overturned. In fact, the city has been conquered many times by foreigners, rebels and imperial armies. It has been destroyed, rebuilt, destroyed again, emptied of inhabitants, repopulated and rebuilt, only to be destroyed again by the occasional natural disaster.

History

The area has been inhabited for about 5000 years, and a number of prehistoric sites have been discovered in or around Nanjing. There are also sites which date back to the Shang and Zhou dynasties.

The city's strategic position, guarded by the surrounding hills and rivers, is the source of both its prosperity and its troubles. The

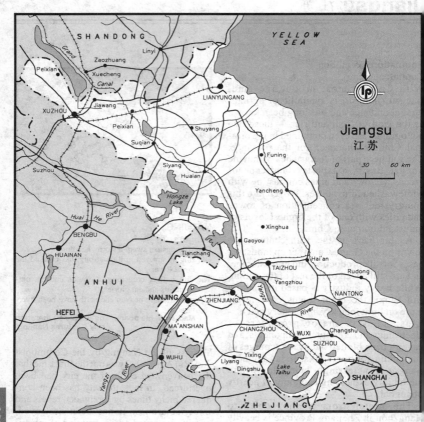

Yangzi narrows here and a bit further east begins to form a delta, so Nanjing became a focus of trade and communications along one of China's greatest water routes.

The city's recorded history dates back to the Warring States Period (476-221 BC) when several states battled for its control, one overcoming the other and using Nanjing as a bastion from which to attack a third state, only to be defeated. This confusing situation was finally put to an end by the Qin Dynasty (221-207 BC); the Qin State defeated all the other states and united the country. From this period on, Nanjing grew in importance as the administrative centre of the surrounding area.

Qin rule ushered in a period of stability for the city, and during the Western and Eastern Han dynasties which succeeded the Qin, Nanjing grew as an important regional centre. In 220 AD the Eastern Han collapsed and three new states emerged. Nanjing became the capital of the state of Wu in the south when the emperor moved his court here, taking advantage of the strategic position on China's waterways and its fort, which appeared impregnable.

The Wu rulers seemed to have learned as

little from history as those before them. They were overthrown by the Jin who rose in the north, who in turn were overthrown by a military strongman who set himself up as the first emperor of the Song Dynasty.

The early part of the 6th century was an inauspicious time to be in Nanjing. There was a terrible flood in 507, a great fire in 521 which destroyed a huge section of the imperial palace, a pestilence in 529 and another flood in 533. There were peasant rebellions in 533, 541, 542 and 544, and the upheaval was compounded by the strains imposed by large numbers of refugees and immigrants from the north.

To top it off, in 548 AD the army of General Hou Jing, who was originally allied with but now plotted to overthrow the southern emperor, attacked Nanjing and in a wave of gratuitous violence looted the city, raped the women and killed or conscripted the other inhabitants. Hou Jing took the city but after a series of palace intrigues also wound up dead.

Meanwhile in the north another general, Wen Di, who had usurped the throne of the reigning Northern Zhou Dynasty, established himself as the first emperor of the Sui Dynasty and set out on a war against the south. Nanjing fell to his army in about 589. Wen Di chose to establish his capital at Xi'an and to eradicate once and for all any claims of the south to the throne of a now united China. Wen completely demolished all the important buildings of Nanjing, including its beautiful palaces, and the city ceased to be important. Although it enjoyed a period of prosperity under the long-lived Tang Dynasty, it gradually slipped back into obscurity.

Ming Dynasty Nanjing's brightest day came in the 14th century with the overthrow of the Yuan Dynasty by a peasant rebellion led by Zhu Yuanzhang. The rebels captured Nanjing in 1356 and went on to capture the Mongol capital at Beijing in 1368. Zhu took the name of Hong Wu and set himself up as the first emperor of the Ming Dynasty (1368-1644). Under Hong Wu, Nanjing was

established as the capital, partly because it was far from the north and safe from sudden barbarian attacks, and partly because it was in the most wealthy and populous part of the country. A massive palace was built, huge walls were raised around the city, and construction of other buildings proceeded at a furious pace. The city became a manufacturing and administrative metropolis and a centre of learning and culture.

However, the next Ming emperor, Yong Le, moved his capital to Beijing in 1420. Nanjing's population was halved and the city declined in importance. It was another bad century – the city suffered a succession of fires, famines, floods, typhoons, tornadoes and even a snowstorm said to have lasted 40 days. If Nanjing was down then, the Manchus to the north were up and fighting. In 1644 Beijing fell to the army under the Chinese rebel Li Zicheng, who then found himself facing a Manchu invasion. The north of China was conquered by the invaders, and though various pretenders to the Ming throne tried to hold out in Nanjing and other places in the south, in time they were all overcome. Although Nanjing continued as a major centre under the Qing, nothing more of note happened until the 19th and 20th centuries.

The Opium wars were waged right to Nanjing's doorstep in 1842 when a British naval task force of 80 ships sailed up the Yangzi River, took the city of Zhenjiang and arrived at Nanjing in August. Threats to bombard Nanjing forced the Chinese to sign the first of the 'unequal treaties' which opened several Chinese ports to foreign trade, and forced China to pay a huge war indemnity and officially cede the island of Hong Kong to Britain.

Just a few years later, one of the most dramatic events in China's history focused attention on Nanjing – the Taiping Rebellion (1851-64) succeeded in taking over most of southern China. This Chinese Christian army gained attention in the West but its success against the Qing worried the Western powers, who preferred to deal with the corrupt and weak Qing rather than the united and strong Taipings. After 1860 the Western

JIANGSU

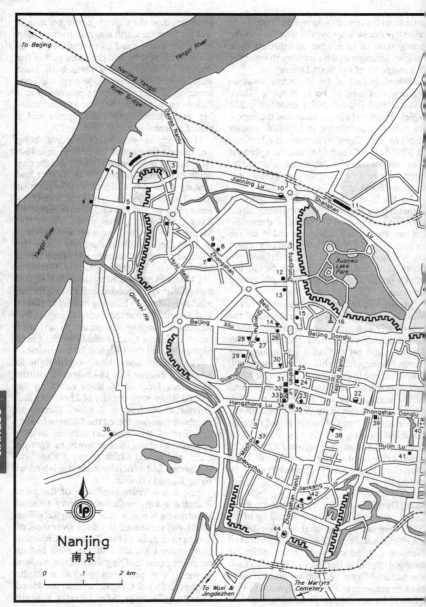

To Beijing

Yangzi River

Nanjing Yangzi
River Bridge

Daqiao Nanlu

Yangzi River

Qinhuai He

Jianning Lu

Shanshan Lu

Zhongyang Lu

Xuanwu
Lake Park

Hutu Beilu

Zhongshan

Beilu

Shanghai Lu

Beijing Xilu

Beijing Donglu

Zhongshan Nanlu

Taiping Nanlu

Guangzhou Lu

Zhongshan

Hangzhong Lu

Zhongshan Donglu

Mochou Lu

Ruijin Lu

Shengzhou Lu

Jiankang Lu

Zhongshan Nanlu

To Wuxi &
Jingdezhen

The Martyrs'
Cemetery

Nanjing
南京

0   1   2 km

JIANGSU

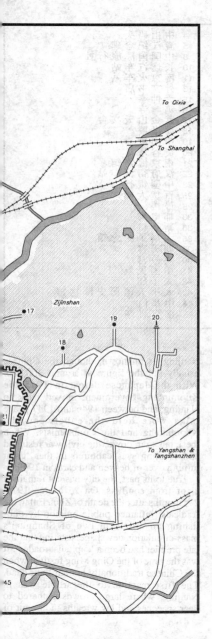

■ PLACES TO STAY

3   Daqiao Hotel
6   Shuangmenlou Hotel
7   Nanjing Hotel
9   Hongqiao Hotel
12 Xuanwu Hotel
24 Jingu Hotel
27 Nanjing University/
    Foreign Students' Dormitory
29 Nanjing Normal University/
    Nanshan Hotel
31 Central Hotel
32 Shengli Hotel
34 Jinling Hotel
39 Xihuamen Hotel

▼ PLACES TO EAT

14 Maxiangxing Restaurant
28 Black Cat Cafe
30 Sprite Freeze
38 Sichuan Restaurant

    OTHER

1   No 4 Dock
2   Nanjing West Railway Station
4   Zhongshan Dock
5   Monument to the Crossing of the
    Yangzi River
8   CITS
10 Long Distance Bus Station
11 Nanjing Railway Station
13 Foreign Languages Bookstore
15 Bell Tower
16 Jiming Temple
17 Zijinshan Observatory
18 Tomb of Hong Wu
19 Sun Yatsen Mausoleum
20 Linggu Pagoda
21 Nanjing Museum
22 Hanfu Jie Bus Station
23 Bank of China
25 Department Store
26 Drum Tower
33 Main Post Office
35 Xinjiekou Traffic Circle
36 Memorial of the Nanjing Massacre
37 Chaotian Palace
40 Ruins of the Ming Palace
41 CAAC
42 Fuzimiao
43 Taiping Museum
44 Zhonghua Gate
45 Nanjing Airport

JIANGSU

■ PLACES TO STAY

3 大桥饭店
6 双门楼宾馆
7 南京饭店
9 虹桥饭店
12 玄武饭店
24 金谷大厦
27 南京大学的外国留学生宿舍
29 南京师范大学的南山宾馆
31 中心大酒店
32 胜利饭店
34 金陵饭店
39 西华门饭店

▼ PLACES TO EAT

14 马祥兴菜馆
28 黑猫餐馆
30 梧州酒家
38 四川酒家

OTHER

1 四号码头
2 南京西站

4 中山码头
5 渡江纪念碑
8 中国国际旅行社
10 长途汽车站
11 南京火车站
13 外文书店
15 大钟亭
16 鸡鸣寺
17 紫金山天文台
18 明陵
19 中山陵
20 灵谷塔
21 南京博物馆
22 汉府街汽车站
23 中国银行
25 百货大楼
26 鼓楼
33 邮电局
35 新街口
36 大屠杀纪念馆
37 朝天宫
40 明故宫
41 中国民航
42 夫子庙
43 太平天国历史博物馆
44 中华门
45 南京机场

powers allied themselves with the Qing and the counteroffensive began. By 1864 the Taipings had been encircled in their capital Nanjing. A Qing army helped by British army regulars like General Charles Gordon (of Khartoum fame) and various European and US mercenaries besieged and bombarded the city for seven months, finally capturing it and slaughtering the Taiping defenders. Hong Xiuquan, the Taiping leader, committed suicide and the rebellion ended.

The Manchus were overthrown in 1911 and Sun Yatsen established a republic with its capital first at Beijing but later at Nanjing. In 1927 Chiang Kaishek ordered the extermination of the Communists, and Yuhuatai Hill to the south of the city was one of the main execution sites. In 1937 the Japanese captured Nanjing and set about butchering the population. Just how many people died in what became known as the 'Rape of

Nanjing' is unknown, though the Chinese usually put the figure at around 300,000. With the Japanese defeat in 1945 the Kuomintang government moved back to Nanjing, and between 1946 and 1947 peace talks were held there between the Kuomintang and the Communists. When these talks ran down, the civil war resumed and Nanjing was captured in that 'great turning over of heaven and earth in 1949'.

True to its past, the city has not remained aloof from conflicts. On 25 March 1976, 2½ months after the death of Zhou Enlai, the 'radicals' inflamed public opinion by publishing an article in two of Shanghai's mass-circulation newspapers stating that the late premier had been a 'capitalist roader'. It was the time of the Qing Ming festival when the Chinese traditionally honour their dead. The first reaction to the article was in Nanjing, where large crowds gathered to hear speeches and lay wreaths in honour of

Zhou. Slogans and posters were put up, a protest march took place through the streets and Zhang Chunqiao (later vilified as a member of the Gang of Four) was named and attacked. The story goes that the carriages of Beijing-bound trains were daubed with messages and slogans so that people in the capital would know what was happening in Nanjing, and that these contributed to the Tiananmen Incident.

Nanjing Today Today, Greater Nanjing is a metropolis with a population of around 4½ million. Despite being something of a political backwater in national terms, the city is one of China's major cultural centres and has developed into an important industrial base for the Chinese motor vehicle, electronics and machine tool industries. Nanjing is a very green and pleasant place, with broad boulevards lined with thousands of trees, giving relief from the oppressive summer heat for which the city is justifiably known as one of China's 'Three Furnaces'. The city is a major centre for education in China and has a large student population drawn from all parts of Jiangsu Province and beyond. It also has a sizable community of foreign students, most involved in Chinese-language studies at Nanjing University and Nanjing Normal University.

Orientation

Nanjing lies entirely on the southern bank of the Yangzi River, bounded in the west by Zijinshan (Purple Mountain). The centre of town is a traffic circle called Xinjiekou, where some of the hotels – including the Jinling Hotel – and most tourist facilities are located. Nanjing railway station and the main long-distance bus station are in the far north of the city. The historical sights – including the Sun Yatsen Mausoleum, Linggu Temple and the tomb of the first Ming emperor Hong Wu – are mainly around Zijinshan, on Nanjing's eastern fringe.

The city has experienced long periods of prosperity – evident in the numerous buildings which successive rulers built – and their tombs, steles, pagodas, temples and niches lay scattered throughout the city. If you can get hold of a copy, *In Search of Old Nanking* by Barry Till and Paula Swart (Joint Publishing Company, Hong Kong, 1982) will give you a thorough rundown. Unfortunately, much of what was built has been destroyed or allowed to crumble into ruins.

Information

CITS This office (☎ 631125) is at 202/1 Zhongshan Beilu. They have a free map with places of interest to tourists shown in English.

Money The Bank of China is at 3 Zhongshan Donglu, just east of Xinjiekou traffic circle. You can also change money at the Jinling and Central hotels.

Post & Telecommunications The main post office is at 19 Zhongshan Lu, just north of Xinjiekou. The more upmarket tourist hotels also offer postal services. There is a large telephone and telegram office just north of the Drum Tower traffic circle.

Maps Several different versions of the local transport map are available from newspaper kiosks and street hawkers around Nanjing. Although now a bit out of date, a glossy map in English covering central Nanjing can sometimes be spotted at hotel or tourist shops.

Early Remains

Nanjing has been inhabited since prehistoric times. Remains of a prehistoric culture have been found at the site of today's Drum Tower in the centre of the city and in surrounding areas. About 200 sites of small clan communities, mainly represented by pottery and bronze artefacts dating back to the late Shang and Zhou dynasties, have been found on both sides of the Yangzi.

In 212 AD, at the end of the Eastern Han period, the military commander in charge of the Nanjing region built a citadel on Qinglingshan in the west of Nanjing. At that time the mountain was referred to as Shitoushan (Stone Head Mountain) and so

JIANGSU

the citadel became known as the Stone City. The wall measured over 10 km in circumference. Today, some of the red sandstone foundations can still be seen.

Ming City Wall

Nanjing enjoyed its golden years under the Ming, and there are numerous reminders of the period to be found. One of the most impressive is the Ming city wall measuring over 33 km – the longest city wall ever built in the world. About two-thirds of it still stands. It was built between 1366 and 1386, by over 200,000 labourers. The layout is irregular, an exception to the usual square walls of these times, because much of it is built on the foundations of earlier walls which took advantage of strategic hills. Averaging 12 metres high and seven metres wide at the top, the wall was built of bricks supplied from five Chinese provinces. Each brick had stamped on it the place it came from, the overseer's name and rank, the brickmaker's name and sometimes the date. This was to ensure that the bricks were well made; if they broke they had to be replaced. Some stone bricks were used, but on the whole they were clay.

Ming City Gates

Some of the original 13 Ming city gates remain, including Heping Gate (hépíng mén) in the north and Zhonghua Gate (zhōnghuá mén) in the south. The city gates were heavily fortified and, rather than being the usual weak points of the defences, they were defensive strongholds. The Zhonghua Gate has four rows of gates, making it almost impregnable; it could house a garrison of 3000 soldiers in vaults in the front gate building. Today some of these vaults are used as souvenir shops and cafes, and are wonderfully cool in summer. Zhonghua Gate can be visited, but Heping Gate is now used as barracks.

Ming Palace Ruins

(mínggùgōng) 明故宫
Built by Hong Wu, the Ming Palace is said to have been a magnificent structure after

which the Imperial Palace in Beijing was modelled. Almost nothing remains of the Ming Palace except five marble bridges lying side by side and known as the Five Dragon Bridges, the old ruined gate called Wu Men, and the enormous column bases of the palace buildings. There are also some stone blocks and a little stone screen carved with animals and scenery.

The palace suffered two major fires its first century and was allowed to fall into ruins after the Ming court moved to Beijing. The Manchus looted it, and during the Taiping Rebellion the bombardment of Nanjing by Qing and Western troops almost completely destroyed the palace.

Drum Tower

(gǔlóu) 鼓楼
Built in 1382, the Drum Tower lies roughly in Nanjing's centre, in the middle of a traffic circle on Beijing Xilu. Drums were usually beaten to give directions for the change of the night watches and, in rare instances, to warn the populace of impending danger. The Nanjing tower originally contained numerous drums and other instruments used on ceremonial occasions, though now only one large drum remains. The ground floor is used for exhibitions of paintings and calligraphy.

Bell Tower

(zhōnglóu) 钟楼
North-east of the Drum Tower, the Bell Tower houses an enormous bell, cast in 1388 and originally situated in a pavilion on the west side of the Drum Tower. The present tower dates from 1889 and is a small two-storey pavilion with a pointed roof and upturned eaves.

Chaotian Palace

(cháotiān gōng) 朝天宫
Chaotian Palace was originally established in the Ming Dynasty as a school for noble children who received instruction here in court etiquette. Most of today's buildings, including the centrepiece of the palace, a Confucian temple, date from 1866 when the whole complex was rebuilt.

Top: On the track, Emeishan, Sichuan (JO)
Left: Dazu Grotto carvings, Dazu, Sichuan (CT)
Right: Worshippers, Wenshu Monastery, Chengdu, Sichuan (CT)

Top: Workers in field and village, Dali, Yunnan (RI'A)
Bottom: Stone Forest, Shilin, Yunnan (RN)

Outside on the small lane running between the canal and the southern wall of the palace is a market selling bric-a-brac. On weekends rows of men sit here at tables playing *xiàngqí* (Chinese chess). At the end of a tiny alley immediately behind the palace is the Jiangsu Province Kunju Theatre *(jiāngsū shěng kūnjùyuàn)*, where excellent – if rather infrequent – performances are held. *(Kunju* is a regional form of classical Chinese opera which developed in the Suzhou-Hangzhou-Nanjing triangle. It is similar to, but slower than, Peking opera and is performed with colourful and elaborate costumes.)

The palace entrance gate is on Mochou Lu on bus route No 4, two stops west from Xinjiekou.

Taiping Museum
(tàipíng tiānguó lìshǐ bówùguǎn)
太平天国历史博物馆
Hong Xiuquan, the leader of the Taipings, had a palace built in Nanjing, but the building was completely destroyed when Nanjing was taken in 1864. All that remains is a stone boat in an ornamental lake in the Western Garden, inside the old Kuomintang government buildings on Changjiang Lu, east of Taiping Lu.

The Taiping Museum is housed in the former mansion of the Hongs' 'Eastern Prince' Yang Xiuqing. The garden next to the mansion is called Zhan Yuan and originally belonged to the first Ming emperor.

The museum has an interesting collection of documents, books and artefacts relating to the rebellion. Most of the literature is copied, the originals being kept in Beijing. There are maps showing the northward progress of the Taiping army from Guangdong, Hong Xiuquan's seals, Taiping coins, cannon balls, rifles and other weapons, and texts which describe the Taiping laws on agrarian reform, social law and cultural policy. Other texts describe divisions in the Taiping leadership, the attacks by the Manchus and foreigners, and the fall of Nanjing in 1864.

Fuzimiao
(fūzǐ miào) 夫子庙
Fuzimiao is in the south of the city, centred around the site of an ancient Confucian temple. It was a centre of Confucian study for over 1500 years. Fuzimiao has been damaged and rebuilt repeatedly, and what you see here today are newly restored late Qing Dynasty structures or wholly new buildings reconstructed in traditional style. The main Temple of Confucius is behind on the small square in front of the canal. Five minutes' walk north-west from here are the Imperial Examination Halls, where scholars spent months – or years – in tiny cells studying Confucian classics in preparation for civil service examinations.

Today, Fuzimiao has become Nanjing's main amusement quarter, and is a particularly lively and crowded place on weekends and public holidays. There are restaurants, silk stores, souvenir shops, art exhibitions, tacky side-shows in old halls and a bookseller stocking ancient Chinese manuscripts.

You can get to the Fuzimiao area from Nanjing West railway station by bus No 16, from the docks by trolley-bus No 31, and from Xinjiekou by bus No 2.

Memorial of the Nanjing Massacre
(dàtúshā jìniànguǎn) 大屠杀纪念馆
The exhibits at the memorial hall document the atrocities committed by Japanese soldiers against the civilian population during the occupation of Nanjing in 1937. They include pictures of actual executions, many taken by Japanese army photographers, and a gruesome viewing hall built over a mass grave of massacre victims. Also on display is furniture used at the signing of Japan's surrender to China – the disproportionately smaller and lower table and chairs given to the Japanese officers carried an unmistakable message.

The exhibits conclude on a more optimistic note, with a final room dedicated to the post-1945 Sino-Japanese reconciliation. The memorial hall is open daily from 8.30 am to 5.00 pm, and entry costs Y2. It's in the city's south-western suburbs on bus route No 7.

JIANGSU

Xuanwu Park

(xuánwǔ gōngyuán) 玄武公园

This park is almost entirely covered by the waters of a large urban lake, but you can walk along causeways or take a boat out to its central forested islands, where there are teahouses, a zoo and a children's fun park. A long path goes around the shores of Xuanwu Lake, beside the old city walls for much of its length. The park's central location makes it a convenient place to escape the hustle – but not necessarily the bustle – of central Nanjing. You can enter Xuanwu Park from the main gate off Zhongyang Lu.

Yangzi River Bridge

(nánjīng chángjiāng dàqiáo) 南京长江大桥

One of the great achievements of the Communists, and one of which they are justifiably proud, is the Yangzi River Bridge at Nanjing which was opened on 23 December 1968. One of the longest bridges in China, it's a double-decker with a 4500-metre-long road on top and a 6700-metre-long railway line below.

The story goes that the bridge was designed and built entirely by the Chinese after the Russians marched out and took the designs with them in 1960. Given the immensity of the construction it really is an impressive engineering feat, before which there was no direct rail link between Beijing and Shanghai.

Monument to the Crossing of the Yangzi River

(dùjiāng jìniàn bēi) 渡江纪念碑

Standing in the north-west of the city on Zhongshan Beilu, this monument erected in April 1979 commemorates the crossing of the river on 23 April 1949 and the capture of Nanjing from the Kuomintang by the Communist army. The characters on the monument are in the calligraphy of Deng Xiaoping.

Nanjing Museum

(nánjīng bówùguǎn) 南京博物馆

Just west of Zhongshan Gate on Zhongshan Lu, the Nanjing Museum houses an array of artefacts from Neolithic times through to the Communist period. The main building was constructed in 1933 with yellow-glazed tiles, red-lacquered gates and columns in the style of an ancient temple.

An interesting exhibit is the burial suit made of small rectangles of jade sewn together with silver thread, dating from the Eastern Han Dynasty (25-220 AD) and excavated from a tomb discovered in the city of Xuzhou in northern Jiangsu Province. Other exhibits include bricks with the inscriptions of their makers and overseers from the Ming city wall, drawings of old Nanjing, an early Qing mural of old Suzhou, and relics from the Taiping Rebellion.

Just east of the museum is a section of the Ming city wall with steps leading up to it from the road. You can walk along the top only as far as Qianhu Lake, where a section of wall has collapsed into the water.

Tomb of Hong Wu

(míng xiàolíng) 明孝陵

This tomb lies east of the city on the southern slope of Zijinshan. Construction began in 1381 and was finished in 1383; the emperor died at the age of 71 in 1398. The first section of the avenue leading up to the mausoleum is lined with stone statues of lions, camels, elephants and horses. There's also a mythical animal called a *xiezhi* which has a mane and a single horn on its head; and a *qilin* which has a scaly body, a cow's tail, deer's hooves and one horn. The second section of the tomb alley turns sharply northward and begins with two large hexagonal columns. Following the columns are pairs of stone military men wearing armour, and these are followed by pairs of stone civil officials. The pathway turns again, crosses some arched stone bridges and goes through a gateway in a wall which surrounds the site of the mausoleum.

As you enter the first courtyard, a paved pathway leads to a pavilion housing several steles. The next gate leads to a large courtyard where you'll find the 'Altar Tower' or 'Soul Tower' – a mammoth rectangular stone structure. To get to the top of the tower, go to the stairway in the middle of the structure.

Behind the tower is a wall, 350 metres in diameter, which surrounds a huge earth mound. Beneath this mound is the tomb vault of Hong Wu, which has not been excavated.

Sun Yatsen Mausoleum
(zhōngshān líng) 中山陵

For many Chinese, a visit to Sun Yatsen's tomb on the slopes of Zijinshan just east of Nanjing is something of a pilgrimage. Sun is recognised by the Communists and the Kuomintang alike as the father of modern China. He died in Beijing in 1925, leaving behind an unstable Chinese republic. He had wished to be buried in Nanjing, no doubt with greater simplicity than the Ming-style tomb which his successors built for him. But less than a year after his death, construction of this immense mausoleum began.

The tomb itself lies at the top of an enormous stone stairway, 323 metres long and 70 metres wide. At the start of the path stands a

Lion statue at Sun Yatsen Memorial

stone gateway built of Fujian marble, with a roof of blue-glazed tiles. The blue and white of the mausoleum were meant to symbolise the white sun on the blue background of the Kuomintang flag.

The crypt is at the top of the steps at the rear of the memorial chamber. A tablet hanging across the threshold is inscribed with the 'Three Principles of the People' as formulated by Dr Sun: nationalism, democracy and people's livelihood. Inside is a seated statue of Dr Sun. The walls are carved with the complete text of the *Outline of Principles for the Establishment of the Nation* put forward by the Nationalist government. A prostrate marble statue of Sun seals his coffin. In fact, it's not known if Sun's body is still in the tomb; the story goes that it was carted off to Taiwan by the Kuomintang and has been there ever since.

Zijinshan
(zǐjīnshān) 紫金山

Most of Nanjing's historical sights – the Sun Yatsen Memorial and Tomb of Hong Wu included – are scattered over the southern slopes of Zijinshan, a high forested hill at the city's eastern fringe.

The **Beamless Hall** is one of the most interesting buildings in Nanjing. In 1381, when Hong Wu was building his tomb, he had a temple on the site torn down and rebuilt a few km to the east. Of this temple only the Beamless Hall (so called because it is built entirely of bricks) remains. The structure has an interesting vaulted ceiling and a large stone platform where Buddhist statues used to be seated. In the 1930s the hall was turned into a memorial to those who died in the 1926-28 revolution. One of the inscriptions on the inside wall is the old Kuomintang national anthem.

A road leads either side of the Beamless Hall and up two flights of steps to the **Pine Wind Pavilion**, originally dedicated to the goddess of mercy as part of the Linggu Temple. Today it houses a small shop and teahouse.

The **Linggu Temple** *(línggǔ sì)* and its memorial hall to Xuan Zang is close by; after

JIANGSU

you pass through the Beamless Hall, turn right and follow the pathway. Xuan Zang was the Buddhist monk who travelled to India and brought back the Buddhist scriptures. Inside the memorial hall is a 13-storey wooden pagoda model which contains part of his skull, a sacrificial table and a portrait of the monk.

Close by is the **Linggu Pagoda** (*línggǔ tǎ*), which was built in the 1930s under the direction of a US architect as a memorial to Kuomintang members who died in the 1926-28 revolution. It's a nine-storey octagonal building 60 metres high.

Day Tour

It's possible to combine all of Zijinshan's sights into a single day trip that includes the Tomb of Hong Wu and the Sun Yatsen Mausoleum. You can take bus No 20 from the Drum Tower and get off at the western end of the Avenue of Stone Animals, two stops before the bus reaches the Tomb of Hong Wu. Alternatively, take bus No 9 from just west of Xinjiekou (opposite the Jinling Hotel) and get off at the avenue's eastern end, one stop before the Sun Yatsen Mausoleum. From there you can continue uphill on foot (or in summer by shuttle bus) to the tomb, the mausoleum and the sights around Linggu Pagoda.

Places to Stay – bottom end

The cheapest beds are at the *Nanjing University/Foreign Students' Dormitory* (*nánjīng dàxué/wàiguó liúxuéshēng sùshè*), a large white-tiled building on Shanghai Lu, just south of Beijing Xilu. Here doubles with communal facilities including kitchen cost Y36 or Y17 per bed – only slightly more than the long-term boarders pay. The best way to get there is to take the No 13 bus from the railway or the long-distance bus station, or you can take a No 3 trolley-bus down Zhongshan Lu and get off just after Beijing Lu.

If it's full, you could try the *Nanjing Normal University/Nanshan Hotel* (*nánjīng shīfàn dàxué nánshān bīnguǎn*). This place also serves mainly as accommodation for foreign students, but often lets out vacant rooms to non-students for US$10 a double with private bathroom. To get there from the Nanjing University dorm, walk half a km south along Shanghai Lu. Turn right into a short market lane, then take the first road left to the main gate of Nanjing Normal University. The hotel is 500 metres inside the campus compound, up to the left from the large grassy quadrangle.

Another bottom-end possibility is the *Daqiao Hotel* (*dàqiáo fàndiàn*). It's in the far north-west of the city at the corner of Daqiao Nanlu and Jianning Lu, and frequented by backpackers from Hong Kong and Japan. A bed in a basic triple costs Y18, or Y30 in a double with attached bathroom, though the loud and cheerful reception staff are generally open to a bit of friendly bargaining. You can get there on a No 10 bus either westbound from the railway station or from the Yangzi ferry terminal.

The only other budget hotel open to foreigners is the *Xihuamen Hotel* (*xīhuámén fàndiàn*), 1½ km east of Xianjiekou on Zhongshan Donglu. The minimum foreigners' rate for a double is Y70. To get there take bus No 5 east from Xinjiekou; the entrance to the hotel compound is almost opposite the 'Panda' factory.

Places to Stay – middle

The *Shuangmenlou Hotel* (☎ 805961) (*shuāngménlóu bīnguǎn*) at 185 Huju Beilu is one of the rambling Chinese garden-style hotels that has seen a few new wings added over the years. Their lowest rate for a double is Y128. To get there from the main railway station or long-distance bus station take a No 10 bus west on Jianning Lu, get off at Daqiao Nanlu and then take a No 21 south on Huju Beilu. Take bus No 16 from near the Yangzi ferry terminal and get off at the second traffic circle.

The *Shengli Hotel* (☎ 648181) (*shènglì fàndiàn*) at 75 Zhongshan Lu near the Jinling Hotel charges Y129 for doubles and Y182 for triples. That seems a bit overpriced for what's offered, but at least the hotel is in a central location and the restaurant is good.

From the railway station take trolley-bus No 33 or from the Yangzi ferry terminal take bus No 16.

Near the CITS office at 202 Zhongshan Beilu is the *Hongqiao Hotel* (☎ 301466) *(hóngqiáo fàndiàn)* which caters largely to tour groups. At US$26 for a simple triple and US$28 for a standard double (including other charges), it offers good value for money. From the railway station, you can take bus No 13 or trolley-bus No 32, and from the Yangzi ferry terminal bus No 16. Across the road at 259 Zhongshan Beilu you'll find the *Nanjing Hotel* (☎ 634121) *(nánjīng fàndiàn)*, the city's oldest tourist establishment. Here you'll pay US$60 for a nice double in a garden setting.

The unexciting Taiwanese joint venture, *Jingu Hotel* (☎ 411888) *(jīngǔ dàshà)*, at 132 Zhongshan Lu diagonally opposite the Central Hotel, charges US$45 for a standard double. The entrance is just off the main street.

Much nicer is the *Xuanwu Hotel* (☎ 303888) *(xuánwǔ fàndiàn)*, a tower block at 193 Zhongyang Lu opposite the Jiangsu Exhibition Hall. It has quite nice doubles overlooking Xuanwu Park starting at US$48. Trolley-bus No 33 south from the long-distance bus or main railway station goes right past it.

Places to Stay – top end

The new *Central Hotel* (☎ 400888, 400666) *(zhōngxīn dàjiǔdiàn)* at 75 Zhongshan Lu near the corner with Huaqiao Lu has a wide range of rooms and prices, from US$77 for a standard double to US$1980 (including service charge) for the presidential suite.

The 36-storey *Jinling Hotel* (☎ 742888) *(jīnlíng fàndiàn)* at Xinjiekou is still the tallest of Nanjing's growing number of tower blocks. The all-inclusive rate for a double starts at US$110, progressing to US$2070 for the ultra-super-luxurious 'Jinling Suite'. The hotel's numerous amenities include a sauna, fitness centre and swimming pool, and at street-level there's a shopping arcade stocking just about any consumer item you're likely to want to buy. The Jinling also

has a good medical service that charges only for prescriptions. Even if you can't afford to stay here, it's worth taking the lift up to the hotel's Sky Palace, the first revolving restaurant in China. From here you can spot the sights of Nanjing, from the Yangzi Bridge to the Sun Yatsen Mausoleum. The cafe on the mezzanine charges only Y12 for a cappuccino and is a good place to relax. At night there's live music. If this place is within your budget you'll probably arrive by taxi anyway, but plebs can get here on one of the many bus routes that run via Xinjiekou.

Places to Eat

Some of Nanjing's livelier eating houses are in the Fuzimiao quarter. The *Yongheyuan Restaurant* (☎ 623836) *(yǒnghéyuán chádiǎnshè)* at 122 Gongyuan Jie specialises in sweet and savoury steamed pastries. Nearby is the *Lao Zhengxing Restaurant (lǎo zhèngxìng càiguǎn)* at 119 Gongyuan Jie, just east of the main square by the river, serves typical lower-Yangzi cuisine and was a favourite of Kuomintang officers before the war. You can get your fingers greasy at Fuzimiao's new *Kentucky Fried Chicken* restaurant *(kěndéjī zhájī)* as well.

In summer there is an excellent night market at the intersection just south of Xinjiekou, where you can get cheap street food. Here a *shāguō* hotpot or a bowl of noodles washed down with a bottle of the malty local Yali beer will cost you around Y4.

If you feel like mingling with Nanjing's overseas student crowd, try the *Black Cat Cafe (hēimāo cānguǎn)*. It's just opposite Nanjing University at No 1 Huaxin Xiang, on a tiny laneway running off Shanghai Lu. The Black Cat stays open late – often after midnight – and house specialties include 'potato croquettes', pancakes and Western-style breakfasts. The *Sprite Freeze (wúzhōu jiǔjiā)* on Guangzhou Lu, 20 metres west from the intersection with Zhongshan Lu, is another foreigners' hang-out, and – encouragingly – is also quite popular with Nanjing locals. It serves a range of good, cheap Chinese dishes and has bilingual menus.

Worth visiting more for the view than for

its food is the vegetarian restaurant at *Jiming Temple*, high on a hill overlooking Xuanwu Park. It's very cheap, but is open only for midday meals. The *Baiyuan Restaurant* on the northernmost island in Xuanwu Lake is a bit more upmarket, but it's another good place to relax.

The *Maxiangxing Restaurant* (☎ 635807) *(qīngzhēn mǎxiángxìng càiguǎn)* at No 5 Zhongshan Beilu serves good cheap Muslim cuisine completely free of the pig fat often used for frying in conventional Chinese cookery. The main restaurant is upstairs in a green and cream building on the Drum Tower traffic circle.

A good place to try local specialties is the *Jiangsu Restaurant* (☎ 623698) *(jiāngsū jiǔjiā)* at 26 Jiankang Lu near the Taiping Museum. Nanjing pressed, salted duck is slathered with roasted salt, steeped in clear brine, baked dry and then kept under cover for some time; the finished product should have a creamy coloured skin and red, tender flesh.

The *Dasanyuan* (☎ 641027) *(dàsānyuǎn jiǔjiā)* at 38 Zhongshan Lu has been recommended for its Cantonese-style cuisine. If you can get a table, the *Sichuan Restaurant* (☎ 643651) *(sìchuān fàndiàn)* at 171 Taiping Lu is not bad either – but scrutinise the bill before you pay.

The Shuangmenlou and Nanjing hotels have their own reasonably priced restaurants with Western menu in English. The Central Hotel and the Jinling Hotel (which has some seven restaurants including the revolving *Sky Palace)* have some of the city's finest food.

Getting There & Away

Air Nanjing has regular air connections to over 20 Chinese cities, including flights to: Beijing (Y500, three to six daily); Canton (Y610, daily); Shanghai (Y140, daily); Xi'an (Y550, three a week); and Chengdu (Y800, four a week), as well as Guilin, Hankou and Huangshan. There are also daily flights to/from Hong Kong.

The main CAAC office (☎ 649275) is at 52 Ruijin Lu (near the terminal of bus route No 4), but you can also buy tickets at the CITS office or at the Jinling or Central Hotel.

Bus The long-distance bus station is west of the main railway station, south-east of the wide bridged intersection with Zhongyang Lu. From here you can get direct buses to Hefei (Y13), Hangzhou (Y22), Yangzhou (Y8) and Zhenjiang (Y8) as well as Changzhou, Wuxi, Huangshan. Other shorter routes leave from the smaller regional bus stations at Hanfu Jie, near Zhonghua Gate and east of Nanjing railway station.

Train The foreigners' booking office is on the right as you approach the railway station, near the entrance to the soft-sleeper waiting room; it's open from 8 to 11.30 am and from 2 to 5 pm. Nanjing is a major stop on the Beijing-Shanghai railway line; there are several trains a day in both directions. Heading eastwards from Nanjing, the line to Shanghai connects with Zhenjiang, Changzhou, Wuxi and Suzhou.

An efficient daily express service runs between Nanjing and Shanghai, using two modern double-decker trains. The No 1 leaves Nanjing at 8.26 am and arrives in Shanghai at 12.20 pm; the No 15 departs at 9.57 am and gets in at 2.41 pm. From Shanghai, the No 2 leaves at 1.40 pm and arrives in Nanjing at 5.42 pm; the No 16 departs Shanghai at 4.30 pm and gets in at 9.26 pm. The Nos 1 and 2 stop only at Wuxi, while the Nos 15 and 16 also stop at Suzhou. All cars are air-con and a no-smoking rule is vigorously enforced. The one-way foreigner-price fare is Y55 (soft seat) or Y27.50 (hard seat).

There is no direct rail link to Hangzhou; you have to go to Shanghai first and then pick up a train or bus. Alternatively, there is a direct bus from Nanjing to Hangzhou. Likewise, to get to Canton by rail you must change trains at Shanghai.

Heading west, there is a direct rail link to the port of Wuhu on the Yangzi River. If you want to go further west along the river then the most sensible thing to do is take the ferry.

Boat There are several departures daily from

Nanjing's Yangzi River port downriver (eastwards) to Shanghai and upriver (westwards) to Wuhan (two days), including a few boats to Chongqing (five days). Most ferries leave from No 4 dock (sìhào mǎtóu), one km north of Zhongshan dock at the western end of Zhongshan Beilu.

Some Chinese-price fares in yuan are:

Destination	2nd Class	3rd Class	4th Class	Duration
Shanghai	73	34	26	16 hours
Jiujiang	84	40	29	30 hours
Wuhan	93	43	36	40 hours
Yichang	226	105	81	3 days
Chongqing	397	18	14	6 days

Getting Around

Taxis wait for customers outside the more upmarket hotels; beware of frequent overcharging. You can get to Xinjiekou, in the heart of town, by jumping on a No 1 bus or a No 33 trolley-bus from the railway station, or a No 10 or No 34 trolley-bus from the Yangzi docks. The airport is not far away in the south-east of the city; CAAC and many of the hotels run buses there. The taxi fare to Xinjiekou should be about Y25, although drivers try to charge foreigners at least Y40 for this short trip.

Nanjing's broader streets are divided into three 'p' zones – pedestrian, pedal and petrol – so bikes are a safe and fast way to go. The CITS office at No 202/1 Zhongshan Beilu rents out bicycles for Y20 a day – they're not bad bikes, but a rip-off for that price.

AROUND NANJING
Qixia Temple
(qíxiá sì) 栖霞寺

Qixia Temple lies 22 km north-east of Nanjing. It was founded by the Buddhist monk, Shao Shezhai, during the Southern Qi Dynasty, and is still an active place of worship. Qixia has long been one of China's most important monasteries, and even today is one of the largest Buddhist seminaries in the country. There are two main temple halls: the Maitreya Hall, with a statue of the Maitreya Buddha sitting cross-legged at the entrance, and behind this the Vairocana Hall,

housing a five-metre-tall statue of Vairocana. Behind the temple is a small seven-storey stone pagoda built in 601 AD, and rebuilt during the late Tang period. The upper part has engraved Sutras and carvings of the Buddha; around the base, each of the pagoda's eight sides depicts Sakyamuni. Paths lead through the forest up to small temples and pavilions on Qixiashan itself, from where you can see the Yangzi River. You reach Qixia from Nanjing by public bus from the Drum Tower bus station or by private minibus from the eastern side of the railway station.

Yangshan Quarry
(yángshān bēicái) 阳山碑材

The quarry at Yangshan, 25 km east of Nanjing, was the source of most of the stone blocks cut for the Ming palace and statues of the Ming tombs. The attraction here is a massive tablet partially hewn from the rock. Had the tablet been finished it would have been almost 15 metres wide, four metres thick and 45 metres high! The base stone was to be 6½ metres high and 13 metres long. One story goes that Ming Dynasty emperor Hong Wu wished to place the enormous tablet on the top of Zijinshan. The gods had promised their assistance to move it, but when they saw the size of the tablet even they gave up and Hong Wu had to abandon the project. It seems, however, that Yong Le, the son of Hong Wu, ordered the tablet to be carved; he planned to erect it at his father's tomb. When the tablet was almost finished he realised there was no way it could be moved.

You can get to Yangshan from the bus station on Hanfu Jie (east of Xinjiekou) on bus Nos 9 and 20. Buses to the thermal-springs resort at Tangshanzhen pass Yangshan on the way.

Buddhist Grottoes

The Buddhist grottoes lie about 20 km east of Nanjing. The earliest caves date from the Qi Dynasty (479-502 AD), though there are others from a number of succeeding dynasties right through to the Ming.

GRAND CANAL
(dàyùnhé) 大运河

The original Grand Canal, like the Great Wall, was not one but a series of interlocking projects from different eras. The earliest parts were dug 2400 years ago in the north to facilitate troop movements. During the Sui Dynasty, the ruthless Emperor Yang Di conscripted a massive workforce to link his new capital of Luoyang to the older capital of Chang'an (Xi'an). Then he extended the project to Hangzhou in less than a decade, making it possible for junks to go along the Yangzi, up the canal, and on to ports along the Yellow River – a trip that might take up to a year.

The canal at that time linked four major east-west running rivers: the Huang (Yellow), Yangzi, Huai and Qiantang. It thus gave China a major north-south transport route, and linked the compass points. It has been said that the canal, the longest artificial waterway in the world, was built by 'a million people with teaspoons'. In fact some estimate closer to five million people, but by even the crudest mathematics the cost in lives must have been enormous.

The emperor was not so much interested in unification as subjugation. Grain from the rich fields of the south was appropriated to feed the hungry armies in the northern capitals. During the Tang Dynasty 100,000 tonnes of grain were transported annually to the north – long chains of imperial barges loaded with tax grain plied the waterways.

During the 13th century, Kublai Khan used the work of his predecessors for much the same purpose, and he did a bit of remodelling to bring the northern terminal up to Beijing, his capital. Marco Polo noted that boats were pulled along by horses with long harnesses which walked along the banks of the canal. In this way large quantities of corn and rice were shipped northward. He wrote:

This magnificent work (the canal) is deserving of admiration; and not so much from the manner in which it is conducted through the country, or its vast extent, as from its utility and the benefit it produces to those cities which lie in its course.

Apart from bringing prosperity to the towns along its course, the canal was also a means by which the sybaritic emperors would move from point A to point B. At one stage during the Emperor Qianlong's reign, it was suggested that the grain fleets be removed from the canal so as to allow the imperial pleasure-cruisers a freer passage.

As time went by, sections of the canal fell into disuse or were engulfed by flooding from the Yellow River. In this century the growth of railways eclipsed the need for water transport. By 1980, silt, poorly planned dams, watergates and irrigation systems, or plain atrophy had reduced internal waterways mileage in China to a third of that in the 1960s.

Imperial Revival
In 1980, the Grand Canal suddenly became a tourist attraction. A flat-bottomed cruiser

Grand Canal
大运河

with air-conditioning and all mod cons materialised out of Wuxi, and passengers coughed up several thousand dollars for a week-long run from Yangzhou to Suzhou, including overnight stopovers at the towns along the way.

Since the 'opening' hundreds of groups have made the trip. CITS has added a new concept – the Dragon Boat, a replica of an imperial barge with carvings, antique furniture, and a high-class restaurant on board. Tourists can dress up like emperors and strut about nibbling at the delicacies served on imperial tableware. Since then, several more boats have been added, and more are planned.

The way things are going, the tourist boats might become the only passenger ships left on the canal. Chinese travellers have little interest – most prefer to get around by faster, more modern means of transport – bus, train and air.

The Beijing-Hangzhou canal meandered almost 1800 km. Today perhaps half of it remains seasonally navigable. The Party claims that, since Liberation, large-scale dredging has made the navigable length 1100 km. This is an exaggeration. Canal depths are up to three metres and canal widths can narrow to less than nine metres. Put these facts together, realise that there are old stone bridges spanning the route, and you come to the conclusion that it is restricted to fairly small flat-bottomed vessels.

The section of the canal from Beijing to Tianjin has been silted up for centuries. A similar fate has befallen most sections from the Yellow River to Tianjin. The stretch from the Yellow River to Peixian (in northern Jiangsu Province) is highly dubious and is most probably silted up from the Yellow River's flooding. Jining, which lies between these two points, was once a prosperous cloth producer; the canal there now lies idle and the town is served by rail.

The canal itself is polluted with oil slicks and doubles as the local garbage bin, sewer and washing machine. There's still plenty to look at on the water: moss-stricken canal-side housing, houseboats, barges, and

glimpses of life at the water's edge like women pounding their washing and men fishing.

Touring the Canal

Heading south from the northern Chinese plains, the canal really picks up at **Peixian**. There are two Peixians – this one is in the far north-central part of Jiangsu Province near the border with Shandong. It lies east of the town of Xuzhou, to which it is linked by a railway line. Peixian is closed, but a tributary canal runs past Xuzhou, feeding into the Grand Canal.

Continuing south, you come to **Huaian** (no rail link). It's open not because of the canal but because it's Zhou Enlai's home town. Tourists (mostly Overseas Chinese) usually stop only to visit his former residence, but there are a couple of other places of interest including pavilions and pagodas. The plaster and tile housing typical of areas south of the Yangzi now give way to mud and thatched buildings. The canal runs deep here and is eminently navigable.

Further south is **Yangzhou** below which the canal passes through locks into the Yangzi. The section from Peixian to Yangzhou is part of a bold plan to divert water from the Yangzi and the rainy south to the arid, drought-racked provinces of Shandong, Hebei, Henan and Anhui. The route is also needed to ship coal to energy-hungry Shanghai from major coal producer Xuzhou. The plan, to be completed in the early 1990s, calls for dredging the section from Yangzhou to Xuzhou to a depth of four metres and a width of 70 metres at the bottom, so that 2000-tonne vessels can pass. A double ship lock is being built at Huaian. So it seems the old canal still has its major uses. The water, it appears, will be provided for irrigation as far north as Jining in Shandong Province.

South of the Yangzi the picture is much brighter, with year-round navigation. The Jiangnan section of the canal (Hangzhou, Suzhou, Wuxi, Changzhou, Danyang, Zhenjiang) is a skein of canals, rivers and branching lakes. Just as interesting as the

Grand Canal are the feeder canals, many of them major thoroughfares in their own right, but sometimes it's difficult to tell which is the Grand Canal, since people may point to any canal and call it that.

Canal Ferries

Travellers have done the route from Hangzhou to Suzhou on overnight passenger boats (with sleeping berths) or on daytime 150-seater ferries. Some people regard this as the highlight of their China trip.

Others have found the boats dirty, crowded and uncomfortable, with a fair part of the trip taken up by views of high canal banks. Some words of advice: you need a good bladder since the toilets are terrible; you need to bring some food; and try and get a window seat, both to see the scenery and to escape the many smokers on the boat. But again, these old boats are falling into disuse.

One reader wrote:

The boat is terrible, dirty, cramped; its windows just above the waterline make it hard to see anything, but the 'toilet' won the prize as the worst in all China. It was a large bucket that was not emptied during our trip, which took 14 hours (including two hours when we were stopped by fog, which is very common in fall and winter).

Another wrote that the canal voyage was 'the highlight of our trip...a filthy but picturesque slice of life in China'.

Estimated times for the sections south of the Yangzi are:

Section	Journey Time
Hangzhou to Suzhou	14 hours, overnight berth or day boat
Suzhou to Wuxi	5-6 hours, early morning day boat
Wuxi to Changzhou	4-5 hours
Changzhou to Zhenjiang	8-9 hours with a possible break in Danyang

It's possible to break the journey about halfway from Hangzhou to Suzhou at the fine canal town of **Jiaxing** which is also linked by rail to Shanghai or Hangzhou. It has textile and food-processing factories and

deals in silk and rice. The pavilion to the south-east of the town, on an island lake, is reputed to be where founding members of the Chinese Communist Party sheltered when disturbed by Shanghai police in 1921. There are other connections running through Lake Taihu.

YANGZHOU
(yángzhōu) 杨州

Yangzhou, at the junction of the Grand Canal and the Yangzi River, was once an economic and cultural centre of Southern China. It was home to scholars, painters, storytellers, poets and merchants in the Sui and Tang dynasties, but little remains of the greatness that Marco Polo witnessed. He served there as Kublai Khan's governor for three years and wrote that:

Yangui has twenty-four towns under its jurisdiction, and must be considered a place of great consequence...the people are idolators, and subsist by trade and manual arts. They manufacture arms and other munitions: in consequence of which many troops are stationed in this part of the country.

Buried outside the town at Leitang, in a simple mound of earth, is Emperor Yang Di, the ruthless tyrant who completed the construction of the Grand Canal during the Sui Dynasty (518-618 AD). Yang Di is said to have levied exorbitant taxes, starved his subjects, and generally been very nasty. The emperor's throne was usurped by members of a powerful noble family who were to found the Tang Dynasty, and Yang Di was strangled by his own generals at Yangzhou in 618.

To the north-west of Yangzhou once stood the Maze Palace, a labyrinth of bronze mirrors and couches with concubines. Yang Di is supposed to have torn about here in a leopard-skin outfit, turning one night into 10 before he finally emerged to deal with affairs of state. The building was burned down, and on the ruins a structure called Jian (Warning) Building, a reminder for future generations, was erected. Still there, near Guanyin Hill, it is now used as a museum of Tang relics.

During the Qing Dynasty (1644-1911), Yangzhou got a new lease of life as a salt-trading centre, and Emperor Qianlong set about remodelling the town in the 18th century. All the streets leading to the town gates were lined with platforms where story-tellers recited chapters from famous novels (the repertoire was reputed to be 30 novels). The period also saw a group of painters known as the 'Eight Eccentrics' break away from traditional methods, creating a style of natural painting that influenced the course of art in China. Merchants and scholars favoured Yangzhou as a retirement home.

The town was badly battered during the Taiping Rebellion in the 19th century, and the Cultural Revolution didn't help much either. Nor have huge sums of money been lavished on phoney temple restoration, as is the case in Beijing. The result is that what you get to see nowadays is probably a shadow of its former glory.

Be that as it may, Yangzhou is one of the quaintest and most picturesque places in all of Jiangsu Province. Unlike Suzhou, Yangzhou is not swamped by tourist hordes, motor vehicles, factories, air pollution, high-rise office towers and a host other new developments plaguing modern China. No doubt, modernisation with all its attendant social ills will eventually come to Yangzhou, but for the moment this place is a rare island of peace and charm in one of China's bus-tling coastal provinces. Yangzhou is well worth your time.

Before charging out in search of tourist sites, take a while to explore the town. Yangzhou is a delightful town for walking. The relative absence of motor vehicles (for how much longer, we wonder) is a key attrac-tion. Guoqing Lu, running in a north-south direction through the centre, is a pleasant tree-shaded street jam-packed with shops and bicycles.

Canals

The town's busy waterlife attracted the atten-tion of 18th-century travellers; Yangzhou used to have 24 stone bridges spanning its network of canals. Although the modern bridges are made out of concrete, these are still good vantage points from which to view canal life.

You might like to investigate the environs a short way out of town. The Grand Canal actually passes a little to the east of Yangzhou. The bus No 2 terminal in the north-east is a boat dock. Bus No 4 runs over a bridge on the canal. There are two ship locks to the south of Yangzhou.

North-east of the town, across the Grand Canal, is the Jiangsu Water Control Project, a large-scale plan for diverting water from the Yangzi for irrigation, drainage, power and navigation. It was completed in 1975 with foreign assistance.

Ge Garden
(gèyuán) 个园

On Dongguan Lu, this garden was land-scaped by the painter Shi Tao for an officer of the Qing court. Shi Tao was an expert at making artificial rocks; the composition here suggests the four seasons.

He Garden
(héyuán) 何园

Alias Jixiao Mountain Villa, the He Garden was built in the 19th century. It contains rockeries, ponds, pavilions and walls inscribed with classical poetry.

Wenfeng Pagoda
(wénfēng tǎ) 文峰塔

Just south-west of the bus station, this pagoda can be scaled to the seventh level (assemble at 9 am, get out your grappling-hooks; highly recommended). It offers a bird's-eye view of the flotsam, jetsam and sampans along a canal, as well as an over-view of the town. Made of brick and wood, it's been rebuilt several times.

Shouxi Lake Park
(shòu xīhú) 瘦西湖

This is the top scenic spot in Yangzhou – in the western suburbs on the bus No 5 route. 'Shouxi' means 'slender west' as opposed to the 'fat west' lake in Hangzhou. In China fat signifies happy and slender means beautiful,

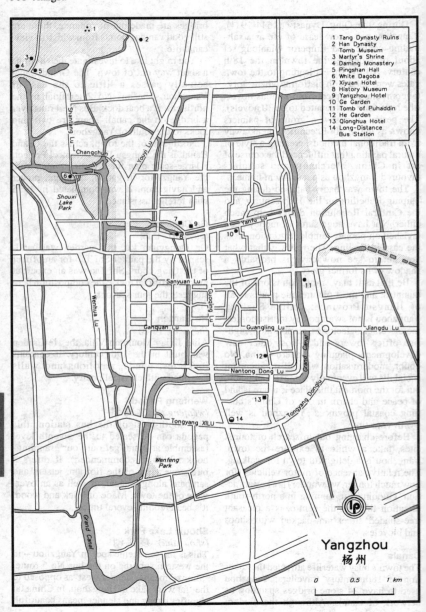

1 Tang Dynasty Ruins
2 Han Dynasty
  Tomb Museum
3 Martyr's Shrine
4 Daming Monastery
5 Pingshan Hall
6 White Dagoba
7 Xiyuan Hotel
8 History Museum
9 Yangzhou Hotel
10 Ge Garden
11 Tomb of Puhaddin
12 He Garden
13 Qionghua Hotel
14 Long-Distance
   Bus Station

Shantang Lu

Changchun Lu

Yowi Lu

Shouxi
Lake
Park

Yanfu Lu

Sanyuan Lu

Guoqing Lu

Wenhua Lu

Ganquan Lu

Guangling Lu

Jiangdu Lu

Grand Canal

Nantong Dong Lu

Tongyang Donglu

Tongyang XILU

Wenfeng
Park

Grand Canal

Yangzhou
杨州

0   0.5   1 km

1 唐城遗址
2 汉墓博物馆
3 烈士墓墓
4 大明寺堂
5 平山堂
6 白塔
7 西园饭店
8 杨州市博物馆
9 杨州宾馆
10 个园
11 普哈丁墓园
12 何园
13 琼花大厦
14 杨州汽车站

but this park verges on the emaciated and is desperately in need of rejuvenation.

It offers an imperial dragon-boat ferry, a restaurant and a white dagoba (dome-shaped shrine) modelled after the one in Beihai Park in Beijing. The highlight is the triple-arched, five-pavilion Wutang Qiao, a bridge built in 1757. For bridge connoisseurs it's rated one of the top 10 ancient Chinese bridges.

Emperor Qianlong's fishing platform is in the park. It is said that the local divers used to put fish on the poor emperor's hook so he'd think it was good luck and provide some more funding for the town.

Daming Monastery
(dàmíng sì) 大明湖
The name means 'Great Brightness Temple', though Emperor Qianlong renamed it Fajing Temple in 1765 when he dropped in for a visit. The monastery was founded over 1000 years ago and subsequently destroyed and rebuilt. Then it was destroyed right down to its foundations during the Taiping Rebellion; what you see today is a 1934 reconstruction. It's nice architecture even so, and – if you time it right – you'll find the shaven-headed monks engaged in religious rituals.

The original temple is credited to the Tang Dynasty monk Jianzhen, who studied sculpture, architecture, fine arts and medicine as well as Buddhism. In 742 AD two Japanese monks invited him to Japan for missionary

work. It turned out to be mission impossible. Jianzhen made five attempts to get there, failing due to storms. The fifth time he ended up in Hainan. On the sixth trip, aged 66, he finally arrived. He stayed in Japan for 10 years and died there in 763 AD. Later, the Japanese made a lacquer statue of Jianzhen, which in 1980 was sent to Yangzhou.

The Chinese have a wooden copy of this statue on display at the Jianzhen Memorial Hall. Modelled after the chief hall of the Toshodai Temple in Nara (Japan), the Jianzhen Memorial Hall was built in 1974 at Daming Monastery and was financed by Japanese contributions. Special exchanges are made between Nara and Yangzhou; even Deng Xiaoping, returning from a trip to Japan, came to the Yangzhou Monastery to strengthen renewed links between the two countries.

Near the monastery is Pingshan Hall *(píngshān táng)*, the residence of the Song Dynasty writer Ouyang Xiu, who served in Yangzhou.

Tomb of Puhaddin
(pǔhādīng mùyuán) 普哈丁墓园
This tomb contains documents regarding China's contacts with the Muslims. It's on the east bank of a canal on the bus No 2 route. Puhaddin came to China during the Yuan Dynasty (1261-1378) to spread the Muslim faith, and spent 10 years in Yangzhou, where he died. There is a mosque in Yangzhou.

History Museum
(yángzhōu shì bówùguǎn) 杨州市博物馆
The museum lies to the north of Guoqing Lu, near the Xiyuan Hotel. It's in a temple originally dedicated to Shi Kefa, a Ming Dynasty official who refused to succumb to his new Qing masters and was executed. The museum contains items from Yangzhou's past. A small collection of calligraphy and paintings of the 'Eight Eccentrics' is displayed in another small museum just off Yanfu Lu near the Xiyuan Hotel.

Places to Stay
Cheapest and closest to the bus station is the

JIANGSU

Qionghua Hotel (☎ 231321) *(qiónghuā dàshà)* on Xuning Lu. You won't have any trouble spotting the multistorey tower which is conspicuously incongruous with its surroundings. Doubles cost Y120.

The garden-style *Xiyuan Hotel* (☎ 344888) *(xīyuán fàndiàn)* at 1 Fengle Shanglu is said to have been constructed over the site of Qianlong's imperial villa. This place certainly has imperial-style character, though it's not for the rock-bottom budget traveller. Doubles/triples cost Y150/180. From the bus station take bus No 8.

Just next door is the *Yangzhou Hotel* *(yángzhōu bīnguǎn)*, the prime tourist joint where doubles cost a cool Y260.

Places to Eat

The big wining and dining area is at the intersection of Guoqing Lu (which runs north from the bus station) and Ganquan Lu. Yangzhou has its own cuisine but, except for a special banquet, you might have trouble finding it. Try the *Caigenxiang Restaurant* *(càigēnxiāng fàndiàn)*, 115 Guoqing Lu. How about buns with crab-ovary stuffing? Along Guoqing Lu and Ganquan Lu are small bakeries and cafes which sell steamed dumplings, noodles, pastries and other goodies – you can see the stuff being kneaded right behind the counter.

Both of the previously mentioned hotels have dining rooms. The *Xiyuan Hotel* harbours a restaurant with great food, including local specialties like famous Yangzhou-style fried rice.

Another great place for local cuisine is the *Fuchun Teahouse (fùchūn cháguǎn)*, in an alley off Guoqing Lu. It's open from 6 am to 7 pm and offers a vast selection of delicious snacks and teas.

Things to Buy

The centre is full of shoe shops and housewares, but there's no sign of the lacquerware, jade, paper-cuts, woodcuts, embroidery or painting that Yangzhou is supposed to be famous for. Maybe that's a blessing – for a famous resort, Yangzhou is relatively free of tacky souvenir shops. But

if tourist junk is what you're after, there are a few shops catering to this need:

Arts & Crafts Factory, west of Xiyuan Hotel
Friendship Store, Guoqing Lu
Lacquer Factory *(qīqì chǎng)*, which makes inlaid lacquer screens with translucent properties, due east of Xiyuan Hotel
Jade Factory *(yùqì chǎng)*, 6 Guangchumenwai Jie
Block Printing Coop, with handbound woodblock printed classics
Yangzhou Antique Store *(yángzhōu wénwùdiàn)*, opposite the Yangzhou Hotel
Renmin Department Store.

Getting There & Away

The nearest airport is in Nanjing. The railway line also gave Yangzhou a miss, which perhaps explains why the city is missing out on China's current tourist and industrial tidal wave. The railway station nearest Yangzhou is in Zhenjiang.

From Yangzhou there are buses to Nanjing (2½ hours), Wuxi, Suzhou and Shanghai. Most frequent (about every 15 minutes) are minibuses from Zhenjiang (Y8, 1½ hours) with fascinating amphibious crossings of the Yangzi). These depart from in front of Zhenjiang railway station – don't let the pedicab drivers convince you otherwise.

Getting Around

The sights are at the edge of town. If you're in a hurry you might consider commandeering a 'turtle' (motortricycle) – they can be found outside the bus station. The central area can easily be covered on foot. The pedicab drivers hanging out in front of the Xiyuan Hotel are con artists asking Y30 or more to go to the bus station (the real fare is Y5), so flag one down on the street.

Bus Nos 1, 2, 3, 5, 6 and 7 terminate near the long-distance bus station. Bus No 1 runs from the bus station up Guoqing Lu and then loops around the perimeter of the inside canal, returning just north of the bus station. Bus No 4 is an east-west bus and goes along Ganquan Lu.

ZHENJIANG
(zhènjiāng) 镇江
Zhenjiang takes its character not from the Grand Canal but from the Yangzi, which it faces. In other words, it's large, murky and industrial. The old silk trade still exists, but is overshadowed by car and shipbuilding and by textile and food-processing plants. It's a medium-sized place with 300 factories, and is home to well over 300,000 people.

Attempts have been made to 'humanise' the city by planting trees along the streets. The sights are pleasant enough since they're removed from the industrial eyesores. To the south are densely wooded areas, mountains and temples tucked away in bamboo groves but they are difficult to get to by local bus.

The city's history goes back some 2500 years. Its strategic and commercial importance, as the gateway to Nanjing, is underlined by the fact that the British and the French established concessions here. Don't be deterred by your first view of Zhenjiang from the railway station; the older part of town is a picturesque area with busy streets, small enterprises, people, bicycles and timber houses.

Information
The Jingkou Hotel has both a CITS (☎ 233387) and a CTS (☎ 231663) office.

Jiaoshan
(jiāoshān) 焦山
The 'three mounts of Zhenjiang', vantage points strewn along the Yangzi, are the principal sights. The temple complexes on each are among the oldest gracing the river, and date back 1500 years.

Also known as Jade Hill because of its dark green foliage (cypresses and bamboo), Jiaoshan is to the east on a small island. There's good hiking here with a number of pavilions along the way to the top of the 150-metre-high mount, from where Xijiang Tower gives a view of activity on the Yangzi. At the base of Jiaoshan is an active monastery with some 200 pieces of tablet engravings, gardens and bonsai displays. Take bus No 4 to the terminal, then a short walk and a boat ride.

Beigushan Park
(běigùshān gōngyuán) 北固山公园
Also on the No 4 bus route, this hill has the Ganlu Temple *(gānlù sì)* complex featuring a Song Dynasty pagoda which offers expansive views of town. It was once six storeys high but is now four, having been vandalised by Red Guards.

Jinshan Park
(jīnshān gōngyuán) 金山公园
This hill has a temple arrayed tier by tier with connecting staircases on a hillside – a remarkable design. Right at the top is the seven-storey octagonal Cishou Pagoda that gives an all-embracing view of the town, the fishponds immediately below and the Yangzi beyond. There are four caves at the mount: Buddhist Sea *(fáhǎi)*, White Dragon *(báilóng)*, Morning Sun *(zhàoyáng)*, and Arhat *(luóhàn)*. Fahai and Bailong caves feature in the Chinese fairy tale *The Story of the White Snake*. West of the base, within walking distance, is No 1 Lifespring Under Heaven. The spring waters of Jiangsu were catalogued by Tang Dynasty tea expert Lu Yu (No 2 is Wuxi, No 3 is Hangzhou). Take bus No 2 to Jinshan.

Museum
(bówùguǎn) 博物馆
A fourth 'mount' of interest between Jinshan and the centre of town is the old British Consulate, which is now a museum and gallery. It houses pottery, bronzes, gold, silver, Tang Dynasty paintings, and a separate section with photographs and memorabilia of the Japanese war. Its retail outlet sells calligraphy, rubbings and paintings. The museum is on the bus No 2 route, and is set high over a very old area of winding stone-laid alleys that go down to boat docks on the Yangzi. It's well worth investigating on foot.

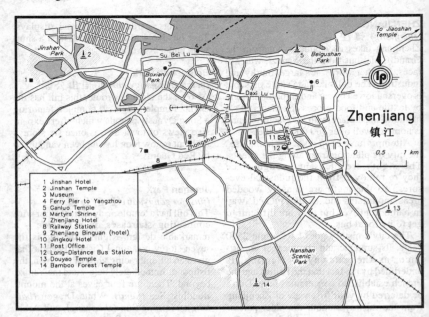

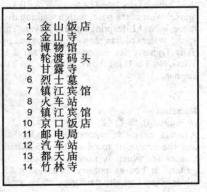

1 金山饭店
2 金山寺
3 博物馆
4 轮渡码头
5 甘露寺
6 烈士墓
7 镇江宾馆
8 火车站
9 镇江口宾馆
10 京口饭店
11 邮电局
12 汽车站
13 都天庙
14 竹林寺

Bamboo Forest Temple
(zhúlín sì) 竹林寺

At the southern end of town in an area known as Nanshan Scenic Park *(nánshān fēngjǐng qū)* is the Bamboo Forest Temple. As temples go, it won't qualify as the biggest or best in China, but the setting amongst the trees and hills is impressive. It's a relaxing spot, the only problem being that regular buses don't go there. Bus Nos 6 and 21 come close and can let you off at the base of the mountain, but from there you'll have to walk a couple of km, hitch, or get a taxi or (hopefully) a minibus.

Places to Stay – middle

Just straddling the line between budget and mid-range accommodation, the *Jingkou Hotel* (☎ 224866; fax 236393) *(jīngkǒu fàndiàn)* charges Y100/120 for singles/doubles. This is also where CTS/CITS has its offices. Officially, the hotel's address is 407 Zhongshan Xilu, but you enter the compound from a gate on Binhe Lu which borders a small river.

The *Zhenjiang Hotel* (☎ 235291) offers the convenience of being on the square right in front of the railway station. You can hear the trains all night and light sleepers might possibly be annoyed, though we found it not too noisy and somewhat aesthetic. The rooms are very comfortable and the staff mostly polite. Single rooms theoretically start from Y60, but foreigners are forced into plusher doubles costing Y150. Suites cost Y280.

Places to Stay – top end

The *Zhenjiang Hotel* (☎ 233888; fax 236425) *(zhènjiāng bīnguǎn)* at 92 Zhongshan Xilu is within walking distance of the railway station. Very obviously designed for Hong Kongers, the high prices are matched only by the bad interior decorating. Bright lights are a major feature – you could wear sunglasses at night in the hotel's aircraft-hanger style lobby or restaurant. Still, the facilities are cushy, with karaoke, business centre and blood-spattered Hong Kong videos beamed to each room. This luxury costs Y280.

The *Jinshan Hotel* (☎ 232970) *(jīnshān fàndiàn)*, 1 Jinshan Xilu, is the place to stay for tour groups. The location is relatively isolated and the building more closely resembles a motel – it started life as an Australian pre-fab. The hotel is a 10-minute walk around the artificial lake near Jinshan Temple, at bus No 2 terminal. Doubles cost from Y200.

Places to Eat

There's a pastry shop near the crossroads in the centre of town, and dumpling houses and noodle shops near the railway stations. The central *Jingjiang Hotel* *(jīngjiāng fàndiàn)* at 111 Jiefang Lu, reputedly has the best food in town; the ground floor has mainly jiaozi and baozi, but upstairs you can get enormous main courses very cheaply.

Things to Buy

There's a very fine Arts & Crafts Store *(gōngyìpǐn dàlóu)* at 191 Jiefang Lu which stocks embroidery, porcelain, jade and other artefacts. It may have some antiques.

Getting There & Away

Bus The long-distance bus station is in the south-east corner of the city centre. There are buses from Zhenjiang to Nanjing and a bus-ferry combination to Yangzhou. You can also get buses to Yangzhou from the front of the main railway station.

Train Zhenjiang is on the main Nanjing-Shanghai line, 3½ hours by fast train to Shanghai, and an hour to Nanjing. Some of the special express trains don't stop at Zhenjiang. Otherwise, there is a grand choice of schedules so check the timetable at the station. Most hotels offer a train booking service and can get sleepers.

Boat A more offbeat means of departure is via the ferries on the Grand Canal or the Yangzi River, but these are infrequent.

Getting Around

The city is ideal for day-tripping. Almost all the transport (including local buses, buses to Yangzhou, taxis and motortricycles) is conveniently close to the railway station.

Bus No 2 is a convenient tour bus. It goes east from the station along Zhongshan Lu to the city centre where the department stores, antique shop and post office are. It then swings west into the older part of town where some specialty and second-hand stores are to be found, goes past the former British consulate, and continues on to Jinshan, the terminal.

Bus No 4, which crosses the No 2 route in the city centre on Jiefang Lu, runs to Ganluo Temple and Jiaoshan in the east.

YIXING COUNTY

(yíxīng xiàn) 宜兴县

Yixing County to the west of Lake Taihu *(tàihú)* has enormous tourist potential and provides a chance to get out of the cities. There are fertile plains, tea and bamboo plantations, and undulating mountains with large caves and grottoes. The real prize, however, is the spectacular potteries of Dingshu village. Although busloads of Chinese tourists descend daily on the county from Wuxi, Nanjing and Shanghai, along with Western group tours on day trips, Yixing County has seen very few individual travellers.

The town of Yixing is *not* the place to go – you're likely to end up being the main attraction yourself. It's a small town (with about 50,000 residents) where the main business of selling noodles, zips, steamed bread, pigs' feet, pots and pans, tools and sunglasses, is all done out on the main street which terminates at the forbidding gates of the Yixing Guesthouse.

You'll probably end up in Yixing town one way or another since the only tourist hotel is there and the buses pass through. The attractions of Yixing County are all within a 30-km range of the town. The pottery town of Dingshu can be done as a day or half-day trip.

If you have time, explore the north-east end of Yixing town with its heavy concentration of comic-book hire places (it's not just kids doing the reading) and all manner of strange transactions down side streets. This and more can be seen in Dingshu. The Confucius Temple at the north-west end of Yixing town which was in poor condition is being renovated.

Karst Caves
(shíhuī yándòng) 石灰岩洞

There are a number of these to the south-west of Yixing township, and they're a cut above average. The drab interiors are lit by the standard selection of coloured neon, but you may wish to supplement this with a torch for navigation. The caves are very wet, so take your raincoat, too. The countryside around the caves is attractive and actually worth more time than the underground. The Mandarin word for cave is *shāndòng*.

Shanjuan Cave *(shànjuǎn dòng)* This cave is embedded in Snail Shell Hill (Luoyanshan), 27 km south-west of Yixing. It covers an area of roughly 5000 sq metres, with passages of 800 metres – enough to make any speleologist delirious. It's divided into upper, middle and lower reaches, plus a water cave. An exterior waterfall provides special sound effects for this weird set.

Entry is via the middle cave, a stone hall with a 1000-metre floor space. From here you can mount a staircase to the snail's shell, the upper cave, or wander down to the lower and water caves. In the water cave, you can jump in a rowing boat for a 120-metre ride to the exit, called 'Suddenly-see-the-Light', where a restaurant, hotel, teahouse, Zhuling village and goodness knows what else await you. Good luck!

There are, of course, many legends associated with the caves – mostly about former resident hermits. One was the hermit Zhu Yingtai. At the exit is a small pavilion which she used as her 'reading room'. Zhu, as the story goes, being a Jin Dynasty female, was not permitted to attend school, so she disguised herself as a male student and took up residence in the caves.

Every piece of stalagmite and stalactite in the cave is carefully catalogued – whether it be a moist sheep, a soggy plum, a cluster of bananas or an elephant. If the commentary is in Chinese, just exercise your imagination – that's what they did.

Buses run to Shanjuan from Yixing. The trip takes one hour and costs hardly anything.

Zhanggong Cave *(zhānggōng dòng)* Nineteen km south of Yixing town are three-score chambers within caves, large and small, divided into upper and lower reaches. Their size is comparable to Shanjuan's, but the layout is different. This is upside-down caving. What you do is scale a small hill called Yufengshan from the inside, and come out on the top, with a splendid view of the surrounding countryside with hamlets stretching as far as Lake Taihu.

There are two large grottoes in this bunch of caverns. The more impressive is the Hall of the Dragon King. From here you make your way through the Dry Nostril Cave, pause to clear your sinuses, and work up to the aforementioned exit.

A little further south of Zhanggong is the Yunutan, or Jade Maiden Pond.

Buses to Zhanggong from Yixing take half an hour. From Zhanggong you can pick up a passing bus to Linggu – the end of the line.

Around Yixing　宜兴地区

1　Aquatic Breeding Farm
2　Yixing Hotel
3　Chuanbei Tea Plantation
4　Furongsi Tea Plantation
5　Shanjuan Cave
6　Yunûtan Pool
7　Purple Sandware Factory
8　Zhanggong Cave
9　Yangxian Tea Plantation
10　Linggu Cave
11　Bamboo Sea

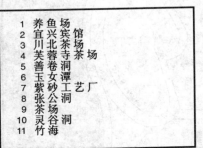

1　养鱼场
2　宜兴宾馆茶场
3　川北茶寺洞潭茶场
4　芙蓉卷女潭工艺厂
5　善玉洞
6　紫张砂公场
7　紫张砂公场洞
8　张公洞
9　茶谷洞
10　灵谷洞
11　竹海

If you're stuck for transport, try to get to Dingshu village, from where bus connections are good.

Linggu Cave *(línggǔ dòng)* Eight km down a dirt road from Zhanggong Cave, Linggu is the largest and least explored of the three caves. You could easily get lost in this one and not because of the scenery either. The cave has six large halls arrayed roughly in a semicircle, and it's a long, deep forage.

Near the Linggu Cave is the Yanxian Tea Plantation *(yánxiàn cháchǎng)*, with bushellots laid out like fat caterpillars stretching into the horizon, and the odd tea villa in the background. The trip is worth it for the tea fields alone.

There are buses to Linggu from Zhanggong (see the Zhanggong Cave section).

Places to Stay

The *Yixing Guesthouse (yíxīng fàndiàn)* caters chiefly to cadres holding meetings. The guesthouse is at the end of Renmin Lu on the southern edge of Yixing town. If there's not a rash of meetings, or a rare tour bus assault, the guesthouse will be empty. It's a large building, with gardens and some luxury living.

The guesthouse is a half-hour walk from Yixing bus station; turn right from the station, follow the main road south along the lakeside, cross three bridges and turn left, then right again to the guesthouse gates.

The long stretch across the bridges is the same road that runs to Dingshu, so if your bus goes to Dingshu ask the driver to let you off closer to the guesthouse. If you don't mind the stroll, and want to see the main drag of Yixing town, another way of getting to the guesthouse is to walk three blocks straight ahead from the bus station, turn right onto Renmin Lu, and keep walking until you hit the guesthouse.

Places to Eat

The guesthouse has a dining room. If you don't mind 500 people at your table (perhaps staring at you, not their food), there are small restaurants opposite the bus station. Along

Renmin Lu you'll find some baked food and dumplings.

Getting There & Away

There are buses from Yixing to Wuxi (2½ hours), Shanghai, Nanjing and Suzhou.

For the adventurous, there are a number of unexplored routes to and from Yixing County. A suggestion is to get there in the conventional manner, and try your luck on a different route out. Pottery is transported via canals and across Lake Taihu to Wuxi and it might be possible to transport yourself likewise. Highways skirt Lake Taihu, eventually running to Suzhou, Shanghai and Hangzhou. If you took a bus to Changxing, a slow branch-line railway leads from there to Hangzhou. At the southern end of the lake is a cross-over point, Huzhou. A little way north of this, on Lake Taihu, is Xiaomeikou, where ferry routes are marked on the map as leading to Wuxi across the lake, and to Suzhou via Yuanshan and Xukou.

Getting Around

There are no local buses in Yixing. There are buses to the sights out of town and all of them

end up in the bus stations of either Yixing town or Dingshu. There are frequent connections between the two stations. Hitchhiking is a possibility.

DINGSHU (JINSHAN)

(dīngshǔ, jīnshān) 丁蜀 / 金山

In Yixing County they not only grow tea, they make plenty of pots to put it in. Small towns in China can be utterly engrossing if they specialise in some kind of product, as Dingshu does.

The town has been a big pottery producer since the Qin and Han dynasties; some of the scenes you can witness here, especially at the loading dock that leads into Lake Taihu, are timeless. Almost every local family is engaged in the manufacture of ceramics, and behind the main part of town half the houses are made of the stuff. Dingshu is *the* pottery capital of China. There are also important porcelain-making plants in Jingdezhen, Handan, Zibo and parts of Guangzhou, but few handle the wide range of ceramics that Dingshu does.

Dingshu is about 25 km south of Yixing town and has two dozen ceramics factories

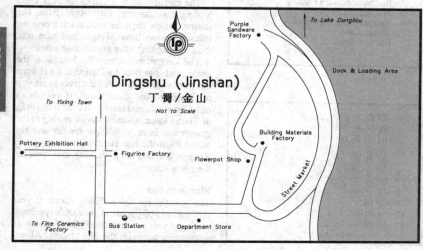

Dingshu (Jinshan)
丁蜀/金山

Not to Scale

To Yixing Town

Pottery Exhibition Hall

Figurine Factory

To Fine Ceramics Factory

Bus Station

Department Store

Flowerpot Shop

Building Materials Factory

Street Market

Purple Sandware Factory

To Lake Donglou

Dock & Loading Area

producing more than 2000 varieties of pottery – quite an output for a population of 100,000. Among the array of products are the ceramic tables and garbage bins that you find around China, huge jars used to store oil and grain, the famed Yixing teapots, and the glazed tiling and ceramic frescoes that are desperately needed as spare parts for tourist attractions – the Forbidden City in Beijing is one of the customers.

Dingshu is also known as Jinshan. The characters for Jinshan usually appear on bus timetables, so ask for that place if Dingshu draws a blank.

Things to See & Do

The 'pottery-house' end of Dingshu is a good 40 minutes from the bus station, but there's plenty to amuse you en route. You can get into the factories if you persist. In theory, each factory has a retail outlet; you can march in and say you're looking for the shop. If you have the money to sling around, CITS in Yixing town can get you into the factories of your choice at a price of their choice. Contact CITS at the Yixing Guesthouse. The following sights can be seen as a three-hour walking tour.

The logical place to get your bearings in Dingshu is the **Pottery Exhibition Hall** (*táocí zhǎnshìchǎng*). To get there turn left from the bus station and veer right past a small corner store.

The exhibition hall is the large, solid building which looks rather like a palace, five minutes up the street on your left. You can view two floors and several wings of pottery and get a good idea of what might be a good purchase. The exhibits are well presented, but taking photos isn't appreciated. There are free markets nearby selling pottery.

Opposite the hall is a **Figurine Factory** (*táocí gōngchǎng*) which produces things like kitsch lampstands. Yet even this factory is experimenting with glazes like tigerskin and snowflake, which is the secret of Dingshu.

Technology got off to a great start here when they introduced the new improved Dragon Kiln over 1000 years ago. Some distance north of the Exhibition Hall is the **Ceramics Research Institute** (*táocì yánjiūsuǒ*).

Backtrack to the bus station. By now you're an expert on Dingshu pots, so ignore the little retail shop on the corner! If you go straight down the street past the bus station, you'll get to the centre of town. En route, you pass two retail outlets. The second one has celadon-ware on the top floor, but you're better off loading up on the way back.

Proceed about 10 minutes from here and you'll see a yellow police box, backed by a large billboard poster. Take the alley to the right and you'll stumble into a very unusual market which runs along the banks of a small canal.

Dingshu Pottery

If you follow the market up, you'll arrive at a boat-loading dock where you begin to get an idea of the scale of things. Concrete housing here is enlivened with broken ceramic tiling, and other lodgings are constructed entirely of large storage jars and pottery shards.

Further past the dock is the **Purple Sandware Factory** where they'll probably slam the door in your face. The dullish brown stoneware produced here (mostly teapots and flowerpots) is prized the world over and dates back about 1000 years. Made from local clays, the teapots have a large and diverse export market, which might have a lot to do with their remarkable properties and aesthetic shapes. They retain the flavour and fragrance of tea for a long time; it's said that after extended use with one type of tea, no further tea leaves are necessary.

The teapots glaze themselves a darker, silkier tea-stain brown colour. It's claimed that the Purple Sands pots can be placed over a direct flame or be shoved in boiling water without cracking (though it's a different story if you drop one on the floor).

From the Purple Sands you can return to town by a different route. Go back towards the dock and take a right fork. This brings you to another road and, if you look left, you will spot the **Building Materials Factory**. This is a large operation which makes glazed tiles, garbage bins, ceramic tables and pottery pavilions. The production of pottery for civic and military use was what really got Dingshu off the ground, and is still the mainstay. Pottery is now produced for sanitation purposes, construction, daily use and the tourist industry – as well as throwing together a pavilion here, or re-tiling a temple there.

Near the gates of the Building Materials Factory is a small retail outlet selling flowerpots and the bonsai arrangements in them. Some other factories around Dingshu are the **East Wind** (garbage bins) and the **Red Star** (glazed vats, stools, tables).

Things to Buy

Pottery in Dingshu is dirt cheap, and valued by the serious as *objets d'art*. Tea sets are so cheap you could afford one for your hotel room. The same pots and cups can be found around Yixing County, but not with the same variety, quality, or price.

Further down the line (Wuxi, Suzhou, Shanghai), the price doubles and the selection narrows. By the time it gets to Hong Kong, the same tea set could cost 10 times more – quite a jump, but it did get it there in one piece.

Also on sale, and something that can be lugged out, are flowerpots, figurines and casseroles. The casseroles are supposed to make the meat tender.

Getting There & Away

There are direct buses from Dingshu to Yixing (20 minutes, with departures about every 20 minutes from 6 am to 5 pm), Wuxi (2½ hours), Zhenjiang and Nanjing.

WUXI & LAKE TAIHU
(wúxī, tàihú) 无锡太湖

Just north of Suzhou is Wuxi, a name that means 'tinless' – the local tin mine that dated back to around 1066-221 BC was exhausted during the Han Dynasty (206 BC-220 AD), not that the locals especially cared. A stone tablet dug out of Xishan hill is engraved, 'Where there is tin, there is fighting; where there is no tin, there is tranquillity'. And indeed there was tranquillity. Like Suzhou, Wuxi was an ancient silk producer, but it remained a sleepy backwater town barely altered by the intrusion of the Grand Canal (though it did once or twice come into the spotlight as a rice-marketing centre).

In this century Wuxi made up for the long sleep. In the 1930s Shanghai businesspeople backed by foreign technicians, set up textile and flour mills, oil-extracting plants, and a soap factory. After Liberation, textile production was stepped up considerably and light and heavy industry boomed. Monstrous housing developments sprang up to accommodate a population that had surpassed Suzhou's. There are hundreds of factories and an emphasis on electronics, textiles, machine manufacturing, chemicals, fishing,

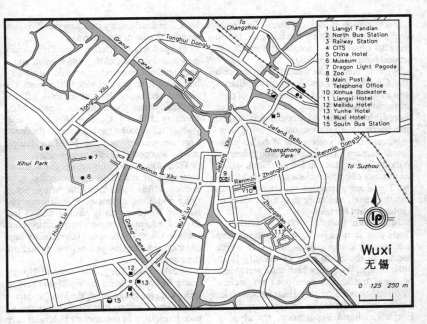

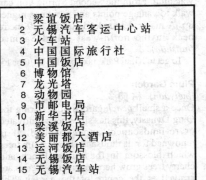

and agricultural crops serving the Shanghai market.

Just outside Wuxi, Lake Taihu is a freshwater lake with a total area of 2200 sq km and an average depth of two metres. There are some 90 islands, large and small, within it. Junks with 'all sails set' gracefully ply the waters – a magnificent nostalgic sight.

The fishing industry is very active, catching over 30 varieties. Fish breed in the shoals, and women float around in wooden tubs, harvesting water-chestnuts. On the shores are plantations of rice, tea with mulberry and citrus trees. Suitable rocks are submerged in the lake for decades, and when they're sufficiently weathered are prized for classical garden landscaping. To the northwest of the lake are hilly zones, to the south-east is a vast plain. The whole area with its fertile soil, mild climate and abundant rainfall is referred to as 'the land of fish and rice'.

Orientation

Wuxi is divided into two sections, five to 10 km apart; the hotel situation is not good in either. Because of the town's earlier stunted growth, there are few 'historical relics' and the main attraction is a natural one – Lake

Taihu – which is out of town. The main tourist sights are out by the lakeside. If you want to observe the locals, the canal life around town is interesting.

Wuxi is shaped like a heart, with an aorta (the Grand Canal) and loads of capillaries (canals). Central Wuxi is a landscape of concrete apartment blocks, factories and an incredible number of department stores, interspersed with busy canals.

Never mind – vestiges of Wuxi's former charm remain. The main thoroughfare of Wuxi is, in fact, the old Grand Canal, which sees plenty of bottlenecks and frenzied activity. There are numerous waterways cutting into the canal, and more than a fair share of vantage-point bridges.

Just down from the railway station is Gongyun Bridge with a passenger and loading dock close by – it's well worth seeing. In the north-west of the city is an older bridge, Wuqiao, which has a great view of canal traffic and overlooks an ancient pavilion stranded on tiny Huangbudun Isle. Traffic will come at you from all directions. For a firsthand experience, try zipping around in a small boat – there are at least three boat stations within the city.

Information

The CITS office is in a building facing the square in front of the main railway station. Unfortunately, they do not sell railway tickets or have any useful information. The best they can do is sell you an air ticket for flights out of Shanghai on China Eastern Airlines.

Xihui Park

(*xīhuì gōngyuán*) 锡惠公园

Enormous and nebulous Xihui Park is west of the city. The highest point in the park, Huishan hill, is 75 metres above sea level. If you climb the Dragon Light Pagoda (*lóngguāng tǎ*), the seven-storey octagonal structure at the top, you'll be able to take in a panorama of Wuxi and Taihu. The brick and wood pagoda was built during the Ming Dynasty, burned down during the Qing Dynasty, and rebuilt in the spring many years

later. For sunrises, try the Qingyun Pavilion, just to the east of the pagoda.

The park has a collection of pavilions, snack bars and teahouses, along with a small zoo, a large artificial lake, and a cave that burrows for half a km from the east side to the west. The western section of the park rambles off into Huishan, where you'll find the famous Ming Dynasty Jichang Garden (*jìchàng yuán*) ('Ming' refers to the garden layout – the buildings are recent), and the Huishan Temple nearby was once a Buddhist monastery.

What follows for this area is the standard catalogue of inscribed stones, halls, gates and crumbled villas from the Ming, Song, Qing and Tang dynasties. (Sometimes you have to wonder who is pulling whose leg. There are so many copies, permutations and fakes in China it's hard to know exactly how old the things are that you're looking at. Still, the copies are nice.)

Speaking of Tang, the Second Spring under Heaven (*tiānxià diè'r quán*) is here so bring your tea mugs, or try the local teahouse brew. The Chinese patronise this watering hole to indulge in the ancient hobby of carp watching. From the Second Spring you can walk to vantage points and pavilions higher up. A major detour leads to the 329-metre peak in the north-west called Sanmao (*huīshān*).

To get to Xihui Park, take bus No 2, 10 or 15.

Plum Garden

(*méiyuán*) 梅园

Once a small *peach* garden built during the Qing Dynasty, this has since been renovated or re-landscaped, and expanded. It is renowned for its thousands of red plum trees which blossom in the spring. Peach and cherry trees grow here too, and rockeries are arrayed at the centre of the garden. The highest point is Plum Pagoda, with views of Taihu. The garden is near the Wuxi bus No 2 terminal.

Li Garden

(*lǐyuán*) 蠡园

This place is always packed out by the locals. As Chinese gardens go, this one is a goner.

The whole thing goes beyond bad taste – a concrete labyrinth of fishponds, walkways, mini-bridges, a mini-pagoda, and souvenir vendors hawking garish plaster and gilded figurines. Inside the garden, on the shore of Taihu, is a tour-boat dock for cruises to other points.

Turtle Head Isle
(guītóuzhǔ) 龟头渚
So named because it appears to be shaped like the head of a turtle, it is not actually an island but being surrounded on three sides by water makes it appear so. This is the basic scenic strolling area where you can watch the junks on Lake Taihu.

You can walk a circuit of the area. If you continue along the shore, you come to the ferry dock for the Sanshan Isles, passing Taihujiajue Archway and Perpetual Spring Bridge (chángchūn qiáo). A walkway leads to a small lighthouse, near which is an inscribed stone referring to the island's name and several pavilions. The architecture here, like that in the Li Garden, is mostly copies of the classical examples. Inland a bit from the lighthouse is Clear Ripples (Chenglan) Hall, a very nice teahouse from where you get a view of the lake.

Further along the south coast are similar vantage points: Jingsong Tower, Guangfu

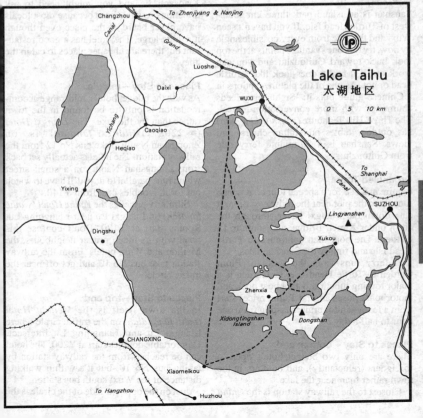

Temple and the 72 Peaks Villa. The highest point of Guitouzhu is the Brightness Pavilion (*guāngmíng tíng*) with all-round vistas. Back past the entrance area is a bridge leading to Zhongdu Island, which has a large workers' sanatorium – no visits without prior appointment.

To get to Guitouzhu, take bus No 1 to its terminal, or take the ferry from the dock near Plum Garden. The Chinese like to make a cycling trip out of it – the road is pleasant, with no heavy traffic. A possible shortcut is around the back of Zhongdu Island leading back towards Taihu Hotel.

Three Hills Isles
(*sānshān*) 三 山

Sanshan is an island park three km southwest of Turtle Head Isle. If you haven't seen Wuxi and the lake from every possible angle by now, try this one. Vantage points at the top look back toward Guitouzhu and you can work out if it really does look like a turtle head or not. As one of the picture captions in a Chinese guide puts it: 'Sightseeing feeds chummies with more conversation-topics'. The Three-Hill Teahouse (*sānshān cháguǎn*) has outdoor tables and rattan chairs, and views. Sanshan is a 20-minute ferry ride from Guitouzhu.

Organised Tours

Inquire at CITS for a special tour boat which runs from the pier near the railway station. It cuts down the Liangxi River (through the city), under Ximen Bridge, and south to Li Garden. The boat then continues to Turtle Head Isle and finally the Sanshan Isles.

A ferry runs from the south of Plum Garden to Turtle Head Isle. Li Garden is a major touring junction with a boat dock and motorboat cruises around Taihu; prices start from a few yuan for cruises lasting from one hour to half a day.

Places to Stay – bottom end

There are only two budget hotels open to foreigners (reluctantly), and both are in the town rather than near the lake.

Closest to the railway station is the *China Hotel* (*zhōngguó fàndiàn*) on Tongyun Lu. Doubles start at Y60. Unfortunately, this place is nearly always full because of the ultra-convenient location.

You can almost always get a bed at the *Liangyi Hotel*, in part because the hotel is stuck down an obscure alley that's difficult to find, and also because taxi drivers confuse this place with the very similarly named (but pricier) Liangxi Hotel. Although the staff are somewhat reluctant to take foreigners, they will do so if you're polite (we managed to stay here, and enjoyed it too). Decent doubles cost Y64 but you'd better have exact change in FEC since the only change they have is RMB. The name of the alley is Xiaosanli Jie and you might need to ask directions several times because most locals have never heard of the place even though it's quite large. The hotel has a good restaurant but there are cheaper places to eat in the alley.

Places to Stay – middle

As with the budget hotels, mid-range accommodation is only to be found in the town rather than by the lake. The *Liangxi Hotel* (☎ 226812) (*liángxī fàndiàn*) is on Zhongshan Nanlu. Take bus No 12 from the railway station. The hotel is actually set back from Zhongshan Nanlu, on a small street which runs parallel to it; you'll have to watch out for it. Doubles cost from Y140.

Similarly priced is the *Yunhe Hotel* (*yùnhé fàndiàn*) on Liangxi Lu near Liangqing Lu. Rooms start at Y120. Don't confuse this hotel with its much pricier neighbours, the Meilidu and Wuxi hotels. From the railway station take bus No 10 and get off near the traffic circle.

Places to Stay – top end

In the town itself is the *Meilidu Hotel* (*měilìdū fàndiàn*) on the traffic circle where Liangxi Lu and Liangqing Lu intersect. Comfortable doubles start at Y200. The hotel can be reached from the railway station by taking bus No 10, but it's within walking distance of the Wuxi south bus station.

Just on the opposite side of the circle is the

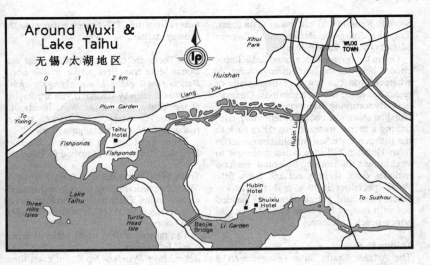

Around Wuxi & Lake Taihu
无锡/太湖地区

four-star *Wuxi Hotel* (*wúxī fàndiàn*). Doubles start from Y300.

All the other tourist hotels are around the lakeside. The *Taihu Hotel* (☎ 667901) (*táihú fàndiàn*) has a large restaurant, telecommunications office, bank and souvenir shop, and overlooks Lake Taihu. Its air-con dining rooms serve Taihu seafood and Wuxi specialties. Three special lakeside villas are for foreign convalescents receiving treatment. The hotel is one of the key centres for group tour activity, and offers boat touring and luxury bus itineraries. Prices start in the Y200 range. The place is a bit awkward to get to – take bus No 2 to the terminal, then walk for about 20 minutes.

Just next door is the *Yangguang Hotel* (*yángguāng fàndiàn*), a Hong Kong joint-venture charging similar upmarket prices.

The *Hubin Hotel* (☎ 668812) (*húbīn fàndiàn*) on Liyuan Lu is a high-rise tour-bus hotel. It charges from Y240 a double. There are 356 beds, air-con, and a full range of facilities including a bar. Take bus No 1 from the railway station.

The *Shuixiu Hotel* (☎ 668591) (*shuǐxiù fàndiàn*) is next to the Hubin Hotel. Doubles cost from around Y200, with pricier rooms

affording a view over the lake. It's an Australian joint-venture and it shows – this squat Australian prefab has koalas and kangaroos crawling over the curtains. Take bus No 1 from the railway station.

The four hotels by the lake are designed for group tours – there are precious few shops out there beyond the hotel gift shops, so stock up on essentials. Anglers can drop out of the hotels toting fishing licences, tackle and bait, cruise around Lake Taihu and have their catches cooked back at the hotel. A rubbing is made first as a memento so you can have your fish and eat it too! Amateurs are parcelled off to the fish ponds for an easy catch.

Places to Eat

The *China Restaurant (zhōngguó fàndiàn)* is recommended for its large servings and low prices. To get there, proceed directly from the railway station and across the bridge; it's on your left, second block down, on the ground floor of the China Hotel, which faces Tongyun Lu.

Other eating places can be found in the markets off Renmin Lu. The stretch along Zhongshan Lu (from the First Department

Store to Renmin Lu) has lots of restaurants. Try the *Jiangnan Restaurant (jiāngnán càiguǎn)* at 435 Zhongshan Lu.

Out in the boondocks, around Lake Taihu, choose between the hotel dining rooms, or whatever you can scrounge from stalls or teahouses at the tourist attractions. One particularly fortifying discovery was a packet of Huishan shortcake cookies (delicious), continuing a tourist tradition that dates back to the 14th century when Buddhist monasteries from Huishan hillsides doled them out to vegetarians in transit. Seasonal seafood includes crab, shrimp, eel and fresh fish. Wuxi specialties include pork ribs in soy sauce, bean curd, a kind of pancake padded out with midget fish from Lake Taihu, and honey-peach in season.

Things to Buy

The Arts & Crafts Store *(gōngyì měishù ménshìbù)* is at 192 Renmin Lu. The Dongfanghong Emporium *(dōngfānghóng shāngdiàn)* is nearby. The First Department Store *(dìyī bǎihuò shāngdiàn)* is at the top end of Zhongshan Lu. The Huishan Clay Figurine Factory *(huìshān níǒu gōngchǎng)* is near Xihui Park.

Silk products and embroidery are good buys. Apart from the places already mentioned, try the merchants in the side streets. Dongfanghong Square is the busiest shopping area.

There are some remarkably ugly clay figurines for sale around the place. A peasant folk art, they were usually models of opera stars, and after a little diversion into revolutionary heroes are back to opera and story figures again. (Wuxi has its own form of opera deriving from folk songs.) The 'Lucky Fatties' are obese babies – symbols of fortune and happiness and just the thing to fill up your mantelpiece with.

Getting There & Away

Air Wuxi has no airport, but you can book flights out of Shanghai on China Eastern Airlines from the Wuxi CAAC office. CAAC's minuscule ticket office is next to the Wuxi Hotel, but most locals purchase air tickets from the CITS branch adjacent to the railway station.

Bus There are two long-distance bus stations. Most travellers arrive at the north station *(wúxī qìchē kèyùn zhōngxīn zhàn)* next to the railway station. If you are staying at the Yunhe, Meilidu or Wuxi hotels, it's more convenient to use the south station *(wúxī qìchē zhàn)* on Liangqing Lu.

There are buses to Shanghai, Suzhou, Dingshu, Yixing and Yangzhou (Y10).

Train Wuxi is on the line from Beijing to Shanghai, with frequent express and special-express trains. There are trains to Suzhou (40 minutes), Shanghai (1¾ hours) and Nanjing (2¾ hours).

The railway station ticket office is a real mess. Foreigners are supposed to buy their tickets from Window No 2, but even there you can expect to spend nearly an hour fighting the queue. At the other windows it's even worse. If you have the right ticket, there is a soft-seat waiting room which will help preserve your sanity.

Boat With such a large lake there is a wealth of scenery and some fascinating routes out of the town. Yixing and Suzhou lie almost on the lake, Changzhou lies north-west of Wuxi on the Grand Canal, and Hangzhou lies inland but is accessible from Wuxi.

From Wuxi there are many boat routes running along smaller canals to outlying counties as well as boats across Lake Taihu and along the Grand Canal. There are many daily boats to Yixing and Changzhou. There is another route through the Wuxi canals, across Lake Taihu and down south through a series of canals to Hangzhou. Alternatively, you can take a boat across Lake Taihu to Huzhou on the southern side and then take a bus to Hangzhou. Huzhou, where there's a tourist service, lies at the junction of routes to Shanghai, Hangzhou and Huangshan. Just north of the town is Xiaomeikou, the ferry dock. North-west of Huzhou is Changxing, and a branch-line railway running to Hangzhou.

Another interchange point for boating is at Zhenxia on the east side of Xidongtingshan Isle. From Zhenxia there are connections to Wuxi, and to Xukou near Suzhou.

Since Wuxi itself covers an area of 400 sq km which is open without a permit, day-tripping along the canals is not technically out of bounds, and there's nothing to stop you from travelling between Hangzhou, Yixing, Jiaxing, Huzhou, Wuxi and Suzhou. A variety of motorboats plies these routes, including two-deck motor barges with aircon, soft seats, a restaurant and space for over 100 passengers. You may see some Chinese-designed passenger hovercraft.

Getting Around

There are about 15 local bus lines. An alternative for faster connections is to grab a motortricycle – there are ranks at the main railway station.

Bus 2 runs from the railway station, along Jiefang Lu, across two bridges to Xihui Park, then way out to Plum Garden, stopping short of the Taihu Hotel. Bus No 2 almost crosses the bus No 1 route at Gongnongbing Square.

Bus No 1 starts on Gongnongbing Lu, and runs to Li Garden and the Hubin and Shuixiu hotels. The actual terminal of bus No 1 is further on across a bridge to the scenery on Turtle Head Isle.

A good tour bus is No 10, which does a long loop around the northern part of the city area, taking in four bridges, Xihui Park and the shopping strip of Renmin Lu.

SUZHOU

(sūzhōu) 苏州

Suzhou's history goes back 2500 years, give or take a hundred – it's one of the oldest towns in the Yangzi basin. With the completion of the Grand Canal in the Sui Dynasty, Suzhou found itself strategically sited on a major trading route, and the city's fortunes and size grew rapidly.

Suzhou flourished as a centre of shipping and grain storage, bustling with merchants and artisans. By the 12th century the town had attained its present dimensions, and if you consult the map, you'll see the layout of the old town. The city walls, a rectangle enclosed by moats, were pierced by six gates (north, south, two in the east, two in the west). Crisscrossing the city were six north-south canals and 14 east-west canals. Although the walls have largely disappeared and a fair proportion of the canals have been plugged, central Suzhou retains its 'Renaissance' character.

A legend was spun around Suzhou through tales of beautiful women with mellifluous voices, and through the famous proverb, 'In Heaven there is Paradise, on earth Suzhou and Hangzhou'. The story picks up when Marco Polo arrived in 1276. He added the adjectives 'great' and 'noble', though he reserved his finer epithets for Hangzhou. The wanderer's keen memory tells us that there were astonishing numbers of craftspeople and rich merchants, as well as great sages, physicians and magicians. He writes:

Moreover I tell you quite truly that there are six thousand bridges of stone in this city, below the greater part of which one galley or two could well pass.

He muses that if the inhabitants had turned their talents to the military arts, they would easily have overrun the whole province. But no, they were totally preoccupied with raising silkworms:

They have vast quantities of raw silk, and manufacture it, not only for their own consumption, all of them being clothed in dresses of silk, but also for other markets.

Indeed, by the 14th century Suzhou had established itself as the leading silk producer in the nation. Although Polo's estimate of 6000 bridges is a bit on the wild side, a map made 150 years before his visit shows 359 bridges, as well as 12 pagodas, more than 50 temples and numerous bathhouses. The town became a spot favoured by the Chinese aristocracy, pleasure-seekers, the leisured, famous scholars, actors and painters who set

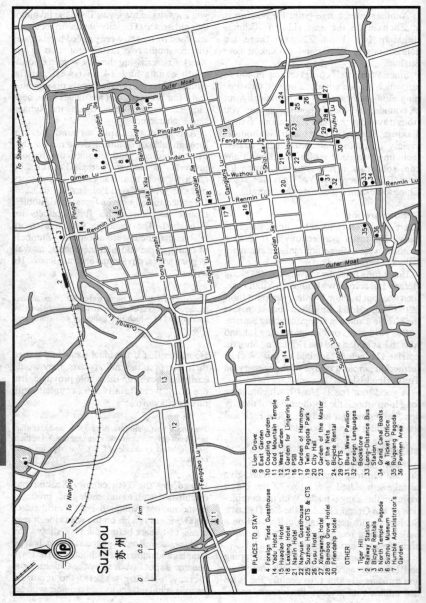

Suzhou
苏州

To Shanghai

To Nanjing

Outer Moat

Pingjiang Lu

Fenghuang Jie

Lindun Lu

Qimen Lu

Wuzhou Lu

Renmin Lu

Outer Moat

Renmin Lu

Dongbei Jie

Baita Donglu

Baita Xilu

Pingqi Lu

Dong Zhongshi

Guanqian Jie

Gangqang Jie

Daoqian Jie

Jinade Lu

Shiquan Jie

Shizi Jie

Zhuhui Lu

Sudong Lu

Guang Lu

Fengqiao Lu

JIANGSU

0   0.5   1 km

PLACES TO STAY

- 4 Foreign Trade Guesthouse
- 14 Yadu Hotel
- 15 Huaqiao Hotel
- 18 Lexiang Hotel
- 21 Nanlin Hotel
- 25 Nanyuan Guesthouse
- 25 Suzhou Hotel, CITS & CTS
- 26 Gusu Hotel
- 27 Xiangwang Hotel
- 28 Bamboo Grove Hotel
- 30 Friendship Hotel

- 8 Lion Grove
- 9 East Garden
- 10 Coupling Garden
- 11 Cold Mountain Temple
- 12 West Garden
- 13 Garden for Lingering In
- 16 PSB
- 17 Garden of Harmony
- 19 Twin Pagoda Park
- 20 City Hall
- 23 Garden of the Master of the Nets
- 24 Bicycle Rental
- 29 CYTS
- 31 Blue Wave Pavilion
- 32 Foreign Languages Bookstore
- 33 Long-Distance Bus Station
- 34 Grand Canal Boats & Ticket Office
- 35 Ruiguang Pagoda
- 36 Panmen Area

OTHER

- 1 Tiger Hill
- 2 Railway Station
- 3 Bicycle Rentals
- 5 North Temple Pagoda
- 6 Suzhou Museum
- 7 Humble Administrator's Garden

about constructing villas and garden retreats for themselves.

At the height of Suzhou's development in the 16th century, the gardens, large and small, numbered over 100. If we mark time here, we arrive at the town's tourist formula today – 'Garden City, Venice of the East' – a medieval mix of woodblock guilds and embroidery societies, whitewashed housing, cobbled streets, tree-lined avenues and canals.

The wretched workers of the silk sweatshops, protesting against paltry wages and the injustices of the contract hire system, were staging violent strikes even in the 15th century, and the landlords shifted. In 1860 Taiping troops took the town without a blow. In 1896 Suzhou was opened to foreign trade, with Japanese and international concessions. During WW II, it was occupied by the Japanese and then by the Kuomintang. Somehow Suzhou slipped through the worst ravages of the Cultural Revolution.

For some lively action, you really can't miss the bridges over the main moat; they offer great vantage points and often host impromptu markets. CITS tours are really

your only option if you want to get into a silk-reeling, silk-weaving or silk-printing mill. There is also an embroidery factory, a jade-carving factory and a sandalwood-fan factory – all within the central area.

Over 600,000 people live here, and numerous enterprises have sprung up, including electronics, machine building, optical instruments, ferro-concrete boat manufacturing and chemical industries. And that, in a nutshell, is the problem. Suzhou still maintains its charming parks, gardens and temples, but Marco Polo would not recognise the place with its motor vehicles, high-rise office buildings, department stores, tourist junk shops and other signs of modernisation. Nevertheless, the town is still worth visiting – at least compared to Shanghai, you could easily call Suzhou relaxing. However, if it's serenity you want, make your stop in Suzhou brief and allocate more time for quiet Yangzhou further to the northwest.

Information

Both CITS (☎ 222681; fax 233593) are CTS (☎ 225583; fax 225931) are in a separate

JIANGSU

building in the Suzhou Hotel compound. The PSB office is at 7 Dashitou Xiang. The Bank of China is at 490 Renmin Lu, but all of the major tourist hotels have foreign-exchange counters as well.

North Temple
(běi sìtǎ) 北寺塔

The North Temple has the tallest pagoda south of the Yangzi – at nine storeys it dominates the north end of Renmin Lu. You can climb it for a fine aerial view of the town and the farmland beyond, which grows tea, rice and wheat. The factory chimneys, the new pagodas of Suzhou, loom on the outskirts, and so does the haze and smoke they create.

The temple complex goes back 1700 years and was originally a residence. The pagoda has been burned, built and rebuilt. Made of wood, it dates from the 17th century. Off to the side of it is Nanmu Hall, which was rebuilt in the Ming Dynasty with some of its features imported from elsewhere. There is a nice teahouse with a small garden out the back.

Suzhou Museum
(sūzhōu bówùguǎn) 苏州博物馆

Situated some blocks east of the pagoda, near the Humble Administrator's Garden, the museum was once the residence of a Taiping leader, Li Xiucheng. It's a good place to visit after you've seen something of Suzhou as it helps fill in the missing bits of the jigsaw as you retrace the town's history.

The museum offers some interesting old maps (Grand Canal, Suzhou, heaven & earth), a silk and embroidery exhibition room (with Qing silk samples), Qing Dynasty steles forbidding workers' strikes, and relics unearthed or rescued from various sites around the Suzhou District (funerary objects, porcelain bowls, bronze swords).

Suzhou Bazaar
(sūzhōu shāngchǎng) 苏州商场

The area surrounding Guanqian Jie is riddled with restaurants, specialty shops, theatres, street vendors, hairdressing salons, noodle dispensaries, silk merchants and sweet shops. This maze of back alleys, the main shopping thoroughfare of Suzhou, is a strolling area with neither bicycles nor buses allowed on Guanqian Jie by day. The bazaar is also the restaurant centre of the city.

Temple of Mystery
(xuánmiàoguān) 玄妙观

The heart of Suzhou Bazaar is the Taoist Temple of Mystery. It was founded in the 3rd century (during the Jin Dynasty and laid out between 275 and 279 AD) with additions during Song times. From the Qing Dynasty onwards, the bazaar fanned out from the temple with small tradespeople and travelling performers using the grounds. The enormous Sanqing Hall, supported by 60 pillars and capped by a double roof with upturned eaves, dates from 1181. It was burnt and seriously damaged in the 19th century. During the Cultural Revolution, the Red Guards squatted here before it was transformed into a library. Today it's been engulfed by the souvenir shops; the square in front of it hosts all manner of outdoor industries including shoe repairing, tailoring and bike parking.

Gardens
(huāyuán) 花园

Suzhou's gardens are looked upon as works of art – a fusion of nature, architecture, poetry and painting designed to ease the mind, move it, or assist it. Unlike the massive imperial gardens, the classical landscaping of Suzhou reflects the personal taste of officials and scholars south of the Yangzi. Rich officials, once their worldly duties were performed, would find solace here in kingdoms of ponds and rockeries. The gardens were meant to be enjoyed either in solitary contemplation or in the company of a close circle of friends with a glass of wine, a concert, poetry recital or a literary discussion.

The key elements of the gardens are rocks and water. There are surprisingly few flowers and no fountains – just like the Zen gardens of Japan, they give one an illusion of a natural scene with only moss, sand and rock. These microcosms were laid out by master

Top: Pagoda in Black Dragon Park, near Kunming, Yunnan (Strauss)
Left: Lijiang Valley, Yunnan (Strauss)
Right: Bamboo fish traps, Erhai Lake, Yunnan (Strauss)

Top: Child in pouch on mother's back, Shapin, Yunnan (RI'A)
Bottom: Piling on the poultry for market (Strauss)

craftspeople and changed hands many times over the centuries. The gardens suffered a setback during the Taiping Rebellion in the 1870s, and under subsequent foreign domination of Suzhou. Efforts were made to restore them in the 1950s but during the so-called Horticultural Revolution gardeners downed tools as flowers were frowned upon. In 1979 the Suzhou Garden Society was formed, and an export company was set up to promote Suzhou-designed gardens. A few of the gardens have been renovated and opened to the public.

Each garden is meant to be savoured at a snail's pace. Remember that the flowers are best left unpicked if the garden is to be preserved. The thing to do is take along a Sunday newspaper, a pot of tea, a deck chair, a sketch pad and a bath sponge. Having said that, let us add that it is very hard to wax contemplative when there are thousands of other visitors (mostly Chinese, an amiable enough lot – mostly taking photos of each other or sketching the foliage). Old-timers come here to relax. The size of the crowds depends on the weather, the day of the week, and the garden. The gardens are usually open from early morning to dusk (from 7.30 am to 5 pm), and admission is a few jiao.

A footnote on gardening in Suzhou: the common people, not having the resources for larger gardens, work at arranging miniatures (potted landscapes, courtyard cultivation). Suzhou, in fact, is the one place in China where you can count on real flowers instead of plastic. If there are any artificial ones, they will at least be silk. As you're strolling the streets it's worthwhile looking for plebeian miniatures. Potted landscapes are sold in various shops, so you can actually buy a piece of Suzhou – but what are you going to do with it?!

Humble Administrator's Garden (zhuó-zhèng yuán) Many consider this Suzhou's second-best garden (after the Garden of the Master of the Nets).

Built in the early 1500s, this was a private garden belonging to Wang Xianchen, a censor with a chequered history. Some say he was demoted to Suzhou, some claim he extorted the money to have the garden constructed, others that the garden was lost to pay a gambling debt by his son.

The garden is also known as the 'Plain Man's Politics Garden', deriving from the quotation, 'To cultivate one's garden to meet one's daily needs, that is what is known as the politics of the plain man'.

There's a five-hectare water park with streams, ponds, bridges and islands of bamboo. You can sense the painter's hand in its design, meant to mimic parts of rural South China. Strong emphasis in Suzhou gardens is given to scenery not found locally. The whole garden is divided into east, middle and west sections though there's nothing of great interest in the East Garden. The Middle Garden is the best. From the Ming Dynasty Distant Fragrance Hall (yuǎn-xiāng táng), you can get a view of everything through lattice windows.

In the same area are the Suzhou Museum and several silk mills.

Lion Grove (shīzilín) Just up the street from the Humble Administrator's Garden, this one-hectare grove was constructed in 1350 by the monk Tian Ru and other disciples as a memorial to their master Zhi Zheng. Zhi, it appears, was some kind of cave dweller, and his last fixed address was c/o 'Lion Cliff', Tianmushan, Zhejiang Province. The garden has rockeries that evoke leonine forms. The walls of the labyrinth of tunnels bear calligraphy from famous chisels.

Garden of Harmony (yíyuán) A small Qing Dynasty garden owned by an official called Gu Wenbin, this one is quite young for a Suzhou garden. It has assimilated many of the features of other gardens and blended them into a style of its own. The garden is divided into eastern and western sections linked by a covered promenade with lattice windows. In the east are buildings and courtyards. The western section has pools with coloured pebbles, rockeries, hillocks and pavilions. The garden is off Renmin Lu, just south of Guanqian Jie.

Blue Wave Pavilion (cānglàngtíng) A bit on the wild side with winding creeks and luxuriant trees, this is one of the oldest gardens in Suzhou. The buildings date from the 11th

1	Canglangshengji Arch
2	Lotus Waterside Pavilion
3	Steles
4	Waterside House
5	Pavilion of Imperial Stele
6	Toilet
7	Buqi Pavilion
8	Pavilion for Admiring Fish
9	Canglangting Garden
10	Wenmiaoxiang House
11	Qingxiang Hall
12	Shrine of 500 Sages
13	Enlightened Way Hall
14	Yangzhi Pavilion
15	Cuilinglong Houses
16	Kanshan Tower
17	Yaohuajingjie House

1	沧浪胜迹坊
2	面水莲亭
3	碑纪
4	面水轩纪
5	御碑纪
6	公厕
7	步砌亭处
8	观鱼亭
9	沧浪妙香亭
10	闻香馆
11	清香名贤祠
12	五百道堂
13	明仰止亭
14	翠玲珑
15	看山楼
16	瑶华仙境
17	

Blue Wave Pavilion (Canglangting)
沧浪厅

century although there has been rebuilding following damage more than a few times. Originally the home of a prince, the property passed into the hands of the scholar Su Zimei who gave it its name. The one-hectare garden attempts to create optical illusions with the scenery both outside and inside – you look from the pool immediately outside to the distant hills.

Enlightened Way Hall *(míngdào táng)*, the largest building, is said to have been a site for delivery of lectures in the Ming Dynasty. On the other side of Renmin Lu, close by, is the former Confucian Temple.

Garden of the Master of the Nets *(wǎngshī yuán)* This is the smallest garden in Suzhou – half the size of Canglangting, and a tenth the size of Zhuozheng. It's so small, it's hard to find, but well worth the trouble since it's better than the others combined.

This garden was laid out in the 12th century, abandoned, then restored in the 18th

century as part of the residence of a retired official. According to one story, he announced that he'd had enough of bureaucracy and would rather be a fisherman. Another explanation of the name is that it was simply near Wangshi Lu.

The eastern part of the garden is the residential area – originally with side rooms for sedan-chair lackeys, guest reception and living quarters. The central part is the main garden. The western part is an inner garden where a courtyard contains the Spring-Rear

Cottage *(diànchūn yí)*, the master's study. This section and the study, with its Ming-style furniture and palace lanterns, was duplicated and unveiled at the Metropolitan Museum of Art in New York in 1981.

A miniature model of the whole garden, using Qingtian jade, Yingde rocks, Anhui paper, Suzhou silk and incorporating the halls, kiosks, ponds, blossoms and rare plants of the original design, was produced especially for a display at the Pompidou Centre in Paris in 1982.

The most striking feature of Wangshi is its use of space. Despite its size, the scale of the buildings is large, but nothing appears cramped. A section of the buildings is used by a cooperative of woodblock artists who find the peaceful atmosphere congenial to work. The entrance is a narrow alley just west of the Suzhou Hotel.

Garden for Lingering In *(liúyuán)* Extending over an area of three hectares, Liuyuan is one of the largest Suzhou gardens, noted for its adroit partitioning with building complexes. It dates from the Ming Dynasty and managed to escape destruction during the Taiping Rebellion. A 700-metre covered walkway connects the major scenic spots, and the windows have carefully selected perspectives. The walkway is inlaid with calligraphy from celebrated masters. The garden has a wealth of potted plants. Outside Mandarin Duck (Yuanyang) Hall is a 6½-metre-high Lake Tai piece – it's the final word on rockeries. The garden is about one km west of the old city walls. The bus there will take you over bridges that look down on the busy water traffic.

West Garden Temple
(xīyuán sì) 西园
About 500 metres west of Liuyuan, this temple was built on the site of a garden laid out at the same time as Liuyuan and then donated to the Buddhist community. The temple was destroyed in the 19th century and entirely rebuilt; it contains some expressive Buddhist statues.

Cold Mountain Temple
(hánshān sì) 寒山寺
One km west of Liuyuan, this temple was named after the poet-monk Hanshan, who lived in the 7th century. It was repeatedly burnt down and rebuilt, and holds little of interest except for a stele by poet Zhang Ji immortalising nearby Maple Bridge and the temple bell (since removed to Japan). However, the fine walls and the humpback bridge are worth seeing. The temple was once the site of lively local trading in silk, wood and grain. Not far from its saffron walls lies the Grand Canal. To get to the temple take bus No 4 to the terminal, cross the bridge and walk to the No 6 bus route; or take bus No 5 and then connect with No 6.

Tiger Hill
(hǔqiūshān) 虎丘山
At the Tiger Hill parking lot (the bus No 5 terminal) we counted 15 Chinese tour buses, six minibuses, five Toyotas, three Shanghai taxis and two Kingswoods (modified with drawn curtains), so it seemed like a popular, interesting place. Actually, Tiger Hill is disappointing. It's an artificial hill, 36 metres high, set in a park of 20 hectares. King He Lu, founding father of Suzhou, who died in the 6th century BC, is buried near the top of the hill. A white tiger is said to have appeared to guard the tomb; hence the name.

Many Arthurian-type legends exist about Tiger Hill. There's a sword-testing stone with a crack in it, split by He Lu. According to legend, He Lu is buried with his 3000 swords. A thousand builders were reputedly bumped off after making the tomb so that its secrets would not be revealed. Tiger Hill Pagoda *(hǔqiū tǎ)*, which was finished in 961 AD, has been leaning for several centuries. This century it split and had to be re-stabilised. Work has been done to reinforce the foundation now that the tilt has reached over two metres. Concrete piles have been driven into the ground around the base, rather like staking in a flowerpot.

Places to Stay – bottom end
We can tell you which place *used to be* the

cheapest and best – without a doubt it was the *Lexiang Hotel* (☎ 223898) *(lèxiāng fàndiàn)* where dorm beds were Y25 and doubles Y180. The problem is that the hotel was being renovated at the time of our visit, and it's likely that prices will be renovated when it reopens. It's hard to imagine that there will still be dorms, but we can always hope. The Lexiang Hotel is right in the centre at 18 Dajing Xiang, an alley which runs off Renmin Lu near the Guanqian markets. To get there take bus No 1 from the railway station.

Places to Stay – middle

Closest to the railway station (not a particularly attractive neighbourhood but convenient) is the *Foreign Trade Guesthouse (wàimào bīnguǎn)*, 684 Renmin Lu, has good-looking doubles/triples for Y120/130.

The south-eastern corner of town has a goldmine of mid-range accommodation. One to consider is the *Friendship Hotel* (☎ 773518) *(yǒuyí bīnguǎn)*, Zhuhui Lu. All rooms are doubles with private bathroom and are very comfortable. An 'ordinary' double is Y130 and a 'standard' is Y170. Suites cost Y260.

Just down the street is the newly opened *Xiangwang Hotel* (☎ 231162) *(xiāngwáng bīnguǎn)*. All doubles cost Y130. The hotel is on the north-western corner of Xiangwang Lu and Zhuhui Lu.

Walk around the corner and you'll reach the entrance of the *Gusu Hotel* (☎ 224689; fax 779727) *(gūsū fàndiàn)*, 5 Xiangwang Lu Shiquan Jie. The building is a bleak-looking Australian prefab on the outside but it's a decent two-star hotel on the inside. Doubles cost Y160.

The *Nanlin Hotel* (☎ 224641; fax 231028) *(nánlín fàndiàn)* is at 22 Gunxiufang off Shiquan Jie. Its very pleasant gardens include a small section with outdoor ceramic tables and chairs. Doubles cost Y176 or Y275. The hotel is convenient to the long-distance bus station and boat dock. The Nanlin is not to be confused with its more expensive neighbour, the Nanyuan.

The *Huaqiao Hotel* (☎ 334011) *(huáqiáo fàndiàn)* on Sanxiang Lu on the western side of town has doubles starting at Y160. Don't confuse this place with the neighbouring and more expensive Yadu Hotel.

Places to Stay – top end

The *Suzhou Hotel* (☎ 224646) *(sūzhōu fàndiàn)*, 115 Shiquan Jie, is the home of CITS. It offers air-con luxury, with a full range of services including a Friendship Store branch, theatre and extensive gardens. Doubles – including fridge and bathroom – start at Y258. This hotel accepts American Express, Visa, Master and Great Wall credit cards.

The *Nanyuan Guesthouse* (☎ 227661; fax 238806) *(nányuán bīnguǎn)*, 249 Shiquan Jie, is inside a walled garden compound. Room prices are Y316, Y690 and a sobering Y1725.

The *Yadu Hotel* (☎ 731888) *(yǎdū dàjiǔdiàn)*, 147 Sanxiang Lu, is an upmarket place in the western area of town. Figure on over Y350 for a 'basic' double.

The *Bamboo Grove Hotel* (☎ 225601; fax 235723) *(zhúhuī bīnguǎn)* on Zhuhui Lu gives all the comforts for prices starting at Y488.

Places to Eat

Suzhou Bazaar is the restaurant centre of the city. A seasonal specialty is a strange, hairy crab, steamed with soy sauce and ginger. The crabs are caught at a freshwater lake seven km north-east of Suzhou in early autumn. The resulting feast is an annual event; Nanjingers and Shanghainese make the trip to Suzhou to sample it. There are prices to suit all wallets. You can stuff your gills for Y5 in a noodle shop, or blow your inheritance in the Songhelou Restaurant.

The *Songhelou Restaurant* (☎ 777003) *(sōnghè lóu)* at 141 Guanqian Jie is the most famous restaurant in Suzhou: Emperor Qianlong is supposed to have eaten there. The large variety of dishes includes squirrel fish, plain steamed prawns, braised eel, pork with pine nuts, butterfly-shaped sea cucumber, watermelon chicken and spicy duck. The waiter will insist that you be parcelled off to the special 'tour bus' cubicle at the back where an English menu awaits. The Songhelou runs from Guanqian Jie to an alley behind, where tour minibuses pull up. Travellers give it mixed reviews.

In the alley at the back of the Songhelou (Taijian Long) are numerous large, crowded prole restaurants. The *Shanghai Laozhengxin* (☎ 225357) is at No 19, *Jinghua Jiulou* is at No 21, *Wangsi Jiujia* is at No 27 and *Yuandachang Caiguan* is at No 29.

A pot of tea is the correct thing to drink with your meal. Suzhou has two native teas: Biluochun Green (Snail Spring Tea) and Jasmine.

There are a couple of other places worth trying. The *Xinjufeng Restaurant* (☎ 773794) *(xīnjùfēng càiguǎn)* at 615 Renmin Lu serves variations on duck and chicken, and regional specialties. The restaurants in the *Suzhou* and *Nanlin* hotels serve local delicacies like Suzhou almond duck and phoenix shrimp.

Entertainment

Try the barber shops and hairdressing salons on Guanqian Jie. No kidding – these places have the brightest lights and the most action in the early evening. As you're walking along, peep over the curtains of the salons to discover China's great beauty secrets. There are also a few dance halls scattered around the same district.

Suzhou has other nightlife, with over a dozen theatres and some storytelling houses. Suzhou Pingtan (ballad singing and storytelling) is where you can hear those sweet voices worked to their fullest. Most of the after-hours activity takes place south of Guanqian Jie. There's a theatre at the Suzhou Hotel which occasionally has live shows.

Things to Buy

Suzhou-style embroidery, calligraphy, painting, sandalwood fans, writing brushes and silk underclothes are for sale nearly everywhere, probably even in the gift shop of your hotel.

Another Suzhou specialty is hair-embroidery. The technique uses human hair worked onto a silk backing. Suzhou embroidery is ranked among the top four needle-styles in China. There's also *kèsī*, which mixes raw and boiled-off silk in the weaving process, and is known as 'carved silk'. It was once reserved for imperial robing and can be bought in painting-scrolls or as waistbands and other items.

Although the Arts & Crafts Research Institute *(gōngyì měishù yánjiūsuǒ)* is not open to tourists, there is some fascinating activity going on there. In 1981, 32-year-old Shen Weizhong carved the world's smallest buddha – three mm tall, with fingers as thin as hair, and a smiling face that can only be seen through a microscope. Another worker carved words onto the hair of a panda. (Now you know how they come up with those bus maps!)

Forgetting artistic pursuits for a moment, check out the Suzhou Foreign Languages Bookstore near the long-distance bus station. This place has a treasure trove of English-language paperbacks – just the thing to preserve your sanity in hard-seat hell when all your fellow passengers stare at you and spit for 12 hours. Most of the books are Signet classics, and though they appear to be imported, prices are much lower than in the West.

Getting There & Away

Air Suzhou does not have an airport, but China Eastern Airlines (☎ 222788) *(dōngfāng hángkōng gōngsī)* has a ticket office for booking flights out of Shanghai.

Bus The long-distance bus station is at the south end of Renmin Lu. Considering that Suzhou is relatively prosperous and supposedly a major tourist attraction, the bus station is surprisingly primitive. There are connections between Suzhou and just about every major place in the region including Shanghai, Hangzhou, Wuxi, Yangzhou and Yixing.

Train Suzhou is on the line from Nanjing to Shanghai. To Shanghai takes about 1¼ hours, to Wuxi 40 minutes and Nanjing 3¼ hours. For long-distance sleepers, ask your hotel or try CITS.

Boat There are boats along the Grand Canal to Wuxi and to Hangzhou. It's basically only foreigners who use them these days – the Chinese prefer the bus or train.

Boats from Suzhou to Hangzhou depart daily at 5.50 am and at 5.30 pm. The fare is Y9.50 to Y11.40 for a seat on the day boat and Y22.30 to 58.50 for a sleeper on the night boat, depending on the class. The trip takes about 14 hours. Boats from Hangzhou to Suzhou depart at 5.50 am and 5.30 pm.

Boats to Wuxi depart from Suzhou at 6.10 am and at noon. The trip takes around five hours. Boats to Suzhou depart from Wuxi at 6.20 am and noon. The fare is Y2.50 for a seat.

Getting Around

Bus The main thoroughfare is Renmin Lu with the railway station off the northern end, and a large boat dock and long-distance bus station at the southern end.

Bus No 1 runs the length of Renmin Lu. Bus No 2 is a kind of round-the-city bus, while bus No 5 is a good east-west bus. Bus No 4 runs from Changmen directly east along Baita Lu, turns south and runs past the east end of Guanqian Jie and then on to the Suzhou Hotel.

Taxi Taxis and motorcycle taxis congregate outside the main railway station, down by the boat dock at the southern end of Renmin Lu, and at Jingmen (Nanxin Bridge) at the western end of Jingde Lu. They also tend to hover around tourist hotels. Although taxis are equipped with meters, the drivers never use them so establish the fare before setting out. Like elsewhere in China, the pedicab drivers are almost more trouble than they are worth.

Bicycle You can rent a bike from a shop just opposite the entrance to the Suzhou Hotel. Another bike rental place is at the very northern end of Renmin Lu, just east of the railway station.

AROUND SUZHOU

Some of the local buses go for a considerable distance, such as bus No 11. You could hop on one for a ride to the terminal to see the enchanting countryside.

Grand Canal

(dàyùn hé) 大运河

The canal proper cuts to the west and south of Suzhou, within a 10-km range of the town. Suburban bus Nos 13, 14, 15 and 16 will get you there. In the north-west, bus No 11 follows the canal for a fair distance. Once you arrive, it's simply a matter of finding yourself a nice bridge, getting out your deck chair and watching the world go by. Unfortunately, parking yourself for too long could make you the main tourist attraction for hordes of Chinese spectators.

Precious Belt Bridge

(bǎodài qiáo) 宝带桥

This is one of China's best, with 53 arches, the three central humpbacks being larger to allow boats through. It straddles the Grand Canal, and is a popular spot with fisherfolk. The bridge is not used for traffic – a modern one has been built alongside – and is thought to be a Tang Dynasty construction named after Wang Zhongshu, a local prefect who sold his precious belt to pay for the bridge's construction for the benefit of his people. Precious Belt Bridge is about five km south-east of Suzhou. Bus No 13 will set you on the right track.

Lake Taihu Area

The following places can all be reached by long-distance buses from the station at the south end of Renmin Lu.

Lingyanshan *(língyán shān)* This is 15 km south-west of Suzhou. There are weirdly shaped rocks, a temple and pagoda (molested by Red Guards), and panoramas of mulberry trees, fertile fields and Lake Taihu in the distance.

The now active Buddhist monastery has a

'Tibetan feel'. It's set aloft a large hill, though in these parts 'large' is relative to totally flat. The monastery dates back to the Ming Dynasty. It was shut down during the Cultural Revolution but was permitted to reopen in 1980.

Lingyanshan is a lovely place to cycle to, though along the way you pass some nightmarish scenes of industrial pollution (these can be intriguing in their own bizarre way).

Tianpingshan *(tiānpíng shān)* This is 18 km south-west and has more of the same – plus some medicinal spring waters.

Guangfu Twenty-five km to the south-west, bordering the lake, Guangfu has an ancient seven-storey pagoda and is dotted with plum trees.

Dongshan *(dōngshān)* Forty km to the south-west, this place is noted for its gardens and the Purple Gold (Zijin) Nunnery, which contains 16 coloured clay arhats and is surrounded by Lake Taihu on three sides.

Xidongtingshan Island *(xīdòngtíng shān)* This town, also called Xishan, is a large island 60 km south-west of Suzhou. Getting there involves a 10-km ferry ride. Eroded Taihu rocks are 'harvested' here for landscaping. Take a bus from opposite Suzhou railway station to Luxian, then catch a ferry across to Zhenxia.

Changshu *(chángshú)* Fifty km north-east of Suzhou, this town is noted for its lace making. To the north-west of the town is Yushan, with historical and scenic spots, including a nine-storey Song pagoda.

Luzhi In this town on the water, 25 km east of Suzhou, the canals provide the main means of commuting – in concrete flat-bottomed boats. The old Baosheng temple has arhats, although that is probably not why you should come here. You could try your luck getting to places like this via canals from small docks in Suzhou.

XUZHOU
(xúzhoū) 徐州

Xuzhou does not fall into the category of a canal town, though a tributary of the Grand Canal passes by its north-eastern end. The history of the town has little to do with the canal – Xuzhou is basically a railway junction with little to see beyond a couple of temples. Oh yes, there is something else – the coal mines. If you should accidentally get stuck here on your way to somewhere else, the following sights might keep you amused for a couple of hours:

Dragon in the Clouds Hill
(yúnlóng shān) 云龙山

This hill has half the scenery of Xuzhou: the Xinghua Temple, several pavilions, and a stone carving from the Northern Wei Dynasty. If you climb to the top of the hill, to the Xinghua Temple, there's a magnificent panorama of the concrete boxes that compose the Xuzhou valley and the mountains that encircle it. There are even orchards out there somewhere. Set in a grotto off the mountainside is a giant gilded buddha head, the statue of the Sakyamuni Buddha. The park itself has an outdoor shooting gallery, and peanuts and ice-lolly sticks littering the slopes. The hill is a 10-minute walk west of the Nanjiao Hotel, or take bus Nos 2 or 11.

Monument to Huaihai Campaign Martyrs
(huáihǎi zhànyì lièshì jìniàntǎ)
淮海战役烈士纪念塔

This revolutionary war memorial and obelisk, which was opened in 1965, is in a huge wooded park at the southern edge of town. The Huaihai battle was a decisive one fought by the People's Liberation Army from November 1948 to January 1949. The obelisk is 38½ metres high and has a gold inscription by Chairman Mao approached by a grand flight of stairs leading up to it. The nearby Memorial Hall contains an extensive collection of weaponry, photos, maps, paintings and memorabilia – over 2000 items altogether – as well as inscriptions by important heads of state, from Zhou Enlai to

Deng Xiaoping. The grounds, 100 acres of pines and cypresses, are meant to be 'symbolic of the evergreen spirit of the revolutionary martyrs'. The park is on the bus No 11 route.

LIANYUNGANG
(liányúngǎng) 连云港

The town is divided into port and city sections. Yuntai Hill is the 'scenic spot' overlooking the ocean, and there are some salt mines along the shores, as well as a Taoist monastery. The mountain is reputed to be the inspiration for the Flowers and Fruit Mountain in the Ming Dynasty classic *Journey to the West* (but three other places in China make the same claim). Other sights include the 2000-year-old stone carvings at Kung Wangshan. There's an International Seamen's Club, Friendship Store, CITS office and several hotels.

Getting There & Away

CAAC flies between Lianyungang and Beijing (Y350), Canton (Y780) and Shanghai (Y240). Buses along the east coast connect Lianyungang with Shanghai. From Xuzhou, a branch line runs east to the major coastal port of Lianyungang (a six-hour ride).

Shandong 山东

Population: 80 million
Capital: Ji'nan

Shandong (*shāndōng*), the turtle-head bobbing into the Yellow Sea, is a slow starter. The province is relatively poor and beset with economic problems, not the least of which is the rotten Yellow River which can't decide where to void itself. The river has changed direction some 26 times in its history and flooded many more times. Six times it has swung its mouth from the Bohai Gulf (north Shandong) to the Yellow Sea (south Shandong), and wreaked havoc on the residents.

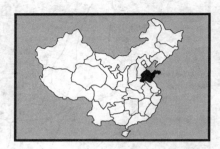

Back in 1899 the river flooded the entire Shandong Plain, a sad irony in view of the two scorching droughts which had swept the area that same year and the year before. Add to that a long period of economic depression, a sudden influx of demobilised troops in 1895 after China's humiliating defeat in the war with Japan, and droves of refugees from the south moving north to escape famines, floods and drought. Then top it off with an imperial government in Beijing either incapable or unwilling to help the local people, and foreigners whose missionaries and railroads had angered the gods and spirits. All this created a perfect breeding ground for a rebellion, and in the last few years of the 19th century the Boxers arose out of Shandong and their rebellion set all of China ablaze.

Controlling the monstrous river that started it all is still going to take a fair bit of dike building. The other major problem is overpopulation. Shandong, with an area of just 150,000 sq km, is the third most populated province after Henan and Sichuan. And to make matters harder, about two-thirds of Shandong is hilly, with the Shandong massif (at 1545 metres, Taishan is the highest peak) looming up in the south-west, and another mountain chain over the tip of the Shandong Peninsula. The rest is fertile plains.

The Germans got their hands on the port of Qingdao in 1898 and set up a few facto-ries. Shandong Province subsequently took a few quantum leaps towards industrialisation. The leading industrial town today is still Qingdao; the capital, Ji'nan, takes second place. Zibo, the major coal-mining centre, is also noted for its glassworks and porcelain. The Shengli Oilfield, opened in northern Shandong in 1965, is the second-largest crude oil source in China. As for railway lines, you can count them on the fingers of one hand, but the Shandong Peninsula has some first-class harbours with good passenger links, and there is a dense network of top-notch roads.

Travellers tend to gloss over this province, which is unfortunate since it has quite a bit to offer. Besides the tourist attractions, an added bonus is that some places (notably Tai'an and Qufu) have very cheap hotels, a godsend for budget travellers in increasingly expensive China. Another impressive feature of this province is that the people (with the notable exception of pedicab drivers) seem to be extremely friendly to foreigners. And for those who partake, beer, wine and mineral water from Qingdao, Laoshan and Yantai are the pride of the nation.

JI'NAN
(jì'nán) 济南

Ji'nan, the capital of Shandong Province, presides over a number of outlying counties

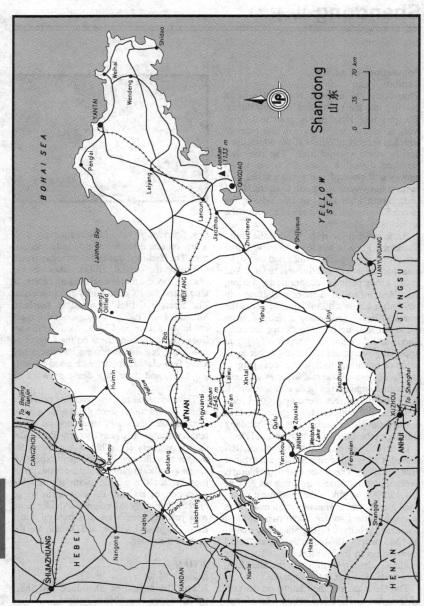

Shandong 山东

SHANDONG

and has a population of around two million in the city proper. The old city had two sets of walls – if you look at the map, you can see the squarish moats that once surrounded them and the inner wall bounded by the springs of Ji'nan. The Communists pulled down the Ming walls in 1949.

The area has been inhabited for at least 4000 years, and some of the earliest reminders of this are the eggshell-thin pieces of black pottery unearthed in the town of Longshan, 30 km east of Ji'nan. Modern development in Ji'nan stems from 1899 when construction of the Ji'nan to Qingdao railway line began. The line gave the city a major communications role when completed in 1904. The Germans had a concession near the railway station after Ji'nan was opened up to foreign trade in 1906. Foreign missions were set up here and industrialisation took place under the Germans, the English and the Japanese. Steel, paper, fertiliser, cars and textiles are now produced here. The city is also an important educational centre.

As for tourism, Ji'nan is about as interesting as watching paint dry. The most frequent visitors are Overseas Chinese with Shandong ancestry. Some come to visit relatives, others make the pilgrimage to reassert their ethnic pride, but increasingly the motive is to sniff out business opportunities – Ji'nan is, after all, the capital and wealthiest place in the province. It's also a friendly city, although for most travellers, Ji'nan serves as a transit point to Shandong's greater glories, specifically Taishan, Qingdao and Qufu.

Information

CITS There is an office (☎ 615858) in the Qilu Hotel, but Ji'nan CITS caters mainly to tour groups.

JITS The Ji'nan International Travel Service (JITS) (☎ 612864), at 117 Jing 7 Wei 4-Lu, offers better service than CITS and has a more centrally located office. The main reason to visit this office is to obtain train tickets. With one day's notice the staff can usually get soft sleepers to anywhere, but hard sleepers may require three or four days' notice unless you're unusually lucky.

Money The Bank of China (☎ 611854) is in Building 10, Shangye Jie, in the eastern part of town.

Bookshops It may be worth digging through the limited selection at the Foreign Languages Bookstore (☎ 612542) at 227 Jing-4 Lu.

Thousand Buddha Mountain
(*qiānfóshān*) 千佛山
The statues were disfigured or just disappeared during the Cultural Revolution, but new ones are gradually being added – Overseas Chinese visitors often donate money to this worthy cause. Thousand Buddha Mountain is on the south side of town. Bus Nos 2 and 31 go there – get off at Qianfoshan Lu.

Shandong Provincial Museum
(*shāndōng bówùguǎn*) 山东省博物馆
The museum was recently refurbished and moved to a new site on the south end of town adjacent to the Thousand Buddha Mountain. The museum is divided into history and nature sections – tools, *objets d'art*, pottery, musical instruments.

Golden Ox Park
(*jīnniú gōngyuán*) 金牛公园
This park on the north side of town is notable for a temple built on a hillside and the city zoo (*jì'nán dòngwùyuán*). Bus Nos 4, 5, 33 and 35 stop here.

You can make a side trip from here a few km to the north of the No 4 bus terminal to see the dike of the Yellow River. That's on the dull side, but you pass by some dusty villages where the locals are engaged in various kinds of back-breaking labour.

Daguanyuan Market
(*dàguānyuán shìchǎng*) 大观园市场
Ji'nan's largest market is a good place to browse around. A couple of blocks to the east is the Ji'nan People's Market (*jì'nán rénmín shāngcháng*).

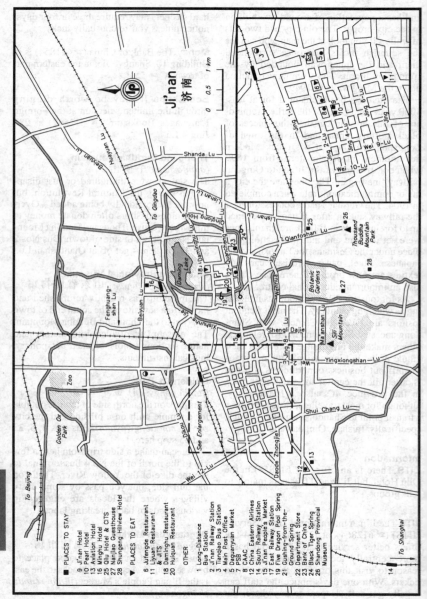

Ji'nan
济南

PLACES TO STAY
9 Ji'nan Hotel
10 Pearl Hotel
13 Aviation Hotel
16 Minghu Hotel
26 Qilu Hotel & CITS
27 Nanjiao Guesthouse
28 Shungeng Hillview Hotel

PLACES TO EAT
6 Jufengde Restaurant
11 Liyuan Restaurant & JITS
18 Daminghu Restaurant
20 Huiquan Restaurant

OTHER
1 Long-Distance Bus Station
2 Jinan Railway Station
3 Tianqiao Bus Station
4 Main Post Office
5 Baguanyuan Market
7 PSB
8 CAAC
12 China Eastern Airlines
14 South Railway Station
15 Ji'nan People's Market
17 East Railway Station
19 Five Dragon Pool Spring
21 Gushing-from-the-Ground Spring
22 Department Store
23 Bank of China
24 Black Tiger Spring
25 Shandong Provincial Museum

Mystery of the Springs

Ji'nan's 100-plus springs are often quoted as the main attraction, so let's set the record straight on this one. The four main parks-cum-springs are Black Tiger Spring (*hēihǔquán*), Pearl Spring (*zhūquán*), Five Dragon Pool (*wǔlóngtán*) and Gushing-from-the-Ground Spring (*bàotúquán*), all marvellous names but hardly accurate as adjectives. Twenty years ago they might have sprung but now they've virtually dried up. The reasons given vary – droughts, pollution from factories, increased industrial

and domestic use and, more quietly, the digging of bomb shelters outside the city.

Daming Lake (*dàmíng hú*) is also affected by this malaise, which the authorities are attempting to 'correct'. Daming Lake has several minor temples, a few teahouses and a restaurant. At Gushing-from-the-Ground Spring there is a small memorial museum dedicated to the 11th-century patriotic poet, Li Qingzhao.

Places to Stay

The accommodation situation for foreigners borders on the absurd. Ji'nan has many fine hotels that would be perfectly acceptable – even more than perfectly acceptable – elsewhere in China. However, most are off-limits to foreigners. These places sit half empty while foreigners shuttle around town encountering 'all full' signs at the few hotels where they can stay. Most of the places catering for foreigners are far from the centre, which is fine if you arrive by tour bus but not so fine if you're walking with a backpack. The limited selection means not only living in an inconvenient location, but also paying high prices. If you find a hotel room for under Y150 in Ji'nan, you're doing well.

Although you aren't likely to find a place to stay for free, one traveller reports such an experience:

Luckily I met the son of a cadre who asked me if I had any foreign video tapes. No, I didn't – how silly of me not to have stocked up in Hong Kong. He shuffled me round to a few dreary tour spots, offered me a place to stay for the night and took me to dinner with his girlfriend. He was, I guess, trying to impress her with his broken English – he certainly impressed her with the price of the meal. I stayed the night in his spacious apartment, finding out how cadres' sons live – high! They have enough money, or access to it, to create a generation gap between themselves and their parents.

The *Aviation Hotel* (☎ 664441, 664443) (*hángkōng dàshà*), 626 Jing 10-Lu, has doubles starting at Y110. Being a bit far from the centre, this place usually has vacancies. Rooms are comfortable and the staff are friendly. Bus No 9 from the centre will get you here, or about Y15 by motortricycle. The hotel is right behind the China Eastern Airlines ticket office.

The *Ji'nan Hotel* (☎ 738981) *(jì'nán fàndiàn)* at 240 Jing 3-Lu has one of the most central locations. Doubles start at Y150 – cheap by Ji'nan standards.

Just next door is the *Pearl Hotel* (☎ 732888; fax 390028) *(zhēnzhū dàjiǔdiàn)*, 164 Jing 3-Lu. This three-star place charges Y200 and up for a double.

The *Nanjiao Guesthouse* (☎ 613931) *(nánjiāo bīnguǎn)*, at 2 Ma'anshan Lu, is out on the south end of town. Expect to pay something like Y250 for a double. Getting to the hotel requires effort – bus No 34 from the centre and then a hike up a hill. It was, so the story goes, flung up for an impending visit by Mao, who then decided to skip Ji'nan.

The *Shungeng Hillview Hotel* (☎ 615901; fax 615288) *(shùngēng shānzhuāng)* is in the same neighbourhood, off Shungeng Lu. Doubles cost Y230 to Y287. Bus No 33 stops nearby.

The *Qilu Hotel* (☎ 266888, 266981) *(qílǔ bīnguǎn)* is the flashy tourist spot in town and home of CITS. Doubles start at Y350. It's on Jing 10-Lu right next to Thousand Buddha Mountain Park *(qiānfóshān gōngyuán)*.

Just north of the east railway station is the *Minghu Hotel* (☎ 556688) *(mínghú dàjiǔdiàn)* on Beiyuan Lu. This three-star place has rooms for around Y260 to Y290.

Places to Eat

Although Ji'nan isn't especially worth visiting for the fine food, with effort you can ferret out some decent fare. One of the better known eating establishments in town is the *Huiquan Restaurant* (☎ 610391) *(huìquán fàndiàn)*, 22 Baotuquan Beilu, which features sweet and sour carp from the Yellow River (served while still breathing so you know it's fresh!). Good Shandong food can be had at *Jufengde Restaurant (jùfēngdé fàndiàn)* at the intersection of Wei 4-Lu and Jing 3-Lu. Just outside the south gate of Daming Lake Park is the *Daminghu Restaurant (dàmínghú fàndiàn)* which also serves Shandong food. Next to JITS is the good but

pricey *Liyuan Restaurant* (☎ 626629) *(lìyuán fànzhuāng)*, at Jing 7 Wei 4-Lu.

Like elsewhere in China, the railway station area has numerous stalls, and you can always get yourself a bottle of 16% proof Tsingtao Red and hope you'll be too far gone to notice the food.

Getting There & Away

Air There are international flights (technically charters) three times a week between Hong Kong and Ji'nan. Domestic flights go from Ji'nan to Beijing (Y200), Canton (Y820), Fuzhou, Shanghai (Y420), Shenyang (Y450), Xiamen (Y700) and Yantai (Y200).

The CAAC ticket office (☎ 733191) *(mínháng shòupiàochù)* is at 348 Jing 2 Wei-Lu. China Eastern Airlines (☎ 764445, 766824) *(dōngfāng hángkōng gōngsī)* is at 408 Jing 10-Lu. Both offices sell the same tickets.

Bus At the moment, Ji'nan has at least three bus stations. The main long-distance bus station *(chángtú qìchē zhàn)* in the north of town has buses to Beijing and Qingdao. The Tianqiao bus station *(tiānqiáo qìchē zhàn)* is near the main railway station (currently being rebuilt) and has minibuses to Tai'an. Just in front of the east railway station *(huǒchē dōngzhàn)* is where you catch minibuses to Qufu and rural areas near Ji'nan.

Train At the time of writing, the situation with railway stations was very confused. Ji'nan Railway Station *(jìnán huǒchē zhàn)* was in the process of being rebuilt, with all trains being diverted to either the south station *(huǒchē nánzhàn)* or the east station *(huǒchē dōngzhàn)*. Trains stopping at one station do not stop at the other. With the opening of the new station (whenever that happens), everything will be rearranged. In the meantime, be absolutely certain about where your train departs from when you purchase a ticket.

Ji'nan is a major link in the east China rail system, with over 30 trains passing through daily. From Ji'nan there are direct trains to Beijing (six hours) and Shanghai (13 hours). The trains from Qingdao to Shenyang which pass through Ji'nan side-step Beijing and go through Tianjin instead. There are direct trains from Ji'nan to Qingdao and Yantai in Shandong Province, and to Hefei in Anhui Province. There are also direct Qingdao-Ji'nan-Xi'an-Xining trains.

Getting Around

To/From the Airport There are two airports in Ji'nan, but nearly all flights use the new international airport (*mínháng jì'nán jīcháng*). This is 40 km east of the city, but a new freeway makes it possible to cover the distance in just 40 minutes. You can catch an airport bus from the CAAC ticket office – try not to miss it because a taxi will cost over Y100!

The old airport (*zhāng zhuāng jīcháng*) is gradually being phased out of use, but it's good to know about it mainly so you don't wind up there by mistake!

Bus & Motortricycle There are about 25 urban and suburban bus lines in Ji'nan, running from 5 am to 9 pm, and two late-night lines (east-west and north-south) finishing at midnight. There are also plenty of motortricycles.

AROUND JI'NAN

Ji'nan itself isn't notable for magnificent scenery, but the surrounding area is slightly better.

Four Gate Pagoda
(*sìméntǎ*) 四门塔

Thirty-three km south-east of Ji'nan, near the village of Liubu, are some of the oldest Buddhist structures in Shandong. There are two clusters, one a few km north-east of the village and the other to the south. Shentong Monastery, founded in the 4th century AD, holds the Four Gate Pagoda, which is possibly the oldest stone pagoda in China and dates back to the 6th century. Four beautiful light-coloured buddhas face each door. The Pagoda of the Dragon and the Tiger (*lónghǔtǎ*) was built during the Tang Dynasty. It stands close to the Shentong Monastery and is surrounded by stupas. Higher up is the Thousand Buddha Cliff (*qiānfóyá*), that has carved grottoes with some 200 small buddhas and half a dozen life-size ones.

Bus No 22 from the centre heads due south on Yingxiongshan Lu to Four Gate Pagoda. There are some tourist buses on this route, departing from Ji'nan at 8 am and returning at 3 pm.

Divine Rock Temple
(*língyánsì*) 灵岩寺

This temple is set in mountainous terrain in Changqing County, 75 km from Ji'nan. It used to be a large monastery that served many dynasties (the Tang, Song and Yuan, among others) and had 500 monks in its heyday. On view is a forest of 200 stupas commemorating the priests who directed the institution. There's also a nine-storey octagonal pagoda as well as the Thousand Buddha Temple (*qiānfódiàn*) which contains 40 fine, highly individualised clay arhats – the best Buddhist statues in Shandong.

Buses to Divine Rock Temple depart from Daguanyuan Market in the centre. The one-way trip takes up to three hours. Some buses terminate at Wande Station (which is south of Ji'nan and 10 km from Divine Rock Temple) from where you get another bus. If you latch onto a Chinese tour group, tourist buses depart around 7.30 am and return about 4 pm.

TAI'AN
(*tài'ān*) 泰安

Tai'an is the gateway town to the sacred Taishan, possibly the best sight in all of Shandong. Apart from this, Tai'an is notable as the home town of Jiang Qing, Mao's fourth wife, ex-film actress and notorious spearhead of the 'Gang of Four', on whom all of China's ills are now blamed. She was later airbrushed out of Chinese history and committed suicide in May 1991.

SHANDONG

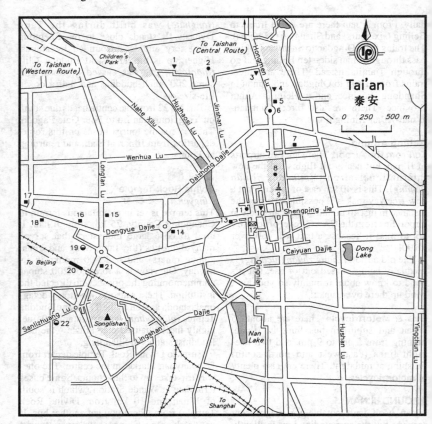

Information

The CITS office (☎ 337020; fax 332240) is on the 5th floor of the Taishan Guesthouse. It's one of the most helpful and friendly CITS offices in China. They offer an interesting qigong tour for Y15 with an English-speaking guide – this tour has become very popular with travellers. The PSB (☎ 224004) is just up the road from the main post office on Qingnian Lu.

Dai Temple

(dai miào) 岱庙

This temple is south of the Taishan Guest-house. It was the pilgrims' first stopover and an ideal place to preview or recap the journey. It once functioned solely for that purpose, being a resting spot for the hiking emperors. The temple is a very large one of 96,000 sq metres, enclosed by high walls. The main hall is the Temple of Heavenly Blessing (Tiangong), dating back to 1009 AD. It towers some 22 metres high and is constructed of wood with double-roof yellow tiling.

The Tiangong was the first built of the 'big three' halls (the others being Taihe Hall at the Forbidden City, and Dacheng Hall at Qufu).

■   PLACES TO STAY

5   Taishan Guesthouse & CITS
7   Taishan Grand Hotel
13 Overseas Chinese Hotel
14 Waimao Dasha (hotel)
15 Longtan Binguan (hotel)
16 Liangmao Dasha (hotel)
17 Baiyun Binguan (hotel)
18 Tiedao Binguan (hotel)
21 Tai'an Binguan (hotel)

▼   PLACES TO EAT

1   Jinshan Seafood Restaurant
3   Dafugui Restaurant
4   Sinaike Restaurant
10 Buyecheng Restaurant

    OTHER

2   Martyrs' Tomb
6   Daizong Archway
8   Museum
9   Dai Temple
11 PSB
12 Post Office
19 Minibuses to Ji'nan &
    Bus No 3 (to Taishan)
20 Railway Station
22 Long-Distance Bus Station

■   PLACES TO STAY

5   泰山宾馆 / 中国国际旅行社
7   泰山大酒店
13 华侨大厦
14 外贸大厦
15 龙潭宾馆
16 粮贸大厦
17 白云宾馆
18 铁道宾馆
21 泰安宾馆

▼   PLACES TO EAT

1   金山渔村
3   大富贵酒店
4   斯奈克酒店
10 不夜城

    OTHER

2   烈士陵园
6   岱宗坊
8   博物馆
9   岱庙
11 公安局外事科
12 邮局
19 往济南汽车 / 三路汽车
20 火车站
22 长途汽车站

It was restored in 1956. Inside is a 62-metre-long fresco running from the west to east walls depicting the god of Taishan on his outward and return journeys. In this case the god is Emperor Zhen Zong, who had the temple built. Zhen Zong raised the god of Taishan to the rank of emperor and there is a seven-metre-high stele to celebrate this in the western courtyard. The fresco has been painstakingly retouched by artisans of succeeding dynasties and, though recently restored, is in poor shape – but a majestic concept nonetheless.

The temple complex has been repeatedly restored; in the late 1920s, however, it was stripped of its statues and transmogrified into offices and shops. Later it suffered damage under the Kuomintang. It is gradually coming back together, not as a temple but as an open-air museum with a forest of 200-odd steles. One inscribed stone, originally at the summit of Taishan, is believed to be over 2000 years old (Qin Dynasty). It can be seen at the Eastern Imperial Hall, along with a small collection of imperial sacrificial vessels. Out-of-towners flock to Taishan Temple to copy the masterful range of calligraphy and poetry styles. Also moved from the summit is a beautiful bronze pavilion.

Around the courtyards are ancient cypresses, gingkos and acacias. At the rear of the temple is a bonsai garden and rockery. By the cypress in front of Tiangong Hall, locals and visitors can indulge in a game of luck. A person is blindfolded next to a rock, has to go around the rock three times anti-clockwise, then three times clockwise, and try and grope towards the cypress, which is

SHANDONG

20 steps away. They miss every time. Outside the main temple gates, if it's the right season, street hawkers sell watermelons with the display pieces deftly cut into rose shapes.

Organised Tours

Worth considering is the CITS tour to Buyang village *(bùyáng zhuāng)*, a chance to meet the locals and see how Chinese rural life is lived. It's not a fake tourist village, but the real thing. Besides seeing how the farmers live and work, you can also have an opportunity to learn simple Chinese cooking, notably how to make dumplings and corn-flour pancakes (the latter are as thin as paper). If you're interested, a visit to a Chinese school and retirement home is thrown in, and you can go fishing with the locals and spend the night in a farmer's home. The itinerary can be arranged according to your needs. The cost depends on group size, length of visit and number of meals eaten. For a one-day trip with 10 people, figure on Y40 each, or Y60 if only four to six people. Ask at CITS for details.

Places to Stay

There's some very good news here. It seems that the Tai'an PSB doesn't give a hoot where you stay – if you're willing to put up with the grotty plumbing, and the staff are willing to put up with you, then you can choose whichever dump offers the best deal.

The most popular place in town with budget travellers is not a dump at all, but the three-star *Taishan Guesthouse* (☎ 224678) *(tàishān bīnguǎn)*, a five-storey complex with souvenir shops, a bank and a restaurant. What makes it popular is the dormitory, which costs Y35 per person. It's a good place to round up a small group for an assault on the mountain. Comfy doubles with private bath are also available for Y140. The hotel is four km from the railway station and just a short walk from the start of the central route trail up Taishan. You can deposit your bags at the hotel's luggage room while you climb the mountain. To get to the hotel, take bus No 3 (Y0.10) or the No 3 minibus (Y0.80) from the railway station to the second-last

stop. A taxi is Y10, or you can charter a whole minibus for the same price.

The *Liangmao Dasha* (☎ 228212) is one block from the railway station. Like many of the cheapie places in Tai'an, it suffers from the usual leaky plumbing and sporadic hot water, but is otherwise OK. Doubles with private bath cost Y48. We were impressed by a sign in the hotel offering safety tips to travellers:

- Safety Needing Attention!
- Be care of depending fire
- Sweep away six injurious insect
- Pay attention to civilisation

The *Waimao Dasha* (☎ 222288) on Dongyue Dajie is one of the better-appointed budget hotels, though the building is showing signs of falling apart. Rooms are Y80.

Around the railway station is a collection of very cheap hotels (see map for locations) featuring bad plumbing and echo-chamber acoustics but very low prices. Among those on offer are the *Longtan Binguan, Tai'an Binguan, Tiedao Binguan* and *Baiyun Binguan*.

The *Taishan Grand Hotel* (☎ 227211) *(tàishān dàjiǔdiàn)* on Daizhong Dajie charges Y140 for a double. When it opened, this place was one of the finest hotels in town, but at the moment it's suffering from lack of maintenance and seems to be going downhill fast.

Geared towards the luxury tourist market, the *Overseas Chinese Hotel* (☎ 228112) *(huáqiáo dàshà)* on Dongyue Dajie offers cushy accommodation starting at Y220.

Places to Eat

Tai'an is not known for its fine cuisine – among the local specialties are scorpion *(xiēzi)* and semi-cooked sweet and sour carp from the Yellow River (the fish is still breathing while it stares at you from the plate). If all this makes you into a vegetarian, you'll probably enjoy the 'stretch-silk apple' *(básī píngguǒ)*. If you decide you can't live without meat after all, try the 'fragrant crisp chicken' *(xiāngsū jī)*. You can sample most of these local dishes at *Buyecheng Restaurant (bùyèchéng)*, which is in an alley just east of the PSB.

Many travellers keep to the set menus in the dining hall of the *Taishan Guesthouse*. The Western breakfast leaves much to be desired, but enormous Chinese set dinners are very reasonable. There's no dearth of restaurants around town, but after Taishan your legs may not let you go hunting (if in need, Tai'an does a roaring trade in walking sticks, many neatly crafted from gnarled pieces of wood).

There are many restaurants along Hongmen Lu (the street leading up to the mountain from the Dai Temple). Just up from the Taishan Guesthouse on Hongmen Lu is a US joint-venture fast-food place, *Sinaike Restaurant (sīnàikè fàndiàn)*. Just across the street, the *Dafugui Restaurant (dàfùguì jiǔdiàn)* serves expensive Shandong and Shanghai-style food. Get your breathing fish at the *Jinshan Seafood Restaurant (jīnshān yúcūn)*, just off Huzhaosi Lu.

Getting There & Away
Bus Tai'an can be approached by road from either Ji'nan or Qufu and is worth combining with a trip to the latter.

The Tai'an-Qufu buses depart from the long-distance bus stations in both cities (two hours, eight buses daily). There might be a couple of odd minibuses which run only when full, but the public buses on this route aren't bad. The highway is in excellent condition.

Although there are a few large public buses connecting Tai'an to Ji'nan, these are overcrowded horrors and you're better off travelling by minibus (Y8, 1½ hours). In Ji'nan, departures are from the Tianqiao bus station. In Tai'an, minibuses to Ji'nan depart from right in front of the railway station.

Train There are more than 20 express trains running daily through Tai'an, with links to Beijing, Harbin, Shenyang, Nanjing, Shanghai, Xi'an, Zhengzhou, Qingdao and Ji'nan.

Tai'an station is about 1¼ hours down the line from Ji'nan, but some special expresses don't stop at Tai'an. The town is a nine-hour ride from Beijing, 11 hours from Zhengzhou and nine from Nanjing. Check the schedule to avoid arriving at some unpleasant hour like 3 am.

Tai'an and Taishan make good stopovers on the way south from Qingdao to Qufu and Shanghai. The trip takes about 9½ hours.

Getting Around
Getting around is easy. The long-distance bus station is near the railway station, so all local transport is directed towards these two terminals. There are three main bus routes. Bus No 3 runs from the Taishan central route trailhead to the western route trailhead via the railway station, so that just about covers everything. Buses No 1 and 2 also end up near the railway station. Minibuses run on the same routes and are more comfortable, but they leave the station only when full. You can commandeer a minibus and use it as a taxi.

Taxis and pedicabs can be found outside the railway station – the drivers practically kidnap any foreigner they see. Expect the usual problems of overcharging, lying (the place across the street 'very far') and so forth.

TAISHAN
(tàishān) 泰山
Also known as Dai, Taishan is the most revered of the five sacred mountains of China, adopted in turn by Taoists, Buddhists, Confucianists and Maoists. From its summit imperial sacrifices to heaven and earth were offered. In China's long history, only five emperors dared to climb Taishan – Emperor Qianlong scaled it 11 times. From its heights Confucius uttered the dictum, 'The world is small'; Mao lumbered up and commented on the sunrise: 'The East is Red'.

Poets, writers and painters have found Taishan a great source of inspiration and extolled its virtues, but today one is left wondering what natural beauty is left. A long string of worshippers has left its tributes on

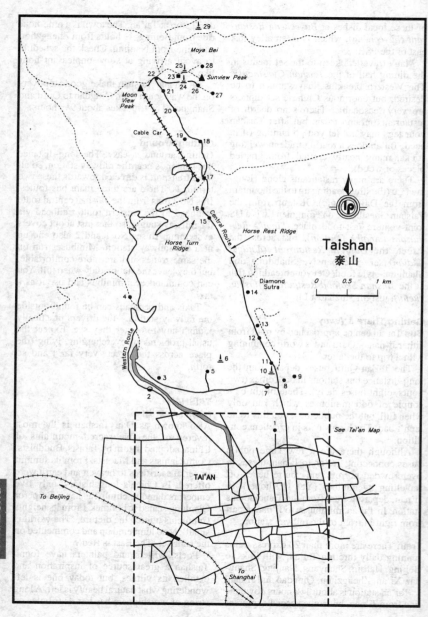

29

Moya Bei

25
28
22 23 24 ▲ Sunview Peak
21 26
▲ Moon 20 27
View
Peak

Cable Car 19

18

17

16
15 Central Route

Horse Rest Ridge
Horse Turn
Ridge

Taishan
泰山

0   0.5   1 km

Diamond
Sutra 14

4

13
12
11
6 10
5 9
3 8
7
2

1

See Tai'an Map

TAI'AN

To Beijing

To
Shanghai

1	Martyrs' Tomb	1	烈士陵园
2	Trailhead for Western Route (No 3 Bus West Terminal or No 2 Bus)	2	三路众汽车西终站
3	Everyman's Bridge & Tomb of Feng Yuxiang	3	大众桥
4	Longevity Bridge	4	长寿桥
5	Puzhao Monastery	5	普照寺
6	Memorial Temple	6	记念寺
7	Trailhead for Central Route (No 3 Bus East Terminal)	7	三路汽车东终站
8	Cloud Empress Pool	8	云母池
9	Tiger Mountain Reservoir	9	虎山水库
10	Guandi Temple	10	关帝庙
11	Red Gate Palace	11	红门
12	10,000 Immortals Pavilion	12	万仙楼
13	Monument to Revolutionary Heroes	13	革命烈士记念碑
14	Doumu Hall	14	斗母宫
15	Hutian Pavilion	15	壶天阁
16	Skywalk Bridge	16	步天桥
17	Zhongtianmen Gate, Guesthouse & Cable Car	17	中天门宾馆 / 空中索道
18	Cloud Bridge	18	云步桥
19	Five Pine Pavilion	19	五松亭
20	Pine Facing Pavilion	20	对松亭
21	Archway to Immortality	21	开松仙坊
22	Nantianmen Gate (South Gate to Heaven)	22	南天门
23	Shenqi Guesthouse	23	神憩宾馆
24	Azure Clouds Temple	24	碧霞祠
25	Jade Emperor Temple	25	玉皇顶
26	Bridge of the Gods	26	仙人桥
27	Zhanlu Terrace	27	占鲁台
28	Gongbei Rock	28	拱北石
29	Rear Temple	29	后石坞

the slopes – calligraphy cut into rock faces, temples, shrines, stairs – to which modern history has added revolutionary memorials, guesthouses, soft-drink vendors, photo booths, a weather station and the final insult – a cable car.

No matter – the pull of the supernatural (legend, religion and history rolled into one) is enough. The Princess of the Azure Clouds (Bixia), a Taoist deity whose presence permeates the temples dotted along the route, is a powerful cult figure for the peasant women of Shandong and beyond. Tribes of wiry grandmothers come each year for the ascent, a journey made more difficult by their bound feet. Their target is the main temples at the summit, where they can offer gifts and prayers for their progeny. It's said that if you climb Taishan you'll live to be 100, and some of the grandmothers look pretty close to that already. For the younger set, Taishan is a popular picnic destination. Tourists – foreign and Chinese – gather on the cold summit at daybreak in the hope of catching a perfect sunrise. In ancient Chinese tradition, it was believed that the sun began its westward journey from Taishan.

As the old Chinese saying goes: 'The journey of a thousand miles begins with a single step'. On Taishan there are some 6000 of them that you'll remember clearly. The mountain is relatively small, but the steps are the kind that get your heart pounding. You and 5000 other climbers, that is! After a while, you realise that what you're looking at is not the mountain but the pilgrims toiling

SHANDONG

up it. The hackwork of China – the carting of concrete blocks, water, produce, goods – is a common sight on city streets, but nowhere does it appear more painful than on the sheer slopes of this mountain. Porters with weals on their shoulders and misshapen backs plod up the stairway to heaven with crates of drinks, bedding and construction for the hotels and dining halls further up. It's a time-honoured tradition, a job passed from father to son, and the cable car seems to have done little to alter it. The idea, as we understood it, was to use the cable car to transport passengers by day, and cargo by night. One wonders how many backs were broken in the building of the temples and stone stairs on Taishan over the centuries, a massive undertaking accomplished without mechanical aids.

All in all, as you may have surmised, Taishan is not the mountain-climbing experience you might expect it to be, and it is not a particularly scenic beauty. But if you accept that, it's an engrossing experience and certainly worthwhile. It will certainly exercise the other five walking muscles you haven't used in the streets already. The trip down, by the way, is even more strenuous for the legs.

Weather Conditions

The peak tourist season is from May to October. But remember that conditions vary considerably on the mountain compared with sea-level Tai'an.

The mountain is frequently enveloped in clouds and haze, which are more prevalent in summer. The best times to visit are in spring and autumn when the humidity is low, though old-timers say that the clearest weather is from early October onwards. In winter the weather is often fine but very cold.

On average, there are 16 fine days in spring, eight in summer, 28 in autumn and 35 in winter. But take care – due to weather changes, you're best advised to carry warm clothing in a small day-pack with you, no matter what the season. You can freeze your butt off on Taishan, though you can hire

padded overcoats. The average seasonal temperatures in degrees Celsius are:

	Winter	Spring	Summer	Autumn
Taishan	-3	20	24	20
Summit	-9	12	17	12

Climbing Taishan

The town of Tai'an lies at the foot of Taishan and is the gateway to the mountain (see the Tai'an section).

By Foot Climbing the mountain costs you a Y40 entrance fee – presumably the cash is used to maintain the concrete steps, temples, pavilions, gates and other decorations.

Upon arrival you have several options, depending on your timing. There are three rest stops to bear in mind: Taishan Guesthouse, at the base of the trail; Zhongtianmen Guesthouse, halfway up; and the Shenqi Guesthouse on top of Taishan.

You should allow at least two hours for climbing between each of these points – a total of eight hours up and down, at the minimum. Allowing several more hours would make the climb less strenuous and give you more time to look around on top. If you want to see the sunrise, then dump your gear at the railway station or the Taishan Guesthouse in Tai'an and time your ascent so that you'll reach the summit before sundown; stay overnight at one of the summit guesthouses and get up early next morning for the famed sunrise (which, for technical reasons, may not be clearly forthcoming).

Chinese tourists without time or money at their disposal sometimes scale at night (with torches and walking sticks) to arrive at the peak in time for sunrise, descending shortly thereafter. Unless you have uncanny night vision or four hours of battery power, this particular option could lead to you getting lost, frozen, falling off a mountainside, or all three.

There are two main paths up the mountain: the central and the western, converging midway at Zhongtianmen Gate. Most people go up via the central path (which used to be the imperial route and hence has more cultural sites) and down by the western path. Other trails run through orchards and woods.

Taishan is 1545 metres above sea level, with a climbing distance of 7½ km from base to summit on the central route. The elevation change from Zhongtian Gate to the summit is approximately 600 metres.

By Minibus Minibuses run from the Tai'an Railway Station to Zhongtianmen Gate, halfway up Taishan, with several departures each morning. Occasional group tour minibuses run from the Taishan Guesthouse too.

Zhongtianmen Gate is less than five minutes' walk from the cable car (kōng zhōng suǒ dào), which holds 30 passengers and takes eight minutes to travel from Zhongtian Gate to Wangfushan, near Nantian Gate. This is China's first large cableway. The cable cars operate in both directions. The fare is Y26 one way, or Y53 for a round trip.

Buses come down the mountain hourly between 1 and 5 pm, but don't count on the schedule or the seats.

Central Route

On this route you'll see a bewildering catalogue of bridges, trees, towers, inscribed stones, caves, pavilions and temples (complex and simplex). Half the trip, for Chinese people at least, is seeing the colossal amount of calligraphy scoring the stones en route. Taishan, in fact, functions as an outdoor museum of calligraphic art, with the prize items being the Diamond Sutra (or Stone Valley Sutra) and the Moya Bei at the summit, which commemorates an imperial sacrifice.

The climb proper begins at **No 1 Archway Under Heaven** at the mountain base. Behind that is a stone archway overgrown with wistaria and inscribed 'the place where Confucius began to climb'. **Red Gate Palace**, standing out with its wine-coloured walls, is the first of a series of temples dedicated to the Princess of the Azure Clouds,

who was the daughter of the god of Taishan. It was rebuilt in 1626.

Doumu Hall was first constructed in 1542 and has the more poetic name of Dragon Spring Nunnery; there's a teahouse inside.

Continuing through the tunnel of cypresses known as Cypress Cave is **Horse Turn Ridge**, where Emperor Zhen Zong had to dismount and continue by sedan chair because his horse refused to go further – smart horse! Another emperor rode a white mule up and down the mountain and the beast died soon after the descent (it was posthumously given the title of general and its tomb is on the mountain).

Zhongtianmen Gate (Midway Gate to Heaven) is the second celestial gate. Beyond Cloud Bridge and to the right is the place where Emperor Zhen Zong pitched his overnight tents. A little way on is **Five Pine Pavilion** where, one day back in 219 BC, Emperor Qin Shihuang was overtaken by a violent storm and was sheltered by the kind pines. He promoted them to the 5th rank of minister; though the three you see are, of course, not the same ministers!

On the slopes higher up is the **Welcoming Pine** with a branch extended as if to shake hands. Beyond that is the **Archway to Immortality**. It was believed that those passing through it would become celestial beings. From here to the summit, emperors were carried in sedan chairs – eat your hearts out!

The third celestial gate is **Nantianmen** (South Gate to Heaven). That, and the steep pathway leading up to it, are symbolic of Taishan and of Shandong itself; the picture pops up on covers of books and on Shandong maps.

On arrival at Taishan Summit (dàidǐng) you will see the **Wavelength Pavilion** (a radio and weather station) and the Journey to the Stars Gondola (the cable car). If you continue along Paradise Rd, you'll come to **Sunset Statue** (where a frozen photographer sits slumped over a table with the view beyond dutifully recorded in sunrises and clipped in front of him).

Welcome to Taishan Shopping Centre.

SHANDONG

Here you'll see fascinating Chinese antics on the precarious rock lookouts – go and check out the **Bridge of the Gods**, which is a couple of giant rocks trapped between two precipices.

The grandmothers' long march ends at the **Azure Clouds Temple** *(bìxiácí)* where small offerings of one sort or another are made to a bronze statue, once richly decorated. The iron tiling on the buildings is intended to prevent damage by strong wind currents, and on the bronze eaves are *chiwen*, ornaments meant to protect against fire. The temple is absolutely splendid, with its location in the clouds, but its guardians are a trifle touchy about you wandering around, and parts of it are inaccessible. Little is known of the temple's history but we do know that it cost a fortune to restore or make additions, as was done in the Ming and Qing dynasties. The bronze statuette of the Princess of the Azure Clouds is in the main hall.

Perched on the highest point (1545 metres) of the Taishan plateau is **Jade Emperor Temple**, with a bronze statue of a Taoist deity. In the courtyard is a rock inscribed with the elevation of the mountain. In front of the temple is the one piece of calligraphy that you can really appreciate – the **Wordless Monument**. This one will leave you speechless. One story goes that it was set up by Emperor Wu 2100 years ago – he wasn't satisfied with what his scribes came up with, so he left it to the viewers' imaginations.

The main sunrise vantage point is a springboard-shaped thing called **Gongbei Rock**; if you're lucky, visibility could extend to over 200 km, as far as the coast. The sunset slides over the Yellow River side. At the rear of the mountain is **Rear Rocky Recess**, one of the better-known spots for viewing pine trees; there are some ruins tangled in the foliage. It's a good place to ramble and lose the crowds for a while.

Western Route

On this route there's nothing of note in the way of structures, but there's considerable variation in scenery, with orchards, pools and flowering plants. The major scenic attraction is **Black Dragon Pool** which is just below **Longevity Bridge** (between the bridge and West Brook Pavilion) and is fed by a small waterfall. Swimming in the waters are some rare, red-scaled carp which are occasionally cooked for the rich. Mythical tales revolve around this pool, said to be the site of underground carp palaces and of magic herbs that turn people into beasts. Worth looking into is the **Puzhao Monastery**, founded 1500 years ago along the base of the mountain.

Places to Stay & Eat

The *Zhongtianmen Guesthouse* (☎ 226740) *(zhōngtiānmén bīnguǎn)* is a halfway house at Zhongtian Gate. Rooms are comfortable but a tad expensive at Y180 for a double. Provided no-one brings a portable stereo or karaoke system, it's a very quiet place.

The *Shenqi Guesthouse* (☎ 223866) *(shénqì bīnguǎn)* is a three-star hotel on the summit costing Y250 for a double – expensive, but you're paying for the view. The hotel provides extra blankets and rents out fashionable People's Liberation Army-style overcoats. There's even an alarm bell which tells you when to get up for sunrise. (If you wonder where all those amazing old women go, it seems that there are lodgings – possibly former monasteries – tucked down side trails.)

Snacks, drinks and the like are sold on the mountain trail, and the hotel has a pricey restaurant.

QUFU
(qūfù) 曲阜

As well as being the birthplace of Confucius, Qufu, with its blending of stone, wood and fine imperial architecture, is an oasis of culture and elegance. It's an excellent stopover worth one or two days, and is quiet, with real birds and grass. There's plenty to see and you can see it all on foot without the hassles of transport or big-city complications. But there is one annoying hassle about the place – the ubiquitous street vendors who chase foreigners down the street yelling 'hello postcard, hello map, hello...' Oddly, 'change money' has not yet entered the local vocabulary. The vendors are thickest around the bus station and entrances to temples and other sites, but you can get away from them in places like the Confucian Forest.

Following a 2000-year-old tradition, there are two fairs a year in Qufu – in spring and autumn, when the place comes alive with craftspeople, healers, acrobats, pedlars, poor peasants and that new symbol of modernisation, camera-clicking tourists.

Information

The CITS office (☎ 412491) is in the Xingtan Hotel, ridiculously located in a remote area south of town far from anything of interest to travellers. Just as well, since this CITS caters almost exclusively to tour groups. There are no train or air tickets on sale here, since neither comes to Qufu.

Confucius Temple

(kǒng miào) 孔庙

The temple started out as a simple memorial hall and mushroomed into a complex one-fifth the size of Qufu. It is laid on a north-south axis, and is over one km long. The main entrance is **Star Gate** *(língxīngmén)* at the south, which leads through a series of portals emblazoned with calligraphy. The third entrance gateway, with four bluish characters, refers to the doctrines of Confucius as heavenly bodies which move in circles without end; it is known as the Arch of the Spirit of the Universe.

Throughout the courtyards of the Confucius Temple, the dominant features are the clusters of twisted pines and cypresses, and row upon row of steles. The tortoise tablets record in archaic Chinese such events as temple reconstructions, great ceremonies or tree plantings. There are over 1000 steles in the temple grounds, with inscriptions from Han to Qing times – the largest such collection in China. The creatures bearing the tablets of praise are actually not tortoises but *bixi*, dragon offspring legendary for their strength. The tablets at Qufu are noted for

their fine calligraphy; a rubbing once formed part of the dowry for a Kong lady.

Roughly halfway along the north-south axis is the **Great Pavilion of the Constellation of Scholars**, a triple-roofed, Jin Dynasty, wooden structure of ceremonial importance dating from 1190. Further north through Dacheng Gate and to the right is a juniper planted by Confucius – or so the tablet in front of it claims. The small Xingtan Pavilion up from that commemorates the spot where Confucius is said to have taught under the shade of an apricot tree.

The core of the Confucian complex is **Dacheng Hall** which, in its present form, dates back to 1724; it towers 31 metres high on a white marble terrace. The reigning sovereign permitted the importation of glazed yellow tiling for the halls in the Confucius Temple, and special stones were brought in from Xishan. The craftspeople did such a good job on the stone dragon-coiled columns that it is said they had to be covered with silk when the emperor came to Qufu lest he felt that the Forbidden City's Taihe Hall paled in comparison.

The hall was used for unusual rites in honour of Confucius. At the beginning of the seasons and on the great sage's birthday, booming drums, bronze bells and musical stones sounded from the hall as dozens of officials in silk robes engaged in 'dignified dancing' and chanting by torchlight. The rare collection of musical instruments is displayed, but the massive stone statue of the bearded philosopher has disappeared – presumably a casualty of the Red Guards.

At the extreme north end of the Confucius Temple is **Shengjidian**, a memorial hall containing a series of stones engraved with scenes from the life of Confucius and tales about him. They are copies of an older set which date back to 1592.

In the eastern compound of the Confucian Temple, behind the Hall of Poetry and Rites, is **Confucius' Well** (a Song-Ming reconstruction) and the **Lu Wall** where the ninth descendant of Confucius hid the sacred texts during the anti-Confucian persecutions of Emperor Qin Shihuang. The books were discovered again in the Han Dynasty (206 BC–220 AD) and led to a lengthy scholastic dispute between those who followed a reconstructive version of the last books, and those who supported the teachings in the rediscovered ones.

Confucianism

Qufu is the birth and death place of the sage Confucius (551-479 BC) whose impact was not felt in his own lifetime. He lived in abject poverty and hardly put pen to paper, but his teachings were recorded by dedicated followers (in the *Analects*). His descendants, the Kong family, fared considerably better.

Confucian ethics were adopted by subsequent rulers to keep the populace in line, and Confucian temples were set up in numerous towns run by officials. Qufu acquired the status of a holy place, with the direct descendants of Confucius as its guardian angels.

The original Confucian Temple at Qufu (dating from 478 BC) was enlarged, remodelled, added to, taken away from and rebuilt. The present buildings are from the Ming Dynasty. In 1513 armed bands sacked the temple and the Kong residence, and walls were built around the town between 1522 and 1567 to fortify it. These walls were recently removed, but vestiges of Ming town planning, like the Drum and Bell towers, remain.

More a code that defined hierarchical relationships than a religion, Confucianism has had a great impact on Chinese culture. It teaches that son must respect father, wife must respect husband, commoner must respect official, officials must respect their ruler, and vice versa. The essence of its teachings are obedience, respect and selflessness, and working for the common good.

One would think that this code would have fitted nicely into the new order of Communism. However, it was swept aside because of its connections with the past. Confucius was seen as a kind of misguided feudal educator, and clan ties and ancestor-worship were viewed as a threat. In 1948 Confucius' direct heir, the first-born son of the 77th generation of the Kong family, fled to Taiwan, breaking a 2500-year tradition of Kong residence in Qufu.

During the Cultural Revolution the emphasis shifted to the youth of China (even if they were led by an old man). A popular anti-Confucian campaign was instigated and Confucius lost face. Many of the statues at Qufu also lost face (literally) amidst cries of 'Down with Confucius, down with his wife!' In the late '60s a contingent of Red Guards descended on the sleepy town of Qufu, burning, defacing and destroying. Other Confucian edifices around the country were also attacked. The leader of the Guards who ransacked Qufu was Tan Houlan. She was jailed for that in 1978 and was not tried until 1982. The Confucius family archives appear to have survived the assaults intact.

Confucian ethics have made something of a comeback, presumably to instil some civic-mindedness where the Party had failed. Confucianism is finding its way back into the Shandong school system, though not by that name. Students are encouraged once again to respect their teachers, elders, neighbours and family. If there's one thing you discover quickly travelling in China, it's that respect among the Chinese has fallen to pieces. With corruption at the top of the system, the cynical young find it difficult to reciprocate respect; the elderly remain suspicious of what has passed and afraid of the street fights and arguments.

In 1979 the Qufu temples were reopened and millions of yuan were allocated for renovations or repairs. Tourism is now the name of the game; if a temple hasn't got a fresh coat of paint, new support pillars, replaced tiling or stonework, a souvenir shop or photo merchant with a Great Sage cardboard cut-out, they'll get round to it soon. Some of the buildings even have electricity, with speakers hooked up to the eaves playing soothing flute music. Emanating from the eaves is some real music – you have to stop and listen twice to make sure – yes, real birds up there! Fully a fifth of Qufu's 50,000 residents are again claiming to be descendants of the Great Sage, though incense burning, mound-burial and ancestor-worship are not consistent with the Party line.

Whether Confucianism can take fresh root in China is a matter for conjecture, but something is needed to fill the idealist void. A few years ago a symposium held in Qufu by Chinese scholars resulted in careful statements reaffirming the significance of Confucius' historical role, and suggesting that the 'progressive' aspects of his work were a valuable legacy which had also been cited in the writings of Mao Zedong. Confucius too, it seems, can be rehabilitated. ∎

Confucius Mansions
(kǒng fǔ) 孔府

Built and rebuilt many times, the Mansions date from the 16th-century Ming Dynasty, with recent patchwork. The place is a maze of 450 halls, rooms and buildings, and getting around it requires a compass – there are all kinds of side passages to which servants were once restricted.

The Mansions are the most sumptuous aristocratic lodgings in China, indicative of the Kong family's former great power. From the Han to the Qing dynasties, Confucius' descendants were ennobled and granted privileges by the emperors. They lived like kings themselves, with 180-course meals, servants and consorts. Confucius even picked up some posthumous honours.

The town of Qufu, which grew around the Mansions, was an autonomous estate administered by the Kongs, who had powers of taxation and execution. Emperors could drop in to visit – the Ceremonial Gate near the south entrance was opened only for this event. Because of royal protection, copious quantities of furniture, ceramics, artefacts, costumery and personal effects survived and some may be viewed. The Kong family archives, a rich legacy, also seem to have survived, and extensive renovations of the complex have been made.

The Mansions are built on an 'interrupted' north-south axis. Grouped by the south gate are the former administrative offices (taxes, edicts, rites, registration, examination halls). To the north on the axis is a special gate – Neizhaimen – that seals off the residential quarters (used for weddings, banquets, private functions). East of Neizhaimen is the Tower of Refuge where the Kong clan could gather in case the peasants turned nasty. It has an iron-lined ceiling on the ground floor, and a staircase that is removable to the 1st floor. Grouped to the west of the main axis are former recreational facilities (studies, guest rooms, libraries, small temples). To the east is the odd kitchen, ancestral temple and the family branch apartments. Far north is a spacious garden with rockeries, ponds and bamboo groves. Kong Decheng, the last of

the line, lived in the Mansions until the 1940s when he hightailed it to Taiwan.

Confucian Forest
(kǒng lín) 孔林

North of the Confucius Mansions, about 2½ km up Lindao Lu, is the Confucian Forest, the largest artificial park and best-preserved cemetery in China. This timeworn route has a kind of 'spirit-way' lined with ancient cypresses.

It takes about 40 minutes to walk, 15 minutes by pedicab or else use bus No 1 (infrequent!). On the way, look into the Yanhui Temple *(yán miào)* which is off to the right and has a spectacular dragon head embedded in the ceiling of the main hall, and a pottery collection. The route to the forest

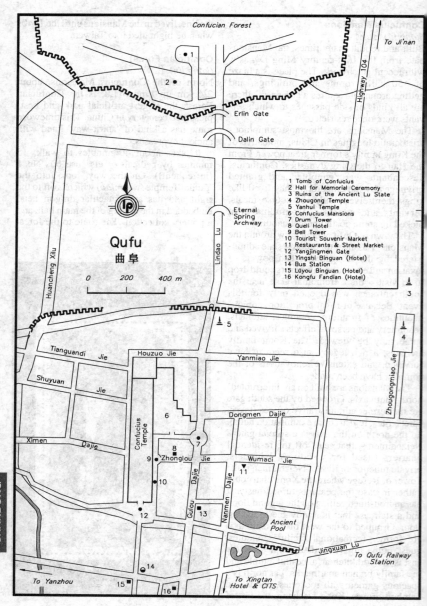

Confucian Forest

To Ji'nan

Highway 104

Erlin Gate

Dalin Gate

Eternal
Spring
Archway

Lindao Lu

Qufu
曲阜

0   200   400 m

1 Tomb of Confucius
2 Hall for Memorial Ceremony
3 Ruins of the Ancient Lu State
4 Zhougong Temple
5 Yanhui Temple
6 Confucius Mansions
7 Drum Tower
8 Queli Hotel
9 Bell Tower
10 Tourist Souvenir Market
11 Restaurants & Street Market
12 Yangjingmen Gate
13 Yingshi Binguan (Hotel)
14 Bus Station
15 Lüyou Binguan (Hotel)
16 Kongfu Fandian (Hotel)

Huancheng Xilu

Tianguandi Jie

Houzuo Jie

Yanmiao Jie

Shuyuan   Jie

Zhougongmiao Jie

Ximen   Dajie

Confucius Temple

6

Dongmen Dajie

Zhonglou Jie

Wumaci Jie

9

10

Gulou Dajie

Nanmen Dajie

11

12

13

Ancient
Pool

14

15   16

Jingxuan Lu

To Yanzhou

To Xingtan
Hotel & CITS

To Qufu Railway
Station

SHANDONG

passes through the Eternal Spring Archway, its stone lintels decorated with coiled dragons, flying phoenixes and galloping horses dating from 1594 (Ming Dynasty). Visitors, who needed permission to enter, had to dismount at the Forest Gates.

The pine and cypress forest of over 20,000 trees, planted by followers of Confucius, covers 200 hectares and is bounded by a wall 10 km long. Buried here is the Great Sage himself and all his descendants. Flanking the approach to Confucius' Tomb are a pair of stone panthers, griffins and larger-than-life guardians. The Confucian tumulus is a simple grass mound enclosed by a low wall, and faced with a Ming Dynasty stele. Nearby are buried his immediate sons. Scattered through the forest are dozens of temples and pavilions, and hundreds of sculptures, tablets and tombstones.

Mausoleum of Shao Hao
(shǎo hào líng) 少昊陵
Shao Hao was one of the five legendary emperors supposed to have ruled China 4000 years ago. His pyramidal tomb, four km north-east of Qufu, dates from the Song Dynasty and is made of large blocks of stone, 25 metres wide at the base, six metres high, with a small temple on top. Some Chinese historians believe that Qufu was built on the

ruins of Shao Hao's ancient capital, but evidence to support this is weak.

Places to Stay – bottom end
Qufu PSB takes a relaxed view – many of the cheaper hotels are permitted to accept foreigners, though they may not necessarily allow you to stay in the really grotty rooms. These cheap hotels have signs written in Chinese characters only – you'll need to learn to recognise the characters, find someone to guide you, or make educated guesses. Don't expect the staff to speak any English in these places either. Nevertheless, cheap hotels are not hard to find – there are literally dozens in Qufu.

An excellent place to stay in the budget range is the *Yingshi Binguan* on Gulou Dajie, south of the Drum Tower. A two-bed dormitory costs Y40 per person, or you can book the whole room for Y80. These rooms have private bath.

Close to the bus station, on the corner with Datong Lu, is the *Kongfu Fandian*. Singles/doubles cost Y80/100.

Many of the others are scattered around the bus station. If you don't get lucky straight away, stand near the station saying 'binguan' and one of the enterprising old women will surely guide you to a nearby hotel for perhaps a Y2 tip.

Places to Stay – middle
The upmarket place in town is the *Queli Hotel* (☎ 411300; fax 412022) (quèlǐ bīnshè), 1 Queli Jie, where singles cost Y120 and doubles are Y190 – the height of luxury.

The *Xingtan Hotel* (☎ 411719) (xìngtán bīnguǎn) was built in a ridiculous site far south of town – nowhere near the areas of interest to visitors. With its high prices (Y150 and up) and remote location, it's obvious that this place is aimed at tour groups with a chartered bus. Individual travellers should probably look elsewhere.

Places to Eat
The food in Qufu is generally of poor quality. The best deals for low prices and reasonable quality seem to be the street markets. The

touristy market just south of Confucius Mansions is one spot, but there is a wider selection on Zhonglou Jie, east of the Queli Hotel.

The name of the Great Sage is being invoked in unexpected ways – Sankong (Three Confucius) Beer is the local brew. Can Confucius Fried Chicken be far behind?

Things to Buy

Whatever else you can say about Confucianism, it's good business. Next to the Confucius Temple there are some free-marketeers selling everything from Confucius T-shirts to Great Sage cigarette lighters.

Actually, much of what's on sale is not related in any way to Confucius or Qufu – some items you might care to look at are personalised carving on chops and ballpoint pens while you wait. The ballpoint pen engraving, done with a kind of gold leaf, can be ordered in dragon designs – with the name of a friend added it makes an excellent gift. For calligraphy lovers, the gift shop inside the Confucius Temple sells stele rubbings.

Getting There & Away

A sign on the Qufu-Tai'an highway says 'You will out of Qufu – a nice trip to you'. Perhaps not perfect English, but it's the thought that counts.

Bus Buses and minibuses run between Qufu and the railway station about once every 30 minutes throughout the day. The large public buses cost Y1 but are packed to the hilt – much better to take the minibuses for Y5. Minibuses also run later, sometimes as late as 11 pm if there are passengers. Minibuses will also serve as taxis if you pay them enough. There are also minibuses to Yanzhou, but these are somewhat less frequent.

There are direct buses from Qufu to Tai'an (Y7, two hours, eight departures daily) and direct buses from Qufu to Ji'nan (three hours, 13 departures daily).

The bus station in Qufu looks almost like a temple from the outside – you might have trouble recognising it if you don't know the

Chinese characters for *qiche zhan*. On the inside it's like a typical Chinese bus station, though there is more tourist junk for sale here than usual. Two nice things we can say about the place – it's usual to give the best seats to foreigners (bus tickets have seat numbers) and the staff force everyone to line up and board in numerical order. We're not sure if this is an expression of Confucianism, but compared with the usual wrestling competitions at Chinese bus stations, it's certainly much appreciated!

Train The situation is a little confused – there's no station in Qufu itself. When a railway project for Qufu was first brought up, the Kong family petitioned for a change of routes, claiming that the trains would disturb the Great Sage's tomb. They won – the clan still had pull in those days – and the nearest tracks were routed to Yanzhou, 13 km to the west of Qufu. But the railway builders didn't give up, and finally constructed another station about six km east of Qufu, though still nothing in Qufu itself.

When you want to buy a train ticket to Qufu, just say 'Qufu' and if the ticket clerk says *meiyou*, try saying 'Yanzhou'. Qufu (Yanzhou) is on the line from Beijing to Shanghai. There's a fair selection of trains, but some special express trains don't stop here; others arrive at inconvenient times like midnight. Qufu is somewhat less than two hours by train from Tai'an, three from Ji'nan, about seven from Nanjing, and about nine hours from Kaifeng.

CAAC is next in line to disturb the sage's tomb, with an airport planned at Qufu. But for the moment, the trains are the fastest way of getting here.

Getting Around

There are only two bus lines and service is not frequent. Probably most useful for travellers is bus No 1 which travels along Gulou Dajie and Lindao Lu in a north-south direction, connecting the bus station area with the Confucian Forest. Bus No 2 travels east-west along Jingxuan Lu. Pedicabs are a more reliable way of getting around, but expect the usual price hassles.

ZOUXIAN
(zōuxiàn) 邹县

This is the home town of Mengzi (formerly spelled Mencius; 372-289 BC) who is regarded as the first great Confucian philosopher. He developed many of the ideas of Confucianism as they were later understood. Zouxian is an excellent place to visit – far more relaxed than Qufu. Zouxian is just to the south of Qufu, a short hop on the train from Yanzhou or by bus from Qufu. A visit can easily be done as a day trip.

ZIBO
(zībó) 淄博

Zibo is a major coal-mining centre on the railway line east of Ji'nan. Over two million people live in this city, which is noted for its glassworks and porcelain. Not far from Zibo, at Linzhi, a pit of horses dating back some 2500 years was excavated. They are older than the horses at Xi'an and with one big difference – they are the remains of actual animals. So far, 600 horse skeletons, probably dating from Qi times (479-502 AD), have been discovered. Horses and chariots indicated the strength of the state, so it's not surprising that they were buried in the course of their master's funeral. About 90 horse skeletons are on display in the pit.

QINGDAO
(qīngdǎo) 青岛

Qingdao is an unexpected replica of a Bavarian village, plonked on the Bohai Gulf – a city of red-tiled roofs and European angles, shapes and echoes, right down to the gardens. Or rather, it *was* like that. Time is taking its toll – the old German dwellings are not what they're cracked up to be or, alternatively, they're more cracked up than you'd expect them to be. Renovation work is sorely needed, but the local government is working mostly on putting up new concrete high-rises in an attempt to 'modernise' the city. Nevertheless, Qingdao is worth seeing – like

Shanghai, it evokes an eerie feeling of *déjà vu*.

Qingdao was a simple fishing village until 1897 when German troops landed (the killing of two German missionaries having given them sufficient pretext). In 1898 China ceded the town to Germany for 99 years, along with the right to build the Shandong railways and to work the mines for 15 km on either side of the tracks.

The Germans developed Qingdao as a coaling station and naval base, and when the Ji'nan to Qingdao railway line was finished in 1904, harbour facilities blossomed, electric lighting appeared, the brewery (established 1903) belched beer, and a modern town arose. It was divided into European, Chinese and business sections. The Germans founded missions and a university and, before long, Qingdao rivalled Tianjin as a trading centre, its independence from China maintained by a garrison of 2000 soldiers.

For a city with such a short history, Qingdao has seen a lot of ping pong. In 1914 the Japanese occupied it, in 1922 the Chinese wrested it back, but it fell to the Japanese again in 1938 and was then recaptured by the Kuomintang. The official history states that the people of Qingdao engaged in heroic struggles against the imperialists and the Kuomintang, and that industrial production has increased more than 10-fold since 1949.

The latter claim is not exaggerated, and it might well be an underestimate. Behind the innocuous facade of a beach resort is a monstrous mess of factories – the newer ones sport Korean flags, an indication of the recent tidal wave of investment flowing into Shandong Province from South Korea. Not only does Qingdao brew up the nation's drinking supplies but it is also the largest industrial producer in Shandong, concentrating on diesel locomotives, automobiles, generators, machinery and light industry (watches, cameras, TVs, textiles). It has a population of 1½ million, though its jurisdiction spreads over 5900 sq km and another 3½ million people.

If you ignore the megalopolis behind it –

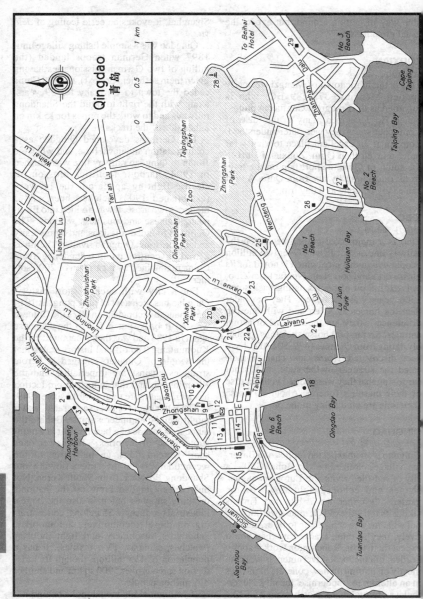

Qingdao 青岛

■ PLACES TO STAY

1 Peace Hotel
2 Friendship Store & Hotel
4 Jingshan Hotel
9 Qingdao Hotel
14 Overseas Chinese Hotel
15 Railway Hotel & Railway Station
16 Qingdao Pharmaceutical
   Building (hotel)
17 Zhanqiao Guesthouse
20 Xinhao Hill Hotel
22 Dongfang Hotel
24 Haiqing Hotel
25 Yellow Sea Hotel &
   China Eastern Airlines
26 Huiquan Dynasty Hotel & CITS
27 Badaguan Hotel
29 Haitian Hotel

OTHER

3 Passenger Ferry Terminal
5 Brewery
6 Local Ferry
7 Xinhua Bookstore
8 Chunhelou Restaurant
10 Catholic Church
11 Bank of China
12 Main Post Office
13 PSB
18 Huilan Pavilion
19 Longshan Underground Market
21 Protestant Church
23 Qingdao Museum
28 Zhanshan Temple

■ PLACES TO STAY

1 和平宾馆
2 友谊商店
4 晶山宾馆
9 青岛饭店
14 华侨饭店
15 铁道大大厦
16 医药大大厦
17 栈桥宾馆
20 信号山迎宾馆
22 东方饭店
24 海青宾馆
25 黄海饭店 / 东方航空公司
26 汇泉王朝大酒店 /
   国际旅行社诚
27 八大关宾馆
29 海天大酒店

OTHER

3 青岛港客运站
5 青岛啤酒厂
6 青岛轮渡站
7 新华书店
8 春和楼饭店
10 天主教堂
11 中国银行
12 邮电局
13 公安局外事科
18 回澜阁
19 龙山地下商业
21 基督教堂
23 青岛博物馆
28 湛山寺

and most do – Qingdao has remarkable charm and is colourful for a Chinese city (irony intended). One can indulge in the guessing game of who once occupied its German mansions, or how they operated. The present function of the larger edifices is a combination of naval base, cadre playground and sanatorium. The town is a favourite for rest and recuperation, and for top-level meetings.

Qingdao means 'green island', and the waterfront promontory, backed by undulating hills, is a true garden city. The misty beauty of the place is unmistakable, with the visual stimulation of the sea, the parks and the patterns of boats and mansions. In the

German end of town, you can't see much of the industrial zones so they don't spoil the view, although the new beachfront high-rises are a real eyesore. Sauntering along the esplanade is the thing to do in Qingdao as is, of course, sunbaking. Sadly, swimming is no longer recommended – the sea water has a colour not unlike the beer which has made this city famous, though we haven't compared the taste.

For a town that produces such copious quantities of beer, wine and spirits, Qingdao is pretty dead at night – not a drunk in sight, and lights out at nine, though hotels try to

SHANDONG

whoop it up with karaoke bars. And there is one form of old-style 'entertainment' which appears to have made a comeback.

After more than two months of travelling in China, I was never approached by prostitutes – that is, until I got to Qingdao. No sooner had I checked into my room at the Beihai Hotel than there was a knock on my door. I opened it to find a miniskirted young woman offering her 'massage' services for sale. I turned down her offer, then headed out to see the sights of the city. Less than an hour later, I was approached by another prostitute just opposite the PSB. I'm not sure whether this is an old tradition or a sign of China's modernisation.

Information

CITS This office (☎ 279215) is in the Huiquan Dynasty Hotel at 9 Nanhai Lu, but they're not particularly helpful to individual travellers. Try them for tours of the brewery, shell-carving factory and locomotive factory or for comic relief.

PSB This office (☎ 262787) is at 29 Hubei Lu, very close to the Overseas Chinese Hotel. The entrance to the compound is a beautiful old German building with a clock tower, but the ugly office block behind it is where the PSB does its business.

Money The budget hotels don't have moneychangers (except the thieves on the street) but luxury hotels can fulfil this need. The Bank of China is at 62 Zhongshan Lu.

Post The main post office is just south of the Bank of China on Zhongshan Lu.

Beaches

(hǎishuǐ yùchǎng) 海水浴场

Along the coast there are six beaches, all with fine white sand. Taking the setting into account, they're hard to beat. The swimming season is from June to September, when the beaches are crowded, but there's also the possibility of fog and rain from June to August. Water temperature is soupy (and so is the water colour) but the sea breezes are pleasant. Beaches are sheltered and have changing sheds (you can hire demure swim-

suits), shower facilities, photo booths, stores and snack bars. Swimming areas are marked off with buoys and Bondi Beach-style shark nets, lifeboat patrols, lifeguards and medical stations. Your chances of drowning at Qingdao, in other words, are absolutely nil. Don't pass up Qingdao in other seasons – spring and autumn bring out the best in local foliage and there are some spectacular flowers.

Just around the corner from the railway station is the **No 6 Bathing Beach**. This strip is particularly lively early in the morning when joggers, fencers, taiji exponents, old men reading newspapers and a few frisbee players turn out. Street-stall breakfast queues form, and there's a busy cottage industry that involves picking over the rocks and beach at low tide. Most of the Chinese people are on vacation and it's a welcome relief to see them so relaxed.

The **Huilan Pavilion** *(huílán gé)*, on a jetty thrusting into the sea, holds occasional art & craft exhibitions – it's worth the stroll, anyhow. Continuing east, around the headland past the lighthouse is Lu Xun Park *(lǔ xùn gōngyuán)* which has the combined **Marine Museum & Aquarium**. The Marine Museum has stuffed and pickled sea life. The Aquarium has sea life that would be better off stuffed or pickled, or in someone's soup. These tiny buildings are billed as the most famous of their kind in China; we'd hate to see the other ones.

Never mind, you're now at the start of the **No 1 Bathing Beach**. While it's no Cable Beach (Western Australia), it's certainly flash for China, and bodies of all shapes and sizes jam the sands in summer. This is the largest beach in Qingdao, with a 580-metre stretch of fine sand, lots of facilities, multi-coloured bathing sheds, restaurants (where you can munch prawns to 'Waltzing Matilda' on the Muzak), ridiculous dolphin statues, and high-rise blocks rather like a Chinese version of Surfer's Paradise. Plonk yourself down on the sand and all sorts of odd people will come up to you. This is the hang-out of the Chinese 'winter swimmers' whose marvellous sun-bronzed physiques don't step into the water until winter; they are said to make bad husbands because they're always at the beach. The beach also has PSB 'moral guardians' who ensure that gymnastics between consenting couples don't get out of hand.

Past the Huiquan Dynasty Hotel and the Ocean Research Institute is the Badaguan *(bādàguān)* area, well known for its sanatoriums and exclusive guesthouses. The spas are scattered in lush wooded zones off the coast, and the streets, named after passes (Badaguan literally means 'Eight Passes Area'), are each lined with a different tree or flower. On Jiayuguan Lu it's maples and on Zhengyangguan it's myrtles. The locals simply call them Peach St, Snowpine St or Crab Apple St. The gardens here are extremely well groomed.

As you head out of the Eight Passes Area, bathing beaches 2 and 3 are just east, and the villas lining the headlands are exquisite. **No 2 Beach** is smaller, quieter and more sheltered than No 1 and is preferred when No 1 is overloaded. Facing No 2 are sanatoriums – but at the western headland is a naval installation, so don't take short cuts.

At the eastern end of the No 2 beach is the former German Governor's Residence. This castle-like villa, made of stone, is a replica of a German palace. It is said to have cost 2,450,000 taels of silver. When Kaiser Wilhelm II got the bill, he immediately recalled the extravagant governor and sacked him.

Xinhao Park
(xìnhàoshān gōngyuán) 信号山公园
Qingdao's city parks are amongst the best in China, and probably more worthwhile than the crowded and polluted beaches.

Xinhao Park harbours one of Qingdao's most astounding pieces of German architecture, the Xinhao Hill Hotel *(xìnhàoshān yíng bīnguǎn)*. At the highest point in the park are the three red golfball-shaped towers known as the 'mushroom buildings' *(mógu lóu)*. Climb up here for an impressive view – it will give you a perspective of just how many

old German buildings with red-tiled roofs still exist!

Just across the street from the eastern side of the park on Daxue Lu is what looks like a temple complex, but proves to be the Qingdao Museum *(qīngdǎo bówùguǎn)* with a collection of Yuan, Ming and Qing paintings.

The Longshan Underground Market *(lóngshān dìxià shāngyè jiē)* is an amazing shopping arcade built in a tunnel right under the park. The entrance to the arcade is on Longshan Lu at the south-west corner of Xinhao Park near the Protestant church.

Other Parks
North of the Huiquan Dynasty Hotel is **Zhongshan Park** *(zhōngshān gōngyuán)*, which covers 80 hectares, has a teahouse and temple and in springtime is a heavily wooded profusion of flowering shrubs and plants. The city zoo *(dòngwùyuán)* is also within the park's boundaries.

The mountainous area north-east of Zhongshan Park is called **Taipingshan Park** *(tàipíngshān gōngyuán)*, an area of walking paths, pavilions and the magnificent Zhanshan Temple *(zhànshān sì)*. This is the best place in town for hiking.

Just west of Zhongshan Park is **Qingdaoshan Park** *(qīngdǎoshān gōngyuán)*. A notable feature of this hilly park is Jingshan Fort *(jīngshān pàotái)*.

Churches
(jiàotáng) 教堂
Off Zhongshan Lu, up a steep hill, is a structure now known simply as the Catholic Church *(tiānzhǔ jiàotáng)* – its double spires can be spotted a long way off. The church is active and services are held on Sunday mornings.

Perhaps not surprisingly, the other main church in town is the Protestant Church *(jīdū jiàotáng)*, a single-spired structure with a clock tower. This church is near the south-west entrance of Xinhao Park by the Longshan Underground Market.

Brewery

(qīngdǎo píjiǔchǎng) 青岛啤酒厂

No guide to Qingdao would be complete without a mention of the brewery, tucked into the industrial part of town, east of the main harbour. Tsingtao Beer ('Tsingtao' is the old spelling for Qingdao) has gained a worldwide following.

The brewery was established early this century by the Germans who still supply the parts for 'modernisation' of the system. The flavour of the finest brew in Asia comes from the mineral waters of nearby Laoshan. First exported in 1954, the beer received the national silver medal for quality in China (as judged by the National Committee on Wines & Liquors in 1979). Pilgrimages to the brewery are reserved for tour groups, but if you want to visit, the best bet would be to approach CITS at the Huiquan Dynasty Hotel to organise a guide and taxi (don't count on it though). Some people have simply fronted up at the factory and been shown around. Otherwise the drink is on tap in town, it's cheap enough in the stores and it's sold all over China.

If you're into factories, Qingdao has many besides those that make booze. Factory tours might give you a chance to observe jade carving, shell carving, locomotives and embroidery. Inquire at CITS.

Places to Stay – bottom end

The *Railway Hotel* (☎ 269963) *(tiědào dàshà)*, 2 Tai'an Lu, is right in front of the railway station. The 24-storey hotel has 224 rooms, including dormitories for Y30 and Y38. Doubles cost Y156 and Y188. The 2nd floor has a reasonable Chinese restaurant but no English menu – the staff just giggle when English is spoken.

The *Friendship Hotel* (☎ 227021) *(yǒuyí bīnguǎn)* is in the same building as the Friendship Store, next door to the Passenger Ferry Terminal on Xinjiang Lu. The Friendship Hotel is popular with budget travellers, though it's in a dumpy neighbourhood. Doubles are Y60. The plumbing is temperamental – expect lukewarm rather than hot water for your evening bath. If you arrive by

Qingdao by boat, the hotel is just a step away. If you arrive by train then it's a bit complicated. First take bus No 6 along Zhongshan Lu to the northern terminal, where it turns around. Then walk back under an overhead bridge near the terminal, turn right, and – if you can find the stop – take the No 21 bus for one stop north. If you can't find it then just walk the last stretch (Qingdao buses are too horrendously crowded to even contemplate taking two in a row).

In the same neighbourhood, but more pleasant, is the *Jingshan Hotel (jīngshān bīnguǎn)* on Xiaogang 2-Lu. Dormitories (a shared double room) cost Y60, or you can book the whole room for Y120. The hotel is a five-minute walk from the Passenger Ferry Terminal.

Straddling the border between budget and mid-range accommodation, the *Qingdao Pharmaceutical Building (yīyào dàshà)* is the large high-rise on No 6 beach with the circular 'VW' sign on the roof. You can't beat the location, even if the building is incongruous with the setting. Singles/doubles cost Y96/120 but there are no dormitories. Prices might shoot up during the summer peak season.

Places to Stay – middle

The *Haiqing Hotel (hǎiqīng bīnguǎn)* on Laiyang Lu near the waterfront is small but comfortable. Singles/doubles cost Y100/ 120.

The *Zhanqiao Guesthouse* (☎ 270502) *(zhànqiáo bīnguǎn)* at 31 Taiping Lu is a marvellous old colonial villa facing the waterfront. Doubles are Y185.

The *Qingdao Hotel* (☎ 268771; fax 262464) *(qīngdǎo fàndiàn)* is at 53 Zhongshan Lu but the entrance is around the corner on Qufu Lu. Just down the street from the Catholic church, the location couldn't be more central. At Y200 for a double, it just barely qualifies as mid-range accommodation. If you have a Chinese student ID, the Chinese price (half of what foreigners usually pay) is a bargain. The adjoining Cantonese restaurant is one of Qingdao's best.

The *Peace Hotel* (☎ 223231) *(hépíng*

bīnguǎn) is behind the Friendship Store near the Passenger Ferry Terminal on Xinjiang Lu. While convenient if you have an early ferry to catch, at Y150 it's overpriced for the facilities and ugly neighbourhood.

The *Beihai Hotel* (☎ 365832) *(běihǎi bīnguǎn)* is somewhat inconvenient – eight km from the railway station in a not too attractive part of town. Doubles cost Y150. You can get there on bus No 31.

Places to Stay – top end

The *Overseas Chinese Hotel* (☎ 279092) *(huáqiáo fàndiàn)*, 72 Hunan Lu, is near the railway station. It's very popular due to the central location but seems ridiculously over-priced at Y245 for the cheapest double.

The *Dongfang Hotel* (☎ 265888; fax 262741) *(dōngfāng fàndiàn)*, 4 Daxue Lu, is a favourite hang-out for privileged cadres and Overseas Chinese. Room prices start at a modest Y241.

The *Yellow Sea Hotel* (☎ 270215) *(huánghǎi fàndiàn)*, 75 Yan'an 1-Lu, is a 19-storey luxury tower to the north-west of the Huiquan Dynasty Hotel. This plush place has doubles starting at Y380.

The *Badaguan Hotel* (☎ 372168; fax 371383) *(bādàguān bīnguǎn)*, 19 Shan-haiguan Lu, is adjacent to the No 2 Beach and has doubles starting at Y373. The hotel also operates 26 marvellous renovated German villas at various places around town – prices on request.

The *Haitian Hotel* (☎ 366185) *(hǎitiān dàjiǔdiàn)*, 39 Zhanshan Dalu, is a four-star hotel at the No 3 Beach and is often packed out with tour groups from Taiwan. Doubles cost Y580 and up.

The high-rise *Huiquan Dynasty Hotel* (☎ 279215) *(huìquán wángcháo dàjiǔdiàn)* at 9 Nanhai Lu, presides over the No 1 Beach. Double rooms at this four-star hotel start at Y570.

For a change of pace, try the incredible *Xinhao Hill Hotel* (☎ 266209; fax 261985) *(xìnhàoshān yíng bīnguǎn)*, 26 Longshan Lu in Xinhaoshan Park. This old German mansion is worth visiting just to photograph the outside, which is perfectly restored. Wad-

dling in all this history is not cheap – rooms cost Y400, Y800 and Y1600, but at least the staff are friendly.

Places to Eat

Zhongshan Lu has several notable restaurants. The top one is the *Chunhelou* (☎ 227371) *(chúnhélóu)*, 146 Zhongshan Lu. The seafood is pricey but the Tsingtao beer is served in real pint mugs.

For morning baozi and cakes, go to the rather illustrious-looking *Tianfu Restaurant* (☎ 225205) *(tiānfǔ jiǔjià)*, 210 Zhongshan Lu, near the northern end of the street. It's open from 6.30 am.

There are some cafes, sidewalk stalls and upmarket canteens such as the *White Spray* *(báilànghuā)* near the Huiquan Dynasty Hotel. They serve large plates of things like prawns, dumplings and bean curd – none of which are particularly inspiring. Take potluck – that's what the signs say.

Next to the Qingdao Hotel on Qufu Lu (just off Zhongshan Lu) is the *Cantonese Restaurant (yuè càitīng)*, which is *the* place for morning dim sum.

Alcohol in this town is plentiful and cheap. There's a huge stock of Tsingtao Red in the department stores on Zhongshan Lu.

Things to Buy

Immediately to the south of the railway station is the Hualian Commercial Building *(huálián shāngshà)*, crammed to the rafters with consumer abundance (even edible bread!). By comparison, the Friendship Store (near the Passenger Ferry Terminal) looks sick.

The busiest shopping district is along Zhongshan Lu, which has an antique store at No 40, and the Arts & Crafts Service Department at the northern end.

Getting There & Away

Air There are so-called international 'charter flights' which follow a regular published schedule – four times weekly between Qingdao and Hong Kong. There are plans to add direct flights from Qingdao to Seoul, South Korea.

SHANDONG

Domestic flights connect Qingdao to Beijing (Y320), Canton (Y930), Changsha (Y540), Chengdu (Y850), Harbin (Y560), Ningbo (Y430), Shanghai (Y350), Shenzhen (Y1290), Wenzhou (Y540), Wuhan and Xiamen (Y790).

The CAAC office (☎ 286047) is at 29 Zhongshan Lu. The booking office of China Eastern Airlines (☎ 270215) is adjacent to the Yellow Sea Hotel at 75 Yan'an 1-Lu.

Bus Buses and minibuses to Yantai depart from the railway station area (Y21) and take 3½ hours for the journey. Buses to Ji'nan cost about Y40 and take eight hours. There are several buses daily to Nanjing (Y50). An air-con bus to Beijing departs at 2 pm, costs Y82 and takes 16 hours.

Train All trains from Qingdao go through the provincial capital of Ji'nan, except for the direct Qingdao to Yantai trains. There are two direct trains daily to Beijing (17 hours). Sleepers are very hard to get without assistance from CITS or your hotel, and most likely you'll have to settle for an expensive soft sleeper.

Direct trains to Shenyang (about 26 hours) pass through Ji'nan and Tianjin, sidestepping Beijing. There are direct trains to Xi'an (about 31 hours) which continue to Lanzhou and Xining.

Trains to Dalian and to Shanghai (about 24 hours) will take almost the same time as the boats. There is one train daily to Shanghai. The train is much more expensive than the boat – there's a foreigners' mark-up on the train but not on the boat.

Train No 506 to Yantai departs from Qingdao at 10.10 am, arriving in Yantai at 4.26 pm (over six hours!). It's faster going the other way – train No 508 departs Yantai at 4.46 pm and arrives in Qingdao at the awful time of 8.52 pm. Doing this route by bus is quicker and more convenient.

Boat There are regular boats from Qingdao to Dalian and Shanghai. There are usually five classes on these boats, including four, six and eight-berth cabins, plus special class, which is about twice the price of 1st class.

The boat to Dalian (on the Liaoning Peninsula), across the Bohai Gulf, is the best way to get there from Qingdao. (It's a long way by train.) The boat takes 26 hours and leaves every four days, but sometimes there can be gaps of up to eight days. The boat is comfortable and fares range from Y27 in 5th class to Y152 in 1st class.

You could also take a bus or train from Qingdao to Yantai and catch the boat from Yantai to Dalian. See the Yantai section for more details.

The daily boat from Qingdao to Shanghai takes about 27 hours. Fares range from Y24 in 5th class to Y233 in special class. The ship is clean and comfortable, and has friendly and helpful staff.

Boats from Qingdao to Canton do exist but are not frequent. Fares range from Y81 in 5th class to Y391 in special class.

In Qingdao, tickets can be bought in the Passenger Ferry Terminal near the Friendship Store.

Getting Around

To/From the Airport Qingdao's airport is 30 km from the city. Taxi drivers ask Y90 for the journey. Buses leave from the China Eastern Airlines ticket office next to the Yellow Sea Hotel, but *ask* first about the schedule – it's not frequent.

Bus Most transport needs can be catered for by the bus No 6 route, which starts at the north end of Zhongshan Lu, runs along it to within a few blocks of the main railway station and then east to the area above No 3 Beach. The No 6 bus stop closest to the main railway station seems to be the one on Zhongshan Lu, just north of the street leading to the Catholic Church.

AROUND QINGDAO

Forty km east of Qingdao is **Laoshan** *(láoshān)*, a mountain area covering some 400 sq km. It's an excellent place to go hiking or climbing – the mountain reaches an elevation of 1133 metres. Historical sites and scenic spots dot the area, and the local product is Laoshan mineral water. The Song Dynasty Taiqing Palace (a Taoist monastery) is the central attraction; there are paths leading to the summit of Laoshan from there. With such a large area there's plenty to explore. Due north of the Taiqing Palace is Jiushui, noted for its numerous streams and waterfalls.

An early morning bus runs from Qingdao railway station to the Taiqing Palace. Other travel agents around Qingdao have more extended itineraries, including an overnight stop in Laoshan, but it's probably hard to crash these tours unless you speak Chinese.

YANTAI
(yāntái) 烟台

Yantai, alias 'Zhifu' (at one time spelled 'Chefoo'), is a busy ice-free port on the northern coast of the Shandong Peninsula. Like Qingdao it grew from a defence outpost and fishing village but, although opened for foreign trade in 1862, it had no foreign concessions. Several nations, Japan and the USA among them, had trading establishments there and Yantai was something of a resort area at one time. Since 1949 the port and naval base at Yantai have been expanded and, apart from fishing and trading, the town is a major producer of wines, spirits and fruits. *Yantai* means 'smoke-terrace': wolf-dung fires were lit on the headland to warn fishing fleets of approaching pirates, a practice that continued during the Opium wars.

Information

There is a CTS office (☎ 25625) in the crumbling edifice next to the Overseas Chinese Guesthouse. If you can wake up the staff (we couldn't even find the staff, though the door was open), they might be able to sell you a ticket on the Weidong Ferry to South Korea. As for train tickets, ask the service desk at your own hotel if you want a sleeper.

Things to See

Apart from drinking and building sand castles, there's very little to see or do. Group tours are corralled off to a fish-freezing factory, a brandy distillery or the orchards behind the town. Yantai's beaches are not the greatest – they're unsheltered and prone to heavy wind-lashing.

The main one is hemmed in at the southwest side by an industrial complex and a naval establishment. **Beach No 2**, out by the Zhifu Hotel, is smaller and more pleasant, but difficult to get to.

A convenient tour of the town can be done on local bus No 3 which leaves from the square near the boat and railway stations. The bus cuts through Yantai, taking in the older parts of town (which are being eaten away by apartment blocks and factory chimneys), and goes past the odd colonial edifice and newer sections. It takes half an hour to get to **Yantaishan Park** (Yantai Hill) and then turns around at the Yantai Hill terminal. If you get off at the terminal and follow a stone wall from there up to the headland, you get a nice view of the naval dockyards, heavy shipping and even navy manoeuvres. There's a plush hotel here, and though the sign says 'Welcome You', this doesn't apply to foreigners.

If you carry on round the headland, you hit the esplanade at **No 1 Beach** where there is some distinctively European architecture – former foreign trading or resort housing. You can continue to the bus No 1 route, which will take you back into town.

Tiny **Yuhuangding Park** has a pleasant pagoda (sometimes featured on glossy tourist brochures) and not much else.

The **museum** *(bówùguǎn)* is not world famous but you can kill 20 minutes there if you have nothing better to do.

Places to Stay – middle

While there are many cheap and conveniently located hotels, almost none will accept foreigners. Six hotels are designated for foreign guests, and most are in rotten locations and charge high prices.

The best deal in town is the *Golden Shell Hotel* (☎ 226150) *(jīnbèi dàjiǔdiàn)*, at 172 Beima Lu, a 10-minute walk from the railway station. It's relatively small for a tourist hotel (by China's standards), but

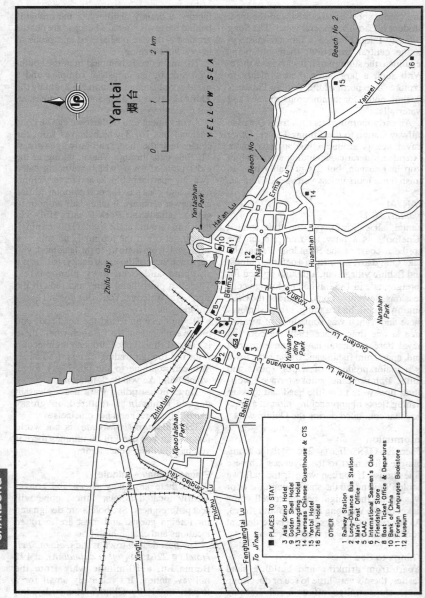

YELLOW SEA

Yantai
烟台

Beach No 2

Beach No 1

Zhifu Bay

Yantaishan Park

Nanshan Park

To Ji'nan

PLACES TO STAY

3 Asia Grand Hotel
9 Golden Shell Hotel
13 Yuhuangding Hotel
14 Overseas Chinese Guesthouse & CTS
15 Yantai Hotel
16 Zhifu Hotel

OTHER

1 Railway Station
2 Long-Distance Bus Station
4 Main Post Office
5 CAAC
6 International Seamen's Club
7 Friendship Store
8 Boat Ticket Office & Departures
10 Bank of China
11 Foreign Languages Bookstore
12 Museum

■ **PLACES TO STAY**

3 亚细亚大酒店
9 金贝大酒店
13 毓璜顶宾馆
14 华侨宾馆/中国旅行社
15 烟台大酒店
16 芝罘宾馆

OTHER

1 火车站
2 长途汽车站
4 电信大楼
5 中国民航
6 国际海员俱乐部
7 友谊商店
8 烟台港客运站
10 中国银行
11 外文书店
12 博物馆

inside it's very clean and comfortable. Doubles cost Y120.

The *Yuhuangding Hotel* (☎ 244401; fax 242788) *(yùhuángdǐng bīnguǎn)* on Yuhuangding Xilu is opposite a small park by the same name. Plush doubles are Y160, and even plusher suites cost Y298. From the railway station area you can reach the hotel on bus No 7.

The high-rise *Zhifu Hotel* (☎ 248421; fax 248289) *(zhīfu bīnguǎn)* has been built about eight km from the station in a pleasant beach area. It's a nice place but a transport disaster. You need two buses to get there (Nos 1 and 5) – the first one stops two blocks away from the railway station (by the post office) and the last one is a rare species indeed. Otherwise it's hitching or jumping the laundry bus which runs into town from the hotel every morning. In other words, you could end up commuting by taxi which eliminates whatever small savings you gain by staying here. Not that it's dirt cheap at Y180 for a double. There's nothing in the vicinity of the hotel except the No 2 Beach, about 10 minutes' walk away, a set menu in the dining hall and

a conference room for 200, which is for reclusive meetings.

Places to Stay – top end
The *Overseas Chinese Guesthouse* (☎ 224431) *(huáqiáo bīnguǎn)* overlooks the city from its hillside perch at 15 Huanshan Lu. Notable for its karaoke bar and home of CTS, the hotel is often booked out by ethnic Chinese from South Korea and Taiwan. Doubles cost Y260 for foreigners. Take bus No 7 to the terminal – the hotel is about 300 metres beyond. Taxis want at least Y10 from the railway station.

The *Asia Grand Hotel* (☎ 247888; fax 242625) *(yàxìyà dàjiǔdiàn)*, 116 Nan Dajie, is indeed grand, though not cheap – doubles cost Y260. The hotel is a 10-minute walk south-west of the railway station, making it one of the few in Yantai with a convenient location.

The *Yantai Hotel* (☎ 248468; fax 248169) *(yāntái dàjiǔdiàn)* has the highest prices and second-worst location in the city, yet it's often full. Doubles cost Y396 to Y462, while suites can go for over Y800. The hotel is over six km east of the railway station, and if you can afford these prices you can also afford a taxi to get there.

Places to Eat
The *Yantai Fandian* is both a hotel (foreigners forbidden) and a restaurant (foreigners allowed). It's sandwiched between the railway station and the boat station. There are three rooms: the central one is the cheapest and has a mass of proletarian clientele with about four chairs between them – it's stand-up noodles, dumplings, beggars and bowls of hot water. The other two sections have beer, and bigger and meatier dishes – and chairs. Just on the east side of the Yantai Fandian is a line-up of closet-sized noodle shops and bars.

In the likely event that you're staying at the *Golden Shell Hotel*, you might want to eat there – the restaurant is reasonably priced and the food is excellent.

The *International Seamen's Club*

(☎ 245348) *(hǎiyuán jùlèbù)* is just south of the railway station on Beima Lu.

All around the Seamen's Club are a number of bars sporting English – apparently a fair number of foreigners pass this way. As for alcohol, you can buy the stuff anywhere, including inside the railway station. It's very cheap, and there's some evil-looking substance that can remove the paint from a car. Yantai is famous for rose-petal wine *(méiguījiǔ)*, brandy *(báilándì)* and red and white wines – renowned brands are Yantai Red, Weimeisi Wine and Jinjiang Brandy.

Things to Buy
Yantai has a remarkably well-stocked Friendship Store *(yǒuyí shāngdiàn)*, no doubt an attempt to cash in on the sailors and hordes of South Korean visitors. The herbal medicine section is particularly rich – stock up on deer antlers, pearl powder, bee pollen and snake gall bladder. Other items for sale include pricey artwork and porcelain vases, but we were most interested in the food section. The Friendship Store is almost directly opposite the railway station.

Getting There & Away
Air There are flights connecting Yantai to Beijing (Y290), Canton (Y1040), Harbin, Ji'nan (Y200), Shanghai (Y420), Shenyang (Y300), Shenzhen (Y1190), Wuhan and Xiamen (Y870).

Bus There are frequent buses and minibuses between Yantai and Qingdao. The large buses cost Y21, though they often ask for an extra Y5 for 'large luggage', which seems to include a backpack. Minibuses cost Y25. In both Qingdao and Yantai, buses congregate in front of the railway stations and depart when full. The journey takes 3½ hours on an excellent highway.

Train The Yantai-Qingdao train (only one daily and slower than the bus) terminates in Qingdao – it does not carry on to Ji'nan. By contrast, there are four trains daily in each direction between Yantai and Ji'nan (about eight hours), bypassing Qingdao completely

and continuing on to Tianjin, Beijing or Shanghai. There are express trains to Beijing (about 17½ hours) and a direct but slow train to Shanghai.

Boat The rail trip to Dalian, on the Liaoning Peninsula, takes a circuitous route. Faster are the daily boats from Yantai. From Yantai to Dalian costs Y120 (1st class), Y70 (2nd class, two-bed cabin), Y40 (3rd class, four-bed cabin), Y30 (4th class, eight to 10-bed cabin) and Y21 (5th class, which you'd rather not know about). The boat leaves Yantai at 8 pm and arrives in Dalian at 6 am the next day. There are other boats between Yantai and Tianjin (berthing at Tianjin's Tanggu Harbour) which run once every five days.

Getting Around
Yantai's airport is 15 km south of the city. A taxi should cost about Y40 from the railway station area. Most taxi drivers expect foreigners to pay quadruple the going rate. The skeletal bus system is slow but sure – get a bus map for Y1 and work it out.

PENGLAI
(pénglái) 蓬莱
About 65 km north-west of Yantai by road is the coastal castle of Penglai, a place of the gods which is often referred to in Chinese mythology. The castle *(pénglái gé)* is perched on a clifftop overlooking the sea and is about 1000 years old. Like much of China's architecture, the castle had been allowed to fall apart, but recently has been fully restored. It's fair to say that this is China's most beautiful castle, and is worth a visit if you've got the time and don't mind the out-and-back ride to get there.

Besides the castle, Penglai is famous for an optical illusion which the locals claim appears every few decades. The last full mirage seen from the castle was in July 1981 when two islands appeared, with roads, trees, buildings, people and vehicles. This phenomenon lasted about 40 minutes (if it had lasted any longer, little red flags and factory chimneys would no doubt have appeared!).

There are some pebbly beaches in the area, but Penglai isn't considered ideal for bathing.

The most popular place to stay is the *Penglaige Guesthouse* (☎ 3192) *(pénglàigé bīnguǎn)* on Zhonglou Beilu. Some small restaurants cater for the domestic tourist market, with seafood being the specialty.

Penglai is a two-hour bus ride from Yantai. Minibuses to Penglai depart from in front of the Yantai railway station.

WEIHAI
(wēihǎi) 威海

About 60 km east of Yantai by road is the obscure port city of Weihai. The British had a concession here around the turn of the century, though little remains today to remind you of its colonial heritage.

Weihai is hardly a place to linger in – it not only lacks scenery, but is horribly expensive. Nevertheless, the port sees plenty of tourist traffic thanks to the opening of a passenger ferry service to Inchon in South Korea.

Rather few foreigners spend any length of time in Weihai, but many transit through here in both directions. It's preferable to arrive in Weihai by boat rather than depart this way – otherwise you may get stuck here for the night while waiting for the boat to depart the next day. Since the boat from Korea arrives in Weihai at 9 am, you'll have no problem getting a bus out of town – we suggest you do so as soon as possible. Hotel prices for foreigners are ridiculous – around Y500! At that price it would be cheaper to fly to Korea.

The introductory Getting There & Away chapter has all the details of the ferry (prices, timetable and so forth).

If you arrive in Weihai without having purchased a ferry ticket in advance, the place to go (immediately upon arrival!) is CITS (☎ 226210, 226490; fax 226058), at 44 Dongcheng Lu. Minibuses run from the ferry terminal in Weihai directly to Yantai and Qingdao.

Hebei 河北

Population: 53 million
Capital: Shijiazhuang

Wrapping itself around the centrally administered municipalities of Beijing and Tianjin is the province of Hebei *(héběi)*. It is often viewed either as an extension of Beijing, the red-tape maker, or of Tianjin, the industrial giant. This is not far off the mark since, geographically speaking, they take up a fair piece of the pie. In fact, Tianjin used to be Hebei's capital, but when that came under central government administration the next largest city, Shijiazhuang, replaced it.

Topographically, Hebei falls into two distinct parts: the mountain tableland to the north, where the Great Wall runs (and also to the western fringes of the province), and the monotonous southern plain. Agriculture – mainly wheat and cotton growing – is hampered by dust storms, droughts (five years in a row from 1972 to 1977) and flooding. These natural disasters will give you some idea of the weather. It's scorching and humid in summer, and freezing in winter, with dust fallout in spring and heavy rains in July and August.

Coal is Hebei's main resource and most of it is shipped through Qinhuangdao, an ugly port town with iron, steel and machine industries.

As far as tourist sights go, there's the beach resort of Beidaihe, and Chengde with its palaces and temples. Shijiazhuang – the capital city – is a waste of time.

Apart from all these, the best thing to see is the Great Wall, which spans the province before meeting the sea at the exotic market town of Shanhaiguan.

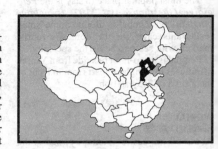

SHIJIAZHUANG
(shíjiāzhuāng) 石家庄

Shijiazhuang is a railway junction town about 250 km south-west of Beijing and, in spite of being the capital of the province, it's the odd town out in Hebei. Its population is around one million, but at the turn of the century it was just a small village with 500 inhabitants and a handful of buildings. With the construction of the Beijing to Wuhan line in 1905 (financed by a Belgian company) and the Shijiazhuang to Taiyuan line which was finished in 1907 (a Russian-French project) the town rapidly expanded to a population of 10,000 in the 1920s.

Shijiazhuang has the biggest officer training school in China; it's about two km west of the city. After the Beijing protests and subsequent killings in 1989, all the new students from Beijing University were taken to this 're-education camp' for a one-year indoctrination.

Shijiazhuang is an industrial city and the tomb of Dr Norman Bethune is just about all there is to see. Otherwise it's only useful as a transit point or a staging area for sights within the region.

Information
The China Youth Travel Service, or CYTS (☎ 615961) – a competitor of CITS – is in room 230 of the Hebei Guesthouse.

If you're staying in a hotel with no foreign exchange counter, try the Bank of China at 118 Zhongshan Zhonglu.

Revolutionary Martyrs' Mausoleum
(lièshì língyuán) 烈士陵园

The guerrilla doctor Norman Bethune (1890-1939) is interred here: there is also a photo

HEBEI

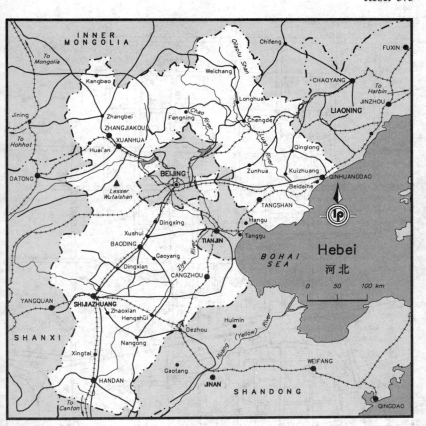

and drawing display depicting his life and works, and a white memorial. Bethune is the most famous 'foreign devil' in China since Marco Polo. Actually, most Chinese people don't know who Polo is, but they all know Bethune *(bái qiúēn)*. He goes down in modern history as the man who served as a surgeon with the Eighth Route Army in the war against Japan, having previously served with the Communists in Spain against Franco and his Nazi allies. Bethune is eulogised in the reading of Mao Zedong Thought: 'We must all learn the spirit of absolute selflessness from Dr Norman Bethune'.

In China, 'Bethune' is also synonymous with 'Canada' – it's about all the Chinese tend to know about the country, and bringing up the name makes for instant friendship if you're Canadian.

More than 700 army cadres and heroes buried in the cemetery died during the Resistance against Japan, the War of Liberation and the Korean War. The area is a large park; in the central alley is a pair of bronze Jin Dynasty lions dating from 1185. The Martyrs' Mausoleum is on Zhongshan Lu, west of the railway station. There is also a statue of Bethune in the courtyard of the

Shijiazhuang 石家庄

PLACES TO STAY
4 Huaien Hebei Hotel
6 Silver Spring Hotel
8 Huadu Dasha (hotel)
9 Luyou Binguan (hotel)
10 Wujing Zongdui Zhaodaisuo (hotel)
11 International Hotel
13 Hebei Guesthouse & CYTS

OTHER
1 Revolutionary Martyrs' Mausoleum
2 Post Office
3 Railway Station
5 Yongan Market
7 Long-Distance Bus Station
12 Teachers' University

Bethune International Peace Hospital a bit further west of the cemetery.

Places to Stay

You'll hardly have to look for a hotel in Shijiazhuang – the hotels will be looking for you. Touts in front of the railway station pounce on any likely looking prospect, often fighting each other in their zeal to kidnap a potential customer. The touts are harmless and can even be useful, but there is one problem – you'll be shown placards with hotel names (in Chinese), photos of rooms and room prices. The problem is that these are Chinese prices – big-noses are often required to pay double price in FEC, and dorms will be off limits. This is not the case in every hotel, but it's the usual policy. The touts may not even know this, so don't automatically assume that you've been lied to if prices aren't as advertised.

Wujing Zongdui Zhaodaisuo (☎ 632713, 632242) is one of the cheapest places that accepts foreigners – the reason why it can take foreigners probably has something to do with the fact that the building is owned by the military. Doubles cost Y40 to Y80 and RMB are accepted. The facilities were a bit tattered at the time of our visit but limited renovation was under way – this could mean higher prices in future, though it seems unlikely that this place will become an upmarket hotel. The building is on Guangming Lu just behind the railway station – you can walk there in 10 minutes. When you exit the station, turn left and walk to Yuhua Lu – use the underpass to get past the railway tracks then up the steps (to your left) to reach Guangming Lu. As yet, the hotel has no English sign.

Lüyou Binguan (☎ 334357) is good value, with doubles for Y118. There is no English sign identifying the hotel except one that says 'Welcome', but there are plenty of bright lights illuminating the building at night. The hotel is on the south-east corner of Zhonghua Dajie and Cang'an Lu. Bus No 3 from the railway station stops nearby.

Huadu Dasha (☎ 334805; fax 333629) is the pride and joy of Shijiazhuang – the tallest building in town. This one is a favourite with the railway station touts, but the advertised cheap dorms are off limits to foreigners. Room prices for doubles/triples are Y100/150 plus 10% – not bad for the cushy standard of accommodation.

The *Silver Spring Hotel (yínquán fàndiàn)* is a mid-range hotel near the railway station. The convenient location and recently remodelled rooms accounts for the prices – doubles range from Y140 to Y190.

Just next door is the even fancier *Hualian Hebei Hotel* (☎ 725991) *(huálián héběi fàndiàn)* where doubles start from Y140.

The *International Hotel* (☎ 647888) *(guójì dàshà)* has long been a haven for geriatric tour groups rather than backpackers. Doubles cost Y260.

The *Hebei Guesthouse* (☎ 615961; fax 614092) *(héběi bīnguǎn)* is the most prestigious address in town. It's a modern eight-storey block with two restaurants and a bar. Doubles begin at Y160 and range all the way up to Y4500 for the presidential suite. The hotel is at 23 Yucai Jie – bus No 6 from the railway station stops nearby.

Places to Eat

Just on the north side of the Silver Spring

Hotel is a long commercial street called the *Yong'an Market*. Here you'll find lots of good eats at rock-bottom prices from both street stalls and indoor restaurants. There is another line-up of street stalls just in front of the railway station but these seem to operate only in the evening. Upstairs in the railway station itself is a large karaoke and restaurant which supplies much of Shijiazhuang's nightlife.

Getting There & Away
CAAC connects Shijiazhuang to Beijing (Y180), Canton (Y910), Xi'an (Y350) and Shanghai (Y560). Shijiazhuang is a major rail hub with comprehensive connections: there are lines to Beijing (about four hours), Taiyuan (about five hours), Dezhou (about five hours) and Canton.

Getting Around
The long-distance bus station is north-east of the railway station and within walking distance. From there you can get buses to sights outside Shijiazhuang. Within the city there are 10 bus lines.

AROUND SHIJIAZHUANG
There's nothing spectacular in this part of Hebei, but there are a few places that you can visit.

Zhengding
(zhèngdìng) 正定
Ten km north of Shijiazhuang, this town has several temples and monasteries. The largest and oldest is the Longxing Monastery *(lóngxīng sì)*, noted for its huge, 20-metre-high bronze buddha dating from the Song Dynasty almost 1000 years ago. The multi-armed statue is housed in the Temple of Great Mercy, an impressive structure with red and yellow galleries.

Zhaozhou Bridge
(zhàozhōu qiáo) 赵州桥
There's an old folk rhyme about the four wonders of Hebei which goes:

The Lion of Cangzhou
The Pagoda of Dingzhou
The Buddha of Zhengding
The Bridge of Zhaozhou

The bridge is in Zhaoxian County, about 40 km south-east of Shijiazhuang and two km south of Zhaoxian town. It has spanned the Jiao River for 1300 years and is possibly the oldest stone-arch bridge in China (another, believed older, has recently been unveiled in Linying County, Henan Province).

Putting the record books aside, Zhaozhou Bridge is remarkable in that it still stands. It is 50 metres long and 9.6 metres wide, with a span of 37 metres; the balustrades are carved with dragons and mythical creatures. Credit for this daring piece of engineering goes to a disputed source but, according to legend, the master mason Lu Ban constructed it overnight. Astounded immortals, refusing to believe that this was possible, arrived to test the bridge. One immortal had a wagon, another had a donkey, and they asked Lu Ban if it was possible for them both to cross at the same time. He nodded. Halfway across, the bridge started to shake and Lu Ban rushed into the water to stabilise

it. This resulted in donkey-prints, wheel-prints and hand-prints being left on the bridge. Several more old stone bridges are to be found in Zhaoxian County.

Cangyanshan

(*cāngyánshān*) 苍岩山

About 78 km south-west of Shijiazhuang is a scenic area of woods, valleys and steep cliffs dotted with pagodas and temples. The novelty here is a bizarre, double-roofed hall sitting on a stone arch bridge spanning a precipitous gorge. It is known as the Hanging Palace, and is reached by a 300-step stairway. The palace dates back to the Sui Dynasty. On the surrounding slopes are other ancient halls.

Xibaipo

(*xībǎipō*) 西柏坡

In Pingshan County, 80 km north-west of Shijiazhuang, was the base from which Mao Zedong, Zhou Enlai and Zhu De directed the northern campaign against the Kuomintang from 1947 to 1948. The original site of Xibaipo village was submerged by the Gangnan Reservoir and the present village has been rebuilt close by. In 1977 a Revolutionary Memorial Museum was erected. Xibaipo has become a tourist trap, but it's still fun to visit.

CHENGDE

(*chéngdé*) 承德

Chengde is an 18th-century imperial resort area, also known as Jehol. It's billed as somewhere to escape from the heat (and now the traffic) of summers in the capital and boasts the remnants of the largest regal gardens in China.

Chengde remained an obscure town until 1703 when Emperor Kangxi began building a summer palace here, with a throne room and the full range of court trappings. More than a home away from home, Chengde turned into a sort of government seat, since where the emperor went his seat went too. Kangxi called his summer creation Bishu Shanzhuang (Fleeing-the-Heat Mountain Villa).

By 1790, during the reign of his grandson Qianlong, it had grown to the size of Beijing's Summer Palace and the Forbidden City combined. Qianlong extended an idea started by Kangxi, to build replicas of minority architecture in order to make envoys feel comfortable. In particular he was keen on promoting Tibetan and Mongolian Lamaism, which had proved to be a useful way of debilitating the meddlesome Mongols. The Mongolian branch of Lamaism required one male in every family to become a monk – a convenient method of channelling manpower and ruining the Mongol economy. This helps explain the Tibetan and Mongolian features of the monasteries north of the summer palace, one of them a replica of the Potala Palace in Lhasa.

So much for business – the rest was the emperor's pleasure: the usual bouts of hunting, feasting and orgies. Occasionally the outer world would make a rude intrusion into this dream life. In 1793, British emissary Lord Macartney arrived, and sought to open trade with China. Qianlong dismissed him with the statement that China possessed all things and had no need of trade.

Chengde has very much slipped back into being the provincial town it once was, its grandeur long decayed, its monks and emperors long gone. The population of over 150,000 is engaged in mining, light industry and tourism. The Qing court has left them a little legacy, but one that needs working on. The palaces and monasteries are tattered – Buddhist statues are disfigured, occasionally beyond recognition, or locked up in dark corners, windows are bricked up, columns are reduced to stumps and the temples are mere facades, impressive from the outside but shells inside.

All this is being restored, in some cases from the base up, in the interests of a projected increase in tourism. It's on the cards that Chinese and Western restaurants, high-class shops, evenings of traditional music (with instruments copied from those rescued from tombs around China) and horse riding will be introduced. Meanwhile there's absolutely nothing wrong with ruins – it's just a matter of changing your expectations.

HEBEI

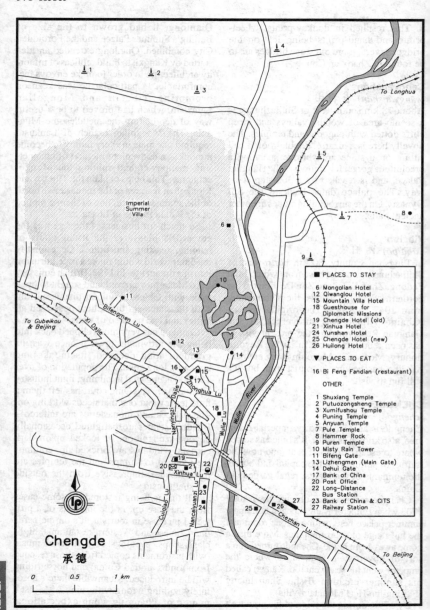

PLACES TO STAY
6 Mongolian Hotel
12 Qiwanglou Hotel
15 Mountain Villa Hotel
18 Guesthouse for
    Diplomatic Missions
19 Chengde Hotel (old)
21 Xinhua Hotel
24 Yunshan Hotel
25 Chengde Hotel (new)
26 Huilong Hotel

PLACES TO EAT
16 Bi Feng Fandian (restaurant)

OTHER
1 Shuxiang Temple
2 Putuozongsheng Temple
3 Xumifushou Temple
4 Puning Temple
5 Anyuan Temple
7 Pule Temple
8 Hammer Rock
9 Puren Temple
10 Misty Rain Tower
11 Bifeng Gate
13 Lizhengmen (Main Gate)
14 Dehui Gate
20 Bank of China
22 Long-Distance
    Bus Station
23 Bank of China & CITS
27 Railway Station

Chengde
承德

0   0.5   1 km

HEBEI

227484) at 6 Nanyuan Donglu, next to the Yunshan Hotel in a green sheet-metal building that looks temporary but isn't. Like most residents of Chengde, the staff are very friendly and helpful. The PSB (☎ 223091) is on Wulie Lu.

The Bank of China is right next to the Yunshan Hotel and CITS. There is another Bank of China on the north side of Zhonghua Lu near the intersection with Nanyingzi Dajie.

Imperial Summer Villa
(bìshǔ shānzhuāng) 避暑山庄
Otherwise known as 'Fleeing-the-Heat Mountain Villa', this park covers 590 hectares and is bounded by a 10-km wall. Emperor Kangxi decreed that there would be 36 'beauty spots' in Jehol; Qianlong delineated 36 more. That makes a total of 72, but where are they? At the north end of the gardens the pavilions were destroyed by warlords and Japanese invaders, and even the forests have suffered cutbacks. The park is on the dull side, and hasn't been very well maintained. With a good deal of imagination you can perhaps detect traces of the original scheme of things, with landscaping borrowed from the southern gardens of Suzhou, Hangzhou and Jiaxing, and from the Mongolian grasslands. There is even a feature for resurrecting the moon, should it not be around – a pool shows a crescent moon created by the reflection of a hole in surrounding rocks.

Passing through Lizhengmen, the main gate, you arrive at the Front Palace, a modest version of Beijing's palace. It contains the main throne hall, the Hall of Simplicity and Sincerity, built of an aromatic hardwood called nanmu and now a museum displaying royal memorabilia, arms, clothing and other accoutrements. The emperor's bedrooms are fully furnished. Around to the side is a door without an exterior handle, through which the lucky bed partner for the night was ushered before being stripped and searched by eunuchs.

The double-storey Misty Rain Tower, on the north-west side of the main lake, was an

Chengde has nothing remotely approaching Beijing's temples, in case you were expecting something along those lines.

The dusty, small-town ambience of Chengde is nice enough and there's some quiet hiking in the rolling countryside. Chinese speakers are apparently delighted with the clarity of the local dialect (maybe because they can actually hear it in the absence of traffic).

Information
You'll find the CITS (☎ 226827; fax

imperial study. Further north is the Wenjin Chamber, built in 1773 to house a copy of the *Sikuquanshu*, a major anthology of classics, history, philosophy and literature commissioned by Qianlong. The anthology took 10 years to put together. Four copies were made but three have disappeared; the fourth is in Beijing.

Ninety per cent of the compound is taken up by lakes, hills, mini-forests and plains, with the odd vantage-point pavilion. At the northern part of the park the emperors reviewed displays of archery, equestrian skills and fireworks. Horses were also chosen and tested here before hunting sorties. Yurts were set up on the mock-Mongolian prairies (a throne, of course, installed in the emperor's yurt) and picnics were held for minority princes. So, it's a good idea to pack a lunch, take your tent and head off for the day...the yurts have returned for the benefit of weary tourists.

Eight Outer Temples
(*wàibā miào*) 外八庙

To the north and north-east of the imperial garden are former temples and monasteries. So how many are there? The count started off at 11 many years ago, then plummeted to five (Japanese bombers, Cultural Revolution), and now the number varies between five and nine. The outer temples are from three to five km from the garden's front gate; a bus No 6 taken to the north-east corner will land you in the vicinity.

The surviving temples were built between 1750 and 1780. The Chinese-style Puren Temple and the vaguely Shanxi-style Shuxiang Temple have been totally rebuilt. Get there in the early morning when the air is crisp and cool and the sun is shining on the front of the temples – that's the best time to take photos. Some of the temples are listed here in clockwise order.

Putuozongsheng Temple (*pǔtuózōng shèng zhī miào*)
Putuozongsheng (Potaraka Doctrine), the largest of the Chengde temples, is a mini-facsimile of Lhasa's Potala. It was built for the chieftains from

Xinjiang, Qinghai, Mongolia and Tibet to celebrate Qianlong's 60th birthday and was also a site for religious assemblies. It's a solid-looking fortress, but is in bad shape – parts are inaccessible or boarded up and gutted by fire. Notice the stone column in the courtyard inscribed in Chinese, Tibetan, Mongolian and Manchurian scripts.

Xumifushou Temple (*xūmǐfúshòu zhī miào*)
Xumifushou (the Temple of Sumeru, Happiness and Longevity) was built in honour of the sixth Panchen Lama, who visited in 1781 and stayed here. It incorporates elements of Tibetan and Han architecture and is an imitation of a temple in Shigatse, Tibet. At the highest point is a hall with eight gilded copper dragons commanding the roof ridges, and behind that sits a glazed-tile pagoda.

Puning Temple (*pǔníng sì*)
Puning (the Temple of Universal Tranquillity) is also modelled on a Tibetan temple. It was built to commemorate Qianlong's victory over Mongol tribes when the subjugated leaders were invited to Chengde. A stele relating the victory is inscribed in Tibetan, Mongol, Chinese and Manchu. The main feature is an Avalokitesvara towering 22 metres; this wooden buddha has 42 arms with an eye on each palm. The temple appears to be used as an active place of worship.

Anyuan Temple (*ānyuǎn miào*)
Only the main hall remains of Anyuan (the Temple of Far Spreading Peace) – a copy of a Xinjiang temple. It contains Buddhist frescoes in a very sad state.

Pule Temple (*pǔlè sì*)
Pule (the Temple of Universal Happiness) is definitely the most interesting of the temples. You can scramble along the banks of the nearby rivulet to a road that leads off near a pagoda at the garden wall.

The temple was built in 1776 for visits of minority envoys (Kazakhs among them). It's in much better shape than the other temples and has been retiled and repainted. At the rear of the temple is the unusual Round

Pavilion, reminiscent of Beijing's Temple of Heaven, which has a magnificent ceiling.

You can hike to Hammer Rock *(bàngchuíshān)* from Pule. It has nothing to do with sharks – the rock is meant to resemble an upside-down hammer. There are commanding views of the area from here. Other scenic rocks to add to your collection include Toad Rock and Monk's Hat Hill. The hiking is pleasant and the scenery is good.

Organised Tours

The only practical way to see all the tourist sights in one day is to take a tour by minibus. Most of these tours start out at 8 am, but a few begin in the afternoon just after lunch, around 1.30 pm. The cheapest sightseeing bus tours cost around Y20 but are Chinese-speaking only. Foreigners are usually welcome to tag along but the tour leaders would be much happier if you could speak Chinese.

The cheapest tours depart from the Lizhengmen Hotel *(lìzhèngmén lǚguǎn)* – this hotel is for Chinese people only but foreigners can join their tours. The tours run daily during the high season (around May through October) but might only be twice weekly during the winter.

The Mountain Villa Hotel also does tours. These cost around Y30 to Y40 per person. If no tour is available, this hotel can also arrange a car and driver for a personalised tour – this costs Y100 or so and several travellers can split the cost.

Pricey tours are available from CITS in Beijing. A complete tour to Chengde costs Y1000 (two days) for one person, but gets cheaper as the group size increases.

Places to Stay

A personal favourite is the *Mountain Villa Hotel* (☎ 223501) *(shānzhuāng bīnguǎn)*, 127 Lizhenmen Lu. The Stalinist architecture evokes mixed reactions, but this place certainly has character. Doubles cost Y75 to Y160. The more expensive rooms are large enough to hold a party in – perhaps that's why they come equipped with mahjong tables. Hotel reps try to capture travellers at

the railway station and provide free transport by minibus – otherwise, take bus No 7 from the railway station and then a short walk; the hotel is opposite the entrance to the Imperial Summer Villa.

The old *Chengde Hotel* (☎ 225179) *(chéngdé bīnguǎn)* on Nanyingzi Dajie has comfortable doubles on Y40 and Y50. Bus No 7 from the railway station drops you right outside the hotel.

There are two hotels called the Chengde Hotel – the one close to the railway station on Chezhan Lu is the new *Chengde Hotel* (☎ 227373; fax 224319) *(chéngdé dàshà)*. This is a decidedly upmarket place – doubles cost Y120, Y150 and Y180.

The *Xinhua Hotel* (☎ 225880) *(xīnhuá fàndiàn)*, 4 Xinhua Beilu, is a reliable cheapie with rooms for Y72.

The *Yunshan Hotel* (☎ 226171) *(yúnshān fàndiàn)* at 6 Nanyuan Donglu is a modern tourist hang-out and home to CITS. Doubles cost Y180.

The *Huilong Hotel* (☎ 232422; fax 232404) *(huìlóng dàshà)* on Chezhan Lu is the newest place in town. Rooms cost Y120, Y200 and Y400.

Also at the top end is the *Guesthouse for Diplomatic Missions* (☎ 441807) *(wàijiāo rényuán bīnguǎn)*, on Wulie Lu. Doubles cost Y170.

There are two hotels just within the walls of the Imperial Summer Villa. On the west side is the *Qiwanglou Hotel (qǐwànglóu bīnguǎn)* built in Qing Dynasty style. It's a three-star hotel with doubles for Y180. Further north and on the east side is the *Mongolian Hotel (měnggǔbāo)* where doubles cost between Y120 and Y180. It's designed in yurt style with air-con, carpet, telephone, and TV – not even Genghis Khan had it this good.

Places to Eat

If you're staying at or near the Mountain Villa Hotel, the nearby *Bi Feng Restaurant* is about 100 metres to your left as you exit the hotel. It has fine Chinese food and cheap prices. It's a friendly, family-run business – there's no English menu so just point to something being eaten by others and it's sure to be good.

There are two main market streets – one just west of the long-distance bus station, and the other just north of the post office. The local specialty is food made from haws (the fruit of the hawthorn), such as wine, ice-cream and sweets. Chengde Pule beer has an interesting flavour – perhaps it's the mountain water. There are lots of trolleys around town dispensing tasty baked turnip. Fresh almonds are grown locally – the almond juice sold in plastic containers is also a Chengde product.

The Chinese restaurant on the 2nd floor of the *Yunshan Hotel* has delicious food in generous portions, and is amazingly cheap, considering the sumptuous surroundings. There is a Western restaurant on the 1st floor of the hotel but, as the Chinese say, it's 'horse-horse tiger-tiger' (so-so).

Getting There & Away
Bus Although there are some long-distance buses between Chengde and Beijing, this is generally not the way to do it – most travellers go by train.

Train The regular approach to Chengde is by train from Beijing. The fast train (No 11) departs from Beijing at 7.17 am and arrives in Chengde at 11.51 am. Soft seat for tickets for foreigners costs Y66 – this is a non-smoking car! The same train gets renamed No 12 when it returns to Beijing, leaving Chengde at 2.31 pm. The one-way trip takes less than five hours. There are slower trains which take over seven hours. Tickets for trains leaving Chengde are only sold on the day of departure. Your hotel can buy your ticket, but this usually requires a small fee and you need to trust the staff with your passport (or old expired passport).

An unexplored route to or from Chengde is the train from Jinzhou, which is in Liaoning Province on the way to Shenyang. There are also trains direct from Chengde to Dandong, via Jinzhou and Shenyang; sleepers are available even though the train originates in Beijing.

Getting Around
There are occasional taxis and pedicabs around town, but most travellers wind up using the minibuses. There are half a dozen bus lines but the only ones you'll probably need to use are the No 7 from the station to the old Chengde Hotel, and the No 6 to the outer temples grouped at the north-east end of town. The service is infrequent – you might have to wait 30 minutes or more.

Another good way to get around town and to the outer temples is on a bicycle; there is a rental place opposite the old Chengde Hotel – other rental places pop up periodically – ask at your hotel.

BEIDAIHE, QINHUANGDAO & SHANHAIGUAN DISTRICT
A 35-km stretch of coastline on China's east coast, this district borders the Bohai Sea.

Beidaihe
(běidàihé) 北戴河
This seaside resort, opened to foreigners in 1979, was built by Westerners but is now popular with both Chinese and non-Chinese. The simple fishing village was transformed when English railway engineers stumbled across it in the 1890s. Diplomats, missionaries and business people from the Tianjin concessions and the Beijing legations hastily built villas and cottages in order to indulge in the new bathing fad.

The original golf courses, bars and cabarets have disappeared, though there are signs that these will be revived in the interests of the nouvelle bourgeoisie. An article a few years ago in the *People's Daily* suggested: 'It does much good to both body and mind to putt and walk under fresh air'.

Something jars about this place, though the setting is right enough – hills, rocks, beaches, pine forests, a sort of Mediterranean flavour. The buildings appear too heavy to the modern eye, and lacking in glass. Then there's the occasional out-of-place Swiss alpine villa or some columnar structure better suited to Rome or Athens.

But who cares about the architecture? Then, as now, Beidaihe is an escape from the

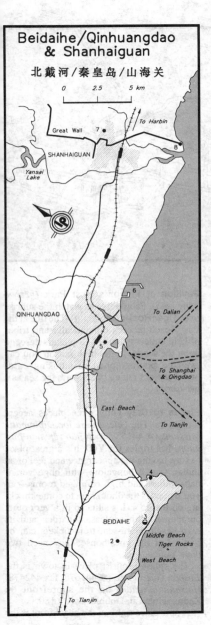

Beidaihe/Qinhuangdao & Shanhaiguan

北戴河/秦皇岛/山海关

0   2.5   5 km

1	Beidaihe Railway Station
2	Lianfengshan Park
3	Bus Station
4	Pigeon's Nest
5	Seamen's Club
6	Oil Wharf
7	First Pass Under Heaven
8	Old Dragon Head

1	北戴河火车站
2	联峰山公园
3	海滨汽车站
4	鸽子窝公园
5	海员俱乐部
6	油港
7	天下第一关
8	老龙头

hassles of Beijing or Tianjin. Kiesslings, the formerly Austrian restaurant, sells excellent pastries and seafood in the summer. The cream of China's leaders congregate at the summer villas, also continuing a tradition – Jiang Qing and Lin Biao had villas here, and Deng Xiaoping is said to have a heavily guarded residence.

Just to make sure nothing nasty comes by in the water, there are shark nets. It's debatable whether sharks live at this latitude – maybe they're submarine nets. Army members and working heroes are rewarded with two-week vacations at Beidaihe. There are many sanatoriums where patients can get away from the noise of the city.

The village comes to life only in the summer (from June to September), when it's warm and fanned by sea breezes and the beaches are jammed. The average June temperature is 21°C (70°F). In January, by contrast, temperatures rest at -5°C (23°F).

Beaches There are three beaches at Beidaihe: West Beach, Middle Beach and East Beach. Rank and ethnic divisions once applied when using these beaches – the West Beach was reserved for foreigners, the

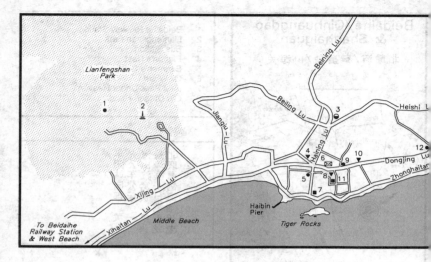

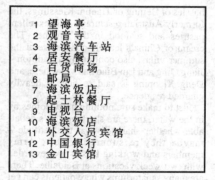

1 望海亭寺
2 观音寺
3 海滨汽车站
4 居安餐厅
5 百货商场
6 邮局
7 海滨饭店
8 起士林餐厅
9 电视台
10 海滨饭店
11 外交人员宾馆
12 中国银行
13 金山宾馆

Middle Beach for Chinese cadres and the like, and the East Beach for sanatorium patients – but this system appears to have been abandoned.

Other Sights There are various hikes to vantage points with expansive views of villas or the coast. Some notable viewing places include the Sea-Viewing Pavilion *(wànghǎi tíng)* at **Lianfengshan Park** *(liánfēngshān gōngyuán)*, about 1½ km north of the beach. Right on the shoreline is the **Eagle**

Pavilion at Pigeon's Nest Park *(gēziwō gōngyuán)*. People like to watch the sunrise over **Tiger Rocks** *(lǎohǔ shí)*. The tide at the East Beach recedes dramatically and tribes of kelp collectors and shell-pickers descend upon the sands. In the high season you can even be photographed in amusing cardboard-cut-out racing boats, with the sea as a backdrop.

Places to Stay Only three places accept foreigners. The *Guesthouse for Diplomatic Missions* (☎ 441587) *(wàijiāo rényuán bīnguǎn)* has triples for Y60. It's a great place to stay, having the appearance and feel of an Indian tourist bungalow with huge verandahs, pillars and high-ceilinged rooms – all you'd need is the dhobi man to come knocking on the door. It's situated in a very quiet compound with a pleasant garden and its own beach. Hard-seat train tickets can be booked at the guesthouse; they need two days' notice.

The splashy tourist place in town is the *Jinshan Guesthouse* (☎ 441678; fax 442478) *(jīnshān bīnguǎn)* on the shorefront on Zhonghaitan Lu. Doubles cost Y180.

A new place right on the beachfront is the

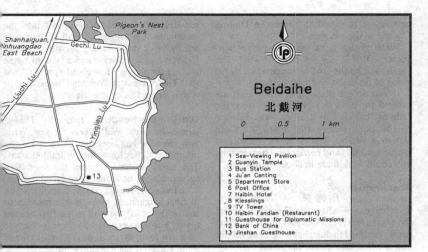

Map legend:
1 Sea-Viewing Pavilion
2 Guanyin Temple
3 Bus Station
4 Ju'an Canting
5 Department Store
6 Post Office
7 Haibin Hotel
8 Kiesslings
9 TV Tower
10 Haibin Fandian (Restaurant)
11 Guesthouse for Diplomatic Missions
12 Bank of China
13 Jinshan Guesthouse

Haibin Hotel (☎ 441373) *(hǎibīn fàndiàn)*. At the time of our visit, it was closed (too early for the season) but will open during summer.

Beidaihe provides a scenic backdrop to money-losing hotels that belong to individual work units. There is an Air Force Hotel, Tangshan Coal Workers' Hotel, National Traffic Bureau Hotel, etc. These hotels are closed to all others and sit empty even during peak season, then suddenly fill to overflowing when the work unit has a meeting in Beidaihe. The exclusive villas are reserved for cadres.

Places to Eat In season, seafood is served in the restaurants. There's the *Beihai Fanzhuang* near the markets and the neighbouring *Ju'an Canting*, which does a mean beef platter *(niúròu tiěbǎn)*. The *Haibin Restaurant* near the Broadcasting Tower is also good.

Near the Guesthouse for Diplomatic Missions is *Kiesslings (qǐshìlín cāntīng)*, which is a relative of the Tianjin branch, only operating from June to August – the bakery is outstanding.

Entertainment There may be some nightlife at the Guesthouse for Diplomatic Missions.

Things to Buy The free market behind the bus terminal has the most amusing high-kitsch collection of sculptured and glued shellwork this side of Dalian – go and see. Handicrafts such as raffia and basketware are on sale in the stores. Some of these shops sell good maps of the area too.

Getting Around There are a couple of short-run buses in Beidaihe, such as the one from the town centre to Pigeon's Nest (in summer only). Much of Beidaihe is small enough to walk around. Minibuses are easy to flag down and you can use them as taxis – negotiate the fare in advance.

There are a couple of bicycle rentals around town; look for rows of bikes. They charge about Y5 per day, and you have to leave a deposit or identification.

Qinhuangdao
(qínhuángdǎo) 秦皇岛
Qinhuangdao is an ugly port city that you'd have to squeeze pretty hard to find tourist attractions in. It has an ice-free harbour, and

petroleum is piped in from the Daqing Oilfield to the wharves.

Water pollution makes the beach a non-starter – this is *not* the place to visit. The locals will be the first to suggest you move along to Beidaihe or Shanhaiguan.

If you do get stuck here, most needs are catered for on a bus No 2 route from the railway station. This runs the short distance to the port, where the Seamen's Club (*hǎiyuán jùlèbù*) has a hotel, restaurant (some seafood) and bar/store. Alternatively, you could walk there in about 15 minutes.

Shanhaiguan

(*shānhǎiguān*) 山海关

Shanhaiguan is where the Great Wall meets the sea. In the 1980s this part of the wall had nearly returned to dust, but it has been rebuilt and is a first-rate tourist drawcard.

Shanhaiguan is a city of considerable charm, and well worth your time. It was a garrison town with a square fortress, four gates at the compass points, and two major avenues running between the gates. The present village is within the substantial remains of the old walled enclosure, making it a picturesque place to wander around. The scenic hills to the north add to the effect. Shanhaiguan has a long and chequered history – nobody is quite sure how long or what kind of chequers – plenty of pitched battles and blood, one would imagine.

First Pass Under Heaven (*tiānxià dìyī guān*) Also known as the East Gate (*dōng-mén*), this magnificent structure is topped with a two-storey, double-roofed tower (Ming Dynasty, rebuilt in 1639). The calligraphy at the top (attributed to the scholar Xiao Xian) reads 'First Pass Under Heaven'. The words reflect the Chinese custom of dividing the world into civilised China and the 'barbarians'. The barbarians got the better of civilised China when they stormed this gate in 1644. An intriguing mini-museum in the tower displays armour, dress, weaponry and pictures. A short section of the wall attached to the East Gate has been rebricked; from this vantage point you can

see decayed sections trailing off into the mountains. On top of the wall at the tower are souvenir shops selling First Pass Under Heaven handkerchiefs, and a parked horse waiting for photos. How about a pair of 'First Pass Under Heaven Wooden Chopsticks' or some 'Brave Lucky Jewellery'?

Old Dragon Head (*lǎo lóng tóu*) This is where the Great Wall meets the sea. What you see now has been reconstructed – the original wall has long since crumbled away. The name is derived from the legendary carved dragon head that once faced the sea. It's a four-km hike or taxi ride from the centre of Shanhaiguan. A more viable route is to follow (by road) the wall to the first beacon tower. You can get part-way there by bicycle on a dirt road, and will pass a small village set in some pleasant countryside.

Yansai Lake (*yànsāi hú*) The lake is also known as Stone River Reservoir (*shíhé shuǐkù*). It's just six km to the north-west of Shanhaiguan. The reservoir is 45 km long and tourists can go boating here. Give them a few years and it could be another Guilin.

Mengjiangnü Temple (*mèngjiāngnǚ miào*) Six km east of Shanhaiguan (with a regular bus service from the South Gate) is the Mengjiangnü Temple, a Song-Ming recon-struction. It has coloured sculptures of Lady Meng and her maids, and calligraphy on Looking for Husband Rock.

Meng's husband, Wan, was press-ganged into wall building because his views conflicted with those of Emperor Qin Shihuang. When winter came the beau-tiful Meng Jiang set off to take her husband warm clothing, only to discover that he had died from the backbreaking labour. Meng tearfully wandered the Great Wall, thinking only of finding Wan's bones to give him a decent burial. The wall, a sensitive soul, was so upset that it collapsed, revealing the skeleton entombed within. Overcome with grief, Meng hurled herself into the sea from a conveniently placed boulder.

Places to Stay The cheapest place to stay is the *North Street Hotel* (*běijiē zhāodàisuǒ*)

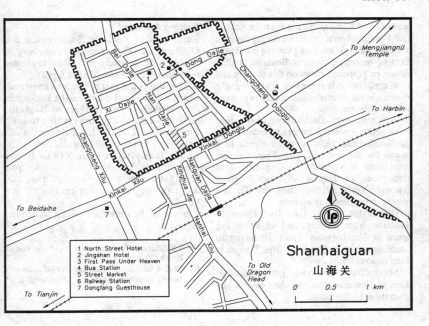

Shanhaiguan
山海关

1 North Street Hotel
2 Jingshan Hotel
3 First Pass Under Heaven
4 Bus Station
5 Street Market
6 Railway Station
7 Dongfang Guesthouse

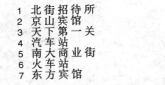

1 北街招待所
2 京山宾馆
3 天下第一关
4 汽车站
5 南大商业街
6 火车站
7 东方宾馆

where doubles are Y50. The spacious rooms come with fans and a private bathroom. The hotel is right near the First Pass Under Heaven (East Gate).

Also in the same neighbourhood is the *Jingshan Hotel* (☎ 551130) (*jīngshān bīnguǎn*), a beautiful place with doubles for Y90 – highly recommended, at least in the off season.

A new place is the *Dongfang Guesthouse* (*dōngfāng bīnguǎn*) on Xinkai Xilu – it's so new that it wasn't yet open during our visit. It's large and nice-looking, but not so attrac-

tive as the other places within the city walls. Still, it's worth considering if your other options are packed out.

Getting There & Away

Air There is an airport at Qinhuangdao, but flights are infrequent – air service is chartered and used mostly by cadres on their way to 'meetings' at the beachside in Beidaihe. There are flights to Beijing (Y200) and Shanghai (Y670).

Train The three stations of Beidaihe, Qinhuangdao and Shanhaiguan are accessible by train from Beijing, Tianjin or Shenyang (Liaoning Province). The trains are frequent but don't always stop at all three stations or always arrive at convenient hours. The usual stop is Shanhaiguan; several trains skip Beidaihe.

One factor to consider is that the hotels at Shanhaiguan are within walking distance of the railway station, whereas at Beidaihe the nearest hotel is at least 10 km from the station. This is no problem if you arrive during daylight or early evening – there are plenty of minibuses meeting incoming trains at Beidaihe station. However, you can't count on this at night and a taxi could be quite expensive. If you're going to arrive in the dead of night, it's better to do so at Shanhaiguan.

Departing from Shanhaiguan also makes some sense – when it comes to ticket sales, the Shanhaiguan railway station should be a model for the rest of China. They've tried something new here – having sufficient employees on duty at all times to meet demand. Not only that, they actually sell tickets rather than say *meiyou*.

The fastest trains take five hours to Beidaihe from Beijing, and an extra 1½ hours to Shanhaiguan. From Shenyang to Shanhaiguan is a five-hour trip. Tianjin is three to four hours away.

Alternatively, you could get a train that stops at Qinhuangdao and then take a bus from there to Beidaihe.

Getting Around

Buses connect Beidaihe, Shanhaiguan and Qinhuangdao. These generally run every 30 minutes from around 6 or 6.30 am to around 6.30 pm (not guaranteed after 6 pm).

Minibuses are faster and less crowded, and can be flagged down easily. But watch out for the minibus drivers at Beidaihe railway station – the drivers like to drop foreigners off at the front door of their hotel for Y15 or so – the regular fare is Y1, so you're paying an extra Y14 to go one more block. To avoid this hassle, pay your fare when everyone else does and don't say anything about getting off at a hotel.

Some of the important public bus routes are:

No 5 Beidaihe railway station to Beidaihe Middle Beach (30 minutes)

Nòs 3 & 4 Beidaihe to Qinhuangdao (45 minutes), then to Shanhaiguan (another 15 minutes)

Beijing 北京

Population: nine million

Beijing: home to stuffy museums and bureaucrats, puffy generals and privileged elitists, host to disgruntled reporters and diplomats; a labyrinth of doors, walls, tunnels, gates and entrances, marked and unmarked. As far away as Ürümqi they run on Beijing's clock; around the country they chortle in *putonghua*, the Beijing dialect; in remote Tibet they struggle to interpret the latest half-baked directives from the capital. In 1983 the Chinese government announced that if the Dalai Lama were to return he'd be posted – where else? – to a desk job in Beijing. This is where they move the cogs and wheels of the Chinese universe, or try to slow them down if they're moving in the wrong direction.

All cities in China are equal, but some are more equal than others. Beijing has the best of everything in China bar the weather: the best food, the best hotels, the best transport, the best temples. But its vast squares and boulevards, its cavernous monoliths, militaristic parades, ubiquitous police, luxury high-rises and armies of tourists may leave you with the impression that Beijing is China's largest theme park. Foreign residents sometimes call it 'the Los Angeles of China' – traffic-choked freeways plus a surreal imitation of Hollywood and Disneyland. It's a fast-changing city – traces of its former character may be found down the back alleys where things are a bit more to human scale.

In 1981 locals gazed in awe at imported colour TV sets displayed behind plate glass at the Beijing Department Store on Wangfujing. In 1983 the same window sported a fashion display direct from Paris. Upstairs in the same store, a Western mannequin modelled a miniskirt and see-through top, nipples clearly visible – the Chinese again stared in awe. Ronald Reagan and the Queen of England have dropped into the neighbourhood; Western rock groups have held jam sessions with their Chinese counterparts nearby. At McDonald's on Wangfujing, the Chinese queue up to buy cheeseburgers – it's just about the only place in China where they queue up. Further up Wangfujing there's a parking problem: cadre limos congregate at the restaurants for evening banquets and there's nowhere to go except up on the footpath. Out on the footpath, street vendors sell everything from steamed bread to rhino horn aphrodisiacs. The hotels around Wangfujing all have discos – young Chinese women dance with Western men, only to be interrogated by the PSB for doing so.

Perhaps nowhere else in China is the generation gap more visible. Appalled by the reforms, many older people still try to defend Chairmen Mao and the years of sacrifice for the socialist revolution. Many young people disdain socialism and are more interested in money, motorbikes, fashion, sex and rock music – not necessarily in that order.

Among the Chinese, Beijing is the promised land. Poor peasants flock to the city in search of the elusive pot of gold at the end of the rainbow – most wind up camped out on the pavement in front of the main railway station. The government tries to encourage them to go home, but the lure of the capital proves too enticing.

Tourists often enjoy Beijing – the city offers plenty to see and do, and you can't beat

589

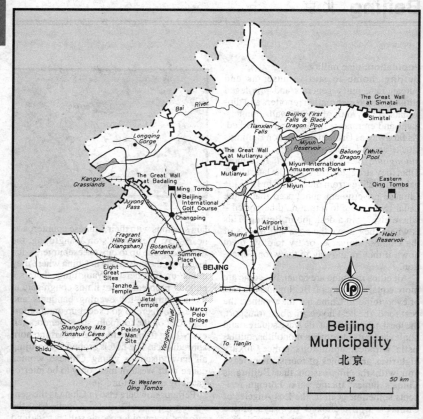

Beijing
Municipality
北京

0   25   50 km

the food or shopping. Those who have slugged it out in hard-seat trains and ramshackle buses through the poverty-stricken interior of China appreciate the creature comforts of Beijing. Other foreigners, having passed their time only in Beijing without seeing the rest of China, come away with the impression that everything is hunky-dory in the PRC and that the Chinese are living high. The Chinese they encounter may, in truth, be doing so.

Group tourists are processed through Beijing in much the same way as the ducks are force-fed on the outlying farms. The two

usually meet on the first night over the dinner table where the phenomenon known as the Jetlag Duck Attack overtakes the unwary traveller. Meanwhile, out in the embassy ghettos long-term foreigners complain that they're losing their Chinese-language skills due to lack of contact.

When the International Olympic Committee came to town to check out Beijing's bid for the 2000 Olympics, locals had their heat and hot water turned off – the government didn't want the Committee to see the pollution caused by burning coal. Street urchins were bussed out of town during the three-day visit; workers were stopped and fined for gobbing on the footpath; streets were cleaned, potholes were patched and squatters' shacks were bulldozed; many were prohibited from driving their vehicles so the Committee would see no traffic jams. For all its seeming liberalism, Beijing keeps an iron fist on its residents.

Whatever impression you come away with, Beijing is not a realistic window on China. It's too much of a cosmetic showcase to qualify. It is, however, a large, relatively clean city, and with a bit of effort you can get out of the make-up department. In between the wide boulevards and militaristic structures are some historical and cultural treasures.

History

Beijing is a time-setter for China, but it actually has a short history as Chinese time spans go. Although the area south-west of the city was inhabited by cave dwellers some 500,000 years ago, the earliest records of settlements date from around 1000 BC. It developed as a frontier trading town for the Mongols, Koreans and tribes from Shandong and central China. By the Warring States Period it had grown to be the capital of the Yan Kingdom and was called Ji, a reference to the marshy features of the area. The town underwent a number of changes as it acquired new warlords, the Khitan Mongols and the Manchurian Jurchen tribes among them. What attracted the conquerors was the strategic position of the town on the edge of the North China Plain. During the Liao Dynasty Beijing was referred to as Yanjing (capital of Yan), still the name used for Beijing's most popular beer.

Beijing's history really gets under way in 1215 AD, the year that Genghis Khan burned all that had gone before him and slaughtered everything in sight. From the ashes emerged Dadu (Great Capital), alias Khanbaliq, the Khan's town. By 1279 Genghis's grandson Kublai had made himself ruler of most of Asia, and Khanbaliq was his capital. Until this time, attempts at unifying China had been centred around Luoyang and Chang'an

(Xi'an). With a lull in the fighting from 1280 to 1300, foreigners managed to drop in along the Silk Road for tea with the Great Khan – Marco Polo even landed a job.

The Mongol emperor was informed by his astrologers that the old city site of Beijing was a breeding ground for rebels, so he shifted it slightly north. The great palace he built no longer remains, but here is Polo's description:

Within these walls...stands the palace of the Great Khan, the most extensive that has ever yet been known...The sides of the great halls are adorned with dragons in carved work and gold, figures of warriors, of birds and of beasts...On each of the four sides of the palace there is a grand flight of marble steps...The new city is of a form perfectly square...each of its sides being six miles. It is enclosed with walls of earth...the wall of the city has twelve gates. The multitude of inhabitants, and the number of houses in the city of Kanbalu, as also in the suburbs outside the city, of which there are twelve, corresponding to the twelve gates, is greater than the mind can comprehend.

Oddly enough, Polo's description could well have been applied to the later Ming city; the lavish lifestyle of the great Khan set the trend for the Ming emperors. Polo goes on to recount what happened on Tartar New Year's Day:

On this occasion, great numbers of beautiful white horses are presented to the Great Khan...all his elephants, amounting to five thousand, are exhibited in the procession, covered with housings of cloth, richly worked with gold and silk.

Polo was equally dazzled by the innovations of gunpowder and paper money. These were not without their drawbacks. In history's first case of paper-currency inflation the last Mongol emperor flooded the country with worthless bills. This, coupled with a large number of natural disasters, provoked an uprising led by the mercenary Zhu Yanhang, who took Beijing in 1368 and ushered in the Ming Dynasty. The city was renamed Beiping (Northern Peace) and for the next 35 years the capital was shifted to Nanjing. To this day the Kuomintang regime on Taiwan refers to Beijing as 'Beiping' and recognises Nanjing as the capital.

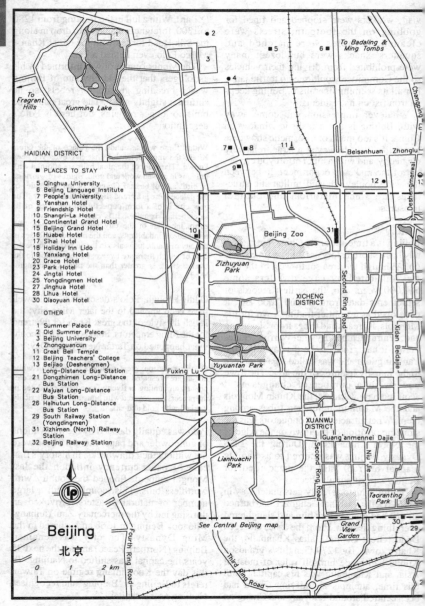

To Badaling & Ming Tombs

Changping Lu

To Fragrant Hills

Kunming Lake

HAIDIAN DISTRICT

Beisanhuan Zhonglu

Deshengmenwai

■ PLACES TO STAY

5 Qinghua University
6 Beijing Language Institute
7 People's University
8 Yanshan Hotel
9 Friendship Hotel
10 Shangri-La Hotel
14 Continental Grand Hotel
15 Beijing Grand Hotel
16 Huabei Hotel
17 Sihai Hotel
18 Holiday Inn Lido
19 Yanxiang Hotel
20 Grace Hotel
23 Park Hotel
24 Jingtai Hotel
25 Yongdingmen Hotel
27 Jinghua Hotel
28 Lihua Hotel
30 Qiaoyuan Hotel

OTHER

1 Summer Palace
2 Old Summer Palace
3 Beijing University
4 Zhongguancun
11 Great Bell Temple
12 Beijing Teachers' College
13 Beijiao (Deshengmen)
    Long-Distance Bus Station
21 Dongzhimen Long-Distance
    Bus Station
22 Majuan Long-Distance
    Bus Station
26 Haihutun Long-Distance
    Bus Station
29 South Railway Station
    (Yongdingmen)
31 Xizhimen (North) Railway
    Station
32 Beijing Railway Station

Beijing Zoo

Zizhuyuan Park

XICHENG DISTRICT

Second Ring Road

Xidan Beidajie

Fuxing Lu

Yuyuantan Park

XUANWU DISTRICT

Guang'anmennei Dajie

Niu Jie

Lianhuachi Park

Second Ring Road

Taoranting Park

See Central Beijing map

Grand View Garden

Beijing
北京

0   1   2 km

Fourth Ring Road

Third Ring Road

30
29

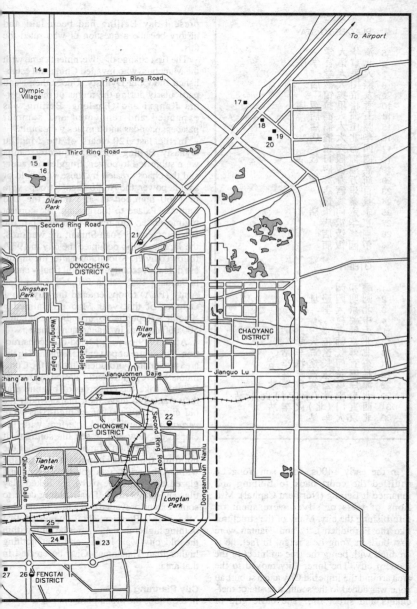

To Airport

Fourth Ring Road

Olympic
Village

14

17

18

19

20

Third Ring Road

15

16

Ditan
Park

Second Ring Road

21

DONGCHENG
DISTRICT

Jingshan
Park

Wangfujing Dajie

Dongsi Beidajie

Ritan
Park

CHAOYANG
DISTRICT

Chang'an Jie

Jianguomen Dajie

Jianguo Lu

32

22

CHONGWEN
DISTRICT

Second Ring Road

Dongsanhuan Nanlu

Qianmen Dajie

Tiantan
Park

Longtan
Park

25

24

23

27

26

FENGTAI
DISTRICT

■ PLACES TO STAY

5 清华大学
6 北京语言学院
7 人民大学
8 燕山大酒店
9 友谊宾馆
10 香格里拉饭店
14 五洲大酒店
15 圆山大酒店
16 华北宾馆
17 四海宾馆
18 丽都假日饭店
19 燕翔饭店
20 新万寿宾馆
23 百乐酒店
24 景泰宾馆
25 永定门饭店
27 京华饭店
28 丽华饭店
30 侨园饭店

OTHER

1 颐和园
2 圆明园遗址
3 北京大学
4 中关村
11 大钟寺
12 北京师范大学
13 北郊长途汽车站
21 东直门长途汽车站
22 马圈长途汽车站
26 海户屯公共汽车站
29 北京南站/永定门火车站
31 西直门(北)火车站
32 北京火车站

In the early 1400s Zhu's son Yong Le shuffled the court back to Beiping and renamed it Beijing (Northern Capital). Millions of taels of silver were spent on refurbishing the city. Many of the structures like the Forbidden City and Tiantan were first built in Yong Le's reign. In fact, he is credited with being the true architect of the modern city. The Inner City moved to the area around the Imperial City and a suburban zone was added to the south, a bustle of merchants and street life. The basic grid of present-day Beijing had been laid and history became a question of who ruled the turf.

The first change of government came with the Manchus, who invaded China and established the Qing Dynasty. Under them, and particularly during the reigns of the emperors Kangxi and Qianlong, Beijing was expanded and renovated and summer palaces, pagodas and temples were built.

In the last 120 years of the Manchu Dynasty Beijing and subsequently China were subjected to power struggles, invaders and the chaos created by those who held or sought power: the Anglo-French troops who in 1860 marched in and burnt the Old Summer Palace to the ground; the corrupt regime under Empress Dowager Cixi; the Boxers; General Yuan Shikai; the warlords; the Japanese who occupied the city in 1937; followed by the Kuomintang after the Japanese defeat. A century of turmoil finally ended in January 1949 when People's Liberation Army (PLA) troops entered the city. On 1 October of that year Mao proclaimed a 'People's Republic' to an audience of some 500,000 citizens in Tiananmen Square.

After 1949 came a period of reconstruction. The centre of power has remained in the area around the Forbidden City, but the Communists have significantly altered the face of Beijing. Like the emperors of bygone eras they wanted to leave their mark. Under the old city-planning schemes high-rises were *verboten* – they would interfere with the emperor's view and lessen his sunlight. It was also a question of rank – the higher the building the more important the person within. The aristocrats got decorations and glazed tiling and the plebs got baked clay tiles and grey bricks. This building code to some extent prevailed over the 'house that Mao built'. Premier Zhou suggested that nothing higher than 45 metres be built within the old city wall limits, and that nothing higher than Tiananmen Gate be erected in that area.

City Planning
In the 1950s the urban planners got to work.

Down came the commemorative arches, and blocks of buildings were reduced to rubble to widen Chang'an Jie and Tiananmen Square. From 1950 to 1952 the outer walls were levelled in the interests of traffic circulation. Soviet experts and technicians poured in, which may explain the Stalinesque features on the public structures that went up. Meanwhile industry, negligible in Beijing until this time, was rapidly expanded. Textiles, iron and steel, petrochemicals and machine-making plants were set up and Beijing became a major industrial city with pollution to match. The situation was exacerbated by the fact that most of the city's greenery had been ripped up. Five and six-storey housing blocks went up at a brisk pace but construction was of poor quality and it still didn't keep pace with the population boom. Agricultural communes were established on the city outskirts to feed the influx of people.

In 1982 the Central Committee of the Party adopted a new urban construction programme for Beijing, a revised version of the 1950s one. They faced tremendous challenges. On the one hand they wanted to continue the building of new roads and the widening of old streets; on the other hand they wanted to preserve the character of the old city and the historical sites. The population of the Beijing area, already well over nine million, is to be limited to 10 million by the year 2000, with four million in the metropolis, 2½ million in satellite towns and 3½ million in farming areas. Many new residential zones are being constructed in 12- to 16-storey blocks, but supply never meets demand and the standard of building is shoddy. In some cases the water pressure does not go above the 3rd storey, and there are usually no lifts (or sufficient electricity to run them).

The plan calls for a limit to industrial construction, a halt to the growth of heavy industry and a shift to self-sufficient food production in the outlying counties. For the moment the self-sufficiency programme appears to be working, with extended use of greenhouses for the winter months. Another major priority shift is environmental. A massive tree-planting campaign is under way which aims to turn some 50% of the metropolitan area into recreational zones. This, however, will mean less farmland and the mushrooming of buildings in satellite locations.

Small businesses, once the mainstay of Beijing's economy, have re-emerged after having been almost wiped out in the rush to collectivise. To solve a huge unemployment problem the government has offered incentives for the self-employed such as tax exemptions and loans. Those with initiative are faring better than average; some earn incomes above Y500 a month, and privately run repair services such as those for bicycles, shoes and watches now outnumber state and collective-owned ones in Beijing.

Climate

The city is not blessed with congenial weather. Autumn (from September to October) is the best time to visit: there's little rain, it's neither dry nor humid, and the city wears a pleasant cloak of foliage. Winter can be interesting if you don't mind the cold; although the temperature can dip as far as -20°C and can freeze your butt off, parts of the capital appear charming in this season. The subdued winter lighting makes the place very photogenic – the cold, dry air makes for good visibility. Winter clothing is readily available – the locals wear about 15 layers. If the wind races down the wide boulevards like Chang'an there's a particularly nasty wind-chill factor. Spring is short, dry and dusty. From April to May a phenomenon known as 'yellow wind' plagues the capital – fine dust particles blown from the Gobi Desert in the north-west sandpaper everything in sight, including your face. The locals go around with mesh bags over their heads. In the 1950s the government ordered the extermination of the city's birds, which led to an insect population boom. They then ordered the insects' habitats (grass and other greens) to be dug up, which led to even more dust being set loose. In summer (June, July and August) the average temperature is 26°C

– very hot – and there's sticky humidity with heavy rains and mosquitoes in July.

Orientation

The city limits of Beijing extend some 80 km, including the urban, the suburban, and the nine counties under its administration. With a total area of 16,800 sq km, Beijing municipality is roughly the size of Belgium.

Though it may not appear so to the visitor in the shambles of arrival, Beijing has a very orderly design. Long, straight boulevards and avenues are crisscrossed by a network of lanes. Places of interest are either very easy to find if they're on the avenues, or impossible to find if they're buried down the narrow alleys *(hútòng)*.

This section refers to the chessboard of the central core, once a walled enclosure. The symmetry folds on an ancient north-south axis passing through Qianmen (Front Gate). The major east-west road is Chang'an Jie (Avenue of Eternal Tranquillity).

As for the street names: Chongwenmen-wai Dajie means 'the avenue (dajie) outside (wai) Chongwen Gate (Chongwenmen)'; whereas Chongwenmennei Dajie means 'the avenue inside Chongwen Gate' (that is, inside the old wall). It's an academic exercise since the gate and the wall in question no longer exist.

Streets are also split along compass points: Dongdajie (East Avenue), Xidajie (West Avenue), Beidajie (North Avenue) and Nandajie (South Avenue). These streets head off from an intersection, usually where a gate once stood.

A major boulevard can change names six or eight times along its length, so intersections become important. The buses are also routed through these points. It therefore pays to study your gates and intersections, and familiarise yourself with the high-rise buildings (often hotels) which serve as useful landmarks to gauge your progress along the chessboard. Other streets are named after bridges, also long gone, like the Bridge of Heaven (Tianqiao), and after features such as old temples which are still there.

Officially, there are three 'ring roads' around Beijing, circumnavigating the city centre in three concentric circles. The first (innermost) ring road is really a joke – just part of the grid around the Forbidden City. However, the second ring road *(èrhuán)* and third *(sānhuán)* should be taken seriously – they're multi-lane freeways which serve as rapid transit corridors (by taxi) if you avoid rush hour. Construction of a fourth ring road *(sìhuán)* is underway.

In imperial days Beijing's parks were laid out at the compass-points: west of the Forbidden City lies Yuetan Park, north lies Ditan, south lies Taoranting and east is Ritan. South-east of the Forbidden City is the showpiece of them all, Tiantan Park.

Information

CITS The main travel office is at the Beijing Tourist Building (☎ 5158570; fax 5158603), 28 Jianguomenwai Dajie, buried behind the New Otani Hotel near the Friendship Store. The other important branch office is in the Beijing International Hotel (☎ 5120509; fax 5120503), north of the railway station at 9 Jianguomennei Dajie. There are many other smaller branch offices in some of the large hotels – these plug Great Wall tours and do not offer the full range of CITS services.

Overall, Beijing CITS deserves honourable mention for being one of the *worst* in China. On the one hand, Beijing CITS can come in handy for booking air tickets, theatre tickets and possibly some day tours like the Underground City. On the other hand, the service charges for just about everything else border on the absurd. Even worse is the tendency of CITS staff to sell scarce railway tickets out the back door to their friends and relatives who are professional ticket scalpers. This particularly applies to the Trans-Siberian trains – getting a ticket (or even a straight answer) from this office is like pulling teeth. For domestic trains don't even waste your time with CITS, but go directly to the Foreigners' Booking Office in the main railway station. Ditto for flights – you'll do better by going directly to the airlines. Bookings for the Shanghai-Hong Kong ferry cannot be made at Beijing CITS;

you have to telephone Shanghai to make the reservation.

To be fair, within this sea of avarice are a few shining islands of honesty and competence. Unfortunately, the rare CITS employees who sincerely try to offer friendly service at fair prices are rewarded with a transfer – possible venues include the Gobi Desert or an oil drilling platform in the South China Sea.

There is an English-speaking 24-hour Beijing Tourism Hotline (☎ 5130828). This service can answer questions and listens to complaints.

PSB This (☎ 5122471) is at 85 Beichizi Dajie, the street running north-south at the eastern side of the Forbidden City. It's open Monday to Friday from 8.30 to 11.30 am and 1 to 5 pm, and on Saturday from 8.30 to 11.30 am; it's closed on Sunday.

Money – Warning! If you attempt to transact black-market exchanges with the young men who solicit you on the street, you will *certainly* be ripped off. We had similar warnings in the previous edition of this book, but it seems our advice was not heeded, so we are strengthening the warning here. Repeat – these guys are not moneychangers, they are *thieves*, and dangerous thieves at that. Just outside the Qiaoyuan and Longtan hotels are gangs of the slimiest low-life in Beijing. Both customers and 'moneychangers' have been beaten. Shortly before we went to press, a gang member outside the Qiaoyuan Hotel was beaten to within an inch of his life by some foreigners who had been ripped off, but this has only made the gang meaner. Now knives are flashed – that no-one has been killed here (yet) is a miracle. The police don't want to be involved – they are too busy fighting counter-revolutionary students and accepting bribes from street vendors.

So a word of caution – if you must change money on the black market (and let's face it, most budget travellers do), then there are two cardinal rules you must obey. The first is to change only with women – they could short-change you, but there have been no reports

yet of female gangs flashing knives and beating customers. Second, change only with someone who is indoors – in a shop, street stall, etc. People who run businesses in a fixed location have their reputation to uphold and can't run away, but mobile street operators have no such concerns.

As for legal money-changing, all hotels – even most budget ones – can change travellers' cheques or US dollars cash.

If you want to cash travellers' cheques and receive US dollars cash in return (necessary if you're going to Russia or Mongolia), this can be done at CITIC, International Building *(guójì dàshà)*, 19 Jianguomenwai Dajie adjacent to the Friendship Store. Other major currencies (eg Hong Kong dollars, Japanese Yen) are available here. CITIC will advance cash on major international credit cards. There is a useful branch of the Bank of China on Dong'anmen Dajie – just to the east of the Forbidden City in Wangfujing near the Foreign Languages Bookstore – which offers many of the same services as CITIC but isn't as friendly.

Post & Telecommunications The international post & telecommunications building is on Jianguomen Beidajie, not far from the Friendship Store. It's open from 8 am to 7 pm. All letters and parcels marked 'Poste Restante, GPO Beijing' will wind up here. The staff even file poste-restante letters in alphabetical order, a rare occurrence in China, but you pay for all this efficiency – there is a Y1 fee charged for each letter received! Overseas parcels must be posted here; a counter sells wrapping paper, string, tape and glue. There's also an international telegraph and telephone service.

There is a small but convenient post office in the CITIC building. Another useful post office is in the basement of the China World Trade Centre.

Most of the tourist hotels sell stamps and some even have 'mini' post offices. You can send overseas packages from these as long as they contain printed matter only.

United Parcel Service (☎ 4994100, 4672278), or UPS, has several service centres for posting express documents and parcels abroad. Most convenient is their office on the ground floor of the Scite Tower on Jianguomenwai (opposite CITIC building). An express service is also offered by DHL (☎ 4662211), Federal Express (☎ 5011017) and TNT Skypak (☎ 4652227).

The Telegraph Building is open 24 hours a day on Xichang'an Jie. Further west on Fuxingmennei Dajie is the International Telephone Office, open daily from 7 am to midnight. However, most of your telecommunication needs can be met at large hotels.

Maps English-language maps of Beijing are handed out for free at the big hotels. They're often part of an advertising supplement for various companies whose locations are, of course, also shown on the map. These maps usually have no Chinese characters but are still very useful for getting around.

It's better to fork out a few RMB for a bilingual map which shows bus routes. These are available from the Friendship Store and hotel gift shops.

If you can deal with Chinese character maps, you'll find a wide variety to choose from. It's impossible for us to say which one is best because new editions printed by different companies are issued every couple of months – this new free-market competition in the map-making business has certainly improved quality. Street vendors hawk these maps near the subway stations, entrances to parks and other likely places.

The *Beijing Shiqutu* is a huge wall map in Chinese, probably the best map available of the city. It's great for decorating your wall, but isn't convenient to carry around on the street.

If you want fine detail in portable form, the best solution is to an atlas. The *Beijing Street Directory & Map (běijīng shìqū xiángtú)* is excellent – everything is in English and Chinese. This is available from the Foreign Languages Bookstore. The Xinhua Bookstore on Wangfujing Dajie sells an even more detailed atlas called *Beijing Shenghuo Dituce*, but this one is in Chinese characters only.

All maps of Beijing which are published in China use the simplified characters. If you have a fondness for the traditional form, buy a Beijing map in Hong Kong.

Embassies Beijing is not a bad place to stock up on visas. You may also need to visit your embassy to replace a stolen or soon-to-expire passport. These bureaucratic quests can sometimes be accomplished in other Chinese cities – there are US, Australian, UK, Czech, French, German, Hungarian, Italian, Japanese, Polish, Russian and Singaporean consulates in Shanghai. There are also US, Japanese, Polish and Thai consulates in Canton, and a US consulate in Shenyang. See the chapters on those cities for details.

In Beijing there are two main embassy compounds: Jianguomenwai and Sanlitun (see the relevant maps under the Visas & Embassies section in the Facts for the Visitor chapter). For a complete list of embassies in Beijing with addresses and phone numbers, see the Facts for the Visitor chapter at the beginning of this book. A visit to embassyland is a trip in itself – sentry boxes with Chinese soldiers, fancy residences for the diplomats and fancy stores, restaurants, discos and nightclubs for entertainment.

The Jianguomenwai Compound is in the vicinity of the Friendship Store. The Sanlitun Compound is several km to the north-east, near the Great Wall Sheraton Hotel.

Visa photos can be obtained from a number of sources – quickest is probably the photo booth in the CITIC building next to the Friendship Store. More professional passport photos can be processed at the photo shops on Wangfujing Dajie.

Medical Services The Sino-German Policlinic (☎ 5011983) *(zhōngdé zhěnsuǒ)* has Western-trained doctors and is one of the most popular medical clinics with foreigners. Emergency service is available 24 hours a day, but there are regular office hours and it's often a good idea to call first for an appointment – the staff speak good English. This clinic is a good place to get those odd vaccinations like rabies and hepatitis B, and dental service is also available. The clinic is downstairs in Landmark Tower B-1, adjacent to the Sheraton Great Wall Hotel.

Beijing Union Medical College (xiéhé yīyuàn) has a 24-hour emergency room (☎ 5127733 ext 217) (jízhěn shì) and a foreigners' clinic (☎ 5127733 ext 251) (wàishìbàn gōng shì). The address is 1 Shifuyuan, Wangfujing.

There is a foreigners' clinic at the Friendship Hospital (☎ 4221122) (yǒuyí yīyuàn), 95 Yongan Lu. The hospital is on the west side of Tiantan Park in the Tianqiao area. Normal outpatient business hours are from 8 to 11.30 am and from 2.30 to 5 pm.

Asia Emergency Assistance is for those really big emergencies. The service is not cheap, but this place can even dispatch a small aircraft to evacuate injured persons from remote areas. There are several branch offices – the Beijing Alarm Centre (☎ 5053521; fax 5053526) is in room 1010 of the China World Trade Centre (guómào dàshà) at 1 Jianguomenwai. The Hong Kong Alarm Centre (☎ (852) 8107881; fax 8450395) can also be contacted for medical evacuation services. The service is available 24 hours a day.

Warning – Police Beijing is the most xenophobic of all Chinese cities. While the Beijing PSB doesn't necessarily look to cause trouble with foreigners, they can and will create international incidents over trivial nonsense if you cross them. Avoiding trouble is usually straightforward, if you understand what the rules are.

The most important rule is that Western men cannot 'insult' Chinese women – 'insult' seems to be a Chinese idiom for 'have sex with'. Actually, it's not even necessary to actually touch the woman – just the appearance of being 'too intimate' can lead to problems. If a Western man rides in a taxi with a Chinese woman, there is a good chance that the taxi will be pulled over, ID cards checked and, if the woman is a Chinese national, the woman will probably be arrested and the man may have his passport

confiscated. We personally know one Westerner who was beaten by the police when he tried to prevent them from hauling away his girlfriend, who in fact was a Hong Kong Chinese. Because the society is very male-oriented, Western women getting involved with Chinese men is viewed far less seriously and seldom causes problems with the PSB.

Beijing has far more police than you at first realise – most are dressed in plain clothes. One of the prime duties of the plain-clothes PSB is to follow journalists talk to. There are also video cameras placed at strategic locations all over Beijing – you can spot them up in the trees along major boulevards. The video tapes were used as evidence to prosecute student activists and sympathisers after the 1989 protests at Tiananmen Square.

There are also civilian 'snitch squads' who watch foreigners and report suspicious activities to the police. This has led to some spectacular blunders:

The police receive a tip – a Western man has a Chinese woman in his hotel room. At 3 am the hotel staff unlock the door of the Westerner's room without knocking and the police barge in. Acting with as much diplomacy as a bull in a China shop, the cops drag the naked couple out of bed – the man is totally bewildered and the woman is screaming hysterically while trying to cover her nude body. Then the police discover she's Japanese, not Chinese – they leave without offering any explanation or apology. As it turns out, the two are married.

On the other hand, there is no reason to be overly paranoid. Foreign men can talk to Chinese women in public places like restaurants, buses or on the street without fear. Most Beijingers are friendly – however, they dare not be 'too friendly'.

Admission Fees Beijing has recently adopted a poorly thought-out policy regarding the admission fees which foreigners are charged for parks, scenic spots, etc. This is now causing big headaches for travellers, so it's something you need to be aware of.

To understand the new policy, you need to realise that in many parks, museums and

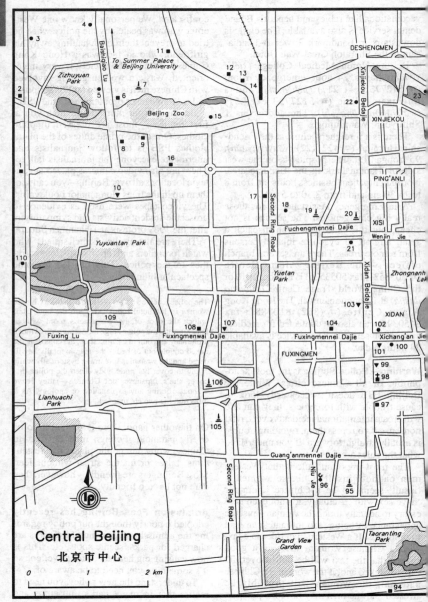

Central Beijing
北京市中心

0   1   2 km

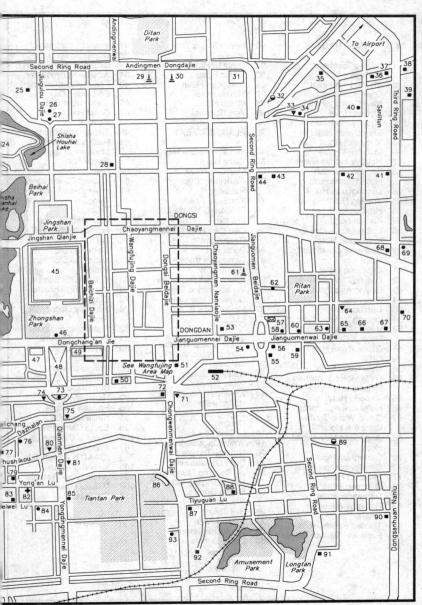

Ditan Park

Second Ring Road

Andingmenwai

Jugulou Dajie

Andingmen Dongdajie

To Airport

25 ■

26 ■
27 ●

Shisha
Houhai
Lake

24

Beihai
Park

Shisha
anhai
ke

Jingshan
Park

Jingshan Qianjie

45

Zhongshan
Park

46 ●

Dongchang'an Jie

47

48

49

74
73

75

lichang

Dazhalan

77

76 ●

80

hushikou

79

Yong'an Lu

83
82

eiwei Lu

84 ●

85

Tiantan Park

Qianmen Dajie

81

Yongdingmennei Dajie

DONGSI

Chaoyangmennei   Dajie

Wangfujing Dajie

Beichizi Dajie

Dongsi Beidajie

Chaoyangmen Nanxiaojie

Jianguomen Beidajie

Second Ring Road

29 ⟂   ⟂ 30   31

32

33 ▼ ● 34

35

36 ■ 37

38

39

Third Ring Road

Sanlitun

40 ●

43 ■
44 ■

42 ■   41 ■

68 ■
69 ●

61 ⟂

62 ■

Ritan
Park

64 ▼

65 ■ 66 ■ 67 ■

70 ■

DONGDAN

53 ●

Jianguomennei Dajie

54 ●

57
58 ▼

⊠ 60 ● 63 ●

56 ■
55 ■ 59 ■

Jianguomenwai Dajie

See Wangfujing
Area Map   51 ■

50 ■   72

52

71 ▼

Chongwenmennai Dajie

89

86

88 ■

Tiyuguan Lu

87 ●

93 ●

92 ■

Amusement
Park

Longtan
Park

91 ■

90 ■

Dongbinhe Nan

Second Ring Road

■ PLACES TO STAY

1 Beijing Teachers' College
2 Shangri La Hotel
6 Olympic Hotel
8 New Century Hotel
9 Xiyuan Hotel
11 Zhongyuan Hotel
12 Shangyuan Hotel
13 Xizhimen Hotel
16 Mandarin Hotel
17 Holiday Inn Downtown
25 Bamboo Garden Hotel/Restaurant
28 Lůsongyuan Hotel
35 Yuyang Hotel
36 Huadu Hotel
37 Kunlun hotel
38 Lufthansa Centre & Kempinski Hotel
39 Sheraton Great Wall Hotel
41 Zhaolong Hotel
42 Chains City Hotel
43 Beijing Asia Hotel
44 Swissotel
50 Capital Hotel
51 Jinlang Hotel
53 Beijing International Hotel & CITS
55 Gloria Plaza Hotel & CITS
56 New Otani Hotel
59 CVIK Hotel & Yaohan Department Store
65 Jianguo Hotel
66 Hotel BeijingToronto
67 China World Trade Centre & Hotel
68 Jingguang New World Hotel
70 Guanghua Hotel
72 Chongwenmen Hotel
77 Far East Hotel
78 Qianmen Hotel
79 Dongfang Hotel
83 Rainbow & Beiwei hotels
87 Tiantan Sports Hotel
88 Parkview Tiantan Hotel

90 Leyou & Hua Thai hotels
91 Longtan Hotel
92 Traffic Hotel
94 Qiaoyuan Hotel
97 Yuexiu Hotel
104 Minzu Hotel
108 Yanjing Hotel

▼ PLACES TO EAT

10 Muslim Restaurants
33 Pizza Hut
64 Mexican Wave
71 Bianyifang Duck Restaurant
74 Kentucky Fried Chicken & Vie de France
75 Qianmen Roast Duck Restaurant
80 Pizza Hut
81 Gongdelin Vegetarian Restaurant
99 Kaorouwan Restaurant
101 Vie de France Bakery
103 Quyuan Restaurant
107 McDonald's II

OTHER

3 China Grand Theatre
4 Central Nationalities Institute
5 National Library
7 Wuta Temple
14 Xizhimen (North) Railway Station
15 Beijing Exhibition Centre
18 Lu Xun Museum
19 White Dagoba Temple
20 Guangji Temple
21 Dizhi Cinema Hall
22 Xu Beihong Museum
23 Song Qingling Museum
24 Prince Gong's Residence
26 Bell Tower
27 Drum Tower
29 Confucius Temple
30 Lama Temple

31 Russian Embassy
32 Dongzhimen Long-Distance Bus Station
34 Australian Embassy
40 Friendship Supermarket
45 Forbidden City
46 Tiananmen Gate
47 Great Hall of the People
48 Tiananmen Square
49 History Museum & Museum of the Revolution
52 Beijing Railway Station
54 Ancient Observatory
57 International Post & Telecommunications Office
58 International Club
60 Friendship Store & CITIC
61 Black Temple
62 Yabao Lu Clothing Market
63 Xiushui Silk Market
69 Chaoyang Theatre
73 Qianmen
76 Sun City Department Store
82 Friendship Hospital
84 Tianqiao Theatre
85 Natural History Museum
86 Hongqiao Market
89 Majuan Long-Distance Bus Station
93 Harmony Club
95 Fayuan Temple
96 Niujie Mosque
98 South Cathedral
100 Shoudu Cinema
102 Aviation Building (CAAC & Airport Bus)
105 Tianning Temple
106 White Cloud Temple
109 Military Museum
110 TV Tower

85	自然博物馆
86	红桥商场
89	马圈长途汽车站
93	幸福俱乐部
95	法源寺
96	牛街礼拜寺
98	南堂
100	首都电影院
102	民航营业大厦
105	天宁寺
106	白云观
109	军事博物馆
110	电视台

other tourist sites (the Forbidden City being a good example) there are numerous halls and pavilions within the compound, and each one has its own admission gate charging separate fees. The locals have the option of buying a general admission ticket for the compound and then buying separate tickets for each pavilion, or just one high-priced all-inclusive ticket which grants admission to every pavilion. For foreigners, the first option is eliminated – the staff want you to buy the all-inclusive ticket, whether you want it or not. This usually works out to be much more expensive than buying separate tickets, especially if you don't want to visit each and every building, pavilion and chamber.

Even more irritating is the fact that you might not want to visit *any* buildings, even though you're paying to do so. Tiantan Park, for example, is a mellow place you could visit every morning just to go jogging, do taiji exercises, watch the children play or whatever. It's unlikely that you'll want to tour the park's pavilions every morning – but as soon as the staff see your foreign face, they want you to buy the all-inclusive tourist ticket which costs over 10 times as much as the general admission ticket for the park.

The goal of the new pricing policy is supposed to be 'convenience' – it's assumed that foreigners would prefer to buy just one ticket rather than many separate ones. Perhaps it is convenient, but it leads to arguments with the ticket-booth staff – like with FEC, those who invented this idiotic scheme gave no thought to the likely results.

At most (but not all) places it's optional – you can buy the general admission ticket rather than the expensive all-inclusive tourist ticket. This is true for Beihai Park, for example, but at the Summer Palace you don't have the option. At some parks where you have a choice of two tickets, making your wishes known to the staff can be a problem if you don't speak Chinese. Many foreigners become exceedingly upset when they realise they've overpaid by 10 times for a ticket when it wasn't necessary – the bitter arguments that sometimes ensue haven't helped Beijing's image in the eyes of foreign tourists.

It's useful to know the correct vocabulary. The all-inclusive tickets are *tàopiào* in Chinese. The general admission tickets are called 'door tickets' *(ménpiào)* or 'common tickets' *(pǔtōngpiào)*.

Tiananmen Square
(tiān'ānmén guǎngchǎng)
天安门广场

Although it was a gathering place and the location of government offices in the imperial days, the square is Mao's creation, as is Chang'an Jie leading to it. This is the heart of Beijing, a vast desert of paving and photobooths. The last major rallies took place here during the Cultural Revolution when Mao, wearing a Red Guard armband, reviewed parades of up to a million people. In 1976 another million people jammed the square to pay their last respects to him. In 1989, army tanks and soldiers cut down pro-democracy demonstrators here. Today the square is a place, if the weather is conducive, for people to lounge around in the evening and to fly decorated kites and balloons for the kiddies. Surrounding or studding the square are a strange mish-mash of monuments past and present: Tiananmen (Gate of Heavenly Peace), the History Museum & Museum of the Revolution, the Great Hall of the People, Qianmen (Front Gate), the Mao Mausoleum and the Monument to the People's Heroes.

If you get up early you can watch the flag-raising ceremony at sunrise, performed by a troop of PLA soldiers drilled to march at precisely 108 paces per minute, 75 cm per pace. The same ceremony in reverse gets performed at sunset, but you can hardly see the soldiers from the throngs gathered to watch.

Tiananmen Gate
(tiān'ānmén) 天安门
Tiananmen, or 'Gate of Heavenly Peace', is a national symbol which pops up on everything from airline tickets to policemen's caps. The gate was built in the 15th century and restored in the 17th. From imperial days it functioned as a rostrum for dealing with or proclaiming to the assembled masses. There are five doors to the gate, and in front of it are seven bridges spanning a stream. Each of these bridges was restricted in its use, and only the emperor could use the central door and bridge.

It was from the gate that Mao proclaimed the People's Republic on 1 October 1949, and there have been a few alterations since then. The dominating feature is the gigantic portrait of Mao, the required backdrop for any photo the Chinese take of themselves at the gate (whether they like him or not). To the left of the portrait is a slogan 'Long Live the People's Republic of China' and to the right 'Long Live the Unity of the Peoples of the World'. The grandstands are used for major reviews and can seat 20,000.

Photography is big at Tiananmen – the Chinese aspire to visit the heart of the nation almost like the Muslims aspire to visit Mecca, and Chinese schoolkids grow up singing 'I Love Tiananmen Beijing'.

You pass through Tiananmen Gate on your way into the Forbidden City (assuming you enter from the south side). There is no fee for walking through the gate, but to go upstairs and look down on the square costs a whopping Y30 for foreigners, Y10 for Chinese. It's hardly worth it – you can get a similar view of the square from inside Qianmen Gate for a fraction of the price.

Qianmen
(qiánmén) 前门
Silent sentinel to the changing times, Qianmen (Front Gate) sits on the south side of Tiananmen Square. The gate was not built as an entrance to the square or Mao Zedong's nearby mausoleum – it's one of the few old gates left with a much longer history than the preceding. Qianmen guarded the wall division between the ancient Inner City and the outer suburban zone, and dates back to the reign of Emperor Yong Le in the 15th century. With the disappearance of the city walls, the gate sits out of context, but it's still an impressive sight and a great landmark to get around by.

Qianmen actually consists of two gates. The southern one is called Arrow Tower *(jiàn lóu)* and the rear one is Zhongyang Gate *(zhōngyángmén*, also called *chéng lóu)*. You can go upstairs into Zhongyang Gate; it's certainly worth the Y2 admission price. There are plans to open the Arrow Tower to visitors, but at the time of writing it still hadn't happened.

Great Hall of the People
(rénmín dàhuì táng) 人民大会堂
This is the venue of the rubber-stamp legislature, the National People's Congress. It's open to the public when the Congress is not sitting – to earn some hard currency it's even rented out occasionally to foreigners for conventions! These are the halls of power, many of them named after provinces and regions of China and decorated appropriately. You can see the 5000-seat banquet room where Nixon dined in 1972, and the 10,000-seat auditorium with the familiar red star embedded in a galaxy of lights in the ceiling. There's a sort of museum-like atmosphere in the Great Hall, with *objets d'art* donated by the provinces, and a snack bar and restaurant. The hall was completed over a 10-month period, from 1958 to 1959.

The hall is on the west side of Tiananmen Square and admission costs a mind-boggling Y30.

Monument to the People's Heroes

(rénmín yīngxióng jìniàn bēi)
人民英雄纪念碑

On the southern side of Tiananmen Square, this monument was completed in 1958 and stands on the site of the old Outer Palace Gate. The 36-metre obelisk, made of Qingdao granite, bears bas-relief carvings of key revolutionary events (one relief shows the Chinese destroying opium in the 19th century) as well as appropriate calligraphy from Mao Zedong and Zhou Enlai. In 1976 the obelisk was the focus of the 'Tiananmen Incident' when hundreds of thousands gathered here to protest the tyranny of the Gang of Four and to mourn the death of Zhou Enlai.

Mao Zedong Mausoleum

(máo zhǔxí jìniàn táng) 毛主席纪念堂

Behind the Monument to the People's Heroes stands this giant mausoleum built to house the body of Chairman Mao. Mao died in September 1976, and the mausoleum was constructed over a period of 10 months from 1976 to 1977. It occupies a prominent position on the powerful north-south axis of the city, but against all laws of geomancy this marble structure faces north. At the end of 1983 the mausoleum was re-opened as a museum with exhibitions on the lives of Zhou Enlai, Zhu De, Mao and the man he persecuted, Liu Shaoqi. Mao's body still remains in its place.

Whatever history will make of Mao, his impact on its course will remain enormous. Easy as it now is to vilify his deeds and excesses, many Chinese show deep respect when confronted with the physical presence of the man. Putting a couple of museums into the mausoleum was meant to knock Mao another rung down the divine ladder. Nevertheless the atmosphere in the inner sanctum is one of hushed reverence, with a thick red pile carpet muting any sound. Foreigners are advised to avoid loud talk, not crack jokes or indulge in other behaviour that will get you arrested.

Photos are prohibited inside the mausoleum and you have to check cameras and bags at the shed outside the entrance. The mausoleum is open daily from 8.30 to 11.30 am and occasionally from 1 pm to 3.30 pm. Join the enormous queue of Chinese sightseers, but don't expect more than a quick glimpse of the body as you file past the sarcophagus. At certain times of year the body requires maintenance and is not on view. The story goes that the Chinese had problems embalming Mao and had to call the Vietnamese to the rescue (Ho Chi Minh was also embalmed). The Vietnamese learned their embalming techniques from the Russians, but the Russians were no longer willing to help the Chinese after the Sino-Soviet split of the mid-1960s. Perhaps the Vietnamese didn't do a very good job because many visitors say Mao's body looks like it's made out of plastic.

CITS guides freely quote the old 7:3 ratio on Mao that first surfaced in 1976: Mao was 70% right and 30% wrong. This is now the official Party line. His gross errors in the Cultural Revolution, it is said, are far outweighed by his contributions. What young people think of him now is quite another matter.

Whatever Mao might have done to the Chinese economy while he was alive, sales of Mao memorabilia are certainly giving the free market a boost these days. At the souvenir shacks outside the mausoleum you can pick up Chairman Mao key rings, thermometers, face towels, handkerchiefs, sun visors, address books and cartons of cigarettes.

Forbidden City

(zǐjìn chéng) 紫禁城

The Forbidden City, so called because it was off limits for 500 years, is the largest and best-preserved cluster of ancient buildings in China. It was home to two dynasties of emperors, the Ming and the Qing, who didn't stray from this pleasure-dome unless they absolutely had to.

The Forbidden City is open daily from 8.30 am to 5 pm – last admission tickets are sold at 3.30 pm. Two hundred years ago the admission price would have been instant death, but this has dropped considerably to

Y45 FEC for foreigners and Y10 RMB for Chinese. The Y45 ticket allows admission to all the special exhibition halls, but if you pay Chinese price these cost extra, although it would still work out much cheaper if you could get Chinese price – that appears to be nearly impossible at the Forbidden City unless you have Asian features, even if you possess legitimate student cards. By way of compensation, your Y45 includes rental of a cassette tape player and tape for a self-guided tour – the tape player requires a refundable Y100 deposit, but you can use your own Walkman instead. For the tape to make sense you must enter the Forbidden City from the south gate and exit from the north. The tape is available in a number of languages, including English, German, Japanese, French, Spanish, Italian, Korean, Russian, Cantonese and, of course, Mandarin Chinese.

It's worth mentioning that many foreigners get Tiananmen Gate confused with the Forbidden City entrance because the two are physically attached and there are no signs in English. As a result, some people wind up purchasing the Tiananmen Gate admission ticket by mistake, not realising that this only gains you admission to the upstairs portion of the gate. To find the Forbidden City ticket booths, keep walking north until you can't walk any further without paying.

The basic layout was built between 1406 and 1420 by Emperor Yong Le, commanding battalions of labourers and craftspeople – some estimate up to a million of them. From this palace the emperors governed China, often rather erratically as they tended to become lost in this self-contained little world and allocated real power to the court eunuchs. One emperor devoted his entire career to carpentry – when an earthquake struck (an ominous sign for an emperor) he was delighted, since it gave him a chance to renovate.

The buildings now seen are mostly post-18th century, as with a lot of restored or rebuilt structures around Beijing. The palace was constantly going up in flames – a lantern festival combined with a sudden gust of Gobi wind would easily do the trick, as would a fireworks display. There were also fires deliberately lit by court eunuchs and officials who could get rich off the repair bills. The moat around the palace, now used for boating, came in handy since the local fire brigade was considered too common to quench the royal flames. Some of the emperors enjoyed the spectacle of fires, but Emperor Jiajing was so disturbed by them that he ordered a hall built in honour of the 'Fire-Pressing God'. Three fires caused by lightning broke out during his reign, including the biggest of the lot in 1557. A century later, in 1664, the Manchus stormed in and burned the palace to the ground.

It was not just the buildings that went up

THE PALACE MUSEUM   ¥ 18.00

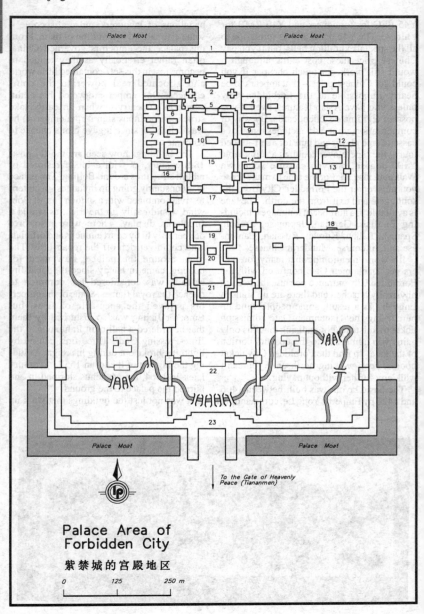

Palace Moat

Palace Moat

1

2

3

4

5

6

7

8

9

10

11

12

13

14

15

16

17

18

19

20

21

22

23

To the Gate of Heavenly
Peace (Tiananmen)

Palace Area of
Forbidden City

紫禁城的宫殿地区

0   125   250 m

1	Gate of Divine Military Genius (Shenwumen)
2	Hall of Imperial Peace
3	Thousand Autumns Pavilion
4	Exhibition of Ming & Qing Dynasty Arts & Crafts
5	Imperial Garden (Yuhuayuan)
6	Western Palaces Nos 16, 17 & 18
7	Palace of Eternal Spring (Changchungong)
8	Palace of Earthly Tranquility (Kunninggong)
9	Exhibition of Ceramics
10	Hall of Union (Jiaotaidian)
11	Exhibition of Jewellery (Hall of the Cultivation of Character)
12	Hall of the Cultivation of Character
13	Exhibition of Paintings (Hall of Imperial Supremacy)
14	Exhibition of Bronzes
15	Palace of Heavenly Purity (Qianqinggong)
16	Hall of Mental Cultivation (Yangxindian)
17	Gate of Heavenly Purity (Qianqingmen)
18	Nine Dragon Screen
19	Hall of Preserving Harmony (Baohedian)
20	Hall of Middle Harmony (Zhonghedian)
21	Hall of Supreme Harmony (Taihedian)
22	Supreme Harmony Gate (Taihemen)
23	Meridian Gate (Wumen)

1	神武门
2	钦安殿
3	千秋亭
4	明清工艺美术馆
5	御花园
6	宫廷史迹陈列
7	长春宫
8	坤宁宫
9	陶瓷馆
10	交泰殿
11	珍宝馆
12	养性殿
13	绘画馆
14	青铜器馆
15	乾清宫
16	养心殿
17	乾清门
18	九龙壁
19	保和殿
20	中和殿
21	太和殿
22	太和门
23	午门

in smoke, but rare books, paintings, calligraphy – anything flammable. In this century there have been two major lootings of the palace: first by the Japanese forces, and second by the Kuomintang who, on the eve of the Communist takeover in 1949, removed thousands of crates of relics to Taiwan, where they are now on display in Taipei's National Palace Museum – considered one of the top three museums in the world. The gaps have been filled by bringing treasures, old and newly discovered, from other parts of China.

The palace is so large (720,000 sq metres, 800 buildings, 9000 rooms) that a permanent restoration squad moves around repainting and repairing. It's estimated to take about 10 years to do a full renovation, by which time the beginning is due for repairs again. The complex was opened to the public in 1949.

The palace was built on a monumental scale, one that should not be taken lightly. Allow yourself a full day for exploration, or perhaps several separate trips if you're an enthusiast. The information given here can only be a skeleton guide; if you want more detail then tag along with a tour group for explanations of individual artefacts. There are plenty of Western tour groups around – the Forbidden City has 10,000 visitors a day. Tour buses drop their groups off at Tiananmen and pick them up again at the north gate; you can also enter the palace from the east or west gates. Even if you had a separate guidebook on the Forbidden City, it would be rather time-consuming to match up and identify every individual object, building and so forth – a spoken guide has more immediacy.

On the north-south axis of the Forbidden City, from Tiananmen at the south to Shenwumen at the north, lie the palace's ceremonial buildings.

Restored in the 17th century, **Meridian Gate** (Wumen) is a massive portal which in former times was reserved for the use of the emperor. Gongs and bells would be sounded upon royal comings and goings. Lesser mortals would use lesser gates – the military used the west gate, civilians used the east gate. The emperor also reviewed his armies from here, passed judgement on prisoners, announced the new year calendar and surveyed the flogging of troublesome ministers.

Across **Golden Stream**, which is shaped to resemble a Tartar bow and is spanned by five marble bridges, is **Supreme Harmony Gate** (Taihemen). It overlooks a massive courtyard that could hold an imperial audience of up to 100,000.

Raised on a marble terrace with balustrades are the **Three Great Halls**, the heart of the Forbidden City.

The **Hall of Supreme Harmony** (Taihedian) is the most important and the largest structure in the Forbidden City. Built in the 15th century and restored in the 17th century, it was used for ceremonial occasions such as the emperor's birthday, the nomination of military leaders, and coronations. Flanking the entrance to the hall are bronze incense burners. The large bronze turtle in the front is a symbol of longevity and stability – it has a removable lid and on special occasions incense was lit inside so that smoke billowed from the mouth.

To the west side of the terrace is a small pavilion with a bronze grain-measure and to the east is a sundial; both are symbolic of imperial justice. On the corners of the roof, as with some other buildings in the city, you'll see a mounted figure with his retreat cut off by mythical and real animals, a story that relates to a cruel tyrant hung from one such eave.

Inside the hall is a richly decorated Dragon Throne where the emperor would preside (decisions final, no correspondence entered into) over trembling officials. The entire court had to hit the floor nine times with their foreheads; combined with the thick veils of incense and the battering of gongs, it would be enough to make anyone dizzy. At the back of the throne is a carved Xumishan, the Buddhist paradise, signifying the throne's supremacy.

Behind Taihedian is the smaller **Hall of Middle Harmony** (Zhonghedian) which was used as a transit lounge for the emperor. Here he would make last-minute preparations, rehearse speeches and receive close ministers. On display are two Qing Dynasty sedan chairs, the emperors' mode of transport around the Forbidden City. The last of the Qing emperors, Puyi, used a bicycle and altered a few features of the palace grounds to make it easier to get around.

The third hall is the **Hall of Preserving Harmony** (Baohedian) used for banquets and later for imperial examinations. It now houses archaeological finds. The Baohedian has no support pillars, and behind it is a 250-tonne marble block carved with dragons and clouds which was moved into Beijing on an ice path. The outer housing surrounding the Three Great Halls was used for storing gold, silver, silks, carpets and other treasures.

The basic configuration of the Three Great Halls is echoed by the next group of buildings, smaller in scale but more important in terms of real power. In China, real power traditionally lies at the back door, or in this case, the back gate.

The first structure is the **Palace of Heavenly Purity** (Qianqinggong), a residence of Ming and early Qing emperors, and later an audience hall for receiving foreign envoys and high officials.

Immediately behind it is the **Hall of Union**, which contains a clepsydra – a water clock with five bronze vessels and a calibrated scale. Water clocks date back several thousand years but this one was made in 1745. There's also a mechanical clock on display, built in 1797, and a collection of imperial jade seals.

At the northern end of the Forbidden City is the **Imperial Garden**, a classical Chinese garden of 7000 sq metres of fine landscaping, with rockeries, walkways and pavilions. It's a good place to take a breather, with snack bars, toilets and souvenir shops. Two more gates lead out through the large **Gate of Divine Military Genius** (Shenwumen).

The western and eastern sides of the Forbidden City are the palatial former living quarters which once contained libraries, temples, theatres, gardens, even the tennis court of the last emperor. These buildings now function as museums requiring extra admission fees, but the foreigners' all-inclusive ticket covers it. Opening hours are irregular and no photos are allowed without prior permission. Special exhibits sometimes appear in the palace museum halls – check the *China Daily* for details.

On the western side of the Forbidden City, towards the north exit, are the six **Western Palaces** which were living quarters for the empress and concubines. These are kept in pristine condition, displaying furniture, silk bedcovers, personal items, and fittings such as cloisonné charcoal burners.

Of particular interest is the **Palace of Eternal Spring** (Changchungong), decorated with mural scenes from the Ming novel *A Dream of Red Mansions*. This is where the Empress Dowager Cixi lived when she was still a concubine.

Nearby is the **Hall of Mental Cultivation** (Yangxindian), a private apartment for the emperors. It was divided into reception rooms, a study where important documents were signed and a bedchamber at the rear.

On the eastern side of the City, six more palaces duplicate the rhythms and layout of those on the west. There are museums here for bronzes, ceramics, and Ming Dynasty arts & crafts. Further east is a display of gold and jade artefacts and Ming and Qing paintings, sometimes augmented with Song and Yuan paintings. Just south, protecting the gateway to two of the palaces, is the polychrome **Nine Dragon Screen** built in 1773.

A few more interesting aspects of the Forbidden City include the watchtowers which stand on top of the walls at the four corners of the city. Structural delights, they have three storeys, are double-roofed and measure 27½ metres high.

In the south-west of the Forbidden City is **Zhongshan Park** (*zhōngshān gōngyuán*),

otherwise known as Sun Yatsen Park. It was laid out at the same time as the palace. Here you'll find the **Altar of Land and Grain**, which is divided into five sections, each filled with earth of a different colour (red, green, black, yellow and white) to symbolise all the earth belonging to the emperor. There is also a concert hall and a 'modernisation' playground in the park.

The **Workers' Cultural Palace** (*láodòng rénmín wénhuà gōng*) in the south-east sector of the Forbidden City is a park with halls dating from 1462 which were used as ancestral temples under the Ming and Qing; they come complete with marble balustrades, terraces and detailed gargoyles. The park is now used for movies, temporary exhibits, cultural performances and the occasional mass wedding. There's boating at the north end and skating in winter on the frozen moat.

A Day in the Life...

Four hundred years ago the Jesuit priest Matteo Ricci spent 20 years in China, much of that time at the imperial court in Beijing. He recorded in his diary:

Just as this people is grossly subject to superstition, so, too, they have very little regard for the truth, acting always with great circumspection, and very cautious about trusting anyone. Subject to this same fear, the kings of modern times abandoned the custom of going out in public. Even formerly, when they did leave the royal enclosure, they would never dare to do so without a thousand preliminary precautions. On such occasions the whole court was placed under military guard. Secret servicemen were placed along the route over which the King was to travel and on all roads leading into it. He was not only hidden from view, but the public never knew in which of the palanquins of his cortège he was actually riding. One would think he was making a journey through enemy country rather than through multitudes of his own subjects and clients.

Zhongnanhai
(*zhōngnánhǎi*) 中南海
Just west of the Forbidden City is China's new forbidden city, Zhongnanhai. The interior of the compound is off limits to tourists, but you can gawk at the entrance. The name means 'the central and south seas' in this case after the two large lakes in the compound.

The southern entrance is via Xinhuamen (Gate of New China) which you'll see on Chang'an Jie; it's guarded by two PLA soldiers and fronted by a flagpole with the red flag flying. The gate was built in 1758 and was then known as the Tower of the Treasured Moon.

The compound was built between the 10th and 13th centuries as a sort of playground for the emperors and their retinue. It was expanded during Ming times but most of the present buildings only date from the Qing Dynasty. After the overthrow of the imperial government and the establishment of the Republic it served as the site of the presidential palace.

Since the founding of the People's Republic in 1949, Zhongnanhai has been the site of the residence and offices of the highest-ranking members of the Communist Party. People like Mao Zedong, Zhou Enlai, Liu Shaoqi and Zhu De have all lived and worked in the area. The offices of the Central Committee of the Communist Party and of the State Council, the Central People's Government and the Military Commission of the Party Central Committee are here.

Prior to the arrival of the new batch of tenants Zhongnanhai had been the site of the emperor's ploughing of the first symbolic furrow of the farming season, and the venue for imperial banquets and the highest examinations in martial arts. Empress Dowager Cixi once lived here; after the failure of the 1898 reform movement she imprisoned Emperor Guangxu in the Hall of Impregnating Vitality where, ironically, he later died. Yuan Shikai used Zhongnanhai for ceremonial occasions during the few years of his presidency of the Chinese Republic; his vice-president moved into Guangxu's death-house.

City Behind the Wall

If ceremonial and administrative duties occupied most of the emperor's working hours, then behind the high walls of the Forbidden City it was the pursuit of pleasure which occupied much of his attention during the evening. One of the imperial bedtime systems was to keep the names of royal wives, consorts and favourites on jade tablets near the emperor's chambers – sometimes as many as 50 of them.

By turning the tablet over, the emperor made his request for the evening, and the eunuch on duty would rush off to find the lucky lady. Stripped naked and therefore weaponless, she was gift-wrapped in a yellow cloth and piggybacked over to the royal boudoir, to be dumped at the feet of the emperor. The eunuch recorded the date and time to verify legitimacy of a possible child.

Financing the affairs of state probably cost less than financing the affairs of the emperor – keeping the pleasure-dome functioning drew heavily on the resources of the empire. During the Ming Dynasty there were an estimated 9000 maids of honour and 70,000 eunuchs serving the court. Apart from the servants and the prize concubines there were also the royal elephants to keep. These were gifts from Burma and were stabled south-west of the Forbidden City. Accorded rank by the emperor, when an elephant died, a period of mourning was declared. Periodically the elephant keepers embezzled the funds intended for elephant chow. When this occurred, the ravenous pachyderms went on a rampage.

While pocketing this cash was illegal, selling elephant dung for use as shampoo was not, and it was believed to give hair extra sheen. Back in the harem the cosmetic bills piled up to 400,000 taels of silver. Then, of course, the concubines who had grown old and gone out of active service were still supposed to be cared for. Rather than cut back on expenditure, the emperor sent out eunuchs to collect emergency taxes whenever money ran short.

As for the palace eunuchs, the royal chop was administered at the Eunuch Clinic near the Forbidden City, using a swift knife and a special chair with a hole in the seat. The candidates sought to better their lives in the service of the court but half of them died after the operation. Mutilation of any kind was considered grounds for exclusion to the next life, so many eunuchs carried their amputated appendages around in pouches, believing that at the time of death the spirits might be deceived into thinking of them as whole. ∎

Summer Palace
(yíhéyuán) 颐和园

This is one of the best sights in Beijing – don't miss it! The Summer Palace is an immense park containing some newish Qing architecture. The site had long been a royal garden and was considerably enlarged and embellished by Emperor Qianlong in the 18th century. He deepened and expanded Kunming Lake with the help of 100,000 labourers – and reputedly surveyed imperial navy drills from a hilltop perch. It was later abandoned.

Empress Dowager Cixi began rebuilding in 1888 using money that was supposedly reserved for the construction of a modern navy – but she did restore a marble boat that sits immobile at the edge of the lake. She had this ugly thing fitted out with several large mirrors and used to dine at the lakeside.

In 1900 foreign troops, annoyed by the Boxer Rebellion, had another go at roasting the Summer Palace. Restorations took place a few years later and a major renovation occurred after 1949, by which time the palace had once more fallen into disrepair.

The original palace was used as a summer residence, an escape from the ferocious heat. The residents of the Forbidden City packed up and decamped here for their holidays, so the emphasis is on cool features – water, gardens, hills. It was divided into four sections: court reception, residences, temples and strolling or sightseeing areas. Three-quarters of the park is occupied by Kunming Lake, and most items of structural interest are towards the east or north gates.

The main building is the Hall of **Benevolence & Longevity**, just off the lake toward the east gate. It houses a hardwood throne and has a courtyard with bronze animals. In it the emperor-in-residence handled state affairs and received envoys.

Along the north shore of the lake is the **Long Corridor**, over 700 metres long, which is decorated with mythical scenes. If the paint looks new it's because a lot of pictures were whitewashed during the Cultural Revolution.

On artificial **Longevity Hill** are a number of temples. The **Pavilion of Precious Clouds** on the western slopes is one of the few structures to escape destruction by the Anglo-French forces. It contains some elaborate bronzes. At the top of the hill sits the Buddhist **Temple of the Sea of Wisdom**, made of glazed tiles; good views of the lake can be had from this spot.

Other sights are largely associated with Empress Cixi, like the place where she kept Emperor Guangxu under house arrest, the place where she celebrated her birthdays, and exhibitions of her furniture and memorabilia. A very Disneylandish atmosphere pervades this 'museum'; tourists can have their photos taken, imperial dress-up fashion.

The Tingliguan Restaurant serves imperial banquet food – fish from Kunming Lake, velvet chicken, dumplings – on regal tableware lookalikes. It has a splendid alfresco location and exorbitant prices, and is housed in what was once an imperial theatre; nowadays there are attached souvenir shops.

Another noteworthy feature of the Summer Palace is the 17-arch bridge spanning 150 metres to South Lake Island; on the mainland side is a beautiful bronze ox. Also note the Jade Belt Bridge on the mid-west side of the lake; and the Garden of Harmonious Interest at the north-east end which is a copy of a Wuxi garden.

You can get around the lake by rowing boat. Boating and swimming are popular pastimes for the locals (windsurfing for the richer ones) and in winter you can skate on the lakes. As with the Forbidden City Moat, it used to be a common practice to cut slabs of ice from the lake in winter and store them for summer use.

The park is about 12 km north-west of the centre of Beijing. The easiest way to get there is to take the subway to Xizhimen (close to the zoo), then a minibus for Y3. Bus No 332 from the zoo is slower but will get you there eventually. Lots of minibuses return to the city centre from the Summer Palace, but get the price and destination settled before departure. You can also get there by bicycle

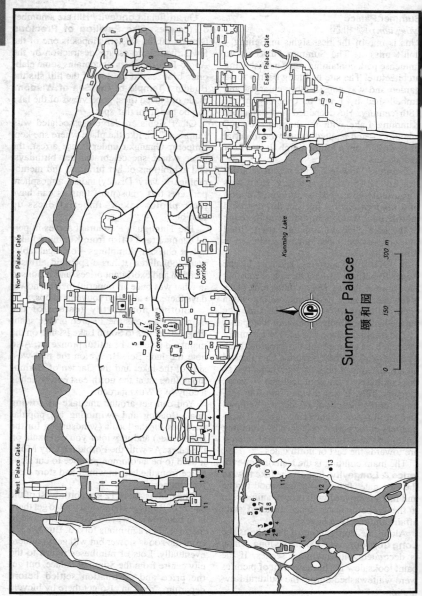

Summer Palace
颐和园

East Palace Gate

North Palace Gate

West Palace Gate

Kunming Lake

Long Corridor

Longevity Hill

300 m

150

0

1	Marble Boat
2	Ferry Dock
3	Listening to the Orioles Restaurant
4	Long Corridor
5	Pavilion of Precious Clouds
6	Hall of Buddhist Tenants
7	Temple of the Sea of Wisdom
8	Temple of Buddhist Virtue
9	Garden of Harmonious Interest
10	Hall of Benevolence & Longevity
11	Rowing Boat Dock
12	Pavilion of Knowing in the Spring
13	Bronze Ox
14	Jade Belt Bridge

1	清晏船
2	码头馆
3	听鹏馆
4	长廊
5	排云殿
6	香崇宗印之阁
7	智慧海
8	佛香阁
9	谐趣园
10	仁寿殿
11	划船码头
12	知春亭
13	铜牛
14	玉带桥

– it takes about 1½ to two hours from the centre of town. Rather than taking the main roads, it's far more pleasant to cycle along the road following the Beijing-Miyun Diversion Canal.

Foreigners are charged Y15, payable in either RMB or FEC. This ticket does *not* get you into everything – there are some additional fees inside. Admission for Chinese costs Y2 – foreigners need to be a Beijing resident with valid ID to get this price.

Old Summer Palace
(yuánmíngyuán) 圆明园

The original Summer Palace was laid out in the 12th century. By the reign of Emperor Qianlong, it had developed into a set of interlocking gardens. Qianlong set the Jesuits to work as architects for European palaces for the gardens – elaborate fountains and baroque statuary.

In the second Opium War (1860), British and French troops destroyed the place and sent the booty abroad. Since the Chinese pavilions and temples were made of wood they did not survive fires, but a marble facade, some broken columns and traces of the fountains stick out of the rice paddies.

The ruins have long been a favourite picnic spot for foreigners living in the capital and for Chinese twosomes seeking a bit of privacy. More recently, the government has decided to slowly restore the gardens, moats

and buildings. It's uncertain yet just how far the restoration will go – will it be allowed to remain as ruins or will it become another tourist circus like the Ming Tombs? At present, it's still a very worthwhile place to visit but it can be crowded on Sundays.

The site covers a huge area – some 2½ km from east to west – so be prepared to do some walking. There are three entrance gates to the compound, all on the south side. The western section is the main area, Yuanmingyuan. The south-eastern corner of the site is the Beautiful Spring Garden (Yichunyuan). The eastern section is the Eternal Spring Garden (Changchunyuan) – it's here that you'll find the Great Fountain Ruins, considered the best-preserved relic in the palace and featured prominently in the tourist brochures.

Minibuses connect the new Summer Palace with the old one, for about Y2. There are some slower but pleasant trips you can do around the area by public transport. Take bus No 332 from the zoo to the Old Summer Palace and to the Summer Palace; change to bus No 333 for the Fragrant Hills; change to bus No 360 to go directly back to the zoo.

Another round-trip route is to take the subway to Pingguoyuan (the last stop in the west) and then take bus No 318 to the Fragrant Hills; change to No 333 for the Summer Palace, and then to No 332 for the zoo.

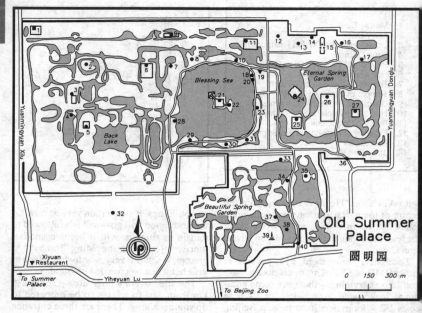

History Museum & Museum of the Revolution

(zhōngguó gémìng lìshǐ bówùguǎn)
中国革命历史博物馆

If you don't count the Forbidden City and other palaces, this is Beijing's largest museum. Housed in a sombre building on the east side of Tiananmen Square, access was long thwarted by special permission requirements. From 1966 to 1978 the museum was closed so that history could be reassessed in the light of recent events.

The presentation of history poses quite a problem for the Chinese Communist Party (CCP). It has failed to publish anything of note on its own history after it gained power, before, during or since the Cultural Revolution. This would have required reams of carefully worded revision according to what tack politics (here synonymous with history) might take – so it was better left unwritten.

There are actually two museums here combined into one – the Museum of History

and the Museum of the Revolution. Explanations throughout most of the museums are, unfortunately, entirely in Chinese, so you won't get much out of this labyrinth unless you're particularly fluent or pick up an English-speaking student. (This situation applies to Beijing's museums in general.) An English text relating to the History Museum is available inside.

The History Museum contains artefacts and cultural relics (many of them copies) from year zero to 1919, subdivided into primitive communal groups, slavery, feudalism and capitalism/imperialism, laced with Marxist commentary. Without a guide you can discern ancient weapons, inventions and musical instruments.

The Museum of the Revolution is split into five sections: the founding of the CCP (1919-21), the first civil war (1924-27), the second civil war (1927-37), resistance against Japan (1937-45) and the third civil war (1945-49).

In 1978 a permanent photo-pictorial exhibit of the life and works of Zhou Enlai became a star attraction, and in 1983 there was an exhibit tracing the life of Liu Shaoqi. PLA soldiers are occasionally taken through the museums on tours; they snap to attention, open portable chairs and sit down in unison for explanations of each section. Whatever spiel they're given would probably be engrossing if you had someone to translate for you. There is an admission fee of Y3.

Military Museum

(jūnshì bówùguǎn) 军事博物馆

Perhaps more to the point than the Museum of the Revolution, this traces the genesis of the PLA from 1927 to the present and has some interesting exhibits: pictures of Mao in the early days, mind-boggling Socialist Realist artwork, captured US tanks from the Korean War and other tools of destruction. All explanations are in Chinese only. You must check your bags at the door, presumably to prevent you from liberating a Sherman tank or MIG aircraft.

The museum is on Fuxing Lu on the western side of the city; to get there take the subway to Junshibowuguan. Admission costs Y2.

Natural History Museum

(zìrán bówùguǎn) 自然博物馆

This is the largest such museum in China. The four main exhibition halls are devoted to flora & fauna, ancient fauna and human evolution. One of the more impressive features is a complete dinosaur skeleton. There is also plenty of pickled wildlife, though nothing worse than what you see for sale in some of the street markets. Some of the exhibits were donated by the British Museum, the American Museum of Natural History and other foreign sources.

The Natural History Museum is in the Tianqiao area, just west of Tiantan Park, just north of the park's west gate entrance. Admission costs Y2. The museum is open daily except Monday, from 8.30 am until 4 pm.

Lu Xun Museum

(lǔ xùn bówùguǎn) 鲁迅博物馆

Dedicated to China's No 1 Thinking Person's Revolutionary, this museum contains manuscripts, diaries, letters and inscriptions by the famous writer. To the west of the museum is a small Chinese walled compound where Lu Xun lived from 1924 to 1926. The museum is off Fuchengmennei Dajie, west of the Xisi intersection on the north-western side of the city.

China Art Gallery

(zhōngguó měishù guǎn)
中国美术馆

Back in the post-Liberation days one of the safest hobbies for an artist was to retouch classical-type landscapes with red flags, belching factory chimneys or bright red tractors. You can get some idea of the state of the arts in China at this gallery. At times very good exhibitions of current work including photo displays are held in an adjacent gallery. Check the *China Daily* for listings. The arts & crafts shop inside has an excellent range of woodblock prints and papercuts. The gallery is west of the Dongsi intersection.

Xu Beihong Museum

(xú bēihóng jìniàn guǎn) 徐悲鸿纪念馆

Here you'll find traditional Chinese paintings, oils, gouaches, sketches and memorabilia of the famous artist, noted for his galloping horse paintings. Painting albums are on sale, as well as reproductions and Chinese stationery. The museum is at 53 Xinjiekou Beidajie, Xicheng District.

Song Qingling Museum

(sòng qìnglíng gùjū) 宋庆龄故居

Madam Song was the wife of Sun Yatsen, the founder of the Republic of China. After 1981 her large residence was transformed into a museum dedicated to her memory and to that of Sun Yatsen. The original layout of the residence is unchanged and on display are personal items and pictures of historical interest. The museum is on the north side of Shisha Houhai lake.

National Library

(běijīng túshūguǎn) 北京图书馆（新馆）

This holds around five million books and four million periodicals and newspapers, over a third of which are in foreign languages. Access to books is limited and access to rare books is even rarer, though you might be shown a microfilm copy if you're lucky. The large collection of rare books includes surviving imperial works such as the *Yong Le Encyclopedia* and selections from the old Jesuit library. Of interest to Ming-Qing scholars is the special collection, the *Shanbenbu*. The library is near the zoo. The old Beijing Library is near Beihai Park on the south side. Beijing University Library also has a large collection of rare books but you aren't likely to get into this place.

Capital Museum & Library
(*shǒudū túshūguǎn*) 首都图书馆
Actually, it's part of the Confucius Temple complex. The museum houses steles, stone inscriptions, bronzes, vases and documents. This place is within walking distance of the Lama Temple. The easiest way to get there is by subway to the Yonghegong station.

Jingshan Park
(*jǐngshān gōngyuán*) 景山公园
North of the Forbidden City is Jingshan (Coal Hill), which contains an artificial mound made of earth excavated to create the palace moat. If you clamber to the top pavilions of this regal pleasure garden you get a magnificent panorama of the capital and a great overview of the russet roofing of the Forbidden City. On the east side of the park is a locust tree where the last of the Mings, Emperor Chongzhen, hanged himself (after slaying his family) rather than see the palace razed by the Manchus. The hill supposedly protects the palace from the evil spirits – or dust storms – from the north, but didn't quite work for Chongzhen.

Entrance to Jingshan Park is a modest Y0.30, or you can pay over 30 times as much for a souvenir 'tourist passport ticket' – fortunately, this is optional.

Beihai Park
(*běihǎi gōngyuán*) 北海公园
Approached by four gates, and just northwest of the Forbidden City, Beihai Park is the former playground of the emperors. It is rumoured to have been the private pleasure domain of Jiang Qing, widow of Mao who, until her death in May 1991, was serving a life sentence as No 1 of the Gang of Four. The park covers an area of 68 hectares, half of which is a lake. The island in the lower middle is composed of the heaped earth dug to create the lake – some attribute this to the handiwork of Kublai Khan.

The site is associated with the Great Khan's palace, the belly-button of Beijing before the creation of the Forbidden City. All that remains of the Khan's court is a large jar made of green jade, in the Round City near the south entrance. A present given in 1265, and said to have contained the Khan's wine, it was later discovered in the hands of Taoist priests who used it to store pickles. In the Light Receiving Hall, the main structure nearby, is a 1½-metre-high white jade buddha inlaid with jewels – a gift from Burma to Empress Dowager Cixi.

From the 12th century on, Beihai Park was landscaped with artificial hills, pavilions, halls, temples and covered walkways. In the present era the structures have been massively restored and Beihai Park is now one of China's best examples of a classical garden. Dominating Jade Islet on the lake, the White Dagoba is a 36-metre-high pop-art 'Peppermint Bottle' originally dating from 1651. It was put up for a visit by the Dalai Lama and was rebuilt in 1741. It's believed that Lamaist scriptures, robes and other sacred objects are encased in this brick-and-stone landmark.

On the north-east shore of the islet is the handsome double-tiered Painted Gallery – with unusual architecture for a walkway. Near the boat dock is the Fangshan Restaurant, dishing up recipes favoured by Empress Cixi. She liked 120-course dinners with about 30 kinds of desserts. The restaurant is expensive and high class, and reservations are necessary (but check out the decor!). Off to one side, however, is a snack bar that dispenses royal pastries much more cheaply.

From this point you can catch a barge to the north-west part of the park or, if energetic, double back and hire a rowing boat (there's another rowing-boat hire place on the north-west side). The attraction on the north side is the Nine Dragon Screen, five metres high and 27 metres long, made of coloured glazed tiles. It's one of the three most famous ones in the PRC, and is in good shape. The screen was to scare off evil

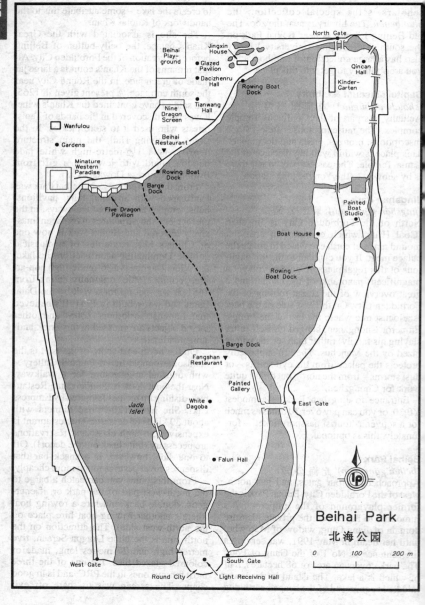

North Gate

Beihai
Playground

Jingxin
House

Glazed
Pavilion

Dacizhenru
Hall

Rowing Boat
Dock

Qincan
Hall

Kinder-
Garten

Nine
Dragon
Screen

Tianwang
Hall

Wanfulou

Beihai
Restaurant

Gardens

Minature
Western
Paradise

Rowing Boat
Dock

Barge
Dock

Painted Boat
Studio

Five Dragon
Pavilion

Boat House

Rowing
Boat Dock

Barge Dock

Fangshan
Restaurant

Painted
Gallery

Jade
Islet

White
Dagoba

East Gate

Falun Hall

West Gate

South Gate

Round City

Light Receiving Hall

Beihai Park

北海公园

0   100   200 m

spirits; it stands at the entrance to a temple which has disappeared. To the south-west of the boat dock on this side is the Five Dragon Pavilion dating from 1651, where the emperors liked to fish or camp out at night to watch the moon.

On the east side of the park are the 'gardens within gardens'. These waterside pavilions, winding corridors and rockeries were summer haunts of the imperial family, notably Emperor Qianlong and Empress Cixi. They date back some 200 years, with structures like the Painted Boat Studio and the Studio of Mental Calmness. Until 1980 the villas were used as government offices.

Beihai Park is a relaxing place to stroll around, grab a snack, sip a beer, rent a rowing boat or, as the Chinese do, cuddle on a bench in the evening. It's crowded at weekends. Some people dive into the lake when no-one's around – swimming is not permitted. In winter there's skating. This is nothing new in China – skating apparently goes back to the 18th century when Emperor Qianlong reviewed the imperial skating parties here.

Tiantan Park
(tiāntán gōngyuán) 天坛公园
The perfection of Ming architecture, Tiantan (the Temple of Heaven) has come to symbolise Beijing. Its lines appear on countless pieces of tourist literature (including your five jiao tourist bill), and as a brand name for

Temple of Heaven

a wide range of products from Tiger Balm to plumbing fixtures. In the 1970s the complex got a facelift and was freshly painted after pigment research. It is set in a 267-hectare park, with four gates at the compass points, and bounded by walls to the north and east. It originally functioned as a vast stage for solemn rites performed by the Son of Heaven who came here to pray for good harvests, seek divine clearance and atone for the sins of the people.

With this complicated mix in mind, the unique architectural features will delight numerologists, necromancers and the superstitious – not to mention acoustic engineers and carpenters. Shape, colour and sound take on symbolic significance. The temples, seen in aerial perspective, are round, and the bases are square, deriving from the ancient Chinese belief that heaven is round, and the earth is square. Thus the north end of the park is semicircular and the south end is square (the Temple of Earth is on the northern compass point and the Temple of Heaven on the southern compass point).

Tiantan was considered highly sacred ground and it was here that the emperor performed the major ceremonial rites of the year. Just before the winter solstice, the emperor and his enormous entourage passed down Qianmen Dajie to the Imperial Vault of Heaven in total silence – commoners were not permitted to view the ceremony and remained cloistered indoors. The procession included elephant chariots, horse chariots and long lines of lancers, nobles, officials and musicians, dressed in their finest, flags fluttering. The next day the emperor waited in a yellow silk tent at the south gate while officials moved the sacred tablets to the Round Altar, where the prayers and sacrificial rituals took place. The least hitch in any part of the proceedings was regarded as an ill omen, and it was thought that the nation's future was thus decided. This was the most important ceremony although other excursions to Ditan (Temple of Earth) also took place.

Round Altar The five-metre-high Round

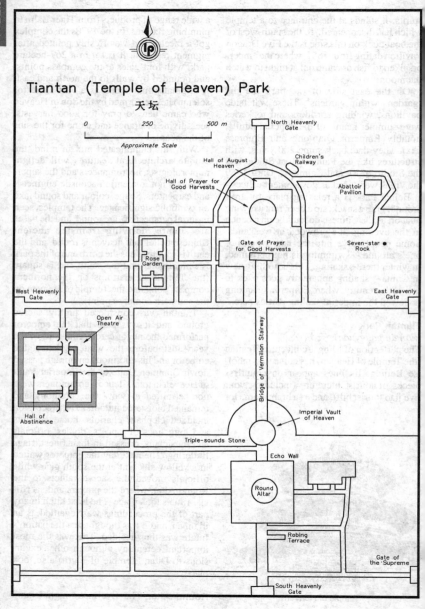

Tiantan (Temple of Heaven) Park
天坛

0   250   500 m

Approximate Scale

North Heavenly Gate

Children's Railway

Hall of August Heaven

Hall of Prayer for Good Harvests

Abattoir Pavilion

Gate of Prayer for Good Harvests

Seven-star Rock

Rose Garden

West Heavenly Gate

East Heavenly Gate

Open Air Theatre

Bridge of Vermilion Stairway

Hall of Abstinence

Imperial Vault of Heaven

Triple-sounds Stone

Echo Wall

Round Altar

Robing Terrace

Gate of the Supreme

South Heavenly Gate

Altar was constructed in 1530 and rebuilt in 1740. It is composed of white marble arrayed in three tiers, and its geometry revolves around the imperial number nine. Odd numbers were considered heavenly, and nine is the largest single-digit odd number. The top tier, thought to symbolise heaven, has nine rings of stones, each ring composed of multiples of nine stones, so that the ninth ring has 81 stones. The middle tier – earth – has the 10th to 18th rings. The bottom tier – humankind – has the 19th to 27th rings, ending with a total of 243 stones in the largest ring, or 27 times nine. The number of stairs and balustrades are also multiples of nine. If you stand in the centre of the upper terrace and say something, the sound waves are bounced off the marble balustrades, making your voice appear louder (nine times?).

Echo Wall Just north of the altar, surrounding the entrance to the Imperial Vault of Heaven, is the Echo Wall, 65 metres in diameter. This enables a whisper to travel clearly from one end to your friend's ear at the other – that is, if there's not a group tour in the middle.

In the courtyard are the Triple Echo Stones. If you stand on the first one and clap or shout, the sound is echoed once, on the second stone twice, and on the third, three times. Should it return four times, you will almost certainly not get a railway ticket that day, or any other day that is a multiple of three.

Imperial Vault of Heaven This octagonal vault was built at the same time as the Round Altar, and is structured along the lines of the older Hall of Prayer for Good Harvests, though it is smaller. It used to contain tablets of the emperor's ancestors, which were used in the winter solstice ceremony. Proceeding up from the Imperial Vault is a walkway: to the left is a molehill composed of excess dirt dumped from digging air-raid shelters and to the right is a rash of souvenir shops.

Hall of Prayer for Good Harvests (*qí nián diàn*) The main structure of the whole complex is the Hall of Prayer for Good Harvests, a magnificent piece mounted on a three-tiered marble terrace. Built in 1420, it was burnt to cinders in 1889 and heads rolled in apportioning blame. The cause seems to have been lightning. A faithful reproduction based on Ming architectural methods was erected the following year, using Oregon fir for the support pillars.

The four pillars at the centre represent the seasons, the 12 in the next ring denote the months of the year, and the 12 outer ones are symbolic of the day, broken into 12 'watches'. Embedded in the ceiling is a carved dragon, a symbol of royalty. The patterning, carving and gilt decoration of this ceiling and its swirl of colour is a dizzy sight – enough to carry you into the Seventh Heaven.

In fact it looks peculiarly modern, like a graphic from a sci-fi movie of a spaceship about to blast into hyperspace. All this is made more amazing by the fact that the wooden pillars ingeniously support the ceiling without nails or cement – for a building 38 metres high and 30 metres in diameter, a stunning accomplishment of carpentry. Capping the structure is a deep blue umbrella of tiles with a golden knob and two complementary eaves.

If you buy the general admission ticket for Tiantan Park (Y1), you need to pay extra to see the Hall of Prayer for Good Harvests. If you buy the overpriced tourist ticket (Y10), admission to everything is included.

Other Tiantan, it should not be forgotten, is also a park and a meeting place. Taiji enthusiasts assemble at the gates in the morning and head off for their favourite spots, some practising snatches of opera en route. There are also nice floral exhibits; along the east wall is a poultry and food market.

I had my best moments in Beijing here – at 6.30 in the morning, watching taiji, dancing to Western music and some other games that people played. This is how Beijing awakes. It became 'just another Chinese parkland' by 9 am as the tourists started to break the magic.

Kees Bikker

Ditan Park

(dìtán gōngyuán) 地坛公园

Although 'Ditan' sounds just like the Chinese word for 'carpet', in this case it means 'Temple of the Earth'. The park was built around 1530 as a place for the emperors to sacrifice lesser beings to keep on good terms with the earth god. The park experienced many years of neglect, but reopened in 1984 as a sort of activity centre for the elderly. The park is just north of the magnificent Lama Temple.

Ritan Park

(rìtán gōngyuán) 日坛公园

Ritan means 'Temple of the Sun' and it's one of Beijing's older parks, having been built in 1530. The park was built as an altar for ritual sacrifice to the sun god. Situated practically right in the middle of Jianguomenwai embassyland, it's a big hit with diplomats, their families and other notables who like to rub elbows with important foreigners. The Ritan Restaurant is in the park and serves jiaozi in an older-style pavilion – this place is very popular with Westerners for snacks.

Yuetan Park

(yuètán gōngyuán) 月坛公园

The name means 'Temple of the Moon'. This is another one of Beijing's sacrificial parks, where the emperors reduced the surplus population to appease the moon god. These days the Yuetan is notable for the Emei Restaurant on the north side of the park, which serves hot Sichuan food with no compromise for foreign palates – Sichuan food addicts prefer it to the Sichuan Restaurant itself.

Yuyuantan Park

(yùyuāntán gōngyuán) 玉渊潭公园

Off to the west of Yuetan Park is Yuyuantan (Jade Hole Pool). The park is notable for the palatial Diaoyutai State Guesthouse, the stomping ground of visiting diplomats and high-ranking cadres. Tourists wandering around the main gate will be politely told to get lost. Just to the south side of the park is the immense TV tower, one of Beijing's most prominent landmarks. The park is just north of the Military Museum.

Taoranting Park

(táorántíng gōngyuán) 陶然亭公园

Taoranting (Happy Pavilion) Park is in the southern part of Beijing. The park dates back to at least the Qing Dynasty, when it gained fame chiefly because it was one of the very few accessible to the masses (most of the others were the private playgrounds of the emperors). In keeping with this tradition, the park is conveniently located just north of the Qiaoyuan Hotel, the centre of Beijing's backpacker community. From the hotel, cross one of the pedestrian bridges over the sewage canal and you're practically there.

Zizhuyuan Park

(zǐzhúyuàn) 紫竹园

The park's name means 'Purple Bamboo', a reference to some of what has been planted here. This place doesn't have much history to distinguish it, being mainly former paddy fields, but during the Ming Dynasty there was a Temple of Longevity *(wànshòu sì)* at this site. The park is pleasant enough and there is a reasonably large lake which makes a good venue for ice skating in winter. Zizhuyuan is in a prestigious neighbourhood just west of the zoo.

Longtan Park

(lóngtán gōngyuán) 龙潭公园

Longtan (Dragon Pool) Park is of chief interest to budget travellers staying at the nearby Longtan Hotel – visit at dawn to see outstanding taiji performances.

The west side of Longtan Park has recently been converted into the Beijing Amusement Park, a world of balloons, cotton candy and nauseating rides (don't eat Sichuan food before getting on the Spider). If this appeals to you, at least avoid it on weekends and holidays.

Grand View Garden

(dàguān yuán) 大观园

At the south-western corner of town is Grand View Garden, also known as Daguanyuan

Park. Unlike most of Beijing's parks, which date back to imperial days, this one is new – construction started in 1984 and was completed four years later. The park was built as a replica of the family gardens described in the Chinese novel *The Dream of the Red Chamber*, written by Cao Xueqin. The book is a Chinese classic written in the late 18th century. While the park is not steeped in history, it could be of interest if you've read the novel. Otherwise, just kick back and enjoy the birds and the trees.

Beijing Zoo
(běijīng dòngwùyuán) 北京动物园
For humans the zoo is OK – an enormous park, pleasant lakes, good birds – but after you've been there you'll probably look as distressed as the animals. No attempt has been made to re-create their natural environments – they live in tiny cages with little shade or water. The Panda House, right by the gates, has four dirty specimens that would be better off dead – you'll be happier looking at the stuffed toy pandas on sale in the zoo's souvenir shop. Parents can buy their children miniature plastic rifles with which they can practise shooting the animals. The children also enjoy throwing rocks at the monkeys and jabbing them with sticks – some of the monkeys fight back by throwing their faeces.

The zoo is in the north-western corner of the city; the former Ming Dynasty garden was converted to a zoo in 1908. It contains 400 species and is the largest in China. Some rare animals reside here, including golden monkeys from Sichuan, Yangzi alligators, wild Tibetan donkeys, the snow leopard and the black-necked crane.

Near to the zoo are the Beijing Planetarium and the bizarre Soviet-style Beijing Exhibition Hall (irregular industrial displays, theatre, Russian restaurant) which looks like some crazed Communist architect's wedding-cake decoration.

Admission is a modest Y1, but there is a Y2 charge for the Panda House and other extra charges for special exhibits.

Getting to the zoo is easy enough – take the subway to the Xizhimen station. From there, it's a 15-minute walk to the west or a short ride on any of the trolley-buses.

Lama Temple
(yōnghégōng) 雍和宫
This is by far the most colourful temple in Beijing – beautiful gardens, stunning frescoes and tapestries, incredible carpentry. Get to this one before you're 'templed out' – it won't chew up your day.

The Lama Temple is the most renowned Tibetan Buddhist temple within China, outside Tibet itself (a carefully worded statement!). North-west of the city centre toward Andingmen, it became the official residence of Count Yin Zhen after extensive renovation. Nothing unusual in that – but in 1723 he was promoted to emperor, and moved to the Forbidden City. His name was changed to Yong Zheng, and his former residence became Yonghe Palace. The green tiles were changed to yellow, the imperial colour, and – as was the custom – the place could not be used except as a temple. In 1744 it was converted into a lamasery, and became a residence for large numbers of monks from Mongolia and Tibet.

In 1792, Qianlong, having quelled an uprising in Tibet, instituted a new administrative system involving two gold vases. One was kept at the Jokhang Temple in Lhasa for determining the reincarnation of the Dalai Lama (under the supervision of the Minister for Tibetan Affairs), and the other was kept at the Lama Temple for the lottery for the Mongolian Grand Living Buddha. The Lama Temple thus assumed a new importance in ethnic minority control.

The lamasery has three richly worked archways and five main halls strung in a line down the middle, each taller than the preceding one. Styles are mixed – Mongolian, Tibetan and Han, with courtyard enclosures and galleries.

The first hall, **Lokapala**, houses a statue of the Maitreya (future) Buddha, flanked by celestial guardians. The statue facing the back door is Weituo, guardian of Buddhism, made of white sandalwood. Beyond, in the courtyard, is a pond with a bronze mandala depicting Xumishan, the Buddhist paradise.

The second hall, **Yonghedian**, has three figures of Buddha – past, present and future.

The third hall, **Yongyoudian**, has statues of the Buddha of Longevity and the Buddha of Medicine (to the left). The courtyard following it has galleries with some nandikesvaras – joyful buddhas tangled up in multi-armed close encounters. These are coyly draped lest you be corrupted by the

Buddha - portrait of the Avalokitesvara in the Lama Temple

sight, and are to be found in other esoteric locations.

The **Hall of the Wheel of Law**, further north, contains a large bronze statue of Tsongkapa (1357-1419), founder of the Yellow Sect, and frescoes depicting his life. This Tibetan-style building is used for study and prayer.

The last hall, **Wanfu Pavilion**, has an 18-metre-high statue of the Maitreya Buddha in his Tibetan form, sculpted from a single piece of sandalwood and clothed in yellow satin. The smoke curling up from the yak-butter lamps transports you momentarily to Tibet, which is where the log for this statue came from.

In 1949 the Lama Temple was declared protected as a major historical relic. Miraculously it survived the Cultural Revolution without scars. In 1979 large amounts of money were spent on repairs and it was restocked with several dozen novices from Inner Mongolia, a token move on the part of the government to back up its claim that the Lama Temple is a 'symbol of religious freedom, national unity and stability in China'. The novices study Tibetan language and the secret practices of the Yellow Sect.

The temple is active again, though some question whether or not the monks in tennis shoes are really monks or members of the PSB. Prayers take place early in the morning, not for public viewing, but if you inquire discreetly of the head lama you might be allowed to return the following morning. No photography is permitted inside the temple buildings, tempting as it is – in part due to the monkish sensitivity to the reproduction of Buddha images, and partly to the postcard industry. The temple is open daily, except Monday, from 9 am to 4 pm. You can get there by subway to the Yonghegong station.

Confucius Temple & Imperial College

(kǒng miào) 孔庙

Just down the hutong opposite the gates of the Lama Temple is the former Confucius Temple and Imperial College *(guózijiān)*. The Confucius Temple is the largest in the land after the one at Qufu. The temple was re-opened in 1981 after some mysterious use as a high-official residence and is now used as a museum – in sharp contrast to the Lama Temple.

The forest of steles in the temple courtyard look forlorn. The steles record the names of those successful in the civil service examinations (possibly the world's first) of the imperial court. To see his name engraved here was the ambition of every scholar, but it wasn't made easy. Candidates were locked in cubicles (about 8000 of them) measuring roughly 1½ by 1½ metres for a period of three days. Many died or went insane during their incarceration.

The Imperial College was the place where the emperor expounded the Confucian classics to an audience of thousands of kneeling students, professors and court officials – an annual rite. Built by the grandson of Kublai Khan in 1306, the former college was the only institution of its kind in China; it's now the Capital Library. Part of the 'collection' are the stone tablets commissioned by Emperor Qianlong. These are engraved with 13 Confucian classics – 800,000 characters or 12 years' work for the scholar who did it. There is an ancient 'Scholar-Tree' in the courtyard.

Great Bell Temple

(dàzhōng sì) 大钟寺

The biggest bell in China, this one weighs a hefty 46½ tonnes and is 6¾ metres tall. The bell is inscribed with Buddhist sutras, a total of over 227,000 Chinese characters.

The bell was cast during the reign of Ming Emperor Yong Le in 1406 and the tower was built in 1733. Getting the bell from the foundry to the temple proved problematic – back in those days it wasn't possible to contract the job out to a Hong Kong company. A shallow canal had to be built which froze over in winter – the bell was moved across the ice by sled.

Within the grounds of the monastery are several other buildings (besides the Bell Tower itself). This includes the Guanyin Hall, Sutra-keeping Tower, Main Buddha

Hall and Four Devas Hall. This monastery is one of the most popular in Beijing and was re-opened in 1980.

The Great Bell Temple is almost two km due east of the Friendship Hotel on Beisanhuan Xilu.

Wuta Temple
(wǔtǎ sì) 五塔寺
This is an Indian-style temple with five pagodas, first constructed in 1473 from a model presented to the court. The temple underwent a major renovation in 1761, was burned to the ground by foreign troops in 1900, partially rebuilt, then closed during the Cultural Revolution. It has once again been restored and re-opened.

The temple is north-west of the zoo and somewhat difficult to find – take Baishiqiao Lu north from the zoo for almost one km to a bridge, and turn east to the temple, which lies in the middle of a field.

White Dagoba Temple
(báitǎ sì) 白塔寺
The dagoba can be spotted from the top of Jingshan, and is similar (and close to) the one in Beihai Park. It was used as a factory during the Cultural Revolution but reopened after restoration in 1980. The dagoba dates back to Kublai Khan's days and was completed with the help of a Nepalese architect, though the halls date only from the Qing Dynasty. It lies off Fuchengmennei Dajie.

Guangji Temple
(guǎngjì sì) 广济寺
The Guangji (Universal Rescue) Temple is on the north-western side of Xisi intersection, and east of the White Dagoba Temple. It's in good shape and is the headquarters of the Chinese Buddhist Association. It is said to contain some of the finest Buddhist statues in China and may be open to the public.

Niujie Mosque
(niújiē lǐbài sì) 牛街礼拜寺
In the south-western sector of Beijing, south of Guang'anmennei Dajie, is a Muslim residential area with a handsome mosque facing

Mecca. Niujie (Ox St) is an area worth checking out with a feel all its own. In a lane further east of the mosque is the Fayuan (Source of Law) Temple. The temple was originally constructed in the 7th century and is still going strong – it's now a Buddhist college, and is open to visitors.

White Cloud Temple
(báiyúnguān) 白云观
This is in a district directly south of Yanjing Hotel and west of the moat. It was once the Taoist centre of North China and the site of temple fairs. Check a map for directions. Walk south on Baiyun Lu and cross the moat. Continue south along Baiyun Lu and turn into a curving street on the left; follow it for 250 metres to the temple entrance. Inside are several courtyards, including a pool, bridge, several halls of worship and Taoist motifs.

Further south of the White Cloud Temple is the Tianningsi pagoda, looking pretty miserable in a virtual industrial junkyard. The temple that was once attached has disappeared.

Black Temple
(zhìhuà sì) 智化寺
So nicknamed because of its deep blue tiling, this is a pretty example of Ming architecture (dating from 1443) but there's nothing else of note. If you strain over the bus map, looking north of the main railway station, you will find a hutong called Lumicang, which runs east off Chaoyangmen Nanxiaojie (about 1½ km north of the station). The temple is at the east end of Lumicang. The coffered ceiling of the third hall of the Growth of Intellect Temple is not at the east end of Lumicang – it's in the USA. Lumicang hutong had rice granaries in the Qing Dynasty.

Cathedrals
East Cathedral *(dōngtáng)* This building at 74 Wangfujing was built on the site of the house of the Jesuit priest Adam Schall. It was founded in 1666 and was later used by the Portuguese Lazarists. It has been rebuilt several times and is now used as a primary

school during the week; Catholic services are held early on Sunday mornings.

South Cathedral (*nántáng*) On Qianmen at the Xuanwumen intersection (north-east side) above the subway station, the South Cathedral is built on the site of Matteo Ricci's house (first built 1703 and destroyed three times since then).

North Cathedral (*běitáng*) Also called the Cathedral of Our Saviour, it was built in 1887, but was badly damaged during the Cultural Revolution and converted to a factory warehouse. It was re-opened at the end of 1985 after restoration work was completed. The cathedral is at Xishiku, in Xicheng (West District).

Underground City
(*dì xià chéng*) 地下城
In the late 1960s, with a Soviet invasion apparently hanging over them, the Chinese built huge civil defence systems, especially in northern China. This hobby started before 1949 when the PLA used the tunnelling technique to surprise the enemy. Pressed for space, and trying to maximise the peacetime possibilities of the air-raid shelters (aside from the fact that the shelters are useless in the event of nuclear attack), Beijing has put them to use as warehouses, factories, shops, restaurants, hotels, roller-skating rinks, theatres and clinics.

It's not one of the most inspiring sights in Beijing, but CITS has tours to the Underground City for Y10, often combined with a visit to the Mao Mausoleum. The section you see on the brief tour is about 270 metres long with tunnels at the four, eight and 15-metre levels. It was constructed by volunteers and shop assistants living in the Qianmen area – about 2000 people and 10 years of spare-time work with simple tools – though the shelters were planned and construction was supervised by the army. The people reap a few benefits now such as preferential treatment for relatives and friends who can stay in a 100-bed hotel, use of the warehouse space – and there's a few bucks to be made

from tourists. Some features of the system you can see are the telecommunications and first-aid rooms and ventilation system.

There are roughly 90 entrances to this particular complex. The guide claims that 10,000 shoppers in the Dazhalan area can be evacuated to the suburbs in five minutes (what about the other 70,000?!) in the event of an attack. Entrances are hidden in shops – the one you descend by is an ordinary-looking garment shop. It's got the flavour of a James Bond movie with a bit of the apocalypse thrown in. A terse lecture is given by a Civil Air Defence man at the end, complete with fluorescent wall map – oh, and a cup of tea before you surface.

If you want to give the CITS tour a miss then there are two bits of the underground city that are easy to get to yourself – the subway and the Dongtian Underground Restaurant.

Dongtian Restaurant The Dongtian (Cave Heaven) Restaurant is just north of Chang'an Jie at 192 Xidan Beidajie, eastern side – look for a display of pictures of subterranean scenes that mark the entrance. Descending 60 steps, you'll come to four small dining rooms, all served by the same restaurant. They have the decor of an American greasy-spoon truck-stop as interpreted by a crazed neoclassical Sino-Italian decorator.

Dongtian is one of about a dozen underground restaurants operating in Beijing. What better way to get there than by subway? Take the tube to Xuanwumen, then hop on a bus north for about two stops.

Chang'an Inn Next to the Dongtian, but not accessible to the public (you can try) is the Chang'an Inn with its 400 beds. There are some 100 underground hotels in Beijing with a total of 10,000 beds. While the views may not be great, the rooms are insulated by several metres of earth from traffic noise, dust, wind and pesky mosquitoes. Young Chinese honeymooners visiting the capital can rent one of the Chang'an Inn's special Double Happiness rooms, decorated with bright red calligraphy wishing them joys when they surface and re-enter the real world. As the Chinese saying goes, 'Make one thing serve two purposes'.

Beijing Subway *(dì xià tiě lù)* The Beijing Subway runs 15 to 20 metres underground and is a major link in the air-raid shelter system, providing fast evacuation of civilians to the suburbs. The east-west line, though opened in 1969, was for a time restricted to Chinese with special passes – foreigners were not permitted to use it until 1980. Like most subways it loses money – several million yuan per year. One reason is that it employs a lot of people who give orders but do very little work. Unlike most other subways the crime rate is low (there is the odd pickpocket), graffiti is nonexistent, it's very clean, and messy suicides are said to be rare (one every couple of years supposedly). The 'Underground Dragon' is mostly tiled, and has austere marble pillars. Some platforms are enlivened with brushwork paintings, illuminated ads – and, surprise, surprise, Hong Kong-based advertising in English only.

A good way to familiarise yourself with urban and suburban Beijing is to hop off the subway at random, explore, and pop back down again. It's only four jiao per ride, you can't get lost, and it gives you some very fast first impressions of different sectors of Beijing, painlessly. The subway is open from 5.30 am to 10.30 pm and trains run every few minutes. It can get very crowded but it sure beats the buses!

Ancient Observatory
(gǔguān xiàngtái) 古观象台

One interesting perspective on Beijing is the observatory mounted on the battlements of a watchtower, once part of the city walls. Dwarfed by embassy housing blocks, it lies in a wilderness of traffic loops and highways just west of the Friendship Store; it's on the south-west corner of Jianguomennei Dajie and the second ring road. The views alone are worth the visit. This is one of the sights that you can visit in safety – small in scope, interesting, some English explanation. The observatory dates back to Kublai Khan's days when it was north of the present site. The Great Khan, as well as later Ming and Qing emperors, relied heavily on astrologers before making a move.

The present Beijing Observatory was built from 1437 to 1446, not only to facilitate astrological predictions but also to aid seafaring navigators. Downstairs are displays of navigational equipment used by Chinese shipping. On the 1st floor are replicas of five 5000-year-old pottery jars, unearthed from Henan Province in 1972 and showing painted patterns of the sun. There are also four replicas of Han Dynasty eave tiles representing east, west, north and south. There is a map drawn on a wooden octagonal board with 1420 stars marked in gold foil or powder; it's a reproduction of the original, which is said to be Ming Dynasty but is based on an older Tang map. Busts of six prominent astronomers are also displayed.

On the 'roof' is a variety of astronomical instruments designed by the Jesuits. The Jesuits, scholars as well as proselytisers, found their way into the capital in 1601 when Matteo Ricci and company were permitted to work with Chinese scientists. The emperor was keen to find out about European firearms and cannons from them.

The Jesuits outdid the resident Muslim calendar-setters and were given control of the observatory, becoming the Chinese court's advisors. Of the eight bronze instruments on display (including an equatorial armilla, celestial globe and altazimuth), six were designed and constructed under the supervision of the Belgian priest Ferdinand Verbiest, who came to China in 1659 to work at the Qing court. The instruments were built between 1669 and 1673, and are embellished with sculptured bronze dragons and other Chinese craftwork, a unique mix of east and west. The azimuth theodolite was supervised by Bernard Stumpf, also a missionary. The eighth instrument, the new armilla, was completed in 1754. It's not clear which of the instruments on display are the originals.

During the Boxer Rebellion, the instruments disappeared into the hands of the

French and the Germans. Some were returned in 1902, while others came back under the provisions of the Treaty of Versailles (1919). Bertrand Russell commented that this was 'probably the most important benefit which the treaty secured to the world'. The observatory the Jesuits set up in Shanghai was used for meteorological predictions, and is still used for that purpose. The Jesuits even had some influence over architecture in Beijing, and designed the Italian rococo palaces at the Old Summer Palace (destroyed in 1860) using Versailles as a blueprint.

More recently, government officials were caught off guard when local and foreign rock bands got together and staged a dance party in the ancient tower. The observatory is open daily except Monday from 9 to 11 am and from 1 to 4 pm.

Beijing University
(běidà) 北京大学

Beijing University and Qinghua University *(qīnghuá dàxué)* are the most prestigious institutes in China. Beida was founded at the turn of the century; it was then called Yanjing University and was administered by the USA. Its students figured prominently in the 4 May 1919 demonstrations and the later resistance to the Japanese. In 1953 the university moved from Jingshan to its present location. In the 1960s the Red Guards first appeared here and the place witnessed some scenes of utter mayhem as the battles of the Cultural Revolution took place.

Beijing University has a beautiful campus, so it's a pity you can't visit it. At one time it was open to foreigners, but students from this school were leaders in the democracy protests of 1989. Since then, the students have been kept on a tight leash and foreign influences are being kept out. The policy could change at any time, but at the time of writing, foreigners required special permission to visit the campus. Such permission is difficult to obtain.

Beijing has about 50 colleges and universities. An intriguing one is the Central Nationalities Institute *(mínzú xuéyuàn)*, just north of the zoo. The institute trains cadres for the regions where ethnic minorities live.

Beijing University is on the bus No 332 route from the zoo, or about a 45-minute bike ride from the city centre.

Blockbuster Bicycle Tour
A suggested itinerary is as follows:

Taoranting Park – Natural History Museum – Dazhalan – Qianmen – Tiananmen Square – History Museum & Museum of the Revolution – Great Hall of the People – Tiananmen Gate – Forbidden City – Beihai Park – Jingshan Park – Song Qingling Museum – Drum Tower – Bell Tower – Confucius Temple – Lama Temple – China Art Gallery – Wanfujing – Kentucky Fried Chicken or McDonald's – Tiantan Park – Home?

Obviously this is far too much to attempt in one day, and it's not recommended that you see everything unless you have only one whirlwind day to dive-bomb the capital. The Forbidden City alone is worth a full day's exploration. But if you start out early (at dawn) you can see a good chunk of town and take in some of Beijing's many moods.

Nonstop cycling time is about two hours – Chinese bike, Western legs, average pace.

The starting point is your hotel – if you're staying at low-priced accommodation this means the south end of town. Almost directly north of the Qiaoyuan Hotel and the lovely sewage canal is **Taoranting Park**, one of several venues for crack-of-dawn taiji exercises. Join the crowd if you wish, or watch from a respectful distance. You can't bring the bike into the park, so pay your small surcharge and leave it with the attendant.

One big block to the east is Yongdingmen Dajie, just another name for the southern end of Qianmen Dajie. Turn north here and you'll eventually find the west entrance of Tiantan Park on your right side. The park is certainly worth exploring, but you can do that some other day. Right now, our goal is just a little to the north, the **Natural History Museum** on the east side of Yongdingmen Dajie.

After you've had your dose of natural history, continue north to where Yongdingmen Dajie becomes Qianmen Dajie. Coming

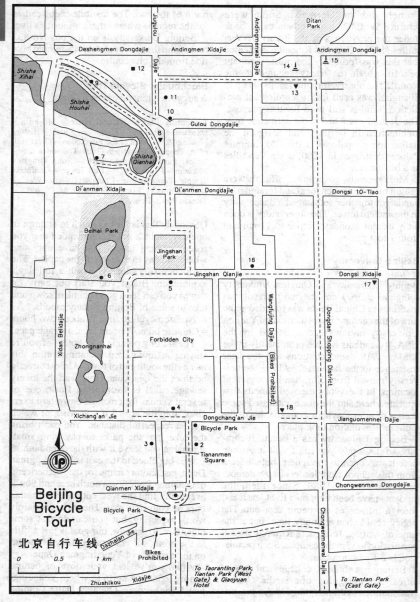

Ditan Park

Deshengmen Dongdajie   Andingmen Xidajie   Andingmennei Dajie   Andingmen Dongdajie

Jiugulou

Andingmennei Dajie

Dajie

14 ⊥   ▼ 15

Shisha
Xihai

■ 12

● 9

Shisha
Houhai

● 11

13 ▼

10 ●

8 ●
▼   Gulou Dongdajie

● 7   Shisha
Qianhai

Di'anmen Xidajie   Di'anmen Dongdajie   Dongsi 10-Tiao

Beihai Park

Jingshan
Park

16 ●

Xidan Beidajie

● 6   Jingshan Qianjie   Dongsi Xidajie

5 ●   17 ▼

Zhongnanhai   Forbidden City   Wangfujing Dajie
(Bikes Prohibited)

Dongdan Shopping District

18 ▼

Xichang'an Jie   Dongchang'an Jie   Jianguomennei Dajie

4 ●

Bicycle Park

● Bicycle Park
3 ●   ● 2

**Beijing
Bicycle
Tour**

Tiananmen
Square

北京自行车线

Qianmen Xidajie   1

Chongwenmen Dongdajie

Bicycle Park

Chongwenmennei Dajie

Dazhalan Jie

0   0.5   1 km

Bikes
Prohibited

To Taoranting Park,
Tiantan Park (West
Gate) & Qiaoyuan
Hotel

Zhushikou   Xidajie

To Tiantan Park
(East Gate)

1	Qianmen
2	History Museum & Museum of the Revolution
3	Great Hall of the People
4	Tiananmen Gate
5	Forbidden City Rear Gate
6	Beihai Park Main Entrance
7	Prince Gong's Residence
8	Kaorouji Restaurant
9	Song Qingling Museum
10	Drum Tower
11	Bell Tower
12	Bamboo Garden Hotel
13	Confucius Restaurant
14	Confucius Temple
15	Lama Temple
16	China Art Gallery
17	Kentucky Fried Chicken
18	McDonald's

1	前门
2	中国革命历史博物馆
3	人民大会堂
4	天安门
5	故宫北门
6	北海公园北门
7	恭王府
8	北京烤肉季
9	宋庆龄故居
10	鼓楼
11	钟楼
12	竹园宾馆
13	孔子餐厅
14	孔庙
15	雍和宫
16	中国美术馆
17	肯德基家乡鸡
18	麦当劳

up on your left is **Dazhalan**, one of Beijing's most intriguing hutongs. Bikes cannot be ridden into this particular hutong, though you can explore most others on two wheels.

Slightly more than a stone's throw to the north is **Qianmen**, the front gate to the vast expanse of **Tiananmen Square**. Traffic is one way for north-south avenues on either side of the square. If you want to go to Tiananmen, dismount after the archway and wheel the bike to the parking areas along the sidewalk. Bicycles cannot be ridden across Tiananmen Square (apparently tanks are OK), but you can walk the bike. Nearby are the **History Museum, Museum of the Revolution, Great Hall of the People, Mao's Mausoleum, Tiananmen Gate** and the **Forbidden City**.

Over to the west side of the Forbidden City you're heading into the most sensitive part of the capital – the **Zhongnanhai Compound**. On the right, going up Beichang Jie, you pass some older housing that lines the moat. On the left is a high wall that shields from view the area where top Party members live and work (it was decided not to rip down this section of the old walls). In 1973, when the new wing of the Beijing Hotel shot up, the PSB suddenly realised that guests with binoculars could observe activity in Zhong-

nanhai, so a fake building was erected along the western wall of the Forbidden City to short-circuit that possibility. Indeed, mysterious buildings abound in this locale (and on the strip back at the traffic lights along the way to Jingshan Park), including private theatres for viewing foreign films and so on.

Then it's **Beihai Park**, which by this time of day should be bustling with activity. You can exercise your arms as well as your legs by hiring a rowing boat. There's a cafe near the south gate overlooking Beihai Lake, where you can get beer, coffee, tea or cold drinks.

Back on the bike and you'll soon reach **Jingshan Park**. There's bicycle parking by the entrance. Jingshan Park is a splendid place to survey the smog of Beijing, get your bearings with 360° views, and enjoy a good overview of the russet roofing of the Forbidden City opposite. There are snack bars both in the park and at the north end of the Forbidden City.

North of Jingshan Park it gets a bit tricky. You want to get off the main road into the small alleys running around the Shisha Hai Lakes. Worth checking out is **Prince Gong's Residence** (*gōngwángfǔ*), which lies more or less at the centre of the arc created by the lakes running from north to south. It's reputed to be the model mansion for Cao Xueqin's 18th-century classic, *A Dream of Red Mansions* (translated as *The Story of the Stone* by David Hawkes, Penguin, 1980). It's one of the largest private residential compounds in Beijing, with a nine-courtyard layout, high walls and elaborate gardens. Prince Gong was the son of a Qing emperor.

The lake district is steeped in history; if you consult a Beijing map you'll see that the set of lakes connects from north to south. In the Yuan Dynasty, barges would come through various canals to the top lake (Jishuitan), a sort of harbour for Beijing. Later the lakes were used for pleasure-boating, and were bordered by the residences of high officials.

The larger lake to the north-west is the Shisha Houhai (Lake of the Ten Back Monasteries). Below that is the Shisha Qianhai (Lake of the Ten Front Monasteries).

Also around the lakes you'll find the **Song Qingling Museum**, the retirement residence of Sun Yatsen's respected *taitai* (wife).

Make a small detour here. If you go northeast through the hutongs you will arrive at the Bamboo Garden Hotel (*zhúyuán bīnguǎn*), which is a wonderful illustration of the surprises that hutongs hold. This was originally the personal garden of Sheng Xuanhuai, an important Qing official. There are exquisite gardens, beautiful courtyards, renovated compound architecture, and expensive restaurant (English menu, alfresco in summer). It's a quiet place to sip a drink.

Another small detour brings you to the Kaorouji Restaurant – not necessarily the cheapest place to get your roast chicken, but the balcony dining in summer is pleasant enough.

Back on the main drag and you come to the **Drum Tower** (*gǔlóu*). It was built in 1420 and has several drums which were beaten to mark the hours of the day – in effect Big Ben of Beijing. Time was kept with a water clock. It's in pretty sad shape, but an impressive structure nonetheless with a solid brick base. Occasional exhibitions take place here since the tower is connected with local artisans.

Behind the Drum Tower, down an alley directly north, is the **Bell Tower** (*zhōnglóu*),

---

Hutong Hopping

A completely different side of Beijing emerges in the *hutongs* or back lanes. The original plan of the city allowed for enclosed courtyards buried down alleys, and though the politics have changed, many of the courtyards remain. Given the choice between a high-rise block and a traditional compound, most residents of Beijing would opt for the latter. The compounds have loads more character – and offer courtyards to grow vegetables in.

There are over 3000 hutongs in Beijing, so there's a lot out there to discover. The word derives from Mongolian and means a passageway between tents or yurts. Many of the hutongs are named after markets (fish, pig, rice, sheep) or trades (hats, bowstrings, trousers) once conducted along them. Others took their names as the seats of government offices, or specialised suppliers to the palace (granaries, red lacquer, armour). Yet others were named after dukes and officers.

Around the Forbidden City of yore there were some unusual industries. Wet-Nurse Lane was full of young mothers who breastfed the imperial offspring. They were selected from around China on scouting trips four times a year. Clothes-Washing Lane was where the women who did the imperial laundry lived. The maids, grown old in the service of the court, were packed off to far-away places for a few years so that their intimate knowledge of the royal undergarments would be out of date by the time they got round to talking to their friends about it.

Walking along the hutongs kind of destroys the advantage of a lightning visit, and may well lead to you acquiring a Chinese entourage. Charging off on a bicycle is the best way to go. If you see an interesting compound, you can stop and peer in – maybe even be invited in; the duller bits you can cruise by. ∎

which was originally built at the same time as the Drum Tower, but burnt down. The present structure is 18th-century, and the gigantic bell which used to hang there has been moved to the Drum Tower. Legend has it that the bellmaker's daughter plunged into the molten iron before the bell was cast. Her father only managed to grab her shoe as she did so, and the bell's soft sound resembled that of the Chinese for 'shoe' (*xié*). The same story is told about a couple of other bells in China.

Back on the road and you'll reach the former **Confucius Temple & Imperial College**, now a museum/library complex. Unless you can read stele-calligraphy, you probably won't spend much time here. A stele standing in the hutong ordered officials to dismount at this point but you can ignore that.

By contrast, just down the road is the **Lama Temple**, one of Beijing's finest. Along the way to the Lama Temple you might pass through several decorated lintels; these graceful archways (*páilóu*), which commemorate mandarin officials or chaste widows, were ripped out of the thoroughfares of Beijing in the 1950s. The reason given was the facilitation of traffic movement. Some have been relocated in parks. The ones you see in this hutong are rarities.

This is the northernmost point of today's journey (you're still with us, aren't you?). Head south now, and if you're still ready for another museum there's the **China Art Gallery**, a slight detour to the west at the northern end of Wangfujing. Unfortunately, Wangfujing itself is closed to cyclists, so back to the east on Dongsi Dajie and you'll find Kentucky Fried Chicken. If the Colonel's fried chicken delights aren't what you had in mind, you could try McDonald's, at the southern end of Wangfujing. No matter what you think of the food, these restaurants are at least as popular as the Forbidden City.

Launch yourself into the sea of cyclists, throw your legs into cruising speed, and cycle the length of Dongdan south to the east entrance of **Tiantan Park**. If this is still Day One of your bike tour, you'll probably be too exhausted to walk inside to see the Temple of Heaven – well, there's always tomorrow. From this point, you're well positioned to head home (wherever that is – probably one of the budget hotels in the southern end of the city).

Golf

The art of poking a white ball around a lawn enjoys considerable prestige value in face-conscious China. If your face needs a lift, check out the Beijing International Golf Course (☎ 9746388) (*běijīng guójì gāo'ěrfū qiú cháng*). This Chinese-Japanese joint-venture opened in mid-1986. The 18-hole golf course is 35 km north of Beijing close to the Ming Tombs in Changping County, and the course was used during the 1990 Asian Games. Pushing that little ball around is not cheap, but the course is in good condition and the scenery is spectacular. Visitor fees are Y250 on weekdays, Y300 on weekends and public holidays. You can rent a set of golf clubs for Y70 and spiked golf shoes for Y50.

There is another golf course, Airport Golf Links, (*jīcháng gāo'ěrfū qiú cháng*) just north of Capital Airport.

Horseback Riding

Several horseback riding parks (*qímǎ cháng*) have opened to the north-west of Beijing in the Western Hills. The nearest is the Fragrant Hills, but the best of the lot is Kangxi Grasslands (see the Around Beijing section). Prices are reasonable, especially the further out you get from the city.

Organised Tours

Northern China is blotted with the huge municipal areas of Beijing and Tianjin, each of which contains some of China's prime tourist attractions.

CITS operates a number of high-priced tours to destinations outside Beijing (Great Wall and Ming Tombs, Y130, including guide and lunch). You can dispense with the guides and food and go for the Chinese tour-bus operators who offer the same tour for Y25.

The tours operated out of the Qiaoyuan Hotel are popular. An alternative is the tour buses which leave from the north-western side of the Chongwenmen intersection, across the road from the Chongwenmen Hotel. Tickets for these tours can be bought at the same place, from the parked minibus labelled 'booking office'.

Typical tours take in the Great Wall and Ming Tombs; Western Hills and Summer Palace; Western Hills and Sleeping Buddha Temple; Tanzhe Temple; Yunshui Caves; Zhoukoudian; and Zunhua (Eastern Qing Tombs). Tours further afield to Chengde (three days) and Beidaihe (five days) are possible.

Places to Stay – bottom end

Hotels Hotels offering budget accommodation are almost entirely concentrated in the southern side of the city. While a bit far from the centre of things, transport along the second and third ring roads makes it reasonably fast to get there, at least by taxi. Buses and minibuses from the Beijing railway station are also frequent.

Beijing's best known backpacker's hostel is the *Qiaoyuan Hotel (qiáoyuán fàndiàn)* on Dongbinhe Lu in the south of the city near the Yongdingmen railway station. There are different phone numbers for the front building (☎ 3038861) and rear building (☎ 3012244).

Dorm beds are Y25, doubles cost from Y60 to Y80 with shower. The rear building is more luxurious but it must be made out of corn flakes – it's falling apart even though it's brand new.

The problem with this place is incompetent management – broken plumbing, sneering employees, 'no beds available' in the dorms when the dorms are empty, no one on duty when you want to check out, etc.

There have been frequent reports that the foreign-exchange counter in the lobby rips off travellers by sticking a few RMB notes into the pile of FEC when you cash a travellers' cheque.

On the other hand, we need to add that many travellers have provoked the staff and contributed to the ill will – keep your temper in check to make it easier for yourself and those who come after you.

By way of compensation, there are numerous privately run services for travellers just outside the hotel – cheap restaurants, bike hire, laundry service, etc. In summer, the area becomes a true travellers' hang-out right down to the banana muesli pancakes and thieving black-market moneychangers.

To get there take bus No 20 or 54 from the main Beijing railway station to the terminal (Yongdingmen). Or from just north of the Chongwenmen Hotel take trolley-bus No 106 to the terminal. From the Yongdingmen terminal, walk for about five minutes to the west following the big highway next to the canal. There are also minibuses for Yongdingmen which leave from opposite the main railway station; these cost Y5 and depart when full. From the airport, the cheapest route is to take the airport bus to the second stop (Swissotel, next to a subway station), then take the subway to Beijing railway station and finally bus Nos 20 or 54 to Yongdingmen.

A lot of people dislike the Qiaoyuan, but there are alternatives. One is the *Jingtai Hotel* (☎ 7212476, 7224675) *(jǐngtài bīnguǎn)* at 65 Yongwai Jingtaixi, a small alley running off Anlelin Lu in the south of the city. Dorm beds cost Y20; doubles/triples without bath Y50/60; doubles with bath Y70, Y90 and Y120. The hotel is clean and pleasant, has hot water all day, and a bar that serves cold beer. From the railway station take bus No 39 to the first stop after it crosses the canal – the name of the bus stop is *Puhuangyu*. From there, you've got a 10-minute walk west on Anlelin Lu. Alternatively, bus No 45 will drop you off at the intersection of Yongdingmennei Jie and Anlelin Lu, also a 10-minute walk from the hotel. Bus No 25 goes right down Anlelin Lu and will drop you off near the hotel – this bus both terminates and starts at the Anlelin Lu's east end. The Jingtai will (reluctantly) accept payment in RMB.

Just a two-minute walk from the Jingtai Hotel is the *Yongdingmen Hotel* (☎ 7212125, 7213344) *(yǒngdìngmén fàndiàn)* at 77

Anlelin Lu. This place is not as good as the Jingtai, but if you arrive during the busy season and the Jingtai is packed out, it beats sleeping on the streets. Doubles/triples are Y58/75 – RMB are accepted, reluctantly. Take bus No 39 from the railway station.

The *Jinghua Hotel* (☎ 7222211) (*jīnghuá fàndiàn*) is on Nansanhuan Xilu, the southern part of the third ring road around Beijing. It's an adequate and friendly place to stay, but the neighbourhood, with its ugly apartment blocks, may leave you cold. Doubles with private bath cost Y50 and Y65. Bus Nos 2 and 17 from Qianmen drop you off nearby. This place is also very convenient for the Haihutun long-distance bus station (buses to cities south of Beijing).

Within walking distance of the Jinghua is the *Lihua Hotel* (☎ 7211144) (*lìhuá fàndiàn*), 71 Yangqiao, Yongdingmenwai. Dorms cost Y25 and doubles are Y90. Bus No 343 is the easiest to get you there but No 14 will also do.

The *Longtan Hotel* (☎ 7711602; fax 7714028) (*lóngtán fàndiàn*), 15 Panjiayuan Nanli, Chaoyang District, is an excellent alternative to all of the preceding and many budget travellers now stay here. The staff are friendly and there is a good (but not cheap) restaurant. Beds go for Y30 in three-bed rooms or Y20 in a five-bed room, and paying in RMB is possible – the communal baths deserve honourable mention for being in extraordinarily good condition. Doubles cost Y80. The hotel is opposite Longtan Park in the south of the city, close to a hospital. Bus No 51 (to the last stop) lets you out near the hotel, but bus No 63 from the railway station is somewhat more frequent. Beware of the rip-off moneychangers hanging around the car park – they are thieves.

The *Traffic Hotel* (☎ 7011114) (*jiāotōng fàndiàn*), 35 Dongsi Kuaiyu Nanjie, has 82 comfortable rooms but no dorms. Doubles with shared bath are Y60; with private bath it's Y96. The hotel is in a narrow alley running south from Tiyuguan Lu – signs in English point the way. Bus No 41 runs on Tiyuguan Lu and drops you off at the alley's entrance.

University Dormitories Typical prices are Y30 for dormitories, Y60 for doubles. Most of these places have no beds – just Japanese style tatami mats – but they're reasonably comfortable. There are some problems with staying in these places – they aren't hotels, so staff are only on duty from around 8 am to 5 pm with the usual two-hour lunch break. Few staff speak English, and if you start arguing with them about FEC and dirty toilets, you'll be asked to leave. They really don't have to take foreigners, so be on your best behaviour here or risk getting kicked out. They provide no special amenities like laundry service or bike rentals, but they often have cheap student cafeterias, although these are only open for short hours, like 5 to 6 pm. Overall, it's usually better to stay in the budget hotels, but the university hostels offer an alternative if the hotels are packed out. And finally, we've had complaints from travellers that some of their small items have been nicked from their rooms, apparently by the staff working in some of these places.

One possible place to stay with a very central location is the *Central Institute of Fine Arts* (☎ 554731) (*zhōngyāng měishù xuéyuàn*), at 5 Xiaowei Hutong in an alley off of Wangfujing near the Beijing Hotel. The main problem with this place is that it's too popular – beds are hard to get, so give them a call first. This school built the now famous 'Goddess of Democracy' which came to symbolise the democracy movement during the Tiananmen protests in 1989. From the railway station take bus 103 to Wangfujing. After you enter the gate of the campus, go to the 8th floor of the building on your left.

One other university that accepts foreigners is the *Beijing Language Institute* (☎ 2017798) (*běijīng yǔyán xuéyuàn*), 15 Xueyuan Lu, Haidian District. Many foreigners come here to study Chinese. Bus No 331 stops in front of the school.

Other possibilities include the *Beijing Teachers' College* (*běishīdà*), *People's University* (*rénmín dàxué*) and *Qinghua University* (*qīnghuá dàxué*), all in the northern part of the city.

Places to Stay – middle

Oddly enough, bargaining for a room is usually more successful in the mid-range hotels than in the budget places. Many travellers report getting discounts of 30% or more, at least during the off-season. Just remember that bargaining in Beijing should be done in a friendly manner.

The *Tiantan Sports Hotel* (☎ 7013388; fax 7015388) (*tiāntán tǐyù bīnguǎn*), 10 Tiyuguan Lu, Chongwen District. The hotel derives its name from its position between Tiantan Park and the gymnasium. It hosts sports-minded group tours but will take whoever else turns up. The hotel has a YMCA tinge to it but is a bright, airy place in a good location with friendly staff; doubles cost Y130. It has a good Indonesian restaurant. To get there take the subway one stop from the main railway station to Chongwenmen, then bus Nos 39, 41 or 43.

Beiwei Hotel (☎ 3012266; fax 3011366) (*běiwěi fàndiàn*), 13 Xijing Lu, Xuanwu District – on the western side of Tiantan Park. Take the subway to Qianmen, then bus No 5 south; you can take bus No 20 direct from the main railway station. Standard rooms are Y130, superior Y150 and suites Y200. This place belongs to the neighbouring Rainbow Hotel but is cheaper.

Lusongyuan Hotel (☎ 4011116, 4030416) (*lǔsōngyuán bīnguǎn*), 22 Banchang Hutong, Dongcheng District. Doubles cost Y160, the staff are very friendly and the place is highly recommended. The problem is that it's difficult to find. When you

---

Temple of Heaven Crashpad

Getting a cheap bed in Beijing wasn't always as easy as stumbling into the Qiaoyuan Hotel and smiling at the bleary-eyed receptionist. Back in 1983, when we were researching the first edition of this book, dormitory accommodation was hard to come by and to get it often required some aggressive arm-wrestles with uncooperative hotel managers. Michael Buckley witnessed the creation of such a dormitory.

Scene 1 The meeting room, ground floor, Tiantan Sports Hotel. I roll in at 11 pm – good timing – the next hotel is miles off, and the manager knows even before he picks up the phone that everything else in town is chock-a-block. After a laborious wait, he allows me a couch in the meeting room. Two more travellers, I discover, are already snoozing on the couches within. Cost is Y3 per night per couchette. Three days later, travellers discover there is another meeting room on the 4th floor – the word spreads.

Scene 2 A traveller strides straight past the manager, backpack on. 'Where are you going?' he demands. 'To the meeting room,' she answers, taking the stairs three at a time, not looking back, unrolls sleeping bag on arrival. Manager scratches head – she didn't even bother to ask if there were any rooms free. Manager, driven crazy by travellers' preference for the low-priced meeting rooms, transforms the one on the 4th floor into a dorm with camp beds, Y8, men only. Female travellers quickly point out the injustice – a conference is held, where else, in the ground-floor meeting room and, amazingly enough, a third meeting room is found (2nd floor) and designated a women's dorm. Both of these former meeting rooms, now established dorms, are large and filled with camp beds entirely surrounded by facing armchairs, a somewhat surreal decor.

Scene 3 Word has spread along the travellers' grapevine as far as Hong Kong, but CITS has received neither news nor reservations. A fresh group of travellers steps into the Tiantan off the Trans-Siberian and heads straight for the dorms – later they set up a disco near the restaurant. The manager has given up denying that the dorms exist: the camp beds are given a shakedown, spruced up, and the price jumps to Y10.

Scene 4 Much later. The dorms are full, *really* full. I am sharing a room with two people, one sleeping on the floor. I pass the desk as two travellers argue with the manager, refusing to believe the dorms are really really full, otherwise known as 'aw-full'. The room I'm in is large – space for two more on the floor, so I offer the travellers the option if they get stuck and tell them the room number. When I return in the evening, there are about seven travellers in the room arguing with the manager about floor space, and I quietly slip back out again. Ah yes, time to leave Beijing before another crashpad is created. ■

approach the hutong from either end, it doesn't seem that there could be a building of such high standard halfway down – but rest assured, the hotel does exist. The hutong is one way and many taxi drivers are reluctant to drive down it in the wrong direction, but others are perfectly willing to do so. The hotel is directly north of the China Art Gallery, second hutong north of Di'anmen, turn left – bus No 104 from Beijing railway station comes close.

Chongwenmen Hotel (☎ 5122211; fax 5122122) *(chóngwénmén fàndiàn)*, 2 Chongwenmen Xi Dajie. This good, mid-range place has a very central location that makes the five-star hotels jealous. Standard rooms are Y190, suites Y260 to Y300.

The *Yuexiu Hotel* (☎ 3014499; fax 3014609) *(yuèxiù dàfàndiàn)*, 24 Xuanwumen Dong Dajie, is a few blocks south of the Xidan shopping district and CAAC. Economy doubles are Y130, standard Y150, superior Y160, deluxe Y180 and suites Y240 to Y370. It's a bargain for such a well located hotel of this standard.

Leyou Hotel (☎ 7712266; fax 7711636) *(lèyóu fàndiàn)*, 13 Dongsanhuan Nanlu, Chaoyang District, east of Longtan Park (south-east Beijing). A decent mid-range hotel with 171 rooms with doubles for Y130, Y150, Y180 and Y280. Take bus No 28 or 52 to the terminus.

The *Far East Hotel* (☎ 3018811; fax 3018233) *(yuǎndōng fàndiàn)*, 90 Tieshuxie Jie, Qianmenwai, Xuanwu District, is actually on the west end of Dazhalan (south-west of Qianmen). It's an excellent location. With double rooms costing Y75 to Y140, this place would qualify as budget accommodation except that the cheap rooms are almost always full. The pricier rooms still aren't a bad deal.

Huabei Hotel (☎ 2022266) *(huáběi dàjiǔdiàn)*, 3 Gulouwai Huangsi Dajie, is in north-central Beijing (north of Ditan Park). Singles are Y160, doubles Y200 to Y320, triples Y240. This place is popular with the Taiwanese, which means they crank up the karaoke at night.

The *Sihai Hotel* (☎ 5006699) *(sìhǎi*

bīnguǎn), Liugongfen, Dongzhimenwai, is close to the Holiday Inn Lido and the airport. Despite this, doubles are only Y120, making it the best deal in this neighbourhood. The desk staff seem friendly enough.

The *Guanghua Hotel* (☎ 5018866; fax 5016516) *(guānghuá fàndiàn)*, 38 Donghuan Beilu, Chaoyang District, is just down the road from the China World Trade Centre on Jianguomenwai. At Y170 for a double, it's dirt cheap for this neighbourhood, but it's also a possible target for renovation and future high prices.

Dongfang Hotel (☎ 3014466; fax 3044801) *(dōngfāng fàndiàn)*, 11 Wanming Lu (south of Qianmen). Standard doubles are Y198, superior rooms cost Y258. It's good value for the high standard and central location.

The *Shangyuan Hotel* (☎ 8311122) *(shàngyuán fàndiàn)*, Xie Jie, Xizhemenwai, Haidian District, is near the Xizhimen (north) railway station. Doubles are only Y120, which explains why it's usually full.

The *Xizhimen Hotel* (☎ 8327755) *(xīzhímén fàndiàn)*, 42 Xie Jie, is also next to the Xizhimen railway station. Doubles are Y108 – excellent value but, like its neighbour, this hotel is almost perpetually full.

Places to Stay – top end

Keeping up with the top-end hotels in Beijing is like skiing uphill. No sooner does one extravaganza open its doors than the ground-breaking ceremony is held for an even more luxurious pleasure palace.

Foreign experts and students should be delighted to know that the Holiday Inn Lido Hotel offers rooms for US$20 per night (green card specials) if you have the right credentials. Ditto for many Swiss-owned hotels (give *Swissotel* a try).

The *Beijing Hotel* (☎ 5137766; fax 5137307) *(běijīng fàndiàn)*, 33 Dong Chang'an Jie, is the most central hotel in the capital and is therefore highly prized by visitors and dignitaries. Standard rooms cost Y460, superior Y920 and suites Y1610. Even at those rates, it's still significantly cheaper than renting an apartment or office in pricey Beijing and rooms are often leased out on a long-term basis. The roof of the west wing commands a great view of Tiananmen Square and the Forbidden City.

Passing the Beijing Hotel we noticed that there was a huge sign (in English and Chinese) over the entrance saying 'The Beijing Hotel Welcomes Its 1.5 Millionth Visitor!' The staff, dressed in neat uniforms, were all waiting in the freezing cold. The steps were covered in red carpet and there were plants and flowers everywhere. About 20 photographers were waiting to record this event. We speculated as to who would be the lucky guest and concluded that whoever it was, he or she was unlikely to be the 1.5 millionth visitor who casually entered the swinging doors and asked to register.

Our theory was confirmed when a large black limousine came up, stopped and had the door opened by a porter. The cameras started clicking and out stepped the most ragged peasant we saw in all of Beijing. He was warmly welcomed into the hotel and brought through the swinging doors. Without further delay – after the disappearance of the camera crews – the lucky 'guest' reappeared through the swinging doors and disappeared back into the black limo, presumably never to see the Beijing Hotel again. Within minutes the carpet and flowers disappeared into the back of a van. I'd love to have known how this obviously staged event was reported in the press.

Brian Malone

An unusual place to stay is the *Hua Thai Apartment Hotel* (☎ 7716688; fax 7715266) *(huátài fàndiàn)*, Jinsong Dongkou (southeast Beijing). It's unusual because you actually get an apartment with kitchen and other home-like facilities. This place might be worth considering if you're planning a long stay and have a sufficient budget. Twin rooms are Y300; a room with four beds costs Y400.

The *China World Hotel* (☎ 5052266; fax 5053167) *(zhōngguó dàfàndiàn)* is at 1 Jianguomenwai Dajie, east of the Friendship Store. Also known as the World Trade Centre, this is one of the finest places in Beijing. And it should be with standard rooms at Y1035 and suites for Y1408. Despite the price, it's often full.

The *Friendship Hotel* (☎ 8498888; fax 8498866) *(yǒuyí bīnguǎn)*, 3 Baishiqiao Lu, is halfway between the Beijing Zoo and the Summer Palace. Originally built in 1954 for Soviet advisors, the place has been upgraded substantially. Facilities are legendary, including the Olympic-size swimming pool (open to all), theatre, tennis courts, 1900 rooms – you practically need a map to find your way around. Standard rooms cost Y517, superior Y748 and suites are Y1265-6210.

The *Jianguo Hotel* (☎ 5002233; fax 5002871) *(jiànguó fàndiàn)*, 5 Jianguomenwai Dajie. Opened in 1982, this was China's first joint-venture hotel. The Chinese staff of about 600 have no spittoons and are not allowed newspapers, cigarettes, naps or even chairs, but can rake in as much as three times an ordinary Beijinger's salary. Superior rooms are Y540, deluxe Y570, suites Y747 to Y920.

There are plenty of other upmarket places to stay in the capital. The following choices are presented in alphabetical order:

Beijing Asia Hotel (☎ 5007788; fax 5008091) *(yàzhōu dàjiǔdiàn)*, 8 Xinzhong Xijie, Gongren Tiyuchang Beilu. Convenient for disembarking airport bus, and near to Dongsishitiao subway station. Standard rooms cost Y345, deluxe Y374, suites Y690 to Y3450.

Beijing Grand Hotel (☎ 2010033; fax 2029893) *(yuánshān dàjiǔdiàn)*, 20 Yumin Dongli, Deshengmenwai, Xicheng District (north-central Beijing near Ditan Park). Taiwanese management; 187 rooms; standard Y288, superior Y316 and deluxe Y403.

Capital Hotel (☎ 5129988; fax 5120323) *(shǒudū bīnguǎn)*, 3 Qianmen Donglu (east of Qianmen – convenient location). Standard Y345, superior Y1035, deluxe Y1495, suites Y2472 to Y11,500 – plus 10% service charge.

Chains City Hotel (☎ 5007799; fax 5007668) *(chéngshì bīnguǎn)*, 4 Gongren Tiyuchang Donglu, Chaoyang District (east central Beijing). Standard Y288, superior Y402.

Continental Grand Hotel (☎ 4915588; fax 4910106) *(wǔzhōu dàjiǔdiàn)*, 8 Beichen Donglu, Beisihuan Lu, Andingmenwai (in the Asian Games Village). Opened in 1990, this amazing place has 1259 rooms and resembles a city in itself. Standard rooms are Y348, superior Y406 and suites Y870 to Y1740.

CVIK Hotel (☎ 5123388; fax 5123542) *(sàitè fàndiàn)*, 22 Jianguomenwai Dajie (across from Friendship Store), 341 rooms. Standard Y345 plus 10% service charge.

Gloria Plaza Hotel (☎ 5158855; fax 5158533) (*kǎilái dàjiǔdiàn*), 2 Jianguomennan Dajie (short distance south-west of the Friendship Store). Standard Y375, superior Y690, deluxe Y920 – plus 10% service charge.

Grace Hotel (☎ 4362288; fax 4361818), (*xīn wànshòu bīnguǎn*), 8 Jiangtai Xilu, Chaoyang District, on the road to the airport in north-east Beijing. Standard singles/doubles Y490/546, superior Y690, deluxe Y863, suites Y1438 to Y2013.

Great Wall Sheraton (☎ 5005566; fax 5003398) (*chángchéng fàndiàn*), Dongsanhuan Beilu (north-east Beijing). Deluxe doubles are Y512; five stars.

Holiday Inn Crowne Plaza (☎ 5133388; fax 5132513) (*guóji yìyuàn huángguān jiàrì fàndiàn*), 48 Wangfujing Dajie, Dengshixikou. Standard Y690, superior Y748, suites Y834 to Y2012 – plus 15% service charge.

Holiday Inn Downtown (☎ 8322288; fax 8320696) (*jīndū jiàrì fàndiàn*), 98 Beilishi Lu, Xicheng District. Actually not right downtown, but on the west side of the second ring road near the Fuchengmen subway station. Standard singles/twins Y270/305; three stars.

Holiday Inn Lido (☎ 5006688; fax 5006237) (*lìdū jiàrì fàndiàn*), Jichang Lu, Jiangtai Lu, on the road to the airport in north-east Beijing. Outstanding facilities include one of the best delicatessens and bakeries in Beijing – if you don't stay here, at least eat here. Standard Y260, superior Y316, suite Y1495 – plus 15% surcharge.

Hotel Beijing-Toronto (☎ 5002266; fax 5002022) (*jīnglún fàndiàn*), 3 Jianguomenwai Dajie (east of the Friendship Store). Standard Y375, deluxe Y431 – plus 15% surcharge. Great buffets!

Hotel New Otani (☎ 5125555; fax 5125346) (*chángfù gōng*), 26 Jianguomenwai Dajie (directly opposite the International Club), 512 rooms. Standard singles/doubles Y690/805, deluxe Y805/920, suites Y1320 to Y2590.

Huadu Hotel (☎ 5001166; fax 5001615) (*huádū fàndiàn*), 8 Xinyuan Nanlu, north-east Beijing. Nice but somewhat overpriced. Standard Y260, superior Y300, suites Y400 – plus 10% surcharge.

International Hotel (☎ 5126688; fax 5129972) (*guóji fàndiàn*), 9 Jianguomennei Dajie. Home to CITS ticket office and very convenient for Beijing main railway station. Standard singles/doubles Y345/431, suites Y546 to Y3450.

Jingguang New World Hotel (☎ 5018888; fax 5013333) (*jīngguǎng xīn shìjiè fàndiàn*), Jingguang Zhongxin, Hujialou, Chaoyang District (east Beijing). An incredible five-star glass tower with indoor pool. Standard Y805, superior Y920, deluxe Y1092, suites Y2185 to Y5750.

Jinlang Hotel (☎ 5132288; fax 5125839) (*jīnláng*

dàjiǔdiàn), 75 Chongnei Dajie, Dongcheng District (one block west of Beijing main railway station). Singles/doubles Y357/391 – overpriced, but you're paying for the convenient location.

Kunlun Hotel (☎ 5003388; fax 5003228) (*kūnlún fàndiàn*), 2 Xinyuan Nanlu, Chaoyang District (north-east Beijing). Standard rooms cost Y380 plus 15% service charge.

Mandarin Hotel (☎ 8319988; fax 8312136) (*xīndàdū fàndiàn*), 21 Chegongzhuang Lu, south of the Beijing Zoo; 354 rooms; economy rooms Y316, standard Y437, superior Y506, deluxe Y794, suite Y1080; four stars.

Minzu Hotel (☎ 6014466; fax 6014849) (*mínzú fàndiàn*), 51 Fuxingmennei Dajie (west of CAAC and Xidan). Standard Y276, superior Y316. Don't confuse this place with the palatial Nationalities Cultural Palace just next door, an exclusive cadre hang-out off limits to foreigners.

New Century Hotel (☎ 8492001; fax 8319183) (*xīn shìjì fàndiàn*), 6 Shoudu Tiyuguan Nanlu, south-west of Beijing Zoo. Standard Y690, superior Y748, deluxe Y776, suites Y1208 to Y8050. Taiwanese, Japanese & French restaurants, a gleaming white high-rise.

Novotel (☎ 5138822; fax 5139088) (*sōnghè dàjiǔdiàn*), 88 Dengshikou, Dongcheng District (north part of Wangfujing). Superior Y518, deluxe Y633, suites Y805.

Olympic Hotel (☎ 8316688; fax 8318390) (*aòlínpīkè fàndiàn*), 52 Baishiqiao Lu, Haidian District, just north-west of the Beijing Zoo. Standard Y345, superior Y690, deluxe Y1380. Cold architecture – looks like a giant CD player.

Palace Hotel (☎ 5128899; fax 5129050) (*wángfǔ fàndiàn*), 8 Jinyu Hutong, Wangfujing. A five-star hotel notable for the Watson's pharmacy is in the basement. Standard rooms are Y920.

Park Hotel (☎ 7212233; fax 7211615) (*bǎilè jiǔdiàn*), 36 Puhuangyu Lu in the far south of Beijing. The hotel itself is in an incredibly dumpy neighbourhood and is definitely not worth the price. Doubles cost Y256.

Parkview Tiantan Hotel (☎ 7012277; fax 7016833) (*tiāntán fàndiàn*), 1 Tiyuguan Lu, Chongwen District (east of Tiantan Park). Standard Y310, superior Y345, suite Y690 – plus 10% service charge.

Peace Hotel (☎ 5128833; fax 5126863) (*hépíng bīnguǎn*), 3 Jinyu Hutong, Wangfujing. Standard Y431, superior Y460, deluxe Y805, suites Y4600.

Qianmen Hotel (☎ 3016688; fax 3013883) (*qiánmén fàndiàn*), 175 Yong'an Lu (south-west of Qianmen). Standard Y260, suites Y400 to Y800. Has bicycle rentals – a relative bargain and good place to stay

Rainbow Hotel (☎ 3012266; fax 3011366) (*tiānqiáo bīnguǎn*), Xijing Lu, Xuanwu District (south-west of Qianmen). Standard Y231, superior Y330 – a popular place to stay.

Sara Hotel (☎ 5136666; fax 5134248) *(huáqiáo dàshà)*, 2 Wangfujing Dajie. Superior Y805, deluxe Y920, suites Y1035 to Y4600. Raging disco and Mexican restaurant.

Shangri-La Hotel (☎ 8412211; fax 8418002) *(xiānggé līlā fàndiàn)*, 29 Zhizhuyuan Lu, Haidian District (west of Zizhuyuan Park). Superior Y718, deluxe Y977, suites Y1150-2012 – plus 15% service charge.

Swissotel (☎ 5012288; fax 5012501) *(běijīng gǎng'aò zhōngxīn)*, Gongren Tiyuchang Beilu & Chaoyangmen Bei Dajie. Convenient for disembarking airport bus, and near Dongsishitiao subway station; 454 rooms; superior Y520, deluxe Y575, suites Y690 to Y2875 – all plus 15% surcharge.

Taiwan Hotel (☎ 5136688; fax 5136896) *(táiwān fàndiàn)*, 5 Jinyu Hutong, Wangfujing. Economy Y260, standard Y288, deluxe Y345, suites Y632 to Y747. For such a high standard and top-notch location, it's a relative bargain.

Tianlun Dynasty Hotel (☎ 5138888; fax 5137866) *(tiānlún wángcháo fàndiàn)*, 50 Wangfujing Dajie. Standard Y357 plus 10% service charge. The 'aircraft-hanger' interior decorating is positively weird – the front desk is on the 3rd floor.

Xiyuan Hotel (☎ 8313388; fax 8314577) *(xīyuàn fàndiàn)*, 1 Sanlihe Lu, immediately south of the Beijing Zoo; 709 rooms; singles/doubles Y400/575; four stars.

Yanjing Hotel (☎ 8326611; fax 8326130) *(yānjīng fàndiàn)*, 19 Fuxingmenwai Dajie (west Beijing). Standard Y220, superior Y242, deluxe Y330.

Yanshan Hotel (☎ 2563388; fax 2568640) *(yānshān dàjiǔdiàn)*, 138A Haidian Lu near the Friendship Hotel in far north-west Beijing. Twin rooms cost Y380 plus 15% service charge.

Yanxiang Hotel (☎ 4376666; fax 4376231) *(yānxiáng fàndiàn)*, 2A Jiangtai Lu, Dongzhimenwai, on the road to the airport in north-east Beijing. Doubles cost Y260. Three stars. This is a cadre hang-out – lots of guards and guns, but no doubt about the security! This hotel tends to be almost always full.

Yuyang Hotel (☎ 4669988; fax 4666638) *(yúyáng fàndiàn)*, Xinyuan Xili, Chaoyang District (north-east Beijing). Standard singles/doubles Y430/490, superior Y518/575, deluxe Y575/633, suites Y1150 to Y2300.

Zhaolong Hotel (☎ 5002299; fax 5003319) *(zhàolóng bīnguǎn)*, Dongsanhuan Beilu & Gongren Tiyuchang Beilu (east Beijing on the third ring road). Standard Y316, deluxe Y661, suites Y3450 to Y5750 – all plus 10% surcharge.

Zhongyuan Hotel (☎ 8318888; fax 8319887) *(zhōngyuàn bīnguǎn)*, 18 Xie Jie, Gaoliangqiao,

Xizhimenwai. It's north-west of the Xizhimen (north) railway station in a somewhat isolated spot; 414 rooms; superior Y430, deluxe Y488, villas Y546, suites Y805 to Y2243. Some nice villas around a swimming pool in addition to main high-rise.

Places to Eat

In a daring denunciation of cadre corruption, Chinese rock musician Cui Jian wrote the 'Official Banquet Song':

I'm a big official, so I eat and drink, eat and drink;
To the Mongolian restaurant we go for hotpot;
To Quanjude for Beijing duck;
Anyway, it's not my money;
So eat and drink and all be merry!

In 1949 Beijing had an incredible 10,000 snack bars and restaurants; by 1976 that number had dwindled to fewer than 700. Restaurants, a nasty bourgeois concept, were all to have been phased out and replaced by revolutionary dispensaries dishing out rice. We could hazard some wild guesses about what happened to some of the chefs – they were allocated jobs as bus drivers while the bus drivers were given jobs as chefs.

The newly permitted free enterprise system has generated an explosion of privately owned eateries. Most of the regional and minority styles are represented in the capital – there is certainly ample variety for the average gastronome and there's no way you'll get through them all.

Eating out in the capital is a true adventure, one that should be seized with both chopsticks. While you can eat at almost any time, lunch hours can be problematic – at noon the restaurants pack out, but by 1 pm the staff usually like to shut down for the requisite afternoon nap.

Table Manners Forget those! We speak here of the popular prole section of a restaurant – waiters are in the nasty habit of intercepting foreigners and detouring them to private cubicles where the furniture is plusher, crowds are nonexistent, prices skyrocket and the kitchen is exactly the same. Any number of tactics will be employed to steer you away from the popular section. Never mind, throw yourself in anyway. Fighting for your meal increases the appetite, and your table company will be congenial enough once you manage to land a seat. Order by pointing to your neighbour's dishes. At the established restaurants you can reserve tables by phoning ahead. This will mean cubicles, banquet-style and more expensive food, although some dishes can only be obtained by phoning ahead with a group order.

Cheap Eats Snacks can be found at roadside stalls, especially around breakfast time. Also try the market areas, and the ground floor of restaurants (the masses section). Small vendors are making a comeback, ever since the return of the ice-cream soda in 1980 after an absence of 14 years. In fact a health problem exists with the unsupervised production of popsicles by home entrepreneurs.

Travellers residing in the Qiaoyuan Hotel or thereabouts can choose from a wide selection of cheapie restaurants which have sprung up to milk the backpacker market. English menus are a nice feature in this neighbourhood, and the locals have learned to make decidedly un-Chinese specialties such as banana muesli. There are so many restaurants clustered in the alleys around the hotel that it's hard to know where to start – all are good. Some popular ones include the *Candlelight*, *Monkey* and *Pink House*.

The Qianmen area in bygone Beijing had the largest concentration of snack bars, and is a good place to go hunting. Down Qianmen Dajie is the *Zhengmingzhai Cakeshop*. The *Jinfeng* at 157 Qianmenwai sells Beijing-style baozi dumplings.

The *Duyichu* at No 36 Qianmen and close to Dazhalan is an ancient restaurant serving *shaomai* (steamed dumplings).

Off the beginning of Dazhalan on Liangshidian hutong is *Zhimielou*, which sells dragon-whisker noodles – strands as fine as silk, an old Qing recipe.

For baozi and jiaozi try the *Hongxinglou* at 1 Beiwei Lu on the west side of the Temple of Heaven. It also serves shaomai and noodles. Twenty different kinds of jiaozi (in season) can be ordered and there's even frozen take-away. The crowded ground floor has two kinds of jiaozi, beer and cold cuts. The next floor has jiaozi and Shandong-style seafood and pork dishes. The seafood is not cheap, but if you stick to jiaozi this can be a very inexpensive place to eat.

The *Ritan Park Restaurant* to the north of the Friendship Store has classy jiaozi and Western snacks. It's patronised by Westerners and housed in a classical-style building.

The Donganmen Night Market gets going from around 6 to 9 pm daily. All sorts of cheap eats from pushcarts are available. The night market is at the northern end of Wangfujing.

Specialties Northern cuisine specialties are Beijing duck, Mongolian hotpot, Muslim barbecue and imperial food. Imperial cuisine is served up in the restaurants of Beihai Park, the Summer Palace and the Fragrant Hills – very expensive, but go for the cheaper snacks. Mongolian hotpot is a winter dish – a brass pot with charcoal inside it is placed at the centre of the table and you cook thick strips of mutton and vegetables yourself, fondue fashion, spicing as you like. Muslim barbecues use lamb, a Chinese Muslim influence; shish kebabs are called *shashlik*.

Beijing duck is the capital's famous invention, now a production line of sorts. Your meal starts at one of the agricultural communes around Beijing where the duck is pumped full of grain and soybean paste to fatten it up. The ripe duck is lacquered with molasses, pumped with air, filled with boiling water, dried, and then roasted over a fruitwood fire. The result, force-fed or not, is delicious.

We forgot to mention that the poor duck is killed somewhere along the line. In fact, the story goes that the original roast duck was not killed. In Chang'an, where the dish is said to have been devised 1200 years ago, two nobles placed live geese and ducks in an iron cage over a charcoal fire. As the heat increased the thirsty birds would drink from a bowl filled with vinegar, honey, malt, ginger and salt until they passed away.

A warning – the ducks get their revenge. We don't know why, but foreigners pigging out on Beijing duck for the first time have a tendency to get very ill from the experience. Whether this is caused by some sinister plot hatched by the ducks or simple overeating, we aren't sure. Nevertheless, go easy the first time – your initial duck dinner should be a small one, and if you don't wind up in the emergency room then you might consume more the second time around.

Beijing Duck Otherwise known as the 'Big Duck', the *Qianmen Quanjude Roast Duck Restaurant* (☎ 7011379) *(qiánmén quànjùdé kǎoyādiàn)* is at 32 Qianmen Dajie, on the east side, near Qianmen subway. This is one of the oldest restaurants in the capital, dating back to 1864. Prices are moderate, and there's a cheaper section through the right-hand doorway. Same duck, same kitchen. The cheap section is very crowded – if you don't get there by 6 pm, forget it. Beer is brewed on the premises. The duck is served in stages. First come boneless meat and crispy skin with a side dish of shallots, plum sauce and crepes, followed by duck soup made of bones and all the other parts except the quack. Language is not really a problem; you just have to negotiate half or whole ducks. The locals will show you the correct etiquette, like when to spit on the floor.

The *Beijing Hotel* has a number of top-class restaurants. Of interest is the genial west-wing dining room on the 7th floor, where you can get Beijing duck. Some think

the food's not up to scratch, but perhaps their taste buds are more finely tuned than most. Other gourmet novelties like bear paws are served if you've got the bucks.

The *Bianyifang Duck Restaurant* (☎ 7012244) *(biànyìfǎng kǎoyādiàn)* is at 2 Chongwenmenwai Dajie. This place uses a slightly different method of preparation – a closed oven.

Sichuan The place to go is the *Sichuan Restaurant* (☎ 336356) *(sìchuān fàndiàn)* at No 51 Rongxian Hutong. To get there go south from Xidan intersection (where Xidan meets Chang'an), turn left into a hutong marked by traffic lights and a police-box, and continue along the hutong till you find the grey wall entrance. contrast to the bland interiors and peeling paint of most of the capital's restaurants, this one is housed in the sumptuous former residence of Yuan Shikai (the general who tried to set himself up as an emperor in 1914). The compound decor is spectacular, and the several dining rooms will clean out your wallet very fast. For cheaper food continue to the back of the courtyard, veer right, and there it is, a dining room with good meals for a few yuan per head if you're sharing dishes. You'll need some drinks for this one! It's a good idea to bring your own in case they've run out (or better still, a flask of yoghurt to cool the flames). The food is out of this world: fiery pork, explosive prawns, bamboo shoots, bean curd (tofu), beef dishes, some seafood, and side dishes of cucumber. In the more expensive parts of the restaurant there's more variety, but the back dining room will sate the appetite.

Another favourite haunt is the *Emei Restaurant* (☎ 863068) *(éméi fàndiàn)* on Yuetan Beijie, on the north side of Yuetan Park, which is about three km west of the Forbidden City; it has very cheap, hot Sichuan food and friendly staff.

Next to the *Qianmen Roast Duck Restaurant* you'll find the *Lili* (☎ 751242) *(lìlì cāntīng)* at 30 Qianmen. The Sichuan-style spicy chicken and hot noodles with peanuts and chillies are very good. They serve some of the best dumplings in Beijing too.

Also try the *Shuxiang* (☎ 545176) *(shǔxiāng cānguǎn)* just across the street from Chongwenmen Hotel.

Hunanese The *Quyuan* (☎ 662196) *(qǔyuán jiǔlóu)* is at 133 Xidan Beidajie north of Chang'an, west side, in a red-fronted building by an overhead bridge. The Hunan food served here is hot and spicy like Sichuan cuisine. If the French can do it with frogs, how often do you get a chance to digest dog? Anyone for hot dog? On the menu is onion dog, dog soup (reputed to be an aphrodisiac) and dog stew. For those with canine sensibilities, perhaps a switch to Hunan-style duck spiced with hot pepper, or some seafood, and several styles of noodles. The desserts with lychees are good; they can be varied or custom-made if you phone in advance. The food is cheap and the management nice.

The *Xiangshu* (☎ 558351) *(xiāngshǔ cāntīng)* is on the Wangfujing side of Dongfeng Market. The food is a combination of Sichuan and Hunan, highly recommended. Try the Xiangshu for the 'silver-thread rolls' which are Beijing's best pastry.

Mongolian Hotpot & Muslim Barbecue *Kaorouwan* (☎ 657707) *(kǎoròuwǎn fànzhuāng)* at 102 Xuanwumennei, south of Xidan intersection, on the east side of the street, serves Muslim barbecues, and you can do your own skewers if the wind is blowing in the right direction.

Hongbinlou (☎ 655691) *(hóngbīnlóu fànzhuāng)* at 82 Xi Chang'an Jie, just east of Xidan intersection, serves shashlik (kebabs), Beijing duck and Mongolian hotpot. Lamb banquets can be ordered in advance.

Shoudu Kaorouji (☎ 445921) at 37 Shichahai is difficult to find but worth it in summer. Go to the Drum Tower *(gǔlóu)* area, turn into a hutong to the left immediately before the Drum Tower as you go north, and follow it down to the lakeside. The dowdy, windowless interiors of most Chinese restaurants make you feel boxed, but here you've got a view of the lake, the alleys and the activity in the area. In summer, tables are moved onto the balcony. This is a place for potless hotpot and Muslim barbecue.

Shanghai If this greasy cuisine appeals to you, try *Laozhengxing* (☎ 5112148) *(lǎozhèngxīng fàndiàn)* at 46 Qianmen Dajie. This place serves the whole range of Shanghai-style seafood including fish, eel, and hairy crabs when in season.

Cantonese *Guangdong Restaurant* (☎ 894881) *(guǎngdōng cāntīng)* in the Xijiao market opposite the zoo serves up Beijing duck and Cantonese-style cuisine, including turtle and snake.

Other Chinese Just across the street from the Confucius Temple is a restaurant called – you guessed it – the *Confucius Restaurant*. It looks like it would bankrupt any budget traveller and is crawling with staff, but a meal for four people with dessert and tea costs around Y120, or Y30 per person.

Huaiyang Fanzhuang at 217 Xidan Beidajie has a Jiangsu-cuisine section serving hairy crab in season.

Shaguoju Restaurant (☎ 661126) *(shāguōjū fànzhuāng)*, in a tacky building at 60 Xisi Nandajie, is further north toward the Xisi intersection. Pork is served in many forms, some dishes in earthenware pots; the food is cheap.

Kangle Restaurant (☎ 443884) *(kānglè fàndiàn)* at 259 Andingmennei is further east of the Drum Tower near the Jiaodaokou intersection. This place serves up Fujian and Yunnan styles of food. Expensive 'across-the-bridge noodles' must be ordered in advance for a minimum of four people. Also try Yunnan-style steamed chicken, seafood and *san bu zhan* (sweet sticky pudding).

Russian Overall, the Russian food here is not too good, but you may find it a welcome break from the noodle and rice dishes. The *Moscow Restaurant* (☎ 894454) *(mòsīkē cāntīng)* is on the west side of the Soviet-designed Exhibition Centre in the zoo district. The vast interior has chandeliers, a high ceiling and fluted columns. Foreigners are shuffled to a side room overlooking the zoo (which has, by the way, no connection with the menu). The food gets mixed reviews, but it's definitely Russian – borsch, cream prawns au gratin, pork à la Kiev, beef stroganoff, black bread, soups and black caviar, moderately priced.

Western All the large tourist hotels serve Western food of varying quality and price. Travellers pining for a croissant or strong coffee will be pleased to know that Beijing is the best place in China to find such delicacies.

Good bets for Western meals are the *Beijing* and *Minzu* hotels. The *Jianguo Hotel* serves Holiday Inn, California home-style cooking at greater than Californian prices. Check the ads in the *China Daily* for novelty events; anyone for a Texas spare-rib barbecue at the *Great Wall Sheraton Hotel*?

Alfredo's in the Sara Hotel (*huáqiáo dàshà*), 2 Wangfujing Dajie, is a Mexican restaurant by day. In the evening, there are often live bands and loud music – especially on Mondays after 10 pm – and the place becomes more of a dance bar. Otherwise, it's sedate enough and the food is fine. The cook is indeed from Mexico, but the prices are Beijing luxury hotel-style.

Similar fare can be had at *Mexican Wave* (☎ 5063961) on Dongdaqiao Lu near the intersection with Guanghua Lu. Dongdaqiao Lu is the major north-south road between the Friendship Store and the Jianguo Hotel on Jianguomenwai. Mexican Wave serves set lunches (Western not Mexican food) from noon until 2.30 pm; dinners (Mexican style) are from around 6 pm onwards. The prices are definitely not for backpackers.

Within the caverns of the enormous Lufthansa Centre (just north of the Great Wall Sheraton) is *Paulaner Brauhaus*, an excellent German restaurant. This place brews its own genuine German beer! Don't confuse this place with the other Brauhaus in

the China World Trade Centre – the latter is a bar only, not a restaurant.

In 1982 a group of Beijing chefs set about reviving the imperial pastry recipes. They even went so far as to dig up the last emperor's brother to try their products out on. The same year, an Overseas Chinese outfit was permitted to start up a snack bar specialising in South-East Asian snacks. Snacking is where you can experience the free market. Jobless youths have carved out small businesses for themselves, and there are licensed family-owned restaurants. The other person you'll meet is the snacker, someone who can't afford a full-course meal. It will cost you next to nothing to sample these places, all highly educational.

French *Maxim's of Paris* (☎ 5122110) (*bālí mǎkèxīmǔ cāntīng*) is not just in Paris – a branch can be found within the precincts of the Chongwenmen Hotel. The joint China-French venture initiated by Pierre Cardin opened in October 1983 with the understanding that the Chinese would take it over after 10 years. Now that the deadline has passed, the place has gone sharply downhill – not recommended. The deteriorating standard of food and service has *not* been accompanied by a commensurate drop in price. Dinner for two – *sacré bleu* – is a cool Y200 or so, excluding that Bordeaux red or the Alsatian Gerwürtzraminer. However, the pissoir is reputed to be the best in China.

Muslim This type of cuisine is not only excellent, but dirt cheap if you know the right place to look for it. The right place is a little street called Baiwanzhuangxi Lu in a neighbourhood known as Ganjiakou (not far south of the zoo). This is where Beijing's Uigur minority congregates – if you didn't know better you'd swear you were walking down a side street in Ürümqi.

Restaurants here are very specialised – the way to eat is to collect some Uigur bread (outstanding stuff!) from the stalls, then sit down in a tea shop or restaurant and order Uigur tea (contains sugar and salt plums), some vegetable dishes, noodles and kebabs (*shashlik*). You'll probably have to collect your meal from several proprietors – one restaurant won't have the full range of goodies. It's often best to eat with a small group (two to four persons) so you can get several dishes and sample everything. Alternatively, you can just drift from stall to stall sampling as you go.

This is a true haven for budget travellers – prices in this neighbourhood are dirt cheap.

Indonesian The *Shanghai Jakarta Restaurant* in the Tiantan Sports Hotel dishes up decent Indonesian-style food like *gado-gado*.

Indian This style of cooking hasn't yet taken Beijing by storm, but there is at least one decent restaurant serving sub-continent cuisine. The *Holiday Inn Downtown (jīndū jiàrì fàndiàn)* at 98 Beilishi Lu in the Xicheng District is where you can get your chappatis and tandoori chicken. The tariff will run about Y100 per person – the food is outstanding, the service rotten.

Vegetarian The Yangzhou-style *Gongdelin Vegetarian Restaurant (gōngdélín sùcài-guǎn)* at 158 Qianmen Dajie is probably the best in the city. It gets rave reviews and serves up wonderful veggie food with names to match. How about the 'peacock in pride' or 'the fire is singeing the snow-capped mountains'? The helpings are generous, the prices low and the staff friendly.

Fast Food From the day of its grand opening in 1992, *McDonald's (màidānglào)* has been all the rage with Beijingers, who easily outnumber the foreigners eating here. Though prices are low, this is one of Beijing's most prestigious restaurants, the venue for cadre birthday parties and a popular hang-out for the upper crust. There are separate lines for RMB and FEC, but everyone can pay with RMB – not surprisingly, there's no waiting at the FEC counter. A plastic Ronald McDonald sits on a bench just outside the door – Chinese queue up to be photographed with him. McDonald's occupies a prime piece of real estate on the corner of Wangfujing and Dongchang'an Jie, just east of the Beijing Hotel. Business has been so good that a

second (but smaller) branch opened in 1993 at the Chang'an Market on Fuxingmenwai Dajie near the Yanjing Hotel.

By comparison, *Kentucky Fried Chicken (kěndéjī jiāxiāng jī)* enjoys a much longer history in Beijing, having spread its wings in 1987. At the time of its opening, it was the largest KFC in the world. The colonel's smiling face is just across the street from Mao's mausoleum in Tiananmen Square – if this doesn't make the late Chairman turn over in his grave, nothing will. A smaller Kentucky Fried has hatched one block east of Wangfujing on the south-western corner of Dongsi Xi Dajie and Dongsi Nan Dajie.

Pizza Hut (bìshèngkè) has arrived on the Beijing fast-food scene with two branches. One is on Dongzhimenwai Dajie in the Sanlitun area (next to the Australian Embassy). The other hut is less conspicuous – it's at 33 Zhushikou Xi Dajie, the second major road south of Qianmen (first big road south of Dazhalan Dajie).

Shakey's Pizza (xǐkè měishì cāntīng) has entered the pizza wars with a branch on Dongchang'an Jie just east of the Wangfujing McDonald's.

Carl's Jr (kèlì hànbǔbāo) and *Dairy Queen (dílì bīngqílín)* occupy the same building on the south-eastern corner of Wangfujing and Jinyu Hutong near the Taiwan Hotel. On Sundays, Chinese dressed as clowns are hired to draw in business.

Uncle Sam's is on the south side of Jianguomenwai. It's just east of CITS but don't let that ruin your appetite – this place seems to do a pretty good business. Food is mixed Western and Chinese, not bad though it gets mixed reviews from travellers.

You've heard of Maxims – Beijing's fast food equivalent is *Minim's*. No joke; it's one door down from its famous big sister in the Chongwenmen Hotel. Lots of tin-foil and surly staff, but for a few yuan they'll put a burger, pizza or sandwich into the microwave oven for you. Mediocre coffee, OK chocolate mousse, and the tomato soup in a cup is not bad.

Supermarkets Despite the abundance of

cheap Chinese restaurants, self-catering in the capital is certainly a reasonable idea – no other way to satisfy those sudden urges for peanut butter, Dutch cheese and Vegemite on French rolls. Or whatever.

Beijing has several notable supermarkets, the best being Hong Kong or Japanese joint-ventures, and at most of them you can pay in RMB – the 'express FEC line' is for suckers. The best of the bunch is *Yaohan* on the south side of Jianguomenwai, across the street from the CITIC building and adjacent to Scite Tower – the supermarket is in the basement.

On the eastern fringe of Jianguomenwai is the China World Trade Centre – go down into the basement to find a fully fledged *Well-come* supermarket, imported lock, stock and shopping carts from Hong Kong. The Well-come slogan 'low everyday prices' doesn't quite describe the situation in Beijing, but you'll find all the familiar goodies right down to the 'No Frills Dried Lemon Peel'.

Just next to the CITIC building is the *Friendship Store* – when you enter the building turn sharply right to find the food section. The supermarket is decidedly mediocre, but new competition may force an improvement soon.

If you're out in Sanlitun embassyland, there's a small *Friendship Supermarket* serving the diplomatic (and not so diplomatic) crowd – the selection is limited but you can score chocolate chip cookies and other imported delicacies. The store is at 5 Sanlitun Lu. In the same neighbourhood just north of the Great Wall Sheraton Hotel is the enormous *Lufthansa Centre* – yes, it is a ticket office for a German airline, but also a multistorey shopping mall. There is a supermarket of sorts in here, but you may have a hard time finding the food amongst the Walkmans, computers and colour TVs.

Bakeries Chinese bread is about as tasty as a wet sponge, but a few entrepreneurs in Beijing have started to introduce edible baked goods to the masses. Most of the customers are foreigners, but some of the locals are beginning to catch on and you can expect the number of European-style bakeries to multiply.

One fine effort in this direction is *Vie de France (dà mòfáng miànbāo diàn)*, which boasts genuine croissants and prices a fraction of what you'd pay in Paris. This bakery currently has two branches – one is at the Qianmen Zhengyang Market, just southwest of Chairman Mao's Mausoleum and adjacent to the enormous Kentucky Fried Chicken. The other branch is on the southeast corner of Xidan and Xichang'an Dajie, across the street from the CAAC office.

Within the confines of the *Friendship Store*, there is a bakery off to the right as you enter the store. Prices here are also very low but the selection is limited.

Another place to look are some of the big hotels – a few have sent the staff off to Europe for a wintertime crash course in making German black bread and Danish pastries. Unfortunately, hotel prices tend to be outrageous. The deli in the *Holiday Inn Lido* is a good example – Y20 or so for a slice of delectable chocolate cake.

Entertainment

Discos *Alfredo's* in the Sara Hotel *(huáqiáo dàshà)* at 2 Wangfujing Dajie is normally a mellow Mexican restaurant, but on Monday nights after 9 pm or so, the heavy metal is rolled out and the volume is turned up loud enough to shatter a taco chip, not to mention eardrums. The foreign bands (Filipino, US and who knows?) keep the disco floor thumping until the wee hours of the morning. This is mostly a hang-out for Westerners – Chinese are few in number here but you do see the odd Hong Konger or Beijing counter-revolutionary. There is no cover charge but you are expected to buy a couple of pricey drinks.

The *Harmony Club (xìngfú jùlèbù)* is a sort of Chinese and foreign counter-culture club offering hard rock music on Saturday nights. It's an unusual place, built in a former bomb shelter, which at least solves problems with noisy neighbours. This place attracts a lot of young people despite the Y30 cover charge. The Harmony Club is in hutong just south of the East Gate of Tiantan Park – go down the stairs to enter.

Bars The *Brauhaus* in the China World Trade Centre on Jianguomenwai is a small bar with occasional live rock bands. There are just a few tables and drinks are expensive, but there's no cover charge and it is popular with the foreign community. This place shouldn't be mistaken for the Paulaner Brauhaus in the Lufthansa Centre, which is a German restaurant.

The *Pig & Whistle* (☎ 5006688 ext 1976) on the ground floor of the Holiday Inn Lido is the most British thing in Beijing besides the UK Embassy. Opening hours are from 5 pm until 1 am on weekdays, and from noon until 1 am on weekends and holidays.

Clubs Sporting, recreational and club facilities are to be found in the Friendship Hotel and the International Club. The International Club can be dull during the daytime – a place with signs telling you what not to do – but it livens up in the evening. There are tennis courts, billiard tables, a full-sized swimming pool, a bowling alley (a bummer – you have to set up your own pins) and a bar/restaurant (it's debatable whether the chef isn't in fact a can opener).

Major hotels have swimming pools, tennis courts and other amenities which are open to nonguests who pay the requisite fees. Many places charge daily admission fees, but others offer discounts if you pay on a monthly basis. The Shangri-la Hotel, for example, charges Y450 per month for the use of the pool and exercise rooms.

Cultural Events Back in the days of Mao, 'cultural events' often meant revolutionary operas featuring evil foreign and Kuomintang devils who eventually were defeated by heroic workers and peasants inspired by the Little Red Book. Fortunately, performances have improved considerably. The *China Daily* carries a listing of cultural evenings recommended for foreigners – also worth checking is the *Beijing Weekend* published once weekly. Offerings include concerts, theatre, minority dancing and some cinema. You can reserve ahead by phoning the box office via your hotel, or pick up tickets at CITS (for a surcharge) – or take a risk and just roll up at the theatre.

Entertainment is cheap compared to the West, but prices are rising. Beijing is on the touring circuit for foreign troupes, and these are also listed in the *China Daily*. They're somewhat screened for content, but they've been beefing up what's available. When Arthur Miller's *Death of a Salesman* was acted out by Chinese at the Capital Theatre, it was held over for two months by popular demand.

The same theatre staged some avant-garde Chinese theatre. It put on two plays by Gao Zingjian, incorporating theatre of the absurd and traditional Chinese theatrical techniques. One of the plays, *Bus-stop*, is based on eight characters who spend 10 years at the bus stop to discover that the service was cancelled long ago. That's either a vicious comment on the Beijing bus service, or a sly reference to Gao's stint in re-education camp during the Cultural Revolution – or else it's a direct steal from Samuel Beckett or Luigi Pirandello.

In the concert department they've presented Beethoven's Ninth played on Chinese palace instruments, such as tuned bells copied from those found in an ancient tomb. Other classical instruments are being revived for dance-drama backings. Bizarre performances are often staged for foreign tour groups and some of these have to be seen to be believed. Perhaps trial runs before touring overseas with cultural shows tailored to Western tastes? Some of this stuff would go down great in Las Vegas.

Television, if you're that kind of addict, brings many different types of entertainment directly into your hotel room – if you have the right kind of room. There are a number of satellite channels, and if you have the proper electronic hookups you can enjoy Western movies and perhaps some naughty Japanese video. Programmes (not the naughty ones) are listed in the *China Daily*. CCTV and Beijing TV are the two local stations, which broadcast mostly in Chinese except for daily English and Japanese lessons. TV is actually a good way of studying Chinese, especially the kids' programmes with fascinating forms of Chinese animation.

As elsewhere in China, karaoke has had a heavy impact. There's no need to list the karaoke venues here – there are so many that you'll have a hard enough time avoiding them. Remember that some of the karaoke places try to cheat foreigners in a big way, with outrageous service charges for 'talking to the hostesses'. Some of the hostesses hang out on the street near their place of employment and try to trick unsuspecting males (even domestic tourists) into going inside for 'a few drinks' – the bill for a couple of Cokes could amount to six months' wages for the average Chinese worker.

As for other events, you might like to delve into items listed in the local newspapers. If you can read Chinese or get a translation you can find out about sporting events, puppet theatre, storytelling and local cinema. These may be sold out, but scalpers do a roaring trade.

You can even set yourself up as an English teacher at the Beijing 'English corner' in Purple Bamboo Park, near the Capital Stadium in the Haidian District.

Movies (*diànyǐng*) Film is out of the boring stage and starting to delve into some contemporary issues, even verging on Cultural Revolution aftershock in a mild manner. The International Club near the Friendship Store shows Chinese films with English subtitles or simultaneous translation into English, every Saturday night at 7 pm. The Rainbow Hall in the International Hotel (☎ 5129960 ext 1883) also has Chinese films with English subtitles, but only shows these once every two weeks on Saturday nights. Ditto for the Great Wall Sheraton Hotel (☎ 5005566 ext 2280). The Friendship Hotel shows old foreign and Chinese films (with simultaneous translation) every Friday night.

Or you can just dive in with the locals at the Dahua Cinema (*dàhuá diànyǐng yuàn*) at 82 Dongdan Beidajie. Another one of Beijing's trendy movie houses is the Shoudu Cinema (*shǒudū diànyǐng yuàn*), 46 Xichang'an Dajie (near Xidan and CAAC). Another very fashionable place is the Dizhi Cinema Hall (*dìzhì lǐtáng*), 30 Yangrou Hutong, which is just west of Xisi Nandajie (the northern end of Xidan) – this place also has a dance hall, karaoke (ugh!) bar and hall for playing snooker. Less trendy but perhaps more educational is the Tuxin Cinema (☎ 8415566 ext 5727), actually inside the National Library (*běijīng túshūguǎn*) which is just north of Zizhuyuan Park in north-west Beijing.

Opera (*píngjù*) It used to be the Marx Brothers, the Gang of Four and the Red Ballet – but it's back to the classics again these days. Beijing opera is one of the many forms of the

Opera mask

Beijing Opera

Beijing opera is usually regarded as the *crème de la crème* of all the opera styles prevalent in China. Traditionally it's been the opera of the masses. In some ways it's very similar to the ancient Greek theatre, with its combination of singing, dialogue, acrobatics and pantomime, the actors wearing masks and the performance accompanied by loud and monotonous rhythms produced with percussion instruments. The themes are usually inspired by disasters, natural calamities, intrigues or rebellions. Many have their source in the fairy tales and stock characters and legends of classical literature. Titles like *The Monkey King, A Drunken Beauty* and *A Fisherman's Revenge* are typical.

The music, singing and costumes are products of the opera's origins. Formerly, Beijing opera was performed mostly on open-air stages in markets, streets, teahouses or temple courtyards. The orchestra had to play loudly and the performers had to develop a piercing style of singing which could be heard over the throng. The costumes are a garish collection of sharply contrasting colours because the stages were originally lit by oil lamps.

The movements and techniques of the dance styles of the Tang Dynasty are similar to those of today's Beijing opera. Provincial opera companies were characterised by their dialect and style of singing, but when these companies converged on Beijing they started a style of musical drama called *kunqu*. This developed during the Ming Dynasty, along with a more popular variety of play-acting with pieces based on legends, historical events and popular novels. These styles gradually merged by the late 18th and early 19th centuries into the Beijing opera we see today.

The musicians usually sit on the stage in plain clothes and play without written scores. The erhu is a two-stringed fiddle which is tuned to a low register, has a soft tone and generally supports the huqin, another two-stringed fiddle tuned to a high register. The yueqin, a sort of moon-shaped four-stringed guitar, has a soft tone and is used to support the erhu. Other instruments are the *sheng* (reed pipes) and the *pipa* (lute), as well as drums, bells and cymbals. Last but not least is the *ban*, a time-clapper which virtually directs the band, beats time for the actors and gives them their cues.

There are four types of actors' roles: the *sheng, dan, jing* and *chou*. The sheng are the leading male actors and they play scholars, officials, warriors, etc. They are divided into the *laosheng* who wear beards and represent old men, and the *xiaosheng* who represent young men. The *wensheng* are the scholars and the civil servants. The *wusheng* play soldiers and other fighters, and because of this are specially trained in acrobatics.

The dan are the female roles. The *laodan* are the elderly, dignified ladies such as mothers, aunts and widows. The *qingyi* are aristocratic ladies in elegant costumes. The *huadan* are the ladies' maids, usually in brightly coloured costumes. The *daomadan* are the warrior women. The *caidan* are the female comedians. Traditionally, female roles were played by male actors.

The jing are the painted-face roles, and they represent warriors, heroes, statesmen, adventurers and demons. Their counterpart is the *fujing*, ridiculous figures who are anything but heroic. The chou is basically the clown. The caidan is sometimes the female counterpart of this male role.

Apart from the singing and music, the opera also uses acrobatics and mime. Few props are used, so each move, gesture or facial expression is symbolic. A whip with silk tassels indicates an actor riding a horse. Lifting a foot means going through a doorway. Language is often archaic Chinese, music is ear- splitting (bring some cotton wool), but the costume and make-up are magnificent. The only action that really catches the Western eye is a swift battle sequence – the women warriors involved are trained acrobats who leap, twirl, twist and somersault into attack.

There are numerous other forms of opera. The Cantonese variety is more 'music hall', often with 'boy meets girl' themes. Gaojia opera is one of the five local opera forms from Fujian Province and is also popular in Taiwan, with songs in the Fujian dialect but influenced by the Beijing opera style.

Strange as it may sound, Chinese music is actually quite closely related to Western music. The 12 notes worked out by the ancient Chinese correspond exactly to those of the ancient Greeks (on which Western music is based). Although most Chinese musical instruments were introduced from India and central Asia, Chinese music is tonally closer to Western music. Western music, however, uses groupings (scales) of eight notes whereas Chinese music uses groupings of five notes. The five-note scale is one of the main reasons Chinese music sounds different from Western music. The other important difference (shared with Indian music) is a lack of harmony, generally considered very important in Western music. ■

art and the most famous, but it's only got a short history. The year 1790 is the key date given; in that year a provincial troupe performed before Emperor Qianlong on his 80th birthday. The form was popularised in the West by the actor Mei Lanfang (1894-1961) who played *dan* or female roles, and is said to have influenced Charlie Chaplin. There is a museum devoted to Mei Lanfang at 9 Huguosi Lu, in western Beijing.

Earlier in the century, teahouses, wine shops and opera were the main nightlife in Beijing; of these, only the opera has survived (just). The opera bears little resemblance to its European counterpart. The mixture of singing, dancing, speaking, mime, acrobatics and dancing can go on for five or six hours; an hour is usually long enough for a Westerner. Plots are fairly basic so the language barrier is not really a problem – the problems are the music, which is searing to Western ears, and the acting, which is heavy and stylised.

When you get bored after the first hour or so, and are sick of the high-pitched whining, the local audience is with you all the way – spitting, eating apples, breast-feeding an urchin on the balcony, or plugging into a transistor radio (important sports match?). It's a lively prole audience viewing entertainment fit for kings.

Another problem is trying to find a performance that really is Beijing opera. All you can do is patiently troop around the theatre circuit until you hit the one that's still dishing up the real thing. Most performances start around 7 or 7.30 pm.

The most reliable (but most expensive) performances are put on for foreigners nightly at the Liyuan Theatre (☎ 3016688 ext 8860 or 8986) – this is in fact inside the Qianmen Hotel (*qiánmén fàndiàn*) at 175 Yong'an Lu. Ticket prices depend on seat location, starting at Y8. For Y20 you can sit at a table and enjoy snacks and tea while watching the show. For Y40 you get better snacks and a table with better location. Performances here last just one hour with sporadic translations flashed on an electronic signboard – the distorted attempts at English

translations are often funnier than the dialogue.

At other theatres, performances are less regular and attempts at translation usually nonexistent, but tickets typically cost only around Y5 depending on seat location. A good place to try is the Jixiang Theatre (*jíxiáng guānyuàn*) on Jinyu Hutong, just east of Wangfujing – it's next to Dairy Queen and across the road from the Taiwan Hotel. In the same neighbourhood is the Capital Theatre (*shǒudū jùcháng*) on the north end of Wangfujing, just south of the Sara Hotel. Also worth trying is the Tianqiao Theatre (*tiānqiáo jùcháng*) at 30 Beiwei Lu just west of Tiantan Park. The largest opera hall in the city is the China Grand Theatre (*zhōngguó jùyuàn*), just north of the Shangri-La Hotel in north-west Beijing.

Drama Something closer to the Western version of tragic-comic theatre enjoys a small but dedicated following in Beijing. There are performances almost every night at the Qingyi Theatre (☎ 553672, 556029) (*qīngyì jùcháng*) at 15 Dongchang'an Jie in the Dongcheng District. Shows get under way around 7 pm. Check the *China Daily* for the current schedule.

Acrobatics (*tèjì biǎoyǎn*) Two thousand years old, and one of the few art forms condoned by Mao, acrobatics is the best deal in town. You can forget CITS, forget railway stations, forget hotels, forget language problems. Magic!

Acts take place in various locations, normally advertised in the *China Daily*. The International Club (☎ 5322188) (*guójì jùlèbù*) at 21 Jianguomenwai Dajie (west of the Friendship Store) has performances for Y15. Another venue for acrobatics is the Chaoyang (*cháoyáng xìyuàn*) at Dongsanhuan Beilu and Chaoyang Beilu out in the north-eastern part of the city. Shows start around 7 pm and acts change nightly. For a rundown on some popular acrobatic stunts see the Shanghai chapter.

Song & Dance Shows These come in different varieties, from Western style to Chinese or occasionally in the style of China's ethnic minorities. They advertise in the *China Daily*, but these shows are sometimes cancelled even if advertised in the newspapers.

One likely venue for song and dance shows is the Capital Theatre *(shǒudū jùcháng)* (☎ 550978) at 22 Wangfujing Dajie. There is another Capital Theatre (☎ 5123492) *(shǒudū tǐyùguǎn)* which has a different name in Chinese – it's on Baishiqiao Lu. Both places are worth checking out.

There are also song and dance shows at the Gloria Plaza Hotel (☎ 5158855) *(kǎilái dàjiǔdiàn)*, 2 Jianguomennan Dajie (close to the Friendship Store).

Cinemas There are about 50 cinemas in the capital showing a mix of Chinese and foreign films. Some good bets are the Dazhalan Cinema *(dàzhàlán xìyuàn)* on Dazhalan Jie; the Jixiang at 14 Jinyu Hutong, off Wangfujing; and the Chaoyang *(cháoyáng xìyuàn)*, at Dongsanhuan Beilu and Chaoyang Beilu out in the east part of the city.

Parks If you arrive early in the morning you can watch taiji and fencing exercises, or perhaps opera singers and musicians practising. It's well worth investigating the very different rhythms of the city at this time. Temporary exhibitions take place in the parks, including horticultural and cultural ones, and there is even the odd bit of open-air theatre, as well as some worthy eating establishments. If you take up residence in Beijing, the parks become very important for preserving sanity. They are open late too, typically until 8 pm.

Things to Buy

There are several notable Chinese shopping districts offering abundant goods and low prices: Wangfujing, Qianmen (including Dazhalan hutong), Xidan and Dongdan. Pricier but more luxurious shopping areas can be found in the embassy ghettos of Jianguomenwai and Sanlitun. There are also some specialised shopping districts – Liulichang, Hongqiao Market and Zhongguancun.

Tourist attractions like the Forbidden City as well as major hotels have garish souvenir shops stocking arts & crafts. Otherwise, specialty shops are scattered around the city core. Stores are generally open from 9 am to 7 pm seven days a week; some are open from 8 am to 8 pm. Bargaining is not a way of life in the stores, but on the free market it certainly is.

Down jackets are one of the best bargains you can find in Beijing, essential survival gear if you visit northern China in the winter. Good buys are stationery (chops, brushes, inks), prints, handicrafts, clothing and antiques). Small or light items to buy are silk scarves, silk underwear, T-shirts, embroidered purses, papercuts, wooden and bronze buddhas, fold-up paper lanterns and kites.

The following is a description of the shopping districts and bargains to be had.

Wangfujing *(wángfújǐng)* This prestigious shopping street is just east of the Beijing Hotel – it's a solid block of stores and a favourite haunt of locals and tourists seeking bargains. Westerners now call it 'McDonald's St' due to the restaurant which occupies the south-east corner of the main intersection. In pre-1949 days it was known as Morrison St, catering mostly to foreigners. The name Wangfujing derives from a 15th-century well, the site of which is now occupied by the offices of the *People's Daily*.

Wangfujing's biggest emporium is the Beijing Department Store *(běijīng bǎihuò dàlóu)*. It was once the city's largest – it's been surpassed in size by some of the new tourist palaces, but you can't beat this place for price and variety.

Of prime interest to foreign travellers is the Foreign Languages Bookstore (No 235). This is not only *the* place in China to buy English-language books, but check out the music tape section upstairs. There is also a Xinhua Bookstore (No 212) next to McDonald's – most of the books are in Chinese but the map department upstairs is well worth your attention.

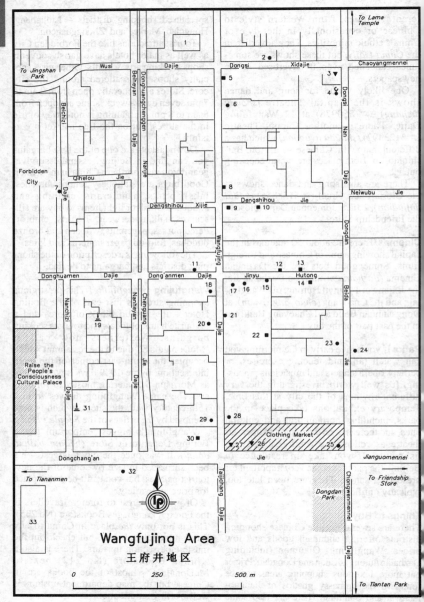

To Lama Temple

Chaoyangmennei

To Jingshan Park

Wusi   Dajie   Dongsi   Xidajie

Beichizi

Beiheyan   Dajie

Donghuangchenggen   Nanjie

Dongsi   Nan   Dajie

Forbidden City

Qihelou   Jie

Dengshihou   Xijie

Wangfujing

Dengshihou   Jie

Neiwubu   Jie

Dongdan

Donghuamen   Dajie

Dong'anmen   Dajie

Jinyu   Hutong

Beida   Jie

Nanchizi   Dajie

Chenguang   Jie

Nanheyan   Dajie

Raise the People's Consciousness Cultural Palace

Clothing Market

Dongchang'an

Jie

Jianguomennei

To Tiananmen

Tajiichang   Dajie

Chongwenmennei   Dajie

Dongdan Park

To Friendship Store

To Tiantan Park

Wangfujing Area
王府井地区

0   250   500 m

■ PLACES TO STAY

5	Sara Hotel
8	Holiday Inn Crowne Plaza
9	Tianlun Dynasty Hotel
10	Novotel Hotel
12	Taiwan Hotel
13	Peace Hotel
14	Palace Hotel & Watson's
22	Central Institute of Fine Arts
30	Beijing Hotel

▼ PLACES TO EAT

3	Kentucky Fried Chicken
16	Carls Jr
17	Dairy Queen
26	Shakey's Pizza
27	McDonald's

OTHER

1	China Art Gallery
2	CAAC Booking Office
4	Mosque
6	Capital Theatre
7	PSB
11	Bank of China
15	Jixiang Theatre
18	Foreign Languages Bookstore
19	Pudu Temple
20	Beijing Department Store
21	Dong'an Bazaar
23	Beijing Union Medical College
24	Dahua Cinema
25	Dongdan Vegetable Market
28	Xinhua Bookstore
29	China Photo Studio
31	Huangshicheng Temple
32	Shanghai Airlines
33	History Museum & Museum of the Revolution

■ PLACES TO STAY

5	华侨大厦
8	国际艺苑皇冠假日饭
9	天伦王朝饭店
10	松鹤大酒店
12	台湾饭店
13	和平宾馆
14	王府饭店／屈臣氏
22	中央美术学院
30	北京饭店

▼ PLACES TO EAT

3	肯德基家乡鸡
16	克力汉堡包
17	迪利冰淇淋
26	喜客美式餐厅
27	麦当劳

OTHER

1	中国美术馆
2	中国民航售票处
4	清真寺
6	首都剧场
7	公安局外事科
11	中国银行
15	吉祥戏院
18	外文书店
19	普渡寺
20	北京百货大楼
21	东安市场
23	协和医院
24	大华电影院
25	东单菜市场
28	新华书店
29	中国照相
31	皇史成
32	上海航空公司售票处
33	中国历史革命博物馆

Wangfujing is the place to go to buy film, though the Friendship Store also offers very competitive prices. You can even find slide film here, but check the expiration dates.

If you're into arts & crafts, it's worth looking into the Beijing Arts & Crafts Service Department at 200 Wangfujing.

Wangfujing is also a good place to go for photoprocessing. Print film can be processed in one hour and the quality isn't bad. The Beijing Hotel and International Club also do processing, but at a higher price. Slides can also be developed but the quality varies from acceptable to abysmal. If your slides mean anything to you, wait until you get home to have them processed. Wangfujing is also a good place to obtain passport-type photos of yourself in a hurry.

If there's anything you think is impossible to buy in Beijing, check out Watson's *(qūchénshì)*, in the basement of the Palace Hotel on Jinyu Hutong (east of Wangfujing). This place sells every vitamin known to humanity, sunscreen (UV) lotion, beauty creams, tampons and the widest selection of condoms in China. Prices are in FEC but you can use RMB for a surcharge (sometimes this works out cheaper depending on the current black-market rate).

Xidan *(xīdān)* Officially known as Xidan Beidajie, this street aspires to be a little Wangfujing. There are fewer foreign tourists here and the shops tend to cater mainly to the local market. Biggest of the bunch is the Xidan Shopping Centre *(xīdān gòuwù zhōngxīn)*, offering everything from imported Swiss chocolate to fashionable hairdos.

Qianmen & Dazhalan *(qiánmén hé dàzhàlán)* If Wangfujing is too organised for you, the place to go and rub shoulders with the proletariat is Dazhalan, a hutong running west from the top end of Qianmen. It's a heady jumble of silk shops, department stores, theatres, herbal medicine, food and clothing specialists and some unusual architecture. The hutong is really more of a sight than a place to shop, but you might find something that catches your eye.

Dazhalan has a definite medieval flavour to it, a hangover from the days when hutongs sold specialised products – one would sell lace, another lanterns, another jade. This one used to be called Silk Street. The name Dazhalan refers to a wicket-gate that was closed at night to keep undesirable prowlers out.

In imperial Beijing, shops and theatres were not permitted near the city centre, and the Qianmen-Dazhalan District was outside the gates. Many of the city's oldest shops can be found along or near this crowded hutong.

Just off the beginning of Dazhalan at 3 Liangshidian Jie is Liubiju, a 400-year-old pickle-and-sauce emporium patronised by discriminating shoppers. Nearby is the Zhimielou Restaurant, which serves imper-

ial snacks. On your right as you go down Dazhalan is a green concave archway with columns at No 5; this is the entrance to Liufuxiang, one of the better-known material and silk stores and a century old.

Dazhalan at one time had five opera theatres. The place used to be thronged with theatre-goers both day (cheap rehearsals) and night (professionals). The nightlife lingers on with two performing theatres, and pedicab men wait for the post-theatre crowds as the rickshaw drivers did many years ago. No 1 Dazhalan was once a theatre.

Another famous shop is the Tongrentang at No 24, selling Chinese herbal medicines. It's been in business since 1669, though it doesn't appear that way from the renovations. It was a royal dispensary in the Qing Dynasty, and derives its pills and potions from secret prescriptions used by royalty. All kinds of weird ingredients – tiger bone, rhino horn, snake wine – will cure you of anything from fright to encephalitis, or so they claim. Traditional doctors are available on the spot for consultation; perhaps ask them about fear of railway stations (patience pills?).

Dazhalan runs about 300 metres deep off the western end of Qianmen. At the far end where the hubbub dies down is a bunch of Chinese hotels, and if you sense something here...yes, you're right, Dazhalan was the gateway to Beijing's red-light district. The brothels were shut down in 1949 and the women packed off to factories.

Towards the western end of Dazhalan is one of the best department stores on the whole street – Sun City *(tàiyáng chéng)*, but the sign is in Chinese characters only.

Qianmen Dajie, and Zhushikou Xidajie leading off to the west, are interesting places to meander. On Qianmen Dajie there are pottery stores at Nos 99 and 149, minority musical instruments at Nos 18 and 104, and a nice second-hand shop at No 117. At 190 Qianmen Dajie you'll find the Army Store, just the place to stock up on green PLA overcoats and Snoopy hats.

Liulichang *(liúlíchǎng)* Not far to the west of Dazhalan is Liulichang, Beijing's antique street. Although it's been a shopping area for quite some time, only recently has it been dressed up for foreign tourists. The stores here are all designed to look like an ancient Chinese village – this makes for good photography, even if you don't buy anything. Plenty of the entrepreneurs hang out a sign in English advising you that they accept American Express, JCB and so on. Almost everything on sale looks antique – most are fakes. There is, of course, nothing wrong with buying fakes as long as you're paying the appropriate prices. Overall, you'll probably do better antique-hunting if you stick to Hongqiao Market or, better yet, the weekend antique market in Tianjin which is particularly impressive at weekends.

Jianguomenwai *(jiànguómēnwài)* The Friendship Store *(yǒuyí shāngdiàn)* at 17 Jianguomenwai (☎ 5003311) is the largest in the land – this place stocks both touristy souvenirs and everyday useful items. Not long ago, it was *the* place to shop in Beijing – so exclusive that only foreigners and cadres were permitted inside.

These days anyone can go in, and for good reason – business is fading fast due to competition from Yaohan, Lufthansa Centre and Chinese department stores which offer a wider selection of goods at the same or lower prices. As a result, the Friendship Store is increasingly trying to appeal to the local market – prices have dropped.

The top floor carries furniture, carpets, arts & crafts – in short, the overpriced touristy junk. On the middle floor are clothing items, fabrics, cosmetics, toys and appliances. The ground floor is where the really useful items are found – tinned and dried foods, tobacco, wines, spirits, coffee, Chinese medicines and film. The book and magazine section is a gold mine for travellers long-starved of anything intelligent to read. To the right are a supermarket and deli. There is a cafe on the ground floor – the atmosphere is ambient but prices are too high, and business is being siphoned off by nearby competitors.

Chinese-made goods can be paid for with RMB but imports require FEC. The demand for FEC is the main reason why this store is losing business, but the management seem indifferent.

Yaohan *(bābǎibàn)* is a huge Japanese department store with an enormous selection – the best deal is the supermarket and restaurant in the basement. There are, of course, lots of pricey luxuries on offer: the latest fashion, makeup and perfumes. Kitchenwares are in basement No 2. Yaohan is on the south side of Jianguomenwai, opposite the CITIC building. Everything can be purchased in RMB.

The Xiushui Silk Market *(xiùshuǐ dōngjiē)* is on the north side of Jianguomenwai between the Friendship Store and the Jianguo Hotel. Because of the prestigious location amidst the luxury hotels, this place is elbow to elbow with foreign tourists at times – go early to avoid crowds and forget it on Sundays. This market is one of the best places to pick up good deals in upmarket clothing – everything from silk underwear and negligees to leather moneybelts. Bargaining is expected here, though it's sometimes difficult because of all the foreign tourists willing to throw money around like water.

At the northernmost end of the Xiushui Silk Market are a few shops behind the stalls selling silk carpets. Having searched for carpets in India and China, some of these were the best value I found. A two by 1½ metre carpet retailed from Y3000 and upwards, which is truly excellent value if you delight in the artistry of such things. The cost of these in the West is frightening! Even the Friendship Store had a decent assortment of carpets, though the ones in the alley were a better buy.

Neil Richardson

Ritan Park is north of the Friendship Store – on the west side of the park and intersecting with it at a 90° angle is Yabao Lu Clothing Market. This place is enormous – no Beijing department store could hope to match the variety and low prices on offer here, but bargaining is *de rigueur*. To borrow a slogan from US country stores, 'If you don't find it here, you don't need it'.

Sanlitun (*sānlǐtún*) The Sanlitun embassy district is in north-east Beijing, close to the Great Wall Sheraton Hotel. Like Jianguomenwai, the stores here are decidedly upmarket, but almost everything can now be bought with RMB and prices are not too outrageous.

Lufthansa Centre falls into a category by itself – it's Beijing's first flashy multistorey shopping mall. The Lufthansa Centre (*yānshā shāngchéng*) is also known as the Kempinski Hotel (*kǎibīnsījī fàndiàn*). You can buy everything here from computer floppy disks to bikinis (but who in China wears the latter?). A supermarket is in the basement.

Hongqiao Market (*hóngqiáo shìchǎng*) This very interesting market is the place to look for antiques, both real and fake. Most of the goods are under 100 years old, so they may not meet the textbook definition of 'antique' – this is no big deal as long as you're not paying antique prices. There are plenty of reasonably priced second-hand goods here.

Besides the old stuff, there are intriguing specialty items – you can buy a Little Red Book for Y20 (be sure to bargain). A favourite buy for foreigners is a 'youth of China' alarm clock with a picture of a rosy-cheeked female Red Guard enthusiastically waving the Little Red Book.

Hongqiao Market is at the north-east corner of Tiantan Park across from the Yuanlong Silk Shop.

Zhongguancun (*zhōngguāncūn*) This is Beijing's hi-tech district, but unless you're stocking up on laser eye-surgery equipment, the real attraction here is the computer shops. However, we do not recommend that you buy a computer here unless you are going to live in Beijing for a while – you'll find lower prices, better quality and a wider selection in Hong Kong. On the other hand, foreigners living in Beijing report that most of the shops here are good about honouring their warranties – an important consideration, since

sending a machine to Hong Kong for service is time-consuming and expensive

All this having been said, Zhongguancun has enough accessories and specialised items to interest any computer freak. Much of the world's Chinese-language software originates in this neighbourhood, including that which was used to produce this book. Pirating software is a big local industry too – if interested, be aware that most Chinese software is copy-protected and much of the pirated programmes infected with computer viruses.

Just off Zhongguancun is the shopping district for low-tech consumer goods (music tapes, clothing, food, etc), known as Haidian Tushucheng.

Zhongguancun is in the Haidian District in the north-western part of Beijing, not far from the Summer Palace.

Getting There & Away

Getting to Beijing is no problem – one of those rail or air lines will lead you to the capital sooner or later. The real problem is getting away, and your exodus is best planned well in advance. There are planes from Beijing to numerous destinations but most travellers will probably leave the city by train – get in early to get a sleeper.

Air You can get to just about anywhere in the world from Beijing. Many travellers make use of the direct flight to Hong Kong with CAAC or Dragonair. If purchased in Beijing, the ticket costs Y1366 in economy class, or HK$1850 if bought in Hong Kong. The big obstacle – flights are booked solid for weeks in advance in both directions! It's a little better in off-season (winter) but during summer the waiting list is a month long – or longer. A cheaper alternative is a flight to Canton or Shenzhen, but these are typically booked out a week or more in advance.

For more information about international flights to Beijing, see the introductory Getting There & Away chapter in this book.

The partially computerised CAAC ticket office (☎ 4014441 for domestic reservations; ☎ 4012221 for international reservations;

and ☎ 554415 for inquiries) is at 117 Dongsi Xidajie.

The CAAC aerial web spreads out in every conceivable direction, with daily flights to major cities and quite a few minor ones. For the most current information, get a CAAC timetable. The following table shows domestic flights and fares from Beijing.

Destination	Fare	Destination	Fare
Baotou	Y290	Beihai	Y1190
Canton	Y980	Changchun	Y470
Changsha	Y730	Changzhou	Y510
Chengdu	Y850	Chongqing	Y820
Dalian	Y360	Dandong	Y420
Fuzhou	Y840	Guilin	Y920
Guiyang	1020	Haikou	Y1250
Hailar	Y650	Hangzhou	Y600
Harbin	Y510	Hefei	Y480
Hohhot	Y240	Huangshan	Y580
Jilin	Y520	Ji'nan	Y200
Kunming	Y1130	Lanzhou	Y680
Lhasa	Y1690	Lianyungang	Y350
Mudanjiang	Y720	Nanchang	Y700
Nanjing	Y500	Nanning	Y1100
Ningbo	Y670	Qingdao	Y320
Qinhuangdao	Y200	Qiqihar	Y630
Shanghai	Y590	Shantou	Y950
Shenyang	Y320	Shenzhen	Y1170
Shijiazhuang	Y180	Taiyuan	Y260
Tianjin	Y120	Tongliao	Y320
Ulanhot	Y460	Ürümqi	Y1410
Wenzhou	Y790	Wuhan	Y570
Xiamen	Y890	Xi'an	Y520
Xining	Y890	Yan'an	Y410
Yantai	Y290	Yinchuan	Y550
Zhanjiang	Y1200	Zhengzhou	Y350

The *Capital Airport Hotel* (☎ 4564562) (*shǒudū jīchǎng bīnguǎn*) is one km from the airport terminal. Although not especially recommended, you could find yourself here if your flight is delayed. Supposedly, the airline should pick up the tab if the delay is their fault, but don't count on it. Singles/doubles are Y110/150.

CAAC goes by a variety of aliases (Air China, China Eastern Airlines, etc), but you can buy tickets for all of them at the Aviation Building, 15 Xichang'an Jie, (☎ domestic 6013336, international 6016667). You can purchase the same tickets at the CAAC office in the China World Trade Centre or from the numerous other CAAC service counters like the one in the Beijing Hotel. You can also buy air tickets from CITS in the International Hotel if you can tolerate their AIM (Avarice, Insolence and *Meiyou*).

Inquiries for all airlines can be made at Beijing International Airport (☎ 552515). The individual offices of airlines are:

Dragonair
  1st floor, L107, World Trade Tower, 1 Jianguomenwai (☎ 5054343; fax 5054347)
Aeroflot
  Hotel Beijing-Toronto, Jianguomenwai (☎ 5002412)
Air France
  2716 China World Trade Centre, 1 Jianguomenwai (☎ 5051818)
Alitalia
  Room 139, Jianguo Hotel, 5 Jianguomenwai (☎ 5002233 ext 139)
All Nippon Airways
  Room 1510, China World Trade Centre, 1 Jianguomenwai (☎ 5053311)
Asiana Airlines
  Room 134, Jianguo Hotel, 5 Jianguomenwai (☎ 5002233 ext 134)
British Airways
  Room 210, 2nd floor, SCITE Tower, 22 Jianguomenwai (☎ 5124070)
Canadian Airlines
  Room 135, Jianguo Hotel, 5 Jianguomenwai (☎ 5003950)
Finnair
  SCITE Tower, 22 Jianguomenwai (☎ 5127180)
Iran Air
  Room 701, CITIC Building, 19 Jianguomenwai (☎ 5124940)
JAL Japan Airlines
  Ground floor, Changfugong Office Building, Hotel New Otani, 26A Jianguomenwai (☎ 5130888)
JAT Yugoslav Airlines
  Room 414, Kunlun Hotel, 2 Xinyuan Nanlu (☎ 5003388 ext 414)
LOT Polish Airlines
  Room 102, West Wing Office Block, China World Trade Centre, 1 Jianguomenwai (☎ 5050136)
Lufthansa
  Lufthansa Centre, 50 Liangmaqiao Lu (☎ 4654488)
MIAT Mongolian Airlines
  CITIC Building, 19 Jianguomenwai (☎ 5002255)
Malaysian Airline System
  Lot 115A/B Level One, West Wing Office Block, China World Trade Centre (☎ 5052681)

Northwest Airlines
  Room 104, China World Trade Centre, 1
  Jianguomenwai (☎ 5053505)
Pakistan International
  Room 106, China World Trade Centre, 1
  Jianguomenwai (☎ 5051681)
Philippine Airlines
  12-53 Jianguomenwai (☎ 5323992)
Qantas
  5th floor, Hotel Beijing-Toronto, 3
  Jianguomenwai (☎ 5002235)
Romanian Air Transport
  Room 109, Jianguo Hotel, 5 Jianguomenwai
  (☎ 5002233 ext 109)
SAS-Scandinavian Airlines
  18th floor, SCITE Tower, 22 Jianguomenwai
  (☎ 5120575)
Singapore Airlines
  Room 109, China World Trade Centre,
  Jianguomenwai (☎ 5052233)
Swissair
  Room 201, SCITE Tower, 22 Jianguomenwai
  (☎ 5123555)
Thai International
  Room 207, SCITE Tower, 22 Jianguomenwai
  (☎ 5123881)
United Airlines
  Room 204, SCITE Tower, 22 Jianguomenwai
  (☎ 5128888)

Bus Many foreigners don't think so, but you can indeed arrive in Beijing by bus. The advantage over the train (besides cost) is that it's easier to get a seat on buses. In general, arriving by bus is easier than departing mainly because when leaving it's very confusing to try and figure out which bus station has the buses you need.

The basic rule is that long-distance bus stations are on the perimeter of the city in the direction you want to go. The four major ones are at Dongzhimen (north-east), Haihutun (south), Beijiao (north – also called Deshengmen) and Majuan (east). In addition, there is a tiny bus station in the car park in front of Beijing railway station – this is where you catch buses to Tianjin and the Great Wall at Badaling. Another tiny bus station is in the car park of the Workers' Stadium – this is mainly geared towards buses for destinations within Beijing Municipality (like Miyun Reservoir).

One of the more useful stations is Haihutun on the southern side of Beijing. It's

at the intersection of Nansanhuan Zhonglu (the southern part of the third ring road) and Nanyuan Lu (which is what Qianmen Lu is called in the far south of town). Long-distance buses from here head to cities such as Qingdao and Shanghai.

Beijiao station is on the north side of the city. It's one km north of the second ring road on Deshengmenwai Dajie, and is often referred to as 'Deshengmen station'. Some long-distance buses depart from here. Otherwise, you might need to take bus No 345 from Deshengmen to the terminus (Changping) from where you can get other long-distance buses.

Train Over 95% of foreigners arriving or departing by train do so at the Beijing main railway station (*běijīng huǒchē zhàn*). There are also two other stations of significance in the city, Yongdingmen (the south railway station) and Xizhimen (the north railway station). There are plans on the drawing board to build an as-yet-unnamed west railway station.

There is a Foreigners' Ticketing Office at the main Beijing railway station. Enter the station and it's to the rear and left side – there's a small sign in English saying 'International Passenger Booking Office'. The ticketing office is inside the foreigners' waiting room. It's open daily, from 5.30 to 7.30 am and 8 am to 5.30 pm, and from 7 pm to 12.30 am. At least those are the official times – foreigners have often found the staff unwilling to sell tickets in the early morning. Whether or not you get a ticket here is potluck – sometimes the staff are friendly and helpful, at other times downright hostile. They sometimes have timetables for sale in English, but usually not. There are lockers inside the waiting room, often full, in which case you'll have to use the left-luggage rooms outside the station (exit station and car park, then to the right). Tickets can be booked several days in advance. Your chances of getting a sleeper (hard or soft) are good so long as you book ahead.

You can pay in RMB at the Foreigners' Ticketing Office provided you have a genuine (or genuine-looking) red card. Getting a Chinese person to buy your ticket from the regular ticket windows involves major tactical difficulties -- mainly that the ticket windows, some two dozen of them, can't be seen half the time for the crowds! Nevertheless, there are some Chinese who make a modest living purchasing tickets and reselling to foreigners for a mark-up (but still cheaper than FEC price).

The following is a table of approximate travel times and train fares out of Beijing for hard seat, hard sleeper and soft sleeper. Variations may arise because of different

Destination	(Approx.) Travel Time (hours)	Soft Sleeper (Y)	Hard Sleeper (Y)	Soft Seat (Y)	Hard Seat (Y)
Baotou	15	257	135	-	83
Beidaihe	6	127	-	64	42
Canton	35	563	296	-	182
Changchun	17	325	170	-	105
Changsha	23	419	220	-	135
Chengde	5	-	-	66	44
Chengdu	34	507	265	-	163
Chongqing	40	521	274	-	169
Dalian	19	331	170	-	105
Datong	7	135	71	66	43
Fuzhou	43	638	335	-	206
Guilin	31	521	274	-	169
Guiyang	49	609	320	-	197
Hangzhou	24	440	231	-	142
Harbin	17	378	198	-	122
Hefei	19	310	155	-	90
Hohhot	12	211	111	-	69
Ji'nan	9	172	91	85	56
Jilin	19	331	171	-	99
Kunming	59	746	392	-	241
Lanzhou	35	474	249	-	154
Liuzhou	34	563	296	-	182
Luoyang	14	246	129	-	79
Nanchang	36	473	238	-	138
Nanjing	20	334	176	-	108
Nanning	39	625	328	-	202
Qingdao	17	267	140	132	86
Qinglongqiao	2	83	37	14	9
Shanghai	17	459	241	-	148
Shenyang	11	257	135	128	83
Shijiazhuang	4	120	-	51	34
Suzhou	25	361	181	-	105
Tai'an	10	187	99	-	61
Taiyuan	11	178	90	-	52
Tianjin	2	93	-	34	21
Turpan	72	833	437	-	269
Ürümqi	75	849	446	-	275
Xi'an	22	347	182	-	112
Xining	44	497	250	-	145
Yantai	18	284	143	-	83
Yanzhou	12	211	111	-	69
Yinchuan	25	368	193	-	119

Travel Times & Train Fares from Beijing

routings of different trains. For example, the journey to Shanghai can take between 17 and 25 hours depending on the train.

Getting Around
To/From the Airport The airport is 25 km from the Forbidden City, but add another 10 km if you're going to the southern end of town.

For Y8 you can catch the airport shuttle bus from the Aviation Building (*mínháng dàshà*) on Xi Chang'an Jie, Xidan District – this is the location of Air China and China North-West Airlines, but it's *not* the same place as the CAAC office. The bus departs on the opposite side of the street (south side of Xichang'an Jie), not from the car park of the Aviation Building.

At the airport, you can catch this shuttle bus in front of the terminal building – buy the bus ticket from the counter inside the terminal building, not on the bus itself. The bus terminates at the Aviation Building in Xidan, but makes several stops en route – get off at the second stop (Swissotel-Hong Kong Macau Centre) if you want to take the subway.

A taxi from the airport to the Forbidden City area costs around Y70, or Y100 to the Qiaoyuan Hotel area in the southern side of town.

Bus Sharpen your elbows, chain your money to your underwear and muster all the patience you can – you'll need it. Overstuffed buses are in vogue in Beijing, and can be particularly nauseating at the height of summer when passengers drip with perspiration. They're cosy in winter if you haven't frozen to the bus stop by the time the trolley arrives, but difficult to exit from – try the nearest window. Fares are typically two jiao depending on distance, but often it's free because you can't see (let alone reach) the conductor.

There are about 140 bus and trolley routes, which make navigation rather confusing, especially if you can't see out of the window in the first place. Bus maps are listed in the Information section earlier in this chapter.

Buses run from around 5 am to 11 pm. A minor compensation for the crowding is that the conductor rarely gets through to you. Bus stops are long and far between. It's important to work out how many stops to go before boarding. Avoid these sardine cans like the plague at rush hours or on holidays.

Buses are routed through landmarks and key intersections, and if you can pick out the head and tail of the route, you can get a good idea of where the monster will travel. Major terminals occur near long-distance junctions: the main Beijing railway station, Dongzhimen, Haihutun, Yongdingmen, Qianmen. The zoo (Dongwuyuan) has the biggest pile-up, with about 15 lines, since it's where inner and outer Beijing get together.

One or two-digit bus numbers are city core, 100-series buses are trolleys, and 300-series are suburban lines. If you can work out how to combine bus and subway connections, the subway will speed up part of the trip. Some useful buses are:

No 1 travels east-west across the city along Chang'an, from Jianguo Lu to Fuxing Lu

No 5 travels the north-south axis, from Deshengmen/Gulou and down the west side of the Forbidden City to Qianmen; it ends at Youanmen

No 44 follows the Circle Line subway in a square on the ring road

No 15 zigzags from the Tianqiao area (west of Tiantan Park) to the zoo and passes several subway stops

No 7 runs from the west side of Qianmen gate to the zoo (Dongwuyuan)

No 20 zigzags from the main Beijing railway station to Yongdingmen station via Chang'an and Qianmen Dajie. This bus gets you to the Qiaoyuan Hotel.

No 54 runs from the main Beijing railway station, terminates at Yongdingmen station and (like bus No 20) is an ideal way to get to the Qiaoyuan Hotel

No 10 trolley runs from the main railway station to the zoo via Chongwenmen, Wangfujing, Art Gallery, Jingshan and Beihai parks

No 106 runs from Dongzhimenwai via Chongwenmen Dajie to Yongdingmen station

No 116 travels from the south entrance of Tiantan Park up Qianmen Dajie to Tiananmen, east along Chang'an to Dongdan and directly north on Dongdan to the Lama Temple – a good sightseeing bus

No 332 covers Dongwuyan (zoo), Minzuxueyuan (Institute for Nationalities), Weigongcun, Renmindaxue (People's University), Zhongguancun, Haidian, Beijingdaxue (Beijing University) and Yiheyuan (Summer Palace). There are actually two Nos 332: regular and express – both make good sightseeing buses. The express bus has fewer stops and is at the head of the queue near the zoo.

Subway *(dì xià tiě)* The Underground Dragon is definitely the best way of travelling around. Trains can move at up to 70 km/h – a jaguar compared to the lumbering buses. The subway is also less crowded per sq cm than the buses, and trains run at a frequency of one every few minutes during peak times. The carriages have seats for 60 and standing room for 200. Platform signs are in Chinese and pinyin. The fare is a flat five jiao regardless of distance. The subway is open from 5 am to 10.30 pm.

Circle Line This 16-km line presently has 18 stations: Beijingzhan (railway station), Jianguomen, Chaoyangmen, Dongsishitiao, Dongzhimen, Yonghegong, Andingmen, Gulou Dajie, Jishuitan, Xizhimen (the north railway station and zoo), Chegongzhuang, Fuchengmen, Fuxingmen, Chang-chun Jie, Xuanwumen, Heping Lu, Qianmen and Chongwenmen.

East-West Line This line has 12 stops and runs from Xidan to Pingguoyuan which is – no, not the capital of North Korea – but a western suburb of Beijing whose name translates as 'Apple Orchard'. It takes 40 minutes to traverse the length of the line. The stops are Xidan, Nanlishilu, Muxudi, Junshibowuguan (Military Museum), Gongzhufen, Wanshoulu, Wukesong, Yuquanlu, Babaoshan, Bajiaocun, Guchenglu and Pingguoyuan. It takes 40 minutes to traverse the length of the line. It's a five-minute walk between station B on the East West Line and station 13 on the Circle Line and there is no direct connection between them.

Bicycle The scale of Beijing is suddenly much reduced on a bike, which can also give you a great deal of freedom. Beijing is as flat as a chapatti. An added advantage is that Beijingers will ride up alongside you to chat. You can check your bearings with them, but it's not claustrophobic like being on the pavement, and you can break off at any time. Just push those pedals!

Bicycles can be hired at the Qiaoyuan Hotel for about Y3 per day. Another good place is the bike shop near the Chongwenmen intersection, on the north side at No 94.

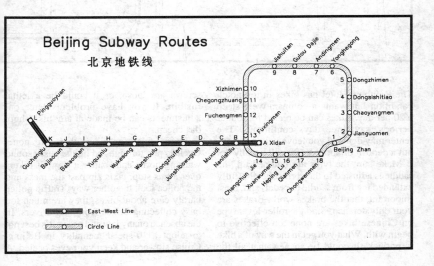

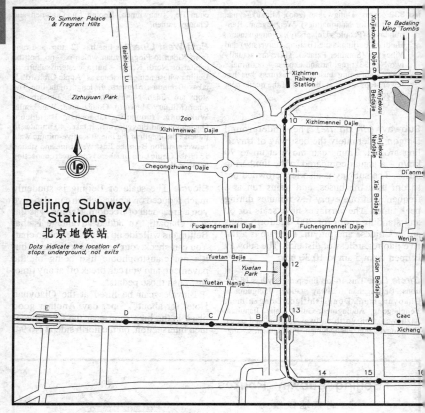

To Summer Palace
& Fragrant Hills

Baishiqao Lu

Zizhuyuan Park

Zoo

Xizhimenwai   Dajie

Chegongzhuang Dajie

Beijing Subway Stations
北京地铁站

*Dots indicate the location of
stops underground, not exits*

Fuchengmenwai Dajie

Yuetan Bejie

Yuetan
Park

Yuetan Nanjie

E   D   C   B

Xizhimen
Railway
Station

Xinjiekouwai Dajie   9

To Badaling
Ming Tombs

Xinjiekou
Beidajie

10   Xizhimennei Dajie

Xinjiekou
Nandajie

11

Xisi Beidajie

Di'anme

Fuchengmennei Dajie

Wenjin J

Xidan Beidajie

12

13   A

Caac

Xichang'

14   15   16

The Rainbow Hotel has bikes in top-notch condition but wants a comparatively steep Y20 per day. Bikes can be rented for longer periods, say three days continuous. The renter may demand you leave your passport, but a deposit of about Y100 will usually do.

Make sure the tyres are pumped up, the saddle is adjusted to the correct height (fully extended leg from saddle to pedal) and, most important, that the brakes work. Brakes are your only defence – and the roller-lever type on Chinese bikes are none too effective to begin with. What you get in the way of a bike is potluck. It could be so new that all the

screws are loose, or it could be a lethal rustbin. If you have problems later on, adjustments can be made at any bike shop, dirt cheap.

Traffic rules for bikes: there are none. Cyclists pile through red lights, buses sound warning horns and scatter a slew of bikers over a bus stop, taxis zip past the mess and the police look the other way. Traffic police hardly care about bikes, they are much too busy collecting bribes from taxi drivers. In the absence of any law and order, it's best not to adopt a 10-speed mentality in Beijing. Cruise slower and keep your eyes peeled. A

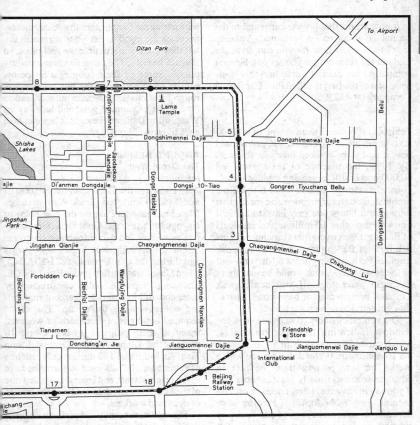

constant thumb on a clear bell is good fun, but nobody takes any notice. You're better off screaming in a foreign language. Insurance – what's that?

Several shopping areas are closed to cyclists from 6 am to 6 pm; Wangfujing is one. Parking is provided everywhere for peanuts – compulsory peanuts since your velo can otherwise be towed away. Beijingese peak hours can be rather astounding – a roving population of three million plus bicycles, a fact explained by the agony of bus rides. This makes turning at roundabouts a rather skilled cycling procedure. If nervous, dismount at the side of the road, wait for the clusters to unthicken, and try again. Beijing in winter presents other problems, like slippery roads (black ice) and frostbite. You need to rug up and be extra careful.

Car Resident foreigners are allowed to drive their own cars in the capital, and to drive the Beijing-Tianjin highway. Most are not permitted to drive more than 40 km from the capital without special permission. Chauffeur-driven cars and minibuses can be hired from some of the major hotels, but why not just rent a taxi by the day for less money?

It now seems that private car rental in the capital is going to be permitted. You are restricted on just how far you can drive, so find out the rules before you set out. Several companies are ready to dive into this business; one of the first is called First Car Rental Company (☎ 4223950).

Taxi In 1986 there were fewer than 1000 taxis available in the capital – if you wanted one, it had to be booked hours in advance. By 1993, the number of taxis exceeded 40,000 and is still increasing rapidly.

In other words, finding a cab is seldom a problem, though surging demand means that during rush hours you may have to battle it out with the other 10 million plus residents of Beijing. One government brochure claims that 80% of Beijing taxis drivers can speak English. Perhaps they meant 80 drivers – out of the total 40,000, that would be just about the right percentage. If you don't speak Chinese, bring a map or have your destination written down in characters.

The vehicles usually have a sticker on the window indicating their per-km charge, which varies all the way from Y1 to Y2 with a Y10 minimum. If you don't get one with a meter, be sure to negotiate the fare in advance. You can usually get a cheaper rate if you say in advance 'I don't need an official receipt' *(wǒ bùbì fāpiào)*. Pricing also depends on size, make, age of car, backway subsidy, air-con, heating, waiting time – we could go on. In general, if you want a cheap ride, search for the oldest, smallest, most decrepit-looking bomb you can. The small micro-buses are usually cheapest. Taxis can be summoned to a location of your choosing or hailed in the streets. They're scarce at certain hours such as drivers' dinner time (from 6 to 8 pm) or the sacred lunchtime siesta.

Beijing taxi drivers, incidentally, pull in around Y500 a month, and there have been reports that some make as much as Y2000. In the nonprofit public sector, bus drivers average just Y150 per month and conductors Y100 per month.

Motortricycle Far cheaper than cars, motortricycles are good to get your adrenalin up, but they usually ask double the real price, so bargain heavily. They can be summoned by phone. Some of their congregation points can be discerned from the bus map; a few rough locations are the main railway station (☎ 555661), Qianmen gate, and halfway up Wangfujing Dajie on the right. They can take ages to arrive, though.

AROUND BEIJING
The Great Wall
(chángchéng) 长城

Also known to the Chinese as the '10,000 Li Wall' (5000 km), the Great Wall stretches from Shanhaiguan Pass on the east coast to Jiayuguan Pass in the Gobi Desert, crossing five provinces and two autonomous regions.

The undertaking was begun 2000 years ago during the Qin Dynasty (221-207 BC), when China was unified under Emperor Qin Shihuang. Separate walls, constructed by independent kingdoms to keep out marauding nomads, were linked up. The effort required hundreds of thousands of workers, many of them political prisoners, and 10 years of hard labour under General Meng Tian. An estimated 180 million cubic metres of rammed earth was used to form the core of the original wall, and legend has it that one of the building materials used was the bodies of deceased workers.

The wall never really did perform its function as a defence line to keep invaders out. As Genghis Khan supposedly said, 'The strength of a wall depends on the courage of those who defend it'. Sentries could be bribed. However, it did work very well as a kind of elevated highway, transporting men and equipment across mountainous terrain. Its beacon tower system, using smoke signals generated by burning wolves' dung, transmitted news of enemy movements quickly back to the capital. To the west was Jiayuguan Pass, an important link on the Silk Road where there was a Customs post of sorts, and where unwanted Chinese were ejected through the gates to face the terrifying wild west.

Marco Polo makes no mention of China's greatest tourist attraction. Both sides of the wall were under the same government at the time of his visit, but the Ming Great Wall had not been built. During the Ming Dynasty a determined effort was made to rehash the whole project, this time facing it with bricks and stone slabs – some 60 million cubic metres of them. They created double-walling running in an elliptical shape to the west of Beijing, and did not necessarily follow the older earthen wall. This Ming project took over 100 years, and the costs in human effort and resources were phenomenal.

The wall was largely forgotten after that, but now it's reached its greatest heights as a tourist attraction. Lengthy sections of it have been swallowed up by the sands, claimed by the mountains, intersected by road or rail, or simply returned to dust. Other bits were carted off by local peasants to construct their own four walls – a hobby that no-one objected to during the Cultural Revolution. The depiction of the wall as an object of great beauty is a bizarre one. It's really a symbol of tyranny, like the Berlin Wall used to be.

Badaling Great Wall *(bādálǐng cháng-chéng)* Most foreigners see the wall at Badaling, 70 km north-west of Beijing at an elevation of 1000 metres. It was restored in 1957 with the addition of guard rails. The section is almost eight metres high with a base of 6½ metres and a width at the top of almost six metres. It runs for several hundred metres, after which, if you keep going, are the unrestored sections where the crowds peter out. Originally the wall here could hold five horsemen riding abreast – nowadays it's about 15 tourists walking abreast.

Unfortunately, if you take a tour bus or train from Beijing you hit peak hour, and you only get a little over an hour at the wall. Many are dissatisfied with such a paltry time at one of the most spectacular sights in the PRC. The solution is to take one-way tours or public transport, spend the time you want, and then figure out a way to get back (you can negotiate a minibus ride for around Y10). Some people take their sleeping bags

and picnic baskets, head off from the crowds and camp out overnight.

The Great Wall Circle Vision Theatre was opened in 1990 – a 360° amphitheatre showing 15-minute films about the Wall. You get to hear about the Wall's history and legends – narration is in English or Chinese and other languages may be added later.

To get up on top of the wall, there is an admission fee of Y15. The Wall also has a cable car, which costs Y55 for foreigners (only Y5 with student card).

You can spend plenty more for a trashy 'I Climbed the Great Wall' T-shirt, a talking panda bear doll, a cuckoo clock that plays 'The East is Red' or a plastic reclining buddha statue with a lightbulb in its mouth. For an additional fee you can get your snap-shot taken aboard a camel and pretend to be Marco Polo – though he wasn't tethered to a wall. There's a story attached to the camel. In 1981 when the director Labella was filming the travels of Polo, the commune that owned the camel refused to move it from the camera's field of view unless they were paid the day's lost earnings. The bill came to Y2000!

If you're hungry, you won't have to look far for food – everything from yoghurt to Beijing duck is available.

Getting There & Away There are cheapie Chinese tours departing from a number of venues. Some depart from the south side of Tiananmen Square (near Kentucky Fried Chicken). Others depart from the car park in front of the Beijing Railway Station (west side of station), but don't get confused with the buses heading for Tianjin (which depart from the exact same spot). You can also catch buses from the car park of the Workers' Stadium *(gōngrén tǐyùguǎn)* – this is on Gongren Tiyuchang Beilu next to the Beijing Asia Hotel and the Dongsishitiao subway station. Departures are only in the morning, around 7.30 to 8 am. Tours cost about Y15 or so, but you often have to bargain and there is sometimes the sickening tendency to try raising the price after you're halfway to the wall. Make sure you understand just what time the tour returns to Beijing unless you want to find another way back. Some tour operators have nice air-con buses; others have older vehicles that appear to date back to the Qing Dynasty.

CITS, CTS, big hotels and everyone else in the tourist business does a tour to Badaling. Prices border on the ridiculous, with some hotels asking over Y300 per person.

Local buses also ply the route to the wall but it's slow going; take bus Nos 5 or 44 to Deshengmen, then No 345 to the terminal (Changping), then a numberless bus to the wall (alternatively, bus No 357 goes part way along the route and you then hitch). Another route is bus No 14 to Beijiao long-distance bus station, which is north of Deshengmen, then a numberless bus to the wall. Going on local buses saves some money but it's a headache even if you speak Chinese.

You can reach the wall by express train from Beijing main railway station, getting off at Qinglongqiao. There are actually three stations within one km of the wall – Qinglongqiao, New Qinglongqiao and Badaling, but the first is by far the closest to your destination. Qinglongqiao station is notable for the statue of Zhan Tianyou, the engineer in charge of building the Beijing-Baotou line. No trains stop at all three stations and many only stop at Qinglongqiao. If you're coming from the direction of Hohhot or Datong you could get out at Qinglongqiao, look around the wall and then continue the same day to Beijing. Your ticket will still be valid for the last stretch to Beijing and you can safely dump your bags in the left-luggage room at Qinglongqiao station while you look around.

There's another approach by slower local trains from Xizhimen (north railway station) in Beijing which stops at Badaling or Qinglongqiao and continues to Kangzhuang. There are several trains on this route with different departure times – check times at the station. One train leaves Xizhimen around 8.10 am and arrives at Badaling at 10.50 am. It departs from Badaling around 2.11 pm and arrives at Beijing at 4 pm. The return fare is about Y20. At Xizhimen station there is a special booking office for this train – tickets are sold only on the day of departure. It is also possible to catch train No 527 at 9.40 am from Yongdingmen (south railway station) and get off at Juyongguan station, but then you'll have to walk several (pleasant) km to the wall. Badaling station is one km from the wall. The Badaling line is quite a feat of engineering; built in 1909, it tunnels under the wall.

A microbus-style taxi to the wall and back will cost at least Y250 for an eight-hour hire with a maximum of five passengers – you are expected to buy lunch for the driver. Considering that this works out to less than Y60 per person, it's certainly not unreasonable.

Mutianyu Great Wall *(mùtiányù chángchéng)* To take some of the pressure off crowded Badaling, a second site for Great Wall viewing has been opened at Mutianyu, 90 km north-east of Beijing. This part of the wall is less of a carnival than Badaling, but the recent addition of souvenir shops and a cable car is starting to attract armadas of tour buses. Nevertheless, Mutianyu is the place most preferred by individual travellers and is still much less crowded than Badaling.

Getting There & Away The Qiaoyuan Hotel operates a minibus directly to the wall at Mutianyu for Y40, which is about the easiest way to get there. A small number of Chinese tour buses also go to Mutianyu – look for them near the Kentucky Fried Chicken near Tiananmen Square, the Beijing railway station or the Workers' Stadium. Entrance to the wall at Mutianyu costs Y15. The cable-car ride costs Y30 one way for Y40 for the return trip.

To go by yourself is complicated and doesn't save much money. If you're starting from the Qiaoyuan Hotel area, take bus No 106 (from Yongdingmen) to Dongzhimen (last station). From there walk across the street to the long-distance bus station and take a bus to Huairou, then it's another 20 km by local minibus (these are scarce), taxi or bicycle.

Simatai Great Wall (*sīmǎtái chángchéng*) If you prefer your Wall without the benefit of handrails, cable cars and tacky souvenir shops, Simatai is the place to go. Of all the parts of the wall near Beijing which are open to tourism, the 19-km section at Simatai is the least developed (for now). Many consider this part of the wall to be the most beautiful.

This section of the wall dates from the Ming Dynasty and has some unusual features like 'obstacle-walls', which are walls-within-walls used for defending against enemies who'd already scaled the Great Wall. There are 135 watchtowers at Simatai, the highest being Wangjinglou. Small cannon have been discovered in this area, as well as evidence of rocket-type weapons such as flying knives and flying swords.

Simatai is not for the chicken-hearted – this section of the wall is very steep. A few slopes have a 70° incline and you need both hands free, so bring a day-pack to hold your camera and other essentials. One narrow section of footpath has a 500-metre drop – it's no place for acrophobiacs.

An early Western visitor was Lord Macartney, who crossed nearby Gubei Pass on his way to Chengde in 1793. His party made a wild guess that the wall contained almost as much material as all the houses in England and Scotland.

In the early 1970s a nearby PLA unit destroyed about three km of the wall to build barracks, setting an example for the locals, who used the stone from the wall to build houses. The story goes that in 1979 the same unit was ordered to rebuild the section torn down.

A small section of the wall at Simatai has already been renovated, but most of it remains in its non-commercialised crumbling condition. Seeing the wall *au natural* is a sharp contrast to Badaling and Mutianyu, which are so well restored that you may get the impression the wall was built just yesterday to serve CITS tour groups. Perhaps it was.

There is a small restaurant at the car park near the base of the wall, and at the present time prices are still reasonable. It's not a bad idea to come prepared with some snacks and water. There is a Y10 admission charge.

Besides those already mentioned, other parts of the wall open to foreigners are the stretches at Jiayuguan in Gansu Province, Shanhaiguan in Hebei Province and Huang-yaguan in Tianjin Municipality. Details for visiting these parts of the wall are covered in the relevant chapters of this book.

Getting There & Away Simatai is 110 km north-east of Beijing, and due to the far distance and lack of tourist facilities, getting there is not particularly convenient unless you arrange your own transport. Hiring a microbus taxi for the day would cost at least Y300, but getting a group together makes it more affordable. Buses to Simatai cost Y20 for the round-trip and depart just once daily from the Dongzhimen bus station at 7 am. The journey takes from two to three hours, and the bus departs Simatai at 3 pm (but ask to be sure).

Tombs
(*líng*) 陵

Dying is a big deal in China, especially if you're an emperor. Since they had to go, the royal families decided to go in style. Around Beijing are three major tomb sites – each tomb holds (or held) the body of an emperor, his wives, girlfriends and funerary treasures. All of the tombs have been plundered at one time or another, but recent efforts at restoration have benefited China's cultural pride, not to mention the tourist industry.

The three tomb sites around Beijing open to tourists are the Ming Tombs, the Western Qing Tombs and the Eastern Qing Tombs. Of the three, the Ming Tombs are by far the most frequently visited.

Ming Tombs (*shísān líng*) The general travellers' consensus on the tombs is that you'd be better off looking at a bank vault, which is, roughly, what the tombs are. The scenery along the way is charming, though, and the approach through a valley is rewarding.

The seven-km 'spirit way' starts with a triumphal arch, then goes through the Great Palace Gate, where officials had to dismount, and passes a giant tortoise (made in 1425) bearing the largest stele in China. This is followed by a guard of 12 sets of stone animals. Every second one is in a reclining position, legend has it, to allow for a 'changing of the guard' at midnight. If your tour bus driver whips past them, insist on stopping to look – they're far more interesting than the tombs – because the drivers like to spend half an hour at the Ming Tombs Reservoir, which is dead boring. Beyond the stone animals are 12 stone-faced human statues of generals, ministers and officials, each distinguishable by their headgear. The stone figures terminate at the Lingxing Gate.

Dingling was the first of the tombs to be excavated and opened to the public. In total, 13 of the 16 Ming emperors are buried in this 40-sq-km area, which is why another name for this site is the Thirteen Tombs. Besides Dingling, two other tombs, Changling and Zhaoling, are open to the public.

Dingling, the tomb of Emperor Wan Li (1573-1620), is the second-largest tomb. Over six years the emperor used half a million workers and a heap of silver to build his necropolis and then held a wild party inside the completed chambers. It was excavated between 1956 and 1958 and you can now visit the underground passageways and caverns. The underground construction covers 1195 sq metres, is built entirely of stone, and is sealed with an unusual lock stone. The tomb yielded up 26 lacquered trunks of funerary objects, some of which are displayed on site; others have been removed to Beijing museums and replaced with copies.

Wan Li and his royal spouses were buried in double coffins surrounded by chunks of uncut jade. The jade was thought to have the power to preserve the dead (or could have bought millions of bowls of rice for starving peasants), so the Chinese tour literature relates. Meanwhile cultural relics experts as

well as chefs are studying the ancient cookbooks unearthed from Dingling with a view to serving Wan Li's favourite dishes to visitors, using replicas of imperial banquet tableware. Until they figure that one out, you might have to be content with the amusing cardboard cut-outs and other props used by Chinese photographers at the site.

The Changling tomb was started in 1409 and took 18 years to complete. This is the final resting place of Emperor Yong Le. According to the story, 16 concubines were buried alive with his corpse. This was the second of the Ming Tombs to be excavated and opened to the public.

Zhaoling is the ninth of the Ming Tombs – it was opened to visitors in 1989. This is the tomb of Emperor Longqing and three of his wives. Longqing died in 1572.

Admission to the Ming Tombs costs Y15 for foreigners, but a student card reduces it to Y2.

Getting There & Away The tombs lie 50 km north-west of Beijing and a few km from the small town of Changping. The tour buses usually combine them with a visit to the Great Wall. You can also get there on the local buses. Take bus Nos 5 or 44 to Deshengmen terminal. West of the flyover is the terminal of bus No 345 which you take to Changping, a one-hour ride. Then take bus No 314 to the tombs (or hitch the last stretch).

Changping main railway station is on the main Beijing-Baotou railway line. There is another station, Changping north station, which is closer to the Ming Tombs, but relatively few trains stop there.

The Ming Tombs

It's only fair to mention that many people consider the Ming Tombs a wipeoff. 'What a monumental disappointment!' said one letter. 'There isn't anything down there, and you pay just to walk into a four-storey deep hole and back out again.' Another letter complained that 'other than seeing that they knew how to make deep excavations in China several centuries ago, there is nothing to justify the trip'.

Perhaps true, but that's a bit like saying that all the Great Wall proves is that the Chinese were capable of putting one brick on top of another for a very long distance. There may not be anything inside the tombs, but like the Wall and the Mao Zedong Mausoleum, it's interesting to see the product of an incredible amount of human labour.

Aware of the fact that many visitors have found the tombs disappointing, the Beijing municipal government is busy dressing up the area. New facilities include a golf course, the Dingling Museum (with a wax Genghis Khan), the Nine Dragons Amusement Park, Aerospace Museum, archery and rifle range, shops, cafes, a 350-room hotel, swimming pool, aquarium, camping ground, picnic area, a fountain (with 200-metre waterjet), fishing pier (on the Ming Tombs Reservoir) and a bicycle racing velodrome. There are also helicopter rides over the tombs and the nearby Great Wall. Plans call for the construction of additional facilities, including a horseracing track, cross-country skiing area and Mongolian yurts for use as a summer hotel.

Western Qing Tombs (*qīng xī líng*) These tombs are in Yixian County, 110 km southwest of Beijing. If you didn't see enough of Dingling, Yuling, Yongling and Deling, well, there's always Tailing, Changling, Chongling and Muling – the latter four being part of Xiling.

The tomb area is vast and houses the corpses of the emperors, empresses and other members and hangers-on of the royal family. The tomb of Emperor Guangxu (Chongling) has been excavated – his was the last imperial tomb and was constructed between 1905 and 1915.

Eastern Qing Tombs (*qīng dōng líng*) The Eastern Qing Tombs area is Death Valley – five emperors, 14 empresses and 136 imperial consorts. In the mountains ringing the valley are buried princes, dukes, imperial nurses, and so on.

The approach to the tomb area is a common 'spirit way', similar to that of the Ming Tombs but with the addition of marble-arch bridges. The materials for the tombs come from all over China, including 20-tonne logs pulled over iced roads, and giant stone slabs.

Two of the tombs are open. Emperor Qianlong (1711-99) started preparations when he was 30, and by the time he was 88 had used up 90 tonnes of silver. His resting place covers half a sq km. Some of the beamless stone chambers are decorated with Tibetan and Sanskrit sutras; the doors bear bas-relief bodhisattvas.

Empress Dowager Cixi also got a head start. Her tomb, Dingdong, was completed some three decades before her death. The phoenix, symbol of the empress, appears above that of the dragon (the emperor's symbol) in the artwork at the front of the tomb – not side by side as on other tombs. Both tombs were plundered in the 1920s.

In Zunhua County (*zūnhuà xiàn*), 125 km east of Beijing, the Eastern Qing Tombs have a lot more to see in them than the Ming Tombs – although you may be a little jaded after the Forbidden City. Of course, the scenery helps make the visit worthwhile.

The only way to get there is by bus and it's a long ride. Tour buses are considerably more comfortable than the local rattle-traps and take three or four hours to get there; you have about three hours on site. It may be possible to make a one-way trip to Zunhua and then take off somewhere else rather than go back to Beijing. A little way north along the road to Chengde is a piece of the Great Wall.

Halfway to Zunhua the tour bus makes a lunch stop at Jixian, more interesting than Zunhua. Jixian is in Tianjin Municipality – see the Tianjin chapter for full details.

Western Hills
(*xī shān*) 西山
Within striking distance of the Summer Palace, and often combined with it on a tour, are the Western Hills, another former villa-resort area. The part of the Western Hills closest to Beijing is known as the Fragrant Hills. This is the last stop for the city buses – if you want to get further into the mountains, you'll have to walk, cycle or take a taxi.

Fragrant Hills Park (*xiāngshān gōngyuán*) You can scramble up the slopes to the top of Incense-Burner Peak, or take the crowded cable car. From the peak you get an all-embracing view of the countryside. The cable car is a good way to get up the moun-

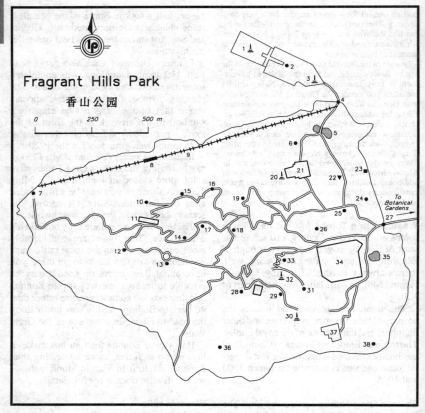

Fragrant Hills Park
香山公园

0   250   500 m

To Botanical Gardens

tain, but it tends to spray you with black grease – an umbrella might be helpful! Starting from the Fragrant Hills, you can hike further into the Western Hills and leave the crowds behind.

The Fragrant Hills area was also razed by foreign troops in 1860 and 1900 but a few bits of original architecture still poke out. A glazed-tile pagoda and the renovated Temple of Brilliance *(zhāo miào)* – a mock-Tibetan temple built in 1780 – are both in the same area. The surrounding heavily wooded park was a hunting ground for the emperors, and once contained a slew of pavilions and

shrines, many of which are now being restored. It's a favourite strolling spot for Beijingers and destined to become another Chinese Disneyland – the cable car is probably a sign of things to come. For those who can afford the ticket, it's possible to stay here at the pricey Xiangshan Hotel.

A bicycle trip to the Fragrant Hills is beautiful but exhausting. There are a couple of ways of getting to the Fragrant Hills by public transport: bus No 333 from the Summer Palace, bus No 360 from the zoo, and bus No 318 from Pingguoyuan (the last stop in the west on the subway).

1	Vajra Throng Pagoda
2	Sun Yatsen Memorial Hall
3	Temple of Azure Clouds
4	North Gate
5	Spectacles Lake
6	Unbosoming Chamber
7	Incense Burner Peak
8	Middle Station
9	Cable Car
10	Stele of Western Hills Shimmering in Snow
11	Platform
12	Sun Facing Cave
13	Jade Sceptre Cliff
14	Moonlight Villa
15	Tiered Cloud Villa
16	Fourth Jade Flower Villa
17	Pavilion of Varied Scenery
18	Jade Flower Villa
19	Hibiscus Hall
20	Glazed Tile Pagoda
21	Temple of Brilliance
22	Pine Forest Restaurant
23	Xiangshan Villa
24	Administrative Office
25	Peak Viewing Pavilion
26	Pavilion of Scattered Clouds
27	East Gate
28	Jade Fragrance Hall
29	White Pine Pavilion
30	Xiangshan Temple Site
31	Halfway Pavilion
32	Temple of Red Glow
33	Eighteen Turns
34	Xiangshan Hotel
35	Jingcui Lake
36	Red Leaf Forest
37	Twin Lakes Villa
38	See Clouds Rise

1	金刚宝座塔
2	孙中山纪念堂
3	碧云寺
4	北门
5	眼镜湖
6	见心斋
7	香炉峰
8	中站
9	缆车
10	西山晴雪览
11	平台
12	朝阳洞
13	玉笏山
14	森玉山庄
15	栖月山庄
16	梯花四院
17	玉景花亭山庄
18	多花山庄
19	玉芙蓉亭馆
20	琉璃塔
21	昭庙
22	松林餐厅
23	香山别墅
24	管理处
25	望云亭
26	多云门亭
27	东门
28	玉香馆
29	白松亭
30	香山寺遗址
31	半山亭
32	洪光寺
33	八盘
34	香山宾馆
35	静翠湖
36	红叶林
37	双清别墅
38	看云起

Azure Clouds Temple (*bìyún sì*) Within walking distance of the North Gate of Fragrant Hills Park is the Azure Clouds Temple, whose landmark is the Diamond Throne Pagoda. Of Indian design, it consists of a raised platform with a central pagoda and stupas around it. The temple was first built in 1366, and was expanded in the 18th century with the addition of the Hall of Arhats, containing 500 statues representing disciples of Buddha. Dr Sun Yatsen's coffin was placed in the temple in 1925 before being moved to Nanjing. In 1954 the govern-

ment renovated Sun's memorial hall, which has a picture display of his revolutionary activities.

Temple of the Sleeping Buddha (*wòfó sì*) About halfway between the Fragrant Hills and the Summer Palace is the Temple of the Sleeping Buddha. During the Cultural Revolution the buddhas in one of the halls were replaced by a statue of Mao (since removed). The draw card is the huge reclining buddha, five metres long, cast in copper. The history books place it in the year 1331 but it's most likely a copy. Its weight is unknown but could be up to 50 tonnes. Pilgrims used to make offerings of shoes to the barefoot statue.

Xiangshan Botanical Gardens (*xiāngshān zhíwù yuán*) About two km east of Fragrant Hills Park and just to the south of the Temple of the Sleeping Buddha is the recently opened Botanical Gardens. At present, the gardens are under development and it's hard to say whether it's worth your trouble to visit. Seeing that this is Beijing and the government is determined to make it a showcase, the gardens could eventually be spectacular.

Badachu
(*bādàchù*) 八大处
Directly south of the Fragrant Hills is Badachu, the Eight Great Sites, also known as Eight Great Temples (*bādà sì*). It has eight monasteries or temples scattered in wooded valleys. The Second Site has the Buddha's Tooth Relic Pagoda, built to house the sacred fang and accidentally discovered when the Allied army demolished the place in 1900.

Take bus No 347, which runs there from the zoo (it crosses the No 318 route). Alternatively, you could take the east-west subway line to the last stop at Pingguoyuan and catch a taxi from there.

Tanzhe Temple
(*tánzhè sì*) 潭柘寺
About 45 km directly west of Beijing is Tanzhe Temple, the largest of all the Beijing temples, occupying an area 260 metres by 160 metres. The Buddhist complex has a long history dating back as early as the 3rd century (Jin Dynasty); structural modifications date from the Liao, Tang, Ming and Qing dynasties. It therefore has a number of features – dragon decorations, mythical animal sculptures and grimacing gods – no longer found in temples in the capital.

Translated literally, 'Tanzhe' means 'Pool Cudrania' – the temple takes its name from its proximity to the Dragon Pool (*lóng tán*)

and some rare Cudrania (*zhè*) trees. Locals come to the Dragon Pool to pray for rain during droughts. The Cudrania trees nourish silkworms and provide a yellow dye. The bark of the tree is believed to cure women of sterility, which may explain why there are so few of these trees left at the temple entrance.

The temple complex is open to the public daily from 8.30 am until 6 pm.

Getting There & Away To get there take bus No 336 from Zhanlanguan Lu, which runs off Fuchengmenwai Dajie north-west of Yuetan Park. Take this bus to the terminal at Mentougou and then hitch. A direct route is bus No 307 from Qianmen to the Hetan terminal and then a numberless bus to the temple. Alternatively, take the subway to Pingguoyuan, bus No 336 to Hetan and the numberless bus to the temple.

Jietai Temple
(*jiètái sì*) 戒台寺
About 10 km south-east of the Tanzhe Temple is a similar but smaller compound, Jietai Temple. The name roughly translates to mean Temple of Ordination Terrace. The temple was built during the Tang Dynasty, around 622 AD, with major improvements made by later tenants during the Ming Dynasty. The main complex is dotted with ancient pines, all of which have quaint names – Nine Dragon Pine is claimed to be over 1300 years old.

It's roughly 35 km from Jietai Temple to Beijing, and a journey out here is usually combined with a visit to Tanzhe Temple.

Marco Polo Bridge
(*lúgōuqiáo*) 卢沟桥
Publicised by the great traveller himself, the Reed Moat Bridge is made of grey marble, is 260 metres long, and has over 250 marble balustrades supporting 485 carved stone lions. First built in 1192, the original arches were washed away in the 17th century. The bridge is a composite of different eras, widened in 1969 – it spans the Yongding River near the little town of Wanping.

Long before CITS, Emperor Qianlong

also did his bit to mote the bridge. In 1751 he put his calligraphy to use and wrote some poetic tracks about Beijing's scenic wonders. His 'Morning Moon Over Lugou Bridge' is now engraved into stone tablets and placed on steles next to the bridge. On the opposite bank is a monument to Qianlong's inspection of the Yongding River.

Despite the publicity campaign by Polo and Qianlong, the bridge wouldn't have rated more than a footnote in Chinese history were it not for the famed 'Marco Polo Bridge Incident' which ignited a full-scale war with Japan. On the night of 7 July, 1937, Japanese troops illegally occupied a railway junction outside Wanping – Japanese and Chinese soldiers started shooting at each other, and that gave Japan enough of an excuse to attack and occupy Beijing. The Chinese were more than a little displeased, especially since Japan had already occupied Manchuria and Taiwan. The Marco Polo Bridge Incident is considered by many as the date of China's entry into WW II.

A relatively recent addition to this ancient site is the 'Memorial Hall of the War of Resistance Against Japan', built in 1987. Also on the site is the Wanping Castle, the Daiwang Temple and a tourist hotel.

You can get to the bridge by taking bus No 109 to Guang'anmen and then catching bus No 339. By bicycle it's about a 16-km trip (one way).

Peking Man Site
(zhōukǒudiàn) 周口店
Site of the primeval Peking Man, Zhoukoudian Village is 48 km south-west of Beijing. There's an 'Apeman Cave' here on a hill above the village, several lesser caves and some dig sites. There is also a fossil exhibition hall – you'd have to be a fossil to stay here for more than 15 minutes. There are three sections to the exhibition hall – prehuman history, the life and times of Peking Man, and a section dealing with recent anthropological research. There are ceramic models, stone tools and the skeletons of prehistoric creatures.

The exhibition hall (☎ 9310278) is open daily from 9 am to 4 pm, but check before you go. You could get a suburban train from Yongdingmen station and get off at Zhoukoudian. Another possibility is a bus from the Haihutun bus station (on the corner of Nansanhuan Zhonglu and Nanyuan Lu). If combined with a trip to Tanzhe Temple and Marco Polo Bridge, approaching by taxi is not unreasonable. Pricey CITS or CTS tours to the site are available according to demand.

There is a guesthouse on the site, though it seems to be intended more for locals than foreign tourists.

There is an interesting story attached to the Peking Man skull. Early this century, villagers around Zhoukoudian found fossils in a local quarry and took them to the local medicine shop for sale as 'dragon bones'. This got back to Beijing, and archaeologists – foreign and Chinese – poured in for a dig. Many years later, a molar was extracted from the earth, and the hunt for a skull was on. They found him in the late afternoon on a day in December 1929, *Sinanthropus Pekinensis* – a complete skull-cap. The cap was believed to be over half a million years old – if so then it rates as one of the missing links in the evolutionary chain. Research on the skull was never carried out. When the Japanese invaded in 1937 the skull-cap was packed away with other dig results and the whole lot vanished. The Chinese accused the Americans, the Americans accused the Japanese, and the mystery remains. Other fragments surfaced from the site after 1949, but no comparable treasure was found.

Kangxi Grasslands
(kǎngxī cǎoyuán) 慷西草原
The grasslands are actually in a beautiful hilly region 80 km north-west of the city. This is considered the best place in Beijing municipality for horseback riding. It is possible to spend the night there in a Mongolian yurt.

Miyun Reservoir
(mìyún shuǐkù) 密云水库
Some 90 km north-east of Beijing is Miyun Reservoir, the city's water supply and largest lake in Beijing Municipality. Since this is drinking water, swimming is prohibited, but the lake is impressive for its scenery.

Chinese entrepreneurs know a good thing when they see it, and Miyun Reservoir has now acquired a number of commercial recreation sites. Most important is the Miyun International Amusement Park (*mìyún guójì yóulè cháng*), not on the lake itself but 20 km to the south-east in the town of Miyun. Facilities include a merry-go-round, monorail, automobile race track and souvenir shops.

If the carnival atmosphere gets to be too much, there are less touristy scenic sites around the reservoir. On the east side of the lake is White Dragon Pool (*bái lóng tán*). While also being developed for tourism, it retains much of its former charm. During the Qing Dynasty, emperors on their way to Chengde would drop in for a visit, so the area is dotted with temples and pavilions which recently have been renovated.

Right in front of the dam is In Front of the Dam Park (*bàqián gōngyuán*), though this is mainly just a place for tourists to get their pictures taken. On the shores of the reservoir itself is a Holiday Resort Village (*dùjià cūn*). North-west of Miyun Reservoir are less-visited scenic spots, including Black Dragon Pool (*hēi lóng tán*), Beijing First Waterfall (*jīngdū dìyī pùbù*), Tianxian Waterfall (*tiān-xiān pùbù*) and Cloud Peak (*yúnfēng shān*).

Trains running to Chengde stop at Miyun. Buses to Miyun depart from the car park of the Workers' Stadium on Gongren Tiyuguan Beilu near the Dongsishitiao subway station.

Haizi Reservoir
(*hǎizi shuǐkù*) 海子水库

At the far eastern end of the Beijing Municipality is Haizi Reservoir, a relatively recent artificial creation hardly ever visited by tourists. Not that there is all that much to see here. The reservoir is distinguished by the fact that it was the site of the aquatic sports (water-skiing, etc) during the 1990 Asian Games.

Due to the games (which were poorly attended), the area has decent recreation facilities, though it's hard to say whether everything will be kept in good nick or be allowed to become dilapidated. At present, modern amenities include the Jinhai Hotel (*jīnhǎi bīnguǎn*) and Jinhai Restaurant (*jīnhǎi cāntīng*). There is a pier (*yóuchuán*

mǎtóu) where you can sometimes catch a cruise across the lake to the aquatic sports area (*shuǐshàng yùndòng cháng*). The shore of the reservoir is dotted with a few recently constructed pavilions. Nearby is Jinghaihu (Golden Sea Lake) Park.

Not being next to any railway line, getting here requires a substantial detour for most travellers. It would be conceivable for tour groups heading out to the Eastern Qing Tombs to stop at Haizi Reservoir along the way.

Shidu
(*shídù*) 十渡

This is Beijing's answer to Guilin. The pinnacle-shaped rock formations, small rivers and general beauty of the place make it a favourite spot with expatriates like foreign students, diplomats and businesspeople.

Shidu means 'ten ferries' or 'ten crossings'. Shidu is 110 km south-west of central Beijing. At least before the new road and bridges were built, it was necessary to cross the Juma River 10 times while travelling along the gorge between Zhangfang and Shidu village.

Places to Stay The Longshan Hotel (*lóngshān fàndiàn*) is opposite the railway station and is the relatively upmarket place to stay in Shidu itself (but that will change soon!). Another place in Shidu is simply called the Shidu Lüguan but doesn't take foreigners – at least not until the renovation is complete.

Down near Jiudu (the 'ninth ferry') there is a camping ground, conveniently located on a flood-plain.

There is a cheap hotel in Liudu (*liùdù lüguǎn*) which will probably not take foreigners until it becomes renovated and pricey.

Getting There & Away This is one of the few scenic areas outside Beijing which can be easily reached by train. Departures are from the south railway station (Yongdingmen) near the Qiaoyuan Hotel – not to be confused with Beijing's main station. If you take the morning train, the trip can be done in one day. The schedule is as follows:

Route	Train No	Depart	Arrive
Yongdingmen-Shidu	595	6.07 am	8.40 am
Yongdingmen-Shidu	597	5.40 pm	8 pm
Shidu-Yongdingmen	596	6.41 pm	9.03 pm
Shidu-Yongdingmen	598	10.41 am	1.05 pm

Yunshui Caves

(yúnshuǐ dòng) 云水洞

The caves are in the Shangfang mountains, not far north of the highway between the Peking Man Site and Shidu. Don't expect to be the first human to explore these depths – there are coloured lights, souvenir shops and snack bars. About one km to the east of the cave entrance is the Doulü Temple, a large monastery complex in the foothills.

Longqing Gorge

(lóngqìngxiá) 龙庆峡

About 90 km north-west of Beijing is Longqing Gorge, a canyon in Yanqing County. The gorge was probably more scenic before the dam and consequent reservoir flooded out the area. Row-boating and hiking are the big attractions during summer. From mid-December to the end of January this is the site of Beijing's Ice Lantern Festival *(bīngdōng jié)*. Similar to the more well-known and longer-lasting festival at Harbin, the 'lanterns' are huge ice carvings into which coloured electric lights are inserted. The effect (at least during the night) is stunning. Children (including adult children) can amuse themselves on the ice slide.

This being a night-time event, there are tactical problems with getting there and staying there during the Ice Lantern Festival. The ride takes two hours each way – chartering a taxi is expensive but the cost can be divided amongst a group of travellers. Most visitors go and return the same day – the one hotel in Longqing Gorge packs out during festival time, though this situation might improve with time if new places are built.

Tianjin 天津

Population: eight million

Like Beijing and Shanghai, Tianjin *(tiānjīn)* belongs to no province – it's a special municipality, which gives it a degree of autonomy, but it's also closely administered by the central government. The city is nicknamed 'Shanghai of the North' – a reference to its history as a foreign concession, its heavy industrial output, its large port and its Europeanised architecture. Foreigners who live there now often call it 'TJ' – an abbreviation which mystifies the Chinese.

History

The city's fortunes are, and always have been, linked to those of Beijing. When the Mongols established Beijing as the capital in the 13th century, Tianjin first rose to prominence as a grain-storage point. Pending remodelling of the Grand Canal by Kublai Khan, the tax grain was shipped along the Yangzi River, out into the open sea, up to Tianjin, and then through to Beijing. With the Grand Canal fully functional as far as Beijing, Tianjin was at the intersection of both inland and port navigation routes. By the 15th century, the town was a walled garrison. In the 17th century Dutch envoys described the city thus:

The town has many temples; it is thickly populated and trade is very brisk – it would be hard to find another town as busy as this in China – because all the boats which go to Beijing, whatever their port of origin, call here, and traffic is astonishingly heavy.

For the sea-dog Western nations, Tianjin was a trading bottleneck too good to be passed up. In 1856 Chinese soldiers boarded the *Arrow*, a boat flying the British flag, ostensibly in search of pirates. This was as much of an excuse as the British and the French needed. Their gunboats attacked the forts outside Tianjin, forcing the Chinese to sign the Treaty of Tianjin (1858), which opened the port up to foreign trade and also legalised the sale of opium. Chinese reluctance to take part in a treaty they had been forced into led the British and French to start a new campaign to open the port to Western trade. In 1860 British troops bombarded Tianjin in an attempt to coerce the Chinese into signing another treaty.

The English and French settled in. Between 1895 and 1900 they were joined by the Japanese, Germans, Austro-Hungarians, Italians and Belgians. Each of the concessions was a self-contained world with its own prison, school, barracks and hospital. Because they were so close together, it was possible to traverse the national styles of architecture in the course of a few hours, from Via Vittorio Emanuele to Cambridge Road. One could cross from the flat roofs and white housing of the Italian concession, pass the Corinthian columns of the banks along the Rue de France, proceed down to the manicured lawns of Victorian mansions, and while away the wee hours of the morning dancing at the German Club (now a library).

This palatial life was disrupted only in 1870 when the locals attacked the French-run orphanage and killed, among others, 10 of the nuns – apparently the Chinese thought the children were being kidnapped. Thirty years later, during the Boxer Rebellion, the foreign powers levelled the walls of the old Chinese city.

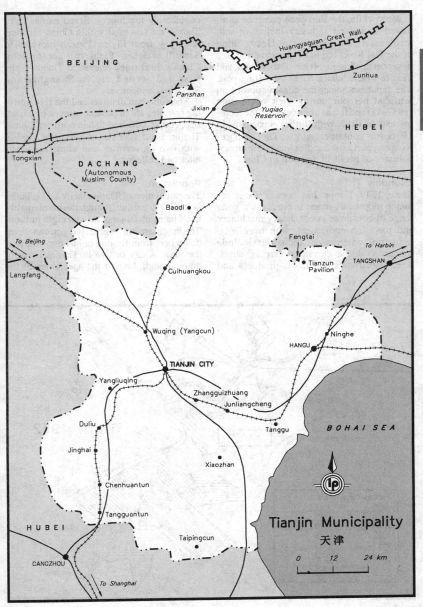

Tianjin Municipality
天津

Meanwhile, the European presence stimulated trade and industry including salt, textiles and glass manufacture. Heavy silting of the Hai River led to the construction of a new port at Tanggu, 50 km downstream, and Tianjin lost its character as a bustling port. The Japanese began the construction of an artificial harbour during their occupation (1937-45) and it was completed by the Communists in 1952, with further expansions in 1976 for container cargo. The Tanggu-Xingang port now handles one of the largest volumes of goods of any port in China.

Economy

Since 1949 Tianjin has been a focus for major industrialisation. It produces a wide range of consumer goods, heavy machinery and precision equipment, with over 3000 industrial enterprises. Industries include rubber products, elevators, carpets, autos, steel, electronics, chemical products and engineering machinery. Brand names from Tianjin are favoured within China for their quality – from Flying Pigeon bicycles to Seagull watches. Plans call for opening China's third stock market in Tianjin – the first and second are in Shanghai and Shenzhen respectively.

The suburban districts and the five outlying counties are important sources of wheat, rice, cotton, corn and fish in northern China. Tianjin itself is a major education centre, with two universities and numerous institutes and colleges.

Population

The population of Tianjin's city and suburbs is some 5½ million, though the municipality itself takes in a total of around eight million. The hotels are impossible, but you can travel down here from Beijing in just two hours on the train. A day or two in Tianjin is really quite enough. One of the specialties of the

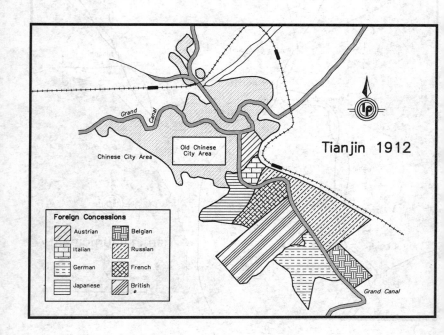

Tianjin 1912

Grand Canal

Chinese City Area

Old Chinese City Area

Grand Canal

Foreign Concessions

Austrian
Italian
German
Japanese
Belgian
Russian
French
British

place is the two-day kite-flying festival held in early April or late September.

Information

The CITS office (☎ 314831) is at 22 Youyi Lu, just opposite the Friendship Store. The PSB (☎ 223613) is at 30 Tangshan Dao, and the Bank of China (☎ 312020) is at 80 Jiefang Beilu. You'll find the international post office, known as the Dongzhan post office, next to the main railway station; overseas parcels can be mailed and long-distance phone calls can be made here. For letters, there is another post office conveniently located on Jiefang Beilu, a short walk north of the Astor Hotel. The Foreign Languages Bookstore (☎ 318187) *(wàiwén shūdiàn)* at 182 Machang Dao is worth a look to stock up on English-language novels for those long train rides.

Antique Market
(gǔwán shìcháng) 古玩市场
Depending on your tastes, the antique market is the best sight in Tianjin even if you're not into collecting second-hand memorabilia. Just the sheer size and variety of this market makes it fascinating to stroll around. Amongst the many items on sale are stamps, silver coins, silverware, porcelain, clocks, photos of Mao, Cultural Revolution exotica (no guns though) and old books.

In China, the one thing you can be certain of is that you can't be certain of anything, especially history, since it is subject to frequent revision according to the politics of the time. Nevertheless, if true, the history behind this market is fascinating. According to the locals, much of what is on display at the antique market was seized during the Cultural Revolution and warehoused – the government is now slowly selling the stuff off to vendors who in turn resell it in Tianjin. These goods supposedly come from all over China. Many of the items carry stickers on the back indicating when, where and from whom the goods were seized.

Just why everything wasn't all immediately destroyed is subject to speculation – possibly it was to be used as evidence at political trials, or maybe some official was a closet antique buff. Or just maybe the Red Guards were aware of the potential resale value. Of course, not all that you see is real – there are indeed fake antiques, fake stickers and so on.

The market is active seven days a week. On weekdays it occupies only a section of central Shenyang Dadao, but on weekends it expands enormously, spilling out into side streets in every direction. It's open from 7.30 am to around 3 pm – get there at 8 am for the widest selection. Sunday morning is best and foreigners residing in Beijing come down here for the day just to shop.

Ancient Culture Street
(gǔ wénhuà jiē) 古文化街
The Ancient Culture Street is an attempt to recreate the appearance of an ancient Chinese city. Besides the traditional buildings, the street is lined with vendors plugging every imaginable type of cultural goody from Chinese scrolls, paintings and chops to the latest heavy-metal sounds on CD. During certain public holidays, street operas are staged here.

Within the confines of the street is the small Tianhou Temple *(tiānhòu gōng)*. Tianhou (Heaven Queen) is the goddess of the sea, and is known by various names in different parts of China (Matsu in Taiwan, Tin Hau in Hong Kong). It is claimed that Tianjin's Tianhou Temple was built in 1326, but has seen a bit of renovation since then.

The Ancient Culture Street is a major drawcard for tourists, both foreigners and locals. The street is in the north-western part of town.

Confucius Temple
(wén miào) 文庙
On the north side of Dongmennei Dajie, one block west of the Ancient Culture St, is Tianjin's Confucius Temple. It was built in 1463 during the Ming Dynasty. The temple, and Confucianists in general, took a beating during the Cultural Revolution. In 1993 the buildings were restored and opened to the public.

TIANJIN

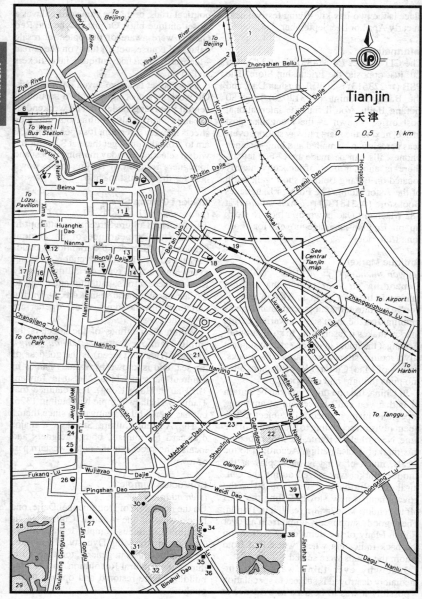

Tianjin
天津

0   0.5   1 km

1 To Beijing
To Beijing
Zhongshan Beilu
Xinkai River
Beiyun River
Ziya River
Jinzhongie Dajie
Kunwei Lu
Zhongshan Lu
3
2
6 To West Bus Station
Nanyunhe Nanlu
5
4
7
Beima
8 Lu
9
Shizilin Dajie
Zhenli Dao
Hongxing Dao
To Lüzu Pavilion
Xima Lu
Huanghe Dao
Nanma Lu
10
11
Xinkai Lu
12
Rongji Dajie
13
18
19
See Central Tianjin map
Nankaima
Nanmenwai Dajie
15
14
Befan Dao
16
17
To Airport
Zhangguizhuang Lu
Liuwei Lu
Changjiang
To Changhong Park
Nanjing Lu
21
Nanjing Lu
20 Shiyijing Lu
To Harbin
Weijin River
Weijin Lu
Xinxing Lu
Chengdu Lu
23
Jieten Nanlu
Dagu Nanlu
Hai River
To Tanggu
24
25
Machang Dao
Shaoxing Lu
22
Guangdong Lu
Qiangzi River
26
Wujiayao Dajie
Fukang Lu
Pingshan Dao
Weidi Dao
39
Dongxing Lu
30
Jinz Gonglu
27
34
Youyi Lu
38
Jianshan Lu
Shuishang Gongyuan
28
31
33
35
37
Dagu Nanlu
29
32
Binshui Dao
36

TIANJIN

■ PLACES TO STAY

20	Furama Hotel
21	Friendship Hotel
31	Sheraton Hotel
33	Crystal Palace Hotel
35	Tianjin Grand Hotel
36	Geneva Hotel
38	Park Hotel

▼ PLACES TO EAT

8	Eardrum Fried Spongecake Shop
13	Yanchunlou Restaurant
14	Quanjude Restaurant
15	Food Street
39	18th Street Dough Twists Shop

OTHER

1	Beining Park
2	North Railway Station
3	Xigu Park
4	Zhongshan Park
5	Dabeiyuan Monastery
6	West Railway Station
7	Grand Mosque
9	North East Bus Station
10	Ancient Culture Street
11	Confucius Temple
12	5th Subway Exit
16	Zhou Enlai Memorial Hall
17	Nankai Park
18	Buses to Beijing
19	Main Railway Station
22	Renmin Park
23	Foreign Languages Bookstore
24	Tianjin University
25	Nankai University
26	South Bus Station
27	TV Tower
28	Shuishang Park
29	Zoo
30	Natural History Museum & Cadre Club
32	Cadre Club Park
34	Friendship Store
37	Children's Park

■ PLACES TO STAY

20	富丽华大酒店
21	友谊宾馆
31	喜来登大酒店
33	水晶宫饭店
35	天津宾馆
36	津利华大酒店
38	乐园饭店

▼ PLACES TO EAT

8	耳朵眼炸糕店
13	燕春楼饭庄
14	全聚德烤鸭店
15	食品街
39	桂发祥麻花店

OTHER

1	北宁公园
2	北火车站
3	西沽公园
4	中山公园
5	大悲院
6	西火车站
7	清真寺
9	东北角发车站
10	古文化街
11	文庙
12	地下铁第五站
16	周恩来记念馆
17	南开公园
18	往北京汽车站
19	天津火车站
22	人民公园
23	外文书店
24	天津大学
25	南开大学
26	八里台发车站
27	电视台
28	水上公园
29	动物园
30	自然博物馆 / 干部俱乐部
32	干部俱乐部公园
34	友谊商店
37	青年儿童活动中心

Grand Mosque

(qīngzhēn sì) 清真寺

Although it has a distinctly Chinese look, this large mosque is an active place of worship for Tianjin's Muslims. The mosque is on Dafeng Lu, not far south of the west railway station.

Dabeiyuan Monastery

(dàbēiyuàn) 大悲院

This is one of the largest and best-preserved temples in the city. Dabeiyuan was built between 1611 and 1644, expanded in 1940, battered during the Cultural Revolution and finally restored in 1980. The temple is on Tianwei Lu in the northern part of the city.

Catholic Church

(xīkāi jiāotáng) 西开教堂

This is one of the most bizarre-looking churches you're likely to see. Situated on the southern end of Binjiang Dao, the twin onion domes form a dramatic backdrop to the 'Coca-Cola Bridge' (a pedestrian overpass crossing Nanjing Lu). It's definitely worth a look. Church services are now permitted again on Sundays, which is about the only time you'll have a chance to look inside.

Earthquake Memorial

(kàngzhèn jìniàn bēi) 抗震纪念碑

Just opposite the Friendship Hotel on Nanjing Lu is a curious, pyramid-shaped memorial. Though there's not much to see here, the memorial is a pointed reminder of the horrific events of 28 July 1976, when an earthquake registering eight on the Richter scale struck north-east China.

It was the greatest natural disaster of the decade. Tianjin was severely affected and the city was closed to tourists for two years. The epicentre was at Tangshan – that city basically disappeared in a few minutes. Five and six-storey housing blocks have been constructed on the outskirts of Tianjin as part of the rehousing programme.

Hai River Park

(hǎihé gōngyuán) 海河公园

Stroll along the banks of the Hai River (a popular pastime with the locals) and see photo booths, fishing, early-morning taijiquan, opera-singing practice and old men toting birdcages. The Hai River esplanades have a peculiarly Parisian feel, in part due to the fact that some of the railing and bridge work is French.

Tianjin's sewage has to go somewhere and the river water isn't so pure that you'd want to drink it, but an attempt has been made to clean it up and plant trees along the embankments. Tianjin's industrial pollution horrors are further downstream and are not included in the tour, but Chinese tourists make their contribution by throwing drink tins and plastic bags into the river.

It's not Venice, but there are tourist boat cruises on the Hai River which commence from a dock not far from the Astor Hotel. The boats cater to Chinese tourists more than foreigners and therefore tend to run mainly during summer weekends and other holiday times.

At the north end of town are half a dozen canals that branch off the Hai River. One vantage point is Xigu Park. Take bus No 5, which runs from near the main railway station and passes by the west station.

TV Tower

(diànshì tái) 电视台

The pride and joy of Tianjin residents, the TV tower dominates the horizon on the south side of town. Besides its functional purpose of transmitting TV and radio broadcasts to the masses, tourists can go upstairs for a whopping Y80 fee. While the tower looks impressive from the ground, views from the top aren't spectacular in the daytime – after all, Tianjin's flat landscape of old buildings isn't exactly the eighth wonder of the world. However, the view is better at night if the sky is clear.

The TV tower is also topped by a revolving restaurant, but you're liable to get indigestion when you see the bill.

Shuishang Park

(shuǐshàng gōngyuán) 水上公园

This large park is in the south-western corner of town, not far from the TV tower. The name in Chinese means 'water park' –

over half the surface area is a lake. The major activity here is renting rowboats and pedal boats.

It's one of the more relaxed places in busy Tianjin, though not on weekends, when the locals descend on the place like cadres at a banquet. The park features a Japanese-style floating garden and a decent zoo.

Getting to the park from the railway station requires two buses. Bus No 8 to the last stop gets you close. From there, catch bus No 54, also to the last stop, just outside the park entrance.

Art Museum
(yìshù bówùguǎn) 艺术博物馆
This museum is easy to get to and is pleasant to stroll around. The gallery is housed in an imposing rococo mansion and has a small but choice collection of brush paintings, painting and calligraphy from bygone eras on the ground floor, and folk-art products such as New Year pictures, Zhang family clay figurines and Wei family kites from the Tianjin area on the 2nd floor. The top floor features special displays.

The Art Museum is at 77 Jiefang Beilu, one stop on bus No 13 from the main railway station.

Other Museums
There are five or so other museums in Tianjin and none are really worth the trouble unless you're an enthusiast. The Natural History Museum *(zìrán bówùguǎn)* is down the fossil-end of town at 206 Machang Dao.

The History Museum *(lìshǐ bówùguǎn)* over on the south-eastern side of the Hai River, at the edge of a triangular park called the No 2 Workers' Cultural Palace *(dì èr gōngrén wénhuà gōng)*, contains 'historical and revolutionary relics of the Tianjin area'.

Guangdong Guild Hall *(guǎngdōng huì guǎn)*, also known as the Museum of Opera, is considered of historical importance because Sun Yatsen gave an important speech there in 1922.

Zhou Enlai Memorial Hall
(zhōu ēnlái jìniàn guǎn)
周恩来纪念馆
Zhou Enlai grew up in Shaoxing in Zhejiang Province, but he attended school in Tianjin, so his classroom is enshrined and there are photos and other memorabilia from his youth (1913-17). The memorial is on the western side of the city in the Nankai District, in the eastern building of Nankai School.

Streetscapes
Far more engrossing than any of the preceding is the fact that Tianjin itself is a museum of European architecture from the turn of the century. One minute you're in little Vienna, turn a corner and you could be in a London street, hop off a bus and you're looking at some vintage French wrought-iron gates or a neo-Gothic cathedral.

If you're an architecture student, go no further – Tianjin is a textbook of just about every style imaginable, a draughtsperson's nightmare or a historian's delight, depending on which way you look at it. Poking out of the post-earthquake shanty rubble could be a high-rise castle of glass and steel; and anyone with a sense of humour will be well satisfied with some of the uses to which the bastions of the European well-to-do have been put.

Tianjin traffic is equally mixed: horse carts, cyclists with heavy loads struggling to make it across an intersection before an ambush from a changing light cuts them off, a parent with a kid in a bicycle sidecar. Judiciously selected buses will take you through as many former concessions as you want – and, presuming you have a window seat, this kind of random touring will be quite rewarding, architecturally speaking.

Chinatown
We couldn't resist this misnomer. The old Chinese sector can easily be identified on the bus map as a rectangle with buses running around the perimeter. Roughly, the boundary roads are: Beima (North Horse), Nanma (South Horse), Xima (West Horse) and Dongma (East Horse). Originally there was

TIANJIN

one main north-south street, crossing an east-west one within that (walled) rectangle.

Within this area you can spend time fruitfully exploring the lanes and side streets where traditional architecture remains, and perhaps even find a dilapidated temple or two. Basically, though, this is a people-watching place, where you can get glimpses of daily life through doorways. All along the way are opportunities to shop, window shop and eat to your heart's content.

Places to Stay

If there is any city in China that will make you feel like a 'foreign devil', Tianjin is it. There are heaps of decent hotels of high standard which have been placed off limits to foreigners, examples being the *Chang Cheng Binguan*, *Tianjin Dajiudian* and the *Baihui Fandian*. However, these places *do* accept Overseas Chinese.

For the big noses, prices border on the ridiculous. So unless you've got an Asian face, heaps of money, or ingratiate yourself into one of the university residences (or a church or bathhouse?), you may end up back at the station. A smart move is to dump your luggage at the station (there's a 24-hour left luggage office) so if worse comes to worst, you can stay up late somewhere without having to cart your gear around. Ideally, make Tianjin a day trip from Beijing.

The only mid-range place accepting foreigners is the *Tianjin Grand Hotel* (☎ 359000; fax 359822) *(tiānjīn bīnguǎn)* on Youyi Lu, Hexi District. And grand it is: 1000 beds in two high-rise blocks built in 1960, but now showing signs of age. No doubt the day of renovation (and higher prices) will come, but at present doubles cost Y120, Y150 and Y240. Take bus No 13 from the main railway station. But be forewarned: because of the 'cheap' prices, it's often full, with many of the rooms permanently occupied by foreigners and locals setting up 'temporary' offices.

Also on the cheaper end by Tianjin standards is the *Park Hotel* (☎ 809818; fax 802042) *(lèyuán fàndiàn)*, 1 Leyuan Lu, east of the Friendship Store and, as the name implies, near a park. Doubles cost Y253,

Y297 and Y417. Rooms are very comfortable and the in-house Golden Lotus Restaurant is topnotch.

The *Tianjin No 1 Hotel (tiānjīn dìyī fàndiàn)* (☎ 310707; fax 313341) is at 158 Jiefang Beilu. It's got a bit of old world charm, which perhaps will make you feel better about having to fork out Y380 for a double. Some travellers have managed to negotiate the tab down to Y190 after exhaustive bargaining and poverty-pleading sessions. The No 1 is an old colonial building diagonally opposite the Hyatt Hotel. The spacious rooms have their own bathrooms, and the staff are fairly amiable. Take bus No 13 three stops from the main railway station and walk south.

The *Friendship Hotel* (☎ 310372) *(yǒuyí bīnguǎn)* charges rather unfriendly prices – doubles are Y402 and Y460. It's a renovated nine-storey Holiday Inn-type place often stocked with foreign business people. The hotel is at 94 Nanjing Lu.

One of the most glamorous places in town is the 346-room *Crystal Palace Hotel* (☎ 310567; fax 310591) *(shuǐjīnggōng fàndiàn)* on Youyi Lu. Doubles start at Y575. Facilities include a swimming pool, tennis court, health club and French restaurant.

Also in the neighbourhood is the *Geneva Hotel* (☎ 342222; fax 349854) *(jīnlìhuá dàjiǔdiàn)*, 30 Youyi Lu, where doubles cost Y383. The hotel is in the rear – the front side of the building is the World Economy & Trade Exhibition Centre, one of the most perverse architectural nightmares in China. Some foreign residents living in Tianjin have suggested that the architect should be tried as a war criminal.

Also somewhat peculiar-looking is the *Hyatt Hotel* (☎ 318888; fax 310021) *(kǎiyuè fàndiàn)* at 219 Jiefang Beilu overlooking the Hai River. Superior/deluxe rooms cost Y632/690 and suites begin at Y805 – plus 10% service charge.

The *Astor Hotel* (☎ 311112; fax 316282) *(lìshùndé fàndiàn)* at 33 Tai'erzhuang Lu, dates from early this century but has been completely refurbished. Doubles cost from Y440 to Y505. The hotel is near the Hyatt.

On the east bank of the Hai River not far from the Astor is the fancy *Furama Hotel (fùlìhuá dàjiǔdiàn)*. Rooms at this luxury tower start at Y690.

The *Sheraton Hotel* (☎ 343388; fax 358740) *(xǐláidēng dàjiǔdiàn)* is on Zijinshan Lu in the south of Tianjin. The hotel offers a special price of Y545 (plus 15% service charge), which includes accommodation, buffet breakfast and free laundry service, and there's no charge for the airport shuttle (international flights only). Oh yes – and a free copy of the *China Daily*.

Places to Eat

There are some wonderful digestibles in Tianjin. If you're staying longer, you can get a small group together, phone ahead and negotiate gourmet delights. 'Tianjin flavour' specialties are mostly in the seasonal seafood line and include crab, prawns, cuttlefish soup and fried carp.

The place to go is *Food Street (shípǐn jiē)*, a covered alley with two levels of restaurants. Old places close and new ones open all the time here, but there are approximately 40 to 50 restaurants on each level. You need to check prices – some of the food stalls are dirt cheap but a few upmarket restaurants are almost absurdly expensive. You can find some real exotica here, like snake (expensive), dogmeat (cheap) and eels (mid-range). Mexican food fans take note: this is the only place in China where we found bags of nacho chips for sale! Food Street is a couple of blocks south of Nanma Lu, about one km west of the centre.

Rongji Dajie is an alley just one block north of Food St and also boasts a fair share of restaurants. The *Quanjude* (☎ 750046) is at 53 Rongji Dajie. Upstairs are banquet rooms with moderate to expensive prices. Seafood is expensive (like sea cucumber, a delicacy that chefs love to foist on foreigners). Beijing duck and Shandong food are also served.

Directly opposite the Quanjude is the *Yanchunlou* (☎ 752761) at 46 Rongji Dajie. It serves Muslim food, lamb dishes and hotpot in winter.

Brownies (bāngní zhàjī) doesn't sell brownies – it's a Canadian-built fast-food restaurant, Tianjin's answer to Kentucky Fried Chicken. It's proven popular with both Chinese and foreigners. It's at the northern end of Binjiang Dao near Quanyechang Department Store.

Just down the street from Brownies is *Franco's Italian Fast Food (yìqílín)*. Specialties here include pizza, spaghetti and real Italian ice cream. This place is doing raging business with the foreign community in Tianjin.

The *Tianjin Roast Duck Restaurant* (☎ 702660) *(tiānjīn kǎoyā diàn)* is at 146 Liaoning Lu in the city centre. You can get Beijing duck here – either the full works or a cheaper basic duck. This place has Mao Zedong's seal of approval (one doesn't really know if that's positive or positively embarrassing advertising these days) and on the restaurant walls are a couple of black & white photos of a relaxed-looking Mao talking to the chefs and autographing the visitors' book.

The *Chuansu Restaurant* (☎ 705142) is at 153 Changchun Dao, between Xinhua Lu and Liaoning Lu, very close to the Tianjin Roast Duck. Spicy hot Sichuan food is the specialty here but other styles are also on the menu.

King of the dumpling shops is *Goubuli* (☎ 700810) *(gǒubùlǐ)* at 77 Shandong Dao, between Changchun Lu and Binjiang Dao. Very crowded, this place serves some of the finest dumplings in the nation – so you might as well dine in style, and it won't cost you an arm or a leg to do so. You can back up the dumplings with tea, soup or beer, and you get upper-crust lacquered chopsticks with which to spear the slippery little devils on your plate. The shop has a century-old history.

The staple of the maison is a dough bun, filled with high-grade pork, spices and gravy, that disintegrates on contact with the palate. Watch for the baozi with the red dot since this indicates a special filling like chicken or shrimp. 'Goubuli' has the alarming translation of 'dogs won't touch them' or

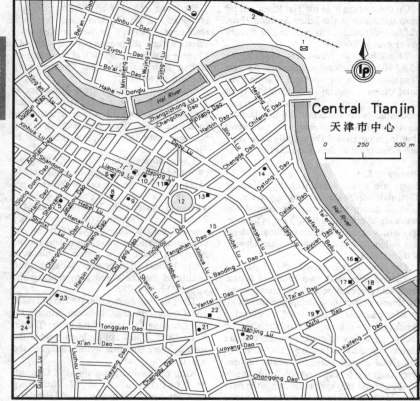

Central Tianjin
天津市中心

0   250   500 m

'dog doesn't care'. The most satisfying explanation of this seems to be that Goubuli was the nickname of the shop's founder, a man with an extraordinarily ugly face – so ugly that even dogs were turned off by him. Former US President George Bush often ate here when he was ambassador to China.

A permanent cake box clipped to a bicycle rack is one of the eccentricities of Tianjin residents – and a prerequisite for a visit to friends. Yangcun rice-flour cake is a pastry produced in Wuqing County suburbs since the Ming Dynasty, so they say. It's made from rice and white sugar.

The *Eardrum Fried Spongecake Shop* *(ěrduǒyǎn zhàgāo diàn)* takes its name from its proximity to Eardrum Lane. This shop specialises in cakes made from rice powder, sugar and bean paste, all fried in sesame oil. These special cakes have been named (you guessed it) 'eardrum fried spongecake'.

Another Tianjin specialty that takes its name from a shop's location is the *18th Street Dough-twists (máhuā)*. The street seems to have been renamed 'Love Your Country St' *(àiguó dào)*, and the famous shop also seems to have a new label *(guìfā xiáng máhuā diàn)*. However, the dough-twists – made

TIANJIN

PLACES TO STAY

11 Guomin Hotel
13 Dongfang Hotel
16 Astor Hotel
17 Tianjin No 1 Hotel
18 Hyatt Hotel
22 Friendship Hotel

▼ PLACES TO EAT

6 Chuansu Restaurant
8 Goubuli Restaurant
19 Kiessling's Bakery

OTHER

1 Dongshan Post Office
2 Main Railway Station
3 Buses to Beijing
4 Tianjin Department Store
5 Antique Market
7 Quanyechang Department Store
9 Binjiang Shangsha Department Store
10 Xinhua Bookstore
12 Zhongxin Park
14 Bank of China
15 PSB
20 International Building
21 Earthquake Memorial
23 International Market
24 Catholic Church

PLACES TO STAY

11 国民大酒店
13 东方饭店
16 利顺德大饭店
17 天津第一饭店
18 凯悦饭店
22 友谊宾馆

▼ PLACES TO EAT

6 川苏菜馆
8 狗不理总店
19 起士林餐厅

OTHER

1 邮政公寓
2 天津火车站
3 往北京汽车站
4 百货大楼
5 古玩市场
7 劝业场
9 滨江商厦
10 新华书店
12 中心公园
14 中国银行
15 公安局外事科
20 国际大厦
21 抗震纪念碑
23 国际商场
24 西开教堂

from sugar, sesame, nuts, vanilla – still taste the same. This is one form of Chinese junk food worth trying.

Kiesslings Bakery (qǐshìlín cāntīng), built by the Austrians back in foreign concession days (1911), is a Tianjin institution. It's at 33 Zhejiang Lu, south-west of the Astor Hotel. From the railway station it's the fourth stop on the No 13 bus route.

Foreign residents of Tianjin with a bit of cash like to pig out every Sunday at the *Sheraton Hotel*, which does a mean buffet from 11 am until 2 pm. It costs Y90 FEC (no student cards accepted), so don't eat breakfast if you want to get the maximum benefit. On other days there are also lunch and dinner buffets with prices ranging from Y30 to Y60 – sometimes they serve pizza!

The *Hyatt Hotel* also does a memorable breakfast buffet. This one costs Y40 and can fill you up for the rest of the day.

Should you wish to fortify a main meal, an ice cream or a coffee, Tianjin produces a variety of liquid substances. There's Kafeijiu, which approximates to Kahlua, and Sekijiu, which is halfway between vodka and aviation fuel.

Shopping Districts

Tianjin's shopping centres are tourist attractions in themselves, particularly if you've been on the road for a while in outback China.

A massive shopping drag extends from the west station south via **Beima Lu**, where it meets another shopping drag coming from the north railway station called **Dongma Lu**. The sprawl of shops snake down the length of **Heping Lu** as far as Zhongxin Park.

If you make your way on foot along Nanma Lu, the southern fringe of 'Chinatown', you'll arrive at the top end of Heping Lu. Going south on Heping, you will find a busy alley, **Rongji Dajie**, leading off to the right – plenty of delectable edibles here, but try to save some space in the lower intestines for Food Street, one block to the south.

The city centre buzzes with activity until late in the evening. It's crammed with theatres, specialty shops, restaurants, large department stores and ice-cream parlours. The street to walk on is **Binjiang Dao**, with alleyways and other shopping streets gathered around it – there's something like eight whole blocks of concentrated shopping. Binjiang Dao also has the most active night market.

You can find just about anything – from silk flowers to a hot bath – in the many boutiques, curio stores and emporiums. The area is particularly lively between 5 and 8 pm, when the streets are thronged with excited shoppers and in-going theatre fans.

A trip to Tianjin will quickly reassure you that China is serious about competing in the textile business. On Binjiang Dao there are over 100 street stalls selling mostly clothing, plus many more permanent-looking stores. The chief department store on this street is the **Binjiang Shangsha** – the only large store in the whole city which seems to have trained the staff to give polite and helpful service.

At the southern end of Binjiang Dao is the four-storey International Market *(guójì shāngchǎng)*. It's one of Tianjin's best department stores and features a fine supermarket. Don't confuse it with the International Building *(guójì dàshà)* at 75 Nanjing Lu. On the 2nd floor is the best supermarket in all of Tianjin – a clone of Hong Kong's finest. The ground floor has the best bakery in the city.

Also worth looking into is the **Friendship Store** *(yǒuyí shāngdiàn)* on Youyi Lu in the southern end of town. The ground floor has

a notable supermarket – rare items on sale here include imported peanut butter and Diet Coke.

Locals look for everyday Chinese consumer products in the **Tianjin Department Store** *(bǎihuò dàlóu)* at 172 Heping Lu. All along Heping Lu you'll find other smaller stores – it's a good general shopping street.

The four traditional arts & crafts in Tianjin are New Year posters, clay figurines, kites and carpets. You can also go hunting for antiques and second-hand goods – Tianjin is less picked-over than Beijing.

The **Quanyechang** (Encouraging Industrial Development Emporium) is an old but large department store and is at the corner of Heping Lu and Binjiang Lu. Besides selling a large variety of consumer goods, the emporium has two theatres and some electronic amusement facilities. The original, smaller Quanyechang has a fascinating balcony interior. If you follow the galleries around they will eventually lead into the main seven-storey block. The older section was founded in 1926.

Things to Buy

Tianjin is considered famous for four types of locally made items: carpets, New Year posters, kites and clay figurines.

Rugs & Carpets If you're serious about carpets (that's serious money!) the best bet is to get to a factory outlet. There are eight carpet factories in the Tianjin Municipality. Making the carpets by hand is a long and tedious process – some of the larger ones can take a proficient weaver over a year to complete. Patterns range from traditional to modern. The No 3 Carpet Factory (☎ 281712) *(tiānjīn dìtǎn sānchǎng)*, 99 Qiongzhou Dao, is in the Hexi District. Small tapestries are a sideline.

Kites Kites are not easily found. Again it's better to go directly to the source, which is the Arts & Crafts Factory (☎ 272855) *(tiānjīn gōngyì měishùchǎng)* at the western end of Huanghe Dao, in the Nankai District. The Wei kites were created by master craftsman Wei Yuan Tai at the beginning of the century, although the kite has been a traditional toy in China for thousands of years.

One story has it that Mr Wei's crow kite was so good that a flock of crows joined it aloft. The body of this line is made of brocade and silk; the skeleton is made of bamboo sticks. Wings can be folded or disassembled, and will pack into boxes (the smaller ones into envelopes). Different kite varieties are made in Beijing, where there is a Kite Arts Company and a Kite Society. One member, Ha Kuiming, made a kite with a diameter of eight metres, which needed two men to hold it back once it got going.

Clay Figurines The terracotta figures originated in the 19th century with the work of Zhang Mingshan: his fifth-generation descendants train new craftspeople. The small figures take themes from human or deity sources and the emphasis is on realistic emotional expressions. Master Zhang was reputedly so skilful that he carried clay up his sleeves on visits to the theatre and came away with clay opera stars in his pockets. In 1900, during the Boxer Rebellion, Western troops came across satirical versions of themselves correct down to the last detail in uniforms. These voodoo dolls were ordered to be removed from the marketplace immediately!

Painted figurines are now much watered down from that particular output; the workshop is at 270 Machang Dao, Hexi District (southern end of Tianjin). The Art Gallery on Jiefang Lu has a collection of earlier Zhang family figurines.

New Year Posters A batch of these is also on display at the art gallery. They first appeared in the 17th century in the town of Yangliuqing, 15 km west of Tianjin proper. Woodblock prints are hand-coloured, and are considered to bring good luck and happiness when posted on the front door during the Lunar New Year – OK if you like pictures of fat babies done in Day-Glo colour schemes. Rarer are the varieties that have historical, deity or folk-tale representations. There's a

salesroom and workshop on Changchun Jie, between Xinhua Lu and Liaoning Lu.

Other There are second-hand stores selling mostly chintz, though some older fur clothing can be found. A few of these stores are in the city centre; also try Dongma Lu. The Yilinge Antique Store at 161 Liaoning Lu has bronzes, ceramics, carvings, paintings and calligraphy, and will engrave seals or arrange artist-commission work. The Wenyuange at 191 Heping Lu is another curio store, mainly dealing in hardwood furniture, and will arrange packing, Customs and delivery.

Getting There & Away

Air CAAC (☎ 704045, 705888) is at 242 Heping Lu. Tianjin has daily flights to Beijing, though it seems crazy to fly – the time spent getting to and from the airport on either end plus airport check-in and security procedures (and CAAC's typical delays) means flying is usually slower than a direct Beijing-Tianjin bus trip.

Domestic flights go from Tianjin to Beijing (Y120), Canton (Y980), Chengdu (Y820), Fuzhou (Y810), Haikou (Y1170), Nanjing (460), Shanghai (Y570), Shantou (Y960), Shenzhen (Y1100), Wenzhou (Y780), Xiamen (Y860) and Xi'an (Y500).

Dragonair and CAAC both offer direct flights between Hong Kong and Tianjin for HK$1850. CITS is Dragonair's ticket sales agent in Tianjin.

Bus The opening of the Beijing-Tianjin Expressway has greatly reduced travel time between the two cities – the journey takes about three hours. Buses to Beijing depart from in front of the Tianjin main railway station. Costs depend on bus size, but average around Y15. In Beijing, catch the bus to Tianjin from the western side of the car park in front of the Beijing main railway station. The bus has two great advantages over the train: there are no hassles in buying a ticket, and you are guaranteed a seat.

There are three long-distance bus stations, with buses running to places that the average foreign traveller will have little interest in. Bus stations are usually located partway along the direction of travel. The south bus station *(bālĭtái fāchē zhàn)* is on the north-eastern edge of the Shangshui Park, which is south-west of the city centre – this is where you get buses to Tanggu. The west bus station *(xīzhàn fāchē zhàn)* is at 2 Xiqing Dao near Tianjin west railway station.

Of possible interest to travellers is the north-east bus station *(dōngbĕijiǎo fāchē zhàn)*, which has the most destinations and the largest ticket office. It's very close to the Ancient Culture Street, just west of the Hai River in the north end of Tianjin. Bus No 24 from the city centre will land you in the general vicinity. From the north-east bus station you can get buses to Jixian, Fengtai (Tianzun Pavilion) and Zunhua (to name just a few places). If you're the sort of person who likes to see everything along the way, a road route worth considering (also served by rail) is from Tianjin to Beijing via Jixian.

Train Tianjin is a major north-south rail junction with frequent trains to Beijing, extensive links with the north-eastern provinces, and lines southwards to Ji'nan, Nanjing, Shanghai, Fuzhou, Hefei, Yantai, Qingdao and Shijiazhuang.

There are three railway stations in Tianjin: main, north and west. Ascertain the correct station. For most trains you'll want the main station. Some trains stop at both main and west, and some go only through the west station (particularly those originating in Beijing and heading south). Trains heading for north-eastern China often stop at the north station.

If you have to alight at the west station, bus No 24 connects the west station to the main station, passing through the central shopping district.

The main station is one of the cleanest and most modern in China. Foreigners can avoid the horrible queues by purchasing tickets on the 2nd floor at the soft-seat ticket office.

Express trains take just under two hours for the trip between Tianjin and Beijing. Local trains take about 2½ hours.

Boat Tianjin's harbour is Tanggu, 50 km (30 minutes by train) from Tianjin proper. This is one of China's major ports, offering a number of possibilities for arriving and departing by boat. See the Tanggu section for details.

Car Foreigners with their own cars (diplomats, resident business people, etc) are permitted to drive along the Beijing-Tianjin highway.

Getting Around

To/From the Airport From the centre, it's about 15 km to Tianjin's Zhangguizhuang Airport. Taxis ask for Y30 or more for the trip. There is a bus from the CAAC ticket office.

Bus A pox on local transport in this city! Tianjin is one of the most confusing places you can take on in China, and things are compounded by the fact that your visit there may turn, by necessity, into a very short one. Your chances of getting on a bus at rush hour are about 2% – and you'll get a unique chance to find out what it feels like to be buried alive in a pile of people. If you must use a bus, try and ambush it at the point of origin.

Key local transport junctions are the areas around the three railway stations. The main (that is, the east) station has the biggest collection: bus Nos 24, 27 and 13, and further out toward the river are Nos 2, 5, 25, 28, 96. At the west station are bus Nos 24, 10 and 31 (Nos 11 and 37 run past west station); at the north railway station are bus Nos 1, 7 and 12.

Another major bus terminal point is around Zhongxin Park, at the edge of the central shopping district. From here you'll get bus Nos 11 and 94, and nearby are bus Nos 9, 20 and 37. To the north of Zhongxin Park are bus Nos 1, 91, 92, 93.

A useful bus to know is the No 24, which runs between the main station and the west station 24 hours a day. Also noteworthy is No 8 – it starts at the main railway station, then zig-zags across town before finally terminating at Nankai University in the southern part of town.

With the exception of bus No 24, buses run from 5 am to 11 pm.

Underground The subway *(dìxià tiělù)* can be useful – it runs all the way from Nanjing Lu to the west railway station and costs five jiao per ride. Tianjin's subway opened in 1982; the cars shuttle back and forth on a single track. There's nothing to see down in the depths except the subterranean bathroom tiling, but it saves a lot of trauma with the buses.

Taxi Taxis can be most readily found near the railway station and around tourist hotels. The cost is from Y1.20 to Y2 per km with a Y10 minimum, and is seldom more than Y20 for any destination within the city. Most drivers prefer not to use the meters, so get the fare engraved in stone before heading out.

Tianjin has many motortricycle – these cost about Y10 to Y15 for anywhere in the city. They are particularly useful for manoeuvring through the narrow, traffic-clogged streets in the centre.

AROUND TIANJIN

Were it not for the abysmal hotel situation, Tianjin would make a fine staging point for trips directly north (to Jixian, Zunhua, Tangshan, Beidaihe and the Great Wall at Huangyaguan), and a launching pad for roaring into the north-east (Manchuria). Preliminary bus tours have been set up for some northern routes, but it's expensive stuff. About the only other place within the Tianjin Municipality that sees many foreign tourists is Tanggu.

Tanggu
(tánggū) 塘沽

There are three harbours on the Tianjin municipality stretch of coastline: Hangu (north), Tanggu-Xingang (centre) and Dagang (south). Tanggu is about 50 km from Tianjin proper.

This is one of China's major international seaports, kept open by ice-breakers in winter. The harbour is where 'friends from all over the world' come to drop anchor – and get ripped-off by outrageously overpriced hotels and con-artist moneychangers. There are a few odd sights around town which could possibly keep you amused for a few hours, but Tanggu is no place to linger.

Nevertheless, you will find foreigners lingering here – not travellers, but business people. Tanggu is booming – many export-oriented industries have set up shop here. The chief focus of all this frenetic activity is the Economic & Technology Development Zone *(jīngjì jìshù kāifā qū)*. Should you decide to wander around this area in the north part of Tanggu, you'll see plenty of factories, but also fancy residences and shops catering for the mostly foreign and Overseas Chinese investors and technical experts.

As for touristy sights, the city is most proud of its Bohai Children's World *(bóhǎi értóng shìjiè)*. It's actually a little better than it sounds – attractive buildings in a park setting on an island in the middle of the harbour.

The other famous spot in town is Dagu Fort *(dàgū pàotái)* on the south bank of the Hai River. The fort was built during the Ming Dynasty, sometime between 1522 and 1567. The purpose was to protect Tianjin from foreign invasions. It may have worked for a while, but considering how easily the Europeans overran the place during the 19th century, it was not exactly a smashing success.

As for shopping and entertainment, there's a Friendship Store and International Seamen's Club just next to the harbour.

For reasons not fully understood (by us), Tanggu has a very heavy public security presence. Many of the cops are in plain clothes, but if you're astute, you'll notice the PSB vehicles – long, white licence plates with black lettering, except for the first two letters which are red. For what it's worth, there is a local rumour that Tanggu is the PSB headquarters.

Places to Stay As in Tianjin, economical accommodation is impossible to come by without knowing someone. If arriving in Tanggu by ship, it's best to hop on the first

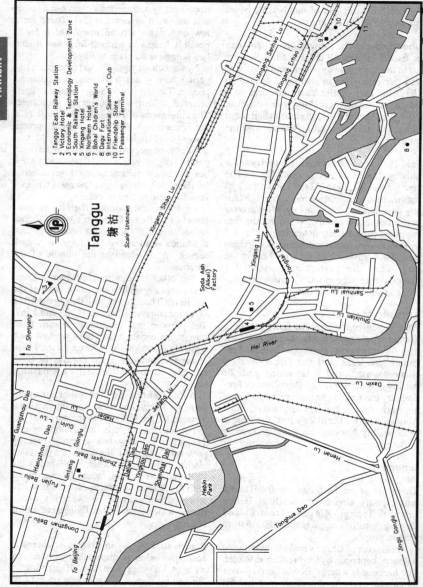

Tanggu 塘沽

Scale Unknown

1 Tanggu East Railway Station
2 Victory Hotel
3 Economic & Technology Development Zone
4 South Railway Station
5 Xingang Hotel
6 Northern Hotel
7 Bohai Children's World
8 Dagu Fort
9 International Seamen's Club
10 Friendship Store
11 Passenger Terminal

To Shenyang

To Beijing

Xingang Sanhao Lu
Xingang Erhao Lu
Xingang Yihao Lu

Xingang Sihao Lu

Xingang Lu

Yonghe Lu

Sanhuai Lu

Shuixian Lu

Daxin Lu

Henan Lu

Soda Ash (Alkali) Factory

Hai River

Hebei Lu
Jietang Lu
Gulin Lu
Gonglu
Jintang
Zhongxin Lu
Dalian Dao
Yingkou Dao
Shanghai Dao

Guangzhou Dao
Hangzhou Beilu
Fujian Beilu
Dongshan Beilu

Tonghai Dao

Jingu Gonglu

Hebin Park

1	塘沽东火车站
2	胜利宾馆
3	经济技术开发区
4	塘沽南火车站
5	新港宾馆
6	北方宾馆
7	渤海儿童世界
8	大沽炮台
9	国际海员俱乐部
10	友谊商店
11	新港客运站

train to Beijing or Beidaihe unless you've got money to burn.

There are four hotels in the city which accept foreigners; the *Xingang Hotel* (☎ 985440) (*xīngǎng bīnguǎn*), Northern Hotel (☎ 982990) (*běifāng bīnguǎn*), Victory Hotel (☎ 985833) (*shènglì bīnguǎn*) and International Seamen's Club (☎ 973897) (*guójì hǎiyuán jùlèbù*). See the Tanggu city map for exact locations.

Getting There & Away Train is certainly the preferred way to go, but there are buses to Tanggu from Tianjin's south long-distance bus station. The main railway line to northeast China runs from Beijing to Harbin via Tianjin and Tanggu. In other words, it's a heavily travelled route with frequent service. Trains cover the 50 km from Tianjin to Tanggu in just 30 minutes. The route passes by salt-works which furnish roughly a quarter of the nation's salt.

Tanggu's harbour was renamed 'New Harbour' (*xīngǎng*) – you catch ferries at the New Harbour passenger ferry terminal (*xīngǎng kèyùn zhàn*).

For travellers, probably the most interesting ships are the international passenger ferries. There is one plying the route between Inchon, South Korea and Tianjin, while another goes to Kobe, Japan. See the Getting There & Away chapter for more details about prices and times.

Boats to Dalian depart 12 times a month. The trip takes around 20 hours. Boats to Yantai depart about four times a month. The

trip takes about 30 hours. Because of the large numbers of passengers on the boats, it's recommended that you stick to 4th class or higher. The liners are comfortable, can take up to 1000 passengers, and are equipped with a bar, restaurant and movies.

In Tianjin, tickets can be bought at 5 Pukou Jie. This tiny street runs west off Taierzhuang Lu and is difficult to find. Pukou Jie is roughly on the same latitude as the enormous smokestack which stands on the opposite side of the river.

Tickets can also be purchased at Tanggu port opposite the Tanggu Theatre, but in Tianjin it's safer to buy in advance.

Tangshan
(tángshān) 塘山
Tangshan was devastated in the earthquake of July 1976 and has since been rebuilt. Over 240,000 people (almost a fifth of Tangshan's population at that time) were killed in the quake and over 160,000 seriously injured; with casualties from Beijing and Tianjin added, the total figures are considerably higher. A new Tangshan has risen from the rubble. As early as 1978 it was claimed that industrial output (steel, cement, engineering) was back to 1976 levels. The present population of the city is around 1½ million. You could stop off in Tangshan for a few hours en route by train from Beijing to Beidaihe. There are direct trains between Tanggu and Tangshan.

Jixian
(jìxiàn) 蓟县
Jixian is rated as one of the 'northern suburbs' of Tianjin, though it's actually 125 km from Tianjin city proper – the Jixian area is about 90 km due east of Beijing.

Near the city's west gate is the Temple of Solitary Joy *(dúlè sì)*. At 1000 years' vintage, the main multistorey wooden structure, the Avalokitesvara Pavilion, qualifies as the oldest such structure in China. It houses a 16-metre-high statue of a bodhisattva with 10 heads which rates as one of China's largest terracotta statues. The buddha dates back to the Liao Dynasty and the murals inside are from the Ming Dynasty. The complex has been restored in the interests of mass tourism.

Just east of Jixian is Yuqiao Reservoir (*yúqiáo shuǐkù*), easily the most attractive body of water (not counting the sea) in Tianjin Municipality.

Getting There & Away One way of getting to Jixian is to join a tour from Beijing to the Eastern Qing Tombs and Zunhua – see the Beijing section for details. However, this will normally only give you a brief lunch stop in Jixian before pushing on to the tombs. There are also regular long-distance buses from Beijing.

Buses from Tianjin's north-east bus station go to Jixian. There is also a direct Tianjin-Jixian rail link.

Panshan
(*pánshān*) 盘山

To the north-west of Jixian is Panshan, a collection of hills ranked among the 15 famous mountains of China. Emperor Qianlong was claimed to have been so taken with the place that he swore he never would have gone south of the Yangzi River had he known Panshan was so beautiful.

The emperor aside, don't expect the Himalayas. Nevertheless, it's still a lovely area, dotted with trees, springs, streams, temples, pavilions and various other ornaments.

The hills are 12 km north-west of Jixian, 150 km north of Tianjin and 40 km west of the Eastern Qing Tombs in Hebei Province. A suburban-type train runs to Jixian from

Tianjin; you can also get there by bus from Tianjin's north-east bus station.

Great Wall at Huangyaguan
(*huángyáguān chángchéng*)
黄崖关长城

At the very northern tip of Tianjin Municipality (bordering Hebei Province) is Huangyaguan (Yellow Cliff Pass). This is where Tianjin residents head to view the Great Wall. This section of the wall is 41 km long before it crumbles away on each end – the part open to tourists was restored in 1984. In addition to the original structures, a museum was added along with the 'Hundred Generals Forest of Steles'.

Huangyaguan is 170 km north of Tianjin city. Buses go to the wall mostly on weekends, with early morning departures from Tianjin's Dongbeijiao bus station or sometimes from the main railway station.

Tianzun Pavilion
(*tiānzūn gé*) 天尊阁

You'd have to be a real temple and pavilion enthusiast to come way out here to see this place. Nevertheless, it's rated as one of Tianjin's big sights. The Tianzun (Heaven Respect) Pavilion is three storeys tall – locals are proud to tell you that it remained standing when everything else nearby was reduced to rubble by the 1976 Tangshan earthquake.

The pavilion is near Fengtai in Ninghe County, on the eastern border of Tianjin Municipality and Hebei Province. Buses to Fengtai depart from Tianjin's north-east bus station.

THE
NORTH-EAST

The North-East

Steam trains, ice cream, dusty roads, mud houses, Mao statues, chimney stacks, logging towns, Soviet-clone hotels, red maples, snowcaps...Manchuria, the north-east, is relatively unvisited by travellers, but has played more than its fair share in the tumultuous events of 20th-century China.

HISTORY

Historically, Manchuria has been the birth-place of the conquerors. Maybe there's something about the inhospitable geography of this region that drives successive waves of people southwards, among them the Mongols and the Manchus. At the turn of this century Manchuria was a sparsely populated region, but it had rich, largely untapped resources. Both the Russians and the Japanese eyed it enviously. After the Chinese were defeated by the Japanese in the Sino-Japanese War of 1894-95, the Liaoning Peninsula was ceded to Japan. Japan's strength alarmed the other foreign powers, Russia among them, and Japan was forced to hand the peninsula back to China. As a 'reward' for this intervention, the Russians were allowed to build a railway across Manchuria to their treaty port of Port Arthur (Lüshun). The Russians moved troops in with the railway, and for the next 10 years effectively controlled north-east China.

The Russo-Japanese War of 1904-05 put an end to Russia's domination of Manchuria. The land battles were fought on Chinese soil, and when the Russians surrendered Japan gained control of the trans-Manchurian railway and Port Arthur. Meanwhile, the overall control of Manchuria moved into the hands of Zhang Zuolin. When the Russo-Japanese War broke out Zhang had been a bandit-leader in control of a large and well-organised private army. Lured by promises of reward, he threw his lot in with the Japanese and emerged from the war with the strongest Chinese army in Manchuria. By the time the Qing Dynasty fell he held 'the

power of life and death' in southern Manchuria, and between 1926 and 1928 ran a regional government recognised by foreign powers. Zhang was ousted by the Kuomintang's Northern Expedition which unified southern and northern China, and he was forced to retire.

Zhang's policy in Manchuria had been to limit Japan's economic and political expansion, and eventually to break Japan's influence entirely. But by the 1920s the militarist Japanese government was ready to take a hard line on China. To them, the advantages of seizing Manchuria were enormous; here was an area of land three times as large as Japan but with a third of her population – an area of undeveloped mines and timber, and vast agricultural possibilities.

Zhang Zuolin was assassinated (both the Japanese and the Kuomintang have been blamed for this one); control of Manchuria passed to his son, Zhang Xueliang, with the blessing of the Kuomintang government in Nanjing. The Japanese invasion of Manchuria began in September 1931, and the weak Kuomintang government in Nanjing either couldn't or wouldn't do anything about it. Chiang Kaishek urged 'reliance' (whatever that meant) on the League of Nations and continued to organise his annihilation campaigns against the Communists. Manchuria fell to the Japanese, who renamed it the independent state of Manchukuo – a Japanese puppet state. The exploitation of the region began in earnest: heavy industry was established and extensive railway lines were laid.

The Japanese occupation of Manchuria was a fateful move for the Chinese Communist forces locked up in Shaanxi. The invasion forced Zhang Xueliang and his 'Dongbei' (North-Eastern) army out of Manchuria – these troops were eventually moved into central China to fight the Communists. Up until the mid-1930s Zhang's loyalty to

Chiang Kaishek never wavered, but he gradually became convinced that Chiang's promises to cede no more territory to Japan and to recover the Manchurian homeland were empty ones. Zhang made a secret truce with the Communists, and when Chiang Kaishek flew to Xi'an in December 1936 to organise yet another extermination campaign against the Communists, Zhang had Chiang arrested. Chiang was only released after agreeing to call off the extermination campaign and to form an alliance with the Communists to resist the Japanese. Chiang never forgave Zhang and later had him arrested and taken to Taiwan as a prisoner – he wasn't permitted to leave Taiwan until 1992.

1945 & After

When WW II ended the north-east suddenly became the focus of a renewed confrontation between the Communist and Kuomintang troops. In February 1945 the meeting of Allied leaders at Yalta discussed the invasion of Japan. Roosevelt was anxious that the Russians should take part, but in return for Soviet support Stalin demanded that Mongolia (part of the Chinese empire until 1911) should be regarded as independent (in fact, a Soviet satellite) and that Soviet rights in Manchuria, lost to Japan, should be restored – that meant the restoration of Soviet control over trans-Manchurian railways, the commercial port of Dalian and the naval base of Port Arthur (Lüshun).

Chiang Kaishek wished to keep the Russians favourably disposed and began negotiations for a treaty with the USSR on the basis of the Yalta agreements. A treaty was eventually signed which pledged that each side would work together in close and friendly collaboration and 'render each other every possible economic assistance in the post-war period' – Stalin had sold out the Communists and thrown Soviet support behind the Kuomintang.

At the Potsdam Conference of July 1945 it was decided that all Japanese forces in Manchuria and North Korea would surrender to the Soviet army; those stationed elsewhere would surrender to the Kuomintang.

After the A-bombs obliterated Hiroshima and Nagasaki in August 1945 and forced the Japanese government to surrender, the Soviet armies moved into Manchuria, engaging the Japanese armies in a brief but bloody conflict. The Americans started transporting Kuomintang troops by air and sea to the north, where they could take the surrender of Japanese forces and regain control of north and central China. The US navy moved in to Qingdao and landed 53,000 marines to protect the railways leading to Beijing and Tianjin and the coal mines which supplied those railways.

The Communists, still in a shaky truce with the Kuomintang, also joined the rush for position. Although Chiang Kaishek told them to remain where they were, the Communist troops marched to Manchuria on foot, picking up arms from abandoned Japanese depots as they went. Other Communist forces went north by sea from Shandong. In November 1945 the Kuomintang attacked the Communists even while US-organised peace negotiations were taking place between the two. That attack put an end to the talks.

All these moves came within days of the Japanese surrender. The Soviet troops established themselves along the railways and main cities. Since the Kuomintang troops could not move in to replace them by the agreed date of mid-November, Chiang asked the Russians to stay in the cities to prevent the Chinese Communist forces from entering the Soviet-controlled zones. The Russians complied and did not withdraw until March 1946 when the Kuomintang troops were finally installed.

In the meantime the Russians stripped the Manchurian cities of all the Japanese military and industrial equipment. Whole factories including machinery, machine tools and even office furniture were dispatched by train to the USSR; even the railway tracks were taken up and shipped out; and gold in the Manchurian banks was taken away. The Russians remained in Port

Arthur and Dalian, and the last of the US troops were not withdrawn until March 1947, though Qingdao (in Shandong Province) continued to be used by the US navy.

The Rise of the Communists

The Communists occupied the countryside, setting in motion their land-reform policies, which quickly built up their support among the peasants. There was a tremendous growth of mass support for the Communists, and the force of 100,000 regulars who had marched into Manchuria rapidly grew to 300,000, as soldiers of the old Manchurian armies that had been forcibly incorporated into the Japanese armies flocked to join them. Within two years the Red Army had grown to 1½ million combat troops and four million support personnel.

On the other side, though the Kuomintang troops numbered three million and had Soviet and US arms and support, its soldiers had nothing to fight for and either deserted or went over to the Communists – who took them in by the thousands. The Kuomintang armies were led by generals whom Chiang had chosen for their personal loyalty to him rather than for their military competence; Chiang ignored the suggestions of the US military advisers whom he himself had asked for.

In 1948 the Communists took the initiative in Manchuria. Strengthened by the recruitment of Kuomintang soldiers and the capture of US equipment, the Communists became both the numerical and material equal of the Kuomintang. Three great battles led by Lin Biao in Manchuria decided the outcome. In the first battle of August 1948, the Kuomintang lost 500,000 people. In the second battle (from November 1948 to January 1949) whole Kuomintang divisions went over to the Communists who took 327,000 prisoners.

The Kuomintang lost seven generals who were killed, captured or deserted; seven divisional commanders crossed sides. The third decisive battle was fought in the area around Beijing and Tianjin; Tianjin fell on 23 January and another 500,000 troops came across to the Communist camp. It was these victories which sealed the fate of the Kuomintang and allowed the Communists to drive southwards.

CLIMATE

The weather tends to extremes in the north-east – mostly cold. Up in Harbin, come January, they'll all be huddled round their coal-burning stoves drinking vodka – and so would you be if it was -30°C outside, with howling Siberian gales. Activity slows to a crunch in this snowflake-spitting weather, while the animals pass the season over totally and sensibly hibernate.

This is not to say that you should avoid winter in North-East China, but merely to suggest that it would be a damn good idea! If, however, you know how to deal with the cold, January and February offers the added attractions of winter sports and various 'ice festivals'. You'll be able to get around more freely from May to September. Mohe, in northern Heilongjiang, holds the record for the coldest temperature recorded in China, a mere -52.3°C.

ECONOMY

The north-east is being developed into an industrial powerhouse. Between the smoke-stacks is enough empty prairie to support large state-run wheat farms with all the potential to make this China's bread-basket. To preserve the ailing forests – the last great timber reserves in the PRC – zones (less than 1% of China's total land area) have been placed off limits to hunters and lumberjacks. A vigorous tree-planting campaign is under-way.

Of the three north-eastern provinces – Liaoning, Heilongjiang and Jilin – Liaoning is China's richest in natural resources. It has large deposits of coal and iron ore, as well as magnesium and petroleum. It also has the heaviest industry and the densest rail network. While there is much hoopla about this year's production of knitted under-wear exceeding that of last year by x per cent, exceeding that of 1980 by xx per cent and exceeding that of 1949 by xxx per cent, the PRC has kept very quiet on the subject of industrial pollution.

Those keen on delving into heavy industry and the accompanying soot, grime and fallout, can find no better place than Benxi in Liaoning Province. Seeing this aspect of China is probably as valid as visiting its temples, but success at getting into the factories is not guaranteed. In lieu of an expensive CITS liaison it pays to befriend a high-ranking factory worker.

TOURISM

Tourism in the north-east is the proverbial 'good news, bad news'. The good news (for the Chinese at least): tourism and the resultant revenues are increasing year by year. Offerings dangled for well-heeled visitors ranging from backpacking, fishing, hunting, birdwatching, skiing and ice skating.

The bad news: most of the north-east is monotonous. There are only two small, reasonably accessible places whose natural beauty stands out – the Changbaishan mountains (Changbaishan Nature Reserve) along the North Korean border, and Jingbo Lake in Heilongjiang. Unfortunately, most of the visitors lack any environmental consciousness – the impact of mass tourism on these places amounts to tonnes of rubbish decorating the scenic landscapes. While some good birdwatching areas near Qiqihar are more or less in well-preserved condition, the dismal fact is that most of the north-east has been given over to agriculture and industry. Temples, museums and other cultural edifices are few and far between.

The industrial city landscapes are supposed to look (starkly) beautiful in winter with photogenic blacks and whites, and some extra-sooty greys. If you can survive the cold, Harbin has an interesting ice festival in winter. Deep in the woods north-east of Harbin, CITS organises hunting, bicycling and winter-sports expeditions. A few whitewater enthusiasts have rafted down the Erdao Songhua River in Jilin. In Bei'an (Dedu County), way up north of Harbin, a set of volcano crater lakes, caves and a volcano museum have opened, but it gets rather poor reviews from visitors. All in all, the north-east remains a place for specialised interests including pharmacology, ornithology and metallurgy.

Hotel prices are absurdly high in the north-east. Dormitories are almost nonexistent; except in Harbin which is slightly cheaper, bottom-end accommodation starts

Oroqen women embroidering wolf skins

at Y170 per night for a double room but Y250 is bare minimum in Dalian! Despite the high prices, 'service' (we use the term loosely) is abysmal. The PSB certainly hasn't helped by placing many perfectly acceptable hotels off limits to foreigners. The most enjoyable parts are out in the backwoods where you get the opposite treatment – very spartan places to stay but really friendly, helpful locals.

Not surprisingly, you won't bump into many Westerners in the north-east – most tourists are Chinese, Overseas Chinese and a smattering of Japanese pursuing special interests like buying ginseng and eating bear paws. The only Western faces you are likely to see are Russian smugglers and occasional business travellers looking to score a great buy in chemicals or iron ore.

SKIING

Don't expect to find another St Moritz or Aspen, but you can pursue the art of sliding downhill in China. You're advised to bring your own equipment. The Chinese make wood and fibreglass skis; you could hire some, but the quality and size of boots and so on cannot be vouched for.

Twenty km from Jilin town (in Jilin Province, east of the capital Changchun) are the Songhua Lake skifields of Daqingshan, with a 1700-metre cableway, lounge, drying rooms and restaurant. Another skifield is at Tonghua, where championships have been held. In Heilongjiang there's the Qingyun skifield, in Shangzhi County, south-east of Harbin; it has a cableway, a guesthouse with room for 350 people, and stone cottages. North of Shangzhi, and approachable by bus, is the Yanzhou County skifield. There's snow for a long time – the main season is from late November to early April.

Another possibility is cross-country skiing, which probably makes more sense given the lack of mountains in the north-east. The Chinese themselves are not much into this – despite all the martial arts movies, aerobic-type exercise has never been particularly popular in China, even more so now with half the population addicted to cigarettes. If you want to tour the north-east on cross-country skis, you will almost certainly need to bring all of your own equipment.

THE EAST IS STEAM

For train enthusiasts, a trip through some parts of China can be like a trip back through time. The following article was sent to us by Patrick Whitehouse for our first edition. We've updated it a bit, and additional info and updates from train buffs are very welcome.

The first railway in China was the line from Shanghai to Woosung, built by foreign capital. Negotiations for its construction began in 1865 and, after fierce opposition, the first eight km out of Shanghai were completed in 1876. The line was pushed on until a Chinese person was knocked down and killed, and the resulting riots caused the whole line to close. Subsequently the Chinese government bought and re-opened it but, after completing payments in 1878, they closed the line, took up the permanent way, and sank it in the sea with all the rolling stock and equipment!

A few lines were built within the next decade but it was not until after the Sino-Japanese War in 1894 that railway building really got going. With the formation of the Chinese Republic in 1912 came nationalisation, and considerable construction took place in the next two decades. The Japanese made their mark on the Manchurian railways after 1931. Their influence extended into China as the country was overrun during WW II; a high proportion of locomotives and rolling stock in operation after the war was of Japanese manufacture or design. During this period a large number of US-built locomotives were sent to China to help rehabilitate the railways, and many of these survive as Class 'KD' 2-8-0s. At the time of Liberation China's railways lay in ruins after 15 years of war. Before 1935 the country had approximately 20,000 km of railway, but by 1949 less than half of it was in working order.

The new government was faced with the gigantic task of reconstructing its war-torn network. The first five-year plan envisaged the building of 55 new railways and the reconstruction or double-tracking of 29 existing lines. In the first 15 years, to 1964, the length of operating railways was estimated to have reached 35,000 km; today the total length is close to 40,000 km and still expanding – only Tibet is without at least some railway facility. There was hardly any signalling 15 years ago; today, China Railways have some of the most modern and sophisticated signalling. Before WW II China imported practically all its rolling stock, equipment and supplies; now it manufactures its own. About 500 locomotives are built each year.

Sad to say, steam is on its way out, a victim of changing technology and environmental concerns.

China was the last country to continue manufacturing steam locomotives, but the last such factory was finally closed in 1989. At first China imported diesels from France and Romania – now the Chinese can make their own. Nevertheless, the steam engines are too numerous to simply scap, so they will be maintained until it's no longer economical to do so. At least for the next decade, if not longer, train buffs will still be able to enjoy the aesthetics of the old steam locomotives in China – enjoy it while you can.

Another major development plan calls for main line electrification. Today a small proportion of lines have wire (Baoji to Chengdu; Yangpingquan to Xiangfan). Also being electrified are the Beijing-Baotou and the Guiyang-Kunming lines. Shortages of electricity though may hamper continued electrification of the trains. The system employed is power-hungry – 25,000 V AC single-phase 50 Hz, with overhead conductor. The French electrical industry has assisted in the initial development of electrification, although the Chinese were quick to clone the technology and are now self-reliant in most respects.

The Chinese are continuing to expand the network of tracks, with much of the work being paid for by loans from the Asian Development Bank. Some of the new lines do not belong to the mammoth money-losing China Railway Administration, but are instead owned by provincial governments. Guangdong Province is keen to make its train lines operate at a profit, which means charging higher prices for passengers and freight. There is even talk of privatisation, but that still seems a long way off.

Three grateful Brits joined a small party of Australians in an official 'rail visit' to Manchuria. As always in China, we were treated as honoured guests – and if our dedication to railways was deemed to be slightly unusual, this was never made known. On this trip everything really begins at Shenyang, the capital of Liaoning Province, and both the largest industrial centre and the communications hub of north-east China. From the rail-fan's point of view, Shenyang is one of the most important rail centres in the country. Six lines converge on the city, and with the coal traffic from Fushun and other mines in the area, with the inbound iron ore and outbound steel to and from nearby Anshan, and with the chemical and manufacturing goods flowing from and through Shenyang itself, freight traffic is plentiful – and in China that means steam!

Space forbids a detailed description of the Fushun mine complex with its attendant steam and electrified railway system – except to say that it's immense. The highlight of the visit to Shenyang was Sugintun steam depot, which is all freight and consequently almost 100% 'QJ' class 2-10-2s, and 'JS' class 2-8-2s. Like most Chinese depots, Sugintun shed is fully equipped to carry out heavy repair work, but not boiler fitting. The 'two-star' attractions were found hidden away. These were two Japanese Pacifics sitting at the back

of the shed – a class 'SL8' No 296 (in steam) and a class 'SL7' (very dead). Both were prewar Manchurian express classes of note, the former being used on the Port Arthur (Luda, near Dalian) to Harbin overnight service on the South Manchurian Railway, and the latter between Port Arthur and Shenyang. The 'SL7s' made their trip with fully air-conditioned trains (some of the first in the world) and ran at an average speed of 110 km/h (68.75 mph).

From Shenyang we journeyed to Jilin, behind steam 'SL' class Pacifics hauling 12 bogies of about 518 tonnes, which is a good load for these engines over a steeply graded route. At least eight sizable rivers are bridged during the trip. As foreign guests we travelled extremely comfortably in a soft-class coach with tea on hand at any time from the blue-uniformed coach attendant. Jilin provided an opportunity for that most relaxing of railway pursuits – railway sauntering, at a place called Dragon Pond Hill station. Locomotive variety here was classes 'QJ' 2-10-2, 'JF' 2-8-2 and, on the passenger runs, 'RM' Pacifics.

At Changchun, further along the line, there are two railway factories: a Locomotive Works and a Passenger Coach Works. The Locomotive Works built the first of the big 'Heping' (Peace) steam locomotives, as well as the power cars for the Beijing subway. The Passenger Coach Works was built in 1957 to help overcome the shortage of passenger stock and today builds lightweight coaches for 160 km/h operation, deluxe coaches and sleeping cars. The plant has been modernised and expanded since 1978; technological aid comes from Japan's largest railway vehicle builders, Nippon Sharyo Seizo Kaisha. The Locomotive Works and the Carriage Works have been visited by foreigners, as have the social complex with its schools, housing and hospital. Other Changchun joys included line-side photography and an early-morning visit to the steam shed. The latter was so fantastic – clean engines, variety and hospitality – that I just stood there in the sunshine for a moment and said out loud, 'I just don't believe it!' In addition to the usual tender engines, the depot sported two different classes of 2-6-4T Class 'DB2' No 89, a Japanese-built locomotive dating from 1934-36, and 'DB1' No 28, an Alco of 1907. The main classes based here are the 'QJ' 2-10-2, 'RM' 4-6-2 and 'SL' 4-6-2, with a shed allocation for around 100. As with Sugintun depot, Changchun was equipped for overhauls at 100,000-km intervals. A heavy general overhaul is carried out on steam locomotives at the main works after 300,000 km.

Our last stop northwards was Harbin, some 500 km north of Vladivostok. Winter comes to Harbin early and line-side photography included snow scenes, albeit dull ones from the weather point of view. Even so, it was impossible not to be thrilled by the sight of heavy double-headed freights hauled by thundering 'QJs', headlights on in the gloom, pounding up the bank at Wang Guang on their way south. Of particular interest was one of China's three named engines – *General Zhu De*, No 2470. Passenger trains were 'RM' hauled.

At a further shed there was another gem hiding in the yard – a Tangshan-built 2-6-2T of 1949-50, No PL275. Harbin is the area freight depot containing the usual high quota of 'QJs' (the last steam locomotives to be built in China). The shed itself dates from 1899 and has a working staff of some 2600 for the 100% steam allocation of approximately 100 locomotives. Winter is the busy season as the roads become impassable, and 70 locomotives from the shed are in daily service, with an equal number coming in for servicing.

Suffice it to say that our visit covered only a small section of China's rail network, but along the way we saw a great deal of Manchuria. Help was always at hand, and we were fortunate enough to find interpreters and guides who showed a positive interest in our hobby – purchasing technical books and crawling over engines for special identification points. One guide had worked his service out on the installation of the Tan Zam Railway ('Uhuru' or 'Freedom' Railway). The Tan Zam Railway was completed in 1975, linking Zambia's copper mines with Tanzania's ports, thus enabling the two countries to bypass the usual South African export routes. Twenty thousand Chinese worked on the project alongside 36,000 Africans. That particular guide had some fascinating stories to tell.

More and more of the steam engines are being relegated to hauling freight in northern backwaters. Narrow gauge steam railways operate keep the lumber industry rolling in places like Yichun, Dailing, Langxiang and Nancha. The mining region around Jiamusi employs steam to haul the ore. CITS in Harbin offers railway tours which take in these remote areas.

Patrick Whitehouse
Millbrook House Ltd
England, 1984

Liaoning 辽宁

Population: six million
Capital: Shenyang
SHENYANG
(shěnyáng) 沈阳

A major industrialised and prosperous city, Shenyang is the cradle of the Manchus, and started as a trading centre for nomads as far back as the 11th century, becoming established as the capital in the 17th century. With the Manchu conquest of Beijing in 1644, Shenyang became a secondary capital under the Manchu name of Mukden, and a centre of the ginseng trade.

The city was occupied by the Russians around the turn of the century as part of their 'railway colonialism', and was a key battleground during the Sino-Japanese War (1904-05). Shenyang rapidly changed hands – in turn dominated by warlords, the Japanese (1931), the Russians (1945), the Kuomintang (1946) and the Chinese Communist Party (1948).

Shenyang is the centre of the Liaoning Province Industrial Effort; six major rail lines converge on the city, including freight lines from Anshan, the steel giant, and Fushun, the coal capital. The industrial output of Shenyang rivals that of Shanghai and includes machinery, aircraft, trams, textiles, pharmaceuticals, rubber products – you name it. The latest products can be viewed at the Liaoning Industrial Exhibition Hall, and factory visits are on the group-tour agenda.

Information

You'll find the CITS (☎ 646501) in a building about 100 metres north of the Phoenix Hotel. The PSB is just off the traffic circle on Zhongshan Lu near the Mao statue. The Bank of China is at 75 Heping Beidajie. The main post office is at 32 Zhongshan Lu, Section 1.

Odd as it might seem, Shenyang has a US consulate (☎ 220057; fax 220074) at 40 Lane 4, Section 5, Sanjing Jie, Hepingqu. In the same lane are also the Japanese and North

Korean consulates. The Russian Consulate is in the Phoenix Hotel.

Mao Statue (Zhongshan Square)
(zhōngshān guǎngchǎng) 中山广场

Of all the unusual statues in north-east China (Soviet war heroes, mini-tanks on top of pillars...), this Mao statue takes the cake. Like some kind of strange machine, it zooms out of Red Flag Square, a giant epoxy-resin Mao at the helm, flanked by vociferous peasants, soldiers and workers. The last word on the personality cult and the follies of the Cultural Revolution, this is a rare item, erected in 1969. The statue is in Zhongshan Square at the intersection of Zhongshan Lu and Nanjing Beijie.

North Tomb
(běilíng) 北陵

This is the finest sight in Shenyang. Set in a huge park, the North Tomb is the burial place of Huang Taiji (1592-1643), who founded the Qing Dynasty (although he did not live to see the conquest of China). The tomb took eight years to build, and the impressive animal statues on the approach to it are reminiscent of the Ming tombs. The larger buildings, used as barracks by various warlords, are in a state of disrepair, though some attempt has been made to restore them. The central grassy mound area is known as

LIAONING

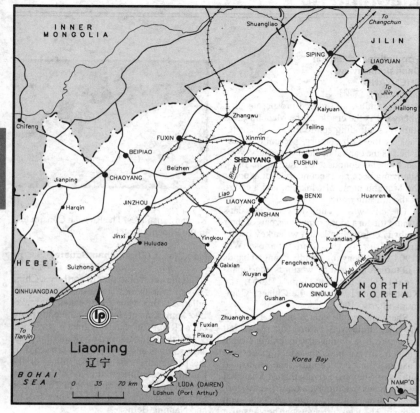

Zhaoling. To get to the North Tomb take bus No 220 from the railway station, bus No 213 from the Imperial Palace or bus No 6.

East Tomb
(dōnglíng) 东陵

Also known as Fuling, this tomb is set in a forested area eight km from Shenyang. Entombed here is Nurhachi, grandfather of Emperor Shunzhi who launched the invasion of China in 1644. Nurhachi is entombed with his mistress. Construction of the tomb started in 1626 and took several years to complete, with subsequent additions and renovations.

It's similar in layout to the North Tomb, but smaller, and is perched on a wooded hilltop overlooking a river. To get to the East Tomb take bus No 18 from the Imperial Palace and then walk.

Imperial Palace
(gùgōng) 故宫

This is a mini-Forbidden-City model in layout, though it's far smaller and the features are Manchu. The main structures were started by Nurhachi and completed in 1636 by his son, Huang Taiji.

Straight through the main gate at the far

end of the courtyard is the main structure, the octagonal Dazheng Hall with its coffered ceiling and an elaborate throne. It was here that Emperor Shunzhi was crowned before setting off to cross the Great Wall in 1644. In the courtyard in front of the hall are the Banner Pavilions, formerly administrative offices used by tribal chieftains.

They now house displays of 17th and 18th-century military equipment – armour, swords and bows. The central courtyard west of Dazheng Hall contains a conference hall, some living quarters, and some shamanist structures (one of the customs of the Manchus was to pour boiling wine into a sacrificial pig's ear, so that its cries would attract the devotees' ancestors). The courtyard to the western fringe is a residential area added on by Emperor Qianlong in the 18th century, and the Wenshu Gallery to the rear housed a copy of the Qianlong anthology.

The palace functions as a museum, with exhibitions of ivory and jade artefacts, musical instruments, furniture, and Ming and Qing paintings. Admission is Y5 and there are extra charges to visit some of the pavilions. You must leave bags at the door and photography is prohibited inside. The captions to exhibits are all in Chinese. If you've visited the Forbidden City in Beijing, Shenyang's Imperial Palace may be a disappointment, but history buffs may find it interesting. It's in the oldest section of the city; bus No 10 from the south railway station will get you there.

Places to Stay

All the provinces in the north-east have attempted to 'standardise' prices for foreigners. Liaoning pitches in with single rooms starting at Y150 FEC – even this would be considered 'budget accommodation'. You may be able to improve on this, but it can be tough.

If you're desperate for something cheap, you can try the *North-East University of Technology* (☎ 393000) (*dōngběi gōng xuéyuàn*) near Nanhu Park – foreigners are sometimes allowed to stay but it's certainly not guaranteed. If you arrive late in the day,

forget it. Take trolley-bus No 11. Another university that sometimes takes foreigners is *Liaoning University* (☎ 462541) (*liáoníng dàxué*) on Chongshan Lu across from Bainiao Park. Bus No 205 stops there.

The *Hua Sha Hotel* (☎ 733423) (*huáshà fàndiàn*) is a stone's throw from the railway station at 3 Zhongshan Lu, Section 1. Singles/doubles are Y150/180. While it looks a bit tattered on the outside, the rooms are in good shape and it's one of the best deals in town. The hotel has a foreign-exchange counter and restaurant, though you'll probably do better to eat outside.

The *Zhongxing Hotel* (☎ 338188; fax 804096) (*zhōngxīng bīnguǎn*) is at 86 Taiyuan Beijie, right in the main market area a couple of blocks south of the railway station. You can't miss the hotel – it's a brick-red pyramid-shaped skyscraper towering over the market. From the outside it looks frightfully expensive, but it's not (by Shenyang standards). Singles are Y140, doubles range from Y200 to Y260 and suites are Y300 to Y600. There is an additional 10% surcharge. If you stay here, shopping will be no problem – the ground floor houses a supermarket.

The *Dongbei Hotel* (☎ 368120) (*dōngběi fàndiàn*), is at 100 Tianjin Beijie – one block south of Taiyuan Beijie, the main shopping street. It's also known as the Dongning Hotel. It's a old place and doesn't look like it should be expensive, but rooms are ridiculously high priced at Y240 for a double. You can try bargaining, but if they won't come down then give it a miss.

The giant statue of Mao in Zhongshan Square faces the *Liaoning Hotel* (☎ 729166; fax 729103) (*liáoníng bīnguǎn*) – looks almost like he's waving to guests in the hotel lobby. The hotel was constructed in 1927 by the Japanese and boasts 77 suites, a billiard room with slate tables, and art nouveau windows – in short, old but elegant. Doubles cost Y300 and Y350.

The fanciest place in the centre is the *Zhongshan Hotel* (☎ 333888; fax 339189) (*zhōngshān dàjiǔdiàn*), a gleaming white 27-storey monolith at 65 Zhongshan Lu. It's

LIAONING

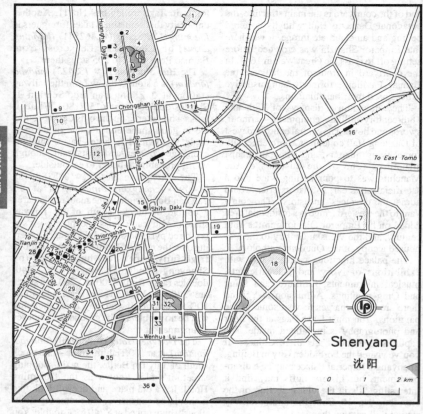

become a major drawcard for Overseas Chinese – you'll hear more Cantonese and Taiwanese spoken in the lobby than Mandarin. The 257 guest rooms and suites have a starting price tag of Y440.

The *Liaoning Mansions* (☎ 665501) *(liáoníng dàshà)* is at 1 Huanghe Dajie, Section 6, going towards the North Tomb. It's a long way from the railway station and therefore tends to serve tour groups. This enormous Soviet-style place looks like Communist Party headquarters (maybe it is). Rooms are a relative bargain at Y188, but it's extremely popular and often full.

The *Phoenix Hotel* (☎ 646501; fax 665207) *(fènghuáng fàndiàn)*, 109 Huanghe Nandajie, is just north of the Liaoning Mansions. This is a major staging area for tour groups, with all the modern amenities and the prices to go with it. Singles are Y265, doubles range from Y345 to Y547 and suites cost Y1110. It's 10 km from the railway station; it costs about Y15 by taxi from the railway station to the hotel.

The *Friendship Hotel* (☎ 601122; fax 600132) *(yǒuyí bīnguǎn)* is at 1 Huanghe Beidajie, Huangguqu, north of the Phoenix Hotel. It's villa-style and geared towards

■ PLACES TO STAY

3	Friendship Hotel
6	Phoenix Hotel
7	Liaoning Mansions
23	Liaoning Hotel
24	Zhongshan Hotel
25	Dongbei Hotel
26	Zhongxing Hotel
27	Hua Sha Hotel

▼ PLACES TO EAT

| 14 | Xinweizhai Roast Duck Restaurant |

OTHER

1	Hang Dynasty Memorial
2	Zhaoling
4	Beiling (North Tomb) Park
5	CITS
8	Park Entrance
9	Liaoning University
10	Bainiao Park
11	North Pagoda
12	Bitang Park
13	North Railway Station
15	City Hall
16	East Railway Station
17	East Pagoda Park
18	Zoo
19	Imperial Palace
20	Bank of China
21	PSB
22	Mao Statue
28	South Railway Station
29	Zhongshan Park
30	US Consulate
31	Foreign Languages Bookstore
32	Qingnian (Youth) Park
33	Liaoning Stadium
34	Nanhu (South Lake) Park
35	North East University of Technology
36	Shenyang Sports Centre

LIAONING

■ PLACES TO STAY

3	友谊宾馆
6	风凰饭店
7	辽宁大厦
23	辽宁宾馆
24	中山大酒店
25	东北饭店
26	中兴宾馆
27	华厦饭店

▼ PLACES TO EAT

| 14 | 新味斋烤鸭店 |

OTHER

1	烈士陵园
2	昭陵
4	北陵公园
5	中国国际旅行社
8	公园门口
9	辽宁大学
10	百鸟公园
11	北塔
12	碧塘公园
13	北火车站
15	市政府
16	东站
17	东塔公园
18	动物园
19	故宫
20	中国银行
21	公安局外事科
22	毛主席像
28	沈阳火车站
29	中山公园
30	美国领事馆
31	外文书店
32	青年公园
33	辽宁体育馆
34	南湖公园
35	东北工学院
36	沈阳体育中心

cadres – foreigners can stay but aren't particularly welcome. Doubles cost Y286.

Places to Eat

The area around the railway station has numerous noodle and rice places, and is the best bet for budget travellers.

If you're looking to eat upmarket, you might want to try *Xinweizhai Roast Duck*

Restaurant (xīnwèizhāi kǎoyā diàn), one of Shenyang's famous houses. It's on a small street called Beishichang Jie, which runs off Shifu Dalu. The restaurant can be reached on bus No 325, but really isn't too convenient unless you take a taxi – from almost anywhere, it's too far to walk. Another option is to eat at the pricey hotel restaurants.

Entertainment
The Shenyang Acrobatic Troupe is one of China's best and definitely worth chasing up. Ask about tickets at the Zhongxing Hotel. CITS also knows where, when and how much.

Things to Buy
The Zhongxing Hotel is part of an enormous complex called the Zhongxing Commercial Centre – it could easily compete with some of Beijing's finest department stores. The building fronts Taiyuan Jie, which is the major shopping street. Just a few paces south of the Hua Sha Hotel is an enormous collection of clothing stalls – you can get dressed in the latest for a pittance here.

Getting There & Away
Air The CAAC office (☎ 363705) is at 31 Zhonghua Lu, Section 3. There are twice-weekly flights between Hong Kong and Shenyang. Aeroflot has an office in the Phoenix Hotel and offers international flights to Irkutsk. A combined Moscow-Irkutsk-Shenyang-Beijing air ticket will save you US$700 compared with a direct Moscow-Beijing flight.

At Shenyang's airport the departure tax for domestic flights is Y20. Flights and fares from Shenyang to other Chinese cities are:

Destination	Fare	Destination	Fare
Beijing	Y320	Canton	Y1300
Changchun	Y140	Changsha	Y1090
Chengdu	Y1170	Chongqing	Y1060
Dalian	Y180	Dandong	Y120
Fuzhou	Y1020	Haikou	Y1560
Hangzhou	Y920	Harbin	Y250
Hohhot, Jilin	Y190	Ji'nan	Y450
Kunming	Y1460	Lanzhou	Y950
Mudanjiang	Y310	Nanjing	Y820
Nanning	Y1380	Ningbo	Y990
Shanghai	Y680	Shantou,	
Ürümqi,		Shenzhen	Y1500
Wenzhou	Y1130	Xiamen, Xi'an	Y840
Yantai	Y300		

Train From Shenyang to Beijing takes nine hours; to Changchun is five hours; to Harbin, nine hours; to Dandong, five hours; and to Dalian, six hours.

The situation with railway stations is tricky – there is a north station (*běi zhàn*) and south station (*nán zhàn*). The south station used to be the main station, but now trains alternate equally between the two stations so you'll have to check the timetable or ask to be certain where you're departing from. In the south station, tickets for the following day can be booked upstairs (the ground floor ticket office is the usual scrum).

Getting Around
Shenyang cabs are equipped with meters but the drivers prefer not to use them. About Y15 to Y20 is sufficient for 10 km.

AROUND SHENYANG
Qianshan (*qiānshān*) is about 50 km from Shenyang. Its name is an abbreviation for Qianlianshan (Thousand Lotuses Mountain).

According to legend, there was once a fairy who wanted to bring spring to the world by embroidering pretty clouds on lotuses. Just as she was making the 999th lotus, the gods found it, accused her of stealing the clouds and had her arrested. The fairy put up a fight and during the struggle all the lotuses dropped to earth, where they immediately turned into green hills. In memory of the fairy, people began to call the mountain 'Thousand Lotuses Mountain' or just Qianshan. Later, when a monk arrived and actually counted the peaks he discovered there were only 999, so he built an artificial one to make a round number.

You can hike around the hills, which have a scattering of Tang, Ming and Qing temples. The mountain, which gets very crowded on Sundays and public holidays, is steep in parts; it takes about three hours to reach the summit. At the southern foot of the mountain (approached along a different bus route) are the Tanggangzi Hot Springs. The last Qing emperor, Puyi, used to bathe here with his empresses.

Places to Stay

Tanggangzi's hot springs are piped into ordinary baths, and there's a sanatorium for those with chronic diseases – there is some hotel accommodation here.

There are several other places to stay at Qianshan: to the right of the park entrance is the *Qianshan Binguan*. The *Lucui Binguan* is in a pleasant spot about 100 metres into the park on the right. Taoist temples on the hills also accept guests overnight.

Getting There & Away

Qianshan takes two hours to reach by bus from the Shenyang long-distance bus station. Another approach is from Anshan, which is 25 km from the mountain – take bus No 8 from a side street about 50 metres in front of Anshan station. If you just want to make a day trip, luggage can be left at the station. The last bus in either direction leaves at 6.30 pm.

The bus drops you off at the entrance to the Qianshan park. Food, drink, Qianshan T-shirts, locally made clickers and knobbly walking sticks are available from hawkers. Maps can be bought from hawkers near the gate or from the ticket office.

DALIAN

(dàlián) 大连

Dalian has been known by a variety of names – Dalny, Dairen, Lüshun, and Luda. Lüshun is the part further south (formerly Port Arthur, now a naval base), and Lüshun and Dalian comprise Luda. In the late 19th century the Western powers were busy carving up pieces of China for themselves. To the outrage of Tsar Nicholas II, Japan gained the Liaoning Peninsula under an 1895 treaty (after creaming Chinese battleships off Port Arthur in 1894). Nicholas II gained the support of the French and Germans and managed to get the Japanese to withdraw from Dalian; the Russians got the place as a concession in 1898, and set about constructing the port of their dreams and an alternative to the only partially ice-free port of Vladivostok.

To Russia's further dismay, however, the Japanese made a comeback, sinking the Russian East Asia naval squadron in 1902, and decimating the Russian Baltic squadron off Korea in 1905. The same year, Dalian passed back into Japanese hands, and the Japanese completed the port facilities in 1930. In 1945, the Soviet Union reoccupied Dalian and did not withdraw definitively until 10 years later.

Dalian is a major port, on a par with Tianjin; Dalian's harbour facilities have been expanded and deepened, with a new harbour completed in 1976 for oil tankers (with a pipeline coming in from Daqing). The city is also an industrial producer in its own right with shipbuilding, petroleum refining, food-processing, diesel engineering and chemical, glassware, and textile industries. These developments have polluted Dalian Bay and affected the fishing enterprises, but efforts are being made to clean it up with waste treatment and oil-reclaiming ships.

Dalian was the first of the 14 open coastal cities to offer a package of attractive terms to foreign investors who had expressed great dissatisfaction with previous discriminatory practices.

It has also become China's 'first rat-free city'. With military precision, local residents planned an intensive eradication campaign and chose April 1986 (when the rats were celebrating peak powers of performance and pregnancy) as the time of assault. A team of rodent specialists from Liaoning Province was later called in for an official inspection of the city.

The *China Daily* reported that the inspection method involved the spreading of talcum powder in favourite rat haunts such as grain depots, shops, factories, schools, ports, etc. After 21 days of powdering, only 0.353% of the total powdered space showed paw prints. The inspection showed that the density rate of rats in key areas of the city met the country's 2% requirement: 0.46% at the harbour, 0.16% at the railway station and 0.83% at the airport. Sounds like the rats had packed their bags and were hastily emigrating by boat, train or plane!

The city of Dalian is remarkably clean,

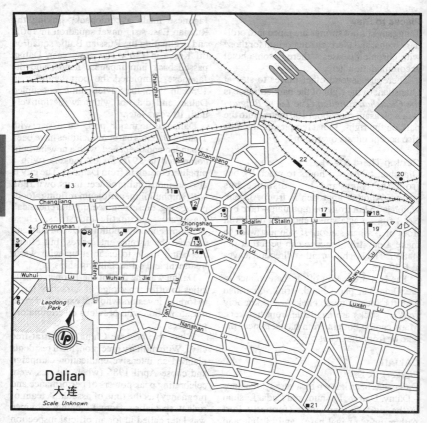

Dalian
大连
Scale Unknown

orderly and attractive. The infrastructure seems adequate and the city feels atypically uncrowded. The credit for this goes to Dalian's Municipal Construction Planning Department, which has made a real effort at replacing the previously ugly matchbox buildings with eye-pleasing structures. Unfortunately, the planners have done nothing about the hotel situation in Dalian, except to raise prices.

Information

CITS This office (☎ 3635795) is on the 4th floor, 1 Changtong Jie, on the west side of

Laodong Park near the Civil Aviation Hotel and CAAC.

PSB This is just to the north-east of Zhongshan Square.

Money You should be aware that Dalian's luxury hotels will *not* change money for people staying elsewhere – this service is for hotel guests only. You can try giving a false room number, but some hotels (the Holiday Inn for example) actually check the records before allowing you to change money. The Bank of China is at 9 Zhongshan Square.

■ PLACES TO STAY

3	Holiday Inn
4	Nongken Hotel
5	CAAC & Civil Aviation Hotel
9	Eastern Hotel
11	Dalian Hotel I
13	Dalian Hotel II
14	Grand Hotel
16	International Hotel
17	Furama Hotel
19	Friendship Store & Hotel
21	Nanshan Hotel

▼ PLACES TO EAT

| 7 | Dajiale Fast Food Restaurant |
| 18 | International Seamen's Club |

OTHER

1	North Railway Station
2	Dalian Railway Station
6	CITS
8	Bus to Dandong
10	Post Office
12	Bank of China
15	PSB
20	Harbour Passenger Terminal
22	East Railway Station

■ PLACES TO STAY

3	九州饭店
4	农垦宾馆
5	民航大厦
9	东方饭店
11	大连饭店
13	大连宾馆
14	大连博览大酒店
16	国际大酒店
17	富丽华大酒店
19	友谊商店 ／ 宾馆
21	南山宾馆

▼ PLACES TO EAT

| 7 | 大家乐快餐厅 |
| 18 | 海员俱乐部 |

OTHER

1	大连北站
2	大连火车站
6	中国国际旅行社
8	往丹东汽车站
10	邮局
12	中国银行
15	公安局外事科
20	大连港客运站
22	大连东站

LIAONING

Post & Telecommunications The post and telephone office is at 10 Zhongshan Square, near the Bank of China.

Stalin Square

(sīdàlín guǎngchǎng) 斯大林广场

Stalin seems to be held in high esteem in this part of China. The square commemorates liberation from Japan in 1945 and the memorial was set up in 1954. During the Cultural Revolution, Stalin Square was used for political rallies. It's on the west end of Zhongshan Lu (on the south side) near city hall.

Other Attractions

For the individual traveller, access to the port facilities (probably one of Dalian's top sights) is limited. You'll have to be content with the large **Natural History Museum** *(zìrán bówùguǎn)* behind the station, with its stuffed sealife. It's open on Tuesday, Thurs-

day, Saturday and Sunday from 8 am to 4 pm. **Laodong Park** *(láodòng gōngyuán)*, in the centre of town, offers good city views. There's also an assortment of **handicraft factories**, whose products include glasswork and shell mosaic.

Places to Stay – bottom end

Dalian competes with Tianjin for the title of 'most expensive city in China'. Prices are an absolute rip-off in most hotels. The few hotels which do charge reasonable prices are permanently full. You can try your luck at the low-end of the hotel battlefield, but if this fails you may find yourself booking a seat on the first hard sleeper (even soft sleeper) to anywhere – it's definitely cheaper than most Dalian hotels.

There is one ray of hope. Some colleges in Dalian will allow foreigners to stay in the dormitories. The problem is one of supply and demand – when they say they're full, they mean it. If you do get in, it can be very cheap – as low as Y10 for a bed but conditions can be horrendous. Representatives from the schools often congregate around the railway station exits about 6 pm – these people may even have a bus to bring you to the school.

One school which says they will accept foreigners is the *Military Medical College* (☎ 2681712 ext 4271) (*jūnyī xuéxiào*). This place is a long way south-east of the centre – take trolley No 102 and get off at the stop called Xiuyue Jie. Bus No 21 to the terminal also gets you there. It's worth calling first to see if they have space, but it's Chinese-speaking only.

Besides the schools, your next-best hope is the *Friendship Hotel* (☎ 2634121) (*yǒuyí bīnguǎn*). This is on the 3rd floor, above the Friendship Store at 137 Sidalin Lu. Doubles cost Y100 – it's not really expensive, but the problem is that it's forever full. You could try arriving at 6 am or so and wait until someone checks out, but you might have to join a queue of other hopefuls.

Places to Stay – middle

The *Eastern Hotel* (*dōngfāng fàndiàn*) is at 28 Zhongshan Lu, not far from the railway station. At Y160, it's no bargain but still cheaper than most Dalian hotels. For that reason, this place is also almost always full.

The seven-storey *Dalian Hotel I* (☎ 2633171) (*dàlián fàndiàn*) is at 6 Shanghai Lu. Singles/doubles go for Y136/175. Again, it tends to book out solid. It's worth noting that there is another Dalian Hotel, with the same name in English but a different Chinese name. The designation of 'I' and 'II' is our own – the Dalian Hotel II is very expensive.

The *Nongken Hotel* (*nóngkěn bīnguǎn*) is a one-star dump charging three-star prices. Doubles cost Y250. It looks like a Chinese-only hotel (there is no English sign), but foreigners can stay here. Since it's so absurdly expensive for such grotty rooms, there are usually vacancies when other hotels

are full. It's on Zhongshan Lu just east of the CAAC office.

Places to Stay – top end

The vast majority of Dalian hotels are top end, at least in price if not in quality. Prices are at least as high as those in Europe and the USA, if not higher. The rooms are comfortable but the level of service is, with few exceptions, abysmal. Not surprisingly, these places often have plenty of vacant rooms while the cheap places are packed out solid.

The *Dalian Hotel II* (☎ 2633111) (*dàlián bīnguǎn*) is at 7 Zhongshan Square. It's an ancient building with a renovated interior. Doubles cost a cool Y418. This hotel was used in a scene in the movie *The Last Emperor*. No doubt when Emperor Puyi was here, the rates were lower.

One of the newest places in town is the *Grand Hotel* (*bólǎn dàjiǔdiàn*) on Jiefang Jie behind the Dalian Hotel. Doubles here start at Y465.

The *Nanshan Hotel* (☎ 2638751) (*nánshān bīnguǎn*), 56 Fenglin Jie, Zhongshanqu, has a dozen villas tucked into very pleasant gardens. It once had the atmosphere of a country club, but has now been renovated and resembles a battleship. Doubles start at Y500. To get there take the round-the-city unnumbered bus; or take tramcar No 201 and then change to bus No 12 or walk uphill.

The *International Hotel* (☎ 2634825) (*guójì dàjiǔdiàn*), 9 Sidalin Lu, has doubles for Y460 plus a 10% service charge.

The *Civil Aviation Hotel* (*mínháng dàshà*) is run by CAAC and is next to their ticket office. Doubles cost a whopping Y582. If you're booked on one of CAAC's hopelessly delayed flights, you might even get to stay here for free.

The *Furama Hotel* (☎ 2630888; fax 2804455) (*fùlìhuá dàjiǔdiàn*) at 74 Sidalin Lu is the glitziest hotel in town, with 500 rooms. It's an Overseas Chinese hang-out and even has its own Friendship Store. Doubles start from Y765 plus 15% surcharge.

The *Holiday Inn* (☎ 2630538) (*jiǔzhōu fàndiàn*) costs Y632 for a single. It's unique among Dalian's luxury hotels in that it is convenient – right next to the railway station. It's not unique in having sneering, surly staff.

Another possibility is the *Bangchuidao Guesthouse* (☎ 2635131) *(bàngchuídǎo bīnguǎn)* to the east of the town on the coast. It's next to an exclusive beach and there is no way to reach it except by taxi. A lot of tour groups stay here.

Places to Eat

The *Dajiale Fast Food Restaurant (dàjiālè kuài cāntīng)* is next to the long-distance bus terminal. The name means 'everybody happy', and despite the 'fast food' stigma, the cuisine is Chinese, not hamburgers. The restaurant is notable for showing pirated rock music videos. Prices are low.

People make the trip to Dalian to gorge themselves on seafood. The *Haiwei Seafood Restaurant (hǎiwèi fàndiàn)*, near the railway station at 85 Zhongshan Lu, serves prawns, sea cucumbers and other exotic marine wildlife. Tianjin Jie is the wining-dining-shopping street within walking range of the railway station.

The *International Seamen's Club (hǎiyuán jùlèbù)*, on the east end of Sidalin Lu, has several dining sections on the 2nd floor. It's not cheap, but you can have a peaceful plate of fried dumplings *(guōtiē)*. *Xinghai Park*, out by the beachfront, has a kind of elevated clubhouse with beach umbrellas – specialties include giant prawns, fish and beer, and in season there's an open-air view overlooking the windsurfers and sunbathers.

Dalian is a prime apple-growing region – you can sample fresh fruit from the stalls all around the railway station.

Entertainment

The Copacabana of Dalian is the International Seamen's Club, open until 10.30 pm, with dining and banquet rooms, a bar where sailors doze with their stale beers to the chirp of video-game machines, and a disco. It has a full-size theatre with weekend offerings – Beijing opera or perhaps a film or an acrobat show.

Getting There & Away

Air Dalian has both domestic and international air connections. CAAC and Dragonair fly to/from Hong Kong for HK$2050. CAAC and All Nippon Airways go to Tokyo and Fukuoka. Dragonair (☎ 2638238 ext 601) has an office on the 6th floor of the International Hotel, 9 Sidalin Lu. Nippon Airways (☎ 2639744) also has its office in the International Hotel, but you can book through CITS. CAAC is at 143 Zhongshan Lu next to the Civil Aviation Hotel. Domestic flights and fares are:

Destination	Fare	Destination	Fare
Beijing	Y360	Canton	Y1120
Changsha	Y900	Chengdu,	
Fuzhou	Y840	Chongqing	Y1000
Haikou,		Harbin	Y430
Hangzhou	Y580	Kunming	Y1290
Nanjing	Y460	Shanghai	Y530
Shantou	Y1010	Shenyang	Y180
Shenzhen	Y1500	Ürümqi	Y1840
Wenzhou	Y1080	Xiamen	Y960

Bus There are buses to Dandong, Fushun and Jinzhou. The government-run long-distance bus station is one block south of the railway station. There is a private bus station just next to CITS. These buses are slightly cheaper, but don't look as safe. Book your ticket peacefully the day before or arrive at the last minute and fight for it. Several buses leave daily for Dandong between 6 and 8 am. There is one night bus at 8 pm. The trip takes nine hours

Train There are nine trains daily to Shenyang and the trip takes six hours. From Shenyang there are direct trains to Beijing and Harbin.

A useful train to know about is No 303, which departs from Dalian at 11.48 pm, arriving in Jilin (via Shenyang) the next day at 5.22 pm. It's useful because a sleeper on this train will save you a night's accommodation in horribly expensive Dalian. The other nice feature of this train is that it's usually very easy to get a hard sleeper (Y125 to Jilin).

Foreigners can book tickets on the 2nd floor of the railway station at window No 5

– it's FEC but there is usually no queue and no waiting! If you're taking the evening train, you have to book after 6 pm but ask just to be sure.

Boat The booking office is at the boat terminal, east of the Seamen's Club, and has a left-luggage office (modern facilities, too). Providing you have a ticket, you can sleep in the comfy building beside the booking office. Since the railway lines from Dalian have to go all the way round the peninsula before proceeding south, boats can actually save you time as well as money.

There are boats to Yantai or Shanghai daily, to Qingdao every other day, to Canton every four to six days, to Tanggu (the port of Tianjin) every four to six days. There are other departures to Weihai, Longkou, Shidao and Yingkou. To Shanghai it takes about 40 hours, to Qingdao it's about 28 hours, and to Yantai about eight hours. Even 3rd class is comfortable, but avoid cargo class. Meals are available and seasickness pills are free.

Getting Around
To/From the Airport The airport is 15 km from the centre and taxi drivers ask Y40 or more for the journey.

Bus Bus No 13 runs from the railway station area, behind the Friendship Store, and to the boat terminal. Tramcar No 201 starts from the railway station, heads in the same direction as bus No 13, but turns south before the Friendship Store and proceeds east (it's good for getting part of the way to the Nanshan Hotel). There is a round-the-city bus with no number, but the characters for circle route (*huán lù*) appear on the destination sign. This bus is useful for a tour through Dalian.

Taxi Drivers have meters but seldom use them. It's usually a flat Y10 for anywhere within the city.

AROUND DALIAN
Dalian is actually a health resort of sorts, so beaches (*hǎishuǐ yùchǎng*) with their attached parks are the attraction. The beach five km to the south-east is for Western VIPs and is bordered by the exclusive Bangchuidao Guesthouse. **Laohutan Park** (*lǎohǔtān gōngyuán*) has a rocky beach that's rather poor for swimming (you can get there on bus No 102 from the city centre).

Small **Fujiazhuang Beach** (*fùjiāzhuāng hǎishuǐ yùchǎng*) is the best – it has fine sand and rock outcrops in the deep bay, and is excellent for swimming but has few facilities. Like the other beaches, this one has a sanatorium nearby; the patients sometimes venture out in their pyjamas to assist rubber-booted fishing crews hauling in their catch. The beach is a fair way out of town – take bus No 102 and then change to bus No 5.

Five km to the south-west is Xinghai Park & Beach (*xīnghǎi gōngyuán*) – it's crowded and a little on the slimy side, but it's got a good seafood restaurant (take bus No 2, or else take tramcar No 201 and then change to tramcar No 202).

BENXI
(*běnxī*) 本溪
About two hours' drive south-east of Shenyang is Benxi, an iron, steel and coal-mining town with a cement works. Liaoning Province accounts for one-tenth of national coal production, with eight large-scale mining areas.

Benxi is notable as one of the most polluted cities in the world – astronauts have commented that the Great Wall and Benxi's pollution were the two recognisable human-made features of China that could be seen from outer space. Big chimneys belch flames and thick black smoke – it's a scene straight from hell. It makes interesting photography though. The train between Shenyang and Dandong stops here briefly – long enough for most travellers.

The main reason some tourists traipse out to Benxi is to see the **Benxi Water Cavern** (*běnxī shuǐdòng*) 27 km east of town. There are boat trips through the cave. It's chilly inside but you can hire an overcoat. The Chinese have given the stalactites and stalagmites weird names, and the associated stories may require an almighty leap of imagination.

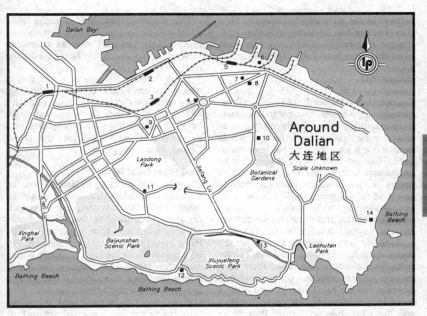

Around
Dalian
大连地区
Scale Unknown

1	Shahekou Railway Station	1 沙河口站
2	North Railway Station	2 大连北站
3	Dalian Railway Station	3 大连火车站
4	Dalian Hotel	4 大连饭店
5	East Railway Station	5 大连东站
6	Harbour Passenger Terminal	6 大连港客运站
7	International Seamen's Club	7 海员俱乐部
8	Friendship Store & Hotel	8 友谊商店/宾馆
9	CAAC	9 中国民航
10	Nanshan Hotel	10 南山宾馆
11	TV Tower	11 电视台
12	Fujiazhuang Resort	12 付家庄景区
13	Military Medical College	13 军医学校
14	Bangchuidao Guesthouse	14 棒棰岛宾馆

BINGYU VALLEY
(bīngyù gōu) 冰峪谷

According to CITS, this is Liaoning's answer to Guilin and Yangshuo. The valley has a number of towering, vertical rock formations with a river meandering between them. It's pretty, but it's not likely to replace Guilin on the travellers' circuit. Still, you might want to have a look.

The valley is 250 km north-east of Dalian. Take a bus from the long-distance bus station to Zhuanghe *(zhuānghé)*, a town about halfway between Dalian and Dandong. Then take another bus to Bingyu Scenic Area *(bīngyù fēngjǐn qū)*. There is a very basic hotel or you can camp for Y25, tent included.

DANDONG
(dāndōng) 丹东

Dandong lies at the border of Liaoning Province and North Korea. Along with Dalian and Yingkou, this is one of the three key trading and communication ports for the whole north-eastern area. The city has been designated one of Liaoning's major export production centres and the production of things like wristwatches, knitwear, printing and foodstuffs is going up. This is the home of Ganoderma – wrinkle-killer face cream made from a rare and expensive mushroom. You can buy tussah silk at the silk factory.

Dandong isn't a cultural Mecca, but it's clean, leafy, easy to cover and doesn't suffer from overcrowding. However, there isn't much to see here other than the view of North Korea across the Yalu River. Many travellers come here to continue onwards to Tonghua and the Changbaishan Nature Reserve in Jilin Province.

Information

The CITS office (☎ 27721) is inside the Dandong Guesthouse and will supply a brochure but no maps. Maps are available only from Xinhua Bookstore, near the post office. They show hardly any street names and therefore aren't too useful, but at least the bus routes are shown.

Things to See

Dandong's chief attraction is its location on the North Korean border (for information on visiting North Korea from Dandong, see Sinuiju, in the Around Dandong section).

The **Yalu River Park** *(yālü jiāng gōngyuán)* is a favourite picnic site, full of photographers trying to squeeze Mum, Dad, kids, Granma and Granpa into the standard 'I visited the Sino-Korean border' shot which has to include the bridge as a backdrop. You can even get your portrait taken in the cockpit of a Chinese MIG fighter.

The **Jinjiangshan Park** *(jǐnjiāng shān gōngyuán)* is close to Dandong Guesthouse. From the top of the park there's a panoramic view of the city and North Korea across the river.

North Korean TV operates one station which you can easily receive in Dandong. They speak only in Korean, but if you can't understand what they're saying, that might be a blessing – the station functions as a personal portrait studio for 'the Great Leader, Kim Il-sung'.

Yalu River Boat Ride

If you want to get close to North Korea, an amusing boat ride will take you down the middle of the Yalu River, which is the boundary line. Boats leave at about 9 am (more often on weekends) from a pier at the Yalu River Park. Photography is not allowed. The boat passes under the bridge, runs to within 10 metres of the Korean side, and then makes a long loop back down the Chinese side to the pier. There's nothing stunning about what you see: rusty tubs being welded, antiquated tubs being loaded, cheerful schoolkids waving, a steam engine chuffing across the bridge. Sinuiju itself is deliberately hidden behind an embankment topped with trees, to keep foreigners with binoculars and telephoto lenses from stealing North Korea's military secrets.

There are, in fact, two bridges – well, one and a half. The original steel-span bridge was 'accidentally' strafed in 1950 by the Americans, who also 'accidentally' bombed the airstrip at Dandong. The Koreans have dismantled this bridge as far as the mid-river boundary line. All that's left is a row of piers on the Korean side and half a bridge (still showing shrapnel pockmarks) on the Chinese side. The present bridge runs parallel to the old one.

Places to Stay

The *Friendship Guesthouse (yǒuyí bīnguǎn)*, a 10-minute walk south of the railway station, is a great place to stay – rooms cost Y100 and are very clean, with a view of the river. The problem is that it's permanently

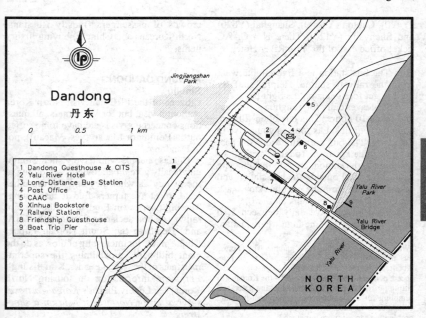

Dandong
丹东

0   0.5   1 km

1 Dandong Guesthouse & CITS
2 Yalu River Hotel
3 Long-Distance Bus Station
4 Post Office
5 CAAC
6 Xinhua Bookstore
7 Railway Station
8 Friendship Guesthouse
9 Boat Trip Pier

Jingjiangshan Park

Yalu River Park

Yalu River Bridge

Yalu River

NORTH KOREA

1	丹东宾馆 ／中国国际旅行社
2	鸭绿江大厦
3	长途汽车站
4	邮局
5	中国民航
6	新华书店
7	火车站
8	友谊宾馆
9	旅游码头

'all full'. The hotel isn't very large and seems to be a popular hang-out for cadres, so maybe it really is full.

The *Yalu River Hotel* (☎ 25901) *(yālü jiāng dàshà)*, 87 Jiuwei Lu, is a shiny, Sino-Japanese joint-venture with 300 rooms in the centre of town. Prices are steep, with doubles starting at Y260.

The *Dandong Guesthouse* (☎ 27312, 27313) *(dāndōng bīnguǎn)* is at 2 Shanshang Jie, about two km or half an hour's walk uphill from the railway station. Apart from its inconvenient location, the mixture of main buildings and villas set in a park is pleasant. Doubles start at Y250 but can be bargained down to Y150 or less after much wrangling and showing of student ID. The rooms all have TV, but if you turn off the telly it's just serenading crickets and the lonesome whistling of steam locomotives shunting outside.

Places to Eat
The *Dandong Guesthouse* offers pricey (FEC only) and unexciting food, including Western breakfasts. The food scene is more lively downtown, where the free-enterprise merchants have set up red lanterns and neon lights to attract passers-by. At a pinch you can get food at the stalls in the railway station, which are open all night.

Getting There & Away
Air There are regular flights to Beijing

(Y420), Canton (Y1400), Shanghai (Y620) and Shenyang (Y120). There is a CAAC ticket office east of the Yalu River Hotel.

Bus The bus station is a five-minute walk from the railway station. Helpful staff try hard to get foreigners on the right bus.

A bus leaves daily for Tonghua at 6.30 am and takes 10 hours. This bus often fills up, so book your ticket as soon as you arrive in Dandong. The bus normally drops off passengers three km from Tonghua station. To continue to the station, cross to the opposite side of the road outside the bus station and take a city bus from the next bus stop – ask for the railway station (huǒchē zhàn).

Several buses leave daily between 5.10 and 6.40 am for the nine-hour trip to Dalian.

Whichever bus you take, it's a gamble. The express bus trip from Dalian to Dandong was some ride. About 10 minutes after departure – considering the speed, perhaps I should say take-off – the Korean girl sitting in front of me was already looking green and fumbling for the window catch. Her well-meaning companions insisted that the best solution for her problem was to eat more tomatoes.

Meanwhile the driver decided to improve his banshee act by using not only his double air-horns but also the outside loudspeaker to harangue traffic in front. His tactic was to move up within three inches of the back bumper of the vehicle in front and then scream in Chinese, 'Move it, move it! Let the vehicle behind overtake!'. Donkey-carts, walking tractors, jeeps – all scattered like buckshot.

The Korean girl succumbed to motion sickness and threw up out of the window. Since the window was very small, the girl had quite a struggle before she finally managed to get her head outside. Traffic coming from the other direction came within a hair's breadth of knocking her block off. The driver kept flying along, turned the internal loudspeaker on and blasted the girl: 'Hey you behind! Get your head in! Get it in! Observe safety! Observe safety!'. While his voice rose to a frenzy, he turned in his seat to look back and the bus swayed violently.

Train There are direct trains to Dandong from Shenyang and Changchun; the trip from Shenyang takes five hours. The combination train from Pyongyang to Moscow and Pyongyang to Beijing passes through Dandong on Saturday at about 3 pm. Buy a platform ticket and watch the international crowds of passengers (mostly Russians, North Koreans and Chinese) buying luxury items.

AROUND DANDONG
Sinuiju
Citizens of the PRC can visit North Korea without a visa, but for Westerners, all questions concerning visas etc have to be sorted out in Beijing or Macau (yes, Macau!), not in Dandong.

Chinese people who have visited Sinuiju universally give it bad reviews – 'nothing to see or buy' is what they say. On the other hand, most Westerners find it fascinating. The big posters (in English) in the Sinuiju railway station declaring 'Death to the USA' and 'Death to the South Korean Puppet Clique' make for interesting photos, as do the giant billboards proclaiming the superhuman feats of the 'Great Leader, Kim Il-sung'. For more information on touring North Korea, see Lonely Planet's *Korea – a travel survival kit* or *North-East Asia on a shoestring*.

Getting There & Away There are four buses weekly from Dandong to Sinuiju. There are also twice-weekly international trains passing through Dandong and Sinuiju from Beijing to Pyongyang, the capital of North Korea. Dandong CITS arranges quickie excursions across the Yalu River to the Korean city of Sinuiju on the other side of the bridge.

Fenghuangshan
About 52 km north-west of Dandong is the town of Fengcheng. The nearby mountain, Fenghuangshan, is 840 metres high and dotted with temples, monasteries and pagodas from the Tang, Ming and Qing dynasties. The Fenghuang Mountain Temple Fair takes place in April and reportedly attracts thousands of people. Fenghuangshan is one hour from Dandong by either train or bus. The express train does not stop here, but you do get a view of the mountain.

Top: Genghis Khan's mausoleum, Dongshen, Inner Mongolia (Strauss)
Bottom: Tibetan children, Xiahe, Gansu (CL)

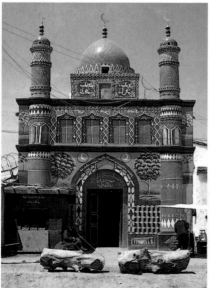

Top: Karakoram Highway, near Tashkurgan, Xinjiang (CB)
Left: Mosque at Ürümqi, Xinjiang (AS)
Right: Taking care of business, Kashgar, Xinjiang (CT)

Wulongbei Hot Springs
(wǔlóngbēi wēnquán)
The springs are about 20 km north of
Dandong on the road to Fengcheng. There's
a guesthouse here and you could try the
springs.

Dagushan
Dagushan, where there are several groups of
Taoist temples dating from the Tang
Dynasty, lies close to the town of Gushan –
about 90 km south-west of Dandong.

Jilin 吉林

Capital: Changchun
CHANGCHUN
(chángchūn) 长春
Changchun, with its broad leafy avenues, is a well laid-out but rather dull city. The Japanese, who developed it as the capital of 'Manchukuo' between 1933 and 1945, built the uninspiring militaristic structures. In 1945 the Russians arrived in Changchun on a looting spree; when they departed in 1946, the Kuomintang moved in to occupy the cities of the north-east, only to find themselves surrounded by the Communists in the countryside. The Communists had assembled a formidable array of scrounged and captured weaponry, even former Japanese tanks and US jeeps, and Changchun saw more than a few of them in action. The Communists took over the city in 1948.

China's first car-manufacturing plant was set up here in the 1950s with Soviet assistance, starting with 95-horsepower Jiefang (Liberation) trucks, and moving on to make bigger and better things like the Red Flag limousines. CITS can arrange a tour. Lesser factories (tractor, locomotives, train coach, carpet, fur, wood-carving) may be accessible.

Travellers have little reason to visit Changchun except to use it as a transit point to someplace else. The hotel situation is awful – all cheap places are off limits to foreigners.

Information
The CITS office (☎ 647052) is adjacent to the Changbaishan Hotel in the Bank of China Building. The PSB is on the south-west corner of Renmin Square near the Bank of China.

The Bank of China is on the 3rd floor of the rear building of the Changbaishan Hotel complex. There is another Bank of China on the north-west corner of Renmin Square (*rénmín guǎngchǎng*), which is at the intersection of Xi'an Dajie and Sidalin Dajie.

The post office is on Sidalin Dajie, two blocks south of the railway station.

Puppet Emperor's Palace & Exhibition Hall
(wěihuánggōng) 伪皇宫
No, this place has nothing to do with seeing puppet shows. Henry Puyi was the last person to ascend to the dragon throne. He was two years old at the time and was forced to abdicate just six years later when the 1911 revolution swept the country. He lived in exile in Tianjin and in 1935 was spirited away to Changchun by the Japanese invaders and set up as the 'puppet emperor' of Manchukuo in 1932. He lived in Changchun for the next 14 years. Puyi was captured by the Russians in 1945 and was only returned to China sometime in the late 1950s, where he was allowed to work as a gardener at one of the colleges in Beijing. He died of cancer in 1967, thus ending a life which had largely been governed by others. His story was the basis for the award-winning film *The Last Emperor*.

South Lake Park
(nánhú gōngyuán) 南湖公园
The largest park in the city is South Lake Park. It has the usual ponds, pavilions and wooden bridges and is right near the

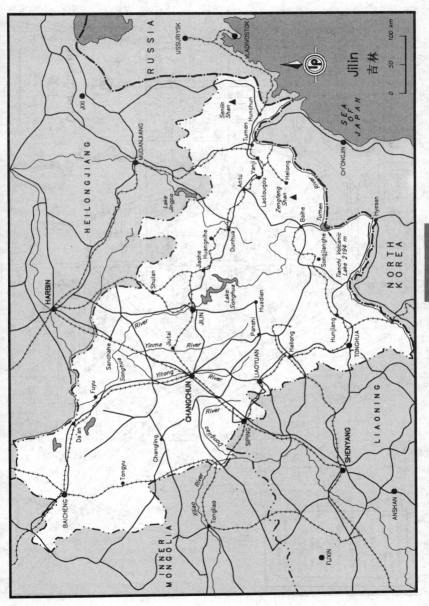

JILIN

JILIN

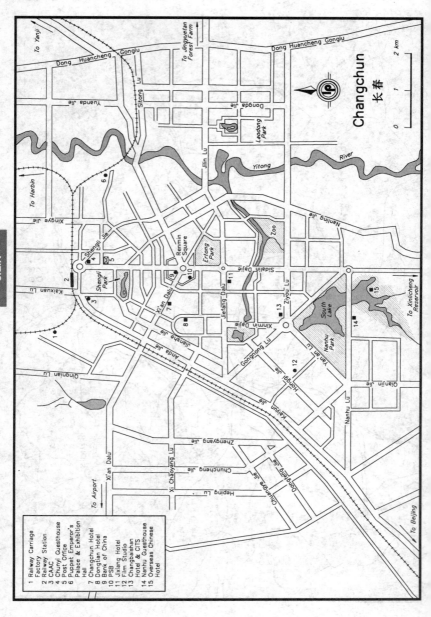

Changchun 长春

1 Railway Carriage
  Factory
2 Railway Station
3 CAAC
4 Chunyi Guesthouse
5 Post Office
6 Puppet Emperor's
  Palace & Exhibition
  Hall
7 Changchun Hotel
8 Dongtian Hotel
9 Bank of China
10 PSB
11 Jixiang Hotel
12 Film Studio
13 Changbaishan
  Hotel & CITS
14 Nanhu Guesthouse
15 Overseas Chinese
  Hotel

1	客车工厂
2	火车站
3	中国民航
4	春谊宾馆
5	邮局
6	伪皇宫
7	长春宾馆
8	洞天宾馆
9	中国银行
10	公安局外事科
11	吉香宾馆
12	长春电影制片厂
13	长白山宾馆／中国国际旅行社
14	南湖宾馆
15	华侨饭店

Changbaishan Hotel. From the station, take trolley-bus No 62 or 63.

Changchun Film Studio
(chángchūndiànyǐng zhìpiànchǎng)
长春电影制片厂
The studio got its start during the civil war, making documentaries. You aren't likely to get inside unless you join a CITS tour, but a Chinese tour may be possible.

Places to Stay
The prices foreigners are expected to pay for accommodation in Changchun are nothing short of insane. Considering that Changchun has so little to offer, with such expensive hotel rooms it's not surprising that most foreigners give this city a miss.

On the south side of town, there are two universities which *might* let you stay in their dormitories, but this depends on the stars and the wind direction. The two campuses are the *North-east Normal University (dōngběi shīfàn dàxué)* and *Jilin Polytechnic University (jílín gōngyè dàxué)*, both on Sidalin Dajie, nine km from the railway station – take bus No 6.

The *Chunyi Guesthouse* (☎ 279966; fax 860171) *(chūnyí bīnguǎn)*, 2 Sidalin Dajie, is one block south of the railway station. They charge Y245 for big, pleasant double rooms with private bath. The staff are friendly.

The main tourist place is the *Changbaishan Hotel* (☎ 883551; fax 882003) *(chángbáishān bīnguǎn)*. Doubles cost Y290. CITS is in the Bank of China building behind the hotel. Take trolley-bus No 62 or 63.

The *Changchun Hotel* (☎ 822661) *(chángchūn bīnguǎn)*, 10 Xinhua Lu, is a short walk west of Renmin Square. Doubles cost Y260.

The *Jixiang Hotel (jíxiáng dàjiǔdiàn)* is on Jiefang Dalu and gets rather few foreign visitors. Doubles cost Y240.

The main cadre hang-out is the exclusive *Nanhu Guesthouse (nánhú bīnguǎn)*, where doubles cost from Y240 to Y3400, and villas cost a trifling Y1500.

Places to Eat
Mouth-watering banquet fare will undoubtedly surface in the classier hotels for a hefty price, but on the streets the level of sanitation will quickly cure your hunger pangs without you having to eat anything at all! The restaurants around the railway station are probably your best bet for a fast and cheap meal. English menus are as rare as a cheap hotel room in Changchun.

Getting There & Away
Air There are flights to Beijing (Y470), Canton (Y1440), Chengdu (Y1310), Hangzhou (Y1000), Nanjing (Y760), Shanghai (Y850), Shenyang, Shenzhen (Y1630) and Xiamen (Y1280). The CAAC office (☎ 39772) is at 2 Liaoning Lu, close to the railway station.

Bus You can catch buses to Jilin (2½ hours, Y13) from in front of the railway station. These depart about once every 20 minutes throughout the day.

Train At the time of writing, the railway station was being rebuilt and everything was a mess. Hopefully it will be sorted out by the time you get there. We found that buying tickets in RMB was entirely possible at the railway station without showing any sort of student ID, but sleepers are impossible to come by unless bought through a hotel or CITS (paying FEC).

There are frequent trains heading north to Harbin (four hours) and south to Shenyang (five hours). Trains are also frequent to Jilin, and there is an overnight train for Yanji (departs 6.40 pm, arrives 6.30 am), which is the route you take to Changbaishan.

JILIN
(jílín) 吉林

East of Changchun is the city of Jilin. A Chinese pamphlet puts it in a nutshell:

Under the guidance of Chairman Mao's revolutionary line, it has made rapid progress in industrial and agricultural production...From a desolate consumer city, Kirin (Jilin) has become a rising industrial city with emphasis on chemical and power industries.

The city of Jilin today is home to 1.3 million people. For travellers, the area is mainly of interest for its winter sports and scenery – if you can survive the cold.

Information

The CITS office (☎ 453773) is in the Xiguan Hotel. Their competitor, CYTS (☎ 456787) is in the Dongguan Hotel.

Most hotels *do not* change money despite the big sign at the reception desks saying 'Foreign Exchange'. The only place that reliably changes money is the Bank of China, adjacent to the Milky Way Hotel.

Ice-Rimmed Trees
(shù guà) (wù sōng) 树挂 / 雾凇

Three large chemical plants were built after 1949. The Fengman Hydroelectric Station, built by the Japanese, disassembled by the Russians and put back together by the Chinese, fuels these enterprises, and provides Jilin with an unusual tourist attraction: water passing from artificial Songhua Lake through the power plant becomes a warm, steamy current that merges with the Songhua River and prevents it from freezing. Overnight, vapour rising from the river meets the - 20°C weather, causing condensation on the

branches of pines and willows on a 20-km stretch of the bank. During the Lunar New Year (late January to mid-February), hordes of Japanese and Overseas Chinese come for the resulting icicle show. To reach this hydroelectric station, take bus No 9 from the roundabout north of the Xiguan Hotel.

Wen Temple
(wén miào) 文庙

Just east of the Jiangcheng Hotel is the Wen Temple, Jilin's largest. It's also known as the Confucius Temple *(kǒng miào)*. From the railway station take bus No 13.

Beishan Park
(běishān gōngyuán) 北山公园

If you need a little exercise, Beishan Park is a hilly area on the west side of town with temples, pavilions, forests and footpaths. The scenery is mellow enough and preferable to Jilin's industrial smokestacks. On the west side of the park is Taoyuan Mountain, which is worth a short hike.

Bus No 7 from the railway station terminates right in front of the park entrance. If you're on a local train, the Beishan railway station is near the park.

Other Sights

In 1976, the Jilin area received a heavy meteorite shower, and the largest bit, weighing 1770 kg, is on view in the meteorite exhibition hall (take bus No 3 from outside the Dongguan Hotel).

It's possible to visit the Jilin Special Products Research Centre *(lóngtánshān lùchǎng)*, where there is a deer park, ginseng garden and a collection of sables. Take bus No 12 from the station and get off on the other side of the bridge over the Songhua River.

Ice Lantern Festival
(bīngdēng jié) 冰灯节

Jilin, like Harbin, has an ice lantern festival, held at Jiangnan Park on the south side of the Songhua River. Locals claim that Jilin invented the ice lantern festival and Harbin copied it. True or not, Harbin's displays are now considered to those of Jilin, but competition between the two cities should produce better ice sculptures.

Places to Stay

Accommodation is overpriced in Jilin but it's not as extreme as the situation in nearby Changchun. It's likely to be most difficult to find a place to stay in January, the peak season for viewing the ice-rimmed trees.

The *Dongguan Hotel* (☎ 454272) (*dōng-guān bīnguǎn*), 223 Songjiang Lu, is the cheapest but it's hardly a bargain. Threadbare rooms for foreigners cost Y170 – Chinese pay less than a third this price. On the other hand, the restaurant on the 2nd floor offers good food at reasonable prices. The hotel is about three km from the station – take trolley-bus No 10 or a taxi for Y10.

Adjacent to the Dongguan Hotel is the upmarket *Jiangcheng Hotel* (☎ 457721) (*jiāngchéng bīnguǎn*). Living conditions are cosy here, but the Y240 price for a double may cause you to hesitate.

Perhaps the best deal in town is the *Milky Way Hotel* (☎ 241780; fax 241621) (*yínhé dàshà*), 175 Songjiang Lu. At least, it's a good deal if you get one of the standard rooms for Y180. Suites cost Y280. This hotel is notable for having a friendly manager who speaks good English.

The *Xiguan Hotel* (☎ 243141) (*xīguān bīnguǎn*), at 661 Songjiang Lu, is about seven km from the station. Take bus No 1 from the station to its terminal beside a roundabout; from there it's about a two-km walk along the riverside. This place is inconvenient to reach without a taxi. Doubles start at Y220.

Getting There & Away

Air There is an international flight from Jilin to Seoul, South Korea via Tianjin. CAAC flies between Jilin and Beijing (Y520), Canton (Y1490), Shanghai (Y900) and Shenyang (Y190).

Bus There are buses between Jilin and Changchun approximately once every 20 minutes throughout the day. The trip takes 2½ hours and costs Y13. The long-distance bus station (*chà lù xiāng*) is one long block west of the railway station.

Train There is a direct rail service between Jilin and Changchun about once every hour in each direction. There are also direct trains to Harbin (four hours) and Yanji.

Getting Around

Although taxis congregate around the railway station and seem to be plentiful on the streets, they are often occupied – allow plenty of time to get where you want to go. Rates are a flat Y10 anywhere within the city.

AROUND JILIN

If you want to try some elementary ski slopes, there's the **Songhuahu Qingshan Ski Resort** (*sōnghuā hú qīngshān huá xuě cháng*) at 935 metres elevation, 16 km southeast of Jilin and just east of Fengman. Any hotel in Jilin can provide further details about snow conditions, lift operation, transport and hire of equipment. There is also a hotel at the ski resort.

During the summer weekends and holidays, the lake (*sōnghuā hú*) is a popular hang-out for locals.

TIANCHI

(*tiānchí*) 天池

Tianchi – the Lake of Heaven – is in the Changbaishan (Ever-White Mountains) Nature Reserve. The reserve is China's largest, covering 210,000 hectares of dense virgin forest. The forest is divided into a semi-protected area where limited lumbering and hunting are permitted, and a protected area where neither is allowed. Because of elevation changes, there is wide variation in animal and plant life. From 700 to 1000 metres above sea level there are mixed coniferous and broad-leaf trees (including white birch and Korean pines); from 1000 to 1800 metres, there are cold-resistant coniferous trees such as dragon spruce and fir; from 1800 to 2000 metres is another forest belt; above 2000 metres it's alpine tundra, treeless and windy. For the

JILIN

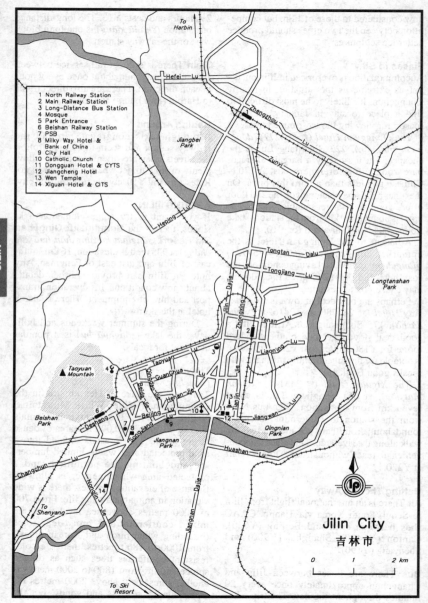

1 North Railway Station
2 Main Railway Station
3 Long-Distance Bus Station
4 Mosque
5 Park Entrance
6 Beishan Railway Station
7 PSB
8 Milky Way Hotel &
  Bank of China
9 City Hall
10 Catholic Church
11 Dongguan Hotel & CYTS
12 Jiangcheng Hotel
13 Wen Temple
14 Xiguan Hotel & CITS

To Harbin

Hefei Lu
Zhengzhou Lu
Jiangbei Park
Zunyi Lu
Heping Lu
Tongtan Dalu
Tongjiang Lu
Longtanshan Park
Jilin Dajie
Zhongxing
Yanan Lu
Liaoning Lu
Taoyuan Mountain
Taoyuan Lu
Qingshao Lu
Guanghua Lu
Hunan Jie
Beida Jie
Tian Jie
Beishan Park
Desheng Lu
Beijing Lu
Songjiang Lu
Jiangwan
Qingnian Park
Jiangnan Park
Huashan Lu
Changchun Lu
Nordin Jie
Jiangnan Dajie

To Shenyang

To Ski Resort

Jilin City
吉林市

0   1   2 km

1	吉林火车北站
2	吉林火车站
3	岔路乡乡
4	清真寺
5	正门
6	北山火车站
7	公安局外事科
8	银河大厦/中国银行
9	市政府
10	天主教堂
11	东关宾馆/中国青旅行社
12	江城宾馆
13	文庙
14	西关宾馆/国际旅行社

budding natural scientist there's plenty to investigate. Some 300 medicinal plants grow within the reserve (including winter daphne, Asia bell and wild ginseng); and some very shy animal species make their home in the mountain range (the rarer ones being the protected cranes, deer and Manchurian tiger).

The reserve is a recent creation, first designated in 1960. During the Cultural Revolution all forestry and conservation work was suspended, and technical and scientific personnel were dispersed to menial jobs. Locals had a free-for-all season on the plant and animal life during this period.

Although Changbaishan was only opened to foreigners in 1982, it has been on the Chinese tour map for some time, with something like 40,000 visitors from the north-eastern provinces arriving each year between July and September. It's become particularly popular with South Koreans since 1992, when diplomatic relations with China were established.

Tianchi, at an elevation of 2194 metres, is the prime scenic spot. It's a volcanic crater-lake, five km from north to south, 3½ km from east to west, and 13 km in circumference. It's surrounded by jagged rock outcrops and peaks; three rivers run off the lake, with a rumbling 68-metre waterfall – the source of the Songhua and Tumen rivers.

Between 11 am and noon the tour buses

roll up to disgorge day-trippers who pose heroically for photos in front of the waterfall, stampede up the mountain, take a lakeside breather and then rush down again between 1 and 2 pm. The beauty of the place is badly marred by picnic detritus, smashed glass and discarded film wrappers.

Apart from midday, when the day-trippers take over, this is a peaceful place to stay for a couple of days and hike around. However, hiking at the lake itself is limited by the sharp peaks and their rock-strewn debris, and by the fact that the lake overlaps the Chinese-North Korean border – there's no tourist build-up yet on the Korean side. Cloud cover starts at 1000 metres and can be prevalent. The highest peak in the Changbaishan range is 2700 metres.

Enchanting scenery like this would not be complete in the Chinese world without a legend or mystery of some sort. Of the many myths, the most intriguing is the origin of the Manchu race. Three heavenly nymphs descended to the lake in search of earthly pleasure. They stripped off for a dip in the lake; along came a magic magpie which deposited a red berry on the dress of one of the maidens. When she picked it up to smell it, the berry flew through her lips into her stomach. The nymph became pregnant and gave birth to a handsome boy with an instant gift of the gab. He went on to foster the Manchus and their dynasty.

Dragons, and other things that go bump in the night, were believed to have sprung from the lake. In fact, they're still believed to do so. There have been intermittent sightings of unidentified swimming objects – China's own Loch Ness beasties or aquatic yetis or what have you. Tianchi is the deepest alpine lake in China – plumbed to a depth estimated at between 200 and 350 metres. Since it is frozen over in winter and temperatures are well below zero, it would take a pretty hardy monster to survive (even plankton can't). Sightings from the Chinese and North Korean sides point to a black bear, fond of swimming, and oblivious to the paperwork necessary for crossing these tight borders. On a more profound note, Chinese couples throw coins into the lake, pledging that their love will remain as deep as Tianchi, and as long-lived.

Access to the Changbaishan area has improved in recent years, but it's still a remote backwater and getting there is expeditionary. If you're planning to hike off the beaten tourist trail, it's advisable to bring

JILIN

dried food, sunscreen lotion, frog-oil tonic and other medical supplies, plus good hiking gear. High altitude weather is very fickle – no matter how warm and sunny it is in the morning, sudden high winds, rain, hail and dramatic drops in temperature are entirely possible by afternoon. In other words, hope for the best but be prepared for the worst.

The hot-spring bathhouse, where water from lake and underground sources is mixed, is close to the hotels. It costs Y1 for a communal dip and Y5 for a private cubicle. If you cross the nearby river via either the tree trunk or the bridge lower down, there's a forest path which leads to the dark, brooding Lesser Tianchi Lake.

Places to Stay

There are many cheap places to stay but all are off limits to foreigners. Big noses are herded into one of five official tourist hotels, all charging a standard Y220 FEC. At present, your options include the *Birch Hotel* (*yuèhuá lóu*), the *Nature Reserve Bureau Hotel* (*bǎohù jú bīnguǎn*), *Meilinsong Guesthouse* (*měilínsōng bīnguǎn*), *Yalin Hotel* (*yǎlín bīnguǎn*) and the *Tianchi Hotel* (*tiānchí fàndiàn*). The Tianchi Hotel is the largest but the Meilinsong Hotel is the only one open during the off-season.

If you have a sleeping bag, camping is a possibility though technically against the rules. Be prepared for possible thunderstorms and try to find a place far from curious Chinese spectators.

In Changbaishan, none of the cheap guesthouses would take me in and the staff were most unhelpful. I had my own tent and camped by Lesser Tianchi Lake together with a Danish guy I met on the bus from Baihe. Camping is not permitted but no officials bothered us. There were many curious Chinese tourists of course. The place was quite badly littered and the rusty pedal-boats in the lake disturbed the silence with their squeaking.

Getting There & Away

The *only* season when there's public transport access (when the road from Baihe to Changbaishan isn't iced over) is from late June to September. A winter trip is not

impossible, though you might need to rent a snowmobile, or at least a jeep with tyre chains. Chinese hikers come to see the autumn colourings – so the peak season with a high local turnover is from mid-July to mid-August.

There are two 'transit points' to Changbaishan: Antu and Baihe. Starting from Changchun, the route via Antu is faster and more common. Before you go, get a weather forecast from someone in Jilin, Changchun or Shenyang (during July and August will be no problem). Allow about five days for the round trip from, say, Shenyang. Tour buses go up the mountain in July and August, but at other times you may have trouble finding a bus from Baihe. The only other local transport is logging trucks and official jeeps – the latter are expensive to rent, and the drivers of the former are very reluctant to give rides.

Via Antu There are trains to Antu from Changchun – the trip takes 10 hours. The evening train departs from Changchun at 6.40 pm. There are sleepers available on this train, but you might have to book them all the way to Yanji. If you arrive in Antu at night you can sleep in the station waiting room. There is also a small hotel in Antu.

Buses for Baihe depart from 7.20 to 10.30 am. You can also get buses to Baihe from Yanji (further down the railway line) but then you'll have to backtrack. From Antu it takes five hours to travel the 125 km. Unless you arrive early in Baihe, you may find yourself waiting till the next morning for transport to Changbaishan, a further 40 km.

Special tourist buses run from Antu to the Changbaishan Hot Springs area in July and August – some of these have a three-day package trip, but you'll be with a mob of noisy, camera-clicking tourists. There are some trains from Shenyang to Antu.

Via Baihe Baihe is the end of the line as far as trains go – a scrapyard for locos. To get to Baihe from Jilin, Changchun or Shenyang, you must take a train or bus to Tonghua and then change to a train for Baihe. The morning train leaves Shenyang at 6.30 am for

Tonghua. From Dandong, there are buses to Tonghua departing at 6.30 am.

The two daily trains between Tonghua and Baihe have two steam locos (one pushing, the other pulling); there are no sleepers, only carriages with soft seats (green velvet) and hard wooden benches (ouch!). The 500-series trains take 10 hours of chuggalugging to cover the 277 km between Tonghua and Baihe. If you're overnighting, it's worth paying extra for soft seat in lieu of a sleeper. The soft-seat waiting room at Tonghua station is the lap of luxury. Look for the sign saying 'soft-seat waiting room' beside the packed hard-seat waiting room, and ring the red bell.

The early morning train arrives in Baihe at 5.20 am and is met by an excursion bus (*yóulǎn chē*), which takes you about three km into the town with its grubby shacks for breakfast before a change of buses for the two-hour trip to the mountain. Buses usually return from the mountain at 2 pm. There are several cheap places to stay in town, all within a few minutes of the bus station.

Buses leave between 5.30 and 6.40 am for Antu and Yanji. The bus bounces past tobacco fields, villages with thatched roofs and log chimneys, stockaded gardens, pigs on mud heaps and howling dogs. Allow five hours to Antu or seven hours to Yanji. Close to Yanji, watch out for an airfield with low-flying, antique MIG fighters (Chinese copies) practising scrambles – the Soviet Union is just a few minutes' flying time away.

Getting Around

The authorities have been constructing roads and bridges in the Tianchi area to improve access for tourism and for forestry and meteorological stations. Buses normally continue past the hotels and the hot-spring bathhouse before dropping passengers off close to the waterfall. From here to the lake is about an hour's hike.

An alternative route for getting from the hotels to Tianchi is to backtrack north for about one km to the crossroads and take the road right (east). It winds on higher and higher, finally turning south, bringing you up onto the ridge of the east side of the valley. The road ends by the meteorological station where you have a splendid view of the lake. From here you head west towards a triangular peak – beyond that small peak it's possible to scramble down to the lake and ford the stream above the waterfall, but take care! Now you are at the end of the main track and can join the crowd back to the hot springs. This walk can be easily completed in one day, but it's always best to get an early start.

AROUND TIANCHI

The Changbaishan region presents you with some possibilities for shaking off the cities and traipsing through the wilderness, and gives you some good reasons for doing so: virgin forest, babbling brooks, and some rough travel and rough trails, as well as rough toilets – if you can find one.

The whole zone is the Yanbian (Chaoxian) Korean Autonomous Prefecture. The local people – of Korean descent – are often indistinguishable in dress from their Chinese counterparts. If you visit this area around mid-August, you can join in the 'Old People Festival'. The Koreans are a fairly lively lot, who enjoy eating spiced cold noodles and dog meat, and singing and dancing – and offering hospitality. They can also drink you under the table. Yanbian has the greatest concentration of Korean and Korean-Han groups in China, mostly inhabiting the border areas north and north-east of Baihe, extending up to Yanji.

Transport by rail is faster, as opposed to spine-jangling dirt roads. Apart from public buses the only other means of getting around is by jeeps or logging trucks. Off the main track, the trains are puffing black dragons, possibly of Japanese vintage. The fittings are old and the uncrowded trains have no sleepers.

Food in general leaves a lot to be desired – in the Korean places you can get by on cold noodles topped with a pile of hot spices or some meat and egg.

In a Tonghua restaurant I was rather relieved when two beggars fought it out and wolfed down the remaining grey dumplings on my plate – I was feeling off-colour from the ones I'd already eaten. A bus lunch-stop along the way yielded a hell's kitchen, with pig's heads bloodying the floor, fires going in corners, and mysterious concoctions bubbling away in cauldrons.

YANJI
(yánjí) 延吉

Yanji is the capital of the Yanbian Autonomous Zone – both Korean and Chinese languages are spoken here, and some semblance of traditional costume and custom is maintained. The surrounding countryside is sprinkled with clusters of thatched cottages. However, there's nothing to see in Yanji; it should be considered mainly a transit point.

Information

The CITS office (☎ 515018, 517906) at 19 Gongyuan Jie Yanxi Lu arranges expensive day trips to see a genuine Korean family and a Korean museum.

Places to Stay

The *Yanji Binguan* is cheap in winter but doubles prices between June and August. Some travellers prefer the *Minzu Fandian*, which has helpful staff and down-to-earth prices. Both hotels are about 40 minutes from the station on foot, or ask the bus driver to drop you nearby if you're coming from Baihe. There's a train from Yanji to Tumen at 5.49 am.

Getting There & Away

Yanji's airport has occasional flights to Changchun for Y180. There are buses between Yanji and Baihe, the starting point for the trip to Tianchi. Since Yanji lies on the railway line between Antu and Tumen (and thence to Mudanjiang in the south-east of Heilongjiang Province) it should not be too difficult to drop in for a visit.

TUMEN
(túmén) 图门

Tumen is a small city on the North Korean border. You could spend a few hours there strolling through the riverside park, or climb the hill for an elevated view of the border area.

The *Dongfang Fandian*, close to the station, charges Y15 for a dorm bed. The *Tumen Binguan* charges Y50.

The most convenient train departs from Tumen at 8.23 am heading for Mudanjiang; it takes 6½ hours and costs Y10 (soft seat).

HUNCHUN
(húnchūn) 珲春

An isolated backwater if there ever was one, Hunchun – just east of Tumen and the North Korean border – may yet have its day in the sun. There has been all sorts of talk about a 'free trade zone' encompassing this part of China plus Vladivostok in Siberia and part of North Korea. While the North Korean border remains as sealed as ever, a new rail link opened to Siberia in 1993. The train connects the Siberian town of Khasan to Hunchun. Foreigners can indeed make this crossing, but obtaining the necessary tourist visa for Russia is problematic for most Western nationalities.

Heilongjiang 黑龙江

Capital: Harbin

HARBIN

(hā'ěrbīn) 哈尔滨

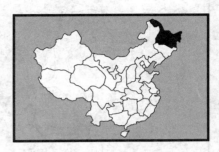

As the provincial capital, Harbin is the educational, cultural and political centre of Heilongjiang. The city now has a population of three million, but at one time it used to be a quiet fishing village on the Songhua River – the name in Manchu means 'place for drying nets'.

In 1896 the Russians negotiated a contract for putting a railway line through Harbin to Vladivostok (and Dalian). The Russian imprint on the town remained in one way or another until the end of WW II; by 1904 the 'rail concession' was in place, and with it came other Russian demands on Manchuria. These were stalled by the Russo-Japanese War (1904-05), and with the Russian defeat the Japanese gained control of the railway. In 1917 large numbers of White Russian refugees flocked to Harbin, fleeing the Bolsheviks; in 1932 the Japanese occupied the city; in 1945 the Soviet Army wrested it back for a year and held it until 1946 when the Kuomintang troops were finally installed, as agreed by Chiang Kaishek and Stalin.

Harbin has not been totally peaceful since the end of WW II – during the Cultural Revolution, rival factions took to the air to drop bombs on one another.

As the largest former Russian settlement outside the former USSR, Harbin has been acutely aware of Soviet colonial eyes, which explains the large-scale air-raid tunnelling in the city. With the collapse of the USSR in 1991, the tunnels have not been maintained and are likely to be used as warehouses or wine cellars.

With the end of Sino-Soviet tensions, cross-border tourism has seen a small boom. You are likely to see Russian faces on the streets of Harbin these days. Their chief motive for visiting the PRC is not tourism, but 'business', otherwise known as smuggling. From Russia they bring an odd selection of goods – deer antlers, live puppies (heavily drugged and stuffed into their luggage), dirty pictures and occasional nasty things like weapons. From China, they buy all manner of consumer goods – clothing, coffee, cosmetics and other items which Russia no longer seems capable of producing. Some of the smugglers supplement their incomes by ripping off other smugglers – the PSB doesn't seem to care what the Russians do to each other as long as Chinese nationals are not involved.

Harbin today is largely an industrial city. As for tourism, winter is the peak season when mostly Overseas Chinese and Japanese tour groups flock to see the Ice Lantern Festival. Hong Kongers and Taiwanese are particularly drawn to Harbin because of the opportunity to see snow and ice – many come unprepared for the -40°C weather, and are reportedly so blown away by the cold that they never set foot north of the Tropic of Cancer again.

While here, put wandering around the market areas and the streets high on your list. There's a very different kind of architectural presence in Harbin – Soviet spires, cupolas and scalloped turreting. The area known as Daoliqu, near Zhongyang Dajie, is good to investigate.

Harbin has several dozen Orthodox churches *(dōngzhèng jiàotáng)*, but most were ransacked during the Cultural Revolu-

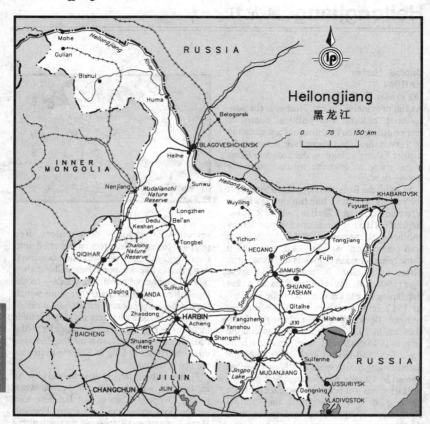

Heilongjiang
黑龙江

0   75   150 km

tion and have since been boarded up or converted for other uses. A few stray onion-domes punctuate the skyline.

The Daoliqu District, in the section toward the banks of the Songhua River, also has the best specialty shops and some market activity, and is worth your time on foot. Another shopping and market area is to be found north-east of the International Hotel, a short walk away at Dazhi Dajie.

Information

The CITS office (☎ 221655) is in a separate building in the grounds of the Swan Hotel *(tiāné fàndiàn)*, at 73 Zhongshan Lu on the No 3 bus route. CITS can arrange specific tours for diverse needs and tastes, including elderly health build-up, bicycling, Chinese law, trade unions, steam locos, hunting, welding technology, honey production etc.

CITS can also arrange tours in the Heilong River area (see that section for details).

The PSB is on Zhongyang Dajie in the centre. The Bank of China is on Hongjun Jie near the International Hotel. The post office is on the corner of Dongda Zhijie and Fendou Lu. The telecommunications office is also on Fendou Lu, two blocks from the post office.

Children's Railway
(értóng gōngyuán) 儿童公园

This railway in the Children's Park was built in 1956. It has two km of track plied by a miniature diesel pulling seven cars with seating for 190; the round trip (Beijing-Moscow?) takes 20 minutes. The crew and administrators are kids under the age of 13.

Stalin Park
(sīdàlín gōngyuán) 斯大林公园

Down by the river, this is a tacky strip stacked with statues; it's the main perambulating zone, with recreation clubs for the locals. A 42-km embankment was constructed along the edge to curb the unruly Songhua River – hence the surreal-looking Flood Control Monument *(fánghóng jìniàn tǎ)* which was built in 1958. The sandy banks of the Songhua take on something of a beach atmosphere in summer, with boating, ice-cream stands and photo booths. It's possible to travel on tour boats arranged through CITS but you might like to investigate local docks for a quick sortie down the Songhua.

During winter the river becomes a road of ice (when it's one metre thick it can support a truck) and the Stalin Park/Sun Island area is the venue for hockey, skating, ice-sailing, sledding and sleighing – equipment can be hired.

Sun Island
(tàiyángdǎo gōngyuán) 太阳岛公园

Opposite Stalin Park and reached by a ferry hop is Sun Island, a sanatorium-recreational zone still under construction. The island covers 3800 hectares and has a number of artificial features – a lake, hunting range, parks, gardens, forested areas – all being worked on to turn this into Harbin's biggest touring attraction. In summer there's swimming and picnics; in winter it's skating and other sports. There are a number of restaurants and other facilities on Sun Island.

Japanese Germ Warfare Experimental Base – 731 Division
(rìběn xìjūn shíyàn jīdì)
日本细菌实验基地

If you haven't visited concentration camps such as Belsen or Auschwitz, a similar lesson in the horrors of extermination can be learnt at this base.

In 1939 the Japanese army set up a top-secret, germ-warfare research centre here. Japanese medical experts experimented to their hearts' content on Chinese, Soviet, Korean, British and other prisoners. Over 4000 were exterminated in bestial fashion: some were frozen or infected with bubonic plague, others were injected with syphilis, and many were roasted alive in furnaces.

When the Soviets took back Harbin in 1945, the Japanese hid all trace of the base. The secret would probably have remained buried forever, but a tenacious Japanese journalist dragged out the truth only recently. Japan's medical profession was rocked by the news that some of its leading members had a criminal past which had hitherto escaped detection. Another disturbing angle to the story was the claim that the Americans had granted freedom to the perpetrators of these crimes in return for their research data. To get there, take bus No 338 from the main railway station to the terminal, which is close to the district of Pingfangqu (about 10 km).

Steam Locomotives
(zhēngqì jīchē) 蒸汽机车

For this, you'll need to organise a tour through CITS and be prepared to pay the tariff. Harbin is the centre of northern China's working network of steam locomotives, even though they're being phased out. There is a steam locomotive depot and marshalling yard in Harbin, but ask CITS about tours to areas employing narrow gauge steam locomotives (Jiamusi, Yichun, etc).

Other Attractions
The **Retirement Home for Foreigners** *(wàiqiáo yǎnglǎo yuàn)* at 1 Wenjing Jie is unique in China. Koreans, Americans, Japanese, Russians or stateless persons spend their last years here. Many of them have interesting tales to tell and many were stranded here as a result of wars and were unable to return to their homeland (the White Russians for example). A few were born in

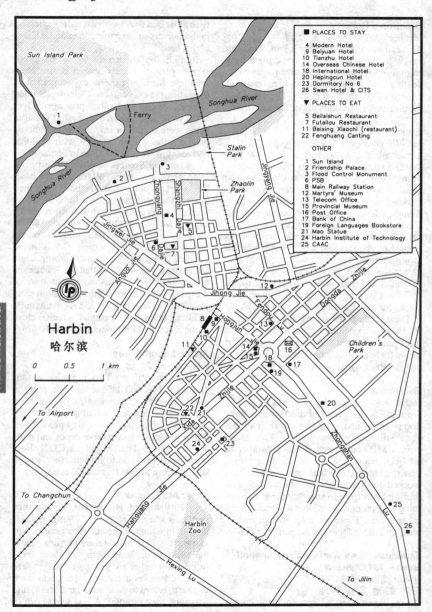

Sun Island Park

Songhua River

Songhua River

Ferry

Stalin Park

Zhaolin Park

Jingyang Jie

Zhongyang

Shangzhi Dajie

Jingwei Jie

Dajie

Anguo Jie

Harbin
哈尔滨

0   0.5   1 km

Jihong Jie

Dongda Zhijie

Fendou Jie

Hongjun

Jie

Zhijie

Children's Park

To Airport

Fujin Jie

To Changchun

Hanguang Jie

Harbin Zoo

Hexing Lu

Changshan Lu

To Jilin

■ PLACES TO STAY
4   Modern Hotel
9   Beiyuan Hotel
10 Tianzhu Hotel
14 Overseas Chinese Hotel
18 International Hotel
20 Hepingcun Hotel
23 Dormitory No 6
26 Swan Hotel & CITS

▼ PLACES TO EAT
5   Beilaishun Restaurant
7   Futailou Restaurant
11 Beixing Xiaochi (restaurant)
22 Fenghuang Canting

OTHER
1   Sun Island
2   Friendship Palace
3   Flood Control Monument
6   PSB
8   Main Railway Station
12 Martyrs' Museum
13 Telecom Office
15 Provincial Museum
16 Post Office
17 Bank of China
19 Foreign Languages Bookstore
21 Mao Statue
24 Harbin Institute of Technology
25 CAAC

HEILONGJIANG

PLACES TO STAY

4 马迭尔宾馆
9 北苑饭店
10 天竹宾馆
14 华侨饭店
18 国际饭店
20 和平村宾馆
23 第六宿舍
26 天鹅饭店 / 中国国际旅行社

PLACES TO EAT

5 北来顺饭店
7 福泰楼饭店
11 北兴小吃
22 凤凰餐厅

OTHER

1 太阳岛
2 友谊宫
3 防洪纪念塔
6 公安局外事科
8 哈尔滨火车站
12 东北烈士馆
13 电信局
15 省博物馆
16 邮局
17 中国银行
19 外文书店
21 毛主席像
24 哈尔滨工业大学
25 中国民航

of town has relics from the anti-Japanese campaign.

Things to Buy

If you're heading into the sub-Siberian wilds, Harbin is the northernmost place in China where you'll be able to stock up English-language books. The selection is limited, but worth looking into is the Foreign Languages Bookstore (☎ 475385), 26 Jinwei Jie, Daoliqu District.

Harbin is famous for furs (mink, etc), deer antlers and other products which are sure to infuriate animal rights activists – if you get upset by these things, give the department stores a miss. You might, however, want to take a look at the Siberian ginseng, though prices aren't really cheap because the locals recognise the export value.

Festivals

If you don't mind the cold, then try not to miss Harbin's main drawcard, the Ice Lantern Festival (*bīngdēng jié*) in Zhaolin Park. Officially, it's held from 5 January to late February, though in reality it may start a week earlier and spill into March. Fanciful sculptures are made in the shapes of animals, plants, buildings or motifs taken from legends. Some of the larger ones have included a crystalline ice bridge and an ice elephant that children could mount from the tail in order to slide down the trunk. At night the sculptures are illuminated from the inside with coloured lights, turning the place into a temporary fantasyland. There are ice festivals held in other Chinese cities, but Harbin's is considered the best.

In warmer times, there's the Harbin Music Festival, a 12-day event that takes place in July (it was suspended during the Cultural Revolution).

Places to Stay

The only dormitory we know of has no name, but we've dubbed it *Dormitory No 6* because of the street address. See the map for details on how to get there. Essentially, you need to take bus No 11 from the railway station and get off by the Mao statue. Walk down the

China and even had citizenship during the Kuomintang era, but lost it when the Communists came to power because they had the wrong racial background. Needless to say, as time goes on the foreigners here are becoming fewer and fewer.

The **Provincial Museum** (*shěng bówùguǎn*) is opposite the International Hotel and has some boring historical and natural history sections; the **Industrial Exhibition Hall** is dead boring; the **zoo** (*dòngwùyuán*) is lukewarm but does have some Manchurian tigers and red-crowned cranes. The **Martyrs' Museum** (*dōngběi lièshì guǎn*) in the centre

HEILONGJIANG

street opposite the Mao statue until you reach the third alley on your right. There're buildings No 4 and No 5, but No 6 has no number. However, it does have the symbol of the China Railway Administration by the doorway. Go to the 5th floor to find the dormitory. There are no showers, but clean blankets and towels are supplied.

We need to mention that there have been a few disturbing reports of arguments over prices – it seems the staff demand more money on departure, or else there are some misunderstandings due to the language barrier. Try to get it written down clearly and be sure you don't hand over your passport as security! Travellers have stayed here recently for as little as Y10.

The *Beiyuan Hotel* (☎ 340128, 340263) *(běiyuàn fàndiàn)* directly faces the railway station. This enormous place dishes up doubles for Y91 and Y140, payable in RMB. Unfortunately, it's often filled to the rooftop with Russians visiting Harbin 'on business'. There have been reports of thefts from rooms – the most likely suspects are some of the guests rather than the Chinese staff. If you stay here, keep your valuables with you or store them in the left-luggage rooms at the railway station.

As you exit the railway station, just off to your right is the 19-storey *Tianzhu Hotel* (☎ 3432725, 343720) *(tiānzhú bīnguǎn)*. This is an excellent place to stay. Although doubles cost Y180, RMB is accepted. The ground floor has an active karaoke restaurant and a good shop with exquisite pastries.

The *Hepingcun Hotel* (☎ 220101) *(hépíngcūn bīnguǎn)* at 109 Zhongshan Lu is a new place offering salubrious accommodation for Y200. The hotel is topped by a revolving restaurant. Take bus or minibus No 103 from the railway station.

The *International Hotel* (☎ 341441; fax 325651) *(guójì fàndiàn)*, 124 Dazhi Jie, is just off of Hongjun Jie less than one km from the railway station. Doubles are Y300. It's run-down and overpriced – only the location is good.

The *Overseas Chinese Hotel* (☎ 341341; fax 323429) *(huáqiáo fàndiàn)* is at 52 Hongjun Jie, even closer to the railway station than the International. This place often packs out with Hong Kongers and Taiwanese in pursuit of snow and business opportunities. Doubles cost Y218.

The *Swan Hotel* (☎ 220201; fax 224895) *(tiāné fàndiàn)*, 73 Zhongshan Lu, is the classiest place in town. Doubles range from Y240 to Y340. It's a nice place to stay, but is a long way from the station. CITS is installed in the same compound and CAAC is nearby. Minibus No 103 running down Zhongshan Lu can take you to the hotel for Y2.

The *Modern Hotel* (☎ 415845; fax 414997) *(mǎdié'ěr bīnguǎn)* is not modern at all – it's an old place with plenty of character. Doubles start at Y180, but beware of overcharging in the hotel's restaurant. The hotel is at 129 Zhongyang Dajie in Daoliqu District, Harbin's most colourful neighbourhood.

The *Friendship Palace Hotel* (☎ 416146) *(yǒuyí gōng bīnguǎn)* is a classy place at 57 Youyi Lu, next to the Songhua River. Doubles start at Y220.

Places to Eat

A practice almost unique to Harbin is that red lanterns hang above the door outside every restaurant. It's a rating system – the more lanterns, the higher the standard and price. It's very convenient for budget travellers – if you see five lanterns out the front, you'd better avoid the place unless you want to splurge.

The *Har Har Le Restaurant (hāhālè fàndiàn)* is in the same building as the Overseas Chinese Hotel. It's cafeteria-style, with good food and cheap prices; there's no need to look at menus – just point to what you want.

As you exit the railway station, turn right down the main drag, pass the Tianzhu Hotel, and turn right at the first street (a small dead-end alley). Here you will find *Beixing Xiaochi* (sign only in Chinese), a great little two-lantern restaurant. The Chinese salad *(jiācháng liángcài)* is outstanding, but everything else on the menu is tasty.

The *Fenghuang Canting* is small but has

great food and is very popular. It's off Xida Zhijie (see map).

There are a couple of places around Stalin Park. On the edge of Zhaolin Park at 113 Shangzhi Dajie, Daoliqu District, is the *Beilaishun Restaurant* (☎ 419027) *(běilái-shùn fàndiàn)* serving Muslim beef and mutton dishes upstairs and also hotpot in winter. The *Futailou Restaurant* (☎ 417598) *(fútàilóu fàndiàn)* at 19 Xi Shisandao Jie serves Beijing roast duck and other dishes, but you need to order two days in advance for regional specialties.

As for the hotels, the *International* sells a lot of expensive exotica. Anyone for grilled bear paws? Or some stewed moose nose with monkey-leg mushrooms? This place seems to be popular with Soviet tourists.

If you visit Sun Island, you can get a good meal at the *Sun Island Restaurant (tàiyáng-dǎo cāntīng)*.

Getting There & Away

Air CAAC and Aeroflot both offer international flights to Khabarovsk in Siberia. From Khabarovsk it is supposed to be possible to get connecting flights to Japan and South Korea, but be aware that Aeroflot is notoriously unreliable. Checked luggage on this airline also has a tendency to disappear.

Another international flight being rumoured to exist (someday) will connect Harbin to Choibalsan in Outer Mongolia. Don't hold your breath waiting.

Domestic flights and fares from Harbin are:

Destination	Fare	Destination	Fare
Beijing	Y510	Canton	Y1550
Changsha	Y1190	Chengdu	Y1350
Chongqing,		Fuzhou	Y1240
Dalian	Y430	Haikou	Y1850
Hangzhou	Y1040	Heihe	Y260
Kunming	Y1750	Nanjing	Y880
Ningbo	Y1010	Qingdao	Y560
Shanghai	Y920	Shenyang	Y250
Shenzhen	Y1650	Ürümqi	Y1920
Wenzhou	Y1290	Xi'an	Y1020
Xiamen	Y1360	Yantai	Y550

CAAC (☎ 222337) has its office at 87 Zhongshan Lu, close to the Swan Hotel. Aeroflot (☎ 241441) has an office in the International Hotel, although it seems to be closed when it's supposed to be open.

Harbin's airport tax is possibly the highest in China – a walloping Y45 for domestic flights.

Bus There is a long-distance bus station near Sankeshu railway station which takes care of a large proportion of bus departures. Other buses depart from the main railway station.

Train There are frequent departures to Beijing, Shanghai and points in between. Harbin to Changchun takes four hours; to Shenyang, nine hours; to Beijing, 18 hours. Rail connections to Qiqihar, Mudanjiang and Jiamusi are regular but slow.

For travellers on the Trans-Siberian railway, Harbin is a possible starting or finishing point.

Boat Boat services operate from mid-April to late November. A regular service between Harbin and Jiamusi takes 27 hours. Buy tickets from the boat dock on Bei Qidao Jie.

Getting Around

To/From the Airport Harbin's airport is 46 km from town and the journey takes at least one hour, half of which is spent in the traffic-clogged streets near the city centre.

Buses depart for the airport from the CAAC office and cost Y8 – buy tickets on the bus, not inside the office. Buses depart about 2½ hours before scheduled flight departure times.

Taxi drivers congregate around the CAAC office and are as persistent as flies – they practically try to pull you off the bus and into their taxis. Don't believe some of the low fares they may quote you (Y30, etc) – the fare suddenly gets jacked up to reality (Y100) halfway to the airport, and if you don't agree to the change you get dumped out in the middle of nowhere. If you want to go by taxi, it's better to arrange it at the railway station (bargaining is mandatory). However, the sole advantage of booking a taxi at the CAAC office is that you could conceivably share it with some other people heading to the airport.

If you are taking the 7.30 am flight to Beijing, you need to be at the CAAC office at 5 am to catch the bus. Since local buses and taxis don't run at 4.30 am, about the only way you can manage this is to stay at the nearby Swan Hotel, which is within walking distance of CAAC. Unfortunately, the Swan Hotel is not cheap.

Bus There are over 20 bus routes in Harbin; buses start running at 5 am and finish at 10 pm (9.30 pm in winter). The most useful one is likely to be No 103 – there is both a minibus and a big bus on this route. The minibus costs Y2 and is far superior to the sardine-tin large buses. Bus No 1 or trolley-bus No 3 will take you from the hotel area to Stalin Park.

Boat CITS has a boat tour along the Songhua River which lasts 2½ hours, but it's definitely a summer-only event.

AROUND HARBIN

Skiers can head for Shangzhi, some 100 km or so from Harbin, but it's best to bring your own equipment and first check with CITS in Harbin that the lift is operating.

MUDANJIANG

(mǔdānjiāng) 牡丹江

A nondescript city of about a million people, Mudanjiang's only interest to travellers is its function as a staging post for visits to nearby Jingbo Lake (see next section).

If you have to spend a night in Mudanjiang, turn right outside the station (right over the railway bridge) and walk for 20 minutes to the Beishan Hotel (☎ 25734) (běishān bīnguǎn), on Xinhua Lu opposite the park. CITS is in the Mudanjiang Hotel (☎ 25633) (mǔdānjiāng bīnguǎn) on Guanghua Jie.

Getting There & Away

There are flights from Mudanjiang to Beijing (Y720), Canton (Y1670), Shanghai (Y990) and Shenyang (Y310). The usual approach by rail to Mudanjiang is from Harbin, though you could also come from the direction of Yanji.

JINGBO LAKE

(jìngbó hú) 镜泊湖

The name means 'mirror lake', and it's probably the most impressive sight in Heilongjiang. The lake covers an area of 90 sq km; it's 45 km long from north to south, with a minimum width of 600 metres and a maximum of six km, and is dotted with islets. The nature reserve encompasses a strip of forest, hills, streams, pools and cliffs around the lake and there is a lava cave in the area. The main pastime is fishing (the season is from June to August); tackle and boats can be hired (prices negotiable). Different varieties of carp (silver, black, red-tailed, crucian) are the trophies.

It's best to avoid peak season (July and August) – autumn is nice when the leaves are changing colour. Get out on the lake in a rowing boat – there are loads of stars at night.

Be sure to visit the Diaoshuilou Waterfall (20 metres high, 40 metres wide). Some foreigners like to come here and amaze the Chinese by diving into the pools. The waterfall is north of Jingbo Villa and within easy hiking distance of it.

The whole area is dotted with forests, hills, pavilions and rock gardens, offering rich opportunities for pleasant walks around the lake. Unfortunately, during the peak summer season you'll have to hike through the jostling mob of photo posers, litter collectors and knick-knack sellers. The Chinese say it's only fun when it's crowded.

The name Mirror Lake comes from a legend related to a wicked king who sent his minister out every week to find a beautiful girl – if the girl didn't suit him, he'd have her killed. A passing monk gave the king a mirror to aid in the selection, saying that this mirror would retain the reflection of a true beauty, even after she turned away. The minister duly trotted off, found a beautiful girl at the lake, and discovered that the mirror test worked. The king immediately asked for the lady's hand. 'What is the most precious thing in the world?' asked the girl. The king thought for some time. 'Power,' he replied. Upon hearing this, the girl threw the mirror into the lake, a storm broke out, and she vanished.

Places to Stay

The centre of operations is *Jingbo Villa* (*jìngbó shānzhuāng*), at the north end of the lake, and the new *Jingbo Lake Hotel* (*jìngbó hú bīnguǎn*). There are other, cheaper hotels around the lake but they aren't allowed to take foreigners.

Getting There & Away

The best approach is by rail from Harbin. Take a train to Dongjing (*dōngjīng*). From there, it's one hour by minibus to the lake.

Some trains only go as far as Mudanjiang. If you get off at Mudanjiang, it's three hours by bus to Jingbo Lake. Buses depart between 6 and 7 am from the square in front of Mudanjiang station, in summer only (from June to September). There are two or three trains a day between Harbin and Mudanjiang.

From Mudanjiang and Dongjing, there are also slower connections by rail to Tumen (one train daily, about six hours), Suifenhe (one train daily, five hours from Mudanjiang) and Jiamusi (two trains a day, about 10 hours).

There are flights between Mudanjiang and Harbin once a week for Y100 – the same flight continues to Beijing.

SUIFENHE
(*suīfēnhé*) 绥芬河

This town achieved commercial importance in 1903 with the opening of the South Manchurian railway, which was a vital link in the original Trans-Siberian route running from Vladivostok to Moscow via Manchuria.

The railway was later re-routed via Khabarovsk to Vladivostok and Nakhodka. In recent years, cross-border trade has livened up here and there's even some Russian tourism. The grandiose nickname of 'Little Moscow of the East' certainly suits the Russian atmosphere in Suifenhe, there's little else to do unless you like a lusty Sino-Soviet friendship evening when, according to a local tourist brochure, Soviet visitors sing 'Evening in Suburban Moscow'. Although the whole place is Chinese, most of the buildings are Russian leftovers in the elegant, gingerbread style from the turn of the century – reminders of pre-Revolutionary times.

With the requisite visas, you can indeed cross the border to Russia and reach Vladivostok from here, but obtaining the necessary bits of paper is a monumental task.

Getting There & Away

There's one train daily (at 6.45 am) from Mudanjiang to Suifenhe; the trip takes about six hours and the train returns from Suifenhe at 1.12 pm.

There is an international passenger train beginning (or ending) at Primorye (Siberia), connecting Pogranichny (Grodekovo) with Suifenhe. Pogranichny is a small town which borders China near Suifenhe, 210 km away from Vladivostok. Pogranichny is connected by bus and taxi with Ussuriisk and Vladivostok. Suifenhe is connected with Harbin and Mudanjiang by rail. The train from Pogranichny to Suifenhe runs daily, and one-way tickets cost US$10. As this is the cheapest way to China, the train is usually packed out with Russian traders and their cargoes of deer antlers, drugged puppies and vodka.

DONGNING
(*dōngníng*) 东宁

This obscure town near the southernmost corner of Heilongjiang is notable for only one thing – a bus connection that can get you to Vladivostok in Siberia. However, a Russian tourist visa is necessary – a difficult thing to come by.

The bus connects the Russian town of Pokrovka (180 km from Vladivostok) with Dongning. Make local inquiries about the schedule. At the time of writing, the bus was jammed- packed.

WUDALIANCHI
(*wǔdàliánchí*) 五大连池

Wudalianchi, which means 'the five large connected lakes', is a nature reserve and health spot which has also been turned into a 'volcano museum'. Many Chinese will tell you that Wudalianchi isn't worth the effort to get there, but basically it depends on whether or not you're a hot springs fanatic.

This area has a long history of volcanic activity. The most recent eruptions were during 1719 and 1720 when lava from craters blocked the nearby Bei River and formed this series of five barrier lakes. The malodorous mineral springs are the source of legendary cures and thus the No 1 attraction for hordes of chronically sick, who slurp the waters or slap mud onto themselves. To increase blood pressure, immerse your feet in a basin of the water; to decrease blood pressure, immerse your head. Baldness, cerebral haemorrhages, skin diseases and gastric ulcers are a few of the ailments helped by drinking the water or applying mud packs. Some of the cures are only temporary.

As for the volcanoes themselves, don't come expecting Mt Fuji or Krakatau. Basically, the volcano museum has steam fumaroles, hot springs, a little geothermal activity here and there but not much else.

To liven up the scenery, there is a sort of Ice Lantern Festival like the one in Harbin, only this one is year-round. The ice sculptures are inside caves which have a steady temperature of -10°C even during summer. Coloured lights inside the sculptures illuminate the psychedelic effect.

Foreigners are expected to stay at the increasingly expensive *Dragon Spring Hotel* (*lóngquán bīnguǎn*).

To reach Wudalianchi, take a six-hour train ride northwards from Harbin to Bei'an, where there are regular buses covering the 60 km to the lakes.

HEILONG RIVER BORDERLANDS
(*hēilóngjiāng biānjìng*) 黑龙江边境
Much of the north-eastern border between China and Siberia follows the course of the Heilongjiang (Black Dragon River), also known to the Russians as the Amur River. Most places along this river are open to foreigners but ask the PSB anyway just to be

---

The Oroqen
The Oroqen minority lived, until recently, the nomadic life of forest hunters. Recent estimates put their numbers at about 4000, scattered over a vast area. Their traditional tent, called a *xianrenzhu*, is covered with birch bark in the summer and deerskin in the winter. Hunting as well as the raising of reindeer are still their main activities. A major source of income is deer hunting since the deer's embryo, antlers, penis and tail are highly prized in Chinese medicine.

The Oroqen lifestyle is changing rapidly, although they retain their self-sufficiency. Boots, clothes and sleeping bags are made from deerskins; baskets, eating utensils and canoes are made from birch bark; horses or reindeer provide transport. Their food consists mostly of meat, fish and wild plants. Oroqens are particularly fond of raw deer liver washed down with fermented mare's milk. Meat is often preserved by drying and smoking.

Interesting facets of their religion included (and probably still do to a lesser degree) a belief in spirits and consulting shamans. It was once taboo to kill bears. If this happened, perhaps in self-defence, a complicated rite was performed to ask the bear's 'forgiveness' and its bones were spread in the open on a tall frame of willow branches. This 'wind burial' was also the standard funeral for a human. Our word 'shaman' means an 'agitated or frenzied person' in the Manchu-Tungus language. Such persons could enter a trance, become 'possessed' by a spirit and then officiate at religious ceremonies.

It's hard to determine how much of their culture the Oroqens have kept. Official publications trumpet stories of a wondrous change from primitive nomadism to settled consumerism complete with satellite TV. Meng Pinggu, a probably fictional Oroqen, was quoted in the *China Daily*; 'Now we Oroqens can see movies at home'.

The Oroqens – China's Nomadic Hunters by Qiu Pu (Foreign Languages Press, Beijing, 1983) is a surprisingly informative publication, provided you skip the political salad dressing. ∎

sure – international borders and ethnic minority areas are sensitive places. It should be possible to see some Siberian forest and the dwindling settlements of northern tribes such as the Oroqen, Ewenki, Hezhen and

In Harbin the CITS office runs boat tours between Huma, Heihe and Tongjiang. Telescopes on the boats will give you a better look at Russian settlements or even at Blagoveshchensk, a large Russian port opposite Heihe.

Assuming you have at least two weeks to spare and are flexible about transport, an independent trip should also be viable during the summer – take some iron rations and insect repellent. Connections between Harbin and this region include the fast option of a flight to Heihe, the much slower option of a train at least as far as Jagdaqi, possibly further, and, of course, buses to the ends of the wilderness.

Mohe
(mòhé) 漠河

Natural wonders are the attraction at Mohe, China's northernmost town, sometimes

Oroqen man

known as the 'Arctic of China'. In mid-June, the sun is visible in the sky for as long as 22 hours. The northern lights (aurora borealis) are another colourful phenomenon seen in the sky at Mohe. China's lowest absolute temperature of -52°C was recorded here in 1965; on normal winter days temperatures of -40°C are common.

During May 1987 this area was devastated by China's worst forest fire in living memory. The towns of Mohe and Xilinji were completely gutted, more than 200 people died and over one million hectares of forest were destroyed.

Try for a permit at the PSB in Jagdaqi *(jiāgédáqí)* in Inner Mongolia. To reach Mohe would require a rail trip north from Jagdaqi to Gulian, followed by a 34-km bus ride.

Heihe
(hēihé) 黑河

Heihe's claim to fame is that it borders Russia. Due to the recent thawing in relations between the two countries, there is a steadily increasing amount of cross-border trade and even a fledgeling tourist industry. Chinese tour groups now are able to cross the border to Blagoveshchensk. Soviet tourists visiting Heihe like to eat Chinese food and stock up on goods which are scarce or nonexistent in Siberia. Chinese tourists don't find much to buy in Russia, but are impressed to see a city where nobody spits and people actually stand in line.

There are still problems for foreigners wishing to visit Blagoveshchensk. A Russian tourist visa is needed, and a re-entry visa for China would also be necessary. All this must be arranged in Beijing, not in Heihe. In theory, one could cross the border at Blagoveshchensk and take a train 109 km to Belogorsk, which is on the Trans-Siberian Railway, then continue on to Europe. This would require a tourist visa with advance booking at hotels – typical Russian bureaucracy which has stymied any attempts to create a tourist industry. You are required to pay for all hotels in advance and rates are exorbitant. Furthermore, the Russian travel agency, Intourist, has no hotel in either Blagoveshchensk or Belogorsk which they are willing to book Westerners into. Consequently, they will not issue a visa for those places. Therefore, the most you might be able to manage is a day trip from Heihe to Blagoveshchensk and back again. In other words, if you want to do the Trans-Siberian, you'll have to depart from Beijing, not Heihe. Perhaps this will change some day, but don't hold your breath.

Flights between Harbin and Heihe exist but are infrequent. Boats also connect Heihe with Mohe and Tongjiang, but the railway does not reach this far north.

Tongjiang
(tóngjiāng) 同江

Tongjiang lies at the junction of the Songhua and Heilong rivers. They swell to a combined width of 10 km but their respective colours, black for the Heilong and yellow for the Songhua, don't mix until later.

The Hezhen minority, a mere 1300 people, lives almost entirely from fishing in this region. A local delicacy is sliced, raw fish with a spicy vinegar sauce. Apart from carp and salmon, the real whopper here is the huso sturgeon *(huáng yú)* which can grow as long as three metres and weigh up to 500 kg!

Tongjiang has boat and bus connections with Jiamusi; boats also connect with Heihe.

Fuyuan
(fǔyuǎn) 抚远

The earliest sunrise in China starts at 2 am in Fuyuan. Close to Fuyuan is the junction of the Heilong and Wusuli rivers. On the Soviet side is the city of Khabarovsk; on the Chinese side, there's the tiny outpost of Wusu, which has 20 inhabitants who see visitors only during the salmon season in September.

JIAMUSI
(jiāmùsī) 佳木斯

North-east of Harbin is Jiamusi. Once a fishing village, it mushroomed into a city of half a million people. It now smelts aluminium, manufactures farm equipment and

refines sugar, and has a paper mill, plastics factory and electrical appliances factory.

Things to See

Among the sights are **Sumuhe Farm**, in the suburbs of Jiamusi. This farm grows ginseng and raises over 700 head of sika and red deer for the antlers. Martens, close kin to the weasel, are also raised. It's not really such a strange combination – in fact the 'three treasures' of the north-east are ginseng, deer antlers and sable pelts. Each of these are also well represented further south in Jilin Province, where production is largely domesticated. Wild ginseng from the Changbaishan area fetches astronomical sums on the Hong Kong market.

A curious item in the north-eastern pharmacopoeia includes frog oil, taken from a substance in the frog's ovary. These and other ingredients will arrive in soups or with stewed chicken if a banquet is ordered at a ritzy hotel. (Non-banquet food on grease-laden dining tables is abysmal in the north-east region, so a visit to the local medicine shop is obligatory for stays of more than a week's duration.)

The **New Friendship Farm** is about 110 km east of Jiamusi on the railway line, a state-run frontier enterprise that is the pride of Heilongjiang – the pioneers who built it arrived in the 1950s and now number around 100,000, organised into numerous agricultural brigades.

The **Village of Fools** is not the pride of Heilongjiang. It's in Huachuan County to the east and north-east of Jiamusi. Cretins and bearers of bulbous goitre are studied at Jiamusi Medical College – the cause of their problems is suspected to be a dietary deficiency.

Places to Stay

The *Huibin Hotel* (☎ 28171) *(huìbīn fàndiàn)* on Zhanqian Lu is near the railway station. CITS packs the tourists into the *Jiamusi Hotel* (☎ 26971) *(jiāmùsī bīnguǎn)* on Guangfu Lu.

Getting There & Away

Jiamusi is connected by rail to Harbin (15

hours), Dalian and Mudanjiang. Steamers ply the Songhua River so it may be possible to travel between Harbin and Jiamusi by water.

DAQING
(dàqìng) 大庆

Daqing is an oil-boom town which appeared in the swamplands in 1960. This is one of those triumph-of-the-spirit towns, and demonstrates China's awesome ability to mobilise large numbers of people for the cause. The first drilling began in the 1950s with Soviet technical assistance; when the Russians withdrew in 1959, the Chinese decided to carry on alone. Shortly after, the first well gushed, and a community of tents, wooden shanties and mud housing erupted in the sub-zero wilderness. By 1975, Daqing was supplying 80% of the PRC's crude oil, but production has since tapered off. Most of the oil is piped to the coast near Dalian.

The town centre of Daqing is a recent creation – an administrative, economic and cultural sector, with residential and office buildings, a library, stores, 'modernisation' playground, exhibition halls and green-houses. But much of Daqing might be described as a massive suburbia – some 8000 oil wells with small communities attached are scattered throughout the 5000-sq-km area – the population of the Daqing area has swelled to one million. A few scarce foreigners with an interest in oil wells drop in – CITS likes to show off new model sections of the Daqing area such as medical facilities, the school or recreational props. Foreigners are herded into the overpriced *Daqing Hotel* (☎ 61294) *(dàqìng bīnguǎn)*.

QIQIHAR
(qíqíhā'ěr) 齐齐哈尔

Qiqihar is the gateway to the Zhalong Nature Reserve, a bird-watching area 35 km to the south-east. It's also one of the oldest settlements in the north-east. The town itself is industrialised, with a population of over a million, and produces locomotives, mining equipment, steel, machine tools and motor vehicles. There's not much to see here – a zoo, a stretch of riverside and the ice-carving festival from January to March.

The CITS office (☎ 72016) is in the Hubin Hotel and the staff are very friendly. They can give you a lot of advice about the best places for watching birds.

Places to Stay

The *Hubin Hotel* is one of the cheapest places accepting foreigners. The more modern *Crane City Hotel* (☎ 472669) – behind the Hubin at 4 Wenhua Dajie – is pricey. You can reach the Hubin Hotel on trolley-bus No 15 – it's seven stops from the railway station.

Getting There & Away

There are flights between Qiqihar and Beijing (Y630), Canton (Y1610) and Shanghai (Y1020). Qiqihar is linked directly by rail to Beijing (about 22 hours) via Harbin (about four hours).

ZHALONG NATURE RESERVE
(zhálóng zìrán bǎohù qū)
扎龙自然保护区

The Zhalong Reserve is at the north-west tip of a giant marsh, and is made up of about 210,000 hectares of reeds, moss and ponds. It lies strategically on a bird-migration path

中国人民邮政

which extends from the Soviet Arctic, around the Gobi Desert, and down into South-East Asia, and some 180 different species of bird are found there, including storks, swans, geese, ducks, herons, harriers, grebes and egrets. The tens of thousands of winged migrants arrive from April to May, rear their young from June to August, and depart from September to October.

Birds will be birds – they value their privacy. While some of the red-crowned cranes are over 1½ metres tall, the reed cover is taller. The best time to visit is in spring before the reeds have a chance to grow.

The nature reserve, one of China's first, was set up in 1979. In 1981 the Chinese Ministry of Forestry invited Dr George Archibald (director of the ICF, the International Crane Foundation) and Wolf Brehm (director of Vogelpark Walsrode, West Germany) to help set up a crane centre at Zhalong. Of the 15 species of cranes in the world, eight are found in China, and six are found at Zhalong. Four of the species that migrate here are on the endangered list: the red-crowned crane, the white-naped crane, the Siberian crane and the hooded crane. Both the red-crowned and white-naped cranes breed at Zhalong (as do the common and demoiselle cranes), while hooded and Siberian cranes use Zhalong as a stopover.

The centre of attention is the red-crowned crane, a fragile creature whose numbers at Zhalong (estimated to be 100 in 1979) were threatened by drainage of the wetlands for farming. The near-extinct bird is, ironically, the ancient symbol of immortality and has long been a symbol of longevity and good

Tigers

China has three subspecies of tiger: the Bengal, the South China and the North-Eastern or Manchurian. All told there are no more than 400 tigers left in China.

The South China subspecies is the most endangered and numbers only about 50 in the wild and about 30 in zoos both in China and abroad. (Even when India launched its Project Tiger in 1973 there were 1800 Royal Bengal tigers left in its territory – a number that was considered perilously low.) Unlike the Bengal and Manchurian tigers, which are found in several countries, the South China tiger is peculiar to China. Its plight began in the 1950s, with indiscriminate hunting and deforestation. At that time tigers were still fairly numerous in many southern provinces, especially in Hunan, Fujian, Guizhou and Jiangxi. Throughout the '50s and early '60s there were 'anti-pest' campaigns and many areas had their entire tiger populations wiped out. Today the subspecies exists only in the mountainous regions of south-west and south-east Hunan, and in northern Guangdong.

The Manchurian tiger seems doomed since it now numbers only 30 in the wilds of Jilin and Heilongjiang; zoos account for about 100 more and some are still found in Russia and North Korea.

The exact number of Bengal tigers in China is not known; they live in the Xishuangbanna Autonomous Region and southern Yunnan near Myanmar (Burma) and Laos, in a few counties in western Yunnan bordering Myanmar, and in the subtropical mountainous region of south-eastern Tibet and neighbouring Assam.

In Mengxian County on the Yellow River, Henan province, an old man named He Guangwei makes a living by catching the big cats *barehanded* – with a bit of help from the martial arts. In over 50 years he's captured at least 230 leopards and seven tigers, as well as killing 700 wild boars and 800 wolves.

If you do happen to come across one of the beasties, his advice is to go for the muzzle between the eyes and the nose. 'A quick hard blow there will make its eyes water, and it stops to rub them, but the blow must be sharp and accurate – if several blows aren't effective, you're in trouble.' If you do get into trouble, he further advises 'You have to kick the animal quickly and hard in vulnerable places like the ears or the belly, but this usually kills the animal, so I don't do it unless my life is at stake.'

Good luck. ∎

luck in the Chinese, Korean and Japanese cultures. With some help from overseas experts, the ecosystem at Zhalong has been studied and improved, and the number of these rare birds has risen. A small number of hand-reared (domesticated) red-crowned and white-naped cranes are kept in a pen at the sanctuary for viewing and study. On the eve of their 'long march' southwards in October, large numbers of cranes can be seen wheeling around, as if in farewell. The birds have been banded to unlock the mystery of their winter migration grounds (in either Korea or southern China).

Since the establishment of the International Crane Foundation (ICF), George Archibald and Ron Sauey have managed to create a 'crane bank' in Wisconsin, USA, stocking 14 of the 15 known species. They've even convinced the North Koreans to set up bird reserves in the mine-studded demilitarised zone between North and South Korea, and the travel baggage of these two countries includes suitcases full of Siberian crane-eggs picked up in Moscow (on one trip a chick hatched en route was nicknamed 'Aeroflot'). Last on the egg-list for the ICF is the black-necked crane, whose home is in remote Tibet and for whom captive breeding may be the final hope.

Places to Stay

The modest *Zhalong Hotel* has dormitories for Y15, double rooms for Y50, and offers tours through the freshwater marshes of the reserve for Y40 per day, in flat-bottom boats. The area is mainly of interest to the patient binoculared and rubber-booted ornithologist.

Getting There & Away

Zhalong is linked to Qiqihar by a good road, but there's not much traffic along it. There are occasional buses – you'll have to inquire to find them. The other alternative is to get a taxi, which will cost around Y30 after some bargaining. Hitching may be possible.

THE
SOUTH-WEST

The South-West

INTRODUCTION

The south-west of China is a region of immense mountains and precipitous cliffs, covered by dense subtropical forests, and cut through by mountain rivers fed by melting snows. This is China's backyard jungle, with fertile basins, exotic flora & fauna, rapids, jagged limestone pinnacles, caverns, and peaks on the edges of the Tibetan Plateau. For centuries, communication by river was hazardous because of the rapids, and communication by road assumed heroic feats of human engineering and endurance. A turbulent history lies behind the brooding landscapes, especially in Yunnan and Sichuan where tribal kingdoms have long resisted Han Chinese and colonial encroachment.

The ancestors of Emperor Qin Shihuang conquered the regions now known as Sichuan, and after he became emperor he had his engineers build a road linking what is now Chengdu to Chongqing and to the regions further south. This road stretched 1600 km from the capital at Xianyang (near modern-day Xi'an). A third of its length is said to have been a 150-cm-wide wooden balcony cantilevered out from the sheer cliff, supported by wooden brackets driven into the rock face. Despite this new means of communication, and the creation (on paper) of new administrative divisions, the chiefs of the people south of Sichuan in the areas now known as Guizhou and Yunnan continued to rule the region themselves. In the later Han period they were given titles and ranks as tribute bearers to the imperial court, and gifts of silk in return for 'protecting' the southern borders of the Chinese empire – but their loyalty to the empire was mainly an invention of the Han and later Chinese historians.

After the fall of the Han Dynasty another thousand years was to pass before much of the south-west could be effectively integrated into the empire, and even then it continued to revert to independence at every opportunity. In the mid-13th century the region was almost pounded into final submission – this time by the Mongol armies of Mangu Khan. When the Mongol rule collapsed in 1368 the south-western regions once again broke with the north; Sichuan was won back by a Ming military expedition in 1371 and then Yunnan the following year. Again, when the Manchus invaded in the 17th century it was the south-western regions which held out the longest – partly due to their geographical location and partly due to inclination. When the Qing Dynasty collapsed in 1911, the south-west was one of the first areas to break with the central government.

RAILWAYS

The story of the modern south-west is the story of the railways. In 1875, a British survey team set out from Bhamo, in upper Burma. The British dream was to link Bhamo with Shanghai, easily 3000 km away. At about the same time, China's first railway tracks were coming out of Shanghai. They proceeded a short distance before they were torn up by superstitious mobs; an even worse fate befell the survey captain from Bhamo. By the early 1900s, various foreign railway gauges – Russian, Japanese, Anglo-American, German, Belgian-French – were running from the treaty ports as far as was necessary for trading and exploiting raw materials, but the south-west was almost forgotten. The only spur was a narrow-gauge French line, completed in 1910, linking Hanoi with Kunming. During WW II another spur was added in Guangxi, trailing off toward Guizhou. The first major link was the Baoji-Chengdu line (1956), which connected with the Chengdu-Chongqing line (1952), and thus with what for centuries was the south-west's lifeline, the Yangzi River.

The railway lines that today's travellers take for granted were completed with great difficulty and loss of life over recent decades. More than 5000 km of added track have sliced literally months off travel time in the south-west. The crowning achievement is the Kunming-Chengdu line. It took some 12 years to make and was completed in 1970, after workers bored through solid rock and bridged deep ravines and treacherous rivers.

Extension of existing railway lines continues to be a major priority in the south-west. The thaw in Sino-Vietnamese relations has led to plans to revitalise the rail links between Nanning and Hanoi and Kunming and Hanoi. In Yunnan, a rail link is on the drawing boards between Kunming and Dali.

Apart from Sichuan, the south-west region is relatively underpopulated. Since its (substantial) natural resources remain largely untapped, the mainstay is agriculture. Its industrial contribution to China as a whole is therefore negligible. The opening of the Chengdu-Kunming line has boosted various industries (including the manufacture of iron, steel, farm machinery and chemical fertilisers) in the cities along the way. It has also caused a gravitation of population to the railway havens. This railway line can be added to China's list of impossible projects that have become fact.

GETTING THERE & AROUND
Itineraries
Distances are stretched in the south-west (from Guangzhou to Kunming is 2216 km by train) and the only way to speed it up is to fly between some points or cut out destinations. The well-worn (and proven) route is to take a boat from Canton to Wuzhou, then a bus to Guilin, and then to travel by train via Guiyang to Kunming, Emei, Chengdu, and Chongqing. From Chongqing people usually take the Yangzi ferry to Yichang or further. You can also proceed directly from Guiyang to Chongqing. Another option is to bypass

the Yangzi trip and head directly to Xi'an from Chengdu.

Air
A favourite plane trip is from Canton to Guilin. It costs only Y250, and gives you an amazing view of the landscape as you fly in. The view is virtually guaranteed since CAAC will not take off if there is a rain cloud in the sky (though that can lead to lengthy delays). One of the newer services for tourists in Guilin is a flight over the karst formations – but you can get an aerial tour by flying there in the first place. You should also remember that the train ride from Canton to Guilin takes 20 hours(!) while flying takes 1½ hours. The other useful flight is from Guilin to Kunming which costs Y355 and takes 1½ hours as compared with 33 hours on the train.

Many savvy travellers interested only in south-west China fly in directly from Bangkok or Chiang Mai to Kunming on one of the weekly CAAC flights or twice weekly Thai flights, making Kunming a base for exploring the south-west. This saves having to get to Guilin, Guiyang or Kunming from Canton. There are also Dragonair flights from Dhaka. Another novel entry route into the south-west is from Vietnam, via the town of Langsön, to Nanning in Guangxi Province. There are direct trains from Nanning to Guilin, a journey of around seven hours.

An exit to consider is the flight from Kunming to Bangkok or Rangoon, or from Nanning to Hanoi, but these all need to be planned well in advance. See the Getting There & Away chapter for the difficulties of getting to Myanmar and Vietnam.

Train
Trains, the horrors of hard-seat travel in the south-west, are a pain in the neck. The problems arise, as they always do, with hard-class seating. No person in their right mind would want to endure hard-seat travel for more than 12 hours – although some masochistic travellers have survived 48-hour ordeals and

arrived somewhat dazed, to put it mildly. Hard sleeper is very comfortable (no crowding permitted), but the tickets may require as much as four days of waiting to get. In a place like Kunming, where you're likely to spend several days anyway, this is OK – just book a ticket out of the place immediately upon arrival.

If you wish to speed things up and carry on regardless, there's a slight chance of being able to upgrade your hard seat to a hard sleeper once you're on the train. This is eminently possible in northern China but not in the south-west. Soft-class sleepers will be available, but most low-budget travellers find them prohibitively expensive. You could try for a soft seat, which is about the same price as a hard-sleeper ticket, but the trains in the south-west don't seem to include this class very often.

Apart from lack of sleepers, crowding is another big problem. Sichuan has the highest population of any province in China and Yunnan has the fewest railway lines so, at times, it seems that a whole quarter of humankind is hurtling down those tracks. Often the train is packed out before it even gets to the south-west, having loaded up in Shanghai. (The No 79 Shanghai-Kunming express is a good example – if you get on board at Guilin you have about zero hope of getting a hard sleeper, and you may not even get a soft sleeper.)

On some trains hard-seat carriages have people hanging from the rafters, watering their turtles in the washbasins, spitting everywhere. On one train two Westerners almost came to fisticuffs with locals over musical chairs in the unreserved section. If a foreigner got up to go to the toilet, a local would take the seat and refuse to budge; if the same displaced foreigner tried to pull the same stunt, all hell would break loose. At night, people are toe-to-toe in the aisles, or curled in foetal positions on the furniture. Hong Kongers refer to a phenomenon known as 'fishing' – which is when your head bobs up and down all night, with intermittent jerks.

One has to retain one's sense of humour in such situations – it pays to distract yourself. Compensation can be found in the sheer magnificence of the scenery along much of the route – you should try to travel by day as much as possible to downplay the discomfort of night. The Chengdu-Baoji train, for our money, is one of the most scenic rides. The Kunming-Chengdu route can be disappointing: engineering marvel that it is, it has tunnels every few metres (427 tunnels and 653 bridges to be exact, 40% of the route) – and these plunge one into a darkness that precludes any attempt to talk, read or view the landscape.

Since the actual act of travelling in the south-west eats up so much of your time there, some strategy is called for. It's better to stop in fewer places, get to know people and leave time for decent train reservations (intermediary stations are not empowered to issue hard-sleeper tickets). If you want to upgrade from hard seat to hard sleeper, check with the conductor in the car immediately behind the dining car – where his or her office is.

If you're really in a bind in hard-class seating, can't upgrade and you've had all you can take, consider getting off at some intermediary station; tickets can be valid for up to seven days, and no re-purchase is necessary – you just use the same ticket to hop back on the next train heading in your direction. You'll be back in the same situation on the next train, but at least you'll get a refreshing night's sleep out of the stop (the 1st-class waiting room at the station can be wonderfully comfortable upon a midnight arrival). Another booster is to hang out in the dining-car after meal time – the staff may let you stay or they may kick you out, but it's worth a try.

Food supplies on south-west trains are not the greatest – you should stock up like a squirrel for the long journey ahead where possible (coffee, fruit, bread, chocolate?). Don't forget to carry a large mug, like every Chinese passenger does (enamel- coated metal mugs are best, since they don't break). The endless supply of hot water from the boiler at one end of every passenger car is useful not only for brewing tea or coffee but

Faces from Xinjiang (CB)

Top: Roadworks equipment, Khunjerab Pass, Xinjiang (CB)
Bottom: Shepherds & flock approaching Sunday market, Kashgar, Xinjiang (Strauss)

for making instant noodle soups, which can be purchased in larger railway stations.

Approximate rail prices can be calculated using the distance tables in the introductory Getting Around chapter. A hard-sleeper ticket from Guilin to Kunming will cost you around Y88 (Chinese price) – if you can get Chinese price, and if any hard sleepers are available.

Boat

An unexplored option is boating. The hover-craft from Hong Kong considerably speeds up the trip to Wuzhou, and from Wuzhou it is possible to navigate to Nanning (this would be a very slow trip, but possibly a scenic one – larger boats anchor in mid-stream due to difficulties with rapids).

Guangxi 广西

Population: 40 million
Capital: Nanning

Guangxi *(guǎngxī)* first came under Chinese sovereignty when a Qin Dynasty army was sent southwards in 214 BC to conquer what is now Guangdong Province and eastern Guangxi. Like the rest of the south-west the region had never been firmly under Chinese control; the eastern and southern parts of Guangxi were occupied by the Chinese, while a system of indirect rule through chieftains of the aboriginal Zhuang people prevailed in the west.

The situation was complicated in the northern regions by the Yao (Mien) and Miao (Hmong) tribespeople, who had been driven there from their homelands in Hunan and Jiangxi by the advance of the Han Chinese settlers. Unlike the Zhuang, who easily assimilated Chinese customs, the Yao and Miao remained in the hill regions, often cruelly oppressed by the Han. There was continuous trouble with the tribes, with major uprisings in the 1830s and another coinciding with the Taiping Rebellion.

Today the Zhuang are China's largest minority, with well over 15 million people (according to a 1990 census) concentrated in Guangxi. Although they are virtually indistinguishable from the Han Chinese, the last outward vestige of their original identity being their linguistic links with the Thai people, in 1955 Guangxi Province was reconstituted as the Guangxi Zhuang Autonomous Region. Besides the Zhuang, Miao and Yao minorities, Guangxi is home to smaller numbers of Dong, Maonan, Mulao, Jing (Vietnamese – Gin) and Yi peoples.

The province remained a comparatively poor one until the present century. The first attempts at modernising Guangxi were made during 1926-27 when the 'Guangxi Clique' (the main opposition to Chiang Kaishek within the Kuomintang) controlled much of Guangdong, Hunan, Guangxi and Hubei.

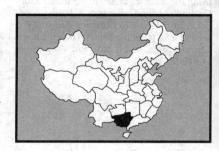

After the outbreak of war with Japan, the province was the scene of major battles and substantial destruction. Guangxi still remains one of China's less affluent provinces, though you might be forgiven for not realising this if you only visited the major population centres of Nanning, Liuzhou, Wuzhou and Guilin, where industry, trade and foreign investment have brought great changes over recent years.

Guangxi's most famous attraction is Guilin, perhaps the most eulogised of all Chinese sightseeing areas. While most travellers spend some time in the nearby town of Yangshuo, very few make it to other parts of Guangxi, and the province remains largely unexplored. For the adventurous, there are minority regions in the northern areas bordering Guizhou and less touristed karst rock formations like those in Guilin on the Zuo River not far from Nanning. Guangxi also offers the opportunity of taking advantage of the recently opened border crossing with Vietnam at the town of Pingxiang, a route that so far has only seen a trickle of Western travellers.

NANNING
(nánníng) 南宁

Nanning (population 2½ million) is one of those provincial centres that provide an insight into just how fast China is develop-

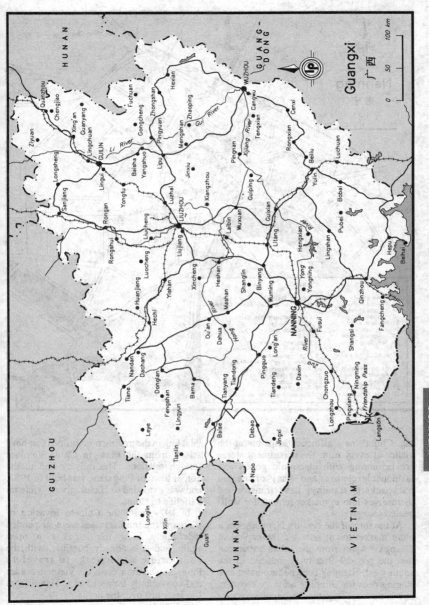

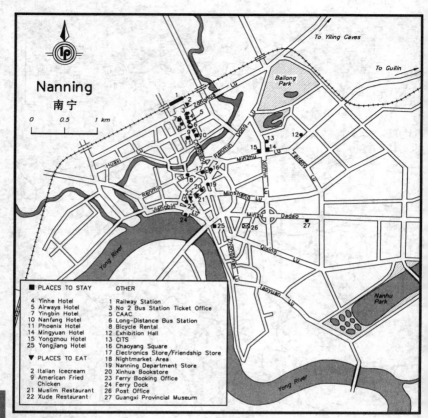

Nanning
南宁

0   0.5   1 km

To Yiling Caves

To Guilin

Bailong Park

To Guilin

Yong River

Nanhu Park

Yong River

■ PLACES TO STAY	OTHER
4 Yinhe Hotel	1 Railway Station
5 Airways Hotel	3 No 2 Bus Station Ticket Office
7 Yingbin Hotel	5 CAAC
10 Nanfang Hotel	6 Long-Distance Bus Station
11 Phoenix Hotel	8 Bicycle Rental
14 Mingyuan Hotel	12 Exhibition Hall
15 Yongznou Hotel	13 CITS
25 Yongjiang Hotel	16 Chaoyang Square
	17 Electronics Store/Friendship Store
▼ PLACES TO EAT	18 Nightmarket Area
	19 Nanning Department Store
2 Italian Icecream	20 Xinhua Bookstore
9 American Fried Chicken	23 Ferry Booking Office
21 Muslim Restaurant	24 Ferry Dock
22 Xude Restaurant	26 Post Office
	27 Guangxi Provincial Museum

ing. China's new affluence leaps out at the visitor at every turn: the department stores are brimming with electronic goods and fashionable clothes, and many of the old backpackers' standbys have transformed themselves into upmarket retreats for well-heeled tour groups.

At the turn of the century Nanning was a mere market town; now it's the capital of Guangxi. Apart from the urban expansion that the post-1949 railway induced in the south-west, Nanning became important as a staging post for shipping arms to Vietnam, and is now set to gather in importance as a vital link in the trading possibilities that have arisen from the thaw in China-Vietnam foreign relations. The railway line to the border town of Pingxiang was built in 1952, and was extended to Hanoi, giving Vietnam a lifeline to China.

In 1979, with the Chinese invasion of Vietnam, the train services were suspended indefinitely. Today the line is set to open again, and it is already possible, with the appropriate paperwork, to travel to Pingxiang by train, cross the Vietnam border and continue by train or bus to Hanoi from Langsön just over the border.

■ PLACES TO STAY

4 银和大厦
5 中国民航酒店
7 迎南宾大酒店
10 南方大宾馆
11 凤凰园饭店
14 明园饭店
15 邕州饭店
25 邕江饭店

▼ PLACES TO EAT

2 意大利冰淇淋
9 华越美餐馆
21 清真饭店
22 继德餐厅

OTHER

1 火车站
3 第二国民航客运售票处
5 中国民航
6 南宁汽车站
8 出租自行车
12 展览馆
13 中国国际旅行社
16 朝阳广场
17 南宁市友谊商店
18 夜市
19 南宁百货大楼
20 新华书店
23 客运码头售票处
24 南宁客运码头
26 电信大楼
27 广西省博物馆

The population of Nanning is more than 63% Zhuang, though for the most part it is impossible to distinguish them from their Han counterparts. The only colourful minorities you're likely to encounter in town are the occasional Miao and Dong selling silver bracelets and earrings on the overhead pedestrian passes near the railway station.

There's not a lot to see in Nanning, but it's likely to become an important transit point for travellers moving on to Vietnam. To do this you will need to have organised the appropriate visa in Hong Kong or Beijing (by the time you have this book in your hands there may be a Vietnam visa issuing office in Kunming). Rumours that it is possible to organise a visa in Nanning are just that; the service is for Chinese only.

Information

CITS The office (☎ 206025) is about 100 metres up the road from the main entrance to the Mingyuan Hotel. Like most CITS offices nowadays they are geared to the needs of tour groups, and apart from handing out a couple of brochures will provide little in the way of assistance for individual travellers.

Guangxi Provincial Museum

(*guǎngxī bówùguǎn*) 广西省博物馆
Down on Minzu Dadao, the museum is worth a browse if you have time on your hands. It's a very eclectic collection, rambling its way through 50,000 years of Guangxi history through to the Opium wars. There's an emphasis on minority artefacts, if your tastes run in this direction. To get there, take a No 6 bus, which runs along Chaoyang Lu from the railway station, into Minzu Dadao and past the museum. Opening hours are 8.30 to 11.30 am and 2.30 to 5 pm.

Bailong Park

(*báilóng gōngyuán*) 白龙公园
Also known as Renmin Park, the park has now reverted to its old name 'Bailong', which means White Dragon. It's a pleasant enough place for a stroll, with a lake, a couple of pagodas, a restaurant and boat hire. Close to the main entrance is a flight of stairs leading up to a viewing platform complete with funny mirrors and an old cannon. Entrance to the park is Y0.2, and it's open until 10.30 pm.

GUANGXI

Nanhu Park

(nánhú gōngyuán) 南湖公园

In the south of the city, Nanhu Park has a children's play area, boat hire and a Chinese medicinal herb garden. It's nothing to get particularly excited about, but it beats queuing up for tickets at the railway station. Bus No 2 will take you there from Chaoyang Lu.

Dragon Boat Races

As in other parts of the south-west (and Guangdong and Macau), Nanning has Dragon Boat races on the fifth day of the fifth lunar month (sometime in June) in which large numbers of sightseers urge the decorated rowing vessels along the Yong River. Those aboard are coordinated by a gong-player.

Places to Stay – bottom end

The old backpacker stand-bys have gone decidedly upmarket and the best hunting ground for affordable accommodation nowadays is the railway station area (more convenient anyway).

Opposite the railway station is the *Yingbin Hotel (yíngbīn fàndiàn)* with basic singles/doubles for Y18/36. There's no English sign for this place, but they take foreign guests all the same. A little further up Chaoyang Lu, next to the CAAC booking office, is the *Airways Hotel (mínháng fàndiàn)*, which is probably the pick of the cheapies. Dorm beds are Y10, singles are Y30 and doubles range from Y36 to Y52, the latter having attached bathrooms. If the Airways is full, head to *Phoenix Hotel (fènghuáng bīnguǎn)* across the road. A bed in a triple with shared bathroom in the south wing will set you back just Y8. Otherwise singles/doubles with attached bathroom are available for Y36/60.

Places to Stay – top end

Nanning has not got a lot in the way of real top-end accommodation, but if you're prepared to spend Y140 or more for your creature comforts there are a few options available. In the railway station area the *Yinhe Hotel (yínhé dàshà)* and the *Nanfang Hotel (nánfāng dàjiǔdiàn)* both have top-rate singles/doubles with air-con, satellite TV and attached bathrooms for Y140.

Less conveniently located, the *Yongjiang Hotel* (☎ 208123) *(yōngjiāng fàndiàn)* has comfortable air-con doubles for Y90. Other options include the *Yongzhou Hotel* (☎ 202338) *(yōngzhōu fàndiàn)*, which has doubles ranging from Y80 to Y180, and the *Mingyuan Hotel* (☎ 202986) *(míngyuán fàndiàn)*, an upmarket monster where the cheapest doubles start at Y180 and range up to Y300 for a suite.

Places to Eat

If you are in the railway station area on Chaoyang Lu, you can't miss the *American Fried Chicken* restaurant. It's run by some young Vietnamese Americans of Chinese extraction (figure that one out), and the friendly staff serve up some surprisingly good food. They are particularly energetic in chasing away the Dickensian beggars that stumble into the place, and this along with interesting mixture of Nanning trendies and bewildered Communist cadres makes for an interesting experience in itself.

For some excellent food and cheap beer try the *Muslim Restaurant (qīngzhēn fàndiàn)*. There is no English menu here, but the staff are friendly and will probably let you into the kitchen to point out what you want. The north end of the restaurant specialises in noodles, while the south end has rice dishes. Just down the road from the Muslim Restaurant is the *Xude Restaurant (jìdé cāntīng)*, with more traditional Chinese fare and exceptionally friendly staff – they'll probably drag you in off the street if you're walking past.

Nanning, like Guilin and Liuzhou, is famous for its dog hotpot, and while most travellers are inclined to give doggy dishes a miss it's worth at least taking a wander through the canine cuisine district just over the Chaoyang Stream and south of Chaoyang Lu. In the evenings this area teems with roadside stalls specialising in dog hotpot *(gǒuròu huǒguō)*.

Getting There & Away

Air CAAC flies four times a week to Canton, four times weekly to Beijing, three times weekly to Kunming (Y410), to Shanghai (Y870) on Fridays, to Shenzhen (Y460) thrice weekly and to Guilin (Y190) thrice weekly. Other flights available include Chengdu (Y510), Shenyang, Hanoi, Hong Kong and a twice-weekly Antonov flight to Beihai. The CAAC office (☎ 23333) is at 82 Chaoyang Lu. The Nanning Air Service Co (☎ 202911) has direct flights to Hong Kong on Wednesdays and Fridays. Tickets can be booked at CITS, 40 Xinmin Lu.

Bus Daily buses to Wuzhou, from Nanning's long-distance bus station, cost Y51 and take up to 11 hours. Buses to Canton are Y58 and take 18 hours (although it's a gruelling trip, this is the cheapest way to get to Canton from Nanning).

There are also regular buses to Liuzhou (Y27, five hours) and Beihai (Y17, three hours). Buses to Pingxiang take around three hours and cost Y15.20, while Fangcheng buses cost Y12.50. An interesting though rigorous option is the bus service to Kunming via Guangnan. Very few travellers have made this trip, and if you have trouble getting tickets for it at the long-distance bus station, try the No 2 bus station – there are ticket offices with friendly staff opposite the railway station.

Tickets to Guangnan just over the Guangxi-Yunnan border are Y48, while direct Kunming tickets cost Y67. The roads are bad and the whole journey can take up to 36 hours.

Train Trains bound for Beijing allow for connections with Liuzhou, Guilin, Changsha, Wuhan (Hankou) and Zhengzhou. Other major destinations with direct rail links with Nanning are Beijing, Shanghai and Xi'an. There are also direct connections with Zhanjiang (14 hours) in Guangdong Province. Zhanjiang is a coastal town with ferry connections to Hainan Island.

Direct trains from Nanning to Guilin take around seven hours and cost Y46 for a hard-seat ticket. There are various trains leaving for Liuzhou throughout the day. Hard-seat tickets for the four-hour trip cost Y28.

There is a service to Chongqing via Guiyang every other day. It's around 12 hours to Guiyang and another eight hours on to Chongqing. Hard-sleeper tickets to Guiyang are around Y70; to Chongqing Y108.

Trains for Pingxiang (No 511) leave at 10.40 am and arrive at 5.05 pm – all things considered an early morning bus would be a better option.

Boat Leaving Nanning by boat is possible if you have time on your hands; boats are slower and less frequent than the equivalent bus trips. When the river level is sufficiently high, there are boats daily to Canton leaving at 8 pm. The boat journey takes in Hengxian, Guiyang, Guiping, Pingnan, Shengxian, Wuzhou and finally Canton. It takes 36 hours to Wuzhou at a cost of Y48, while Canton takes 48 hours at a cost of Y78.

Getting Around

There are bicycle-hire places on Chaoyang Lu close to the railway station. The signs are in Chinese only, but for the closest place to the railway station look for the mysterious English sign that says 'gauzyangz lijfazdingh' (!). Bikes here are Y0.4 per hour, while the next place, a little up the road next door to the Yu Feng Restaurant, charges Y0.5 per hour.

Alternative modes of transport exist in the abundant taxis and motorcycle taxis (a ride on the back of a motorcycle). Both require hard-headed bargaining, but if you can manage this the motorcycle taxis can be a fairly economical way of getting quickly from A to B.

AROUND NANNING
Yiling Caves & Wuming
(*yílíng yán*) 伊岭岩

Twenty-five km to the north-north-west of Nanning are the Yiling Caves, with their stalagmites and galactic lights; 15 minutes is enough for the caves, but the surrounding countryside is worth exploring.

Wuming is 45 km from Nanning, on the

GUANGXI

same road that leads to the Yiling Caves. There are CITS-organised visits to the local Two-Bridge Production Brigade which you probably won't get on. A few km further up the line is Lingshui Springs, which is a big swimming pool.

To get to either Wuming or the Yiling Caves, take a minibus from the square on the left-hand side of Chaoyang Lu just over the Chaoyang Stream.

Jintiancun

There are a couple of cultural sights along the way, but nothing of note. Just 25 km north-west of Guiping is Jintiancun, the wellspring of one of the weirdest chapters in Chinese history:

Hong Xiuquan, a schoolteacher possibly suffering from hallucinations generated by an illness, declared himself the brother of Jesus Christ and took upon himself the mission of liberating China from the Manchus.

These were the seeds of the Taiping Rebellion (1850-64), which sought to distribute land equally among all Chinese and to establish equality between the sexes. The extremely puritanical Christian sect that Hong developed eventually established a standing army of over a million which swept across 17 provinces in an effort to defeat the Qing Dynasty, at the loss of 20 million lives.

After Hong's army was finally surrounded by Qing forces in Nanjing in 1864, he committed suicide along with nearly 100,000 of his followers.

Zuo River Scenic Area

(zuǒjiāng fēngjǐngqū) 左江风景区

The recently opened Zuo River area, around 190 km south-east of Nanning, provides the opportunity to see karst rock formations like those in Guilin, with the added attraction that this area is home to around 80 groups of Zhuang minority rock paintings. The largest of these is in the area of Mt Huashan *(huāshān bìhuà)*, which has a fresco 40 metres in height and 220 metres across.

Scholars maintain that the paintings have at least a 200-year history, and in design they have a similar appearance to the 'primitive' look of some Guizhou batiks. This area is still relatively unexplored by Western travellers, and for the time being the easiest way

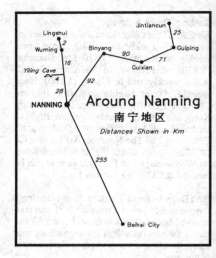

to see the area would be to join a CITS-organised tour.

Alternatively, take a bus from the Nanning square on Chaoyang Lu to Ningming City Wharf *(níngmíng xiànchéng mǎtóu)*, and from there haggle to join up with one of the boat tours. This area is officially open, so there should be accommodation available in Ningming.

Pingxiang

(píngxiáng) 凭祥

Pingxiang is the staging post for onward transport to Vietnam. It's basically a border trading town, and after you've taken a wander through the bustling markets there's not a lot to see. Several hotels in town accept foreigners, and the main one is next door to the long-distance bus station.

Nevertheless, there's no real need to stay in Pingxiang. An early morning bus from Nanning's long-distance bus station will get you into Pingxiang before midday, and at this point you should be able to hitch a lift to the Friendship Pass *(yǒuyì guān)* on the Vietnamese border.

There will be minibuses and private transport running from around the long-distance bus station – you shouldn't have to pay more than Y5 for a ride. From the Friendship Pass it's a 10-minute walk to Vietnam and some of the most unwelcoming border guards you're ever likely to have encountered – some US dollars might speed up proceedings, but it would be best to reserve this option as a last resort. Onward transport to Hanoi by train or bus is via the Vietnamese town of Langsön.

Beihai
(běihǎi) 北海

Beihai is a coastal town that sees very few Western travellers. It's probably worth a couple of days, providing you don't expect too much of the beaches, rated by some as the best in China. One option might be to stop over here before travelling on by bus to Zhanjiang, from where there is onward ferry transport to Haikou on Hainan Island.

Beihai is the main centre for an area that has been designated the Binhai Tourism Area. It includes the towns of Hepu (28 km Beihai), Qinzhou (108 km) and Fangcheng (153 km). Both Beihai and Hepu are renowned for their pearls, a popular buy for visiting Chinese tourists. The closest beach to Beihai is the Yin Beach *(yíntān)*.

Places to Stay For accommodation, try the *Beihai Yingbinguan (běihǎi yíngbīnguǎn)* on 32 Beibuwan Zhonglu close to the long-distance bus station. Other possibilities include

the *Beihai Binguan (běihǎi bīnguǎn)* at 6 Beibuwan Donglu and the *Fulihua Hotel (fùlìhuá dàjiǔdiàn)* on Chating Lu.

Buses to Beihai are available from Nanning, Liuzhou and Guilin – see the Getting There & Away sections for these cities for more information.

GUILIN
(guìlín) 桂林

Guilin has always been famous in China for its scenery and has been eulogised in innumerable literary works, paintings and inscriptions since its founding. For all that, and despite the fact that for the Chinese Guilin is rated the most beautiful spot in the world – the world of course meaning China – most Western visitors find it a big disappointment.

The stunning limestone peaks are not much in evidence on Guilin's polluted and congested streets, and the town's motley assortment of tourist sights sport exploitative FEC entry fees. Accommodation rates have soared with the advent of large-scale overseas Chinese tourism, and most backpackers give the town a miss in favour of Yangshuo, just over an hour's minibus journey away.

The city was founded during the Qin Dynasty and developed as a transport centre with the building of the Ling Canal which linked the important Pearl and Yangzi river systems. Under the Ming it was a provincial capital, a status it retained until 1914 when

Nanning became the capital. During the 1930s and throughout WW II Guilin was a Communist stronghold and its population expanded from about 100,000 to over a million as people sought refuge here. Today it's the home of over 300,000.

While it's worth spending a day cycling around Guilin, it's not really such a good idea to spend much longer than this. A combination of heat, hazy skies, industry, congested streets, enormous crowds and tourism hype make Guilin one of China's most overrated travel experiences. If you don't want to be disappointed, hightail it down to the finer scenery and unhurried pace of Yangshuo and the villages around it.

Information & Orientation

Most of Guilin lies on the western bank of the Li River. The main artery is Zhongshan Lu, which runs roughly parallel to the river on its western side. At the southern end of this street – that is, Zhongshan Nanlu – is Guilin railway station, where most trains pull in. Zhongshan Lu itself is a rapidly developing stretch of tourist-class hotels, opulent department stores and expensive restaurants – a good place for a browse, but be careful about where you stop off for a bite to eat.

Closer to the centre of town is Banyan Lake to the west of Zhongshan Lu, and Fir Lake on the eastern side. Further up around the Zhongshan Lu/Jiefang Lu intersection, you'll find the CITS office, the PSB and places to hire bicycles, as well as one of Guilin's original upmarket hotels and landmarks, the large Li River Hotel.

Jiefang Lu runs east-west across Zhongshan Lu. Heading east, it runs over Liberation (Jiefang) Bridge to the large Seven Star Park, one of the town's chief attractions. This is also where you'll find the upscale Ramada Renaissance Riverside Hotel. Most of the limestone pinnacles form a circle around the town, though a few pop up within the city limits.

For the best views of the surrounding karst formations you either have to climb to the top of the hills or get out of the town altogether. The peaks are not very high and are often obscured by the buildings – the best views are from the top of the Li River Hotel.

CITS The office (☎ 222648) is at 14 Ronghu Beilu, facing Banyan Lake. The staff are friendly and reasonably helpful.

PSB This office is on Sanduo Lu, a side street which runs west off Zhongshan Lu, in the area between Banyan Lake and Jiefang Lu.

Money The main branch of the Bank of China is on Ronghu Beilu and this is where you will have to go if you want a cash advance on your credit card. For changing money and travellers' cheques the other branch on the corner of Shanghai Nanlu and Zhongshan Nanlu next to the railway station is adequate. Alternatively, tourist hotels, including the Hidden Hill, have foreign-exchange services which you can usually use even if you're not staying at the hotel. The black market for FEC has cooled considerably in Guilin in recent years, and it's better to keep your FEC for Yangshuo, where there's more demand and less chance of being ripped off.

Post & Telecommunications The post and telecommunications building is on Zhongshan Lu. There is a second post office on the north corner of the large square in front of the railway station; it has a convenient direct-dial international telephone service that is considerably cheaper than dialling from the business centres of the tourist hotels and much more reliable than the hit-and-miss services offered in Yangshuo. Some of the large hotels, such as the Li River Hotel, have post offices.

Solitary Beauty Peak
(dúxiù fēng) 独秀峰
The 152-metre pinnacle is at the centre of the town. The climb to the top is steep but there are good views of the town, the Li River and surrounding hills. The nephew of a Ming emperor built a palace at the foot of the peak in the 14th century, but only the gate remains.

The site of the palace is now occupied by a teachers' college.

Bus No 1 goes up Zhongshan Lu past the western side of the peak. Alternatively, take bus No 2, which goes past the eastern side along the river. Both buses leave from Guilin railway station.

Wave-Subduing Hill
(fúbō shān) 伏波山

Close to Solitary Beauty and standing beside the western bank of the Li River, this peak offers a fine view of the town. Its name is variously described as being derived from the fact that the peak descends into the river, blocking the waves, and from a temple that was established here for a Tang-Dynasty general who was called Fubo Jiangjun, the wave-subduing general.

On the southern slope of the hill is Returned Pearl Cave *(huánzhū dòng)*. The story goes that the cave was illuminated by a single pearl and inhabited by a dragon; one day a fisher stole the pearl but he was overcome by shame and returned it.

Near this cave is Thousand Buddhas Cave *(qiānfó dòng)*, a typically Chinese exaggeration – there seem to be a couple of dozen statues at most, dating from the Tang and Song dynasties. Bus No 2 runs past the hill.

Seven Star Park
(qīxīng gōngyuán) 七星公园

Seven Star Park is on the eastern side of the Li River. Cross Liberation Bridge *(jiěfàng qiáo)* and the Ming Dynasty Flower Bridge to the park.

The park takes its name from its seven peaks, which are supposed to resemble the star pattern of the Ursa Major (Big Dipper) constellation. There are several caves in the peaks, where visitors have inscribed graffiti for centuries – including a recent one which says, 'The Chinese Communist Party is the core of the leadership of all the Chinese People'. It takes a lot of imagination to see the 'Monkey Picking Peaches' and 'Two Dragons Playing Ball' in the stalagmites and stalactites. Otherwise, try the pitiful zoo.

To get to the park take bus No 9, 10 or 11 from the railway station. From the park, bus No 13 runs back across the Li River, past Wave-Subduing Hill and down to Reed Flute Cave.

Reed Flute Cave
(lúdí yán) 芦笛岩

Ironically, the most extraordinary scenery Guilin has to offer is underground. If you see nothing else then try not to miss the Reed Flute Cave – rather like a set from *Journey to the Centre of the Earth*. At one time the entrance to the cave was distinguished by clumps of reeds used by the locals to make musical instruments, hence the name.

One grotto, the Crystal Palace of the Dragon King, can comfortably hold about 1000 people, though many more crammed in here during the war when the cave was used as an air-raid shelter. The dominant feature of the cave is a great slab of white rock hanging from a ledge like a cataract, while opposite stands a huge stalactite said to resemble an old scholar. The story goes that a visiting scholar wished to write a poem worthy of the cave's beauty. After a long time he had composed only two sentences and, lamenting his inability to find the right words, turned to stone.

The other story is that the slab is the Dragon King's needle, used as a weapon by his opponent the Monkey King. The Monkey King used the needle to destroy the dragon's army of snails and jellyfish, leaving their petrified remains scattered around the floor of the cave. You can no doubt invent your own stories.

The cave is on the north-western outskirts of town. Take bus No 3 from the railway station to the last stop. Bus No 13 will take you to the cave from Seven Star Park. Otherwise, it's an easy bicycle ride. For a guided tour try tagging on to one of the Western tour groups. Try to avoid the cave in the tourist (carnival) season, when the magic goes on holiday. The extortionate entry fee of Y15 FEC puts many sensible travellers off.

Other Hills
Time to knock off a few more peaks. North

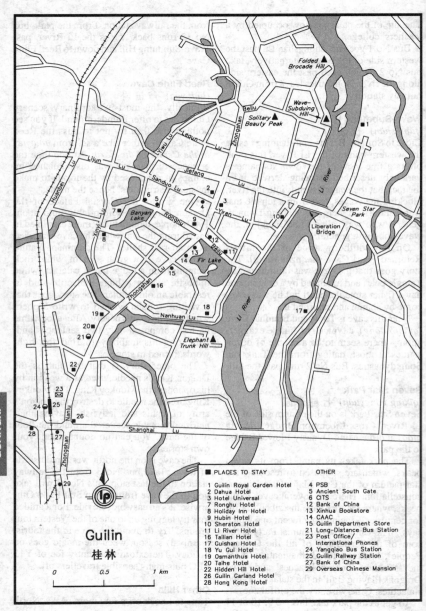

Guilin

桂林

0   0.5   1 km

PLACES TO STAY

1 Guilin Royal Garden Hotel
2 Dahua Hotel
3 Hotel Universal
7 Ronghu Hotel
8 Holiday Inn Hotel
9 Hubin Hotel
10 Sheraton Hotel
11 Li River Hotel
16 Talian Hotel
17 Guishan Hotel
18 Yu Gui Hotel
19 Osmanthus Hotel
20 Taihe Hotel
22 Hidden Hill Hotel
26 Guilin Garland Hotel
28 Hong Kong Hotel

OTHER

4 PSB
5 Ancient South Gate
6 CITS
12 Bank of China
13 Xinhua Bookstore
14 CAAC
15 Guilin Department Store
21 Long-Distance Bus Station
23 Post Office/
   International Phones
24 Yangqiao Bus Station
25 Guilin Railway Station
27 Bank of China
29 Overseas Chinese Mansion

GUANGXI

of Solitary Beauty is **Folded Brocade Hill** (diécǎi shān). Climb the stone pathway which takes you through the Wind Cave, with walls decked with inscriptions and Buddhist sculptures. Some of the damage to faces on the sculptures is a legacy of the Cultural Revolution. Great views from the top of the hill. Bus No 1 runs past the hill.

There's a good view of **Old Man Hill** (lǎorén shān), a curiously shaped hill to the north-east, from Wave-Subduing Hill. The best way to get there is by bicycle as buses don't go past it. At the southern end of town, one of Guilin's best known sights is **Ele-phant Trunk Hill** (xiàngbí shān) which stands next to the Li River. It's basically a large lump of rock with a big hole in it.

At the southern end of Guilin, **South Park** (nán gōngyuán) is a pretty place. You can contemplate the mythological immortal who is said to have lived in one of the caves here; look for the his statue.

There are two lakes near the city centre, **Banyan Lake** (róng hú) on the western side and **Fir Lake** (shān hú) on the eastern side. Banyan Lake is named after an 800-year-old banyan tree on its shore. The tree stands by the restored South City Gate (nán mén) originally built during the Tang Dynasty.

A word of warning about hiking in the hills: in remote areas it would probably be best not to hike alone.

Places to Stay – bottom end

There's a real shortage of budget accommodation in Guilin, the lower end of the market being served primarily by Yangshuo. The first option for most backpackers who want to spend an evening in Guilin is the *Overseas Chinese Hotel (huáqiáo dàshà)*, where a bed in a clean three-bed room is Y25. There are also doubles available for Y40 with shared bathroom and Y60 with private bathroom.

The only other budget option in Guilin is the *Dahua Hotel (dáhuá jiǔdiàn)*, a 20-minute hike north of the railway station up Zhongshan Lu. Dorms with TV and attached bathroom cost Y25 and doubles with the same features cost Y70. Triples are also available at Y85. It's a friendly place, though it would probably be a good idea to avoid the slightly sleazy coffee shop with its partitioned cubicles and bevy of female attendants.

Places to Stay – middle

The only real difference between most of the lower-end and middle-range hotels is that the former have dormitory accommodation. The *Hidden Hill Hotel* (☎ 333540) (yǐnshān fàndiàn) on Zhongshan Nanlu a few minutes' walk north of the railway station, with a foreign-exchange service and restaurant, has doubles ranging from Y80 to Y120

GUANGXI

and not much else available. If it's a double you want, you'd probably be better off at the Dahua, where the rooms are similar but cheaper.

Close to the long-distance bus station is the *Taihe Hotel* (☎ 335504) *(tàihé fàndiàn)*. Doubles cost Y120 and triples are also available from Y120. Opposite the railway station, the *Guilin Garland Hotel* (☎ 332511) *(kǎiyuè jiǔdiàn)* is a better deal with comfortable doubles with attached bathrooms for Y98.

Up on Ronghu Beilu the *Hubin Hotel* (☎ 222837) *(húbīn fàndiàn)* has basic singles/doubles for Y60 and triples for Y70. Air-con doubles with attached bathroom are also available for Y90.

Places to Stay – top end

At the lower end of the top range is the *Yu Gui Hotel (yùguì bīnguǎn)*, a derelict kind of place opposite the Elephant Hill Park. Singles here start at Y120, while doubles range from Y160 to Y200.

Not far from the railway station and in a different league altogether is the Hong Kong-managed *Hong Kong Hotel* (☎ 335753) *(xiāngjiāng fàndiàn)*. Doubles range from US$50 to US$60, and the hotel is complete with shopping facilities, bicycle rental, sauna and a revolving restaurant on the 19th floor. Also not far from the railway station, on Zhongshan Lu, is the *Osmanthus Hotel* (☎ 332261) *(dānguì dàjiǔdiàn)* with doubles in the western wing ranging from US$60 to US$80 and the same in the eastern wing from US$30 to US$45.

The *Ronghu Hotel* (☎ 223811) *(rónghú fàndiàn)* at 17 Ronghu Lu once catered only for Overseas Chinese. Indeed, you practically needed a map of the hotel grounds and a fluent command of the local dialect to find the reception desk! Since then a new wing has been added, the range of clientele expanded and room prices have shot up. Singles start at Y160 and doubles range from Y200 to Y300. Doubles can be converted into triples by the addition of an extra bed at a charge of Y40. It's a bit inconveniently located unless you have a bicycle.

The *Li River Hotel* (☎ 222881) *(lǐjiāng fàndiàn)* at 1 Shanhu Beilu was once the main tourist hotel in Guilin. It's right in the middle of town and the roof provides a panoramic view of the encircling hills. Standard doubles are US$50 and a deluxe room will set you back US$70; there are no singles available. It has the full works: post office, barber, bank, restaurants, tour groups and bellboys in monkey suits.

The US-style *Holiday Inn Hotel* (☎ 223950) *(guìlín bīnguǎn)* at 14 Ronghu Nanlu has doubles posted at US$80, but when occupancy is low you can negotiate this to US$50 or less. Another brand-name place is the *Ramada Renaissance Riverside Hotel* (☎ 442411) on Yanjiang Lu near Seven Star Park. Rooms start here at US$75.

Opposite Elephant Trunk Hill is the flash four-star *Guishan Hotel (guìshān jiǔdiàn)*, where rooms start at US$100 a night. The Guishan also hires apartments in the compound that go for as low as US$300 a *month*. The foreign-managed *Sheraton Guilin Hotel* (☎ 443388) *(wénhuá dàjiǔdiàn)* at 9 Binjiang Nanlu has rates starting at US$90.

Places to Eat

Guilin food is basically Cantonese. Traditionally the town is noted for its snake soup, wild cat or bamboo rat, washed down with snake-bile wine. You could be devouring some of these animals into extinction. The pangolin (a sort of Chinese armadillo) is a protected species but still crops up on restaurant menus. Other protected species include the muntjac horned pheasant, mini-turtle, short-tailed monkey and gem-faced civet. Generally the most exotic stuff you should come across is eels, catfish, pigeons and dog.

Unfortunately, overseas Chinese with fistfuls of dollars have pushed many restaurant prices into Hong Kong/Taipei levels, and the problem is compounded by overcharging in the smaller restaurants. If prices are not listed make a point of asking first.

If you are just after a quick bite to eat, your best bet is to wander north of the railway station up Zhongshan Lu. There are a couple of places between the railway station and the long-distance bus station with reasonable prices and English menus. Don't worry too much about finding these places; the staff normally dash into the crowd and drag you off the street. There's a restaurant that won't break the budget on the near right corner of Zhongshan Lu and Nanhuan Lu. It has semi-decent coffee that comes in dainty little teapots.

Just north of the Osmanthus Hotel on Zhongshan Lu is *Beer Street*, a half-indoor, half-outdoor place with a good variety of Chinese dishes and cold beer at fair prices.

The Overseas Chinese Mansion has a cosy little coffee shop that's quite reasonable. Next door is a small restaurant with cheap Western breakfasts.

The Chinese restaurant in the Grand Hotel has fabulous dim sum – it's very popular among Taiwanese tourists. For reasonably priced upper-end meals and excellent coffee try the revolving restaurant on the 19th floor of the Hong Kong Hotel. Pots of percolated coffee are good value here at Y10.

Getting There & Away

Guilin is connected to many places by air, bus, train and boat. Give serious thought to flying in or out of this place, as train connections are not good.

Air CAAC has an office (☎ 223063) at 144 Zhongshan Lu, just to the south of the intersection of Zhongshan Lu and Shahu Beilu. Guilin is well connected to the rest of China by air and destinations include: Beijing, Y920; Shanghai, Y700; Hangzhou (Zhejiang), Y610; Xiamen (Fujian), Y440; Canton (Guangdong), Y300; Shenzhen (Guangdong), Y370; Guiyang (Guizhou), Y210; Chongqing (Sichuan), Y340; Kunming (Yunnan), Y430; Chengdu (Sichuan), Y480; Xi'an (Shaanxi), Y550; Lanzhou (Gansu), Y830; Ürümqi (Xinjiang), Y1690; Nanning (Guangxi), Y190; Hong Kong (Y850).

Probably the most popular travellers' option is the Guilin-Kunming flight, which saves considerable travelling time and saves mucking about trying to get tickets on a train that is frequently booked out.

Bus For short local runs (ie Yangshuo), minibuses depart regularly from the railway station. Buses to Yangshuo should set you back Y6, and the trip takes just over an hour.

The long-distance bus station is just south of the railway station on Zhongshan Lu. Buses to Longsheng run through the day approximately hourly from 7 am to 5.20 pm; one bus a day goes to Sanjiang at 8.40 am; buses to Xingping leave approximately hourly from 9 am to 4.30 pm; two buses a day run to Beihai at 7 am and 8.40 am; buses for Xing'an leave at 9.40, 11.40 am and 3.40 pm. Buses for Liuzhou leave at 6.40 am, and in Liuzhou it is possible to connect with buses for Nanning.

For Wuzhou and Canton both ordinary and deluxe buses are available – the deluxe buses offer a bit more legroom, a feature not to be sneezed at over a long distance, though it's a comfort that nearly doubles the price of the trip. Buses to Canton leave at 2, 3, and 3.30 pm; deluxe buses cost Y71.80 and ordinary buses Y44.50. Buses for Wuzhou leave at 8.20 am, 5.30 and 7 pm; deluxe buses cost Y42.60 and ordinary buses Y29.20. There is also a bus service leaving for Zhuhai at 12.20 pm.

Behind the railway station is the Yangqiao long-distance bus station, where buses and minibuses leave on a regular basis for Longsheng and Sanjiang among other places.

Train There are useful train connections to Guilin, but some of these (like the Kunming-Guiyang-Guilin-Shanghai route) tend to involve long hauls on unbelievably crowded carriages. Guilin railway station has a separate ticket office for foreigners; this means you'll have to pay tourist price but at least you avoid the impossible queues and will normally be able to pick up a ticket. By the time you have this book in your hands there should also be an advance booking office in Yangshuo.

Direct trains out of Guilin include those to Kunming (about 33 hours); Beijing (50 hours); Canton (16 hours); Shanghai (35 hours); Xi'an (35 hours); Guiyang (18 hours); Zhanjiang, Guangdong (about 13 hours); Changsha, Jiangsu (12 hours); Liuzhou (four hours) and Nanning (seven hours). For Chongqing change trains at Guiyang.

There are two trains a day to Kunming: one starts from Shanghai; the other from Canton. In either case the trains are generally very crowded. The 'Friendly Youth' ticket counter at Guilin station seems to have no problems in supplying hard-sleeper tickets providing you are happy to pay tourist prices in FEC, though these are usually for the train from Canton, which gets to Guilin between 2 and 3 am. Tourist-price tickets from Guilin to Kunming are Y90 for hard seat, Y185/346 for hard/soft sleeper.

There is a direct train to Canton. Tourist-price fares are Y81 for hard seat, Y116/230 for hard/soft sleeper. Otherwise you have to stop at Hengyang and change trains. The indirect route will take about 24 hours and fares are slightly cheaper.

Getting Around
To/From the Airport A taxi to the airport costs a minimum of Y30, but this will require some determined bargaining and probably Chinese language skills. Most of the hotels in Yangshuo can organise an airport taxi for Y60 – not too bad if there are three or four of you. There are also CAAC buses from the city office to the airport for Y5, but these tend to run on an infrequent basis – check with the CAAC office for times.

Bus & Taxi Most of the city buses leave from the terminal at Guilin railway station and will get you to many major sights, but a bicycle is definitely better.

Taxis are available from the major tourist hotels for Y15 per trip, depending on the distance. Pedicabs charge Y3 to Y5 per trip.

Bicycle Bicycles are definitely the best way to get around Guilin. There has been a proliferation of bicycle-hire shops over the last few years – just look along Zhongshan Lu for the signs. There are a couple near the long-distance bus station, one next to the

Overseas Chinese Hotel and another on the grounds of the Li River Hotel. Most charge between Y7 and Y10 per day and require Y200 or your passport as security.

Boat A popular tourist trip is the boat ride from Guilin down the Li River to Yangshuo. Although this is still popular with tour groups (whole fleets of boats do the run daily in the high season), low-budget travellers have been put off by the exorbitant ticket prices, which presently come in at Y220 FEC including a bus trip back to Guilin from Yangshuo.

Much cheaper, and arguably more interesting, boat trips are available in Yangshuo, and it makes more sense to travel by minibus to Yangshuo and organise a trip there. Tickets for Guilin boat trips can be bought at the CITS office or at any tourist hotel. The boats leave from a dock on the Li River about 100 metres north of Elephant Trunk Hill.

AROUND GUILIN
The Ling Canal (*líng qú*) is in Xing'an County, about 70 km north of Guilin. It was built during the 2nd century BC in the reign of the first Qin emperor, Qin Shihuang, to transport supplies to his army. The canal links the Xiang River (which flows into the Yangzi) and the Tan River (which flows into the Pearl River), thus connecting two of China's major waterways.

You can see the Ling Canal at **Xing'an**, a market town of about 30,000 people, two hours by bus from Guilin. There are three daily buses from the long-distance bus station leaving at 9.40, 11.40 am and 3.40 pm. The town is also connected to Guilin by train. Two branches of the canal flow through the town, one at the north end and one at the south. The total length of the Ling Canal is 34 km.

YANGSHUO
(*yángshuò*) 阳朔
Just 1½ hours from Guilin by bus, Yangshuo has, along with Dali in Yunnan, become one of those legendary backpacker destinations

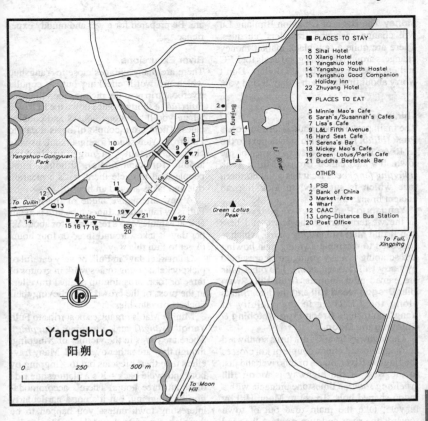

PLACES TO STAY
8 Sihai Hotel
10 Xilang Hotel
11 Yangshuo Hotel
14 Yangshuo Youth Hostel
15 Yangshuo Good Companion
   Holiday Inn
22 Zhuyang Hotel

PLACES TO EAT
5 Minnie Mao's Cafe
6 Sarah's/Susannah's Cafes
7 Lisa's Cafe
9 L&L Fifth Avenue
16 Hard Seat Cafe
17 Serena's Bar
18 Mickey Mao's Cafe
19 Green Lotus/Paris Cafe
21 Buddha Beefsteak Bar

OTHER
1 PSB
2 Bank of China
3 Market Area
4 Wharf
12 CAAC
13 Long-Distance Bus Station
20 Post Office

Yangshuo
阳朔

that most travellers have heard about long before they even set foot in China. It's a tiny country town set amidst limestone pinnacles, and makes a great laid-back base from which to explore other small villages in the nearby countryside.

Give Guilin itself a miss, head down to Yangshuo, hire a mountain bike and find out what the Guilin landscape is really all about. A lot of people have even stayed overnight in the villages, and if you want to go camping on the mountains you shouldn't have any problem. It's probably not permitted to camp out, but who's going to climb a 200-metre peak to bring you down? There are caves in the peaks, unlit by fairy lights, many no doubt untrod by human feet.

Information

CITS There's an office on the grounds of the Yangshuo Hotel and another office next to the Sihai Hotel. You can get useful maps of Yangshuo and the surrounding area which show villages, paths and roads. The staff are helpful and friendly, though travellers seldom avail themselves of their services – enterprising locals working from the cafes are generally more in touch with the needs of independent travellers.

Money The Bank of China on Binjiang Lu will change cash and travellers' cheques. There are quite a few black-market money changers around offering good deals for FEC and even better deals for US dollars. Don't worry about finding them – they'll find you.

Things to See

The main peak in Yangshuo is **Green Lotus Peak** (*bìlián fēng*), which stands next to the Li River in the south-eastern corner of the town. It's also called Bronze Mirror Peak (*tóngjìng fēng*) because it has a flat northern face which is supposed to look like an ancient bronze mirror.

Yangshuo Park (*yángshuò gōngyuán*) is in the western part of the town, and here you'll find **Man Hill** (*xīláng shān*), which is supposed to resemble a young man bowing and scraping to a shy young girl represented by **Lady Hill** (*xiǎogū shān*). The other hills are named after animals: **Crab Hill, Swan Hill, Dragon Head Hill** and the like. Sights along the Li River in the vicinity of Yangshuo include **Green Frog Watching & Enjoying the Moon**.

The highway from Guilin turns southward at Yangshuo and after a couple of km crosses the Jingbao River. South of this river and just to the west of the highway is **Moon Hill** (*yuèliang shān*), a limestone pinnacle with a moon-shaped hole. To get to Moon Hill by bicycle, take the main road out of town towards the river and turn right on the road about 200 metres before the bridge. Cycle for about 50 minutes – Moon Hill is on your right and the views from the top are incredible!

A series of caves have been opened up not far from Moon Hill: the **Black Buddha Caves** (*hēifó dòng*). If you head out to Moon Hill, you will undoubtedly be intercepted and invited to visit the caves. It's theoretically possible to walk through the mountain and come out on the other side, though locals report that it takes at least three to four hours (and how do you get back to your bicycle?). Tours cost in the vicinity of Y15 per head, though prices go down the more of you there

are. Be prepared for a wet and muddy experience.

River Excursions

There are many villages close to Yangshuo which are worth checking out. A popular riverboat trip is to the picturesque village of **Fuli** (*fùlì*) a short distance down the Li River, where you'll see stone houses and cobbled lanes. There are a couple of boats a day to Fuli from Yangshuo (foreigners are usually charged Y8, but you might try looking around for local boats), although most people tend to cycle there – it's a pleasant ride and takes around an hour.

A new alternative mode of transport to Fuli is by inner-tube. Inner-tube hire is available at Minnie Mao's restaurant for about Y3 per day. It takes around three or four hours to get to Fuli this way.

On market days in Fuli, be very careful of pickpockets; young males work in groups of three or four, brushing up against travellers in the press of the crowd and relieving their pockets of valuables.

Minnie Mao's organises boat trips to Fuli, **Yangti** (*yángtí*) and Xingping (*xīngpíng*). There are caves in the vicinity of Xingping, though they are rather overrated. Many travellers take their bicycles out to Xingping by boat and cycle back – it's a picturesque ride of about three hours. There's accommodation in Xingping, but it's not a particularly interesting town unless you happen to be there on a market day. Minnie Mao's also offers rafting trips and kayak hire, both popular options in the warm summer months.

Markets

Villages in the vicinity of Yangshuo are best visited on market days, and these operate on a three-day, monthly cycle. Yangshuo is on the same cycle as Xingping. Thus, markets take place every three days starting on the first of the month for Baisha (1, 4, 7, etc), every three days starting on the second of the month for Fuli (2, 5, 8, etc), and every three days starting on the third of the month for Yangshuo and Xingping (3, 6, 9, etc). There are no markets on the 10th, 20th, 30th and 31st of the month.

Places to Stay

The three most popular places to stay in Yangshuo are the *Yangshuo Youth Hostel*, opposite the bus station, the *Good Companion Holiday Inn* just not far from the youth hostel, and the *Sihai Hotel* (also known as the Good Companion Holiday Inn just to confuse things) nestled in among all the travellers' hang-outs on Xi Jie. All three offer very similar standards and can be noisy – the Yangshuo Youth Hostel and the Good Companion because of trucks hurtling down the main road to Guilin, and the Sihai because of late-night drinking binges by travellers in the cafes below.

The Yangshuo Youth Hostel has some of the friendliest staff in town, and until recently even had a sign posted explaining their enlightened views on casual sex. Beds in a five-bed dorm cost Y4 or Y7, the latter being for a room with an attached bathroom. Singles/doubles/triples with attached bathroom are Y10/24/30. The Good Companion Holiday Inn is often full and has dorm beds for Y5 and beds in doubles/triples for Y9/7.

The Sihai Hotel is popular mainly for its convenience to the cafes on Xi Jie, and apart from the noise in the evenings and the dampness of the rooms in the winter months there's little to complain about. The Sihai has 'luxury' doubles for Y20 per person as well as singles/doubles/triples with shared bathroom for Y10/16/21.

Travellers coming in on the night bus from Wuzhou are often dropped off outside the *Zhuyang Hotel*. It's actually not a bad place to stay. Singles with attached bathroom are Y20, while doubles range from Y24 to Y30. A bed in a triple costs Y10.

The *Xilang Hotel*, which is set back from the street and very quiet at night, gets neglected by many travellers and tends to be more popular with Chinese. Despite this, it's a friendly place with reasonable rates. Singles are Y8 and doubles/triples with attached bathroom are Y14/8 per bed.

The *Yangshuo Hotel* is shabbily upmarket, offering damp doubles with attached bathroom for Y30, and air-con doubles/triples for Y70/84. Triples with attached bathroom are also available at Y12 per bed.

Places to Eat

Xi Jie teems with tiny cafes offering interesting Chinese/Western crossovers as well as perennial travellers' favourites such as banana pancakes, muesli and pizza. For anyone who has been wandering around China for a while it's a good chance to have a break from oily stir-fried vegetables.

Undoubtedly the most popular of the cafes is *Lisa's*. Lisa herself is a wonderful host, and travellers rave about her Tibetan coffee and dishes like the duck & potato. Lisa's often gets crowded early in the evening, but there are plenty of other places worth trying.

L&L Fifth Avenue just across the road has some of the best Chinese food in Yangshuo as well as a very authentic bolognese (*yìdàlì miàn*); they also show movies in the evening. A little further along Xi Jie are *Sarah's*, *Susannah's* and *Minnie Mao's*.

Other popular places include the cluster of cafes up on the corner of Xi Jie and the main road: *Green Lotus*, *Paris Café* and *Buddha Beefsteak Bar*. They all have outdoor seating and are good places to sit and watch the world go by. The menu at the Paris Café offers local coffee followed by the comment 'not recommended'.

The places on the main road are where some of Yangshuo's original cafes started. They don't enjoy the popularity of some of the places on Xi Jie, but cafes like *Slims*, *The Hard Seat*, *Serena's* and *Mickey Mao's* are all friendly spots for a meal or a cup of coffee.

If you get tired of the 'international' spots, hop over to the narrow street east of and parallel to Xi Jie; here you'll find a number of *yóutiáo* (fried breadsticks) and noodle vendors.

Things to Buy

Yangshuo has developed into a good place to do some souvenir shopping and most travellers end up buying at least something while they are in town. Good buys include silk jackets (at much cheaper prices than in Hong Kong), hand-painted T-shirts, scroll paintings, batiks (from Guizhou) and name chops. Everything on sale should be bargained for. The paintings available in Yangshuo, for example, are generally poor quality (even if you think they look good) and a starting price of Y200 can easily go down to at least Y100.

If you are in the market for a chop, bear in mind that it is not the size of the stone that is important in determining a price but quality of the stone itself. Often the smaller pieces are more expensive than the hefty chunks of rock available. The three best places (according to locals) for chops in Yangshuo are L&L Fifth Avenue, the hole-in-the-wall place next to Lisa's, and Minnie Mao's. Generally the prices offered for chops are fair and require less bargaining than other items.

Getting There & Away

Air The closest airport is in Guilin, and there is now a CAAC office in Yangshuo with a computerised booking service. This will save mucking about with CITS or making a trip into Guilin. Check the Guilin Getting There & Away section for details on the flights available. The office is opposite the Guilin long-distance bus station.

Bus There are frequent buses and minibuses running to Guilin through the day. The best option is the minibus service which operates from the square in front of the bus station. Buses leave as soon as they fill up, which takes anywhere from five to 15 minutes, and the trip takes a little over an hour. They charge Y6.

If you're heading to Canton you can take a bus/boat combination from Yangshuo; buses to Wuzhou leave at 6.40 am and 5.30 pm and cost Y30. The morning bus allows you to connect with the evening boat from Wuzhou; the evening bus is less convenient as it leaves you to sit out in the wee small hours of the morning waiting for the first boat of the day. It is possible to book onward boat connections to Canton in Yangshuo but only for 3rd-class tickets. If you want your own 2nd-class cabin you should book in Wuzhou when you arrive – there are usually cabins available for the 8 pm night boat for Y66 (around double the price of a 3rd-class ticket).

It is also possible to book the Wuzhou-Hong Kong hovercraft in Yangshuo. Both CITS and the Yangshuo Youth Hostel sell a combined bus/boat ticket for Y240 FEC. Most people catch the morning bus and overnight in Wuzhou, though accommodation is not included in the price of the ticket.

Other destinations from Yangshuo's long-distance bus station include Liuzhou, for which buses leave at 6.50 and 7.40 am and cost Y21.50. Buses direct to Canton leave at 5 pm and cost Y56. It's reportedly a hellish journey, but the quickest way of getting to Canton short of flying.

Train The nearest railway station is in Guilin. A number of cafes around Yangshuo will organise train tickets at reasonable prices, and CITS can organise foreigner's price tickets. For Kunming, an option recommended by CITS is a deal whereby you bus to Liuzhou and travel on by hard sleeper to Kunming. The whole deal is Y250 FEC. At the time of writing there were plans to open an advance rail booking office in Yangshuo.

Getting Around

Yangshuo itself is small enough to walk around without burning up too many calories, but if you want to get further afield then hire a bicycle. Just look for rows of bikes and signs near the intersection of Xi Jie and the main road. The charge is about Y3 per day. Mountain bikes are also available at Y6 a day.

LI RIVER
(lǐ jiāng) 漓江
The Li River is the connecting waterway between Guilin and Yangshuo and is one of the main tourist attractions of the area. A thousand years ago a poet wrote of the scenery around Yangshuo: 'The river forms a green gauze belt, the mountains are like blue jade hairpins'. The 83-km stretch

between the towns is hardly that but you do see some extraordinary peaks, sprays of bamboo lining the riverbanks, fishers in small boats and picturesque villages.

As is the Chinese habit, every feature along the route has been named. **Paint Brush Hill** juts straight up from the ground with a pointed tip like a Chinese writing brush. **Cock-fighting Hills** stand face to face like two cocks about to engage in battle. **Mural Hill** just past the small town of Yangti is a sheer cliff rising abruptly out of the water; there are supposed to be the images of nine horses in the weathered patterns on the cliff face.

Tour boats depart from Guilin from a jetty about 100 metres north of Elephant Trunk Hill each morning at around 7.30 am. The trip takes about six hours round trip and costs a phenomenal Y220 FEC. Many people find that the time drags by the end. It's probably not worth it if you're going to be spending any length of time in Yangshuo, unless you decide to overnight in Xingping at the halfway point. Back in Yangshuo, buses meet the incoming boats to take passengers on to Guilin, pausing at a tourist market and photo stop near Moon Hill.

Xingping
(xīngpíng) 兴坪

This scenic little town sits on the banks of the Li River about three hours upstream from Yangshuo. The mountain scenery around Xingping is even more breathtaking than around Yangshuo and there are many unexplored caves in the area. People residing in some of the caves manufacture gunpowder for a living.

Few travellers spend the night in Xingping, but it's certainly worth considering a stay here. One small hotel sits on a point that juts out into the river; basic rooms are Y10 per person. A couple of doll's house restaurants with bilingual menus keep everyone fed (take care that they don't overcharge).

Getting There & Away Some travellers come to Xingping by boat from Yangshuo and then pedal back to Yangshuo on bicycles

they've hired and brought on the boat. The boat costs Y20 per person (tourist price, you may be able to get a lower fare) and takes 2½ to four hours depending on the river level. Minnie Mao's can organise boat tickets for you.

The 25-km Yangshuo-Xingping road winds through rice fields, lush vegetable gardens and gnarled peaks and only takes a couple of hours by bike, going slowly. By bus (Y2.90) it's only 45 minutes to an hour away.

LONGSHENG & SANJIANG
(lóngshèng/sānjiāng) 龙胜/三江

Around three hours by bus to the north-west of Guilin, Longsheng and Sanjiang are close to the border of Guizhou Province and are a good introduction to the rich minority cultures of this province. The Longsheng area is home to a colourful mixture of Dong, Yao and Miao minorities, while Sanjiang is mainly Dong.

Longsheng's main attractions are its rice terraces (tītián) and a nearby hot spring. The hot spring (wēnquán) is a tacky highlight of Chinese tours of the area and can be safely missed. Local buses running out to the hot spring, however, pass through rolling hills sculptured with precipitous rice terraces and studded with Yao minority villages. The area is reminiscent of Banaue in northern Luzon, Philippines. It's possible to desert the bus around six or seven km from the hot spring and take off into the hills for some exploring. The locals are generally very friendly.

Sanjiang itself is a drab kind of town with loudspeakers blasting out propaganda day and night, but there are Dong villages in the vicinity. The main sight is the **Chengyang Wind & Rain Bridge** (chéngyáng qiáo) to the west of town on the road to the railway station. It's possible to walk out there in around 30 minutes.

Longsheng and Sanjiang are best visited with an overnight stay in each. Trying to do either as a day trip from Guilin would leave you with no time to get out of town and see the sights.

GUANGXI

Places to Stay & Eat

At present there is only one hotel in Longsheng that accepts foreigners: *Longsheng Hotel (lóngshèng bīnguǎn)*. To get there, walk downhill from the bus station and turn right to cross the bridge into town. Turn left at the first intersection and it's on your right. Beds in a double with attached bathroom are Y24. There's a decent restaurant next door to the hotel, and a number of places selling noodles near the bus station.

Accommodation in Sanjiang is no less basic than in Longsheng. The best option is probably *The Hostel of the Department Store (sānjiāng bǎihuò zhāodàisuǒ)*, which is on the opposite corner to the long-distance bus station. Four-bed dorms cost Y4; doubles Y5.50 per bed; and singles with attached bathroom cost Y8.

The *Hostel of the People's Government of the Sanjiang Dong Autonomous Region*, as it proclaims itself, is a filthy rat-infested hole with doubles for Y12. The hotel reverberates to the sound of propaganda between the hours of 6 am and 10 pm. To get there, follow the road that runs between the Department Store Hostel and the bus station uphill and bear left.

There are numerous little restaurants of the pick-and-choose variety around the bus station. Next to the Department Store Hostel on the 2nd floor is the *Deyi Restaurant*, with staff who will probably panic when you walk in. The food is good though.

Getting There & Away

It's best to catch a bus to Longsheng, overnight there and catch a minibus or public bus on to Sanjiang the next day. In Guilin there are buses and minibuses running to Longsheng from the long-distance bus station, the Yangqiao bus station (behind the railway station) and from the railway station. The long-distance bus station has buses approximately on the hour between 7 am and 5.20 pm. Buses from the railway station and the Yangqiao bus station are less frequent but do the trip a little faster.

From Longsheng to Sanjiang there are minibuses running from the intersection next to the bridge just down the road from the bus station. The fare is Y5 and the journey takes around 1½ hours.

The Sanjiang bus station has buses back to Guilin at 7.20 and 9.30 am, and buses to Liuzhou at 7 and 8 am. There are three buses a day to Longsheng at 7.40 and 10.30 am and at 12.40 pm. Travelling from Sanjiang to Guizhou is possible but slow and arduous. One possibility is to take a train to Tongdao in Hunan Province and from there travel onwards by bus to Liping in Guizhou (there are minibuses running to the railway station half hourly through the day).

The other possibility is to do the trip slowly by public buses, via Longe, Zhaoxing and on to Liping. Buses to Longe in Guizhou leave at 8.30 am and will probably arrive just in time for you to have missed the only bus on to Liping. If so, you will have to overnight in Longe (the only hotel is in the bus station and costs Y5 for a double) and carry on at 11 am the following day to Liping. See the Guizhou chapter for more information on this interesting region.

LIUZHOU

(liǔzhōu) 柳州

Liuzhou, with a population of over 730,000, is the largest city on the Liu River and an important south-west China railway junction. The place dates back to the Tang Dynasty, at which time it was a dumping ground for disgraced court officials. The town was largely left to its mountain wilds until 1949, when it was transformed into a major industrial city. Today it is Guangxi's most important industrial city, a good enough reason as any to leave it to its own devices.

Liuzhou is Guilin's poor cousin with similar but less impressive karst scenery on the outskirts of town. If you didn't think much of Guilin, the chances are you'll be even less impressed with Liuzhou. It's an unwelcoming town with limited accommodation (most of the hotels will shoo you away with cries of 'no foreigners') and almost nothing to see.

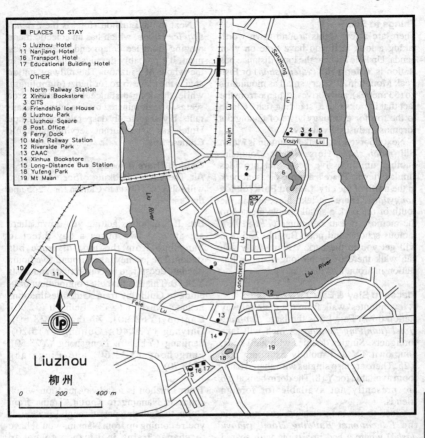

■ PLACES TO STAY

5 Liuzhou Hotel
11 Nanjiang Hotel
16 Transport Hotel
17 Educational Building Hotel

OTHER

1 North Railway Station
2 Xinhua Bookstore
3 CITS
4 Friendship Ice House
6 Liuzhou Park
7 Liuzhou Sqaure
8 Post Office
9 Ferry Dock
10 Main Railway Station
12 Riverside Park
13 CAAC
14 Xinhua Bookstore
15 Long-Distance Bus Station
18 Yufeng Park
19 Mt Maan

Liuzhou

柳州

0   200   400 m

■ PLACES TO STAY

5 柳州饭店
11 南疆饭店
16 交通饭店
17 教育大厦

OTHER

1 柳北站
2 新华书店
3 中国国际旅行社

4 冰屋公园
6 谊州广场
7 柳州邮电局
8 柳州电运车站
9 航运码头
10 火车站公园
12 江滨公园
13 民航售票处
14 新华书店
15 汽车总站公园
18 鱼峰山
19 马鞍

Things to See

There are a few sights around town worth taking a look at if you have time on your hands. Up Feie Lu near the long-distance bus station is **Yufeng Hill** (*yúfēng shān*) or Fish Peak Mountain. It's very small as mountains go (33 metres), and derives its name from the fact that it looks like a 'standing fish'. Climb to the top for a smoggy vista of Guangxi's foremost industrialised city.

Next door to Fish Peak Mountain is **Maan Hill** (*mǎān shān*), Horse Saddle Mountain, another unimpressive peak that provides similar views. There's a more pleasant park in the north of the city: **Liuhou Park** (*liǔhòu gōngyuán*). There's a lake here, and in the south of the park a small temple erected to the memory of Liu Zongyuan (772-819), a famous scholar and poet. Bus No 2, 5 or 6 will get you to the park. Alternatively you can walk there from the long-distance bus station in around 20 minutes.

Places to Stay & Eat

A few minutes' walk from the main railway station down Feie Lu is the large *Nanjiang Hotel* (*nánjiāng fàndiàn*), which will take foreigners. Singles/doubles with hard beds, your own TV and mouldy bathroom cost Y25. There are also singles with shared bathroom available for Y18. The dorm beds at Y6 are presently not available for foreign friends.

Close to the long-distance bus station is the *Educational Building Hotel* (*jiàoyù dàshà*) where a bed in a triple with shared bathroom is Y12 and doubles with attached bathroom are Y56. Right next door to the long-distance bus station is the *Transport Hotel*, which despite its English sign does not take foreigners. This may change and it might be worth inquiring as to the latest developments; doubles are Y30 and beds in a triple are Y13.50.

The *Liuzhou Hotel* (*liǔzhōu fàndiàn*) is the best of Liuzhou's dismal hotels. Singles/doubles with attached bathroom cost Y54/64. To get there take a bus No 2 to the Liuhou Park, turn right into Youyi Lu and look out for the hotel on the right.

Next to the Liuzhou Hotel is the *Friendship Ice House*, which has an eclectic menu ranging from ice cream and coffee to dog meat. It's probably the nicest place to eat in the whole of Liuzhou. The railway station area is the place to go for jiaozi (dumplings), while the long-distance bus station area seems to be dominated by dog hotpot restaurants. If you get really desperate, the Liuzhou Hotel has a restaurant serving palatable Chinese fare.

Getting There & Away

Air The CAAC booking office on Feie Lu will sell you a ticket to Canton for Y245 and that's it.

Bus If Liuzhou is getting you down, there are at least two buses a day direct to Yangshuo from the long-distance bus station. The journey takes around five hours (the bus doesn't go to Guilin first) and costs Y14.70. This is a far better option than travelling to Guilin by train. Other destinations include Wuzhou (Y33), Beihai (Y32.90), Canton (Y62.90), Zhuhai (Y78.60), Guiyang (Y20.40), Guiping (Y15.20), Sanjiang (Y17.50), Longsheng (Y23.50), Fangcheng (Y33.60) and Pingxiang (Y38.70).

Train Liuzhou is a railway junction which connects Nanning to Guilin. Trains from Guilin to Kunming pass through Liuzhou. If you're coming up from Nanning you'll have to change trains in Liuzhou to get to Kunming. All trains heading out of Nanning pass through Liuzhou, and you could hook up with any one of these to get to a number of major destinations. Possibilities include Beijing, Shanghai, Canton, Xi'an, Guiyang and Changsha.

The hard-seat fare from Liuzhou to Guilin is around Y18, and the trip takes approximately four hours. Hard-seat tickets for the four-hour trip to Nanning are Y28.

Getting Around

Liuzhou is uncomfortably large – forget about walking round it, particularly at the height of summer when the place is like a blast furnace! Unfortunately, there don't seem to be any bicycle-hire places about either. Pedicabs, motortricycles, motorcycle taxis and taxis can be found at the bus station outside the railway station. Bus No 2 will take you to the Liuzhou Hotel. Bus No 4 heads south through the karst peaks and might be a good tour bus. Bus maps can be bought from sidewalk hawkers. Bus No 11 links the long-distance bus station to the main railway station.

WUZHOU

(*wúzhōu*) 梧州

Situated at major and minor river junctions, Wuzhou was an important trading town in the 18th century. In 1897 the British dived in there, setting up steamer services to Canton, Hong Kong and later Nanning. A British consulate was established – which gives some idea of the town's importance as a trading centre at the time – and the town was also used by British and US missionaries as a launching pad for the conversion of the heathen Chinese.

The period after 1949 saw some industrial development with the establishment of a paper mill, food-processing factories, and machinery and plastics manufacturing, among other industries. During the Cultural Revolution, Guilin and the nearby towns appear to have become battlegrounds for Red Guard factions claiming loyalty to Mao. In something approaching a civil war half of Wuzhou was reportedly destroyed.

Today, Wuzhou has some fine street markets, tailors, tobacco, herbs, roast duck and river life to explore. Wuzhou also has one of Guangxi's more unusual sights in the Snake Repository.

For the most part travellers transit for a few hours in Wuzhou on the popular trip from Canton to Guilin/Yangshuo, taking a boat from Canton to Wuzhou and then a bus to Yangshuo or Guilin. An overnight stop here isn't the end of the world, however. There are a couple of pleasant parks around town and some interesting street life, though

Wuzhou is by no means one of Guangxi's major attractions.

Information

The post office is on Nanhuan Lu, just before the bridge. Good maps of the city, with bus routes, are available from shops near the ferry dock (for Canton and Nanning) and long-distance bus station. CITS has an office at the Beishan Hotel, but you shouldn't have to deal with them at all if you're just passing through – all onward tickets can easily be purchased at the boat dock or bus station.

Snake Repository

(*shécáng*) 蛇仓

Wuzhou has the largest snake repository in all of south-west China, a major drawcard for overseas Chinese tourists and a sight that pulls in the occasional Western traveller. More than one million snakes are transported annually to Wuzhou (from places like Nanning, Liuzhou and Yulin) for export to the kitchens of Hong Kong, Macau and other snake-devouring parts of the world. They're kept in cages at a storehouse in the north-east section of town. To get there, take the road that runs away from the river next to the Wuzhou Hotel; it's about one km away. You might be lucky/unlucky enough to catch one of the snake and cat fights staged for visiting groups of overseas Chinese tourists. The repository is open daily; it's closed for lunch from 11.30 am to 2.30 pm.

Western Bamboo Temple

(*xīlán yuán*) 西竹寺

Just north of town in the Xilan Park is the Western Bamboo Temple, where around 20 Buddhist nuns live. The vegetarian restaurant is highly rated by travellers who have taken the time to wander up here, though it's only open for lunch. You can walk to the temple along Zhongshan Lu (bear left at Dongzheng Lu) from the bus station area in about half an hour.

Sun Yatsen Park

(*zhōngshān gōngyuán*) 中山公园

Just north of the river up Zhongshan Lu, Sun

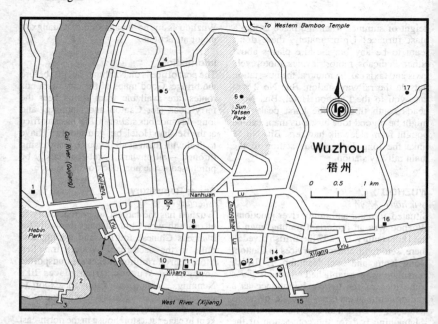

■ PLACES TO STAY

1 Hebin Hotel
4 Beishan Hotel
10 Yuanjiang Hotel
11 Xinxi Hotel
16 Wuzhou Hotel

OTHER

2 Yuanjiang Pavilion
3 Ferry Dock (for Hong Kong)
5 Museum
6 Sun Yatsen Memorial Hall
7 Post Office
8 Bank of China
9 Waterside Restaurants
12 Long Distance Bus Station
13 Long Distance Bus Station
14 Ferry Tickets (for Canton & Nanning)
15 Ferry Dock (for Canton & Nanning)
17 Snake Repository

■ PLACES TO STAY

1 河滨饭店
4 北山饭店
10 鸳江酒店
11 新西旅店
16 梧州大酒店

OTHER

2 鸳江亭
3 往香港船
5 博物馆
6 中山纪念堂
7 邮电局
8 中国银行
9 河边餐厅
12 客运站
13 客运站
14 梧州港客运站码头
15 客运站
17 蛇仓

Yatsen Park is worth a look, if you have time on your hands, as the site of China's earliest memorial hall for the founder of the Republic of China. The hall was constructed in 1928 and commemorates an important speech given by Sun Yatsen in Wuzhou.

Places to Stay

The steady flow of Hong Kong Chinese into Wuzhou has pushed hotel prices up, and in a couple of places, room rates are quoted in HK dollars. If you want or need to overnight in Wuzhou, the best choice is the *Yuanjiang Hotel (yuānjiāng jiŭdiàn)* on Xijiang Lu, a five-minute walk down from the bus station and ferry dock area. Singles/doubles with attached bathroom range from Y35/55, while singles/doubles with common washing facilities are Y25/35. There are also dorm-style triples for Y20. Close by is the gloomy *Xinxi Hotel (xīnxī lǚdiàn)*, with similar rates, dingier rooms and less friendly staff.

If both of the above hotels are full (not likely), try the *Hebin Hotel (hébīn fàndiàn)*, west across the Gui River near the bridge. Doubles cost around Y80 a night, but it's a bit of a concrete hulk. The only reason you'd really want to stay here is if you're catching the early morning hovercraft to Hong Kong (see Getting There & Away in this section).

Previously the top spot in town, the *Beishan Hotel (běishān fàndiàn)*, at 12 Beishan Lu up Dazhong Lu to the north of the city centre, is better off given a miss. It's overly expensive for what they offer. It's also a fair trudge out of town.

Wuzhou's newest hotel, the *Wuzhou Hotel* (☎ 222193) *(wúzhōu dàjiŭdiàn)*, is already showing signs of wear and tear, although the lifts are still working, at least. Even if you've got money to throw around, it's still not particularly good value. The cheaper rooms are generally booked out, and foreign guests will be directed to the standard doubles, which start at HK$332. The cheapest doubles start at HK$132, but they are hard to get. About the best thing here is the coffee shop in the lobby (see the following Places to Eat section).

Places to Eat

There's no shortage of small restaurants, especially in the vicinity of the boat docks and bus station. The illuminated mirages by the riverbank are floating restaurants à la Aberdeen (Hong Kong) with extravagant names such as *Water City Paradise*.

If that doesn't appeal to you, there are other small restaurants along the eastern bank of the Gui River on Guijiang Erlu. For a slightly upmarket snack and a cup of coffee after a long bus or boat journey head over to the ground-floor coffee shop at the *Wuzhou Hotel*. A good cup of coffee costs only Y4, and the food is not bad either. Ask them about their bolognese *(yìdàlì miàn)* – the chef trained in one of Guilin's top hotels.

Getting There & Away

Bus Buses from Wuzhou to Yangshuo leave from the two bus stations to the left of the ferry dock area (for Canton and Nanning) and cost Y32.60. Buses leave at 7.20, 8.20 and 11.30 am, and at 6.40 pm, making it generally possible to connect with bus from any of the boats coming in from Canton. Hovercrafts to Hong Kong connect with the 6.40 pm bus. There are also bus connections to Liuzhou (Y63.60), Nanning (Y66.80), Guilin (Y51), Canton (Y55.20) and Shenzhen (Y78.90).

The bus trip from Wuzhou to Yangshuo takes seven hours, with another two hours to Guilin. The scenically impressive marathon from Wuzhou to Nanning takes around 12 hours on a good run.

Boat There is a hovercraft boat service between Wuzhou and Hong Kong on odd days of the month (1, 3, 5, 7 etc), leaving at 7 am and arriving in Hong Kong at around 3 pm on the same day.

CITS and the Yangshuo Youth Hostel in Yangshuo can arrange tickets for the trip; for more details see the Yangshuo Getting There & Away section and the Getting There & Away chapter at the start of this book.

Boats to Canton leave at 3, 6 and 8 pm and the cheapest tickets are for the crowded (but bearable) dorm-style accommodation at Y32.70. Two-bed/four-bed cabins are Y66/47, although these last two options are not available on all boat services.

There are daily (assuming the river level is sufficiently high) boats to Nanning (Y49, 36 hours). Tickets can be bought from the booking office opposite the ferry dock area.

GUANGXI

Guizhou 贵州

Population: 26 million
Capital: Guiyang

Until recent times Guizhou (*guìzhōu*) was one of the most backward and sparsely populated areas in China. Although the Han Dynasty set up an administration in the area, the Chinese merely attempted to maintain some measure of control over the non-Chinese tribes who lived here, and Chinese settlement was confined to the north and east of the province. The eastern areas were not settled until the 16th century, when the native minorities were forced out of the most fertile areas. Another wave of Chinese immigration in the late 19th century brought many settlers in from overpopulated Hunan and Sichuan. But Guizhou remained impoverished and backward, with poor communications and transport.

When the Japanese invasion forced the Kuomintang to retreat to the south-west, the development of Guizhou began; roads to the neighbouring provinces were constructed, a rail link was built to Guangxi, and some industries were set up in Guiyang and Zunyi. Most of the activity ceased with the end of WW II, and it was not until the construction of the railways in the south-west under Communist rule that some industrialisation was revived.

Mountains and plateaus make up some 87% of Guizhou's topography, which has an average altitude of 1000 metres above sea level. A recent drive to increase income from tourism has seen the opening of many remote regions of Guizhou, but for the most part they remain unexplored. The star attraction close to Guiyang is the Huangguoshu Falls, China's biggest. The neighbourhood also presents opportunities for hiking and stumbling around some of China's all-too-little-visited villages.

About 75% of the population is Han and the rest a flamboyant mixture of minorities such as Miao, Bouyei, Dong, Yi, Shui, Hui, Zhuang, Bai, Tujiao and Gelao. Between

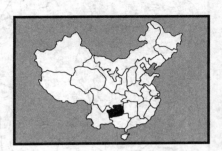

them these minorities celebrate nearly 1000 festivals each year which preserve fascinating customs and elaborate skills in architecture, dress and handicrafts.

Recent analyses in the Chinese press have provided grim warnings about backwardness and poverty. Eight million of the province's population live below the national poverty line. Between 60% and 70% of the population are illiterate and nearly 50% of the villages are not accessible by road.

However, in typical Han fashion the blame was laid at the door of the minorities, who were castigated for 'poor educational quality'; more self-righteous arguments were levelled at cave-dwellers because 'the temptations of modern life have failed to lure these Miao out of their dark, unhealthy cave'. These self-sufficient minorities living without TV, radio, electricity etc are certainly poor, but they show few signs of embracing consumer life and throwing away their cultural identity as a reward for assimilation with the Han.

The province's most famous export is Maotai liquor, named for the village of its origin in Renhuai County. This fiery white spirit is sold in distinctive white bottles with a diagonal red label. Millions of Chinese tuned in to national TV in 1972 when Zhou Enlai and Richard Nixon toasted each other

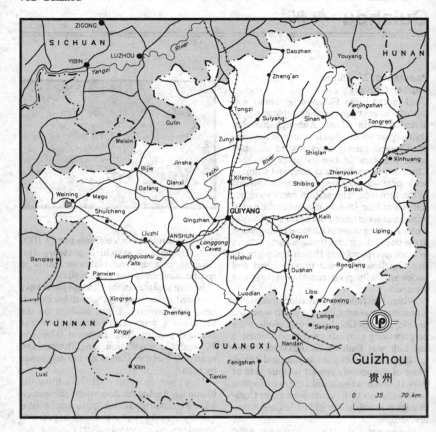

Guizhou
贵州

0   35   70 km

GUIZHOU

with three successive cups of Maotai. Guizhou is also, like Yunnan, a major tobacco-producing area.

Surprisingly for a province so rich in minority culture, Guizhou is neglected by most travellers. One of the reasons is probably the difficulty of travel in the province. Very little English is spoken and it is unusual to bump into other travellers even in Guiyang. For anyone who takes the plunge, however, travel is cheap and invariably rewarding, easily rivalling the much more popular attractions of Yunnan.

The south-east of Guizhou in particular deserves more attention from adventurous travellers. Around 72% of the population in this region is Miao, Dong and a mixture of other minorities. Those who strike off from Guilin to Guiyang by local buses, for example, will find themselves travelling through countless tiny villages with drum towers and wind and rain bridges. With the exception of the buses and trucks that ply the roads, life in this part of China seems to go on as it has for centuries past.

FESTIVALS

Festivities amongst the minorities in

Guizhou offer plenty of scope for exploration. Festivals take place throughout the lunar calendar at specific sites and are technicolour spectaculars which can feature bullfighting, horse racing, pipe playing, comic opera, singing contests and gigantic courting parties.

There are several festivals in Guiyang during the first lunar month (usually February or March), fourth lunar month (around May) and sixth lunar month (around July). Some of these take place in Huaxi.

Another town open to foreigners is Kaili, on the railway line east of Guiyang. A profusion of festivals is held in nearby minority areas such as Lei Gongshan, Xijiang, Danxi, Qingman and Panghai. The town of Zhijiang, about 50 km from Kaili, is also a festival location.

Further east on the railway line is Zhenyuan, recently opened to foreigners, which is renowned for its festivals between April and July. This town was once an important staging point on the ancient post road from central China to South-East Asia.

GUIYANG
(guìyáng) 贵阳

Guiyang, the capital of Guizhou Province, has a mild climate all year round; its name means 'Precious Sun' and may be a reference to the fact that the sun rarely seems to shine through the clouds and drizzle. Despite this, Guiyang remains a much underrated Chinese city. Most travellers give the place a miss, but it's worth lingering for a day or so. There's good food available, lively market and shopping areas and a few interesting sights around town.

A few old neighbourhoods and temples remain and with some effort the place can be appreciated for the funky conglomeration of town and village that it is. Guiyang is also a jumping-off point for the Huangguoshu Falls or via Kaili to the minority areas of the south-east.

Orientation

Guiyang is a sprawling kind of place that at first glance seems to lack a centre of any kind. It doesn't take long to get on top of things, however.

Zunyi Lu heads up from the railway station and links up with Zhonghua Lu, the road that cuts through the centre of town and is home to Guiyang's main shopping area. Yan'an Lu intersects Zhonghua Lu, and it is here that you will find the Bank of China, CITS, the long-distance bus station and, on the other end, the expensive Guiyang Plaza Hotel. There are more hotels further up Zhonghua Lu near the intersection with Beijing Lu.

Information

CITS This office is at 11 Yan'an Zhonglu (☎ 525873) and is one of China's few genuinely helpful and friendly branches of CITS. It's probably partly due to the fact that very few foreigners ever call into the place.

Money The Bank of China is up on the intersection of Zhonghua Zhonglu and Yan'an Zhonglu, not far from CITS. Closer to the railway station, CAAC also has a foreign-exchange counter. The Guiyang Plaza Hotel has an efficient exchange service, though the hotel is quite a trudge from the railway station at the end of Yan'an Donglu.

Post & Telecommunications The post and telecommunications building is up on the intersection of Zunyi Lu and Zhonghua Lu. You can make international phone calls here. It all looks very chaotic, but if you stand around looking confused someone will probably take you by the hand and help you queue-jump. International calls get priority, and most of the locals queuing are making long-distance calls.

Bookshop There's a branch of the Xinhua Foreign Languages Bookstore on Yan'an Donglu. It's not particularly well stocked, but if you're desperate for reading material there should be something worth picking up. They also stock material on Guizhou's minorities, though most of it is pretty unreadable.

PLACES TO STAY

1. Guizhou Park Hotel
2. Bajiaoyan Hotel
3. Yunyan Hotel
4. Qianling Hotel
6. Guiyang Plaza Hotel
17. Jinqiao Hotel
26. Overseas Chinese Friendship Guesthouse
28. Chaoyang Hotel

PLACES TO EAT

15. Jiangnan Dumplings
16. Maike Fast Food Restaurant
27. Guizhou Beijing Duck Restaurant

OTHER

5. Museum
7. Advance Rail Ticket Office
8. Foreign Language Bookstore
9. Xinhua Foreign Language Bookstore
10. CITS
11. Long-Distance Bus Station
12. Huajia Pavilion
13. Wen Chang Pavilion
14. Department store
18. Post & Telecommunications
19. Qianming Temple
20. Jiaxiu Pavilion
21. People's Square/Mao Statue
22. CAAC
23. Guizhou Exhibition Centre
24. Chaoyang Cinema
25. Guizhou Gymnasium
29. Railway Station

Guiyang

贵阳

0   250   500 m

Dangers & Annoyances Guiyang has a reputation among Chinese as one of China's most dangerous cities for theft. It's probably a good idea to be particularly careful at night. The railway station is a favoured haunt of pickpockets, and travellers have reported problems in the station. Take care.

Things to See

The distinctive architectural characteristic of Guiyang's handful of Mussolini-modern buildings is the columns – like the ones at the Provincial Exhibition Hall. The main street, Zunyi Lu, leading north from the railway station harbours one of the largest glistening white statues of Mao Zedong in China. For details on the scenic bus tour around the city, see the Getting Around section.

Qianlingshan Park (*qiánlíng shān gōngyuán*) is worth a visit for its forested walks and for the late Ming Dynasty **Hongfu Monastery** (*hóngfú sì*). The monastery has a vegetarian restaurant, making the park a good place to head out to for lunch. From the Jinqiao Hotel take a No 10 bus and from the railway station area take a No 2 bus. The park is open from 8 am to 6 pm.

Guiyang's two other park attractions – **Huaxi Park** (*huāxī gōngyuán*) and **Nanjiao Park** (*nánjiāo gōngyuán*) – are nothing to get particularly excited about, and if you are short of time give them a miss. Both of them have caves and strolling areas. Not far from the CAAC office is the **Hebin Park** (*hébīn gōngyuán*), a nondescript place with nothing of real interest.

Guiyang is a pleasant enough place to stroll around (if it's not raining), and apart from the markets and shopping district there are a few pavilions and pagodas scattered around town. These include the **Wen Chang Pavilion**, **Jiaxiu Pavilion**, **Huajia Pavilion** and the **Qianming Temple**. Check the map for their locations. They're all within easy walking distance of the centre of town.

Places to Stay – bottom end

Unfortunately budget accommodation is in short supply in Guiyang. Contrary to popular opinion the 1st-class waiting room upstairs in the railway station is not a place to crash out, and if you try it you'll be asked to leave.

If you don't mind dirt and noise you can try the *Chaoyang Hotel* (*cháoyáng fàndiàn*) on Zunyi Lu just a a few minutes' walk from the railway station. There are dorm beds here for Y10 and doubles for Y45. It's a chaotic kind of place with Tibetans on the steps outside selling bits of dried tiger (!), but it's probably OK for an overnight stay.

The *Overseas Chinese Friendship Guesthouse* (*qiáoyì dàjiǔdiàn*) was closed for

GUIZHOU

renovations at the time of writing, and is likely to be fairly pricey whenever it is resurrected. The only other moderately priced option available for foreigners is the *Jinqiao Hotel* (☎ 27921) *(jīnqiáo fàndiàn)*, inconveniently located on Ruijin Zhonglu, a good 25 minutes' walk from the railway station. Four-bed dorms here cost Y20; doubles with bathroom are Y88; and suites are available from Y172. Buses No 1 and 2 run from the railway station past the hotel.

Places to Stay – middle

Most of Guiyang's accommodation is mid-range in standard, even if some of the prices quoted for rooms are definitely top end. Pick of the bunch in terms of value for money is the *Sports Hotel* (☎ 522470) *(tǐyù bīnguǎn)* on the grounds of the Guizhou Gymnasium. It's next door to the big restaurant on the railway station side of the complex. Enormous and very clean doubles with TV and bathroom start from Y110. If you want a night of comfort they're well worth the money. The hotel is just a short walk from the railway station.

Other mid-range options generally represent far less value for money. The *Guiyang Plaza Hotel* (☎ 627047) *(jīnzhù dàjiǔdiàn)* is basically an attempt to produce a homegrown Holiday Inn lookalike. The result is not that bad, if you like that kind of thing. There's an exchange place, a coffee shop, restaurants and shops. Singles/doubles/triples cost Y220/380/400. You might be able to wangle a discount here.

Up on the corner of Zhonghua Beilu and Beijing Lu are three hotels catering to the well-heeled. The cheapest of the bunch is the *Bajiaoyan Hotel* *(bājiǎoyán fàndiàn)*. It has clean doubles with bathroom from Y140 and suites from Y240. Close by, the *Yunyan Hotel* (☎ 623324) *(yúnyán bīnguǎn)* is an unfriendly Chinese monster with rip-off prices. Singles/doubles cost Y160 and triples cost Y300. The *Guizhou Park Hotel* (☎ 622888) *(guìzhōu fàndiàn)* is the lap of luxury, with standard doubles starting at US$52. Ask about the presidential suite for

US$368 – maybe they have special rates for backpackers.

Finally, the inconveniently located *Hua Xi Hotel* (☎ 551129) *(huāxī bīnguǎn)*, an old official tourist hotel, is 20 km south-west of the city, halfway to the airport. The dun-coloured buildings are on a hill in a landscaped and mini-forest area. Rooms cost Y120, but determined bargaining often pays dividends. There are cheap dorms available, but the staff are not keen to let them to foreigners. Basically this place is so far from everything that it's better off avoided. Getting there requires taking a No 2 bus to Hebin Park *(hébīn gōngyuán)* and changing there to a No 21 to Huaxi Park *(huāxī gōngyuán)*. From there, the hotel is a five-minute walk to the south.

Places to Eat

Guiyang, like Kunming, is a great city for snack tracking. Just follow Zunyi Lu up to Zhonghua Nanlu and peer into the side alleys for noodle, dumpling and kebab stalls.

Next door to the Sports Hotel on the grounds of the Guizhou Gymnasium is an excellent Chinese restaurant with fairly reasonable prices. Try their chicken and peanuts dish *(gōngbǎo jīdīng)*. There's no English menu, but it's a popular place so there should be a representative selection of what's available on other diners' tables.

North of the post and telecommunications building, Zhonghua Nanlu is a dumpling shop that is worth a special recommendation. The *Jiāngnán jiǎoziguǎn* has great steamed dumplings *(zhēngjiǎo)* and the specialty of the house is chicken soup *(qìguōjī)*; interesting sweets are also available. Prices are very reasonable. Not far away on the other side of the road is the trendy *Maike Fast Food Restaurant (màikè hànbǎo kuàicān)*, which serves sandwiches and hamburgers; the food is not that bad.

For a special night out, try the *Guizhou Beijing Duck Restaurant (guìzhōu běijīng kǎoyādiàn)*, across the road from the Chaoyang Hotel near the railway station. The duck here is really excellent, and although you'll be looking at around Y40 for a whole duck it's money well spent.

Getting There & Away

Air The CAAC office (☎ 522300) is at 170 Zunyi Lu. The flights from Guiyang include: Beijing (Y1020, daily); Canton (Y420, daily); Haikou, Hainan Island (Y460, Sunday); Kunming, Yunnan (Y230, Sunday); Guilin, Guangxi (thrice weekly); Shanghai (Y850, twice weekly); Wuhan, Hubei (Y460, Sunday); Chengdu, Sichuan (Y260, thrice weekly); Chongqing, Sichuan (Y160, twice weekly); Xi'an, Shaanxi (Y470, once weekly); Xiamen, Fujian (Y630, Sunday); and Changsha, Hunan (Y340, twice weekly).

Bus The long-distance bus station is quite a long way from the railway station, and if you're looking at getting out of Guiyang quickly you're better off using the bus services that operate from the railway station. There are two buses a day to Xingyi (from where there are onward buses to Kunming) at 10.20 am and 8 pm for Y25. Minibuses run through the day every 20 minutes for Anshun, Kaili and Zunyi. Standard buses run approximately every hour to Kaili for Y14.

It's also possible to take tour buses to Huangguoshu Falls from the railway station. They depart at 7 am and cost Y25. If you don't want to stay overnight at the falls, this would probably represent the most hassle-free way of getting out there. There are also buses running from the long-distance bus station to Huangguoshu, Kaili, Zunyi and Liping (south-east of the province). Take bus No 1 or 2 from the railway station to the long-distance bus station.

Train Direct trains run to Kunming, Shanghai, Guilin, Liuzhou (Guangxi), Nanning (Guangxi), Zhanjiang (Guangdong) and Chongqing. Fares from Guiyang are: Kunming (Y86, hard sleeper); Anshun (Y18, hard seat); and to Nanning (Y108, hard sleeper).

There doesn't seem to be much of a black market for train tickets in Guiyang, but you can try hanging around at the railway station and see what happens.

Getting Around

If you want to do a city-loop tour, then across the square from the railway station are two round-the-city buses, Nos 1 and 2. They follow the same route but No 2 goes clockwise while No 1 goes anti-clockwise. These buses will get you to most places (bar the Hua Xi Hotel) – the round trip from the railway station costs Y0.80 and takes about 45 minutes. You can get a good window seat since you get on at the terminal; the same cannot be said if you choose to alight at random for a foot-sortie. The main shopping street is on the bus No 1 route heading north, but this area is more fun to explore on foot.

ANSHUN
(ānshùn) 安顺

Anshun, once an opium-trading centre, remains the commercial hub of western Guizhou but is now known for its batiks. The town's main attraction is the **Wen Temple** *(wénmiào)*, north-east of the railway station. The temple which dates back to the Ming Dynasty underwent restoration work in 1668.

Spending a day or two in Anshun isn't the worst of fates. The karst valley setting is pleasant and some of the narrow streets are lined with interesting old wooden houses. It is also the best place from which to visit Huangguoshu Falls and Longgong Caves.

CITS (☎ 3173) has an office at the Hongshan Hotel which organises trips to Huangguoshu and the surrounding area. From town, the bus station and the railway station are four and three km away respectively. The Hongshan Hotel minibus charges about Y5 per person for transfer to the railway station.

Places to Stay

Near the bus station are a couple of convenient places. The *Xixiushan Hotel (xīxiùshān bīnguǎn)* just around the corner and up the road from the bus station has cheap dorm beds but is sometimes reluctant to let to

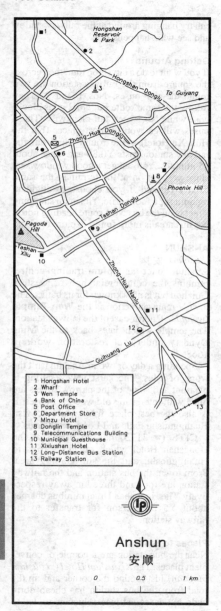

1 虹山宾馆
2 码头
3 文庙
4 中国银行
5 邮电局
6 百货大楼
7 民族饭店
8 东林寺
9 邮电大楼
10 市招待所
11 西秀山宾馆
12 长途汽车站
13 火车站

1 Hongshan Hotel
2 Wharf
3 Wen Temple
4 Bank of China
5 Post Office
6 Department Store
7 Minzu Hotel
8 Donglin Temple
9 Telecommunications Building
10 Municipal Guesthouse
11 Xixiushan Hotel
12 Long-Distance Bus Station
13 Railway Station

Anshun
安顺

0   0.5   1 km

foreigners. Doubles cost around Y40. Behind the bus station, a guesthouse, the *qìchēzhàn zhāodàisuǒ*, has very cheap six-bed dorms. Again, they are often not keen on taking foreigners.

The *Minzu Hotel (mínzú fàndiàn)* on Tashan Donglu, on the eastern side of town near the highway to Guiyang, has doubles for Y45. Ask about rooms in the old building *(jiùlóu)*, which is substantially cheaper. There's a Muslim restaurant on the 2nd floor.

The main tourist joint, inconveniently located on the northern outskirts of Anshun, is the *Hongshan Hotel* (☎ 23435) *(hóngshān bīnguǎn)*, on 39 Baihong Lu. It's definitely lacking in the electricity and plumbing departments, but it's solid. The hotel gardens overlook an artificial lake. This place should be given a miss as its cheapest rooms are now Y135.

Getting There & Away

Bus The simplest option is probably the minibuses that run to Anshun from the Guiyang railway station. They run every 20 minutes and cost Y12. Alternatively, you can head out to the long-distance bus station, where buses run approximately on the hour between 7 am and noon.

Adventurous travellers might want to consider travelling onwards from Anshun to Kunming by bus or vice versa. From Anshun the first stop is Panxian, where you'll need to stay overnight. From Panxian there is

GUIZHOU

onward transport to Qujing (Yunnan) and from there are frequent buses to Kunming.

An even better alternative is travelling from Anshun or Huangguoshu to Xingyi in the south-west of Guizhou. Xingyi is worth a visit in itself, and there are direct buses from there to Kunming (12 hours). From Anshun to Xingyi, it takes around six hours. There are probably other ways of doing this trip. Check your map and be imaginative. If you can make it to Yunnan, onward transport to Kunming should be no problem.

Train Most of the trains running between Guiyang and Anshun at present arrive in Anshun in the evening. One exception is the No 571 which runs between Guiyang and Dawan. It departs at 8.17 am and arrives in Anshun at 11 am. From Anshun, Huangguoshu Falls and Longgong Caves are 46 and 32 km away respectively. There are usually minibuses operating from the railway station to either of these for Y5, though prices are fairly flexible and may require a little bargaining.

If you're thinking of travelling onwards from Anshun to Kunming by train, bear in mind that it's almost impossible to get hold of hard-sleeper tickets in Anshun itself. If comfort is important to you, you'll be better off heading back to Guiyang and organising your ticket there.

AROUND ANSHUN
Huangguoshu Falls
(*huángguǒshù dàpùbù*) 黄果树大瀑布
Located 43 km south-west of Anshun, China's premier cataract reaches a width of 81 metres, with a drop of 74 metres into the Rhinoceros Pool. For a preview, there is a drawing of the falls on the 10-fen Foreign Exchange Certificate (FEC). Huangguoshu provides an excellent chance to go rambling through the superb rural minority areas on foot.

Once you're there, you'll have no transport problems as everything you need is within walking range or, if you wish to go further, hiking range. Take a raincoat if you're off to the waterfalls and a warm jacket or sweater if you're descending into caves, which can be chilly.

The thunder of Huangguoshu Falls can be heard for some distance, and the mist from the falls carries to the local villages during

the rainy season, which lasts from May to October. The falls are at their most spectacular about four days after heavy rains. The dry season lasts from November to April, so during March and April the flow of water can become a less impressive trickle.

The main falls are the central piece of a huge waterfall, cave and karst area, covering some 450 sq km. It was only explored by the Chinese in the 1980s as a preliminary to harnessing the hydroelectric potential. They discovered about 18 falls, four subterranean rivers, and 100 caves, many of which are now being gradually opened up to visitors.

At the edge of the falls is **Water Curtain Cave** (*shuǐlián dòng*), a niche in the cliffs which is approached by a slippery (and dangerous) sortie wading across rocks in the Rhinoceros Pool – from the cave you'll get an interior view of the gushing waters through six 'windows'.

One km above the main falls is **Steep Slope Falls** (*dǒupō pùbù*), which is easy to reach. Steep Slope Falls is 105 metres wide and 23 metres high, and gets its name from the crisscross patterning of sloping waters. Eight km below Huangguoshu Falls are the **Star Bridge Falls** (*tiānxīng qiáo*).

Huangguoshu (Yellow Fruit Tree) is in the Zhenning Bouyei and Miao Autonomous County. The Miao are not in evidence around the falls, but for the Bouyei, who favour river valleys, this is prime water country. The Bouyei are the 'aboriginals' of Guizhou. The people are of Thai origin and related to the Zhuangs in Guangxi. They number two million, mostly spread over the southwestern sector of Guizhou Province. Bouyei dress is dark and sombre, with colourful trimmings; 'best' clothes come out on festival or market days. The Bouyei marry early, usually at 16, but sometimes as young as 12. Married women are distinguished by headgear symbols.

The Bouyei are very poor, showing signs of malnutrition and wearing clothes that are grubby and tattered. The contrast with the postcard minority image of starched and ironed costumes, or the ring-of-confidence sparkling teeth is obvious. The Bouyei tribespeople are also shy and suspicious of foreigners.

Batik (cloth wax-dyeing) is one of the skills of the Bouyei. The masonry at Huangguoshu is also intriguing – stone blocks comprise the housing, but no plaster is used; the roofs are finished in stone slates.

There is a Bouyei festival in Huangguoshu lasting 10 days during the first lunar month (usually February or early March).

Longgong Caves

About 32 km from Anshun is a spectacular series of underground caverns called **Longgong** (*lónggōng*), or Dragon Palace, which form a network through some 20 mountains. Charter boats tour one of the largest water-filled caves, often called the 'Dragon Cave'. The caverns lie in Anshun County, at the Bouyei settlement of Longtan (*lóngtǎn zhài*) (Dragon Pool). Other scenic caves in the vicinity include **Daji Dong**, **Chuan Dong** and **Linlang Dong**.

Places to Stay & Eat

At the bus park near the Huangguoshu Falls are some food stalls. Below them, down the cliff, is a teahouse and souvenir shop. The viewing area for the falls is a short downhill walk from the bus park. Further away from the bus park is *Huangguoshu Guesthouse* (*huángguǒshù bīnguǎn*), which is only for foreigners. Clean rooms with bathroom start at Y30 per person. Its decent restaurant charges from Y5 to Y30 for set meals; buy tickets at the reception desk.

Just before the bridge on the way into town from Anshun is the *Tianxing Hotel* (*tiānxīng fàndiàn*) with cheaper accommodation for Y15 per person. Other dosshouses in the village with no facilities charge Y2 per night, but the authorities may require foreigners to stay in one of the sanctioned hotels.

Getting There & Away

You can get to Huangguoshu Falls and Longgong Caves from either Guiyang or Anshun. If you miss the 7 am direct bus to the falls from the Guiyang long-distance bus station, you can catch a bus or a train to Anshun and hitch up with a minibus there. Minibuses run every 20 minutes from the Guiyang railway station to Anshun, a distance of 106 km from Guiyang. Another direct option is a bus running from Guiyang to Dailang. Buses leave from the Guiyang long-distance bus station every half hour between 8 and 10 am and pass through Anshun, Zhenning and Huangguoshu.

Alternatively, local tour buses leave from the Guiyang railway station at 7 am. They take in both the falls and Longgong Caves for Y25.

From the Anshun long-distance bus station there's a 7.40 am bus to Huangguoshu; the 7, 7.20 am and noon buses to Zhenfeng all pass through Huangguoshu, as do the 7.20 and 11.30 am buses to Qinglong. There are also minibuses running from in front of Anshun railway station to Huangguoshu and Longgong.

There's a local bus from Huangguoshu to Guiyang at 12.30 pm; other buses depart from Huangguoshu for Anshun at 10.30 am, 2, 3, 4 and 4.30 pm. These will probably connect with trains leaving Anshun for Guiyang or Kunming.

KAILI
(kāilì) 凯里

Around 195 km almost directly east of Guiyang, Kaili is a fairly uninspiring kind of place, but it's the gateway to the minority areas of south-eastern Guizhou. The bus journey between here and Liping in the far south-east of Guizhou takes you through some of the most fascinating minority regions in this part of China. It should be possible to stop over in some of these towns without arousing the ire of local PSB agents.

Particularly recommended are Leishan, Yongle and Rongjiang. Liping is a good base for exploring nearby Dong villages. Buses also run from Kaili to the Miao area of Shibing, from where there are cruises on the Wuyang River, something that the local tourist authorities are promoting heavily. This whole area sees very few Western travellers.

Things to See

There's really not a great deal in this category. There's a pagoda in the **Dage Park** *(dàgé gōngyuán)*, which is not surprising as the park's name means 'big pagoda park'. The only other thing to check out is the drum tower down in **Jinquanhu Park** *(jīnquánhú gōngyuán)*. In the south of town is the moderately interesting **Minorities Museum** *(zhōu mínzú bówùguǎn)*.

Festivals

Kaili and the areas around it are host to a large number of minority festivals. One of the biggest is the Lusheng Festival, held from 11 to 18 of the first lunar month. The *lusheng* is a reed instrument used by the Miao people. Activities include playing the lusheng (of course), dancing, drumming, bull fighting and horse racing. Participants are said to number 30,000. The festival is held in Danxi.

A similar festival is held midway through the seventh lunar month in Qingman. Participants number 20,000. The Miao new year is celebrated on the first four days of the 10th lunar month in Kaili, Guading, Danxi and other Miao areas by some 50,000 people.

Places to Stay

Cheap accommodation is not that easy to come by in Kaili. South of the long-distance bus station is the *Shiyou Guesthouse (shíyóu zhāodàisuǒ)* with doubles for Y20, but it is often full. Not far from there is the *Yunpanpo Hotel (yíngpānpō bīnguǎn)* which has two-bed dorms for Y20 in the old wing and more upmarket doubles in the new wing for Y100 and upwards. To find this place, look for a big gate opposite the Minority Souvenir Shop, enter and follow the road up and to the right.

The *Zhenhua Guesthouse (zhènhuá zhāodàisuǒ)* was not taking foreigners at the time of writing, but it might be worth checking on the latest situation. The only other option is the *Kaili Hotel (kǎilǐ bīnguǎn)* down in the south of town.

GUIZHOU

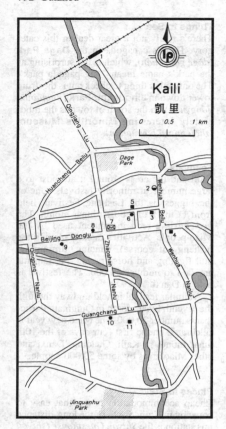

1 Railway Station
2 Long-Distance Bus Station
3 Shiyou Guesthouse
4 Zhenhua Guesthouse
5 Yunpanpo Hotel
6 Minorities Souvenir Shop
7 Post Office
8 Bank of China
9 PSB
10 Minorities Museum
11 Kaili Hotel

Getting There & Away

Numerous trains pass through Kaili, but it's probably easiest to travel by bus if you're coming from Guiyang. There are buses on the hour (from 8 am to 4.30 pm) running from the railway station for Y14. There are also numerous buses from Guiyang long-distance bus station for the same price. Buses take three to four hours. The Yunpanpo Hotel runs a comfortable minibus from the hotel to the Guizhou Gymnasium in Guiyang at 7 am for Y30. The same bus heads back to Kaili at around 1 pm. Look for it at the main entrance to the gymnasium.

The Kaili long-distance bus station has frequent buses to Guiyang, Shibing, Zhenyuan, Rongjiang, Liping and Congjiang.

AROUND KAILI

The minority areas of south-eastern Guizhou are relatively unexplored by Western travellers, and the following are some places that are worth checking out. Very little English is spoken in this part of the world and you're not likely to bump into many other travellers, but if that's your kind of thing strike off somewhere on a local bus.

Shibing & Zhenyuan

(shībǐng/zhènyuán) 施秉/镇远

Shibing is basically an overgrown Miao village that offers opportunity for walks in the surrounding countryside and visits to even smaller Miao villages. The major attraction in the area are cruises on the **Wuyang River** *(wǔyáng hé)*, which pass through Guilin lookalike countryside (karst rock formations) before ending up in Zhenyuan. From here you could take a bus back to Shibing or Kaili, or a bus on to Tianzhu, which in turn offers the interesting prospect of an undoubtedly rough bus journey down to Jinping and on to Liping. From Liping it is possible to travel (slowly) all the way to Guilin, passing through Dong minority villages en route.

Places to Stay & Eat There's basic accommodation in Shibing at the *Shibing Guesthouse (shībǐng zhāodàisuǒ)*; in Zhenyuan at the *Zhenyuan Guesthouse (zhènyuán zhāodàisuǒ)*. Both are small towns and you'll have no problems finding the hotels.

KAILI TO LIPING
Liping, in the far south-east of Guizhou is a fairly uninteresting town, but the road between it and Kaili is crammed with sights and some beautiful countryside. Ideally, it would be best to get off the bus and spend at least a couple of hours in some of the minority villages like Leishan, Tashi, Chejiang, Rongjiang, Maogong and Gaojin. Most of these towns have Dong wind and rain bridges and drum towers, many of which you'll see from the bus.

Liping has basic accommodation in the *Liping Guesthouse (lìpíng zhāodàisuǒ)* for Y12 for a double. It's down the hill from the bus station on the near right-hand corner of the first intersection. Accommodation in other towns between Liping and Kaili should be a possibility. If you wander around looking lost, someone will either put you on the next bus or take you to the local hotel.

LIPING TO GUILIN
This is really only an option for travellers with time to kill. Buses in this part of the world are very infrequent and travel at a snail's pace over roads that only barely qualify as such. Buses run from Liping to Diping *(dìpíng)* or Longe *(lóngé)* at 7 am. To Longe, it takes around four hours, passing through the town of Zhaoxing *(zhàoxīng)*, an

incredible Dong minority village with a total of five drum towers. There's a hotel in Zhaoxing, and a stop in the village would require you stay in it as there is only one bus a day travelling between here and Longe. Longe, another Dong village, also requires an overnight stop, as the bus on to Sanjiang in Guangxi Province doesn't leave until at least 11 am the next day. From Sanjiang there are buses on to Longsheng or direct to Guilin.

ZUNYI
(zūnyì) 遵 义
Around 163 km north of Guiyang, Zunyi is worth a mention and even possibly a visit for those who have a particular interest in Chinese Communist Party history. For everyone else it's a fairly drab, industrialised Chinese town with few attractions.

Hemmed into the Jiangxi Soviet by Kuomintang forces, on 16 October 1934 the Communists set out on a herculean one-year, 9600-km tramp from one end of China to the other. By mid-December they had reached Guizhou and marched on Zunyi, a prosperous mercantile town. Taking the town by surprise, the Communists were able to stock up on supplies and take a breather. On 15-18 January 1935, the top-level Communist leadership took stock of their situation in the now-famous Zunyi Conference. The resolutions taken largely reflected the views of Mao Zedong, who was elected a full member of the ruling Standing Committee of the Politburo and chief assistant to Zhou Enlai in military planning. It was a crucial factor in Mao's rise to power.

Things to See
The main sight is the **Zunyi Conference Site** *(zūnyì huìyì huìzhǐ)*. It's around four or five km to the south of the railway station and is home to a collection of CCP memorabilia. The meeting rooms and living quarters are also open to the public. It is open daily.

Zunyi Park *(zūnyì gōngyuán)* is the park area across the road from the conference site and **Phoenix Hill Park** *(fènghuángshān gōngyuán)* is not far off. Neither is particu-

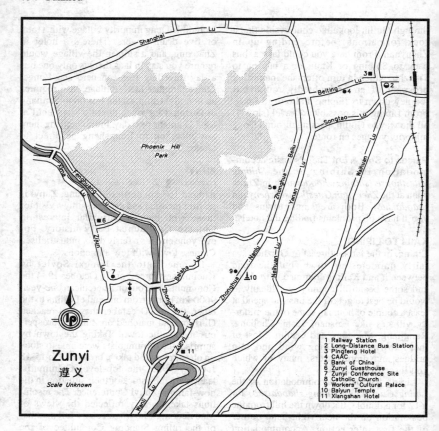

Zunyi
遵义
Scale Unknown

1 Railway Station
2 Long-Distance Bus Station
3 Pingfeng Hotel
4 CAAC
5 Bank of China
6 Zunyi Guesthouse
7 Zunyi Conference Site
8 Catholic Church
9 Workers' Cultural Palace
10 Baiyun Temple
11 Xiangshan Hotel

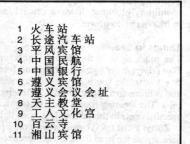

1　火车站　汽车站
2　长途风宾民航行馆
3　平国国义银会议会址
4　中中遵遵天工百湘
5　中遵义银宾馆
6　遵义义会议会址
7　遵义会议会址
8　天主人教文化宫
9　工人文化宫
10　百云寺
11　湘山宾馆

GUIZHOU

larly exciting, but will probably make for a pleasant enough stroll if you have some time to kill.

Places to Stay

Close to the railway station is the *Pingfeng Hotel (píngfēng lǚshè)*, a very basic place with dorms for around Y10. Near the conference site is the official tourist abode, the *Zunyi Guesthouse (zūnyì bīnguǎn)*, costs around Y50 for a double.

Getting There & Away

Zunyi is on the main northern railway line

that connects Guiyang with Chongqing, Chengdu, Shanghai and basically the rest of China. It could be used as a stopover on any of these routes, and a hard-seat ticket is Y18.

Alternatively, buses run in the morning from Guiyang's long-distance bus station. Zunyi's long-distance bus station is in front of the railway station, and there are morning buses from 7 am from here to Guiyang.

XINGYI
(xīngyì) 兴义

Xingyi is mainly a stopover in the far south-west of Guizhou for those travelling between Guiyang and Kunming by bus. The main attraction in the area is the **Maling Gorge** *(mǎlíng héxiágǔ)*. There are steps and walkways cut into the gorge, which is quite precipitous in parts. It's a good idea to bring along a torch to light your way through some of the caves that the path passes through.

Xingyi is an interesting town to wander around, and sights around town include a good minorities' museum. There's only one hotel that takes foreigners (don't worry, you'll get directed to it) and it costs Y15 for a bed in a three-bed dorm.

Getting There & Away

There are two buses a day from in front of the Guiyang railway station at 10.20 am and 8 pm for Y25. It's better to catch the morning bus, as the evening bus will get you to Xingyi *very* early the next morning. From Xingyi, buses to Kunming take around 12 hours. From Kunming's long-distance bus station there are morning buses to Xingyi.

Sichuan 四川

Population: 100 million
Capital: Chengdu

Sichuan *(sìchuān)* is the largest province in China, and also the most heavily populated, with almost 100 million people. It is the eastern region of Sichuan, the great Chengdu plain, that supports one of the densest rural populations in the world, while the regions to the west are mountainous and sparsely populated, mainly by Tibetans. Roughly the size of France, give or take Luxembourg, Sichuan has rich natural resources. Wild mountainous terrain and fast rivers kept it relatively isolated until the present era, and much of the western fringe is still remote. This inaccessibility has made it the site of various breakaway kingdoms throughout Chinese history, and it was here that the beleaguered Kuomintang Party spent its last days before being vanquished to Taiwan. The capital is Chengdu; the largest city is Chongqing, which is also the stepping-stone for the ferry ride down the Yangzi River.

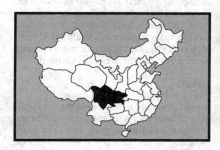

The Chinese often refer to Sichuan as *tiānfǔ zhī guó*, the 'Heavenly Kingdom', a reference to its resources, prosperity and rich cultural heritage. The province continues to get rich, having been at the forefront of China's labouring economic reforms over the last 15 years. Zhao Ziyang, who climbed the giddy heights from First Party Secretary of Sichuan to General Secretary of the Communist Party before being banished from the halls of power in the aftermath of the Tiananmen massacre, made his reputation in Sichuan, instituting pioneering agricultural reforms in the province. These reforms, the so-called 'responsibility system', whereby plots of land were let out to farmers for individual use on the condition that a portion of the crops be sold back to the government, had spread throughout the whole of China by 1984, and its principles have since been applied to the industrial sector.

There is nowhere better to see the fruits of these reforms than Chengdu, the capital of the province. It is without a doubt the most prosperous, liberal and fashionable city in the south-west. There are bustling commercial markets everywhere, the department stores are crowded with the latest consumer goodies, and locals dressed in Hong Kong fashions zip around town on motorbikes and multi-geared mountain bikes.

Meanwhile, worlds away from the scenes of urban renewal and economic reform, the remote mountains of Sichuan, Gansu and Shaanxi provinces are the natural habitat of the giant panda. Of China's 1174 species of birds, 420 species of mammals and 500 species of reptiles and amphibians, this is the one animal which Westerners automatically associate with China. This is probably due in part to the Chinese fondness several years ago for giving them away as presents to foreign governments, but the cute black patches around the eyes help too.

CHENGDU
(chéngdū) 成都

Chengdu is Sichuan's capital, and its administrative, educational and cultural centre, as well as a major industrial base. It boasts a 2500-year history, linked closely with the art & craft trades. During the Eastern Han Dynasty (25-220 AD) the city was often referred to as Jincheng (Brocade City), due to its thriving silk brocade industry. Like

SICHUAN

Sichuan 四川

0   60   120 km

other major Chinese cities, the place has had its share of turmoil. First it was devastated by the Mongols in retaliation for fierce fighting put up by the Sichuanese. From 1644 to 1647 it was presided over by the rebel Zhang Xiangzhong, who set up an independent state in Sichuan, ruling by terror and mass executions. Three centuries later the city was set up as one of the last strongholds of the Kuomintang. Ironically, the name 'Chengdu' means Perfect Metropolis – and today around three million people inhabit the perfect city proper, or three times that if you count the surrounding metropolitan area.

The original city was walled with a moat, gates at the compass points, and the Viceroy's Palace (14th century) at the heart. The latter was the imperial quarter. The remains of the city walls were demolished in the early 1960s, and the Viceroy's Palace was blown to smithereens at the height of the Cultural Revolution. In its place was erected the Russian-style Exhibition Hall. Outside, Mao waves merrily down Renmin Lu; inside, the standard portraits of Marx, Engels, Lenin, Stalin and Mao gaze down in wonder at the masses hurrying about the business of getting rich. (In Beijing's Tiananmen Square, the four portraits have been removed, to be resurrected for special occasions.)

Comparisons between Chengdu and Beijing are tempting – the same city-planning hand at work – but Chengdu is an altogether different place, with far more greenery, overhanging wooden housing in the older parts of town, and a very different kind of energy coming off the streets. One of the most intriguing aspects of the city is that its artisans are back. These small-time basket-weavers, cobblers, itinerant dentists, tailors, houseware merchants and snack hawkers swarm the streets and contribute to the bustling energy of the city. But they are just part of the story. Like the other major cities of China, Chengdu is starting to swagger with a new-found affluence. Travellers just off a bus from Yunnan or Tibet often find themselves rubbing shoulders with rural Chinese to gawk at the opulent interiors of Chengdu's department stores, with their electronic goods, Hong Kong fashions and other trendy consumer items. Chengdu is a city on the verge of a new era.

The best way to come to terms with the city is to strike off on a walk and get off the Beijing-style boulevards. Free markets, flea markets, black markets, pedlar markets, commercial districts, underground shopping malls – you'll stumble over more and more of them with each twist and turn of the back alleys. Around the corner comes a florist shop on wheels – a bicycle laden with gladioli – or you chance upon a meat market, a vegetable market, a spice market, or a side street devoted to a species of household repair. Add to this the indoor food markets, the countless tiny restaurants specialising in Sichuan snacks, the old men walking their song birds or huddled over a game of Go, and you're looking at one of China's most intriguing cities.

Orientation

Chengdu has echoes of boulevard-sweeping Beijing in its grand scale, except that here flowering shrubs and foliage line the expanses. As in Beijing there is a ring road right around the outer city. The main boulevard that sweeps through the centre of everything is Renmin Lu, in its north (*běi*), central (*zhōng*) and south (*nán*) manifestations. The nucleus of the city is the square that interrupts the progress of Renmin Lu, with administrative buildings, the Sichuan Exhibition Hall, a sports stadium and, at its southern extent, a colossal Mao presiding over a city long since oblivious to his presence.

The area where Renmin Nanlu crosses the Jin River, near the Jinjiang and Traffic hotels, has become the city's tourist ghetto. This is where you'll find most of the restaurants and arts & crafts shops catering for foreigners, and even nowadays a couple of pubs.

Finally, Chengdu is a true Asian city in its nonchalant disregard of systematic street numbering and even naming. It's not unusual, when following street numbers in one direction, to meet another set coming the other way, often leaving the poor family in the middle with five sets of numbers over their doorway. Street names, also, seem to change every 100 metres or so. Bear this in mind when you're looking for somewhere in particular, and rely more on nearby landmarks and relative locations on maps than on street numbers and names

Information

CITS Unless you're interested in joining a tour group, there's no real point in bothering the people at CITS. Staff in the Jinjiang Hotel office will give you a cursory glance as you walk in, and if you don't look like you're dripping with money will go back to reading the paper. Staff in the main office (☎ 25042) on Renmin Nanlu opposite the Jinjiang Hotel are much friendlier but can't book train tickets or flights and have been trained to say 'Tibet is closed'. About the only useful thing they can do for you is book Dragon Air flights to Hong Kong. For the kind of help that individual travellers need, you will have to head down to the Flower Garden Restaurant or the YS Restaurant near the Traffic Hotel. There are friendly locals in both these places who, for a price, can help out with all kinds of travel needs.

PSB The office (☎ 26577) is on Xinhua Donglu, east of the intersection with Renmin Zhonglu. This is the place to report thefts etc.

For permits to visit 'closed' areas in Sichuan and visa extensions, you are better off going to the provincial PSB on Wenmiaohou Jie, which is off Jiangxi Jie to the west of the Jinjiang Hotel. Certain members of the staff speak excellent English. This office is open Monday and Wednesday from 8.30 to 11 am and from 3 to 5 pm, and on Saturday from 8.30 to 11 am.

Money All of the hotels mentioned in Places to Stay have foreign-exchange counters. The Jinjiang Hotel has a branch of the Bank of China, but they are usually unwilling to change your money unless you are a guest of the hotel; the Minshan Hotel across the road

is not so fussy. The main branch of the Bank of China is in a huge yellow building up on Renmin Donglu. This is the place for credit card withdrawals and the like.

On the streets in the vicinity of the Jinjiang and Traffic hotels you'll be pestered by hordes of moneychangers – the black-market rate in Chengdu is usually a bit above average, but the usual rules about changing money on the streets apply.

Post & Telecommunications The main post office is on the corner of Huaxingzhen Jie and Shuwa Beijie close to the Cultural Palace in the centre of town. Poste-restante mail is kept behind the window marked 'International Post' – names of addressees for poste-restante parcels are marked on a blackboard.

Poste-restante service at the main post office is generally efficient. Nevertheless, since it's across town from the Jin River tourist area, many tourists have their mail addressed to the Jinjiang Hotel. In our experience this hotel is not an especially good place to receive mail if you're not staying there. If you do attempt to pick up mail at the Jinjiang, be sure to check both the reception desk and the hotel's post office.

The best place in town for making collect calls is in the telecommunications centre, east of the Sichuan Exhibition Centre. You can also make direct-dial overseas calls from here.

Consulates The US Consulate General (☎ 582222) has an office in Chengdu in the west wing of the Jinjiang Hotel.

Maps City bus maps can be found at railway stations, the Jinjiang Hotel and Xinhua bookshops. Three different maps in Chinese provide excellent detail for Sichuan Province, Chengdu city or its surrounding areas. The English 'Tourist Map of Chengdu', available at the Jinjiang Hotel's gift shop, is very useful for city excursions.

Bookshop The Sichuan Foreign Languages Bookshop has mildly captivating tourist

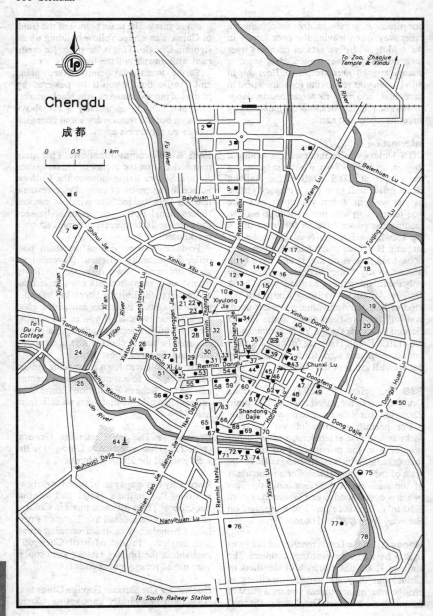

Chengdu
成都

0   0.5   1 km

To Zoo, Zhaojue
Temple & Xindu

Sha River

Fu River

Beierhuan Lu

Jiefang Lu

Fuqing Lu

Beiyuan Lu

Renmin Beilu

Shihui Jie

Xinhua Xilu

Xi'an Lu

Shangtongren Lu

Dongchenggen Jie

Zhonglu

Zhongjie

Xiyulong Jie

Xiyu Jie

Xinhua Donglu

Xishuncheng Lu

Renmin Zhonglu

Chunxi Lu

Dongfeng Lu

Dongyi Huan Lu

Xijiao River

To
Du Fu
Cottage

Tonghuimen

Xiatongren Lu

Renmin Xi Lu

Renmin Donglu

Shandong Dajie

Hongxing Lu

Dong Dajie

Wainan Renmin Lu

Jin River

Wuhouci Dajie

Nan Dajie

Jiangyi Jie

Jinian Qiao Lu

Renmin Nanlu

Xinnan Lu

Nanyihuan Lu

To South Railway Station

SICHUAN

■ **PLACES TO STAY**

3	Chengdu Grand Hotel
4	Jingrong Hotel
5	Tibet Hotel
6	Baifurong Hotel
13	Chengdu Guesthouse
15	Geological Guesthouse
26	Jinhe Hotel
34	Zhufeng Guesthouse
39	Sichuan Hotel
48	Xingchuan Hotel
50	Chengdu Hotel
55	Rongcheng Hotel
56	Yuanding Hotel
65	Jinjiang Hotel
66	Minshan Hotel
68	Binjiang Hotel
69	Black Coffee Hotel
73	Traffic Hotel

▼ **PLACES TO EAT**

12	Zhang Liangfen Bean Jelly Restaurant
14	Longyan Baozi Dumpling Restaurant
16	Guo Soup Balls Restaurant
17	Chen Mapo Doufu Restaurant
22	Rongleyuan Restaurant
36	Dan Dan Noodle Restaurant
42	Shimeixuan Restaurant
45	Yaohua Restaurant
47	Zhenzhu Yuanzi Restaurant
60	Chengdu Restaurant
62	Banna Restaurant
71	Sichuan Restaurant
72	Flower Garden Restaurant

OTHER

1	North Railway Station
2	North Bus Station
7	Ximen Bus Station
8	Tomb of Wang Jian
9	Army Surplus Store

10	PSB
11	Wenshu Monastery
18	Advance Rail Booking Office
19	Fun Park
20	Mengzhuiwan Swimming Pool
21	No 3 Hospital
23	Tape Shop
24	Qingyang Palace (Wenhua Park)
25	Baihuatan Park
27	Sichuan Fine Arts Exihibition Hall
28	Advance Rail Booking Office
29	Chengdu Folk Arts Exhibition Centre ('Hell World')
30	Sichuan Exhibition Centre
31	Mao Statue
32	Municipal Sports Stadium
33	Telecommunications Centre
35	Cultural Palace
37	Hongqi Market
38	Main Post Office
40	Stock Market
41	Jinjiang Theatre
43	Sichuan Foreign Language Bookshop
44	Bank of China
46	Chunxi Commercial District
49	Municipal Museum
51	Renmin Park
52	Sichuan Antique Store
53	Dental Hospital
54	People's Market
57	Provincial PSB
58	Chengdu Department Store
59	Advance Rail Booking Office
61	Friendship Store
63	China Southwest Airlines/Pubs
64	Wuhou Temple (Nanjiao Park)
67	CAAC
70	China Southwest Airlines Booking Office
74	Xinnanmen Bus Station
75	Jiuyanqiao Bus Station
76	Sichuan Museum
77	Sichuan University
78	River Viewing Pavilion Park

literature and general data, as well as the usual collection of English-teaching materials, *Jane Eyre*, US and British short-story collections and Grimm's fairy tales. And while you're here, there's a counter selling watery versions of Western music and traditional Chinese music in cassette form. The store is just down the road south of the Sichuan Hotel on Dongfeng Lu.

Dangers & Annoyances There have been several reports of foreigners becoming targets for rip-offs and theft in Chengdu. In particular there have been a couple of incidents (one foreigner was stabbed) on the riverside pathway between the Jinjiang and Traffic hotels. Take care late at night – it's best not to walk alone.

To avoid getting ripped off by taxis,

■ PLACES TO STAY

3	成都大酒店
4	京蓉宾馆
5	西藏饭店
6	白芙蓉宾馆
13	成都旅馆
15	地质宾馆
26	金河宾馆
34	珠峰宾馆
39	四川川宾馆
48	兴都饭店
50	成蓉饭店
55	蓉园饭店
56	园丁饭店
65	锦江宾馆
66	岷山饭店
68	滨江饭店
69	黑咖啡饭店
73	交通饭店

▼ PLACES TO EAT

12	张凉粉
14	龙眼包子
16	郭汤元
17	陈麻婆豆腐
22	荣乐园
36	担担面
42	食美华饭店
45	耀华珠元餐厅
47	珍珠元子餐厅
60	成都餐厅
62	版纳酒家食馆
71	四川食馆
72	花园食馆

OTHER

1	火车北站
2	城北汽车客运中心
7	西门汽车站
8	王建墓
9	军衣店
10	公安局
11	文殊院
18	火车站售票处
19	市游乐园
20	猛追湾游泳池
21	三医院
23	音像书店
24	青羊宫/文化公园
25	百华潭公园
27	四川美术展览馆
28	火车城售票处
29	鬼
30	省展览像馆
31	毛主席像馆
32	市体育场
33	电话电报大楼
35	文化宫
37	红旗商场
38	市电信局
40	红庙子
41	锦江剧场
43	省外文书店
44	银行大厦商业区
46	春熙路商业区
49	市博物公园
51	人民公店
52	文物科医院
53	牙人民商场
54	省公安局
57	成都百货大楼
58	火车站售票处
59	友谊商店
61	中国西南航空公司
63	武侯祠/南郊公园
64	中国国际旅行社
67	中国西南航空售票处
70	中国南门汽车站
74	新眼桥汽车站
75	九省川博物馆
76	省四川大学
77	四望江楼公园
78	望江公园

pedicab drivers and restaurants, always get the price at the start of proceedings. Pickpockets are common around bus stations, railway stations and post offices, and watch out for gangs who razor your bags on buses (the No 16 bus is the most notorious). It's a good idea to use a money belt.

If you want to play it safe with train tickets, make a note of the ticket numbers. If the tickets are stolen you'll be given replacements, providing you can supply the numbers of the old ones.

Should things get out of hand, ring the Foreign Affairs section (*wàishìkē*) of the

SICHUAN

PSB (☎ 26577). English is spoken and they usually do their best to be of assistance.

Wenshu Monastery
(wénshū yuàn) 文殊院

Wenshu Monastery, which dates back to the Tang Dynasty, is Chengdu's largest and best preserved Buddhist place of worship. It was originally known as Xinxiang Temple, but was renamed after a Buddhist monk who lived there in the late 17th century. It is believed that his presence literally illuminated the monastery. The complex includes 192 buildings, many of them carved with exquisite relief work. It is also home to the Sichuan and Chengdu Buddhist associations.

Perhaps the best thing about the monastery are the bustling crowds of worshippers who flock to the place. It's not often you get to see such an active place of worship in China, and it's well worth the trip. The alley off Renmin Zhonglu, on which Wenshu is located, is a curiosity in itself, with joss-stick vendors, foot-callus removers, blind fortune-tellers with bamboo spills, and flower and firework sellers. In the monastery area, check out the teahouse and vegetarian restaurant – it's a good place for lunch. The monastery is open daily from 8 am to 8 pm, and there's an entry charge of Y0.5.

Tomb of Wang Jian
(wángjiàn mù) 王建墓

In the north-west of town, the Tomb of Wang Jian was until 1942 thought to be Zhu Geliang's music pavilion (see Wuhou Temple, in the following Temple Parks section). The tomb in the central building is surrounded by statues of 24 musicians all playing different instruments, and is considered to be the best surviving record of a Tang Dynasty musical troupe.

Wang Jian (847-918 AD) was a Tang general who established the Former Shu kingdom in the aftermath of the collapse of the Tang in 907 AD. Also featured are relics taken from the tomb itself, including a jade belt, mourning books and imperial seals. The tomb is open daily except Monday, from 9 am to noon and from 2 to 5.30 pm.

Temple Parks

There are a couple of worthwhile temple parks in the city area, all within cycling distance of the Jinjiang and Traffic hotels. They are all open seven days a week from 7.30 am to 6 pm.

West of Mao on the western section of the circular road is **Wénhuà Park** (wénhuà gōngyuán), home to **Qingyang Palace** (qīngyáng gōng). It is the oldest and most extensive Taoist temple in the Chengdu area. The story goes that Laozi, the shadowy high priest of Taoism and reputed author of the Daodejing, The Way and its Power, asked a friend to meet him there. When the friend arrived he saw only a boy leading two goats on a leash...and, in a fabulous leap of lateral thinking, realised the boy was Laozi. The goats are represented in bronze in the rear building on the temple grounds. If the one with only one horn looks slightly ungoatlike, it is because it combines features of all the Chinese zodiac animals: a mouse's ears; a cow's nose; a horse's mouth; the back of a rabbit; a snake's tail; neck of a monkey; and a pig's bum. The solitary horn was borrowed from a dragon. And if you're wondering whether the goat has any goatish qualities at all, take a look at the beard. The other goat can vanquish life's troubles and pains if you stroke its flank.

Qingyang Palace can be combined with a visit to the nearby **Du Fu Cottage** (dùfǔ cǎotáng), erstwhile home of the celebrated Tang Dynasty poet. Something of a rover, Du Fu (712-70 AD) was born in Henan and left his home province to see China at the tender age of 20. He was an official in Chang'an (the ancient capital on the site of modern-day Xi'an) for 10 years, was later captured by rebels after an uprising, and fled to Chengdu, where he stayed for four years. He built himself a humble cottage and penned over 200 poems on simple themes around the lives of the people who lived and worked nearby.

The present grounds – 20 hectares of leafy

bamboo and luxuriant vegetation – are said to be a much enlarged version of Du Fu's original poetic retreat. It's also the centre of the Chengdu Du Fu Study Society, and the Du Fu Museum on the grounds houses 30,000 tomes by and on the poet in 15 languages. Du Fu's statue is accompanied by statues of two lesser poets: Li You and Huang Tingjian. From the time of his death in exile (in Hunan), Du Fu acquired a cult status, and his poems have been a major source of inspiration for many Chinese artists (there are paintings displayed on site).

To the west of the Jinjiang Hotel and next to Nanjiao Park is **Wuhou Temple** (*wǔhóu cí*). Wuhou might be translated as 'Minister of War', and was the title given to Zhu Geliang, a famous military strategist of the Three Kingdoms Period (220-65 AD) immortalised in one of the classics of Chinese literature: *The Tale of the Three Kingdoms*. Curiously, for the Chinese Zhu Geliang is not the main attraction of the temple. The front shrine is dedicated to Liu Bei, Zhu Geliang's emperor. Liu's temple, the Hanzhaolie Temple, was moved here and rebuilt during the Ming Dynasty, but the Wuhou Temple name stuck all the same. Liu is a popular Chinese surname and many Overseas Chinese with the surname make a point of visiting the temple while they are in Chengdu on the glorious off-chance that the emperor is a distant ancestor. If you're here around lunchtime, check out the vegetarian restaurant – there's even an English menu.

In the south-east of town, near Sichuan University is **River Viewing Pavilion Park** (*wàngjiāng lóu*). The pavilion itself is a four-storey Qing wooden structure with a teahouse and restaurant. The park is famous for its lush forests of bamboo. Over 150 types of bamboo from China, Japan and South-East Asia have been collected together here. They range from bonsai-sized potted plants to towering giants, creating a shady retreat in the heat of summer (a cold, damp retreat in winter). The pavilion was built to the memory of Xue Tao, a female Tang Dynasty poet with a great love for bamboo. Nearby is a well, said to be the place where she drew water to dye her writing paper.

Renmin Park
(*rénmín gōngyuán*) 人民公园

This is one Chinese park well worth recommending. It's to the south-west of the city centre. The teahouse here is excellent (see the Places to Eat section), and just near the entrance is the candyseller, producing works of art in toffee. While most of the action is around the entrance, it's worth having a poke around in the park itself. There's a bonsai rockery, a kids' playground, a few swimming pools, and the Monument to the Martyrs of the Railway-Protecting Movement (1911). This obelisk, decorated with shunting manoeuvres and railway tracks, marks an uprising of the people against officers who pocketed cash raised for the construction of the Chengdu-Chongqing line. Since Renmin Park was also at the time a private officer's garden, it was a fitting place to erect the structure.

Sichuan Museum
(*sìchuānshěng bówùguavn*)
四川博物馆

The Sichuan Museum is the largest provincial museum in China's south-west, with more than 150,000 items on display. For historians, the displays of tiled murals and frescoes taken from tombs are of great interest in their depictions of ancient daily activities from agriculture to dance. The museum is closed on Mondays. It's down Renmin Nanlu in the direction of the south railway station, but is within cycling distance of the Jinjiang Hotel.

Sichuan University Museum
(*sìdà bówùguǎn*) 四大博物馆

The museum is on the 1st and 3rd floors of Sichuan University's Liberal Arts building. Founded in 1914 by US scholar D S Dye, it underwent several closings and name changes before re-opening under its current name in 1984. The six exhibition rooms display, on a rotating basis, a collection of over 40,000 items. The collection is particularly strong in the fields of ethnology, folklore and traditional arts. The Tibetan Art Exhibition Room, for example, is designed like a family worship hall and contains Buddha images, thangkas (religious paintings), Tibetan musical instruments and various other cultural artefacts. The ethnology room exhibits artefacts from the Yi, Qiang, Miao, Jingpo, Naxi and Tibetan cultures. The Chinese painting and calligraphy room displays works from the Tang, Song, Yuan, Ming and Qing dynasties. Some labels are in English.

The museum is open Monday to Saturday, from 9 am to noon and from 2.30 to 5.30 pm. The university grounds are within easy walking distance of Jiuyanqiao bus station, next to the Nine-Arch Bridge. A No 35 bus east from Binjiang Lu will terminate near the bridge. From there, walk south across Yihuan Nanlu to the university.

Zoo
(dòngwùyuán) 动物园

Chinese zoos are always slightly depressing experiences, and it's difficult not to compare the lush expansive grounds that the humans get to stroll around in with the concrete bunkers allocated to the exhibits. Still, since Sichuan is China's foremost panda habitat, Chengdu Zoo has the nation's largest collection, and this in itself makes the zoo worth a visit for many travellers. About eight pandas are on hand for observation; during the hottest summer months, however, they're not very active.

The zoo is about six km from Chengdu city centre, and is open from 8 am to 6 pm daily. The best way to get there is by bicycle (around half an hour from the Traffic Hotel). The No 302 bus from the northern railway station, which terminates at the zoo, is almost impossible to find. There are also minibuses running direct to the zoo from the north railway station.

Zhaojue Temple
(zhàojué sì) 昭觉寺

Next door to the zoo, Zhaojue Temple is a Tang Dynasty building dating originally

back to the 7th century. It underwent extensive reconstruction under the supervision of Po Shan, a famous Buddhist monk, during the early Qing, with waterways and groves of trees being established around the temple. The temple itself has served as a model for many Japanese and South-East Asian Buddhist temples. Naturally, it went through hard times during the Cultural Revolution, and has only been restored over the last 10 years. It's worth combining with a trip to the zoo.

Chengdu Folkways Artistic Hall
(guǐchéng) 鬼城

Finally, definitely an offbeat attraction is the 'Demon Gallery' or 'Hell World' just to the west of the Sichuan Exhibition Centre. It's in one of Chengdu's underground bomb shelters and you have to walk underground for a couple of hundred metres before you get to it.

The exhibition itself is a truly Boschean landscape, with demons skewering their hapless victims, simmering them in huge vats, tearing out their tongues and flailing their skin off their bodies – is this where CITS staff end up? The idea is to depict the Chinese 18 levels of hell. The Chinese explanation at the door helpfully suggests that it 'gives vivid and realistic artistic expression to life in Chengdu prior to Liberation'. The exhibition is open daily andcosts Y8 (foreigner's price) entry.

Places to Stay – bottom end

The *Traffic Hotel* (☎ 554962) *(jiāotōng fàndiàn)*, next to Xinnanmen bus station, has for a long time been the main hang-out for backpackers, but prices have been on the rise over recent years. It's clean, comfortable, fairly quiet and close to a number of good dining spots.

A bed in a triple is Y26, with immaculate showers and toilet down the hall. Doubles/triples with satellite TV and private bathroom cost Y84/96. The staff at reception are friendly and there's a notice board with travel information in the foyer. Another useful service here is a baggage room where you can leave heavy backpacks for a few days while you head off to Emeishan, Jiuzhaigou or wherever. To get here from the northern railway station, take trolley-bus No 1 to the far side of the bridge across from the hotel.

For a unique hotel experience in China many travellers spend at least one night in the *Black Coffee Hotel (hēi kāfēi fàndiàn)*, affectionately known by residents as the 'Black Coffin'. It's close to the Jinjiang and Traffic hotels.

Basically it's a bomb shelter which has been converted into an underground hotel, karaoke parlour and bar, and the result of all that work is that staying here is like living in a bomb shelter. It comes in for a lot of flak, but if it wasn't for the state of the washing facilities (long-timers head over to the Traffic Hotel for a shower), it would actually not be a bad place to stay.

Three-bed dorms are Y9 a bed; four-bed dorms are Y4 a bed; and doubles *(with* a vent, as the management proudly points out) are Y30. There's worse accommodation around in China, and if you don't mind (or even enjoy) the slightly sleazy atmosphere and having to wander through the bar to have a shower this might be your ticket.

There *is* other budget accommodation available in Chengdu, but the hotels are less conveniently located than the Traffic and Black Coffee hotels and are not geared up to the needs of foreigners (no bicycle hire for example). If this doesn't worry you, one of the cheapest options around is the *Yuanding Hotel (yuándǐng fàndiàn)*, which is up an alley to the west of Renmin Nanlu. In the new west wing two-room dorms with all mod cons are Y48; singles with bathroom are Y48; and triples are Y24. In the old east wing doubles with attached bathroom are Y24 per bed; triples are Y12; and four-bed dorms are Y7.

Not far from here is the *Rongcheng Hotel* (☎ 22931) *(róngchéng fàndiàn)*, a slightly chaotic kind of place with doubles with bathroom for Y50. There are also triples for Y74 and 'superior doubles' that range from Y100. The *Xingchuan Hotel (xīngchuān fàndiàn)* has similar rates and standards to the Traffic

Hotel, except that they accept RMB here. Doubles with attached bathroom are Y77; triples Y84; and air-con doubles are Y99. They may or may not allow you to stay in the 10-person dorm for Y20.

Finally, only resort to CAAC's *Blue Sky Hotel*, next door to the China Southwest Airlines office on Renmin Nanlu, if everything else is full (highly unlikely). It's fairly unfriendly and no longer particularly cheap. Doubles/triples cost Y88/102.

Places to Stay – middle

Chengdu is pretty short of mid-range accommodation. The only real contender is the Traffic Hotel, which has already been mentioned in the bottom-end section. The *Binjiang Hotel*, not far from the Traffic, used to be a popular mid-range option, but it has gone for a major face-lift, jacked up its prices and gets nothing but bad reports. The same is partly true of the *Tibet Hotel*, which has well and truly renovated itself into the top-end category, though you at least get what you pay for there.

Places to Stay – top end

The *Jinjiang Hotel* (☎ 582222) *(jǐnjiāng bīnguǎn)* at 180 Renmin Nanlu was once the headquarters for all travellers who made it to Chengdu. Nowadays it's strictly a top-end job with standard doubles for US$50. There's not a great deal to recommend it. The coffee shop is not even a very nice place to hang out.

Opposite the Jinjiang on Renmin Nanlu is the newer, 21-storey *Minshan Hotel* (☎ 583333) *(mínshān fàndiàn)*, which does a brisk tour-group business. Modern doubles start at US$60 and suites are US$120. The Minshan has a couple of bars, a teahouse and three restaurants.

Opposite the north railway station is the new *Chengdu Grand Hotel (chéngdū dàjiǔdiàn)*, a plush place designed to attract the roving business account. Prices vary according to demand (they often double when conferences are held in town), but you can reckon on a minimum of Y271 for a standard double, Y181 for a standard single and Y388 for a two-room suite.

Not far down Renmin Beilu is the *Tibet Hotel* (☎ 333988) (*xīzàng fàndiàn*), with very similar rates and standards to the Chengdu Grand Hotel. Just east of the Sichuan Exhibition Centre, the *Sichuan Hotel* (☎ 661115) (*sìchuān bīnguǎn*) is a Chinese-style hotel of the kind you find all over China, except that this one has been remodelled in an attempt to bring it up to international standards. It hasn't been entirely successful. Doubles start at around Y200.

The nearby *Shudu Mansion Hotel* (☎ 673888) (*shǔdū dàshà bīnguǎn*) is more successful in creating the international hotel look, though it seems to get few international customers. Doubles are Y320 and suites are Y550.

Places to Eat

Sichuan cuisine is world famous and in a class of its own. The Chinese claim that it comprises more than 4000 dishes, of which over 300 are said to be famous. It's easily China's hottest and spiciest cuisine, often using *huājiāo*, literally 'flower pepper', a crunchy little item that leaves a numbing and strangely unfamiliar aftertaste – some compare it to spicy detergent. Sichuan chefs have a catch-cry that draws attention to the diversity of Sichuanese cooking styles: *bǎicài, bǎiwèi*, literally 'a hundred dishes, a hundred flavours'.

Whether 'a hundred flavours' is a characteristic Chinese exaggeration or not it is difficult to say. There is, nevertheless, a bewildering cornucopia of Sichuanese sauces and culinary-preparation techniques; in fact, there are so many that you could spend a couple of months eating out in Chengdu and still only have scratched the surface. Some of the more famous varieties are *yúxiāng wèi*, a really tasty fish-flavoured sauce that draws heavily on vinegar, soy sauce and mashed garlic and ginger; *málà wèi*, a numbingly spicy sauce that is often prepared with bean curd (it's a little like having your mouth washed out with soap);

yānxūn wèi, a 'smoked flavour' sauce, of which the most justifiably famous is that used with smoked duck; and, perhaps most famous of all – the hot and sour sauce (*suānlà wèi*). The hot and sour soup, *suānlà tāng*, is eaten throughout China and is great on a cold day.

There are also some well-known Sichuan dishes to look out for. The most famous is spicy chicken fried with peanuts (*gōngbǎo jīdīng*) which is served by almost all the local restaurants. Equally well known is *mápó dòufu* which is bean curd, pork and chopped spring onions prepared in a chilli sauce – there are a couple of restaurants specialising in this dish in Chengdu. A favourite with travellers and worth trying simply for the novelty value is *guōbā ròupiàn*. *Guōbā* refers to the crispy bits of rice, uncannily similar to rice crispies, that get stuck to the bottom of the rice pot – they are put on a plate, and pork and gravy added in front of the diner. Also look out for 'pocket bean curd' (*kǒudài dòufu*), cubes of stuffed bean curd, 'strange taste chicken' (*guài'iwèi jīsī*), diced chicken prepared with 'strange taste' sauce, and 'smoked-tea duck' (*zhāngchá yāzi*).

Famous Restaurants The *Chengdu Restaurant* (*chéngdū cāntīng*) at 134 Shangdong Dajie is one of Chengdu's most famous and authentic Sichuan restaurants – a favourite with travellers. Good atmosphere, decent food, reasonable prices – downstairs is adequate. Try to assemble a party of vagabonds from the hotel before sallying forth, since tables are large, and you get to sample more with a bigger group. It's about a 20-minute walk along a side alley opposite the Jinjiang Hotel. Arrive early.

The *Rongleyuan* (*rónglè yuán*) is at 48 Renmin Zhonglu. It's hard to find – look for a small, red-fronted doorway that leads to a larger courtyard. It has recently undergone a major face-lift and prices have risen accordingly. It's probably best left for a special occasion.

For *guōbā ròupiàn*, you can't beat the *Shimeixuan Restaurant* (*shíměixuān cān-*

tīng) opposite the Jinjiang Theatre on Huaxingzhen Jie. A large plate of the crispy rice in pork and lychee sauce costs around Y10, plenty for two. The restaurant has lots of other great dishes, too, and the proprietors don't seem to mind if you walk through the kitchen and point out what you want. Large, clean dining rooms with wooden tables and ceiling fans make eating here even more enjoyable.

Another main-course restaurant in the heart of the city is the *Yaohua Restaurant* (*yàohuá fàndiàn*) at 22 Chunxi Lu. A visit by Mao himself in 1958 clinched the restaurant's reputation. Among Chinese, the restaurant is also renowned for its Western food – be adventurous and judge for yourself.

Riverside Restaurants Along the south side of the Jin River between the Jinjiang and Traffic hotels is a short string of restaurants and teahouses with outdoor tables. All serve Sichuan specialties as well as Chinese standards and a few Western dishes and are well worth trying; perhaps the best is the *Jinjiang Restaurant*, which offers tasty *mápō dòufu* and *dāndān miàn* (noodles in a spicy peanut sauce) at reasonable prices.

Down at the very end of the row, close to the Traffic Hotel, is the popular *Flower Garden Restaurant*, where travellers talk over Jiuzhaigou adventures or trade tips on getting permits for western Sichuan and beyond.

This is also a good place to inquire about train tickets and 'unauthorised' budget tours of Chengdu and northern Sichuan. The food? Consistently good, from noodles to more elaborate dishes. There are a few Western dishes (breakfasts and sandwiches) on the bilingual menu. Don't miss the peach custard, which is marked on the menu as 'Phoenix & Dragon Soup'.

Also on the same stretch of road and popular with travellers is the *YS Restaurant*. The food here is excellent, and the staff are friendly. Like the Flower Garden, this place also offers some travellers' services.

Vegetarian A special treat for ailing vegetarians is to head out to the Wenshu Monastery, where there is an excellent vegetarian restaurant with an English menu. If you're really keen, you might ride out to the *Monastery of Divine Light* in Xindu, 18 km north of Chengdu, in time for lunch (11 am to noon). For details of the bus service see the Around Chengdu section.

Snacks Many of Chengdu's specialties originated as *xiǎo chī* or 'little eats'. The snack bars are great fun and will cost you next to nothing. In fact, the offerings can be outdone in no other Chinese city – and if you line up several of these places you will get yourself a banquet in stages.

Unfortunately, many of Chengdu's famous snack places are falling prey to the massive reconstruction work that in many areas is tearing the city down and starting from scratch. This is particularly true of the Dongfeng Lu area, though a few places are still hanging in there. We can't promise that all the places marked on the map and mentioned here will still be there by the time you set out in search of them. Take a look anyway – it's worth the effort.

Pock-marked Grandma's Bean Curd (*chén mápō dòufu*) serves *mápō dòufu* with a vengeance. Soft bean curd is served up with a fiery meat sauce (laced with garlic, minced beef, salted soybean, chilli oil and nasty little peppercorns). As the story goes, the madame with the pock-marked face set up shop here (reputed to be the same shop as today's) a century ago, providing food and lodging for itinerant pedlars (the clientele don't seem to have changed a great deal).

Bean curd is made on the premises and costs around Y2 a bowl. Beer is served to cool the fires. Don't worry about the grotty, greasy decor – those spices should kill any lurking bugs. Also served are spicy chicken and duck, and plates of tripe. Situated at 113 Xiyulong Jie, the small white shop has a green front.

The area just east of Xishuncheng Jie on Tidu Jie used to be a good area for snacks but, as this whole part of town had basically been transformed into a vast hole in the ground at the time of the writing, it's difficult to say whether they will ever materialise again. There's a remote possibility that they will reappear in shiny laminex when this area comes to life again as a commercial shopping district.

One place that is still going strong is *Zhenzhu Yuanzi (zhēnzhū yuánzi)*. The beauty of this atmospheric little restaurant is that it has sampler courses that allow you to dip into the whole gamut of the Chengdu snack experience. The Y3 course gives you a range of sweet and savoury items, while the Y5 course is basically the same deal on a grander and more filling scale. Both allow you to sample the specialties of shops that have now folded up – *Zhong shuijiao* and *Lai tangyuan*, to name a couple. The restaurant is east of the Sichuan Hotel on the opposite side of the road.

Hotpot Although it is said to have originated in Chongqing, *huǒguō* or hotpot is very popular in Chengdu. You'll see lots of sidewalk hotpot operations in the older section of town near the Chunxi Lu market as well as along the river. Big woks full of hot, spiced oil (not to be confused with the mild Mongolian version, which employs simmering soup broth) invite passers-by to sit down, pick out skewers of raw ingredients and make a do-it-yourself fondue. You pay by the skewer – it's best to ask the price of a skewer before you place it in the oil. During the winter months the skewered items on offer tend to be meat or 'heavy' vegetables like potatoes. In the summer months lighter, mostly vegetarian fare is the norm.

This stuff is *very* hot, and many non-Sichuanese can't take it. If this is the case, try asking for *báiwèi*, the hotpot for wimps. Chinese (and some travellers) will turn their noses up at this, claiming that it's not the real thing – just ignore them.

Other Generally, eating out in Chinese cities means choosing between Chinese or diabolically prepared Western food. Chengdu has at least one alternative to both of these in the *Banna Restaurant (bǎnnà jiǔjiā)*, where they do Dai minority food. It's a little pricey (figure on Y20 per head at least) by Chinese standards, but the food is excellent.

Unfortunately, there's no English menu and the Chinese menu is almost indecipherable even if you have good Chinese, but you can try asking for *zhúzi niúròu* (curry beef cooked in bamboo) or *yézi jīròu* (curry chicken cooked in a coconut). The rice is prepared in bamboo also and is delicious.

The restaurant decor is almost tasteful, done out in bamboo, and there is live ethnic music during dinner. Cross the bridge from the Traffic Hotel and walk north-east to the first big intersection. The restaurant is on the near left corner.

Teahouses The teahouse, or *chádiàn*, has always been the equivalent of the French cafe or the British pub in China – or at least this was true of the pre-1949 era. Activities ranged from haggling over the bride's dowry to fierce political debate (and sometimes drinking tea). The latter was especially true of Sichuan, which historically has been one of the first areas to rebel and one of the last to come to heel.

Chengdu's teahouses are thus somewhat special – as in other Chinese cities, they were closed down during the Cultural Revolution because they were thought to be dangerous assembly places for 'counter-revolutionaries'. With factional battles raging in Sichuan as late as 1975, re-emergence of this part of daily life has been slow – but you can't keep an old tea addict down! Teahouses sprawl over Chengdu sidewalks (in back-alley sections), with bamboo armchairs that permit ventilation of one's back.

In the past, Chengdu teahouses also functioned as venues for Sichuan opera – the plain-clothes variety, performed by amateurs or retired workers. There's been a revival of the teahouse opera, but such places (and the times of performances) are difficult to locate, so it's best to find a local to take you there (try asking at the Flower Garden or YS restaurants). Other kinds of entertainment include storytelling and musicians, while some teahouses cater entirely for chess players.

Most Chinese teahouses cater for the menfolk, young and old (mostly old), who come to meet, stoke their pipes or thump cards on the table. If you're staying in the Traffic Hotel area, you can't miss the riverside teahouse between the Flower Garden and YS restaurants. This place is always packed with old men playing *wéiqí*, or Go.

A more comfortable setting is the *Renmin Teahouse (rénmín cháguǎn)* in Renmin Park, which is a leisurely tangle of bamboo armchairs, sooty kettles and ceramics, with a great outdoor location by a lake. It's mixed, a family-type teahouse – crowded on weekends. In the late afternoon workers roll up to soothe shattered factory-nerves – and some just doze off in their armchairs. You can do the same. A most pleasant afternoon can be spent here in relative anonymity over a bottomless cup of stone-flower tea at a cost so ridiculous it's not worth quoting. When enough tea freaks appear on the terrace, the stray earpicker, with Q-tips at the ready, roves through, and paper-profile cutters with deft scissors also make the rounds.

A charming indoor family-type teahouse is also to be found in Wenshu Monastery, with a crowded and steamy ambience. Another teahouse worth checking out is in the Jinjiang Theatre, not far from the post office. This place also has performances of Sichuan opera.

Entertainment

Entertainment can be fruitful hunting in Chengdu, but you will have to hunt. If you don't speak Chinese, ask around among the English-speaking staff at the riverside restaurants for entertainment ideas. If something strikes your fancy, get it written down in Chinese, and get a good map location – these places are often hard to find, especially at night. If you have more time, try and get advance tickets. Offerings include teahouse entertainment, acrobatics, cinema, Sichuan opera, Beijing opera, drama, art exhibits, traditional music, storytelling and shadow plays among other things.

Chengdu is the home of Sichuan opera, which has a 200-year tradition and features slapstick dress-up, eyeglass-shattering songs, men dressed as women and occasional gymnastics. There are several opera houses scattered throughout the older sections of town. Some offer only a couple of performances per week while others are open daily.

One of the easier Sichuan opera venues to find is the *Jinjiang Theatre (jǐnjiāng jùyuàn)* on Huaxinzhen Jie, which is a combination of teahouse, opera theatre and cinema. Sichuan opera performances here are frequent and of a high standard – performance times are listed on boards near the entrance (you may have to enlist a Chinese-reading acquaintance to figure out what's what). Mr Lee at the Flower Garden Snack Bar and Qiu Xi at the YS Restaurant both offer Sichuan opera tours in which front-row seats are reserved and the foreigners are taken backstage to meet the actors. Both services get rave reports from travellers.

Pubs Most of Chengdu's boozing options are of the karaoke variety, a form of entertainment that has taken the city by storm. These places tend to be expensive and of limited interest to most Westerners. One place that serves reasonably priced drinks and only offers up the occasional spot of audience participation in the entertainment is *The Pub*, next door to China Southwest Airlines on Renmin Lu. It has emerged as a favourite hang-out for the foreigner population as well as for young hip Chinese. There's usually live entertainment alternating with MTV video clips and it's a good place to hang out in the evenings. It's open late and plays havoc with early morning travel plans (did I say I was catching the 7 am bus to Leshan?).

Things to Buy

Chengdu is home to a host of commercial and shopping districts: the Qingyang Palace Commercial Street; the Shudou Boulevard Commercial Street; the Chenghuang Miao

Electronic Market; the Chunxi Lu Commercial Street; and even, as one locally produced English map indicates, 'Electronic Brain Street – No 1 Ring Road' (in Chinese, electronic brain means 'computer'). Let's assume, however, that you don't want to spend the rest of your life conspicuously consuming in Chengdu's commercial streets; if this is the case, the pick of the bunch for a stroll and a few purchases is Chunxi Lu.

Chunxi Lu is the main shopping artery, lined with department stores, art dealers, secondhand bookshops, stationers, spectacle shops and photo stores. At No 10 is the Arts & Crafts Service Department Store *(chéngdū měishùpǐn fúwùbù)*, dealing in most of the Sichuan specialties (lacquerware, silverwork, bamboo products). This place also has branches in the Jinjiang Hotel, the airport and the Chengdu Folk Arts Exhibition Centre.

The best advice for Chunxi Lu is just to stroll around and dive into any shop that looks interesting. You are almost bound to come up with something you couldn't possibly do without. Look out for the Derentang Chemist, the oldest and largest of all Chengdu's Chinese pharmacies, at the bottom end (south) of the road on the left. The Sichuan Antique Store that used to be on the north end of Chunxi Lu has now moved to a huge new building opposite the Sichuan Fine Arts Exhibition Hall on Renmin Lu. It's worth a visit, and while a lot of the stuff is overpriced there are usually still a few bargains to be had.

Along Renmin Nanlu to the north of the Jinjiang Hotel is a string of antique and handicraft shops. There is some really good stuff in these shops, though it's a good idea to avoid anything with an air of antiquity to it – it's almost definitely fake. Woodcuts are a relatively inexpensive purchase. On the opposite side of the road down next to the Minshan Hotel is a night market with lots of souvenir items on sale. Some of the stuff is not bad, but be prepared for an intense bargaining session if anything catches your eye. Another place for souvenirs is the Municipal

Museum. It has an auction every Sunday morning from 9 am.

Renmin Market *(rénmín shìchǎng)* is a maze of daily necessity stuff – worth poking your nose into but not of great interest for purchases. Further north of that, along Jiefang Zhonglu, are small shops selling fur-lined and sheepskin coats and jackets (as well as heavy PLA-type overcoats) – a good selection, not found in too many other places. There's another place selling army surplus stuff (good for stocking up on warm clothing if you're heading to Tibet or Jiuzhaigou) up on Renmin Zhonglu.

Getting There & Away

Transport connections in Chengdu are more comprehensive than in other parts of the south-west.

Air China Southwest Airlines (☎ 23991) is diagonally opposite the Jinjiang Hotel, and is a good place to purchase tickets between China destinations other than Chengdu. The smaller Sichuan Provincial Airlines also has an office nearby. It flies to many of the same destinations as Southwest, but it's probably a good idea to only use it at a pinch. Its fleet of aircraft mainly comprises Russian hand-me-downs from CAAC.

China Southwest Airlines has plenty of air connections out of Chengdu, including Beijing (Y850); Tianjin (Y820); Harbin, Heilongjiang (Y1350); Shenyang, Liaoning (Y1170); Hangzhou, Zhejiang (Y850); Ürümqi, Xinjiang (Y1130); Xiamen, Fujian (Y950); Canton (Y670); Shenzhen, Guangdong (Y910); Haikou, Hainan Island (Y880); Chongqing, Sichuan (Y160); Guilin, Guangxi (Y480); Guiyang, Guizhou (Y260); Kunming, Yunnan (Y360); Lanzhou, Gansu (Y470); Lhasa, Tibet (Y990); Nanjing, Jiangsu (Y800); Shanghai (Y890); and Xi'an, Shaanxi (Y320).

The most frequently asked question in Chengdu must be 'Can I fly to Lhasa?' Officially the answer is 'No', but this doesn't stop the occasional lucky traveller from waltzing in to the Southwest Airlines office and leaving with a ticket. The trick to this one is having your money ready. If they're willing to sell you a ticket, you're going to have to fork out quick before they change their minds. Forget about rushing off to the bank to change a couple of travellers' cheques. Another trick is asking for a 1st-class ticket. Failing this, you'll either have to join a CITS tour, buy a ticket at nearly twice the standard ticket price from the Flower Garden Restaurant or head over to Golmud and do the trip by bus.

Bus The main bus station, Xinnanmen bus station, next to the Traffic Hotel, sells tickets to most destinations around Sichuan but not to the north. For northern destinations you will need to head over to the Ximen bus station in the north-west of the city.

For Emeishan, the best option is the 9.30 am bus that runs direct to Baoguo Temple. Buy your ticket the day before to ensure a seat. There are frequent buses all morning to Leshan (Y15). For Qingcheng Shan there's a bus at 7.50 am for Y7. Night buses are available to Chongqing at 5 pm; prices vary depending on the condition of the bus, but range from Y39. Other buses include Dazu (6.50 am), Kangding (8.20 am), Rongxian (7.20 and 8.20 am) and Ya'an (hourly from 6.50 am to 2.30 pm).

The Ximen bus station is really only of interest to travellers heading up to Jiuzhaigou or taking the overland route to Xiahe in Gansu Province by way of northern Sichuan. Unlike the Xinnanmen bus station, this place has special foreigner's prices (a surcharge of 70%) and charges in FEC. Buses to Songpan leave at 7.20 am and cost Y33.10 (Chinese price). There are buses running direct from Songpan to Jiuzhaigou. Buses to Maoxian (en route to Songpan) leave at 7.20 am and cost Y19.20 (Chinese price). Other buses include Dujiangyan every 10 minutes for Y4.20 and Qingcheng Shan every 20 minutes from 7.10 to 9.50 am.

The north bus station is west of the railway station and has buses every half hour (Y14.50) and minibuses (Y17.60) to Leshan. There's a morning bus from here to Chongq-

ing at 9 am for Y38.30 and luxury night buses at 5, 5.30 and 6.30 pm for Y74.

Train Getting train tickets out of Chengdu is no easy feat. Many travellers simply give up on the idea and get locals at either the Flower Garden or YS restaurants to fix tickets up for them. This is fine if you don't mind paying extra for their services. Doing it yourself can be time-consuming and frustrating. Some travellers have had success at one of the various advance booking offices around town and others have managed to buy direct from black marketeers at the railway station. The best advice is to give it a try, but if it looks like you're going to be spending all your time in Chengdu chasing a ticket, spend a bit extra and get the locals at the Flower Garden or the YS to arrange it for you. Don't bother with CITS.

For those looking at getting to Lijiang and Dali, there are trains to Panzhihua (also known as Jinjiang) on the Chengdu-Kunming route. There's an early morning (7.50 am) train (No 389), but as this one doesn't get in to Panzhihua until just after midnight it will mean an overnight stay. A better option is the No 321, which leaves Chengdu at 4.15 pm and gets into Panzhihua at 8.50 am the following morning. This will allow you to hook up with a bus or minibus to either Lijiang or Dali and avoid a miserable evening in Panzhihua. The No 93 express leaves at 9.15 pm and gets to Panzhihua at 10.30 am the following day. Hard-sleeper tickets are approximately Y116 for foreigners.

You can use any of the trains headed for Kunming or Panzhihua to get to Emei. Express trains take just under two hours, while fast trains take around three hours. A hard seat should cost Y7. Trains to Kunming take either 23 hours or 29 hours, depending on whether they are fast or express, and the cost is around Y126 for a hard sleeper. Trains to Chongqing take around 12 hours and should cost approximately Y80 for a hard sleeper; Chinese price for a hard seat is Y27.

Other rail options include Canton,

Beijing, Shanghai, Guiyang, Hefei, Xi'an, Ürümqi, Lanzhou and Taiyuan.

Getting Around

Bus The most useful bus is No 16, which runs from Chengdu north railway station to the south railway station, passing by the PSB, the Foreign Languages Bookshop and the Jinjiang Hotel.

Bus maps carry colour coding for trolleys and ordinary buses – bus Nos 1, 2, 3, 4 and 5 can also be trolleys bearing the same number. Trolley-bus No 1 runs from Xinnanmen bus station to Chengdu north railway station. Ordinary bus No 4 runs from the Ximen bus station (north-western end of town) to the south-eastern sector, and continues service until 1 am (most others cease around 9.30 to 10.30 pm).

Bicycle Many of Chengdu's old bicycle hire shops have disappeared, and most travellers hire their bikes these days from the Traffic Hotel. You might try scouting around for other places, but if you're staying in or nearby the Traffic Hotel this is the easiest option.

The usual rules apply – check your bike before you cycle off; some of them are death traps. Also make an effort to park your bike in a designated parking area. Bicycle theft is a problem here as in most Chinese cities.

AROUND CHENGDU
Monastery of Divine Light
(bǎoguāng sì) 宝光寺

This monastery in the north of Xindu County is an active Buddhist temple. It comprises five halls and 16 courtyards, surrounded by bamboo. Pilgrims, monks and tourists head for Xindu, which makes for lively proceedings and attracts a fine line-up of hawkers. The temple was founded in the 9th century, was subsequently destroyed, and was reconstructed in the 17th century.

Among the monastery treasures are a white jade Buddha from Burma, Ming and Qing paintings and calligraphy, a stone tablet engraved with 1000 Buddhist figures (540 AD) and ceremonial musical instruments.

Unfortunately, most of the more valuable items are locked away and require special permission to view them – you may be able to get this if you can find whoever's in charge around here.

The Arhat Hall, built in the 19th century, contains 500 two-metre-high clay figurines representing Buddhist saints and disciples. Well, not all of them: among this spaced-out lot are two earthlings – emperors Kangxi and Qianlong. They're distinguishable by their royal costumes, beards, boots and capes. One of the impostors, Kangxi, is shown with a pockmarked face, perhaps a whim of the sculptor. About one km from the monastery is Osmanthus Lake and its bamboo groves, lotuses, and osmanthus trees. In the middle of the lake is a small memorial hall for the Ming scholar Yang Shengan.

The temple has an excellent vegetarian restaurant where a huge array of dishes is prepared by monastic chefs. The restaurant's opening hours are from 10 am to 3 pm, though it is best to be here around lunch time, when there is more available. The monastery itself is open daily between 8 am and 5.30 pm.

Getting There & Away Xindu is 18 km north of Chengdu: a round trip on a bicycle would be 40 km, or at least four hours' cycling time on a Chinese bike. Alternatively, buses run from the terminal of the No 1 trolley bus in front of the north railway station. The trip takes just under an hour and buses run from 6.20 am to 6.30 pm.

Qingcheng Shan
(qīngchéng shān) 青城山

For those with limited time, Qingcheng Shan, a holy Daoist mountain some 65 km west of Chengdu, is a good alternative to more rigorous climb at Emeishan. The peak is 1600 metres. There are numerous Daoist temples en route to the summit. The Jianfu Temple (jiànfú gōng) at the entrance to the mountain area is probably the best preserved. Of the 500 or so Daoist monks in residence on the mountain prior to 'Liberation', there are now thought to be around 100 left.

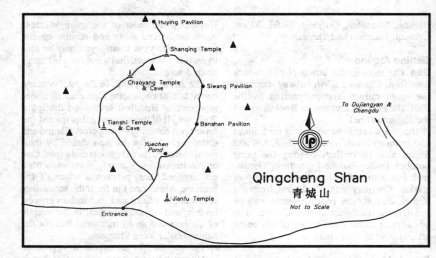

There's accommodation and food available at three spots on the mountain: at the base at Jianfu Temple. About halfway up at Tianshi Cave *(tiānshī dòng)* and at the summit at Shangqing Temple *(shàngqīng gōng)*. Reckon on around Y10 to Y15 per person. Most people ascend by way of Tianshi Cave and descend via Siwang Pavilion and Banshan Pavilion.

The climb to the top is a leisurely four-hour hike, making Qingcheng Shan an ideal day trip from Chengdu. Many travellers, however, prefer to set off around midday, stay overnight at Shangqing Temple and hike up to the summit for the sunrise. This leaves time to walk down and head over to Dujiangyan for the afternoon. There's a Y5 entry charge for the mountain area.

Getting There & Away There are buses to Qingcheng Shan from all three of Chengdu's long-distance bus stations. The Xinnanmen bus station (next to the Traffic Hotel) has buses from 7.50 am. There are more frequent bus services from the Ximen bus station in the west of town (approximately 20 minutes between 7 am and 9.50 am). From the north bus station there are buses from 8.30 am. The fare at all three is around Y7.

From the entrance to the mountain there are buses running back to Chengdu and also to Guanxian for Dujiangyan.

Dujiangyan
(dūjiāngyàn) 都江堰

The Dujiangyan irrigation project, some 60 km north-west of Chengdu, was undertaken in the 3rd century BC to divert the fast-flowing Min River and rechannel it into irrigation canals. The Min was subject to flooding at this point, yet when it subsided droughts could ensue. A weir system was built to split the force of the river, and a trunk canal was cut through a mountain to irrigate the Chengdu plain. Thus the mighty Min was tamed, and a temple was erected to commemorate the occasion in 168 AD. The temple, **Fulong Temple** *(fúlóng guān)*, can still be seen in the Lidui Park *(líduī gōng-yuán)*.

The project is ongoing – it originally irrigated over a million hectares of land, and since Liberation this has expanded to three million hectares. Most of the present dams, reservoirs, pumping stations, hydroelectric works, bridgework and features are modern; a good overall view of the outlay can be gained from **Two Kings Temple** (*èrwáng miào*), which dates back to 494 AD. The two kings are Li Bing, governor of the kingdom of Shu and father of the irrigation project, and his son, Er Lang. Inside is a statue of Li Bing, shockingly lifelike; in the rear hall is a standing figure of his son holding a dam tool. There's also a Qing Dynasty project map, and behind the temple there is a terrace saying in effect, 'Mao was here' (1958).

Dujiangyan gets mixed reports from travellers. Some people love the place, others find the whole idea of visiting a massive irrigation project boring. There's not a great

deal of local flavour, although there is a small teahouse sited on **South Bridge** (*nánqiáo*), near Lidui Park entrance, and visiting the nearby temples is not a bad way to while away an afternoon. The *Liuhe Hotel*, about 15 minutes' walk from the Guanxian bus station, has beds from Y10, though most visitors do Dujiangyan as a day trip.

Getting There & Away Buses run to Guanxian from Ximen bus station in Chengdu every 10 minutes. They cost Y4.20, and the trip takes 1½ hours over bumpy roads. From the Dujiangyan bus terminal it's not a bad idea to catch another bus on to the Two Kings Temple and work your way back. It's also possible to hook up with buses here going to Qingcheng Shan.

Wolong Nature Reserve
(*wòlóng zìrán bǎohùqū*)
卧龙自然保护区
Wolong Nature Reserve lies 40 km northwest of Chengdu, about nine hours of rough roads by bus (via Guanxian). It was set up in the late 1970s and is the largest of the 13 reserves set aside by the Chinese government especially for panda conservation. Of

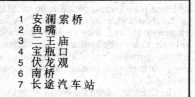

1 安澜索桥
2 鱼嘴
3 二王庙
4 宝瓶口
5 伏龙观
6 南桥
7 长途汽车站

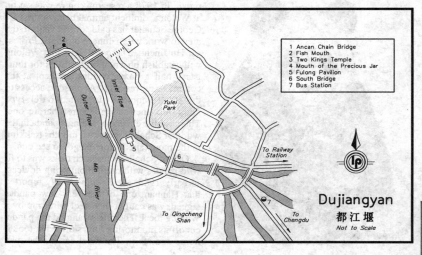

1 Ancan Chain Bridge
2 Fish Mouth
3 Two Kings Temple
4 Mouth of the Precious Jar
5 Fulong Pavilion
6 South Bridge
7 Bus Station

Yulei Park

Outer Flow

Inter Flow

Min River

To Railway Station

To Qingcheng Shan

To Chengdu

Dujiangyan
都江堰
Not to Scale

these 13 reserves, 11 are in Sichuan. The United Nations has designated Wolong as an international biosphere preserve.

Estimates place the total number of giant pandas at a round figure of 1000, most of which are distributed in approximately 28 counties of north and north-western Sichuan (with further ranges in Gansu and Shaanxi). Other animals protected here are the golden monkey, golden langur, musk deer and snow leopard. The reserve is estimated to have some 3000 kinds of plants and covers an area of 200,000 hectares. To the north-west is Mt Siguniang (6240 metres) and to the east it drops as low as 155 metres. Pandas like to dine in the zone from 2300 to 3200 metres, ranging lower in winter.

The earliest known remains of the panda date back 600,000 years. It's stoutly built, rather clumsy, and has a thick pelt of fine hair, a short tail, and a round white face with eyes set in black-rimmed sockets. Though it staggers when it walks, the panda is a good climber, and lives mostly on a vegetarian diet of bamboo and sugar-cane leaves. Mating

season has proved a great disappointment to observers at the Wolong Reserve, since pandas are rather particular. Related to the bear and the raccoon, pandas – despite their human-looking shades – can be vicious in self-defence. In captivity they establish remarkable ties with their keepers after a period of time, and can be trained to do a repertoire of tricks.

The giant panda was first discovered in 1896 in Sichuan, and is headed for extinction. Part of the problem is the gradual diminution of their food supply; in the mid-70s more than 130 pandas starved to death when one of the bamboo species on which they feed flowered and withered in the Minshan mountains of Sichuan. Pandas consume enormous amounts of bamboo, although their digestive tracts get little value from the plant (consumption is up to 20 kg of bamboo a day in captivity). They are carnivorous, but they're slow to catch animals. Other problems are genetic defects, internal parasites and a slow reproductive rate (artificial insemination has been used at Beijing Zoo).

The Chinese invited the World Wide Fund for Nature (whose emblem is the lovable panda) to assist in research, itself a rare move. In 1978 a research centre was set up at Wolong. Eminent animal behaviourist Dr George Schaller has paid several visits to the area to work with Chinese biologist Professor Hu Jinchu. There are signs that Wolong will establish observation facilities for tourists – half a dozen pandas are kept at the commune for research. At present, access to this small community is limited to trek-type tours since the road in is a treacherous one. There is little chance of seeing a panda in the wild; Dr Schaller spent two months trekking in the mountains before he got to see one.

One of Schaller's research tasks was to fit wild pandas with radio-monitoring devices. In early 1983, the *People's Daily* reported that Hanhan, one of the very few pandas tagged, was caught in a steel wire trap by a Wolong local. The man strangled the panda, cut off its monitoring ring, skinned it, took it home and ate it. The meal earned the man

Top: Kashgar Sunday market, Kashgar, Xinjiang (CB)
Left: Spices and beans, Kashgar, Xinjiang (CT)
Right: Melon seller, Sunday market, Kashgar, Xinjiang (RI'A)

Top: A young boy, Tingri West, Tibet (CB)
Bottom: Survival – Potala Palace, Lhasa, Tibet (Strauss)

two years in jail. Since then penalties have increased; in 1990 two Sichuan men who were found with four panda skins were publicly executed.

On a brighter note, directives have been issued forbidding locals to hunt, fell trees or make charcoal in the mountainous habitats of the panda. Peasants in the areas are being offered rewards equivalent to double their annual salary if they save a starving panda.

One way to visit the reserve without opting for an expensive CITS tour is to check with the guys at the Flower Garden Restaurant in Chengdu. If there's enough interest, they are able to organise tours at affordable prices.

EMEISHAN
(éméishān) 峨眉山

Emeishan (Mt Emei), locked in a medieval time warp, receives a steady stream of happy pilgrims with their straw hats, makeshift baggage, walking canes and fans. The monasteries hold sombre Buddhist monks, the tinkle of bells, clouds of incense, and firewood and coal lumped in the courtyards for the winter months.

It is more or less a straight mountain climb, with your attention directed to the luxuriant scenery – and, as in *The Canterbury Tales*, to fellow pilgrims. Admirable are the hardened affiliates of Grannies Alpine Club, who slog it up there with the best of them, walking sticks at the ready lest a brazen monkey dare think them easy prey for a food-mugging. They come yearly for the assault, and burn paper money as a Buddhist offering for longevity. The climb no doubt adds to their longevity, so the two factors may be related. For the traveller itching to do something, the Emei climb is a good opportunity to air the respiratory organs, as well as to observe post-1976 religious freedoms in action, since you are obliged to stay in the rickety monasteries along the route.

One of the Middle Kingdom's four famous Buddhist mountains (the others are Putuo, Wutai and Jiuhua), Emeishan has little of its original temple-work left. The glittering Jinding (Golden Summit) Temple,

with its brass tiling engraved with Tibetan script, was completely gutted by fire. A similar fate befell numerous other temples and monasteries on the mount – war with the Japanese and Red Guard looting have taken their toll.

The original temple structures dated back as far as the advent of Buddhism itself in China; by the 14th century, the estimated 100 or so holy structures housed several thousand monks.

The present temple count is around 20 active after a Cultural Revolution hiatus, bearing only traces of their original splendour. Since 1976 the remnants have been renovated, access to the mountain has been improved, hiking paths widened, lodgings added, and tourists permitted to climb to the sacred summit.

Hiking is spectacular enough. Fir trees, pines and cedars clothe the slopes; lofty crags, cloud-kissing precipices, butterflies and azaleas together form a nature reserve of sorts. The major scenic goal of Chinese hikers is to witness a sunrise or sunset over the sea of clouds at the summit. On the rare afternoon there is a phenomenon known as Buddha's Aureole – rainbow rings, produced by refraction of water particles, attach themselves to a person's shadow in a cloud bank below the summit. Devout Buddhists, thinking this was a call from yonder, used to jump off the Cliff of Self-Sacrifice in ecstasy, so during the Ming and Qing dynasties officials set up iron poles and chain railings to prevent suicides. These days your head can be stuck in a cardboard cutout on the site, and you can be photographed in that same act of attaining nirvana.

Weather
The best season to visit is from May to October. Winter is not impossible, but will present some trekking problems – iron soles with spikes can be hired to deal with encrusted ice and snow on the trails. At the height of summer, which is scorching elsewhere in Sichuan, Emei presents cool majesty. Temperate zones start at 1000 metres.

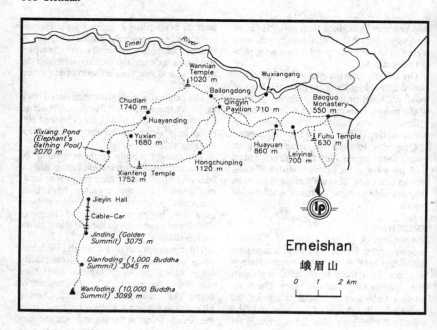

Cloud cover and mist are prevalent, and will most likely interfere with the sunrise. If lucky, you'll see Mt Gongga to the west; if not, you'll have to settle for the telecom tower 'temple' and the meteorological station. Monthly average temperatures in degrees Celsius are:

	Jan	Apr	Jul	Oct
Emei Town	7	21	26	17
Summit	-6	3	12	-1

What to Bring

Emei is a tall one at 3099 metres, so the weather is uncertain and you'd be best advised to prepare for sudden changes without weighing yourself down with a huge pack (steps can be steep). There is no heating or insulation in the monasteries, but blankets are provided (a couple of places have electric blankets nowadays), and you can hire heavy overcoats at the top. Heavy rain can be a problem, calling for a good pair of rough-soled shoes or boots, so you don't go head over heels on the smooth stone steps further up. Flimsy plastic macs are sold by enterprising vendors on the slopes – these will last about 10 minutes before you get wet.

Strange hiking equipment as it may sound, a fixed-length umbrella would be most useful – for the rain, and as a walking stick (scare the hell out of those monkeys by pressing auto-release!). These kinds of umbrellas cost from around Y11 to Y16 in China. If you want to look more authentic you can get yourself a handcrafted walking stick, very cheap – and while you're at it, get a fan and a straw hat too. A torch would be handy. Food supplies are not necessary, but a pocket of munchies wouldn't hurt. Bring toilet paper with you. Luggage can be left at Emei railway station, at the Hongzhushan Hotel, or at one of the monasteries.

Some travellers have become sick from contaminated water supplies on the mountain, so you might consider carrying bottled water.

Ascending the Heights

Baoguo village is the key transport junction, lying between Baoguo Monastery and the Hongzhushan Hotel at the foot of the mountain. You can dump your bags at the Hongzhushan or Xi Xiang hotels for a modest charge. (It may be possible to dump them at the Baoguo Monastery or the Emei town railway station as well.)

Most people start their ascent of the mountain at Wannian Temple *(wànnián sì)* and come down through Qingyin Pavilion. From Baoguo Monastery there are buses running close to Wannian Temple and to Qingyin Pavilion five or six times a day between 7 am and 3 pm; the fare is Y2. In the other direction, buses start running around 8 am and stop at 4 pm.

The bus depot near Qingyin Pavilion also has connections back to Emei town and to Leshan, but there are more running from Baoguo. If you're stuck for connections you may be able to hitch back to Baoguo, otherwise it's a 15-km hike.

For a 'softer' combination, take the bus to Qingyin Pavilion and then walk along the more scenic route via Hongchunping and Yuxian to the Golden Summit. From there you can descend the six km to Jieyin Summit to take a bus back down. If you want to 'cheat' in earnest, see the following Cheating section.

Routes Most people ascend Emeishan via Wannian Temple, Chu Temple, Huayan Summit, Xixiang Pond and on to the summit, and descend from the summit via Xixiang Pond, Xianfeng Temple Hongchunping and Qingyin Pavilion. The paths converge just below Xixiang Pond – there are several small restaurants where the path forks. To give you an idea of the distances involved (remember you are going uphill), the above route pans out as follows.

Wannian Temple (15 km), Xixiang Pond (15 km), Golden Summit (3½ km), Ten Thousand Buddha Summit (3½ km), Golden Summit (15 km), Xixiang Pond (12½ km), Xianfeng Temple (15 km), Hongchunping (six km), Qingyin Pavilion (12½ km),

Leiyin Temple (1½ km), Fuhu Temple (one km), Baoguo Monastery

Duration Two to three days on site is enough. You usually need one day up and one day down. Enough time should be left for a slow-paced descent, which can be more punishing for the old trotters. A hardy Frenchman made it up and down on the same day, but he must have had unusual legs. Chinese and Western sources have some wildly misleading figures on the length and difficulty of the Emei climb. These figures can be attributed to geriatric or Chinese walking times, or ignorance of the buses running to Wannian Temple.

Assuming that most people will want to start climbing from Qingyin Pavilion or Wannian Temple, buses from Baoguo Monastery run close to these points, so that knocks off the initial 15 km. Wannian Temple is at 1020 metres, and the Golden Summit is at 3075 metres. With a healthy set of lungs, at a rate of 200 metres' elevation gain per hour, the trip up from Wannian Temple could be done in 10 hours if foul weather does not develop.

Starting off early in the morning from Wannian Temple, you should be able to get to a point below the Golden Summit by nightfall, then continue to the Golden and Ten Thousand Buddha summits the next day, before descending to Baoguo Monastery. Some people prefer to spend two days up and two days down, spending more time exploring along the way. If you have time to spare, you could meander over the slopes to villages hugging the mountainsides.

On the main routes described above, in climbing time you'd be looking at:

Ascent Qingyin Pavilion (one hour), Wannian Temple (four hours), Xixiang Pond (three hours), Jieyinding (one hour), Golden Summit (one hour), Ten Thousand Buddha Summit

Descent Ten Thousand Buddha Summit (45 minutes), Golden Summit (45 minutes), Jieyin Hall (2½ hours), Xixiang Pond (two hours), Xianfeng Temple (3½ hours), Qingyin Pavilion

Cheating Cheating is a popular pastime on Emei. Old women are portered up on the sturdy backs of young men (likewise, healthy-looking young women are carried up). If this mode of transport isn't your cup of tea, there are also minibuses and buses leaving from the square in front of Baoguo Monastery between 7 and 8 am. They run along a recently made dirt road round the back of the mountain up to Jieyin Hall (2640 metres). From there, it's only 1½ hours to the top. Minibuses (Y10 one way, two hours) and buses (Y6) take about three hours to get up the mountain. Minibuses are usually chartered by prior arrangement.

If even the Jieyin Hall-Golden Summit climb is too much, you can now accomplish this route in about 20 minutes by cable car for Y9 one way, Y15 return.

Places to Stay & Eat

The old monasteries offer food, shelter and sights all rolled into one, and, while spartan, are a delightful change from the regular tourist hotels. They've got maybe as much as 1000 years of character.

You'll probably be asked to pay some ridiculous prices. Bargaining is definitely necessary. Prices range from Y2 in a very large dormitory (10 beds or more) to Y15 per person in a single, double or triple room. It's very difficult to get into the dorms – the staff usually let in only the Chinese. In between are other options like a four-bed room at Y6 per person – again, the Chinese get preference for these. Plumbing and electricity are primitive; candles are supplied. Rats can be a nuisance, particularly if you leave food lying around your room.

There are eight monastery guesthouses – at Baoguo Temple, Qingyin Pavilion, Wannian Temple, Xixiang Pond, Xianfeng Temple, Hongchunping, Fuhu Temple and Leiyin Temple. There's also a host of smaller lodgings at Chu Temple, Jieyin Hall, Yuxian, Bailongdong, the Golden Summit and Huayuan, for instance. The smaller places will accept you if the main monasteries are overloaded. Failing those, you can kip out

virtually anywhere – a teahouse, a wayside restaurant – if night is descending.

Be prepared to backtrack or advance under cover of darkness, as key points are often full of pilgrims – old women two to a bed, camped down the corridors, or camping out in the hallowed temple itself, on the floor. Monasteries usually have halfway hygienic restaurants with monk-chefs serving up the vegetarian fare; from Y2 to Y4 should cover a meal. There is often a small retail outlet selling peanuts, biscuits and canned fruit within the monastery precincts. Along the route are small restaurants and food stalls where you can replenish the guts and the tea mug. Food gets more expensive and less varied the higher you mount, due to cartage surcharges and difficulties.

An exception to the monasteries is the *Hongzhushan Hotel (hóngzhūshān bīnguǎn)*, at the foot of Emeishan. It's got dreary brick and plaster dorm accommodation at Y15 per person. Better villa-type rooms are available for Y30 per person and up. This hotel has a very pleasant dining section which is a 10-minute walk back into the forest. There you can dine on a 2nd-floor balcony, where a set menu costs Y10 (copious servings).

About 400 metres uphill from the Baoguo-Leshan bus station is another place *(Xi Xiang Hotel) (xīxiàng fàndiàn)* where comfortable dorm accommodation is available for Y15 per person. At either of these hotels it's a good idea to book a bed or room in advance so you won't be turned away after you've descended the mountain.

Some notes on the monasteries follow. Most of the ones mentioned are sited at key walking junctions and tend to be packed out. If you don't get in, do check out the restaurant and its patrons.

Baoguo Monastery *(bàoguó sì)* This monastery was built in the 16th century, enlarged in the 17th century by Emperor Kangxi, and recently renovated. Its 3½-metre porcelain buddha, made in 1415, is housed near the Sutra Library. To the left of the gate is a rockery for potted miniature trees and rare plants. There's a nice vegetarian restaurant and teahouse with solid wood tables.

Fuhu Monastery *(fúhǔ sì)* 'Crouching Tiger Monastery', as it is known in Chinese, is sunk in the forest. Inside is a seven-metre-high copper pagoda inscribed with Buddhist images and texts. The monastery was completely renovated recently, with the addition of bedding for 400 and restaurant seating for 200. A stay here costs a bit more than at the average Emeishan monastery but is well worth it if you can get in.

Wannian Monastery *(wànnián sì)* The Temple of 10,000 Years is the oldest surviving Emei monastery (reconstructed in the 9th century). It's dedicated to the man on the white elephant, the bodhisattva Puxian, who is the protector of the mountain. This statue, 8½ metres high, cast in copper and bronze, weighing an estimated 62,000 kg, is found in Brick Hall, a domed building with small stupas on it. The statue was made in 980 AD. Accommodation in the Wannian Temple area is Y10 per person, with good vegetarian food. If it's full, go back towards Qingyin Pavilion to Bailongdong, a small guesthouse.

Qingyin Pavilion *(qīngyīn gé)* Named the Pure Sound Pavilion because of the sound effects produced by rapid waters coursing around rock formations in the area, the temple itself is built on an outcrop in the middle of a fast-flowing stream. There are small pavilions from which to observe the waterworks and appreciate the natural music. Swimming here is possible.

Xixiang Pond *(xǐxiàng chí)* According to legend, the Elephant Bathing Pool is the spot where Puxian flew his elephant in for a big scrub, but there's not much of a pool to speak of today. Being almost at the crossroads of both major trails, this is something of a hangout and beds are scarce. New extensions to the accommodation here hasn't completely solved the problem of pilgrim overload so be prepared to move on.

The monkeys have got it all figured out – Xixiang Pond is the place to be. If you come across a monkey 'tollgate', the standard procedure is to thrust open palms towards the outlaw to show you have no food. The Chinese find the monkeys an integral part of the Emei trip, and like to tease them. As an aside, monkeys form an important part of Chinese mythology – and there is a saying in Chinese, 'With one monkey in the way, not even 10,000 men can pass' – which may be deeper than you think!

Some of these chimps are big buggers, and staying cool when they look like they might make a leap at you is easier said than done. There is much debate as to whether it's better to give them something to eat or to fight them off. One thing is certain, if you do throw them something, don't do it in too much moderation. They get annoyed very quickly if they think they are being undersold.

Woyunan *(wòyún ān)* Just below the summit, the Cloud-Reposing Hermitage was built in 1974, a dark, gloomy, primitive wooden structure. Beds here are among the cheapest on the mountain. The hotel will rent padded cotton overcoats for around Y1 a day. Another shop nearby offers the same deal. These are mostly intended for patrons of the sunrise – on a very clear day (rare) the most spectacular sight is not the sunrise but the Gongga Shan range rising up like a phantom to the west.

Golden Summit *(jīndǐng)* At 3077 metres, the magnificent Golden Summit temple is as far as most hikers make it. It has been entirely rebuilt since being gutted by a fire several years ago. Covered with glazed tile and surrounded by white marble balustrades, it now occupies 1695 sq metres. The original temple had a bronze-coated roof, which is how it got the name Jinding (which can mean 'Gold Top' as well as 'Golden Summit').

Xianfeng Monastery *(xiānfēng sì)* The surroundings are wonderful, backed into rugged cliffs, and the Magic Peak Monastery has loads of character. Try and get a room at the rear, where the floors give pleasant views. It's off the main track so it's not crowded. Nearby is Jiulao Cave, inhabited by big bats.

Getting There & Away

The hubs of the transport links to Emeishan are Baoguo village and Emei town. Emei town itself is best skipped, though it does have markets, a cheap dormitory at the Emei Hotel, a good restaurant, and a long-distance bus station.

Emei town lies 3½ km from the railway station. Baoguo is another 6½ km from Emei town. At Emei station, buses will be waiting for train arrivals – the short trip to Baoguo is Y1 in a minibus, and Y0.60 in a local bus. From Baoguo there are 11 buses a day to Emei town, the first at 7 am and the last at 6 pm – no service during lunch hour. There are also occasional direct buses between Emei and Qingyin for Y5.

There are also direct buses running from Baoguo to Leshan and Chengdu. Four buses a day run from Baoguo to Leshan (37 km), at 8.10 and 9.10 am and at 1.20 and 2.40 pm. The trip takes one hour and the fare is Y3. There are also direct buses from Baoguo to the Big Buddha itself at 9.50 am and 4 pm. There are good bus connections between Leshan and Chengdu. The bus from Baoguo to Chengdu costs Y14 and takes four hours.

Emei railway station is on the Chengdu-Kunming railway line, and the three-hour trip to Chengdu costs Y8 (hard seat, Chinese price). The train from Emei town is more comfortable than the bus, but does not offer the convenience of leaving from Baoguo (trains are also less frequent and timing may be off). You can purchase one-day advance train tickets at two little booths by the pavilion in Baoguo square.

LESHAN

(lèshān) 乐山

The opportunity to delve into small-town life in the PRC should always be followed up. While Leshan is no village, it's on a scale that you can be comfortable with. It's an old town which has parts that have that lived-in-forever look, while the trendiest addition from this century is the odd soda-bar with garish fluorescent tubes, disco music, and patrons huddled over fizzy orange drinks. The hotel situation is good, decent food can

be unearthed and it's a good resting spot for those Emei-weary legs – plus there's a major archaeological site, the Grand Buddha.

Things to See

The **Grand Buddha** *(dàfó)* is 71 metres high, carved into a cliff face overlooking the confluence of the Dadu and Min rivers. It qualifies as the largest Buddha in the world, with the one at Bamian, Afghanistan, as runner-up (besides, the Leshan model is sitting down!). Dafo's ears are seven metres long, insteps 8½ metres broad, and a picnic could be conducted on the nail of his big toe, which is 1½ metres long – the toe itself is 8½ metres long.

This lunatic project was begun in the year 713 AD, engineered by a Buddhist monk called Haitong who organised fund raising and hired workers; it was completed 90 years later. Below the Buddha was a hollow where boatmen used to vanish – Haitong hoped that the Buddha's presence would subdue the swift currents and protect the boatmen, and Dafo did do a lot of good, as the surplus rocks from the sculpting filled the river hollow. Haitong gouged out his own eyes in an effort to protect funding from disappearing into the hands of officers, but he died before the completion of his life's work. A building used to shelter the giant statue, but it was destroyed during a Ming Dynasty war.

Inside the body, hidden from view, is a water-drainage system to prevent weathering, although the stone statue has seen its fair share. Dafo is so old that foliage is trying to reclaim him – flowers growing on the giant hands, a bushy chest, ferns in his topknots, and weeds winding out of his earholes. He gazes down, perhaps in alarm, at the drifting pollutants in the river that presumably come from the paper mill at the industrial end of town (which started large-scale operation in 1979).

Officials are worried about the possibility of a collapse due to soil erosion; one suggestion that has not met with an enthusiastic response is to cover the Buddha with a huge transparent shell.

It's worth making several passes at big

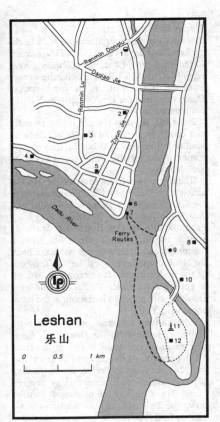

1 Long-Distance Bus Station
2 Dongfeng Hotel
3 Leshan Hotel
4 Jiazhou Guesthouse
5 Municipal Guesthouse
6 Long-Distance Ferry Dock
7 Short-Distance Ferry Dock
8 Jiurifeng Guesthouse
9 Great Buddha
10 Nanlou Guesthouse
11 Wuyou Temple
12 Da Du He Hotel

1 长途汽车站
2 东风饭店
3 乐山宾馆
4 嘉州宾馆
5 市招待所
6 长途码头
7 短途码头
8 就日峰宾馆
9 大佛
10 南楼宾馆
11 乌尤寺
12 大度河饭店

Buddha, as there are all kinds of angles on him. You can go to the top, opposite the head, and then descend a short stairway to the feet for a Lilliputian perspective. A local boat passes by for a frontal view, which reveals two guardians in the cliff side, not visible from land.

To make a round tour that encompasses these possibilities, take the passenger vessel from the Leshan pier. It leaves from the pier every 30 minutes or so at 7 am and 5 pm and costs Y1; sit on the upper deck facing the dock, since the boat turns around when leaving. You pass in close by the Grand

Buddha and the first stop is at the **Wuyou Monastery** (*wūyōu sì*). The monastery dates, like the Grand Buddha, from the Tang Dynasty with Ming and Qing renovations; it's a museum piece containing calligraphy, painting and artefacts, and commands panoramic views. Wuyou also has a hall of 1000 arhats, terracotta monks displaying an incredible variety of postures and facial expressions – no two are alike. The food at the temple's veggie restaurant is cheap and tasty.

You can get off the boat here if you want and go cross-country over the top of Wuyou Hill, continue on to the ferry (Y1) linking it to Lingyun Hill (the suspension bridge has been condemned), and reach the semi-active **Grand Buddha Temple** (*dàfó sì*) which sits near Dafo's head. To get back to Leshan walk south to the small ferry going direct across the Min River.

This whole exercise can be done in less than 1½ hours from the Leshan dock;

however, it's worth making a day of it. If you want to avoid the crowds, you should consider doing this route in reverse, that is, starting with the Dafo Temple and Grand Buddha in the morning and on to Wuyou Monastery in the afternoon.

It would be a mistake to think of Leshan as one big Buddha, for the area is steeped in history. Over 1000 rock tombs were built here in the Eastern Han Dynasty (25-220 AD). By the remains of the town ramparts is an older section of town with cobbled streets and green, blue and red-shuttered buildings; the area around the ferry docks and the old town buzzes with market activity. In season, the markets yield a surprising array of fresh fruit and vegetables, so you can do more than look at them. Further out, by the Jiazhou Hotel, are teahouses with bamboo chairs spilling onto the street.

If you happen to be in town on a Sunday evening, you might like to visit the English Corner which takes place in the riverside park close to the Jiazhou Hotel.

Entry Fees Be prepared to be constantly forking out money when you visit the Grand Buddha. The separate entry fees probably add up to a total of Y20. Some examples are the fee for the Buddha's feet (Y3), the Grand Buddha Temple (Y2), the Buddha (Y3) and a host of little fees for footbridges and so on. Some travellers get very irate about all these hidden costs, but rules is rules!

Places to Stay & Eat

Probably the most popular place with back-packers these days is the *Leshan Educational Research Centre* (☎ 22964) *(lèshān jiàoyù yánjiūsuǒ)* at 156 Liren, around the corner from the bus station in the town centre. Damp doubles here are Y40, triples Y10-15 per person.

Near the Wuyou Temple is the friendly and economical *Da Du He Hotel (dàdù hé fàndiàn)*. Beds cost Y10, but this may require some bargaining; the dining room has good Sichuan food.

There are two Chinese hostelries in the area above the head of the Grand Buddha, *Nanlou Guesthouse (nánlóu bīnguǎn)* and *Jiurifeng Guesthouse (jiùrìfēng bīnguǎn)*. Perhaps due to the Buddha's drainage system, the cliff around here is wet, and the dampness can extend to the rooms. Check the Nanlou's prices to see if they've leapt out of the budget range. It's definitely difficult to get a bed for under Y20 at the Jiurifeng. Doubles with attached bathroom at the latter come in at Y100.

Alternatives to these are two decrepit Chinese guesthouses. The *Dongfeng (dōng-fēng fàndiàn)* has doubles and triples from Y8 per person. At the dull end of town near the bus station is the *Jiading Hotel (jiādìng lǚguǎn)*, which will accept stray foreign faces. The overflow of patrons is stuffed down the hallways, and the washrooms are hard to find (you might throw up when you

see them anyway). Rooms have simple beds and seem to cost Y8 regardless of whether two, three or four people occupy one. There are decaying singles here for Y10.

Top-of-the-line is the *Jiazhou Hotel (jiā-zhōu bīnguǎn)*, which has become rather expensive. Doubles with common bathroom are Y30, while doubles with bathroom attached range from Y80. The dining room serves amazing set dinners for around Y10 – they're only for hotel guests with advance orders, but friends can creep in. The hotel is in a pleasant area; to get there take the town's sole bus line to the terminal.

Getting There & Away

Bus There are three bus stations in Leshan, which is understandably confusing for many travellers. The main one for travellers is the Leshan long-distance bus station. There are numerous daily buses running to Chengdu (the first at 7.20 am and the last at 4.30 pm). The 165-km trip takes over five hours; fares are Y12 in an ordinary bus and Y17 in a soft-seat coach.

One thing to watch out for is the bus's Chengdu destination. Most of the buses run to the Xinnanmen bus station next to the Traffic Hotel, but several run to the north bus station, which is inconvenient for Chengdu's budget accommodation. At the time of writing the 8, 9.30 and 10.50 am and 3 pm buses terminated at the north bus station, while all others went to the Xinnanmen station – check for the latest schedule.

From Emeishan to Leshan is 30 km; buses run to Emei town, Baoguo Temple, or Qingyin Pavilion. Most buses go to Baoguo Temple and there are only two buses a day to Qingyin Pavilion.

There's an express soft-seat coach daily at 7.30 am and 4.40 pm to Chongqing. The trip takes 12 hours and costs around Y70. There's also an early morning ordinary bus at 6.20 am for around Y50.

The other bus stations around town are the Provincial Bus Co *(shěng qìchē yùnshū gōngsī)* and the Lianyun *(liányùn chēzhàn)*. Both have numerous daily departures for Chengdu, Baoguo and Emei. The former is close to the long-distance ferry dock and the latter is about 15 minutes' walk to the north of the ferry dock.

Boat There is a boat to Chongqing, departing Leshan at 7.20 am every four days, but it's difficult to get aboard. The trip takes 36 hours and costs about Y68 in 3rd class. A shorter run to Yibin departs daily at 7 am, and costs Y25 in 3rd class. Yibin is part-way to Chongqing and has a railway station.

Getting Around

Bus There is one bus line in Leshan, running from the bus station to the Jiazhou Hotel. The timetable is posted at the Jiazhou bus stop. The bus runs from 6 am to 6 pm, at roughly 20-minute intervals with no service at lunchtime (about 11.20 am to 1.20 pm). On foot, it's a half-hour walk from one end of town to the other.

Bicycle You can hire a bike just near the bridge across the Min River. The price is Y1 an hour; watch out if you hire overnight as charges continue while you snore, unless otherwise negotiated. Bikes are of limited use if visiting the Grand Buddha since uphill work is required, and the track to Wuyou Hill is a dirt one. However, if you wish to explore the surrounding countryside, the bike will be useful – a suggested start is to continue out of town past the Jiazhou Hotel.

MEISHAN
(méishān) 眉山

Meishan, 90 km south-west of Chengdu by road or rail (it's on the Kunming-Chengdu railway line) is largely of interest to those with a knowledge of Chinese language, literature and calligraphy. It was the residence of Su Xun and his two sons, Su Shi and Su Zhe, the three noted literati of the Northern Song Dynasty (960-1127). Their residence was converted into a temple in the early Ming Dynasty, with renovations under the Qing emperor Hongwu (1875-1909). The mansion and pavilions now operate as a museum for the study of the writings of the

Northern Song period. Historical documents, relics of the Su family, writings, calligraphy – some 4500 items all told are on display at the Sansu (Three Sus) shrine.

CHONGQING
(chóngqìng) 重庆

Chongqing (known in pre-pinyin China as 'Chungking') was opened as a treaty port in 1890, but not many foreigners made it up the river to this isolated outpost, and those who did had little impact. A programme of industrialisation got under way in 1928, but it was in the wake of the Japanese invasion that Chongqing really took off as a major centre; the city was the wartime capital of the Kuomintang from 1938 onwards and refugees from all over China flooded in, swelling the population to over two million. The irony of this overpopulated, overstrained city with its bomb-shattered houses is that the name means something like 'double jubilation' or 'repeated good luck'. Emperor Zhao Dun of the Song Dynasty succeeded to the throne in 1190, having previously been made the prince of the city of Gongzhou; as a celebration of these two happy events, he renamed Gongzhou as Chongqing.

Edgar Snow arrived in the city in 1939 and found it:

...a place of moist heat, dirt and wide confusion, into which, between air raids, the imported central government...made an effort to introduce some technique of order and construction. Acres of buildings had been destroyed in the barbaric raids of May and June. The Japanese preferred moonlit nights for their calls, when from their base in Hankow they could follow the silver banner of the Yangzi up to its confluence with the Jialing, which identified the capital in a way no blackout could obscure. The city had no defending air force and only a few anti-aircraft guns....Spacious public shelters were being dug, but it was estimated that a third of the population still had no protection. Government officials, given advance warning, sped outside the city in their motor cars – cabinet ministers first, then vice-ministers, then minor bureaucrats. The populace soon caught on; when they saw a string of official cars racing to the west, they dropped everything and ran. A mad scramble of rickshaws, carts, animals and humanity blew up the main streets like a great wind, carrying all before it.

The war is over, and today the city is hardly a backwater. Chongqing is rated as the chief industrial city of south-west China, with its production amounting to a fifth of Sichuan's total industrial output. The total metropolitan area has a population of some 13 million; around 2½ million live in the city proper. Chongqing sets itself apart from other Chinese cities by the curious absence of bicycles. There's barely a cyclist to be found, as the steep hills on which the city is built make it coronary country for any would-be cyclist. This is no problem for the visitor. It's quite a pleasant city to stroll around, and even if it's not exactly brimming with 'sights' there's nevertheless a certain picturesque quality to this grey city, built as it is on hills that surround the confluence of two great rivers. For Chinese tourists the 'sights' are usually connected with the Communist Revolution.

Orientation

The heart of Chongqing spreads across a hilly peninsula of land wedged between the Jialing River to the north and the Yangzi River to the south. The rivers meet at the tip of the peninsula at the eastern end of the city.

The central focus of this congested peninsula of winding streets for most visitors is the Liberation Monument, around which most of Chongqing's accommodation is clustered. Getting there from the railway station is a matter of walking or taking a cable car up to Zhongshan Lu. Bus No 405 will take you from here eastwards to the Liberation Monument and No 401 goes to the Chaotianmen Dock area.

Chongqing is a good city for exploring on foot. The distances are manageable, and there's always an interesting alley to duck into. Between the Liberation monument and the Chaotianmen Dock area are a number of steep, laddered alleyways, usually lined with little shops. Also of interest, and within walking distance of the Liberation Monument, are the two cable cars over the Jialing and Yangzi rivers.

Information

CITS The travel service (☎ 350188) has its office in a building in the Renmin Hotel compound. They're a friendly mob but hopelessly disorganised. As is usually the case, you are better off doing things yourself.

PSB The office (☎ 43973) is on Linjiang Lu. Bus No 103 from the front of the Renmin Hotel will take you there. If it's permits for the wilds of northern Sichuan that you are after, wait until you get to Chengdu, where they are more used to dealing with this kind of thing.

Money The main Chongqing branch of Bank of China is on Minzu Lu, just up the road from the Huixianlou Hotel. Most of the hotels also have foreign-exchange counters and, if their rates aren't good enough for you, there is generally a small crowd of hopefuls milling around outside the Huixianlou Hotel. Black-market rates in Chongqing are comparable with those in Chengdu.

Post There is a branch post office on Minzu Lu within walking distance of the Chung King and Huixianlou hotels. Both the Renmin and Chung King hotels offer limited postal services.

Maps Good maps in Chinese are available from street vendors (the ones selling newspapers) around the Liberation Monument area.

Luohan Temple
(*luóhàn sì*) 罗汉寺

Luohan is the Chinese rendering of the Sanskrit 'arhat', which is a Buddhist term referring to people who have released themselves from the psychological bondage of greed, hate and delusion. Built around 1000 years ago, Luohan Temple features a long entrance-way flanked by rock carvings, a hall of painted terracotta arhat sculptures (the usual 500) and a hall containing a large gold Buddha figure. Behind the Buddha altar is an Indian-style jataka mural depicting Prince Siddhartha in the process of cutting his hair to renounce the world.

At its peak, Luohan Temple was home to some 70 monks; there are around 18 in residence these days. The temple is popular with local worshippers, who burn tonnes of fragrant incense. Try and make an effort to call into this temple, even if it's just to take a quick look at the incredibly lifelike arhats.

The vegetarian restaurant here is excellent and very cheap, but it's only open for lunch (approximately 11.30 am to 1.30 pm).

Red Cliff Village
(*hóngyán cūn*) 红岩村

During the tenuous Kuomintang-Communist alliance against the Japanese during WW II, Red Cliff Village outside Chongqing was used as the offices and living quarters of the Communist representatives to the Kuomintang. Among others, Ye Jianying, Zhou Enlai and Zhou's wife Deng Yingchao lived here. After the Japanese surrender in 1945, it was also to Chongqing that Mao Zedong – at the instigation of US ambassador Patrick Hurley – came in August of that year to join in the peace negotiations with the Kuomintang. The talks lasted 42 days and resulted in a formal agreement which Mao described as 'words on paper'.

One of China's better revolutionary history museums now stands at the site, and has a large collection of photos, though none of the captions are in English. A short walk from the museum is the building which housed the South Bureau of the Communist Party's Central Committee and the office of the representatives of the Eighth Route Army – though there's little to see except a few sparse furnishings and photographs.

To get to Red Cliff Village, the best bus to take is the No 104 from its terminal on Beiqu Lu just north of the Liberation monument. Alternatively, Chinese tour buses from the Chaotianmen dock and the railway station take in Red Cliff Village and other Communist sights around town for Y10. Red Cliff Village is open daily from 8.30 am to 5 pm.

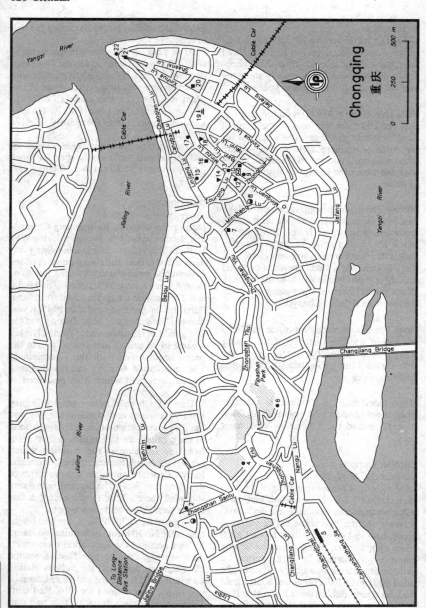

Chongqing 重庆

■ PLACES TO STAY

3	Renmin Hotel
7	Chongqing Guesthouse
11	Yudu Hotel
16	Huixianlou Hotel
20	Chung King Hotel
21	Three Gorges Hotel

▼ PLACES TO EAT

| 14 | Huleyuan Restaurant |
| 18 | Lamb Restaurant |

OTHER

1	Buses to SACO Prisons
2	CAAC
3	CITS
4	Cultural Palace of the Labouring People
5	Railway Station
6	Chongqing Museum
8	Long-Distance Bus Station (for Dazu)
9	Foreign Languages Bookstore
10	Post Office
12	Xinhua Bookstore
13	Liberation Monument
15	PSB
17	Bank of China
19	Luohan Temple
22	Chaotianmen Dock (Booking Hall)

■ PLACES TO STAY

3	人民宾馆
7	重庆宾馆
11	愉都宾馆
16	会仙楼宾馆
20	重庆饭店
21	三峡宾馆

▼ PLACES TO EAT

| 14 | 湖乐园 |
| 18 | 羊肉馆 |

OTHER

1	至中美合作所汽车站
2	中国民船
3	中国国际旅行社
4	劳动人民文化宫
5	火车站
6	博物馆
8	长途汽车站（往大足）
9	外文书店
10	邮电局
12	新华书店
13	解放碑
15	公安局外事科
17	中国银行
19	罗汉寺
22	朝天门码头（售票处）

US-Chiang Kaishek Criminal Acts Exhibition Hall & SACO Prisons

(*zhōngměi hézuòsuǒ jízhōngyíng jiùzhǐ*)
中美合作所集中营旧址

In 1941 the USA and Chiang Kaishek signed a secret agreement to set up the Sino-American Cooperation Organisation (SACO), under which USA helped to train and dispatch secret agents for the Kuomintang government. The chief of SACO was Tai Li, head of the Kuomintang military secret service; its deputy chief was a US Navy officer, Commodore M E Miles.

The SACO prisons were set up outside Chongqing during WW II. The Kuomintang never recognised the Communist Party as a legal political entity, although in theory it recognised its army as allies in the struggle against the Japanese invaders. Civilian Communists remained subject to the same repressive laws, and though these were not enforced at the time, they were not actually rescinded. Hundreds of political prisoners were still kept captive by the Kuomintang in these prisons and others, and according to the Communists many were executed.

Unfortunately, the absence of English captions makes this sight a fairly uninteresting one for most Western visitors. The exhibition hall has lots of photos on display; there are manacles and chains but nothing to ghoul over. The hall is open from 8.30 am to 5 pm and admission is Y2. To get there take bus No 217 from the station on Liziba Lu. It's about a 20-minute ride. Make sure that the driver knows where you want to get off, as the place is not obvious. The SACO

Prisons are a long hour's walk from the hall If you are really keen to see these sights, there are Chinese tour buses leaving from the Chaotianmen dock and railway station areas for Y10. They take in both the hall and the prisons and throw in some other revolutionary sights as well.

Temple Parks

Chongqing's two temple parks get neglected by many visitors, but they are a pleasant enough way to while away an afternoon. **Pipa Shan Park** (*pípáshān gōngyuán*) at 345 metres marks the highest point on the Chongqing peninsula. The Hongxing Pavilion at the top of the park provides good views of Chongqing. The park is open from 6 am to 10 pm.

The **Eling Park** (*éling gōngyuán*) is more of a hike out of town and not really worth a special trip. You can find the Liangjiang Pavilion here.

Bridges

Worth checking out are the enormous Jialing and Yangzi bridges. The Jialing Bridge, which crosses the river north of central Chongqing, was built between 1963 and 1966. It is 150 metres long and 60 metres high and for 15 years was one of the few means of access to the rest of China. The Yangzi Bridge to the south was finished in 1981. In 1989 the new Shimen Bridge over the Yangzi River was completed.

Cable-Car Trips

There are cable cars spanning both of the rivers that cut through Chongqing: the Jialing River and the Yangzi River. The rides provide views of precipitously stacked housing and environment-unfriendly industrial estates. Both are within walking distance of the Liberation Monument. The Jialing River cable car starts from Cangbai Lu, and the Yangzi River cable car starts from Zhongshan Lu.

Chongqing Museum

(*chóngqìng bówùguǎn*) 重庆博物馆
If you are really stuck for something to do you might wander over to the museum. The dinosaur skeletons on display were unearthed between 1974 and 1977 at Zigong, Yangchuan and elsewhere in Sichuan Province. It's open from 9 to 11.30 am and from 2 to 5.30 pm. The museum is at the foot of Pipashan Park in the southern part of town.

Northern Hot Springs

(*běi wēnquán gōngyuán*) 北温泉公园
North-east of the city, overlooking the Jialing River, the Northern Hot Springs are in a large park which is the site of a 5th-century Buddhist temple. The springs have an Olympic-size swimming pool where you can bathe to an audience. There are also private rooms with hot baths – big tubs where the water comes up to your neck if you sit and up to your waist if you stand. Swimsuits can be hired here – they're coloured red, symbolising happiness. There's another group of springs 20 km south of Chongqing but the northern group is said to be better.

To get to the springs, take bus No 306 from the Liberation monument.

Places to Stay – bottom end

Chongqing has a serious shortage of budget accommodation, which means that most travellers get out of town as quickly as possible. Believe it or not, the cheapest dorms in town are the eight-bed rooms at the *Huixianlou Hotel* (☎ 44135) (*huìxiān bīnguǎn*), close to the Liberation Monument, where a bed will set you back Y30. About the best thing that can be said for this place is that it is well located. From the railway station, walk up to Zhongshan Lu and take bus No 405 to the Liberation Monument (*jiěfàng bēi*).

At the time of writing the *Three Gorges Hotel* (☎ 331112) (*sānxiá bīnguǎn*), down by the Chaotianmen dock, had applied to take foreign guests. If the bid was successful this hotel should be able to supply a cheaper alternative to the Huixianlou Hotel. They have basic doubles for Y30 and may be setting up a dorm as well. It would be a good idea to check out the latest situation if you are looking at saving a few yuan.

Places to Stay – top end

Basically, all the hotels in Chongqing charge ridiculous amounts of money. It's probably something to do with limited room for expansion on the crowded peninsula. If you don't mind an expensive stay, the *Renmin Hotel* (☎ 351421) *(rénmín bīnguǎn)* is one of the most incredible hotels in China, and if you don't stay here you have got to at least visit the place.

It's quite literally a palace, with a design that seems inspired by the Temple of Heaven and the Forbidden City in Beijing. The hotel comprises three wings (north, south and east), and these are separated by an enormous circular concert hall that is 65 metres high and seats 4000 people. The hotel was constructed in 1953.

In the north and south wings singles are Y160, while doubles range between Y220 and Y330. The east wing only has doubles for Y220. From the railway station, the best way to get to the hotel is to head up to Zhongshan Lu and catch bus No 401 or 405 to the traffic circle and walk east down Renmin Lu. Alternatively, if you are spending this kind of money for a room, catch a taxi for Y15.

Better in terms of service and value is the *Chung King Hotel* (☎ 349301) *(chóngqìng fàndiàn)*, a joint-venture operation on Xinhua Lu near the Chaotianmen pier area. Singles cost Y160 and doubles range from Y240 to Y330. Facilities include a small gift shop (with a few English titles), foreign exchange, post and telecommunications, taxi and clinic. The hotel has its own shuttle bus to and from the railway station.

The *Chongqing Guesthouse* (☎ 345888) *(chóngqìng bīnguǎn)* on Minsheng Lu has transformed itself into a Chinese-style luxury hotel. Singles/doubles in the old wing are Y220/280, while doubles in the new VIP wing range from US$80. One other well located top-range hotel is the *Yudu Hotel* *(yùdū jiǔdiàn)* close to the Liberation Monument. Singles/doubles are Y160/190.

Finally, on the southern side of the Yangzi, a fair trudge from all the action is the *Yangtze Chongqing Holiday Inn* (☎ 203380) *(yáng-*zǐjiāng jiàrì jiǔdiàn)*, with all the services that you would expect of a Holiday Inn Group hotel. Room rates start at US$75.

Places to Eat

The central business district in the eastern section of the city near the docks abounds with small restaurants and street vendors. For tasty noodles and baozi, check out Xinhua Lu and Shaanxi Lu towards Chaotianmen dock. Behind the Huixianlou Hotel in the vicinity of Luohan Temple and in the area of the Yudu Hotel are some good night markets.

Chongqing's number one specialty is *huǒguō*, or hotpot. Skewers of pre-sliced meat and vegetables are placed in boiling hot, spiced oil. Hotpot is usually priced by the skewer, and while it's usually cheap it's a good idea to check prices as you go along. Although hotpot can be found wherever there are street vendors or small restaurants, Wuyi Lu has the greatest variety and is locally known as *huǒguō jiē*, or 'hotpot street'. Wuyi Lu runs off Minzu Lu between Xinhua Lu and Bayi Lu, a couple of blocks away from the Huixianlou and Chung King hotels. Bayi Lu is also a great street for snack-hunting.

Zourong Lu is a good street for larger, sit-down restaurants when you've got a group and feel like feasting on Sichuanese main courses. Among them is the well-known *Yizhishi Restaurant*, which serves Sichuan-style pastries in the morning and local specialities like tea-smoked duck and dry-stewed fish at lunch and dinner.

The area around Huixianlou Hotel, where most travellers stay, is teeming with restaurants. But if you're stuck for ideas you can try the *Lamb Restaurant (yángròu guǎn)* just up the road from the hotel. All the lamb dishes here are *hot*, but the kebabs aren't too punishing on the taste buds. Also not far away is the *Huleyuan Restaurant (húlè yuán)* with Cantonese-style dim sum in the basement. It's a good place for a late breakfast or lunch.

Of the hotel restaurants, *Chung King Hotel* has the best food – expensive by

Chinese standards but moderately priced for most foreigners. The hotel was in fact built next door to the famous *Chung King Restaurant (chóngqìng fàndiàn)*, which is still going strong. The hotel's coffee shop serves Western breakfasts.

Getting There & Away

Air The CAAC office (☎ 55824) is on the corner of Zhongshan Sanlu and Renmin Lu. You can also book flights at the Chung King Hotel.

Chongqing is connected by air to Beijing (Y820, daily); Canton (Y590, daily); Changsha (Y350, three times a week); Chengdu (Y160, daily); Guilin (Y340, Sundays); Kunming (Y320, daily); Nanjing (Y650, twice weekly); Shanghai (Y770, daily); Xi'an (Y300, four times weekly); Guiyang (Y180, twice weekly); Lanzhou (Y560, once weekly); Qingdao (Y790, twice weekly); Haikou (Y630, daily); Xiamen (Y760, four times a week); Shenyang (Y1060, twice weekly); and Harbin (Y1320, twice weekly).

Air China (CAAC's international line) flies between Chongqing and Hong Kong on Monday, Thursday, and Saturday for Y1100 one way. Tickets can be booked at the CAAC office or at the Chung King Hotel.

Bus The long-distance bus station is on the northern side of the Jialing River, across the Jialing Bridge. Getting to the bus station isn't so straightforward. Take bus No 105 from the intersection of Zhongshan Lu and Renmin Lu, cross the Jialing Bridge, and get off at the terminal. The bus station is further up ahead and you can walk if you're not carrying too much, or take bus No 210 for the last stretch. The bus station has luxury overnight buses to Chengdu for Y74.

Although the long-distance bus station has buses to Dazu, it's such a hike out of town that you are better off hooking up with one of the buses that leave from the Chongqing Peninsula.

Basically there are two options: the first is a company called Kangfulai *(kāngfúlái)*, which has ticketing offices and departure points outside the Chongqing Guesthouse, to the west of the main entrance of the Renmin Hotel and on the eastern side of the railway station; and the second is the long-distance bus station just around the corner from the Liberation Monument.

The Kangfulai buses leave at 8 am, are Y17 and run straight through to Dazu in around five hours, while the long-distance bus station buses leave at 7.30 am, cost Y12 and can take up to six or seven hours.

Train From Chongqing there are direct trains to Shanghai, Xi'an, Guiyang, Nanning (every other day), Chengdu, Zhengzhou, Canton, Beijing and Kunming. For trains to Dazu, there are at least three trains heading for Chengdu from Chongqing between 6 and 9 am. The 6.40 am train gets to Dazu at around 11.10 am; a hard-seat ticket should cost around Y12.

Trains to Nanning go via Guiyang and Liuzhou (five or six hours by bus from Guilin) and take around 32 hours; a hard-sleeper should cost Y124. Trains to Guiyang take around 12 hours and cost Y72 for a hard sleeper. Trains to Shanghai also take in Guiyang, before making a long haul through the sticks to Hangzhou and on to the final destination. The journey takes around 50 hours and costs Y250 for a hard sleeper. To Chengdu, it takes around 11 hours and costs Y80 for a hard sleeper. Trains to Kunming and Panzhihua (for Lijiang and Dali) go via Chengdu, and it makes a lot of sense to break your trip at this point.

If you want to get to Guilin in a hurry you will have to fly – travelling by train requires that you change in Guiyang. Alternatively, you might travel to Liuzhou by train and go on direct to Yangshuo or Guilin by bus.

Boat There are boats from Chongqing down the Yangzi River to Wuhan. The ride is a popular tourist trip, a good way of getting away from the trains and an excellent way to get to Wuhan. For details, see the following section on the Yangzi River as well as the sections on Wuhan, Shanghai and Yueyang.

Another boat option, and one that very few travellers use is the service to Leshan.

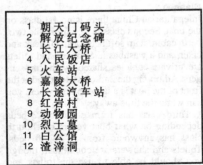

Around Chongqing
重庆地区

0   1   2 km

1 Chaotianmen Dock
2 Liberation Monument
3 Changjiang Bridge
4 Renmin Hotel
5 Railway Station
6 Jialing Bridge
7 Long-Distance Bus Station
8 Red Cliff Village
9 Zoo
10 Martyrs' Cemetery
11 Baigongguan-SACO Prison
12 Zhazhidong-SACO Prison

```
1  码头
2  解放纪念碑
3  长江大桥
4  人民大饭店
5  火车站
6  嘉陵江大桥
7  长途汽车站
8  红岩村
9  动物园
10 烈士公墓
11 白公馆
12 渣滓洞
```

Sorting out just when the boats leave is a bit of a hassle, though officially it is every four days. Third-class tickets are Y155, 4th class Y98 and 5th class Y58.

Getting Around
Buses in Chongqing are tediously slow, and since there are no bicycles they're even more crowded than in other Chinese cities.

Nowadays, as in most other Chinese cities, flagging down a taxi is no problem. They charge Y15 for all runs within the peninsula, but you can expect this to go up rapidly along with everything else.

DOWNRIVER ON THE YANGZI: CHONGQING TO WUHAN
The dramatic scenery and rushing waters of China's greatest river may have been inspirational to many of China's painters and poets, but there was little in the way of inspiration for those with the task of negotiating this dangerous stretch of water's twists and turns. And there was not just danger to contend with; there was also sheer hard work. A large boat pushing upstream often needed hundreds of coolies (trackers), who lined the riverbanks and hauled the boat with long ropes against the surging waters. Even

SICHUAN

today smaller boats can still be seen being pulled up the river by their crews.

The Yangzi is China's longest river and the third-longest in the world at 6300 km, emanating from the snow-covered Tanggulashan mountains in south-west Qinghai and cutting its way through Tibet and seven Chinese provinces before emptying into the East China Sea just north of Shanghai. Between the towns of Fengjie in Sichuan and Yichang in Hubei lie three great gorges, regarded as one of the great scenic attractions of China. The steamer ride from Chongqing to Wuhan is one of the popular tourist trips. It's a nice way to get from Chongqing to Wuhan, a relief from the trains and the scenery is pleasant, but don't expect to be dwarfed by mile-high cliffs! A lot of people find the trip quite boring, possibly because of over-anticipation.

The ride downriver from Chongqing to Wuhan takes three days and two nights. Upriver the ride takes five days – see the Wuhan section for details. One possibility is to take the boat as far as Yichang, which will let you see the gorges and the huge Gezhouba Dam, the most scenic parts.

At Yichang you can take a train north to Xiangfan and another to Luoyang. If you continue the boat ride you can get off at Yueyang and take the train to Canton, or you can carry on to Wuhan. There are also a few boats that go beyond Wuhan, including one all the way to Shanghai, which is 2400 km downriver – a week's journey.

Tickets

You can buy tickets for the boats from CITS in Chongqing or from the booking office at Chaotianmen dock. You'll generally have to book two or three days ahead of your intended date of departure, but some people have arrived, got their tickets and left the same day (there's a direct minibus from the railway station to Chaotianmen for Y3 per person). CITS adds a service charge of Y15 to the price of the tickets, but you may wonder where the service went since they're hopelessly disorganised and never seem to

know just what tickets are available. There is a 70% surcharge for foreigners' tickets.

The main booking office at Chaotianmen dock is open daily from 9 to 11 am and 2.30 to 5 pm. Outside this main hall are several small agencies that also sell marked-up boat tickets; it's worth trying them if the main office doesn't have tickets for the day you want. No-one at CITS, the boat ticket office or the ticket agencies seems willing to sell a foreigner a Chinese-price ticket, whatever documents you carry. The ticket-takers on the boat, however, will accept a Chinese-price ticket if you show proof of residence in China as a foreign expert or student. Hence if you're legitimate, have got the right papers and speak Chinese, you can usually get a local to buy a ticket for you.

Second-class cabins get hopelessly overbooked in the middle of the year when the tour groups are piling into the country, and even the tour groups sometimes end up being relegated to 3rd-class cabins, so don't be surprised if you can't get a ticket at this time of year.

Classes

In egalitarian China there is no 1st class on the boat. Second class is a comfortable two-berth cabin, with soft beds, a small desk and chair, and a washbasin. Showers and toilets are private cubicles shared by the passengers. Adjoining the 2nd-class deck and at the front of the boat is a large lounge where you can while the time away.

Third class has from eight to 12 beds depending on what boat you're on. Fourth class has anywhere from 24 to 40 beds. Toilets and showers are communal, though you should be able to use the toilets and showers in 2nd class. If they don't let you into the 2nd-class area then have a look around the boat; some boats have some toilet cubicles on the lower deck with doors and partitions. There doesn't seem to be any problem just wandering into the lounge and plonking yourself down.

Below 4th class are a couple of large cabins the entire width of the boat that accommodate about 40 people on triple-tiered bunks. In addition, there's a deck class where you can camp out in the corridors, but it's highly unlikely you'll be sold tickets for these classes. If you take one of the large dormitories, remember that this part of China is very cold in winter and very hot in summer. Petty thieves have been reported in the dorms, so keep valuable items safe – particularly at night.

Fares
The pricing in the main booking hall at Chaotianmen dock is very confusing. Firstly there is a 70% surcharge for tickets for foreigners and secondly the prices posted in the hall are generally out of date. The following are the CITS posted prices for the major destinations on the river. Prices should be a little cheaper if you book them yourself.

Destination	2nd Class (Y)	3rd Class (Y)	4th Class (Y)
Yichang	497	242	190
Wuhan (Hankou)	725	313	271
Nanjing	969	461	357
Shanghai	1102	523	404

There are lots of other intermediate destinations including Jiujiang and Wuhu (potential jumping-off points for Lushan and Huangshan) and Nanjing (Jiangsu) on the Shanghai route. Between Nanjing and Wuhan (Hubei) a hydrofoil service cuts travelling time down from 40 hours to just 10 – see the Wuhan section for details.

Departure Times
Boats that terminate in Yichang (Hubei) generally depart Chongqing at 7 or 8 am. Those that go beyond to Shashi and Wuhan depart at 6.30 and 8 am. Fast boats to Shanghai leave at 8 am and slow boats every other day at 9 am. These times can change from season to season depending on the river level, so check at the signboards at the main ticket hall to be sure. On the signboards, Wuhan is listed as Hankou, since this is the district of Wuhan where the boat docks.

You can sleep on the boat the night before departure for Y16 – which is cheaper than the Huixianlou Hotel and easier than getting up early and hoofing it down to the pier. Your ticket should give the number of the pier where your boat will be waiting the night before.

Once you've boarded, a steward will exchange your ticket for a numbered, colour-coded tag that denotes your bed assignment. Hang onto the tag, since it must be exchanged for your ticket at the end of the voyage – without it they won't let you off the boat.

Food
There are a couple of restaurants on the boat. The one on the lower deck caters for the masses and is pretty terrible. The restaurant on the upper deck is quite good, but how much you're charged seems to vary from boat to boat. It's a good idea to bring some of your own food with you. When the boat stops at a town for any length of time, passengers may disembark and eat at little restaurants near the pier.

First Day
For the first few hours the river is lined with factories, though this gives way to some pretty, green terraced countryside with the occasional small town.

Around noon (depending on the boat) you arrive at the town of **Fuling**. The town overlooks the mouth of the Wu River which runs southwards into Guizhou; it controls the river traffic between Guizhou and eastern Sichuan. Near Fuling in the middle of the Yangzi River is a huge rock called Baihe Ridge. On one side of the rock are three carvings known as 'stone fish' which date back to ancient times and are thought to have served as watermarks – the rock can be seen only when the river is at its very lowest. In addition to the carvings, there is a large number of inscriptions describing the culture, art and technology of these ancient times.

The next major town is **Fengdu** (fēngdū). Nearby Pingdushan mountain is said to be

SICHUAN

the abode of devils. The story goes that during the Han Dynasty two men, Yin Changsheng and Wang Fangping, lived on the mountain, and when their family names were joined together they were mistakenly thought to be the Yinwang, the King of Hell. Numerous temples containing sculptures of demons and devils have been built on the mountain since the Tang Dynasty, with heartening names like 'Between the Living and the Dead', 'Bridge of Helplessness' and 'Palace of the King of Hell'.

The boat then passes through **Zhongxian County**. North-east of the county seat of Zhongzhou is the **Qian Jinggou** site where primitive stone artefacts including axes, hoes and stone weights attached to fishing nets were unearthed.

In the afternoon the boat passes by **Shibaozhai (Stone Treasure Stronghold)** on the northern bank of the river. Shibaozhai is a 30-metre-high rock which is supposed to look something like a stone seal. During the early years of Emperor Qianlong's reign (1736-97) an impressive red wooden temple, the Lanruodian, shaped like a pagoda and 11 storeys high, was built on the rock. It houses a statue of Buddha and inscriptions which commemorate its construction.

Around 7 pm the boat arrives in the large town of **Wanxian** where it ties up for the night. Wanxian is the hub of transportation and communications along the river between eastern Sichuan and western Hubei and has traditionally been known as the gateway to Sichuan. It was opened to foreign trade in 1917. It's a neat, hilly town and a great place to wander around for a few hours while the boat is in port. There's a pleasant park around the tower in the centre of town. A long flight of steps leads from the pier up the riverbank to a bustling night market where you can get something to eat or buy very cheap wickerwork baskets, chairs and stools.

Second Day

Boats generally depart Wanxian before dawn. Before entering the gorges the boat passes by (and may stop at) the town of **Fengjie**. This ancient town was the capital of the state of Kui during the Spring and Autumn and Warring States periods from 770 to 221 BC. The town overlooks the Qutang Gorge, the first of the three Yangzi gorges. Just east of Fengjie is a one km-long shoal where the remains of stone piles could be seen when the water level was low. These piles were erected in the Stone and Bronze ages, possibly for commemorative and sacrificial purposes, but their remains were removed in 1964 since they were considered a danger to navigation. Another set of similar structures can be found east of Fengjie outside a place called Baidicheng.

At the entrance to the Qutang Gorge is **Baidicheng** or White King Town on the river's northern bank, 7½ km from Fengjie. The story goes that a high official proclaimed himself king during the Western Han Dynasty, and moved his capital to this town. A well was discovered which emitted a fragrant white vapour; this struck him as such an auspicious omen that he renamed himself the White King and his capital 'White King Town'.

The spectacular **Sanxia** (Three Gorges), Qutang, Wu and Xiling, start just after Fengjie and end near Yichang, a stretch of about 200 km. The gorges vary from 300 metres at their widest to less than 100 metres at their narrowest. The seasonal difference in water level can be as much as 50 metres.

Qutang Gorge (*qūtáng xiá*) is the smallest and shortest gorge (only eight km long), though the water flows most rapidly here. High on the north bank, at a place called Fengxiang (Bellows) Gorge, are a series of crevices. There is said to have been an ancient tribe in this area whose custom was to place the coffins of their dead in high mountain caves. Nine coffins were discovered in these crevices, some containing bronze swords, armour and other artefacts, but they are believed to date back only as far as the Warring States Period.

Wu Gorge (*wū xiá*) is about 40 km in length and the cliffs on either side rise to just over 900 metres. The gorge is noted for the Kong Ming tablet, a large slab of rock at the foot of the Peak of the Immortals. Kong

Ming was prime minister of the state of Shu during the period of the Three Kingdoms (220-280 AD). On the tablet is a description of his stance upholding the alliance between the states of Shu and Wu against the state of Wei. **Badong** is a town on the southern bank of the river within the gorge. The town is a communications centre from which roads span out into western Hubei Province. The boat usually stops here.

Xiling Gorge (*xīlíng xiá*) is the longest of the three gorges at 80 km. At the end of the gorge everyone crowds out onto the deck to watch the boat pass through the locks of the huge **Gezhouba Dam**.

The next stop is the industrial town of **Yichang**, at about 3 pm if the boat is on time. From here you can take a train north to Xiangfan, where you can catch a train to Luoyang. Yichang is regarded as the gateway to the Upper Yangzi and was once a walled city dating back at least as far as the Sui Dynasty. The town was opened to foreign trade in 1877 by a treaty between Britain and China, and a foreign concession area was set up along the river front to the south-east of the walled city. Near the Yichang railway station you can take bus No 10 to **White Horse Cave** (*báimǎdòng*). For Y2, you can boat and walk through caverns with impressive stalactites and stalagmites. Five minutes' walk from the other end is an equally impressive place – **Three Visitors Cave** (*sānyǒudòng*), along with a cliff trail that overlooks the Yangzi River.

After leaving Yichang, the boat passes under the immense **Changjiang Bridge** at the town of **Zhicheng**. The bridge is 1700 metres long and supports a double-track railway with roads for trucks and cars on either side. It came into operation in 1971.

The next major town is **Shashi**, a light-industrial town. As early as the Tang Dynasty Shashi was a trading centre of some importance, enjoying great prosperity during the Taiping Rebellion when trade lower down the Yangzi was largely at a standstill. It was opened up to foreign trade in 1896 by the Treaty of Shimonoseki between China and Japan, and though an area outside the town

was assigned as a Japanese concession it was never developed. About 7½ km from Shashi is the ancient town of **Jingzhou**, to which you can catch a bus.

Third Day

There is absolutely nothing to see on the third day; you're out on the flat plains of eastern China, the river widens immensely and you can see little of the shore. The boat continues down river during the night and passes by the town of **Chenglingji**, which lies at the confluence of Lake Dongting and the Yangzi River. East of Lake Dongting is the town of **Yueyang**, which you'll reach at around about 6 am. If the boat is on time then you'll get into **Wuhan** late that afternoon, around 5 pm. (For details on Yueyang and Wuhan and the Yangzi River between Wuhan and Shanghai, see the separate sections in this book.)

DAZU
(*dàzú*) 大足

The grotto art of Dazu County, 160 km north-west of Chongqing, is rated alongside China's other great Buddhist cave sculpture at Dunhuang, Luoyang and Datong. Historical records for Dazu are sketchy. The cliff carvings and statues (with Buddhist, Taoist and Confucian influences) amount to thousands of pieces, large and small, scattered over the county in some 40-odd places. The main groupings are at Beishan (North Hill) and the more interesting Baoding. They date from the Tang Dynasty (9th century) to the Song (13th century).

The town of Dazu is a small, unhurried place. It's also been relatively unvisited by Westerners, and the surrounding countryside is superb.

Beishan
(*běi shān*) 北山

Beishan is about a 30-minute hike from Dazu town – aim straight for the pagoda visible from the bus station. There are good overall views from the top of the hill. The dark niches hold small statues, many in poor condition; only one or two are of interest.

Niche No 136 depicts Puxian, the patron saint (male) of Emeishan, riding a white elephant. The same niche has the androgynous Sun and Moon Guanyin. Niche 155 holds a bit more talent, the Peacock King. According to inscriptions, the Beishan site was originally a military camp, with the earliest carvings commissioned by a general.

At Beishan there's a Y1 entry fee for the park area and a further Y10 entry fee for the sculptures. The park is open from 8 am to 5 pm.

Baoding
(bǎodǐng shān) 宝顶山

Fifteen km north-east of Dazu town, the Baoding sculptures are definitely more interesting than those at Beishan. The founding work is attributed to Zhao Zhifeng, a monk from an obscure Yoga sect of Tantric Buddhism. There's a monastery with nice woodwork and throngs of pilgrims. On the lower section of the hill on which the monastery sits is a horseshoe-shaped cliff sculptured with coloured figures, some of them up to eight metres high. The centrepiece is a 31-metre-long, five-metre-high reclining buddha, depicted in the state of entering nirvana, the torso sunk into the cliff face – most peaceful.

Statues around the rest of the 125-metre horseshoe vary considerably: Buddhist preachers and sages, historical figures, realistic scenes (on the rear of a postcard one is described as 'Pastureland – Cowboy at Rest'), and delicate sculptures a few cm in height. Some of them have been eroded by wind and rain, some have lost layers of paint, but generally there is a remarkable survival rate (fanatical Red Guards did descend on the Dazu area bent on defacing the sculptures, but were stopped – so the story goes – by an urgent order from Zhou Enlai).

Baoding differs from other grottoes in that it was based on a preconceived plan which incorporated some of the area's natural features – a sculpture next to the reclining buddha, for example, makes use of an underground spring. Completion of the sculptures is believed to have taken 70 years, between 1179 and 1249 AD. It's easy to spend a few hours wandering around this area. Showpieces are the enormous reclining buddha and, inside a small temple on the carved cliff, the Goddess of Mercy, with a spectacular gilt forest of fingers (1007 hands if you care to check). Each hand has an eye, the symbol of wisdom. But besides the major attractions there are countless minor details that will capture your attention.

Minibuses to Baoding leave Dazu town every 20 minutes or so through the day, though they start to thin out by about 4 pm; the fare is Y1.50, but the locals will probably try to charge you Y5. The last bus departs Baoding for Dazu at around 6 pm. The sites are open from 8 am to 5 pm, and there's a Y10 foreigners' price entry charge. As you pass by in the bus, keep an eye on the cliff faces for solo sculptures that may occasionally pop up.

Places to Stay & Eat

The Dazu Guesthouse (dàzú bīnguǎn) is the official abode for foreigners. It divides into two wings (with a new three-star wing under construction). The old wing is the first you come to when you turn off the main road, and it has doubles for Y15 per bed. Even though it's attached to the guesthouse, the Chinese name at the entrance is the xiàn zhāodàisuǒ or the County Guesthouse. The new wing is up the road and to the right. Doubles here with attached bathroom and air-con are Y90, or Y70 without air-con.

If you come in to Dazu from Chongqing tell the driver you want to get off at the Dazu Hotel – just call out dàzú bīnguǎn. Coming from this direction the hotel is up a small street to the right. If you come from Chengdu, turn left out of the bus station, cross over a bridge and bear to the right. The turn off for the hotel is about 500 metres up the road on the left.

Finding a bite to eat in Dazu is no problem. There are a number of good Chinese restaurants of the pick and choose variety on the same stretch of road as the new of the Dazu Guesthouse. Back on the main road moving in the direction of the bus station, there's a similar place on the left-hand side. The fare differs little from place to place, and there's no real point making particular recommendations.

Getting There & Away

Bus There are several options by bus. The first is the direct bus from Chongqing to Dazu which leaves at 7.20 am from Chongqing's north-west bus station; there are seven buses a day, the fare is Y15, and the trip takes five to seven hours depending on whether there is a lunch break. The second is the Kangfulai (KFL) bus company, which has three ticket offices and pickup points: next to the Chongqing Guesthouse, the railway station and the Renmin Hotel.

Tickets with KFL cost Y17 and buses depart at 8 am. There are also two buses a day to Dazu at 7.30 and 9.50 am from the long-distance bus station close to the Liberation Monument; tickets are Y12. Buses from Chengdu to Dazu leave from the Xinnanmen bus station next to the Traffic Hotel at 6.50 am. The journey takes around 10 hours and the fare is Y33.

From Dazu there are onward buses to Chongqing and Chengdu. Buses run on the half hour from 6 am to 4.30 pm between Dazu and Chongqing and cost Y12. For Chengdu there are two buses a day at 7 am and 8 pm, and tickets cost Y24. The night bus is best avoided. It arrives in Chengdu at around 4 am and terminates at the north railway station – it also often putters off ahead of schedule.

Train To get to Dazu by train, you should drop off the Chengdu-Chongqing railway line at Youtingpu town (five hours from Chongqing, seven hours from Chengdu), which is the nearest stop to Dazu. Despite the fact that the town is around 30 km from Dazu, train timetables refer to it as Dazu station. See the Train section of the Chongqing Getting There & Away section for more information on trains to Dazu. There are frequent minibuses running from the railway station to Dazu.

WESTERN SICHUAN & THE ROAD TO TIBET

Literally the next best thing to Tibet are the Sichuan mountains to the north and west of Chengdu – heaps of whipping cream that rise above 4500 metres, with deep valleys and rapid rivers. Tibetans and Tibetan-related peoples (Qiang) live by herding yaks, sheep and goats on the high-altitude Kangba Plateau Grasslands to the far north-west. Another zone, the Zoigê Grassland (north of Chengdu, towards the Gansu border) is over 3000 metres above sea level. Closer to Chengdu, the Tibetans have been assimilated, speak Chinese and have little memory of their origins, although they're regarded as a separate minority and are exempt from birth control quotas. Further out, however, Tibetan customs and clothing are much more in evidence.

Towns on the Kangba Plateau experience cold temperatures, with up to 200 freezing days per year; summers are blistering by day and the high altitude invites particularly bad sunburn. Lightning storms are frequent from May to October; cloud cover can shroud the scenic peaks. On a pleasanter note, there appear to be sufficient hot springs in these areas to have a solid bath along the route.

A theme often echoed by ancient Chinese poets is that the road to Sichuan is harder to travel than the road to heaven. In the present era, with the province more accessible by road, we can shift the poetry to Tibet and the highway connecting it with western Sichuan.

The Sichuan-Tibet Highway, begun in 1950 and finished in 1954, is one of the world's highest, roughest, most dangerous and most beautiful roads. The highway has been split into northern and southern routes. The northern route (2412 km) runs via Kangding, Ganzi and Dêgê before crossing the boundary into Tibet. The southern route (2140 km) runs via Kangding, Litang and Batang before entering Tibet.

While getting to Tibet is currently no problem, the land route between Chengdu and Lhasa is closed to foreigners for safety reasons. Some 'palefaces' have succeeded and arrived intact in Lhasa. The less fortunate were some Americans and Australians on the back of a truck which overturned close to Dêgê; one member of the group lost half an arm and another member sustained multiple injuries to her back. It took several days for medical help to be sent and even longer before the injured could be brought back to Chengdu.

It is possible to do the trip by local buses, but foreigners will have problems getting hold of tickets and are likely to be turned back en route. This may all change, however. In early '93 at least one Hong Konger came through the whole way on local buses, and three Swiss successfully rode their motor bikes from Lhasa to Chengdu. It might be worth asking around for the latest on this route.

A couple of years ago there was a legendary crate, the Chengdu-Lhasa bus, which suffered countless breakdowns and took weeks to arrive. In 1985, a monumental mudslip on the southern route took out the road for dozens of km and the service was discontinued. Trucks are the only transport travelling consistently long hauls on this highway. The major truck depots are in Chengdu, Chamdo and Lhasa. Trucks usually run from Lhasa or from Chengdu only as far as Chamdo, where you have to find another lift. The police have now clamped down on truckers giving lifts to foreigners; there is rumoured to be a sign in Chinese near Dêgê which warns drivers not to take foreigners. Certainly at Dêgê itself, there is a checkpoint on the bridge where guards turn back foreigners. If drivers are caught, they could lose their licences or receive massive fines. Foreigners caught arriving from Chengdu are often fined and always sent back. If you're arriving from Tibet nobody gives a damn.

In sum, the odds are stacked much higher against you when travelling into, rather than out of, Tibet. Whatever you do, bear in mind the risk and equip yourself properly with food and warm clothing. For information on Tibet and Qinghai see the separate chapters in this book. The Sichuan-Tibet Highway is given in-depth coverage in Lonely Planet's *Tibet – a travel survival kit*.

At present, the bus service on the Sichuan-Tibet Highway only seems to function well as far as Kangding. The Exit-Entry Administration Office of Chengdu's PSB hands out permits to Kangding, Ganzi and Dêgê and other towns in the Garzê (Ganzi) Autonomous Prefecture fairly regularly. Some travellers have followed the highway across the Kangba Plateau to the following places.

Kangding (Dardo)
(kāngdìng) 康定

Kangding (2620 metres) is a small town nestled in majestic scenery. Swift currents from the rapids of the Zhepuo River give Kangding hydropower, the source of heating and electricity for the town. There is a daily bus service from Chengdu's Xinnanmen bus station to Kangding via Ya'an and Luding.

Towering above Kangding is the mighty peak of Mt Gongga (7556 metres) – to behold it is worth 10 years of meditation, says an inscription in a ruined monastery by the base. The mountain is apparently often covered with cloud so patience is required for the beholding. It sits in a mountain range, with a sister peak just below it towering to 5200 metres. Pilgrims used to circle the two for several hundred km to pay homage.

Mt Gongga is on the open list for foreign mountaineers – in 1981 it buried eight Japanese climbers in an avalanche. Known conquests of this awesome 'goddess' are those by two Americans in 1939, and by six Chinese in 1957.

Things to See There are three or four lamaseries in town in various stages of reconstruction. The most active is **Nanwu Monastery** *(nánwù sì)* in the western part of the town on the northern bank of the Zhepuo River. The **Kangding Monastery** *(kāngdìng sì)* is in the centre of town not far from the bus station. The **Kangding Lamasery** *(kāngdìng dàlāmāsì)* is the most picturesque, sitting on a mountain 500 metres above the northern side of town; the five pavilions and surrounding trails afford good views of Kangding and nearby snow peaks.

Places to Stay & Eat There are at least two hotels that accept foreigners in Kangding. For convenience, most travellers stay in the hostelry opposite the bus station. This place has dorm beds for Y5. If you follow the river that runs through town upstream you'll come to the *Paramount Hotel*. This hotel has a restaurant, though like everywhere else in Kangding the food is pretty terrible. There are a couple of noodle shops in the bus station area.

Moxixiang

(móxīxiāng) 磨西乡

There's not much to recommend this little urban aggregation in the middle of nowhere, but if you are headed for **Hailuogou Glacier Park** this is where you'll have to stay. There are two hotels here. The first is the *Bus Station Hotel (qìchēzhàn zhāodàisuǒ)*, which has beds for Y10. There's another place a little up the road, which has beds for the same rates. The latter has ponies for hire. The going rate for ponies is around Y35 to Y40 per day.

There's a reception office for Hailuogou Glacier Park next door to the Catholic church (you can't miss it – it has a steeple with a cross on the top). This place also has ponies and guides for hire, and sells tickets for the glacier. As for the church, its principal claim to fame is that Mao slept in it on the Long March.

Getting There & Away Buses from Kangding to Moxixiang leave at 1 pm and cost Y10.30. From Moxixiang there are buses back to Kangding and on to Luding. Many travellers who come up here to visit Hailuogou set out by way of Kangding and Moxixiang and return by way of Luding. From Luding there are buses to Chengdu for around Y35. Buses from Moxixiang to Luding leave at 7 am and cost Y10.

Hailuogou Glacier Park

(hǎiluógōu) 海罗沟公园

Hailuogou Glacier Park is part of Mt Gongga and is the lowest glacier in Asia. The main glacier (No 1 Glacier) is 14 km in length and covers an area of 16 sq km. It's relatively young as glaciers go: around 1600 years. Guides from the town of Moxixiang lead inexpensive four to seven-day pony treks along glacier trails (which are virtually impossible to follow without a guide). This trip has become much more accessible over recent years, but it's still a good idea to come prepared. Bring warm clothing and good sunglasses with you as a minimum. There is food and drink available en route, but it's still worth bringing some high-calorie food with you.

If you are on a pony you can do the entire trip through to the No 3 Camp in around seven to eight hours. On foot you would be better off doing the trip over two days, though it's probably possible to make it to the No 3 Camp in one day if you keep up a brisk pace.

From Moxixiang the path follows the Yanzigou River. Just after Moxixiang you'll be stopped by the park entrance, where they charge Y24. From here it's a straightforward walk or ride (if you are on a pony) around 11 km to the **No 1 Camp** *(yīhào yíngdì)*, which is at 1940 metres. En route you'll cross a rickety bridge over the river. The distance to the next camp is around six km.

At the **No 2 Camp** *(èrhào yíngdì)* (2620 metres) the path leaves the river valley and passes through lush rainforest for around five km. At the **No 3 Camp** *(sānhào yíngdì)* there is a sign notifying visitors that you should take a guide to the glacier itself. Pony guides from Moxixiang do not qualify. From the No 3 camp the first stop is the **Glacier Viewing Platform** *(bīngchuān guānjǐngtái)* at 3000 metres. From here you can see the **Glacier Tongue** to the left and to the right the **No 2 Glacier**. From the platform it is possible to continue on via a path that runs alongside the glacier to the **Glacier Waterfall Viewing Platform** *(bīngchuān pùbù guānjǐngtái)*.

Just how far you get from the No 3 Camp will depend entirely on weather conditions. If you are after spectacular views of Mt Gongga from the glacier it will probably pay to build a couple of extra days into your schedule.

Places to Stay & Eat There is cheap accommodation and places to pitch a tent at each of the camps en route to the glacier, and both the No 1 and No 2 camps have hot springs if you are in need of a soak. Some people do the walk slowly (three or four hours a day), overnighting at each of the camps. But it is equally possible to head straight up to the No 3 Camp, where there is chalet-style accommodation for four people for Y70. Naturally you can't expect any showering facilities up here – save your dirt for the hot springs lower down.

The camps all sell some food and drinks. Mineral water, soft drinks and beer are all available.

Getting There & Away Hailuogou is accessible via the town of Moxixiang, which in turn can be reached by bus from Kangding. See the previous entry on Moxixiang for details.

Luding
(lùdìng) 泸定
Luding is around halfway between Kangding and Moxixiang, and is an interesting alternative return route to Chengdu if you are just in this region for Hailuogou Glacier Park. Luding is famous throughout China as the site of what is commonly regarded as the most glorious moment of the Great March. The key element in this is the Luding Bridge, a chain suspension affair high over the Dadu River.

In May 1935 the Communist troops were approaching the Luding Bridge, only to discover that Kuomintang troops had beat them to it, removed the planks from the bridge and had it covered with firepower. In response, 20 Communist troops crossed the bridge hand by hand armed with grenades and then proceeded to overcome the Kuomintang troops on the other side. As one reader who wrote in put it: 'it sounds like the A Team!' This action allowed the Long March to continue before the main body of the Kuomintang forces could catch up with them.

The **Luding Bridge** *(lùdìng qiáo)* is in the south of town. The original bridge was first constructed in 1705 and was an important link in the Sichuan-Tibet road. On the main street in town you might want to look out for the **Luding Bridge Revolutionary Artifacts Museum** *(lùdìngqiáo gémìng wénwù chénlièguǎn)*, which houses a collection of some 150 items left behind by members of the Long March.

Places to Stay & Eat There are a few hotels in Luding. The *Luding Hotel* has an English sign and is just down the road from the bus station. Beds in a triple here cost Y12. Some of the rooms have verandas with views of the river. Other places around town with similar rates are the *County Guesthouse (xiàn zhāodàisuǒ)* and the *Bus Station Hotel (chēzhàn lǚguǎn)*.

Getting There & Away From Luding there are buses to Moxixiang (Y10), Kangding (Y18) and direct to Chengdu (Y32). Buses to Chengdu leave at 7 am.

Ganzi
(gānzī) 甘孜
The capital of the Ganzi (Garzê) Tibetan Autonomous Region sits high in a Cholashan mountain valley (3800 metres) north-west of Kangding, and is populated by mostly Tibetans and Khampas. Very few Westerners have sojourned here, though as the Xining-Chengdu route between Qinghai and Sichuan becomes more popular it may yet get its due. For now it's little more than an intermediate stop between Sêrxu and Kangding for travellers in a hurry to reach 'civilisation' after the rigours of the Xining-Sêrxu road.

The **Ganzi Lamasery** *(gānzī sì)* just north of the town's Tibetan quarter is worth a visit for views of the Ganzi valley, although it's not a particularly spectacular structure.

The *Ganzixian Hotel* has beds for Y10, a decent dining room, friendly staff and plenty of hot water.

For details on the trip north to Xining via Sêrxu, see the Xining to Chengdu section in the Qinghai chapter.

Dêgê
(dégé) 德格

This is the last town on the Chengdu-Lhasa highway before it enters Tibet proper. The 250-year-old **Bakong Scripture Printing Lamasery** houses an extensive collection of Tibetan scriptures of the five Lamaist sects which are revered by followers the world over. Under the direction of the abbot are some 300 workers; housed within the monastery are over 200,000 hardwood printing plates. Texts include ancient works on astronomy, geography, music, medicine and Buddhist classics. A history of Indian Buddhism, comprising 555 woodblock plates, is the only surviving copy in the world (written in Hindi, Sanskrit and Tibetan). Protecting the monastery from fire and earthquake is a guardian goddess, a green Avalokitesvara.

Litang
(lǐtáng) 理塘

West of Kangding on the southern route to Tibet is Litang, which at 4700 metres is 1000 metres higher than Lhasa and a few hundred metres short of the world record for high towns (Wenchuan, on the Tibet-Qinghai Plateau). Litang rests at the edge of a vast grassland. A trading fair and festival lasting 10 days is held here annually beginning on the 13th day of the sixth lunar month; it's sponsored by the Panchen Lama.

NORTHERN SICHUAN

The Aba (Tibet & Qiang) Autonomous Prefecture of northern Sichuan is perhaps the most Tibetan area of the province and doesn't require any special permits from the Chengdu PSB.

Jiuzhaigou
(jiǔzhàigōu) 九寨沟

In northern Sichuan, close to the Gansu border, is Jiuzhaigou (literally: Nine Stockade Gully), which was 'discovered' in the '70s and is now being groomed for an annual influx of 300,000 visitors. In 1984, Zhao Ziyang made the famous comment which all Sichuanese tourism officials love to quote: 'Guilin's scenery ranks top in the world, but Jiuzhaigou's scenery even tops Guilin's'.

Jiuzhaigou, which has several Tibetan settlements, offers a number of dazzling features – it is a nature reserve area (with some panda conservation zones) with North-American-type alpine scenes (peaks, clear lakes, forests). Scattered throughout the region are Tibetan prayer wheels and *chortens*, Tibetan stupas. The remoteness of the region and the chaotic transport connections have kept it clean and relatively untouristed.

Despite the good intentions of the authorities, all this looks certain to change fast. A helicopter landing pad is under construction even though the mountain ranges between Chengdu and Jiuzhaigou are not ideal terrain for helicopters. Tourism officials are already going one step further and planning an airport for small jets.

You should calculate between a week and 10 days for the round trip by road. It takes from two to three days to get there and you can easily spend three or four days, or even weeks, doing superb hikes along trails which cross spectacular scenery of waterfalls, ponds, lakes and forests – just the place to rejuvenate polluted urban senses.

The entrance to Jiuzhaigou National Park is close to the Yangdong Hotel. From there a dirt road runs as far as the Nuorilang Falls where the road splits: branch right for Swan Lake; branch left for Long Lake. Nuorilang is becoming a tourist centre of sorts. From Yangdong to Nuorilang is 14 km, Nuorilang to Long Lake is 18 km, Nuorilang to Rizi is nine km, Rizi to Swan Lake is eight km.

Jiuzhaigou and Huanglong are both around 3000 metres in altitude. Between October and April snow often cuts off access for weeks on end. Make sure you take warm clothing. Food can be abysmal so take iron rations with you. The rainy season lasts from June to August.

Roads in these regions are dangerous so don't expect more than minimum standards of vehicle, driver or road maintenance.

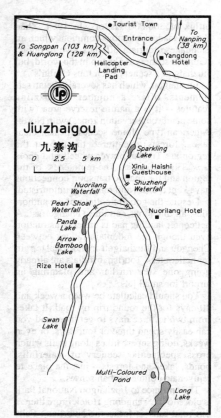

Jiuzhaigou
九寨沟

0   2.5   5 km

To Songpan (103 km) & Huanglong (128 km)

• Tourist Town
Entrance
To Nanping (38 km)
Yangdong Hotel
Helicopter Landing Pad

Sparkling Lake
Xiniu Haishi Guesthouse
Nuorilang Waterfall
Shuzheng Waterfall
Pearl Shoal Waterfall
Nuorilang Hotel
Panda Lake
Arrow Bamboo Lake
Rize Hotel
Swan Lake
Multi-Coloured Pond
Long Lake

Shock horror stories circulating recently about Jiuzhaigou included one about a minibusload of Hong Kongers who reported sighting a UFO; another busload plunged over a precipice, killing all 20 passengers. An outbreak of plague in the area caught two more Hong Kongers, who were immediately cremated.

Transport is not plentiful – if you board en route rather than catching a bus at its originating point, be prepared for some tough competition for seats. To maximise your chances of a seat on a bus out of Jiuzhaigou, it's best to book your ticket three days in advance at the entrance to the reserve. Hitching has been known to work.

Huanglong
(huánglóng) 黄龙

This valley, studded with terraced, coloured ponds (blue, yellow, white and green) and waterfalls, is about 56 km from Songpan, on the main road to Jiuzhaigou. The Yellow Dragon Temple *(huánglóng sì)* and the surrounding area were designated a national park in 1983. The most spectacular terraced ponds are behind the temple, about a two-hour walk from the main road. Huanglong is almost always included on the itinerary for a Jiuzhaigou tour, but some people find it disappointing and prefer an extra day at Jiuzhaigou. An annual Miao Hui (Temple Fair) held here around the middle of the sixth lunar month (roughly mid-August) attracts large numbers of traders from the Qiang minority.

Places to Stay
It will probably be necessary to overnight in Songpan before travelling on to Jiuzhaigou. In Jiuzhaigou itself most travellers prefer to head up into the park, where there is cheaper Tibetan-style accommodation.

In Songpan, three small hostelries offer doubles, triples and five-bed rooms; prices average Y7 to Y10 per bed. The *Songpan Guesthouse* is a current favourite for its friendly service.

In Jiuzhaigou, the state-run *Rizi Guesthouse* hotel *(rìzé zhāodàisuǒ)* and the better, privately run *Xiniu Haishi Guesthouse (xīniú hǎishí sùshè)* compete happily for FEC. The *Yangdong Hotel (yángdóng zhāodàisuǒ)* has become expensive, with beds ranging in price from Y25.

There is Tibetan-style accommodation from around four km into the park. Further up again, near the Nuorilang Falls, is the *Minzulou Tibetan Guesthouse*, a wooden building with basic but friendly accommodation for around Y5 per person. If you take the right fork in the road just before the Nuorilang Guesthouse, there is more Tibetan accommodation. The further you are prepared to traipse for your bed, the cheaper prices get. Tourists usually put up at the *Nuorilang Hotel (nuòrìláng zhāodàisuǒ)*, where there's a tourist office. Rooms are around Y25 per person.

In Huanglong National Park are several small guesthouses with beds for Y5 or less – no frills, just hard beds and maybe a coal burner in the winter. The *Huanglong Hotel (huánglóng zhāodàisuǒ)* has slightly more upmarket accommodation. It's down at the entrance to the park.

Nobody has a decent word for food in this region. Chengdu would be a good place to stock up.

Getting There & Away

Warning The ticket office at the Ximen bus station in Chengdu requires that foreigners present a PICC (People Insurance Company of China) card certifying that they're carrying a PICC insurance policy for bus travel in northern Sichuan (the same applies for most of Gansu Province further north). This policy apparently follows from a lawsuit brought upon the Chinese government by the family of a Japanese tourist who was killed in a bus crash in the Jiuzhaigou area. The card costs Y20 for one month's cover and is available from the PICC office *(zhōngguó rénmín bǎoxiǎn gōngsī)* on Shudu Dadao (Renmin Donglu), just down the road from the Hongqi Market in Chengdu. There are English speakers in the office. The bus station won't accept any other type of travel insurance. It's a good idea to have this card with you at all times while travelling in northern Sichuan – any bus driver could ask to see it.

Bus Until helicopters and jets send shock waves over Jiuzhaigou, the local bus remains the best means of transport. It can be taken in one dose or as part of a bus/train combination. Several intriguing routes follow.

The buses going directly north from Chengdu (Ximen bus station) to Songpan leaves at 7 am, takes 12 hours and costs Y66 (foreigner's price). There is usually no problem for onward travel from Songpan to Jiuzhaigou (2½ hours), though the same

cannot be said of Huanglong, for which there are seldom buses. From Jiuzhaigou, however, there are often tour buses that take in Huanglong as a stopover on the way back to Chengdu.

Alternatively, it is possible to travel direct to Jiuzhaigou by taking a bus to Nanping and getting off 41 km before the bus reaches its final destination. The roads on this journey are notoriously bad, and you will need to stopover en route. The bus leaves from the Ximen bus station at 7.20 am and overnights in Maowen. Next to the bus station is the *Renmin Hotel*, with inexpensive three-bed dorms. You should reach Jiuzhaigou around 6 or 7 pm the following day. If you nod off and miss the entrance to Jiuzhaigou, you will have to overnight in Nanping and backtrack the next day. Buses to Nanping cost around Y80 for foreigners.

Bus/train combinations are more troublesome, but can be done. The most popular option is to travel north on the Chengdu-Baoji railway line as far as Zhaohua, where you will have to stay overnight. From Zhaohua there are usually tour buses to both Jiuzhaigou and Huanglong in the height of the tourist season, but if this isn't the case you can either bus to Nanping and overnight there before doing the final 41 km the next morning or take a Chengdu-bound bus to Jiuzhaigou. Buses for Chengdu go via Nanping and Jiuzhaigou (check to be certain). It's a good idea to book your onward bus ticket as soon as you get into Zhaohua. The road between Zhaohua and Nanping is notoriously dangerous – this is not a trip for those with no stomach for adventurous travel.

Another train/bus option is to take a train or bus to either Mianyang or Jiangyou, both north of Chengdu. Then take a bus to Pingwu, where you can change for a bus to Jiuzhaigou. This road is reportedly superior to the one between Zhaohua and Nanping.

Tours During the summer, various companies in Chengdu operate tours to Jiuzhaigou. Some include side trips in the general region. The most welcome customers are Hong

Kongers, who tend to travel in miniature armies and can easily book out a whole bus. Most of the trips are advertised for a certain day, but the bus will only go if full. If you are unlucky you may spend days waiting. Find out exactly how many days the trip lasts and which places are to be visited. If you're not sure about the tour company, avoid paying in advance. If there's a booking list, have a look and see how many people have registered. You can register first and pay before departure.

A standard tour includes Huanglong and Jiuzhaigou, lasts seven days and costs an average of Y500 to Y600 per person. There are longer tours which include visits to the Tibetan grassland areas of Barkam and Zöige. Prices vary according to the colour of your skin, availability of FEC and the scruples of the companies involved. Check to see what the guys at the Flower Garden restaurant in Chengdu are offering as a starter and use this as a basis for checking out other tours.

In Songpan, you can also arrange pony treks to nearby Munigou, where there is a waterfall, hot springs and temple – and few tourists. The cost is Y50 per person per day, plus a nominal charge for tents and bedding. Both the Flower Garden and YS restaurants just down from the Traffic Hotel offer pony treks in this region. They are both reliable operators.

Apart from the two above restaurants, the following places in Chengdu have been known to offer tours: Ximen bus station, travel agencies in the Traffic Hotel, the Jinjiang Hotel and CITS. The latter two are the most expensive. There is also an agency next to the north railway station

A word of warning. Several tour operators in Chengdu have been blacklisted by Hong Kong travellers for lousy service, rip-offs and rudeness. Ask around among travellers to pinpoint a reliable agency.

Chengdu to Xiahe

This journey has emerged as a popular back-door route into Gansu Province for many travellers. Those who have done this route in the winter months don't recommend it. The roads often become impassable and temperatures plummet way past the tolerance levels of most mere mortals. Even in good weather, you need to give yourself at least five days to do the trip, more if you want to poke around some monasteries or make a side trip to Jiuzhaigou.

The first leg is from Chengdu to Songpan (see the Jiuzhaigou section for details on getting there and away). Most travellers take a side trip from Songpan to Jiuzhaigou at this point. From Songpan you can travel onwards to Zöige (nuòěrgài), where you will need to overnight. There is some confusion as to the status of Zöige for individual travellers, and many travellers have been required to purchase a travel permit on arrival. Don't worry too much about it; the PSB will find you if they think it's important. The local hotel charges Y20 for a double or Y8 in the dorm. From the cinema in town it is possible to walk up the hills and visit a couple of monasteries. There are superb views from up here.

Zöige has two bus stations at either end of town with buses back to Songpan and on to Luqu and Hezuo on alternating days. If you can't get an onward ticket for the next day at one, try the other. From Zöige most people travel on to Hezuo, though Luqu is another possibility. Hezuo is only a few hours from Xiahe, and you should be able to make the trip the following morning.

From Xiahe you have the option of travelling on to Lanzhou or taking the more unusual option of travelling on to Xining in Qinghai Province via Tongren.

Yunnan 云南

Population: 34 million
Capital: Kunming

Geographically, Yunnan *(yúnnán)* is the most varied of all of China's provinces, with terrains as widely divergent as tropical rainforest and icy Tibetan highlands. It is also the sixth-largest province in China and the home of a third of all China's ethnic minorities and half of all China's plant and animal species.

When Qin Shihuang and the Han emperors first held tentative sway over the south-west, Yunnan was occupied by a large number of non-Chinese aboriginal peoples who lacked any strong political organisation. But by the 7th century AD the Bai people had established a powerful kingdom, the Nanzhao, south of Dali. Initially allying its power with the Chinese against the Tibetans, this kingdom extended its power until, in the middle of the 8th century, it was able to challenge and defeat the Tang armies. It took control of a large slice of the south-west and established itself as a fully independent entity, dominating the trade routes from China to India and Burma. The Nanzhao kingdom fell in the 10th century and was replaced by the kingdom of Dali, an independent state which lasted until it was overrun by the Mongols in the mid-13th century. After 15 centuries of resistance to northern rule, this part of the south-west was finally integrated into the empire as the province of Yunnan.

Even so it remained an isolated frontier region, with scattered Chinese garrisons and settlements in the valleys and basins, a mixed aboriginal population occupying the uplands, and various Dai (Thai) and other minorities along the Lancang (Mekong) River. Like the rest of the south-west, it was always one of the first regions to break with the northern government. Today, however, Yunnan Province looks to be firmly back in the Chinese fold; it is a province of 34 million people, including a veritable constel-

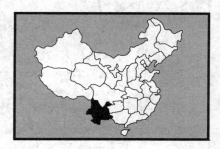

lation of minorities (24 registered): the Zhuang, Hui, Yi, Miao, Tibetans, Mongols, Yao, Bai, Hani, Dai, Lisu, Lahu, Wa, Naxi, Jingpo, Bulang, Pumi, Nu, Achang, Benglong, Jinuo and Dulong. Its chief attraction is, in fact, those pockets of the province that have successfully resisted Chinese influence and exhibit strong local identities. Even Kunming, the provincial capital, has a flavour all its own that seems more than half a world away from Beijing. The province is also well known for its mild climate – the name 'Yunnan' is a reference to this reputation, meaning 'South of the Clouds'.

KUNMING
(kūnmíng) 昆明
History

The region of Kunming has been inhabited for 2000 years. Tomb excavations around Lake Dian to the south of the city have unearthed thousands of artefacts from that period – weapons, drums, paintings, and silver, jade and turquoise jewellery – that suggest a well-developed culture and provide clues to a very sketchy early history of the city. Until the 8th century the town was a remote Chinese outpost, but the kingdom of Nanzhao, centred to the north-west of Kunming at Dali, captured it and made it a secondary capital. In 1274 the Mongols came through, sweeping all and sundry

before them. Marco Polo, who put his big feet and top hat in everywhere, gives us a fascinating picture of Kunming's commerce in the late 13th century:

At the end of these five days journeys you arrive at the capital city, which is named Yachi, and is very great and noble. In it are found merchants and artisans, with a mixed population, consisting of idolaters, Nestorian Christians and Saracens or Mohametans... The land is fertile in rice and wheat...For money they employ the white porcelain shell, found in the sea, and which they also wear as ornaments about their necks. Eighty of the shells are equal in value to...two Venetian groats. In this country also there are salt

springs...the duty levied on this salt produces large revenues to the Emperor. The natives do not consider it an injury done to them when others have connection with their wives, provided the act is voluntary on the woman's part. Here there is a lake almost a hundred miles in circuit, in which great quantities of fish are caught. The people are accustomed to eat the raw flesh of fowls, sheep, oxen and buffalo...the poorer sorts only dip it in a sauce of garlic... they eat it as well as we do the cooked.

In the 14th century the Ming set up shop in Yunnanfu, as Kunming was then known, building a walled town on the present site. From the 17th century onwards the history

Top: Monk with human thighbone trumpet, Lhasa, Tibet (CB)
Left: Prayer flags in the snow, on the road to Nepal, Tibet (CT)
Right: Prayer flags, Tibet (CT)

Top: Monks on the roof of Jokhang Temple, Lhasa, Tibet (CB)
Left: Pilgrim wearing 'gau' (portable shrine) in Lhasa, Tibet (Strauss)
Right: Prayer wheels, Tashilhunpo Monastery, Tibet (CT)

of this city becomes rather grisly. The last Ming resistance to the invading Manchu took place in Yunnan in the 1650s and was crushed by General Wu Sangui. Wu in turn rebelled against the king and held out until his death in 1678. His successor was overthrown by the Manchu Emperor Kangxi and killed himself in Kunming in 1681. In the 19th century, the city suffered several bloodbaths, as the rebel Muslim leader Du Wenxiu, the Sultan of Dali, attacked and besieged the city several times between 1858 and 1868. A large number of buildings were destroyed and it was not until 1873 that the rebellion was finally and bloodily crushed.

The intrusion of the West into Kunming began in the middle of the 19th century when Britain took control of Burma, and France took control of Indochina, providing access to the city from the south. By 1900 Kunming, Hekou, Simao and Mengzi were opened to foreign trade. The French were keen on exploiting the region's copper, tin and lumber resources, and in 1910 their Indochina railroad, started in 1898, reached the city.

Kunming's expansion began with WW II, when factories were established here and refugees fleeing the Japanese poured in from eastern China. To keep the Japanese tied up in China, Anglo-American forces sent supplies to Nationalist troops entrenched in Sichuan and Yunnan. Supplies came overland on a dirt road carved out of the mountains in 1937-38 by 160,000 Chinese with virtually no equipment. This was the famous Burma Road, a 1000-km haul from Lashio to Kunming (today, the western extension of Kunming's Renmin Lu, leading in the direction of Heilinpu, is the tail end of the Road).

In early 1942 the Japanese captured Lashio, cutting the line. Kunming continued to handle most of the incoming aid during 1942-45 when US planes flew the dangerous mission of crossing the 'Hump', the towering 5000-metre mountain ranges between India and Yunnan. A black market sprang up and a fair proportion of the medicines, canned food, petrol and other goods intended for the military were siphoned off into other hands.

Kunming Today

The face of Kunming has been radically altered since then, with streets widened, office buildings and housing projects flung up. With the coming of the railways, industry has expanded rapidly, and a surprising range of goods and machinery available in China now bears the 'made in Yunnan' stamp. Kunming also has its own steel plant. The city's produce includes foodstuffs, trucks, machine tools, electrical equipment, textiles, chemicals, building materials and plastics.

Kunming's total population is around 3½ million, though only a million or so inhabit the urban area. At most, minorities account for 6% of Kunming's population, although the farming areas in the outlying counties have some Yi, Hui and Miao groups native to the area. Also calling Kunming home are some 150,000 Vietnamese refugees from the Chinese-Vietnamese wars and border clashes that started in 1977.

There's very little to see in the way of sights in Kunming. It is, however, a great place to wander around on foot, once you get off the wide boulevards. It is unfortunate that much of Kunming's charm is under threat: like much of China, in recent years the city has been treated to a major face-lift. For the locals this spells 'progress', but for Western visitors in search of the old Kunming it means that the quaint back alleyways lined with fascinating wooden buildings are rapidly disappearing. Fortunately there is enough still standing to make it worth getting lost in the backstreets, but how long it will stay this way is anyone's guess.

Nevertheless, despite the proliferating high-rises and luxury hotels (Kunming has been designated a Special Tourism Centre), the city remains an interesting place to linger for a few days. There is some great food available, and the streets are vibrant with shoppers, pedlars, roadside masseurs, karaoke stalls and the occasional street performer.

At an elevation of 1890 metres, Kunming has a milder climate than most other Chinese cities, and can be visited at any time of year. Light clothes will usually be adequate, but

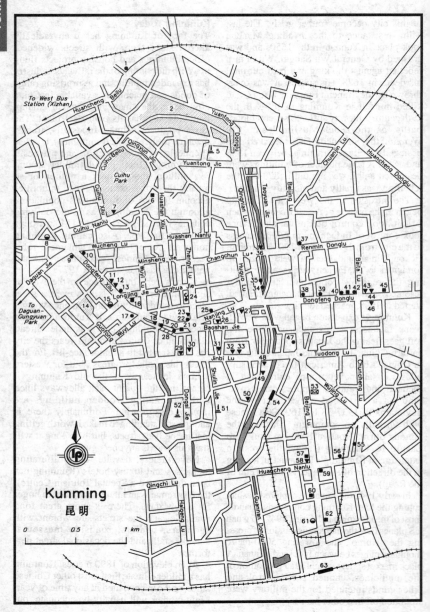

To West Bus
Station (Xizhan)

Cuihu
Park

To Daguan-
Gungyuan Park

Kunming
昆明

0   0.5   1 km

PLACES TO STAY

6 Cuihu Guesthouse
16 Yunnan Hotel
21 Spring City (Chuncheng) Hotel
41 Kunming Hotel
45 Camellia Hotel
57 Kunhu Hotel
59 Golden Dragon Hotel
60 King World Hotel
62 Three Leaves Hotel/Groove Garden

PLACES TO EAT

7 Laozhiqing Restaurant
11 Blue Skies Duck Restaurant
12 Shanghai Noodle Restaurant
18 Qiaoxiangyuan Restaurant
23 Ice Cream Shop
26 Beijing Restaurant
27 Minsheng Restaurant
28 Muslim Restaurants
29 California Noodle King USA
30 Yunnan Across the Bridge Noodles Restaurant
31 Chuanwei Sichuan Restaurant
32 Nanlaisheng Coffee Shop
33 Mengbai Across the Bridge Noodles
36 Yingjianglou Muslim Restaurant
43 Yunnan Typical Local Food Restaurant
44 New Land Restaurant
46 Cooking School
48 Guanshengyuan Restaurant
49 Pan Se Seng Restaurant
50 Yingjianglou Restaurant (No 2)
58 Happy Cafe

OTHER

1 Yunnan Minorities Institute
2 Kunming Zoo
3 North Railway Station
4 Yunnan University
5 Yuantong Temple
8 Xiaoximen Bus Station
9 Yunnan Arts & Crafts Store
10 Dongfeng Department Store
13 Arts Theatre
14 Guofang Sports Ground
15 Wacang Lu Minibuses (for Western Hills, Bamboo Temple etc)
17 Yunnan Provincial Museum
19 Wuhua Mansions Department Store
20 Kunming United Airlines
22 Kunming Department Store
24 Ancient Mosque
25 Xinhua Bookstore
34 Yunnan Antique Store
35 Foreign Languages Bookstore
37 Bank of China
38 Post & Telephone Office
39 Golden Triangle Bar
40 Shanghai Airlines
42 CAAC
47 PSB
51 East Pagoda
52 West Pagoda
53 International Post Office
54 South Railway Station
55 Thai Airways
56 CITS
61 Long-Distance Bus Station
63 Main Railway Station

it's wise to bring some woollies during the winter months, when temperatures can suddenly drop, particularly in the evenings – there have even been a couple of light snowfalls in recent years. There's a fairly even spread of temperatures from April to September. Winters are short, sunny and dry. In summer (from June to August) Kunming offers cool respite, although rain is more prevalent then.

Orientation

The jurisdiction of Kunming covers 6200 sq km, including four city districts and four rural counties (which supply the city with fruit and vegetables). The centre of the city is the traffic circle at the intersection of Zhengyi Lu and Dongfeng Lu. This is where you'll find the local trendies, cinemas, karaoke bars and department stores overflowing with the latest fashions and electronic goods. Surprisingly, it is still possible to find rows of old wooden houses in nearby neighbourhoods. To the south-west of the intersection down to Jinbi Lu there are some interesting old alleys and some great places to eat. Jinbi Lu itself is a fascinating tree-lined street crowded with shops and restaurants.

■ PLACES TO STAY

6 翠湖宾馆
16 云南饭店
21 云春城饭店
41 昆明饭店
45 茶花宾馆
57 昆湖饭店
59 金龙饭店
60 锦华大酒店
62 三叶饭店

▼ PLACES TO EAT

7 老知食馆
11 蓝天烤鸭店
12 上海面园店
18 桥香园饭店
23 冰淇淋店
26 北京饭店
27 民生饭店
28 清真饭店
29 美国加州牛肉面大王店
30 云南过桥米线
31 川味饭店
32 南来盛咖啡馆
33 蒙白过桥米线
36 映江楼饭店
43 根兴大陆饭店
44 新学厨饭店
46 冠生园饭店
48 斑色酒村
49 映江楼饭店
50 快乐食馆
58

OTHER

1 云南少数民族学院
2 昆明动物站园
3 火车南北大学
4 云南通大寺
5 圆门
8 小云西工艺美术汽车客运站服务部
9 东南风百货商店
10 艺术剧院
13 国体育场
14 南路防仓省小型车站
15 瓦云南博物馆
17 五华大厦
19 昆明联合航空公司
20 昆明百货商店商店
22 南城清书古寺
24 新华文物店店
25 云外南文书行
34 中国电银局
35 邮政酒吧
37 金角海国际航空公司
38 上中民航售票处
39 公安国塔塔
40 东西寺寺
42 国际南火车空公司旅行社
47 明泰国际航空
51 长途汽车总站
52 火车站
53
54
55
56
61
63

To the north of the intersection are Cuihu Park, a pleasant place for a wander, Yuantong Temple and the Kunming Zoo, the inhabitants of which, like those of most Chinese animal incarceration sites, would probably be better off put out of their misery. East of the intersection is Kunming's major north-south road, Beijing Lu. At the southern end is the main railway station and a few hotels that are popular with travellers. At about the halfway point Beijing Lu is intersected by Dongfeng Donglu, which is where the other popular hotel for travellers, the Camellia, can be found.

Information

CITS The travel service (☎ 313 2895) is just east of Beijing Lu on Huancheng Nanlu. Like CITS offices elsewhere in China, this one emphasises group tours and is not able to offer a lot of assistance to individual travellers. It does, however, hand out some information in the form of pamphlets and so on.

CITS books international plane tickets and has tour buses to destinations around Kunming. Some travellers have successfully made reservations by telex to Beijing for tickets on the Trans-Siberian.

PSB This is at 525 Beijing Lu and is open from 8 to 11.30 am and from 2 to 5.30 pm. It's a tiny office with a small plaque in English on the wall outside. The officers on duty in the Foreign Affairs branch usually speak excellent English and are quite friendly.

Money The Kunming, Green Lake, Camellia, King World, Sakura Holiday Inn and Golden Dragon hotels each have foreign-exchange counters. Changing in the hotels is generally more convenient than trudging up to the Bank of China on Renmin Donglu. The highest concentration of moneychangers is in front of the Kunming Hotel, but be very careful of rip-offs – they occur frequently by sleight of hand. Rates are usually among the best in China, especially for US dollars. Beware of moneychangers handing you back a US$100 bill and telling you it's a fake – it has often been discreetly swapped for a US$1 bill.

Post & Telecommunications There is an international post office on the east side of Beijing Lu. It's halfway between Tuodong Lu and Huancheng Nanlu and has a very efficient poste restante and parcel service – this is where poste restante mail ends up. Every poste restante letter or parcel that comes in is listed in a ledger that's kept on the counter. To claim a letter, you must show your passport or ID. At least one of the clerks speaks English. You can also make telephone calls here. There is another post office to the north of this one, on Beijing Lu near the intersection with Dongfeng Donglu.

With Kunming's hotels in the grip of a renovation frenzy, it's probably not a good idea to use a hotel as a poste restante address unless you are absolutely sure that it is still standing and will be open.

Maps There are at least five varieties of map, some with a smattering of English names, available from hotels and the Foreign Languages Bookstore. The *Kunming Tourist Map* has street and hotel names in English and shows bus lines. Arguably the best of the maps is the one available outside the long-distance bus station, although the English content is minimal. An excellent Chinese map of Yunnan is also available at the same place.

Medical Services The Yan'an Hospital *(yán'ān yīyuàn)* is on Jiaosanqiao Lu, about one km north-east of the Kunming Hotel – there's a foreigners' clinic (☎ 22390) on the 1st floor of the outpatients' building.

Tang Dynasty Pagodas

To the south of Jinbi Lu are two Tang pagodas, of which the West Pagoda *(xīsì tǎ)* is a must-see. The East Pagoda *(dōngsì tǎ)* was, according to Chinese sources, destroyed by an earthquake; Western sources say it was destroyed by the Muslim revolt. It was rebuilt in the 19th century, but there's little to see. Far more interesting is the West Pagoda. It's on Dongsi Jie, a bustling market street – you'll probably have to walk your bicycle through the crowds. The West Pagoda has a compound that is a popular spot for old people to get together, drink tea and play cards and mahjong. It's easy to spend an hour or so here sipping tea and watching the action.

Yunnan Provincial Museum

(yúnnánshěng bówùguǎn) 昆明省博物馆
The museum, on Wuyi Lu, houses an exhibition centred around Yunnan's minorities, as well as a collection of artefacts from tomb excavations at Jinning on the southern rim of Lake Dian. All things considered, the museum is probably not worth the foreigner's entry fee of Y5. The exhibits are for the most part fairly tacky – shop mannequins dressed in minority colours and fuzzy photographs of minority festivals. There's a shop on the 2nd floor with some reasonably priced batiks and paintings. The museum is closed on Sunday.

Yuantong Temple

(yuántōng sì) 圆通寺
The Yuantong Temple, to the north-east of the Green Lake Hotel, is the largest Buddhist complex in Kunming, and is a target for

pilgrims. It is over 1000 years old, and has seen many renovations. Leading up to the main hall from the entrance is an extensive display of flowers and potted landscapes. The central courtyard holds a large square pond intersected by walkways and bridges, and has an octagonal pavilion at the centre. To the rear of the temple a new hall has been added, enshrining a statue of Sakyamuni, a gift from the king of Thailand. Watch out for pickpockets outside the temple and for the elderly women inside who do their best to stop foreigners taking pictures of the Buddhist statuary.

Zoo
(dòngwùyuán) 动物园
Close to Yuantong Temple is the zoo, and as Chinese zoos go it's not too shabby. The grounds are pleasantly leafy and high up, and provide a bird's-eye vista of the city. Most travellers find the animals' living conditions depressing – animal lovers are better off giving the place a miss.

Cuihu Park
(cuìhú gōngyuán)
A short distance south-west of the zoo, the Cuihu Park needn't be high on your agenda but it is worth taking a stroll in. Sunday sees the park at its liveliest, when it is host to an English Corner and to free Chinese opera performances.

Ancient Mosque
(nánchéng qīngzhēn gǔsì) 清真寺
Today, while Kunming's Buddhist shrines, desecrated during the Cultural Revolution, are humming with renovations for the tourist trade, the local Muslim population seems to have been left out of the action. The 400-year-old Ancient Mosque, a ramshackle building at the city centre next to the Kunming Department Store at 51 Zhengyi Lu, was turned into a factory during the Cultural Revolution. Today, it's worth calling in and taking a look at how the restoration work is coming along. The West Pagoda tends to be a livelier congregation spot for local Muslims, however.

Organised Tours
Several tour outfits cover the area faster than public minibuses would, but you must be prepared to pay for it. They generally feature a lot of sights that most Western travellers find rather boring, like the Black Dragon Pool and various caves (a national obsession). More central sights like Yuantong Temple are just a short bicycle ride away – it hardly makes sense to join a tour to see them. Many of the tour operators no longer take foreigners on their tours (only China could get away with institutionalised racism of this kind) – perhaps there have been problems in the past.

The Xiyuan Hotel, at the western shores of Lake Dian, has scenic boat tours which may or may not be an interesting afternoon

---

Kunming's Muslims
Unlike Muslims in other parts of China, who generally formed settlements at the termini of trade routes used by Arab traders, Yunnan's sizable Muslim population dates back to the 13th-century Mongol invasion of China. Ethnically indistinguishable from the Han Chinese, the *hui*, as Muslims are known, have had an unfortunate history of repression and persecution, a recent low-point being the years of the Cultural Revolution. The Cultural Revolution failed to spark off a revolt of any kind, though unsuccessful protests were registered in Beijing. The turbulent years of the mid-nineteenth century, which witnessed the massive Taiping and Nian rebellions, were another matter. Heavy land taxes and disputes between Muslims and Han Chinese over local gold and silver mines triggered a Muslim uprising in 1855.

The Muslims made Dali the centre of their operations and laid siege to Kunming, overrunning the city briefly in 1863. Du Wenxiu, the Muslim leader, proclaimed his newly established kingdom Nanping Guo, or the Kingdom of the Pacified South. But the Muslim successes were short-lived. In 1873 Dali was taken by Qing forces and Du Wenxiu was captured and executed, having failed in a suicide attempt. ∎

outing. There are various tours to the Stone Forest running from in front of the railway station, a ticket office just down from the Golden Dragon Hotel on Beijing Lu and from the Three Leaves Hotel – avoid them. You'll spend the whole morning rummaging around in caves that demand exorbitant foreigner's price entrances, followed by a marathon midday lunch. If you're lucky you may even get an hour or so in the Stone Forest before being whisked back to Kunming. That said, the occasional traveller has come back satisfied with the experience – an interesting initiation into Chinese tourism rituals.

Places to Stay – bottom end

Most of the bottom-end hotels listed in this section also have mid-range accommodation, while most of the old mid-range hotels have gone upmarket in pursuit of the tourgroup dollar.

The most popular travellers' hang-out these days is the *Camellia Hotel (cháhuā bīnguǎn)* on Dongfeng Donglu. This is a friendly place with 24-hour hot water, bicycle hire and a poste restante. Beds in a dorm cost Y10, while basic singles/doubles are Y40. More upmarket doubles with TV and attached bathroom are also available, ranging from Y120 to Y200, though few foreigners use them.

The *Three Leaves Hotel (sānyè fàndiàn)* is a short walk from Kunming main railway station and directly opposite the long-distance bus station on Beijing Lu. At the time of writing the hotel was undergoing renovations, which normally spells one thing: massive price hikes. This is a shame, as it used to be the next best thing to the Camellia, and had bus services to Dali and Xishuangbanna. If you arrive at the railway station or the long-distance bus station, check the place out to see what the latest is.

The *Kunhu Hotel* (☎ 3133737) *(kūnhú fàndiàn)* is a bit farther up Beijing Lu from the railway station, just north of Huancheng Nanlu and the Golden Dragon Hotel. The hotel has been declining in popularity with travellers due to the surliness of the staff and

apparently arbitrary decisions about the availability of rooms – sometimes they accept foreigners, sometimes they don't. Beds in five-bed dorms cost Y10, and there are singles/doubles with attached bathroom for Y40, though these are seldom available. The best rooms available are the air-con doubles in the new wing for Y80; they have 24-hour hot water and are pretty good value for money. The hotel is two stops from the railway station on bus No 3, 23 or 25.

The rambling *Yunnan Hotel* (☎ 3130258) *(yúnnán fàndiàn)* on Dongfeng Xilu, near the Yunnan Provincial Museum and the Zhengyi Department Store, was Kunming's first tourist hotel. Nowadays it's mostly inhabited by mainland Chinese on private or government business. It's an unfriendly place and is only recommended in the unlikely event of everything else being booked up. Triples cost Y42, while doubles with attached bathroom range from Y80 to Y120.

Close to the Yunnan Hotel is the *Spring City Hotel (chūnchéng fàndiàn)*. Not many foreigners stay here, but it has some clean, cheapish rooms. Beds in a seven-room dorm cost Y18, while beds in a triple are Y22. There are also doubles with attached bathroom available for Y88.

Places to Stay – top end

With the new emphasis on Kunming as a tourism centre, the local authorities seem hell-bent on imposing luxury standards on all mid-range accommodation. Most of the old mid-range hotels have undergone or are undergoing extensive renovations, and prices have risen accordingly. Places like the Cuihu Guesthouse have brought in Western management and chefs, and the Kunming Hotel has made an uncompromising break with its more plebeian past.

The *Kunming Hotel* (☎ 3162063) *(kūnmíng fàndiàn)* at 145 Dongfeng Donglu has a north and a south wing; both are fairly expensive, though the south wing is the cheaper of the two. Only doubles are available in the north wing, and prices range from Y330 for a standard room (TV, air-con, bathroom, etc) up to Y1500 for a deluxe suite. The south wing has singles for Y95 and doubles from Y155 to Y240. The hotel has some useful facilities: CITS/poste restante, post office, photocopying, bike hire, a good restaurant and a couple of shops. To get there from the main station, take bus No 23 to the intersection of Dongfeng Lu and Beijing Lu, and then take a bus east or walk. From the west bus station *(xīzhàn)* take bus No 5.

Diagonally opposite the Kunming Hotel is Kunming's latest super-luxury monster: the *Holiday Inn Sakura (yīnghuā jiǎrì jiǔdiàn)*. It is presently the best of Kunming's hotels, sporting some excellent restaurants, a super-chic disco and the best breakfast in town. You can expect the usual Holiday Inn standards and room rates (US$80 to 90 for a double).

The *Cuihu Guesthouse* (☎ 5155788) *(cuìhú bīnguǎn)* is at 16 Cuihu Nanlu. It's at the edge of an older section of Kunming and is quiet and pleasant. At the time of writing the Cuihu was undergoing extensive renovations and prices were set to jump. You should reckon on Y400 for a double here. The hotel's location should make it a good option if you are in the market for top-range accommodation. Bus No 1 runs between the west bus station and the centre of town via the Cuihu. From Beijing Lu, take bus No 2.

Down on Beijing Lu, the *Golden Dragon Hotel* (☎ 3133015) *(jīnlóng fàndiàn)* is a Hong Kong-China joint venture. Only doubles are available and these start at US$50. Superior rooms are available at US$60, while suites scale the giddy heights of US$600 (plus 10% service charge). A 15% discount is sometimes available on request. Both CAAC and Dragonair have offices here and there is a business centre on the premises as well. The Golden Dragon, once Kunming's premiere upmarket hotel, is gradually losing custom to the other new hotels around Kunming and some complain that standards are slipping. The coffee shop on the 1st floor has a reasonable bolognese and the coffee at Y10 allows for refills.

Down the road from the Golden Dragon is another classy luxury hotel: the *King World Hotel* (☎ 3138888) *(jǐnhuá dàjiǔdiàn)*.

Doubles range from US$60 for a standard to US$90 for a superior suite. The hotel features an expensive revolving restaurant (the highest above sea level in China, the hotel proudly points out) on the top floor.

Places to Eat

Kunming has some great food, especially in the snack line. Regional specialties are herb-infused chicken in an earthenware steampot *(qìguōjī)*, Yunnan ham *(xuānwèi huǒtuǐ)*, across-the-bridge noodles *(guòqiáo mǐxiàn)*, goat cheese *(rǔbǐng)* and various Muslim beef and mutton dishes. Some travellers wax enthusiastic about toasted goat cheese, another local specialty. It probably depends on how long you've been away from civilisation – the cheese is actually quite bland and sticks to your teeth.

Gourmets with money to burn may perhaps be interested in a whole banquet based on Jizhong fungus (mushrooms) or 30 courses of cold mutton, not to mention fried grasshoppers or elephant trunk braised in soy sauce.

The chief breakfast in Kunming, as throughout most of Yunnan, is noodles (choice of rice or wheat), usually served in a meat broth with a chilli sauce.

Local Specialties There are several eating places near the Kunming and Camellia hotels on Dongfeng Donglu that feature bilingual menus. The *Cooking School* on Dongfeng Lu specialises in local fish and vegetable dishes, and gets the thumbs down from everyone who eats there. The *Olympic Restaurant* (east of the Cooking School and so named because of its proximity to the stadium) is another place that is best avoided. Locals claim that it has been investigated by the PSB on numerous occasions for over-charging customers and for its faltering hygiene standards. One of the best options on Dongfeng Donglu is the *Yunnan Typical Local Food Restaurant*. It has a good range of dishes, including across-the-bridge noodles. Almost next door is the *New Land Restaurant*, another good place to eat.

Several small restaurants in the vicinity of

Yunnan University's main gate are highly recommended, especially the popular *Tong Da Li Restaurant*. Coming out of the Yunnan University gate, go left on the main road and then take the first left onto a small back street; Tong Da Li is the first restaurant on the right. This area is about 15 minutes' walk north from the Green Lake Hotel.

Two of the better-known places for steampot chicken are the *Spring City Hotel* and the *Dongfeng Hotel*, around the corner of Wuyi Lu and Wucheng Lu, in the direction of the Cuihu Guesthouse. Try the 2nd floor of the Spring City Hotel, though service can be bad there. Several small, private restaurants on Beijing Lu opposite the long-distance bus station sell cheaper versions of steampot chicken. Steampot chicken is served in dark-brown Jianshui County casserole pots, and is imbued with medicinal properties depending on the spicing – caterpillar fungus *(chóngcǎo)*, pseudo-ginseng or gastrodia.

The best Hui or Chinese Muslim food in Kunming is reportedly served at the *Yingjianglou Muslim Restaurant* (☎ 3165198) *(yìngjiānglóu fàndiàn)* at 360 Changchun Lu. It's still running strong after many years and can be found in an interesting, bustling part of town. An English menu is available and one of the staff speaks English. Try the cold sliced beef – it comes with a delicious sauce. There's also another Yingjianglou on the small lane at the southern end of Huguo Lu.

Yunnan's best-known dish is across-the-bridge noodles. You are provided with a bowl of very hot soup (stewed with chicken, duck and spare ribs) on which a thin layer of oil is floating, along with a side dish of raw pork slivers (in classier places this might be chicken or fish) and vegetables, and a bowl of rice noodles. Diners place all of the ingredients quickly into the soup bowl, where they are cooked by the steamy broth.

Across-the-bridge noodles is the stuff of which fairy tales are made, as the following story proves:

Once upon a time there was a scholar at the South Lake in Mengzi (Southern Yunnan) who was attracted by the peace and quiet of an island there. He settled into a cottage on the island, in preparation for official examinations. His wife, meanwhile, had to cross a long wooden bridge over the lake to bring the bookworm his meals. The fodder was always cold in winter by the time she got to the study bower. Oversleeping one day, she made a curious discovery – she'd stewed a fat chicken and was puzzled to find the soup still hot, though it gave off no steam – the oil layer on the surface had preserved the temperature of the broth. Subsequent experiments showed that she could cook the rest of the ingredients for her husband's meal in the hot broth after she crossed the bridge.

It is possible to try across-the-bridge noodles in innumerable restaurants in Kunming. Prices generally vary from Y5 to Y15 depending on the side dishes provided. It's usually worth spending a bit more, because with only one or two condiments it lacks zest.

A good restaurant to try Kunming's famous noodle dish is the *Minsheng Restaurant (mínshēng fàndiàn)*. Prices are either Y5 or Y10, but you'll almost certainly be pressured into taking the Y10 option – relax, it's worth it. Close to the Yunnan Provincial Museum and set back from the main road a little is the *Qiaoxiangyuan Restaurant (qiáoxiāng yuán)*. The noodles here are also very good and are similarly priced to those of the Minsheng Restaurant.

The *Yunnan Across-the-Bridge Noodles Restaurant (guòqiáo mǐxiànguǎn)* on Nantong Jie serves huge bowls at rock-bottom prices. The decor is, shall we say, basic – the predominant noise is a chorus of hissing and slurping; tattered beggars circulate among the stainless-steel-topped tables, pursued by management. Never mind the beggars or the decor – the food is absolutely delicious! The atmosphere, as can be imagined, is very different from the tourist hotels, where the same fare will cost you exponentially more.

A more recent phenomenon in Kunming is the discovery of ethnic cuisines. At present there are at least two Dai minority restaurants in Kunming. The food is spicy and uses sticky rice as its staple. Popular with overseas students studying in Kunming is the *Laozhiqing Restaurant (lǎozhīqīng shíguǎn)* next to the main entrance to Cuihu Park. It's an open-fronted place complete with miniature chairs. The *Pan Se Seng Restaurant* is a bit more upmarket and features karaoke and live music in the evenings, but it's a good place for lunch. There's no English menu, but the staff are very friendly and willing to help out. It's another place to try Dai cuisine, an opportunity you won't get again unless you head down to Xishuangbanna.

Finally, a few doors down from the Kunhu Hotel on Beijing Lu is the *Happy Cafe*. It used to be known as the Pizza Hut, and is a good place to find other travellers. The English menu features all the traveller's favourites, and the pizzas aren't bad at all. Almost next door is the *Yuelai Cafe*, another popular place to hang out.

Continental Breakfast For the best coffee in town, seek out the wooden stools of the *Nanlaisheng Coffee Shop (nánláishèng kāfēiguǎn)* at No 299 Jinbi Lu. This is the place to get a cup of *real*, heart-starting coffee. Cakes and breads are also available, though the French breads that the shop once sold are no longer in evidence. Coffee tickets and bread are sold at the front of the shop; take your coffee ticket into the kitchen at the back to pick up the black, freshly brewed coffee (milk costs extra, sugar is free). This is a good place to meet local foreign residents.

The big hotels all sport coffee shops. For a no-holds-barred breakfast buffet, head down to the *Holiday Inn*, where you can eat as much as you can stuff in for Y40. The ground-floor coffee shop in the *Golden Dragon Hotel* is not quite in the same league, but the coffee is good; it seems a little steep at Y10, but it becomes better value for money after a few refills. There are also cakes and snacks available. The Happy Cafe close by also serves good coffee and breakfast sets.

Other Chinese There is a string of eateries on Xiangyun Jie between Jinbi Lu and Dongfeng Donglu. At the Dongfeng end at No 77 is the *Beijing Restaurant (běijīng fàndiàn)* with northern-style seafood, chicken and duck. At the Jinbi end of Xiangyun Jie is the *Chuanwei Restaurant (chuānwèi fàndiàn)*, which serves Sichuan-style chicken, spicy bean curd, hot pork, duck and seafood. In between are lots of street vendors and small private restaurants.

Pick of the pleb restaurants is the *Shanghai Noodle Restaurant (shànghǎi miànguǎn)* at 73 Dongfeng Xilu, in a yellow-fronted building. To the left side you'll get cheap noodles; to the right are steampot chicken, cold cuts and dumplings. Just a few doors up is the *Blue Skies Duck Restaurant (lántiān kǎoyādián)*. It's a good place to sample some inexpensive duck dishes.

Snacks Kunming used to be a good place for bakeries, but many of these seem to be disappearing. Exploration of Kunming's backstreets might turn up a few lingerers, however.

In the vicinity of the long-distance bus station and in many of the side streets running off Beijing Lu it is possible to come across sidewalk noodle shops. Generally you get a bowl of rice noodles for around Y1 and a bewildering array of sauces to flavour the broth with – most of them are hot and spicy.

Another place to go snack-hunting is Huguo Lu, north of Nantaiqiao, for simmering noodle bars and a teahouse. The intersection of Changchun and Huguo yields lots of small eateries. Also try Baoshan Jie, an east-west street running between Zhengyi Lu and Huguo Lu – Baoshan is also a good place to seek out other across-the-bridge noodle restaurants. In fact, this whole area is a hub of restaurant activity. The stretch of Daguan Jie from Dongfeng to Huancheng is a busy free market, and in season you'll get fruit – mangoes, pineapples, 'ox-belly' fruit from Xishuangbanna, and pears from the Chenggong orchards or from Dali.

Hotel Food The *Kunming Hotel* has a restaurant on the ground floor of the new wing which has good food, reasonable prices and fairly friendly and efficient service (occasionally the harried servers forget to bring a dish). The menu includes Yunnan specialties and Western breakfasts as well as Chinese standards.

The *Camellia Hotel* has a similar restaurant set-up, also quite good. The bar-lounge area makes a pleasant meeting spot.

At the *Green Lake Hotel* there is a bar and cafe on the 3rd floor, a Western restaurant on the 5th floor and a Chinese restaurant on the 2nd floor. The food in these places has a good reputation. The Green Lake is in the process of making a leap into the luxury hotel range and chefs have been brought in from overseas to supervise the restaurant food. You can expect prices to go up accordingly.

Entertainment

If you're not an ardent fan of karaoke bars, the nightlife options for Kunming are fairly dismal – but then again where aren't they in China? The most popular foreigners' hangout is the *Groove Garden* next to the Three Leaves Hotel. It's a tiny place with seating at the bar and in a dark room upstairs. If it all looks a little seedy, don't be put off. The staff are extremely friendly and their beer is the cheapest in town. It's Y2.50 for a local beer, but take a plunge and splash out on the Ginseng beer (Y15) for an interesting taste experience.

Some travellers have reported the existence of the *Love Bean Bar* somewhere near the Cuihu Park. We never managed to stumble across it, but it's reportedly another place with an interesting mix of foreign and Chinese clientele. Not far from the Camellia Hotel, the *Golden Triangle Bar* sounds promising, but is an expensive place for a drink by Chinese standards.

You might be able to chase up minority dancing displays (more often held for the benefit of group tours), travelling troupes or Yunnan Opera. CITS sometimes has information on these events. The Arts Theatre on Dongfeng Xilu is a likely venue.

Already mentioned in the Cuihu Park entry are the Sunday afternoon performances of Yunnan Opera in the park.

Things to Buy

You have to do a fair bit of digging to come up with inspiring purchases in Kunming. Yunnan specialties are jade (related to Burmese), marble (from the Dali area), batik, minority embroidery (also musical instruments and dress accessories) and spotted brass utensils.

Other crafts to consider are some of the basic utilitarian items that are part of everyday Yunnanese life: the large bamboo waterpipes for smoking angel-haired Yunnan tobacco, local herbal medicines (Yunnan White Medicine *(yúnnán báiyào)* is a blend of over 100 herbs and is highly prized by Chinese throughout the world) and the *qìguō* or ceramic steampot.

Yunnanese tea is also an excellent buy and comes in several varieties, from bowl-shaped bricks of smoked green tea called *tuōchá*, which have been around since at least Marco Polo's time, to leafy black tea that rivals some of India's best.

One of the main shopping drags is Zhengyi Lu, which has the Zhengyi Department Store, the Overseas Chinese Department Store and the Kunming Department Store, but these mainly sell consumer goods. Other shopping areas are Jinbi Lu by the Zhengyi Lu intersection (lots of small specialty shops), and Dongfeng Donglu, between Zhengyi Lu and Huguo Lu.

The Kunming Arts & Crafts Shop *(gōngyì měishù fúwùbù)*, on Qingnian Lu, has some batik, pottery, porcelain and handicrafts, but it's pretty dull. Better to look among the privately run shops on Beijing Lu and Dongfeng Donglu. Outside the Kunming Hotel you will probably be ambushed by minority women flogging their handiwork – bargain if you want a sane price. Both the Green Lake and Kunming hotels sell batik which you can also find in Dali. Delve into the smaller shops around Jinbi Lu if you're into embroidery. For Yunnan herbal medicines, check the large pharmacy on Zhengyi Lu (on the east side, several blocks up from the Kunming Department Store). The southern end of Beijing Lu also has a few herbal medicine shops.

Kunming is a fairly good place to stock up

on film. Fuji and other film can be bought at the larger tourist hotels.

Getting There & Away

Air CAAC (☎ 3137465) is at 146 Dongfeng Donglu, next door to the Kunming Hotel. It's best to book your flights directly at CAAC, especially if you want a flight out the next day. The other CAAC office in the Golden Dragon Hotel can also take bookings and issue tickets but not for the next day. As well as internal flights, CAAC also has international flights to: Hong Kong (Y900, four times a week); Bangkok (Y950, Wednesday); Rangoon (Y1240, Wednesday); and Vientiane (Y850, Saturday).

For internal flights, alternatives to CAAC are Shanghai Airlines (☎ 3038502), close to CAAC on Dongfeng Donglu, which has flights to Shanghai (Y840), and United Airlines on Dongfeng Xilu, which has flights to Beijing (Y888).

Thai Airways (☎ 3133315) has three weekly flights to Chiang Mai (Y770) and Bangkok (Y950). The office is at 32 Chuncheng Lu. It's definitely necessary to reconfirm your flight, as travellers are frequently bumped off flights and left stranded. Dragonair (☎ 3133104) has an office in the Golden Dragon Hotel and has twice-weekly (Thursday and Sunday) flights to Hong Kong for Y900.

Kunming is well connected by air to the rest of China, and most flights (even Xishuangbanna and Mangshi) are on Boeing 737s. Possible flights include Beijing (Y1130, daily); Shanghai (Y1020, daily); Canton (Y570, daily); Nanning (Y410, daily except Monday); Haikou (Y520, daily except Monday); Xiamen (Y840, four times a week); Chengdu (Y360, daily); Chongqing (Y320, daily except Friday); Xi'an (Y610, thrice weekly); Lanzhou (Y870, twice weekly); Shenyang (Y1460, thrice weekly); Harbin (Y1750, Monday); Wuhan (Y680, twice weekly); Shenzhen (Y870, daily except Monday); Simao (Y240, thrice weekly); Jinghong (Banna) (Y340, daily); Mangshi (Dehong) (Y350, daily); Nanjing (Y930, thrice weekly); Hangzhou (Y860,

twice weekly) and Qingdao (Y1180, twice weekly).

Kunming's air connections have been much improved by the use of Boeing 737s and a wider availability of flights, so it's often possible to book flights to Xishuangbanna, the Dehong region and most other popular destinations at short notice. However, the availability of flights out of Kunming depends on the season, so it pays to book at least a week in advance.

During April (Water-Splashing Festival) and summer, the air connection for Xishuangbanna (Jinghong) can be booked rock solid for two to three weeks, and the CAAC office jammed with maniacs pushing, shoving and trying to pull rank. At times like this it is best to make your plans for Xishuangbanna as flexible as possible: consider the bus option, or book your flight several weeks ahead and spend the intervening time in Dali or elsewhere.

Bus The bus situation in Kunming can be a little confusing at first. There seem to be buses leaving from all over the place. However, the long-distance bus station on Beijing Lu is the main centre of operations, and this is the best place to organise bus tickets to almost anywhere in Yunnan or further afield. Exceptions to this are more local destinations like Lake Dian. A further exception is the bus trip to Xishuangbanna, for which many travellers use the bus service from the Three Leaves Hotel (check to see whether this service is still operating in the aftermath of the hotel's renovations).

The most popular bus routes from Kunming are Dali, Lijiang, Jinghong (in the Xishuangbanna prefecture in the south) and the Dehong prefecture (in the west). The long distances involved have made sleeper buses a popular option over recent years. These have reclining seats or even double-tiered bunks in some cases. If you're looking at an overnight trip, they are definitely worth the extra cost. Very few travellers go straight from Kunming to Lijiang; it makes better sense to take a sleeper bus to Dali first and then move on to Lijiang. The long-distance bus station has buses to Xiaguan, from where you can get a minibus or a local bus to Dali, a 30-minute trip.

There are numerous night buses to Xiaguan from 6.30 pm, and prices range from Y33 for an ordinary bus to Y70 for a sleeper. For the longer Lijiang trip, buses leave at 1 pm and prices range from Y55 to Y65 – the latter has reclining seats, but it's still a long and uncomfortable journey. Buses for Jinghong in Xishuangbanna take around 24 hours, and the trip includes an overnight stop. Buses leaving at 6 am should arrive the following day in Jinghong at around 4 pm. Buses from the Three Leaves Hotel leave at 6 am and cost Y44. From the long-distance bus station buses leave at 7.20 and 7.45 am and cost Y45 or Y50 – the latter is a marginally more comfortable bus with slightly more legroom and a 'better class' of passenger (less spitting and chain-smoking).

Both options for getting to the Dehong region involve long hauls, so it's worth considering doing at least one leg of the trip by air (to Mangshi). Buses leave for Baoshan from the long-distance bus station at 2.30 and 6.30 pm and cost Y65. The journey takes around 15 hours and is pretty punishing. Buses direct to Ruili take even longer (24 hours), but sleeper buses are available for this trip at Y145. Ordinary and deluxe buses cost Y95 and Y125 respectively.

It is possible to travel by bus to several destinations in neighbouring provinces from the long-distance bus station. Buses to Guiyang (in Guizhou Province) leave at 7.45 am, take around 24 hours and cost Y39. It is possible to break the trip by travelling first to Xingyi (Y24 – buses leave at 7.20 am), an interesting town just over the border, and staying overnight there. Another interesting option is the bus service to Nanning in Guangxi Province. The bus station is not keen on selling tickets for this route to foreigners, but if you meet resistance buy a ticket to Guangnan, a border town with onward connections to Nanning. Buses to Nanning cost Y67 and buses leave at 7.45 pm. The trip can take anything up to 36 hours.

Finally, the long-distance bus station also has buses running to the Stone Forest, and this is probably the best way to visit it. For further information see the Stone Forest Getting There & Away section.

Train Rail options out of Kunming include Beijing (via Guiyang, Changsha and Zhengzhou), Shanghai (via Liuzhou, Guilin, Guiyang and Hangzhou), Canton (also via Liuzhou, Guilin and Guiyang) and Chengdu and Chongqing (via Panzhihua, or Jinjiang as it is also known).

During peak season Kunming can become a real trap for railway travellers. Make a point of booking your tickets at least four days in advance. The advance booking office a couple of doors down from the Chuncheng Hotel is only worth a try if you queue there at 6.30 am. The ticket office in the main station sells tickets from 6.30 pm for trains departing the next day, but these are a real rarity. Unless you can get your hands on a black-market ticket (there doesn't seem to be much of a market for them in Kunming), getting hold of a ticket at local prices is almost impossible.

If you are heading for Guilin, it's sometimes possible to escape the railway congestion by flying to Nanning and then taking a train or bus to Guilin, although for a little more money you can fly direct to Guilin.

Kunming-Shanghai trains travel via Guiyang, Guilin, Zhuzhou, Nanchang and Hangzhou. The whole trip (3069 km) takes just over 60 hours. A tourist-price hard sleeper for Guilin costs Y180, while onwards to Shanghai costs around Y360. For Beijing, via Guiyang, Changsha and Zhengzhou (3182 km), a hard sleeper will set you back Y366. For Chongqing, trains pass through Guiyang, taking around 24 hours; a hard sleeper costs Y158. Alternatively you might travel to Panzhihua (Jinjiang), from where the No 86/83 train leaves daily for Chongqing via Chengdu at 6.30 pm, though this is a much more round-about way of doing things. Canton trains take 49 hours and cost Y276 for a hard sleeper. A hard-sleeper train from Kunming to Guiyang (13½ hours) costs Y98 (take the Beijing or Shanghai train or the No 324, which leaves at 4.29 pm). Trains to Emei (21 hours) cost Y128; on the same route, Chengdu (25 hours) costs Y140.

Getting Around

Most of the major sights are within a 15-km radius of Kunming. Local transport to these places is awkward, crowded and time-consuming; it tends to be an out-and-back job, with few crossovers for combined touring. If you wish to take in everything, you'd be looking at something like five return trips, which would consume three days or more. You can simplify this by pushing Black Dragon Pool, Anning Hot Springs and the Golden Temple to the background, and concentrating on the trips of high interest – the Bamboo Temple and Western Hills, both of which have decent transport connections with special express buses in the mornings. Lake Dian presents some engrossing circular-tour possibilities on its own. Better yet, buy a map, hire a good bicycle and tour the area by bike.

Bus The best option for getting out to the sights around Kunming is to head over to Wacang Lu, the first street on the left on Dongfeng Xilu after the Yunnan Provincial Museum. Minibuses run here to all the major sights, including the Golden Temple, Black Dragon Pool, Bamboo Temple, Lake Dian, Daguan Park and the Western Hills. Buses run through the day as soon as they are full, and they fill up fairly quickly in the mornings. Getting a minibus back is normally no problem either. They save considerable time and effort in sorting out the complicated system of local buses running out of town, and get to their destinations a lot quicker too.

For anyone set on using the local bus system, some options include the No 10 to the Golden Temple and No 6 to the Dragon Gate in the Western Hills, both from Xiaoximen bus station; the No 24 from Kunming railway station to Haigeng Park; and the No 4 from the Zoo to Daguan Park.

Bicycle Bikes are a fast way to get around town. Both the Kunming and Camellia hotels offer what's fast becoming a national standard rental rate of Y10 per day. The bikes for hire at the Happy Cafe look like they've seen better days, and if two or three people have been there before you in the morning the supply of bikes will be exhausted anyway.

AROUND KUNMING
Golden Temple
(*jīndiàn*) 金殿

This Taoist temple is perched amid a pine forest on Phoenix Song Mountain, 11 km north-east of Kunming. The original was carted off to Dali; the present one dates from the Ming Dynasty and was enlarged by General Wu Sangui, who was dispatched by the Manchus in 1659 to quell the uprisings in the region. Wu Sangui turned against the Manchus and set himself up as a rebel warlord, with the Golden Temple as his summer residence.

The pillars, ornate door frames, walls, fittings and roof tiles of the 6½-metre temple are all made of copper; the entire structure, laid on a white Dali marble foundation, is estimated to weigh more than 300 tonnes. In the courtyard are ancient camellia trees. At the back is a 14-tonne bronze bell, cast in 1423. The gardens around the temple offer secluded areas for picnicking. In the compound are teahouses and a noodle stand.

To get there take bus No 10 from the Xiaoximen bus station or a minibus from Wacang Lu. Many travellers ride hired bikes to the temple – it's fairly level going all the way to the base of the hill. Unless you come by minibus, you'll have to climb an easy hill path to the temple compound.

Black Dragon Pool
(*hēilóng tán*) 黑龙潭

Eleven km north of Kunming is this uninspiring garden, with old cypresses, dull Taoist pavilions and no bubble in the springs. But the view of the surrounding mountains from the garden is inspiring. Within walking distance is the **Kunming**

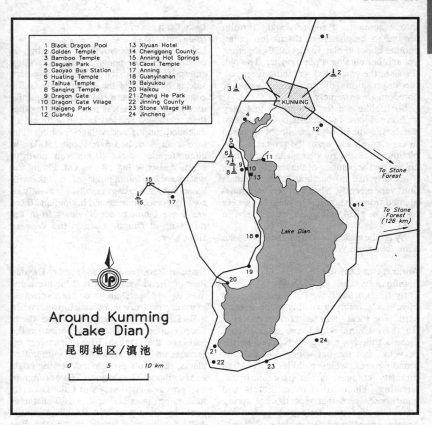

Around Kunming (Lake Dian)
昆明地区/滇池

0   5   10 km

1 Black Dragon Pool
2 Golden Temple
3 Bamboo Temple
4 Daguan Park
5 Gaoyao Bus Station
6 Huating Temple
7 Taihua Temple
8 Sanqing Temple
9 Dragon Gate
10 Dragon Gate Village
11 Haigeng Park
12 Guandu
13 Xiyuan Hotel
14 Chenggong County
15 Anning Hot Springs
16 Caoxi Temple
17 Anning
18 Guanyinshan
19 Baiyukou
20 Haikou
21 Zheng He Park
22 Jinning County
23 Stone Village Hill
24 Jincheng

KUNMING

To Stone Forest

To Stone Forest (126 km)

Lake Dian

Botanical Institute, where the collection of flora might be of interest to specialists. Minibuses run here frequently from Wacang Lu.

Bamboo Temple
(qióngzhú sì) 笻竹寺

Twelve km north-west of Kunming, this temple dates back to the Tang Dynasty. Burned down and rebuilt in the 15th century, it was restored from 1883 to 1890 when the abbot employed the master Sichuan sculptor Li Guangxiu and his apprentices to fashion 500 *luohan* (arhats or 'noble ones'). These life-size clay figures are stunning – either very realistic or very surrealistic – a sculptural tour de force.

Down one huge wall come the incredible surfing buddhas, some 70-odd, riding the waves on a variety of mounts – blue dogs, giant crabs, shrimp, turtles, unicorns. One gentleman has metre-long eyebrows; another has an arm that shoots clear across the hall to the ceiling.

In the main section are housed row upon row of standing figures. The statues have been done with the precision of a split-second photograph – a monk about to chomp into a large peach (the face contorted almost into a scream), a figure caught turning around to emphasise a discussion point, another about to clap two cymbals together, yet another cursing a pet monster. The old, the sick, the emaciated – nothing is spared; the expressions of joy, anger, grief or boredom are extremely vivid.

So lifelike are the sculptures that they were considered in bad taste by his contemporaries (some of whom no doubt appeared in caricature), and upon the project's completion Li Guangxiu disappeared into thin air. As for the bamboo of the temple's name, it actually had no bamboo on the grounds until very recently, when bamboo was transplanted from Chengdu. The main halls were restored in 1958 and again, extensively, in 1981.

By far the easiest way to get there is to take a minibus from Wacang Lu.

Anning Hot Springs
(*ānníng wēnquán*) 安宁温泉

Forty-four km south-west of Kunming, most travellers sensibly give this place a wide berth. The local tourist authorities proclaim (in their Chinese-language promotional material) the hot spring as 'No 1 under the heavens', but the hot spring and the surrounding area, which includes some Miao minority villages, is not particularly interesting. There are various hotels and guesthouses here that pipe the hot spring water into the rooms, but reports have it that couples are not accepted in some of them – this rule may have changed. Nearby, and possibly worth a look, is the Caoxi Monastery. It's over the river and couple of km or so to the south in a bamboo grove on Cong Hill.

If you're determined to see for yourself, be warned – unless you can find a minibus at Wacang Lu, getting to the hot springs is tricky. Take a No 5 bus from the Kunming Hotel westwards to the Nantaiqiao bus station, cross the road and change to a No 18 bus. The No 18 only runs twice a day, at 8 am and 2 pm. The last stop is Anning. In the afternoon, buses run back to Kunming at 2 and 4 pm.

Lake Dian
(*diān chí*) 滇池

Lake Dian, to the south of Kunming, is dotted with settlements, farms and fishing enterprises around the shores; the western side is hilly, while the eastern side is flat country. The southern end of the lake, particularly the south-east, is industrial, but other than that there are lots of possibilities for extended touring and village-crashing. The lake is an elongated one, about 150 km in circumference, about 40 km from north to south, and covering 300 sq km. Plying the waters are *fanchuan*, pirate-sized junks with bamboo-battened canvas sails. It's mainly an area for scenic touring and hiking, and there are some fabulous aerial views from the ridges up at Dragon Gate in the Western Hills.

Daguan Park (*dàguān gōngyuán*) Daguan Park or Grand View Park is at the northernmost tip of Lake Dian, three km south-west of the city centre. It dates back to 1682, when a Buddhist temple was constructed there. Shortly after, in 1690, work began on the park and the Daguan Tower. It covers 60 hectares and includes a nursery with potted plants, children's playground, rowing boats and pavilions. The **Daguan Tower** (*dàguān lóu*) provides good views of Lake Dian. Its facades are inscribed with a 180-character poem by Qing poet Sun Ranweng rapturously extolling the beauty of the lake. Bus No 4 runs to Daguan Park from Yuantong Temple via the city centre area.

At the north-east end of the park is a boat dock where an 8 am departure takes you from Daguan to Haikou on Lake Dian, passing by Dragon Gate Village. The boat departs from Haikou for Daguan at 2 pm and the one-way trip takes four hours. One-hour boat trips on the lake are possible from Daguan Park.

From Haikou you can catch bus No 15, which runs back to the Xiaoximen terminal in Kunming. You should also be able to connect with a minibus to get back to Kunming. Bus No 15 departs Xiaoximen for Haikou at 8 and 10 am, and at 12.30 and 4 pm; it returns from Haikou at 10.30 am, and at 12.30, 3 and 7.30 pm.

Western Hills (*xī shān*) The Western Hills spread out across a long wedge of parkland on the western side of Lake Dian; they're also known as the 'Sleeping Beauty Hills' – a reference to their undulating contours, which are thought to resemble a reclining woman with tresses of hair flowing into the sea. The path up to the summit passes a series of famous temples – it's a steep approach from the north side. The hike from Gaoyao bus station at the foot of the Western Hills to Dragon Gate takes 2½ hours. If you're pushed for time, there's a connecting bus from Gaoyao to the top section, or you could take a minibus direct from Wacang Lu in Kunming to Dragon Gate. Alternatively, it is also possible to cycle to the Western Hills in about 1½ hours – to vary the trip, consider doing the return route across the dikes of upper Lake Dian.

At the foot of the climb, about 15 km from Kunming, is **Huating Temple** (*huátíng sì*), a country temple of the Nanzhao kingdom believed to have been constructed in the 11th century, rebuilt in the 14th century, and extended in the Ming and Qing dynasties. The temple has some fine statues and excellent gardens.

The road from the Huating Temple winds from here up to the Ming Dynasty **Taihua Temple** (*tàihuá sì*), again housing a fine collection of flowering trees in the courtyards, including magnolias and camellias.

Between the Taihua Temple and Sanqing Taoist Temple near the summit is the **Tomb of Nie Er** (1912-36) (*nièěr zhīmù*), a talented Yunnan musician. Nie composed the national anthem of the PRC before drowning in Japan en route for further training in the Soviet Union.

The **Sanqing Temple** (*sānqīng gé*) near the top of the mountain was a country villa for a prince of the Yuan Dynasty, and was later turned into a temple dedicated to the three main Taoist deities.

Further up is **Dragon Gate** (*lóngmén*), a group of grottoes, sculptures, corridors and pavilions hacked from the cliff between 1781 and 1835 by a Taoist monk and coworkers, who must have been hanging up there by their fingertips. At least that's what the locals do when they visit, seeking out the most precarious perches for views of Lake Dian. The tunnelling along the outer cliff edge is so narrow that only one or two people can squeeze by at a time, so avoid public holidays! One of the last grottoes is dedicated to the deity who assisted those preparing for imperial exams – there is graffiti on the walls from grateful graduates, but nowadays the Chinese use it as a urinal.

From Kunming to the Western Hills the most convenient mode of transport is again the minibuses at Wacang Lu. You can take your pick of Dragon Gate (ask for *lóngmén*) or a service to the Western Hills (ask for *xīshān*). Alternatively, real travellers might like to avail themselves of the local bus service: take bus No 5 from the Kunming Hotel to Xiaoximen bus station, and then change to bus No 6, which will take you to the Gaoyao bus station at the foot of the hills.

From the Western Hills to Kunming you can either take the bus or scramble down from the Dragon Gate area directly to the lakeside along a zigzag dirt path and steps that lead to Dragon Gate Village. A narrow spit of land leads from here across the lake. At the western side of the 'spit' is a nice fish restaurant with simple food, wooden hut, fish from the lake – just go into the kitchen to organise some tasty food. Continuing across the land spit, you arrive at a narrow stretch of water which is negotiated by a tiny ferry. It's worthwhile hanging around here to see what passes by as this is the bottleneck of the lake, and junks, fishing vessels and other craft must come through.

Having made the short ferry crossing, you proceed by foot through a village area to Haigeng Park, where you can pick up a minibus for the run back to Wacang Lu.

The tour can easily be done in reverse; start with a minibus to Haigeng Park, walk to Dragon Gate Village, climb straight up to Dragon Gate, then make your way down through the temples to the Gaoyao bus station, where you can get bus No 6 back to the Xiaoximen station. Alternatively, bus No 33 runs along the coast through Dragon Gate Village, or you can take the early-morning boat from Daguan Park.

Haigeng Park (*hǎigěng gōngyuán*) On the north-eastern side of the lake, the local tourist authorities have high hopes for Haigeng. Minority villages are being constructed here with the aim of finally representing all 26 of Yunnan's minorities. It might end up being an expensive cultural experience for the visitor, with a Y10 general entry fee and Y5 per village. Besides the villages, the park has a small beach with swimming and a mini-resort area (roller-skating, restaurants, snacks, and you can hire airbeds for lounging around on the lake). Travellers' responses to the whole deal are fairly mixed, with some writing it off as a tacky attempt to cash in on the interest in local minorities and others claiming it is one of Kunming's premiere sights. If you're at all averse to tourist board fabrications of ethnic cultures, give the place a miss and spend an extra day in Xishuangbanna or Dehong, where you can see the real thing.

Again, the best way to get to Haigeng is by a minibus from Wacang Lu. Take bus No 24 from Kunming main bus station on Beijing Lu.

Zheng He Park (*zhènghé gōngyuán*) At the south-east corner of the lake, this park commemorates the Ming Dynasty navigator Zheng He (known as Admiral Cheng Ho throughout most of the world). A mausoleum here holds tablets describing his life and works. Zheng He, a Muslim, made seven voyages to over 30 Asian and African countries in the 15th century in command of a huge imperial fleet (for details, see the section on the town of Quanzhou in Fujian Province).

Bus No 21 from the Xiaoximen station terminates at the phosphate fertiliser factory near Gucheng at the south-west side of the lake, and north-west of Zheng He Park. From here it may be possible to hike along the hills

to the bus No 15 terminal at Haikou; bus No 15 will take you back to Xiaoximen station.

Jinning County (*jìnníng xiàn*) This is the site of archaeological discoveries from early Kunming, and you'll find it at the southern end of the lake. Bronze vessels, a gold seal and other artefacts were unearthed at Stone Hill, and some items are displayed at the Provincial Museum in Kunming. Bus No 14 runs to Jinning from Xiaoximen station, via Chenggong and Jincheng.

Chenggong County (*chénggòng xiàn*) This is an orchard region on the eastern side of the lake. Climate has a lot to do with Kunming's reputation as the florist of China. Flowers bloom all year round, with the 'flower tide' in January, February and March – which is the best time to visit. Camellias, azaleas, magnolias and orchids are not usually associated with China by Westerners although many of the Western varieties derive from south-west China varieties. They were introduced to the West by adventuring botanists who carted off samples in the 19th and 20th centuries. Azaleas are native to China – of the 800 varieties in the world, 650 are found in Yunnan. During the Spring Festival (February/March) a profusion of blooming species can be found at temple sites around Kunming – notably Taihua, Huating and Golden temples, as well as Black Dragon Pool and Yuantong Hill.

Bus No 13 from Kunming's Xiaoximen station runs to Chenggong via Jincheng; departures from Xiaoximen are at 7.30 and 8 am, and at 2, 2.30, 4.30 and 5 pm. The bus leaves Chenggong for Xiaoximen at 9.30 and 10 am, and at 4 and 4.30 pm.

STONE FOREST
(*shílín*) 石林
The Stone Forest, around 120 km south-east of Kunming, is a massive collection of grey limestone pillars, split by rain water and eroded to their present fanciful forms, the tallest standing 30 metres high. Marine fossils found in the area suggest that it was

once under the sea. Legend has it that the immortals smashed a mountain into a labyrinth for lovers seeking some privacy – and picnicking Chinese couples take heed of this myth (it can get busy in there!).

The maze of grey pinnacles and peaks, with the odd pool, is treated as an oversized rockery, with a walkway here, a pavilion there, some railings along paths and, if you look more closely, some mind-bending weeds. The larger formations have titles like Baby Elephant, Everlasting Fungus, Baby Buffalo, Moon-Gazing Rhino, Sword Pond. The maze is cooler and quieter by moonlight, and would enthral a surrealist painter.

There are actually several stone forests in the region – the section open to foreign tourists covers 80 hectares. Twelve km to the north-east is a larger (300-hectare) rock series called Fungi Forest, with karst caves and a large waterfall.

The Stone Forest is basically a Chinese tourist attraction and some Westerners find it grossly overrated on the scale of geographical wonders. The important thing, if you venture there, is to get away from the main tourist area – within a couple of km of the centre are some idyllic, secluded walks.

The villages in the Lunan County vicinity are inhabited by the Sani branch of the Yi tribespeople. Considering that so many other 'ethnic' areas of Yunnan are now open, you could be disappointed if you make the trip just to see the Sani branch of the Yi tribespeople who live in this area. Their craftwork (embroidery, purses, footwear) is sold at stalls by the entrance to the forest, and Sani women act as tour guides for groups. Off to the side is Five-Tree Village, which is an easy walk and has the flavour of a Mexican pueblo, but the tribespeople have been somewhat influenced by commercialism. For those keen on genuine village and farming life, well, the Stone Forest is a big place – you can easily get lost. Just take your butterfly net and a lunch box along and keep walking – you'll get somewhere eventually.

There is a Y5 entry fee for foreigners into the main Stone Forest. Getting into other sections costs Y2.

Activities

The Shilin and Yunlin hotels put on Sani song-and-dance evenings – usually when there are enough tourists around. Surprisingly, these events turn into good-natured exchanges between Homo Ektachromo and Sani Dollari, and neither comes off the worse for wear. The short performances display ethnic costumery and musical instruments. Years ago the hotels charged a small fee for the performances; recently they've been admitting tourists for free (once tourism picks up again the fees will probably be reinstated). The performances start around 8.30 pm. The Torch Festival (wrestling, bullfighting, singing and dancing) takes place on 24 June at a natural outdoor amphitheatre by Hidden Lake.

Places to Stay

The *Shilin Hotel (shílín bīnguǎn)*, near the main entrance to the Stone Forest, is a villa-type place with souvenir shop and dining hall. A double room costs Y100, a single Y60, and there are triples available for Y20 per bed. Similar in size and room rates is the *Yunlin Hotel (yúnlín fàndiàn)*, which is off the road that forks to the right in front of the entrance. In addition to Y60 singles and Y100 doubles, the Yunlin has concrete cells with soft beds for Y10 per person. These cheaper rooms have an attached washing area where you can bathe using a metal basin; toilets are down the hall. Both the Yunlin and Shilin hotels cater mostly for Overseas Chinese tour groups.

Near the bus terminal are several smaller hotels with basic rooms for Y10 per person – these have similar bathing facilities to the Y10 rooms at the Yunlin but are not as clean.

Places to Eat

Several restaurants next to the bus terminal specialise in duck roasted in extremely hot clay ovens with pine needles. A whole duck costs Y15 and takes about 20 minutes to cook – have the restaurant staff put a beer in their freezer and it'll be just right when the duck comes out. The ducks are massaged with a local sesame oil mixture before roasting.

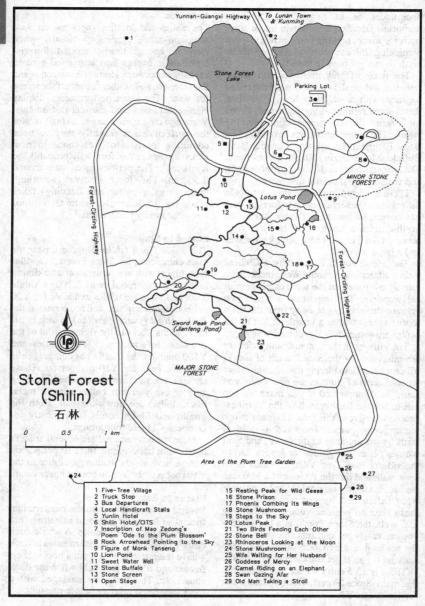

Yunnan-Guangxi Highway · To Lunan Town & Kunming

Stone Forest Lake

Parking Lot

Stone Forest (Shilin)

石林

MINOR STONE FOREST

Lotus Pond

Forest-Circling Highway

Sword Peak Pond (Jianfeng Pond)

MAJOR STONE FOREST

Area of the Plum Tree Garden

0   0.5   1 km

1 Five-Tree Village
2 Truck Stop
3 Bus Departures
4 Local Handicraft Stalls
5 Yunlin Hotel
6 Shilin Hotel/CITS
7 Inscription of Mao Zedong's Poem 'Ode to the Plum Blossom'
8 Rock Arrowhead Pointing to the Sky
9 Figure of Monk Tanseng
10 Lion Pond
11 Sweet Water Well
12 Stone Buffalo
13 Stone Screen
14 Open Stage

15 Resting Peak for Wild Geese
16 Stone Prison
17 Phoenix Combing its Wings
18 Stone Mushroom
19 Steps to the Sky
20 Lotus Peak
21 Two Birds Feeding Each Other
22 Stone Bell
23 Rhinoceros Looking at the Moon
24 Stone Mushroom
25 Wife Waiting for Her Husband
26 Goddess of Mercy
27 Camel Riding on an Elephant
28 Swan Gazing Afar
29 Old Man Taking a Stroll

<!-- Chinese glossary box -->

#	
1	村车站摊宾馆
2	木车车艺林宾馆
3	五卡汽工云石
4	工云石梅簇僧
5	林林梅簇僧子
6	石泳石擎石池井牛风
7	石梅石池井牛风
8	泳石擎石阶峰渡食 天
9	唐僧子水水屏场雁监夙芝天花鸟钟牛年夫音驼鹅步从容
10	狮子水水屏场雁监凤
11	甜小石舞落石凤灵岔莲双
12	小水水屏场雁监凤
13	石水屏场雁监凤芝
14	舞场雁监凤芝天
15	落雁监凤芝天花
16	石凤凤石天花鸟
17	凤夙芝石阶峰渡 翅
18	灵芝天花鸟钟牛
19	岔天花鸟钟牛年
20	莲花鸟钟牛年夫 渡
21	双鸟钟牛年夫音 食
22	石钟牛年夫音望 月芝
23	犀牛年夫音望灵
24	万年夫音石灵芝
25	望夫音石石
26	观音石石象
27	骆驼鹅骑远 象
28	天鹅绒远嘱
29	漫步从容

Near the main Stone Forest entrance is a cluster of food vendors that purvey a variety of pastries and noodles from dawn to dusk. The *Shilin Hotel* and *Yunlin Hotel* offer fixed-price meals that aren't bad. The Y15 dinner at the Yunlin Hotel includes 12 different dishes, rice, tea and beer – quite a bargain. Western breakfasts are available at either hotel for around Y6.

Getting There & Away

There is a variety of options for getting to the Stone Forest. In all cases the trip takes around 3½ hours one way. If you know exactly how long you intend to stay, book return transport in advance in Kunming. It's best to take an overnight stop in the Forest for further exploration – though if you're just looking at the Forest itself then a day trip will do.

Bus The best way to get to the Stone Forest is to head down to the long-distance bus station in Kunming and buy a one-way ticket for Y13. Buses leave at 7.45 and 8 am. Alternatively, the west bus station has two buses a day, at 7.15 am and 1.30 pm. It is possible to buy return tickets here. The Kunming Hotel and Three Leaves Hotel sell tickets for tour buses to Shilin for Y20, but if you take this option you'll be stuck with a boring tour that takes in at least three caves en route (Y10 FEC entry for each); once you've pigged out on the obligatory lunch, you'll be lucky to have had two hours wandering around the forest. It's much better to buy the tickets at the long-distance bus station and leave yourself the option of staying overnight or returning the same day, as you please.

To get from the Stone Forest to Kunming, take one of the local buses leaving at 7 am and between 2.30 and 3.30 pm (check for the schedule, as it changes from time to time) from the bus parking lot. If you came in from the west bus station, return buses leave at 7.30 am and 3 pm. There are also departures at 1 pm from the Shilin Hotel. These may be pre-booked, but empty seats can usually be found due to passengers staying overnight. You could also try hitching back to Kunming from the Stone Forest.

Bus & Train The old French narrow-gauge line that runs all the way from Kunming to Hanoi (Chinese trains now terminate at Hekou near the Vietnamese border) is an interesting alternative way of getting to Shilin. Trains bound for Kaiyuan stop at the town of Yiliang, which is only 45 minutes by bus from Shilin. Stations along the way sport steep roofs and painted shutters in the French style. Train Nos 311 and 313 travel by night, arriving at midnight and 1 am respectively. A more sensible option is the No 501, which leaves at 7 am from the North Railway Station (*běi zhàn*). Buses from Yiliang are infrequent (be prepared for a wait of couple of hours), and often only go as far as Lunan, from where you will have to hitch to Shilin. There are plans to open the line all the way to Hanoi before 1997, and with the consequent increased traffic this may become a more viable route then.

LUNAN
(lùnán) 路南

Lunan is a small market town about 10 km from the Stone Forest. It's not worth making a special effort to visit, but if you do go, try and catch a market day (Wednesday or Saturday), when Lunan becomes a colossal jam of donkeys, horse carts and bicycles. The streets are packed with produce, poultry and wares, and Sani women are dressed in their finest.

To get to Lunan from the Stone Forest, head back towards Kunming and take the first major crossroads left, then the second crossroads straight on but veering to the right. You'll have to hitch a truck or hire a three-wheeler (Y3 to Y5 or some foreign cigarettes for a 20-minute ride). Plenty of trucks head that way on market day, some from the truck-stop near the Forest.

XIAGUAN
(xiàguān) 下关

Xiaguan lies at the southern tip of Erhai Lake, about 400 km west of Kunming. It was once an important staging-post on the Burma Road and is still a key centre for transport in north-west Yunnan. Xiaguan is the capital of Dali prefecture and was previously known as Dali. This confuses many travellers, who think they are already in Dali, book into a hotel and head off in pursuit of a banana pancake only to discover they haven't arrived yet. Nobody stays in Xiaguan unless they have an early bus the next morning. Walk out of the long-distance bus station when you arrive, turn left and take the first street on the left. Just up from the corner are local buses running to the real Dali – if you want to be sure, ask for dàlǐ gùchéng (Dali Old City). The trip takes 20 minutes and costs Y0.80.

Things to See
Xiaguan has developed into an industrial city specialising in tea processing, cigarette making and the production of textiles and chemicals. There is little to keep you here other than transport connections.

There are good views of the lake and mountains from **Erhai Park** (érhǎi gōngyuán). You can reach the park by boat. A larger boat runs round the lake; get details at the Xinqiao ferry terminal (xīnqiáo mǎtóu), the pier beside the new bridge.

Places to Stay
Some travellers end up staying a night in Xiaguan in order to catch an early morning bus from the long-distance bus station. If this is the case, there are three hotels close to the bus station, all much of a muchness.

Right next to the bus station is the *Keyun Hotel* (kèyùn fàndiàn). They have four-bed dorms for Y10 a bed, triples for Y15 a bed and doubles for Y36. Singles cost Y25. More upmarket singles/doubles with attached bathroom are also available at Y50/66. Turn left out of the bus station and on the far corner of the first left is the *Dali Hotel* (dàlǐ fàndiàn), which has similar rates and standards. Four-bed dorms cost Y10 a bed, while singles/doubles are Y25/36. Diagonally opposite (back towards the long-distance bus station) is the *Xiaguan Hotel* (xiàguān bīnguǎn), which is probably the most upmarket of the three. Basic triples are available for Y15 per bed and doubles with bathroom are Y70.

Getting There & Away
For the moment the only transport option available is bus, but this is all set to change. An airport is being built close to Xiaguan, and will provide air links with Kunming; a railway link with Kunming is also under construction. Xiaguan should fare well, but it remains to be seen how the small town of Dali will cope with the ensuing deluge of visitors.

Unless you're making for one of the typical traveller destinations (ie Kunming or Lijiang), you'll probably have to head into the Xiaguan long-distance bus station to organise your onward transport. There's really no point in coming here to organise a bus ticket for Kunming as there are services available from Dali itself, but for the record buses leave from 6.30 to 7 am and 6.30 to 7 pm. Prices range from Y36 for a creaking, bone-jarring ordinary bus to Y83 for a sleeper with two-tiered bunks – take your pick.

Other bus options include Baoshan for Y11.60 (seven hours; buses leave at 7, 7.30 and 11.30 am) and Mangshi (Luxi) for Y23.10 (13 hours; buses leave at 7.30 am). If you're heading into the Dehong region, it would make more sense to give Mangshi a miss and get a bus direct to Ruili – buses leave at 6.30 am, take 15 hours and cost Y29.70. The Ruili journey is not only long, it's also fairly rugged. Consider breaking the journey up by staying overnight in Baoshan.

For the interesting possibility of buses from Xiaguan to Xishuangbanna, it looks like travellers are just going to have to be patient and wait. Despite rumours to the contrary, this route is still not open. When we questioned them about it, the PSB in Kunming mumbled something about 1997 (seems to be the magical year in which everything in China is going to open up and become easy – something to do with Hong Kong?). Buses definitely run to Simao, leaving at 6.30 am, but even if you get a ticket (very unlikely) you will probably be picked up at the first checkpoint, fined, given a spanking and sent back to Xiaguan.

For Mt Jizu (Chicken-Foot Mountain) buses run to Binchuan at 7 and 8 am and at 1.40 and 2.30 pm. Buses for Lijiang (these stop in Dali to pick up passengers, and tickets can also be booked in Dali) leave at 7 and 7.30 am. Finally, it is possible to go by bus from Xiaguan to Zhongdian, though it would make far more sense to head to Lijiang first and rest up there for a couple of days. Buses leave at 6.30 and 7 am and cost Y18.40.

AROUND XIAGUAN

All of Dali prefecture is open nowadays, so you shouldn't have any problems with nasty PSB officials if you wander off the beaten track. The chief attraction for travellers is Mt Jizu, an ancient Buddhist pilgrimage site.

Mt Jizu
(jīzú shān)

Mount Jizu, or, to translate its Chinese name, Chicken-Foot Mountain, is one of China's sacred mountains and a major attraction for Buddhist pilgrims, both Chinese and Tibetan. At the time of the Qing Dynasty there were approximately 100 temples on the mountain and somewhere in the vicinity of 5000 resident monks. The Cultural Revolution's anarchic assault on the traditional past did away with much that was of interest on the mountain, though renovation work on the temples has been going on since 1979. Today, it's estimated that more than 150,000 tourists and pilgrims clamber up the mountain every year to watch the sunrise. Jinding, or the 'Golden Summit', is at a cool 3240 metres so you will need some warm clothing.

Sights along the way include the **Zhusheng Temple** (zhùshèng sì), about an hour's walk up from the bus stop at Shazhi. This is the most important temple on the mountain. **Zhongshan Temple** (zhōngshān sì), about halfway up the mountain, is a fairly recent construction and holds little of interest. Just before the last ascent is the **Huashou Gate** (huáshǒu mén). At the summit is the **Lengyan Pagoda**, a 13-tier Tang Dynasty pagoda that was restored in 1927, and some basic accommodation at the **Jinding Temple** next to the pagoda – a sleeping bag might be a good idea at this altitude.

To reach Mt Jizu from Xiaguan you should first take a bus to Binchuan, which is 70 km east of Xiaguan. Buses leave at 7 and 8 am and 1.40 and 2.30 pm. From Binchuan take another bus or minibus to the foot of mountain. If you turn up in Binchuan, the locals will probably guess your destination. During peak tourist season there may be a direct bus between Xiaguan and Shazhi, the village at the foot of Mt Jizu.

Accommodation is available at the base of the mountain, about halfway up and on the summit. A popular option for making the ascent is to hire a pony. The ponies were originally used to carry supplies up until a local hit on the idea of hiring them out to the big noses with the bulging wallets. Travellers who have done the trip claim it's a lot of fun.

Some travellers have hiked from Wase on the eastern shore of Erhai Lake to Mt Jizu. It is certainly a possibility, but it isn't recommended, and should only be undertaken by experienced hikers. Locals in Dali claim that it is easy to get lost in the mountainous terrain and in bad weather the hike could turn into a bad experience. Take care, and talk to locals in Dali about your plans before you go.

Weishan
(wēishān)

Weishan is famous for the Taoist temples on nearby Mt Weibao *(wēibǎo shān)*. There are reportedly some fine Taoist murals here. It's 61 km due south of Xiaguan so it could be done as a day trip. You might have to convince the ticket clerk at Xiaguan bus station that you are not taking this route to Xishuangbanna.

Yongping
(yǒngpíng)

Yongping is 55 km south-west of Xiaguan on the old Burma Road. The Jinguang Monastery *(jīnguāng sì)* is the attraction here.

DALI
(dàlǐ) 大理

Dali lies on the western edge of Erhai Lake at an altitude of 1900 metres, with the imposing Cangshan mountain range (average 4000 metres) behind it. The main inhabitants of the region are the Bai, who number about 1½ million according to a 1990 census.

The Bai people have long-established roots in the Erhai Lake region, being thought to have settled the area some 3000 years ago. In the early 8th century they grouped together and succeeded in defeating the Tang imperial army, establishing the Nanzhao kingdom. The kingdom held power, exerting considerable influence throughout south-west China and even, to a lesser degree, south-east Asia (the kingdom controlled upper Burma for much of the 9th century), through to the mid-13th century when it fell

before the undefeatable Mongol hordes of Kublai Khan. It was this event that brought Yunnan back into the imperial Chinese ambit.

For much of the five centuries in which Yunnan governed its own affairs, Dali was the centre of operations, and the old city still retains a historical atmosphere that is hard to come by in other parts of China. Certainly the area has become a Mecca for travellers looking for a rest from the rigours of China travel, but it's easy enough to escape the crowds on the narrow backstreets lined with old stone houses.

Basically, Dali is a perfect place to tune out for a while and forget about trains, planes and bone-jarring buses. The stunning mountain backdrop, Erhai Lake, the old city, cappuccini, pizzas and the herbal alternative (you can pick it yourself) to cheap Chinese beer make it, alongside Yangshuo, one of the few places in China where you can well and truly forget about China.

Orientation

Dali is a midget-sized city which has preserved some cobbled streets and traditional stone architecture within its old walls. Unless you are in a mad hurry (in which case use a bike), you can get your bearings just by taking a walk for an hour or so. It takes about half an hour to walk from the South Gate across town to the North Gate. Many of the sights around Dali couldn't be considered stunning on their own, but they do provide a destination towards which you can happily dawdle even if you don't arrive.

Abstract maps of Dali and the Erhai Lake area are available at the reception desks of the two hotels – there may be a third by the time you read this.

Information

PSB This is at the northern end of the block behind the No 2 Guesthouse. Previous goodwill has been overtaxed by some travellers, so this is no longer the place to get a second or third visa extension.

Money The Bank of China is in the centre of

town, at the corner of Huguo Lu and Fuxing Lu. If you've got US dollars, Dali is an excellent place to change them into RMB – there are some *very* good rates available, especially if you're prepared to haggle. The Bai women in traditional moneychanger's attire will find you – don't worry about looking for them.

Post & Telecommunications The post office is on Fuxing Lu, with the Bank of China nearby across Huguo Lu. This is the best place to make international calls. The staff are friendly and you can dial yourself – it beats spending all day getting wired on Tibetan coffee at the Tibetan Cafe while waiting for the staff to place your call.

Dali Museum
(dàlǐ bówùguǎn) 大理博物馆

This small collection of archaeological pieces relating to Bai history is nothing to get particularly excited about, but certainly worth a browse in between coffees or fruit shakes on Huguo Lu. There's an interesting permanent art exhibition at the back of the museum, featuring various artists who have leapt onto the Yunnan school of art bandwagon.

Three Pagodas
(sān tǎsì) 三塔

Standing on the hillside behind Dali, the pagodas look pretty, particularly when seen reflected in the nearby lake. They are, in fact, among the oldest standing structures in south-western China. The tallest of the three, Qianxun Pagoda, has 16 tiers that reach a height of 70 metres. It was originally erected in the mid-9th century by Xi'an engineers. It is flanked by two smaller pagodas that are 10-tiered and measure 42 metres high each.

The temple behind the pagodas, Chongsheng Temple, is laid out in the traditional Yunnanese style, with three layers of buildings lined up with a sacred peak in the background. The temple has been recently restored and converted into a museum that chronicles the history, construction and renovation of the pagodas. Also on exhibit are

marble slabs that have been cut and framed so that the patterns of the marble appear to depict landscapes.

Festivals

If you don't mind crowds, probably the best time to be in Dali is during the Third Moon Fair *(sānyuè jié)*, which begins on the 15th day of the third lunar month (usually April) and ends on the 21st day. The origins of the fair lie in its commemoration of a fabled visit by Guanyin, the Buddhist Goddess of Mercy, to the Nanzhao kingdom. Today it's more like an extra festive market, with people from all over Yunnan arriving to buy, sell, and make merry.

The Three Temples Festival *(ràosānlíng)* is held between the 23rd and 25th days of the fourth lunar month (usually May). The name of the festival refers to making a tour of three temples – and this is basically what the participants do. The first day involves a walk from Dali's South Gate to the Xizhou Shengyuan Temple at the foot of Mt Wutai. Here the walkers stay up until dawn, dancing and singing, before moving on to Jingui Temple at the shore of the Erhai Lake. The final day involves walking back to Dali by way of Majiuyi Temple.

The Torch Festival *(huǒbǎ jié)* is held on the 24th day of the sixth lunar month (usually July). Flaming torches are paraded at night through homes and fields. Other events include firework displays and dragon-boat racing.

Places to Stay

Dali's a wonderful place to visit, but the accommodation situation in both the town's hotels is dismal. It's not so much the standards – most travellers are used to these by the time they get to Dali – as the fact that the hotels are exactly what the Chinese authorities seem to think hotels should be: big, characterless, draughty institutions run by surly staff who act as though they're doing you a favour every time they unlock your door for you.

Just about everyone who makes it to Dali heads for the *No 2 Guesthouse (dìèr*

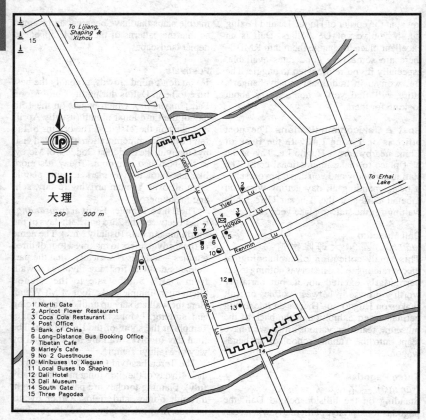

Dali 大理

0   250   500 m

To Lijiang,
Shaping &
Xizhou

To Erhai
Lake

1 North Gate
2 Apricot Flower Restaurant
3 Coca Cola Restaurant
4 Post Office
5 Bank of China
6 Long-Distance Bus Booking Office
7 Tibetan Cafe
8 Marley's Cafe
9 No 2 Guesthouse
10 Minibuses to Xiaguan
11 Local Buses to Shaping
12 Dali Hotel
13 Dali Museum
14 South Gate
15 Three Pagodas

zhāodàisuǒ) on Huguo Lu in the centre of town. It has little to recommend it: you'll need to start queuing early for the one hour or so of hot water in the evening, and the staff seem even more fed up with the place than the guests, but the rates are fairly reasonable. The rooms in a courtyard to the right of the reception are cheapest at Y8 for a bed in a dorm. Check that your door locks before you take a room there, however. These old rooms have seen better days and are not very thief-proof. In the newer section of the hotel, which was undergoing extensive, and noisy, renovations on our last visit, dorms range from Y10-12, depending on the number of beds in the room. There are also singles available for Y27, but with no bathroom.

On the last occasion on which I stayed at the No 2 Guesthouse, as usual all the foreign guests came dashing back at the magical hour of 6.30 pm for their hot shower...only to discover that the girl with the keys to their rooms had beaten them all to it and was taking a marathon, Paris-to-Dakka-rally of a shower that must have left her cleaner than a sterilised catheter. In the meantime a couple of dozen foreigners milled around outside in the hall, so tantalisingly close and yet so far from their towels, blocks of soap, rubber ducks and toothbrushes. The next day I booked into the Dali Hotel.

The *Dali Hotel (dàlǐ bīnguǎn)* on Fuxing Lu is the sole alternative to the No 1 Guesthouse, and it's not much better really. Two good things can be said about it: firstly, the staff are psychologically at an argumentative disadvantage because of the exceeding silliness of their fake Bai minority headdresses (usually held in place with a rubber band); and secondly, you have to walk for 10 minutes or so to get to the cafes on Huguo Lu – the exercise will give you the illusion of having earned your banana pancake.

The three-bed dorms at the back are a good deal at Y12 and, surprisingly, are used by very few travellers – they are in a pleasant old wooden building. Standard doubles with an attached bathroom and a TV are Y70. It's Y100 for doubles with air-con, and if you want a telephone too you'll have to pay Y120 – you can ring all around Dali with your phone (if it works): when we asked whether it was possible to use the phones for international calls they looked at us as if we had asked whether the interstellar landing pod had been installed yet.

Places to Eat
The top section of Huguo Lu, clustered around the entrance to the No 2 Guesthouse, is where most of the travellers' hang-outs are. Most of them are good value for money,

and have good food and pleasant staff, all of which are a welcome relief if you've been on the road for a while. If you're a misanthropic type and want to avoid the other travellers, you can eat with the locals in any number of Chinese restaurants around town – they are also more likely to have English menus here than in other parts of China.

It's difficult to make recommendations; as in Yangshuo restaurants wax and wane in popularity for all kinds of reasons. (Interestingly, Lisa of Lisa's restaurant, easily the most popular restaurant in Yangshuo, opened a 'branch' in Dali that at the time of writing at least had completely failed to take off.) The biggies when we were in town last were the *Tibetan Cafe*, especially for breakfast, and *Marley's Cafe* for afternoon drinks (the seats outside get the sun), the Sunday Bai minority feasts and late-night carousing.

The longest-running restaurant in town, the *Coca Cola Restaurant*, is still going strong and serving the best pizzas and Mexican food around. The Coca Cola has a book exchange and rental service (the sale prices are high to discourage people from buying the books and exhausting the library – a point that seems too complex for many travellers to grasp), and Darren (from the US) and Xiangxia, who run the place, are a mine of useful information on Dali. Getting there involves a five-minute walk down Huguo Lu, which means that it gets less crowded than a lot of the other places.

Basically, it's a good idea to move around a bit and share your patronage around. Most of the cafes have decent food and they all try hard to please. If you're a fan of Japanese food, try the *Happy Cafe* next door to the Tibetan – it serves the Japanese travellers' market and is a good place to meet wandering souls from Tokyo, Osaka and so on.

Things to Buy
Dali is famous for its marble, and while a slab of the stuff in your backpack might slow you down a bit, local entrepreneurs produce everything from ashtrays to model pagodas

YUNNAN

in small enough chunks to make it feasible to stow one or two away in your pack.

Huguo Lu has become a mini Khao San Rd in its profusion of clothes shops. It won't take you long to decide whether the clothes are for you or not – you could outfit yourself for a time-machine jaunt back to Woodstock here – but bear in mind that the shopkeepers can also make clothes to your specifications, so you're not necessarily just stuck with the flower-power ready-made stuff. Prices are very reasonable.

Most of the 'silver' jewellery sold in Dali is really brass. Occasionally it actually is silver, though this will be reflected in the starting price. The only advice worth giving, if you're in the market for this kind of thing, is to bargain hard.

Batik wall hangings have become popular in Dali. One place down from No 2 Guesthouse on Huguo Lu has a good collection, but don't believe the proprietors of the shop (a couple from somewhere in northern China) when they tell you they make the stuff themselves and start justifying the extortionate prices they charge by telling how many hours they worked on a piece. Most of the batik, as in Yangshuo, comes from Guizhou where it can be bought for a song.

Getting There & Away

Public buses stop outside the Dali Hotel on Fuxing Lu at 7.20 am, on their way from Xiaguan to Lijiang. Tickets are available at the booking office on the corner of Huguo Lu and Fuxing Lu – this place charges Y18 FEC for tickets, which is not the case in Xiaguan. It's an interesting six- to seven-hour trip with some amazing scenery en route. There's a stop for breakfast at around 9 am – dig into some of the worst Chinese food you're ever likely to come across.

Polish-made Autosan buses to Kunming leave from diagonally opposite the post office on Fuxing Lu at 6.30 am and 6 pm. The trip takes 11 hours and tickets cost Y44. The deluxe Ikarus service to Kunming leaves at 6 am and 6 pm and costs Y55. Tickets for either bus should be purchased in advance at the ticket office (corner of Fuxing Lu and

Huguo Lu), which is open from 7.30 am to 8 pm. Attempts by this office to take your FEC should be resisted – they are not authorised to do so. If you find this annoying, go to Kunming from Xiaguan, where the long-distance bus station still accepts RMB.

Minibuses to Xiaguan leave frequently (when full) during the day from the corner of Renmin Lu and Fuxing Lu. The price is Y1. Alternatively, take the public bus for Y0.80.

Getting Around

Bikes are the best way to get around. Prices average Y3 per day. The No 2 Guesthouse has the largest selection of bikes for hire – an important consideration if you're doing some long-distance cycling and you need to find a good bike.

The government-run travel service at the gate of the No 2 Guesthouse has tours to sights around Dali. When deciding whether to use this service or not you might want to consider that its introduction involved the PSB harassing the very popular independent tours running from various cafes in town. Government monopolies and squeezes on private enterprise are still alive and well in China. It might be worth checking at Marley's to see if the private tours, which included visits to remote villages, have survived.

AROUND DALI
Goddess of Mercy Temple
(guānyīn táng) 观音堂
The temple is built over a large boulder said to have been placed there by the Goddess of Mercy to block an invading enemy's advance. It is five km south of Dali.

Erhai Lake
(érhǎi hú) 洱海
The lake is a 40-minute walk from town or a 10-minute downhill zip on a bike. You can watch the large junks or the smaller boats with their queue of captive cormorants waiting on the edge of the boat for their turn to do the fishing. A ring placed round their necks stops them from guzzling the catch.

From Caicun, the lakeside village east of

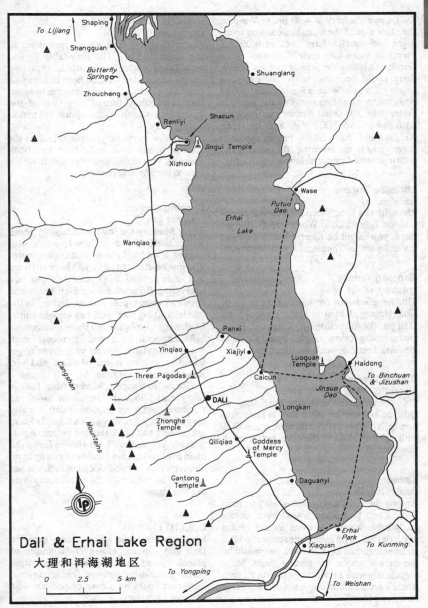

Dali & Erhai Lake Region
大理和洱海湖地区

0   2.5   5 km

Dali, there's a ferry at 4.30 pm to Wase on the other side of the lake. You can stay overnight and catch a ferry back at 6.00 am. Plenty of locals take their bikes over. Since ferries crisscross the lake at various points, there could be some scope for extended touring. Close to Wase is Putuo Island (*pǔtuó dǎo*) with the Lesser Putuo Temple (*xiǎopǔtuó sì*). Other ferries run between Longkan and Haidong, and between Xiaguan and Jinsuo Island. Ferries appear to leave early in the morning (for market) and return around 4 pm; timetables are flexible.

Zhonghe Temple
(*zhōnghé sì*)
Zhonghe is a long, steep hike up the mountainside behind Dali. When you finally get there, you might be received with a cup of tea and a smile. Then again, you might not.

Gantong Temple
(*gǎntōng sì*) 甘通寺
This temple is not far south of the town of Guanyintang, which is about six km from Dali in the direction of Xiaguan. From Guanyintang follow the path uphill for three km. Ask friendly locals for directions.

Qingbi Stream
(*qīngbì xī*) 青碧溪
This scenic picnic spot near the village of Qiliqiao is three km from Dali in the direction of Xiaguan. After hiking four km up a path running close to the river, you'll reach three ponds.

Xizhou
(*xǐzhōu*) 喜洲
Among the 101 things to do while you're in Dali, a trip to Xizhou would have to rate fairly high. It's an old town around 25 km north of Dali, with even better preserved Bai architecture than Dali. A local bus would be the easiest option for getting there, but a bicycle trip with an overnight stop in Xizhou (there's accommodation in town) would also be a good idea.

Butterfly Spring
(*húdié quán*) 蝴蝶泉
Butterfly Spring is a pleasant spot about 30 km north of Dali. The inevitable legend associated with the spring is that two lovers committed suicide here to escape a cruel king. After jumping into the bottomless pond, they turned into two of the butterflies which gather here en masse during May.

If you're energetic you could bike to the spring. Since it is only four km from Shaping, you could also combine it with a visit to the Shaping market.

Shaping Market
(*shāpíng gǎnjí*)
Every Monday the town of Shaping, about 30 km north of Dali, is host to a colourful market. It's a good place to take some snaps. The market starts to rattle and hum at 10 am and ends around 2.30 pm. You can buy everything from tobacco, melon seeds and noodles to meat, pots and wardrobes. In the ethnic clothing line, you can look at shirts, headdresses, embroidered shoes and money-belts. Expect to be quoted ridiculously high prices on anything you set your eyes on, get into a bargaining frame of mind, and you should have a good time.

Getting to Shaping Market from Dali is fairly easy. Both the hotels in town run minibuses out there on market day. Usually they leave at 9 pm, though it's a good idea to ask around and book the day before. Alternatively you can walk up Huguo Lu to the main road and catch a local bus from up here, although bear in mind that market day is not going to be the ideal time to take a spin on the local buses.

DALI TO LIJIANG
Most travellers take a direct route between Dali and Lijiang. However, a couple of places visited by Chinese tourists might make interesting detours for foreigners. Transport could be a case of potluck with buses or hitching.

Jianchuan

(jiànchūan) 剑川

This town is 92 km north of Dali on the Dali-Lijiang road. Approaching from the direction of Dali, you'll come to the small village of Diannan about eight km before Jianchuan. At Diannan, a small road branches south-west from the main road and passes through the village of Shaxi (23 km from the junction). Close to this village are the Shibaoshan Grottoes *(shíbǎoshān shíkù)*. There are three temple groups: Stone Bell *(shízhōng)*, Lion Pass *(shīzi guān)* and Shadeng Village *(shādēng cūn)*.

Heqing

(hèqìng) 鹤庆

About 46 km south of Lijiang, Heqing is on the road which joins the main Dali-Lijiang road just above Erhai Lake at Dengchuan. In the centre of town is the Yunhe Pavilion, a wooden structure built during the Ming Dynasty.

LIJIANG

(lìjiāng) 丽江

North of Dali, bordering Tibet, is the town of Lijiang with its spectacular mountain backdrop. Lijiang is the base of the Naxi (also spelt Nakhi and Nahi) minority, who number about 278,000 in Yunnan and Sichuan. The Naxi are descended from Tibetan nomads and lived until recently in a matriarchal society. Women still seem to run the show, certainly in the old part of Lijiang.

The Naxi matriarchs maintained their hold over the men with flexible arrangements for love affairs. The *azhu* (friend) system allowed a couple to become lovers without setting up joint residence. Both partners would continue to live in their respective homes; the boyfriend would spend the nights at his girlfriend's house but return to live and work at his mother's house during the day. Any children born to the couple belonged to the woman, who was responsible for bringing them up. The father provided support, but once the relationship was over, so was the support. Children lived with their mothers; no special effort was made to recognise paternity. Women inherited all property, and disputes were adjudicated by female elders. The matriarchal system

appears to have survived around Yongning, north of Lijiang.

There are strong matriarchal influences in the Naxi language. Nouns enlarge their meaning when the word for 'female' is added; conversely, the addition of the word for 'male' will decrease the meaning. For example, 'stone' plus 'female' conveys the idea of a boulder; 'stone' plus 'male' conveys the idea of a pebble.

Naxi women wear blue blouses and trousers covered by blue or black aprons. The T-shaped, traditional cape not only stops the basket always worn on the back from chafing, but also symbolises the heavens. Day and night are represented by the light and dark halves of the cape; seven embroidered circles symbolise the stars. The sun and moon used to be depicted with two larger circles, but these have gone out of fashion.

The Naxi created a written language over 1000 years ago using an extraordinary system of pictographs. The most famous Naxi text is the Dongba classic in 500 volumes. Dongba were Naxi shamans who were caretakers of the written language and mediators between the Naxi and the spirit world. The Dongba religion eventually absorbed itself into an amalgam of Lamaist Buddhism, Islam and Taoism. The Tibetan origins of the Naxi are confirmed by references in Naxi literature to Lake Manasarovar and Mt Kailas, both in Western Tibet.

Yunnan was a hunting ground for famous foreign plant-hunters such as Kingdon Ward, Forrest and Joseph Rock. Joseph Rock, an Austro-American, lived almost continuously in Lijiang between 1922 and 1949. Rock is still remembered by some locals. A man of quick and violent temper, he required a special chair to accommodate his corpulent frame. He burdened his large caravans with a gold dinner service and a collapsible bathtub from Abercrombie & Fitch. He also wrote a definitive guide to Hawaiian flora before devoting the rest of his life to researching Naxi culture and collecting the flora of the region.

The Ancient Nakhi Kingdom of Southwest China (Harvard University Press, 1947) is Joseph Rock's definitive work; the two volumes are heavy-duty reading. For a lighter treatment of the man and his work, take a look at *In China's Border Provinces: The Turbulent Career of Joseph Rock, Botanist-Explorer* by J B Sutton (Hastings House, 1974).

Another venerable work on Lijiang worth reading if you can find it is *The Forgotten Kingdom* by Peter Goulart (John Murray Co, 1955). Goulart was a White Russian who studied Naxi culture and lived in Lijiang from 1940 to 1949.

Orientation

Lijiang is a small town in a beautiful valley. The main attractions are in the surrounding area, so use a bike to get out of town to the mountains, where you can hike around. You may need time to acclimatise to the height (2400 metres).

Your initial response when you pull into the new bus station and start the long trudge up to the square might be 'Get me out of here!' First impressions of Lijiang are likely to be of an underwhelming, dusty Chinese town, especially if you've just come from Dali. It's not until you get into the old town – a delightful maze of cobbled streets, rickety old wooden buildings, gushing canals and the hurly-burly of market life – that you realise Lijiang is more than a boring Chinese urban sprawl in the middle of nowhere. The approximate line of division is Lion Hill, the bump in the middle of town that's topped by a radio mast. Everything west of the hill is the new town, and everything east of the hill is the old town.

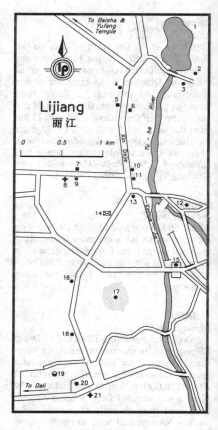

Information

Information is available at the foreigner cafes on Mao Square.

The PSB is opposite the Lijiang Guesthouse, though some travellers have also been sent up to another office next to the north bus station. There seems to be no problem extending visas in Lijiang.

The Bank of China is on Xin Dajie almost opposite the intersection of the road that leads off to the Lijiang Hotel and the PSB. It is now possible to change travellers' cheques there.

Old Town

Crisscrossed by canals and a maze of narrow streets, the old town is not to be missed. Arrive by mid-morning to see the market square full of Naxi women in traditional dress. Parrots and plants adorn the front porches, old women sell griddle cakes in front of tea shops, men walk past with hunting falcons proudly keeping balance on their gloved fists, more old women energetically slam down the trumps on a card table

1	Black Dragon Pool Park
2	Shop & Dongba Museum
3	Dongba Research Institute
4	Yunling Theatre
5	No 2 Guesthouse & North Bus Station
6	Mao Statue
7	Lijiang Guesthouse
8	Hospital
9	PSB
10	Bank of China
11	Xinhua Bookstore
12	Naxi Musical Performances
13	Cinema
14	Post Office
15	Market Square
16	Bicycle Hire
17	Radio Mast
18	Sports Ground
19	Long-Distance Bus Station
20	Yunshan Hotel
21	Country Hospital

1	黑龙潭公园
2	商店/东巴博物馆
3	东巴研究所
4	云岭剧场
5	第二招待所
6	毛主席广场
7	丽江宾馆
8	门诊所
9	二公安局
10	中国银行
11	新华书店
12	纳西音乐
13	电影院
14	邮电局
15	四出街
16	出租单车
17	狮子山
18	体育场
19	长途汽车站
20	云杉饭店
21	县医

in the middle of the street. You can buy embroidery and lengths of striped cloth in shops around the market.

Above the old town is a beautiful park which can be reached on the path leading past the radio antenna. Sit on the slope in the early morning and watch the mist clearing as the old town comes to life.

Black Dragon Pool Park
(hēilóngtán gōngyuán) 黑龙潭公园

The park is on the northern edge of town. Apart from strolling around the pool, you can visit the Dongba Research Institute, which is part of a renovated complex on the hillside. There is a museum here, but you will have to pay Y2 to have a guide show you around, and her explanations are in Chinese. At the far side of the pond are renovated buildings used for an art exhibition, a pavilion with its own bridge across the water and the Ming Dynasty Wufeng Temple. Entry to the park costs Y1.

Museum of Naxi Culture

Mr Xuan Ke, a Naxi scholar who spent 20 years in labour camps following the suppres-

sion of the Hundred Flowers movement, has turned his family Lijiang home into a small repository for Naxi and Lijiang cultural items. Besides clothing and musical instruments (including an original Persian lute that has been used in Naxi music for centuries), his home displays Dr Joseph Rock's large, handmade furniture and has a small library of out-of-print books on Lijiang. Dr Rock was a close family friend.

Xuan Ke speaks English and is always willing to discuss his original ideas about world culture (for example, that music and dance originated as rites of exorcism). His home is in the old town, around the corner from the No 40 Restaurant.

Festivals

The 13th day of the third moon (late March or early April) is the traditional day to hold a Fertility Festival (why not?).

July brings Huoba Jie *(huǒbǎ jié)*, the Torch Festival also celebrated by the Bai in the Dali region. The origin of this festival can be traced back to the intrigues of the Nanzhao kingdom, when the wife of a man the king did away with in a fire eluded the romantic entreaties of the same king by leaping into a fire.

Places to Stay

The first place you'll come across when you arrive in town is the *Yunshan Hotel (yúnshān fàndiàn)*, also known as the *No 3 Guesthouse*, next to the new bus station. If it wasn't for its slightly inconvenient location in a boring part of town, it would undoubtedly be the best place to stay in Lijiang – unless you are really pinching the pennies, in which case go straight to the No 2 Guesthouse. The Yunshan has beds in a four-bed dorm for Y6; three-bed dorms are Y8 with B&W TV and Y15 with colour TV, and there are very comfortable two-bed dorms with attached bathroom for Y20.

The very basic *No 2 Guesthouse (dièr zhāodàisuǒ)* next to the old north bus station is the budget option, with hard dorm beds for Y6. Beds in doubles are Y10 per person with shared bathroom or Y22 per person with private bathroom. The upmarket dorm beds are over in the west wing, and will set you back Y8 a night. Threats of an airport have led to a flurry of hotel construction work in Lijiang, and the No 2 Guesthouse, determined not to miss out on the action, is doing its own bit for China's foreign currency reserves. By the time you have this book in your hands the new wing will have opened, with rooms ranging in price from Y40 to Y100.

The *Lijiang Guesthouse (No 1 Hotel) (dìyī zhāodàisuǒ)* has more comfortable four-bed dorms for Y10 per bed; triples are also available for Y28 a bed with bathroom and Y12 without. A double without bathroom costs Y28, double with bathroom Y72. The hotel has two blocks; the one at the back is deluxe. The Hotel Service Bureau is on your left when you come out of the lobby. This is the place to ask about hiring a vehicle, and you might like to look at the excellent map on their wall. Next door to the Service Bureau is the shower room – ask at the reception desk for the precise opening time. To the right of the showers, a few doors down, is the bike depot.

Places to Eat

Like Dali, Lijiang has a legion of small, family-operated restaurants catering to the fantasies of China backpackers. Kitchens are tiny and waits are long (if one of the ubiquitous Dutch tour groups is in town, forget it), but the food is usually interesting. There are always several 'Naxi' items on the menu, including the famous 'Naxi omelette' and 'Naxi sandwich' (goat cheese, tomato and fried egg between two pieces of local baba flatbread). Try locally produced *yinjiu*, a lychee-based wine with a 500-year history – it tastes like a decent semi-sweet sherry.

Mao Square Most people stumble across the restaurants lining Mao Square first. *Peter's*, run by Crystal, a former opera diva, distinguishes itself as far and away the most popular of the foreigner restaurants here. Whether this will remain the case is difficult to say as Crystal and her Alaskan husband, Tom, were off to Alaska, leaving the restaurant in the hands of Crystal's family. *Ma Ma Hu* and *Salvadore's* are two other restaurants on the square that deserve more custom than they get: good food, friendly people – don't be intimidated into not eating elsewhere if you ate first at Peter's. Incidentally, Peter's has opened a *Peter's 2* next door to the new bus station, a venture that seems destined for failure: it's in a dismal location, and the cafe itself is fairly dismal too.

Old Town There are also some great places to eat in the old part of town. *Mimi's Cafe* comes up tops for its friendly service and wonderful atmosphere. When you turn into the old quarter you'll see English signs advertising it and the *No 40 Restaurant*. Service is slow at the latter, but they have a great room upstairs which kind of makes the wait worthwhile. Also in the old part of town, look out for *Kele* on the opposite side of the canal; it's run by a friendly young Naxi woman.

Other Elsewhere around Lijiang and off the travellers' circuit look out for places serving *baba*, the Lijiang local specialty – thick flatbreads of wheat, served plain or stuffed with meats, vegetable or sweets. Morning is the best time to check out the baba selection. In the old town, you can buy baba from street vendors. Close to the cinema is a place which serves only baba, noodles and *doujiang*, the standard soya bean drink – a very inexpensive and filling breakfast. There are several smaller restaurants just before the entrance to the Black Dragon Lake Park. Xin Dajie has several pastry shops.

Entertainment

One of the few things you can do in the evening in Lijiang is attend performances of the Naxi orchestra. Performances are held nightly in a beautiful old building just inside the old town, usually from 7.30 to 9.30 pm. What's distinctive about the group is not only that all 16 to 18 members are Naxis, but that they play a type of Taoist temple music that has been lost elsewhere in China. The pieces they perform are supposedly faithful renditions of music from the Han, Song and Tang dynasties, played on original instruments (in most of China such instruments didn't survive the Communist revolution). This is a very rare chance to hear Chinese music as it must have sounded in classical China. Xuan Ke usually speaks for the group at performances, explaining each musical piece and describing the instruments. There are taped recordings of the music available for Y10.

You can usually turn up on your own and watch a performance, though no-one will assist you in this endeavour – the cafes and the hotels seem to be united in keeping the location of the venue a secret, probably so that they can take you there personally and earn a cut of the takings. Check the Lijiang map for its rough coordinates and listen for the twangings of mysterious instruments as you grope your way up the alley in the darkness.

There are plans to hold musical performances at the Yunling Theatre next to the No 2 Guesthouse. Ask around to see if they have come to fruition.

Getting There & Away

The bus situation in Lijiang is complicated by the existence of two bus stations. If you're staying up at the Lijiang Hotel or the No 2 Guesthouse, check to see what's on offer at the north bus station before making the long trek down to the new bus station. Be warned: sometimes the north bus station sells tickets for buses running from the new bus station. There should be a connecting bus from the north station if this is the case, but it would be a good idea to check – ask at one of the cafes on Mao Square if you're really confused.

Buses for Dali can be booked at the north station even though they come into the new station from the other direction. They leave at 7 and 11 am, take around six hours and cost Y18. The other most popular options are the Kunming and Jinjiang (for rail connections with Chengdu) bus services from the new long-distance bus station in the south of town. Buses for Kunming leave at 7 am (Y40), or at 7 pm (Y58 or Y82); the latter is a sleeper. Jinjiang buses leave at 7 am which, failing a major breakdown (not in *China*) will allow you to connect with the 6.30 pm train to Chengdu (Y28, arriving around 10 am next morning). Unless current policy changes, it is not possible for foreigners to book tickets of any kind for the train here, though Chinese can book hard-seat tickets. Reason: so that the railways can try and rip you off for a Y240 FEC soft sleeper to Chengdu. During the rainy season (July to September), the Lijiang-Jinjiang road is often washed out and Chengdu-bound travellers have no alternative but to return to Kunming to catch a train or plane onward.

Other buses from the south long-distance bus station include those to Zhongdian (Y12.90), Daju (Y4.80) and Qiaotou (Y2.10).

Getting Around

The modern part of town is a tedious place to walk around. The old town, however, is best seen on foot. Bike hire is readily available around town – at the Mao square, at the hotels and down near the long-distance bus station.

Lijiang (nicknamed 'Land of Horses') is famous for its easily trained horses, which are usually white or chestnut with distinctive white stripes on the back. It might be possible to arrange an excursion on horseback.

AROUND LIJIANG
Monasteries

Lijiang's monasteries are Tibetan in origin and belong to the Red Hat sect. Most of them were extensively damaged during the Cultural Revolution and there's not much monastic activity to be seen nowadays. Nevertheless, most of them are worth hopping on a bicycle and heading out of town for a look.

Puji Monastery (*pǔjí sì*) Around five km north-west of town (on a trail that passes the two ponds to the north of town) are a few monks at the Puji Monastery who are usually happy to show the occasional stray traveller around.

Yufeng Monastery (*yùfēng sì*) This small lamasery is on a hillside about five km past the town of Baisha. The last three km of the track require a steep climb. If you decide to leave your bike at the foot of the hill, don't leave it too close to the village below – the local kids have been known to let the air out of the tyres!

The monastery sits at the foot of Mt Yulongxue and was established in 1756. The monastery's main attraction nowadays is the 'camellia tree of 10,000 blossoms' (*wànduǒ shānchá*). Ten thousand might be something of an exaggeration, but locals claim that the tree produces at least 4000 between February and April. A monk on the grounds risked his life to keep the tree secretly watered during the years of the Cultural Revolution.

Fuguo Monastery (*fùguó sì*) Also not far from Baisha village, this was once the largest of Lijiang's monasteries. In the monastery compound look out for the Hufa Hall; the interior walls have some interesting frescoes (see the Frescoes section).

Wenbi Monastery (*wénbǐ sì*) The Wenbi Monastery involves a fairly steep uphill ride to the south-west of Lijiang. The monastery itself is not that interesting, but there are some good views and pleasant walks in the near vicinity.

Frescoes

Lijiang is famed for its temple frescoes. Most travellers are probably not going to want to spend a week or so traipsing around seeking them out, but it may be worth checking out one or two of them. For the most part the frescoes were carried out during the 15th and 16th centuries by Tibetan, Naxi, Bai and Han artists. Many of them were subsequently restored during the later Qing Dynasty. They depict variously Taoist, and Chinese and Tibetan Buddhist themes and can be found on the interior walls of temples in the area. The best example is said by experts to be the fresco in Baisha's Dabaoji Hall.

To find examples of the frescoes, in Baisha ask around for the **Dabaoji Hall** (*dàbǎojī gōng*), the **Liuli Temple** (*liúlí diàn*) or the **Dading Pavilion** (*dàdìng gé*). In the nearby village of Longquan (*lóngquán*) frescoes can also be found on the interior walls of the **Dajue Temple** (*dàjué gōng*). See the preceding Fuguo Monastery entry for further frescoes.

Baisha
(*báishā*) 白沙

Baisha is a small village on the plain north of Lijiang in the vicinity of several old temples (see the preceding Frescoes section). Before Kublai Khan made it part of his Yuan Empire (1279-1368), it was the capital of the Naxi kingdom. It's hardly changed since then and though at first sight it seems nothing more than a desultory collection of dirt roads and stone houses, it offers a close-up glimpse of Naxi culture for those willing to spend some time nosing around.

The star attraction of Baisha will probably

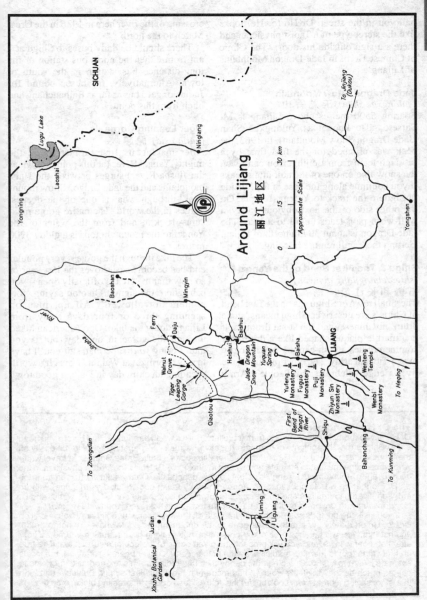

Around Lijiang
丽江地区

SICHUAN

To Jinjiang
(Dukou)

Lugu Lake

Yongning

Laoshai

Ninglang

Yongshen

Approximate Scale

0   15   30 km

Jinsha River

Baoshan

Mingyin

Ferry

Daju

Baishui

Heishui

Jade Dragon
Snow Mountain

Yuquan
Spring

Baisha

LIJIANG

Wenteng
Temple

Walnut
Grove

Tiger
Leaping
Gorge

Yufeng
Monastery

Fuguo
Monastery

Puji
Monastery

To Heping

Qiaotou

Zhiyun Sin
Monastery

Wenbi
Monastery

To Zhongdian

First
Bend of
Yangzi
River

Shigu

Baihanchang

To Kunming

Judian

Liming
Liguang

Xinzha Botanical
Garden

hail you in the street. Dr Ho (or He) looks like the stereotype of a Taoist physician and there's a sign outside his door: 'The Clinic of Chinese Herbs in Jade-Dragon Mountains of Lijiang'.

Jade Dragon Snow Mountain
(yùlóngxuě shān) 玉龙雪山

Soaring 5500 metres above Lijiang is Mt Satseto, also known as Yulongxue Shan (Jade Dragon Snow Mountain). In 1963, the peak was climbed for the first time by a research team from Beijing. You can reach the snow line on one of the adjoining peaks if you continue along the base of the hillside but ignore the track to Yufeng Temple. On the other side of the next obvious valley, a well-worn path leads uphill to a lake. The Jade Dragon is about 30 km north of Lijian. Getting there will require hitching.

Shigu & The First Bend of the Yangzi
(shígǔ/chángjiāng dìyīwān)
石鼓和长江第一湾

The small town of Shigu sits on the first bend of China's greatest river. Shigu means 'stone drum' in Chinese, and the stone drum itself is a marble plaque shaped like a drum that commemorates a 16th-century Naxi victory over a Tibetan army. The other plaque on the river's edge celebrates the People's Army

crossing of the river here in 1936 in the Great March to the north.

There should be daily buses to Shigu at 7 am from either the north bus station or the long-distance bus station in the south of town. Alternatively, try buses bound for Judian or get a bus as far as Baihanchang and hitch from this point.

Tiger Leaping Gorge
(hǔtiào xiá) 虎越峡

After making its first turn at Shigu the mighty Yangzi River (at this point known as the Jinsha River) surges between the Haba mountains and the Jade Dragon Snow mountains, through what is one of the deepest gorges in the world. The entire gorge measures 16 km, and from the water of the Yangzi to the mountain tops is a giddy 3900 metres.

The hike through the gorge is very popular and has become easier over the last year or so now that the area is officially open – you can ignore the sign at Qiaotou saying 'foreigners not allowed'. All up, plan on spending three or four days away from Lijiang doing the hike. One American hiked through the gorge in one day, but if you didn't bring *your* superman suit you'll have to stay overnight at Walnut Grove. It's worth spending an extra day in Daju, a good town

---

The Dr Ho Phenomenon

Dr Ho gets extremely mixed reports from travellers, but it's worth bearing in mind before you head out to Baisha that the majority of them are negative: words like 'charlatan' seem to roll easily off the tongue after a visit. It's not entirely the venerable doctor's fault. Bruce Chatwin, a travel writer who was among the first to stumble across and mythologise Dr Ho as the 'Taoist physician in the Jade-Dragon Mountains of Lijiang', is at least partly responsible. Chatwin did such a romantic job on Dr Ho that he was to subsequently appear in every travel book (including this one) with an entry on Lijiang; journalists and photographers turned up from every corner of the world; and Dr Ho, previously an unknown doctor in an unknown town, had achieved worldwide renown.

If you visit, the doctor's son Baisha will drag you off the street for your obligatory house-call on Dr Ho. Unfortunately the attention has gone to the doctor's head somewhat – try not to hold it against him. You will be shown as many press clippings proving his international fame as your attention span allows, and you will probably be given some of the doctor's special tea. The true market value (not to mention medicinal value) of this tea has never been ascertained, but locals estimate Y0.20 to Y0.50. Dr Ho has the canny trick of handing out his tea and asking guests to pay as much as they think it's worth. It has made him the wealthiest soul in Baisha – although this is not saying a great deal. Look out for the John Cleese quote: 'Interesting bloke; crap tea'. ∎

to poke around in with a great place to stay in the Tiger Leaping Gorge Hotel.

Hiking Through the Gorge The first thing to do is to check with Peter's or Mimi's cafes (or wherever is now the hip place to hang out) for the latest gossip on the mini trek, particularly the transport side of things, which is where problems arise. It's difficult to recommend which end of the gorge to start at (Qiaotou or Daju), but we will say this: while finishing at Qiaotou has the advantage of easier transport links back to Lijiang, you should consider the fact that, even if you have to wait a day or two for a bus to Lijiang from Daju, there are much worse places to hang around for a couple of days.

Ideally you should do the walk in two days. From Qiaotou walk north from the China Hotel, which is where the bus from Lijiang drops you off and where you'll stay overnight if you came in on the 1 pm bus. Cross the bridge, turn right and you are on the Tiger Leaping Gorge trail. A six- to eight-hour walk will bring you to the small town of Walnut Grove. This is the approximate halfway point, and there are two hotels nestled among the walnuts. At the moment the *Summer Mountain Spring Guesthouse*, which has beds for Y2, is the best of the two, but remember that things change – take a look at the alternatives. Food and beer are also available here, though not bottled water; bring your own.

The next day's walk is slightly shorter at four to six hours. The first two or three hours should bring you to a plateau that is more or less opposite Daju. The trail divides here and you should be careful to take the steep path leading up to a village. From here there is a path that descends down to the ferry.

The ferry and its sinister Neanderthal cave-dwelling helmsman were, until recently when the ferry crossing price was regulated at Y5, collectively the much-cursed bane of Tiger Leaping Gorge trekkers. The last instalment in the saga was that a party of Dutch travellers put together a petition signed by various injured parties to the effect that the ferryman was a petty crook. The petition was lodged at the Kunming and Lijiang PSB, so there's always the possibility he

has been publicly shot and that river crossings are now executed without the assistance of a ferry...or, better still, by a peaceable old ferryman with a sincere conviction in the moral justice of equal fares for foreigners and Chinese alike...but it's unlikely.

From the ferry drop-off point to Daju is a fairly straightforward walk to the south. The Tiger Leaping Gorge Hotel, Daju's premiere vacationer's residence, costs Y2.5 a bed and is on the left-hand side as you walk southward out of town; it's about 600-700 metres from the department store. It has good food and is a good place to hang out for at least a day. If you're doing the walk the other way round and heading for Qiaotou, walk north through town, aiming for the white pagoda at the foot of the mountains.

Warning Many travellers have become sick on the Tiger Leaping Gorge trek. It's probably a good idea to bring your own bottled water.

Getting There & Away Buses run to Qiaotou daily from the south long-distance bus station in Lijiang at 1 pm for Y5.50 (the No 2 shuttle bus runs from the north station at 12.45 pm to connect with it), and theoretically minibuses run every second day from Daju back to Lijiang for Y10. The Jade Dragon Mountain Travel Service in Daju will charge you Y20 for the same ticket. Doing it in reverse is possible: check in the foreigner cafes for details of the Daju minibus service or alternatively check at the north bus station, which has a bus service every five days.

Lugu Lake
(lúgŭ hú) 泸沽湖
This remote lake overlaps the Yunnan-Sichuan border and is a centre for several Tibetan, Yi and Mosu (a Naxi subgroup) villages. The Mosu still practise matriarchy, and many of the Naxi customs now lost in Lijiang are still in evidence here. The lake itself is fairly high at 2685 metres and is usually snowbound over the winter months. Several islands on the lake can be visited by

dugout canoe, which can be rented for Y3 to Y4 per day. Twelve km west of the lake is **Yongning Monastery** *(yŏngníng sì)*, a lamasery with at least 20 lamas in residence.

Places to Stay & Eat When you arrive at Lugu Lake there are three hotels in the vicinity of the bus drop-off point. None of them are places you are likely to remember fondly in years to come. They all charge between Y3 and Y5 for a bed in a double, and there are no showers. Food is available, but is recommended only as a buffer against malnutrition – little fish, potatoes and eggs are the order of the day.

A popular option with travellers is the Tibetan-style lodge about ½ km in the direction of Yongning. Look for a red Chinese sign next to a shop, turn right and follow the path through some fields. Beds here are Y8 – it's slightly more expensive than the other places, but at least it has some character. There's also food and beer (you'll need the beer if you're going to eat the food) available in the lodge.

Finally, there is also a guesthouse in Yongning, which makes a good base from which to hike out to the nearby hot spring *(wēnquán)*. The guesthouse is the tallest building in town and easily sought out.

Getting There & Away From Lijiang it's a nine-hour bus trip to Ninglang, the Lugu County seat. There are at least three places to stay in town, though most people stay at the Government Guesthouse, with beds for Y12. From Ninglang it's another four or five hours by bus to Lugu Lake. There are two bus stations on the main street quite close to one another. Check in both for the next bus to Lugu. There is also an English speaker in the Government Guesthouse who is usually happy to provide information.

Some travellers have tried hiking from Yongning on to Muli in Sichuan Province, from where there is bus transport to Xichang on the Kunming-Chengdu line. But be warned: it's a dangerous route with no accommodation. You'll need to bring a tent, a warm sleeping bag and all your own pro-

visions. There's also no reason to expect the Tibetan tribespeople (all armed) you come across en route to be friendly either. One Canadian traveller we met had a frightening experience with locals while hiking this route and headed back to Yongning. Most travellers head back to Lijiang the same way they came.

ZHONGDIAN
(zhōngdiàn) 中甸

Located 198 km north-west of Lijiang, Zhongdian was officially opened on 1 December 1992. It's likely to become a popular destination for more hardy travellers looking at a rough five- or six-day journey to Chengdu through Tibetan townships and rugged mountain terrain, or for those looking to slip into Tibet by the back door. There are rumours that the Yunnan route into Tibet will open up in coming years, but it is unlikely, given the dangers of the route.

Whether it is worth a trip in itself is a difficult question. If you don't have time to make it into Tibet, Zhongdian, a principally Tibetan town with a heavy Han overlay and a sprinkling of Bai, Hui (Muslim) and Naxi, is worth taking a look at. It's perhaps worth visiting in combination with the Tiger Leaping Gorge trek. Start at Daju and then take a bus from Qiaotou at the end of the trek to Zhongdian. The bus journey from Qiaotou takes only three or four hours.

Zhongdian is at 3200 metres and very close to the Tibetan border. About an hour's walk from town to the north is the Jietang Songlin Monastery *(jiétáng sōnglín sì)*, a major Tibetan monastery complex with several hundred monks.

Places to Stay & Eat
It gets cold in Zhongdian, particularly between November and March, and the only place in town that supplies electric blankets is the *Yongsheng Hotel (yŏngshēng fàndiàn)*. Dorm beds here cost Y8 to Y10. Next to the bus station is the *Transport Hostel (jiāotōng zhāodàisuǒ)* where you can get a bed for Y5. If these are full, try the *Agricultural Implements Hostel (nóngjù zhāodàisuǒ)*, which

deserves full marks for its imaginative name at least. Beds here are Y5. There is also a hotel next to the post office with singles and doubles at very reasonable prices.

Up in the north of town are some Sichuan-style restaurants and a little place cranking out pretty good dumplings. South of the bus station, just before the post office you can find a state-run restaurant, as well as a Tibetan and Naxi restaurant. Be wary of hotpot meals – numerous travellers have been ripped off by locals charging ridiculous sums. Check the price of everything when you order.

Getting There & Away

Buses for Zhongdian leave daily from Lijiang's south long-distance bus station and take six to seven hours. Another alternative is to travel from Xiaguan, from where buses leave daily at 7 and 7.30 am and take around 11 hours. There are also several buses a day from Qiaotou, at the southern end of the Tiger Leaping Gorge trek. Finally, you can head straight to Zhongdian from Kunming, a 1½-day bus ordeal that might appeal to the certifiably insane.

Onward travel from Zhongdian offers some interesting possibilities. The one that is no longer illegal is the arduous bus-hopping trek to Chengdu, in Sichuan. If you're up for this you're looking at minimum of five to six days' travel at some very high altitudes – you'll need warm clothes. The first stage of the trip is Zhongdian to Derong (*déróng*) just over the Sichuan border, a journey of around seven hours; from Derong head for Xiangcheng (*xiāngchéng*) (six hours) and from here on to Daocheng (*dàochéng*) (four hours) or straight to Litang (*lǐtáng*) (10 hours), although you may be forced to stay overnight in Daocheng. From Litang it's 12 hours to Kangding (*kāngdìng*) and another 12 hours on to Chengdu. Accommodation on the way is rough and your fellow passengers are likely to be chain-smoking phlegm removalists whose idea of fun is leaving the windows open and letting the sub-zero mountain breezes ruffle their hair. Have fun!

The other destination from Zhongdian is Tibet and, who knows, by the time you have this book in your hands the miraculous may have occurred and this route may be open – don't count on it, though. For more information on this route see the Road Routes section of the Tibet chapter.

AROUND ZHONGDIAN

There are probably numerous as yet unexplored possibilities for trips out of Zhongdian. At present the two most popular options are **Baishui Tai** (*báishuǐ tái*) and **Mt Meilixue** (*méilǐxuě shān*). The former is a limestone deposit plateau 108 km to the south-east of Zhongdian with some breathtaking scenery and Tibetan villages en route. Mt Meilixue straddles the Yunnan Tibetan border, and at 6740 metres rates as Yunnan's highest peak. Getting to the mountain can be a problem in the winter months. If you are planning to head to Mt Meilixue, try and combine it with a visit to Deqin (*déqīn*), the last major town before the mountain. There is an important Tibetan monastery here. Reports indicate that it is closed to foreigners, but this is probably set to change now that Zhongdian is open.

Getting There & Away

Transport to sights around Zhongdian are still pretty touch and go. If it is possible to rustle up a group of travellers with similar interests, there are jeeps and minibuses for hire for Y250 to Y350 per day.

JINJIANG

(*jīnjiāng*) 金江

Jinjiang is the tiny railhead for the large town of Panzhihua, just over the border in Sichuan Province.

Accommodation in this jolly little hamlet is provided courtesy of various fleapits, the most convenient of which for hassling for tickets is the *Railway Hotel* (*tiělù lǚxíngshè*). It's directly opposite the railway station; beds in a clean triple cost Y8, Y5.5 in a four-bed room and Y12.20 in a double. Make an effort to get on a train before you book in anywhere.

For travellers Jinjiang is an important

junction for the Lijiang-Chengdu route. To reach Jinjiang from Chengdu, one of the better trains is the No 85/84 which leaves Chengdu at 7.05 pm and reaches Jinjiang at 10.32 am the next day. This will give you time to get to Lijiang without having to stay overnight in Jinjiang. A hard sleeper for this trip costs Y116. At Jinjiang station the minibus drivers are likely to assault you in droves for the trip to Lijiang – you shouldn't pay more than Y20 for a ticket.

Travelling in the other direction, from Lijiang to Chengdu, you can forget about getting train tickets of any kind before you get to Jinjiang. The bus station in Lijiang won't sell them to you and there doesn't seem to be a black market for them either. To make matters worse this is a busy line and even the hard-seat tickets get booked out from time to time. Most travellers coming in from Lijiang on the morning bus make it in time to connect with the No 86/83 to Chengdu departing at 6.32 pm. If you want anything other than a hard seat, look for the entrance to the toilet to the right of the inquiries booth, turn left into the door just in front of the toilet (remember, this is China), and to the back of the courtyard on the right-hand side is an office selling hard-sleeper (Y116) and soft-sleeper (Y240) tickets. If you miss the 6.32 pm train, there are other trains to Chengdu at 8.55 pm and 2.15 am. If you stay overnight in Jinjiang (highly unrecommended) the first train the next day leaves at 2.30 pm.

XISHUANGBANNA REGION
(xīshuāngbǎnnà) 西双版纳

The region of Xishuangbanna is in the deep south of Yunnan Province, next to the Myanmar and Laotian borders. The name Xishuangbanna is a Chinese approximation of the original Thai name, *Sip Sawng Panna* (12 rice-growing districts). Xishuangbanna Dai Autonomous Prefecture, as it is known officially, is subdivided into the three counties of Jinghong, Menghai and Mengla. Mengla County is still closed to foreign tourists at present and permits seem to be a bit

hit or miss, though they can be applied for at the PSB office in Jinghong.

Theoretically, all of Xishuangbanna, with the exception of Mengla, is open to foreign travellers, but this doesn't stop the PSB pulling over the occasional foreigner on a remote stretch of road and fining them. Travel permits in this part of the world are just a scam – if you get one, take a look at the Destinations entry...it's almost always left blank. But when it comes down to it, a travel permit, at Y20, is cheaper than a fine, which is normally Y50.

About half the 650,000-strong population of this region are Dai; another 25% or so are Han Chinese and the rest are a hotchpotch of minorities which includes the Miao, Zhuang, Yao and lesser-known hill tribes such as the Aini, Jinuo, Bulang, Lahu and Wa.

The Dai people are concentrated in this pocket of Yunnan and exercise a clear upper hand in the economy of Xishuangbanna. During the Cultural Revolution many Dai people simply voted with their feet and slipped across the border to join their fellow Dai who are sprinkled throughout Thailand, Laos, Myanmar and Vietnam. Not only the Dai but also most of the other minorities in these areas display a nonchalant disregard for borders and authority in general.

The Dai are Buddhists who were driven

Yao minority person

Xishuangbanna
西双版纳

0   25   50 km

Approximate Scale

To Simao

Zhengnuo

Mengyang

Bajiao Ting

Jinghong   Mangjao

Gasa

Menghai   Nannuoshan   Manfeilong

Jinuo

Menglun

Ganlaba
(Menghan)

Jingbo

Lancang

(Mekong)

River

Luosuo

River

YUNNAN

Xiaojie

Damenglong

M Y A N M A R
(B U R M A)

Mekong River

southwards by the Mongol invasion of the 13th century. The Dai state of Xishuang-banna was annexed by the Mongols and then by the Chinese, and a Chinese governor was installed in the regional capital of Jinglan (present-day Jinghong). Countless Buddhist temples were built in the early days of the Dai state and now lie in the jungles in ruins. During the Cultural Revolution Xishuang-banna's temples were desecrated and destroyed. Some were saved by being used as granaries, but many are now being rebuilt from scratch. Temples are also recovering their role, with or without official blessing,

as village schools where young children are accepted for religious training as monks.

To keep themselves off the damp earth in the tropical rainforest weather, the Dai live in spacious wooden houses raised on stilts in the classic style, with the pigs and chickens below. The common dress for Dai women is a straw hat or towel-wrap headdress; a tight, short blouse in a bright colour; and a printed sarong with a belt of silver links. Some Dai men tattoo their bodies with animal designs. Betel-nut chewing is popular and many Dai youngsters get their teeth capped with gold; otherwise they are considered ugly.

Ethnolinguistically, the Dai are part of the

very large Thai family that includes the Siamese, Lao, Shan, Thai Dam and Ahom peoples found scattered throughout the river valleys of Thailand, Myanmar, Laos, north Vietnam and Assam. The Xishuangbanna Dai are broken into four subgroups, the Shui Dai, Han Dai, Huayai Dai and Kemu Dai, each distinguished by variations in costume. All speak the Dai language, which is quite similar to Lao and northern Thai dialects. In fact Thai is as useful as Chinese once you get off the beaten track a little, and you might have fun with a Thai phrasebook (Lonely Planet produces one). The written language of the Dais employs a script which looks like a cross between Lao and Burmese.

Like Hainan Island, Xishuangbanna is home to many unique species of plant and animal life. Unfortunately, recent scientific studies have demonstrated the devastating effect of previous government policies on land use; the tropical rainforest areas of Hainan and Xishuangbanna are now as acutely endangered as similar rainforest areas elsewhere on the planet. The jungle areas that remain still contain dwindling numbers of wild elephants (200), tigers, leopards and also golden-haired monkeys. The Tropical Institute in Jinghong has gardens with a limited selection of plants, which give an idea of the spectacular plant life in the deep forests, but foreign visitors are not welcome.

In recent years Xishuangbanna has become China's own mini-Thailand, and the Han Chinese tourists have been heading down in droves for the sunshine, Dai minority dancing, water splashing festivals (held daily nowadays), and other typical elements of Chinese tourist culture such as the 'forest of one tree', the 'king of tea trees' and other trees that suggest something less prosaic than a mere tree.

Xishuangbanna has wet and dry seasons. The wet season is between June and August, when it rains ferociously almost every day. From September to February there is less rainfall but thick fog descends during the late evening and doesn't lift until 10 am or even later at the height of winter. Between May and August there are frequent and spectacular thunderstorms.

Between November and March temperatures average about 19°C. The hottest months of the year are from April to September, when you can expect an average of 25°C.

Festivals

Festivals celebrated by the Dai attract hordes of foreigners and Han Chinese. The Water-Splashing Festival held around mid-April (usually 13-15 April) washes away the dirt, sorrow and demons of the old year and brings in the happiness of the new. The first day of the festival is devoted to a giant market. The second day features dragon-boat racing (races in Jinghong are held on the Mekong River below the bridge), swimming races and rocket-launching. The third day features the water-splashing freakout – be prepared to get drenched all day by the locals. In the evenings there is dancing, launching of hot-air paper balloons and game-playing.

The festivities attract loads of tourists, so all the planes will be booked out, but the bus may be an alternative. Hotels in Jinghong town are booked solid, but you could stay in a nearby Dai village and commute. Festivities take place all over Xishuangbanna, so you might be lucky further away from Jinghong.

During the Tanpa Festival in February, young boys are sent to the local temple for initiation as novice monks. At approximately the same time (between February and March), Tan Jing Festival participants honour Buddhist texts housed in local temples.

The Tan Ta Festival is held during the last 10-day period of October or November, with temple ceremonies, rocket launches from special towers and hot-air balloons. The rockets, which often contain lucky amulets, blast off with a curious droning sound like mini-space shuttles before exploding high above; those who find the amulets are assured of good luck.

The farming season (from July to October) is the time for the Closed-Door Festival, when marriages or festivals are banned. Traditionally, this is also the time of year that men aged 20 or older ordain as monks for a period of time. The season ends with the Open-Door Festival, when everyone lets their hair down again to celebrate the harvest.

SIMAO
(*sīmáo*) 思茅

Simao, an uninteresting little town, used to be Xishuangbanna's air link with the outside world. Nowadays Jinghong has its own airport and very few travellers stop here. True, the occasional traveller flies from Kunming to Simao and does the final leg to Jinghong by bus, but it's doubtful whether it's worth the effort really. The scenery between Simao and Jinghong is not exactly a Sumatran jungle, and if you're travelling further afield from Jinghong you'll get to see plenty of Xishuangbannan scenery anyway.

Getting There & Away
Air The CAAC office (☎ 2234) is just off the main street at the northern corner of Hongqi Square. It's open from 8 to 11 am and from 2.30 to 5.30 pm; it's closed on Saturday afternoon and on Sunday.

When the airport is operative, there are flights between Kunming and Simao. The fare is Y240 and flights depart three days a week.

Bus It's almost unheard of for travellers to go to Simao by bus, though most pass through briefly on the way from Kunming to Jinghong or vice versa. There are buses from Simao to Baoshan and Xiaguan, but this route is still off limits for foreigners. Checkpoints are frequent on this road, and you're unlikely to get through without detection.

JINGHONG
(*jǐnghóng*) 景洪

Jinghong, the capital of Xishuangbanna prefecture, lies beside the Lancang River (Mekong River). It's a sleepy town with streets lined with palms, which help mask the Chinese-built concrete boxes until they merge with the stilt-houses in the surrounding villages. It doesn't have much to keep you beyond a couple of days. It's more a base for operations than a place to hang out, though it's not without a certain laid-back charm.

Information
CITS The travel service (☎ 2708) is on the Banna Hotel grounds opposite reception (enter via the stairs on the left). The staff are friendly, but unless you're prepared to fork out for a guided tour there's not much they can do for you. Renting a vehicle has become very expensive (around US$100 a day for a car), and with the advent of the Chinese tourism phenomenon, vehicles have come into short supply anyway.

PSB This is opposite Peacock Park in the centre of town. It's hard not to get the feeling that they are making it all up as they go along here – they'd probably sell you a permit for the coffee shop in the Kunming Holiday Inn if you were stupid enough to go in and ask for one. Try them for permits for Mengla.

Money The Bank of China is on Jinghong Xilu opposite the post office. Load up on RMB before you leave for Xishuangbanna, as there's not much demand for FEC (except at the Banna Hotel, where they smile and say 'FEC only'), and certainly no black market.

Post & Telecommunications The post office is in the centre of town on the intersection of Jinghong west and south roads (Xilu and Beilu). In fact, you should make your phone calls before you get to Xishuangbanna. There are only six lines out of Jinghong, and they are always busy. There are three international phone booths at the Banna hotel, but you could probably count the number of times international calls have ever been successfully placed from them on the fingers of one hand.

Chunhuan Park
(*chūnhuān gōngyuán*) 春欢公园

Chunhuan Park, in the south of Jinghong

YUNNAN

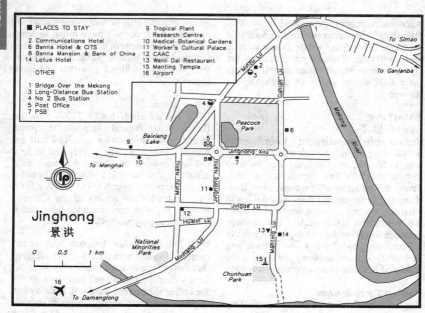

■ **PLACES TO STAY**

2 Communications Hotel
6 Banna Hotel & CITS
8 Banna Mansion & Bank of China
14 Lotus Hotel

OTHER

1 Bridge Over the Mekong
3 Long-Distance Bus Station
4 No 2 Bus Station
5 Post Office
7 PSB

9 Tropical Plant Research Centre
10 Medical Botanical Gardens
11 Worker's Cultural Palace
12 CAAC
13 Wanli Dai Restaurant
15 Manting Temple
16 Airport

Jinghong
景洪

0   0.5   1 km

To Simao
To Ganlanba
To Menghai
To Damenglong

Peacock Park
Baixiang Lake
Jinghong Xilu
Jingde Lu
Hualin Lu
National Minorities Park
Chunhuan Park
Mirzu Lu
Ganlan Lu
Mekong River
Minzu Nanlu
Jinghong Nanlu
Minnang Lu
Manting Lu

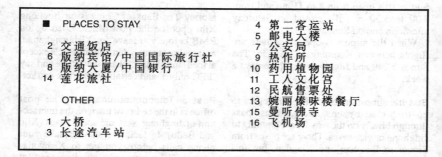

■ **PLACES TO STAY**

2 交通饭店
6 版纳宾馆/中国国际旅行社
8 版纳大厦/中国银行
14 莲花旅社

OTHER

1 大桥
3 长途汽车站

4 第二客运站
5 邮电大楼
7 公安局
9 热作所
10 药用人文化园
11 工人文化物园宫
12 民航
13 婉丽傣味楼餐厅
15 曼听佛寺
16 飞机场

down past the Dai restaurants, is a fairly poor excuse for an outing. Don't encourage them by paying the Y5 foreigner's price entry; follow the real travellers and continue past the legit entrance, turn right around the park and sneak in this way. The park contains a couple of replica stupas, Dai dancing girls (you'll probably get to see a water-splashing festival – now held daily by popular demand

– if you hang around) and a pitiful elephant in chains. Just before you get to the park entrance is the **Manting Temple** *(mántīng fósì)*. It's claimed to date back 1100 years.

Tropical Plant Research Institute
(rèzuòsuǒ) 热带植物研究所
This is a short bicycle ride out of town. Very few foreigners bother visiting it, which is not

particularly surprising, because there's very little to see unless you hook up with a CITS tour and get into the inner sanctum. The grounds are pleasant enough, however, and make for a scenic five-minute bicycle ride. Look out for the coffee shop that serves great Banna coffee. A little way back towards town and on the opposite side of the road is the **Medicinal Botanical Gardens in Xishuangbanna**. Staff at the gate might try to deter you from entering by telling you it's boring. It's not a trick to keep you out...they're telling the truth.

Peacock Lake
(gănlán bà) 孔雀湖

This artificial lake in the centre of town isn't much but the small park next to it is pleasant. There's also a zoo, but the animals in the zoo are so ferociously baited by onlookers that you can't help feeling depressed by it. The gibbons just sit in their cage with no escape from the jabbing; one ape finally pulled the stick away from its attacker, then threw up its arms and grimaced in perfect imitation of its tormentor. There's a sad bear in a tiny cage, giant salamanders and a pair of huge pythons.

The English Language Corner takes place here every Sunday evening, so this is your chance to exchange views or practise your English with the locals.

Workers' Cultural Palace
(gōngrén wénhuàgōng) 工人文化宫

Evening dances are staged here. Several travellers have raved about the Dance of the Peacock, a traditional Dai dance sometimes staged for visiting dignitaries here or at the Banna Hotel. You might be able to ferret out details from the Banna Hotel reception desk or CITS.

National Minorities Park
(mínzú fēngqíng yuán) 民族风情园

If you come in to Jinghong by plane, you'll pass this place on the way in to town. It's not that far south of the CAAC booking office. On the map of Jinghong provided by the Banna Hotel bicycle hire service it's myste-

riously referred to as the 'Minority Flirtation Expression'. Intrigued? If so, head down on Wednesday or Saturday when, from 7 to 11 pm, there are minority dances and so on. If you don't have a bike, buses run from in front of the long-distance bus station at 7 pm.

Bridge Over the Mekong
(mǐgòng qiáo) 湄公桥

The bridge is no technical wonder, and the views of the river from it are not even that good – but it's there and it is a bridge over the Mekong after all. If rumour is correct, there was an attempt some years ago by a member of a disaffected minority to blow up the bridge. Jinghong is such a splendidly torpid town, it's hard to imagine the excitement. The no-photography rule has been dropped.

Places to Stay

The *Banna Hotel (bǎnnà bīnguǎn)* in the centre of town used to be one of those exceedingly rare Chinese hotels that travellers reminisced about after they had left. Not any more. The Bamboo House, which is where the dorms are, is still a nice spot to lounge in the shade of the surrounding palms, but the views of the Mekong have been swallowed up by the hotel extensions. A bed in the Bamboo House is Y10, while damp doubles with attached bathroom and no air-con are Y45. Air-con doubles are Y100-120, but these rooms in newly constructed annexes to the back of the hotel are falling apart already.

If you're in the market for real basic accommodation with a Dai flavour head down to Manting Lu. It's a long walk from the bus station (around 25 minutes), in the south of town. There are two places here that have been invaded by backpackers: the first is the *Wanli Dai Restaurant (wǎnlì dàiwèilóu cāntīng)* with beds in a triple for Y4 (bathing Dai style with a bucket); and the second is the *Lotus Hotel*, which has doubles with bathroom for Y8 and without for Y6. Unfortunately, the latter is often full. There is no hot water available in either of the Dai hotels;

if this is one of your basic needs you'll have to head up to the Banna Hotel.

There are a couple of other accommodation options that are for the most part neglected by travellers, mainly because they lack atmosphere. The *Communications Hotel (jiāotōng fàndiàn)*, next to the long-distance bus station, has some very good mid-range rooms and cheap dorms. Beds in a four-bed room range from Y6 to Y10, while clean doubles with bathroom and TV cost Y35. There are also upmarket singles available for Y50 that compare favourably with rooms at the Banna Hotel that go for Y100.

Finally, right in the heart of town, the *Banna Mansion (bǎnnà dàshà)* has doubles with air-con and the works for Y88, and triples for Y102. It tends to pick up the overflow when the Banna Hotel is full.

Places to Eat

The 'in' place to eat is the *Wanli Dai Restaurant (wǎnlì dàiwèilóu cāntīng)*, which also has the cheapest accommodation in town. They rarely have anything available at lunchtime, but come evenings this place probably has the best food in all of China. Try their roast fish, eel or roast beef cooked with lemon grass or served with peanut-and-tomato sauce. Vegetarians can order roast bamboo shoot prepared in the same fashion – sublime. Other mouthwatering specialties include fried river moss (sounds rather unappetising but is excellent with beer) and spicy bamboo-shoot soup. Don't forget to try the black glutinous rice. The upstairs balcony is a pleasant place to sit with a beer in the winter and read about the sub-zero temperatures in Beijing.

Actually, the whole of Manting Lu is lined with Dai restaurants, but it seems as if the Westerners have marked the Wanli (particularly the upstairs veranda) as their own and left the rest for the busloads of Chinese tourists who come in every evening. The restaurant next door to the Wanli has live Dai dance performances every evening.

Elsewhere around town is pretty much standard Chinese fare. Walk up from Manting Lu and turn left in the direction of the CAAC booking office and you will find a host of tiny Chinese restaurants; most of them are pretty good for lunch. Next to the bus station there are also some good restaurants – look out for the place specialising in dumplings.

Street markets sell coconuts, bananas, papayas, pomelos (a type of grapefruit), and pineapples. The pineapples, served peeled on a stick, are probably the best in China. The covered market near the Banna Hotel is at its busiest in the morning.

Getting There & Away

Air More flights and bigger planes (737s) mean that it's a lot easier to fly to Jinghong from Kunming than it used to be. It's often even possible to book the day before. In April (Water-Splashing Festival), allow for at least a few days' advance booking, however, as this is a very popular time for Chinese to visit. Flights to Jinghong (Banna) are daily and cost Y340 from Kunming. Flights back are also daily and can be booked at the CAAC booking office in Jinghong. Check at the Banna Hotel reception counter for ticket prices, as tickets are occasionally sold here to foreigners for local prices – a saving of around Y100. The flight takes 50 minutes.

Bus There are daily buses from Kunming to Jinghong. Buses booked at the Three Leaves Hotel cost Y44, leave at 6.40 am and arrive around 4.30 pm the next day (there is an overnight stop on the way). Buses from the main Kunming bus station cost Y45 or Y50, the latter offering a little more legroom. Buses leave at 7.20 am and 7.45 am, and arrive in Jinghong the next day an hour or so later than the buses from the Three Leaves Hotel. Buses back to Kunming are available from the Banna Hotel (you're more likely to have foreign company on the bus if you book here) or from the long-distance bus station. Shock-horror, rattle and shake monsters also run from the No 2 bus station, the downmarket option for real travellers.

If you're torn between the bus and the plane, don't let other travellers give you any crap about missing the scenery on the flight.

There are some good views from the bus window, but nothing that won't stop you nodding off to sleep and certainly nothing much that will make you sit up and decide that the 24 hours of inhaling second-hand smoke and bouncing up and down on a hard seat were worth it.

The towns usually selected by the bus driver for overnight stays along the route are Tongguan and Mojiang. Both have basic transit hotels next to their bus terminals that cost only Y5 for a bed, but there's always a mad scramble for bed assignments among passengers at the reception desk. In Tongguan, you can avoid the crowds by slipping out the back of the large transit hotel to a smaller guesthouse on a hillside. In Mojiang there are a couple of hotels just around the corner from the transit hotel/bus terminal with double rooms for Y10.

In Jinghong buses leave from two locations. The long-distance bus station has buses running to towns around Xishuangbanna, but it is mainly useful for more distant destinations. The best place to get out of Jinghong and explore other parts of Xishuangbanna is the No 2 bus station. Apart from the obvious Kunming option, for which there are numerous buses running through the day from 6 am, the long-distance bus station also has buses running to Baoshan and Xiaguan – which would be interesting if the PSB would let you take them. For buses around Xishuangbanna, the best advice is to head down to the No 2 bus station earlyish and ask around. There are no real timetables. Most of the buses that run locally from the long-distance bus station call in at the No 2 bus station to pick up extra passengers, so you'll get something one way or another.

Getting Around

The Banna Hotel hires out bikes for Y5 a day, and there's a place across the road that is cheaper at Y3. The bikes from the Banna Hotel are better, however.

CITS run a number of tours around Xishuangbanna from their little office at the Banna Hotel. The tours tend to be expensive, but they suit travellers who are on a rushed itinerary and who can't afford the time lost mucking about with public transport. There is a three-day tour that takes in almost all of the region.

AROUND JINGHONG

The possibilities for day trips and longer excursions out of Jinghong are endless. Some travellers have hiked and hitched from Menghai to Damenglong, some have cycled up to Menghai and Mengzhe on mountain bikes (it's almost impossible on bikes without gears), and one French photographer hitched up with a local medicine man and spent seven days doing house calls in the jungle.

Obviously, it's the longer trips that allow you to escape the hordes of Han Chinese tourists and get a feel for what Xishuangbanna is about. But even with limited time there are some interesting possibilities. Probably the best is an overnight (or several nights) stay in Ganlanba (also known as Menghan). It's only around 27 km from Jinghong, and not that hard to cycle to, even on a local bike. The trip takes around two hours or so.

Most other destinations in Xishuangbanna are only two or three hours away by bus, but generally they are not much in themselves – you need to get out and about. Xishuangbanna is one place where you really need a bike, or at the very least some sturdy hiking boots.

Nearby Villages

Before heading further afield, there are numerous villages in the vicinity of Jinghong that can be reached by bicycle. Most of them are the kind of places you happen upon by chance, and it's difficult to make recommendations. On the other side of the Mekong are some small villages, and a popular jaunt involves heading off down Manting Lu – if you go far enough you'll hit a ferry crossing point on the Mekong. There are also villages in this area, and many travellers have been invited into Dai homes for tea and snacks.

Mengyang

(měngyáng) 勐养

Mengyang is 34 km east of Jinghong on the road to Simao. It's a centre for the Hani, Lahu and Floral-Belt Dai. Chinese tourists stop here to see a banyan tree shaped like an elephant.

From Mengyang it's another 19 km to Jinuo, which is home base for the Jinuo minority. Travellers have reported that the Jinuo are unfriendly, so you'll probably have to stay in Mengyang. Some minorities dislike tourists, and if this is the case with the Jinuo they should be left alone.

The Jinuo, sometimes known as the Youle, were officially 'discovered' as a minority in 1979. The women wear a white cowl, a cotton tunic with bright horizontal stripes, and a tubular black skirt. Ear-lobe decoration is an elaborate custom – the larger the hole and the more flowers it can contain the better. The teeth are sometimes painted black with the sap of the lacquer tree, which serves the dual dental purpose of beautifying the mouth and preventing tooth decay or halitosis. Previously, the Jinuo lived in long houses with as many as 27 families occupying rooms on either side of the central corridor. Each family had its own hearth, but the oldest man owned the largest hearth, which was the first at the door. Long houses are rarely used now and it looks like the Jinuo are quickly losing their distinctive way of life.

Ganlanba (Menghan)

(gānlánbà) 橄榄坝

Ganlanba, or Menghan as it's sometimes referred to, lies on the Mekong south-east of Jinghong. In the past the main attraction of Ganlanba was the boat journey down the Mekong from Jinghong. Improved roads sank the popular boat trip (locals prefer to spend an hour on a bus to three hours on the boat), and the only way to travel down the river now is to charter a boat at special tourist prices – at least Y300 FEC.

Nevertheless, Ganlanba remains a wonderful retreat from hectic Jinghong. The town itself is fairly forgettable, but if you come on a bike (it is also possible to hire one in Ganlanba) there is plenty of scope for exploration in the neighbourhood. Check the visitors' book in the Dai Bamboo House for some ideas.

Places to Stay The family-run *Dai Bamboo House* is a house on stilts with a dorm for Y5 per bed and small doubles for Y12; all beds are on the floor in the traditional Dai style. The friendly family serves Dai food on tiny lacquered tables. A previous Japanese guest has drawn a map of the surrounding area to assist with exploration. It's a favourite with everyone who stays here (the only negative comment in the visitors' book was by a Chinese person from Nanjing), and many people end up staying longer than they had intended. It's on the right-hand side (heading away from Jinghong) of the main road that runs through town.

Getting There & Away Now that the boat is gone, it's either bus or bicycle. Buses cost Y4.70 and take just over an hour – which is ridiculous when you consider it's less than 30 km away from Jinghong. It's possible to cycle the distance in a brisk two hours or a leisurely three hours, and it's a pleasant enough ride.

Getting Around The only way to do this is by bicycle or hiking. If you didn't bring your own bike, take the lane next to the Dai Bamboo House and follow it down towards the river. After passing through a small market area you'll reach another main road. On the right hand corner is a bicycle repair shop run by an old man from Sichuan – he has bicycles for hire for Y5 a day.

Around Ganlanba

The stately Wat Ban Suan Men, south-west of town, is said to be 730 years old and is one of the best surviving examples of Dai temple architecture in Yunnan. Follow the road closest to the Mekong southwards out of town and then take a path that follows the river. Check at the Dai Bamboo House for information before you leave.

There are numerous temples and villages in the area that are worth exploring. There's an old decaying temple on the road into town from Jinghong, and to the south of this, overlooking the Mekong, is a white stupa. Most travellers who have spent any time here recommend striking off aimlessly on day trips and seeing what you turn up.

Menglun

(měnglún) 勐仑

Menglun is the next major port of call east of Ganlanba. There's no problem heading over here (you might apply for a permit to be on the safe side), but onward travel might attract the vigilant eye of the Xishuangbanna PSB.

The major attraction for Chinese visitors is the **Menglun Tropical Gardens**. At the time of writing, there was a lot of construction work going on in and around the gardens, which meant that the hotel here was not a very peaceful place to stay. It looks like the authorities plan to turn Menglun into an upmarket tourist attraction, which means it will probably become less of an attractive proposition for solo travellers. The tropical gardens have a Y10 entry fee, and the hotel in the gardens has clean doubles for Y42.

Getting There & Away Four buses a day leave from the main street of Ganlanba to Menglun between 7.30 and 8.30 am. Buses also leave from Jinghong's long-distance bus station at 9 am for Y6.80. Some travellers have also cycled here from Ganlanba. Cycling onwards to Mengla was not recommended at the time of writing because of the PSB. A permit for Mengla should make a difference, but it's hard to say.

Damenglong

(dà měnglóng) 大勐龙

Damenglong is about 70 km south of Jinghong and a few km from the Myanmar border. It's another sleepy village that serves well enough as a base for hikes around the surrounding hills. It's also one of those places where, after three hours of bouncing up and down in a terminally ill bus, you arrive, thinking 'Is this *it*?' The village is not much (it rouses itself somewhat for the Sunday market), but the surrounding countryside, peppered with decaying stupas and little villages, is worth a couple of days' exploration. Unfortunately there's no bicycle hire in town.

Manfeilong Pagoda *(mánfēilóng tǎ)* This pagoda, built in 1204, is Damenglong's premiere attraction. According to legend, the temple was built on the spot of a hallowed footprint left by Sakyamuni, who once visited Xishuangbanna – if you're interested in ancient footprints you can look for it in a niche below one of the nine stupas. Unfortunately, in recent years a 'beautification' job has been done on the temple with a couple of cans of silver paint – it probably sounded like a good idea at the time, but now that the paint has started to flake off it creates a very tacky effect.

If you're in Xishuangbanna in late October or early November, check for the precise dates of the Tan Ta festival. Manfeilong Pagoda is host to hundreds of locals at this time in celebrations that include dancing, rockets, paper balloons and so on.

Manfeilong is easy to get to; just walk back along the main road towards Jinghong for two km until you reach a small village with a temple on your left. From here there's a path up the hill; it's about 20 minutes' walk.

Black Pagoda Just down from the stone mythical beasts that have mysteriously set up camp in the centre of town is a Dai monastery with a path beside it leading up to the Black Pagoda. The pagoda itself is not black at all – it's covered in flaking silver paint. Take a stroll up, but bear in mind that the real reason for the climb is less the pagoda itself than the superb views of Damenglong and the surrounding countryside.

Places to Stay & Eat The officially sanctioned foreigners' residence is the depressing *Damenglong Guesthouse (dàměnglóng zhàodàisuǒ)*. To get there, take the first right down the hill from the bus station and walk up the end of the road to the local government building. The hotel is in the grounds to the left, just past some ornamental frogs. Basic dorm beds are Y6, and that's all the manager (a chronic drunk – hang on to your receipts for the room because he'll claim you didn't pay) is prepared to give foreigners. The toilets and washing facilities are at the back beside a slimy reservoir that looks like it might be harbouring the *Blob*.

The food situation in Damenglong is OK. Just down from the bus station on the right are a couple of decent restaurants. The Chinese signs proclaim them to be Dai restaurants, but it's the old story of going out the back, pointing to your vegies and getting them five minutes later in a little pool of oil.

Just down from the monastery is Damenglong's trendy veranda restaurant: *Restaurant Bueno Vista – good Dai food*. Actually all the words are joined together on the sign, which makes it a little difficult to make out at first. It's a good place to hang out, and the food's not bad. Spare a thought for the hip youngsters lounging around here, three long days from the cosmopolitan, happening city of Kunming.

Getting There & Away There are frequent buses to Damenglong (Y5, 2½ hours) from the No 2 bus station in Jinghong, although it's best to get to the station between 7 and 8 am. Buses for the return trip leave the Damenglong bus station early in the morning and at 1, 2 and 4 pm.

Around Damenglong

The village of Xiaojie, about 15 km before Damenglong, is surrounded by Bulang, Lahu and Hani villages. Lahu women shave their heads; apparently the younger Lahu women aren't happy about this any more and use caps to hide their shaven heads. The Bulang are possibly descended from the Lolo in northern Yunnan. The women wear black turbans with silver decorations; many of the designs are of shells, fish and marine life.

There's plenty of room for exploration in this area, although you're not allowed over the border.

Menghai

(ménghǎi) 勐海

This uninspiring place serves as a centre for trips into the surrounding area. Perched on top of a nearby hill is an atrocious loudspeaker system which pounds the hapless inhabitants with distorted noise. The Sunday market attracts members of the hill tribes and the best way to find it is to follow the early-morning crowds. This is the only time when the town shows signs of life other than the dogs, chickens, pigs and cows cruising the street. There are a couple of drab hotels (Y3 per bed); one is at the main bus station.

Buses and minibuses run from the No 2 bus station in Jinghong to Menghai approximately every hour; the fare is Y3.80 and the trip takes about 90 minutes. Minibuses to Jinghong, Menghun and Jingzhen leave from a minibus centre in Menghai, about one km down the street from the main bus station.

Menghun

(ménghùn) 勐混

This tiny village is about 26 km south-west of Menghai. The Sunday market here begins buzzing around 7 am and lingers on through to noon. The swirl of hill tribes and women sporting fancy leggings, headdresses, earrings and bracelets alone makes the trip worthwhile. Although the market seems to be the main attraction, a temple and footpaths that wind through the lush hills behind the White Tower Hotel are also worth an extra day or two.

Places to Stay & Eat The *Phoenix Hotel* *(fènghuáng fàndiàn)* is very noisy and better off given a miss. It may close down soon anyway. The more secluded *White Tower Hotel* (through the archway to the right of the bus stop) is roomier and quieter; doubles here cost Y8. There are several good Dai restaurants along the main street, including the popular *Bienvenue*.

Getting There & Away Buses from Jinghong to Menghun are very infrequent, though there is at least one a day from the long-distance bus station for Y5.50 in the afternoon. It has a habit of sitting around at the station for half an hour after it's due to leave and then repeating the process five minutes down the road at the No 2 bus station. An alternative option is to catch one of the frequent minibuses from the minibus centre in Menghai for Y3 (45 minutes).

Unless you have a very good bike with gears, cycling to Menghai and Menghun is not a real option. The road up to Menghai is so steep that you'll end up pushing the bike most of the way. Coming back would be fun however.

Intrepid travellers have hitched and hiked all the way from here to Damenglong. This should be no problem, providing you don't inadvertently stray over the Myanmar border at some point. A mountain bike would be the best way to do it. Hitching and walking should take a leisurely seven days.

Jingzhen
(*jǐngzhen*) 景真

In the village of Jingzhen, about 14 km north-west of Menghai, is the **Octagonal Pavilion** (*bājiǎo tíng*), first built in 1701. The original structure was severely damaged during the Cultural Revolution, so the present renovated building isn't exactly thrilling. Take a close look at the new paintings on the wall of the temple. There are some interesting scenes which appear to depict People's Liberation Army (PLA) soldiers causing death and destruction during the Cultural Revolution; adjoining scenes depict Buddha vanquishing PLA soldiers, one of whom is waving goodbye as he drowns in a pond.

Jingzhen is a pleasant rural spot for walks along the river or the fishponds behind the village. Frequent minibuses from the minibus centre in Menghai go via Jingzhen.

Nanluoshan
(*nánluóshān*) 南罗山

Nanluoshan is on the road between Jinghong and Menghai (17 km from Menghai). It's best done as a day trip from Menghai, providing you start early and return to the main road before dusk. The bus will drop you off close to a bridge; cross the bridge and follow the dirt track about six km uphill until you join a newly constructed main road.

About one km before the junction, you'll round a bend in the road and see a fence with a stile and stone benches beyond. This is the turn-off for the steps down to the overrated **King of Tea Trees** (*cháwáng*) – the name says it all! According to the Hani, their ancestors have been growing tea for 55 generations and this tree was the first one planted. The tree is definitely not worth descending hundreds of steps to see; it is half-dead and covered with moss, graffiti and signs forbidding graffiti. A crumbling concrete pavilion daubed with red paint completes the picture.

The new highway has been bulldozed out of the mountain for the comfort of tourists who can now visit the hill tribes further up the mountain. When we were there, the Hani and Lahu villagers were quite friendly. Repeated exposure to tour buses is certain to cause changes. If you leave the main road, there's some pleasant hiking in the area, but don't expect villagers to automatically give you a bed for the night. A Hani villager did invite us into his stilt house for an excellent meal and some firewater that left us wobbling downhill.

The Hani (also known in adjacent countries as the Akha) are of Tibetan origin but according to folklore they are descended from frogs' eyes. They stick to the hills, cultivating rice, corn and the occasional poppy. Trading takes place at weekly markets where the Dai obviously dominate the Hani, who seem only too keen to scamper back to their mountain retreats. Hani women wear headdresses of beads, feathers, coins and silver rings. At one remote market the women were very nervous and it was only when their backs were turned that I could inspect their headdresses, which were constructed with French (Vietnamese), Burmese and Indian coins from the turn of the century.

BAOSHAN REGION
(*bǎoshān dìqū*) 保山地区

Travellers who pass through the Baoshan area tend to do so quickly, generally staying overnight in Baoshan city on the way to Ruili and Wanding, but the area is worth a bit more time than that. There are some worthwhile historical sights, the old quarters of Tengchong and Baoshan make for some good browsing, as in other parts of southern Yunnan distinctive minority groups are in abundance, and the Tengchong area is rich in volcanic activity, with hot springs and volcanic peaks.

As early as the 4th and 5th centuries BC (two centuries before the northern routes through central Asia were established), the Baoshan area was an important stage on the southern Silk Road – the Sichuan-India route. The area did not really come under Chinese control until the time of the Han Dynasty when, in 69 AD, it was named the Yongchang Administrative District.

Baoshan
(bǎoshān) 保山
Baoshan is a small city that's easily explored on foot. There are pockets of traditional wooden architecture still standing in the city area and some good walks in the outskirts of town. It has innumerable specialty products that range from excellent coffee to leather boots and pepper and silk. Tea aficionados

might like to try the Reclining Buddha Baoshan Tea, a brand of national repute.

Information Baoshan is not exactly geared up for a large-scale invasion of foreign visitors, and little in the way of information is available for the place. There's an information booth in the long-distance bus station, where they dispense free Chinese maps. Otherwise, try the travel agency opposite the traffic hotel on Huancheng Donglu. Some English is spoken here and the place is run by friendly staff. The China Bank is next to the Yindou Hotel, and the post office is centrally located not far away.

Things to See Baoshan is an interesting city to wander aimlessly in. The streets are lively and, in many areas, lined with old traditional homes. The major sight within easy walking distance of the centre of town is **Taibao Park** *(tàibǎo gōngyuán)*. It's flanked to the south

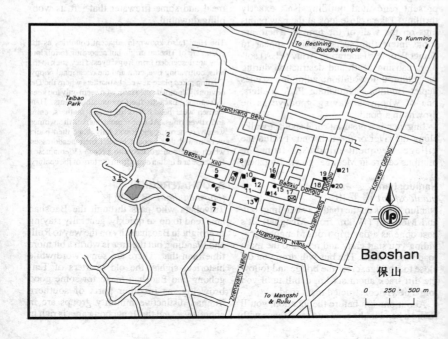

Baoshan
保山

0   250   500 m

by the **Wenbi Pagoda** (*wénbĭ tă*) and to the east by the **Yuhuang Pavilion** (*yùhuáng gé*). All three are worth a look. The Yuhuang Pavilion dates back to the Ming Dynasty and has a small museum next door to it. The small viewing pagodas in the park provide good views of Baoshan, the Wenbi Pagoda and Yiluo Pond. There are paths in the park striking off to the north, west and south. The northern path doubles back to the south eventually and takes you past a very mediocre zoo (keep walking). Continuing to the south you will reach **Yiluo Pond** (*yìluó chí*), also known as the Dragon Spring Pond (*lóngquán chí*). The best thing about the latter are the views of the 13-tiered Wenbi Pagoda.

Places to Stay There are plenty of inexpensive places to stay in Baoshan. Right next to the bus station is the *Traffic Hotel* (*kèyùn zhùsùbù*), which has beds in a clean three-bed dorm for Y10 and in a four-bed dorm for Y7. Another good place with similar rates is the *Lanyuan Hotel* (*lányuàn dàjiǔjiā*), which is two or three minutes down from the bus station on the other side of the road.

Along Baoxiu Xilu are a few sprawling Chinese-style hotels. They all take foreigners and surprisingly all seem fairly friendly even though they're probably uninspiring places to stay. The first is the *Yongchang Hotel* (*yǒngchāng bīnguǎn*), which has dorm beds for Y9. A host of other rooms are available: singles from Y15 to Y100 and doubles from Y22 to Y70 – don't expect anything more than a bed in the cheaper rooms. Not far up the road is the *Lanhua Hotel* (*lánhuā bīnguǎn*), which has beds in four-bed dorms

---

■ PLACES TO STAY

10	Lanhua Hotel
11	Baoshan Guesthouse
12	Yongchang Hotel
16	Yindou Hotel
19	Traffic Hotel
21	Lanyuan Hotel

▼ PLACES TO EAT

| 9 | Across the Bridge Noodle Restaurant |
| 13 | Huizu Shitang Muslim Restaurant |

OTHER

1	Zoo
2	Yuhuang Pavilion
3	Wenbi Pagoda
4	Yiluo Pond
5	PSB
6	Worker's Cultural Palace
7	Youth Palace
8	Cinema
14	Department Store
15	CAAC
17	Post Office
18	Long-Distance Bus Station
20	Baoshan Travel Agency

■ PLACES TO STAY

10	兰花宾馆
11	保山宾馆
12	永昌宾馆
16	银都大酒店
19	客运住宿部
21	兰苑大酒家

▼ PLACES TO EAT

| 9 | 过桥米线 |
| 13 | 回族食堂 |

OTHER

1	动物园
2	玉皇阁
3	文笔塔
4	易罗池
5	公安局
6	工人文化宫
7	青少年宫
8	电影院
14	百货大楼
15	中国民航售票处
17	邮电局
18	汽车总站
20	旅游服务部

The Last Word
In the Baoshan post office the staff were using the postage scales to weigh three deep-fried chickens. It was a unique undertaking (perhaps the stuff of which *Guinness Book of Records* attempts are made), and the customers, who seemed to vaguely approve of the proceedings, waited patiently in line, lighting up cigarettes and grinding their phlegm contentedly into the concrete underfoot. Finally one of the girls dragged herself away from the chickens, sauntered over my way and glanced at my letter. She sighed wearily, as if to say 'not *another* one', and shook her head: 'the address is not central enough – you'll have to write it again'. I refused. She insisted. I refused again. She took a new envelope and placed it in front of me. I ignored it and pushed my original letter towards her again. She eyed it suspiciously and turned it over: 'Your name should be after your address not before it'. I crossed out my name at the head of the address and re-wrote it at the bottom. 'Happy?' I asked her. She scowled, thrust my letter onto the scales and handed it back to me dripping with deep-fried chicken oil. As always, it's the people behind the counter who get the last laugh in China. ∎

for Y6 and three-bed dorms for Y8. Doubles with attached bathroom come in at Y80 and deluxe singles at Y100. The *Baoshan Guesthouse (bǎoshān bīnguǎn)* is where the pedicab drivers will take you if you stumble off the bus looking dazed and confused. It has beds in triples for Y8 and in doubles for Y12, which is not a bad deal. Over in the north wing are slightly upmarket (bathroom attached) doubles for Y60.

Finally, Baoshan may be the place to spend a night in comfort. The *Yindou Hotel (yíndū dàjiǔdiàn)* is a money-making venture set up by the Bank of China. Locals are awed by the fact that it has elevators, but for the footsore, China-weary traveller, this is not all it offers: for Y70 you get a very comfortable carpeted double with international telephone, 24-hour hot water, air-con and satellite TV. If you've been roughing it for a while, it's a good place to have a night off from China.

Places to Eat Baoxiu Lu and the road to the south running parallel to it are good places to seek out cheap restaurants. Look for the place selling dumplings and noodles down the road from the Yindou Hotel towards the bus station. *Huizu Shitang* is a good Muslim restaurant on the opposite corner to the department store. There is also an across-the-bridge noodle restaurant on Baoxiu Xilu that is worth checking out. Give the hotel restaurants a miss. As in Kunming there are

plenty of roadside snacks available. The *Splendid Tea House* in the long-distance bus compound is notable as a place to avoid. It has terrible coffee for Y3, and the owner has a penchant for serenading her guests on a clapped-out karaoke machine at 100 decibels. It is also the entrance for one of the worst discos in China.

Getting There & Away You can fly in and out of Baoshan, though very few Western travellers do; mysteriously, there are no references to this air link in CAAC timetables. Ask in Kunming for details or at the Baoshan CAAC office, which is at 96 Baoxiu Donglu. It's very hard to find – look carefully for it opposite and slightly to the south of the Yindou Hotel: the English sign says 'Baoshan Minhang'. Tickets to Kunming cost Y190. The airport is around nine km south of town.

The Baoshan long-distance bus station is a huge new construction, and there are buses running from here to a host of destinations around Yunnan. There are numerous buses daily to Kunming for Y65. Buses for Xiaguan (Dali) leave at 7 am and cost Y14.80; the journey takes around seven hours. Forget about buses to Simao, Jinghong or Damenglong (yes, buses run there) in Xishuangbanna – foreigners are *verboten*. Other possibilities include Mangshi (Luxi), Tengchong, Yingjiang and Ruili. Buses to the latter leave at 6.30 am, take seven to eight hours and cost Y20.

Getting Around Baoshan can comfortably be explored on foot, which is probably why there is no evidence of bicycle hire stands around town. This is a pity because a bicycle would be the ideal way to get to some of the sights around Baoshan. With any luck, an enterprising local may fill this gap as increasing numbers of foreigners pass through the area.

Around Baoshan

Just 17 km north of town, the Reclining Buddha Temple *(wòfó sì)* is one of the most important historical sights in the near vicinity of Baoshan. The temple dates back to the Tang Dynasty, having a history of some 1200 years. The reclining buddha itself, in a cave to the rear of the temple area, was severely damaged during the Cultural Revolution and has only recently been restored.

The only problem is getting to the temple. Ask at the travel agent opposite the long-distance bus station for the latest on minibuses or local buses. It would be a fairly comfortable bicycle trip if you could get hold of a bike.

Tengchong

(téngchōng) 腾冲

Not many travellers get to this town on the other side of the Gaoligong Mountain range, but it's an interesting place. There are some 20 volcanoes in the vicinity and lively geothermal activity – lots of hot springs. It's also prime earthquake territory, having experienced 71 earthquakes measuring over five on the Richter scale since 1500 AD. The town itself has preserved on a larger scale the kind of traditional wooden architecture that has survived only in pockets in Kunming and Baoshan. It's not exactly Dali, but there's a definite charm to some of the narrow backstreets. The town is at an altitude of 1650 metres and can get quite crisp in the evenings during the winter months.

Information Tengchong has a small travel office on the 2nd floor above the reception office of the Tengchong Guesthouse. It's disorganised and very little English is spoken, but the staff are eager to be of assistance. The post office and the Bank of China are next door to each other on Fengshan Lu, although it would be advisable to change money before you get to Tengchong. There is no market for FEC here.

Things to See There's not exactly a wealth of sights in town but it's worth taking a look at the **Frontier Trade Bazaar of Tengchong** – yes, that's the English sign at the head of the market. It's not as lively as the markets in Ruili, but there's plenty of colour and activity in the mornings. The best street for old buildings is Yingjiang Lu, both the east and west sections. The backstreets running off the western section of Yingjiang Lu make for some good exploring and photographs.

About one km to the south-west of town is the **Laifeng Temple** *(láifēng sì)*. A park was established here in 1981 with a a small museum, photography exhibits and funny mirrors. It's nothing special, but a pleasant enough walk if you have nothing else to do.

Places to Stay & Eat There are not a lot of places to stay in Tengchong. Most of the hotels have a 'no-foreigners' policy. At the time of writing, a new hotel was under construction on Guanghua Lu, and if it takes foreigners this would be the handiest spot to the bus station. Failing this, head up to the *No 4 Government Hotel (sì lǚshè)* on Yingjiang Donglu. It's in what appears to be a bus parking compound. Beds in a four-bed dorm here are Y6, while basic singles are Y10. More upmarket singles/doubles with bathroom and TV are Y20/40. Up on Yingjiang Xilu is the wonderful little *Swan Goose Hotel*. Hassle them to give you a bed – at the time of writing they were not taking foreigners.

The sprawling *Tengchong Guesthouse (téngchōng bīnguǎn)* is in a quiet location but is a long walk from the bus station. They also lock up very securely at night and then disappear just to make sure you can't get out

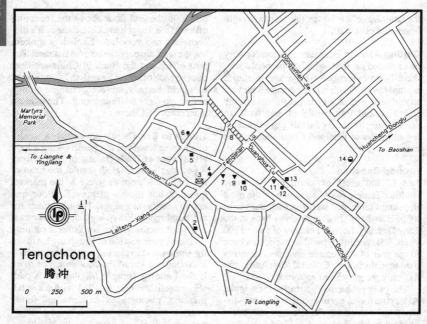

Tengchong

腾冲

0   250   500 m

of the place in the morning for your early morning bus. There are dorm beds available here for Y10 and basic doubles for Y25. The deluxe doubles for Y50 have verandas as well as attached bathrooms and TVs.

The restaurant at the Tengchong Guesthouse seems to be permanently out for lunch, so if you're staying here you'll have to head into town for your victuals. Look out for the *Friendship Restaurant (yǒuyì fàndiàn)* on Fengshan Lu just before Yingjiang Donglu. There's no English sign, but it's an open-fronted place and fairly easy to find. Ask for their delicious Shandong-style steamed dumplings *(zhengjiǎo)* – they are unlike dumplings anywhere else in China. Otherwise head out to the back of the restaurant and invent your own meal.

Just around the corner from the Friendship Restaurant is *Guoying Huishiguan (guóyíng huíshíguǎn)*, a Muslim place with good food. The long-distance bus station area has a lot of noodle vendors, but nothing worth recommending in particular. One place that might be worth trying is the Burmese *Zhongmian Restaurant (zhōngmiàn cāntīng)* on Guanghua Lu, though the Burmese food here looks like it has been heavily Sinicised.

Getting There & Away Tengchong long-distance bus station must be the only bus station in the whole of the south-west that has a board with English information about bus times and prices. Ignore it – it's completely out of date, though it's a nice thought. Ignore the irate scrawlings by foreigners too ('Yingjiang – bullshit Y100 FEC fine!'). You shouldn't have problems with the PSB in this neck of the woods anymore.

Buses run from the long-distance bus station to Baoshan from 6.30 to 11.30 am. The price is Y16.20. The journey should take around eight hours, though it often takes longer. Buses to Ruili run via Yingjiang and Zhongfeng and cost Y12. Alternatively, if you have time on your hands, travel by minibus to Yingjiang (stopping to have a browse in Lianghe on the way), stay overnight there and travel on to Ruili by bus the next day. There are also buses to Mangshi

and to Kunming. The latter is a two-day trip (Y64) with an overnight stop en route.

Getting Around Tengchong is another town that suffers from an absence of bicycle hire stands, although the town itself is small enough to walk around, and the sights outside town are in such hilly terrain that it's doubtful whether anyone would really want to tackle them on a Chinese bicycle.

Around Tengchong

There's a lot to see around Tengchong, but as the area has only recently opened, getting out to the sights, as in Baoshan, is a bit of a problem. Catching buses part of the way and hiking up to the sights is one possibility, but not particularly feasible without good mapping and some ability in Chinese. The Tengchong Guesthouse has tour buses running out to most of the major sights, but of course this means doing it Chinese style.

Heshun Village *(héshùn xiāng)* If you come into Tengchong from Ruili and Yingjiang, just four km before pulling into town you pass through the village of Heshun. It's worth hiking back to take a closer look at the village. The Chinese make much fuss of the fact that it has been set aside as a kind of retirement village for Overseas Chinese, but for the average Western visitor it's likely to be of more interest as a quiet, traditional Chinese village with cobbled streets. There are some great old buildings in the village, providing lots of photo opportunities. You may also get a chance to meet some older English speakers.

Mt Yunfeng *(yúnfēng shān)* Mt Yunfeng is a Taoist mountain dotted with temples and monastic retreats, 47 km to the north of Tengchong. The temples were built in the early 17th century, and the best example is said to be the Yunfeng Temple at the summit. Getting there is not so easy. The nearest town is Gudong *(gúdōng)*, and catching a bus out here and then hitching is certainly one possibility, but if you're less adventurous the tour buses from the Tengchong Guesthouse are probably the best bet.

Volcanoes *(huǒshānqún)* Tengchong County is renowned for its volcanoes, and although they have been behaving themselves for many centuries the seismic and geothermal activity in the area probably indicate that they won't always continue to do so. The closest to town is Mt Ma'an *(mǎān shān)*, around five km to the north-west. It's just south of the main road that runs to Yingjiang. Around 22 km to the north of town, near the village of Gongping, is a cluster of volcanoes: the Kong Mountains *(kōngshān huǒshānkǒu)*. They're a popular destination for Chinese tour groups, and hitching up with one for the ride out there should be no problem. Check at the Tengchong Guesthouse.

Hot Springs The 'Sea of Heat' *(rèhǎi)* as the Chinese poetically refer to it, lies around 12 km to the south-west of Tengchong. As usual there are spas and hot spring hotels in the area. One of the most popular sights for Chinese visitors is a mini-geyser that shoots up spring water half a metre or so at temperatures close to boiling point.

DEHONG REGION
(déhóng zhōu) 德宏

Dehong prefecture, like Xishuangbanna, borders Myanmar and is heavily populated by distinctive minority groups, but for some reason it doesn't seem to have captured travellers' imaginations to the extent that Xishuangbanna has. It's in the far west of Yunnan and is definitely more off the beaten track than Xishuangbanna; you're unlikely to see the busloads of Chinese tourists who have overrun Xishuangbanna in recent years, and even less likely to bump into more than a couple of other backpackers. Most Chinese in Dehong are there for the Myanmar trade that comes through the towns of Ruili and Wanding. Burmese jade is a commodity that many Chinese have grown rich on in recent years, but there are countless other items being spirited over the border that separates China and Myanmar, many of them illicit.

Many minority groups are represented in Dehong, but among the most obvious are the Burmese, the Dai and the Jingpo (known in nearby Myanmar as the Kachin, a minority presently at war with the Myanmar government). Throughout Dehong it is possible to see signs sporting numerous languages: Chinese, Burmese, Dai and English. This is a border region that is getting rich on trade – in the markets you can see old Indian men selling jewellery, tinned fruits from Thailand, Burmese papier maché furniture, young bloods with huge wads of foreign currency, and Chinese plain-clothes police trying not to look too obvious.

Yingjiang
(yíngjiāng) 盈江

Yingjiang is a possible stopover if you're heading to Ruili and Wanding from Tengchong or Baoshan. It's not really worth a special effort (it might be described as a *very*

The Rebel

He slid into the chair opposite me and glanced around nervously. 'The walls have ears,' I almost expected him to say. But no, it was something altogether more mundane: what did I do? I was writing a book about China. 'China? Why not Myanmar?' he asked, looking slightly surprised. I explained that it had been a foolish mistake on my part but, now that I had already started, it was a bit late to change. But my newly acquired friend from Burma wasn't convinced: 'I take you to Kachin rebel camp in Myanmar,' he said. 'We dye your hair black. You wear Chinese clothes. We travel at night. Maybe the border guards they shoot at you – no problem. We take you rebel camp. You write Kachin rebels good people.' After expressing reservations about dyeing my hair, I exchanged business cards with him, and we agreed to keep in touch. ■

pale shadow of Ruili), but the locals are friendly and, even though there's not a lot to do, you can at least sit around and chat with the Kachin rebels.

Things to See There's nothing much really. Take a minibus out to **Gucheng** (*gùchéng*), which means 'old town', to see an old Chinese town. It's only a 20-minute ride, and it's fairly picturesque. Back on the road to Ruili, a couple of km out of town, is an old stupa: **Laomian Pagoda** (*lǎomiàn tǎ*). The name means 'old Burmese stupa/pagoda', which is a fairly accurate description. Locals claim it's a nice place to visit in the evenings 'with someone you care about' – see if you can find the local PSB and invite one of the boys in green along.

Places to Stay & Eat Opposite the long-distance bus station is the drab *State Guesthouse* (*guóyíng lǚshè*). Locals claim it is a den of iniquity, but unfortunately we didn't come across anything particularly iniquitous. It's Y5 for a bed in a five-bed dorm and Y15 for singles and doubles alike. None of the rooms have showers. You also need to take a bit of a hike if you want to use the toilet.

Better still, give the State Den of Iniquity a miss and walk into town (turn right out of the bus station) for the *Yingxiang Hotel* (*yíngxiáng lǚshé*). It's on the right-hand side of the road, just after the road makes a bit of a turn to the right. This clean and friendly place has singles/doubles for Y10/14 and singles with bathroom and TV for Y26. The hot water is solar heated and doesn't really get warm until mid-afternoon.

Yingjiang's answer to the Hilton is the *Great Wall Hotel* (*chángchéng bīnguǎn*), where the cheapest rooms cost Y40 (no carpet!) and the most expensive are Y120. All rooms have their own TVs and bathrooms. To get there, keep walking from the Yingxiang Hotel and turn right at the first major intersection; the Great Wall is on the corner of the next intersection.

Yingjiang is not a gastronomical experience that merits a postcard to mum and dad,

but the cheap noodle stores over near the bus station will keep you alive for another day. Look out for *Ann Hot & Cold*, an effusively friendly little Burmese shop that has samosas, cakes and coffee. It's on the right-hand side around 100 metres down from the bus station. If you're male and you value the contents of your wallet (not to mention your virtue) don't venture into the place with the sign saying 'bar' opposite the Yingxiang Hotel.

Getting There & Away There are buses at 8.30 am to Yingjiang from Ruili. If you take one of these you'll probably be stuck in the place overnight unless you take the one minibus that leaves around 2 pm for Lianghe (an interesting little town), where you can connect with another minibus for Tengchong. The whole trip should cost Y15 and take around three to four hours. If you're coming the other way there are frequent minibuses to Ruili for Y18 and less frequent ordinary buses for Y11. And you can even get a sleeper bus from here to Kunming. Buses for Baoshan leave early in the morning.

Ruili
(*ruìlì*) 瑞丽

Ruili is without a doubt one of the more interesting towns in south-western China. It's just a few km from Myanmar and has a real border-town feel about it. There's a great mix of Han Chinese, minorities and Burmese traders, and travellers tend to linger longer than they intended just for the atmosphere. At first sight it doesn't seem like much, but it's worth giving the place a couple of days. There are some interesting minority villages nearby; the stupas are in much better condition than those in Xishuangbanna, and it's worth travelling onwards to Wanding and Mangshi, either as day trips or as overnight stops.

Information The shop next to the reception area of the Ruili Guesthouse has maps and a brochure on Ruili, but there's very little else in the way of information available. The PSB

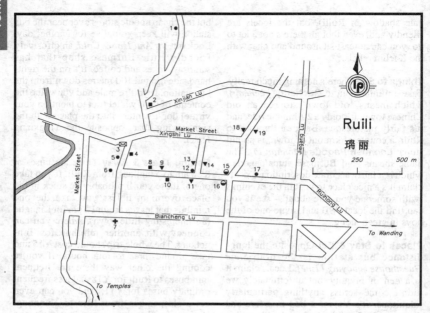

Ruili
瑞丽

0   250   500 m

To Wanding

To Temples

is just up the road from the guesthouse, and the new telecommunications building is just down the road. Telecommunications are better in Dehong than they are in Xishuangbanna, and the Ruili Guesthouse has an international phone booth where you can dial for yourself. The Bank of China is not far from the long-distance bus station.

Ruili is a very good place to do some illicit money changing – US dollars are in much demand for the Myanmar border trade, and with a little haggling very good rates are available. As usual, never hand over your dollars (or FEC) until you've counted your money.

Reportedly a recent development in Ruili is the availability of one-day visas for the Myanmar town of Muse. They cost US$10, and you'll need to ask around on exactly how to organise it.

Things to See There is really not a lot to see in Ruili itself. It's a great town to wander

around in though, and it's so small that you can cover most of it in an hour. The market street in the west of town is the most colourful by day, while by night the market street just round the corner from the Ruili Guesthouse is the liveliest place to hang out. Most of Ruili's sights are outside town, and you'll need a bicycle to get out and see them.

Places to Stay While everywhere else in Dehong and Baoshan has rock-bottom prices for accommodation, Ruili is the exception to the rule. To make matters worse, there are so many Chinese and Burmese coming into town to do business that there is often a shortage of accommodation. When everywhere is full you will often be able to squeeze into one of the hotels that doesn't officially take foreigners – prices are significantly cheaper in these places.

Two hotels that take foreigners and have dormitory accommodation are the *Ruili Guesthouse (ruìlì bīnguǎn)* and the *Mingrui*

■ PLACES TO STAY

2	Ruili Guesthouse
4	Yongchang Hotel
8	Mingrui Hotel
10	Nanyang Hotel

▼ PLACES TO EAT

9	Mianthai Restaurant
11	Panthay Restaurant
13	Noodles & Coffee
14	Restaurants
18	Indian Tea & Pastries Shop
19	Muslim Restaurant

OTHER

1	PSB
3	Post Office
5	Xinhua Bookstore
6	Cinema
7	Hospital
12	Moneychanger Corner
15	Minibus Stand
16	Long-Distance Bus Station
17	Bank of China

■ PLACES TO STAY

2	瑞丽宾馆
4	永昌大酒家
8	明瑞宾馆
10	南洋宾馆

▼ PLACES TO EAT

9	缅泰味饭店
11	缅甸餐厅
13	面条及咖啡
14	餐厅
18	印度茶馆
19	清真食馆

OTHER

1	公安局
3	邮电大楼
5	新华书店
6	电影院
7	医院
12	换钱处
15	小型车站
16	长途汽车站
17	中国银行

Hotel (míngruì bīnguǎn). Both of them are friendly and clean. The Ruili Guesthouse is a pleasant, rambling old edifice that has dorm beds for Y10. Showers and toilets are out the back. The only other accommodation option here are doubles at Y120 – not good value for money. Dorm beds at the Mingrui Hotel are Y12, and doubles with bathroom, TV and carpet are also available for Y80 – the cheapest doubles in town!

The *Yongchang Hotel (yǒngchāng dàjiǔdiàn)* attracts fewer travellers (possibly because it always seems to be full), but is also a comfortable, clean place to stay, with dorm beds at Y10. Standard doubles here are Y120, and suites are also available for Y180. Finally, the *Nanyang Hotel (nányáng bīnguǎn)* is the other officially sanctioned abode for foreigners, though few would be keen on forking out Y120 for the rooms here. Note the sign – 'leave with valuable body please' – and be sure to comply: the hotel has apparently had problems with guests leaving their bodies behind – perhaps as a first instalment on the room bill.

Places to Eat Reports concerning the existence of decent curries in Ruili are greatly exaggerated, but there is some good food available all the same. Take a stroll up the market street around the corner from the Ruili Hotel in the evening and check out all the hotpot stands – as always with hotpot, confirm prices beforehand. Look out for the *Coca Cola Restaurant* in a tiny alley on the left-hand side of the same strip. The people here are very friendly and will cook the things you pick out from their pile of food. At the end of the market street are some Muslim restaurants and a popular Indian tea and pastry shop.

Other places worth checking out are the *Mianthai Restaurant* and, over the road, the *Panthay Restaurant* for great Burmese snacks and so on. The noodle stalls on the street that runs from the moneychanger's corner back to the market street are also very good. Try the noodles and coffee in the first place on the left in the morning.

Entertainment Ruili may be only a small town, but by Chinese standards it packs a lot of punch on the entertainment level. For the Chinese, Ruili has a reputation as one of *the* happening places in Yunnan, and young people with money head down here just for a few nights out. That said, don't expect too much. The discos all close at 11 pm or midnight, and the same is true of the bars. Of the discos, the *Mingrui Disco*, in the basement of the hotel of the same name, is justifiably the most popular. There is a resident Burmese band, disco music and a spot of karaoke. Entry is Y10, but it's worth it for an insight into what the Chinese view as a jiving nightspot.

Adventurous travellers with a few extra yuan might want to try out some of the bars that line the back alleys of the market street close to the Ruili Guesthouse. They look like brothels, with little clusters of heavily made up women sitting outside, but they are not. A few words of advice: if a woman sits with you (this will probably only happen if you are male), you will be expected to buy her a drink (Y30 or more), and you will be served a plate of fruit that you didn't order (Y50) – you can send it back with some friendly but forceful objections. All things considered you're safer in these places if you don't speak Chinese. Some of them look very sleazy. One of the safest is the *Phoenix Bar*, which has an English sign and serves coffee as well as beer.

Getting There & Away Ruili is connected to Kunming by air by way of Mangshi. Flights leave daily, take 50 minutes and cost Y350. There are minibuses leaving direct from the airport for Ruili at a cost of Y17. The trip takes around 2½ hours. Flight reservations for Kunming can be made at the reception desk of the Ruili Guesthouse.

Buses for Kunming leave from the long-distance bus station between 6.30 and 7 am. Prices for the 24-hour journey range from Y95 for an ordinary bus to Y155 for a sleeper. Give the sleeper serious consideration – it is by all accounts a hell of a ride. Buses to Xiaguan (Dali) take 14 hours, leave at 6.30 am and cost Y35. Baoshan is seven to eight hours away; buses leave at 6.30 am and cost Y20. Buses also leave at 6.30 am for Tengchong; the five hour trip costs Y17. There are two buses a day for Yingjiang (at 8.30 am and noon) for Y11.

Minibuses leave for more local destinations from opposite the long-distance bus station. It's about an hour to Wanding (Y7). Other destinations are Jiegao (Y3), Nongdao (Y4) and Zhongfeng.

Getting Around Ruili itself is easily explored on foot, but all the most interesting day trips require a bicycle. Like accommodation, in Ruili bicycles don't come cheap, or at least the deposit doesn't. The only place renting bicycles at present is the Mingrui Hotel. The charge is Y1 an hour or Y10 per day; the deposit is a hefty Y300 or Y200 and your passport, and no amount of arguing will change their minds about it. Make sure you get a receipt, though there have been no reports of deposits disappearing.

Around Ruili

Most of the sights around Ruili can be explored easily by bicycle. It's worth making frequent detours down the narrow paths that lead off the main roads to visit minority villages. The people are friendly, and there are lots of photo opportunities.

Nongan Golden Duck Temple (*nóngān jīnyā tǎ*) A short ride to the south-west of town, the Golden Duck Temple is an attractive stupa in a courtyard. It is said to have been established to mark the arrival of a pair of golden ducks who brought good fortune to what was previously an uninhabited marshy area.

Myanmar Bridge Continue straight ahead from the Golden Duck Temple and you'll reach the Myanmar bridge over the Ruili river or the Shweli river as it's known in Myanmar. The bridge was only completed in August of 1992, and is already ferrying a steady stream of local traffic. On a more controversial note, the bridge is said to be being used for overland shipments of arms from China to the Rangoon government. The bridge itself is nothing much to see and the guards make sure (in a friendly way) that you don't get too close, but travellers can stand on the Chinese end and indulge the perennial fascination with illicit borders.

Temples Just after the Golden Duck Temple is a crossroads. The road to the right leads to the villages of Jiexiang and Nongdao, and on the way are a number of small temples, villages and stupas worth taking a look at. Most of them are not particularly noteworthy and the village life nearby is more interesting – there are often small market areas near the temples.

The first major temple is the **Hansha Temple** (*hánshāzhuàng sì*), a fine wooden structure with a few resident monks. It's set a little off the road but easy to find. Another 15 minutes or so down the road, look out for a white stupa on the hillside to the right. This is **Leizhuangxiang** (*léizhuāngxiāng*), Ruili's oldest stupa, dating back to the middle of the Tang Dynasty. There's a nunnery up on the grounds of the stupa and fantastic views of the Ruili area. Once the stupa comes into view, take the next path to the right that cuts through the fields. There are signs in Chinese and Dai pointing the way, which leads through a couple of Dai villages. You'll need to get off your bicycle and push for the last ascent up to the stupa.

A few km past the town of Jiexiang is the **Denghannong Temple** (*dēnghánnóngzhuāng sì*), a wooden Dai temple with pleasant surroundings. Like the other temples in the area, the effect is spoiled somewhat by the corrugated tin roof.

Nongdao (*nóngdǎo*) Around 26 km southwest of Ruili, the small town of Nongdao is worth an overnight trip. The locals (mainly

Burmese and Dai) don't get all that many foreign visitors and are a friendly lot. There's a solitary hotel in town (you can't miss it) that has doubles for Y10. It would be possible to cycle here, stopping off at some of the temple sights along the way, or take a minibus from Ruili – they leave fairly frequently through the day.

Jiele Golden Pagoda (*jiělè jīntǎ*) A few km to the east of Ruili on the road to Wanding is the Jiele Golden Pagoda, a fine structure that dates back 200 years.

Zhaduo Waterfall (*zhāduó pùbù*) The waterfall is east of Ruili, north of the road to Mangshi. It's probably worth cycling out here for a swim when the weather's hot.

Wanding
(*wǎndīng*) 畹町

Many travellers don't make it to Wanding, or do it only as a day trip. It's not as interesting as Ruili, but there's cheaper accommodation here and it's a nice laid-back place to spend a day or so. Part of the attraction is that the town is right on the Myanmar border, and the Wanding Guesthouse and the Yufeng Hotel provide good views of the hills, small township and occasional stupa over on the Myanmar side.

Information Call in and visit the lovely people at the Wanding Travel Bureau. English is spoken and they really try hard. There's a branch of the Bank of China on the main road that comes in from Ruili. The post office is next door to the Xinhua Bookshop on the same road and can even make international phone calls. It's difficult to say what would happen if you turned up at the PSB in pursuit of a visa extension, but Wanding is an easy-going kind of place and it's hard to imagine it being a problem.

Things to See Check out the colourful market area, a fascinating mix of minority peoples. The main market occurs every five days. The new **Co-operative Border Market** should be finished by the time you

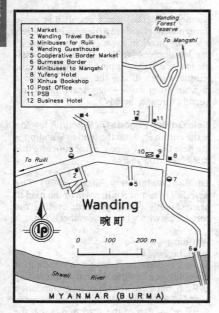

1	Market
2	Wanding Travel Bureau
3	Minibuses for Ruili
4	Wanding Guesthouse
5	Cooperative Border Market
6	Burmese Border
7	Minibuses to Mangshi
8	Yufeng Hotel
9	Xinhua Bookshop
10	Post Office
11	PSB
12	Business Hotel

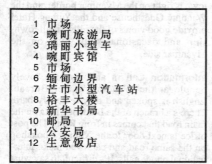

1	市场
2	畹町旅游局
3	瑞丽小型车
4	畹町宾馆
5	市场
6	缅甸边界
7	芒市小型汽车站
8	裕丰大楼
9	新华书局
10	邮局
11	公安局
12	生意饭店

have this book in your hands and should also be worth checking out. Two minutes' walk down from the Yufeng Hotel will see you in Myanmar. The only giveaway is the dilapidated Customs office. Apparently a Belgian couple did a day trip into Myanmar for US$20 late in 1992 (the proceeds were shared by those who failed to notice them

crossing the bridge), but the guards were not interested in allowing a repeat performance when we were in town. Talk to the Wanding Travel Bureau for the latest on this situation.

It's worth climbing up to the north of town to take a look at the **Wanding Forest Reserve** (*wǎndīng sēnlín gōngyuán*). There's a Y0.20 entry charge and some pleasant walks. Avoid the absolutely pathetic zoo, home to three psychotic monkeys, a couple of peacocks and an unidentified ball of fur that was either fast asleep or dead. There were three empty cages here when we visited – the cheapest accommodation option in town for travellers on a shoestring budget. The reserve also has an uninspiring pagoda and a 'quiet resting area' – a novel concept for the Chinese.

The Wanding Travel Bureau can organise river trips for Y35. This includes a barbecue lunch in a minority village. Alternatively, it is possible to catch a lift on a boat with locals by taking a minibus in the direction of Mangshi and getting off at the bridge that connects with the main Ruili-Mangshi road. Travellers have caught boats back to the second bridge closer to Ruili and then hitched back to Ruili or Wanding. Serious haggling is required for boat trips, but hitching by road can be done with the aid of some foreign cigarettes.

Places to Stay & Eat The cheapest place to stay is the clean and friendly *Yufeng Hotel* (*yùfēng dàlóu*). Dorm beds here are Y8 and basic doubles are Y30. The *Wanding Guesthouse* (*wǎndīng bīnguǎn*) is in a rambling building up on the hill with good views of Myanmar. Comfortable doubles with attached bathroom and satellite TV (catch up with the latest MTV video clips on the China-Myanmar border!) are Y50. Triples are also available for Y60. The other option is the *Business Hotel* (*shēngyì fàndiàn*), a dingy little place that was undergoing extensive renovations at the time of writing. It has basic singles/doubles for Y15/30.

The area around the Yufeng Hotel is best for cheap restaurants. Most of them are of the pick-and-choose variety, and are all of a muchness. Next to the Mangshi minibus stop is a good Muslim restaurant. In the mornings try the dumpling stands opposite the turn-off for the Wanding Guesthouse.

Entertainment The disco on the ground floor of the Yufeng Hotel is the place to get down in Wanding. The resident Burmese band alternates with terrible Chinese disco sessions, in which the locals dance in formation.

Getting There & Away Minibuses run to Ruili for Y7 and to Mangshi for Y15. They leave through the day whenever they are full. You shouldn't have to wait more than 15 minutes for a bus to Ruili; buses to Mangshi are less frequent.

Mangshi (Luxi)
(mángshì) 芒市

Mangshi is Dehong's air link with the outside world. If you fly in from Kunming there are minibuses running direct from the airport to Ruili and most people take this option, but there are a few sights in and around Mangshi itself that make dallying

here a day or so worthwhile if you have the time.

Things to See Mangshi is not a particularly big place, and it's interesting just to take a wander round. There are a couple of markets in town and a number of **temples** in the vicinity of the Dehong Guesthouse. Around seven or eight km south of town are the **Fapa Hot Springs** *(fǎpà wēnquán)*; they get good reports from travellers who have cycled out to them. Not far from the Dehong Guesthouse is the **Mangshi Nationalities Palace** *(mínzú wénhuà gōng)*.

1	中国民航
2	汽车站
3	昆明饭店
4	中国银行
5	中国邮局
6	汽车站
7	市场
8	民族文化宫
9	德宏宾馆
10	寺庙

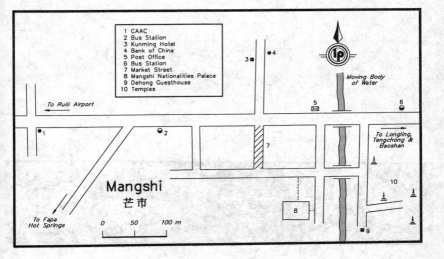

1 CAAC
2 Bus Station
3 Kunming Hotel
4 Bank of China
5 Post Office
6 Bus Station
7 Market Street
8 Mangshi Nationalities Palace
9 Dehong Guesthouse
10 Temples

Moving Body of Water

To Ruili Airport

To Longling, Tengchong & Baoshan

Mangshi
芒市

To Fapa Hot Springs

0   50   100 m

Jamming

'Don't go to the Yufeng Disco,' the locals warned me. 'It's full of Burmese who'll mug you and steal all your money.' Having never been mugged in China, I wandered into the gloomy surroundings of the disco at around 9 pm. Within minutes I had met all the Burmese in the bar, including the band members, who invited me up for a number (all Westerners eat hamburgers and play guitar like ringin' a bell, right?). A few beers got me in the mood, and after much conferring we came up with *Get Back* and *Get Off My Cloud*, the former sung in Burmese because I could only remember the chorus and something about JoJo leaving his home somewhere in Alabama. We cranked up the amps and ripped through our numbers, much to the bewilderment of the audience (who weren't sure whether to foxtrot or to samba), and to the annoyance of two PSB men (who seemed to sense that this was cultural pollution of the highest order). I left the stage to find that my bar tab had been paid by a Burmese business person. ■

Places to Stay & Eat The most popular place to stay is the *Dehong Guesthouse (déhóng bīnguǎn)*. Dorm beds are available here for Y8, while upmarket doubles range up to Y120. The *Kunming Hotel* has similar rates.

There is nothing to write home about on the culinary front, but the food market areas near the Kunming Hotel have good noodle dishes and so on. There are numerous pick-and-choose restaurants around town also.

Getting There & Away There are daily flights (737s) between Mangshi and Kunming for Y350; the flight takes around 50 minutes. Minibuses leave from the airport for the Mangshi CAAC office. It is possible to book or reconfirm flights here, or you could wait until you get to Ruili, where the Ruili Guesthouse offers the same service.

Minibuses connect Mangshi with Ruili and Wanding, both of which cost Y15. There are frequent departures. The long-distance bus station is the place to organise transport for Baoshan, Tengchong, Xiaguan and Kunming.

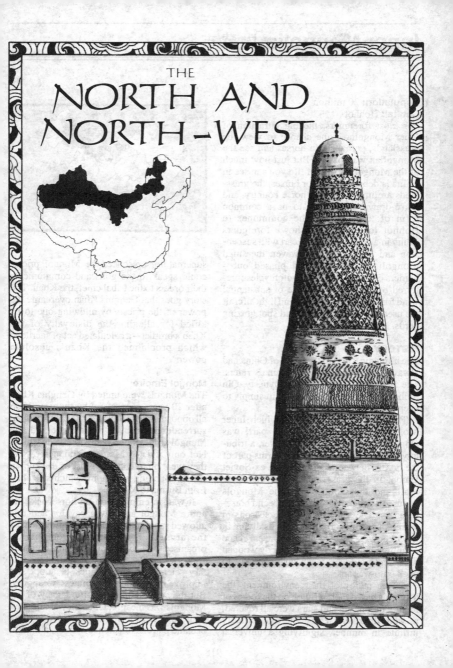

THE
NORTH AND
NORTH-WEST

Inner Mongolia 内蒙古

Population: 20 million
Capital: Hohhot

For most foreigners, the big attraction of Inner Mongolia is the chance to view the grasslands, perhaps ride horses and see the Mongolian way of life. But just how much of the Mongolian way of life you can see in China is debatable. As for horses, the grasslands are indeed perfect horse country, and horse-drawn carts seem to be a common form of transport on the communes (a Hohhot tourist leaflet shows foreigners riding in a decorated camel cart with suspension and truck tyres). However, the small Mongolian horse is being phased out – herders can now purchase motorcycles (preferred over bicycles because of substantial wind force), and helicopters and light aircraft are used to round up steers and spot grazing herds.

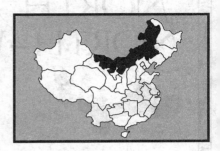

HISTORY

The nomadic tribes to the north of China had always been a problem for China's rulers. The first emperor of the Qin Dynasty, Qin Shihuang, had the Great Wall built simply to keep them out.

The Mongol homeland, of which Inner Mongolia *(nèi ménggǔ)* forms part, was along the banks of the Onon River, a tributary of the Amur, which today forms part of the border between China and the ex-Soviet Union. In the grassland beyond the Great Wall and the Gobi Desert the Mongols endured a rough life as shepherds and horse-breeders. They moved with the seasons in search of pastures for their animals, living in tents known as *yurts*. The yurts were made of animal hide usually supported by wooden rods, and could be taken apart quickly to pack onto wagons.

At the mercy of their environment, the Mongols based their religion on the forces of nature: moon, sun and stars were all revered, as were the rivers. The gods were virtually infinite in number, signifying a universal supernatural presence; the Mongol priests could speak to the gods and communicate their orders to the tribal chief, the Khan. The story goes that Genghis Khan overcame the power of the priests by allowing one to be killed for alleging the disloyalty of the Khan's brother – a calculated act of sacrilege which proclaimed the Khan's absolute power.

Mongol Empire

The Mongols were united by Genghis Khan after 20 years of warfare; by the year 1206 all opposition to his rule among the tribes had surrendered or been wiped out and the Mongol armies stood ready to invade China. Not only did the Mongols conquer China, they went on to conquer most of the known world, founding an empire which stretched from Burma to Russia.

It was an empire won on horseback; the entire Mongol army was cavalry and this allowed rapid movement and deployment of the armies. The Mongols were highly organised and expert at planning complex strategies and tactics. They excelled in military science and were quick to adopt and improve on Persian and Chinese weaponry. But the cultural and scientific legacy of the Mongols was meagre. Once they abandoned their policies of terror and destruction, they became patrons of science and art, although

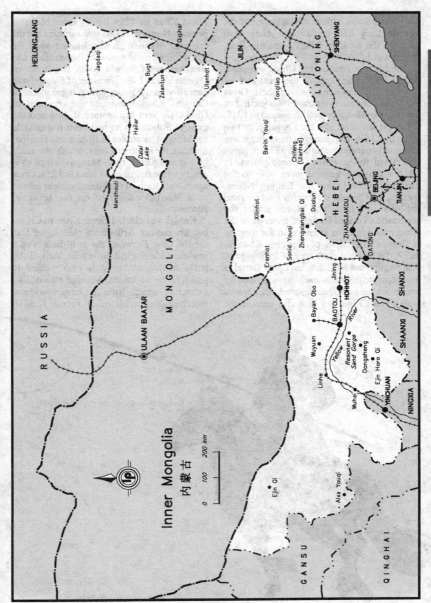

not practitioners. Under the influence of the people they had conquered, they also adopted the local religions – mainly Buddhism and Islam.

The Mongol conquest of China was slow, delayed by campaigns in the west and by internal strife. Secure behind their Great Wall, the Chinese rulers had little inkling of the fury the Mongols would unleash in 1211, when the invasion of China began. For two years the Great Wall deterred them, but it was eventually penetrated through a 27-km gorge which led to the north Chinese plains. In 1215 a Chinese general went over to the Mongols and led them into Beijing. Nevertheless, the Chinese stubbornly held out, and the war in China was placed under the command of one of Genghis' generals so the Khan could turn his attention to the west.

Despite the death of Genghis Khan in 1227, the Mongols lost none of their vigour. The empire had been divided up by Genghis into separate domains, each domain ruled by one of his sons or other descendants. Ogadai was given China and was also elected the Great Khan in 1229 by an assemblage of princes. Northern China was subdued but the conquest of the south was delayed while the Khan turned his attention to the invasion and subjugation of Russia. With the death of Ogadai in 1241, the invasion of Europe was cancelled and Mangu Khan, a grandson of Genghis Khan, continued the conquest of China. He sent his brother Kublai and the general Subotai (who had been responsible for Mongol successes in Russia and Europe) to attack the south of China, which was ruled by the Song emperors. Mangu died of dysentery while fighting in China in 1259. Once again, the death of the Khan brought an end to a Mongol campaign on the brink of success.

Kublai was elected Great Khan in China, but his brother Arik-Boko challenged him for the title. Between the two there was a profound ideological difference. Arik-Boko led a faction of Mongols who wanted to preserve the traditional Mongol way of life, extracting wealth from the empire without intermingling with other races. Kublai,

Inner Mongolian horseman

however, realised that an empire won on horseback could not be governed on horseback and intended to establish a government in China with permanent power concentrated in the cities and towns. The deaths of Kublai's enemies in the 'Golden Horde' (the Mongol faction which controlled the far west of the empire) and the defeat of Arik-Boko's forces by Kublai's generals enabled Kublai Khan to complete the conquest of southern China by 1279. It was the first and only time that China has been ruled in its entirety by foreigners.

The Mongols established their capital at Beijing, and Kublai Khan became the first emperor of the Yuan Dynasty. The Mongols improved the road system linking China with Russia, promoted trade throughout the empire and with Europe, instituted a famine relief scheme and expanded the canal system which brought food from the countryside to the cities. It was into this China that foreigners like Marco Polo wandered, and his book *Description of the World* revealed the secrets of Asia to an amazed Europe.

The Mongols' conquest of China was also to lead to their demise. They alienated the Chinese by staffing the government bureaucracy with Mongols, Muslims and other foreigners. The Chinese were excluded from government and relegated to the level of second-class citizens in their own country. Landowners and wealthy traders were favoured, taxation was high and the prosperity of the empire did little to improve the lot of the peasant. Even though the Mongols did not mix with their Chinese subjects, they did succumb to Chinese civilisation: the warriors grew soft. Kublai died in 1294, the last Khan to rule over a united Mongol empire. He was followed by a series of weak and incompetent rulers who were unable to contain the revolts that spread all over China. In 1368 Chinese rebels converged on Beijing and the Mongols were driven out by an army led by Zhu Yuanzhang, who then founded the Ming Dynasty.

The entire Mongol empire had disintegrated by the end of the 14th century, and the Mongol homeland returned to the way of life it knew before Genghis Khan. Once again the Mongols became a collection of disorganised roaming tribes, warring among themselves and occasionally raiding China until the Qing emperors finally gained control over them in the 18th century.

Divided Mongolia

The eastern expansion of the Russian empire placed the Mongols in the middle of the border struggles between the Russians and the Chinese, and the Russian empire set up a 'protectorate' over the northern part of Mongolia. The rest of Mongolia was governed by the Chinese until 1911, when the Qing fell. For eight years Mongolia remained an independent state until the Chinese returned. Then in 1924 during the Soviet Civil War, the Soviet Communist Army pursued White Russian leaders to Urga (now Ulaan Baatar), where they helped create the Mongolian People's Republic by ousting the lama priesthood and the Mongol princes. The new republic has remained very much under Soviet domination.

During the war between China and Japan in the 1930s and '40s, parts of what is now Inner Mongolia were occupied by the Japanese, and Communist guerrillas also operated there. In 1936 Mao Zedong told Edgar Snow in Yan'an:

As for Inner Mongolia, which is populated by both Chinese and Mongolians, we will struggle to drive Japan from there and help Inner Mongolia to establish an autonomous state...when the people's revolution has been victorious in China, the Outer Mongolian republic will automatically become part of the Chinese federation, at its own will.

But that was not to be. In 1945 Stalin extracted full recognition of the independence of Outer Mongolia from Chiang Kaishek when the two signed an anti-Japanese Sino-Soviet alliance. Two years later, with the resumption of the civil war in China, the Chinese Communists designated what was left to China of the Mongol territories as the 'Autonomous Region of Inner Mongolia'. With the Communist victory in 1949, Outer Mongolia did not join the People's Republic as Mao had said it would. The region remained firmly under Soviet control, though it was relatively benign until the 1960s when China and the USSR suddenly became enemies. Mongolia found itself the meat in the sandwich – more than 100,000 Soviet soldiers poured into Mongolia, effectively turning it into a huge military base.

It was not until 1962 that the border with Outer Mongolia was finally settled, though parts of the far north-east were disputed by the Soviet Union. Then in 1969 the Chinese carved up Inner Mongolia and donated bits of it to other provinces – they were reinstated in 1979. The Chinese seem sufficiently confident about the assimilation of the Mongols to talk about historical absurdities like 'Genghis Khan's Chinese armies' or the 'minority assistance in building the Great Wall'.

In 1981 when an Italian film crew rented the courtyard of Beijing's Forbidden City as a Marco Polo film location (at a reported cost of US$4000 a day – the Chinese originally wanted US$10,000 a day), a splendid assembly of horses and soldiers was laid on, the soldiers portrayed by People's Liberation Army troops. The Chinese claimed the money was secondary and that historical accuracy was the thing at stake. However, they didn't like the Mongols being depicted as hated by the Song Dynasty Chinese they had overrun – after all, that conflicts with the Communist claim that China's minorities get along famously with the Han majority. It's rather an odd claim, since the Great Wall was built to keep out the ethnic minorities (at the time referred to less politely as 'barbarians'). More predictably, the Chinese vetoed some seduction scenes involving Chinese concubines and Mongol lechers.

CLIMATE

Siberian blizzards and cold currents rake the plains in winter – forget it! In winter you'll even witness the phenomenon of snow on the desert sand dunes. Summer (from June to August) brings pleasant temperatures, but the region is prone to occasional thunderstorms. Visiting from May to September is feasible, but pack warm clothing for spring or autumn.

ECONOMY

Much of the Inner Mongolia region comprises vast areas of natural grazing land. The economy is based on stock breeding of cattle, sheep, horses and camels, and the region is the main source of tanned hides, wool and dairy products for China. The Greater Hinggan range makes up about one-sixth of the country's forests and is an important source of timber and paper pulp. The region is also rich in minerals such as coal and iron ore, as you will clearly see if you visit Baotou.

POPULATION & PEOPLE

Just over two million people live in Outer Mongolia. Inner Mongolia stretches across half of northern China and is inhabited by around 20 million people. About 10% of these are Mongols, practitioners of Tibetan Buddhism with some Muslims among them. The rest of the population is made up of mostly Han Chinese (concentrated in Baotou and Hohhot) and minority Huis, Manchus, Daurs and Ewenkis. The Mongolians are very much a minority in Inner Mongolia.

Since 1949 the Chinese have followed a policy of assimilation of the Mongols. The Chinese language became a compulsory subject in schools, the populace was organised into sheep-farming cooperatives and communes, and new railways and roads brought in Chinese settlers.

The Mongolians are scattered throughout China's north-eastern provinces, as well as through Qinghai and Xinjiang. In total, there are some 3½ million Mongolians living in China, and another half a million in Russia.

The 'Inner Mongolia Autonomous Region' enjoys little or no autonomy at all. Since the break-up of the Soviet Union in 1991, Outer Mongolia has been free of Soviet control and is reasserting its nationalism. This has the Chinese worried – nationalistic movements like those in Tibet and Xinjiang do not exactly please Beijing. As a result, The PSB keeps a tight lid on potential real or imagined independence activists.

A smattering of Chinese have ended up on the wrong side of the border; by a Beijing count there are 10,000 ethnic Chinese residing in Outer Mongolia, 6000 of them in Ulaan Baatar. Back in mid-1983 more than 600 were expelled by the Mongolian government and sent to China. Others have left due to the deteriorating conditions of the Mongolian economy and the improvement in China's living standards. There are only about 1000 people living in Ulaan Baatar these days who identify themselves as ethnically Chinese.

HOHHOT
(hūhéhàotè) 呼和浩特

Hohhot became the capital of Inner Mongolia in 1952, when it served as the administrative and educational centre. It was founded in the 16th century and, like the other towns, grew around its temples and lamaseries, which are now in ruins. Hide and wool industries are the mainstay, backed up by machine-building, a sugar refinery, fertiliser plants, a diesel-engine factory and iron and steel production. The population is just over one million if the outlying areas are included.

'Hohhot' means 'blue city' in Mongolian, though many Chinese-speaking locals mistakenly claim it means 'green city'. Perhaps the name refers to the crisp blue skies – this is one of the sunniest parts of China outside of the western deserts. Hohhot is certainly one of China's more pleasant cities and the main entrance point for tours of the grasslands.

Information

CITS & CTS The CITS office (☎ 624494) is in the lobby of the Inner Mongolia Hotel. However, we have found CTS (☎ 626774) to be more helpful for buying train and air tickets and for arranging tours to the grasslands. CTS is on the 3rd floor of the rear building, and employs English, French, German and Japanese speakers.

PSB This is in the vicinity of Renmin Park,

near the corner of Zhongshan Lu and Xilin Guole Lu.

Money Most convenient for changing money are the Bank of China branches inside the Inner Mongolia and Zhaojun hotels. The main branch is on Xinhua Dajie.

Inner Mongolia Museum
(nèi ménggǔ bówùguǎn) 内蒙古博物馆

Well presented and definitely worth a visit, this is the biggest attraction in town. The museum includes a large mammoth skeleton dug out of a coal mine; a fantastic array of Mongolian costumery, artefacts, archery equipment and saddles; and a yurt. The top floors of the museum are sometimes closed. The flying horse on top of the building is meant to symbolise the forward spirit of the Mongolian people. The museum is at 1 Xinhua Dajie and costs only Y0.30.

Five Pagoda Temple
(wǔtǎ sì) 五塔寺

This miniaturised structure dating back to 1740 is now bereft of its temple, leaving the Five Pagodas standing on a rectangular block. The pagodas are built with glazed bricks and are inscribed in Mongolian, Sanskrit and Tibetan. Cut into niches are small Buddhist figures; around the back is a screen wall with an astronomical chart inscribed in Mongolian. The Five Pagodas are on the bus No 1 route.

Dazhao Temple
(dàzhào) 大召

The old part of town directly north of the tomb of Wang Zhaojun has some interesting sights. Down some alleys off a main street is the Dazhao Temple, which has almost fallen apart. The temple is incidental; the main action is on the streets. Around the area of the Dazhao Temple are some fascinating adobe houses, low and squat with decorated glass windows.

Xiletuzhao Temple
(xílètúzhào) 席勒图召

Not far from the Dazhao Temple is the

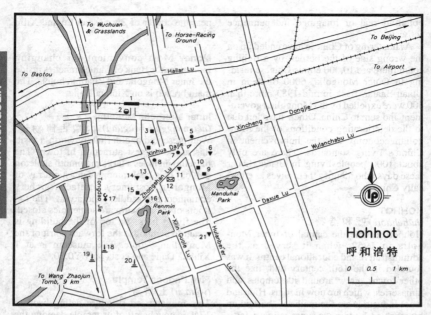

Hohhot

呼和浩特

0   0.5   1 km

Xiletuzhao Temple. It's the stomping ground of the 11th Grand Living Buddha, who dresses in civvies and is apparently active. There's nothing special to see though. The original temple burned down and the present one was built in the 19th century; the Chinese-style building has a few Tibetan touches. The swastika symbols on the exterior have long been used in Persian, Indian, Greek and Jewish cultures – they symbolise truth and eternity (no relation to its mirror image, the Nazi swastika).

Great Mosque
(qīngzhēn dà sì) 清真大寺

North of Xiletuzhao on Tongdao Jie is the Great Mosque, which is not so great – in fact, it's in sad shape. It dates from the Qing Dynasty, with later expansions.

Wang Zhaojun Tomb
(zhāojūn mù) 昭君墓

The tomb of this Han Dynasty concubine to Emperor Yuandi (1st century BC) is a bit of a bore – although it does permit some countryside viewing at the edge of town. It would be more interesting if the tomb was in better condition – presently, it's in rather pathetic shape though perhaps some renovation work will be considered when CITS recognises the hard currency potential. The tomb is nine km from the city on the bus No 14 route.

Organised Tours

Both CITS and CTS turn on the culture in Hohhot, from the grasslands tour to the equestrian displays at the horse-racing ground. Horse-racing, polo and stunt riding are put on for large tour groups, if you latch onto one somehow – otherwise they take place only on rare festive occasions. Likewise with song and dance soirées. Other things you might be able to wangle out of CITS or CTS if combining in-town sights with a grasslands sortie are a visit to the carpet works, or to the underground tunnel-

■ PLACES TO STAY

3 Hohhot Hotel
4 Zhaojun Hotel
9 Inner Mongolia Hotel & CITS
10 Xincheng Hotel
15 Yunzhong Hotel & Minzu Department
   Store

▼ PLACES TO EAT

6 Malaqin Restaurant
11 Yikesai Restaurant
14 Bailingxiang Restaurant
21 Aoni Fried Chicken

OTHER

1 Railway Station
2 Long-Distance Bus Station
5 Bailing Market
7 Inner Mongolia Museum
8 Bank of China
12 Post Office
13 CAAC
16 PSB
17 Great Mosque
18 Xiletuzhao Temple
19 Dazhao Temple
20 Five Pagoda Temple

■ PLACES TO STAY

3 呼和浩特宾馆
4 昭君大酒店
9 内蒙古饭店／中国国际旅行社
10 新城宾馆
15 云中大酒店／民族商场

▼ PLACES TO EAT

6 马拉沁饭店
11 伊克赛酒楼
14 百灵香餐厅
21 奥妮炸鸡店

OTHER

1 火车站
2 长途汽车站
5 百灵商场
7 内蒙古博物馆
8 中国银行
12 邮局
13 中国民航
16 公安局外事科
17 清真大寺
18 席勒图召
19 大召
20 五塔寺

ling system built to evacuate Hohhot residents to the Daqing mountains in the event of a Soviet bear hug.

Festivals

The summer festival known as **Naadam** (*nādámù*) features traditional Mongolian sports such as competition archery, horse racing, wrestling and camel racing. Prizes vary from a goat to a fully equipped horse. The fair has its origins in the ancient Obo-Worshipping Festival (an *obo* is a pile of stones with a hollow space for offerings – a kind of shaman shrine). The Mongolian clans make a beeline for the fairs on any form of transport they can muster, and create an impromptu yurt city. For foreigners, Hohhot is a good place to see the Naadam festivities. The exact date of Naadam varies in China, but is usually around mid-August. It's worth knowing that Naadam is celebrated at a dif-

ferent time in Outer Mongolia – always 11-13 July, which corresponds to the date of Mongolia's 1921 revolution. To find out just when and where Naadam events are being staged, contact the Hohhot CITS or CTS – other branches of CITS in China know very little about Naadam so don't even bother asking in Beijing or Canton.

Places to Stay

The *Hohhot Hotel* (☎ 662200) (*hūhéhàotè bīnguǎn*) is near the railway station and has dorms for Y64 and doubles for Y128. It's a convenient place to stay, but not a particularly nice hotel.

Most budget travellers prefer the *Xincheng Hotel* (☎ 663322) (*xīnchéng bīnguǎn*). It's the cheapest place in town, with nice dorms with three beds each for Y20. Magnificent doubles with private bath go for Y100 and

Y120. With large rooms and tree-shaded spacious grounds, it's rather like living in a park. The gift shop has maps and there are bicycle rentals. It's two km from the railway station. No bus runs from the railway station to the hotel – bus No 20 stops near the hotel, but to catch this bus you must turn left as you exit the railway station and walk a long block to Hulunbei'er Lu. Otherwise, get a taxi for Y10.

Just around the corner from the Xincheng Hotel is the *Inner Mongolia Hotel* (☎ 664233; fax 661479) *(nèi ménggǔ fàndiàn)*, a 14-storey high-rise on Wulanchabu Xilu. This is the home of CITS and CTS, and though the standard is three-star, lack of maintenance is beginning to take its toll. As usual, the problem is plumbing. Dorms in a three-bed room cost Y50 per person; doubles are Y150 and Y200.

The *Yunzhong Hotel* (☎ 668822) *(yúnzhōng dàjiǔdiàn)* is a new place on Zhongshan Xilu, hidden behind the Minzu Department Store. Doubles cost Y140, Y160 and Y220.

The *Zhaojun Hotel* (☎ 662211; fax 668825) *(zhāojūn dàjiǔdiàn)*, 11 Xinhua Dajie, is a fancy Hong Kong joint venture. Everything here works well – the heat, the plumbing – and the staff are very friendly. This is no doubt the best hotel in Inner Mongolia. Of course, luxury is something you pay for – doubles cost Y220 and Y260.

Places to Eat

The Chinese restaurant in the *Inner Mongolia Hotel* plays a dirty trick on foreigners – the English menu has higher prices than the Chinese menu and none of the inexpensive dishes appear on the English menu. Also, the staff are unwilling to tell you what's available, so unless your Chinese reading ability is keen, it's better to eat elsewhere. Cheap local restaurants are in the alley just across the street from the hotel.

The *Malaqin Restaurant (malaqin* means 'horseman') is recommended for both Chinese and Mongolian food. Try the Mongolian hotpot, roasted lamb and kebab. Prices are moderate even though this place

caters to foreign tour groups, and the friendly staff speak some English.

Yikesai (yīkèsài jiǔlóu) and *Bailingxiang (bǎilíngxiāng cāntīng)* restaurants also serve good Mongolian food.

Hohhot's answer to the Colonel (of Kentucky fame) is *Aoni Fried Chicken (àonī zhàjī diàn)* in the southern section of Hulunbei'er Lu.

The *Zhaojun Hotel Restaurant* is good but the price of a good meal is high enough to bankrupt Outer Mongolia.

Entertainment

Just east of the intersection of Xinhua Dajie and Hulunbei'er Lu is the Bailing Market *(bǎilíng shāngchǎng)*. As you face the market, on the right side of the building is a theatre where you can see brilliant Mongolian singing and dancing performances at night. When we went there, we found just four people watching the show – all foreigners! This is despite the fact that the performance was outstanding. It could be that performances are not held every night – we assume that someone actually has to buy a ticket or the show will be cancelled. Tickets are sold at all the big hotels for Y8. If the front desk staff at your hotel seem to know nothing about this, ask CITS or CTS.

Things to Buy

The Minority Handicraft Factory on the southern side of town on the bus No 1 route has a retail shop for tourists. There is a limited selection, but wares include inlaid knife and chopstick sets, daggers, boots, embroidered shoes, costumes, brassware, blankets and curios.

You'll actually find a better selection and lower prices at the Minzu Department Store *(mínzú shāngchǎng)*. It's on Zhongshan Lu where the stairs cross the road. This is also where you'll find the Friendship Store.

Getting There & Away

Air CAAC's office (☎ 664103) is on Xilin Guole Lu. There are flights to Baotou (Y120), Beijing (Y240), Canton (Y1190), Chifeng (Y420), Hailar (Y880), Ulanhot

(Y510) and Wuhan (Y620). There is also an international flight to Ulaan Baatar in Outer Mongolia which costs US$150.

Air tickets between Hohhot and Beijing are harder to buy than the Holy Grail. Try the CTS office – sometimes you get lucky. Otherwise, go directly to CAAC.

Bus There are sporadic bus connections between Hohhot and Datong. Buses to Baotou go once every 30 minutes or so. The most useful bus for travellers is the one to Dongsheng, which departs at 7.40 am.

Train Hohhot is on the Beijing-Lanzhou railway line that cuts a long loop through Inner Mongolia; about 2½ hours out of Beijing you'll pass the eroded ramains of the Great Wall (it looks like a dirt embankment). On the fastest trains Beijing to Hohhot is a 12-hour trip, Datong to Hohhot takes five hours, Baotou to Hohhot is three hours, and Yinchuan to Hohhot is 12 hours. Trains are most frequent between Hohhot and Beijing, less so between Yinchuan and Hohhot, and run only twice a day between Lanzhou and Yinchuan. There are twice-daily connections between Taiyuan and Datong, where a connection to Hohhot can be made.

Unless you have a relative on the inside, getting a sleeper is impossible if you go to the station on your own – even hard-seat tickets seem to take connections! All tickets are sold at the back door – the back door for foreigners is CTS at the Inner Mongolia Hotel (CITS also does it but they seem more bureaucratic).

Getting Around

To/From the Airport Hohhot Airport is about 35 km east of the city. There is a bus from the CAAC booking office. Taxi drivers ask around Y80 for the journey.

Bus You can get a detailed bus map (in Chinese only), which includes surrounding regions, from the hotel gift shops and bookstalls around town. Check with hotel staff for your proposed route. Bus No 1 runs from the railway station to the old part of the city in the south-western corner.

Taxi These are available from the hotels and railway station area. There are no meters, but drivers charge around Y10 between the railway station and the Inner Mongolia Hotel.

Bicycle Hohhot is reasonably small and, weather permitting, you can go a long way on a pair of self-propelled wheels. Bikes can be hired at both the Xincheng and Inner Mongolia hotels, and there are numerous bike stalls along the main road to the left of the station. Prices average Y0.50 per hour, Y2 for half a day, and Y5 for the whole day. A passport or similar ID is required.

AROUND HOHHOT

About 15 km west of Hohhot, the Sino-Tibetan monastery **Wusutuzhao** is hardly worth looking at, but the surrounding arid landscape is spectacular.

About 20 km east of Hohhot, along the airport road, is the **White Pagoda** (*báitǎ*), a seven-storey octagonal tower. The pagoda can be reached by a half-hour suburban train ride, or drop in by taxi if you're on the way to the airport.

THE GRASSLANDS

(*cǎoyuán*) 草原

This is what most travellers come to see in Inner Mongolia. If the price of a tour is too hefty, you can see much the same thing at Dongsheng and even stay there in a yurt for a fraction of what CITS charges. Or if you want to get further out into the grasslands, consider a trip to Hailar or Xilinhot (see those sections later in this chapter).

Organised Tours

Cashing in on the magic attraction of Mongolia is the name of the game here, and tours to the grasslands are organised by the Hohhot CITS and CTS. Both organisations have a stable of vehicles ranging from jeeps to buses to take you out there.

Most of Hohhot's population is Han

Chinese. The Mongolians are out on the grasslands, supposedly roaming around on their horses or drinking milk tea (a mixture of horse's milk and salt) in their yurts. For pure theatre, nothing beats the CITS Grasslands Tour.

As for visions of the descendants of the mighty Khan riding the endless plains, the herds of wild horses, and the remnants of Xanadu, make sure you get a detailed itinerary from CITS so you can decide whether it's worth the price.

The real country for seeing Mongolians in their native habitat is Outer Mongolia, but getting there is both expensive and difficult. Grasslands and yurt dwellings can be seen in other parts of China – in Xinjiang for example. Remember that grass is only green in summer – the verdant pasturelands can turn a shrivelled shade of brown from November to April. Take warm, windproof clothing – there's a considerable wind-chill factor even at the height of summer.

There are three grasslands targeted for CITS and CTS tours: Xilamuren (80 km from Hohhot), Gegentala (170 km away in Siziwang Qi) and Huitengxile (120 km from Hohhot), which is the most beautiful but least visited.

Legally speaking, all tours must be arranged through an authorised travel agency like CTS, CITS or some of the others catering to mainly Chinese tourists (China Comfort Inner Mongolia Travel Service in the Hohhot Hotel). There are some fledgeling private travel agents who try to solicit business in the lobbies of the tourist hotels – you can talk to them and discuss prices.

There are also individual taxi drivers around the railway station who do self-styled grassland tours for around Y200 per person, which includes an overnight stay in a yurt belonging to the driver's family. These unofficial tours are technically illegal and get mixed reviews – one traveller was served a wretched meal in a yurt – cooked over a cow-dung fire – and got food poisoning. As you'll discover if you explore the Mongolian hinterland, sanitation is not a strong point so watch what you eat.

The following prices, quoted by CTS, are payable in FEC:

To Xilamuren

People	1 Day	2 Days	3 Days
1	499	603	751
2-3	275	339	443
4-6	180	246	302
7-10	144	185	234
11-20	116	155	215
over 20	103	150	206

To Gegentala

People	2 Days	3 Days
1	831	985
2-3	462	560
4-6	290	337
7-10	220	280
11-20	208	260
over 20	194	242

To Huitengxile

People	2 Days	3 Days
1	691	839
2-3	388	486
4-6	248	298
7-10	203	254
11-20	175	230
over 20	160	215

Itinerary

Here's a two-day itinerary to give you some idea of the picnics, outings and carnivals in Inner Mongolia.

Day 1 At 2.30 pm, we discover the first day is half over – the tour is by calendar days. After a three-hour drive over the mountains to the grasslands plateau we arrive at Wulantuge commune. The major industry here seems to be shepherding tourists. It's the first commune from Hohhot, so lots of groups are processed through this meatworks. On our arrival, a woman in Mongolian costume (still, however, wearing slacks underneath and a tell-tale pair of tennis shoes) pops out of a door to greet us. Dinner is very good – baozi and meat dishes. The guide motions toward the yurt compound at the edge of town. These are on fixed brick and concrete foundations with 75-watt light bulbs dangling from each yurt-hole. The yurts are only for tourists – the natives live in sensibly thick-walled brick structures. The outhouse is primitive – I'm wondering if the joke is on us, and whether the locals are sitting on porcelain models with flushers. A clammy, damp cold permeates the yurts, sufficient to send an arthritic into spasms.

Day 2 Breakfast is at 8.30 am, a decidedly Western hour. We take advantage of the lull to poke around – post office, school, souvenir shop. There's a large temple structure with Sino-Tibetan features, probably 18th-century, with colonnade, intricate windows and doorways, devilish frescoes – but entry is barred. Part of the complex around it has been turned into a dining hall for receiving the likes of us. At breakfast I ask the guide (who sits at a separate table with the driver) a few questions in relation to the tourist industry, which he either ignores, evades, or pretends not to understand. Back at the yurts are two ruddy-cheeked gentlemen waiting with two moth-eaten animals. The ruddy complexion comes from wind chill – the animals have not weathered it so well. One is, I guess you might call it, yes, a horse. The other is the worst-looking excuse for a camel I've seen. I mean, camels are ugly, but this one had just about fallen apart. It's strictly a mounted picture-taking session; the attendants keep these pathetic specimens on leashes, explaining that they're too dangerous to be ridden solo.

At 9.30 am the driver whips over the grasslands – very nice, peaceful, dirt paths. It's reassuring to see some real grass in China. Hong Kongers get most enthralled about this; there isn't too much of the stuff around Kowloon. We stop to observe a flock of sheep – the shepherd poses for photos. Then, the highlight of the tour, a visit to a typical Mongolian family. They live in a three-room brick dwelling, and there, smack on the wall as you enter, is a giant poster of a koala (New South Wales Tourist Authority) which confirms my impression that perhaps I'd be better off on an Australian sheep farm. The typical family is wearing standard Han ration clothing (did we catch them with their pants down?) but they bring out Mongolian garb for dress-up photo-sessions – for us to dress up, that is. They've obviously given up. Parked out the back is their form of transport – bicycles. It puzzles me why we are brought here when there are yurt dwellers in the area. The only explanation I can think of is that they're further out from the Wulantuge commune, and the driver is too lazy or has been given other directions. Or perhaps any real Mongolian wants nothing to do with CITS – a view with which I can sympathise.

Motoring off again, we visit an *obo*, a pile of stones in the middle of nowhere. When nomads used to gather for mid-May festivals, each would bring a stone and lay it here. We go back to Wulantuge for a banquet-style lunch; a sheep is slaughtered and barbecued, for a surcharge. After lunch, the guide announces that it's time for *xiûxi* – the rest period will be 2½ hours. We wave goodbye to the woman near the yurt compound (as she struggles to get into her Mongolian robes in time), and head back for Hohhot. We arrive around 4.30 that afternoon; the tour is supposed to last until 6 pm and there is a filler of sights around town that I've already seen and which don't require a guide.

In sum, depending on what you've negotiated, your real time on the grasslands amounts to about two hours, plus the drive there and back. You spend a lot of time sleeping, eating, waiting and taking pictures of each other. The three-day itineraries are probably much the same, with feeble archery or song and dance routines thrown in. The best part of the trip is, unexpectedly, the food – the meals were banquet-size and tasty.

XILINHOT
(xílínhàotè) 锡林浩特

Another option for pursuing the topic of the disappearing Mongols is to visit Xilinhot, 500 km north-east of Hohhot as the crow flies. It is the headquarters of the large Xilin Gol League, which is subdivided into 10 districts and over 100 communes. The league covers an area of 172,000 sq km, with a population of under a million – a quarter of whom are Mongolian. The Xilin Gol League was a centre of Mongolian nationalism in the 1930s but today the major occupation is the tending of sheep, cattle, goats, camels and horses – some five million of them – and herding tourists. Heavy industry is minimal, though petroleum deposits have been discovered. Ensconced in Xilinhot is the Beizimiao, a large, dilapidated lamasery in Chinese style dating from the Qing Dynasty.

If you can put up with the avarice and antics of CITS, they have jeep excursions to communes 50 km and 130 km away, with overnight stops in yurts, tea-tasting and campfires. Should you strike a genuine Mongol you might get a cup of their milk tea. It's made of horse's milk and salt, and apparently tastes revolting; it's also most impolite to refuse.

Places to Stay
The hotel in Xilinhot that accepts foreigners is the *Baima Fandian* (☎ 4392) – triple rooms in this 21-room hotel cost an outrageous Y170. CITS is in the same building. Both CITS (☎ 4752) and the manager of the Baima Fandian are intent on squeezing all the cash they can out of foreigners with expensive tours. You can take a local bus or rent a vehicle to visit nearby villages (taxis are hard to come by in this backwater – finding a horse might be easier!). Travelling

outside the town requires another permit, but it's readily available from the PSB in Xilinhot.

Because we speak Chinese and had a lot of luck we could manage in Xilinhot. The CITS is ruled by someone who is interested in your money and nothing more! In Xilinhot itself there is nothing to do. We would advise other tourists to arrange a tour via CITS in Hohhot. Xilinhot isn't worth all the trouble (permits for everything).

Henneke & Erzsebet

Getting There & Away

The bus station in Hohhot is unwilling to sell tickets, so you must fly from Hohhot. There are three flights weekly. Fortunately, you can return overland, though this requires a travel permit *(tōngxíngzhèng)* – none is needed if you fly.

You can leave Xilinhot overland by a combination of bus and train. Xilinhot PSB will readily issue travel permits (smile at them, we want to keep them friendly). To return to Hohhot or Beijing, you must take the bus to Sonid Youqi *(sūnítè yòuqí)* on the Erenhot-Jining railway line. From Sonid Youqi, there is only one train weekly to Jining (Jining is on the Beijing-Hohhot line). At the time of writing, the train departs Sonid Youqi on Saturday, but check with the local authorities in Xilinhot because the schedule could change.

CITS and the Baima Fandian management have been telling travellers that they must exit Xilinhot by taxi for Y2000. Your best bet is to ask at the PSB or the bus company.

BAOTOU
(bāotóu) 包头

The largest city in Inner Mongolia lies on the bleak northernmost reaches of the Yellow River, to the west of Hohhot. The name means 'land with deer' in Mongolian, and though there is still a deer farm outside of Baotou, you are only likely to encounter these creatures on the dinner plate in some of the upmarket restaurants around town.

Previously set in an area of underdeveloped semi-desert inhabited by Mongol herders, Baotou underwent a radical change when the Communists came to power in 1949. In the next decade, a 1923 railway line linking the town with Beijing was extended south-east to Yinchuan, and roads were constructed to facilitate access to the region's iron, coal and other mineral deposits.

Today, Baotou is an industrial community of nearly one million people – despite the showcase Mongolian street signs, nearly the entire population is Han Chinese. The city is not blessed with scenic sights, though for some reason Japanese tour groups continue to throng here and pay high prices for the privilege. Baotou is definitely a city of specialised interests – a couple of nearby monasteries, a steel mill, steam locomotive museum, small sand dunes and a mausoleum dedicated to Genghis Khan. Most of these sights are not in the city itself, but a couple of hours outside the town. Overall, Baotou is a useful transit point and you can keep yourself amused here for a day or so, but if you miss it, don't lose any sleep. The best thing

Inner Mongolian farmer

INNER MONGOLIA

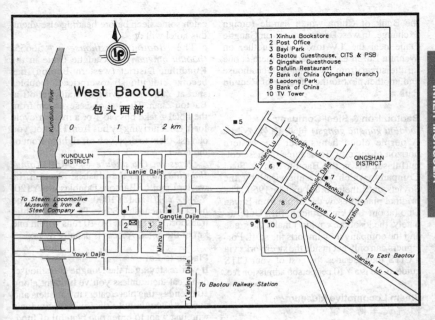

West Baotou
包头西部

1 Xinhua Bookstore
2 Post Office
3 Bayi Park
4 Baotou Guesthouse, CITS & PSB
5 Qingshan Guesthouse
6 Dafulin Restaurant
7 Bank of China (Qingshan Branch)
8 Laodong Park
9 Bank of China
10 TV Tower

KUNDULUN DISTRICT

QINGSHAN DISTRICT

Kundulun River

Tuanjie Dajie

To Steam Locomotive Museum & Iron & Steel Company →

Gangtie Dajie

Youyi Dajie

Minzu Xilu

Fuqiang Lu

Qingshan Lu

Hudemulin Dajie

Wenhua Lu

Minzhu Lu

Kexue Lu

Jianshe Lu

To East Baotou

A'erding Dajie

To Baotou Railway Station

1 新华书店
2 邮局
3 八一公园
4 包头宾馆/中国国际旅行社/公安局
5 青山宾馆
6 大福林饭庄
7 中国银行（青山商业大厦）
8 劳动公园
9 中国银行
10 电视塔

we can say for the place is that the people are very friendly.

Orientation

Baotou is a huge town – 20 km of urban sprawl separate the eastern and western parts of the city. It's the eastern area that most travellers visit because it's useful as a transit hub – the west area has the steel mill and locomotive museum.

The station for the western area is Baotou station *(bāotóu zhàn)*; for the eastern area it's Baotou east station *(bāotóu dōng zhàn)*. The eastern district is called Donghe; the western area is subdivided into two adjacent districts, Qingshan and Kundulun.

Information

CITS This office (☎ 54615; fax 54615) is in the Baotou Guesthouse. The staff are very friendly – some speak English but Japanese seems to be the preferred language here. Besides practising your Japanese, the main reason for dropping in would probably be to arrange a trip to the steelworks. CITS also does tours to the nearby Yellow River, though this is mainly a group activity.

PSB This is in the same compound as the Baotou Guesthouse.

Money None of the hotels have a money-changing desk, but there are four branches of the Bank of China which handle foreign exchange. In west Baotou, one is on Gangtie Dajie near the TV tower and another on Wenhua Lu. In eastern Baotou, there is one up the street from the Donghe Guesthouse and another next to the entrance of Renmin Park.

Baotou Iron & Steel Company
(bāotóu gāngtiě gōngsī) 包头钢铁公司
A purple cloud hangs over the western horizon of the city. The source of these colourful sunsets is the Baotou Iron & Steel Company, which was supervised by the Soviets until their abrupt exit in 1960. The original plan foresaw use of ore from Bayan Obo (about 140 km further north). Unfortunately, the local ore couldn't make the grade and the company now imports the stuff. Foreigners can only get inside the steelworks via a CITS tour. Besides the cost of your CITS guide, there is a Y10 per person admission fee.

Steam Locomotive Museum
蒸汽火车博物馆
(zhēngqì huǒchē bówùguǎn)
The museum is fairly small but there is talk of expanding it. CITS offers tours but you can visit on your own. For foreigners, the admission fee is a steep Y30 per person.

Places to Stay
The *Donghe Guesthouse* (☎ 72541) *(dōnghé bīnguǎn)*, 14 Nanmenwai, is about 15 minutes' walk (or take bus No 5) from Baotou east station. Doubles range from Y40 (two-bed dorm) to Y80 and Y100 for a double with private bath. This place is the most popular with budget travellers and is the only place for foreigners in eastern Baotou.

Your only other alternative for budget accommodation is a dumpy little hotel, the *A'erding Fandian*, next to Baotou station (western Baotou). Doubles are Y25. It's just to your right as you exit the station. The area around the western station is pretty bleak – a couple of shops, foodstalls and not much else. But if you're only staying in Baotou to

catch some sleep before heading elsewhere, this hotel will do.

The *Baotou Guesthouse* (☎ 56655) *(bāotóu bīnguǎn)* on Gangtie Dajie in the Kundulun District (western Baotou) has become ridiculously overpriced. Doubles start at Y280. If arriving by train, get off at Baotou Zhan. The station is seven km from the hotel – take bus No 1 or a motortricycle for Y15. If arriving by bus from Hohhot, you can ask them to drop you off right in front of the hotel.

Qingshan Guesthouse (☎ 34091) *(qīngshān bīnguǎn)* is the plushest place in the western part of Baotou. Doubles are Y120, Y240, Y320 and Y1000. Adjacent to the hotel is a Friendship Store. There is no public transport, though bus No 10 runs within one km of the hotel. Access is usually by taxi.

Places to Eat
If you're staying at the Donghe Guesthouse, don't eat there unless you've brought along 10 friends – this place caters to banquets and doesn't know how to deal with individuals who just want to order one plateful of food. It's much better to go across the street to the *Asia Fast Food Restaurant (yàzhōu kuài cāntīng)* which offers meals for around Y7. Or you can walk down to the railway station where the abundant foodstalls all seem to offer the exact same food.

Over in the western part of town, the big famous place is the *Dafulin Restaurant (dàfúlín fànzhuāng)* about one km from the Qingshan Guesthouse.

Things to Buy
The hotel gift shops stock a small selection of minority handicraft tourist stuff, but Hohhot is a better place to buy this stuff. As China's mineral capital, Baotou would be a good place to find bargains on iron ore, cobalt and lignite, in case you need this stuff.

Getting There & Away
Air CAAC has two ticket offices – one inside the Baotou Guesthouse and another at the Donghe Hotel. There is only one flight a week from Baotou to Canton (Y1040) which

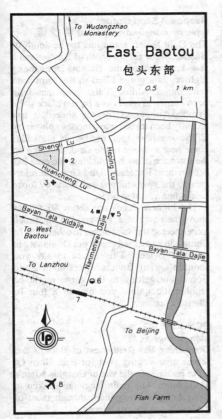

East Baotou
包头东部

0 0.5 1 km

To Wudangzhao Monastery

To West Baotou

To Lanzhou

To Beijing

Shengli Lu

Huancheng Lu

Heping Lu

Bayan Tala Xidajie

Bayan Tala Dajie

Nanmenwai Dajie

Fish Farm

1	Renmin Park
2	Bank of China
3	No 2 Hospital
4	Donghe Guesthouse
5	Asia Fast Food Restaurant
6	Long-Distance Bus Station
7	East Baotou Railway Station
8	Airport

1	人民公园
2	中国二银行
3	第二医院
4	东河宾馆
5	亚洲快餐厅
6	长途汽车站
7	包头东站
8	飞机场

short distance, taxis ask around Y20 for the one-way journey.

Bus Bus Nos 5 and 10 stop close to the Baotou Guesthouse and shuttle between the western and eastern sections of Baotou in 45 minutes. Much more comfortable are the minibuses (zhōngbā) which cost Y2 to Y3 – you board these at the regular bus stops.

Taxi Taxis and motorised tricycles congregate at the railway station and tourist hotels. No meters exist so the fare is negotiable.

AROUND BAOTOU
Wudangzhao Monastery
(wǔdāngzhào) 五当召

The main tourist attraction near Baotou is the large Wudangzhao Monastery, about 2½ hours from the city by bus. This monastery of the Gelukpa (Yellow Sect) of Tibetan Buddhism was built around 1749 in typical Tibetan style with flat-roofed buildings. It once housed 1200 monks. The ashes of seven reincarnations of the monastery's 'living buddha' are kept in a special hall. Today all religious activity is restricted to a handful of

stops off in Wuhan (Y620), one flight weekly to Hohhot (why bother when the bus takes only three hours?). There are also flights to Beijing (Y390) and Xi'an (Y370).

Bus A bus from Baotou east railway station to Hohhot is Y13 for the three-hour trip (an extra Y3 from Baotou west station). The extra fare will be collected on the bus, not when you buy your ticket in Hohhot.

Getting Around
To/From the Airport The airport is two km south of Baotou east station. Despite the

pilgrims and doorkeeper-monks who collect the admission fee.

For the crowds of day-tripping, camera-clicking tourists this is no place for religion. The surrounding hillsides are carpeted with hundreds of smashed bottles and piles of garbage. Try and walk into the hills away from the pandemonium; the site has a peculiar strength in its secretive, brooding atmosphere.

Although the monastery is very crowded with mainly Chinese tourists, it's still worth visiting. Just wait until the whole group gets out of the hall and discover how quickly silence can return.

Getting There & Away The monastery is 70 km north-east of Baotou. Bus No 7 goes to Shiguai – halfway to the monastery – and from Shiguai there are minibuses which do the second leg of the journey.

At 7 am there is a bus direct from the long-distance bus station (east Baotou) to the monastery – no need to change buses. For the return trip, you can catch this same bus from the same place at 4 pm (check with the driver when you arrive). Otherwise, do the minibus shuffle again.

Perhaps the best option are the minibuses which leave from in front of the eastern Baotou railway station and go directly to the monastery for Y5.

There's a basic dorm next to the monastery. CITS organises tours, but you can easily manage on your own. Take a torch if you want to see anything inside the monastery. Admission to the compound is Y3.

Meidaizhao Monastery
(měidàizhào) 美岱召

This monastery is much smaller than Wudangzhao and consequently little visited, although it's more accessible. Meidaizhao is halfway between Baotou and Hohhot, less than half a km north of the main highway (a 10-minute walk). Buses on the Baotou-Hohhot route can drop you off here. Like Wudangzhao, the monastery is devoted to the Gelukpa (Yellow Sect) of Tibetan Buddhism.

Resonant Sand Gorge
(yīméng xiǎng shāwān) 伊盟响沙湾

The Gobi Desert starts just to the south of Baotou. Some 60 km south of Baotou and a few km west of the Baotou-Dongsheng highway is a gorge filled to the brim with sand dunes. Although the gorge has long been known to locals as a barren place to be avoided (no grass for the sheep) it has recently been turned into a money spinner by CITS. Japanese tour groups in particular come here to frolic in the sand. To spice up the romance of such frolicking, the area has been named Resonant Sand Gorge, a reference to the swooshing sound made by loose sand when you step on it.

The highest dunes are about 40 metres above their own base. But you can find much more spectacular sand dunes in other parts of China – in particular, check out Dunhuang in Gansu Province. This is not to say you shouldn't visit Baotou's Resonant Sand Gorge, but getting to the gorge might be problematic unless you are on a tour or charter a taxi.

DONGSHENG
(dōngshèng) 东胜

Dongsheng lies south-west of Baotou and serves as a staging post for Ejin Horo Qi *(yījīn huòluò qí)*, the site of Genghis Khan's Mausoleum. The main language spoken in Dongsheng is Mongolian, though most of the locals can speak Chinese.

There is virtually nothing to see in Dongsheng itself, though the place looks a bit like a Wild West town, with wind, dust, sand and donkeys. A lot of building is going on, but it will probably be a while before they turn it into another Beijing.

If you get an early start, it's possible to reach Dongsheng in the morning, visit the Genghis Khan mausoleum, then return to Dongsheng to spend the night, or possibly all the way back to Baotou or Hohhot the same day (this would be exhausting though).

Information
The CITS office (☎ 26301) is in the Ordos Hotel, a stiff 40-minute walk from the bus

station. English is spoken and the staff are overjoyed to find a real live foreigner to practise with.

Places to Stay

The *Foreign Trade Hotel (wàimào dàjiǔdiàn)* has doubles for Y30, or less with a Chinese student card. As you exit the bus station, turn right and when you reach the first intersection, turn right again, walk 100 metres and the hotel will be on the left.

Many travellers also stay at the cheapie *Yimeng Binguan*, but beware – Chinese on conference junkets and groups sometimes book out this hotel. The staff are friendly though and may direct you elsewhere. Triples can cost as little as Y15. With your back to the bus station, turn right and walk to the first crossroad, then turn left and the hotel is about 100 metres onwards (left-hand side).

The most upmarket place in town is the *Ordos Hotel (☎ 26301) (è'ěrduōsī fàndiàn)* – with doubles for Y120. You might want to drop in here just to cheer up the CITS staff. The *Dongsheng Guesthouse (dōngshèng bīnguǎn)* is another place where many of the tour groups are put up for the night.

Getting There & Away

Most travellers take the bus directly from Hohhot – it departs at 7.40 am, takes 5½ hours and costs Y25. This bus is amazingly comfortable, with videos included. Sit on the right side of the bus for mountain views along the way (or left side on the way back). The bus goes via Baotou but doesn't stop there. Just to the south of Baotou, the bus crosses the Yellow River.

Another route is to go from Baotou. Catch buses to Dongsheng from the long-distance bus station (eastern Baotou). The government-run bus to Dongsheng departs from Baotou at 7.30 am – buy tickets inside the station. If you miss this one, there are unscheduled departures throughout the day from the station area on privately run buses – these depart when full and you buy the tickets on the bus. Typically, these buses run about once every 30 minutes. The journey

from Baotou to Dongsheng takes about 2½ hours.

AROUND DONGSHEN
Genghis Khan's Mausoleum

(chéngjí sīhàn língyuán) 成吉思汗陵园
The mausoleum is a bus trip away from Dongshen, in the middle of nowhere.

In 1954, what are said to be the ashes of the Khan were brought back from Qinghai (where they had been taken to prevent them from falling into the hands of the Japanese) and a large Mongolian-style mausoleum was built near Ejin Horo Qi. As for why the Japanese should want the Khan's ashes, it had to do with Japan's attempted invasion of Mongolia – Japanese propagandists, citing legends that Genghis Khan came from across the sea, claimed that the Mongolian people originated in Japan. This was to assure the Mongolians that reuniting with the Japanese motherland was just like getting together with family. As it turned out, a joint Russian-Mongolian (mostly Russian) force overwhelmingly defeated the Japanese attack on Outer Mongolia in 1939, though the Japanese successfully occupied Inner Mongolia and held it until the war's end in 1945.

The Cultural Revolution did enough damage to the mausoleum to keep the renovators busy for eight years and the result looks new. With the collapse of Soviet domination in 1991, Outer Mongolia has been whipping itself up into a nationalistic fervour and Genghis Khan has been elevated to godlike status. As a result, holy pilgrimages to the mausoleum have become the sacred duty of both Inner and Outer Mongolians. If you want to meet any true Mongolians, this is probably one of the best places in China to do it.

Ceremonies are held four times a year at the mausoleum to honour his memory. Butter lamps are lit, *khadas* (ritual scarves) presented and whole cooked sheep piled high before the Khan's stone statue while chanting is performed by Mongolian monks and specially chosen elders from the Daur nationality.

Photographers outside the mausoleum have robes so you can dress up and have your photo taken posing as the Great Khan. Inside are displays of Genghis Khan's martial gear and statue. Various yurts contain the biers of Genghis and his close relatives. The huge frescoes around the walls are done in cartoon style to depict important stages in the Khan's rise.

The mausoleum gets good reviews from travellers. One traveller wrote to Lonely Planet and said 'I wouldn't have missed it for the world'. Even if you're not a mausoleum fan, the scenery along the way is intriguing. Admission to the mausoleum is Y10 for foreigners.

At the end of the dirt road to the right of the mausoleum's entrance, go one km to reach the temporary residence of the Khan. You can get into this residence on the same ticket you bought for the mausoleum. Nearby is a compound (open only in summer) with nice grasslands, horses, sheep, goats and cows, plus some interesting buildings with traditional clothing, warrior outfits and riding equipment inside – all ready for the Naadam tourist carnival.

Places to Stay

There is a tourist yurt camping ground (*ménggǔbāo*) near the mausoleum, where you can stay for Y30.

The other place is a hostel (*chéngjí sīhàn líng zhāodàisuǒ*) with no English name. However, most visitors elect to stay in Dongsheng and commute to the mausoleum for a day trip.

Getting There & Away

The first bus leaves Dongsheng at 7 am, but there are several throughout the day. The journey from Dongsheng to the mausoleum takes 1½ hours.

Another strategy is to take a bus to Ejin Horo Qi (*yījīn huòluò qí*), which is 25 km from the mausoleum, and then switch to a minibus which takes 30 minutes to complete the journey.

HAILAR

(*hǎilāěr*) 海拉尔

This town in the north-eastern corner of Inner Mongolia has been opened relatively recently and is starting to attract tourists. CITS (☎ 21728) has set up an office here at 2 Shengli Lu and is determined to make this into the hottest new grassland destination. Expensive accommodation is available at the *Humeng Binguan*, but new places are under construction and the competition will, hopefully, bring down costs. There are direct flights between Hailar and Beijing (Y650), or you can reach this place on a long train ride from Harbin.

MANZHOULI

(*mǎnzhōulǐ*) 满洲里

The border town where the Trans-Siberian Railway crosses from China to Russia, the main attraction here is Dalai Lake (*dálài hú*), which unexpectedly pops out of the Mongolian grasslands like an enormous inland sea. This is Inner Mongolia's largest lake, a good area for fishing, bird-watching and minority-watching.

The other big feature is for train buffs – the steam locomotive storage and repair yards in Manzhouli are some of the more impressive in China.

Kublai Khan

CITS (☎ 2976) has established a Manzhouli branch at 121 Erdaojie and is ever ready, willing and able to take you on a tour in return for a sufficient wad of cash. Access to Manzhouli is, of course, by train from Harbin, though if you're doing the Trans-Siberian from Moscow you could conceivably jump off here after passing through Chinese Customs and immigration.

XANADU PALACE
(shàngdū) 上都

About 320 km north of Beijing, tucked away near Duolun in Inner Mongolia, are the remains of Xanadu, the great Kublai Khan's palace of legendary splendour. Marco Polo visited the Khan in the 13th century and recorded his impressions of the palace:

There is at this place a very fine marble palace, the rooms of which are all gilt and painted with figures of men and beasts and birds, and with a variety of trees and flowers, all executed with such exquisite art that you regard them with delight and astonishment.

Round this palace a wall is built enclosing a compass of 16 miles, and inside the Park there are fountains and rivers and brooks, and beautiful meadows, with all kinds of wild animals (excluding such as are of ferocious nature), which the Emperor has procured and placed there to supply food for his gerfalcons and hawks. Moreover (at a spot in the Park where there is a charming wood) he has another

Palace built of cane. It is gilt all over, and most elaborately finished inside. The Lord abides at this Park of his, dwelling sometimes in the Marble Palace and sometimes in the Cane Palace for three months of the year, to wit, June, July and August; preferring this residence because it is by no means hot; in fact it is a very cool place. When the 28th day of August arrives, he takes his departure, and the Cane Palace is taken to pieces.

In the 19th century, Samuel Taylor Coleridge (who never went near the place) stoked his imagination with some opium and composed 'Kubla Khan', a glowing poem about Xanadu that has been on the set menu for students of English literature ever since.

Over the centuries the deserted palace has crumbled back to dust and the site has been visited by very few foreigners. In 1986 a couple of British students, Louisa Slack and William Hamilton-Dalrymple, followed Marco Polo's original route from Jerusalem to Xanadu. The palace remains are close to Duolun, which is off limits to foreigners, so the local PSB ejected the British duo from the region but compassionately arranged their exit via the legendary site, where all photography was forbidden. The PSB officers must have doubted the sanity of the foreigners, who proceeded to chant Coleridge's poem while pouring a small bottle of oil from the Holy Sepulchre in Jerusalem (the same gift Marco Polo had

---

Save the Trees

Straddling the Great Wall is the world's most ambitious reafforestation and afforestation programme – a shelter belt creeping toward its ultimate length of 6000 km. Known as the 'Green Wall', the belt is designed to protect precious farmland from the sands of the Gobi Desert when the winter winds blow. It will eventually stretch from Xinjiang to Heilongjiang (China's last great timber preserve). This huge tree-planting programme is only a small part of the PRC's schedule – there's a similar belt along the south-east coast to break the force of summer typhoons. It's an attempt to reverse the effects of centuries of careless tree-cutting which, combined with slash-and-burn farming, has contributed to disastrous flooding and other ecological catastrophes.

Tree-planting is the duty of every able-bodied person in China. In the early years of the PRC forest cover was decimated to about 9%, but since the formation of the communes and production brigades in 1958, the cover has been raised to almost 13%.

The goal for the year 2000 is 20% cover, which would require tree-planting on 70 million hectares. Planting in the northern frontier zones is done in one-km-wide strips; millions of hectares have already been reafforested, with a survival rate of 55%. Wasteland and barren hills are allocated to rural households for planting and farming (also done on a contract basis), and the government provides seeds, saplings and know-how. ∎

INNER MONGOLIA

once brought for the Khan) onto the dilapidated site of the Khan's throne. According to the students, hardly anything remains of Xanadu.

TOURING OUTER MONGOLIA

It should not be forgotten that Outer Mongolia is an independent country, and this is no doubt the place to go to see genuine Mongolian culture as well as some magnificent natural scenery. A trip to Mongolia can be arranged as part of the Trans-Siberian journey, but it involves considerable bureaucracy. Lonely Planet publishes a guide for Mongolia which will tell you how to visit for the least possible cost. Worth mentioning here is that you should do everything in your power to avoid dealing with the official Mongolian state tourism bureau, Juulchin. If there's any organisation that makes CITS look good, Juulchin is it.

Ningxia 宁夏

Population: four million
Capital: Yinchuan

Ningxia (*níngxià*) was carved out as a separate administrative region in 1928 and remained a province until 1954, when it was absorbed into Gansu Province. In 1958 Ningxia re-emerged, this time as an Autonomous Region with a large Hui population. The boundaries of the region have ebbed and flowed since then – Inner Mongolia was included at one time, but the borders are now somewhat reduced.

Part of the arid north-west of China, much of Ningxia is populated by a few hardy nomads who make their living grazing sheep and goats. Winters are hard and cold, with plummeting temperatures; blistering summers make irrigation a necessity. In fact, the province would be virtually uninhabitable if it were not for the Yellow River, Ningxia's lifeline. Most of the population lives near the river or the irrigation channels which run off of it. These channels were created in the Han Dynasty, when the area was first settled by the Han Chinese in the 1st century BC.

More than four million people live in Ningxia, but only about a third are Hui, living mostly in the south of the province. The rest are Han Chinese. The Hui minority are descended from Arab and Iranian traders who travelled to China during the Tang Dynasty. Their numbers were later increased during the Yuan Dynasty by immigrants from Central Asia. Apart from their continued adherence to Islam, the Hui have been assimilated into Han culture.

In 1958 the building of the Baotou-Lanzhou railway, which cuts through Ningxia, helped to relieve the area's isolation and develop some industry in this otherwise almost exclusively agricultural region.

YINCHUAN
(yínchuān) 银川

Sheltered from the deserts of Mongolia by

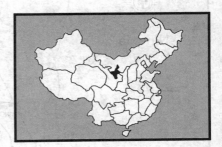

the high ranges of the Helanshan to its west and abundantly supplied with water from the nearby Yellow River, Yinchuan occupies a favoured geographical position in otherwise harsh surroundings. This city was once the capital of the Western Xia, a mysterious kingdom founded during the 11th century.

Orientation

Yinchuan is divided into two parts: a new industrial section close to the railway station, and the old town about four km away, where the hotels and sights are. At the old town's centre is the large Drum Tower, from which the main streets radiate.

Information

The main CITS/CTS office (☎ 544485) is upstairs at 150 Jiefang Xijie. There is also a small CITS office in room 129 of the Ningxia Hotel. The PSB is in a white building on Jiefang Xijie.

The main office of the Bank of China (☎ 543925) is at No 102 Jiefang Jie in a new white-tiled building near the Ningxia Hotel. The post and telephone office is right in the centre of town at the corner of Minzu Jie and Jiefang Jie.

North Pagoda
(běitǎ) 北塔

The North Pagoda (also called the Haibao

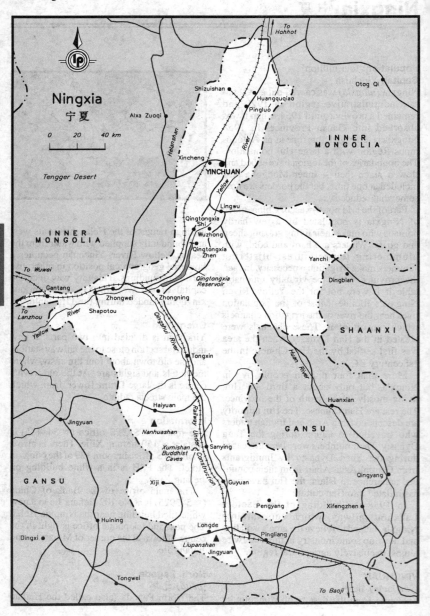

NINGXIA

Pagoda), stands out prominently in the north of the city. Records of the structure date from the 5th century. In 1739 an earthquake toppled the lot, but it was rebuilt in 1771 in the original style. It's part of a monastery which has also been spruced up as a tourist attraction.

There is no public transport out here. Other than walking, you can reach the pagoda by bicycle or taxi. It's 2½ km from the Oasis Hotel.

Regional Museum
(qū bówùguǎn) 区博物馆
The museum is on Jinning Jie, three blocks south of Jiefang Lu, in the old Chengtian Monastery. It has recently been extended, and its collection includes Western Xia and Northern Zhou historical relics as well as material covering the *Hui* culture. Within the leafy courtyard is the **West Pagoda** *(xītǎ)*. The museum is open from 8.30 am to 6.30 pm; it's closed on Monday.

Drum Tower
(gǔlóu) 鼓楼
The Drum Tower stands in the middle of a small intersection several blocks east of the post office. It's a classical Chinese-style building and is worth climbing for a quick look.

Yuhuang Pavilion
(yùhuáng gé) 玉皇阁
This restored 400-year-old building is on Jiefang Jie, one block east of the Drum Tower. The pavilion has a tiny museum whose collection includes two fascinating mummified bodies taken from tombs outside Yinchuan.

South Gate
(nánmén) 南门
This is in the south-east of the city near the long-distance bus station. It's been likened to a scaled-down version of Beijing's Tiananmen – complete with Mao portrait. Despite its lack of grandeur, the South Gate is popular with Chinese tourists as a backdrop for their own portrait shots of Mao.

Mosque
(qīngzhēn sì) 清真寺
The Nanguan mosque is a modern Middle-Eastern style structure showing little Chinese architectural influence, with Islamic arches and dome roofs covered in green tiles. This is Yinchuan's main mosque, and an active place of worship, so don't just stroll in without first asking permission. It's within easy walking distance of the South Gate.

Places to Stay
If you want to stay in the new city, there's the *Alashan Hotel* (☎ 366723) *(ālāshān fàndiàn)*, a friendly Chinese hotel just west of the traffic circle (recognisable by a white statue) at Tie Dongjie and Xincheng Jie. With nice doubles with bath for just Y46, this place is good value. Across the intersection you'll find the *Xincheng Hotel (xīnchéng fàndiàn)*, which has similar rates. The No 1 bus stops almost outside.

The No 1 also stops near the *Oasis Hotel* (☎ 546351) *(lüzhōu fàndiàn)* on Jiefang Xijie, easily distinguished by the 'rocket ship' on the roof. Here, a bed in a triple costs Y10, simple singles/doubles cost Y36/40, and a double with bathroom Y48. Unfortunately the Oasis is often full.

One block south you'll find the *Xinxi Hotel (xìnxī fàndiàn)* which has good dorm beds for Y8, and singles for Y40 with private showers.

The *Ningxia Hotel* (☎ (0951) 545131) *(níngxià bīnguǎn)*, at No 3 Gongyuan Jie near Zhongshan Park is a classy establishment with prices starting at Y100 for a double. Pleasant gardens cover the compound.

At the time of writing, another upmarket place, the *Ningfeng Hotel (níngfēng bīnguǎn)*, diagonally opposite the post office, was nearing completion and will probably offer the best accommodation in Yinchuan.

Places to Eat
Good for street food are the stalls in the backstreets around the long-distance bus station or Xinhua Jie near the museum. On offer are beef and lamb dishes, noodles, fried dumplings and Islamic pastries. A local Hui

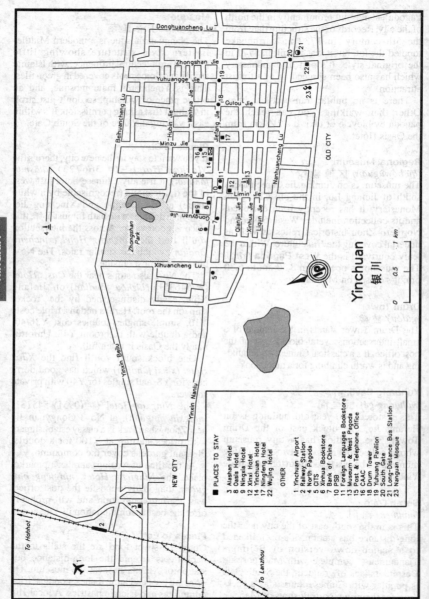

Donghuancheng Lu

Zhongshan Jie

Yuhuangge Jie

Wenhua Jie

Gulou Jie

Hubin Jie

Jiefang Jie

Minzu Jie

Jinning Jie

Limin Jie

Qianjin Jie

Xinhua Jie

Liqun Jie

Gongyuan Jie

Xihuancheng Lu

Beihuancheng Lu

Nanhuancheng Lu

OLD CITY

Zhongshan Park

NEW CITY

Yinxin Beilu

Yinxin Nanlu

To Hohhot

To Lanzhou

Yinchuan
银川

0   0.5   1 km

NINGXIA

PLACES TO STAY
3   Alashan Hotel
8   Oasis Hotel
9   Ningxia Hotel
12   Xinhua Hotel
16   Yinchuan Hotel
17   Ningfeng Hotel
22   Wujing Hotel

OTHER
1   Yinchuan Airport
2   Railway Station
4   North Pagoda
5   CITS
6   Xinhua Bookstore
10   Bank of China
11   Foreign Languages Bookstore
13   Museum & West Pagoda
15   Post & Telephone Office
18   Drum Tower
19   CAAC
20   Yuhuang Pavilion
21   Southern Gate
23   Nanguan Mosque

(wényì cházhuāng), in an old-style building just south-east of Yuhuang Pavilion.

Getting There & Away

Air The main CAAC ticket office (☎ 622143) is at 14 Minzu Beijie. There's also a branch of the CAAC-clone United China Airlines (☎ 631625) at 24 Zhongshan Beilu, north of Jiefang Lu. There are flights connecting Yinchuan with Beijing (Y550, four weekly); and Xi'an (Y280, daily); Taiyuan (Y290, twice weekly); and Lanzhou (Y170, twice weekly). A CAAC bus meets incoming and departing flights; the airport is some 13 km out of town.

Bus The long-distance bus station is in the south-eastern part of town on the square near the South Gate. Regular buses connect Yinchuan with Qingtongxia Shi, Zhongwei, Tongxin, Guyuan and alongside the Great Wall Dingbian in Shaanxi Province. There are also four standard buses each day to Xi'an (via Guyuan, Y53) and one sleeper bus (Y108). There is also one daily bus to Lanzhou (Y38).

Train Yinchuan lies on the Lanzhou-Beijing railway line which runs through Baotou, Hohhot and Datong. There's one express and two slower trains daily in each direction. Express trains from Yinchuan take 10 hours to Lanzhou, and 12 hours to Hohhot.

Getting Around

Yinchuan is not crowded like China's other provincial and regional capitals, and you can usually find a vacant seat on the bus. Bus No 1 runs back and forth along Jiefang Lu in the old town to the railway station. Minibuses also run this route and are a convenient and faster alternative, charging Y2. Yinchuan is an ideal city for bicycling, but renting a bike is not always easy. The Oasis, Xinxi and Ningxia hotels have a few rental bicycles, but only for their own guests – the CITS may be able to help.

■ PLACES TO STAY

3　阿拉善饭店
8　绿洲饭店
9　宁夏宾馆
12　信息饭店
14　银川饭馆
17　宁丰宾馆
22　武警饭店

OTHER

1　银川飞机场
2　火车站
4　北塔
5　中国国际旅行社
6　新华书店
7　中国银行
10　公安局
11　外文书店
13　博物馆和西塔
15　邮电大楼
16　中国民航
18　鼓楼
19　玉皇阁
20　南门
21　长途汽车站
23　清真寺

sweet called 'eight treasures rice' *(bābǎo fàn)* is made from jujubes and rice, pressed together and steam-cooked to form an enormous loaf. Street vendors sell slices with a topping of honey for about Y1.

The *Huanying Islamic Restaurant (huānyíng qīngzhēn fànzhuāng)*, at No 23 Jiefang Jie (next to the Yinchuan Hotel) has some tasty dishes in the section upstairs.

Yinchuan has a number of traditional teahouses where locals meet to chat, play cards or Chinese chess and sip tea. The local blend, called 'three bubbles tea' *(sānpào chà)*, is based on a mix of dried ingredients including persimmons, longans, grapes, walnuts, sesame seeds and Fujian green tea served in a small porcelain bowl with a lid. A generous chunk of rock sugar is thrown in so the brew sweetens gradually. A good place to stop for a cuppa is the *Wenyi Teahouse*

NINGXIA

AROUND YINCHUAN
Helanshan
(hèlánshān) 贺兰山

The mountains of the Helanshan range are clearly visible from Yinchuan. The range forms an important natural barrier against desert winds and invaders alike, with the highest peak reaching 3556 metres. Along the foothills of the Helanshan lie some interesting sights.

About 17 km north-west of Yinchuan is the historic pass village of Gunzhongkou, where there are walking trails up into the surrounding hills. There are scheduled buses to Gunzhongkou only in July and August, when people from the city come up here to escape the summer heat.

Not far to the north of the resort are the Twin Pagodas of Baisikou *(báisìkŏu shuāngtǎ)*, 13 and 14 storeys high and decorated with statuettes of Buddha.

South of Gunzhongkou is the Western Xia Mausoleum *(xīxià wánglíng)*, the main tourist destination in this area. According to legend, the founder of the Western Xia Kingdom, Li Yuanhao, built 72 tombs. One was for himself, others held relatives or were left empty. The Western Xia Kingdom lasted for 190 years and 10 successive emperors, but was wiped out by Genghis Khan. For some reason, the kingdom was not included in *The 24 Histories*, the standard Chinese work on the history of that era. Numerous Chinese scholars have joined the hunt to solve this mystery.

To visit the Twin Pagodas and the mausoleum (or Gunzhongkou out of season) you will have to either join one of the occasional CITS tours or hire a taxi. Because of the area's poor roads, a trip including all three sights would take a full day.

Qingtongxia
(qīngtóngxiá) 青铜峡

Two places go by the name of Qingtongxia: the 'city' (Qingtongxia *Shi*) on the main highway 54 km south of Yinchuan, and the smaller 'town' (Qingtongxia *Zhen*) 29 km further south at the dam built across the

Yellow River in 1962 for hydroelectricity and water diversion.

Near Qingtongxia Zhen is the famous group known as the '108 Dagobas' *(yìbǎi líng bā tǎ)*. The 12 rows of brick pagodas are arranged in a large triangular constellation, standing defiantly above the great artificial lake. Their white vase-like shape contrasts strikingly with the arid slopes above them. Dating from the Yuan Dynasty, it is still not known why they were erected here.

Getting There & Away The 108 Dagobas are best seen as a day trip from Yinchuan. There are many daily buses and minibuses to Qingtongxia Shi, but only two direct buses (at 9 am and 12.30, Y6) to the dam-site town. If you take the 12.30 bus there, on the way back you will have to change buses in Qingtongxia Zhen. Alternatively, take a slow train to the nearby Qingtongxia railway station, then walk or catch a bus to the dam-site. At Qingtongxia Zhen you can either walk over the dam-bridge and then follow paths along the lake shore (1½ hours return), or take a speedboat across (10 minutes, Y10 return).

ZHONGWEI
(zhōngwèi) 中卫

Zhongwei lies 167 km south-west of Yinchuan on the Lanzhou-Baotou railway line. It's sandwiched between the sand dunes of the Tengger Desert to the north and the Yellow River to the south. This is a market town with a plodding, peaceful pace, a complete change from the hurly-burly of most Chinese cities.

Gao Temple
(gāo miào) 高庙

The main attraction in town is the Gao Temple, an eclectic, multipurpose temple which serves Buddhism, Confucianism and Taoism. Built during the 15th century and flattened by an earthquake during the 18th century, it was later rebuilt and expanded several times until being virtually razed again by fire in 1942. Extensive repairs have been made to the present wooden structure whose dozens of towers and pavilions look like parts of a jagged wedding cake. The temple includes a hotchpotch of statues from all three religions, so you can see Gautama Buddha, bodhisattvas, the Jade Emperor and the Holy Mother under one roof. Foreigners' entry tickets cost Y15.

Places to Stay

The *Railway Hotel (tiělù bīnguǎn)*, directly opposite the station, has beds in triples for Y15 and doubles with bathroom for Y30.

The *Yellow River Guesthouse* (☎ 2941) *(huánghé bīnguǎn)* a short way west of the Drum Tower, is Zhongwei's only tourist hotel. Standard doubles go for Y88. The CITS (☎ 2620) has an office on the 4th floor of the 'government wing'. The hotel rents bikes for Y1 per hour.

There's a guesthouse at Shapotou (16 km from Zhongwei) that's nicer than anything in town (see the Shapotou section for details).

Getting There & Away

From Zhongwei there is one daily express and two slower trains to Yinchuan or Lanzhou, and infrequent services to Wuwei in Gansu Province via a direct line west. Zhongwei also has bus connections with Yinchuan and Guyuan.

AROUND ZHONGWEI
Water Wheels
(shuǐchē) 水车

Since the Han Dynasty, water wheels have been a common sight in Ningxia Province and in other regions crossed by the Yellow River. Mechanical pumps have now taken over, though water wheels are occasionally used to pump water from the river down a complicated system of ducts and canals to the fields.

To see some old idle water wheels, ride or bus your way to Yingshui, a village west of Zhongwei on the Shapotou road. From here a dirt road goes seven km to the Yellow River, where a ferry will take you across to Xiaheye. On the other side walk east (left) for about two km to the water wheels near the river.

Leather Rafts
(yángpí fázi) 羊皮筏子

Leather rafts have been a traditional mode of transport on the Yellow River for centuries. They usually served for short crossings, although thousands of rafts were used during the 1950s to freight huge loads of tobacco, herbs or people on a two-week trip covering nearly 2000 km between Lanzhou and Baotou. The largest raft then in use was made from 600 sheepskins, measured 12 metres by seven metres and could carry loads of up to 30 tonnes.

The raft-making process begins with careful skinning of sheep (or sometimes cattle) carcasses. The skins are then soaked for several days in oil and brine before being taken out and inflated. An average of 14 hides are tied together under a wooden framework to make a strong raft capable of carrying four people and four bikes. Single-skin rafts are also used in parts of Gansu and Qinghai, where you either lie on top of your raft or crawl inside while the rafter lies on top to direct your passage across the river. There is usually enough air inside a large cowhide to last for 15 minutes which, reportedly, is about twice the time needed for an average crossing.

Skin rafts are still used quite a bit in western China. You can see them in action on the Yellow River at Shapotou – you could even have a go yourself.

Shapotou Desert Research Centre
(shāpōtóu shāmò yánjiūsuǒ)
沙波头沙漠研究所

Shapotou lies about 16 km west of Zhongwei on the fringe of the Tengger Desert. The Desert Research Centre was founded in 1956 with the task of researching methods to fix or hold back the moving sand dunes from the railway. From 1962 onwards, the researchers have been using the 'chequerboard method' for sand blockage and fixation introduced in the 1950s by a Soviet adviser. Plants are protected inside small chequerboards composed of straw bales which are replaced every five years. Even with this protection, plants still require 15 years for full growth.

Several thousand hectares of land have now been reclaimed to create an impressive ribbon of greenery beside the railway.

If you intend strolling off into the desert, remember that the sun overhead and the hot sand underfoot will grill you at both ends – wear thick-soled shoes and a broad-rimmed hat.

If you decide to stay here, rather than in Zhongwei, the friendly *Shapo Guesthouse* (☎ 2781) *(shāpō shānzhuāng)* is built around a garden courtyard on the banks of the Yellow River. It has cool and cosy doubles with shower for Y36, or Y18 per bed. There's a very small bar/restaurant on the premises.

The road from Zhongwei deteriorates dramatically after Tingshui, and the drive to Shapotou takes about a half an hour. The CITS in Zhongwei often organises tours out here. Otherwise you can charter your own three-wheeler for around Y25, perhaps including a side trip to see the water wheels.

TONGXIN
(tóngxīn) 同心

Tongxin, on the road between Zhongning and Guyuan, has an overwhelmingly *Hui* population. The main attraction is the Great Mosque *(qīngzhēn dàsì)*, a few km south of the bus station, that was built during the Ming Dynasty. One of the largest mosques in Ningxia Province, this is a traditional Chinese wooden structure with Islamic woodcuts and decorations of carved brick.

GUYUAN
(gùyuán) 固原

Guyuan is in the south of Ningxia Province, 460 km from Yinchuan. There is a fine set of Buddhist grottoes at Xumishan *(xūmíshān shíkū)* about 50 km north-west of Guyuan. Xumi is the Chinese version of the Sanskrit word *sumeru*, which means 'treasure mountain'.

Cut into five adjacent peaks are 132 caves containing over 300 Buddhist statues dating

back 1400 years, from the Northern Wei to the Sui and Tang dynasties. The finest Buddhist statues are found in Caves 14, 45, 46, 51, 67 and 70. Cave 5 contains the most famous statue on Xumishan: a colossal Maitreya Buddha, 19 metres high. It remains remarkably well preserved even though the protective tower has long since collapsed and left it exposed to the elements.

Over 60 miniature Buddhist statues and tombs dating from the Han Dynasty have been found in Xiji County, about 60 km west of Guyuan.

There is no regular transport to the caves; to reach the site you'll have to charter a vehicle (minibus or motortricycle), either directly from Guyuan or from Sanying *(sānyíng)*. Sanying is on the main road 40 km north of town near the Xumishan turn-off. Entry to the caves site costs Y10 for foreigners.

Places to Stay

The *Jiaotong Hotel (jiāotōng fàndiàn)* upstairs in the large new long-distance bus station has beds in clean triples for Y20 and doubles with bath for Y60. The *Guyuan Guesthouse (gùyuán bīnguǎn)* on Zhengfu Jie south-east of the bus station has rather better doubles for Y80.

Getting There & Away

A Zhongwei-Baoji (Shaanxi Province) railway line routed through Guyuan is under construction. When completed it will make travelling here much less uncomfortable. At the moment, however, the only way to and from Guyuan is by bus. There are buses from Lanzhou (via Xiji, Y30, nine hours), Tianshui (in Gansu, Y28, eight hours), Xi'an (Y34, 11 hours), Baoji (in Shaanxi, Y26, eight hours) and Yinchuan (Y19, nine hours). The hill country of southern Ningxia has some lovely scenery, the green well-watered valleys contrasting starkly with the region's arid north.

Gansu 甘肃

Population: 20 million
Capital: Lanzhou

Gansu (*gānsù*) is a rugged and barren state, consisting mostly of mountains and deserts. It's hard to imagine that through this narrow corridor China maintained political, cultural and commercial contacts with central Asia and the lands beyond. A frontier with a semi-arid climate, liable to frequent droughts and famines, it has always been on the edge of the empire (except when that empire spilled over into Xinjiang as it did under the Han and the Qing). It was an impoverished region and its inhabitants played little part in the destiny of their country.

However, the famed Silk Road, along which camel caravans carried goods in and out of China, threaded its way through Gansu. The most common export was the highly prized Chinese silk, from which the road took its name. Travellers and merchants from as far away as the Roman Empire entered the Middle Kingdom via this route, using the string of oasis towns as stepping-stones through the barren wastes. Buddhism was also carried into China along the Silk Road, and the Buddhist cave temples found all the way from Xinjiang through Gansu and up through northern China are reminders of the influx of ideas the road made possible.

The Great Wall snaked its way across northern China and into Gansu, finishing up not far past the town of Jiayuguan. All was not peaceful within the wall, however. The Muslim rebellion of 1862 to 1878 was put down with incredible savagery by the Chinese; untold numbers of people, probably millions, were killed and the destruction of cities and property brought the province to ruin – and finally established Chinese control. The century was topped off by a massive famine.

Traditionally the towns of Gansu have been established in the oases along the major caravan route where agriculture is possible. With the coming of modern methods of

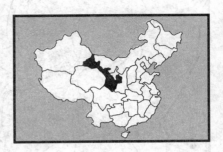

transport, some industrial development and the exploitation of oil, iron ore and coal deposits has taken place. The foothills of the mountainous regions which border Qinghai Province to the south support a pastoral economy based on horses, cattle, sheep and camels. To the north of the 'Gansu corridor' – that narrow part of Gansu that extends north-west from the capital of Lanzhou – lies a barren desert which extends into Inner Mongolia, much of it true desert, some of it sparse grassland.

Well over 20 million people inhabit Gansu. The province has a considerable variety of minority peoples, among them the Hui, Mongols, Tibetans and Kazakhs. The Han Chinese have built their own settlements – places like Jiayuguan and Jiuquan, which have been Chinese outposts for centuries.

Rail – Gansu to Xinjiang

The 1892-km Lanzhou-Ürümqi railway line, completed in 1963, was one of the great achievements of the early Communist regime. It has done much to relieve the isolation and backwardness of this region.

The railway line stretches north-west along the Gansu corridor from Lanzhou to Ürümqi. A new line links Ürümqi to Alashankou on the border of Kazakhstan in the former USSR, and the first train services

GANSU

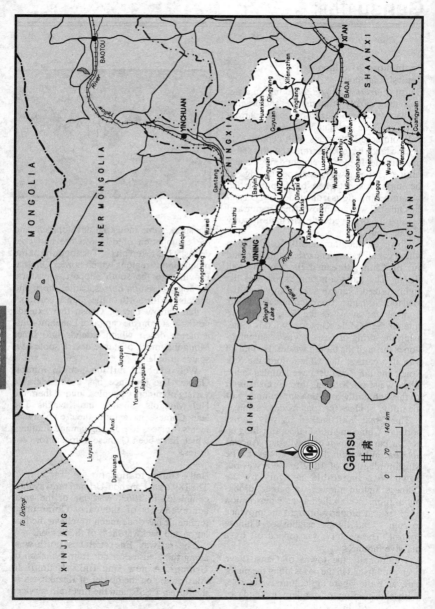

have recently begun between Ürümqi and Alma Ata. The Marco Polos of the railway age usually break the trip at Jiayuguan (the end of the Great Wall) and at Liuyuan, and then take a bus south to the remarkable Buddhist Caves at Dunhuang. Some travellers head directly from Xi'an to Ürümqi, which is a 2½-day trip, and then work their way back down the line, stopping off at the other open towns.

All long-distance services have dining cars serving nourishing – if rather unexciting – rice or noodle-based dishes with vegetables, meat, or eggs. Hot meals in polystyrene boxes (universally disposed of via the nearest open window) are also served from trolleys wheeled through the carriages. Also sold on the train are bottled beer or soft drinks and snacks like peanuts and dried fruit. Food with more variety can be bought from hawkers on the station platforms when the train makes its occasional stops. If you're going straight through to Ürümqi from Lanzhou or Xi'an, it might be worth bringing along extra food (especially fresh fruit) and some boiled or mineral water just in case supplies on the train run out.

As you head westward from Lanzhou the real desolation begins, when the scenery changes to endless rugged stony plains. In places you'll spot the Qilianshan mountain range towards the south-west, so high that its peaks are covered with glaciers and perpetual snow. Every so often along the line you pass a collection of mud huts, a tiny railway station in the middle of nowhere, or a stretch of agricultural land standing in stark contrast to the surrounding desert. The approach to Ürümqi is dramatic: the train passes over rugged mountains and emerges onto an immense plain of grasslands, grazed by horses, sheep and cattle. Far to the north are the snow-capped Tianshan mountains. The grasslands gradually give way to dry desert and an hour or so later you arrive in Ürümqi, with its concrete jungle of apartment blocks, factories and smokestacks.

There are direct expresses to Ürümqi from Chengdu, Shanghai and Beijing, but trains from Beijing via Baotou and Yinchuan (on the Inner Mongolia/Ningxia line) run only as far west as Lanzhou.

LANZHOU
(*lánzhōu*) 兰州

Lanzhou, the capital of Gansu, has been an important garrison town and transport centre since ancient times.

Situated on the major routes along the Gansu corridor into central Asia, westward into Qinghai and Tibet, south into Sichuan and north-west along the Yellow River, Lanzhou was a major centre of caravan traffic into the border regions up until WW II.

The development of Lanzhou as an industrial centre began after the Communist victory and the city's subsequent integration into China's expanding national rail network. During the 1950s, lines from Baoji in Shaanxi and Baotou in Inner Mongolia were extended here, and construction soon began on the Lanzhou-Ürümqi line; a railway line was also built between Lanzhou and Xining. This secured Lanzhou's position as the principal industrial centre in north-west China, causing the city's population to increase more than tenfold within little more than a generation. About 200,000 people lived in Lanzhou in 1949; by 1959 numbers had almost reached a million and today the population is approaching three million.

Although the city has few real attractions, it's a reasonably attractive place for a short visit.

Orientation
Lanzhou is situated at 1600 metres above sea level in a narrow valley surrounded by low mountains. Its location has forced the city to develop westwards in a long urban strip extending for over 20 km along the southern banks of the Yellow River. Central Lanzhou is at the city's eastern end within the triangle formed by the railway station, the large Xiguan traffic circle and The East is Red Square (nowadays often given the more banal name of 'Central Square'). Most of the tourist facilities are here, but the main long-distance bus station, the museum and the

popular Friendship Hotel are all located much further to the west.

Information

CITS The office (☎ 23055 or Jincheng Hotel – 416638 ext 761) is on Nongmin Xiang, the lane running behind the Jincheng Hotel. The staff are helpful and cooperative.

PSB Two offices of the PSB have entry-exit offices issuing visa extensions and Alien Travel Permits. This is quite handy, since it gives you a second local option if you can't get what you want at the first office. The 'provincial' office is at No 38 Qingyang Lu on The East is Red Square. From the main old green-and-while-tiled building at the front, walk left to a separate wing; the office is on the 3rd floor, left of the stairs. The PSB's smaller 'city' office is at No 132 Wudu Lu on the right as you enter the compound.

Money The Bank of China has a new head office (☎ 485354) just north of The East is Red Square on Pingliang Lu. The local black market outside the bank is lukewarm, but more enterprising moneychangers can be found along Xijin Donglu near the Friendship Hotel.

Post & Telecommunications There are post offices across from Lanzhou railway station and at the west bus station. The main post and telephone office is on the corner of Minzhu Donglu and Pingliang Lu. It's open from 8.30 am to 7 pm and has a cheap parcel-wrapping service. A good place to make international collect calls is the telephone and telegram office on the corner of Qingyang Lu and Jinchang Lu. The larger hotels all offer postal services.

Maps The long-format transport maps of Lanzhou mirror the city's stretched-out shape; half a dozen or so versions are sold by street hawkers and the Xinhua Bookstore, but the best is a bilingual map available from CITS and hotel shops.

Gansu Provincial Museum

(*gānsù shěng bówùguǎn*) 甘肃省博物馆
The Provincial Museum is directly across the street from the Friendship Hotel, and is among the best of China's smaller provincial museums.

On the 2nd floor is a newly refurbished exhibition, 'Cultural Relics of the Silk Road'. It starts with Neolithic painted pottery taken from a site 300 km south-east of here at Dadiwan. The Dadiwan culture existed at least 7000 years ago, and is thought by some archaeologists to predate the better-known Yangshuo culture. Some of the Dadiwan pieces bear painted black signs, which are believed to be early forms of pictographic characters. Later Han Dynasty exhibits include a 70-cm long piece of fine embroidered lace and inscribed wooden tablets used to relay messages along the Silk Road. Outstanding is a 1½-metre high Tang-Dynasty warrior made from glaze-coloured earthenware, the largest such piece found yet in China.

Also interesting is a 2nd-century BC gilded silver plate depicting Bacchus, the Greek god of wine, from the Eastern Roman Empire. It was unearthed at Jingyuan, 120 km north-east of Lanzhou in 1989, and is evidence of significant contact between the two distant ancient civilisations.

There is also a bronze replica of a galloping horse with numerous accompanying chariots and mounted horsemen, excavated from the Leitai Han Tomb in Wuwei; the original is now housed in Beijing. Among the Yuan Dynasty relics is a pocket-edition of a Chinese-Tibetan bilingual Buddhist scripture, and a hand-written copy of the Koran with Persian annotations.

On the ground floor are some rather mundane exhibits of Gansu's flora, fauna and geology. Much more interesting is a fossilised skeleton of a giant mammoth unearthed in 1973. There are also fragments of skeletons, teeth and tusks from other extinct members of the pachyderm family.

The museum is open from 9 to 11.30 am and from 2.30 to 5 pm; it's closed on Sunday. Admission for foreigners is Y10.

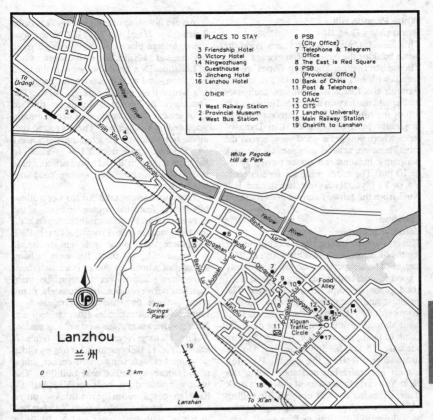

PLACES TO STAY

3 Friendship Hotel
5 Victory Hotel
14 Ningwozhuang Guesthouse
15 Jincheng Hotel
16 Lanzhou Hotel

OTHER

1 West Railway Station
2 Provincial Museum
4 West Bus Station
6 PSB (City Office)
7 Telephone & Telegram Office
8 The East is Red Square
9 PSB (Provincial Office)
10 Bank of China
11 Post & Telephone Office
12 CAAC
13 CITS
17 Lanzhou University
18 Main Railway Station
19 Chairlift to Lanshan

To Ürümqi

Yellow River

Xijin Xilu

Xijin Donglu

White Pagoda Hill & Park

Yellow River

Binhe Lu

Zhongshan Lu

Wudu Lu

Qingyang Lu

Baiyin Lu

Jiuquan Lu

Dongang Lu

Food Alley

Minzhu Lu

Xiguan Traffic Circle

Tianshui Lu

Five Springs Park

Lanzhou 兰州

0   1   2 km

Lanshan

To Xi'an

GANSU

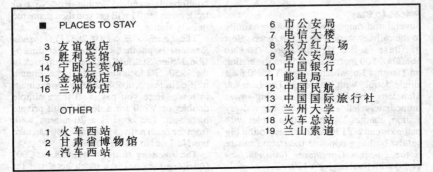

PLACES TO STAY

3 友谊饭店
5 胜利宾馆
14 宁卧庄宾馆
15 金城饭店
16 兰州饭店

OTHER

1 火车西站
2 甘肃省博物馆
4 汽车西站

6 市公安局大楼
7 电信局
8 东方红广场
9 省公安局
10 中国银行
11 中国邮电局
12 中国民航
13 中国国际旅行社
17 兰州大学
18 火车总站
19 兰山索道

White Pagoda Hill
(báitǎ shān) 白塔山

This pleasant, well-managed park is on the north bank of the Yellow River near the old Zhongshan Bridge. The steep slopes are terraced, with lots of small walkways leading through the forest to pavilions, teahouses and a plant nursery on a secluded hillside. On top of the hill is the White Pagoda Temple, originally built during the Yuan Dynasty, from where you get a good view across the city. There are several mosques on the park periphery. In summer it's open from 6.30 am to 10 pm. The entry price for foreigners is Y5, or Y1 if you flash your student card. Bus No 7 from the railway station goes there.

Lanshan
(lánshān gōngyuán)

This mountain range rises steeply to the south of Lanzhou, reaching over 2000 metres. The temperature on top is normally a good 5° cooler than in the valley, so it's a good place to come in hot weather. The quickest and nicest way up is by chairlift from behind Five Springs Park. The chairlift takes about 20 minutes to make the diagonal climb to the upper terminal; it's Y6 to go up but only Y5 for the downward leg. On the summit you'll find the Santai Pavilion *(sāntái gé)*, refreshment stands and a fun park. You can plonk yourself down in a deck chair, sip some tea and observe life rolling on below you. A paved trail zig-zags its way back down to Five Springs Park.

Places to Stay

Several mid-range places in close proximity to the railway station let in foreigners. Best of these is the *Yingbin Hotel (yíngbīn fàndiàn)*, 500 metres down from the station on Tianshui Lu, which charges Y45/90 for a single/double with bathroom. The *Lanzhou Mansions (lánzhōu dàshà)*, the big tower immediately left as you leave the railway station, charges Y40 per bed in triples with bathroom and Y136 for doubles. In the big yellow building opposite the station square is the *Lanshan Guesthouse (lánshān bīnguǎn)* with doubles for Y120.

An old favourite of budget travellers is the *Friendship Hotel* (☎ 334711) *(yǒuyì fàndiàn)*, a large place consisting of two main buildings at 14 Xijin Xilu on the western side of Lanzhou. Don't even bother with the front reception – just walk around to the rear building where they put all foreign guests. The conditions in the small dorms on the 3rd floor are excellent, and are an exceptionally good deal at Y20 per bed. There's round-the-clock hot water in the communal showers too. Doubles range from Y180 to Y220. In the front wing you'll find a post office, a cafe and a well-stocked shop selling food and tourist items.

To get to the hotel take bus No 1 or trolley-bus No 31 from the square in front of the railway station. Private minibuses charge Y2 for the same routes. From the hotel it's a 15-minute walk to the west bus station. If you're arriving by train, the west railway station just around the corner is a much more convenient place to get off than the main Lanzhou railway station; unfortunately, many trains – those from the east terminating at Lanzhou and all expresses from Ürümqi and Xining – *don't* stop at the west railway station.

The *Victory Hotel* (☎ 21509) *(shènglì fàndiàn)* at 133 Zhongshan Lu has an older downmarket west wing on the corner, and a newer more upmarket east building. The west wing has dorm beds for Y12, but it's hard to get a room here unless you're Chinese. The east wing charges Y45 per bed in triples with bathroom, and Y120 for a comfortable standard double. Bus No 1 or trolley-bus No 31 will get you there from the railway station.

The *Lanzhou Hotel* (☎ 28321) *(lánzhōu fàndiàn)* is another of those over-dimensional 'Sino-Stalinist' edifices put up back in the 1950s. Its location on the large Xiguan traffic circle is probably the most convenient in town. Here you pay Y80 for a simple double, or Y240 for a double with private bathroom. The hotel is a 20-minute walk from the main railway station or you can take bus No 1 or No 7 for two stops.

The *Jincheng Hotel* (☎ 416638 ext 200) *(jīnchéng fàndiàn)* is a plush hotel not far from the Lanzhou Hotel. Standard doubles cost Y297 and their suite is Y528. The hotel has shops, a post office, clinic, several restaurants and a lively bar. The dorms are behind the main hotel building on the 4th floor of a separate wing (☎ 416638 ext 487), best reached from the rear gate next to the CITS office. At Y24 per bed, these depressing concrete-floor rooms are poor value, especially compared with the dorms at the Friendship Hotel.

The spacious and sleepily quiet *Ningwozhuang Guesthouse* (☎ 416221 ext 444) *(níngwòzhuāng bīnguǎn)* has doubles from Y200 upwards. Once an exclusive residence for visiting Party cadres, this place has some of the most extensive and well-kept gardens you'll see in any Chinese hotel. Buildings are scattered around the hotel grounds; reception is in the wing ahead on the left as you go through the entrance, and decorated with photos of one-time hotel guests – the president of Mali, a Singapore cabinet minister, a Thai princess.

Places to Eat

The dining hall in the rear building of the *Friendship Hotel* has hearty set meals for Y20 per person. The *Jincheng Hotel* has a reasonably good Chinese restaurant with English menu. Good places for street food are the lane running east from the new Bank of China building, and the market near the railway station.

Several typical Lanzhou specialties are sold on the streets. One is called *ròujiābǐng* – lamb or pork fried with onion, capsicum and a dash of paprika served inside a 'pocket' of flat-bread. For dessert try the local Muslim dish, *tiánpéizi*. It's made by lightly boiling highland barley kernels, then leaving the soaked grains for several days until a mild fermentation occurs. It's served with a sour-sweet milky-white sauce and has a delicious, aromatic flavour.

Getting There & Away

Air CAAC's office (☎ 21964, 28174) is at 46 Donggang Xilu at the corner of a small lane, a five-minute walk west of the Lanzhou Hotel. It's open from 8.30 to 11.30 am and from 3 to 6 pm.

Lanzhou has daily air connections with Beijing (Y690, twice daily), Canton (Y1030), Shanghai (Y950), Xi'an (Y280) and Dunhuang (Y520). There are also less frequent flights to Jiayuguan (Y360), Chengdu (Y470), Guilin (Y830), Ürümqi (Y880), Fuzhou (Y1070), Kunming (Y870) and Hong Kong (Y1850 or HK$2380).

The airport for Lanzhou is at Zhongchuan, 75 km north of the city. CAAC have several airport hotels for people catching early-morning flights. The newer Zhongchuan Hotel (☎ 415926) *(zhōngchuān bīnguǎn)* charges US$40 for a standard double. The cheapest beds are Y50 in doubles with bathroom. High winds often delay flights – and CAAC can find plenty of other excuses.

Bus The west bus station *(qìchē xīzhàn)* handles departures to Linxia, Xiahe and Hezuo. Foreigner-price bus fares out of Lanzhou are relatively expensive, but it's difficult to get them at Chinese prices. There are seven buses per day to Linxia (Y22, 3½ hours), but only one daily bus to Xiahe (Y40, eight hours) leaving at 7.30 am. Linxia is on the way to Xiahe and all buses call in there, so if you can't get on a direct bus to Xiahe take an early bus to Linxia and change there. There are also buses to Wuwei (Y27, seven hours), Zhangye (Y36, 11 hours) and Jiayuguan (Y41, 15 hours). There is a 6 pm sleeper bus *(wòpùchē)* to Jiuquan (Y105, via Wuwei and Zhangye).

Another long-distance bus station on Pingliang Lu not far from the post office has departures mainly for eastern destinations such as Xi'an (Y52), Yinchuan (Y40) and Guyuan (in Ningxia, Y25).

Travel Insurance A new regulation requires foreigners who travel by public bus in Gansu to be ensured with the People's Insurance Company of China (PICC), regardless of whether they have taken out their own travel insurance or not. (Apparently, this follows a successful lawsuit against the Gansu provincial government by the parents of a Japanese

GANSU

tourist who was killed in a bus accident here in 1991. Depending on how you view this matter, the insurance requirement is either an act of collective punishment aimed at all foreigners, or merely a prudent means of covering any future liability claims). In any case, some long-distance bus stations may refuse to sell you a ticket unless you can show them your PICC insurance. The requirement is currently being enforced mainly on routes in and out of Lanzhou and in north-western Gansu.

Travellers have managed to avoid paying insurance by showing someone else's papers when they buy their bus ticket or getting a Chinese person to buy it for them. Some buy the ticket on the bus itself, but drivers often demand a generous 'tip' for their compliance. Frankly, it's less hassle to just buy insurance and forget the whole thing. Private long-distance minibuses appear to be exempt from the travel insurance requirement, however.

In Lanzhou you can buy insurance at the PICC office (☎ 416422 ext 114) at 150 Qingyang Lu, the CITS office and most of the tourist hotels. It costs Y10 for seven days and Y20 for 15 days, plus Y1 for each additional day. CITS and some of the hotels charge an additional Y5 commission.

Train Trains run to Ürümqi; to Beijing via Hohhot and Datong; to Golmud via Xining; to Shanghai via Xi'an and Zhengzhou; and to Beijing via Xi'an and Zhengzhou, or you can go south to Chengdu. Heading west, it takes 18 hours to reach Jiayuguan; 24 hours to Liuyuan; 37 hours to Turpan and 40 hours to Ürümqi.

The station has a separate window for foreigners (No 15), but it's difficult to get anything other than a hard seat. CITS can get you sleeper tickets at one day's notice. Black-market train tickets have become something of a cottage industry in Lanzhou. You simply order a ticket (at the Chinese price plus a small commission) from one of the touts standing around the railway station; they evidently have an 'understanding' with the ticket office staff, and can get hard-seat

tickets within a few minutes. It's advisable to have a Chinese-reading person check the ticket before you pay up.

Sleeper prices for foreigners are: Baotou Y287/151 (soft/hard), Beijing Y474/249, Chengdu Y334/176, Liuyuan Y314/164, Tianshui Y130/68, Ürümqi Y461/242, Xi'an Y218/114.

Getting Around

To/From the Airport Airport buses leave from the CAAC office twice a day at 10 am and 7 pm (Y12 one way). The Jincheng Hotel also runs a coach bus out to the airport. A small taxi (such as a Lada) from central Lanzhou to the airport costs Y150 one way.

Bus The most useful bus routes are No 1 and trolley-bus No 31 running from the railway station past the Victory Hotel, the west bus station and the Friendship Hotel. Private minibuses ply the same routes, charging Y2 for the the longest ride.

Warning: Lanzhou has a reputation as a centre for pickpockets and petty thieves; be especially careful on crowded buses, and at the railway and long-distance bus stations. Minibuses are a safer bet.

Other The city's pedicab and motortricycle drivers are the most disorientated in China – take along a good local street map for their benefit.

AROUND LANZHOU

The **Bingling Si Caves** (*bǐnglíng sì*) are carved into a 60-metre-high canyon beside the Liujiaxia Reservoir on the Yellow River. Isolated by the waters of the dam, this group of 183 Buddhist grottoes has evidently been spared from the vandalism of the Cultural Revolution. A levy now protects the caves from damage during high-water periods. The local cliffs are composed of an eroded and porous rock with numerous natural cavities, giving the area an appearance reminiscent of Australia's Bungle Bungle country.

The oldest caves have been repaired and added to on numerous occasions since they were built during the Western Qin Dynasty. They contain 694 statues, 82 clay sculptures and a number of frescos. Cave 169, containing one buddha and two bodhisattvas, is one of the oldest and best preserved in China. Most of the other caves were completed during the prosperous Tang period. The star of the caves is the 27-metre-high seated statue of Maitreya, the future Buddha.

Depending on which caves you want to see, entry costs Y3, Y10, Y50 or Y150. The cheaper tickets are for the unlocked caves, while the Y150 ticket (one price for foreigners and Chinese) gives you a complete guided tour including the magnificent Caves 169 and 172.

Places to Stay
In Yongjing you can stay at the *Lidian Hotel* (*lìdiàn bīnguǎn*) for Y50 for a good double with bathroom, or the *Huanghe Hotel* (*huánghé bīnguǎn*) for Y30 a room.

Getting There & Away
From Lanzhou to the caves is a 12-hour round trip, half of that time on a bus and half

Buddha at Bingling Si Caves

on a boat. CITS, the nearby Tianma Travel (*tiānmǎ lǚxíngshè*) and Dongfang Travel (*dōngfāng lǚxíngshè*) in the Victory Hotel all run tours to the caves whenever they have enough people; the usual tour price is Y88 (excluding entry tickets), which is quite reasonable.

Unless you take a tour or charter a vehicle, it's not really possible to get to Bingling Si and back in one day. If you organise the trip yourself, you'll probably have to stay overnight in Yongjing, because the boat normally gets back from the caves after the last bus has left for Lanzhou. You can take a 7.30 am bus to Yongjing from the west bus station; later buses leave from outside the west wing of the Victory Hotel at 3 and 5 pm (Y10 local price). The 7.30 bus often arrives just in time for you to catch one of the boats to Bingling Si. The railway line to Yongjing does not carry passenger services.

All boats depart from Liujiaxia, a tiny port half an hour's walk uphill from Yongjing. The trip costs Y40 for foreigners (no student discounts) and takes three hours each way; boats only stay at the caves for one hour – so don't mess about! Food and drink are not available on the boat, so bring some with you. You can also charter a speed boat across the reservoir for Y170 return.

If you're going on to Linxia or Xiahe, you can avoid backtracking to Lanzhou by taking a direct bus to Linxia from the main street of Yongjing (Y7.50, 4½ hours). The bus takes an interesting high route east of the Yellow River through areas settled by the Dongxiang ethnic minority.

MAIJISHAN
(*màijīshān*) 麦积山
Maijishan, a mountain famed for its grottoes, lies south of Tianshui town in south-eastern Gansu Province. The mountain bears some resemblance to a corn rick, hence the name Maijishan (Corn Rick Mountain).

The Maijishan grottoes are one of China's four largest temple groups; the others are at Datong, Luoyang and Dunhuang. The caves date back to the Northern Wei and Song dynasties and contain clay figures and wall paintings. It's not certain just how the artists managed to clamber so high; one theory is that they piled up blocks of wood to the top of the mountain before moving down, gradually removing blocks of wood as they descended. Stone sculptures were evidently brought in from elsewhere, since the local rock is too soft for carving, as at Dunhuang.

Earthquakes have demolished many of the caves in the central section, while murals have tended to drop off due to damp or rain; fire has destroyed a large number of the wooden structures. Parts of the rock wall have now been stabilised with sprayed-on liquid cement.

Catwalks and steep spiral stairs have been built across the cliff face. It's scary to look down, but perfectly safe. Most of the remaining 194 caves can only be seen through wire netting or barred doors – take a torch. Apart from the Qifo Pavilion and the huge buddha statues which are easily accessible, it's hard to get a rewarding peek into many of the caves unless you take a guide. If you want a guide, you had best contact CITS in Tianshui; there are guides available at Maijishan (at the main office uphill from the bus station) for around Y40, but getting an English-speaking one at short notice is not always possible.

Visitors often pause above the statue of Buddha and attempt to throw coins or even cigarettes onto his head. If the objects stay there, so the story goes, the thrower's mind is pure. The visitor may be pure, but Buddha certainly cops a load of rubbish.

The ticket office is about a 15-minute walk uphill from where the bus lets you off. Cameras and bags may not be taken into the caves area – the ticket office has a cheap left-luggage section for this purpose. The caves are open from 9 am to 5 pm. Entry for foreigners costs Y15 (Y5 for students).

To reach the high ridge rising behind the ticket office, follow the road up towards the ticket office, but when you get to the sharp bend to the left, take the forest track to the right. Continue uphill along this trail for about 15 minutes and then look for a path climbing off to the left. If you follow this,

you'll find yourself on a dizzying, knife-edge route with fine views of the grottoes on the cliff face.

Orientation & Information

Tianshui has two sections: the railhead, known as Beidao, and the main city area 20 km to the east, known as Qincheng. Minibuses and public buses run very frequently between the two districts (Y2, 30 minutes each way), but unless you're staying there or have some business with CITS there's no real reason to go to Qincheng. CITS (☎ (0938) 214463) has its main office at 1 Huancheng Donglu on the 3rd floor, and another branch in the Tianshui Hotel.

Maijishan is about 35 km south of Beidao. There are no direct public buses to Maijishan, only public buses from the railway station to Qincheng (bus No 1), and from Qincheng to Maijishan (bus No 5), but you can easily change buses at the turnoff 3 km south of the station (near the Longlin Hotel). There are also many private minibuses that pick up arriving tourists and ferry them straight out to the caves. The trip takes over an hour one way, and on weekends the whole operation can get pretty crowded.

Places to Stay & Eat

The *Government Hostel (zhèngfǔ zhāodàisuǒ)* in the green-tiled building slightly left of the railway station will accept foreigners and is very cheap. Here, the most expensive beds are in doubles with bathroom for Y16.

The *Longlin Hotel* (☎ (0938) 235594) *(lónglín fàndiàn)* is south of the railway station where the Maijishan and Qincheng roads diverge. The hotel entrance is just left (east) around the corner. A reasonable double with attached bathroom costs Y112, or you can take just one bed for exactly half. The dining hall on the ground floor is worth eating at, and there are a few good restaurants outside as well.

The *Tianshui Hotel* (☎ (0938) 212410) *(tiānshuǐ bīnguǎn)* at No 5 Yingbin Lu is still the only luxury hotel. Its location on the Qincheng side of town is a bit inconvenient,

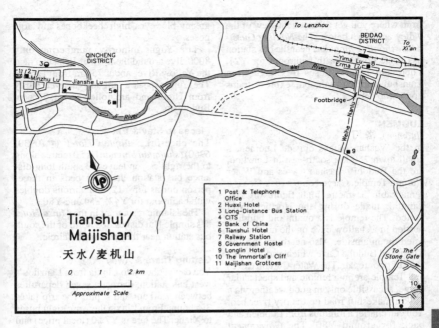

Tianshui/
Maijishan

天水/麦机山

0   1   2 km

Approximate Scale

1 Post & Telephone
   Office
2 Huaxi Hotel
3 Long-Distance Bus Station
4 CITS
5 Bank of China
6 Tianshui Hotel
7 Railway Station
8 Government Hostel
9 Longlin Hotel
10 The Immortal's Cliff
11 Maijishan Grottoes

To The
Stone Gate

GANSU

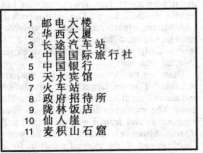

1 邮电大楼厦
2 华西大汽车站
3 长途汽国际旅行社
4 中国国际银行
5 中国天水宾馆
6 天火车站
7 火车站招待所
8 政府林饭店
9 陇人崖
10 仙积山石窟
11 麦积山石窟

since the Maijishan caves are in the opposite direction from the railway station. Minibuses from the railway station can drop you off at the corner just up from the hotel. The rate for a standard double with private bathroom is US$27. There is a restaurant in the hotel itself, and an upmarket place next door.

There are food stalls and cheap restaurants at Maijishan.

Getting There & Away

Tianshui is on the Xi'an-Lanzhou railway line; there are dozens of daily trains in either direction, and all stop here. If you arrive early you can visit Maijishan as a day trip, avoiding the need to stay overnight in Tianshui. From the long-distance bus station in Qincheng there are buses to Lanzhou, Gangu, Guyuan (in Ninxia) and Hanzhong (in south-eastern Shaanxi). Tianshui has a noisy military airport, but apart from occasional charter aircraft there are no CAAC flights here.

GANGU
(gāngǔ) 甘谷

At Gangu, on the railway line 45 km west of Tianshui, is a massive 23-metre tall buddha, high on a cliff overlooking the Wei River. The statue is evidently of Tang Dynasty origin and sports a twirled moustache. A path along a steep ridge leads up past several small temples to a platform below the statue, from where you get an excellent view of the valley and town below. The *Nanling Guesthouse (nánlíng bīnguǎn)* near the bus station has basic doubles with bathroom for Y24. There are regular buses to Gangu from Tianshui and Wushan, but express trains don't stop here.

LUOMEN
(luòmén) 洛门

In the Wushan ranges outside Luomen, a small town 250 km south-east of Lanzhou, are the Buddhist Lashao Caves and Water Curtain Temple. Carved onto a rock face is a remarkable 31-metre high figure of Sakyamuni, made during the Northern Wei period. The temple is a quaint old building nestled in a shallow cave on the nearby forested mountainside. Also nearby is the Ten Thousand Buddha Cave which, sadly, is in a state of poor repair. The Water Curtain Caves and Temple are in a remote and spectacular gorge, accessible only in good weather via a 17-km makeshift road up the dry river bed. You can charter a minibus from Luomen and back for around Y80. The *Government Hostel (zhèngfǔ zhāodàisuǒ)* in Luomen has rooms from Y32.

LINXIA
(línxià) 临夏

Linxia was once an important stop on the Silk Road between Lanzhou and Yangguan. Today the town has a decidedly Muslim *Hui* character, with a large mosque in the centre of town; old men with long stringy beards and white caps shuffle about the streets. In the markets you'll also see carved gourds, daggers, saddlery, carpets, and wrought iron goods. Linxia does a thriving trade in spectacles made with ground crystal lenses and metal frames.

Linxia is also a regional centre for the Dongxiang minority. The Dongxiang minority speak their own Altaic language and are believed to be descendants of 13th-century immigrants from central Asia who were moved forcibly to China after Kublai Khan's conquest of the Middle East. Some have greeny-blue eyes, high cheekbones and large noses.

The Yugur minority, numbering only 8000, live around the town of Jishishan near the Yellow River about 75 km from Linxia. The Yugur speak a language derived partly from Uigur and are followers of Tibetan Buddhism.

Places to Stay & Eat
The cheerful *Shuiquan Hotel* (☎ (0930) 6960) *(shuǐquán bīnguǎn)* is 50 metres along to the right as you leave the south long-distance bus station. It offers beds in three-person dorms for Y12, and various doubles with bathroom for Y42, Y54 and Y80.

The Islamic restaurant in the *Minzu Hotel* has simple Hui dishes. It's north of the south bus station near the large traffic circle.

Getting There & Away
You can get buses to Linxia from Lanzhou's west bus station; there are seven departures between 7.30 am and 4 pm. The trip takes 3½ hours. From Linxia there are eight buses to Xiahe. The fare is Y7.50 (local price) and the trip up takes four hours, the last bus leaving around 2.30 pm. The last bus back to Lanzhou departs at 5 pm. Other useful departures go to Hezuo (four daily), Xining (Y23, several daily, eight hours) and Tongren (in Qinghai, one daily).

There are two long-distance bus stations in Linxia: a newer, larger south bus station and the old north bus station about three km away. The south bus station has most connections to and from Lanzhou, Xiahe and Hezuo. However, direct buses between Lanzhou and Xiahe generally call in for a lunch stop at the north bus station.

XIAHE
(xiàhé) 夏河

Xiahe is one of the most enchanting places to visit in China, especially if you can't get to Tibet. Outside of Lhasa, it's the leading Tibetan monastery town. Indeed, in some ways it's better than Tibet – many Tibetans come here on pilgrimage dressed in their finest, most colourful clothing. The pilgrims,

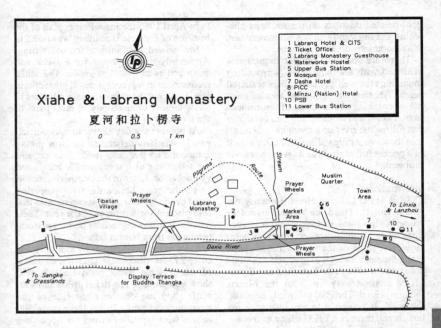

Xiahe & Labrang Monastery
夏河和拉卜楞寺

0   0.5   1 km

1 Labrang Hotel & CITS
2 Ticket Office
3 Labrang Monastery Guesthouse
4 Waterworks Hostel
5 Upper Bus Station
6 Mosque
7 Dasha Hotel
8 PICC
9 Minzu (Nation) Hotel
10 PSB
11 Lower Bus Station

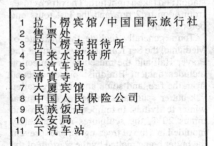

1 拉卜楞宾馆/中国国际旅行社
2 售票处
3 拉卜楞寺招待所
4 自来水招待所
5 上汽车站
6 清真寺
7 大厦宾馆
8 中国人民保险公司
9 民族饭店
10 公安局
11 下汽车站

the monks, the monastery, the mountain scenery – when you enter Xiahe, you feel like you've entered another world.

The religious activity is focused on the Labrang Monastery, one of the six major Tibetan monasteries of the Gelukpa (Yellow Hat sect of Tibetan Buddhism). The others are Ganden, Sera and Drepung monasteries in the Lhasa area; Tashilhunpo Monastery in

Shigatse; and Ta'er Monastery in Huanzhong, Qinghai Province.

Today Xiahe is a microcosm of southwestern Gansu, with the area's three main ethnic groups represented; roughly speaking, Xiahe's population is 45% ethnically Tibetan, 45% Han and 10% Muslim.

Orientation

At 2920 metres above sea level, Xiahe stretches for several km east-to-west along the Daxia River. The Labrang Monastery is roughly halfway along, and marks a division between Xiahe's mainly Han and Hui Chinese eastern quarter and the overwhelmingly Tibetan village to the west.

A three-km pilgrims' way with long rows of prayer wheels and Buddhist shrines circumnavigates the monastery. The route crosses the road just up from the upper bus station and continues along the river, back across the road and around the slopes above Labrang. From here you can see the small gold-painted dagobas on the rooftops glistening magnificently in the afternoon sun. It's a good introduction to Xiahe.

There are some 40 smaller monasteries affiliated with Labrang in the surrounding mountains (as well as many others scattered across Tibet and China) and the area is a great place for hiking in clean, peaceful surroundings. Take warm clothing and rain gear. You can follow the river up to Sangke or head up into the surrounding valleys, but carry a stick or a pocket full of rocks as dogs are a serious problem.

Information

CITS is at the Labrang Hotel (formerly the Xiahe Hotel). There are several banks in Xiahe but no Bank of China, and it is very difficult to change travellers' cheques here. However, some of the small antique shops along the main street will give you a reasonable rate for US$ cash. There is a small post office a short way up from the Minzu (Nation) Hotel. The PSB is directly opposite the hotel. If you need to buy insurance for bus travel, there is a PICC office in a compound just across the first bridge. You can rent bikes at several of the restaurants along the main road for about Y10 a day.

Labrang Monastery

(lābǔlèng sì) 拉卜楞寺
The monastery was built in 1709 by E'angzongzhe, the first- generation Jiamuyang ('living buddha'), who came from the nearby town of Ganjia. It houses six institutes (Institute of Esoteric Buddhism, Higher & Lower Institutes of Theology, Institute of Medicine, Institute of Astrology and Institute of Law). There are also numerous temple halls, 'living buddha' residences and living quarters for the monks.

At its peak the monastery housed nearly 4000 monks, but their ranks were decimated during the Cultural Revolution, when monks and buildings took a heavy beating. The numbers are gradually recovering, and there are about 1700 monks today, drawn from Qinghai, Gansu, Sichuan and Inner Mongolia.

In April 1985 the main Prayer Hall of the Institute of Esoteric Buddhism was razed in a fire caused by faulty electrical wiring. Apparently the fire burnt for a week and destroyed some priceless relics. The hall's reconstruction was completed at great cost in mid-1990, but the monks remain reluctant to allow the use of electricity in most parts of the monastery.

At noon every day senior monks participate in scholarly debates in the large grassy compound on the main road; these debates are something of a spectacle for locals and visitors alike. Later in the afternoon, monks sit on the grass beside the river preparing ritual music for the religious ceremonies that take place at various times of the year. Their musical instruments include horns and trumpets made from human bones.

Entry to the monastery is by tour only and costs Y15 (no discounts). One of the monks, of whom some speak good English, will show you around. The ticket office and souvenir shop are on the right side of the monastery car park. To get there walk 500 metres west (upvalley) from the upper bus station and take a right turn. The office closes from noon to 2 pm, and the last tours end before 4 pm.

Tours generally include the Institute of Medicine, the Ser Kung Golden Temple, the Prayer Hall and the museum. Its collection includes ancient Buddhist pieces rescued from the fire, and some amazingly detailed yak-butter sculptures made for the annual winter festivities. In temperatures of around minus 20°C, the sculptures are delicately moulded in a tub of freezing water to prevent the butter being melted by the warmth of the hands.

Festivals These are important not only for the monks but also for the nomads, who stream into town from the grasslands in multicoloured splendour. Since the Tibetans use a lunar calendar, dates for individual festivals vary from year to year.

The Monlam (Great Prayer) Festival starts three days after the Tibetan New Year, which is usually in February or early March. On the

13th, 14th, 15th and 16th days of this month there are some spectacular ceremonies.

On the morning of the 13th a *thangka* (sacred painting on cloth) of Buddha measuring over 30 metres by 20 metres is unfurled on the other side of the Daxia River from the hillside facing the monastery. This event is accompanied by processions and prayer assemblies. On the 14th there is an all-day session of Cham dances performed by 35 masked dancers, with Yama, the Lord of Death, playing the leading role. On the 15th there is an evening display of butter lanterns and sculptures. On the 16th the Maitreya statue is paraded around the monastery all day.

During the second month (usually starting in March or early April) there are several interesting festivals, especially those held on the seventh and eighth days. Scriptural debates, lighting of butter lamps, collective prayers and blessings take place at other times during the year to commemorate Sakyamuni, Tsong Khapa or individual generations of the 'living buddhas'.

Sangke Grasslands
(*sāngkē cǎoyuán*)

Around and beyond the village of Sangke, 14 km upvalley from Xiahe, is a small lake surrounded by large expanses of open grassland where the Tibetans graze their yak herds. In summer these rolling pastures are at their greenest and have numerous wildflowers – it's a lovely place for walking. The Labrang Hotel has nomad-style tents up on the grasslands where you can stay overnight for around Y30 per bed. The road from Xiahe rises gradually and you can bicycle up in about one hour. You can also get up there by motortricycle for about Y30 return.

Places to Stay

Finding somewhere affordable shouldn't be a problem in Xiahe.

The *Dasha Hotel* (*dàshà bīnguǎn*) near the bridge charges Y20 in quads or Y15 in triples; average doubles with bathroom are Y80. There's hot water for showering at night. Opposite is the *Xinhua Hostel* (*xīnhuá zhāodàisuǒ*), where beds in doubles/triples are Y15/10. The place has a spartan orderliness – there are no showers and only a solitary toilet.

The next place up is the *Waterworks Hostel* (*zìláishuǐ zhāodàisuǒ*), with beds from Y8. (They also have an ultra-basic dorm with beds for just Y4, but it's only intended as a crash-pad for Tibetans). The showers are disgusting and there's no hot water anyway, but you can get yourself clean for Y2 at the public bathhouse a few doors up. They do have a few better doubles for Y25 and Y35. To get there from the upper bus station, head a short way ahead to the small bridge where a dirt lane leads left down to the hostel.

The *Labrang Monastery Guesthouse* (*lābǔlèng sì zhāodàisuǒ*) has beds for Y10 in double and triple rooms. It's run by old monks who potter around and smile a lot. It doesn't have showers, but there's always plenty of hot water from the boiler.

The nicest accommodation in Xiahe is the *Labrang Hotel* (☎ (09412) 21849) (*lābǔlèng bīnguǎn*) by the river a few km upvalley from the village. Originally the head lama's summer residence, it was knocked down by rampaging Red Guards and – a sore point with locals – rebuilt as a tourist hotel during the early 1980s. Nevertheless, it's a very friendly and tranquil place – one of the few hotels in China where you can wake to the gentle sound of a rushing stream.

A double suite with nice bathroom is US$25 a night; other doubles with bathroom cost US$20 and US$12. Beds in ornately painted triples are Y13, and Y11 in an eight-person dorm with communal showers. All rooms are heated in winter and there's hot water in the morning and evening. It's excellent value and recommended if you don't mind staying a bit out of the village. You can get here by motortricycle for about Y5, or walk in 45 minutes. The hotel rents out good pushbikes for Y2 per hour or Y15 a day.

The *Minzu (Nation) Hotel* near the lower bus station was undergoing renovations when we arrived to update this book. The improvements seem likely to nudge this one-time cheap-and-nasty into a rather higher price range.

Places to Eat

The *Labrang Hotel* has a restaurant serving good food. The restaurant downstairs in the *Dasha Hotel* also has some great dishes and a detailed English/Chinese menu. There are a number of simple and cheap Sichuan restaurants along the main street north of the monastery.

The *Tibet Restaurant (zàng cāntīng)* is on the 2nd floor on the left a few minutes' walk up from the Dasha. It was started by a local Tibetan, but has recently been taken over by a Han Chinese newcomer, so it's lost some of its authenticity. On the menu are Tibetan staples like yak-milk yoghurt with honey and *tsampa*. Tsampa is made from yak butter, coarse milk powder and highland-barley flour mixed into a dough with the fingers and eaten uncooked – just the thing to see you through a Himalayan winter. Don't expect to see only vegetarian dishes – as the Dalai Lama himself has said, if the highland Tibetans didn't eat meat they would have starved to death long ago.

Things to Buy

The shops along Xiahe's main street are a surprisingly good place to pick up Tibetan handicrafts. Needless to say, prices are highly negotiable. On sale are yak butter pots, daggers, fur-lined boots, colourful Tibetan shawls, tiny silver teapots, amber products and Tibetan *laba* trumpets. If you're heading off into the hills, consider buying a *gǒubàng*, a heavy tapered metal rod attached to a leather cord and used as a defence against wild dogs – it might also make a useful paperweight. Also on sale are a disturbingly large number of otter, lynx and even endangered snow-leopard hides, poached from the wilds of Qinghai and Tibet.

Getting There & Away

Xiahe is accessible only by bus. Most travellers arrive from Lanzhou, but some visit Xiahe as a stop en route between Gansu and Sichuan. From Lanzhou, there is only one direct daily bus departing from the west bus station at 7.30 am. It's a nine-hour ride, including a stop for lunch at Linxia. If you can't get a direct ticket from Lanzhou to Xiahe, then take a morning bus to Linxia and change there. The road between Linxia and Xiahe is being upgraded, with the eventual aim of making return day trips by tourist coach possible from Lanzhou.

All buses out of Xiahe pass through the lower bus station, so it's most convenient to board there. The direct bus to Lanzhou departs at 6.30 am – if you need to load your luggage onto the roof, turn up a bit earlier. In summer there are eight scheduled daily buses to Linxia between 6 am and 4 pm (Y7.50 local price, 3½ hours), and seven daily buses to Hezuo between 6.30 am and 3.40 pm (including two buses running via Hezuo en route to Maqu). A few private minibuses also leave irregularly for Hezuo and Linxia from along the main street. There's also one bus a day to Tongren (in Qinghai) at 6.30 am.

SICHUAN ROUTE

This scenic route goes via rough dirt roads along the eastern edge of the Tibetan mountains. Although a few buses go all the way from Lanzhou to Chengdu in Sichuan Province, it's best to do it in several stages, stopping at Linxia, Xiahe, Hezuo, Langmusi or Zoigê, a trip taking at least four days. For travel through this area you're supposed to have an Alien Travel Permit and PICC insurance.

All buses pass through Hezuo (*hézuò*), an ugly town of interest only as a transit point. In summer there are six or seven daily buses to Hezuo from Xiahe (Y8, 2½ hours) and Linxia (Y11, three hours). There is only one direct bus a day from Hezuo and Zoigê (Y20, eight hours), but more frequent connections to Luqu (*lùqǔ*), a predominantly Tibetan-speaking village several hours south of Hezuo on the Tao River. Other buses go to Maqu (*mǎqǔ*), which is off the route and closed to foreigners, but on the way Maqu buses pass near to Langmusi (*lángmùsì*), just inside Gansu Province.

Langmusi has two very large Tibetan Buddhist monasteries, each with around 600 monks. Unlike other monastic centres it's not surrounded by a large town, just a small village and many active temples. There's mountainous scenery on all sides and the local people still get around on the back of yaks. It's the most 'Tibetan' place travellers are likely to get to in China. Langmusi has two simple guesthouses with beds for about Y8.

On a highland plateau two hours further south in Sichuan is Zoigê *(ruðěrgài)*, from where it's possible to make a side trip to Jiuzhaigou National Park. From Zoigê it's a full day's journey by bus south to Chengdu.

TIANZHU
(tiānzhù) 天祝

Tianzhu, a predominantly Tibetan-speaking town on the railway line between Lanzhou and Wuwei, is still very much *closed to foreigners*. To go to there you must have an Alien Travel Permit, issued specifically for Tianzhu by the Lanzhou PSB, otherwise you'll be detained while the authorities decide how heavy your fine should be. It's highly unlikely they'll give you a permit

anyway, but even if they do you won't necessarily be welcome with the PSB in Tianzhu itself.

WUWEI
(wǔweī) 武威

Wuwei is the next town on the long Gansu rail corridor and is a pleasant place for a stopover. The famous galloping horse (now at the Museum of Chinese History in Beijing) was recovered in 1969 from a tomb at the Leitai Temple on the northern edge of the city. The local museum is housed in the Wenmiao Temple; its collection includes Han porcelain pieces, millstones, bronze utensils, tiny clay stoves, Northern Wei armour and carved stone tablets. The old Bell Tower in a backstreet behind Dong Dajie can be climbed; at the top is a massive cast-iron bell still in occasional use. The Luoshen Pagoda in the rear of the PSB compound on Beida Jie is also worth a look.

Places to Stay & Eat

The *Liangzhou Hotel (liángzhōu bīnguǎn)* has beds in simple doubles for Y22, and very nice double rooms with bathroom for Y90. The *Tianma Hotel* (☎ (0935) 2356) *(tiānmǎ bīnguǎn)* charges Y158 for standard doubles. It has a CITS office, a money-changing service and a large dining hall downstairs. In the evening a diverse range of street food is available from stalls near the park on Xi Dajie.

Getting There & Away

Wuwei is on the main Lanzhou-Ürümqi railway line. There is also a direct line east from Wuwei via Gantang to Zhongwei in Ningxia – roughly 300 km shorter than journeying via Lanzhou – but only infrequent and slow regional trains run this route. There are also daily buses to Zhongwei (Y25, six hours), Zhangye (Y17, five hours) and Jiayuguan (Y35, 10 hours), as well as some 15 bus departures a day to Lanzhou (7½ hours, Y27, or Y80 sleeper-bus). They'll probably want to see your PICC insurance at the ticket office.

GANSU

GANSU

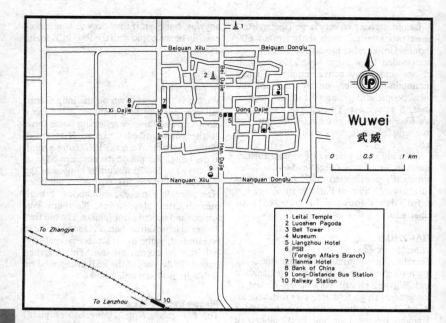

Beiguan Xilu

Beiguan Donglu

Xi Dajie

Dong Dajie

Nanguan Xilu

Nanguan Donglu

To Zhangye

To Lanzhou

Wuwei
武威

0   0.5   1 km

1 Leitai Temple
2 Luoshen Pagoda
3 Bell Tower
4 Museum
5 Liangzhou Hotel
6 PSB
   (Foreign Affairs Branch)
7 Tianma Hotel
8 Bank of China
9 Long-Distance Bus Station
10 Railway Station

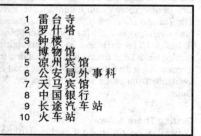

1	雷台寺塔
2	罗什楼
3	钟楼
4	博物馆
5	凉州宾馆
6	公安局外事科
7	天马宾馆
8	中国银行
9	长途汽车站
10	火车站

ZHANGYE

(zhāngyè) 张掖

Zhangye is the biggest town in Gansu north of Wuwei. It was once an important garrison town and a stop on the Silk Road (Marco Polo supposedly spent a year here). Photographs taken at the turn of the century show a still largely intact old city with high defensive walls, but little remains of the original Zhangye today. Definitely worth a visit is the Giant Buddha Temple *(dàfó sì)*, which houses an impressive 34-metre-long sleeping buddha. This clay statue is the largest of its kind in China and was built during the Western Xia period.

At Mati *(mǎtí)*, a beautiful Tibetan village 135 km south of Zhangye in the foothills of the Qilianshan, is the Horse's Hoof Temple *(mǎtí sì)*, built within a high cliff face and accessible only via an amazing passageway through the caves. Just outside Mati are the Thousand Buddha Caves *(qiānfó dòng)*. Mati is still little visited by foreigners, and to visit the area you need an Alien Travel Permit issued by the PSB in Zhangye or Lanzhou. Visitors have to stay overnight in Mati, since there's only one bus there each day.

Places to Stay

The *Ganzhou Hotel* (☎ 2402) *(gānzhōu bīnguǎn)* on Nan Jie charges Y88 for a standard double and Y16 per bed in quads. The only other foreigners' hotel is the *Zhangye Hotel* (☎ 2601) (*zhāngyè bīnguǎn*) at 65 Xianfu Jie, which has beds in small dorms for Y24 and doubles for Y112; this hotel also has a CITS office.

Getting There & Away

All trains running between Lanzhou and

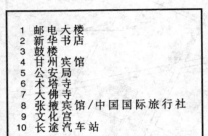

```
1   邮电大楼
2   新华书店
3   鼓楼
4   甘州宾馆
5   公安局
6   木塔寺
7   大佛寺
8   张掖宾馆/中国国际旅行社
9   文化宫
10  长途汽车站
```

Ürümqi stop at Zhangye. The bus to Mati departs from the main long-distance bus station at 2.20 pm and returns to Zhangye the next day at 6.20 am; the trip takes three hours and costs Y7. There are also a number of daily buses from Zhangye south to Wuwei and north to Jiayuguan. However, foreigners are not supposed to travel the latter route by road, apparently due to sensitivity regarding the Long March rocket-launching site near Jiuquan.

JIAYUGUAN

(*jiāyùguān*) 嘉峪关

Jiayuguan (Jiayu Pass) is an ancient Han Chinese outpost. The Great Wall once extended beyond here, but in 1372, during the first few years of the Ming Dynasty, a fortress was built. From then on Jiayuguan was considered the terminal of the wall and the end of the empire.

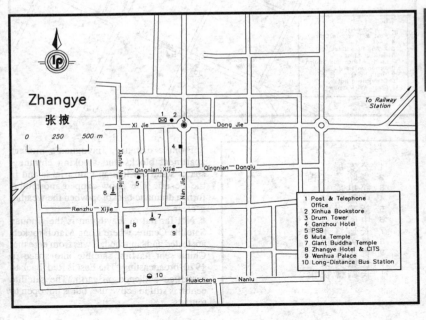

Zhangye
张掖

0   250   500 m

To Railway Station

Xi Jie — Dong Jie
Qingnian - Xijie — Qingnian - Donglu
Renzhu - Xijie
Huaicheng — Nanlu

Xianfu Nanjie
Nan Jie

1 Post & Telephone Office
2 Xinhua Bookstore
3 Drum Tower
4 Ganzhou Hotel
5 PSB
6 Muta Temple
7 Giant Buddha Temple
8 Zhangye Hotel & CITS
9 Wenhua Palace
10 Long-Distance Bus Station

GANSU

Jiayuguan
嘉裕关

To Jiayuguan Fort
(5 km)

To Jiuquan

0   250   500 m

To Railway
Station

Xiangguan Donglu
Xiangguan Xilu
Xinhua Nanlu
Jianshe Xilu

1 PSB
2 Jiayuguan Hotel
3 Post & Telephone Office
4 CAAC
5 Xinhua Bookstore
6 Bank of China
7 Long-Distance Bus Station
8 Xiongguan Hotel
9 Youth Hotel
10 Changcheng Hotel
11 Great Wall Museum

```
1   公安局
2   嘉峪关宾馆
3   邮电局
4   中国民航
5   新华书店
6   中国银行
7   长途汽车站
8   雄关宾馆
9   青年宾馆
10  长城宾馆
11  长城博物馆
```

GANSU

From a distance, Jiayuguan's modern apartment blocks and smoking chimney-stacks stand out like an industrial island in the desert. The snow-capped mountains form a dramatic backdrop when the weather is clear.

Not far out of Jiayuguan is the Jiuquan Satellite Centre, where Long March rockets are tested and launched. It was from here that China sent its first satellite into space in 1970, broadcasting 'The East is Red' back to a startled audience on earth. The satellite centre is still in active use, but is not open to tourists.

Orientation

The Jiayuguan Hotel on the central traffic circle is the town's pivotal point. The main tourist amenities are within convenient walking distance of the hotel. The new long-distance bus station is on a six-way crossroads where the Gansu Highway passes through town. The railway station is four km south of the centre.

Information

CITS CITS (☎ 2632) is in the lobby of the Jiayuguan Hotel. There is another office (☎ 24917 or 25299) on the 2nd floor of the building behind the Changcheng Hotel.

PSB This is in a compound near the Jiayuguan Hotel. Turn right at the hotel gate, then right again at the next corner. The entry-exit office is left from the gateway.

Post There is a post and telephone office diagonally opposite the Jiayuguan Hotel. It's open from 8.30 am to 7 pm.

Money The Bank of China is on Xinhua Lu, 600 metres south of the Jiayuguan Hotel, and is open from 9 am to noon, and from 2.30 to 7.30 pm.

Maps The Xinhua Bookstore on the 3rd floor of a building 300 metres south of the central traffic circle has detailed Chinese maps of Jiayuguan and the surrounding area for Y4.

Jiayuguan Fort

(jiāyùguān chénglóu) 嘉峪关城楼
This is the main attraction of Jiayuguan. The fort guards the pass which lies between the snow-capped Qilianshan peaks and Black Mountain *(hēishān)* of the Mazong range. During the Ming Dynasty this was considered the terminus of the Great Wall, though crumbling fragments can be seen to the west.

The fort was dubbed the 'Impregnable Defile Under Heaven'. Although the Chinese often controlled territory far beyond Jiayuguan, this was the last major stronghold of the empire to the west.

The fort was built in 1372, with additional

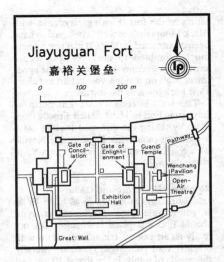

towers and battlements added later. The outer wall is about 733 metres in circumference and almost 10 metres high. At the eastern end of the fort is the Gate of Enlightenment *(guānghuà mén)* and in the west is the Gate of Conciliation *(róuyuǎn mén)*. Over each gate stand 17-metre-high towers with upturned flying eaves. On the inside of each gate are horse lanes leading up to the top of the wall. At the fort's four corners are blockhouses, bowmen's turrets and watchtowers. Outside the Gate of Enlightenment but inside the outer wall are three interesting buildings: the Wenchang Pavilion, Guandi Temple and the open-air theatre stage *(zhàntái)*.

The fort is five km west of Jiayuguan. You can cycle out there in about half an hour, or pick up a motorbike, taxi or minibus outside the Jiayuguan Hotel; for a small taxi, bargain for around Y40 there and back. The fort is open from 8 am to 12.30 pm, and from 2.30 to 6 pm. Foreigners' entry tickets cost Y12.

Overhanging Great Wall

(xuánbì chángchéng) 悬壁长城
The Overhanging Great Wall is seven km north-west of Jiayuguan and almost as inter-

esting as the fort. Linking Jiayuguan with Black Mountain, the wall is believed to have been constructed in 1540. It had since pretty much crumbled to dust but was reconstructed by students in 1987. From the upper tower high on a ridge you get an excellent view back towards the township.

The wall is roughly six km north of Jiayuguan Fort and best visited directly from there by taking the dirt road leading north towards the mountains. If you're on a bicycle it's a rough but very nice ride. It costs Y5 to climb the wall.

Xincheng Underground Gallery

(xīnchéng dìxià huàláng) 新城地下画廊
If you're interested in Chinese art, you should find this place fascinating. It's not really an art gallery, but ancient tombs with original wall paintings. There are literally thousands of tombs in the desert 20 km east of Jiayuguan, but only one is currently open to visitors. The tombs date from approximately 220 to 420 AD (the Wei and Jin periods).

Very few tourists come here, so there are no regular buses. You can hire a minibus for around Y50. The gallery is open continuously from 8 am to 7 pm.

Black Mountain Rock Paintings

(hēishān yánhuà) 黑山岩画
About nine km to the north-west of Jiayuguan are some rock paintings dating back to the Warring States Period (476-221 BC). While they are not as bright or interesting as those in the Xincheng Underground Gallery, they are considerably older – a good place for the true art historian.

There's no public transport out there, so you'll have to make your own way by pushbike, taxi or minibus.

First Beacon Tower

(dìyī dūn) 第一墩
This is the crumbling remains of a tower built on top of a cliff in 1539 at what was once the westernmost edge of the Great Wall. There isn't much to this place now, but you could

include it with a taxi trip to Jiayuguan pass. It's six km south-west of Jiayuguan.

Places to Stay

The *Youth Hotel* (☎ 25833/4) *qīngnián bīnguǎn*), a new place built in an incongruous 'European castle' style, offers the best value in town. It's clean and friendly, with rates ranging from Y16 per bed in triples without bathroom, Y80 for a double with bathroom to Y140 for the suite. There's hot water mornings and evenings. The hotel is on Jianshe Xilu, at the southern end of town. It's a bit far from things, but there are frequent minibuses to the railway station and into town.

On the traffic circle at the centre of town is the *Jiayuguan Hotel* (☎ 26321) *(jiāyùguān bīnguǎn)*. The charge for a double ranges from Y190 to Y230. Beds in simple triples are a relatively expensive Y30 – the hotel meeting room serves as an overflow dormitory at Y20 per couch.

The *Xiongguan Hotel* (*xióngguān bīnguǎn*) down the road on Xinhua Lu has doubles for Y100 and beds in small dorms from Y28. It's a lacklustre affair, though the staff do their best.

Jiayuguan's only luxury accommodation is at the *Chángchéng Hotel* (☎ (09477) 25277) *(chángchéng bīnguǎn)* at No 6 Jianshe Xilu, not far from the Youth Hotel. Its 'dorms' – actually triples with a private bathroom – cost Y100 a bed. Double rooms are Y300 and the suite is Y600. It's got a small bank, a postal service and a swimming pool out the back.

Places to Eat

The local food is certainly nothing to get excited about, but you didn't come to the deserts of western China to eat anyway – face it, you're a long way from Canton! The *Jiayuguan Hotel* restaurant has main-course dishes for around Y10, and there's a sort-of-reasonable place to the right from the hotel gate. The *Youth Hotel* has a canteen serving simple but sound meals. The *Changcheng Hotel* has the only really good restaurant anywhere in Jiayuguan.

Getting There & Away

Air Jiayuguan has a small airport 13 km north-east of the city. There are flights to Dunhuang (Y200, three a week), Lanzhou (Y360, three a week) and Xi'an (Y650, twice weekly). The CAAC office (☎ 26237) is on Xinhua Nanlu a short distance south of the Jiayuguan Hotel.

Bus You can buy bus tickets at a booth right outside the Jiayuguan Hotel as well as the long-distance bus station. If you're going to Dunhuang, you can take one of the five direct daily buses there rather than the longer train/bus option. The 380-km trip takes seven hours and costs Y27. There are also sleeper coaches to Ürümqi (Y170 for a lower berth) and Lanzhou (Y125), but at the time of writing, foreigners were not allowed to travel by road between Jiuquan and Zhangye. Although the town of Jiuquan has little worth seeing, the half-hour trip only costs Y1.80 and buses leave frequently.

Train Jiayuguan lies on the Lanzhou-Ürümqi railway line. There are three expresses and three rapid trains each way daily; it's six hours to Liuyuan and 18 hours to Lanzhou. The large new Jiayuguan railway station has recently replaced the old building beside it, which was hopelessly inadequate.

Getting Around

An airport bus (Y4 one way) from the CAAC office meets all flights.

Minibuses and public buses to the railway station run down Xinhua Lu then past the Changcheng Hotel. The Jiayuguan Hotel and the Youth Hotel have bicycles for rent at Y1 per hour. Bikes are excellent for getting around town, to the fort and (if you don't mind the occasional gulp of dust) to the Hanging Wall too, but you'll need motorised transport for the other sights. Getting together a group of travellers brings down the cost. Taxis, motorbikes and minibuses wait outside the Jiayuguan Hotel. When bargaining the price for a minibus, allow about

Y2 per km – less for longer trips. Apart from the July 1st Glacier, all the sights can be visited in a single day's tour.

AROUND JIAYUGUAN
July 1st Glacier

(qīyī bīngchuān) 七一冰川

The July 1st Glacier lies at 4300 metres, high up in the Qilianshan mountains. Hikers can walk a five-km-long trail alongside the glacier, but at that elevation it gets cold even in summer, so come prepared. The area looks as if it would present a serious challenge even for experienced mountaineers – just getting through the inevitable red tape could be exhausting! The glacier is 120 km south-west of Jiayuguan, so you'll have to organise your own transport out there. To charter a small minibus with three passengers to the glacier costs about Y200 return. If you've got good insurance, you might choose to get there on the back of a motorbike for Y120.

LIUYUAN

(liǔyuán) 柳园

Liuyuan, on the Lanzhou-Ürümqi railway line, is the jumping-off point for Dunhuang. It's a tiny, forlorn-looking town in the middle of the desert and definitely not the sort of place to hang around.

There are six trains daily in each direction. Going east, it takes six hours to reach Jiayuguan and 18 hours to reach Lanzhou. Heading west, it's 13 hours to Turpan and 16 hours to Ürümqi.

Scheduled buses for Dunhuang depart eight times daily from a small bus terminal one block south of the station. There are almost always minibuses parked outside the station waiting to cart off arriving passengers, regardless of what time trains get in. It's a breezy 2½-hour trip by surfaced road, and the fare is Y10.

If you do end up staying the night here, the only accommodation for foreigners is the Liuyuan Hotel *(liǔyuán bīnguǎn)* on the main street right by the bus station; it has dorm beds for Y15 and doubles for Y80.

GANSU

DUNHUANG

(dūnhuáng) 敦煌

Dunhuang is a large oasis in one of China's most arid regions. After travelling for hours towards Dunhuang, the flat, barren desert landscape suddenly gives way to lush green cultivated fields with mountainous rolling sand dunes as a backdrop. The area has a certain haunting beauty, especially at night under a star-studded sky.

However, it's not so much the desert dunes and romantic nights that attract tourists to Dunhuang, but the superb Buddhist art at the nearby Mogao Caves. During the Han and Tang dynasties, Dunhuang was a major point of interchange between China and the outside world, a stopping-off post for both incoming and outgoing trading caravans. These days, Dunhuang's economic fortunes have been revived by tourism – it's one of the leading travel destinations in the country.

Orientation

Dunhuang radiates from the main traffic circle by the post office; all hotels and tourist facilities are within walking distance of this point. The long-distance bus station is a 15-minute walk away on Dingzi Lu.

Information

CITS The main CITS office is on the 2nd floor at the southern end of Dingzi Lu, almost opposite the Western Region Hotel. They also have a branch at the Dunhuang Hotel (Binguan). Since you can't buy train tickets in Dunhuang, there isn't a whole lot they can do for you other than give you bus and train departure times or arrange tours to remote sights such as Yumen Pass.

PSB This is on Xi Dajie, near the Bank of China. It's open from 8 am to noon and from 3 to 6 pm, and is closed on Sunday.

Money The Bank of China is on Xi Dajie, two blocks west of the post office. It's open from 9 am to noon, and from 2.30 to 5.30 pm.

Post & Telecommunications The post and telephone office is on the north-western side of the main traffic circle.

Maps You can buy a cheap map of Dunhuang from street hawkers, at the Dunhuang Hotel (Binguan) or the Xinhua Bookstore. It's all in Chinese, but still useful for basic orientation.

Dunhuang County Museum

(dūnhuáng xiàn bówùguǎn)

敦煌县博物馆

The museum is on Dong Dajie east of the main traffic circle. It's divided into three sections. The first section displays some of the Tibetan and Chinese scriptures unearthed from Cave No 17 at Mogao. The second section shows sacrificial objects from the Han to the Tang dynasties. The third section includes relics such as silks, brocades, bamboo slips and reed torches (for the beacons) from the Yangguan and Yumen passes. A pleasant museum for a browse.

Places to Stay

The *Western Region Hotel (xīyù bīnguǎn)* is a white-tiled building a few doors south of the bus station. They have beds in triples for Y15 and doubles with bathroom for Y50. This is a new place with a fresh feel, and already popular with backpackers for its low prices and convenient location.

Almost directly opposite the bus station is the *Feitian Hotel* (☎ (09474) 22726) *(fēitiān bīnguǎn)*. Their multi-bed dorms cost Y15, and doubles are Y100. It's got nice gardens, and the staff are friendly and helpful.

One block to the north is the smaller *Dunhuang Hotel (Fandian) (dūnhuáng fàndiàn)*, which charges Y15 per bed in simple quads and Y80 for a double with bathroom. This place has clearly seen better days and you can do much better, but it's got character.

The nearby *Mingshan Hotel* (☎ 22132) *(míngshān bīnguǎn)* is a similar old-style place. Hard, solid dorm beds in cramped dorms go for Y12, and simple doubles are Y44, or Y110 with bathroom.

A second, much larger *Dunhuang Hotel (Binguan)* (☎ (09474) 22415, 22538)

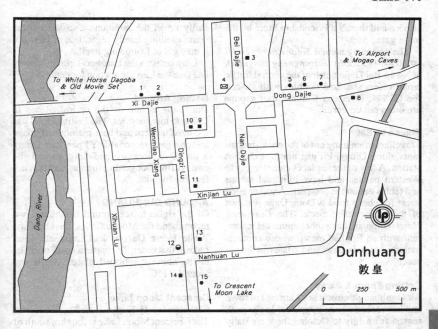

Dunhuang 敦皇

1	PSB
2	Bank of China
3	Solar Energy Hotel
4	Post & Telephone Office
5	Dunhuang County Museum
6	Xinhua Bookstore
7	CAAC
8	Dunhuang Hotel (Binguan)
9	Yangguan Hotel
10	Mingshan Hotel
11	Dunhuang Hotel (Fandian)
12	Long-Distance Bus Station
13	Feitian Hotel
14	Western Region Hotel
15	CITS

1	公安局
2	中国银行
3	太阳能宾馆
4	邮电局
5	敦煌县博物馆
6	新华书店
7	中国民航
8	敦煌宾馆
9	阳关宾馆
10	鸣山宾馆
11	敦煌饭店
12	长途汽车站
13	飞天宾馆
14	西域宾馆
15	中国国际旅行社

GANSU

(dūnhuáng bīnguǎn) is at No 1 Dong Dajie on the eastern side of town. This tourist hotel has a comprehensive range of rooms with major seasonal price variation. Suites have air-con and cost Y340 in the high season (June to September), but only Y200 in the

low season; standard doubles are Y220 (high season) and Y140 (low season); the cheapest dorm beds are Y15. Across the road is the hotel's older northern wing with doubles for Y160/120 and basic triples and quads for Y35/30. The hotel has a ticket-booking service and there's a Friendship Store by the main gate.

The curiously named *Solar Energy Hotel* (☎ (09474) 22306) *(tàiyángnéng bīnguǎn)*, at No 14 Bei Dajie north of the central traffic circle offers standard doubles with air-con for US$44. Overseas Chinese tour groups are often put up here.

Places to Eat
Travellers often hang out at the cheap restaurants along Dingzi Lu just north of the bus station. A few of these places cater largely to Western palates and have bilingual menus and tables out on the footpath. Another good street for cheap food is Dong Dajie just east of the main traffic circle. The *Dunhuang Hotel* (Binguan) has a more upmarket restaurant with an English menu, whose contents include 'camels paw' and 'dates in honey sauce'.

Getting There & Away
Air Dunhuang's airport is 13 km east of town and has recently been upgraded. In the peak season from July to October there are daily flights to/from Lanzhou (Y520) and Xi'an (Y760) and less frequent air services between Beijing and Ürümqi. Flights can be booked at the CAAC booking office (☎ 22389) on Dong Dajie or the Dunhuang Hotel (Binguan).

Bus & Train Buses to Liuyuan (130 km) depart eight times daily from the bus station between 7.30 am and 6 pm. The fare is Y10 and the trip takes about 2½ hours. There are scheduled public buses to Jiayuguan (Y27, seven hours) at 7.30, 9 and 11.30 am, and at 1.30 and 5 pm. Most buses actually go to Jiuquan (a rather boring place), stopping only briefly in Jiayuguan. There are also privately owned minibuses to Jiayuguan and other destinations; these cruise the streets, leaving only when they have enough passengers.

There's one early-morning bus to Golmud (Y36, 13 hours) via a scenic route south across a pass in the Altun Shan. Arrive early enough to store your luggage on the roof. It's

chilly up in the mountains, so keep some warm clothing handy regardless of how hot it may get in Dunhuang itself.

Liuyuan is on the Lanzhou-Ürümqi railway line (see the Liuyuan section for details).

Getting Around
Dunhuang is one of the easiest places in China to hire bicycles. The Feitian Hotel has the most modern and best-maintained bikes, and charges a reasonable Y1 per hour. Doing a bit of exploratory pedalling around the oasis is fine, but getting to most sights is not feasible by bike.

AROUND DUNHUANG
Of the sights to see around Dunhuang, we recommend the Mogao Caves, the Old City, White Horse Dagoba and Crescent Moon Lake in that order. To charter a small minibus to the above-mentioned places you'll pay around Y150.

Crescent Moon Lake
(yuèyáquán) 月牙泉
The Crescent Moon Lake is four km south of the centre of Dunhuang at the Singing Sand Mountains *(míngshāshān)*, where the oasis meets the desert. Springwater trickles up into a depression between huge sand dunes, forming a small, crescent-shaped pond (not to be confused with the concreted storage pool nearby). The climb to the top of the dunes is sweaty work, but the dramatic view back across the rolling desert sands towards the oasis makes the effort worthwhile.

Out here the recreational activities include the predictable camel rides, more novel 'dune surfing' (sand sliding) and paragliding – jumping off the top of high dunes with a shute on your back. Novices may find the idea of sailing high above the evening desert landscape a bit unnerving, but – the Chinese-made gliding gear notwithstanding – soft, loose sand makes even a crash-landing relatively unhazardous. Even so, it might be prudent to look at your insurance policy before you leap! Paragliding costs Y30 a go – that's for one successful flight.

You can ride a bike out to the dunes, but

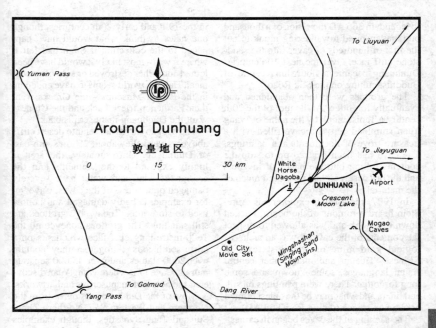

Around Dunhuang
敦皇地区

To Liuyuan

Yumen Pass

0   15   30 km

White Horse Dagoba

DUNHUANG

To Jiayuguan

Airport

Crescent Moon Lake

Mogao Caves

Old City Movie Set

Mingshashan (Singing Sand Mountains)

To Golmud

Yang Pass

Dang River

there's also an evening bus at 6 pm from Dunhuang bus station, returning at 8 pm. The fare is Y7 for the round trip. The admission fee to the lake and dunes area is Y13 for foreigners.

If you go walking off into the dunes in the heat of the day, be sure to carry water – and wear a hat, or you'll fry your brains.

White Horse Dagoba
(báimǎ tǎ) 白马塔
Something of an anticlimax, the dagoba is four km west of town and is easily combined with the trip out to the Old City – Movie Set. It makes a good place for a short bicycle excursion.

Old City – Movie Set
(diànyǐng gǔchéng) 电影古城
This reconstructed Song-Dynasty town, complete with five-metre-high city walls, was built in 1987 as a movie set for a Sino-Japanese co-production titled *Dunhuang*.

Standing isolated out in the desert some 20 km south-west of Dunhuang, from a distance the Old City has a dramatic and strikingly realistic appearance. From close up, though, the place is starting to look a bit shabby; the mud-brick walls are crumbling and the bare yards behind the makeshift facades are scattered with litter – it's vaguely reminiscent of a 'wild west' ghost town. Nevertheless, it's a reasonably interesting place for a short visit.

Chinese minibuses to the Old City leave from the side street one block north of Dunhuang bus station; they charge only Y10, but generally stay far too long. You can get there by bicycle, and will arrive fit and thirsty. Entry costs Y12 (Y6 for students).

Mogao Caves
(mògāo kū) 莫高窟
The Mogao Caves are the most impressive and best-preserved examples of Buddhist cave art anywhere in China, and are the highlight of a visit to Dunhuang. According

to legend, in 366 AD the vision of a thousand buddhas inspired a wandering monk to cut the first of hundreds of caves into the sandstone cliff face. Over the next 10 centuries Dunhuang became a flourishing centre of Buddhist culture on the Silk Road.

The grottoes were then abandoned and eventually forgotten. At the turn of the 20th century a Taoist monk by the name of Wang Yuan stumbled across a cave filled with a treasure trove of documents and paintings. The cave had been bricked up to stop the contents falling into the hands of invaders and the dry desert air had preserved much of the material.

In 1907, the British explorer Sir Aurel Stein heard a rumour of the hoard, tracked down the monk and was allowed to inspect the contents of the cave. It was an archaeological gold mine of Buddhist texts in Chinese, Tibetan and many other central Asian languages, some known and some long forgotten. There were paintings on silk and linen, and what may be the oldest printed book in existence (dating from 868 AD).

The sacking of the caves began in earnest. Stein convinced Wang to part with a large section of the library in return for a donation towards the restoration of some of the grottoes. He carted away 24 packing cases of manuscripts and five of paintings, embroideries and art relics, all of which were deposited in the British Museum. The following year a French explorer, Pelliot, passed through Dunhuang and bought more of the manuscripts from the monk.

He was followed by others from the USA, Japan and Russia, who all carted off their booty. News of the find filtered through to Beijing, and the imperial court ordered the remainder of the collection to be transported to the capital. Many items were pilfered while they sat in the Dunhuang government offices, and Stein reported in 1914 when he returned to the area that fine Buddhist manuscripts were brought to him for sale. He also said that Wang had regretted not taking up his original offer to buy the entire collection.

For the Chinese it's another example of the plundering of the country by foreigners in the 19th and early 20th centuries, though one hates to think what would have happened to the collection if Stein had left it where it was – most likely it would have been looted and either destroyed or sold off piecemeal. Half the world seems to have ended up in the British Museum – the Greeks want their Parthenon frieze back and the Chinese want the Dunhuang manuscripts back.

The Mogao Caves are set into desert cliffs above a river valley about 25 km south-east of Dunhuang. Unfortunately, the area is highly exposed to the elements and the erosion of wind and water have severely damaged quite a few of the caves. Cave 94, for example, is badly damaged and is now used to store junk. Today, 492 grottoes are still standing. The grottoes honeycomb the 1600-metre-long cliff face which sits on a north-south axis. Altogether they contain over 2000 statues and over 45,000 separate murals. Cave 17 is where Wang Yuan discovered the hoard of manuscripts and artworks.

Most of the Dunhuang art dates from the Northern and Western Wei, Northern Zhou, Sui and Tang dynasties, though examples from the Five Dynasties, Northern Song, Western Xia and Yuan can also be found. The Northern Wei, Western Wei, Northern Zhou and Tang caves are in the best state of preservation.

The caves tend to be rectangular or square with recessed, decorated ceilings. The focal point of each is the group of brightly painted statues representing Buddha and the bodhisattvas or Buddha's disciples. The smaller statues are made of terracotta, coated with a kind of plaster surface so that intricate details could be etched into the surface. The walls and ceilings were also plastered with layers of cement and clay and then painted with watercolour. Large sections of the mural are made up of decorative patterns using motifs from nature, architecture, or textiles.

Northern Wei, Western Wei & Northern Zhou Caves The Turkic-speaking Tobas who inhabited the region north of China invaded and conquered the country in the 4th century and founded the Northern Wei

Dynasty around 386 AD. They deliberately adopted a policy of copying Chinese customs and lifestyle. But friction between groups who wanted to maintain the traditional Toba lifestyle and those who wanted to assimilate with the Chinese eventually split the Toba empire in two in the middle of the 6th century; the eastern part adopted the Chinese way of life and the rulers took the dynasty name of Northern Qi. The western part took the dynastic name of Northern Zhou and tried to revert to Toba customs without success. By 567 AD, however, they had defeated the Qi and taken control of all of northern China.

The fall of the Han Dynasty in 220 AD had sent Confucianism into decline. With the turmoil produced by the Toba invasions, Buddhism's teachings of nirvana and personal salvation became highly appealing. The religion spread rapidly under the patronage of the new rulers, and made a new and decisive impact on Chinese art which can be seen in the Buddhist statues at Mogao.

The art of this period is characterised by its attempt to depict the spirituality of those who had achieved enlightenment and transcended the material world through their asceticism. The Wei statues are slim, ethereal figures with finely chiselled features and comparatively large heads. The bodhisattvas in Northern Wei Caves 248 and 257 are a good example of the later Wei. Like the sculptures of the same period at Luoyang, the expressions on the faces of the buddhas and bodhisattvas are benevolently saccharine – Cave 259 of the Northern Wei period is a good example.

The Wei and Zhou paintings at Mogao are some of the most interesting in the grottoes. The figures are simple, almost cartoon-like, with round heads, elongated ears and puppet-like, segmented bodies which are boldly outlined. The female figures are all naked to the waist, with large breasts, which suggests an Indian influence. Northern Zhou Cave 299 shows musicians and dancers in this style, and Cave 290 shows flying celestial maidens. The paintings in Northern Zhou Cave 428 are a good example of this style.

The wall painting in Northern Wei Cave 254, done in the same style, portrays the story of Buddha vanquishing Mara:

One night, Buddha sat beneath a fig tree south of the Indian city of Patna, and entered into deep meditation. Mara, the Evil One, realising that Sakyamuni was on the verge of enlightenment, rushed to the spot. Mara tempted him with desire, parading three voluptuous goddesses before him, but Sakyamuni resisted. Then Mara assailed him with hurricanes, torrential rains and showers of flaming rocks, but the missiles turned to lotus petals. Finally Mara challenged Buddha's right to do what he was doing, but Buddha touched the earth with his fingertip and the roaring it summoned up drove away Mara and his army of demons. Sakyamuni had achieved enlightenment – but Mara was waiting with one last temptation. This time it was an appeal to reason, that speech-defying revelations could not be translated into words and no one would understand so profound a truth as the Buddha had attained; but Buddha said that there would be some who would understand, and Mara was finally banished forever.

The murals tend to be highly detailed and the figures are relatively small. During the Wei Dynasty, portraits of noble patrons began to be depicted alongside the more religious themes that they had sponsored. These figures depict the lifestyle and fashions of the Wei nobles. The men are usually shown in the Chinese robe and the women in a tight-fitting gown with loose sleeves.

Sui Caves The throne of the Northern Zhou Dynasty was usurped by a general of Chinese or mixed Chinese-Toba origin. Prudently putting to death all the sons of the former emperor, he embarked on a series of wars which by 589 had reunited northern and southern China for the first time in 360 years. The Tobas simply disappeared from history, either mixing with other Turkish tribes from central Asia or assimilating with the Chinese.

The Sui Dynasty was short-lived, and very much a transition between the Wei and Tang periods. It did not leave any great masterpieces. Again, the best Sui art was of Buddhist origin. What separates the Sui style from that of the Wei is the rigidity of its sculpture. The figures of the Buddha and bodhisattvas are stiff and immobile; their heads are curiously oversized and their torsos elongated. They wear Chinese robes and show none of the Indian-inspired softness and grace of the Wei figures.

At Mogao the Sui caves are north of the Wei caves. Buddha's disciples Ananda and Kasyapa are both seen here for the first time – see Cave 419, for example. There are also a number of examples of the lotus flower symbol and designs from Middle Asian and Persian brocades. Stories from the life of Buddha provide the main themes of the wall paintings. Other Sui caves include 204, 244, 302 and 427. Some of the paintings show processions of musicians, attendants, wagons and horses.

Tang Caves The reign of the last Sui emperor, Yang Ti, was characterised by imperial extravagance, cruelty and social injustice. Taking advantage of the inevitable peasant revolts which had arisen in eastern China, a noble family of Chinese-Turkish descent assassinated the emperor, took control of the capital, Chang'an, and assumed the throne, taking the dynasty name of Tang.

During the Tang period, China pushed its borders forcefully eastward as far as Lake Balkhash in today's Kazakhstan. Outside trade expanded and foreign merchants and people of diverse religions streamed into the Tang capital of Chang'an. Tang art took on incomparable vigour, moving towards greater realism and nobility of form. Buddhism had become prominent and Buddhist art reached its peak; the proud bearing of the Buddhist figures in the Mogao Caves reflects the feelings of the times, the prevailing image of the brave Tang warrior, and the strength and steadfastness of the empire.

Extravagant robes drape many of the figures, which show an element of sensuality typical of Persian and Indian art. The Tang figures are notable for their overwhelming size and power. The best examples are the colossal buddhas of caves 96 and 130; the one in Cave 96 stands over 30 metres high. The statues can be viewed from platforms constructed in the cave wall opposite their chests and faces. The roof and walls of Cave 130 are adorned with paintings.

The portraits of Tang nobles are considerably larger than those of the Wei and Sui dynasties, and the figures tend to occupy important positions within the murals. In some cases the patrons are portrayed in the same scene as the Buddha.

Unlike the figures of the Wei, Zhou and Sui periods, the Tang figures are realistic with a range of very human expressions. The portrait of a Buddhist nun in Cave 17 and the statue of Buddha's older disciple Kasyapa in Cave 45 are good examples of this. There are also notable exceptions such as the statues in Cave 16 with their heavy eyebrows, long slitted eyes and enormous hands.

Other Tang Dynasty caves include 45, 57, 103, 112, 156, 159, 196, 217, 220, 320, 321, 328 and 329. Cave 156 has an interesting wall mural showing a Tang army on the march and Cave 158 has a huge statue of the dead Buddha with a group of grieving 'foreigners'.

Later Caves The Tang period marked the ultimate development of the cave paintings. During later dynasties the economy around Dunhuang went into decline and the luxuriousness and vigour typical of Tang painting began to be replaced by simpler drawing techniques and flatter figures. However, during the Northern Song period a number of important breakthroughs were made in landscape painting. Wutaishan in Cave 61 is a good example of this style. People are integrated into the landscape and scenery is depicted for its own sake, rather than just as an abstract backdrop.

No 3 is an example of a Yuan Dynasty cave. Cave 346 is an example of a Five Dynasties cave. Cave 55 is another example of a Northern Song construction.

Admission Foreigners have the choice of buying a ticket for Y13 or for Y45; the Y13 ticket lets you see 10 caves, while the Y45 ticket is for 30 caves (give or take a few). Unless you're on a particularly tight budget or have the most passing of interests in Buddhist cave art, the Y45 ticket is definitely worth the extra money.

All visitors must be accompanied by a local guide (included in the admission fee). Even if there are only a few of you, foreigners are generally put into a separate tour group with a guide who speaks English. Otherwise you could round up any foreigners present into a single group and ask to have an English-speaking guide assigned to you.

The caves are open from 8.30 to 11.30 am and from 2 to 3.45 pm. More people tend to turn up for the morning session, but it's longer so you have more time to look around; the afternoon session can be a bit rushed. People sometimes come back a second time to see the caves at a more leisurely pace.

Except for the small niches (most of them in very bad condition or bare of statues and paintings), all the caves have locked gates. Many of the locked caves are in such poor condition that they are simply not worth opening to the general public. Some, like Cave 462 – the Mizong Cave – contain Tantric art whose explicit sexual portrayals have been deemed too corrupting for the public to view. A few caves are in the process of being restored. More than 40 have been cleared for public view.

Photography is strictly prohibited everywhere within the fenced-off caves area, though photos are sometimes permitted after payment of an appropriately large sum of money; cameras and all hand luggage must be deposited at an office near the entrance gate. Shops at the caves and in Dunhuang itself sell comprehensive sets of slides, postcards and books. Most caves are lit only by indirect sunlight from outside, often making it hard to see detail, particularly in the niches. Heavy but low-powered torches (flashlights) can be hired at the ticket office for Y2; if you have your own, bring it.

Getting There & Away The Mogao Caves are 25 km and 30 minutes by bus from Dunhuang. There are only two scheduled public buses daily – the first departs at 8 am

and returns at 11 am. The afternoon bus departs at 1.30 pm and returns at 4 pm. The return fare is Y5 – even if you arrive on the morning bus and take the afternoon bus back. The bus leaves from outside a small ticket office two blocks north of the bus station; buy tickets there or on the bus.

Depending on your bargaining skills, you should be able to hire a taxi out there for around Y50 return, including the driver's waiting time.

Some people ride out to the caves, but be warned that half the ride is through total desert – hot work in summer. The Mogao Hostel *(mògāokū zhāodàisuǒ)* is the only accommodation at the caves; it has rooms for Y30 and does good set meals in the tourist season.

Yang & Yumen Passes
(yángguān, yùménguān) 阳关和玉门关
Some 76 km south-west of Dunhuang is the Yang (South) Pass. Here, Han Dynasty beacon towers marked the caravan route westwards and warned of advancing invaders, but what remains has now largely disappeared under the shifting sands. Nearby are the ruins of the ancient Han town of Shouchang. The Yumen (Jade Gate) Pass, 98 km north-west of Dunhuang, is also known for its ancient ruins.

Caravans heading out of China would travel up the Gansu corridor to Dunhuang; the Yumen Pass was the starting point of the road which ran across the north of what is now Xinjiang Province, and the Yang Pass was the start of the route which cut through the south of the region.

The trip out to both Yang Pass and Yumen Pass takes a whole day. There are irregular tours to the passes – sometimes including a few other sights like the Old City on the way – mainly during the tourist season; inquire at the main CITS or at the Dunhuang Hotel (Binguan). The only other way to get there is by chartered vehicle; count on paying around Y250 all-inclusive for a small minibus.

Xinjiang 新疆

Population: 13 million
Capital: Ürümqi

Xinjiang *(xīnjiāng)* is one of China's 'autonomous regions', inhabited predominantly by the Turkish-speaking Muslim Uigur *(wéiwúěr)* people, whose autonomy from their Chinese overlords is only nominal.

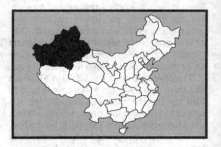

HISTORY

The history of this desolate north-western region has largely been one of continuing wars and conflicts between the native populations, coupled with repeated Chinese invasions and subjugations.

The Chinese were interested in the region for two reasons. Firstly, a lucrative trade plied the 'silk roads' that cut through the oasis towns north and south of the Taklimakan Desert. Along this route camel caravans would carry goods from China to central Asia (from where they eventually found their way to Europe). The trade had been going on at least since Roman days when silk, the principal Chinese export, was prized by fashionable Roman women. Whoever controlled the oasis towns could also tax the flow of goods, so the conquest of Xinjiang was a highly profitable venture.

Secondly, subjugation of the region would help control the troublesome nomadic border tribes, the 'barbarians', who made frequent raids into China to carry off prisoners and booty.

The Chinese never really subdued the region and their hold over it waxed and waned with the power of the central government. The area was constantly subjected to waves of invasions by the Huns and Tibetans, as well as by the Mongols under Genghis Khan, and later on by the Turkic Timur (known as Tamerlane or Tamburlaine in English) at the beginning of the 15th century.

The Han were the first Chinese rulers to conquer Xinjiang. They did so between 73 and 97 AD, even crossing the Tianshan mountains and marching an army of 70,000 people as far as the Caspian Sea, although the Chinese only held onto an area slightly to the east of Lake Balkash. With the demise of the Han in the 3rd century the Chinese lost control of the region until the Tang expeditions re-conquered it and extended Chinese power as far as Lake Balkash.

Qing Dynasty

With the fall of the Tang, the region was once again lost to the Chinese; it was not recovered until the Qing Dynasty, when the second Qing emperor, Kangxi, came to the throne at 16 years of age. His long rule from 1661 to 1722 allowed him enough time to conquer Mongolia and Tibet as well, giving the Chinese power over the largest area ever.

The 19th century was a bloody one of general unrest for Xinjiang, with internal and external threats. A raging rebellion had been staged between the Yellow and Yangzi rivers in 1796, followed by the massive Taiping Rebellion from 1851 to 1864. There were also two major Muslim rebellions: one in Yunnan from 1855 to 1873, and another in the north-west which spread across Shaanxi, Ningxia, Gansu and Xinjiang from 1862 to 1873. Both were put down with extreme savagery by the Chinese. The north-western rebellion had grown out of decades of Chinese misrule, religious controversy, and

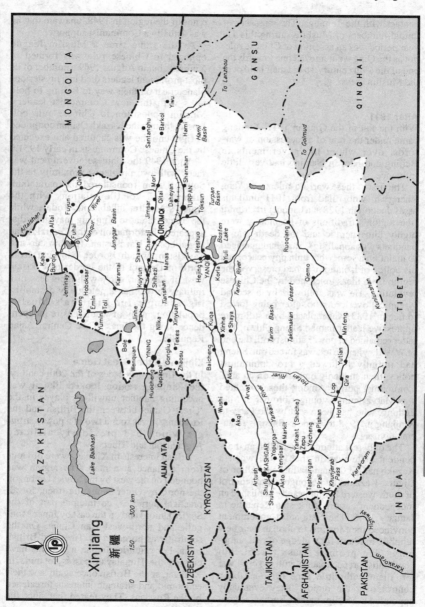

Xinjiang
新疆

XINJIANG

contact with the Taipings. The massacre of untold numbers of Muslims during this 11-year period was an assertion of Chinese rule, but as the Qing went into decline towards the end of the 19th century, so did their hold over the Muslim areas.

After 1911

With the fall of the Qing in 1911, Xinjiang came under the rule of a succession of warlords, over whom the governments in Beijing and later in Nanjing had very little influence.

The first of these warlord-rulers was Yang Zhengxin, who ruled from 1911 until his assassination in 1928 at a banquet in Ürümqi (the region's traditions of hospitality were highly idiosyncratic and the death rate at banquets was appalling). Yang had managed to maintain a somewhat unhappy peace, and his policy of isolationism had preserved the region from ideas unleashed by the Chinese revolution. He was followed by a second tyrannical overlord who, after being forced to flee in 1933, was replaced by a still more oppressive leader named Sheng Shizai. The latter remained in power almost until the end of WW II, when he too was forced out. Sheng had initially followed a pro-Communist policy, then suddenly embarked on an anti-Communist purge. Among those executed was Mao Zemin, a younger brother of Mao Zedong, who had been sent by the Party to Xinjiang in 1938 to work as Sheng's financial adviser.

The only real attempt to establish an independent state was in the 1940s, when a Kazakh named Osman leading a rebellion of Uigurs, Kazakhs and Mongols took control of south-western Xinjiang and established an independent eastern Turkestan Republic in January 1945. The Nationalist government convinced the Muslims to abolish their new republic in return for a pledge of real autonomy. The promise wasn't kept, but Nationalist preoccupation with the civil war left them with little time to re-establish control over the region. They eventually appointed a Muslim named Burhan as governor of the region in 1948, unaware that he was actually a Communist supporter.

At the same time a Muslim league opposed to Chinese rule was formed in Xinjiang, but in August 1949 a number of its most prominent leaders died in a mysterious plane crash on their way to Beijing to hold talks with the new Communist leaders. Muslim opposition to Chinese rule collapsed, though the Kazakh Osman continued to fight until he was captured and executed by the Chinese Communists in early 1951.

After 1949 the Chinese government was faced with two problems: proximity to the Soviet Union (considered the paramount threat), and volatile relations with the region's Muslim inhabitants. Today, while the Soviet threat to Xinjiang may have disappeared, the formation of the Central Asian Republics of Kazakhstan, Kirghyzstan and Tajikistan, which border Xinjiang from north of Ürümqi to the border of Pakistan west of Kashgar, carry with them less of a military threat than a potentially destabilising example for Xinjiang's Muslim population, many of whom desire independence along the lines of the Central Asian Republics.

Xinjiang & the 'Great Game'

In the first few decades of the 20th century, the Xinjiang region looked like it was becoming another unwilling player in the 'Great Game' between the British and the Russians. It was round two of a power struggle which had previously afflicted Afghanistan and Tibet.

British interests in Xinjiang were obvious from a glance at a map. The region was bounded on the west by the Soviet Union, on the north by Outer Mongolia (then, for all practical purposes, an integral part of the Soviet Union) and on the east by Inner Mongolia and north-west Han China. On the south it was bordered by Tibet and British India. For centuries Indian merchants have crossed the Himalayan passes to trade in Kashgar, so the British once again saw their economic and strategic interests threatened by the Russians. They feared that since the

Russians had now spied out the area, they might follow up with a territorial annexation. If there were any such plans, they were stopped by the disastrous Russo-Japanese War of 1904-05, the revolution of 1917, the ensuing civil war and the Nazi invasion of the Soviet Union.

In the end it was the Chinese who won out in the Great Game, without even trying. Today the region bristles with Chinese troops and weapons. Probably the biggest concern for the Chinese government now is renewed Islamic fundamentalism and calls for independence following the independence of the bordering ex-Soviet republics.

GEOGRAPHY

Xinjiang is divided by the east-west Tianshan range into two major regions. To the south of the range is the Tarim Basin, and to the north is the Junggar Basin.

The Tarim Basin, a huge depression whose centre is the sands of the Taklimakan Desert and where streams from the surrounding mountains lose themselves, is bordered to the south by the Kunlunshan range.

Other streams run from the Tianshan range into the Tarim River, which flows eastward and empties into the vast salt marsh and lake of Lop Nur. The boundaries of Lop Nur vary greatly from year to year as a result of climatic variation; it's an area of almost uninhabited poor grassland and semi-desert. Since 1964 the Chinese have been testing nuclear bombs here.

The Taklimakan Desert is a true desert. Cultivation is only possible in the oases of irrigated land centred on the streams flowing into the basin from the surrounding mountains. These oases, largely populated by Uigur people, have had flourishing cultures

---

Foreign Devils on the Silk Road

Adventurers on the road to Xinjiang might well like to reflect on an earlier group of European adventurers who descended on Chinese Turkestan, as Xinjiang was then known, and carted off early Buddhist art treasures by the tonne at the turn of the century. Their exploits are vividly described by Peter Hopkirk in his book *Foreign Devils on the Silk Road – the Search for the Lost Cities & Treasures of Chinese Central Asia* (Oxford Paperbacks, 1984).

The British first began to take an interest in the central Asian region from their imperial base in India. Initially, 'moonshees', local Indian traders trained in basic cartography and surveying, were sent to investigate the region. They heard from oasis dwellers in the Taklamakan Desert of legendary ancient cities buried beneath the sands of the desert. In 1864 William Johnson was the first British official to sneak into the region, visiting one of these fabled lost cities in its tomb of sand close to Hotan. He was soon followed by Sir Douglas Forsyth, who made a report on his exploits: 'On the Buried Cities in the Shifting Sands of the Great Desert of Gobi'. Not long afterwards, the race to unearth the treasures beneath the desert's 'shifting sands' was on.

The first European archaeologist/adventurer to descend on the region was the Swede Sven Hedin. A brilliant cartogapher and fluent in seven languages, Hedin made three trailblazing expeditions into the Taklamakan Desert, unearthing a wealth of treasures and writing a two-volume account of his journeys: *Through Asia*. The second explorer, in pursuit of Buddhist art treasures, was Sir Auriel Stein, a Hungarian who took up British citizenship. Stein's expeditions into the Taklamakan, accompanied by his terrier Dash, were to culminate in his removing a goldmine of Buddhist texts in Chinese, Tibetan and central Asian languages from Dunhuang to the British Museum.

Between 1902 and 1914 Xinjiang saw four German and four French expeditions, as well as expeditions by the Russians and Japanese, all jockeying for their share of the region's archaeological treasures. While these explorers were feted and lionised by adoring publics at home, the Chinese today commonly see them as robbers who stripped the region of its past. Defenders point to the wide-scale destruction that took place during the Cultural Revolution and to the defacing of Buddhist art works by Muslims who stumbled across them. Whatever the case, today most of central Asia's finest archaeological finds are scattered across the museums of Europe. ∎

of their own for 2000 years and were important stopover points on the Silk Road.

They support an irrigated agricultural industry based mainly on food grains and fruit, while the grasslands of the foothills support a pastoral industry based on sheep and horses. The agriculture of places like the Turpan and Hami depressions depends entirely on irrigation, using water drawn from underground streams. Only in the Ili Valley, west of Ürümqi, is rainfall sufficient to support a flourishing agricultural and pastoral industry.

The Junggar Basin has been the centre of extensive colonisation by the Chinese since the 1950s. Large state farms have been established on formerly uncultivated land. The major towns are Ürümqi (the capital of Xinjiang), Shihezi and Manas. Their importance grew with the completion of the Xinjiang railway from Lanzhou to Ürümqi in 1963, the rapid growth in the population, and the exploitation of rich oil resources in the basin.

The Junggar Basin is less arid than the Tarim Basin and is mostly grassland supporting a pastoral population. The people are primarily nomadic Kazakhs or Torgut Mongols, herding sheep, some horses, cattle and camels. The north and north-west of the Junggar Basin are bounded by the Altaishan range of 3000 to 4000-metre-high peaks on the Mongolian border. It's an area of substantial rainfall, and the mountains are either tree-covered or have rich pasturelands. Mainly nomadic Kazakh or Oirat Mongol herders live here.

CLIMATE

Xinjiang's weather tends towards extremes – sizzling summers and frigid winters. As much of the province is desert, humidity is low. Although Ürümqi is tolerable in summer, the Turpan Basin more than deserves the title of 'hottest place in China' with maximums of up to 49°C.

In winter, though, you'll need your woollies in Xinjiang. In Ürümqi the average temperature in January is around -10°C, with minimums of around -30°C. Winter temperatures in Turpan are only about 5°C warmer.

POPULATION & PEOPLE

Xinjiang is inhabited by something like 13 of China's official total of 55 national minorities. One problem for the Chinese is that 50% of their country isn't even inhabited by Chinese, but by minority people who mostly don't like them. What's more, these minority people inhabit regions bordering Vietnam, India, Afghanistan and the Commonwealth of Independent States (ex-USSR) – all places of past or possible future conflict with China.

In 1955 the province of Xinjiang was renamed the Uigur Autonomous Region. At that time more than 90% of the population was non-Chinese. With the building of the railway from Lanzhou to Ürümqi and the development of industry in the region, there was a large influx of Chinese people who now form a majority in the northern area while the Uigurs continue to predominate in the south.

In 1953 Xinjiang had a population of about five million, of whom 3½ million were Uigurs and only a very small number were Han Chinese. By 1970 the number of Hans was estimated to have grown to about four million. There are now over 13 million people in Xinjiang, of whom only about

Kazakh man

seven million are Uigurs. It's a trend that will inevitably continue as the region develops, with the result that the Uigurs will be subjugated and pacified by sheer weight of numbers.

Relations between the Han and the minority people in the region vary. The nomadic Kazakhs were angered by the forced introduction of the communes. About 60,000 of them are supposed to have crossed into the Soviet Union in 1962. This figure represents a sizable proportion of the population, since at present there are only about a million Kazakhs spread across Xinjiang, Gansu and Qinghai. Other groups of Kazakhs escaped to India or Pakistan and were granted political asylum in Turkey, where they were resettled. Chinese relations with the Tajiks (around 26,000) are said to be better.

Unfortunately for the Han Chinese, relations with the fairly numerous minority Uigurs can be best described as volatile. The Chinese have done a great deal to reduce the backwardness of the region, building roads, railways and hospitals, and industrialising the towns. The Chinese presence also prevents the Uigurs from fighting among themselves, which has been a problem whenever centralised rule has toppled. So it's difficult for the Chinese to understand the hostility with which they are greeted. Part of this ill will probably originates from centuries of Chinese misrule and from the savage way in which the 19th-century rebellions were put down; part of it simply because the Uigurs don't have much in common with the Chinese. The Uigur religion is monotheistic Islam, their written script is Arabic, their language is closely related to Turkish, and their physical features are basically Caucasian – many could easily be mistaken for Greeks, southern Italians or other southern Europeans.

Part of the problem may also stem from the intentional or unintentional Chinese policy of blurring the distinctions between Han and Uigur cultures. The recent reintroduction of Arabic script in primary schools is offset by the almost exclusive and hence requisite use of Chinese language at tertiary level. Arabic script has been given a romanised form to speed up the learning process and promote literacy. During the Cultural Revolution mosques were closed – a very sensitive issue with the local devout. With the death of Mao and the rise of a more liberal regime to power, the mosques have since been reopened.

In spite of simmering ethnic tensions, there is little likelihood of Xinjiang ever achieving any real autonomy – the influx of Chinese soldiers and settlers means that it is almost certainly out of the question. However, even now there is some sort of anti-Chinese riot or demonstration in one Xinjiang town or another every year. For many years the Lop Nur (*lóbù bó*) region in the Tarim Basin has been used for nuclear tests. Reports of livestock and locals suffering from radiation poisoning were confirmed when Uigur protesters took to the streets in Xinjiang and even Beijing. In 1990, serious ethnic riots prompted the Chinese to close the Kashgar area to foreigners and seal off the border with Pakistan. It was opened again in 1992. For the Uigurs the Chinese are very much a foreign occupation force.

Minority Nationalities

The minority nationalities of Xinjiang are probably some of the most interesting in China. To the west of Ürümqi, where the Tianshan range divides in two, is the Ili Valley. The population in the valley consists of Kirghiz, Kazakhs and Chinese, and even includes a colony of Sibo (the descendants of the Manchu garrison which was stationed here after the conquests of the 18th century). Another peculiar army to hit Xinjiang was that of the refugee White Russian troops who fled after their defeat in the Russian Civil War. Some settled here and founded scattered colonies.

The most interesting minority has a population of one; in the 1930s there was a bizarre story that T E Lawrence (of Arabia) was active in the British cause against the Russians in Xinjiang, and had gone wandering off with a band of local tribespeople to raise hell and high sandstorms. It was a rumour which continued even after Lawrence's fatal motorcycle accident in Britain in 1936 and is not the least fantastic part of the Lawrence legend.

LANGUAGE

If you have Caucasian features and speak Turkish, you will blend perfectly into Xinjiang, provided you wear the right clothing. Once you leave the beaten path, Russian can sometimes prove even more useful than Chinese! Even if your command of Turkish, Russian or Uigur is minimal, the Uigurs love to hear an attempt being made at their language – it helps them to forget their isolation.

Uigur Mini-Glossary

With no apologies for transliteration, the following are some Uigur words for bargaining, travelling or just passing the time of day:

hello (peace be upon you)
salaam aleikum
how much?
khanj pul?
good
yakshi
not good
yok yakshi
what's your name?
sen ismi nemā?
goodbye
khosh
bus
optus
bus stop
baket
ticket
bilhet
food/restaurant
ash/ashkhana
yes
ah
no
emess

TIME

Xinjiang is several time zones removed from Beijing, which prefers to ignore the fact. Officially, Beijing time applies; in practice, Xinjiang time is used haphazardly for meal times in hotels, bus departures, etc. Xinjiang time is one hour behind Beijing time – however, daylight-saving time is not used, so during the summer Xinjiang time is two hours behind Beijing time. Try and straighten out any confusion by asking whether the stated time is Beijing time *(běijīng shíjiān)*, Beijing daylight-saving time *(xiàlìng shíjiān)* or Xinjiang time *(xīnjiāng shíjiān)*. Kashgar time is one hour behind Xinjiang time.

ÜRÜMQI

(wūlǔmùqí) 乌鲁木齐

The capital of Xinjiang, Ürümqi started to boom after the Communists built the railway line from Lanzhou across the Xinjiang desert. About 950,000 people live here now, 80% of them Han Chinese – the place has always been a Chinese island in a sea of Muslims. The inspired concrete-block architecture of socialist eastern China has been imported lock, stock and barrel, and Ürümqi essentially looks little different from its northern Han-China counterparts 2000 km east. There are few 'sights' as such, but it's an intrinsically interesting place to visit.

Two and a half days up the railway line from Xi'an and in the same country, you couldn't come across a people more different from the Chinese than the Uigurs. Ürümqi is the first place where you'll see these swarthy Turkic descendants in any number. They are larger and heavier than the Han Chinese and many of them could easily pass for southern Italians or Greeks. The Uigur women wear skirts or dresses and brightly coloured scarves, in contrast to the slacks and baggy trousers of the Han Chinese. At arm's distance from the Uigurs are the Han Chinese immigrants as well as the People's Liberation Army (PLA) soldiers, who are not only there to keep an eye on the ex-Soviet republics and maintain Chinese control over Xinjiang, but also to keep the tenuous peace between the Uigurs and the Han. It's hard not to feel you're in the provincial capital of a foreign occupation force.

Orientation

One of the difficulties of finding your way around is that the streets have a notorious habit of changing names every few blocks – a nightmare for mapmakers. Most of the sights, tourist facilities and hotels are scattered across the city, though they're all easily reached on local buses.

The railway and long-distance bus stations are in the south-western corner of the city. There are two candidates for the title of 'city centre': the first is the area around the large Hongshan Department Store where some of the major arteries intersect; the other is in the eastern part of the city, where you'll find the main shopping district, CITS, the PSB and the Bank of China.

Information

CITS This office (☎ 221427) is in a compound on the eastern side of Renmin Square in the drab concrete building on your left as you enter the compound (there's a sign in front of the gate). It's open Monday to Saturday, from 9.30 am to 1 pm and from 4 to 8 pm.

You might want to come here for the entertainment value – seldom will you encounter a more confused CITS office than this one. Each worker quotes you a different price on tickets and gives conflicting information for transport. Some of the staff claim that a certain place is open – others claim it's closed. One traveller making inquiries about travel to Lhasa was told to go to Kashgar and make his way onwards by local bus. Just give the place a miss.

CYTS This outfit has a branch on the 1st floor of the Hongshan Hotel, and they are the pick of the bunch. They can organise train tickets for you and provide maps and other information. They charge 10% of the ticket price for their train ticket service. Try the black market at the railway station yourself first.

Pakistan Tourism Office This is in room 8006 in the Overseas Chinese Hotel. They cannot organise Pakistan visas.

PSB This is a 10-minute walk from the CITS office, in a large government building just to the north-west of Renmin Square.

Money The Bank of China is at 343 Jiefang Nanlu close to Renmin Square. It's open from 10 am to 2 pm and 3.30 to 4.30 pm, and is closed Wednesday and Friday afternoons and all day Sunday. International credit cards are accepted here too. The 'other' money marketeers conveniently prowl this beat. Take bus No 1 from the Overseas Chinese Hotel or the Kunlun Guesthouse.

Post The main post office is a big Corinthian-colonnaded building directly across the traffic circle from the Hongshan Department Store. The foreign section is efficient and has a packing service.

Maps Good maps, in Chinese and showing the bus routes, are available from the railway station, bus station, department stores, post office, bookstores and most of the hotels. The Hongshan Department Store has some excellent maps of Xinjiang.

Xinjiang Autonomous Region Museum
(xīnjiāng wéiwúěr zìzhìqū bówùguǎn)
新疆维吾尔自治区博物馆

Xinjiang covers 16% of China's total land surface. It is inhabited not only by the Han Chinese but also by 13 of China's official total of 55 minority peoples. One wing of the museum contains an interesting exhibition relating to some of the Xinjiang minority groups and it's well worth a look.

Notable among the exhibits are the Daur hats (made from animal heads) with large fur rims – there are about 94,000 Daur people spread across Xinjiang, Inner Mongolia and Heilongjiang. The Tajik exhibition features silver and coral beads supporting silver pendants – the people number about 26,500 and are found only in Xinjiang. There are about 900,000 Kazakhs living in Xinjiang and their exhibition in the museum features a heavily furnished yurt. The Mongol exhibit includes particularly ornate silver bridles and saddles studded with semi-precious stones, stringed

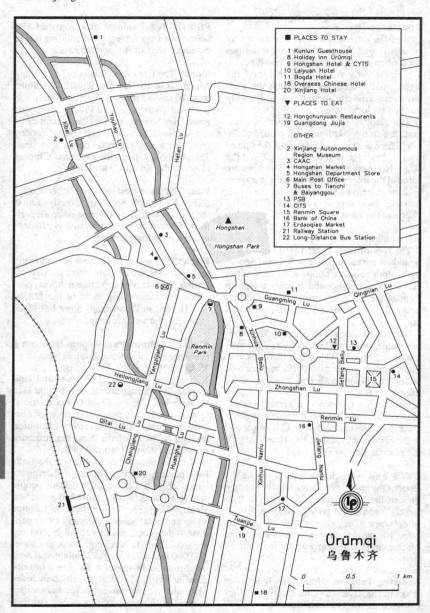

■ PLACES TO STAY

1 Kunlun Guesthouse
8 Holiday Inn Ürümqi
9 Hongshan Hotel & CYTS
10 Laiyuan Hotel
11 Bogda Hotel
18 Overseas Chinese Hotel
20 Xinjiang Hotel

▼ PLACES TO EAT

12 Hongchunyuan Restaurants
19 Guangdong Jiujia

OTHER

2 Xinjiang Autonomous
  Region Museum
3 CAAC
4 Hongshan Market
5 Hongshan Department Store
6 Main Post Office
7 Buses to Tianchi
  & Baiyanggou
13 PSB
14 CITS
15 Renmin Square
16 Bank of China
17 Erdaoqiao Market
21 Railway Station
22 Long-Distance Bus Station

Hongshan

Hongshan Park

Guangming Lu

Qingnian Lu

Xinhua Beilu

Jiefang Beilu

Zhongshan Lu

Renmin Lu

Renmin Park

Heilongjiang Lu

Yangzijiang Lu

Qitai Lu

Changjiang Lu

Huanghe Lu

Xinhua Nanlu

Jiefang Nanlu

Tuanjie Lu

Xibei Lu

Youhao Lu

Hetan Lu

Ürümqi
乌鲁木齐

0   0.5   1 km

XINJIANG

musical instruments and decorated riding boots.

Another wing of the museum has a fascinating section devoted to history. Prime exhibits are the preserved bodies of two men and two women discovered in tombs in Xinjiang, similar to those in the museum at Hangzhou. Also interesting is the collection of multicoloured clay figurines unearthed from Turpan, dating back to the Tang Dynasty. Note the collection of silk fragments with various patterns from different dynasties.

The distinctive Soviet-style building with a green dome is on Xibei Lu, about 20 minutes' walk from the Kunlun Guesthouse. From Hongshan Department Store take bus No 7 for four stops and ask to get off at the museum (bówùguǎn).

Renmin Park

(rénmín gōngyuán) 人民公园
This beautiful, tree-shaded park is about one km in length and can be entered from either the north or south gates. The best time to visit is early in the morning when the Chinese are out here doing their exercises. There are plenty of birds in the park and a few pavilions. Near the north end is a lake where you can hire rowing boats – a pleasant way to relax after dinner. Try to avoid the park on Sunday, when the locals descend on the place in force.

Hongshan Park & Pagoda

(hóngshān gōngyuán) 红山公园
It's not exactly one of the world's eight wonders, but the pagoda sits on top of a big hill just to the north of Renmin Park and affords sweeping views of the city.

Places to Stay – bottom end

The *Hongshan Hotel* (☎ 24761) (hóngshān bīnguǎn) is a good base in the centre of town and is very popular with budget travellers. The dorms cost Y25 in a three-bed room without private bathroom. For Y45, they also have two-bed dorms with private bathroom – these are reasonable value if you don't mind paying a little more for the luxury. The communal showers invariably have long queues – a wait of half an hour is not unusual.

Just around the corner from the Hongshan is the *Bogda Hotel* (bógédá bīnguǎn). Prices here are basically the same as those at the Hongshan, with three-bed dormitories coming in at Y25 per person.

For both these places, from the railway station, take bus No 2 for four stops. You'll then be close to the main post office, which is a short walk from the hotel. From the long-distance bus station, turn right out of the station gates and walk about 150 metres along Heilongjiang Lu until you cross an intersection and reach the stop for bus No 8. Take this bus east for four stops and then switch to either bus No 7 or 17 going north for one stop. If coming from the airport, the China Air CAAC bus drops you off by the post office, close to the hotel.

Given that dorm prices have gone up so much in Ürümqi, the best option for budget travellers is the *Xinjiang Hotel* (☎ 552511) *(xīnjiāng fàndiàn)* at the southern end of Changjiang Lu. It's the only hotel within walking distance of the railway station. Dorms cost Y14 per person and doubles are Y37 per bed. The only rooms here with attached bathroom cost Y150.

The *Overseas Chinese Hotel* (☎ 260845) *(huáqiáo bīnguǎn)* is much further from the town centre than the Hongshan Hotel but still easy to reach from there on bus No 7. Prices here seem to have escalated over recent years, with staff denying the existence of dormitory accommodation. Doubles here look good, but at Y100 they are overpriced.

The *Friendship Hotel* (☎ 264220) *(yǒuyì bīnguǎn)* has a very inconvenient location, about seven km south-east of the railway station. Cadres, who usually arrive in chauffeur-driven limousines, like to stay here. Interestingly, this is the hotel recommended by CITS to budget travellers, which just goes to show how detached from reality they are.

Places to Stay – top end
Yes, the Holiday Inn group have stuck a hotel in the middle of Ürümqi: *Holiday Inn Urumqi* (☎ 218788) *(xīnjiāng jiàrì dàjiǔdiàn)*. Even if you can't afford to stay here, they have great coffee, an excellent breakfast buffet and the wildest disco in western China. Room rates range from US$75 upwards, but significant discounts are available during the quieter winter months.

Not far from the Holiday Inn is another upmarket hotel, though nowhere near in the same league as its massive competitor: the *Laiyuan Hotel* *(láiyuǎn fàndiàn)*. Doubles here range from Y200 to Y500 but, while the rooms are nice, if you are going to spend this kind of money you'd be better off heading over to the Holiday Inn.

Places to Eat
Ürümqi is a good place to try Uigur foods such as shish kebab or noodles with spicy vegetables, beef or lamb *(lāmiàn)*. During the summer, the markets are packed with delicious fruit, both fresh and dried. Try the *Hongshan Market* across from the Hongshan Department Store. An even better place is the *Erdaoqiao Market* near the Overseas Chinese Hotel.

The *Hongchunyuan Restaurant (hóngchūnyuán fàndiàn)*, close to the PSB, is actually a Chinese-only hotel with two restaurants. One serves Chinese food *(zhōng cān)* and the other – called the *Pumpkin Restaurant* – serves Western food *(xī cān)*. The Western restaurant has an English menu – the Chinese restaurant doesn't. Prices are cheap.

Near the Overseas Chinese Hotel is a good Cantonese restaurant called *Guangdong Jiujia*. In the morning they serve dim sum, and Hong Kongers flock to this place. From the Overseas Chinese Hotel, go one block north and turn left – the restaurant is on the left side.

The Holiday Inn has a few restaurants with extremely high standards and prices to match. *Kashgari's* serves up Muslim dishes, while the *Xi Wang Mu* has everything Chinese from Sichuan to Cantonese dim sum. If you've been starved of creature comforts for a while call in in the morning for the breakfast buffet. The restaurant is on the left-hand side of the lobby, and the whole deal, including coffee refills and as much as you can eat is Y40. There's a Delicatessen Corner also on the ground floor retailing stuff like HP Sauce, Horlicks and Honey Pops.

Entertainment
On the 2nd floor of the Holiday Inn is Silks, a disco that's open until 2 am – the cover charge is an exorbitant Y50 if you're not a guest, but if you get there early enough in the evening you might be able to wander in free of charge.

Getting There & Away
Air Ürümqi is connected by air with Beijing (Y1410), Canton (Y1910), Chengdu (Y1130), Xiamen (Y2110), Guilin (Y1695), Tianjin (Y1500), Hangzhou (Y1820) (Y1293), Lanzhou (Y880), Luoyang, Shanghai (Y1820),

Shenyang, Xi'an (Y1150), and Zhengzhou (Y1370).

There are also flights from Ürümqi to the following places in Xinjiang: Aksu, Altai, Fuyun, Hotan, Karamai, Kashgar (Y650), Kuqa (Y320), Khotan and Korla, Qiemo, and Yining (Y280).

There are once-weekly flights to Tashkent for Y1760 and twice-weekly flights to Alma Ata for Y720.

The CAAC office (☎ 217942) is on Youhao Lu, just up the road from the post office; it's open from 10 am to 1.30 pm and from 4 to 8 pm. There's a special foreigners' counter, where they speak English and issue tickets with a minimum of fuss. Bus Nos 1 and 2 go past the office.

Bus The long-distance bus station is in the western part of town. The departure time given on your ticket is normally Beijing time; check if you're not sure. There are buses for most cities in Xinjiang. The most popular destinations for travellers are Turpan, Yining and Kashgar. They demand FEC here and add a 100% foreigner's surcharge to the price of tickets. It's a complete scam: you'll still be sitting on the same crowded, ramshackle contraption as the locals.

Some sample foreigner-price ticket charges are: Shihezi Y18, Altai Y75, Turpan Y23, Kuqa Y79 and Kashgar Y147. An interesting further option is the Alma Ata (ālāmùtú) bus service. The 1052-km trip takes 24 hours straight through with three stops for meals, and costs US$48. Visas are issued on the border at present, but the Chinese government requires that you get an exit permit at the PSB. Check at window No 8 in the bus station for the latest on this service.

Buses to Turpan also run from the Erdaoqiao Market. There's not a great deal to be gained from going here though. They also demand FEC (a tantrum seems to assist in breaking their will) and they charge even more than the public bus station.

It is reportedly possible to travel all the way to Dunhuang by bus. Travel first to Hami, and from there to Liuyuan. From Liuyuan you can take another bus to Dunhuang.

Train From Ürümqi there are eastbound trains at least six times daily. Popular destinations include Beijing via Lanzhou, Yinchuan, Baotou, Hohhot and Datong; to Xi'an via Lanzhou; to Beijing via Xi'an, Zhengzhou and Shijiazhuang; to Shanghai via Xi'an, Zhengzhou and Nanjing; to Chengdu via Lanzhou. Sleeper tickets to Liuyuan cost Y135 (hard) or Y257 (soft); to Beijing Y446 (hard) or Y849 (soft); to Xi'an Y328 (hard) or Y625 (soft); to Lanzhou Y249 (hard) or Y474 (soft); and to Chengdu Y320 (hard) or Y665 (soft). Trains to Alma Ata are also available, though they work out more expensive than travelling by bus.

There is intense competition for tickets at the railway station, where the market has been cornered by a variety of touts both inside and outside the system. Try and book as far in advance as possible and join the queue before 8 am. If you only manage to get a hard-seat ticket, you can sometimes buy hard sleepers on the train for at least part of your journey – provided you queue persistently within a few minutes of the train's departure. If all else fails, head down to CYTS in the Hongshan Hotel.

There is a rail link between Ürümqi and Korla via Daheyan (Turpan station). At present, only 500-series trains (hard seat only) run on this route, which may be scenic but is hardly worth 18 hours of hard-seat travel.

Getting Around

There seems to be nowhere to hire bicycles in Ürümqi, a sorry state of affairs given how spread out the town is. If you resort to the bus system, be warned that there have been numerous reports of pickpocketing and bag slashing on Ürümqi buses – take care.

AROUND ÜRÜMQI
Tianchi
(tiānchí) 天池
Tianchi (Lake of Heaven) is a sight you'll never forget. Halfway up a mountain in the

middle of a desert, it looks like a chunk of Switzerland or Canada that's been exiled to western China. The small, deep-blue lake is surrounded by hills covered with fir trees and grazed by horses. Scattered around are the yurts of the Kazakh people who inhabit the mountains; in the distance are the snow-covered peaks of the Tianshan range, and you can climb the hills right up to the snow line.

The lake is 115 km east of Ürümqi at an elevation of 1900 metres. Nearby is the 5445-metre-high Bogda Feng, the Peak of God. The lake freezes over in Xinjiang's bitter winter and the roads up here are open only in the summer months – a pity, since it would make an excellent place for ice-skating.

Buses leave Ürümqi at around 8 am from both the north and south gates of Renmin Park – the north side is more convenient if you're staying at the Hongshan Hotel. Departures are from where the sign says (in English) 'Taxi Service'. Buy your ticket about 30 minutes ahead of time to ensure getting a seat. The trip takes over three hours. The bus will probably drop you off at the end of the lake – from there it's a 20-minute walk to the hotel on the banks. The bus back to Ürümqi leaves at around 4 pm from a bus park just over a low ridge at the back of the hotel. If you stay overnight you'll have the place pretty much to yourself in the morning and after 4 pm, since most people only come here on day trips. Some people have hitched on trucks to the lake.

A one-way ticket costs Y15. You can buy round-trip tickets – these are valid for any day but you only have a reserved seat if you come back on the same day. If you buy a return ticket and want to come back another day with a reserved seat, it will cost you extra.

The Heavenly Lake Hotel on the banks of the lake is a garish building utterly out of place compared with the blues and greens of the surroundings. There are rooms for six people at Y10 per bed. There are boat cruises on the lake.

The other possibility, of course, is to hike into the hills and go camping – it's a great opportunity, and a rare one in China. The surrounding countryside is absolutely stunning. Follow the track skirting the lake for about four km to the far end and walk up the valley. During the summer, Kazakhs set up yurts in this area for tourist accommodation. Horses are also offered (at Y60 to Y100 per day) for a trek to the snow line. The return trek takes 10 hours. Water is best taken from the spring gushing straight out of the mountain at the edge of the lake rather than further up the valley where humans and livestock have contributed to the liquid.

Baiyanggou
(báiyánggōu) 白扬沟

Baiyanggou, also known as the Southern Pastures, is a vast expanse of grazing land 56 km south of Ürümqi. The land is inhabited by Kazakh herdsmen who graze sheep, cattle and horses here during the summer months.

Curious stories have been told of the gangs of Hong Kong Chinese who come down here by the minibusload. Unused to vast open spaces or to the sight of animals almost in the wild, they leap from the bus and charge at the unsuspecting creatures, who scatter in all directions. A distraught Kazakh herdsman usually rides up waving his arms in the air and shouting abuse, and must be placated by the tour guide with apologies and cigarettes.

It's a 1½-hour ride. The directions for getting there are the same as for Tianchi – at the north and south gates of Renmin Park in Ürümqi there are buses departing at approximately 9 am from where the sign says 'Taxi Service'. There is also a local bus leaving from the bus station close to Lijiaoqiao (see map). There are two buses each day, leaving at approximately 8.40 am and 5.40 pm in the summer, and at 8.30 am and 3.30 pm in the winter.

It is possible to stay up in the pasturelands at some of the Kazakh yurts.

HAMI
(hāmì) 哈密

The town of Hami is a small oasis at the remotest end of China. Known in the past as

Kumul, it was once an important caravan stop on the northern route of the Silk Road. Hami's most famous product is the delicious Hami melon *(hāmì guā)*, highly prized by thirsty train passengers who scramble to buy them during the short stop at Hami station. You can also buy these melons in Turpan.

There are reportedly buses running from Hami to Liuyuan in Gansu Province, making this an interesting alternative route to Dunhuang.

DAHEYAN
(dàhéyán) 大河沿

The jumping-off point for Turpan is a place on the railway line signposted 'Turpan Zhan' *(tǔlǔfān zhàn)*. In fact, you are actually in Daheyan, and the Turpan oasis is an hour's drive south across the desert. Daheyan is not a place you'll want to hang around in, so spare a thought for the locals, who have to eke out a sane living here.

The bus station is a five-minute walk from the railway station. Walk up the road leading from the railway station and turn right at the first main intersection; the bus station is a few minutes' walk ahead on the left-hand side of the road. There are four buses a day to Turpan – two in the morning and two in the afternoon, and the fare is Y2 for the 58-km trip, which takes 1½ hours. The bus gets extremely crowded and it's quite a push-and-shove match to get on. There are lots of trucks on these roads and you may be able to hitch if you miss the bus. If you miss the bus and can't get there hitching, you'll have to spend the night in this exotic outpost. The hotel (Y10 per bed) is behind the bus station.

TURPAN
(tǔlǔfān) 吐鲁番

East of Ürümqi the Taishan mountains split into a southern and a northern range; between the two lie the Hami and Turpan basins. Both are below sea level and receive practically no rain; summers are searingly hot. Part of the Turpan Basin is 154 metres below sea level – the lowest spot in China and the second-lowest depression in the world.

Turpan County is inhabited by about 170,000 people: about 120,000 are Uigurs and the rest mostly Chinese. The centre of the county is the large Turpan oasis. It's little more than a few main streets set in a vast tract of grain fields, and more importantly it's been spared the architectural horrors that have been inflicted on Ürümqi. Most of the streets are planted with trees and are lined with mud-brick walls enclosing mud houses. Open channels with flowing water run down the sides of the streets; the inhabitants draw water from these and use them to wash their clothes, dishes and themselves in.

Of the major towns in Xinjiang visited by foreigners, Turpan and Kashgar remain closest to traditional Uigur culture; Ürümqi and Shihezi are Chinese settlements. Turpan also holds a special place in Uigur history since nearby Gaochang was once the capital of the Uigurs. It was an important staging post on the Silk Road and was a centre of Buddhism before being converted to Islam in the 8th century. During the Chinese occupation it served as a garrison town.

Turpan is a quiet place (one of the few in China) and the Turpan Guesthouse or the Oasis Hotel are good spots to sit underneath the vine trellises and contemplate the moon and stars. The living is cheap, the food is good and the people are friendly, and there are numerous interesting sights scattered around to keep you occupied. Along with Dali and Yangshuo, it's one of the few places in the country where you can relax and withdraw a bit from China. It's also the hottest – the highest recorded temperature here was 49.6°C. Fortunately, the humidity is low – so low that your laundry is practically dry by the time you get it hung up!

Orientation

The centre of the Turpan oasis is little more than a few main roads and a couple of side streets. You'll find the shops, market, long-distance bus station, tourist guesthouse and a couple of plodding donkey carts all within easy walking distance of each other. The centre is called 'Old City' *(lǎochéng)* and the western part is 'New City' *(xīnchéng)*. Most

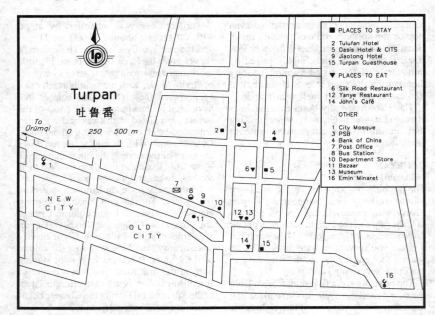

Turpan
吐鲁番

To Ürümqi

0   250   500 m

NEW CITY

OLD CITY

■ PLACES TO STAY

2 Tulufan Hotel
5 Oasis Hotel & CITS
9 Jiaotong Hotel
15 Turpan Guesthouse

▼ PLACES TO EAT

6 Silk Road Restaurant
12 Yanye Restaurant
14 John's Café

OTHER

1 City Mosque
3 PSB
4 Bank of China
7 Post Office
8 Bus Station
10 Department Store
11 Bazaar
13 Museum
16 Emin Minaret

■ PLACES TO STAY

2 吐鲁番饭店
5 绿洲宾馆
9 交通宾馆
15 吐鲁番宾馆

▼ PLACES TO EAT

6 丝路酒家
12 焱焱饭店
14 咖啡馆

OTHER

1 清真寺
3 公安馆
4 中国银行
7 邮局
8 长途汽车站
10 百货商店
11 巴扎(集市)
13 博物馆
16 额敏吐

of the sights are scattered on the outskirts of the oasis or in the surrounding desert.

Information

The CITS office (☎ 22768) is at the Oasis Hotel. The friendly manager is a Uigur and speaks excellent English. The office is open from 10 am to 2 pm, and from 6 to 9 pm. Only CITS has maps of the oasis and the surrounding area. The PSB is one block west of the Bank of China.

The most convenient place to change money is at the Oasis Hotel. There is also a Bank of China about 10 minutes' walk from the hotel (see map). The post office is right near the bus station and the bazaar. More convenient is the post office inside the Oasis Hotel – they can handle parcels.

Bazaar

(nóngmào shìchǎng) 农贸市场

This is one of the most fascinating markets in China – only Kashgar's can match it.

You'll find lots of exotica on sale, including brightly decorated knives, Muslim clothing, delicious flatbread, goats (both living and cooked), and unusual fruits. Bargaining is expected, but it's mostly good-natured, not the usual tug of war experienced elsewhere in China.

The market is across from the bus station, within walking distance of all the hotels. Most travellers visit here the day before heading out on the minibus tours. It's a good place for stocking up on munchies – raisins and peanuts mixed together make good travelling food.

City Mosque
(qīngzhēn sì) 清真寺

There are several mosques in town. The City Mosque, the most active of them is on the western outskirts about three km from the centre. Take care not to disturb the worshippers. You can get here by bicycle.

Emin Minaret
(émǐn tǎ) 额敏塔

Also known as Sugongta, this tower and adjoining mosque is just three km from Turpan on the eastern outskirts of town. It's designed in a simple Afghani style and was built in the late 1770s by a local ruler. The minaret is circular, 44 metres high and tapering towards the top. The temple is bare inside, but services are held every Friday and on holidays.

You could possibly walk or bicycle here from the Turpan Guesthouse, but most people stop here on a minibus tour. Turn left out of the guesthouse and left again at the first crossroad; this road leads straight down to the mosque. There is a hole in the wall at the side of the mosque so you can get into the main building. If you want to climb the minaret you'll have to ask the keeper to unlock the door to the stairway; he lives in the small whitewashed building beside the mosque.

Song & Dance Show

If someone is willing to pay Y400, CITS will organise a performance of traditional Uigur music, song & dance in the courtyard of the Turpan Guesthouse under the trellises. Visiting Japanese tour groups often cough up the money, but they usually have no objection to other travellers watching for free. Most of the singers and dancers are women, but there is usually at least one man. During the summer, the shows are held almost every night from around 10 pm. They're fun nights that usually end up with the front row of the audience being dragged out to dance with the performers, who must rate as some of the liveliest and most colourful people in China.

Places to Stay

The *Turpan Guesthouse (tǔlǔfān bīnguǎn)* was for a long time the most popular hotel in Turpan, but recent renovations and the surliness of the staff have made it a less desirable place to stay. The new wing at the front of the hotel is a real eyesore, and the staff seem to take great pleasure in fining foreigners who pick the grapes (Y30 a time!) – it doesn't stop them grabbing handfuls for themselves. In the shade of the vine trellises is a good place to sit while saturating yourself with beer or cold drinks (try the watermelon juice). Rates are Y15 for a dormitory bed and Y100 and up for a double in one of the new wings.

The *Oasis Hotel (lǜzhōu bīnguǎn)* is the newest of Turpan's hotels, but it already rivals the Turpan Guesthouse in atmosphere. Dorm beds are Y20, though there is talk of pushing this up to Y40 during the busy summer months – try bargaining them down. Doubles range from Y150 to Y200. All rooms, including dorms, have air-con.

The *Jiaotong Hotel (jiāotōng bīnguǎn)* is right next to the bus station and market – a busy, noisy place. Dorms are Y15 and doubles cost Y80.

The *Tulufan Hotel (tǔlǔfān fàndiàn)* doesn't really have a lot going for it, but it does have dorm beds for Y18. Doubles are Y46 per bed and come with an attached bathroom and air-con.

Places to Eat

Opposite the Turpan Hotel is *John's Cafe*,

XINJIANG

which also has a branch in Kashgar. It's a good place to hang out and has an English menu and reasonable prices.

Opposite the Oasis Hotel is the *Silk Road Restaurant* with a menu made up mainly of Chinese dishes with the occasional Muslim dish thrown in for good measure. The area around the *Yanye Restaurant* is also a good place to eat. A couple of the restaurants here have English menus and the staff are all very friendly. A couple of them set chairs outside during the day so that you can sip on a beer.

Getting There & Away
Getting out of Turpan is a confused affair but most people make it to the outside world by some means or another. The nearest airport is at Ürümqi.

Bus The bus station is near the market. Make sure you get to the station an hour before departure, because there is invariably a long queue for tickets. The Uigurs are even worse than the Chinese about standing in line, but Turpan employs an 'enforcer' to keep order – if only more stations would do this! There are buses from here to Ürümqi and to Daheyan.

There are at least four buses daily to Ürümqi plus private minibuses about once every hour. In Turpan, the public buses want FEC! You can often manage to pay in RMB with a student card or some other ID with your picture (try a driver's licence). Try bypassing all these hassles by simply heading out to the back of the bus station and jumping on a bus headed to wherever you're going. There's usually some room left on Ürümqi-bound buses and at least you'll end up paying something more like the local price this way.

It's great scenery along the route to Ürümqi – immense grey sand dunes, and snow-capped mountains visible in the distance. The fare is anywhere from Y15 to Y27 (depending on the mood of conductor or the ticket seller) and the 180-km trip takes four hours.

Train The nearest railway line is the Ürümqi-Lanzhou line, north of Turpan. The nearest station is at Daheyan. (There are four buses daily between Daheyan and Turpan.) There are six trains daily in both directions. If you're travelling between Ürümqi and Turpan, the direct bus is faster and more convenient than the train. The train from Daheyan to Ürümqi takes three hours, from Daheyan to Liuyuan is 13 hours, to Jiayuguan is 19 hours, and to Lanzhou takes 37 hours.

Getting Around
Public transport around Turpan is by minibus, bicycle or donkey cart. Bicycles are most convenient for the town itself. The only place hiring bicycles is the Turpan Guesthouse. Bikes here cost Y15 per day. Minibus drivers usually hang around the hotel gates – negotiate the fare in advance. Donkey carts can be found around the market, but this mode of transport is gradually fading away.

AROUND TURPAN
There are many sights in the countryside around Turpan, and it requires at least a day to see everything of importance.

The only way to see the sights is to hire a minibus for a full day (about 10 hours). You won't have to look for them – the drivers will come looking for you. It's easy to find other travellers to share the expense. Figure on spending at least Y300 for the whole group. The minibuses normally hold six passengers – any more than eight would be uncomfortable. Make sure it's clearly understood which places you want to see. A typical trip should include the Atsana Graves, Gaochang Ruins, Bezeklik Caves, Grape Valley, Emin Minaret, Karez underground irrigation channels, and Jiaohe Ruins (usually in that order).

A few drivers are bad news – they may try to rush you or skip some of the places you want to see – but most are OK. The driver we had last time was great, and we wound up buying him lunch, cold drinks and a large watermelon as a parting gift.

Don't underestimate the desert. In country like this, the sun can fry your brain in less time than it takes to make fried rice. Essential

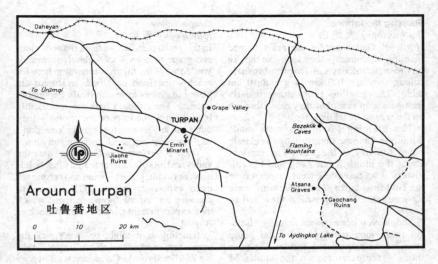

Around Turpan
吐鲁番地区

survival gear includes a water bottle, sunglasses and straw hat. Some UV lotion and Vaseline (or Chapstick) for your lips also come in handy.

There are admission fees to a few of the sites – most cost less than Y10 and all are payable in RMB.

Atsana Graves
(āsītǎnà gǔmùqū) 阿斯塔娜古墓区

These graves, where the dead of Gaochang are buried, lie north-west of the ancient city. Only three of the tombs are open to tourists, and each of these is approached by a short flight of steps which leads down to the burial chamber about six metres below ground level.

One tomb contains portraits of the deceased painted on the walls, while another has paintings of birds. The third tomb holds two well-preserved corpses (one mummy from the original trio seems to have been removed to Turpan's museum) like those in the museums at Ürümqi and Hangzhou. Some of the artefacts date back as far as the Jin Dynasty, from the 3rd to 5th centuries AD. The finds include silks, brocades, embroideries and many funerary objects such as shoes, hats and sashes made of recycled paper. The last turned out to be quite special for archaeologists, since the paper included deeds, records of slave purchases, orders for silk and other everyday transactions.

Gaochang Ruins
(gāochāng gǔchéng) 高昌故城

About 46 km east of Turpan are the ruins of Gaochang, the capital of the Uigurs when they moved into the Xinjiang region from Mongolia in the 9th century. It had originally been founded in the 7th century during the Tang Dynasty and became a major staging post on the Silk Road.

The walls of the city are clearly visible. They stood as much as 12 metres thick, formed a rough square with a perimeter of six km, and were surrounded by a moat. Gaochang was divided into an outer city, an inner city within the walls, and a palace and government compound. A large monastery in the south-western part of the city is in reasonable condition, with some of its rooms, corridors and doorways still preserved.

Flaming Mountains
(huǒyànshān) 火焰山

North of Gaochang lie the aptly named Flaming Mountains – they look like they're on fire in the midday sun. Purplish-brown in colour, they are 100 km long and 10 km wide. The minibus tours don't usually include a stop here, but they drive through on the way to Bezeklik Caves.

The Flaming Mountains were made famous in Chinese literature by the classic novel *Journey to the West*. The story is about the monk Xuan Zang and his followers who travelled west in search of the Buddhist sutra. The mountains were a formidable barrier which they had to cross.

Should you contemplate actually climbing these mountains, you'd better equip yourself with insulated insoles for your shoes – temperatures on the sunbaked surface have been known to reach 80°C – hot enough to fry an egg.

Bezeklik Thousand Buddha Caves
(bózīkèlǐ qiānfó dòng) 柏孜克里千佛洞

On the western side of the Flaming Mountains, on a cliff face fronting a river valley, are the remains of these Buddhist cave temples. All the caves are in dreadful condition, most having been devastated by Muslims or robbed by all and sundry. The large statues which stood at the back of each cave have been destroyed or stolen and the faces of the buddhas ornamenting the walls have either been scrapped or completely gouged out. Particularly active in the export of murals was a German, Albert von Le Coq, who removed whole frescos from the stone walls and transported them back to the Berlin Museum – where Allied bombing wiped most of them out during WW II. Today the caves reveal little more than a hint of what these works of art were like in their heyday.

Photography is forbidden inside the caves, but there isn't much reason to bother. Fortunately, the scenery just outside the caves is fine.

Grape Valley
(pútáo gōu) 葡萄沟

In this small paradise – a thick maze of vines and grape trellises – stark desert surrounds you. Most of the minibus tours stop here for lunch – the food isn't bad, and there are plenty of grapes in season (early September is best). The children here are remarkably friendly and like to pose for photos – they don't ask any money for this so please don't turn them into beggars by offering anything.

There is a winery *(guǒjiǔchǎng)* near the valley and lots of well-ventilated brick buildings for drying grapes – wine and raisins are major exports of Turpan. CITS is trying to organise an annual 'grape festival' which they expect to hold during the third week of August.

Tempting as it might be, don't pick the grapes here or anywhere else in Turpan. There is a Y15 fine if you do. Considerable effort goes into raising these grapes and the farmers don't appreciate tourists eating their profits.

Karez Underground Irrigation Channels
(dìxiàshuǐ) 地下水

The word 'karez' means wells. The wells are sunk at various points to the north of Turpan to collect ground water, which comes from melting snow in the Bogdashan mountains. The ground water then passes through underground channels to irrigate farms in the valley below.

The city of Turpan owes its existence to these vital wells and channels, some of

which were constructed over 2000 years ago. Some of the channels are on the surface, but putting them underground greatly reduces water loss from evaporation. They are fed entirely by gravity, thus eliminating the need for pumps. There are over a thousand wells, and the total length of the channels exceeds 3000 km. It's remarkable to think that this extensive irrigation system was all constructed by hand and without modern building materials. Locals like to boast that this is one of China's greatest public works projects, on a par with the Great Wall and Grand Canal.

There are a number of places to view the channels, but most of the minibus tours stop at one particular spot on the west side of Turpan. Unfortunately, there are a few children here who ask foreigners for money.

Jiaohe Ruins
(jiāohé gùchéng) 交河古城
During the Han Dynasty, Jiaohe was established by the Chinese as a garrison town to defend the borderlands. The city was decimated by Genghis Khan's 'travelling roadshow' but you'd be forgiven if you thought it had been struck by an A-bomb. The buildings are rather more obvious than the ruins of Gaochang though, and you can walk through the old streets and along the roads. A main road cuts through the city, and at the end is a large monastery with figures of the Buddha still visible.

The ruins are around seven to eight km west of Turpan and stand on an island bounded by two small rivers – thus the name Jiaohe, which means 'confluence of two rivers'. During the cooler months it is possible to cycle out here without any problem

Sand Therapy Clinic
(shā liáo zhàn) 沙疗站
Over 5000 people a year – mostly Kazakhs – come to Turpan to get buried up to their necks in the sand. It is believed that the hot sand can greatly relieve the aches of rheumatism. The Sand Therapy Clinic is pretty much an outdoor sandbox, and it only operates from June to August. There's not much

to see here and the minibuses usually don't include this as part of your tour except by special request. If you're plagued by rheumatism, you might want to give this therapy a try.

Aydingkol Salt Lake
(àidīng hú) 艾丁湖
At the very bottom of the Turpan depression is Aydingkol Lake, 154 metres below sea level. The 'lake' usually has little water – it's a huge, muddy evaporating pond with a surface of crystallised salt, but technically it's the second-lowest lake in the world, only surpassed by the Dead Sea in Israel and Jordan.

Most of the tours do not stop here. If you want to see Aydingkol Lake, tell your driver and expect to pay extra for the additional distance.

SHIHEZI
(shíhézi) 石河子
A couple of hours' drive north-west of Ürümqi is the town of Shihezi, or Stony Creek. It's a Chinese outpost and almost all the inhabitants are Hans. The town is officially open to foreigners, but it looks so boring that even a statue would pack up and leave town. The bus between Ürümqi and Yining passes through here.

KUQA
(kùchē) 库车
On the Silk Road between Turpan and Kashgar lies Kuqa. Scattered around the Kuqa region are at least seven Thousand Buddha Caves (qiānfó dòng) which rival those of Dunhuang and Datong. There are also at least four ancient ruined cities in the area.

Kuqa comprises an old city and a much newer Chinese part of town. The Buddhist cave paintings and ruined cities in the area are remains of a pre-Islamic Buddhist civilisation. When the 7th century Chinese traveller Xuan Zang (Hsuan Tsang) passed through Kuqa he recorded that the city's western gate was flanked by two enormous 30 metre Buddha statues and that there were numerous monasteries decorated with beautiful Buddhist frescos in the area. Twelve hundred years later, the German archeologist-adventurers Grünwedel and Le Coq removed many of these paintings and sculptures to Berlin.

Places to Stay
Next to the bus station is a guesthouse *(kùchē qìchēzhàn zhāodàisuǒ)* with doubles for Y10. Hot water is almost non-existent here if you're in need of shower. In town is the Kuqa Guesthouse *(kùchē bīnguǎn)* with beds in a clean double for Y20. Service and facilities here are definitely better here than at the bus station, if such things are important to you.

Getting There & Away
There are flights from Ürümqi for Y320, but it is not possible to fly onwards from Kuqa to Kashgar. You'll have to go back to Ürümqi for this.

Buses from Ürümqi to Kuqa cost Y79 for around 1½ days' travel. From Kuqa it's another 1½ days on to Kashgar by bus. You might be lucky and a get a local-price ticket at the bus station, but don't count on it. There are also buses to Yining.

Getting Around
Kuqa's sights are scattered around the surrounding countryside, and the only way to get to see them is to hire a vehicle. The 3rd floor of the Government Building *(zhèngfu dàlóu)* in the centre of town has a branch of CITS, where you can hire a car for the day for around Y300. A trip out to the Kyzil Thousand Buddha Caves should cost around Y200.

AROUND KUQA
Kyzil Thousand Buddha Caves
(kèzīěr qiānfó dòng) 克孜尔千佛洞
There are quite a lot of Thousand Buddha Caves around Kuqa, but the most important site is this one, around 70 km to the west of Kuqa in Baicheng County. They date back to the 3rd century AD. Although there are more than 230 caves here, at the time of writing only six of the caves were open to public viewing. A no photography rule is in force.

Ruined Cities
(gùchéng) 古城
The closest of the ruined cities to Kuqa can be approached by foot. Pilangcheng is about 15 minutes out of town and is the ancient capital of the region. Around 23 km to the east of Kuqa is the ancient city of Subashi.

HOTAN
(hétián) 和田
At a distance of around 1980 km south-west of Ürümqi by road (via Kashgar), Hotan is one of the remotest parts of Xinjiang. It is also in real desert country at the southern boundary of the Taklimakan Desert. Despite this, it is renowned for its temperate climate (by Xinjiang standards at least), not being subject to such extremes of seasonal temperatures as Turpan or Ürümqi.

As this place was only recently opened, it is still early days for Hotan tourism. You can be sure if you head out here that you will be one of the first.

Like Kuqa, the sights are spread around the surrounding countryside and are of the ruined city variety. Ten km to the west of town are the **Yurturgan Ruins** *(yuètègān yízhǐ)*, the ancient capital of a pre-Islamic kingdom dating back to the 3rd to 8th centuries AD. The **Malikurwatur Ruins** *(málìkèwǎtè gùchéng)* are 12 km south of town, and there are some temples and pagoda-like buildings a further 10 km to the south.

Hotan is renowned for its carpet and silk production. **Jiyaxiang** *(jíyáxiāng)*, a small town 11 km north-east of Hotan still produces hand-woven carpets using looms. Most of the houses in town are tiny, family-run factories. In town itself, on the eastern bank of the Jade Dragon Kashgar River *(yùlóng kāshì hé)*, just north of the road to Qiemo, is a carpet factory.

Places to Stay & Eat
The *Hotan No 1 Guesthouse (hétián dìqū dìyī zhāodàisuǒ)* has basic accommodation,

as well as few more upmarket rooms. The CAAC office is here also. The other option is the Hotan Guesthouse *(hétián bīnguǎn)* is newer and probably more expensive than the No 1.

Visitors to Hotan are advised to take care with the local food. The meals available at both the hotels are reported to be fairly safe, but it's easy to get sick from eating on the street.

Getting There & Away

Hotan is connected by air to Ürümqi. There may also be flights from here to Aksu. Buses from Ürümqi to Hotan generally travel by way of Kashgar and can take as long as five days. It makes more sense to visit Hotan from Kashgar, which is a distance of 509 km. The trip takes one to two days, and buses from Kashgar depart at 8 am. One possibility might be to take a bus from Kashgar to Hotan and then fly back to Ürümqi.

Getting Around

Hiring a vehicle is the only way to get around Hotan's sights. There should be locals with vehicles for hire on the lookout for visiting foreigners. Failing this, try the bus station or the No 7 Bus Co *(dìqī yùnshū gōngsī)*.

KASHGAR
(kāshí) 喀什

Kashgar is a giant oasis 1290 metres above sea level. Like Timbuktu, it's one of those fabled cities that everyone seems to know about but no-one seems to get to. A thousand years ago it was a key centre on the Silk Road, and when Marco Polo passed through he commented that:

The inhabitants live by trade and industry. They have fine orchards and vineyards and flourishing estates. Cotton grows here in plenty, besides flax and hemp. The soil is fruitful and productive of all the means of life. The country is the starting-point from which many merchants set out to market their wares all over the world.

History

In the early part of this century, Kashgar was a relatively major town on the edge of a vast nowhere and separated from the rest of China by an endless sandpit. Traders from India tramped to Kashgar via Gilgit and the Hunza Valley; in 1890 the British sent a trade agent to Kashgar to represent their interests and in 1908 they established a consulate. As with Tibet in the 1890s, the rumours soon spread that the Russians were on the verge of gobbling up Xinjiang.

To most people, Kashgar, which is five or six weeks' journey over 15,000-foot passes from the nearest railhead in India, must seem a place barbarously remote; but for us its outlandish name spelt civilisation. The raptures of arrival were unqualified. Discovery is a delightful process, but rediscovery is better; few people can ever have enjoyed a bath more than we did, who had not had one for 5½ months.

That is how Peter Fleming described his arrival in Kashgar back in 1935, after he and Kini Maillart had spent almost half a year on the backs of camels and donkeys getting there from Beijing. Fleming described the city as being 'in effect run by the secret police, the Russian advisers, and the Soviet Consulate, and most of the high officials were only figureheads'. The rest of the foreign community consisted of the British Consul and his wife, their 15 Hunza guards from the north of Pakistan, and a couple of Swedish missionaries.

Contact with the Soviet Union seemed to make sense given the geographical location of Kashgar. Ethnically, culturally, linguistically and theologically the inhabitants of Kashgar had absolutely nothing in common with the Chinese and everything in common with the Muslim inhabitants on the other side of the border. Whereas it took a five-month camel and donkey ride to get to Beijing and a five-or six-week hike to reach the nearest railhead in British India (although mail runners could do it in two), the Soviet railhead at Osh was more accessible, and from Kashgar strings of camels would stalk westward with their bales of wool, returning with cargoes of Russian cigarettes, matches and sugar.

Rumours and also banquets seemed to be at their most eccentric in Kashgar. Fleming describes his last night there at a banquet given by the city officials:

> ...half in their honour and half in ours...You never know what may happen at a banquet in Kashgar and each of our official hosts had prudently brought his own bodyguard. Turkic and Chinese soldiers lounged everywhere; automatic rifles and executioner's swords were much in evidence, and the Mauser pistols of the waiters knocked ominously against the back of your chair as they leant over you with the dishes.

Speeches made by just about everyone were feverishly translated into English, Russian, Chinese and Turkish, and no-one was assassinated.

Kashgar Today

The Kashgar of today has lost much of the 'romantic' value that made eating there in the '30s a slightly nervous experience. When the Communists came to power the city walls were ripped down and a huge, glistening white statue of Chairman Mao was erected on the main street. The statue stands today, hand outstretched to the sky above and the lands beyond, a constant reminder to the local populace of the alien regime that controls the city.

About 200,000 people live here, and apart from the Uigur majority this number includes Tajiks, Kirghiz and Uzbekh. The number of Han Chinese living here is relatively small – nothing like the horde that dominates Ürümqi, although PLA troops are always conspicuous and there are plenty of Han plain-clothes police.

Nor does it take six months to reach Kashgar now; it's a three-day bus ride from

Ürümqi or you can fly out in a couple of hours if you have more consideration for your bum. No longer as remote, or as fabled, the city sounds like a disappointment – yet the peculiar quality of Kashgar is that every so often you chance on some scene that suggests a different age and a world removed from China.

Kashgar is renowned for playing diabolical tricks on the stomach; it's possibly a bug in the water, but whatever it is, your enjoyment of the place can be ruined.

Some foreign women wandering the streets on their own have been sexually harassed. This may be remotely connected with style of dress or even the town's diet of bawdy films. Whatever the reason, it's best for women travellers to dress as you would in any Muslim country.

In Kashgar, the adults don't gather round foreigners like the Han Chinese, but the Uigur children do – they come in plague proportions. If you've got a camera, spare plenty of film for photos of every kid on the block! A foreign face, rare as it is, is usually assumed to be American, but quite often the locals will ask if you're a Pakistani.

Information

CITS CITS has an office in the Chini Bagh Hotel (☎ 23156), but the staff seem to have little understanding of the needs of individual travellers, so you're probably better off giving it a miss.

Other John's Information & Cafe opposite the Seman Hotel is probably the best place to get the lowdown on travelling to Pakistan and seeing the sights around Kashgar. John himself is a mine of information and he offers competitive rates for minibus and 4WD hire.

Money The Bank of China (☎ 2461) is on Renmin Xilu near the post office. The money-changing brigade will pursue you all over Kashgar. Cash US dollars are snapped up for Sino-Pakistani trade and by Kashgaris preparing for pilgrimage to Mecca.

Maps Fairly accurate maps of Kashgar are available from some of the hotels. There's one (in Chinese) in the waiting hall of the long-distance bus station which may help you orientate yourself.

Sunday Market
(jiàrì jíshì) 假日集市
You should not miss the bumper market that takes place every Sunday on the eastern fringe of town. Hundreds of donkey carts, horseriders, pedestrians and animals thunder into town for a bargaining extravaganza. It's best to just wander at random through the huge market area and watch camels, goats, horses, melons, grapes, hats, knives, beds and doorframes being bought and sold. Beware of pickpockets.

Bazaar
(jíshì) 集市
Sundays excepted, the bazaar is the focus of activity in Kashgar. The main market street can be reached from the lanes opposite the Id Kah Square which run off the main north-south road. Kashgar is noted for the ornate knives sold in the bazaar and by hawkers in the streets. It's also a hat-making centre, and the northern end of the street is devoted entirely to stalls selling embroidered caps and fur-lined headgear. Blacksmiths pound away on anvils, colourful painted wooden saddles can be bought, and you can pick your dinner from a choice line-up of goats' heads and hoofs. Boots are a good buy at around Y35 per pair. The price varies with the number of soles and you should allow three days for them to be finished.

Old Asian men with long thick beards, fur overcoats and high leather boots swelter in the sun. The Muslim Uigur women here dress in skirts and stockings like the Uigur women in Ürümqi and Turpan, but there's a much greater prevalence of faces hidden behind veils of brown gauze. In the evening the Id Kah Square is a bustling marketplace, and numerous market streets lead off from the square.

Some of the best areas for walking are east of the main bazaar and north-west of the Id Kah Mosque. To the south of the centre is a large cluster of mud-brick houses covering a sort of plateau – it's worth a wander round.

Id Kah Mosque
(ài tí gǎ ér qīngzhēn sì) 艾提尕尔清真寺
The Id Kah Mosque is a stark contrast to the Chinese-style mosques in eastern cities like Canton and Xi'an. The Id Kah looks like it's been lifted out of Pakistan or Afghanistan, and has the central dome and flanking minarets which Westerners usually associate with a mosque. Prayer time is around 10 pm, though that may vary throughout the year. During the festival of Korban Bairam, usually held in September and October, pilgrims gather in front of the mosque and gradually twirl themselves into a frenzy of dancing which is driven by wailing music from a small band perched on the mosque's portal.

Smaller mosques are scattered among the houses on the streets around the town centre.

Abakh Hoja Tomb
(xiāngfēi mù) 香妃墓
This strange construction is in the eastern part of the oasis. It looks something like a stubby, multicoloured miniature of the Taj Mahal, with green tiles on the walls and dome. To one side of the mosque is a cemetery, with a rectangular base surmounted by fat, conical mud structures. The tomb is the burial place of Hidajetulla Hoja, a Muslim missionary and saint, and his 72 descendants. It's an hour's walk from the Kashgar Guesthouse, but you should be able to hitch a lift on a donkey cart – just show the driver a photo of where you want to go. The tomb lies on a side street off a long east-west road.

The Chinese call this place the Fragrant Concubine's Tomb *(xiāngfēi mù)* in honour of one daughter of the Hoja clan who was married to the emperor Qianlong. However, her body was later moved to Hebei Province and is not actually entombed here.

Renmin Park & Zoo
rénmín gōngyuán, dòngwùyuán
人民公园和动物园
The park is a pleasant place in which to sit,

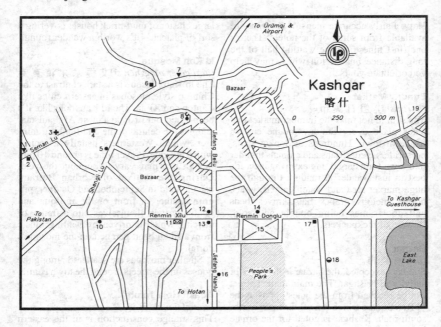

but the zoo is depressing. The kindest thing you could do for some of the animals would be to put a bullet through their heads. In front of the entrance to the park is Renmin Square and on the opposite side of the road is the massive white statue of Mao Zedong.

Places to Stay

The *Seman Hotel* (☎ 2129, 2060) *(sèmǎn bīnguǎn)* is probably the best place to base yourself in Kashgar. It's in the former Soviet consulate on the western edge of town. It's a pleasant place to stay, with relaxing grounds. A double with bathroom costs Y60 – check to make sure the plumbing works. A bed in the dormitory costs Y17 (only available during the summer months). Take a look at the sign outside which modestly points out that the 'Seman Hotel was appraised to be one of the 10 hotels famed for their best service in the world in 1988'. The thing is that the locals actually believe it: 'Staying at

the Seman Hotel? Yes, one of the best hotels in the world'.

The *Chini Bagh Hotel* (☎ 2291, 2103) *(qíníbāhé bīnguǎn)* is probably the next best place to stay, though it gets very noisy in the summer months when it fills up with Pakistani traders. Doubles with bathroom cost Y80; three-bed dorms are Y32; four-bed dorms are Y26; and a bed in a chaotic six-bed room costs Y10. The shower block is a slime pit. Extensive renovations have completely obliterated any of the colonial grandeur the hotel may once have possessed. Western visitors, both male and female, have complained of sexual harassment from Pakistani guests at this hotel.

The *Kashgar Guesthouse* (☎ 2367, 2368) *(kāshí gě'ěr bīnguǎn)* is the top-rated hotel in town and is up to the same good standard of any other basic Chinese tourist hotel further east. The problem with this place is that it's too far from the town centre – the main intersection is a good hour's walk

■ PLACES TO STAY

2	Seman Hotel	色满宾馆
4	Silk Road Hotel	丝绸之路饭店
6	Chini Bagh Hotel	其尼巴合宾馆
17	Tiannan Hotel	天南饭店

▼ PLACES TO EAT

| 1 | John's Information & Cafe | 咖啡馆 |
| 7 | Le Bistro Cafe | 咖啡馆 |

OTHER

3	Minorities Hospital	民族医院
5	PSB	公安局
8	Id Kah Mosque	艾提尕清真寺
9	Id Kah Square	艾提尕广场
10	Bank of China	中国银行
11	Post Office	邮电大楼
12	Cinema	电影院
13	Department Store	百货大楼
14	Mao Statue	毛泽东塑像
15	People's (Renmin) Square	人民广场
16	CAAC	中国民航
18	Long-Distance Bus Station	长途汽车站
19	Sunday Market	星期日市场

away, and there's no bus. Now that donkey carts have been driven off the streets of Kashgar it's not even possible to resort to this mode of transport. Double rooms in building No 1 go for Y100 (with shower and toilet). A bed in a four-bed room in one of the other buildings is Y20, but the building is a real echo chamber. There's a post office, dining rooms, souvenir shops and a small store (just inside the front gate) which sells bottled fruit.

At the time of writing the old Friendship Hotel was undergoing renovations and a name change: it is now known as the *Silk Road Hotel*. This will probably be an excuse to jack up the prices sky high, but it may be worth checking out all the same.

The one other place in town that takes foreigners is the *Tiannan Hotel (tiānnán fàndiàn)* down near the bus station. It's a bit of a dive, but it has bicycle hire, a laundry service and reasonably priced rooms. Beds in a double are Y18, and in a four-bed dorm

Y15. There are also dorms available for Y10, but they're reluctant to give them to foreigners unless you come in a group of four or more. There are also suites for Y120 and twins with bathroom for Y56.

Places to Eat

There are plenty of restaurants around town and the streetside stalls have great local delicacies. The Seman Hotel has a nice little restaurant out the back with tables outside. They rarely have any rice here, but they can cook up great noodle dishes. There are also a couple of good places to eat opposite the Seman Hotel, the pick of them being *John's Information & Cafe*. It has an English menu and very reasonable prices.

Make a point of heading down to *Le Bistro*, just down the road from the Chini Bagh Hotel. This place has good coffee and cakes and an extensive English menu. Even

XINJIANG

the music is not bad. It's run by friendly people and is one of the few places that stay open during the winter months.

It's difficult to say what will happen to the *Oasis Cafe* with all the renovation work going on at the Silk Road Hotel. Prices here had already got expensive, and if the attached Silk Road Hotel goes upmarket, it's likely that the prices at the restaurant will too. Check the place out for the latest.

For a wide variety of Uigur foods, pop into the food market close to the Id Kah Mosque. There you can try shish kebab, rice with mutton, fried fish, samosa (rectangles of crisp pastry enclosing fried mincemeat) and fruit. To the left of the mosque is a teahouse with a balcony above the bustling crowds. Flat bread and shish kebab are sold at the huddle of stalls on the main road, just west of the big square opposite the Mao statue. There are a couple of excellent ice-cream stalls here too – selling very cold and very vanilla ice-cream. There are more ice-cream stalls in the Id Kah Square, and you should find eggs and roast chicken being sold near the main intersection at night. You might also want to consider the following food for thought:

After dark, Kashgar can still get pretty rough. Prices you bartered down while it was still light (i.e. if you're sitting at a stall eating kebabs) mysteriously go back up to Western levels as night falls. Should you complain, the number of Uigurs around you then multiplies rapidly! Always pay *as soon as* you get the goods.

Philip Clarke

Getting There & Away

Air There are daily flights from Kashgar to Ürümqi (Y650). The flight takes slightly under two hours.

The CAAC office (☎ 22113) is on Jiefang Nanlu south of the Id Kah Mosque.

Bus There are buses from the Kashgar long-distance bus station to Ürümqi, Daheyan, Aksu, Hotan, Maralbixi, Khotan, Yengisar, Payziwat, Yopuria, Makit, Yakam and Kargilik. The Kashgar bus station, like its counterpart in Ürümqi, charges a 100% sur-

charge for foreigners' tickets. Oddly, their prices are even more expensive than Ürümqi's. Some sample prices are: Ürümqi Y197; Turpan Y184; Kuqa Y102; and Yining Y170.

The daily bus to Ürümqi travels via Aksu, Korla and Toksun. Tickets can only be bought one day before departure and the bus is scheduled to depart Kashgar at 8 am. The trip takes three days.

The bus to Turpan actually goes to Daheyan, stopping overnight at Aksu and Korla and going straight through Toksun on to Daheyan. The trip takes three days. Daheyan is a small railway town on the line from Lanzhou to Ürümqi, and to get to nearby Turpan there are three buses a day. See the Daheyan section for details.

You won't have access to baggage stored on the roof of the bus during the trip, so take a small bag of essentials on board with you. Be warned that buses don't always run on schedule. You could take four days to do the trip, driving anything between eight and 14 hours a day depending on breakdowns or other factors.

Korla and Aksu are once again officially open to foreigners. The town of Yanqi, 52 km north of Korla, is a possible stopover (by rail or bus) for a visit to Buddhist caves in the area or to the nearby lake, Bagragh Kol (*bósīténg hú*). From Yanqi to the lakeside centre of Bohu is about 12 km. Access to the lake from Bohu could involve a mud-wading expedition, but the fishing villages might be worth a visit. Prices charged for transport can be as high as Y100 per day for a motorised three-wheeler – bargaining is advised. Korla has bus and rail connections with Daheyan (Turpan station), Ürümqi and Yining. Aksu has bus and air connections. The major problem with stopping off on the way between Kashgar and Ürümqi is that you will need great patience to commandeer a seat in buses already packed to the gills.

The road between Xinjiang and Tibet, one of the roughest in the world, passes through the disputed territory of Aksai Chin. This route is not officially open to foreigners; some have hitched unofficially from Lhasa to Kashgar in as little as 16 days, others have taken months. Plenty of foreigners have been fined travelling towards Lhasa from Kashgar, and the PSB's worries about safety are understandable in this instance. *Tibet – a travel survival kit* (Lonely Planet Publications) contains more details on this route, which should not be attempted without full preparations for high-altitude travel. At least two foreigners have died on this route: one was thrown from the back of a truck when it hit a pothole; the other died of a combination of hypothermia and altitude sickness, also while riding on the back of a truck.

The road connection between China and Pakistan via the Karakoram Highway is described later in this chapter.

Getting Around

The city buses are of no use; to get around you have to walk or hire a bike. The most common transport in Kashgar is by bicycle. Donkey carts have been banned from the streets.

The Tiannan Hotel has bike hire, and John's Information & Cafe may also have a bicycle hire service by the time you have this book in your hands. At the very least, someone at the cafe will know where you can hire a bike. Check also at the Seman Hotel.

For jeep and minibus hire, the best place to inquire is John's Information & Cafe. Day tours will set you back around Y250 to Y300.

AROUND KASHGAR
Hanoi
(hànnuòyī gùchéng) 罕诺依古城
The ruins of this ancient city lie about 30 km east of Kashgar. The town reached its zenith during the Tang and Song dynasties but appears to have been abandoned after the 11th century. To get out here you'll probably have to try and hire a jeep at the Kashgar Guesthouse – apparently it's a rough ride to see mediocre rubble.

Three Immortals Buddhist Caves
(sānxiān dòng) 三仙洞
These Buddhist caves are on a sheer cliff on the south bank of the Qiakmakh River about 20 km north of Kashgar. There are three caves, one with frescos which are still discernible. Going to the caves makes a pleasant excursion, but it's not worth it just for the art.

KARAKORAM HIGHWAY
(zhōngbā gōnglù) 中巴公路
This highway over Khunjerab Pass (4800 metres) was opened to foreigners in May 1986 and closed again in April 1990. The official excuse was landslides, but the real reason was a political 'earthquake'. However, in August of the same year it opened again but only for individual travel from Pakistan to Kashgar – from Kashgar to Pakistan required an expensive CITS tour! As of April 1992 the highway was again open to individuals.

From 15 April to late October buses run daily from the Chini Bagh Hotel in Kashgarto Tashkurgan, which is where the Chinese Customs are located. Be warned: although the highway is officially open, it still remains a relatively dangerous trip. Landslides are common, and in 1992 at least one traveller was killed by falling rocks – take your hard hat.

For centuries this route was used by caravans plodding down the Silk Road. Back in 400 AD, the Chinese pilgrim Fa Xian recorded feelings of vertigo:

> The way was difficult and rugged, running along a bank exceedingly precipitous. When one approached the edge of it, his eyes became unsteady; and if he wished to go forward in the same direction, there was no place on which he could place his foot, and beneath were the waters of the river called the Indus.

Khunjerab means 'valley of blood', a reference to local bandits who took advantage of the terrain to plunder caravans and slaughter the merchants.

Nearly 20 years were required to plan, push, blast and level the present road between Islamabad and Kashgar; over 400 road-builders died. The rough section between Kashgar and the Pakistan border still needs a few more years before it can be called a road. Facilities en route are being steadily improved, but take warm clothing, food and drink on board with you – once stowed on the roof of the bus your baggage will not be easily accessible.

Information

For information or advice, contact the Pakistan Tourism Development Corporation, H-2, St 61, F – 7/4, Islamabad, Pakistan. CITS in Ürümqi has no maps, no knowledge of the highway and no interest other than to sell you an outrageously expensive tour.

Once again, John's Information & Cafe in Kashgar is probably the best place to catch up with the latest developments on the highway situation. The CITS office is only interested in hiring minibuses for the trip, and is not forthcoming on the situation with public buses.

A separate guide, *The Karakoram Highway – a travel survival kit* (Lonely Planet Publications), is available.

Visas

Pakistani visas are compulsory for visitors from most Western countries. Visas are *not* given at the border; Hong Kong and Beijing are the closest places to obtain your Pakistan visa, so plan ahead if you want to enter or exit China on this road.

Chinese visas can be obtained in your own country, in Hong Kong or in Islamabad. The Chinese embassy in Islamabad takes three to four days to issue a one-month visa and charges around 250 rupees for US citizens, 550 rupees for Australians or 800 rupees for UK citizens.

Border

Opening & Closing Times These are officially given as 15 April and 31 October respectively. However, the border can open late or close early depending on conditions at the Khunjerab Pass.

Formalities Travel formalities are performed at Sust, on the Pakistan border; the Chinese border post is at Tashkurgan, where there is accommodation available. You probably won't be able to change Pakistan rupees

in Tashkurgan, only Western currencies. But don't worry, Kashgar street marketeers love cash rupees and US dollars.

Routing

The Karakoram Highway stretches between Kashgar and Islamabad. The following chart provides a rough guide to distances and average journey times:

Route	Distance (km)	Duration
Kashgar-Tashkurgan	280	seven hours
Tashkurgan-Pirali	84	90 minutes
Pirali-Khunjerab (Sino-Pakistan border)	35	one hour
Khunjerab-Sust	86	2¼ hours
Sust-Passu	35	45 minutes
Passu-Gulmit	14	20 minutes
Gulmit-Karimabad	37	one hour
Karimabad (Hunza)-Gilgit	98	two hours
Gilgit-Rawalpindi	631	18 hours

From China to Pakistan Buses direct from Kashgar to the Pakistani border post at Sust leave from the Chini Bagh Hotel at about 11.30 am all through the summer. From June to September buses are laid on, but earlier or later in the season there may not be buses on some days. There's an overnight stop in Tashkurgan. The same bus goes on to Sust the next day. Through the summer of 1992 buses cost Y134. You can expect this price to have risen somewhat. There aren't many food stops, so bring a day's water and snacks. CITS provides minibuses for the same route at around Y370 per person. If you take this option, you should be able to negotiate stops for photographs and sightseeing.

Everything that goes on top of the bus is Customs-inspected at Chini Bagh and stays locked up for the entire journey. So carry on whatever you want for the overnight stop, plus whatever you declared to Customs on entering China.

From Kashgar, the bus crosses the Pamir Plateau (3000 metres), passing the foothills of Kongurshan (*gōnggé'ér shān*), which is 7719 metres high, and nearby Muztag-Atashan (*mùshìtǎgé shān*) at 7546 metres. The journey continues through stunning scenery: high mountain pastures with grazing camels and yaks tended by Tajiks who live in yurts. Some travellers have stayed in yurts beside Karakol Lake (kǎlākùlì hú), close to both these mountains. Sven Hedin, the Swedish explorer, nearly drowned in this lake!

The bus stays overnight at Tashkurgan (tǎshíkù'ěrgān), a predominantly Tajik town which could be used as a base to explore the nearby ruined fort, local cemeteries and surrounding high country. This is where the Customs post is now located.

From Tashkurgan (3600 metres) the road climbs higher for the two-hour stretch to Pirali, which isn't worth a stop. If you're on a Pakistani bus, you'll have no need to change buses; if you've taken the local bus from Kashgar, you'll need to change to a Pakistani bus from Pirali onwards.

From Pakistan to China From Rawalpindi to Gilgit (a 15-hour trip) there are six buses daily. An ordinary coach costs about 150 rupees, deluxe around 180 rupees. If you can't stand the pace of the bus ride, the flight between Rawalpindi and Gilgit (at least one flight per day, weather permitting) is about 570 rupees.

From Gilgit to Sust, there's a Northern Areas Transport Company (NATCO) bus which costs 60 rupees; buy your ticket early on the morning of departure – the bus leaves at 8 am. The tourist hotel at Sust charges 25-30 rupees for a bed in the dormitory, or about 60/80 rupees for singles/doubles.

From Sust to Pirali, there's a NATCO bus for 300 rupees. Get your ticket from the NATCO office first thing in the morning – you'll need to show it to Customs. At Pirali everyone changes to a Chinese bus to Kashgar (Y80). This bus stops overnight at Tashkurgan. Trucks offer lifts (negotiate the price); ditto for jeeps. From Tashkurgan to Kashgar takes aeons over an atrocious, boulder-strewn road.

YINING
(yīníng) 伊宁
Also known as Gulja, Yining lies close to the border, about 700 km west of Ürümqi. It is the centre of the Ili Kazakh Autonomous Prefecture.

On the death of Genghis Khan in 1227, his four sons inherited responsibility for the Mongol empire. Chaghatai, the second-eldest, took over a huge area which included Turkestan, Xinjiang and, further south, most of Khorasan. Chaghatai is said to have made his capital at Almalik, close to Yining in the valley of the Ili River.

The Ili Valley became an easy access point for invaders and later for the northern route of the Silk Road, which stretched to the Caspian Sea. Russian and Chinese control over this borderland was at best tenuous. Yining was occupied by the Tsar's troops in 1876 during Yakub Beg's independent rule of Kashgaria. Five years later, the Chinese cracked down on Yakub Beg and Yining was handed back by the Russians. In 1962, there were major Sino-Soviet clashes along the Ili River. In late 1986, the Chinese claimed to have shot six Soviet infiltrators.

Chinese appear uneasy here and warn against staying out after dark, when knives are fast and streets unsafe. They probably do have some problems keeping order in an alien environment. The local Kazakhs and Uzbekhs can be a rough bunch (regularly drunk in the evenings and occasionally involved in street fights) but very friendly towards foreigners, whom they put in a different category from those in authority.

In particular, now that there are direct bus and train services between Ürümqi and Alma Ata there is no real overpowering reason to visit Yining itself. Unless, of course, you're the kind of traveller who revels in far-flung places where nothing seems to work – planes don't arrive, banks run out of money, telephones are perpetually out of order, government workers don't show up for work and much of the population is drunk. Indeed, it seems more like Russia than China.

Information
CITS This office (☎ 22439) is in room 324 of a large administration building at 27 Sidalin Beilu, which is just to the west of the post

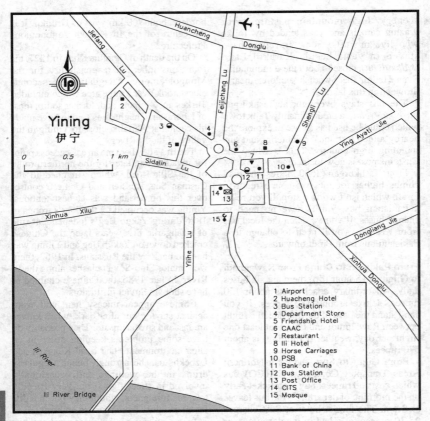

Yining
伊宁

0   0.5   1 km

1 Airport
2 Huacheng Hotel
3 Bus Station
4 Department Store
5 Friendship Hotel
6 CAAC
7 Restaurant
8 Ili Hotel
9 Horse Carriages
10 PSB
11 Bank of China
12 Bus Station
13 Post Office
14 CITS
15 Mosque

XINJIANG

office. You might want to call first to wake up the staff and let them know you're coming.

PSB This is two blocks from the Ili Hotel, near a big radio tower.

Money It would be prudent to bring a sufficient supply of FEC with you rather than to depend on the banks in Yining.

There is a sign by the entrance of the Ili Hotel saying 'Bank of China'. Don't believe it. The actual Bank of China is one block south of the Ili Hotel. When you find it, don't be surprised if they don't have any FEC –

they often run out, and the man in charge of FEC only shows up for work occasionally.

Post The post office is right on the big traffic circle in the centre of town.

Maps The Friendship Hotel sells a map called *A Tourist Guide to Ili*. This map is also available at the Ili Hotel, but the person in charge of map sales hasn't shown up for work for several years.

Things to See

Yining is a grubby place that has a few faded

```
1  飞 机 场
2  花 城 宾 馆
3  长 途 汽 车 站
4  百 货 大 楼
5  友 谊 宾 馆
6  中 国 民 航
7  餐 厅
8  伊 犁 宾 馆
9  马 车
10 公 安 局 外 事 科
11 中 国 银 行
12 长 途 汽 车 站
13 邮 局
14 中 国 国 际 旅 行 社
15 清 真 寺
```

remnants of Russian architecture, but overall there's not much to the town itself. The main attraction here is the local Uigur, Kazakh and Uzbekh culture. The region is semi-arid, but there are many trees and intensive agriculture thanks to heavy water runoff from the nearby Tianshan mountains. The one true scenic spot in this area is **Sayram Lake**, high in the mountains about four hours from Yining – the rest is uninspiring. About six km south of the town centre is a bridge over the Ili River. It's worthwhile leaving the main street and following alleys which pass the occasional Russian-style house with carved window-frames, painted shutters and plaster peeling from ornate designs. The **street-markets** are famous for fruit (especially in August), carpets and leather (boots).

The **Ili Valley** is pretty – the roads are lined with tall birch trees and there are farms everywhere. The best way to get out and see the countryside is to take a horse carriage (*mǎ chē*). These cost about Y10 for a 1½-hour tour. Most of the carriage drivers congregate in an area about one block east of the Ili Hotel. Communication can be a real problem – the drivers are Kazakhs and few speak Chinese – the only English they know is 'change money'.

Places to Stay

Most budget travellers stay in the *Ili Hotel* (☎ 22794) (*yīlí bīnguǎn*) close to the bus

station and the CAAC. The hotel features lovely, tree-shaded grounds, but the staff are incredibly lethargic. Dorms cost Y10 and doubles range from Y40 to Y80. Showers are available sometime in the evening and are turned off at 10 pm – buy shower tickets at the front desk for Y0.50.

The only other place worth considering is the *Friendship Hotel* (☎ 24631) (*yǒuyì bīnguǎn*). It doesn't have all the nice trees of the Ili Hotel, but the rooms are very clean and the staff are not only conscious, but actually friendly! The dorms cost Y18 – there are two beds in each room and an attached bathroom. The main problem with the Friendship Hotel is that it's hard to find – it's down an obscure side-street and the only sign pointing the way is in Chinese.

One other place accepts foreigners – the *Huacheng Hotel* (☎ 2911 ext 296) (*huáchéng bīnguǎn*). Doubles are Y60 and the rooms look decent, but it's too far from everything and there are no cheap dorms.

Places to Eat

The *Ili Hotel* serves filling but unexciting set meals for Y2.70. Buy your meal ticket from the comatose staff at the front desk. Lunch is served around 2 pm.

Go out the main gate of the Ili Hotel, turn right and walk for half a block – there's a small, unnamed restaurant on the left. There's good and cheap food, but lots of hot peppers. If you don't want it hot, say '*búyào làjiāo*'.

Food markets can be interesting places to eat. There's one about 10 minutes' walk south-east of the bus station. Apart from the usual kebabs and flat-bread (nan), there's another type of kebab which is dipped in batter before roasting. When you try it, make sure that they use meat and not mutton fat or it will taste revolting.

On the main street close to the cinema are two food markets on opposite sides of the street, one catering for Chinese tastes, the other for the wild minority population. The Chinese sector does the usual meat and vegetable dishes. The wild side is almost medieval, with restaurant proprietors yelling at you over steaming cauldrons, while drunken customers roll around on benches and tables set outside. The staple foods seem to be mutton stew, kebab and flat-bread.

Getting There & Away

Air It's relatively easy to buy an air ticket from Ürümqi to Yining, but difficult or impossible to get a flight back. The one-way fare is Y176 and the flight takes 1½ hours. Flights run six days a week. If you're determined to fly back to Ürümqi, your best bet is to buy tickets through the hotels. You could also try CITS or go directly to the airport.

The CAAC office is one block west of the Ili Hotel in Yining, but the man in charge seems to be in a coma and the office is normally closed. A lot of foreigners have complained so perhaps things will change – someday.

Figure on spending at least three to four working days to buy an air ticket in Yining. Cancelled and delayed flights are the norm.

Bus Buses leave daily from Ürümqi at 9 am (Beijing summer time) and take two days to get to Yining. Departures from Yining are at 8 am during summer, and at 7 am the rest of the year. You may be able to pay in RMB in Yining. It's best to purchase tickets a day in advance. There are two bus stations in Yining – buses from one station do not stop at the other, so you must buy your ticket from the place from which you want to depart.

Buses run daily to Kashgar via Korla, Kuqa and Aksu. The full trip to Kashgar takes three days and the ticket costs Y93.

AROUND YINING

The large and beautiful **Sayram Lake** (*sàilǐmù hú*) is to the north of Yining. The bus between Ürümqi and Yining makes a 30-minute rest stop here. The bus from Yining to Sayram Lake takes slightly more than three hours.

If you would like to explore this alpine lake, it's possible to spend the night here, though very few travellers do this. The best place to stay is the *Gǔozigōu Zhāodàisuǒ*

where rooms are just Y3. There is one other hotel, the *Sàilǐmù Zhāodàisuǒ*, a terrible place that looks like it might collapse soon. There is food up here, but the selection is limited, so bring what you need.

It is possible to hire horses at the lake and go riding with the Kazakh shepherds. It costs about Y40 for a whole day, but be sure to bargain. The area presents some good hiking opportunities. The water from the lake is considered drinkable, but be careful about contamination around the shoreline from sheep.

VISITING THE EX-SOVIET UNION

In theory, it is possible to travel overland by bus from Yining to Panfilov in Kazakhstan, and then on to Alma Ata. At the time of writing this trip was possible, but prices were rising all the time. The latest standard charge at the time of writing was US$30 by bus to Panfilov and then another US$30 on to Alma Ata, a ridiculous state of affairs when you consider that buses do the trip from Ürümqi for US$48. All things considered, it's probably better to organise things in Ürümqi, where you're much less likely to get ripped off.

Local Kazakhs, Uigurs, Kirghiz, and others who have relatives on the other side of the border make this trip regularly and inexpensively. Previously it was necessary for foreigners making the same trip to have everything pre-booked with Intourist before setting off. Currently this is not the case (though the Russian embassy in Beijing won't tell you this if you inquire), and visas are available on the border. Accommodation in Alma Ata is reportedly very expensive, however.

Buses between Yining and Panfilov run daily from 1 May to 1 October via the border town of Korgas (*hùochéng*), or Khorgos in Russian. This road is actually open all year because of its low elevation, but winter storms could close it for a few days at a time. It's necessary to change buses in Panfilov to reach Alma Ata.

It may or may not be possible to spend the night in Panfilov, though the chances are that you will be forced to travel between Korgas and Alma Ata in one day. This is problematic because the border post is only open from 8.30 am to 4 pm. Crossing the other way into China should be no problem provided you have organised a Chinese visa beforehand, but at present this whole region is an unknown, with very few travellers making the trip. The Trans-Continental rail link between Moscow and Beijing via Ürümqi at least should be fairly straightforward.

One traveller has written in warning of problems with Chinese Customs after entering from Korgas: getting into China was no problem, but when he tried to exit in Shenzhen he was told that he had to return to Korgas and exit there. It took him two days of hassle in Shenzhen to get out of China. If you enter China via Korgas, try and make it clear to the Customs officials that you will not be exiting the country the same way: say the name of the place you plan to exit followed by ...*chūjìng*.

Inquire about the possibility of a crossing between Frunze (the capital of Kirghizstan)

and Kashgar, via Turugart Pass *(tǔ'ěrgǎtè shānkǒu)*. CITS have been quoting prohibitively high rates for doing the journey by car, but other options may become a possibility.

There are also flights (Y720, twice weekly) between Ürümqi and Alma Ata, run jointly by Aeroflot and CAAC. The Alma Ata CAAC office (☎ 330170 or 336956) is in the Otpar Hotel, Gao Erji St.

ALTAI
(ā'lètài) 阿勒泰
This town is near the northernmost tip of Xinjiang, close to the border. Just to the north of Altai is a stunning natural area with peaks over 4000 metres. It may be possible to visit this area now, but transport is reportedly a problem. Whatever the case, Altai itself is open to foreigners. CAAC has flights from Ürümqi four times weekly for Y151 – the flight takes 1½ hours. Since you cannot visit the mountains and forests at this time, it seems rather pointless to go to Altai. Again, we can only hope that things will change.

TIBET AND QINGHAI

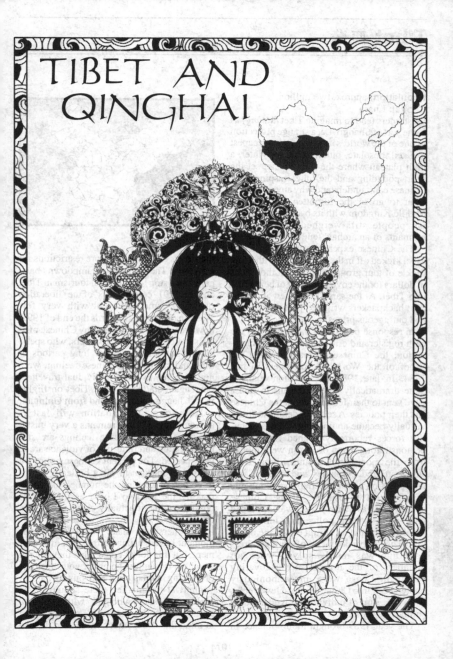

Tibet 西藏

Population: approx. two million
Capital: Lhasa

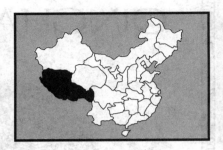

Westerners tend to imagine Tibet *(xīzàng)* as some sort of Shangri-La, a strange projection of one of the world's most barren landscapes: isolated, desolate, bitterly cold in winter, a high plateau where the thin air can set the heart pounding and the lungs rasping. The Chinese can't understand why anyone would want to go to the forgotten end of their Middle Kingdom with its backward, barbarian people still weighed down by the remnants of an archaic feudal culture.

The Chinese experiment with tourism in Tibet kicked off in the early 1980s with a tiny trickle of tour groups dishing out thousands of dollars for the coveted cachet of being first into Tibet. At the same time a few independent backpackers wriggled past the red tape and outrageous prices.

In response perhaps to the tinkling of the cash register and criticism of their administration, the Chinese officially opened the 'Roof of the World' to foreigners in late 1984. In late 1987 the situation changed quite dramatically when Tibetans in Lhasa gave vent to their feelings about the Chinese and their policies. A series of demonstrations virtually became an uprising. Chinese security forces reportedly opened fire on the demonstrators, many of whom were monks from the monasteries around Lhasa. Both sides suffered casualties and at least one police station was reduced to a smoking pile of rubble. The response of the Chinese authorities was swift; Lhasa was swamped with plain-clothes police and uniformed security, who put an abrupt end to the uprising. The embarrassment of foreign press coverage was neatly solved when all members of the foreign media covering events in Lhasa were unceremoniously booted back into China. Within a few weeks, it was the turn of individual travellers to be similarly ejected.

The year 1989 brought more violence in the streets of Lhasa and more restrictions for travellers. The following clampdowns basically put a stop to individual tourism in Tibet and the 1991 'celebrations' of the 'liberation of Tibet' came and went with very few Western observers. Towards the end of 1992, however, despite comments by Chinese officials indicating that backpackers, who spend very little money, stay for long periods of time and stir up anti-Chinese feeling, were not welcome in Tibet, individual travellers once again started to enter Tibet on flights from Chengdu and overland from Golmud.

How long this situation will last is anyone's guess. Tibet remains a very unstable region. Anti-Chinese feelings are still running high and flare-ups of violence are to be expected. The present Chinese policy on individual tourism in Tibet basically seems to be one of keeping the numbers down by making the road to Lhasa as difficult as possible, without actually closing the place off.

Travellers who make it into Tibet at the moment have reasonable freedom of movement, but this doesn't mean that they are not watched. If you just go about your business of visiting monasteries and buying jars of yoghurt at the market, there should be no problems. Visitors who go in with a political agenda are another matter. It's worth bearing in mind that Tibet (much more than the rest of China) is effectively a police state, and political discussions with local Tibetans can have serious consequences.

Despite its Chinese-run administration and the influx of foreign visitors, Tibet retains the fascination of a unique culture quite distinct from that of the Han Chinese. Since full-scale treatment of Tibetan regions would (and should!) take a whole book, Lonely Planet has done just that with its guide *Tibet – a travel survival kit.*

HISTORY

Recorded Tibetan history begins in the 7th century AD when the Tibetan armies were considered as great a scourge to their neighbours as the Huns were to Europe. Under King Songtsen Gampo the Tibetans occupied Nepal and collected tribute from parts of Yunnan Province. Shortly after the death of Gampo the armies moved north and took control of the Silk Road, including the great city of Kashgar. Opposed by Chinese troops, who occupied all of Xinjiang under the Tang Dynasty, the Tibetans responded by sacking the imperial city of Chang'an (present-day Xi'an). It was not until 842 that Tibetan expansion came to a sudden halt with the assassination of the king, and the region broke up into independent feuding principalities. Never again would the Tibetan armies leave their high plateau.

As secular authority waned, the power of the Buddhist clergy increased. When Buddhism reached Tibet in the 3rd century, it had to compete with Bon, the traditional animistic religion of the region. Buddhism adopted many of the rituals of Bon, like the flying of prayer flags and the turning of prayer wheels. These rituals combined with the esoteric practices of Tantric Buddhism (imported from India) to evolve into Tibetan Buddhism.

The religion had spread through Tibet by the 7th century; after the 9th century the monasteries became increasingly politicised, and in 1641 the Gelukpa (the Yellow Hat sect, a reformist movement advocating stringent monastic discipline) used the support of the Buddhist Mongols to crush the Red Hats, their rivals.

The Yellow Hats' leader adopted the title of Dalai Lama, or Ocean of Wisdom; religion and politics became inextricably entwined, presided over by the Dalai Lama – the god-king. Each Dalai Lama was considered the reincarnation of the last, upon whose death the monks searched the land for a newborn child who showed some sign of embodying his predecessor's spirit. The Yellow Hats won the Mongols to their cause by finding the fourth Dalai Lama in the family of the Mongol ruler. The Mongols, however, came to regard Tibet as their own domain and in 1705 ousted the Dalai Lama. Considered a threat to China, the Mongols were targeted by the Qing emperor Kangxi, who sent an expedition to Tibet to expel them. The Chinese left behind representatives to direct Tibetan foreign affairs, and for the next two centuries these Ambans (representatives) maintained a presence, but had scant control in the region.

With the fall of the Qing Dynasty in 1911 Tibet entered a period of independence that was to last until 1950. In that year the People's Liberation Army (PLA) entered the region and occupied eastern Tibet. The Dalai Lama sent a delegation to Beijing which reached an agreement with the Chinese that allowed the PLA to occupy the rest of Tibet but left the existing political, social and religious organisation intact. The agreement was to last until 1959. In that year a rebellion broke out. Just why it happened and how widespread it was depends on whether you believe the Chinese or the Tibetans – in any case the rebellion was suppressed by Chinese troops and the Dalai Lama and his retinue fled to India. Another 80,000 Tibetans crossed the high passes, enduring atrocious conditions to escape into India and Nepal.

Tibet became an 'autonomous' region of China. Over the next few years its political organisation was altered drastically.

China & Tibet

Tibetans and Chinese interpret the history of

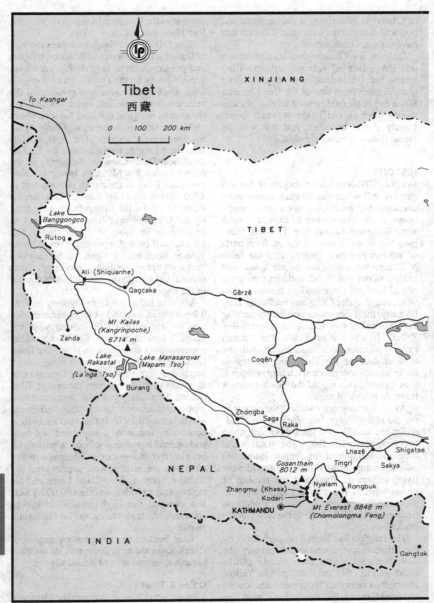

Tibet
西藏

0   100   200 km

To Kashgar

XINJIANG

TIBET

Lake Banggongco

Rutog

Ali (Shiquanhe)

Qagcaka

Gêrzê

Mt Kailas (Kangrinpoche) 6714 m

Coqên

Zanda

Lake Rakastal (La'nga Tso)

Lake Manasarovar (Mapam Tso)

Burang

Zhongba

Saga

Raka

Lhazê

Shigatse

NEPAL

Gosanthain 8012 m

Tingri

Sakya

Zhangmu (Khasa)

Kodari

Nyalam

Rongbuk

KATHMANDU

Mt Everest 8848 m (Chomolongma Feng)

INDIA

Gangtok

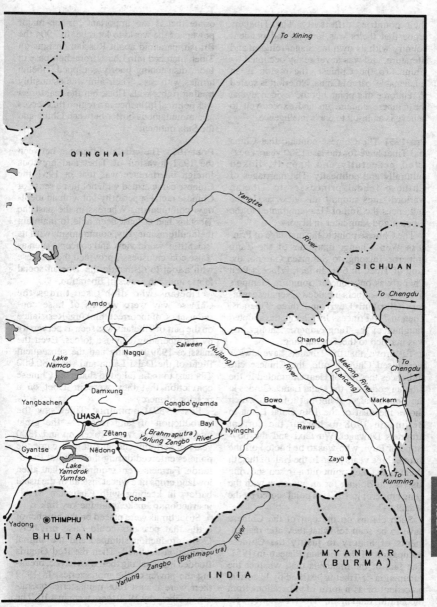

their countries differently. The Tibetans argue that theirs was long an independent country with its own language, religion and literature, and was never really occupied by China. To the Chinese, the region is an 'inalienable' part of China. No effort is spared to reinforce that point, but the 'evidence' that the Chinese conjure up and expect you to believe is an insult to one's intelligence.

Pre-1951 The Chinese contend that China and Tibet have for the last 1300 years coexisted peacefully and happily, linked culturally and politically. The marriages of Chinese feudal princesses to Tibetan warlord-kings support this view, as do the audiences the Son of Heaven granted to the Tibetan god-king later in history.

The Chinese point to the marriage of Princess Wen Cheng, daughter of the Tang emperor Taizong, to Songtsen Gampo, the king of Tibet, in 641. In fact, Princess Wen Cheng was only one of Songtsen Gampo's five wives – others included a Nepalese princess (Bhrikuti Devi) and three Tibetans. Then in 710 Princess Jin Cheng, the adopted daughter of the Tang emperor Zhongzong, was married to the Tibetan king.

To 'prove' that the Tibetans have always recognised Chinese rule, the Chinese cite audiences the Son of Heaven granted to the Tibetan god-king, the Dalai Lama. Guides in the Potala Palace point out a fresco which shows the visit of the 13th Dalai Lama to Beijing in 1908 to honour the corrupt Empress Dowager Wu Cixi and the boy-emperor Puyi, who was to be booted off the throne three years later. In the Hall of the 5th Dalai Lama they point out a fresco showing his visit to Beijing for an audience with the Qing emperor in 1652 – a point scored by the Manchus?

Such claims on the part of the Chinese have to be seen for what they are: realignments of history to justify the Chinese occupation of the Tibetan Plateau in 1951. The fact of the matter is that, whether the occupation of Tibet is justified by historical precedent or as a form of 'liberation' from theocratic feudalism, Tibet occupies real estate that is too important for the major powers of the world to let it be. In 1904 the British, paranoid about Russian designs on Tibet, marched into Lhasa from their base in India dispatching poorly equipped Tibetan armies with ease. Their aim was ostensibly trading rights with Tibet, but the real target was political influence in a region that serves as a mountainous buffer between China and the Subcontinent.

Post-1951 The crucial difference between the 1951 invasion of Tibet and previous foreign interference was that in 1951 the Chinese came armed with not just a sense of Chinese racial superiority but with an ideology: communism. Whereas in the past the Tibetans had at least been able to maintain their cultural integrity, communism, with its 'scientific' world view and concepts such as 'false consciousness', provided the Chinese with a tool to dismantle the Tibetan social fabric under the rules of liberation.

Tibetans who didn't see things the Chinese way were victims of false consciousness, of incorrect thinking. Resistance on the part of Tibetans was seen as perversity by the liberating Chinese forces. Even the massive 1959 uprising and the subsequent flight of the Dalai Lama and some 80,000 Tibetans to India failed to shake the Chinese conviction that they were in Tibet on a mission of mercy.

Post-1959 Communist Tibet saw the introduction of land reform – the great monastic estates were broken up and 1300 years of serfdom ended. But then came the policies enforced during the Cultural Revolution. Farmers were required to plant alien lowland crops like wheat instead of the usual barley, in keeping with Chairman Mao's instruction to 'make grain the key link'.

Strict limits were placed on the number of cattle that peasants could raise privately. Grain production slumped and the animal population declined. Then the Red Guards flooded in, wreaking their own havoc, breaking the power of the monasteries. In 1959 there were at least 1600 monasteries operating in Tibet – by 1979 there were just 10. The

Red Guards disbanded the monasteries and either executed the monks or sent them to work in fields or labour camps.

Although they built roads, schools and hospitals, the Chinese basically made a mess of Tibet – economically at least. Whether your average Tibetan peasant is any better off materially or any happier under the Chinese than under the former theocracy is a matter of opinion. Although the Chinese will never voluntarily relinquish control of Tibet regardless of who or what faction holds power in Beijing, the present regime in Beijing has at least taken steps over the last few years to improve the living conditions in Tibet and relations between the Tibetans and the Chinese.

The Maoist Communist Party chief in Tibet, General Ren Rong, was sacked in 1979. Most of the rural communes were disbanded and the land was returned to private farmers who were allowed to grow or graze whatever they wanted and to sell their produce in free markets. Taxes were reduced and state subsidies to the region increased. Some of the monasteries have been reopened on a limited basis, and the Chinese are wooing the Dalai Lama in the hope that he will return to Tibet. But as his status in the outside world continues to improve, it is becoming increasingly unlikely that he will return to accept what would most likely be an office job in Beijing with the effect of legitimising Chinese rule.

In 1985 the 'celebrations' marking the 20th anniversary of the Tibetan Autonomous Region (TAR) went off like a damp squib. Apart from banning the Western press from the event, the Chinese provided Lhasa with a tight military blanket, including sharp-shooters on the roof of the Potala Palace – the general picture looked more like a nervous show of strength than anything else.

Certainly a most acute problem for Tibet (as for Qinghai and Xinjiang) is a policy of stealthy resettlement: a massive influx of Han settlers from surrounding provinces threatens to oust Tibetans from employment, occupy arable land and swamp the Tibetan culture with that of the Han Chinese. A large part of what's going on is hidden from world view – most reports come through the eyes and ears of Tibetan refugees, who speak of forced abortion and sterilisation.

TIBET TODAY

Since 1987 Tibetans in Lhasa have given vent to their frustrations in a series of anti-Chinese demonstrations that have resulted in untold violence. The Chinese attempt to eradicate a feudal culture and integrate the Tibetan people into the Chinese Motherland has for the most part been a dismal failure, with the Chinese achieving very few converts to their cause.

Despite Chinese efforts to paint a rosy picture of life on the roof of the world, the general feeling, most visitors agree, is of a country under occupation. The Dalai Lama continues to be worshipped by his people, and his acceptance in late 1989 of the Nobel Peace Prize marked a greater sympathy on the part of the Western world for the plight of the Tibetan people.

At present it seems that Tibet's greatest hope lies in the untiring efforts of the Dalai Lama to make world leaders and the public aware of the condition of his country. At the same time, as religious freedoms return to Tibet, the greatest threat to the country comes from continued 'population transfer' from China to Tibet, a policy that the Dalai Lama himself has referred to as 'cultural genocide' for the Tibetan people.

Unfortunately, China's great potential as a trading nation and as a market for Western goods makes many world leaders wary of raising the Tibet issue with China. One can only hope that both Western and Eastern governments come to the realisation that Chinese economic progress can only continue with outside assistance and that foreign pressure might in fact go some way to making Tibet a truly autonomous region.

GEOGRAPHY

Most of Tibet is an immense plateau which lies at an altitude from 4000 to 5000 metres. It's a desolate region broken by a series of east-west mountain ranges, and is completely barren except for some poor grasslands to the south-east. The plateau is bounded to the north by the Kunlunshan range which separates Tibet from Xinjiang Province, and to the south by the Himalayas and their peaks rising over 7000 metres.

The Qamdo region of Tibet in the east is a somewhat lower section of plateau, drained by the headwaters of the Salween, Mekong and Upper Yangzi rivers. It's an area of considerably greater rainfall than the rest of Tibet and the climate is less extreme. In a number of valleys in the south of the country some agriculture (such as growing the country's main crop, barley) is possible – most of the Tibetan population lives in this area. On the uplands surrounding these valleys the inhabitants are mainly pastoralists, raising sheep, yaks and horses.

CLIMATE

The climate in Tibet (and neighbouring Qinghai) sometimes gives the impression that all four seasons have been compressed into one day. In general, summer temperatures are pleasantly warm at midday and drop dramatically in the shade and at night. Winter brings intense cold and fierce winds, although Lhasa sees little snow. The best time to travel is between May and September.

In southern and eastern Tibet, the Himalayas act as a barrier against the rain-bearing monsoons, and rainfall decreases as you travel north. The central region of Tibet sees only 25 to 50 cm of rain a year (Sikkim, by contrast, sees some 500 cm). Snowfall is far less common in Tibet than the name 'Land of Snows' implies. The sun is quick to melt off snowfalls.

Temperatures can vary from below zero during the early morning and evening to a sizzling 38°C at midday. In the north and west of Tibet rainfall becomes even scarcer, but fewer than 100 days in the year are frost-free and temperatures plummet as low as -40°C. Northern monsoons can sweep across the plains for days on end, often whipping up dust storms, sandstorms, snowstorms, or (rare) rainstorms. In the summer, the snow line in the north and east lies between 5000 and 6000 metres; in the south it's even higher, at 6000 metres.

POPULATION

Tibet's population includes Tibetans as well as increasing numbers of Han Chinese settlers and PLA soldiers. Recent Chinese government figures put the total population of Tibet at around 1,900,000, but with the Chinese Government remaining coy about its policy of swamping Tibetan culture through emigration to the Tibetan Plateau such figures should be taken with a grain of

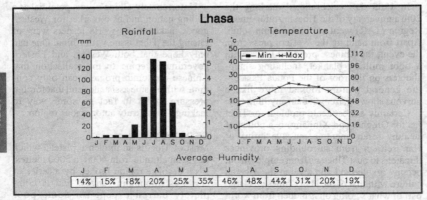

salt. The large influx of Han Chinese settlers is likely to have swollen the actual population of Tibet considerably. Recent reports have also indicated that Han Chinese settlers in Tibet are exempt from the one-child policy, thus promoting a more rapid Sinicisation of the plateau.

There are thought to be some 3,900,000 Tibetans spread out over Tibet, Qinghai, Sichuan, Gansu and Yunnan.

LANGUAGE

Although many Tibetans in the cities have a rudimentary command of Chinese, they are pleased (and try hard not to crack up!) when you make an effort to speak in Tibetan. Out on the desolate plateau, you'll have to use Tibetan. In either case, you might be able to save your bacon with a Tibetan phrasebook such as the Lonely Planet one.

Tibetan Mini-Glossary

The following are some phrases that you might find useful:

hello
　tashi delag
thank you
　thuk ji chay
how are you?
　kuzak de po yinpe?
how much?
　di gatse ray
it's very good
　shidak yak po dhuk
cheers!
　tamdil!

WHAT TO BRING

Department stores in Xining, Golmud and Lhasa have quite a wide selection of warm clothing, but their stock fluctuates so you can't rely on them entirely. Keep the cold at bay with a down jacket, woollen sweater, long underwear, woollen socks, gloves and woolly hat. Protect yourself against the sun with lip salve, sunscreen, sunglasses and something to cover your head.

Trekking is not officially approved in Tibet, but it is feasible for the experienced walker providing you are prepared to be self-sufficient in food, fuel and shelter. Bring equipment suitable for sub-zero temperatures, such as a high-quality down sleeping bag, thermal underwear, ground mat, four-season tent, stove and fuel. (Remember that gas canisters and bottles of methylated spirits may not be welcome on planes.)

The food situation in Lhasa continues to improve, but it's still advisable to bring in any special foods or supplies – if you intend to trek, you'll appreciate the variety.

HEALTH
Acute Mountain Sickness

Most visitors to Tibet and Qinghai – both high-altitude regions with thin air – will suffer some symptoms of Acute Mountain Sickness (AMS). Until your body has become acclimatised to the lack of oxygen you may experience temporary symptoms such as headaches, sleeping difficulties, nausea and dizziness. If any of these persist or worsen, you should immediately descend to a lower altitude and seek medical help. It's rare for AMS to turn really nasty in Lhasa, but if it does, you should check with one of the hospitals there and consider a flight to Chengdu. Certainly, if you intend to do some

Tibetan monk

trekking or mountaineering at higher altitudes, you owe it to yourself to thoroughly understand AMS.

To prepare yourself for higher altitudes, spend the first few days taking your exercise slowly. Drink plenty of liquids (keep your urine a nice pale colour!) to avoid dehydration. Alcohol, tobacco and sedatives are best avoided.

Of the many books available on this subject, *Mountain Sickness: Prevention, Recognition & Treatment* by Peter Hackett (The American Alpine Club) is among the best. If you have any doubts about your health, consult your doctor before you go.

There's no call for instant alarm, but you should not ignore AMS. We met a 65-year-old American with a pacemaker who had taken the bus from Golmud and was happily strolling the streets of Lhasa. On the other hand, the Chinese PSB has reported several foreigners dying from a combination of AMS, cold (hypothermia) and exposure. Oxygen is available at Lhasa tourist hotels – some tourists even carry their own oxygen bags in the streets!

Giardiasis

A nasty stomach bug called *Giardia* has travelled from Nepal to Lhasa, where it treks the intestinal paths of unfortunate foreigners – the locals seem immune. Check with your doctor on the pros and cons of anti-giardiasis drugs such as Tiniba or Flagyl, and take some with you, because they are hard to find in Lhasa. Some of the most poignant notices in Lhasa are those by foreigners urgently seeking these magical medicines – two such foreigners in constant search of relief received the nickname of 'flagylantes'.

Colds

Coughs and colds are common among foreigners, and everyone in Tibet has a runny nose. Keep yourself well supplied with favourite remedies, vitamins and warm clothes. To beat the cold and (most importantly) the dust, join the parade of people wearing surgical or industrial face-masks – the main street in Lhasa sometimes looks like a scene from the movie *M*A*S*H*.

DANGERS & ANNOYANCES

Theft

In Tibet, there has been an increase in theft from foreigners. In Xining, a nimble-fingered gang of pickpockets rides the buses. Sneak thieves operate on the train between Golmud and Xining. In Lhasa, the favourite venues for pickpocketing are the bus station, post office, Barkhor market and hotels. Lhasa also has a chronic problem with bike theft.

Cable locks, sold in most cities in China, are useful for bikes and to secure gear on a train. Moneybelts are essential. If something is stolen, you should obtain a loss report from the nearest PSB, though they may refuse to include details of cash on the loss report.

In the past, several foreigners trekking in the Everest base camp region have reported thefts. Apparently local villagers or nomads who possess very little find the temptation of foreign goodies too great.

Dogs

A word of warning about the dogs which roam in packs around monasteries and towns. Several foreigners have been badly bitten, and we have heard reports of rabies. Keep your distance during the day, and watch your step in the dark. One French visitor got into the habit of detonating Chinese bangers to send the hounds packing!

FOOD

The staple diet in Tibet consists of *tsampa* (roasted barley meal) and butter tea. *Momo* (dumplings filled with meat) and *thukpa* (noodles with meat) are usually available at small restaurants. Tibetans consume large quantities of *chang*, a tangy alcoholic drink made from fermented barley.

Most of the larger towns have restaurants serving Chinese or Muslim dishes. Western foods feature on the menus of some hotels and restaurants catering to backpackers in Lhasa.

Outside the towns you should carry your

own supply of food, since what little is available is often highly priced and poor quality. When entering from Nepal, it's wise to bring food for the journey to Lhasa.

GETTING THERE & AWAY
There is a serious shortage of transport in these regions, and drivers enjoy high status. The three main types of vehicle are bus, truck and 4WD. On some routes there are modern Japanese buses; other routes are covered by battered wrecks which gasp over each high pass as if it's their last. Trucks are often more comfortable, more fun and faster than the bus. Landcruisers are the chariots of the cadres and those foreigners who can afford CITS rates.

Bus prices in Tibet have been doubled, or in some cases trebled, for foreigners. This price hike could be considered acceptable for deluxe buses, but not for the old bangers. Trucks tend to charge the same as buses, but the Chinese government has moved to stop foreigners from hitching on trucks by threatening the drivers with fines or confiscation of their vehicle. (See the Lhasa section for information on 4WD hire.)

In both Tibet and Qinghai, your safety is entirely at the mercy of the vehicle, the driver and the condition of the road surface. Tibetans take their minds off these variables by praying, and you'd be wise to do likewise unless you want to end up a gibbering bag of nerves. Road accidents are frequent and foreigners have been injured or killed in the past.

During the heyday of individual travel, many foreigners introduced their own means of transport. Small groups of mountain bikers commuted along the road between Lhasa and Kathmandu, stopping at the tops of passes to pose for heroic photos among the prayer flags. Although the Chinese border officials do not particularly approve of such activities, a trickle of cyclists and even motorbike riders are again taking to the roads of Tibet, mainly coming up from Kathmandu. Three Swiss riders made it all the way from Kathmandu to Chengdu on BMW bikes before being ordered off the road by the authorities in April 1993.

Tours
Several agencies in Kathmandu and Chengdu (in Sichuan) arrange group tours to Lhasa and Shigatse only. There are no minimum numbers of members required for the tours, but naturally the more of you there are the cheaper it ends up per head. Chengdu CITS were charging Y5420 for one person and Y3370 for 10 or more for a three-day tour with accommodation at the Holiday Inn Hotel in Lhasa. A five-night, six-day tour will set you back Y8400 for one or Y4300 for 10 or more people. You can beat these prices by 25% to 50% at other agencies in Chengdu, but the reality is that these cheaper tours usually advertise more days in the itinerary than you actually end up with or in some other way sell you short.

By mid-'93 the Chinese embassy in Kathmandu was making it as difficult as possible to travel overland to Lhasa. One reliable tour agency with once-weekly departures for an eight-day tour to Lhasa is Arnika (☎ 414594). Tours cost US$900 per person.

LHASA
(lāsà) 拉萨
Lhasa has long been the capital of Tibet and remains the political centre, the most important city and the showpiece of the region. It lies a mere 3683 metres above sea level.

Lhasa is actually two cities: one Chinese and one Tibetan. The Chinese part is the larger and is made up of the same sort of architecture that you see in eastern China. The lively Tibetan side is a ramshackle, scungy place, full of winding streets where the smell of yak butter permeates the air. Towering above the city and encircled by the ugly Chinese blockhouses is the Potala Palace. The other orientation point is the Jokhang Temple, which forms the nucleus of the Tibetan part of town.

Information
As usual, you can forget about calling on CITS for any useful information – rustling up a map strains at the limits of this outfit's

TIBET

Lhasa
拉薩

0   0.5   1 km

To Drapchi &
Sangyip Prisons
(Political Detainees)

To Ganden &
Chamdo (Tsiamdo)

To Lhünzub

To Sera Monastery

To Drepung
& Nechung
Monasteries

To Doilungdêqên &
Gonggar Airport

Lhasa River (Kyi Chu)

Linkuo Beilu

Jiefang Beilu

Tuanjie Lu

Beijing Dongxu

Qingnian Lu

Renmin Lu

Jinzhu Donglu

Duosen Gelu

Beijing Xilu

Minzu Lu

Nordulingka Lu

■ PLACES TO STAY

2   Tibet Hotel
5   Lhasa Holiday Inn
22 Yak Hotel
23 Snowlands Hotel
27 Kirey Hotel
28 Banak Shol Hotel
29 Plateau Hotel
31 Himalaya Hotel

▼ PLACES TO EAT

11 Good Jmells Restaurant
20 Tashi's Restaurant
24 Barkhor Cafe

OTHER

1   Zoo
3   Norbu Lingke
4   Nepalese Consulate
6   CITS
7   Bus Station
8   Bank of China
9   Yak Statue
10 Transmitter Mast
12 Potala Palace
13 CAAC
14 Exhibition Hall
15 Post Office &
    Telecommunications
16 Worker's Cultural Palace
17 Xinhua Bookstore
18 Bus Ticket Office
19 Minibus Stand
21 Lilac Bar
25 Ganden Bus Tickets
26 Jokhang Temple
30 PSB
32 Tibet University

■ PLACES TO STAY

2	西藏宾馆
5	拉萨饭店
22	亚客旅社
23	雪城旅馆
27	吉日旅社
28	八郎学旅社
29	高原旅馆
31	喜玛拉亚宾馆

▼ PLACES TO EAT

11	好味菜馆
20	咖啡馆
24	八廓咖啡馆

OTHER

1	动物园
3	罗布杯卡
4	尼泊尔大使馆
6	中国国际旅行社
7	汽车站
8	中国银行
9	毛牛像
10	电视台
12	布达拉宫
13	中国民航
14	展览馆
15	邮电局
16	劳动人民文化宫
17	新华书店
18	汽车售票处
19	小型车站
21	咖啡馆
25	汽车售票处
26	大昭寺
30	公安局
32	西藏大学

organisational abilities. The best place for the latest on Tibetan individual travel these days is the Yak Hotel or a table in Tashi's Restaurant.

For information or permits relating to trekking or mountaineering, visit the Mountaineering Association at No 8 Linkuo Donglu next to the Himalaya Hotel. The office is on the 2nd floor.

CITS If you're really set on wasting your time here, CITS have an office opposite the Holiday Inn.

PSB There are two offices – one behind the Potala and the other on Linkuo Lu in the direction of Sera Monastery – and they are open Monday to Saturday from 10 am to 1 pm and 4 to 6.30 pm. They are closed on Sunday (though there is always someone on duty to deal with emergencies). The Linkuo Lu branch is the place to do your business. The other gets consistently bad reports, with one unfortunate traveller being given a choice between a Y1000 FEC fine or a jail sentence for having the impudence to waltz in and request a visa extension.

Nepalese Consulate-General The consulate (☎ 22880) is at 13 Norbulingka Lu. Visa-issuing hours are Monday to Saturday, from 9.30 am to 12.30 pm. An exit stamp from the PSB is no longer required. The visa fee is a standard Y125, even if you're blonde and Scandinavian. Bring along the cash with your passport and one photo, and the visa should be ready in a day. The one-month visa is valid for entry within three months.

Some travellers have obtained Nepalese visas on the border at Kodari.

Money The Bank of China is close to the PSB, just behind the Potala. Hours are from 10 am to 1.30 pm and from 4 to 6.30 pm, Monday to Saturday. It's closed on Sunday. Look out for the cryptically subversive sign inside: 'Question authority'. There is a second Bank of China that can handle travellers' cheques between the Kirey and Banak Shol Hotels. The main branch can arrange credit card advances.

The Lhasa Holiday Inn is unobliging about serving those who are not staying at the hotel. Out on the streets, black-market rates for FEC and US dollars are generally very good.

Maps Lhasa maps are available in either Chinese or Tibetan but not in English from Xinhua Bookstore, which has a branch in the centre of town. The Yak Hotel also sells a map put together by a long-term foreign resident for Y1. It's a little out of date, but worth picking up for its exhaustive listings around town.

Medical Services Several hospitals in Lhasa treat foreigners. The Tibetan Autonomous Region People's Hospital and the Regional Military Hospital have been recommended. The Lhasa Holiday Inn may be able to refer you to a doctor at the hotel.

Potala Palace
(bùdǎlā gōng) 布达拉宫

The most imposing attraction of Lhasa is the Potala, once the centre of the Tibetan government and the winter residence of the Dalai Lama. One of the architectural wonders of the world, this immense construction has thousands of rooms, shrines and statues. It dates from the 17th century but is on the site of a former structure built a thousand years earlier. Each day a stream of pilgrims files through this religious maze while chanting, prostrating themselves and offering *khata* (ceremonial scarves) or yak butter.

The general layout of the Potala includes a Red Palace for religious functions and a White Palace for the living quarters of the Dalai Lama. The Red Palace contains many halls and chapels – the most stunning chapels house the jewel-bedecked tombs of previous Dalai Lamas. The apartments of the 13th and 14th Dalai Lamas in the White Palace offer an insight into the high life. The roof has marvellous views, if the monks will let you go there.

The Potala is open Monday and Thursday from 9 am to noon only. Foreigners pay a hefty Y25 admission or engage in a lengthy discussion with the door-keepers about how they misplaced their student card and should only be paying Y8 – it usually works. The long climb to the entrance is not recommended on your first day in town – do something relaxing at ground level. Remember, photography is not officially allowed.

Jokhang Temple
(dàzhāo sì) 大昭寺

The golden-roofed Jokhang is 1300 years old and one of Tibet's holiest shrines. It was built to commemorate the marriage of the Tang princess Wen Cheng to King Songtsen Gampo, and houses a pure gold statue of the Buddha Sakyamuni brought to Tibet by the princess. Here too, pilgrims in their hundreds prostrate themselves in front of the temple entrance before continuing on their circuit. Follow the pilgrims through a labyrinth of shrines, halls and galleries containing some of the finest and oldest treasures of Tibetan art. Some were destroyed during the Cultural Revolution and have been replaced with duplicates. Take a torch if you want a closer look, and avoid getting lost by copying the nomad kids and hanging onto the tresses of the pilgrim in front.

Goddess, Guardian of the Law, Jokhang Temple

TIBET

The Jokhang is best visited early in the morning; you may not be allowed to enter after 11 am. Whatever you do, be considerate to the pilgrims and respect the sacred nature of these places.

Barkhor

The Barkhor is essentially a pilgrim circuit which is followed clockwise round the periphery of the Jokhang. It is also a hive of market activity, an astounding jamboree, a Tibetan-style stock exchange. All round the circuit are shops, stalls, teahouses and hawkers. There's a wide variety of items to gladden a Tibetan heart – prayer flags, block prints of the holy scriptures, earrings, Tibetan boots, Nepalese biscuits, puffed rice, yak butter and incense.

It's worth making several visits here to see the people who roll up from remote parts of Tibet: Khambas from eastern Tibet braid their hair with red yarn and stride around with ornate swords or daggers; Goloks (Tibetan nomads) from the north wear ragged sheepskins, and the women display incredibly ornate hairbands down their backs.

Whether you buy from a shop or a hawker, many of the Tibetan goods on sale have been imported from Nepal and you are most unlikely to find genuine antiques. The prices asked from foreigners have reached absurd heights. Whatever the starting price, be it in RMB or FEC, expect to halve it. Much of the 'turquoise' in the market is, in fact, a paste of ground turquoise and cement – some keen buyers bite the stones and reject them if the teeth leave white scratch marks. Also, bear in mind that Chinese Customs can confiscate antiques (anything made before 1959) if they think you are carrying out 'too much'.

Norbu Lingka

(luóbù línkǎ) 罗布林卡

About three km west of the Potala is the Norbu Lingka, which used to be the summer residence of the Dalai Lama. The pleasant park contains small palaces, chapels and a zoo. For Y2 you can join pilgrims on a tour of the New Palace, built by the 14th Dalai Lama in 1956, which contains vivid murals. The gardens are a favourite spot for picnics.

Exhibition Hall

At the foot of the Potala is the Exhibition Hall, open from 9 am to 4 pm on Monday, Thursday and Sunday only. The historical exhibition has some interesting photos, but draws predictable conclusions about China and Tibet. The rooms devoted to Tibetan ethnography, monastic life, handicrafts and daily life are well worth a visit. It's fun to observe the reaction of nomads on a pilgrimage to Lhasa when they see the exhibition of nomad life. Most of them get a giggle out of seeing their home in a museum – complete with stuffed dog.

Yak Statue

This is not a sight to seek out, but you'll probably wander past the pair of bronze yaks set in the middle of the road just down from the Potala and wonder how they came to be there. They were actually erected in 'celebration' of the 1991 anniversary of the Chinese takeover ('liberation' in China-speak). They have slightly more appeal than your average Mao statue, and that's about the most that can be said for them.

Places to Stay – bottom end

With individual travellers once again thumbing their noses at CITS-sponsored tours and making their own way to Tibet, all the old travellers' stand-bys are doing good business again.

The most popular nowadays is the *Yak Hotel* (*yǎ lǚshè*). It doesn't provide views of the Jokhang like Snowlands does, but it's the best place to catch up with the latest gossip, and the sofas on the verandas are as good a place as any to while away a couple of days doing nothing. The hotel has dorm beds from Y10 and beds in doubles from Y15 to Y60. Check out the beautiful Tibetan style Y30-per-bed doubles if you've got an extra few yuan in your wallet. Hot water is intermittent – keep an ear to the ground. The Yak has a good information board and provides bicycles for hire.

TIBET

Snowlands Hotel (☎ 23687) *(xuěyù lǚguǎn)*, close to the Jokhang Temple, is a friendly place – it was a legend during the days of 'unorganised' travel – with rooms arranged around a courtyard. Beds cost Y10. Ask at reception about luggage storage and bike hire.

The *Banak Shol* (☎ 23829) *(bālángxuě lǚshè)* is on Beijing Donglu near the Barkhor. For reasons that remain mysterious it has slipped from its star status as *the* place to hang out in Lhasa, and it's rare nowadays to bump into a traveller staying here. Despite this, it remains a friendly hotel with a good location. Doubles cost Y22; a bed in a dorm costs Y10. There are showers and luggage storage, and bike hire can be arranged.

The *Kirey Hotel (jírì lǚguǎn)*, close to the Banak Shol, charges from Y8 for dorm beds. Doubles start at Y15 per person. It has great showers and super-friendly staff – all it lacks is atmosphere, and this is no doubt what keeps the crowds at bay.

Inconveniently located down Linkuo Lu is the *Himalaya Hotel (xīmǎlāyǎ fàndiàn)* with doubles for Y60. It's a fairly dull attempt at a mid-range Tibetan-style hotel, and the staff seem suspicious of everyone who comes through the door.

If you scout around town, it is possible to find the kind of Chinese-style accommodation you've become accustomed to elsewhere on your trip, but that's not what people come all the way to Tibet...is it?

Places to Stay – top end

The *Lhasa Holiday Inn* (☎ 32221) *(lāsà fàndiàn)* is the lap of Lhasa luxury and boasts 468 guest rooms. Doubles start at US$55 per room, and triples are US$75. Suites and Tibetan-style rooms are also available, the latter coming in at US$111. Rates are raised by 20% for the busy month of August. During the quieter winter months from 1 November to 31 March there are substantial discounts available that make the triples in particular a good deal if you want to rest up after a hard trip. The facilities include Chinese and Western restaurants, a coffee shop and souvenir shops. A free shuttle

service using minibuses operates between the hotel and the Barkhor. The transport desk arranges day trips to Drepung, Sera or Ganden monasteries (prices range between Y20 and Y100 per person). If you want to hire a taxi, 4WD, minibus or bus, inquire at the transport desk.

The *Tibet Hotel (xīzàng bīnguǎn)* is a few hundred metres up the road from the Lhasa Holiday Inn. Built in mock-Tibetan style, it showed signs of dilapidation within a few months of opening but is still hanging in there. It's more popular with Chinese businesspeople and tour groups than with the foreign set, but the rooms are not bad and offer reasonably good value for money. Doubles start at US$38 in the high season, but like the Holiday Inn the management is open to a little haggling during the low-occupancy winter months.

Places to Eat

Food can be mighty scarce out on the high plateau, but Lhasa offers Chinese, Western, Tibetan and even some Nepalese cuisine.

Indisputably No 1 on the backpackers' dining circuit at present is *Tashi's Restaurant*, just up the road from Snowlands on the corner of Beijing Lu. It's a dingy little establishment that allows you to rub knees with every other foreigner who happens to be in town. The menu consists of bobis, thukpa, momos and cheesecake (pick the odd one out). The back room is for the long-termers – a couple of months in the mountains without a wash and you should earn yourself a place on the back room Tibetan independence debating team.

Apart from Tashi's, where do the travellers go to eat? Nowhere. It's a curious situation, but you're in no way bound to fall into step with the marching orders of backpacker fashion. Snowlands has a very decent pick-and-choose restaurant, but you need to be there early if you want anything to eat. Up the road from the Yak Hotel in the direction of the Potala is the *Lilac Bar*, where they cudgel diners' eardrums with Chinese pop and serve a semi-decent plate of greasy chips. The Banak Shol Restaurant, a travellers' favourite back in the old days of independent travel, is still going under the moniker *Kailash Restaurant*. It's run by a friendly old Tibetan guy, and the food is consistently good. Alternatively, Lhasa also abounds with very good Chinese-style restaurants, an ideologically unsound cuisine in the eyes of many, but good all the same.

One other place that enjoys a trickle of Western patronage is the Nepalese *Good Jmells* (the sign painter had problems with the initial 's' required in the standard English spelling of the word 'smells'). Popular wisdom has it that the only decent thing on the menu is the garlic chicken at Y15. We can't comment on the authority of this piece of folklore, as we went with 17 other foreigners, all of whom ordered garlic chicken. You can take it from us that 18 orders of garlic chicken take quite a long time to prepare.

Finally, for the truly famished and financially solvent, there's a smorgasbord of gastronomical delights at the Holiday Inn. The *Hard Yak Cafe* has yak burgers with French fries at Y34 (30% extra if you pay in RMB) and chocolate mousse and apple strüdel for dessert. The percolated coffee is good too at Y10 including refills. The *Gya Sey Kang* has Sichuan cuisine and the *Himalayan Restaurant* provides Indian meals. The Gya Sey Kang has a breakfast buffet that at Y52 definitely doesn't deliver the goods – you'd be better off spending Y2 for a couple of boiled eggs and a jar of yoghurt at Tashi's.

Getting There & Away

Air Lhasa is not really connected with anywhere in China except Chengdu, a mysterious state of affairs given that China's air links have been expanding so rapidly. The one exception is a once-weekly (Sunday) direct flight to Beijing at Y1690. Chengdu flights leave twice a day at 8 and 8.30 am (figure that one out) and cost Y990. Buses out to the airport leave at 4.30 pm the previous afternoon, providing a major source of revenue for the airport hotel. Flights for Kathmandu operate on Tuesday and Saturday and cost US$190.

The CAAC office (☎ 22417) at 88 Jiefang Lu is fairly well organised, and getting flights at short notice is generally no problem.

Bus The bus station is a deserted monstrosity four km out of town, near the Norbu Lingka. Foreigners are charged double the local price. Buy your tickets several days in advance and roll up early. Alternatively, buy your tickets at the ticket office a few doors down from the Xinhua Bookstore. You definitely won't get a local price ticket here, but it will save you a long trudge.

Beware of well-dressed pickpockets operating around the buses, particularly in the early morning. They push up close, pretending to join the scrum to get on the bus, but instead they pickpocket at lightning speed.

There are daily departures in the early morning for Gyantse (Y53), Shigatse (Y70), Zêtang (Y36.40) and Golmud (Y187). The schedule for buses to Zhangmu (Y155) is a bit hit and miss. There should be a weekly service on Saturday; failing this, buses run every 10 days.

The tickets sold to foreigners at the bus station are foreigner's tickets, and if that's what you paid for you should check that you have actually been issued a foreigner's ticket. There have been reports of bus station staff pocketing the FEC and issuing a Chinese ticket. This can create problems when you board the bus, and is also a problem if you want a refund.

Road Routes Although there are five major road routes to Lhasa, foreigners are officially allowed to use only the Nepal and Qinghai routes.

Nepal Route The road connecting Lhasa with Nepal is officially called the Friendship Highway and runs from Lhasa to Zhangmu (the Chinese border post) via Gyantse and Shigatse. It's a spectacular trip over high passes and across the plateau. If the weather's good, you'll get a fine view of Mt Everest from the Tibetan village of Tingri. From Zhangmu, it's 11 km to the Nepalese border post at Kodari, which has transport connections to Kathmandu.

Accommodation en route is generally fairly basic, but prices are usually reasonable, and as long as you don't mind doing without luxuries like a shower for the duration of your trip there's no great hardship involved. The food situation has also improved greatly in recent years, though it tends to be expensive. It's still a good idea to bring some instant noodles along with you. Warm clothing is an essential.

Very few people do the Nepal trip by local bus nowadays, mainly because you have no control over your itinerary this way. By far the most popular option is renting a 4WD through the Yak Hotel and sorting out a private itinerary with the driver. A popular option is a seven- to eight-day jaunt taking in Gyantse, Shigatse, Sakya, the Everest base camp, Tingri and on to the border. Prices are very reasonable – reckon on around Y700 to Y1000 RMB per person for the 4WD.

The Yak Hotel operation is a reliable option and you can generally trust your driver to hold to a spoken agreement. If you go for one of the other operators in town, it would probably be a good idea to get everything down in writing. Check with the people at the Yak for the latest on permit requirements. At the time of writing, only the Everest base camp required a permit for the above itinerary.

Travelling from Nepal to Lhasa, the only transport for foreigners is arranged through tour agencies. If you already have a Chinese visa, you can try turning up at the border. The occasional traveller slips through (even a couple on bicycles). At Zhangmu (Khasa) you can hunt around for buses, minibuses, 4WDs or trucks heading towards Lhasa.

Qinghai Route An asphalted road connects Xining with Lhasa via Golmud; it crosses the desolate, barren and virtually uninhabited Tibetan Plateau. Theoretically, both Japanese and local Chinese buses do the run, the former including an overnight stop at Amdo. In practice, however, the Japanese buses are often not available and a Chinese bus is the only option. Whatever you do, do not succumb to the blandishments of CITS in Golmud and hire one of their minibuses for the trip. These invariably break down, and if this happens you're likely to be stranded in the middle of nowhere, a far worse scenario than 30-odd hours on a Chinese bus. CITS are not in the habit of recompensing inconvenienced (or dead) travellers either.

Reckon on around 35 hours from Golmud to Lhasa by bus. Chinese buses cost Y470 (three times the local price!) and Japanese buses, when they're available, cost Y520. Paying in RMB is generally no problem if you do things yourself at the bus station and avoid the rapacious Mr Hou at Golmud CITS.

Take warm clothing and food on the bus, since baggage is not accessible during the trip.

Other Routes Between Lhasa and Sichuan, Yunnan or Xinjiang provinces are some of the wildest, highest and most dangerous routes in the world; they are not open to foreigners. If you do travel along them, don't underestimate the physical dangers – take food and warm clothing. The PSB tends to fine those heading into Tibet, but travel in the opposite direction is controlled less. Travel on these routes usually takes several weeks of hitching on trucks, which have a high accident rate. Lonely Planet's *Tibet – a travel survival kit* describes these routes in detail.

Getting Around

To/From the Airport Gonggar Airport is a good two hours by bus from Lhasa, and as all flights leave early in the morning most travellers are forced to take an afternoon bus out to the airport and stay overnight. There is no public transport available from Lhasa that connects with flights to Chengdu or Beijing. CAAC buses leave from the CAAC office every 20 minutes or so between 2.30 and 4.30 pm and cost Y19. The only alternative to this is to hire a 4WD at the Yak Hotel – which works out at around Y50 to Y60 per head if there are five of you – and leave early in the morning.

CAAC buses stop at the official CAAC Hotel, which costs Y40 for a bed in a basic triple or Y50 in a double. Opposite the hotel is the Karaoke Cafe, which is a friendly, if a little grubby, place with four-bed dorms for Y15. There are also doubles ranging from Y20 to Y75. The restaurant here has a bad reputation for ripping travellers off and serving up inedible food. Opposite the check-in area is another small hotel with cardboard boxes for Y15. Nobody has a good word for food out at the airport. Airport tax is Y15 for internal flights, Y60 for flights to Kathmandu.

Other Most of Lhasa can be explored on foot, but for longer excursions bicycle is an excellent way to get around. The Yak Hotel has bicycle hire for Y6 per day. Look for the notice warning travellers about the prevalence of bicycle theft in Lhasa. It's a good idea to have your own lock and chain.

Rickshaws are common in Lhasa, and most trips cost between Y2 and Y3. For trips out to nearby monasteries, there are minibuses. Many travellers end up hitching a ride with tractors for a couple of yuan for places like Sera Monastery.

AROUND LHASA
Monasteries

Prior to 1959, Lhasa had three monasteries which functioned as 'pillars of the Tibetan state'. As part of a concerted effort to smash the influence of these, the Cultural Revolution wiped out the monastic population, which once numbered thousands. The buildings of Ganden Monastery were shelled and demolished. Today, buildings are being reconstructed, and even if Chinese motives in all this are centred more on the tourist dollar than on any notions of religious freedom and making amends for past wrongs it is still gratifying to see that the monasteries are starting to come to life again, although nowhere near the scale on which they once operated.

Drepung (*zhébàng sì*) The Drepung dates back to the early 15th century and lies about seven km west of Lhasa. In its time it was the largest of Tibet's monastic towns and, some maintain, the largest monastery in the world. Today, the total number of monks in residence here has dwindled from 7000 to around 400. Around 40% of the monastery's structures have been destroyed.

Officially, entrance to the monastery is Y15, though the monks on duty usually only take Y7. While exploring the monastery grounds maintain a watchful eye for packs of vicious dogs. A walking stick for beating them off might be a good idea. Bites are not uncommon.

Drepung is easily reached by bike, though most people take a minibus from the stand down the road from the Jokhang. The fare is Y1 to the turnoff and Y2 if you take a minibus up the hill to the monastery itself.

Sera (*sèlā sì*) About four km north of Lhasa, this monastery was founded in 1419 by a disciple of Tsong Khapa. About 300 monks are now in residence, well down from an original population of around 5000. Debating takes place from 3 pm in a garden next to the central assembly hall (Jepa Duchen) in the centre of the monastery.

At the base of a mountain, just east of the monastery, is a Tibetan 'sky burial' site where the deceased are chopped up and then served to vultures. Tourism has reduced this admittedly grisly event to an almost daily confrontation between *domden* (undertakers) and scores of photo-hungry visitors. The reactions of the domden have become very violent. Our advice is to leave the place alone.

An hour's walk will get you up to the monastery, but most people hitch a ride with a tractor for Y1.

Ganden (*gāndān sì*) About 45 km east of Lhasa, this monastery was founded in 1409 by Tsong Khapa. During the Cultural Revolution the monastery was subjected to intense shelling, and monks were made to dismantle the remains. Some 400 monks have returned now, but the reconstruction work awaiting them is huge. For all this, the monastery is still well worth visiting and remains an important pilgrimage site.

Pilgrim buses leave for Ganden from the south-western corner of the Jokhang early in the morning. The ticket office is a small tin structure on the Barkhor circuit and they are not keen on selling tickets to foreigners. Persistence pays off, however. Buy tickets the day before you intend to travel.

YARLUNG VALLEY
(yálǔ liúyù) 雅鲁流域
About 170 km south-east of Lhasa, this valley is considered to be the birthplace of Tibetan culture. Near the adjacent towns of Zêtang and Nêdong, which form the administrative centre of the region, are several sites of religious importance.

Samye Monastery
This lies about 30 km west of Zêtang, on the opposite bank of the Yarlung Zangbo (Brahmaputra River). It was founded in 775 AD by King Trisong Detsen as the first monastery in Tibet. Getting there is complicated, but the monastery commands a beautiful, secluded position.

To reach Samye, catch a bus from Lhasa to Zêtang. Buses leave at 7.40 and 11 am from the bus station. You will be dropped off close to a ferry which functions sporadically and will take you across the river. From there, a tractor, truck or horse and cart will carry you the five km to Samye. There's inexpensive accommodation at the monastery and also in Zêtang.

The question of permits is (as usual) rather confused. The best thing seems to be to head out there. If you're stopped by the PSB in Zêtang they will fix you up with a permit on the spot.

Yumbu Lhakang
About 12 km south-west of Zêtang, Yumbu Lhakang is the legendary first building in Tibet. Although small in scale, it soars in recently renovated splendour above the valley. Get there by hiring a bike or 4WD in Zêtang, or hitch on a tractor.

Tombs of the Kings
At Qonggyai, about 26 km west of Zêtang, these tombs are less of a visual treat; their importance is essentially historical. To get there, hire a 4WD or spend half the day pedalling there and back on a bike.

Places to Stay & Eat
The *Zêtang Hotel* is the newest hotel in the area. It is also the shoddiest, with fittings falling to bits and toilets leaking under the lazy gaze of the staff. Most travellers give the place a miss and head over to the guesthouse. Bikes and 4WDs may be available for hire – depending on the mood of the staff.

The *Zêtang Guesthouse*, close to the hotel, is a standard Chinese guesthouse which charges Y10 per person in a functional double. It may also be possible to hire 4WDs here.

There is also inexpensive accommodation at Samye itself, and this is where most travellers stay. At the time of writing there was even a hotel under construction here. Both Zêtang and Samye have restaurants and shops that will keep you alive for a couple more days.

Getting There & Away
Buses for Zêtang (Y36.40) leave Lhasa two or three times a day. There should be buses at 7.40 and 11 am from the Lhasa bus station. Buses heading back to Lhasa leave from the traffic circle in Zêtang every morning – buy your ticket the day before from a tin shack just south of the traffic circle.

SHIGATSE
(Xigazê), (rìkèzé) 日喀则
The second-largest urban centre in Tibet is Shigatse. This is the seat of the Panchen Lama, a reincarnation of Amitabha (Buddha of Infinite Light), who ranks close to the Dalai Lama. The 10th Panchen Lama, who died in 1989, reportedly of a heart attack, was taken to Beijing during the '60s and lived a largely puppet existence there, visiting Tibet only occasionally.

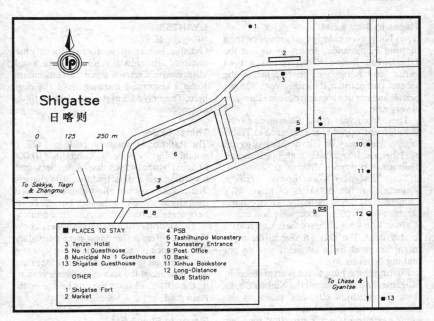

Monastery. Built in 1447 by a nephew of Tsong Khapa, the monastery once housed over 4000 monks, but now there are only 600. Apart from a giant statue of the Maitreya Buddha (nearly 27 metres high) in the Temple of the Maitreya, the monastery is also famed for its **Grand Hall** with its opulent tomb (containing 85 kg of gold and masses of jewels) of the fourth Panchen Lama. Admission costs Y18 and the monastery is open from 9.30 am to 5.30 pm. It's closed on Sunday.

Very little remains of the old Shigatse *dzong* or fortress, but the ruins on the skyline are imposing all the same. It's possible to hike up to the fortress from the pilgrim circuit for good views of the town.

Like everywhere else in Tibet, once you get off the main streets of Shigatse for some exploring, you should maintain a vigilant eye for packs of dogs. The pilgrim circuit is particularly bad.

Things to See

The main attraction in Shigatse is the seat of the Panchen Lama – **Tashilhunpo**

TIBET

Places to Stay & Eat

Everybody, even elderly tour groups coming in from Kathmandu, seems to stay at the Tibetan-run *Tenzin Hotel*. It has a roof terrace and is opposite the market in the Tibetan part of town. It charges from Y15 per person and has doubles and dorms. Hot water is very rare.

The *Municipal No 1 Guesthouse (dìyī zhāodàisuǒ)*, opposite the entrance to Tashilhunpo Monastery, is a basic place also run by Tibetans. It's popular with pilgrims and bedbugs. A bed costs Y10.

The *Shigatse Guesthouse (rìkèzé bīnguǎn)*, on the outskirts of town, is a Chinese-style hotel built for group tours. Doubles for Y100 are poor value and unless it's built into your itinerary there's no reason to stay here. The *Oxygen Bar* in the hotel might be good for a laugh, if you've got nothing better to do.

Finding something to eat is no problem in Shigatse. The area around the Xinhua Bookstore is restaurant city, and many of the places advertise English menus. The *Snowlands Restaurant* on this stretch of road has Tibetan food, but most of the other places are Sichuan Chinese cuisine.

Getting There & Away

Shigatse is an important transport centre with connections to the Nepalese border, western Tibet, Lhasa and Golmud. There are two routes linking Lhasa and Shigatse; the most popular one runs via Gyantse.

Buses to Lhasa cost Y55 and leave daily from the bus station. The trip takes an average of five or six hours, up to 10 hours if you get a run-down bus.

Another possibility is onward travel from Shigatse to the Nepalese border (Zhangmu). Tickets are Y90, and buses leave twice a week. Because the buses actually start out from Shigatse, if you book early it is usually no problem to get a seat.

Buses to Sakya leave on Tuesday, Friday and Saturday from the transport depot opposite the bus station. Buy your ticket (Y32) the day before at 10 am.

GYANTSE

(jiāngzī) 江孜

Gyantse is one of southern Tibet's chief centres, although it's more like a small village which retains some Tibetan charm. Keep a respectful distance from the dogs here. They rave all night and sleep until the afternoon.

Things to See

The **Palkhor Monastery**, built in 1427, is notable for its superb Kumbum (10,000 images) stupa which has nine tiers and, according to Buddhist tradition, 108 chapels. The monks may not allow you to complete the pilgrim circuit to the top, but the lower tiers contain excellent murals. Take a torch.

The **Dzong** (old fort) which towers above Gyantse offers a fine view over the valley. The entrance is usually locked, but you may be able to get the key (for a small fee) from a little house at the foot of the steps leading up the hill; it's close to the tiny bridge on the main road.

Places to Stay & Eat

Most people stay at the *Gyantse Hotel* on the main drag. You can't miss it. Gyantse is a very small place. Dorm beds are Y10, and the hotel also has a restaurant. Another place on the same stretch of road is the *No 1 Guesthouse (dìyī zhāodàisuǒ)*, which has basically the same rates.

You can eat at your hotel, but there are also some good Chinese restaurants out on the main street. A couple of them are run by Sichuanese and the food is *hot*. It's a good idea to check the prices of dishes before ordering.

Getting There & Away

The road from Lhasa splits here: one branch goes to Shigatse; the other heads south into Sikkim via the town of Yadong.

Bus connections to Lhasa usually consist of buses from Shigatse or elsewhere which are passing through. They are often packed solid and you'll be lucky to find a seat for the five-hour ride. The fare is around Y60 on a Japanese bus. Wait for the buses at the crossroads; if a bus stops overnight at the bus station in Gyantse, talk to the driver, who might let you on in the morning.

The same problems apply for travel to Shigatse (Y14, two hours) or the border with Nepal.

Transport to Yadong is scarce, and there's a checkpoint en route where foreigners are ordered to turn back.

SAKYA
(sàjiā) 萨迦

Sakya is 152 km west of Shigatse and about 25 km south of the main road. The huge, brooding monastery at Sakya was Tibet's most powerful 700 years ago and was once the centre for the Sakyapa sect founded in the 11th century. The monastery probably contains the finest collection of Tibetan religious relics remaining in Tibet – the monks may restrict you to a couple of halls. Admission costs Y5.

Places to Stay & Eat At the bus station is the *Bus Station Guesthouse (qìchēzhàn zhāodàisuǒ)* with beds for Y8, and just east of the bus station is the *Sakya County Guesthouse (sàjiāxiàn zhāodàisuǒ)*. There's a restaurant between these two hotels that's not too bad. Failing this, there's a shop selling instant noodles and so on opposite the entrance to the monastery.

Getting There & Away Most people arrange to see Sakya as an overnight stop when they hire a 4WD for the border or to the Everest base camp. It's possible to do it by public transport, but it will take time.

There's a bus from Shigatse to Sakya in the morning on Monday and Thursday; buses returning to Shigatse do so on Tuesday and Friday. Buy your ticket (Y28) the day before.

TINGRI
(dìngrì) 定日

There are in fact two Tingris: new Tingri (Xêgar) and old Tingri (Tingri). New Tingri has a checkpoint and a tourist hotel, and not much else. Old Tingri is a Tibetan town.

There's not much to do here except look for Everest on the skyline, but most travellers use Tingri as a final stopover before heading on to Zhangmu on the Tibetan/Nepalese border. On the right-hand side of the highway is the run-down *Tsultrim Lama Hotel* with beds for Y10. Meals are also available here. The other hotel in town is the *Mt Everest View Hotel* also with beds for Y10. This place has a good dining area.

From Tingri it's three or four spectacular hours to the border – up, up and then down, down, down.

RONGBUK MONASTERY & EVEREST BASE CAMP

Many travellers doing the Lhasa-Kodari trip take in Rongbuk and the Everest base camp as a side trip before heading down to the border. Some people have had problems with their 4WD drivers refusing to drive up to Rongbuk or the base camp because of the condition of the trail. It would make sense to check on this situation in Lhasa before you set off, and make sure that your driver is aware that you expect him to drive up there.

There is dorm accommodation at Rongbuk Monastery, which is about three hours walk from the base camp. Beds cost Y10, and it's a good idea to bring your own food. Monks at the monastery are sometimes willing to sell food, much of it stuff that has been left behind by previous expeditions, but it's probably best not to count on this.

If you are hiking up to the base camp from Rongbuk, you'll know you've reached your destination when you come across a toilet block. For those thinking of hiking the whole way from Xêgar or Tingri, refer to Lonely Planet's *Tibet – a travel survival kit* for detailed hiking information. It's a four-day walk up to Rongbuk.

ZHANGMU
(zhāngmù) 樟木

The last Chinese town you'll see before hitting Nepal has plenty of places to stay and eat, and in some ways represents a better place to spend your last night than Tingri –

TIBET

it's lower (around 2000 metres) and warmer at least. The Chinese-style *Zhangmu Guesthouse* is right next to the border, but back up the hill are privately run places like the *Himalaya Guesthouse* and the *Sunlight Hotel*. The Himalaya Guesthouse is a bizarre place with dorm beds for Y8. The Sunlight has the same rates, while the Zhangmu Guesthouse charges higher FEC rates.

Three twists back up the hill will take you to the Bank of China. This is the place to change your FEC back to US dollars. You will need exchange receipts. It is possible to change RMB for rupees out on the street, but FEC rates are no higher than RMB rates.

ZHANGMU TO KODARI

The last leg of the trip requires a 10-km downhill walk to Kodari. There are usually a few guys hanging around who are willing to carry your pack for you for a small fee. Whether you avail yourself of their services depends on how tired you are. It's not really necessary.

There are at least two shortcuts on the way down. Look for the steep trails that cut straight down the hillside. There are usually locals using them.

Qinghai 青海

Population: approx. four million
Capital: Xining

HISTORY

Qinghai *(qīnghǎi)* used to be part of the Tibetan world – with the exception of the eastern area around the capital of Xining, the region (formerly known as Amdo) was not incorporated into the Chinese empire until the early 18th century.

The province is a sort of Chinese Siberia where common criminals as well as political prisoners are incarcerated. These prisoners have included former Kuomintang army and police officers, 'rightists' arrested in the late 1950s harvesting of the Hundred Flowers, victims of the Cultural Revolution, former Red Guards arrested for their activities during the Cultural Revolution, supporters of the Gang of Four and opponents of the present regime.

Many of the Han Chinese settlers of the region are former prisoners who, because of their prison records, have little or no future in eastern China and so choose to stay in Qinghai.

Although there is a greater degree of consciousness these days in the Western world of the existence of Chinese reform camps, exile (along with execution) remains a popular way of dealing with pesky opponents to the Party line.

GEOGRAPHY

Qinghai Province lies on the north-east border of Tibet and is one of the great cartographical constructions of our time. For centuries this was part of the Tibetan world and today it's separated from the Tibetan homeland by nothing more than the colours on a Chinese-made map.

Eastern Qinghai is a high grassy plateau rising between 2500 and 3000 metres above sea level, and is slashed by a series of mountain ranges whose peaks rise to 5000 metres. It's the source of the Yellow River.

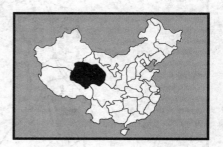

Most of the agricultural regions are concentrated in the east around the Xining area, but the surrounding uplands and the regions west of Qinghai Lake have good pasturelands for sheep, horses and cattle.

North-west Qinghai is a great basin surrounded by mountains. It's littered with salt marshes and saline lakes and afflicted with harsh, cold winters. Parts of it are barren desert, but it's also rich in mineral deposits, particularly oil.

Southern Qinghai is a high plateau 3500 metres above sea level. It's separated from Tibet by the Tanggula range, whose peaks rise to over 6500 metres, and the Yangzi and the Mekong rivers have their source here. Most of the region is grassland and the population is composed almost entirely of semi-nomadic Tibetan herders rearing goats, sheep and yaks.

POPULATION & PEOPLE

The population of Qinghai is a mixture of minorities including the Kazakhs, Mongols and Hui.

Tibetans are found throughout the province and the Han settlers are concentrated around the area of Xining, the provincial capital.

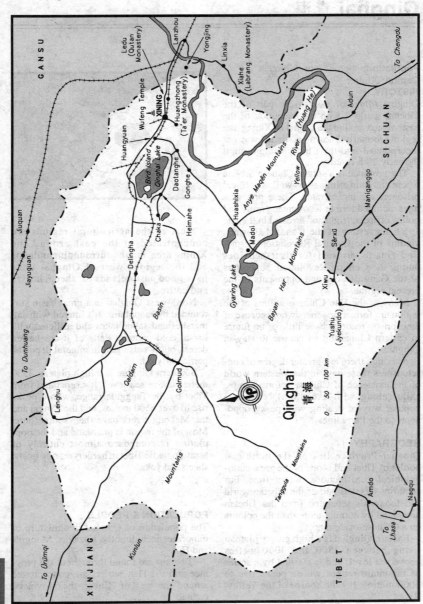

XINING
(xīníng) 西宁

Xining is the only large city in Qinghai and is the capital of the province. It's a long-established Chinese city, and has been a military garrison and trading centre since the 16th century.

Nowadays, it's a stopover for foreigners following the route between Qinghai and Tibet. Perched at 2200 metres elevation on the edge of the Tibetan Plateau, you can pause to consider the direction of your plunge.

Information

The CITS office (☎ 45901 ext 1109) is in the front building of the Xining Hotel *(xīníng bīnguǎn)*. The Qinghai Tourist Corporation *(qīnghǎi lǚyóu zhōng gōngsī)*, in the Qinghai Hotel, can issue travel permits more readily than CITS and seems to be more knowledgeable. You'll find the Public Security Bureau (PSB) on Bei Dajie (see map).

Good maps in Chinese are available at the railway station and at bookstalls around town.

Warning Watch your belongings – theft is common in Xining. Be especially careful of the pickpockets on city buses (No 9 is notorious).

Things to See

Xining has nothing exceptional to see, but it is a convenient staging post for visiting Ta'er Lamasery (Monastery) and Qinghai Lake. (See the Around Xining and Qinghai Lake sections for details.)

The **market** near the West Gate *(xīmén)* is the best sight in town. Stock up on munchies, especially if you're heading to Golmud, Qinghai Lake or over the mountains to Chengdu.

The **Great Mosque** *(qīngzhēn dà sì)* is on Dongguan Dajie. This mosque, built during the late 14th century, is one of the largest in China's north-west and attracts large crowds of worshippers, particularly on Friday.

The **Beishan Temple** *(běishān sì)* is about a 45-minute walk up the mountainside north-west of the Xining Hotel. The hike is pleasant and there's a good view over Xining from the temple.

Places to Stay

If you don't mind spending a little bit extra, the *Yongfu Hotel (yǒngfù bīnguǎn)* just down the road from the railway station is probably the best place to stay in Xining. The staff are extremely friendly and the rooms all have private bathrooms with a regular supply of hot water. A bed in a double costs Y25 and triples are Y20. The coffee shop here is a pleasant place to hang out – the coffee's terrible, but at least it's cheap.

The *Xining Dasha (xīníng dàshà)* is a gloomy kind of place, but it has the advantages of being cheap and close to the station. There's a dorm here for Y6, and doubles range from Y13 to Y26 per bed. If you turn up on your own, they'll probably try and put you into a single for Y57. Take bus No 1 from the station and get off at the second stop. Alternatively, walk – it takes a little over 10 minutes.

The *Xining Hotel* (☎ 45901) *(xīníng bīnguǎn)* is probably better avoided. There are no longer any dorms here, and the rooms that are available are overpriced. The cheapest option is a triple for Y38 per bed. After this doubles start at Y110 and spiral up to Y190 for a suite. If you're still interested, reception is in the building at the rear. Take bus No 9 from opposite the railway station – it's five km.

The new *Qinghai Hotel* (☎ 44888) *(qīnghǎi bīnguǎn)* is Xining's interpretation of a high-class international hotel – they got the room rates right at least. Doubles start at US$40, while the best room in the house fetches a staggering US$1000. The hotel is almost nine km from the railway station – not too convenient unless you want to commute by taxi.

Places to Eat

Some of the cheapest and best meals are available all around the huge market area near the West Gate. This is one of the best markets in China and is also reasonably clean.

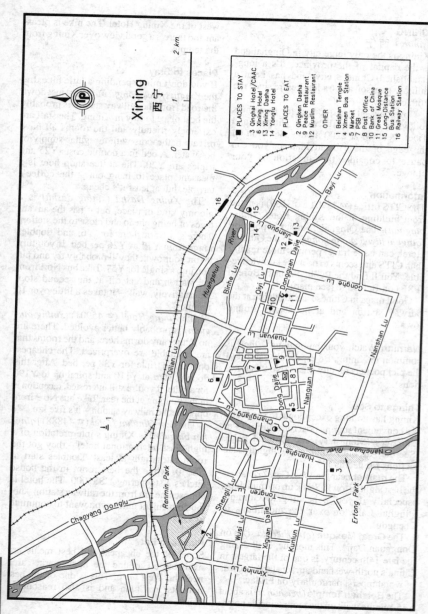

Xining
西宁

0   1   2 km

PLACES TO STAY
3   Qinghai Hotel/CAAC
13 Xining Hotel
13 Xining Dasha
14 Yonglu Hotel

PLACES TO EAT
2   Qingken Dasha
9   Peace Restaurant
12 Muslim Restaurant

OTHER
1   Beishan Temple
4   Ximen Bus Station
5   Market
7   PSB
8   Post Office
10 Bank of China
11 Great Mosque
15 Long-Distance Bus Station
16 Railway Station

The area around the Xining Dasha has good kebab stalls during the evening. Diagonally opposite the Xining Dasha is a good Muslim restaurant. It's next door to the Qilian Mountain Hotel (Chinese only).

If you're staying at the Yongfu Hotel, check out the hotel's restaurant. It has excellent noodle dishes at reasonable prices. Turn left out of the hotel towards the station and it's a few doors down. Just up the road from the hotel are a number of popular Muslim restaurants.

The best place in town for Chinese food is the *Peace Restaurant* (☎ 48069) *(hépíng jiǔjiā)* on Dong Dajie. At the time of writing this place was undergoing renovations, which will probably mean price hikes when it re-opens.

Finally, the Qinghai Hotel has an excellent Chinese restaurant on its 2nd floor. The menu is only in Chinese, but there should be an English speaker on the staff. Considering the quality of the food, it's very good value. Avoid the restaurant at the Xining Hotel.

Getting There & Away

Air The CAAC office is on the 1st floor of the Qinghai Hotel, and it would be difficult to find a more confused office. They don't seem to have any idea of what flights are available from Xining. The proposed flights to Golmud don't seem to have materialised, and at present the only options are Beijing (Y890) and Xi'an (Y360).

Bus The main bus station, opposite the railway station, has daily departures in the morning for Heimahe (near Qinghai Lake), Golmud (1½ days, Y42.80) and the Ta'er Monastery. Between 8.30 am and noon there are three buses running to Tongren. From Tongren it is possible to take onward buses to Xiahe in Gansu Province. There are buses to Lanzhou at 7.30 am. An interesting option might be the bus service to Lenghu *(lěnghú)*, in the north, close to the border with Xinjiang. Theoretically it should be possible to continue on to Ürümqi or *somewhere* in Xinjiang from Lenghu. Locals weren't sure about this, but agreed it *might* be possible.

Some travellers looking for an offbeat Tibetan experience have made the journey from Xining to Chengdu (Sichuan) by bus. The scenery is reportedly stunning and very Tibetan. It's a rough trip requiring nearly a week; accidents occur frequently. Just how long this route will remain open to foreigners is uncertain – probably until someone gets killed. At the time of writing, it was still possible. Don't bother to ask CITS for information about this journey – they told us 'if I were going there, I wouldn't start from here'.

The route to Chengdu is as follows: by bus from Xining to Madoi *(mǎduō)* (two days); Madoi to Xiwu *(xiēwǔ)*; by bus or truck to Sêrxu *(shíqú)* in Sichuan Province; then from Sêrxu to Kangding *(kāngdìng)* (two days); and Kangding to Chengdu (two days). All along the way there are cheap places to stay – the bus company will either put you up at their own hostels or direct you to another hotel.

Train Xining has frequent rail connections to

Lanzhou (4½ hours). Other train connections include Beijing, Shanghai, Qingdao, Xi'an and Golmud. There are two trains to Golmud; the afternoon train does the trip around six hours faster than the morning train. Foreigners have reported thefts on the Golmud train, particularly during the night.

AROUND XINING

One of the six great monasteries of the Yellow Hat sect of Tibetan Buddhism is **Ta'er Lamasery** *(tǎ'ěr sì)*, a large Tibetan monastery in the town of Huangzhong about 26 km south-east of Xining. It was built in 1577 on sacred ground – the birthplace of Tsong Khapa, founder of the Yellow Hat sect. Six temples are open – buy admission tickets from the window close to the row of stupas.

The monastery is noted for its extraordinary sculptures of human figures, animals and landscapes carved out of yak butter. The art of butter sculpture probably dates back 1300 years in Tibet and was taken up by the Ta'er Lamasery in the last years of the 16th century.

It's a pretty place and very popular with the local tourists. Go hiking in the surrounding area or follow the pilgrims clockwise on a scenic circuit round the monastery.

Photography is prohibited inside the temples, and they mean it! Outside the house with the butter statues, the monks have nailed to the wall all the film they have ripped out of cameras.

Overall, Ta'er Lamasery is an interesting sampler for the splendid monasteries of Xiahe or Lhasa.

Places to Stay & Eat The monastery has a couple of buildings which have been converted from monks' quarters into tourist accommodation. Rooms in the wooden buildings are arranged around a courtyard and come complete with gallery and murals. A bed in a three-bed room costs Y10.

The *Ta'er Hotel (tǎ'ěr sì bīnguǎn)* is just opposite the Tibetan hospital and charges Y80 for a double.

The food at the monastery is good. For a

change, take a wander down the hill towards town and try some noodles in a Muslim restaurant. Stalls on the approach road to the monastery sell great yoghurt and peaches.

Getting There & Away Buses to Huangzhong leave from the Sports Complex *(tǐyù chǎng)* just around the corner from the Ximen bus station *(xīmén qìchēzhàn)* in Xining about every 10 minutes between 7 am and 6.30 pm. The 45-minute ride costs Y3. Minibuses also do the trip faster for a fare of Y5.

Catch your return bus or minibus to Xining from the square in Huangzhong.

QINGHAI LAKE
(qīnghǎi hú) 青海湖

Qinghai Lake (Koko Nor), known as the Western Sea in ancient times, is a somewhat surreal-looking saline lake lying 300 km west of Xining and 3200 metres above sea level. It's the largest lake in China and contains huge numbers of fish.

The main attraction is Bird Island – a breeding ground for thousands of wild geese, gulls, cormorants, sandpipers, extremely rare black-necked cranes and many other bird species. Perhaps most interesting are the bar-headed geese. These hardy birds migrate high over the Himalayas to spend winter on the Indian plains, and have been spotted flying at 10,000 metres.

You will only see birds in any quantity during the breeding season between March and early June – worth remembering if you are considering a CITS tour.

It gets chilly at night so bring warm clothing. The lake water is too salty to drink, so be sure and carry a sufficient supply if you intend to do any hiking. There are nomads around the lake – most are friendly and may invite you in for a cup of tea in their tents.

Getting There & Away
North Shore The northern shore of the lake is readily accessible by train. Unfortunately, this is not the part of the lake that has many birds and you might be disappointed if this is all you get to see. Ha'ergai railway station

is the jumping-off point and the lake is an hour's walk away. If you are going to Golmud, you'll get good views of the whole northern shoreline from the train's windows.

Bird Island Most travellers head for Bird Island (*niǎo dǎo*), 360 km from Xining on the south shore of the lake. It's somewhat difficult to reach. The small settlement of Heimahe (*hēimǎhé*), 50 km from Bird Island, is the closest town that has regular public transport to Xining.

In Heimahe there's a sign which shows the way to the state-run hotel where rooms are just Y5. There's a surprisingly good restaurant and a well-stocked shop, but it's wise to bring some supplies anyway from Xining in case you want to do some hiking.

To reach Bird Island, take the road branching north from Heimahe – an occasional bus goes in this direction as far as Shinaihai (*shínǎihài*) (40 km). From there it's a hike or a hitch for 13 km to the Bird Island Hotel

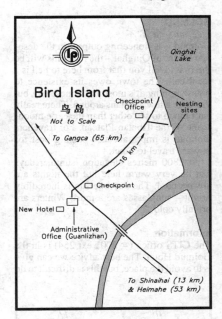

(*niǎo dǎo bīnguǎn*) – it's a boring walk. Dorms cost Y10, the hotel staff are very friendly and the food is good. You must register at the hotel and pay Y5 admission before being shepherded to the island (16 km).

Every Saturday or Sunday during summer, there is a day trip from Xining to Bird Island for only Y40. Buses depart at 7 am from Ximen bus station and return at 9 pm. Book tickets ahead of time as they are sometimes difficult to get hold of. Don't expect a tranquil nature experience – your fellow passengers may be very noisy.

If you can get together a group, it is possible to rent minibuses through the Peace Restaurant (☎ 48069) (*hépíng jiǔjiā*). Go to the 3rd floor to inquire.

CITS organises a three-day trip to Bird Island which costs Y150 (FEC) based on a minimum of 10 passengers. This price is for the bus only – meals and accommodation are an additional Y60 per day.

GOLMUD
(géěrmù) 格尔木

Golmud is a pioneering outpost in the desolate centre of Qinghai – the residents will be the first to tell you that from here to hell is a local call. The town owes its existence to potash mining. It's mostly a Chinese city, but there are a few Tibetans around. There really isn't much to see other than the eerie moonscape of the Tibetan Plateau. For travellers Golmud is important as a staging post for onward travel to Tibet.

At 2800 metres elevation, summer days can be very warm here but the nights are always cool. The daytime sun is incredibly bright – sunglasses are a must. Winters are brutally cold.

Information
The CITS office (☎ 2001 ext 254) is in the Golmud Hotel. The best advice we can give is to avoid the place, but this is difficult to do as Mr Hou, the office head, will probably be waiting for you at the railway station to make sure you don't jump on the nearest bus to Lhasa or try to stay at a non-authorised hotel. Officially, all travellers with their eyes set on Tibet should register with CITS, which will then fax your details through to Lhasa and charge you Y50 for the service. In practice, however, some travellers have gone directly to the Tibet bus station and registered there instead.

CITS will try to get you on to one of their minibuses to Lhasa. Don't do it. Breakdowns are frequent (the minibuses are just not up to the kind of terrain that separates Golmud from Lhasa), and when they occur you're basically up shit creek. There will be no compensation and you'll either have to wait a couple of days for help or hitch onwards – neither is much fun.

There were eight of us in Golmud, and the CITS minibus (just US$20 more than the public bus) sounded like such an easy option that we decided to

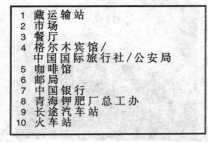

1 Tibet Bus Station
2 Market
3 Restaurant
4 Golmud Hotel, CITS & PSB
5 Best Cafe
6 Post Office
7 Bank of China
8 Potash Company Office
9 Bus Station
10 Railway Station

1 藏运输站
2 市场
3 餐厅
4 格尔木宾馆/
   中国国际旅行社/公安局
5 咖啡馆
6 邮局
7 中国银行
8 青海钾肥厂总工办
9 长途汽车站
10 火车站

go with it. There were problems of course (the bus was being repaired), but Mr Hou suggested that if we went out for drinks with him he'd be able to let us know by the end of the evening.

One drink led to another and before we knew it we were in the Golmud Hotel karaoke bar. Mr Hou wheezed incoherently through a couple of numbers and then danced with each of the girls in our group one by one. Protests cut no ice with Mr Hou – you *do* want to go to Tibet, don't you?

The next day we didn't leave until noon. The driver had apparently spent two hours supplying the minibus with petrol and another two hours washing it down as a result of the mess incurred in the filling up process. Well, that was the story anyway. The first few hours of the trip were great (the girls agreed it was almost worth dancing with Mr Hou for). Seven hours and a snapped chassis later we were standing around in a blizzard.

It's not easy for eight foreigners with huge backpacks to hitch a ride to Lhasa. Big bribes are required. A bit of hysterical screaming doesn't go astray either. If you do manage to get onto a bus, don't expect a seat. The interior of the bus we hooked up with looked like a rugby scrum. 'Mind you give a seat to the foreign guests', shouted the driver into the melee. We spent the next 30 hours standing up. The only stop was at noon the next day for a bowl of noodles.

The PSB is in the Golmud Hotel, where you can also buy a simple map of the city. The Bank of China is on the corner of Kunlun Lu and Chaidamu Lu. You'll find the post office on the corner of Chaidamu Lu and Jiangyuan Lu.

Things to See

The city itself is devoid of scenic spots. It's not unpleasant to walk around, but it doesn't take long to cover the whole town on foot. You might be able to find a taxi to take you to the pasturelands *(cǎoyúan)* on the edge of town. Here the nomads live in yurts and the area has a nice backdrop of snow-capped peaks in the distance.

Places to Stay

There's only one place accepting foreigners, the Golmud Hotel (☎ 2817) *(gé'ěrmù bīnguǎn)*. Dorms in the old building cost Y16, and doubles are Y50 per bed. The staff are unbelievably surly and the hot water supply is erratic. The new wing is more expensive, with triples at Y40 per bed and doubles for

Y60 per bed. There's a free bus service from the railway station to the hotel. Walking takes about 35 minutes.

Places to Eat

Just outside the gate of the Golmud Hotel is the *Golmud Hotel Restaurant*. The food is good and very cheap. Down the road towards the Bank of China is *The Best Cafe*, a friendly place (in Golmud!) with a decent English menu. They'll even make you a disgusting cup of coffee here. It's on the 2nd floor – look for the sign.

Getting There & Away

Air Despite the fact that local maps have a photograph of the airport with what looks like a real aeroplane sitting on its runway, there are still no flights, and it's doubtful whether the much-touted plans to establish a service between Xining and Golmud will ever come to anything. The CAAC office in the Golmud Hotel is a deserted dust-trap full of stacked-up chairs and mattresses. Check in Xining for the latest developments.

Bus The Golmud bus station is just opposite the railway station. The journey from Golmud to Dunhuang is 524 km (Y40, 13 hours). The bus departs at 6.30 am (7.30 am in summer). Foreigners must pay in FEC! Buy your ticket a day in advance. The bus leaves from behind the station, not in front – nobody will bother to tell you this and you could easily miss it. Luggage must be stored on the roof. Be sure to keep a jacket with you – it gets cold in those mountain passes. It's a rough, corrugated road and the screeching music on board will test your eardrums.

There are also daily buses to Xining, but it makes little sense to go this way – the train is faster and smoother. Some foreigners have also had problems buying bus tickets to Xining, even though coming the other way is no problem.

Buses for Lhasa leave from the Tibet bus station on Xizang Lu. There's a special foreigner's section inside where they charge special foreigner's prices – at least they do it with a smile. Prices seem to vary from day

> **Is Tibet Open?**
> Well, no-one in China has the foggiest. Let's just say it's financially prudent to pretend it isn't, even if it really is. Got that? So, for example, in Chengdu they say it's closed, and then they sell everyone expensive tours. In Golmud they'll say it's closed so that they can charge you nearly Y500 to sit in a lurching rustbucket for 35 hours. It's difficult not to conclude that the Y50 registration business isn't just a matter of keeping up appearances. After all, you don't end up with a permit of any kind – you'll be lucky if you get a receipt. ∎

to day, but the average seems to be Y470 on the Chinese bus and Y520 on the Japanese bus (if it's running). To this you'll probably have to add a Y50 registration fee. The tickets are generally payable in RMB, while FEC is required for the registration.

The Japanese buses stop overnight (usually in Amdo), while the Chinese buses do the trip straight through with a couple of meal stops. Either way, the trip takes from 28 to 35 hours and would have to rate as one of the world's worst bus journeys. After five or six hours you'll probably start to lose interest in the scenery, and after 20 hours you'll be grappling with an unhealthy desire to throw yourself off the nearest precipice.

Train From Xining there are two trains, one express and one local. The local runs in the morning, the express in the afternoon. From Golmud back to Xining, the express train runs at around 2 pm, the local train at around 8.30 pm. The express train is around six hours quicker than the local.

An attempt to build a railway from

Golmud to Lhasa was abandoned after it was discovered that it would be necessary to bore a tunnel through an ice-filled mountain. The Chinese consulted the Swiss (the world's best tunnel builders) who concluded it was impossible.

AROUND GOLMUD

Potash is Golmud's reason for existence. Most of the townsfolk work at the **Qinghai Potash Plant** (*qīnghǎi jiáfēichǎng*) 60 km from Golmud – it's not exactly a scenic area, but it's different. Only three such plants exist in the world – this one was built with US technical assistance. Potash is harvested from three reservoirs six metres deep and three sq km in area. Tours of the plant are free. To arrange a visit, drop in at the potash company office in Golmud – the tall, modern steeple building near the railway station. The place you need to find is called the General Engineering Office (*zǒnggōngbàn*). As you approach the plant, the scenery becomes incredibly desolate – not a blade of grass grows in this salty soil.

Index

TEXT

Map references are in **bold** type.

Accommodation 153-156
Adventure Sports 151-152
Air Travel

From Beijing 658-660
To/From China 172-179
Within China 193-196
Aksu (Xin) 1004
Altai (Xin) 1011

Anhui 444-452, **445**
Animals 47-48, 625, 746, 796,
  805, 815-817, 843
Anqing (Anh) 340
Anshun (Gui) 787-789, **788**

1054 Index

Continued from page 4

From the Authors

From Robert I'd like to express my gratitude to a number of French foreign residents of Beijing, including Stephane Beccamel, Pierre Sanavio, Pauline Jubert and Catherine Durand-Drouhim. Also special thanks to computer experts Carlos McEvilly (USA) and Lodewijk Kleijn (Netherlands); Tobin Miller and Melanie Straub, two American students in Tianjin; Rupert Winchester (UK) in Hong Kong; to Shane Nunn (USA), now transplanted to South Korea; Richard Flasher (USA), adventure traveller extraordinaire; and to numerous Chinese people I met along the way, who provided helpful advice, companionship, hospitality and some terrific dumplings.

From Chris Western China is a big place and, if it wasn't for a host of fellow travellers who gave me access to their notes, opinions and experiences, I'd probably still be there. Wen-Ying was a special help here in Puli, checking original Chinese sources for me and helping out with the Chinese character text and map problems. On the road, Mark Withycombe and Annika Anderson were great travel companions who provided useful notes on their travels through Xishuangbanna. Nobby and Juliet, old friends, provided me with an account of their extended travels through south-west China. Special thanks are due to Ludwy from Holland, who gratefully served as my guinea pig on the Kunming-Nanning bus trip and wrote back with an account of his 36-hour ordeal. Darren of Coca Cola Restaurant fame in Dali was generous with his time and assistance and the same is true of Tom Marakow from Peter's Café in Lijiang. Sue Pitt, Shelley Arnold and Yngve Lokas helped me out in Dehong. Lewis Duffy gave me the low down on his exploits hiking around Lugu Lake. Richard & Robin Ruogley, Kashgar foreign residents, helped me out in Xinjiang. Michael Risher, kick-boxing quiet American, joined me in Chongqing, Dazu and Chengdu, and helped me out with info. Adam Pinch and Richard were excellent companions in Yangshuo. Thanks to Stefan Frazier for a reconnaissance trip out to scenic Gonggar Airport. And finally, thanks to the crowd who were with me on the marathon 37-hour no-seats bus from Golmud to Lhasa: Robin, Clint, Anabelle, John, Arethra, Eva and ('israeli 'orrible') Pablo. To all these, and all the countless others whom I have failed to mention, happy travels!

From Clem I would like to acknowledge the assistance of the following people: Rob Nichols (USA), Sabrina Ramage (USA), Jeremy Hamshaw (UK) Penny Kershall (UK) Annie & Stuart (SA), Poh Lay Hoon (Sin) Lee Jong Neung (K) Roland Liu (AUS), Stewart Smith (UK).

Thanks

Thanks to the following travellers and others (apologies if we've misspelt your name) who took the time to write to us about their experiences of China:

Charles Albertson (USA), Alois Amiein (CH), Greg Anderson (AUS), Brigitta Andersson (S), P A Andisides (NZ), Cheryl Armstrong (C), Alison Armstrong (UK), Rachel Arnold (USA), Frederic Aron (F), Alexander Atepolikhin, Keith Bailey (UK), Todd Ballinger (USA), Ralf Banfeld (D), Jeanette Barbieri, Caroline Barnes (UK), Melvin C Bashner (USA), Annabelle Baurichter (NL), Frank Bauroth (USA), Roger Beaud (CH), Guy Beauregard, Darren Bedwell (USA), Hannu Berghall (S), Silas Berry, Jocelyn Paul Bertheau (C), Jane Best (UK), Michael Best, George Beuthin (USA), Minke Binnerts (NL), Thomas Birchler (AUS), Henrietta Bisgood (IRL), Lissa Bouwens, Lawrence Bowles (USA), Thomas Boxler (USA), Roland Brandes (CH), Karen Branen (USA), Guilio Bregliano (I), Robert Brooks (UK), Dr & Mrs R Brown (USA), David Browning (AUS), Dave Bulbeck (UK), Candace Butler (USA), Shane & Adele Caldwell (AUS), Elizabeth Carvalho (AUS), Camina Charly

(F), Pierre Chaux (F), Paul Chu (C), Linda Ciano (USA), David Clapperton (UK), Tom Clarke (AUS), Michael Clarke (UK), David Cohen (UK), Zach Coleman (USA), Bruce Connolly, Cynthia Connolly (USA), Mike Conway (N), Chris Cony (UK), Martin Cooper (HK), Stacey Coppel (UK), Laurence Cox (UK), Philippe Crambert (F), Yael & Danny Cramer (Isr), Jeremy Crawford (UK), R A Cresswell, Anita Crofts (USA), Paul Cullen (AUS), Mr & Mrs Cullen (AUS), P Cullenn (AUS), Elizabeth Cunningham (USA), Richard Davies (UK), Rhidian A Davies (UK), Michael Day (USA), Maxine Degraaf (AUS), Peter Delevett (USA), Brian Dempsey (USA), Marieke den Das (NL), Christopher Dennis (UK), Alek Derom (B), Marc Deshaies (USA), Susie Destner (F), Henry & Jo Dodds (UK), Benedikta Dorer (A), Martin Dudemaine, Neil Dunaetz (USA), Dorothy Dwyer, Sabine Ebel (D), Martin Echsel (A), Ron Edwards (AUS), Anne Mari Ehmsen (DK), Jane Eiseley (USA), Stefan Eklof (S), Misha Elias (UK), Mark Elliott, Drs R & B Engbretsen (USA), Hennele Erzsebet (NL), Rob Etherton, Tim Eyre (UK), Jaap Fahrenfort (NL), DJ & C Fairweather (AUS), Carol Falcett (USA), C Falcetti (USA), Ian Fanning (AUS), Cristina Ferraro (I), John Fettes, Jamie Finch (UK), Jim Fisher (USA), Murray Fitzgerald (AUS), Eric Forday (AUS), Alberto Forneris (I), Alv Terje Fotland (N), Thys Franssen (NL), John Fraser (C), Nancy Gallagher, Andrew Ganner (UK), William Gardner (C), Liz Gay (HK), Eleanor Gayner (USA), Drew Geldart (UK), Wolfram Genssler (D), Dr Barbieri Giovanni (I), Andrew Gledhill, Robert Goldschlager (Isr), Rene Granacher (D), Paula Greenwood (UK), Hildegunde Grueper (D), Jerry Guest (UK), Thierry & Nelly Guichard, Esther Gyssel (NL), Chung-bong Ha (HK), Michael Haeder (D), Barbara Haller (CH), Span Hanna, Tim Hannon (USA), Nick Hare (UK), Pat Harlow (UK), Christopher Harris (USA), A B Harwood (UK), Paul Hattaway, Lukas Havlicek, Reggie Haye, Michelle Haynes (C), Stephane Hennion (F), M Holley (UK), Sharon

Hoo Yuen Mei (Sin), Brad Houk (USA), Wang Hsin (Tai), Doug Hsu (USA), David & Greeba Hughes (UK), Gordon Brent Ingram (C), Mary & Mike Jackson (UK), John Jacobsen (USA), Martha Jaffe (USA), Alan F Jay (C), Louise Jefferies (C), Lars Jensen (DK), Sian Jones (NZ), Dudley Jones (UK), Gregers Jorgensen (DK), Dr Martin Jung (D), Andy Kanter (USA), Michael Kardos (USA), Cristina Katsu (USA), Tricia Kennedy (AUS), Peter Kerby, Fabienne Kern (USA), Brent Kirchner (CA), Lothar M Kirsch (D), Hanan J Kisch (Isr), Shelley Kissil (Isr), Peter Klafka (D), Paul Knight (UK), Jorg Kochendorfer (D), Peter Kolthof (NL), Yin Tong Kon (Sin), Katherine Kongdon (C), Gudrun Koppold (D), Ales Krejci, Jesse & Vivian Kwan (HK), Paule Lamarque (F), Ian Lamont (USA), Sallie Latch, Andrea Ledward (UK), Kevin LeeMarie Lergrange (F), Jo Lerner (B), Elizabeth Lescheid, Lane Leskela, Ran Levy (Isr), I-Ann Lin (USA), Peter Lindgreu (S), Bart Lipkens (B), F P Liposki (AUS), Barbara Lippoln (S), Rhonda Liu, Susan Lively (USA), Florian Loeckle, Pamela Logan (USA), Hose Lomas (Sp), Chris Lorrance (UK), Jill Lundmark (NZ), Christie Lurie (USA), Cath. & Charlie Lyster (UK), Jean Maalouf (F), Cathie Mackenzie (NZ), Pia Madsen (DK), Brian Malone (IRL), Chris Manderson (USA), Ben Manelan, Molly Martell (USA), Steven Martin (UK), Brent Maupin (USA), Randy Mauro (C), Cookie McBride (UK), Siobhan McErlane, Julie McGovern (AUS), Mararetta McIlvane, Nigel McKay (UK), Rosaline C S McKenzie (UK), Andrew Meyer (USA), Tobie Meyer (USA), S J & D Michel (USA), Harold Migee (Tai), Russell Miles (AUS), J Miles (NZ), Graham Millsteed (AUS), Marylise Montandon (CH), Martin Moos (CH), Birgitta Morell (S), Vivienne Morrell (NZ), Michael Mortensen (USA), Kazumi Nakagawa (J), Andrea Nasser, Mr D Naylor (AUS), James Newall (UK), Peta Newbound (AUS), Jim Nichols, Eva Nielsen (DK), Alina Niemi (USA), Ann-Christine Nilsson (S), Holger Norenberg Prof John Norris (USA), Neil O'Brien (NZ), John Oakley

(AUS), Mathias Olafsson (S), Ed Parker (UK), Claude Payen (F), Stig Uffe Pedersen (DK), Tan Tang Penn (M), Geoff Perriman (UK), Bo & Monica Person (S), Mark W Pickens (USA), Cies Pierrot (NL), Renato Piselli (I), Caroline Porter (UK), John Porter (AUS), Brian Powell (UK), Philippe Prevost (F), Karin Purdie (UK), Gunter Quaiber (D), Prof & Mrs D Rankin (UK), C I Read (UK), Lema Rees (USA), Gwyan Rhabyt (USA), Susanne Riedel (D), Zvi Rimalt (Isr), Steve Rippon (UK), Wolfgang Ristl (A), K T Rodwell (UK), Ludovic Ronchaud (F), Ingrid Ronde (NL), Bo Rosen (S), Jeff Rothman (USA), Phil Rush, Oded Salamy (USA), Karen Sam (M), Daniel Say (C), Florian Schmidt (HK), Dr Werner Schultheis (D), Steven Schwankert, Jim Scott (USA), Anatoli Semenov, Becky Semler (USA), Kit Moh Sew (Sin), Mary Seyfang (AUS), Rakefet Shapira (Isr), Hal C Sharpe (USA), Lee Sharrocks (UK), Nick Sheard, Keren Shinar (Isr), Carolina Sierimo (Fin), Graham & Sue Small (NZ), Jeanette Smed (DK), Edward Smith (AUS), Rhona Smith (UK), Lindy Smith (UK), John Sneddon (AUS), Attila Sonmex Jason Soo (C), Dr M E Speechly- Dick (UK), Raina Spencer (UK), Brian Spillane (USA), M W Staats (CH), Richard Staynings (UK), Katryn Steenbeke (B), Margaret Steig (USA), A Steinwachs (D), Suzanne Stevens, Julia Stone (AUS), Thomas Sturm (DK), D Stych (UK), Chiara Subhas (USA), Clayton Tang, Gavin Tanguay (NZ), Syan Tapp (UK), Mary Terry (UK), S Theunissen (NL), Anne Thomas (J), Mitch Thompson, Howard Tillis (C), Celita Tjon (NL), David Tombe (IRL), Megan

Tracy (USA), Claudia Trasancos (AUS), Andrew Tully (AUS), Milan Turner (USA), Andrzej Urbanik, Anne Vallier (F), R & B Vallings (NZ), N C Van Beek (NL), Ingeborg van den Bunder, Cynthia van Ginkel (C), Oscar van Wel (B), Peter Veldhuizen (NL), A Verrall, Michael Walker (C), Carsten Warburg, Geoff Warman (UK), Dorian Weber, Drs Sara & Neil Weiss (Isr), Ronen Werzig (USA), Ken White (AUS), Fiona Whitehead, Trevor Whittington (AUS), Eda Wijtenburg (B), Pierre Willems (B), Vanhaverbeke William, Steve & Claire Willot (AUS), Neil & Rhonda Wilson (AUS), Sarah Winfield (UK), Mark Wishart (AUS), Silkie Wittig (D), Roberto Wolnowicz, Nathan Wong (USA), Deb Wood (USA), Tim Woodward, Choo & Hoolam Woon (AUS), Ben Wrigley (UK), Robert Wyburn (UK), Pat Yale (UK), Hua Yang (Chi), Madeline Yap (AUS), Madeline Yap (AUS), Edward Yersh (C), Martien Ypelaar (NL), R A Zambardino (UK), Ubaldo Zambelli (I), M Zeller (USA), Karolyn Zergen, E P Zuidgeest (NL)

A - Austria, AUS - Australia, B - Belgium, C - Canada, CH - Switzerland, Chi - People's Republic of China, D - Germany, DK - Denmark, Fin - Finland, F - France, HK - Hong Kong, I - Italy, IRL - Ireland, Isr - Israel, J - Japan, Kor - Korea, M - Malaysia, N - Norway, NL - Netherlands, NZ - New Zealand, Sin - Singapore, Sp - Spain, S - Sweden, Tai - Taiwan, T - Thailand, UK - United Kingdom, USA - United States of America

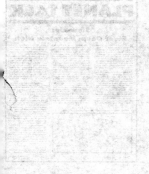

PLANETALK

MONTHLY PLANET PUBLICATIONS

PLANET TALK
Lonely Planet's FREE quarterly newsletter

We love hearing from you and think you'd like to hear from us.

When...*is the right time to see reindeer in Finland?*
Where...*can you hear the best palm-wine music in Ghana?*
How...*do you get from Asunción to Areguá by steam train?*
What...*is the best way to see India?*

For the answer to these and many other questions read PLANET TALK.

Every issue is packed with up-to-date travel news and advice including:

- *a letter from Lonely Planet founders Tony and Maureen Wheeler*
- *travel diary from a Lonely Planet author - find out what it's really like out on the road*
- *feature article on an important and topical travel issue*
- *a selection of recent letters from our readers*
- *the latest travel news from all over the world*
- *details on Lonely Planet's new and forthcoming releases*

To join our mailing list contact any Lonely Planet office (address below).

LONELY PLANET PUBLICATIONS
Australia: PO Box 617, Hawthorn 3122, Victoria (tel: 03-819 1877)
USA: Embarcadero West, 155 Filbert St, Suite 251, Oakland, CA 94607 (tel: 510-893 8555)
TOLL FREE: (800) 275-8555
UK: 10 Barley Mow Passage, Chiswick, London W4 4PH (tel: 081-742 3161)
France: 71 bis rue du Cardinal Lemoine – 75005 Paris (tel: 1-46 34 00 58)

Also available: Lonely Planet T-shirts. 100% heavyweight cotton (S, M, L, XL)

Guides to North-East Asia

Beijing - city guide
Beijing is the hub of a vast nation. This guide will help travellers to find the best this ancient and fascinating city has to offer.

North-East Asia on a shoestring
Concise information for independent low-budget travel in China, Hong Kong, Japan, Macau, North Korea, South Korea, Taiwan and Mongolia.

Hong Kong, Macau & Canton - a travel survival kit
This practical guide has all the travel facts on these three close but diverse cities, linked by history, culture and geography.

Japan - a travel survival kit
Japan combines modern cities and remote wilderness areas, sophisticated technology and ancient tradition. This guide tells you how to find the Japan that many visitors never see.

Korea - a travel survival kit
South Korea is one of the great undiscovered destinations, with its mountains, ancient temples and lively modern cities. This guide also includes a chapter on reclusive North Korea.

Mongolia - a travel survival kit
Mongolia is truly a destination for the adventurous. This guide gives visitors the first real opportunity to explore this remote but newly accessible country.

Seoul - city guide
It is easy to explore Seoul's ancient royal palaces and bustling market places with this comprehensive guide packed with vital information for leisure and business travellers alike.

Taiwan - a travel survival kit
Traditional Chinese ways survive in prosperous Taiwan. This guide has Chinese script and pinyin throughout.

Tibet - a travel survival kit
The fabled mountain-land of Tibet is slowly becoming accessible to travellers. This guide has full details on this remote and fascinating region, including the border crossing to Nepal.

Tokyo - city guide
Tokyo is a dynamic metropolis and one of the world's leading arbiters of taste and style. This guide will help you to explore the many sides of Tokyo, the modern Japanese miracle rolled into a single fascinating, sometimes startling package.

Also available:
Cantonese phrasebook, *Mandarin Chinese* phrasebook, *Korean* phrasebook, *Tibet* phrasebook, and *Japanese* phrasebook.

Lonely Planet Guidebooks

Lonely Planet guidebooks cover every accessible part of Asia as well as Australia, the Pacific, South America, Africa, the Middle East, Europe and parts of North America. There are five series: *travel survival kits*, covering a country for a range of budgets; *shoestring guides* with compact information for low-budget travel in a major region; *walking guides*; *city guides* and *phrasebooks*.

Mail Order

Lonely Planet guidebooks are distributed worldwide. They are also available by mail order from Lonely Planet, so if you have difficulty finding a title please write to us. US and Canadian residents should write to Embarcadero West, 155 Filbert St, Suite 251, Oakland CA 94607, USA; European residents should write to 10 Barley Mow Passage, Chiswick, London W4 4PH; and residents of other countries to PO Box 617, Hawthorn, Victoria 3122, Australia.

Indian Subcontinent
Bangladesh
India
Hindi/Urdu phrasebook
Trekking in the Indian Himalaya
Karakoram Highway
Kashmir, Ladakh & Zanskar
Nepal
Trekking in the Nepal Himalaya
Nepali phrasebook
Pakistan
Sri Lanka
Sri Lanka phrasebook

Africa
Africa on a shoestring
Central Africa
East Africa
Trekking in East Africa
Kenya
Swahili phrasebook
Morocco, Algeria & Tunisia
Arabic (Moroccan) phrasebook
South Africa, Lesotho & Swaziland
Zimbabwe, Botswana & Namibia
West Africa

Central America & the Caribbean
Baja California
Central America on a shoestring
Costa Rica
Eastern Caribbean
Guatemala, Belize & Yucatán: La Ruta Maya
Mexico

Europe
Baltic States & Kaliningrad
Dublin city guide
Eastern Europe on a shoestring
Eastern Europe phrasebook
Finland
France
Greece
Hungary
Iceland, Greenland & the Faroe Islands
Ireland
Italy
Mediterranean Europe on a shoestring
Mediterranean Europe phrasebook
Poland
Scandinavian & Baltic Europe on a shoestring
Scandinavian Europe phrasebook
Switzerland
Trekking in Spain
Trekking in Greece
USSR
Russian phrasebook
Western Europe on a shoestring
Western Europe phrasebook

North America
Alaska
Canada
Hawaii

South America
Argentina, Uruguay & Paraguay
Bolivia
Brazil
Brazilian phrasebook
Chile & Easter Island
Colombia
Ecuador & the Galápagos Islands
Latin American Spanish phrasebook
Peru
Quechua phrasebook
South America on a shoestring
Trekking in the Patagonian Andes
Venezuela

The Lonely Planet Story

Lonely Planet published its first book in 1973 in response to the numerous 'How did you do it?' questions Maureen and Tony Wheeler were asked after driving, bussing, hitching, sailing and railing their way from England to Australia.

Written at a kitchen table and hand collated, trimmed and stapled, *Across Asia on the Cheap* became an instant local bestseller, inspiring thoughts of another book.

Eighteen months in South-East Asia resulted in their second guide, *South-East Asia on a shoestring*, which they put together in a backstreet Chinese hotel in Singapore in 1975. The 'yellow bible' as it quickly became known to backpackers around the world, soon became *the* guide to the region. It has sold well over half a million copies and is now in its 8th edition, still retaining its familiar yellow cover.

Today there are over 140 Lonely Planet titles in print – books that have that same adventurous approach to travel as those early guides; books that 'assume you know how to get your luggage off the carousel' as one reviewer put it.

Although Lonely Planet initially specialised in guides to Asia, they now cover most regions of the world, including the Pacific, South America, Africa, the Middle East and Europe. The list of *walking guides* and *phrasebooks* (for 'unusual' languages such as Quechua, Swahili, Nepali and Egyptian Arabic) is also growing rapidly.

The emphasis continues to be on travel for independent travellers. Tony and Maureen still travel for several months of each year and play an active part in the writing, updating and quality control of Lonely Planet's guides.

They have been joined by over 50 authors, 90 staff – mainly editors, cartographers & designers – at our office in Melbourne, Australia, at our US office in Oakland, California and at our European office in Paris; another five at our office in London handle sales for Britain, Europe and Africa. Travellers themselves also make a valuable contribution to the guides through the feedback we receive in thousands of letters each year.

The people at Lonely Planet strongly believe that travellers can make a positive contribution to the countries they visit, both through their appreciation of the countries' culture, wildlife and natural features, and through the money they spend. In addition, the company makes a direct contribution to the countries and regions it covers. Since 1986 a percentage of the income from each book has been donated to ventures such as famine relief in Africa; aid projects in India; agricultural projects in Central America; Greenpeace's efforts to halt French nuclear testing in the Pacific and Amnesty International. In 1993 $100,000 was donated to such causes.

Lonely Planet's basic travel philosophy is summed up in Tony Wheeler's comment, 'Don't worry about whether your trip will work out. Just go!'.